BENSON *and* HEDGES
CRICKET YEAR
FIFTH EDITION

BENSON and HEDGES
CRICKET YEAR

FIFTH EDITION
SEPTEMBER 1985 TO SEPTEMBER 1986

EDITOR DAVID LEMMON
ASSOCIATE EDITOR TONY LEWIS

PELHAM BOOKS

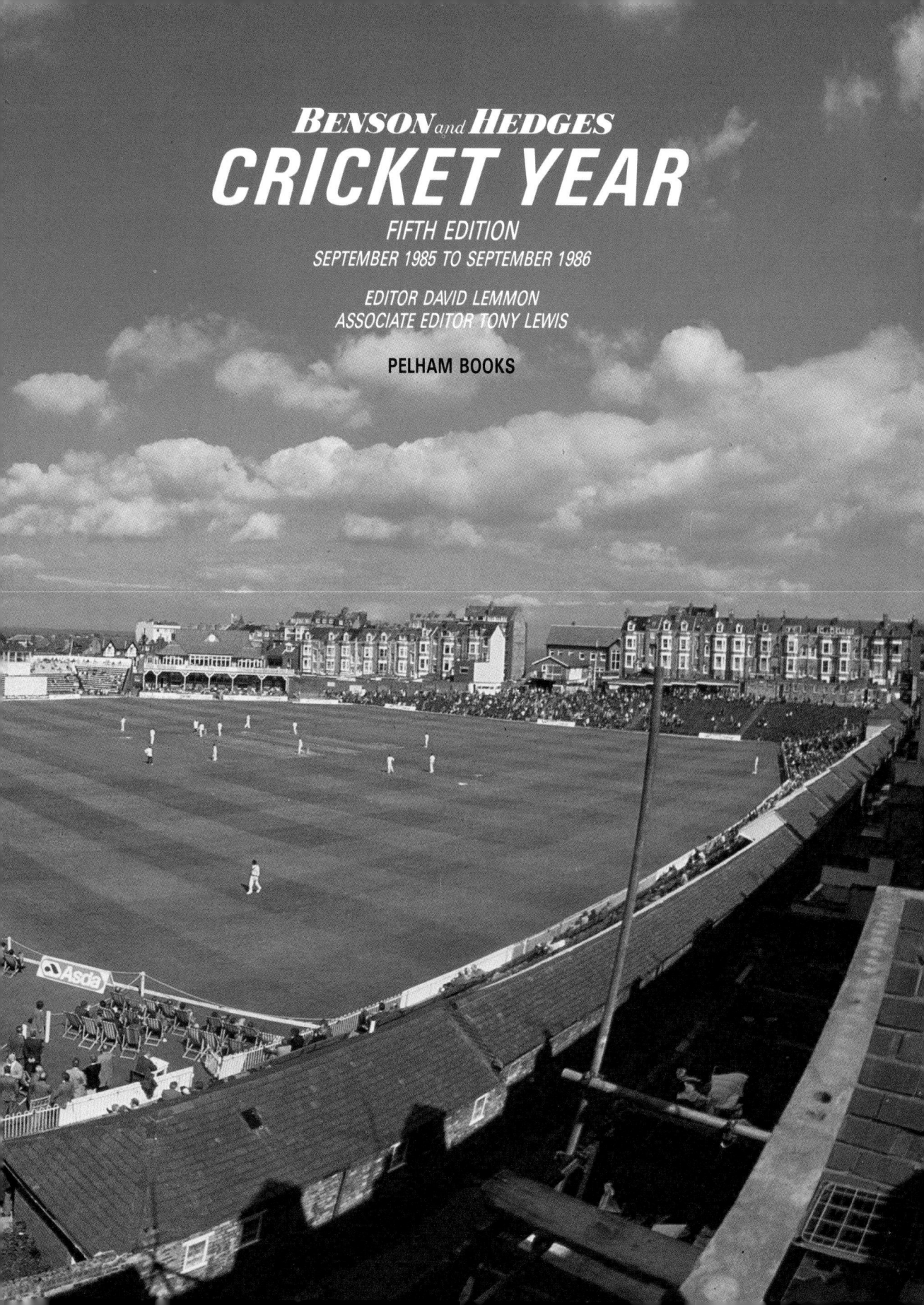

First published in Great Britain by
Pelham Books Ltd
27 Wrights Lane
London W8 5TZ
1986

British Library Cataloguing in Publication Data
Benson and Hedges cricket year. – 5th ed.
1. Cricket – Periodicals
796.358′05   GV911

ISBN 0 7207 1695 0

Filmset in Times and Univers by MS Filmsetting Limited, Frome, Somerset
Printed and bound in Italy by Arnoldo Mondadori

Editor's Note

The aim of *Benson and Hedges Cricket Year* is that the cricket enthusiast shall be able to read through the happenings in world cricket, from each October until the following September (the end of the English season). Form charts are printed and a player's every appearance will be given on these charts, and date and place allow these appearances to be readily found in the text.

The symbol * indicates 'not out' or 'wicket-keeper' according to the context and the symbol † indicates captain.

The editor wishes to express his deepest thanks to Brian Croudy, Brian Heald, Les Hatten, Victor Isaacs, Anthony Lalley, Qamar Ahmed, Peter Sichel, Sudhir Vaidya and John Ward whose advice and help over statistics have been invaluable.

Sponsor's message

1986 was one of those seasons which both enthusiasts and professional players will remember for a variety of reasons. A combination of controversial publicity, disappointing performances and the ever capricious weather conspired to cast a shadow over our National Sport.

As in our previous editions, the 1986 *Benson and Hedges Cricket Year* aims to encapsulate the flavour of the season past, in a comprehensive review and critique of the sport in all nine countries where first-class cricket has been played.

For whichever reason you recall the past season, we hope that this superbly illustrated annual will provide a lasting record of Cricket's most memorable moments.

PAUL RUTHERFORD
Director, Benson and Hedges

Contents

Comment

When writing of the 1921 season Sydney Pardon, editor of *Wisden*, said that there had never been a season so disheartening. England had suffered crushing defeats at Lord's, Nottingham and Leeds, and although two draws had done something to restore self-respect, they afforded but a small consolation. He accepted that England were handicapped by the absence of Hobbs, as they were by the absence of Botham for most of 1986, but 'the fact that thirty players appeared for England in the Test matches last summer is in itself proof that we had not a real eleven, but a series of scratch sides'.

In 1921, England were faced by one of the strongest teams that Australia has ever put into the field. In 1986, England were faced by India who had previously won only one Test match in England, and by New Zealand who had not won a series in this country. In 1921, as Pardon mentions, England fielded thirty players in the Test series. In 1986, if one includes the Texaco Trophy matches and Larkins who was selected but was unable to play because of injury, England called upon twenty-nine players. Sixty-five years ago, England had returned from a five–nil thrashing in Australia. In 1986, England faced India and New Zealand after losing by five Tests to nil in the West Indies. The last two Test matches of 1921 were drawn with England leading on the first innings in both matches. There were three drawn Tests in 1986, but only in the last match, against New Zealand at The Oval, did England lead on the first innings. In 1986, as in 1921, England sacked their captain early in the season but retained him in the side.

If one looks closely at these parallels between the 1921 and 1986 seasons, one must reach the conclusion that English cricket, at international level, suffered its most disheartening season in history in the summer of 1986. When we fell to the Australians in 1921 we were still suffering from the aftermath of a horrendous war. When we were trounced by Bradman's Australians in 1948 a similar excuse could be offered. When West Indies overwhelmed us in 1984 we could forward the reason that we were confronted by a pace attack of unprecedented power which did not always conform to the strictures of Law 42, section 8. What can we offer as a reason for our failures in 1986? Under Gower's captaincy we had succeeded in India in 1984–85 and had outplayed a weak Australian side in the 'Ashes' series of 1985, but those victories had tended to obscure truths on technique and attitude that we would rather remain hidden. They were to be glaringly exposed by Kapil Dev, Chetan Sharma, Maninder Singh and Richard Hadlee in the summer of 1986.

It may seem ungracious to find fault first with the selectors whose task is a difficult one, but one is convinced that in the summer of 1986 they lacked a settled policy. They clutched at straws, influenced by the merest whims of current form which could not be substantiated by a closer scrutiny of the facts. The prime example here is the selection of Moxon as Gooch's fourth opening partner in four Test matches. The Yorkshireman seemingly won his cap on the strength of a century in each innings against the Indian tourists. The fact that the Indians were playing the last match of their tour in a festival atmosphere and that their attack was void of its leading bowlers did not seem to matter. Yet before we take the selectors too much to task on this, let us consider the problems that faced them.

That they were hasty in giving Gatting the captaincy for the series against New Zealand and for the tour of Australia is undeniable, but at the end of the third Test match against India in which Gatting played a good innings after being badly missed early on, the selectors had only four days in which to choose the side for the Texaco Trophy matches against New Zealand, and those four days were filled with the second round of the NatWest Bank Trophy and the Benson and Hedges Cup Final. After the drawn first Test match against New Zealand they had only the four matches in the quarter-finals of the NatWest Bank Trophy to aid them. No wonder they clutched at straws.

It is obvious to all that the fixture list is now so congested with international matches that the growth of young players is being stifled, particularly the development of young bowlers who have never received the help, advice or encouragement that is given to batsmen. In the summer of 1986, a young player of note like Bailey, Hugh Morris, Whitaker or Prichard could have found that in the twenty-four Britannic Assurance County Championship matches which he would hoped to have played, the opposition could have been without their Test players, presumably their best players, in fourteen of those matches. How can a young player hope to be judged or to be tested if he is not competing against the best that is available? How else can he hone his skills?

The example of Australia should be taken as a warning to all. The Sheffield Shield has been all but choked to death by a surfeit of international cricket. Consider what faces the England party on the current tour of Australia which began only three weeks after the end of the England season. A tour lasting four and a half months was to include five Test matches, four of them in a six-week period. The Test series was to be followed by a *minimum* of eight one-day internationals against Australia and West Indies, and after that a four-country limited-over competition in Perth. Could this surfeit of delights, which now dominates the Australian season each year, be the reason why Australia could at present be ranked as seventh out of seven among the Test-playing nations? Can one blame Gooch, with a young family, for turning his back on it. He created no precedent. The New Zealand side that toured England in 1986 did so without Reid and Boock who chose to put domestic commitments first.

One does not question that international matches present cricket with its major source of revenue, but one is concerned that such a lucrative source could be destroyed by excess. An international contest should be a special event, not a weekly meeting.

There were journalists and photographers who were exhausted by the demands made on them by the international programme of 1986. Could not a similar sense of staleness and exhaustion have affected England performances following an emotionally draining tour of the West Indies and a mammoth tour of Australia looming on the horizon.

On the players falls the responsibility for the future health of the game, and if, at times, one was worried on this score, it was because on some occasions one felt that there were those who had lost sight of the fact that the substantial incomes they derive from interests outside the game are entirely dependent upon their commitment to the game itself. The emphasis that television places on international matches and the large audience that it provides can encourage players to expend energy on displaying wares in which they have a commercial interest, and one feels that this is a temptation that should be avoided in future. The TCCB has already acted to prevent players on the tour to Australia having 'ghosted' articles published in the national Press, although why this ban was not extended to include magazines one cannot understand, and perhaps they will act next year to prevent the ostentatious display of watches and the like in the course of a Test match.

If one seems over-concerned, it is because there has been a decline in standards in the last decade and one wishes to prevent further intrusions on the decency, sportsmanship and code of behaviour which shows a concern for other people which are the very fabric of the game. It would be wise to show a desire to preserve standards now, while cricket is booming, rather than wait for a time, as did association football, when the attitude and behaviour of players and the greed of many connected with the game has brought it to a level where desperate measures are needed.

In spite of England's poor showing at Test level, and in spite of some unkind weather, cricket continued to boom in 1986. A capacity crowd watched an enthralling Benson and Hedges Cup Final end in the pouring rain, and tickets for the NatWest Bank Trophy Final and for several days at Test matches were sold out well in advance. Around the county grounds, amid the usual mutterings about committees, selections and selectors, there was a feeling of buoyancy. There was excited talk about the wicket-keeping of Marsh of Kent, the batting of Whitaker, Bailey and Prichard, the bowling of Jarvis, Bicknell and Childs, and the innings that Jesty played for Surrey against Lancashire at The Oval. There was also a general feeling that county cricket is the best of cricket and that it does not get the attention that it deserves, especially by the television companies. Perhaps it is a concern that we should note, and our attention should be more firmly focussed on domestic cricket throughout the world, for where the domestic game is allowed to sicken Test cricket will die.

David Lemmon
October 1986

KINGS of the WILLOW

WIN the TEST with the BEST

Comes the Blind Fury

The season in the West Indies.
Shell Shield. The Grant Geddes Harrison Line
Limited-Over competition.
The England tour. Test and One-Day series.

Port-of-Spain, Trinidad.
(Adrian Murrell)

With all the leading players in the Caribbean for the first time in several seasons and obliged to play in at least two Shell Shield matches to be eligible for selection for the Test squad, domestic cricket in the West Indies in 1986 was restored to its former place of importance. This was gratifying not only for the good of cricket in the area, but also for the sponsors who, justifiably, had expressed concern about the devaluation of the Shell Shield in the past two seasons. The attitude of followers of the game could be gauged from the fact that there was a significant increase in attendances at matches, and the crowd for the Barbados – Jamaica match at Kensington Oval was reported as being the largest ever seen for a Shield match on that ground.

Geddes Grant Harrison Line Trophy

7 January

at Sabina Park, Kingston, Jamaica
Guyana 137 for 8 (A.G. Daley 4 for 26)
Jamaica 138 for 4 (W.W. Lewis 56)

Jamaica (2 pts) won by 6 wickets

8 January

at Mindoo Park, Castries
Windward Islands 108 for 3
Leeward Islands 111 for 5

Leeward Islands (2 pts) won by 5 wickets

The season began with the limited-over competition. Both matches were affected by the weather. In Zone A, Jamaica won comfortably. Daley and E.E. Lewis who hit 39 when Leeward Islands were pressing for runs took the individual awards.

Shell Shield

9, 10 and 11 January

at Sabina Park, Kingston, Jamaica
Guyana 41 (B.P. Patterson 7 for 24) and 202 (R.A. Harper 65, T. Mohammed 57, C.A. Walsh 8 for 92)
Jamaica 126 (R.A. Harper 4 for 37) and 118 for 7 (R.A. Harper 4 for 29)

Jamaica won by 3 wickets
Jamaica 16 pts, Guyana 0 pts

10, 11 and 12 January

at Kensington Oval, Bridgetown, Barbados
Barbados 350 (C.A. Best 179, E.L. Reifer 51 not out, R. Nanan 5 for 82)
Trinidad and Tobago 177 (J. Garner 5 for 55) and 160

Barbados won by an innings and 13 runs
Barbados 16 pts, Trinidad and Tobago 0 pts

at Mindoo Philip Park, Castries
Windward Islands *v.* **Leeward Islands**
Match abandoned
Windward Islands 4 pts, Leeward Islands 4 pts

The Shell Shield opened in sensational fashion when Patterson, in only his second Shield match, and Walsh bowled out Guyana in 15.1 overs before lunch on the first day for the

Patrick Patterson began the Shell Shield season by taking 7 for 24 for Jamaica against Guyana. He won his first Test cap for West Indies during the season. (Adrian Murrell)

lowest score ever recorded in the competition. Both bowlers were aided by some fine close catching, and Guyana were 11 for 7 before Roger Harper, who made 18, and Butts added 20. Jamaica fared only marginally better and were 82 for 7 against the spin of Harper and Butts before Holding, who hit 2 sixes and 4 fours, took them to a lead of 85. An astounding first day ended with Guyana 60 for 3 in their second innings. Timur Mohammed batted soundly, and Harper, who shared a last wicket partnership of 50 with Lambert, hit a belligerent 65 so that Jamaica were left to make 118 to win. Again they faltered to the spinners and slumped to 92 for 7, an improbable victory looming for Guyana, but Daley gave Davidson fine support to clinch the win for Jamaica half an hour before lunch on the third of the four days scheduled for the match.

Sent in to bat, Barbados reached 350 thanks to Best hitting the highest score of his career. He hit a six and 21 fours. Garner, leading Barbados in his first Shield season since 1982, and Marshall capitalised on some injudicious strokes by the visitors who lost their last 9 wickets for 80 runs after they had followed-on 173 runs in arrears.

A sodden outfield made play impossible at Castries although the sun shone for most of the four days.

Geddes Grant Harrison Line Trophy

15 January

at Shaw Park
Guyana 106 for 8
Trinidad and Tobago 108 for 3 (P.V. Simmons 62)

Trinidad and Tobago (2 pts) won by 7 wickets

Courtney Walsh who routed Guyana at Sabina Park, 10 January. He was most unlucky not to win a regular place in the West Indian side. (Adrian Murrell)

Carlisle Best hit 179 against Trinidad. The Barbadian was the only batsman to reach 500 runs in Shell Shield cricket during the season. (Adrian Murrell)

at Kensington Oval, Bridgetown, Barbados

Barbados 276 for 3 (T.R.O. Payne 100 not out, T.A. Hunte 75)
Windward Islands 105 for 7

Barbados (2 pts) won by 146 runs

Simons and Payne won the individual awards in the second round of matches in the limited-over competition which brought the elimination of Guyana and Windwards.

Shell Shield

16, 17, 18 January

at Sabina Park, Kingston, Jamaica

Jamaica 230 (P.J. Dujon 75, W.K.R. Benjamin 5 for 47) and 10 for 0
Leeward Islands 77 (C.A. Walsh 4 for 23) and 162 (E.A.E. Baptiste 58, B.P. Patterson 4 for 37, M.A. Holding 4 for 52)

Jamaica won by 10 wickets
Jamaica 16 pts, Leeward Islands 0 pts

17, 18, 19 and 20 January

at Kensington Oval, Bridgetown, Barbados

Barbados 175 (D.L. Haynes 81, J.T. Etienne 6 for 35) and 338 for 5 dec (D.L. Haynes 112, C.G. Greenidge 59, J. Garner 56, C.A. Best 54)
Windward Islands 94 (M.D. Marshall 4 for 39) and 301 (J.D. Charles 82, L.C. Sebastien 69, M.D. Marshall 6 for 85)

Barbados won by 118 runs
Barbados 16 pts, Windward Islands 0 pts

at Guaracara Park, Pointe-a-Pierre

Trinidad and Tobago 180 (C.G. Butts 5 for 43) and 371 (H.A. Gomes 168 not out, A. Rajah 57, R.A. Harper 4 for 64)
Guyana 149 and 138 (G. Mahabir 4 for 31)

Trinidad and Tobago won by 264 runs
Trinidad and Tobago 16 pts, Guyana 0 pts

The Jamaican pace bowlers again devastated the opposition, and Jamaica and Barbados moved clear at the top of the table.

Put in to bat when play started late because of overnight rain and with parts of the outfield still very damp, Jamaica reached 177 for 5 by the close. Dujon, who hit 6 fours and a six, was the only man to come to terms with a varied attack in which Winston Benjamin, making his debut in first-class competitive cricket (he had played in the Scarborough Festival) was most impressive. Leeward Islands lost 5 wickets for 21 runs in an hour before lunch on the second day, and also lost Kelly who was hit in the mouth by a ball from Patterson and had to retire hurt. He lost two teeth. Benjamin and Ferris added 38 for the last wicket, but could not save the follow-on. Patterson quickly removed Richardson and Richards so that the two Test batsmen shared the indignity of being dismissed twice in the day. Baptiste and Otto added 73 for the 5th wicket, but Otto fell to a good catch in the deep by Daley off Walsh on the last ball of the day, and the following morning, after a delayed start, Leeward Islands lost their last 5 wickets for 17 runs.

Left-arm spinner Javan Etienne took a career best 6 for 35 on the first day in Barbados where the home side contrived

Barbados 1986
First Class Matches

BATTING

	v. Trinidad and Tobago (Bridgetown) 10–12 January 1986		v. Windward Islands (Bridgetown) 17–20 January 1986		v. Leeward Islands (Nevis) 24–27 January 1986		v. Jamaica (Bridgetown) 31 Jan.–3 Feb. 1986		v. Guyana (Essequibo) 6–9 February 1986		v. England XI (Bridgetown) 14–17 March 1986		M	Inns	NOs	Runs	HS	Av
D.L. Haynes	4	—	81	112	118	14	30	65	12	9			5	9	—	445	118	49.44
C.A. Best	179	—	33	54	9	47	78	0	111	7	2	42	6	11	—	562	179	51.09
T.A. Hunte	25	—	12	15	1	39	0	0					4	7	—	92	39	13.14
R.I.C. Holder	0	—	0	5*									2	3	1	5	5*	2.50
T.R.O. Payne	17	—	7	22*	62	18*	38	22	62	9	1	7	6	11	2	265	62	29.44
M.C. Worrell	14	—											1	1	—	14	14	14.00
M.D. Marshall	13	—	2	—			11	17	1	7*			4	6	1	51	17	10.20
G.L. Linton	23	—	1	—	0	0			1	—			4	5	—	25	23	5.00
J. Garner	5	—	17	56	10	20	1	11	44	—	4	23*	6	10	1	191	56	21.22
E.L. Reifer	51*	—											1	1	1	51	51*	—
W.T. Greenidge	10	—	5*	—	0	—	3*	0*					4	5	3	18	10	9.00
N.D. Broomes			0	—	0*	—					11*		3	3	2	11*		11.00
C.G. Greenidge			6	59	90	70	23	30	66	17*			4	8	1	361	90	51.57
S.R. Greaves					21	2	7	0					2	4	—	30	21	7.50
R.O. Estwick					0	2*	8	6			1		3	5	1	17	8	4.25
W.E. Reid							0	3	13*	4*	25	14	3	6	2	59	25	14.75
N.A. Johnson									6		40	56	2	3	—	102	56	34.00
L.N. Reifer									9	0	35	59*	2	4	1	103	59*	34.33
V. Greene									17	—	5	6	2	3	—	28	17	9.33
A.S. Gilkes											52	32	1	2	—	84	52	42.00
M. Innes											28	6	1	2	—	34	28	17.00

	T&T		WI		LI		Jam		Guy		Eng	
Byes	3		3	8	9	8		9	6	4		7
Leg-byes	2		4	3	11	14	8	3	7	4	9	8
Wides	1				2	3						
No-balls	3		4	2	2	2	17	6	10	1	4	8
Total	350		175	338	336	236	224	172	365	62	217	268
Wickets	10		10	5	10	7	10	10	10	4	10	7
Results	W		W		D		W		D		W	
Points	16		16		8		16		8		—	

Catches 15 – T.R.O. Payne (ct 11/st 4)
8 – C.A. Best
6 – C.G. Greenidge
4 – J. Garner, M.D. Marshall and M.C. Worrell (ct 3/st 1)
3 – D.L. Haynes
2 – T.A. Hunte, W.T. Greenidge, N.D. Broomes, L.N. Reifer and subs
1 – R.I.C. Holder, M. Innes and W.E. Reid

BOWLING

	J. Garner	W.T. Greenidge	M.D. Marshall	G.L. Linton	E.L. Reifer	C.A. Best	N.D. Broomes	R.O. Estwick	S.R. Greaves
v. Trinidad and Tobago	15.1-1-55-5	6-0-29-1	16-1-48-3	4-1-12-0	4-0-19-0				
(Bridgetown) 10–12 January	10-4-22-3	8.3-3-25-2	11-3-27-2	10-2-39-3	8-0-31-0	4-0-9-0			
v. Windward Islands	10-3-24-2	5-3-8-1	13-5-39-4	4.4-2-7-2			2-1-6-0		
(Bridgetown) 17–20 January	19-4-82-1	14.1-3-58-2	28-5-85-6	17-1-46-0			11-3-17-0		
v. Leeward Islands	14-4-28-6	12-3-48-2		12.5-3-49-1				8-1-33-1	5-0-25-0
(Nevis) 24–27 January	16-2-40-0	13-2-55-0		7-0-40-0		3-1-4-0	32-6-74-2	20-7-34-0	
v. Jamaica (Bridgetown)	16-1-47-3	5-1-14-1	16-2-35-4					9-2-44-1	
31 January–3 February	23.5-6-42-6		24-4-73-3					7-2-13-0	1-0-2-0
v. Guyana (Essequibo)	8-0-32-2		14-2-39-1	16-2-51-1		12-1-42-0			
6–9 February	9-6-6-0		5-0-7-0	37-6-94-2					
v. England XI	9-4-21-1						1-0-4-0	18-7-38-3	
(Bridgetown) 14–17 March	16-3-31-1					5.3-0-20-1	15-1-44-0	21-1-58-2	
	166-38– 430-30 av. 14.33	63.4-15– 237-9 av. 26.33	127-22– 353-23 av. 15.34	108.3-17– 338-9 av. 37.55	12-0– 50-0 av. —	24.3-2– 75-1 av. 75.00	61-11– 145-2 av. 72.50	83-20– 220-7 av. 31.42	6-0– 27-0 av. —

a M.W. Gatting absent hurt

Larry Gomes hit 168 not out for Trinidad against Guyana at Pointe-a-Pierre. (George Herringshaw)

Thelston Payne hit a hundred for Barbados in the one-day competition and deputised for Dujon as West Indies wicket-keeper in the second Test match. (Patrick Eagar)

some ingenious ways of getting out. Haynes was run out in going for a fourth run and showed such petulance that he later made a public apology. Linton became the first batsman in the West Indies to be given out 'handled ball' when, having played a ball from Collymore down at his feet, he picked the ball up. In their turn Windward Islands fell apart against the Barbadian pace attack, and when Barbados batted again Greenidge, who had just returned from Australia, and Haynes began with a partnership of 143. Haynes hit 13 fours in his 112 and Garner made 56 off 53 balls with 3 sixes and 3 fours. He declared and left the visitors 10 hours in which to make 420. They battled bravely and Sebastien and Charles added 134 for the 5th wicket. The stand was broken when Charles, having survived an lbw appeal, was run out by Best as he lingered out of his ground. Barbados went on to achieve their first victory over Windwards.

Larry Gomes, with 168 in 7½ hours, starred in Trinidad's win over Guyana. The home side recovered from 130 for 9 to dominate the match.

Geddes Grant Harrison Line Trophy

22 January

at Queen's Park Oval, Port of Spain

Jamaica 180 for 9 (O.W. Peters 74)
Trinidad and Tobago 131 (P.V. Simmons 59)

Jamaica (2 pts) won by 49 runs

at Warner Park, Basseterre

Barbados 213 for 8
Leeward Islands 216 for 7

Leeward Islands (2 pts) won by 3 wickets

Holding and S.I. Williams took the individual honours in these matches which meant that Jamaica would play Leeward Islands in the final. In Zone A, Jamaica finished with 4 points, Trinidad and Tobago 2 and Guyana 0. In Zone B, the positions were Leeward Islands 4 points, Barbados 2 and Windward Islands 0.

W.E. Reid	V. Greene	L.N. Reifer	Byes	Leg-byes	Wides	No-balls	Total	Wkts
			7	7	3	13	177	10
			4	3	1		160	10
			6	4		11	94	10
			5	8	3	15	301	10
				6		1	189	10
			2	7		3	256	2
4.2–3–1–1				1		6	142	10
16–2–30–0			17	4		9	181	10
22–2–86–2	21–4–75–2			7		6	332	10
22–7–43–2	21–2–80–2		6	2		7	238	6
8–0–17–1	20–1–72–5	8–0–18–1		1	2	1	171	10
32–8–70–3	27–4–74–2	2–0–8–0		7		4	312	9a
104.2–22–	89–11–	10–0–						
247–9	301–11	26–1						
av. 27.44	av. 27.36	av. 26.00						

Shell Shield

24, 25, 26 and 27 January

at Grove Park, Nevis

Barbados 336 (D.L. Haynes 118, C.G. Greenidge 90, T.R.O. Payne 62) and 226 for 7 dec (C.G. Greenidge 70)
Leeward Islands 189 (R.M. Otto 50, J. Garner 6 for 28) and 256 for 2 (L.L. Lawrence 113, E.E. Lewis 108 not out)

Match drawn
Barbados 8 pts, Leeward Islands 4 pts

at Queen's Park Oval, Port of Spain

Jamaica 191 (C.A. Davidson 67 not out, R. Nanan 4 for 34) and 165 (R. Nana 5 for 52)
Trinidad and Tobago 310 (A.L. Logie 79) and 47 for 0

Trinidad and Tobago won by 10 wickets
Trinidad and Tobago 16 pts, Jamaica 0 pts

at Rose Hall, Berbice

Guyana 502 for 7 dec (T. Mohammed 200 not out, A.F.D. Jackman 83, R.A. Harper 72, C.B. Lambert 61)

Guyana 1986
First Class Matches

BATTING

	v. Jamaica (Kingston) 9–11 January 1986	v. Trinidad (Pointe-à-Pierre) 17–20 January 1986	v. Windward Islands (Berbice) 24–27 January 1986	v. Barbados (Essequibo) 6–9 February 1986	v. Leeward Islands (Bourda) 12–15 February 1986		M	Inns	NOs	Runs	HS	Av
A.A. Lyght	0 9	19 19	20	—			3	5	—	67	20	13.40
C.B. Lambert	0 24	33 3	61	— 47 57	0 48		5	9	—	273	61	30.33
T. Mohammed	1 57	0 4	200*	— 33 6	0 31		5	9	1	332	200*	41.50
A.F.D. Jackman	1 11	25 16	83	— 18 14	67 35		5	9	—	270	83	30.00
R. Seeram	0 7			— 0 6			2	4	—	13	7	3.25
D.I. Kallicharran	0 5	0 15	3	— 5 32*	29 14		5	9	1	103	32*	12.87
R.A. Harper	18 65	7 8	72	— 20 23	32 17*		5	9	1	262	72	32.75
M.R. Pydanna	0 1	9 5		—			2	4	—	15	9	3.75
C.G. Butts	6 0	22 33	17*	— 16 —	1 0		5	8	1	95	33	13.57
R.F. Joseph	4 3			—			1	2	—	7	4	3.50
L.A. Lambert	0* 5*	10 2	—	— 15 —			4	5	2	32	15	10.66
K. Edwards		3 16	3	—			2	3	—	22	16	7.33
C.V. Solomon		13* 1*		— 1 —	1* 1		4	5	3	17	13*	8.50
M.A. Harper			37	— 149* 64*	42 106		3	5	2	398	149*	132.66
S. Bamfield				15 21	13 83		2	4	—	132	83	33.00
F. Sattaur					17 0		1	2	—	17	17	8.50
M. Grenville					7 6*		1	2	1	13	7	13.00
Byes	4 7	10		6								
Leg-byes	1	6 3	5	7 2	4 4							
Wides			1										
No-balls	7 7	2 3		6 7	5 7							
Total	41 202	149 138	502	332 238	218 352							
Wickets	10 10	10 10	7	10 6	10 9							
Results	L	L	W	D	D							
Points	0	0	16	4	4							

Catches 10 – R.A. Harper
9 – C.B. Lambert
6 – D.I. Kallicharran
5 – S. Bamfield

3 – M.A. Harper, T. Mohammed and M.R. Pydanna (ct 2/st 1)
2 – A.F.D. Jackman, L.A. Lambert, C.G. Butts, C.V. Solomon, A.A. Lyght and subs
1 – R. Seeram, K. Edwards, F. Sattaur and M. Grenville

BOWLING

	R.F. Joseph	L.A. Lambert	R.A. Harper	C.G. Butts	D.I. Kallicharran	C.V. Solomon	C.B. Lambert	M.A. Harper	M. Grenville
v. Jamaica (Kingston) 9–11 January	7-1-21-0 3-0-11-0	7-1-26-1 3-1-7-0	15-3-37-4 21-6-29-4	10-3-25-2 12-2-23-1	4.5-1-12-3 14.2-1-35-2				
v. Trinidad and Tobago (Pointe-à-Pierre) 17–20 January		9.3-0-49-1 15-4-43-1	26.5-3-64-4	20-6-43-5 43-9-102-2	16-0-68-3 18-1-63-0	4-0-13-1 20-4-80-3	1-0-3-0		
v. Windward Islands (Berbice) 24–27 January		4-0-21-0 5-0-35-1	20-5-42-3 17-2-48-1	32.3-11-57-6 17.1-4-48-3	14-2-43-1 27-0-84-2	4-0-18-0 17-1-79-3			
v. Barbados (Essequibo) 6–9 February		3-0-14-0	42-13-104-3 5-1-11-0	47.4-11-102-3 13-5-17-1	17-5-43-0 10-4-15-3	24-6-78-4 4-1-9-0		4-1-11-0 2-1-2-0	
v. Leeward Islands (Bourda) 12–15 February			33-7-75-3	39-12-98-5	28.3-7-66-2	9-1-38-0			2-0-19-0
	10-1– 32-1 —	46.3-6– 195-4 av. 48.75	179.5-40– 410-22 av. 18.63	234.2-63– 515-28 av. 18.39	149.4-21– 429-16 av. 26.81	82-13– 315-11 av. 28.63	1-0– 3-0 —	6-2– 13-0 —	

Windward Islands 183 (L.D. John 70, C.G. Butts 6 for 57) and 303 (J.D. Charles 114)

Guyana won by an innings and 16 runs
Guyana 16 pts, Windward Islands 0 pts

Venturing from their own island for the first time, Jamaica slumped badly. Put in to bat, they lost 5 wickets for 48 runs, and only Davidson, batting for over 3 hours and hitting 9 fours, saved them from total rout by a varied attack. Gus Logie also batted for 3 hours to reach his highest score of the season, and he and Gabriel, who played with restraint, put on an invaluable 99 for the 3rd Trinidad wicket. The lower order brought Trinidad a lead of 119, and when Jamaica ended the third day on 126 for 7 the match was virtually decided. Once more it was skipper Nanan who bowled outstandingly for Trinidad. In his 14th season in the Shield he was to take 30 wickets and move past Andy Roberts' record of 180 wickets in the competition. Holding showed anger when given out caught behind on the third day and later, in a television interview, apologised for his outburst.

Barbados moved clear at the top of the table by virtue of their first innings lead in the drawn match with Leeward Islands. Haynes and Greenidge began the match with a stand of 166, Haynes reaching his second century in successive innings and batting for $5\frac{1}{2}$ hours during which time he hit 16 fours. Garner returned his best figures in the Shell Shield, but Leewards just avoided the follow-on. Garner declared 40 minutes before the close of the third day setting the home side 384 to win. They lost Richardson at 43, but Lawrence and Lewis nearly brought about a famous victory with a 2nd wicket stand of 243, a Leeward Islands record. The home side just failed to maintain the necessary momentum.

Timur Mohammed reached the highest score of his career in Berbice. It was the only double century of the season and provided the backbone of the massive Guyana total. The contrasting off-spin of Butts and Harper gave Guyana the match in spite of a fine maiden century by Charles. Butts tended to flight the ball more than Harper who bowled with a flatter trajectory. Kallicharran offered variety with his leg-spin. Shortly before this match Milton Pydanna announced his retirement. He had kept wicket for Guyana since 1971 and his 54 matches were the most played by an individual in the competition.

31 January, 1, 2 and 3 February

at Kensington Oval, Bridgetown

Barbados 224 (C.A. Best 78, M.A. Holding 4 for 38) and 172 (D.L. Haynes 65, A.G. Daley 4 for 46)
Jamaica 142 (P.J. Dujon 69, M.D. Marshall 4 for 35) and 181 (P.J. Dujon 58 not out, J. Garner 6 for 42)

Barbados won by 73 runs
Barbados 16 pts, Jamaica 0 pts

at Warner Park, Basseterre

Leeward Islands 503 for 8 dec (R.M. Otto 165, I.V.A. Richards 132, N.C. Guishard 51 not out, R.B. Richardson 50)
Trinidad and Tobago 302 (A. Rajah 69, A.H. Gray 54 not out, P.V. Simmons 52) and 200 (P.V. Simmons 65, I.V.A. Richards 4 for 80, N.C. Guishard 5 for 84)

Leeward Islands won by an innings and 1 run
Leeward Islands 16 pts, Trinidad and Tobago 0 pts

In a match dominated by bowlers, Barbados beat Jamaica by 73 runs and so won the Shell Shield for the 12th time. Sent in to bat, Barbados built their innings around Best's 78. He began with a six, but thereafter batted with great restraint. Barbados were aided by some poor fielding, the Jamaicans putting down seven catches. Only Dujon, who batted for 168 minutes, withstood the Barbadian attack adequately and the home side took a lead of 82. Haynes batted patiently as the home side's middle order again displayed weaknesses, and Jamaica were asked to make 255 to win. They began the last day on 13 for 0, but Garner had Peters lbw and Powell caught at slip and when Neita was run out Jamaica were 58 for 3. Dujon batted doggedly, but the last 6 wickets fell for 28 runs.

Leewards outplayed Trinidad in St Kitts to gain the first outright victory in matches between the two sides. Nanan

Patrick Patterson wears an anguished look as Haynes edges him through the slips, Barbados v. Jamaica. (Adrian Murrell)

	Byes	Leg-byes	Wides	No-balls	Total	Wkts
	5			9	126	10
	5	8		5	118	7
	4	3		7	180	10
	8	8	2	5	371	10
	1	1	1	8	183	10
	7	2	3	15	303	10
	6	7		10	365	10
	4	4		1	62	4
	4	5		2	305	10

elected to bowl first, but his decision was wrecked when Gray had both openers dropped in his first over. Even so, the home side was 141 for 4 before Otto and Richards added a record 237 for the 5th wicket. Richards played his first significant innings of the season, hitting a six and 16 fours off 146 balls. Otto reached his highest score in first-class cricket, hitting 2 sixes and 14 fours. Trinidad were handicapped in that Gray could bowl only 12 overs because of a back injury. The visitors batted weakly against the off-spin of Richards and Guishard who bowled 138 overs and took 14 wickets between them.

6, 7, 8 and 9 February

at Arnos Vale, St Vincent

Jamaica 98 (S.J. Hinds 6 for 19) and 200 (S.J. Hinds 4 for 40)
Windward Islands 204 (L.C. Sebastien 52, C.A. Walsh 7 for 75) and 95 for 2

Jamaica 1986
First Class Matches

BATTING	v. Guyana (Kingston) 9–11 January 1986		v. Leeward Islands (Kingston) 16–18 January 1986		v. Trinidad (Port of Spain) 24–27 January 1986		v. Barbados (Bridgetown) 31 Jan.–3 Feb. 1986		v. Windward Islands (St Vincent) 6–8 February 1986		v. England XI (Kingston) 13–16 February 1986		M	Inns	NOs	Runs	HS	Av
W.W. Lewis	23	7	13	6*	5	1			15	0			4	8	1	70	23	10.00
F.A. Cunningham	8	20	17	0*			24	34	14	24	14	7	5	10	1	162	34	18.00
G. Powell	7	13	23	—	16	27	0	9	20	40	36	19	6	11	—	210	40	19.09
M.C. Neita	2	5	33	—	6	38	2	12	10	17	66	40	6	11	—	231	66	21.00
G.A. Heron	12	11	12	—			1	4					3	5	—	40	12	8.00
P.J. Dujon	13	0	75	—	9	22	69	58*	2	4	39	31	6	11	1	322	75	32.20
C.A. Davidson	12*	22*	1	—	67*	19	0	20	5	10	30	40	6	11	3	226	67*	28.25
A.G. Daley	0	17*	2	—	21	6	8	3	2	47	14	1	6	11	1	121	47	12.10
M.A. Holding	34	5	21	—	31	3	5	0	3	12			6	9	—	114	34	12.66
C.A. Walsh	1	—	0	—	4	3*	19	4	6	14	0*	0*	6	10	3	51	19	7.28
B.P. Patterson	0	—	2*	—	0	0	1*	2	0*	3*			5	8	4	8	3*	2.00
O.W. Peters					5	5	6	5					2	4	—	21	6	5.25
M.A. Tucker					16	29			14	9			2	4	—	68	29	17.00
L. Cunningham											0	9	1	2	—	9	9	4.50
J.C. Adams									13	3			1	2	—	16	13	8.00
D.C. Dixon											1	6	1	2	—	7	6	3.50
Byes	5	5	2	4	4	8		17		7	2	5						
Leg-byes		8	10		3	4	1	4	6	8	3	2						
Wides			3															
No-balls	9	5	17		4		6	9	1	5	4	5						
Total	126	118	230	10	191	165	142	181	98	200	222	168						
Wickets	10	7	10	1	10	10	10	10	10	10	9†	9						
Result	W		W		L		L		L									
Points	16		16		0		0		0		—							

Catches
17 – P. J. Dujon
7 – M.A. Holding
6 – G. Powell, A.G. Daley and C.A. Davidson
5 – F.A. Cunningham and M.C. Neita
4 – C.A. Walsh and G.A. Heron
3 – B.P. Patterson
2 – W.W. Lewis
1 – J.C. Adams and D.C. Dixon

BOWLING	C.A. Walsh	B.P. Patterson	M.A. Holding	A.G. Daley	M.A. Tucker	D.C. Dixon	J.C. Adams	C.A. Davidson	M.C. Neita
v. Guyana (Kingston)	8–1–13–3	7.1–2–24–7							
9–11 January	19.3–2–92–8	15–3–63–0	8–2–20–2	5–0–19–0					
v. Leeward Islands	12–4–23–4	9–4–18–3	5–0–21–1	2.2–0–9–1					
(Kingston) 16–18 January	8–1–42–1	9.3–2–37–4	8–0–52–4	4–0–24–1					
v. Trinidad and Tobago	22–4–70–2	29–4–82–3	21–6–55–1	13–3–33–2	20–4–64–2				
(Port of Spain) 24–27 January		4–0–15–0	3–1–15–0	1–0–2–0	2–1–15–0				
v. Barbados (Bridgetown)	23–3–74–2	15–3–45–1	12–2–38–4	19–3–59–3					
31 January–3 February	12–4–38–1	17–4–37–2	15–4–39–3	22–10–46–4					
v. Windward Islands	23.3–3–75–7	18–4–48–2	5–2–11–0	12–2–23–1			9–3–34–0		
(St Vincent) 6–8 February	10–0–34–1	5–0–18–0		3–0–18–0			7–1–25–1		
v. England XI	33–9–84–3		13.3–1–44–2	34.2–6–119–3		6–0–28–0	14–2–50–2	5–0–15–0	
(Kingston) 13–16 February	12–2–32–2		16–1–37–1	16–1–37–1		13–1–44–0	8–4–13–0	3–1–5–0	11–2–29–2
	183–33	128.4–26–	80.3–18–	131.4–25–	38–9–	19–1–	22–6–	8–1–	11–2–
	577–34	387–22	295–17	389–16	138–3	72–0	63–2	20–0	29–2
	av. 16.97	av. 17.59	av. 17.35	av. 24.31	av. 46.00	—	av. 31.50	—	av. 14.50

a A.L. Kelly retired hurt

Windward Islands won by 8 wickets
Windward Islands 16 pts, Jamaica 0 pts

at Hampton Court, Essequibo

Guyana 332 (M.A. Harper 149 not out) and 238 for 6 dec. (M.A. Harper 64 not out, C.B. Lambert 57)
Barbados 365 (C.A. Best 111, C.G. Greenidge 66, T.R.O. Payne 62, C.V. Solomon 4 for 78) and 62 for 4

Match drawn

Barbados 8 pts, Guyana 4 pts

Celebrating their win over England a few days earlier, Windward Islands asked Jamaica to bat first on a slow pitch which offered both turn and uneven bounce and bowled them out for 98 with Hinds returning career best figures with his off-breaks. A determined half century by Sebastiẹn,

Barbados win the Shell Shield. Joel Garner looks proud in his first year as captain. (Adrian Murrell)

batting at number 5, helped Windwards to a first innings lead of 106 in spite of Courtenay Walsh producing another splendid performance. The young fast bowler could consider himself desperately unlucky not to have been chosen ahead of team-mate Patterson for a place in the Test side. Jamaica again faltered when they batted a second time and slipped to their fourth Shield defeat at Arnos Vale.

Mark Harper scored 213 runs at Essequibo without being dismissed, but Barbados still took first innings points and generally had the better of a relaxed game. He hit his first century in the Shield, having made his debut in 1976. He hit 5 sixes and 12 fours. Carlisle Best became the only batsman to reach 500 runs in the Shield during the season.

12, 13, 14 and 15 February

at Bourda

Guyana 218 (A.F.D. Jackman 67) and 352 for 9 (M.A. Harper 106, S. Bamfield 83, E. Proctor 4 for 46)
Leeward Islands 305 (L.L. Lawrence 86, R.B. Richardson 55, C.G. Butts 5 for 98)

Match drawn
Leeward Islands 8 pts, Guyana 4 pts

13, 14, 15 and 16 February

at Windsor Park, Rosseau

Windward Islands 207 (I. Cadette 84, R. Nanan 5 for 60, A.H. Gray 5 for 72) and 133 (R. Nanan 4 for 21, G. Mahabir 4 for 42)
Trinidad and Tobago 182 (R. Nanan 61, W. Thomas 4 for 63) and 159 for 6 (D. Williams 50)

Trinidad and Tobago won by 4 wickets
Trinidad and Tobago 16 pts, Windward Islands 5 pts

Byes	Leg-byes	Wides	No-balls	Total	Wkts
4			7	41	10
7	1		7	202	10
2	4		2	77	9a
4	3		7	162	10
	6		14	310	10
			2	47	0
	8		17	224	10
9	3		6	172	10
12	1		9	204	10
			3	95	2
24	7		27	371	10
14	3	1	3	177	5

An opening stand of 138 between Lawrence and Richardson set Leewards towards a first innings lead after Guyana had batted indifferently. Mark Harper hit 2 sixes and 10 fours in his second Shield century and veteran Stephen Bamfield, recalled as wicket-keeper, hit his highest Shield score in a stand of 166 for the 6th wicket. The stand was broken by Proctor, the first Anguillan to play Shell Shield cricket, who took 5 for 85 in his debut match.

The match at Rosseau was a personal triumph for Trinidad skipper Ranjie Nanan. He returned match figures of 9 for 81 which took him to 185 wickets, a new Shield record, and, going in at 64 for 6, hit 61 to restore his side's chances of victory. Mohammed and Williams, a six and 4 fours, gave Trinidad victory on the last day after 4 wickets had fallen for 57. Windwards' defeat was a disappointment to them, but with the retirement of Norbert Phillip and the absence of

Leeward Islands 1986
First Class Matches

BATTING	v. Windward Islands (Castries) 10–13 January 1986	v. Jamaica (Kingston) 16–18 January 1986	v. Barbados (Nevis) 24–27 January 1986	v. Trinidad and Tobago (Basseterre) 31 Jan–3 Feb. 1986	v. England XI (Antigua) 7–10 February 1986	v. Guyana (Bourda) 12–15 February 1986	M	Inns	NOs	Runs	HS	Av
A.L. Kelly	8*	2		24 —	12 16		3	5	1	62	24	15.50
R.B. Richardson	5	1	10	21 50	19 27	55	5	8	—	188	55	23.50
E.E. Lewis	3	30	12	108* 28	6 36	12	5	8	1	235	108*	33.57
R.M. Otto	0	22	50	2º 165	55 92	10	5	8	1	396	165	56.57
I.V.A. Richards	2	5	16	— 132	32		4	5	—	187	132	37.40
S.I. Williams	0	16	45		42 —		3	4	—	103	45	25.75
E.A.E. Baptiste	13	58					1	2	—	71	58	35.50
N.C. Guishard	2	0	1	51* —	54 17	8	5	7	1	133	54	22.16
T.A. Merrick	1	6		0 —			2	3	—	7	6	2.33
W.K.R. Benjamin	14	0	21	— 10*	30 5	16	5	7	1	96	30	16.00
G.J.F. Ferris	21*	8*	8*	— —	2* 11*		4	5	5	50	21*	—
L.L. Lawrence			10	113 19	6 35	86	4	6	—	269	113	44.83
K. Arthurton		9	—		11 13		2	3	—	33	13	11.00
E.T. Willett			0	—			1	1	—	0	0	0.00
M.C.V. Simon				8	16 0	31	4	4	—	45	31	11.25
J.D. Thompson					3 1		1	2	—	4	3	2.00
E.J. Proctor						2 —	1	1	—	2	2	2.00
C. Ambrose						0* —	1	1	1	0	0*	—
Byes		2	4	2 1	4 9	4						
Leg-byes	4	3	6	7 9	8 7	5						
Wides				2	1							
No-balls	2	7	1	3 4	10 18	2						
Total	77	162	189	256 503	236 288	305						
Wickets	9†	10	10	2 8	10 10	10						
Results	Ab.	L	D	W	D	D						
Points	4	0	4	16	—	8						

Catches 11 – M.C.V. Simon (ct 10/st 1) 3 – L.L. Lawrence and N.C. Guishard
5 – R.M. Otto 2 – A.L. Kelly, R.B. Richardson and W.K.R. Benjamin
4 – S.I. Williams and I.V.A. Richards 1 – E.T. Willett, K. Arthurton and E.E. Lewis

† A.L. Kelly retired hurt

BOWLING	T.A. Merrick	W.K.R. Benjamin	E.A.E. Baptiste	G.J.F. Ferris	N.C. Guishard	I.V.A. Richards	E.T. Willett	J.D. Thompson	R.M. Otto
v. Windward Islands (Castries) 10–13 January									
v. Jamaica (Kingston) 16–18 January	16–1–64–2	16.4–5–47–5 0.5–0–6–0	13–4–24–1	8–1–17–0	20–7–42–1	13–2–24–0			
v. Barbados (Nevis) 24–27 January		24.5–6–59–3 17–2–40–1		24–3–64–3 12–5–30–1	36–10–78–1 17.3–4–36–2	10–3–24–0	49–20–91–2 17–5–48–1		
v. Trinidad and Tobago (Basseterre) 31 Jan–3 Feb	12–0–67–3 4–1–16–0	22–5–72–1 1–1–0–1		12–1–40–1 4–0–16–0	38.5–11–75–2 38–15–84–5	25–8–40–3 37–7–80–4			
v. England XI (Antigua) 7–10 February		30.1–11–60–1 17–2–37–3		31–5–91–4	48–7–124–2	30–6–60–0		38–6–93–3	5–1–16–0
v. Guyana (Bourda) 12–15 February		16–3–39–3 13–3–40–2			27–7–55–3 37–7–119–1	1–0–1–0 5–2–7–0			20–2–46–0
	32–2– 147–5 av. 29.40	158.3–38– 400–20 av. 20.00	13–4– 24–1 av. 24.00	91–15– 258–9 av. 28.66	262.2–68– 613–17 av. 36.05	121–28– 236–7 av. 33.71	66–25– 139–3 av. 46.33	38–6– 93–3 av. 31.00	25–3– 62–0 av. —

a E.E. Lewis 3–0–11–0

Winston Davis, who decided to play for Tasmania so denying himself selection for West Indies, they had fared better during the season than they had expected at the outset.

The England party, West Indies, 1986.
Back row, *left to right* – Robinson, Smith, Taylor, Thomas, Edmonds, Ellison, Foster, Downton, French.
Front row, *left to right* – Gooch, Botham, Gatting, Gower (captain), Lamb, Willey and Emburey. (*Adrian Murrell*)

Shell Shield-Final Table

	P	W	L	D	NR	Pts
Barbados (5)	5	3	—	2	—	64
Trinidad and Tobago (1)	5	3	2	—	—	48
Leeward Islands (2)	5	1	1	2	1	32
Jamaica (6)	5	2	3	—	—	32
Windward Islands (4)	5	1	3	—	1	25
Guyana (3)	5	1	2	2	—	24

(1985 positions in brackets)

Geddes Grant Harrison Line Trophy Final

1 March

at Recreation Ground, St John's

Leeward Islands 169 for 8 (I.V.A. Richards 60)
Jamaica 173 for 4 (M.C. Neita 67)

Jamaica won by 6 wickets

The match was reduced to 39 overs. Richards dominated his side's innings although there were some useful lusty blows from Guishard and Benjamin at the close. Neita took the Man of the Match award as Jamaica won with 4.3 overs to spare.

The England party that was selected to tour the West Indies showed two major surprises. David Smith, the Worcestershire, and former Surrey, left-hander, having received much publicity in the press, was chosen for his believed ability to play quick bowling, and Greg Thomas was named as one of the pace bowlers in the side. The selection of Thomas was made on intuition rather than performance, but all Test selectors should be allowed one such gamble. The remainder of the side was fairly predictable although one would have preferred Cowans to Les Taylor, hardly likely to thrive in the West Indies, and Willey and both wicket-keepers could consider themselves a little fortunate to be chosen although French certainly deserved another tour after his yeoman service in India.

For some weeks Gooch hesitated in accepting the TCCB's

R.B. Richardson	C. Ambrose	E.J. Proctor	Byes	Leg-byes	Wides	No-balls	Total	Wkts
								ab
			2	10	3	17	230	10
			4				10	0
			9	11	3	2	336	10
			8	14		2	236	7
			5	3	1	15	302	10
				4	2	2	200	10
3-0-4-0			11	10		8	409	10
17-2-40-5			8	9	1	4	94	8
5-0-19-0	17-1-61-2	12-1-39-1		4		5	218	10
	21-4-79-2	13-1-46-4		4		7	352	9a
25-2–	38-5–	25-2–						
63-5	140-4	85-5						
av. 12.60	*av.* 35.00	*av.* 17.00						

invitation. He seemed angry at reaction to him in the West Indies where he was still seen as the leading protagonist in the South African venture and therefore a supporter of apartheid. Gooch had done nothing to improve the situation by the publication of a 'ghosted' book which had in no way explained or justified his actions. Where there should have been silence, sense and reason on both sides, there was bombast, and politicians in Trinidad and Antigua in particular exploited the situation.

Eventually Gooch was persuaded to join the party and assurances were given. His final acceptance says much for the diplomatic and persuasive powers of the TCCB, but the cloud of uncertainty which had appeared in the days before Christmas was to hover menacingly over the heads of the

Trinidad and Tobago 1986
First Class Matches

BATTING	v. Barbados (Bridgetown) 10–12 January 1986		v. Guyana (Pointe-à-Pierre) 17–20 January 1986		v. Jamaica (Port of Spain) 24–27 January 1986		v. Leeward Islands (Basseterre) 31 Jan.–3 Feb. 1986		v. Windward Islands (Rosseau) 13–16 February 1986		v. England XI (Port of Spain) 28 Feb.–2 Mar. 1986		M	Inns	NOs	Runs	HS	Av
R.S. Gabriel	19	9	45	10	41	35*	2	13	0	20*			5	10	2	194	45	24.25
P.V. Simmons	12	35	0	3			52	65	36	0	24	6	5	10	—	233	65	23.30
A.L. Logie	20	32	38	16	79	—	`5	14	2	0			5	9	—	206	79	22.88
H.A. Gomes	15	11	2	168*			23	6	6	12			5	9	1	243	168*	30.37
P. Moosai	26	20	5	36	25	10*	25	12					4	8	1	159	36	22.71
R. Nanan	6	10	1	1	17	—	0	29*	61	8*	26	—	6	10	2	159	61	19.87
K.C. Williams	39	16	18	29	30	—	0	8					4	7	—	140	39	20.00
D.A. Williams	0	10	37	13	26	—	42	3	2	50	17	—	6	10	—	200	50	20.00
A.H. Gray	4	1	2	15	0*	—	54*	4	4	—	2	—	6	9	2	86	54*	12.28
G.S. Antoine	6*	3*											1	2	2	9	6*	—
G. Mahabir	0	5	17*	0	0	—	6	8	1*	—	2	—	6	9	2	39	17*	5.57
A. Rajah			1	57	49	—	69	30	12	12	12	55*	5	9	1	297	69	37.12
C.R. Rampersad					23	—							1	1	—	23	23	23.00
D.I. Momammed									46	49	6	5	2	4	—	106	49	26.50
D. St Hilaire									2	—			1	1	—	2	2	2.00
M. Richardson											0	1	1	2	—	1	1	0.50
N. Gomez											2	39	1	2	—	41	39	20.50
M. Bedoe											9	—	1	1	—	9	9	9.00
G. Gilman											0*	—	1	1	—	0	0*	—
Byes	7	4	4	8			5		3	1	1	1						
Leg-byes	7	3	3	8	6		3	4	2		5	6						
Wides	3	1		2			1	2			2	1						
No-balls	13		7	5	14	2	15	2	5	7	1	2						
Total	177	160	180	371	310	47	302	200	182	159	109	116						
Wickets	10	10	10	10	10	0	10	10	10	6	10	4						
Results		L		W		W		L		W		D						
Points		0		16		16		0		16		—						

Catches
9 – D.A. Williams (ct 6/st 3)
8 – P.V. Simmons
7 – R.S. Gabriel
4 – A.H. Gray
3 – R. Nanan and G. Mahabir

2 – H.A. Gomes, A.L. Logie,
    C.R. Rampersad, A. Rajah,
    D.I. Mohammed and M. Bedoe
1 – K.C. Williams, P. Moosai and sub

BOWLING	A.H. Gray	K.C. Williams	G.S. Antoine	G.Mahabir	R. Nanan	H.A. Gomes	P.V. Simmons	D. St Hilaire	G. Gilman
v. Barbados (Bridgetown) 10–12 January	20.5–1–75–2	8–1–24–0	17–1–95–1	15–1–69–0	28–3–82–5				
v. Guyana (Pointe-à-Pierre) 17–20 January	17–3–46–2	2–0–6–0		13.1–3–40–3	26–8–51–3				
v. Jamaica (Port of Spain) 24–27 January	12–1–40–2	19–4–48–3		7–1–31–4	10–7–6–1				
	16–2–53–2	10–1–40–3		16–0–50–1	17–3–34–4	3–1–7–0			
	14–3–33–1	6–2–13–1		32–9–55–3	28.5–9–52–5				
v. Leeward Islands (Basseterre) 31 Jan–3 Feb	12–1–53–1	15–0–93–1		42.3–9–138–3	51–9–136–3	3–0–12–0	10–0–61–0		
v. Windward Island (Rosseau) 13–16 February	23–4–72–5			11–4–23–0	29.3–6–60–5	1–0–6–0		3–0–27–0	
	8–0–17–2			12–1–42–4	13.3–2–21–4		6–0–17–0	4–0–24–0	
v. England XI (Port of Spain) 28 February–2 March	24.3–9–50–5			21–6–48–2	28–9–54–3		6–2–18–0		8–1–35–0
	11–2–39–2			2–1–3–0	4–0–12–0				12–1–44–2
	158.2–26–	60–8–	17–1–	171.4–35–	235.5–56–	7–1–	22–2–	7–0–	20–2–
	478–24	224–8	95–1	499–20	508–33	35–0	96–0	51–0	79–2
	av. 19.91	av. 28.00	av. 95.00	av. 24.95	av. 15.39	—	—		av. 39.50

The start of the England tour at Arnos Vale, St Vincent.
(Adrian Murrell)

party throughout the tour which began on a slow pitch at Arnos Vale against a below strength Windward Islands side.

1, 2, 3 and 4 February 1986

at Arnos Vale, St Vincent

England XI 186 (M.W. Gatting 77, D.J. Collymore 5 for 34) and 94 (S.J. Hinds 5 for 21)
Windward Islands 168 (P.H. Edmonds 4 for 38) and 113 for 3

Windward Islands won by 7 wickets

M. Bedoe		Byes	Leg-byes	Wides	No-balls	Total	Wkts
		3	2	1	3	350	10
			6		2	149	10
		10	3		3	138	10
		4	3		4	191	10
		8	4			165	10
		1	9	2	4	503	8
		12	7	1	14	207	10
		8	4		6	133	10
5–0–19–0		5		1	1	229	10
				3	3	101	4
5–0–							
19–0							
—							

Play began half an hour late because of overnight rain. Robinson played on and Smith was bowled behind his legs so that, at lunch, England were 38 for 2. In the afternoon, the tourists were cramped by the off-spin of Hinds and the orthodox left-arm of Etienne and Marshall. Tedious batting was lightened only by Gatting's 77 in under 3 hours. The whole day produced 187 runs in 101 overs as the England innings was brought to a close by Desmond Collymore, left-arm medium pace, with the second new ball.

The pitch gave no encouragement to stroke play, but Windward Islands were aided by an abundance of no-balls from Thomas. Foster was accurate, and Willey and Edmonds exerted a stranglehold on the home batsmen, but the West Indian spinners were to prove more effective than their counterparts.

The English batsmen gave a wretched display. They showed no inclination to attack the spinners, and by the end of the third day, Windward Islands, 77 for 1, were in sight of a victory which was accomplished with little fuss on the last day.

To add to England's woe, Bruce French was bitten by a dog and was unable to play in Antigua.

7, 8, 9 and 10 February 1986

at St John's, Antigua

Leeward Islands 236 (R.M. Otto 55, N.C. Guishard 54) and 288 (R.M. Otto 92, N.A. Foster 4 for 54)
England XI 409 (M.W. Gatting 71, R.T. Robinson 68, A.J. Lamb 64, G.A. Gooch 53, G.J.F. Ferris 4 for 91) and 94 for 8 (R.B. Richardson 5 for 40)

Match drawn

Leeward Islands took the field without Richards, Merrick and Baptiste, and England enjoyed a much better first day in Antigua than they had in St Vincent. Thomas, Ellison and Foster all bowled well so that Leeward Islands were only raised by an 8th wicket stand of 89 between Guishard and Benjamin which was ended when Emburey bowled Benjamin.

England closed the first day at 34 for 0, but Gooch and Robinson, who enjoyed some luck, took the stand to 118 next morning. Except for Gower, who dabbed an off-break from Thompson to slip when he had scored 5, all the English batsmen provided some cheer and when there was a sign of faltering Emburey and Ellison put on 59.

Botham produced a fiery spell, Thomas bowled briskly and aggressively and Foster was again impressive so that England were given every chance of victory by their bowlers. They were left to make 116 in 70 minutes plus 20 overs, a Sunday League afternoon stroll. Leeward Islands were handicapped in that Ferris was unable to bowl, and Richie Richardson opened the attack with his unpretentious, and

Windward Islands 1986
First Class Matches

BATTING

	v. Leeward Islands (Castries) 10–13 January 1986	v. Barbados (Bridgetown) 17–20 January 1986	v. Guyana (Berbice) 24–27 January 1986	v. England XI (St Vincent) 1–4 February 1986	v. Jamaica (St Vincent) 6–8 February 1986	v. Trinidad and Tobago (Rosseau) 13–16 February 1986	M	Inns	NOs	Runs	HS	Av
L.C. Sebastien		6 69	15 29	26 11*	52 —	2 22	5	9	1	232	69	29.00
L.D. John		4 10	70 11	15 22	18 44*	33 44	5	10	1	271	70	30.11
L.A. Lewis		6 24	22 0	3 30	32 —	10 2	5	9	—	129	32	14.33
F.X. Maurice		13 3	0 20				2	4	—	36	20	9.00
J.D. Charles		11 82	1 114	30 24	2 0	0 1	5	10	—	265	114	26.50
S.L. Mahon		4 14		0 12*	24 7*	25 6	4	8	2	92	25	15.33
I. Cadette		5 43	25 15	17 —	18 41	84 5	5	9	—	253	84	28.11
D.J. Collymore		14* 8	7 36	31* —	21 —	3 17	5	9	2	137	36	19.57
J.T. Etienne		7 8	18* 1	4 —	0 —	3 8*	5	8	2	49	18*	8.16
S.J. Hinds		0 6	9 42	1 —	0 —	8* 3	5	8	1	60	42	8.57
S.A.E. Murphy		3 3*	1 7*				2	4	2	14	7*	7.00
T.Z. Kentish			13 1				1	2	—	14	13	7.00
R. Marshall				1 —	9 —	0 2	3	4	—	12	9	3.00
W. Thomas				9 —	6* —	5 5	3	4	1	25	9	8.33
Byes		6 5	1 7	2 6	12	12 8						
Leg-byes		4 8	1 2	4 1		7 4						
Wides		3	1 3			1						
No-balls		11 15	8 15	25 8	9 3	14 6						
Total		94 301	183 303	168 113	204 95	207 133						
Wickets		10 10	10 10	10 3	10 2	10 10						
Results	Ab.	L	L	W	W	L						
Points	4	0	0	—	16	5						

Catches
5 – I. Cadette (ct 4/st 1) and L.A. Lewis
4 – S.J. Hinds, J.D. Charles and R. Marshall
3 – S.A.E. Murphy and J.T. Etienne
2 – W. Thomas, D.J. Collymore, S.L. Mahon and sub
1 – F.X. Maurice, L.D. John and L.C. Sebastien

BOWLING

	D.J. Collymore	S.A.E. Murphy	S.J. Hinds	J.T. Etienne	J.D. Charles	T.Z. Kentish	W. Thomas	R. Marshall
v. Leeward Islands (Castries) 10–13 January								
v. Barbados (Bridgetown) 17–20 January	15-7-36-1	8-0-48-1	10-0-49-0	16.2-8-35-6				
	20-4-59-0	8-0-54-0	29-4-97-2	38-6-114-3	3-1-3-0			
v. Guyana (Berbice) 24–27 January	22-1-75-1	21-2-100-0	34-3-121-3	34-4-118-1	2-0-5-0	24-3-78-0		
v. England XI (St Vincent) 1–4 February	23-4-34-5		22-3-61-2	19-4-37-1			13.5-3-26-1	24-8-26-1
	12-6-17-2		22.5-8-21-5	20-3-37-3			9-2-13-0	
v. Jamaica (St Vincent) 6–8 February	9-0-22-1		12-2-19-6	12-3-24-1			9-0-27-1	
	9-0-27-1		23-9-40-4	19-4-37-1				8-0-17-0
v. Trinidad and Tobago (Rosseau) 13–16 February	12-6-22-1		11-1-46-0	17-2-26-2			24-3-63-4	12.5-4-20-2
	15.5-2-59-3		3-0-13-0	6-2-14-0			15-0-53-3	8-0-19-0
	137.5-30-351-15	37-2-202-1	166.5-30-467-22	181.2-35-445-18	5-1-8-0	24-3-78-0	93.5-11-243-12	52.5-12-82-3
	av 23.40	av 202.00	av 21.22	av 24.72	—	—	av 20.25	av 27.33

RIGHT: *Windward Islands – victors over England. (Adrian Murrell)*

rarely used, seamers. England responded with an horrific batting display, a fusion of panic and ineptitude. Only Robinson reached double figures as the first six batsmen were shot out for 75, Richardson taking his first wickets in first-class cricket.

13, 14, 15 and 16 February 1986

at Sabina Park, Kingston, Jamaica

England XI 371 (M.W. Gatting 80, A.J. Lamb 78) and 177 for 5 dec (A.J. Lamb 60 not out)
Jamaica 222 (M.C. Neita 66) and 168 (P.H. Edmonds 4 for 44)

England XI won by 158 runs

Put in to bat, England made a poor start when Robinson and Gower fell in Holding's opening spell. Robinson was caught in the gully and Gower edged to slip. Their manner of surrender was disturbing.

Gooch was caught behind off Walsh at 56, but Lamb and Gatting raised spirits with a stylish stand of 147. England closed the first day at 329 for 8 and had the better of the second when Taylor captured three wickets and Jamaica were 184 for 5. Jamaica, and West Indies, suffered a blow when Holding retired from the match with a ham-string injury.

There was no batting recovery for Jamaica, but Walsh fought his way back into the West Indies squad with a ferocious spell of bowling during which he accounted for both Gooch and Gower. Lamb again batted well and there were some good shots from Botham who had finished off the Jamaican first innings in a lively manner with some good bowling.

Edmonds spun England to victory on the last day which was encouraging, but the tourists' performance in the field was poor and there was an air of laxity in their play. Other problems pressed upon them. Botham had suffered a groin injury which was to keep him out of the first one-day international, and Gower had seemed completely unable to find form with the bat.

Leeward Islands v. England XI at St John's, Antigua. (Adrian Murrell)

Gooch is ruffled by a bouncer, Jamaica v. England XI. (Adrian Murrell)

	Byes	Leg-byes	Wides	No-balls	Total	Wkts
						ab
	3	4		4	175	10
	8	3	2	2	338	5
		5	1		502	7
	1	1		7	186	10
	4	2	1	4	94	10
		6		1	98	10
	7	8		5	200	10
	3	2		5	182	10
	1			7	159	6

Gooch is spectacularly caught by Dujon, Jamaica v. England XI. (Adrian Murrell)

Gower caught Richards, bowled Patterson 0, first one-day international. (Adrian Murrell)

First One-Day International
WEST INDIES v. ENGLAND

Whatever hopes were raised by the victory over Jamaica were quickly dispelled by the events of the first one-day international. West Indies won the toss and asked England to bat. Thomas and Patterson made their debuts in international cricket while Les Taylor played in his first limited-over international. It was the giant fast bowler Patrick Patterson who dominated the scene.

Within two overs he had made an emphatic entrance in international cricket and established himself as a menace to batsmen in line with Garner, Marshall, Holding, Roberts and the seemingly unending generations of West Indian pace men. Robinson was bowled by a fast, full, straight delivery, and Gower, driving wildly, was caught at first slip. Both batsmen lasted four balls.

It seemed that these disasters to England had been negotiated when Gooch, playing mostly off the back foot, was dropped at slip by Richards who hurt his hand in the process. The score was then 22 and Gooch and Gatting continued to defy the bowling after that, defensively rather than aggressively, but surviving.

The tragedy came for England when the score had reached 47. Gatting attempted to hook a ball from Marshall, seemed undecided in mid-stroke, and was hit full on the bridge of the nose. Gatting was wearing a helmet, but no visor. There had been no overuse of the short pitched ball, and the shot was a legitimate one, as was the delivery. It was a straightforward accident which was to have serious repercussions for England for the remainder of the tour. Gatting was led from the field, and he was later flown back to England for repairs. To add to the misery, the ball which hit him trickled on to the wicket and bowled him.

Gooch was bowled by a splendid delivery, but Lamb and Willey added 62 sensible runs although batsmen could have been excused having no stomach for the fight after the injury to Gatting. Lamb and Willey fell to successive balls. The innings moved peacefully to the end of 46 overs, West Indies having failed by 4 overs to reach the quota expected in 3 hours, 20 minutes. There is, of course, no penalty for slow over-rates in the West Indies.

A target of 146 was hardly likely to worry the West Indian batsmen. Greenidge and Haynes made a positive start before falling in quick succession. Richardson and Gomes then took their side to within 4 runs of victory and then fell at the same score. It meant that England had only been beaten by 6 wickets although, in truth, the gap between the two sides looked far greater.

First Test Match
WEST INDIES v. ENGLAND

Deprived of the batsman who had been far the most impressive in application, technique and temperament, and accorded inadequate practice facilities on a tour of increasingly murmuring hostility from politicians and demonstrators, England entered the first Test match with unease. The victories over India and Australia seemed far distant, and the Indian medium pacers and the Australian bowlers of average county standard were recalled with the nostalgia of blue remembered hills. Certainly the present reality of Patterson, Marshall, Garner and Holding offered darker mountains and threatening storm. David Smith took Gatting's place, the England vice-captain having returned home after his dreadful injury, and Greg Thomas was also called up for his Test debut. The omission of Foster was as

OPPOSITE: *Sabina Park, Kingston, Jamaica. (Adrian Murrell)*

ABOVE: *Gooch bowled Marshall 36, first one-day international. (Adrian Murrell)*

ABOVE: *Gatting plays a ball from Marshall into his face and is out of the tour for several weeks. A grave blow for England. (Adrian Murrell)*

FIRST ONE-DAY INTERNATIONAL – WEST INDIES v. ENGLAND
18 February 1986 at Sabina Park, Kingston, Jamaica

ENGLAND			
G.A. Gooch	b Marshall		36
R.T. Robinson	b Patterson		0
D.I. Gower†	c Richards, b Patterson		0
M.W. Gatting	b Marshall		10
A.J. Lamb	c Greenidge, b Marshall		30
P. Willey	c Richardson, b Marshall		26
P.R. Downton*	lbw, b Garner		8
J.E. Emburey	b Garner		5
N.A. Foster	not out		5
J.G. Thomas	not out		0
L.B. Taylor			
Extras	b 8, lb 2, w 4, nb 11		25
(46 overs)	(for 8 wickets)		145

	O	M	R	W
Garner	10	—	18	2
Patterson	7	—	17	2
Walsh	9	—	42	—
Marshall	10	1	23	4
Harper	10	—	35	—

FALL OF WICKETS
1- 2, 2- 10, 3- 47, 4- 63, 5- 125, 6- 125, 7- 137, 8- 143

WEST INDIES			
C.G. Greenidge	c Downton, b Thomas		45
D.L. Haynes	c Downton, b Foster		35
R.B. Richardson	lbw, b Gooch		32
H.A. Gomes	st Downton, b Willey		19
P.J. Dujon*	not out		3
R.A. Harper	not out		1
I.V.A. Richards†			
M.D. Marshall			
J. Garner			
B.P. Patterson			
C.A. Walsh			
Extras	b 4, lb 2, nb 5		11
(43.5 overs)	(for 4 wickets)		146

	O	M	R	W
Taylor	7	2	17	—
Thomas	8	1	35	1
Foster	10	1	44	1
Emburey	10	3	19	—
Willey	6.5	—	25	1
Gooch	2	2	0	1

FALL OF WICKETS
1- 84, 2- 89, 3- 142, 4- 142

Umpires: D.M. Archer & A. Gaynor

West Indies won by 6 wickets

FIRST TEST MATCH – WEST INDIES v. ENGLAND
21, 22 and 23 February 1986 at Sabina Park, Kingston, Jamaica

ENGLAND

	FIRST INNINGS		SECOND INNINGS	
G.A. Gooch	c Garner, b Marshall	51	b Marshall	0
R.T. Robinson	c Greenidge, b Patterson	6	b Garner	0
D.I. Gower†	lbw, b Holding	16	c Best, b Patterson	9
D.M. Smith	c Dujon, b Patterson	1	(7) c Gomes, b Marshall	0
A.J. Lamb	b Garner	49	c sub (Harper), b Patterson	13
I.T. Botham	c Patterson, b Marshall	15	b Marshall	29
P. Willey	c Dujon, b Holding	0	(4) b Garner	71
P.R. Downton*	c Dujon, b Patterson	2	c Haynes, b Holding	3
R.M. Ellison	c Haynes, b Patterson	9	b Garner	11
P.H. Edmonds	not out	5	lbw, b Patterson	7
J.G. Thomas	b Garner	0	not out	1
Extras	nb 5	5	b 5, nb 3	8
		159		152

	O	M	R	W	O	M	R	W
Marshall	11	1	30	2	11	4	29	3
Garner	14.3	—	58	2	9	2	22	3
Patterson	11	4	30	4	10.5	—	44	3
Holding	7	—	36	2	12	1	52	1
Richards	1	1	0	—				
Richardson	1	—	5	—				

FALL OF WICKETS
1- 32, 2- 52, 3- 54, 4- 83, 5- 120, 6- 127, 7- 138, 8- 142, 9- 158
1- 1, 2- 3, 3- 19, 4- 40, 5- 95, 6- 103, 7- 106, 8- 140, 9- 146

WEST INDIES

	FIRST INNINGS		SECOND INNINGS	
C.G. Greenidge	lbw, b Ellison	58		
D.L. Haynes	c Downton, b Thomas	32	(1) not out	4
J. Garner	c Edmonds, b Botham	24		
R.B. Richardson	lbw, b Botham	7	(2) not out	0
H.A. Gomes	lbw, b Ellison	56		
C.A. Best	lbw, b Willey	35		
I.V.A. Richards†	lbw, b Ellison	23		
P.J. Dujon*	c Gooch, b Thomas	54		
M.D. Marshall	c sub (Emburey), b Ellison	6		
M.A. Holding	lbw, b Ellison	3		
B.P. Patterson	not out	0		
Extras	b 2, lb 4, nb 3	9	nb 1	1
		307	(for no wkt)	5

	O	M	R	W	O	M	R	W
Botham	19	4	67	2				
Thomas	28.5	6	82	2	1	—	4	—
Ellison	33	12	78	5				
Edmonds	21	6	53	—				
Willey	4	—	15	1				
Gooch	2	1	6	—				
Lamb					0.0	—	1	—

FALL OF WICKETS
1- 95, 2- 112, 3- 115, 4- 183, 5- 222, 6- 241, 7- 247, 8- 299, 9- 303

Umpires: D.M. Archer & J.B. Gayle

West Indies won by 10 wickets

cruel as it was incomprehensible. West Indies gave first caps to Carlisle Best, star of the Shell Shield, and to Balfour Patrick Patterson. He was to have a significant influence on the match which, after the first hour, went entirely in favour of the West Indies as England were completely outplayed in every aspect of the game.

Gower won the toss and took the brave, correct action of batting first. The pitch was hard, uneven and with grassy patches. It was well suited to the quicker bowlers of which West Indies had an abundance.

For an hour Gooch and Robinson kept Marshall and Garner at bay. Gooch played very straight and twice hit Garner for 4. It was the advent of Patterson which changed the course of events. Robinson, backing away from a short pitched delivery, guided the ball low to Greenidge's right hand at first slip.

Gower looked discomforted by Patterson's first ball to him, slashed the second over the slips for 6 and repeated the shot to the third ball which went first bounce for 4. He faced ten balls in all before he was leg before to Holding. His innings suggested that England were in a state of shock, and poor Smith, having scored a single off a full toss from Holding, endorsed the feeling as he sparred at a wide delivery, a wretched shot. In the 13th over, England had been 32 for 0. In the 17th, they were 54 for 3.

Gooch had had some fortune against Holding, edging him for 4, but he was generally solid. Lamb improvised bravely, and England lunched at 79 for 3, but in the first over of the afternoon, Gooch lofted a nastily lifting ball into the hands of gully. Botham was sound for a while and then hooked to square leg as Marshall baited the trap.

The rest was dismal and a moroseness settled upon England's cricket which was to be lifted only for fleeting moments in the weeks to come. Lamb alone sold himself dearly. He was bowled by a shooter from Garner. England were all out just before tea. By the close, West Indies had reached 85 without loss although Greenidge had to retire hurt after being hit in the face by a ball from Botham.

Thomas had a fast and encouraging first over in Test cricket, his first ball went off the edge at catchable height through the slips and his second produced a chance to Willey at gully which was missed. Greenidge hit the first three balls of Thomas's second over for boundaries.

West Indies batted scratchily on the second morning, but Gomes nudged and pushed in his usual effective fashion, and Carlisle Best began his Test career by hooking Botham for 6. Best also hooked a thrilling 4 between two long legs that Botham posted and played some generally attractive shots until falling lbw to Willey, the first spinner tried, shortly before tea. By then West Indies were ahead and their lead was growing. Richards was threatening to demolish England when he offered no stroke to Ellison and was lbw.

Ellison gave England hope with 5 wickets which curtailed the West Indies score to manageable proportions. At least it seemed manageable when Gooch and Robinson began England's second innings 148 in arrears, but within a few overs it became gargantuan.

West Indies had closed the second day on 268 for 7, and England captured the last 3 wickets inside an hour on the third morning. By lunch, Gooch and Robinson gone, England had scored 18.

Thereafter, Willey, unorthodox and unattractive, apart, England were torn to shreds. Four of the best fast bowlers that the game has seen bowled at top pace on a wicket which gave them assistance, and they were unfettered by any considerations for Law 42. Nothing should detract from the

Ellison is caught by Haynes off Patterson – congratulations follow. (Adrian Murrell)

Haynes is caught by Downton off Thomas. Genuinely fast, the Welshman made an encouraging start in Test cricket. (Adrian Murrell)

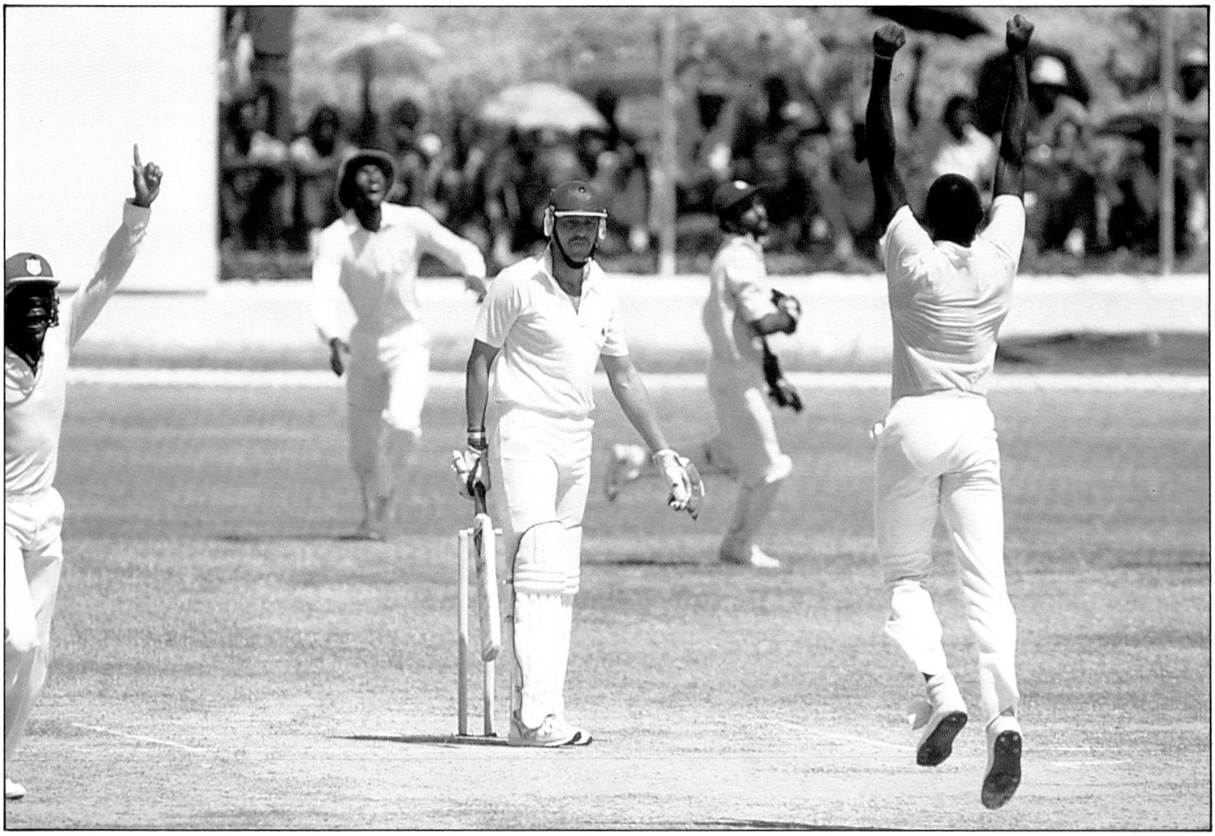

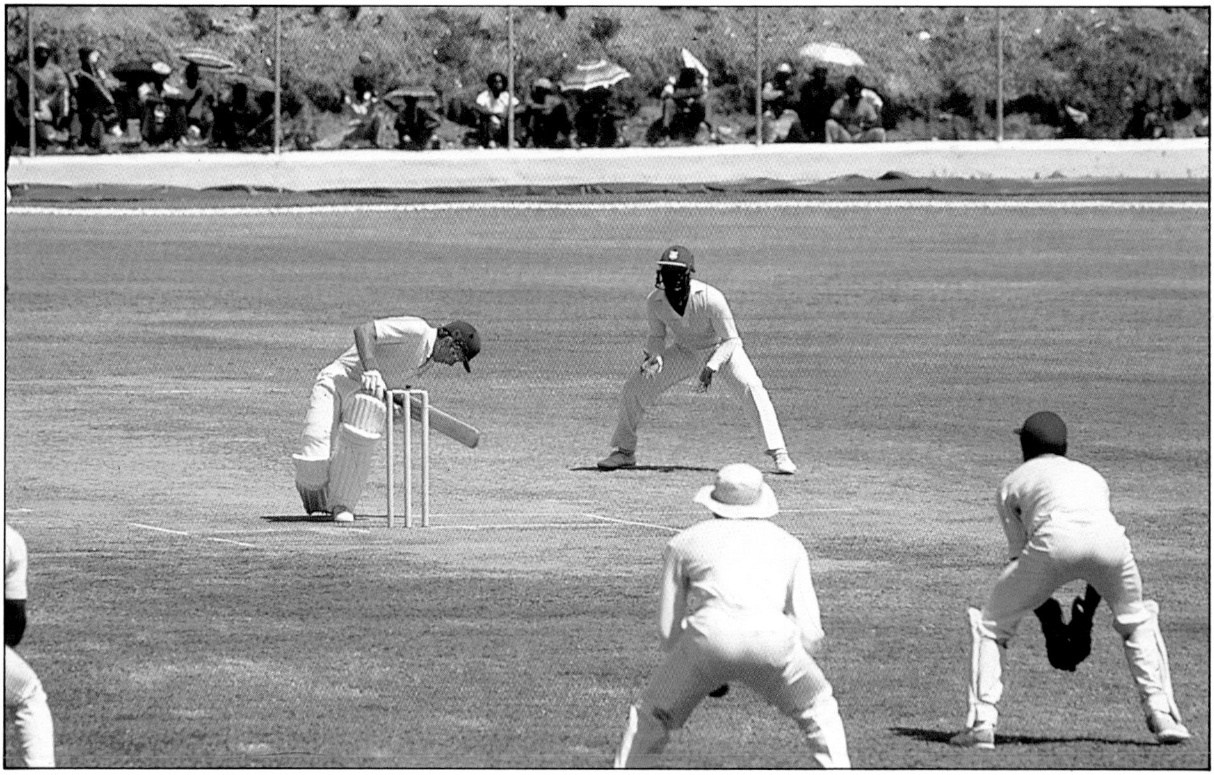

OPPOSITE: *Smith caught Dujon, bowled Patterson 1. Both batsman and bowler were making their Test debuts. (Adrian Murrell)*

West Indian superiority, nor from the greatness of their fast bowlers, but this was cricket without subtlety and if one had only little sympathy for English batsmen of uncertain technique, one had great concern for the future of the game at international level.

28 February, 1 and 2 March 1986

at Queen's Park Oval, Port-of-Spain

England XI 229 (R.T. Robinson 76, A.H. Gray 5 for 50) and 101 for 4 dec

Trinidad and Tobago 109 (N.A. Foster 6 for 54) and 116 for 4 (A. Rajah 55 not out)

Match drawn

After their shattering experience in the first Test the England party moved on to Trinidad in an atmosphere of growing animosity. The threatened boycott of the matches by trade unions and politicians and the organised demonstrations made the England party virtual prisoners in their hotel. Such a situation is hardly suitable preparation for the enjoyment of, and the right attitude to, a game.

Tony Brown, a sensitive, diplomatic and intelligent manager, returned from England where he had flown with Gatting. Brown had suffered a family bereavement, and he brought back with him from England Wilf Slack who had come as replacement for Gatting.

Rain delayed and punctuated the opening day of the match against Trinidad when England, put in to bat, reached

OPPOSITE: *Gower sways under a bouncer. (Adrian Murrell)*

145 for 3. Gooch and Robinson began with a stand of 50, but Slack, possibly weary after his journey, was caught at extra cover for 0 off the 13th ball he received. Gray, out of the reckoning for a Test place, yet as fast as anyone in the England side, took 5 wickets in the innings as the tourists struggled on a difficult wicket.

The home side fared even worse as Foster, ably supported by the accurate Taylor, produced a fine spell and laid waste the middle order.

In the only three-day match of the tour Gower made a challenging declaration, but Rajah's innings denied England victory after Taylor and Foster had made an early breakthrough.

Second One-Day International
WEST INDIES v. ENGLAND

West Indies were without Dujon and Greenidge so that Thelston Payne was brought in as wicket-keeper although he had several superiors in the West Indies, Williams, Worrell and Cadette among them. England gave Slack his first taste of international cricket.

Gower won the toss and asked West Indies to bat. Initially his plan worked well enough. The pitch was good and the bowling was steady, and Best, the emergency opener, scratched for runs. A rain interrupted morning brought the number of overs per side to 37, and by the 28th over, Foster's accuracy, the running out of Best and generally sound cricket had restricted West Indies to 106 for 2.

It was then that Viv Richards joined Richardson in a stand which realised 117 runs off the last 9 overs of the innings. Botham was brought back to bowl when Richards came in and the West Indian captain greeted his friend with a 4 to mid wicket. This was a mere prelude. From 39 balls Richards hit

---

SECOND ONE-DAY INTERNATIONAL – WEST INDIES v. ENGLAND
4 March 1986 at Queen's Park Oval, Port-of-Spain, Trinidad

WEST INDIES					ENGLAND			
D.L. Haynes	b Foster		53		G.A. Gooch	not out		129
C.A. Best	run out		10		I.T. Botham	c Richards, b Garner		8
R.B. Richardson	not out		79		W.N. Slack	c Payne, b Walsh		34
I.V.A. Richards†	c Foster, b Botham		82		A.J. Lamb	b Garner		16
R.A. Harper	not out		0		D.I. Gower†	run out		9
H.A. Gomes					P. Willey	c Richards, b Garner		10
T.R.O. Payne*					D.M. Smith	not out		10
M.D. Marshall					P.R. Downton*			
J. Garner					R.M. Ellison			
C.A. Walsh					J.E. Emburey			
B.P. Patterson					N.A. Foster			
Extras	lb 4, nb 1		5		Extras	b 1, lb 7, nb 6		14
			—					—
(37 overs)	(for 3 wickets)		229		(37 overs)	(for 5 wickets)		230

	O	M	R	W		O	M	R	W
Botham	8	1	59	1	Garner	9	1	62	3
Foster	10	1	42	1	Patterson	6	—	30	—
Ellison	8	—	57	—	Walsh	9	—	49	1
Emburey	8	2	48	—	Marshall	10	1	59	—
Willey	3	—	19	—	Harper	3	—	22	—

FALL OF WICKETS
1- 37, 2- 106, 3- 223

FALL OF WICKETS
1- 9, 2- 98, 3- 143, 4- 170, 5- 187

Umpires: S. Mohammed & C. Cumberbatch

England won by 5 wickets

West Indians swarm to greet their local heroes. (Adrian Murrell)

Gooch in glory – 129 not out in the second one-day international – England's only century of the tour. (Adrian Murrell)

82 runs. It was an innings of such breath-taking dominance as to make even some of the great man's previous feats pale into insignificance. Botham, unwisely, was called upon to bowl the last over, and the over produced 23 runs, including 3 sixes, two of them to Richardson whose magnificent innings was overshadowed by that of the master. Richards was caught at long leg to give Botham some consolation, but, not surprisingly, the England fielding and bowling had wavered considerably during this final, wonderful onslaught.

England took up the challenge of scoring at 6.2 runs an over against the West Indian pace men by sending in Botham to open the innings with Gooch. It could well have worked as a gambit, but Richards held a juggling catch above his head at mid-on off a full blooded stroke. Slack joined Gooch who began to bat with great authority, and they added 89 in 17 overs, a foundation which gave hope that the improbable could be achieved. Seventeen of the runs came from Harper's first over, but it was Gooch's ability to produce exciting scoring strokes off the quicker bowlers, especially Garner, which brought visions of glory.

Slack was out when he attempted a big swing at Walsh, but he had done enough to threaten Robinson's Test place. Lamb was bowled by Garner in the 27th over when the score was 143 so that the task which faced Gooch, and England, was still formidable.

The Essex opener held centre stage. He had driven Walsh for a straight six and treated all bowlers with the disdain that comes of majesty. Marshall was forced to operate with a man on the long off boundary, but Gower sacrificed himself in a mix up, Willey followed soon after and 50 were needed off 5 overs, an enormous task against bowling of quality.

Smith gave sane support and with 4 overs left, 38 were needed. Smith hit Patterson for 4 over long off, and the target for the last two overs was 18 runs. It was vital that Gooch stayed until the end, for it was hardly likely that Downton and the remaining batsmen could achieve this run rate. He had some luck when he edged Marshall for 4, but the last over was reached with 9 runs wanted. Patterson was the bowler.

The first two balls produced singles and the third ball Gooch pulled through mid-wicket for the all important boundary. He took a single off the fourth ball, and he and Smith held a mid wicket conference. Their tactics had been decided. Smith was beaten by a widish delivery from Patterson, but the batsmen scampered through for a single as the ball went through to the wicket-keeper. Gooch aimed a drive at the last ball, but the ball squirted off his pad. The batsmen ran and the ball whistled past the stumps at the bowler's end just as Gooch made his ground to give England their first ever victory in a limited-over international in the West Indies.

Gooch's match-winning innings of 129 was made off 126 balls. He hit 17 fours as well as the six off Walsh. He was named Man of this memorable Match, and England at last had something at which to cheer.

Second Test Match
WEST INDIES *v.* ENGLAND

With Robinson still unfit, England gave a first Test cap to Wilf Slack. Smith, handicapped by sunstroke in the first Test, was omitted so that Emburey could be brought in. Payne, winning his first Test cap, and Walsh replaced the injured Dujon and Holding in the West Indies side.

Richards won the toss and asked England to bat. England would have almost certainly elected to bat first had they won the toss so Richards's decision was based on a desire to put England under pressure rather than any devil to be found in the wicket.

England's troubles began with the second ball of the match when Gooch was hit on the shoulder by a bouncer. He jabbed the next ball for 2 and was well caught at third slip off a tentative shot fourth ball. Within an hour England were 30 for 3. A bright ray of sun for the visitors shone in the hour before lunch when, in 9 overs, Gower and Lamb scored 78 runs. It was to be the only ray of the day for England. These two batsmen, who coped admirably with some fine bowling, were the only two to reach double figures as England succumbed miserably. The England innings, allowing for brief stoppages for showers, had lasted just four hours as it had done in Jamaica.

The day ended with West Indies 67 for the loss of Greenidge, well caught at slip, but not before he had savaged Botham who conceded 39 runs in 5 overs as he unwisely persisted in giving Greenidge practice in hooking. Botham's five inept overs were to hang like an albatross around his neck for the rest of the match and after, as the criticisms of the side began to mount.

Haynes and Richardson were slow into their stride on the second morning, but once they found their touch England suffered. Richardson began to dominate as soon as he had blunted the early threat posed by Thomas and Ellison. He reached 50 off 60 balls with 11 fours. When Botham joined the attack Haynes was soon accelerating. The great all-rounder trundled in, fireless, and his lack of zest seemed symptomatic of much that was wrong with England.

When Edmonds bowled he turned the ball appreciably, but Gower failed to note the sign and at lunch Richardson was 75 not out. In the early afternoon he raced to his hundred, hitting Thomas for successive fours and hooking the next ball for six to move from 84 to 98 in three deliveries.

At 200 for 1, Gower bowled both spinners in conjunction for the first time. The move brought success as Richardson was caught sweeping. Haynes, testing the patience of the crowd, was stumped when he overbalanced, but Downton missed a straight-forward stumping which would have accounted for Best, and the West Indies middle order took their side to a position of total command. Richards hit 34 off 22 balls before falling to a splendid catch at slip off Edmonds. Emburey and Edmonds served England well, but West Indies closed the day at 347 for 8, a lead of 171 and three days remaining.

Marshall hit cleanly to extend the West Indies lead to 223 on the third morning, and England were soon in trouble. In

ABOVE: *'I am monarch of all I survey' – Viv Richards at home. (Adrian Murrell)*

ABOVE: *Gooch is caught in the slips by Carlisle Best. (Adrian Murrell)*

RIGHT: *Slack is run out for 0. (Adrian Murrell)*

Peter Willey is bowled by Marshall. (Adrian Murrell)

the third over of their innings Slack wanted a silly run. Gooch sent him back and he just failed to make his ground.

Earlier events suggested that this would herald an English surrender, but Gower played some enterprising shots and Gooch assumed the role of a rock. They added 80 before Walsh moved a ball back at Gower and hit his off stump. Walsh, who bowled a magnificently hostile spell, also accounted for Gooch just as the England opener was looking

unmovable. Walsh moved a ball into him sharply and had him lbw.

Willey and Lamb combined in a rugged stand, and in spite of Walsh's fine bowling, West Indies, not aided by some sloppy wicket-keeping, were being kept at bay. When bad light ended play early England were 168 for 3 and hopeful.

The hope was maintained as it rained throughout the rest day. It began to evaporate when the sun shone on the fourth day's play. The Lamb/Willey stand continued doggedly, but both fell to deliveries which kept low and Botham was caught behind, well, off Marshall's away swinger so that the last three recognised batsmen were out in the space of 4 overs.

Downton became Malcolm Marshall's 200th Test victim, and there seemed no sting in England's tail until Ellison and Thomas came together at 174 for 9 and proceeded to play with a resource and determination that must have shamed some of their colleagues. They added 72 runs, full of fight and energy, and West Indies were left to make 93 to win. It was an easy task, but at least England had made the match last into the fifth day.

Greenidge fell to Edmonds at 72, and the last day began with West Indies needing another 17. Emburey dismissed Richardson and Gomes in quick succession, but by then it was already too late. Indeed, it was four days too late, for the game had been lost on Friday afternoon.

SECOND TEST MATCH – WEST INDIES v. ENGLAND
7, 8, 9, 11 and 12 March 1986 at Queen's Park Oval, Port-of-Spain, Trinidad

ENGLAND

	FIRST INNINGS		SECOND INNINGS	
G.A. Gooch	c Best, b Marshall	2	lbw, b Walsh	43
W.N. Slack	c Payne, b Marshall	2	run out	0
D.I. Gower†	lbw, b Garner	66	b Walsh	47
P. Willey	c Payne, b Patterson	5	b Marshall	26
A.J. Lamb	c Marshall, b Garner	62	lbw, b Walsh	40
I.T. Botham	c Richardson, b Marshall	2	c Payne, b Walsh	1
J.E. Emburey	c Payne, b Garner	0	c Best, b Walsh	14
P.R. Downton*	c Marshall, b Walsh	8	lbw, b Marshall	5
R.M. Ellison	lbw, b Marshall	4	lbw, b Marshall	36
P.H. Edmonds	not out	3	c Payne, b Garner	13
J.G. Thomas	b Patterson	4	not out	31
Extras	lb 4, nb 14	18	b 20, lb 11, w 1, nb 27	59
		176		**315**

WEST INDIES

	FIRST INNINGS		SECOND INNINGS	
C.G. Greenidge	c Lamb, b Thomas	37	c Lamb, b Edmonds	45
D.L. Haynes	st Downton, b Emburey	67	not out	39
R.B. Richardson	c Downton, b Emburey	102	c Gooch, b Emburey	9
H.A. Gomes	st Downton, b Emburey	30	b Emburey	0
C.A. Best	b Edmonds	22	not out	0
I.V.A. Richards†	c Botham, b Edmonds	34		
T.R.O. Payne*	c Gower, b Emburey	5		
M.D. Marshall	not out	62		
J. Garner	c Gooch, b Emburey	12		
C.A. Walsh	c Edmonds, b Thomas	3		
B.P. Patterson	c Gooch, b Botham	9		
Extras	lb 11, w 1, nb 4	16	lb 2	2
		399	(for 3 wickets)	**95**

	O	M	R	W	O	M	R	W
Marshall	15	3	38	4	32.2	9	94	4
Garner	15	4	45	3	21	5	44	1
Patterson	8.4	—	60	2	16	—	65	—
Walsh	6	2	29	1	27	4	74	4
Richards					7	4	7	—
Gomes					1	1	0	—

	O	M	R	W	O	M	R	W
Botham	9.4	—	68	1				
Thomas	20	4	86	2	5	1	21	—
Ellison	18	3	58	—	3	1	12	—
Edmonds	30	5	98	2	12.3	3	24	1
Emburey	27	5	78	5	10	1	36	2

FALL OF WICKETS
1- 2, 2- 11, 3- 30, 4- 136, 5- 147, 6- 148, 7- 156, 8- 163, 9- 174
1- 2, 2- 82, 3- 109, 4- 190, 5- 192, 6- 197, 7- 214, 8- 214, 9- 243

FALL OF WICKETS
1- 59, 2- 209, 3- 242, 4- 256, 5- 298, 6- 303, 7- 327, 8- 342, 9- 364
1- 72, 2- 89, 3- 91

Umpires: D.M. Archer & C. Cumberbatch

West Indies won by 7 wickets

Richie Richardson on his way to 102. (Adrian Murrell)

Allan Lamb in posture symbolising England's plight. (Adrian Murrell)

14, 15, 16 and 17 March 1986

at Kensington Oval, Bridgetown, Barbados

England XI 171 (V. Greene 5 for 72) and 312 (I.T. Botham 70, P. Willey 60)

Barbados 217 (A.S. Gilkes 52) and 268 for 7 (L.N. Reifer 59 not out, N. Johnson 56)

Barbados won by 3 wickets

The move to Barbados brought little respite to the England party from their problems and growing criticism. The disaffection for the tour by some of the members was apparent. Gooch resented the focus of attention that he had drawn, for he alone seemed to attract the anger of the anti-apartheid demonstrators. Botham, angered by his treatment at the hands of the press, had become something of a recluse, and the party appeared to have splintered into groups as the younger members sought advice and leadership from senior members which did not seem to be forthcoming as factions went their chosen ways.

It is not the policy of this publication to seek scandal or concern itself with non-cricketing matters, but the lack of dedication to practice on the part of some of the side served only to fuel the rumours and accusations that were rife.

For Botham, there must be sympathy. His success as an all-rounder at Test level is unparalleled, and when he fails to maintain the very highest standards that he alone has set he is subjected to severe criticism. At the same time he has not always acted with what would seem to be sense and propriety. Like all public personalities he is in danger of becoming a victim of the publicity that he engenders, and he is, as yet, unable to discern that some who laud him today are likely to be his most severe critics tomorrow. The media, and

television especially, needs instant heroes, and those heroes are dispensed with when they are no longer fashionable.

Amid the controversy there was joy for England as Mike Gatting returned to the West Indies and captained the side in the match against Barbados. It was a short-lived joy, for, after batting well, he was caught at slip off his glove from a ball by the medium pacer Vibert Greene and the ball broke his right thumb. It was the cruellest of luck for the England vice-captain.

Botham was to follow him in injury. He was not at his best as he hit 27 off 36 balls, and in the middle of his fourth over at the start of the Barbados innings he was forced to retire with injured ankle ligaments.

England lost their last 6 wickets for 20 runs in another dismal batting performance, and the provincial side, below strength, closed at 65 for 0. With Willey leading the side, Foster headed the England revival on the second day when he ran out Innes with a fine throw from long leg in the third over. Ellison produced an acrobatic caught and bowled to account for Best, and Payne was bowled by a Taylor shooter. Edmonds bowled commendably and Barbados's lead was restricted to 46 runs.

Left one-and-three-quarter hours batting, England began promisingly, but failed to capitalise on their good start and closed at 67 for 2. Botham batted courageously on the third day, scoring 70 in three hours of application in spite of his damaged ankle. Willey, Ellison and Smith made good contributions and England reached 312 even though Gatting was unable to bat.

Barbados were 80 for 3 at lunch on the last day and an England victory looked probable. Reifer and Johnson batted sensibly, however, and Garner came in to smite the ball cleanly and powerfully so that he and Reifer added the last 46 runs that were needed to give the home side victory. It was a disappointment for England, but there were some positive features from the match that were an encouragement to them.

Third One-Day International
WEST INDIES v. ENGLAND

England's morale sank low again after a dreadful performance in the third one-day international.

Put in to bat, West Indies were given an encouraging start by Greenidge and Haynes. Botham bowled a fine first over, beating Greenidge twice, and Thomas started with a maiden. His second over was all astray, however. He was hit for 3 fours and at the end of 4 overs, West Indies had scored 20. Thomas was withdrawn from the attack, but West Indies reached 60 after 15 overs.

It was Foster who effected the breakthrough; he persuaded Haynes to chop on and had Greenidge caught behind in successive overs. There was to be no respite for England in spite of these successes, for with glorious strokes and audacious running, Richards and Richardson scored 117 in 17 overs. The stand reached its conclusion in the 34th over, bowled by Emburey, as Richards hit 2 fours and 2 sixes before being brilliantly caught off the last ball of the over by Foster on the long off boundary. Had Foster not held the ball high above his head, it would have carried for 6.

THIRD ONE-DAY INTERNATIONAL – WEST INDIES v. ENGLAND
19 March 1986 at Kensington Oval, Bridgetown, Barbados

WEST INDIES									ENGLAND							
C.G. Greenidge	c Downton, b Foster				31				G.A. Gooch	c Dujon, b Garner				6		
D.L. Haynes	b Foster				28				R.T. Robinson	c Richardson,						
R.B. Richardson	b Botham				62					b Marshall				23		
I.V.A. Richards†	c Foster, b Emburey				62				W.N. Slack	c Dujon, b Holding				9		
P.J. Dujon*	c Lamb, b Foster				23				D.I. Gower†	lbw, b Marshall				0		
R.A. Harper	not out				24				A.J. Lamb	c Marshall, b Holding				18		
J. Garner	b Emburey				3				I.T. Botham	c Garner, b Marshall				14		
M.D. Marshall	c and b Botham				9				P. Willey	c Greenidge, b Harper				9		
M.A. Holding	not out				0				P.R. Downton*	b Harper				0		
H.A. Gomes									J.E. Emburey	c Dujon, b Patterson				15		
B.P. Patterson									N.A. Foster	not out				9		
Extras	lb 4, w 2, nb 1				7				J.G. Thomas	c Richards,						
										b Patterson				0		
(46 overs)	(for 7 wickets)				279				Extras	lb 3, w 3, nb 5				11		
									(39 overs)					114		

	O	M	R	W			O	M	R	W
Botham	9	2	39	2	Garner	6	2	6	1
Thomas	7	1	50	—	Patterson	9	1	38	2
Foster	9	—	39	3	Marshall	6	2	14	3
Willey	6	—	21	—	Holding	10	1	29	2
Gooch	6	1	41	—	Harper	8	1	24	2
Emburey	9	—	55	2					

FALL OF WICKETS
1-61, 2-64, 3-181, 4-195, 5-225, 6-239, 7-248

FALL OF WICKETS
1-18, 2-42, 3-42, 4-46, 5-69, 6-81, 7-82, 8-85, 9-113

Umpires: D. Archer & L. Barker

West Indies won by 135 runs

Dujon and Harper made useful, bustling additions, and West Indies could be well satisfied with their score.

Robinson played Patterson for fours off his toes, but Gooch was harshly adjudged, caught behind in the 5th over and the rot set in. Slack managed only three scoring shots in 10 overs, a single and 2 fours in one over from Holding. Robinson grew in frustration as wides appeared to pass unsignalled so he slashed Marshall to deep gully. Gower was lbw to a shooter. Marshall also accounted for Botham who drove to deep mid-off, and Lamb was well caught on the square-leg boundary. It was left to Emburey and Foster to see England to three figures, scant consolation for this miserable batting showing.

Third Test Match
WEST INDIES v. ENGLAND

By winning the toss, England were able to take advantage of the wicket which, it was believed, would give early encouragement to the bowlers. Botham, Thomas and Foster failed to exploit whatever help the pitch offered, however, and West Indies, aided by some sloppy fielding, raced to 113 for 1 at lunch, closing, more sedately, on 269 for 2.

The early breakthrough was achieved by Foster who, in his first over, had Greenidge superbly caught at second slip by Botham, diving to his left. Richardson was instantly aggressive and reached 50 off 44 balls. He was dropped by Gooch at extra cover off Thomas when 55, and he offered a much more difficult chance to Emburey at cover when 85, but otherwise he went serenely to his sixth Test century, an innings full of majesty and of threat to all Test bowlers for some years to come.

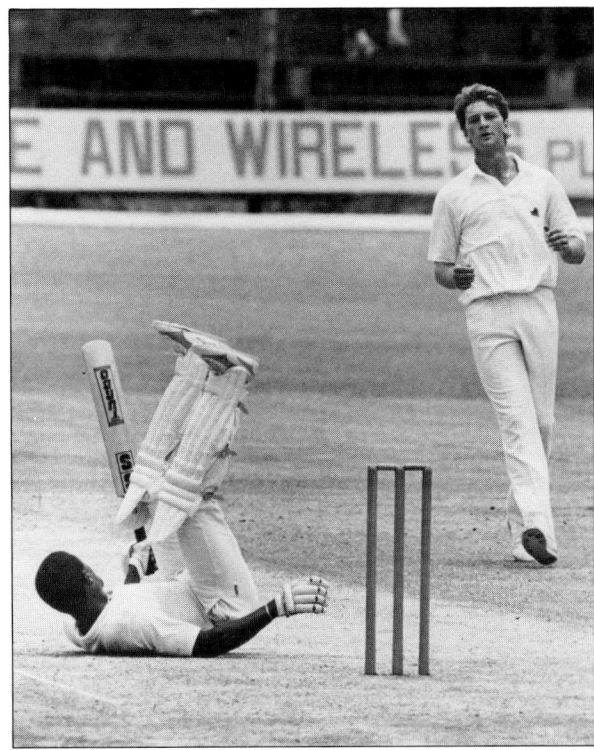

Richardson is on the floor after a Thomas bouncer, but he got up to make 160, his second century in successive Tests. (Adrian Murrell)

responded with two mighty sixes and was to fall to Thomas's first ball after lunch.

Dujon, all grace and charm, hooked Botham to long leg where Slack, fielding for Emburey, took a fine diving catch. Downton also took a good catch, and Thomas had figures of 4 for 14 with the second new ball, but West Indies were past 400 and England faced a stiff task.

It became harder when Robinson played a poor, indecisive shot, the ball lobbing off his glove to the wicket-keeper, and England were 6 for 1. There were fears of another English disintegration, but Gooch and Gower took their side firmly to 110 for 1 by the close, and, momentarily, the match seemed on level terms.

The Sunday pattern was a dismally familiar one. Gower swivelled to hit Marshall for four and nibbled at the next delivery to give a catch behind. Gooch was also caught behind and then the ship sank without trace of survivors. At the start of the day, the follow-on seemed unthinkable; within an hour it loomed as an inevitability. Marshall and Garner did the early damage, and then came Patterson, who had not impressed since the first Test, and Holding. The last 8 wickets fell for 55 runs.

Botham offered hope for a while, batting with a sense of responsibility in spite of being felled by a blow in the ribs from a ball by Holding, but he rashly hooked in the last over

Haynes, badly missed by Edmonds when 51, was caught by the only slip posted an hour before the close. Once again he had been the West Indian anchor man.

The list of walking wounded grew when John Emburey reported sick on the second morning, but before he retired to bed he bowled a tidy spell and accounted for Richardson, lbw sweeping. The spinners crowded Richards, but he

THIRD TEST MATCH – WEST INDIES *v.* ENGLAND
21, 22, 23 and 25 March 1986 at Kensington Oval, Bridgetown, Barbados

WEST INDIES

	FIRST INNINGS	
C.G. Greenidge	c Botham, b Foster	21
D.L. Haynes	c Botham, b Foster	84
R.B. Richardson	lbw, b Emburey	160
H.A. Gomes	c Gower, b Thomas	33
I.V.A. Richards†	c Downton, b Thomas	51
C.A. Best	lbw, b Foster	21
P.J. Dujon*	c sub (Slack), b Botham	5
M.A. Holding	b Thomas	23
M.D. Marshall	run out	4
J. Garner	c Gooch, b Thomas	0
B.P. Patterson	not out	0
Extras	b 2, lb 9, w 3, nb 2	16
		418

ENGLAND

	FIRST INNINGS		SECOND INNINGS	
G.A. Gooch	c Dujon, b Garner	53	b Patterson	11
R.T. Robinson	c Dujon, b Marshall	3	b Patterson	43
D.I. Gower†	c Dujon, b Marshall	66	c Marshall, b Garner	23
P. Willey	c Dujon, b Marshall	5	lbw, b Garner	17
A.J. Lamb	c Richardson, b Marshall	5	c and b Holding	6
I.T. Botham	c Dujon, b Patterson	14	(7) c Dujon, b Garner	21
P.R. Downton*	lbw, b Holding	11	(8) c Dujon, b Holding	26
J.E. Emburey	c Best, b Patterson	0	(9) not out	35
P.H. Edmonds	c Richardson, b Patterson	4	(6) lbw, b Garner	4
N.A. Foster	lbw, b Holding	0	c Richardson, b Holding	0
J.G. Thomas	not out	4	b Patterson	0
Extras	b 4, lb 8, w 2, nb 10	24	lb 1, nb 12	13
		189		199

	O	M	R	W
Botham	24	3	80	1
Thomas	16.1	2	70	4
Foster	19	—	76	3
Edmonds	29	2	85	—
Emburey	38	7	96	1

	O	M	R	W	O	M	R	W
Marshall	14	1	42	4	13	1	47	—
Garner	14	4	35	1	17	2	69	4
Patterson	15	5	54	3	8.4	2	28	3
Holding	13	4	37	2	10	1	47	3
Richards	3	—	9	—	4	1	7	—

FALL OF WICKETS
1- 34, 2- 228, 3- 268, 4- 361, 5- 362, 6- 367, 7- 406, 8- 413, 9- 418

FALL OF WICKETS
1- 6, 2- 126, 3- 134, 4- 141, 5- 151, 6- 168, 7- 172, 8- 181, 9- 185
1- 48, 2- 70, 3- 94, 4- 108, 5- 108, 6- 132, 7- 138, 8- 188, 9- 188

Umpires: D.M. Archer & L. Barker

West Indies won by an innings and 30 runs

before lunch and skied the ball to Dujon who enjoyed a good day. In both senses it was dreadful timing by the great man, but he was to commit a graver act of folly later in the day. By then, England had followed-on.

Gooch and Robinson negotiated the 50 minutes before tea with confidence, but the last session began with Gooch playing on to Patterson in the third over. Robinson played on half an hour later and Gower recklessly sacrificed his wicket, edging carelessly to slip. Lamb and Willey followed in quick succession, and Botham slogged 21 off 32 balls before falling to a wild, rash shot on the last ball of a miserable day for English cricket.

In the earlier part of the day, England had been confronted by high class pace bowling and, conscious of past failure, they had succumbed. In the evening session, they had succumbed as much to their own low morale as anything else. Botham had come to the wicket with 20 minutes remaining, the score 108 for 4, and a rest day beckoning, but he played an innings totally out of context with that situation. It left the impression that the ship was rudderless, a view that was enhanced by the lack of demand on players to practise.

In the Brearley era, under Brearley's insistence, it was the captain and assistant manager who decided that nets were to be voluntary or compulsory only when those two officials said so. Willis, as assistant manager, was an unwise choice for the tour in that he is too close to recent events. With a new captain, facing problems that Brearley never encountered, a stronger line and a fresh approach were needed.

With sensible batting Downton and Emburey held up the West Indians until the stroke of lunch, but defeat had long since been inevitable as had the destination of the Wisden Trophy. There was still pride and passion to play for.

Fourth One-Day International
WEST INDIES v. ENGLAND

In contrast to the fast, uneven, bumpy pitches on which they had so far played, England found themselves struggling to score runs on a slow wicket. The ball came on to the bat, and Marshall, determining that one slip was enough on such a pitch, had Gooch caught at mid-wicket where he had just positioned Richards. For Robinson, who had had a most disappointing tour, the conditions were totally wrong, but he gave the England innings some substance with a dour knock which, had the overs not been limited, would have had more value. After 11 overs, the Notts opener had scored only 4, and his 55 occupied 40 overs. It was an innings that was needed, however, for only a brisk effort from Botham helped England to any sort of respectability. On this wicket, another 35 runs could have given the West Indies problems, but 165 never looked like being adequate.

There was hope for England when Greenidge fell to the second ball of the innings, but 14 were taken off Foster's fifth over, and there was never any doubt as to who would win the match. It appeared that the spinners might make things hard for the West Indies, but Gower delayed using them in

---

FOURTH ONE-DAY INTERNATIONAL – WEST INDIES v. ENGLAND
31 March 1986 at Queen's Park Oval, Port-of-Spain, Trinidad

ENGLAND				WEST INDIES			
G.A. Gooch	c Richards, b Marshall	10		C.G. Greenidge	b Foster	0
R.T. Robinson	b Marshall	55		D.L. Haynes	not out	77
D.I. Gower†	b Walsh	20		R.B. Richardson	c Gooch, b Emburey	31
A.J. Lamb	c Dujon, b Walsh	16		I.V.A. Richards†	not out	50
I.T. Botham	c Harper, b Garner	29		H.A. Gomes		
P. Willey	c Greenidge, b Marshall	6		P.J. Dujon*		
P.R. Downton*	c Greenidge, b Marshall	12		R.A. Harper		
R.M. Ellison	b Garner	5		M.A. Holding		
J.E. Emburey	not out	2		M.D. Marshall		
P.H. Edmonds	b Garner	0		J. Garner		
N.A. Foster				C.A. Walsh		
Extras	b 1, lb 4, w 2, nb 3	10		Extras	lb 7, w 1	8
	(47 overs) (for 9 wickets)	165			(38.2 overs) (for 2 wickets)	166

	O	M	R	W		O	M	R	W
Marshall	9	—	37	4	Foster	6	1	27	1
Garner	9	1	22	3	Ellison	7	—	30	—
Holding	9	1	32	—	Botham	5	—	24	—
Walsh	10	—	25	2	Edmonds	10	1	38	—
Harper	10	—	44	—	Emburey	10	2	31	1
					Gower	0.2	—	9	—

FALL OF WICKETS
1- 15, 2- 49, 3- 88, 4- 126, 5- 138, 6- 154, 7- 161, 8- 165,
9- 165

FALL OF WICKETS
1- 0, 2- 75

Umpires: C. Cumberbatch & S. Mohammed

West Indies won by 8 wickets

tandem, and, in any case, when Richards came in at 75 for 2 in the 22nd over, batting suddenly reached another dimension. He hit the only 3 sixes of the day, and the interest began to drain from the match.

West Indies batted, bowled and fielded far better than England, and once again criticism of the way in which the tour was being conducted was rife. Botham, to the shame of those responsible, was scurrilously treated by the tabloid newspapers whose sales depend upon the sensational revelations of people's private lives, true or otherwise, that they make rather than upon the quality of their cricket reporting. The sadness is that millions of people seem to want such stuff, for these are the papers that they buy.

To add to the woe, Gooch was indicating that, because of political statements, he was unwilling to return to Antigua for the last Test match, and it needed a visit by that eminent diplomat Donald Carr, and some persuasion by Gower, to convince him that he should see the tour through.

Fourth Test Match
WEST INDIES v. ENGLAND

No blame could be attached to the England side for their batting display in the first innings. They asked to bat first on a coarse, green wicket where survival was precarious and life dangerous. It was disgracefully under-prepared for a Test match although, obviously, highly suited to the West Indian pace attack.

Smith, Lamb and Botham, in differing ways, played courageously for England. Smith hit 47 off 80 balls, but he and Lamb fell in successive overs. Gooch had held out for 75 minutes before playing a limp batted shot and steering the ball to slip while Botham, after scoring 38 in a disciplined and relaxed manner, was out to a wild shot.

West Indies closed the first day at 12 for 0, but three wretched overs from Thomas set them on a brisk start on the second morning. Foster had Haynes brilliantly taken at slip by Botham, but the Essex bowler was also erratic, and it was left to Botham and Emburey, 8 overs for 10 runs, to effect economy.

Greenidge fell on the stroke of lunch when he tried to pull a ball from Emburey that did not bounce, and Richardson succumbed when he charged wildly at the off-spinner and missed. Richardson had had one escape when he was dropped by Willey, a difficult chance at cover, off Thomas who continued to offer some very hittable balls.

Greenidge had reached 5000 runs in Test cricket and Richards was to pass 6000. It was the West Indian captain who put his side firmly on top. Emburey had curtailed all batsmen, but Richards lifted him high for six. In 3 hours, off 113 balls, he hit 87 and was out when he missed a Botham inswinger.

West Indies lost 3 wickets in 5 overs in the last hour, and the England bowlers had had a good day in restricting the home side's lead to 71. It was increased to 112 the following morning, but Botham cut down the tail in 3 overs with the

---

FOURTH TEST MATCH – WEST INDIES v. ENGLAND
3, 4 and 5 April 1986 at Queen's Park Oval, Port-of-Spain, Trinidad

ENGLAND

	FIRST INNINGS		SECOND INNINGS	
G.A. Gooch	c Richards, b Garner	14	c Dujon, b Marshall	0
R.T. Robinson	c Marshall, b Garner	0	b Garner	5
D.I. Gower†	c Dujon, b Garner	10	lbw, b Patterson	22
D.M. Smith	c Greenidge, b Patterson	47	lbw, b Holding	32
A.J. Lamb	b Holding	36	b Patterson	11
I.T. Botham	b Holding	38	c Gomes, b Marshall	25
P. Willey	c Richardson, b Garner	10	lbw, b Marshall	2
P.R. Downton*	c Garner, b Marshall	7	not out	11
J.E. Emburey	c Haynes, b Marshall	8	b Holding	0
N.A. Foster	c Richards, b Holding	0	b Garner	14
J.G. Thomas	not out	5	b Garner	0
Extras	b 1, lb 2, w 1, nb 21	25	b 5, lb 7, nb 16	28
		200		**150**

WEST INDIES

	FIRST INNINGS		SECOND INNINGS	
C.G. Greenidge	lbw, b Emburey	42		
D.L. Haynes	c Botham, b Foster	25	(1) not out	17
R.B. Richardson	b Emburey	32	(2) not out	22
H.A. Gomes	c Downton, b Foster	48		
I.V.A. Richards†	lbw, b Botham	87		
P.J. Dujon*	c Downton, b Botham	5		
M.D. Marshall	b Emburey	5		
R.A. Harper	lbw, b Botham	21		
M.A. Holding	b Botham	25		
J. Garner	not out	5		
B.P. Patterson	c Downton, b Botham	3		
Extras	lb 10, w 3, nb 1	14		0
		312	(for no wicket)	**39**

	O	M	R	W	O	M	R	W
Marshall	23	4	71	2	10	2	42	3
Garner	18	3	43	4	9	3	15	3
Patterson	10	2	31	1	9	1	36	2
Holding	14.4	3	52	3	10	1	45	2

	O	M	R	W	O	M	R	W
Botham	24.1	3	71	5	3	—	24	—
Thomas	15	—	101	—				
Foster	24	3	68	2	2.5	—	15	—
Emburey	27	10	62	3				

FALL OF WICKETS
1- 8, 2- 29, 3- 31, 4- 123, 5- 124, 6- 151, 7- 168, 8- 181, 9- 190
1- 0, 2- 30, 3- 30, 4- 75, 5- 105, 6- 109, 7- 115, 8- 126, 9- 150

FALL OF WICKETS
1- 58, 2- 72, 3- 111, 4- 213, 5- 244, 6- 249, 7- 249, 8- 299, 9- 306

Umpires: C. Cumberbatch & S. Mohammed

West Indies won by 10 wickets

second new ball. He finished with figures of 5 for 71, an excellent performance, and this took his tally of Test wickets to 352, only 3 short of Dennis Lillee's record.

England now proceeded to give one of their most miserable batting performances in many years as they showed neither technique nor willingness to cope with high class fast bowling. The misery began third ball when Gooch mishooked. Robinson, the gap between bat and pad growing each innings, was bowled. Patterson left Gower stranded with quick movement, and Lamb fell to a ball which pitched on middle stump and hit the off.

Holding bowled beautifully and had Smith lbw to an inswinger, the batsman offering no stroke. Willey had looked increasingly vulnerable as the tour progressed and, not surprisingly, fell to Marshall. Botham was taken at cover, and Emburey lost his off stump. Garner accounted for Foster and Thomas.

England were all out in 38 overs, and West Indies scored the runs that they required inside half an hour to bring them victory in three days. England's hopes of the second day seemed an age away.

To add to their problems, England lost Peter Willey who was forced to return home with a knee injury.

RIGHT: *Captains of varying fortunes – Gower and Richards leave the field together. (Adrian Murrell)*

FIFTH TEST MATCH – WEST INDIES v. ENGLAND
11, 12, 13, 15 and 16 April 1986 at Recreation Ground, St John's, Antigua

WEST INDIES

	FIRST INNINGS			SECOND INNINGS	
C.G. Greenidge	b Botham	14			
D.L. Haynes	c Gatting, b Ellison	131	(1) run out	70	
R.B. Richardson	c Slack, b Emburey	24	(2) c Robinson, b Emburey	31	
H.A. Gomes	b Emburey	24			
I.V.A. Richards†	c Gooch, b Botham	26	(3) not out	110	
P.J. Dujon*	b Foster	21			
M.D. Marshall	c Gatting, b Gooch	76			
R.A. Harper	c Lamb, b Foster	60	(4) not out	19	
M.A. Holding	c Gower, b Ellison	73			
J. Garner	run out	11			
B.P. Patterson	not out	0			
Extras	b 2, lb 11, w 1	14	b 4, lb 9, w 1, nb 2	16	
		474	(for 2 wkts, dec)	246	

ENGLAND

	FIRST INNINGS			SECOND INNINGS	
G.A. Gooch	lbw, b Holding	51	lbw, b Holding	51	
W.N. Slack	c Greenidge, b Patterson	52	b Garner	8	
R.T. Robinson	b Marshall	12	run out	3	
D.I. Gower†	c Dujon, b Marshall	90	(5) c Dujon, b Harper	21	
A.J. Lamb	c and b Harper	1	(6) b Marshall	1	
M.W. Gatting	c Dujon, b Garner	15	(7) b Holding	1	
I.T. Botham	c Harper, b Garner	10	(8) b Harper	13	
P.R. Downton*	c Holding, b Garner	5	(9) lbw, b Marshall	13	
R.M. Ellison	c Dujon, b Marshall	6	(4) lbw, b Garner	16	
J.E. Emburey	not out	7	c Richardson, b Harper	0	
N.A. Foster	c Holding, b Garner	10	not out	0	
Extras	b 5, lb 6, nb 40	51	b 10, lb 10, w 2, nb 21	43	
		310		170	

	O	M	R	W	O	M	R	W
Botham	40	6	147	2	15	—	78	—
Foster	28	5	86	2	10	—	40	—
Ellison	24.3	3	114	2	4	—	32	—
Emburey	37	11	93	2	14	—	83	1
Gooch	5	2	21	1				

	O	M	R	W	O	M	R	W
Marshall	24	5	64	3	16.1	6	25	2
Garner	21.4	2	67	4	17	5	38	2
Patterson	14	2	49	1	15	3	29	—
Holding	20	3	71	1	16	3	45	2
Harper	26	7	45	1	12	8	10	3
Richards	2	—	3	—	3	1	3	—

FALL OF WICKETS
1- 23, 2- 63, 3- 137, 4- 178, 5- 232, 6- 281, 7- 351, 8- 401, 9- 450
1- 100, 2- 161

FALL OF WICKETS
1- 127, 2- 132, 3- 157, 4- 159, 5- 205, 6- 223, 7- 237, 8- 289, 9- 290
1- 14, 2- 29, 3- 84, 4- 101, 5- 112, 6- 124, 7- 147, 8- 164, 9- 168

Umpires: C. Cumberbatch & L. Barker

West Indies won by 240 runs

England in West Indies 1986
First Class Matches

BATTING	v Windward Islands (St Vincent) 1–4 February 1986		v Leeward Islands (Antigua) 7–10 February 1986		v Jamaica (Kingston) 13–16 February 1986		First Test Match (Kingston) 21–23 February 1986		v Trinidad (Port of Spain) 28 Feb.–1 Mar. 1986		Second Test Match (Port of Spain) 7–12 March 1986		v Barbados (Bridgetown) 14–17 March 1986		Third Test Match (Bridgetown) 21–25 March 1986		Fourth Test Match (Port of Spain) 3–5 April 1986		Fifth Test Match (Antigua) 11–16 April 1986	
G.A. Gooch	27	10	53	0	36	6	51	0	23	12	2	43			53	11	14	0	51	51
R.T. Robinson	9	7	68	32	9	19	6	0	76	6			40	21	3	43	0	5	12	3
D.M. Smith	0	18					1	0	7	23*			24	43			47	32		
M.W. Gatting	77	14	71	8	80	15							36	—					15	1
A.J. Lamb	5	6	64	1	78	60*	49	13			62	40			5	6	36	11	1	1
P. Willey	16	2					0	71	27	10	5	26	8	60	5	17	10	2		
P.R. Downton	16	2	4	10*	4	7*	2	3			8	5			11	26	7	11*	5	13
P.H. Edmonds	14	18*			15*	—			5	7	5*	—	3*	13	3	20	4	4		
N.A. Foster	4	1	14	—			1	—			6*	10	0	0	0	14			10	0*
J.G. Thomas	5	5	1*	1*			0	1*			4	31*			4*	0	5*	0		
L.B. Taylor	4*	0			0	—			8	—			9	0*						
D.I. Gower			5	9	2	11	16	9	43	7	66	47			66	23	10	22	90	21
I.T. Botham			40	4	32	38	15	29			2	1	27	70	14	21	38	25	10	13
J.E. Emburey			38	6	25	—			32	—	0	14			0	35*	8	0	7*	0
R.M. Ellison			21	1	32	—	9	11			4	36	2	45					6	16
W.N. Slack									0	37*	2	0	12	23			0	9	52	8
B.N. French									0	—							0			
Byes	1	4	11	8	24	14		5	5			20		4		1	5		5	10
Leg-byes	1	2	10	9	7	3				3	4	11	1	7	8	1	2	7	6	10
Wides		1		1		1			1	3		1	2		2		1			2
No-balls	7	4	9	4	27	3	5	3	1		14	27	1	4	10	12	21	16	40	21
Total	186	94	409	94	371	177	159	152	229	101	176	315	171	312	189	199	200	150	310	170
Wickets	10	10	10	8	10	5	10	10	10	4	10	10	10	9†	10	10	10	10	10	10
Result	L		D		W		L		D		L		L		L		L		L	

Catches

- 15 – P.R. Downton (ct 12/st 3)
- 10 – G.A. Gooch
- 6 – B.N. French (ct 5/st 1) and I.T. Botham
- 5 – A.J. Lamb and J.G. Thomas
- 4 – M.W. Gatting, R.T. Robinson, D.I. Gower and J.E. Emburey
- 3 – W.N. Slack, P. Willey and subs
- 2 – L.B. Taylor, P.H. Edmonds and N.A. Foster
- 1 – D.M. Smith and R.M. Ellison

† M.W. Gatting absent hurt

BOWLING

	J.G. Thomas	N.A. Foster	P.H. Edmonds	L.B. Taylor	P. Willey	I.T. Botham	R.M. Ellison	J.E. Emburey	M.W. Gatting
v. Windward Islands (St Vincent) 1–4 February	16–4–54–3 / 6–0–15–0	7–3–11–1 / 2–1–4–0	25–5–38–4 / 22–2–48–1	7–1–17–0 / 1–0–2–0	26–8–42–2 / 22.4–6–38–2				
v. Leeward Islands (Antigua) 7–10 February	10–1–37–1 / 17–1–77–2	13–6–33–2 / 20–3–54–4				14–4–51–0 / 9.1–2–28–2	13–1–37–3 / 16–1–49–1	16.2–3–51–3 / 26–6–64–1	3–0–15–1
v. Jamaica (Kingston) 13–16 February			16–4–40–0 / 19–4–44–4	18–2–70–3 / 13–3–28–2		13.2–3–31–2 / 6–1–13–0	15–2–45–2 / 17–4–36–2	19–6–31–1 / 8–2–16–1	
First Test Match (Kingston) 21–23 February	28.5–6–82–2 / 1–0–4–0		21–6–53–0		4–0–15–1	19–4–67–2 / 33–12–78–5			
v. Trinidad and Tobago (Port of Spain) 28 February–2 March		16.4–5–54–6 / 7–3–16–1	1–0–2–0 / 9–1–29–1	14–5–27–3 / 9–1–31–1	5–1–10–1			8–4–15–1 / 9–1–23–0	
Second Test Match (Port of Spain) 7–12 March	20–4–86–2 / 5–1–21–0		30–5–98–2 / 12.3–3–24–1			9.4–0–68–1	18–3–58–0 / 3–1–12–0	27–5–78–5 / 10–1–36–2	
v. Barbados (Bridgetown) 14–17 March		15–3–57–0 / 16–1–69–2		21.3–6–45–3 / 27.4–5–84–2	19.3–4–46–3 / 12–1–38–1	3.3–0–13–0 / 18–1–46–2	15–3–36–3 / 4–1–16–0		
Third Test Match (Bridgetown) 21–25 March	16.1–2–70–4	19–0–76–3	29–2–85–0			24–3–80–1		38–7–96–1	
Fourth Test Match (Port of Spain) 3–5 April	15–0–101–0	24–3–68–2 / 2.5–0–15–0				24.1–3–71–5 / 3–0–24–0		27–10–62–3	
Fifth Test Match (Antigua) 11–16 April		28–5–86–2 / 10–0–40–0				40–6–147–2 / 15–0–78–0	24.3–3–114–2 / 4–0–32–0	37–11–93–2 / 14–0–83–1	
	135–19–547–14 av. 39.07	180.3–33–583–23 av. 25.34	233.4–43–590–18 av. 32.77	93.3–17–259–13 av. 19.92	79.4–17–162–8 av. 20.25	180.5–26–671–15 av. 44.73	162.3–31–513–18 av. 28.50	239.2–56–648–21 av. 30.85	3–0–15–1 av. 15.00

a M.A. Holding absent hurt

M	Inns	NOs	Runs	HS	Av
9	18	—	443	53	24.61
9	18	—	359	68	19.94
5	10	1	195	47	21.66
5	9	—	317	80	35.22
8	16	1	438	78	29.20
7	14	—	259	71	18.50
8	16	3	134	26	10.30
7	12	5	111	20	15.85
7	12	2	60	14	6.00
6	12	6	57	31*	9.50
4	6	2	21	9	5.25
8	16	—	447	90	27.93
8	16	—	379	70	23.68
7	12	2	165	38	16.50
6	11	—	183	45	16.63
4	8	1	134	52	19.14
2	3	—	9	9	3.00

G.A. Gooch	A.J. Lamb	Byes	Leg-byes	Wides	No-balls	Total	Wkts
		2	4		25	168	10
		6			8	113	3
		4	8		10	236	10
		9	7	1	18	288	10
		2	3		4	222	9a
7–3–24–0		5	2		5	168	9
2–1–6–0		2	4		3	307	10
	0.0–0–1–0				1	5	0
3–0–5–0		1	5	2	1	109	10
		1	6	1	2	116	4
			11	1	4	399	10
			2			95	3
			9		4	217	10
		7	8		8	268	7
		2	9	3	2	418	10
			10	3	1	312	10
						39	0
5–2–21–1		2	11	1		474	10
		4	9	1	2	246	2
17–6–	0.0–0–						
56–1	1–0						
av. 56.00	—						

Fifth Test Match
WEST INDIES *v.* ENGLAND

Doubts as to Gower's fitness shrouded the selection of the England side. He had been hit on the wrist by a ball from Marshall in the fourth Test and did not declare himself fit until the morning of the match. David Smith was ruled out because of the recurrence of his back injury, but Mike Gatting was able to play for the first time in the series.

The England management had rightly complained to the West Indian authorities about the pitches on which they had been asked to play the Test series for they were invariably wickets on which the bounce was uneven, but the St John's wicket provided the best batsman's wicket of the tour. Nevertheless, Gower chose to field when he won the toss, believing that the only advantage bowlers would gain from the pitch would be the moisture on the first morning. Unfortunately, England fielded poorly and bowled indifferently so that any help that might have been in the pitch was squandered.

Foster and Ellison could not get their line right, and Foster, a player very much in need of encouragement, saw Haynes missed at slip by Botham when 2. Haynes was also dropped off Emburey when 38, but he went on to make a sober hundred which gave the innings backbone.

Botham beat Greenidge with a full pitched delivery on the off stump and Richardson was taken at short leg off bat and

Wilf Slack – a maiden Test fifty. (Adrian Murrell)

Cable and Wireless Test Series Averages – West Indies v. England

WEST INDIES BATTING

	M	Inns	NOs	Runs	HS	Av	100s	50s
D.L. Haynes	5	9	3	469	131	78.16	1	3
I.V.A. Richards	5	6	1	331	110*	66.20	1	2
R.B. Richardson	5	9	2	387	160	55.28	2	
R.A. Harper	2	3	1	100	60	50.00		1
M.D. Marshall	5	5	1	153	76	38.25		2
C.G. Greenidge	5	6		217	58	36.16		1
H.A. Gomes	5	6		191	56	31.83		1
M.A. Holding	4	4		124	73	31.00		1
C.A. Best	3	4	1	78	35	26.00		
P.J. Dujon	4	4		85	54	21.25		1
J. Garner	5	5	1	52	24	13.00		
B.P. Patterson	5	5	3	12	9	6.00		

Played in one Test: T.R.O. Payne 5; C.A. Walsh 3

ENGLAND BATTING

	M	Inns	NOs	Runs	HS	Av	100s	50s
D.I. Gower	5	10		370	90	37.00		3
G.A. Gooch	5	10		276	53	27.60		4
A.J. Lamb	5	10		224	62	22.40		1
D.M. Smith	2	4		80	47	20.00		
P. Willey	4	8		136	71	17.00		1
I.T. Botham	5	10		168	38	16.80		
W.N. Slack	2	4		62	52	15.50		1
R.M. Ellison	3	6		82	36	13.66		
J.G. Thomas	4	8	4	45	31*	11.25		
J.E. Emburey	4	8	2	64	35*	10.66		
P.R. Downton	5	10	1	91	26	10.11		
R.T. Robinson	4	8		72	43	9.00		
P.H. Edmonds	3	6	2	36	13	9.00		
N.A. Foster	3	6	1	24	14	4.80		

Played in one Test: M.W. Gatting 15 & 1

WEST INDIES BOWLING

	Overs	Mds	Runs	Wkts	Av	Best	5/inns
R.A. Harper	38	15	55	4	13.75	3/10	
J. Garner	156.1	30	436	27	16.14	4/43	
M.D. Marshall	169.3	36	482	27	17.85	4/38	
C.A. Walsh	33	6	103	5	20.60	4/74	
B.P. Patterson	118.1	19	426	19	22.42	4/30	
M.A. Holding	102.4	16	385	16	24.06	3/47	
I.V.A. Richards	20	7	29	0	—		

Bowled in one innings: R.B. Richardson 1-0-5-0; H.A. Gomes 1-1-0-0

ENGLAND BOWLING

	Overs	Mds	Runs	Wkts	Av	Best	5/inns
G.A. Gooch	7	3	27	1	27.00	1/21	
J.E. Emburey	153	34	448	14	32.00	5/78	1
N.A. Foster	83.5	8	285	7	40.71	3/76	
R.M. Ellison	82.3	19	294	7	42.00	5/78	1
J.G. Thomas	86	13	364	8	45.50	4/70	
I.T. Botham	134.5	16	535	11	48.63	5/71	1
P.H. Edmonds	92.3	16	260	3	86.66	2/98	

Bowled in one innings: P. Willey 4 - 0 - 15 - 1; A.J. Lamb 0.1 - 0 - 1 - 0

WEST INDIES CATCHES

16 - P.J. Dujon; 6 - R.B. Richardson; 5 - T.R.O. Payne; 4 - M.D. Marshall and C.A. Best; 3 - C.G. Greenidge, D.L. Haynes and M.A. Holding; 2 - R.A. Harper (plus one as sub), J. Garner, H.A. Gomes and I.V.A. Richards, 1 - B.P. Patterson

ENGLAND CATCHES

8 - P.R. Downton (ct 6/st 2); 6 - G.A. Gooch; 4 - I.T. Botham; 3 - A.J. Lamb and D.I. Gower; 2 - P.H. Edmonds and M.W. Gatting; 1 - R.T. Robinson and W.N. Slack (plus one as sub) sub (J.E. Emburey)

---

pad. Richardson was again not at his best against Emburey. The off-spinner had further success when he hit Gomes's off stump with a ball that turned sharply. Richards seemed intent on hitting only fours, but there was a suggestion that the great man was not middling the ball and when Botham set two fine legs Richards fell for the trap and was out hooking.

England had contained well and West Indies closed the day on 228 for 4. Foster bowled Dujon, off stump, in the second over of the second morning, and Haynes's long innings was brought to an end by Ellison, but Botham was unable to get closer to Lillee's record as West Indies launched a violent attack on the bowling. Marshall hit two huge sixes off Emburey and savaged all bowlers with great power. Harper was quick and enthusiastic, and Holding set about the bowlers gleefully. Botham posted eight men on the boundary, but Holding hit 13 runs off 5 balls before being brilliantly caught by Gower off a skier. The fielder ran back and took the ball over his shoulder. West Indies, aided by some shoddy fielding, ended at 474, scored at more than 3½ an over, yet the first 36 overs of the innings had yielded only 80 runs.

Gooch and Slack went solidly to the close at 40 for 1. West Indies were not shown to good advantage in their petulant attitude over a ball change. The scene was repeated the following morning, and it is a great pity that a side so often on top should react so shamefully when the game and its conduct were not totally in their favour. Richards later apologised to the umpires.

No balls abounded. Gooch was stolid and then composed. Slack almost seemed to be enjoying himself, and the opening partnership realised 127. Sadly, both batsmen fell in quick succession. Holding, in what he stated would be his last Test, employed his long run of rhythmic beauty and beat Gooch on the line of the off stump. Fielders clustered round the bat and Slack clipped Patterson to backward of square leg. Robinson was bowled through a cavernous gap between bat and pad, and Lamb played carelessly.

England were in danger of having to follow on, but Gatting stayed with Gower for a time before he chased a wide ball outside the off stump. Botham was taken at square leg and Downton at extra cover so that Garner had taken 3 wickets in 7 overs. At 237 for 7, the follow on looked more probable every over, and when the new ball was taken 4 overs from the end of the day this probability looked to have been turned into a near certainty as Gower cut Holding into the hands of Garner at gully only to see the big man drop the easiest of catches. England, 263 for 7 at the close, breathed again.

Ellison and Gower took their stand to 52 on the fourth morning, and the indignity of having to follow on was avoided. Ellison, having lasted for 82 brave minutes, was caught at the wicket off Marshall, and Gower, having reached the highest score by an Englishman in the series,

FIRST CLASS AVERAGES

BATTING	M	Inns	NOs	Runs	HS	Av	100s	50s
M.A. Harper	3	5	2	398	149*	132.66	2	1
D.L. Haynes	10	18	3	914	131	60.93	3	5
R.M. Otto	5	8	1	396	165	56.57	1	3
I.V.A. Richards	9	11	1	518	132	51.80	2	2
C.A. Best	9	15	1	640	179	45.71	2	2
L.L. Lawrence	4	6		269	113	44.83	1	1
C.G. Greenidge	9	14	1	578	90	44.46		5
T. Mohammed	5	9	1	332	200*	41.50	1	1
R.B. Richardson	10	17	2	575	160	38.33	2	2
A. Rajah	5	9	1	297	69	37.12		3
R.A. Harper	7	12	2	362	72	36.20		3
L.N. Reifer	2	4	1	103	59*	34.33		1
N.A. Johnson	2	3		102	56	34.00		1
E.E. Lewis	5	8	1	235	108*	33.57	1	
S. Bamfield	2	4		132	83	33.00		1
H.A. Gomes	10	15	1	434	168*	31.00	1	1
C.B. Lambert	5	9		273	61	30.33		2
L.D. John	5	10	1	271	70	30.11		1
A.F.D. Jackman	5	9		270	83	30.00		2
P.J. Dujon	10	15	1	407	75	29.07		4
L.C. Sebastien	5	9	1	232	69	29.00		2
C.A. Davidson	6	11	3	226	67*	28.25		1
I. Cadette	5	9		253	84	28.11		1
T.R.O. Payne	7	12	2	270	62	27.00		2
J.D. Charles	5	10		265	114	26.50	1	1
D.I. Mohammed	2	4		106	49	26.50		
S.I. Williams	3	4		103	45	25.75		
R.S. Gabriel	5	10	2	194	45	24.25		
P.V. Simmons	5	10		233	65	23.30		2
A.L. Logie	5	9		206	79	22.88		1
P. Moosai	4	8	1	159	36	22.71		
M.D. Marshall	9	11	2	204	76	22.66		2
N.C. Guishard	5	7	1	133	54	22.26		2
M.C. Neita	6	11		231	66	21.00		1
K.C. Williams	4	7		140	39	20.00		
D.A. Williams	6	10		200	50	20.00		1
R. Nanan	6	10	2	159	61	19.87		1
D.J. Collymore	5	9	2	137	36	19.57		
G. Powell	6	11		210	40	19.09		
J. Garner	11	15	2	243	56	18.69		1
M.A. Holding	10	13		238	73	18.30		1
F.A. Cunningham	5	10	1	162	34	18.00		
L.A. Lewis	5	9		129	32	14.33		
D.I. Kallicharran	5	9	1	103	32*	12.87		
A.G. Daley	6	11	1	121	47	12.10		

(Qualification – 100 runs, average 10.00)

BOWLING	Overs	Mds	Runs	Wkts	Av	Best	10/m	5/inn
J. Garner	322.1	68	866	57	15.19	6/28		3
R. Nanan	235.5	56	508	33	15.39	5/52		3
M.D. Marshall	296.3	58	835	50	16.70	6/85	1	1
C.A. Walsh	216	39	680	39	17.43	8/92	2	1
R.A. Harper	217.5	55	465	26	17.88	4/29		
C.G. Butts	234.2	63	515	28	18.39	6/57		3
B.P. Patterson	246.5	45	813	41	19.82	7/24		1
A.H. Gray	158.2	26	478	24	19.91	5/50		2
W.K.R. Benjamin	158.3	38	400	20	20.00	5/47		1
M.A. Holding	183.1	34	680	33	20.60	4/38		
S.J. Hinds	166.5	30	467	22	21.22	6/19	2	1
D.J. Collymore	137.5	30	351	15	23.40	5/34		1
A.G. Daley	131.4	25	389	6	24.31	4/46		
J.T. Etienne	181.2	35	445	18	24.72	6/35		1
G. Mahabir	171.4	35	499	20	24.95	4/31		
D.I. Kallicharran	149.4	21	429	16	26.81	3/12		
W.E. Reid	89	11	301	11	27.36	5/72		1
C.V. Solomon	82	13	315	11	28.63	4/78		
N.C. Guishard	262.2	68	613	17	36.05	5/84		

(Qualification – 10 wickets)

LEADING FIELDERS
33 - P.J. Dujon; 20 - T.R.O. Payne (ct 16/st 4); 12 - R.A. Harper and C.A. Best; 11 - M.C.V. Simon (ct 10/st 1); 10 - M.A. Holding

perished the same way after some acrobatics by Dujon.

Marshall then subjected Foster to some unwarranted, unnecessary, uncensured and vicious short pitched bowling, accompanied by the fast bowler's glare, as England added 20 for the last wicket.

As Greenidge had injured himself in the dressing room Richardson opened with Haynes. They went off at a brisk rate and the stand had produced 100 before Richardson fell to Emburey for the sixth time in succession. Haynes, encouraged by some loose bowling on the leg side, hit Ellison for 2 sixes, and he took his aggregate for the series to 469 before responding slowly to a call for a leg-bye and being run out, but by then Richards had claimed centre stage.

From the second ball he received Richards hit a six. From 35 deliveries he made 50, and from the next 21 he made another 50. The massacre of the England bowlers ended when he declared after reaching 110 from only 41 scoring strokes. His century off 56 balls was the quickest century in Test history, beating Jack Gregory's for Australia against South Africa in 1921–22 by 11 balls. Richards hit 6 sixes and 7 fours and did not play a false stroke in an innings which intoxicated his home crowd and stunned his opponents who could only pay homage in awe at the man's brilliance.

His declaration left England to make 411 in 6 hours, 50 minutes, or, more realistically, to survive for that time on a wicket which was still playing well and on which the West Indies had hit 19 sixes. In the fourth over Slack was bowled between bat and pad, and Robinson's wretched tour came to an end a little later when he hesitated and was beaten by Logie's direct hit on the stumps. Ellison, now as night-watchman, found himself at the wicket for the second time on a shell-shocking day, and England closed at 33 for 2.

With sensible batting, Gooch and Ellison survived almost until lunch on the last day. The only danger to England's batsmen on a placid pitch was the occasional ball that would scuttle through low, but if the batsman got on to the front foot, this danger could be avoided. It was such a delivery that dismissed Ellison ten minutes before lunch.

Ellison and Gooch had done all that could have been expected of them as a pair, but Gooch's dismissal after $3\frac{1}{4}$ hours of stubborn defence, lbw as he played back, heralded an horrendous afternoon, a microcosm of much that had gone wrong on the tour. Neither Lamb nor Gatting, whose absence through injury had cast him in the role of missing saviour, suggested permanence. Gower, missed by Marshall off a simple return catch when 2, offered sterner resistance until Harper spun a ball to clip the outside edge as he brought the innings to an ironic end.

Botham, like Gooch, curbed his natural attacking game for half an hour and then saw a ball trickle back on to his stumps. Downton, who had been lucky to hold his place throughout the series, was lbw and Emburey was taken at slip. England had lost ten Test matches in a row to the West Indies, and there seemed little more to be said.

Few came out of the tour with credit. The appointment of Willis as assistant manager was an inspired miscasting, and one can only wonder in perplexity at what reasons were seen for the appointment. To Gower and to Willis, blame must be attached for the inept performances on the field and some of the events off it which stimulated so much adverse publicity. Gower is still learning the art of captaincy. He has had a hard

baptism, and if he is to succeed, he needs to assert his own individual quality of leadership which must include discipline as well as example. More than anything, England's cricket team needs dignity and discipline. We remarked on this following the Test against Sri Lanka at Lord's in 1984, but there are, as yet, no signs of it being achieved.

At the centre of much of the disquiet of the tour were Botham and Gooch although for different reasons. Gooch was caught in a political maelstrom of his own making. It was not simply his trip to South Africa three years ago which fuelled the flames, but some of his actions since. His trip had consequences beyond his comprehension, and he was ill advised to derive further revenue from the South African venture by his 'writings' and statements.

He was subjected to much abuse in the West Indies, but it would have helped the rest of the side more if he could have responded with something other than morose introspection.

He and Botham, in their varying ways, have come far from their roots. They have given much to the game, and derived a great deal from it. They now stand at a point where they have to find added maturity that will enable them to face their responsibilities to the game, to all those connected with it, and not least to themselves.

When West Indies toured England in 1984 we commented on the fact that Law 42, section 8, was consistently violated, and that the spirit of the game was totally ignored, so that spectators came to view the England side as sacrificial animals in a religious, or political, slaughter. We believe this state of affairs still exists, and one ponders on the future of cricket while acknowledging Richards's side as one of the very greatest, certainly in bowling, ever to have stepped into a Test arena.

LEFT: *King Viv – the West Indian captain at his mightiest, a hundred off 56 balls in front of his home crowd. (Adrian Murrell)*

Youth and Joy

The season in Sri Lanka
Sri Lanka *v.* India. Sri Lanka *v.* England 'B'. Sri Lanka *v.*
Pakistan. Three Nations Tournament. Asia Cup.

Ketterama Stadium.
(David Munden)

The 1984–85 season had been a lean one for followers of cricket in Sri Lanka. Two one-day internationals against a New Zealand side on its way to Pakistan were supplemented by two unexpected and unscheduled matches against the England side which had taken a temporary rest from the troubles in India. The Sri Lankan team then played in the two limited-over tournaments in Australia. They did themselves scant justice. Their fielding fell well below its usual high standard and the bowling looked weak. As the tour progressed, the spirits sagged and even the batting lacked lustre.

In spite of the poor form shown on the tour of Australia, Sri Lanka ended the year with a feeling of optimism. A strong Pakistan under-23 side had found formidable opposition in the island and the emergence of young players like Jurangpathy and Mahanama, coupled with the development of pace bowler Rumesh Ratnayake, gave hope that Sri Lanka were close to their first Test victory and the series against India which was scheduled to begin at the beginning of September was eagerly anticipated.

21, 22 and 23 August 1985

at Colombo

Sri Lankan Colts XI 385 for 6 dec (S. Warnakulasuriya 174 not out, R. Jurangpathy 61, A. Ranatunga 51) and 53 for 0
Indians 296 (D.B. Vengsarkar 133, S. Weerasinghe 5 for 114)

Match drawn

Sumithra Warnakulasuriya, 174 not out for the Colts XI against the Indian tourists. A most exciting debutant. (All Sport)

The strength of Sri Lankan's young cricketers was forcibly demonstrated in the opening match of the tour by the Indians. A rather dour first day saw the Colts reach 195 for 3 off 87 overs before bad light ended play. On the second day, opening batsman Sumithra Warnakulasuriya reached a maiden first-class century and finished on 174 which included 2 sixes and 15 fours. There was more impressive batting from Jurangpathy, but Vengsarkar hit a cultured hundred for the tourists and, inevitably, the match was drawn. The disturbing aspect from the Indian point of view was how well the young Sri Lankan batsmen dealt with the leg-spin of Sivaramakrishnan.

First One-Day International
SRI LANKA v. INDIA

The limited-over series series began with a splendid match which saw India gain victory with three balls to spare.

Sri Lanka began cautiously. Only 9 runs came from the first 5 overs, and after 15 overs they had reached only 32. Ravi Ratnayeke and Madugalle fell in quick succession, and Silva was out at 82. Roy Dias and Arjuna Ranatunga then launched a blistering attack upon the bowling which brought 110 runs at more than ten an over. Inspired by Mendis, Sri Lanka plundered 45 off the last 5 overs and appeared to have reached a winning score, but Srikkanth and Shastri gave India just the start they needed with 67 in 17 overs. Azharuddin again failed, but Vengsarkar and Shastri took the score to 135 before Shastri fell to Ranatunga. When Amarnath was out in the thirty-ninth over India were still 42 short of victory.

Vengsarkar's fine innings came to an end in the forty-fourth over with India 8 short of their target. Viswanath scrambled two off the next ball so that 6 runs were needed off the last over. De Mel had bowled disappointingly, erring in line and length in the closing overs, and it was he who was to bowl the final over. His first ball was short and Viswanath cut it for four. The next two deliveries were pushed for singles and India were home with three balls to spare.

Gamini Goonesena named Roy Dias as the Man of the Match for his thrilling batting display, and no one who witnessed this magnificent innings would argue with his choice.

26, 27 and 28 August 1985

at Colombo

Indians 249 (M. Azharuddin 66, R.N. Kapil Dev 58) and 123 for 2 (M. Azharuddin 59 not out)
Sri Lanka Board President's XI 361 for 9 dec (A. Gurusinghe 100 not out, S. Wettimuny 83)

Match drawn

The Indian tourists reached 225 for 6 on the first day off 84 overs and drew most comfort from Azharuddin's first worthwhile innings of the tour and a subdued fifty from Kapil Dev who had missed the opening first-class match with a throat infection. They lost their last 4 wickets in an hour on the second morning. Sidath Wettimuny batted four hours for his 83. He and Madugalle added 77 for the third wicket, but the dismissal of Madugalle saw 3 wickets fall for 2 runs in 15 balls. This brought Asanka Gurusinghe and Guy de Alwis

FIRST ONE-DAY INTERNATIONAL – SRI LANKA v. INDIA
25 August 1985 at Sinhalese Sports Club, Colombo

SRI LANKA				INDIA			
S.A.R. Silva*	c Chetan Sharma, b Shastri		36	R.J. Shastri	c J.R. Ratnayeke,		
J.R. Ratnayeke	c Shastri, b Amarnath		13		b Ranatunga		67
R.S. Madugalle	c and b Ghopal Sharma		3	K. Srikkanth	c de Mel, b Wijesuriya		29
R.L. Dias	b Chetan Sharma		80	M. Azharuddin	b Wijesuriyja		7
A. Ranatunga	b Chetan Sharma		64	D.B. Vengsarkar	c J.R. Ratnayeke,		
L.R.D. Mendis†	not out		29		b R.J. Ratnayeke		89
P.A. de Silva	b Chetan Sharma		4	R.N. Kapil Dev†	c Silva, b J.R. Ratnayeke		24
A.L.F. de Mel	not out		2	S.M. Gavaskar	run out		0
R.J. Ratnayake				M.B. Amarnath	c Silva, b R.J. Ratnayeke		2
R.G.C.E. Wijesuriya				Chetan Sharma	run out		8
V.B. John				S. Viswanath*	not out		7
Extras	lb 10		10	L. Sivaramakrishnan	not out		1
				Ghopal Sharma			
(45 overs)	(for 6 wickets)		241	Extras	lb 6, w 1, nb 1		8
				(44.3 overs)	(for 8 wickets)		242

	O	M	R	W		O	M	R	W
Kapil Dev	9	1	47	—	de Mel	8.3	1	54	—
Chetan Sharma	9	2	50	3	John	9	—	32	—
Ghopal Sharma	9	—	21	1	R.J. Ratnayake	9	—	35	2
Amarnath	8	—	40	1	Wijesuriya	8	—	56	2
Shastri	5	—	35	1	J.R. Ratnayeke	6	—	32	1
Sivaramakrishnan	5	—	38	—	Ranatunga	4	—	27	1

FALL OF WICKETS
1- 34, 2- 40, 3- 82, 4- 192, 5- 227, 6- 231

FALL OF WICKETS
1- 67, 2- 81, 3- 135, 4- 185, 5- 196, 6- 200, 7- 221, 8- 234

India won by 2 wickets

together and they stayed to add 56 before de Alwis fell to Kapil Dev on the last morning. Gurusinghe, yet another of Sri Lanka's talented schoolboys, played with a great sense of maturity and the 18-year old left-hander reached a fine century. There was time for Azharuddin to reach his second fifty of the match before the close. Apart from Azharuddin's batting, India could also be encouraged by Sivaramakrishnan's bowling. He did not bowl on the last morning, but took 3 for 46 in 20 overs on the second day.

First Test Match
SRI LANKA v. INDIA

Kapil Dev won the toss and decided to bat. It proved to be an unwise decision as Indian batsmen struggled throughout the first day to reach 184 for 7 before bad light ended play five minutes early.

They began most uneasily against the lively attack of Asantha de Mel and Rumesh Ratnayake who bowled Srikkanth after half an hour's play. Ratnayake should have had another success, but Azharuddin was dropped at slip by Ranatunga. The miss proved not to be costly, for Azharuddin, looking nothing like the batsman who had flayed the England bowlers ten months earlier, edged Saliya Ahangama's fourth ball in Test cricket to the wicket-keeper. The return of de Mel brought further disaster to India, for Vengsarkar flirted outside the off stump and provided Silva with his second catch while Rajput, after batting for an hour and a half, skied the ball to the wicket-keeper when he mishooked Ahangama. Shastri stayed only half an hour before becoming Silva's fourth victim.

Coming in at 65 for 5, Kapil Dev's response was typical.

He faced only 26 deliveries, but hit 7 fours in an innings of 36 which came in 24 minutes. He was responsible for the entire sixth wicket stand before he too was caught behind off de Mel.

Throughout these catastrophes Gavaskar batted with his usual calm and although Viswanath became de Mel's fourth wicket of the day, he and Chetan Sharma gave a hint of revival as they added 41 before the close. They took their stand to 59, the best of the innings, before Chetan Sharma became the sixth batsman to be caught by Amal Silva who thereby established a Test record for Sri Lanka.

Gavaskar's 342-minute innings came to an end when he was run out and two overs later the innings was over. Sri Lanka's start was as bad as India's had been. Chetan Sharma, showing more pace, control and movement than he had done against England, sent back Wettimuny, Silva and Dias with only 33 scored. Mendis dominated a stand of 85 in ten minutes over two hours and although he fell to Maninder Singh's left-arm spin, Sri Lanka had recovered somewhat at 148 for 4 by the close.

The third day saw Sri Lanka move into a position of total dominance. Madugalle and Ranatunga, who had been 55 and 16 not out respectively over night, both reached centuries, their first in Test cricket, and took their stand to 144 before Madugalle, having hit 10 fours, was caught and bowled by Maninder. Ranatunga was still unbeaten at the close which came at 342 for 7.

Ranatunga added only 2 to his overnight score on the fourth morning and the last three wickets fell for 5 runs. Silva soon claimed his seventh catch of the match, but after Azharuddin had again failed, Rajput and Vengsarkar looked to be taking India to safety in a dour struggle on a docile

FIRST TEST MATCH – SRI LANKA v. INDIA
30, 31 August, 1, 3 and 4 September 1985 at Sinhalese Sports Club, Maitland Place, Colombo

INDIA

	FIRST INNINGS		SECOND INNINGS	
L.S. Rajput	c Silva, b Ahangama	32	c Silva, b Ratnayake	61
K. Srikkanth	b Ratnayake	2	c Silva, b Ratnayake	9
M. Azharuddin	c Silva, b Ahangama	3	lbw, b Ahangama	16
D.B. Vengsarkar	c Silva, b de Mel	6	not out	98
S.M. Gavaskar	run out	51	c de Mel, b Ratnayake	0
R.J. Shastri	c Silva, b de Mel	9	lbw, b Ratnayake	40
R.N. Kapil Dev†	c Silva, b de Mel	36	c sub (Arunasiri), b Ratnayake	6
S. Viswanath*	c E.A.R. de Silva, b de Mel	20	c Silva, b Ratnayake	0
Chetan Sharma	c Silva, b de Mel	38	run out	4
Ghopal Sharma	not out	10	lbw, b Ahangama	1
Maninder Singh	lbw, b Ratnayake	0	b Ahangama	3
Extras	lb 5, w 1, nb 5	11	b 4, lb 3, nb 6	13
		218		251

SRI LANKA

	FIRST INNINGS		SECOND INNINGS	
S. Wettimuny	c Viswanath, b C. Sharma	13		
S.A.R. Silva*	c Azharuddin, b C. Sharma	7	(6) not out	1
R.S. Madugalle	c and b Maninder	103	(5) not out	5
R.L. Dias	c Azharuddin, b C. Sharma	4	(3) c Srikkanth, b Dev	0
L.R.D. Mendis†	c Gavaskar, b Maninder	51	(2) c Dev, b C. Sharma	18
A. Ranatunga	b Shastri	111	(4) run out	15
P.A. de Silva	c Azharuddin, b Shastri	33	(1) c Maninder, b Dev	21
A.L.F. de Mel	c Viswanath, b Dev	16		
R.J. Ratnayake	lbw, b Dev	2		
E.A.R. de Silva	not out	1		
F.S. Ahangama	c Viswanath, b Dev	0		
Extras	lb 5, nb 1	6	lb 1	1
		347	(for 4 wkts)	61

	O	M	R	W	O	M	R	W
de Mel	28	8	64	5	30	3	84	—
R.J. Ratnayake	24.2	8	64	2	41	10	85	6
Ahangama	23	3	60	2	27.3	10	49	3
E.A.R. de Silva	12	5	18	—	15	6	20	—
Ranatunga	10	8	7	—	6	2	6	—

	O	M	R	W	O	M	R	W
Kapil Dev	30.4	8	74	3	4	—	36	2
Chetan Sharma	25	3	81	3	4	—	24	1
Shastri	34	9	70	2				
Maninder Singh	40	12	82	2				
Ghopal Sharma	15	6	35	—				

FALL OF WICKETS
1- 19, 2- 30, 3- 47, 4- 49, 5- 65, 6- 101, 7- 143, 8- 202, 9- 218
1- 23, 2- 54, 3- 130, 4- 130, 5- 188, 6- 206, 7- 206, 8- 220, 9- 229

FALL OF WICKETS
1- 18, 2- 29, 3- 33, 4- 118, 5- 262, 6- 317, 7- 342, 8- 346, 9- 346
1- 38, 2- 39, 3- 44, 4- 58

Umpires: K.B. Francis & J. Felsinger

Match drawn

wicket. In the final session of the day, Rumesh Ratnayake found the edge of Rajput's bat with a lifting ball and three balls later deceived Gavaskar with his slower delivery. India slept uneasily at 153 for 4.

Sri Lanka's hopes of achieving their first Test victory were blighted on the last day when two hours play was lost to rain. Ratnayake, named Man of the Match, revived hopes with 3 wickets in 15 balls. In the sixth over of the delayed afternoon session, he had Shastri lbw, and two overs later his slower ball again proved effective as Kapil Dev mishit to mid-wicket. Viswanath was caught behind second ball which gave Ratnayake a career best 6 for 85 and brought Silva his ninth dismissal, a feat only bettered in Test cricket by Bob Taylor and only equalled by Marsh, Langley and D.A. Murray.

Maninder Singh held up Sri Lanka for 45 minutes as he and Vengsarkar put on 22 for the last wicket. This stand proved decisive in thwarting the home side who were left to make 123 in 11 overs.

Impossible as the target seemed, Sri Lanka attempted the task amid a buzz of excitement. Aravinda de Silva hooked the first ball from Kapil Dev out of the ground and Mendis began with two sparkling fours through extra cover. In four overs, they scored 38, but then the innings lost momentum as

LEFT: *Arjuna Ranatunga hit his first two Test centuries during the season was the most prolific run scorer in Sri Lanka. (All Sport)*

Madugalle – a maiden Test century v. *India at Colombo, September, 1985. (Adrian Murrell)*

Amal Silva – a century in Sri Lanka's first Test victory and 22 dismissals in the three-match Test series, a world record. (Ken Kelly)

3 wickets fell in 8 balls. Ranatunga revived hopes with some brisk running between the wickets, but he was run out, and Madugalle and Silva gave up the chase as the light faded and the match was abandoned with three overs still remaining.

Four players made their debuts in Test cricket in this match – Viswanath and Rajput for India; Asoka de Silva and Ahangama for Sri Lanka.

Second Test Match
SRI LANKA v. INDIA

Sri Lanka brought in Sanjeewa Weerasinghe, a seventeen-year old leg spinner, for his Test debut in place of Asoka de Silva, and India made two changes, Mohinder Amarnath and Laxman Sivaramakrishnan replacing Ghopal Sharma and Maninder Singh.

The first day was a dour affair. Aided by dropped catches, Sri Lanka reached 169 for 1 off 89 overs, six hours of batting. Madugalle was lbw to Chetan Sharma on the second morning without addition to the score, but Dias and Amal Silva put on 60 before Silva was caught behind off Shastri. His 111, his second hundred in four Tests, was made in 492 minutes. It was a dogged innings which laid the foundation of the success that was to come and earned him the Man of the Match award.

Roy Dias and Duleep Mendis now gave the innings a boost with a stand of 99 which ended shortly before tea,

which came at 337 for 4. Dias continued in rich form in the final session and looked set for a sparkling hundred until caught behind off Chetan Sharma at 368. He had hit 11 fours. His dismissal signalled a collapse and the last six wickets fell for 17 runs.

Sri Lanka could not have been disappointed by their total, however, and soon they had taken a firm grip on the game. The fourth ball of the innings saw Rajput edge de Mel to Silva who took an exciting diving catch. Azharuddin survived only two balls before touching the third to the wicket-keeper, and when Vengsarkar was taken at slip, India were 3 for 3, the back of their innings broken.

Nightwatchman Sivaramakrishnan survived the last two overs with eight men clustered round the bat and next day helped Srikkanath to restore some sanity to the Indian batting. It was Srikkanth who was the first to go for a courageous 64 out of 79, and 9 runs later Sivaramakrishnan fell to Ratnayake so that, at 88 for 5, India were in deep trouble again.

Gavaskar and Amarnath scored only 5 runs in the 10 overs they shared together before lunch, and Gavaskar, defending grimly, took 50 minutes to add to his score after the interval. The pair added 90 in 52 overs before, ironically, Gavaskar provided Silva with his first stumping in Test cricket. The former Indian captain had batted for 245 minutes and faced 166 balls. His innings included 7 fours. At the close, India were 210 for 6 and, seemingly, had saved the game.

Lively bowling by the three Sri Lankan seam bowlers brought renewed hope to the home side on the fourth morning as the last four wickets fell for the addition of only 34 runs. Wettimuny and Silva gave Sri Lanka a solid start in their bid for quick runs, but they fell in quick succession. This brought together Aravinda de Silva and Roy Dias.

Aravinda de Silva, promoted to give impetus to the innings, took 33 minutes to get off the mark, and at tea, the pair had added only 48. After the break they launched an astonishing attack upon the bowling which brought 64 in 6 overs. Aravinda de Silva, unquestionably one of the most exciting young batsmen in the world, hit 2 sixes and 9 fours in his first Test fifty, and Dias, who again batted splendidly, was unbeaten when Mendis declared.

Faced with the daunting task of scoring 348 to win, India had reached 16 in the seventh over when bad light ended play. Rajput and Srikkanth seemed in no trouble on the last morning and took the score to 39 before Rajput was lbw to de Mel off the last ball of the fifteenth over. Two balls later Srikkanth was out to Ratnayake and when Vengsarkar, the most successful of the Indian batsmen on the tour, was caught behind for nought, Sri Lanka scented a famous victory.

Azharuddin and Gavaskar took the score to 63 by lunch time, but an hour into the afternoon Sri Lanka again struck two quick blows as both batsmen fell to catches behind the wicket with the score on 84.

Shastri and Amarnath batted cautiously, but at 98, Sri Lanka yet again struck twice in quick succession. Aravinda de Silva took a magnificent catch at forward short leg to dismiss Amarnath and Shastri provided the irrepressible Amal Silva with his fourth catch of the innings.

Kapil Dev and Sivaramakrishnan now threatened to deny Sri Lanka. They resisted 85 minutes, during which time 70 runs were scored, but de Mel, who did so much throughout the series as the experienced member of the Sri Lankan attack, found the edge of Sivaramakrishnan's bat and Silva again swallowed the catch.

Viswanath was lbw third ball and the crowd waited rapturously as the last twenty overs began. They did not have long to wait, for with the second ball of the first of the mandatory overs, Ratnayake deceived Kapil Dev into giving him a return catch. The Indian captain's valiant innings was at an end and Sri Lanka had victory in a Test match for the first time. It was their fourteenth Test match since gaining that status.

Duleep Mendis, whose thoughtful and inspirational captaincy had been a vital factor in his country's success, was quoted as saying, 'This is the finest hour of my cricketing career – it's a dream come true.' It was a dream come true for many of the charming and kindly people who inhabit the island. None was happier than President Junius Jayewardene who watched the play and declared a public holiday in celebration of the famous victory.

SECOND TEST MATCH – SRI LANKA v. INDIA
6, 7, 8, 10 and 11 September 1985 at P. Saravanamuttu Oval, Colombo

SRI LANKA

	FIRST INNINGS		SECOND INNINGS	
S. Wettimuny	run out	19	c Rajput, b C. Sharma	32
S.A.R. Silva*	c Viswanath, b Shastri	111	c Vengsarkar, b Dev	11
R.S. Madugalle	lbw, b C. Sharma	54		
R.L. Dias	c Viswanath, b C. Sharma	95	not out	60
L.R.D. Mendis†	c Shastri, b Amarnath	51	not out	13
A. Ranatunga	lbw, b C. Sharma	21		
P.A. de Silva	c Azharuddin, b C. Sharma	2	(3) b Shastri	75
A.L.F. de Mel	lbw, b Shastri	0		
R.J. Ratnayake	c Sivarama, b Shastri	7		
S. Weerasinghe	b C. Sharma	3		
F.S. Ahangama	not out	0		
	lb 3, w 4, nb 15	22	b 4, lb 6, nb 5	15
		385	(for 3 wkts dec)	206

INDIA

	FIRST INNINGS		SECOND INNINGS	
L.S. Rajput	c Silva, b de Mel	0	lbw, b de Mel	12
K. Srikkanth	c Mendis, b Ahangama	64	lbw, b Ranayake	25
M. Azharuddin	c Silva, b Ratnayake	0	c Silva, b de Mel	25
D.B. Vengsarkar	c Ranatunga, b Ratnayake	1	c Silva, b Ratnayake	0
L. Sivarama-krishnan	c Wettimuny, b Ratnayake	18	(9) c Silva, b de Mel	21
S.M. Gavaskar	st Silva, b Ranatunga	52	(5) c Silva, b Ratnayake	19
M.B Amarnath	c Ahangama, b de Mel	60	(6) c de Silva, b Ratnayake	10
R.J. Shastri	c Silva, b Ahangama	17	(7) c Silva, b Ahangama	4
R.N. Kapil Dev†	c Ratnayake b Ahangama	6	(8) c and b Ratnayake	78
S. Viswanath*	c Wettimuny, b Ratnayake	7	lbw, b Ahangama	0
Chetan Sharma	not out	4	not out	0
Extras	b 4, lb 6, w 1, nb 4	15	lb 2, nb 2	4
		244		198

	O	M	R	W	O	M	R	W
Kapil Dev	32	10	69	—	20	4	73	1
Chetan Sharma	33	3	118	5	13	1	55	1
Shastri	45.3	11	74	3	13	4	41	1
Sivaramakrishnan	31	4	90	—	7	1	27	—
Amarnath	15	2	31	1				

	O	M	R	W	O	M	R	W
de Mel	31	8	63	2	22	4	64	3
R.J. Ratnayake	25.1	5	76	4	23.2	6	49	5
Ahangama	18	3	59	3	14	3	56	2
Weerasinghe	16	7	28	—	3	1	8	—
Ranatunga	5	1	8	1	4	—	19	—

FALL OF WICKETS
1- 74, 2- 169, 3- 229, 4- 328, 5- 368, 6- 372, 7- 375, 8- 375, 9- 379
1- 46, 2- 48, 3- 180

FALL OF WICKETS
1- 0, 2- 1, 3- 3, 4- 79, 5- 88, 6- 178, 7- 218, 8- 229, 9- 238
1- 39, 2- 39, 3- 41, 4- 84, 5- 84, 6- 98, 7- 98, 8- 168, 9- 169

Umpires: S. Ponnadurai & P.W. Vidanagamage

Sri Lanka won by 149 runs

Third Test Match
SRI LANKA v. INDIA

India took the wise step of utilising Shastri's talents more fully and promoted him to open the innings in place of Rajput whose place went to Roger Binny. Maninder Singh's slow left-arm was preferred to the leg-spin of Sivaramakrishnan. Sri Lanka also dropped their leg-spinner and gave a first Test cap to Jurangpathy, an exciting schoolboy batsman and off-break bowler.

Once again India had an uneasy first day after Shastri had fallen at 10, but the middle order showed a greater sense of stability and they closed at 197 for 6. They added another 52 on the second morning and soon had Sri Lanka in trouble as the pace trio of Kapil Dev, Binny and Chetan Sharma reduced them to 80 for 4. Ranatunga and Mendis came together in a stand of 73 in 100 minutes which effected a recovery, and after Ranatunga, who had hit a six and 6 fours, was out, only one more ball was possible before bad light ended play 17 minutes early.

On the third morning, India played their best cricket of the tour. Although Binny was out of the attack through injury, they took the last five Sri Lankan wickets for the addition of only 45 runs and Maninder Singh had his best bowling figures in Test cricket. Srikkanth and Shastri then gave India's second innings a rousing start with a brisk stand of 74 which ended when Srikkanth was lbw after scoring 47 off 40

balls. India ended the day at 149 for 1.

When play resumed on the fourth day Shastri and Amarnath took their second wicket stand to 104 before Shastri became Silva's twenty-second and last dismissal of the series. Amarnath reached a most accomplished century and Kapil Dev was able to declare and leave his side seven hours and twenty overs in which to bowl out the opposition. They could hardly have begun better as Wettimuny, Silva and Madugalle were all back in the pavilion with 34 scored. Dias and Mendis stayed until the close which came at 78 for 3, but Sri Lanka faced defeat.

The day had certainly belonged to India. Amarnath's ninth Test hundred had come off 207 balls and his innings had lasted 395 minutes. Kapil Dev had become India's leading wicket-taker in Test cricket when he had Silva caught behind. It was his two hundred and sixty-seventh Test wicket. Chetan Sharma had begun the collapse when he had Wettimuny caught at slip off his third ball.

India sensed victory, but Mendis and Dias had worked hard to bring Sri Lanka to this point in a Test series and they were not going to surrender easily. Sri Lanka's two leading batsmen, captain and vice-captain, stayed throughout the morning and into the afternoon until a few minutes before tea when Dias was run out. They had added 216, a Sri Lankan fourth wicket record in Test cricket, and Dias had batted for 312 minutes, hitting 17 fours off the 216 balls he received.

THIRD TEST MATCH – SRI LANKA v. INDIA
14, 15, 16, 18 and 19 September 1985 at Asgiriya, Kandy

INDIA

	FIRST INNINGS		SECOND INNINGS	
R.J. Shastri	c Madugalle, b de Mel	6	c Silva, b Ahangama	81
K. Srikkanth	b Ahangama	40	lbw, b Ahangama	47
M.B. Amarnath	lbw, b Ahangama	30	not out	116
D.B. Vengsarkar	run out	62	lbw, b Ahangama	10
M. Azharuddin	c Silva, b Ahangama	25	(6) b Ratnayake	43
S.M. Gavaskar	c Silva, b Ratnayake	49	(7) not out	15
R.N. Kapil Dev†	lbw, b Ahangama	0	(5) b Ranatunga	2
R.M.H. Binny	c de Mel, b Ahangama	19		
Chetan Sharma	c Wettimuny, b de Mel	11		
S. Viswanath*	c Silva, b Ratnayake	4		
Maninder Singh	not out	0		
Extras	lb 1, w 1, nb 1	3	lb 5, w 4, nb 2	11
		249	(for 5 wkts dec)	325

SRI LANKA

	FIRST INNINGS		SECOND INNINGS	
S. Wettimuny	c Viswanath, b Dev	34	c Vengsarkar, b C. Sharma	5
S.A.R. Silva*	lbw, b Binny	19	c Viswanath, b Dev	2
R.S. Madugalle	c and b Binny	5	c Viswanath, b Dev	10
R.L. Dias	c Viswanath, b. C. Sharma	8	run out	106
L.R.D. Mendis†	c sub (Sivaramakrishnan), b Maninder	53	c Gavaskar, b C. Sharma	124
A. Ranatunga	c Vengsarkar, b Maninder	38	b C. Sharma	0
F.S. Ahangama	c Gavaskar, b Maninder	11		
P.A. de Silva	run out	8	(7) not out	29
R. Jurangpathy	c Viswanath, b Dev	1	(8) lbw, b Dev	0
A.L.F. de Mel	c Viswanath, b Maninder	1	(9) not out	9
R.J. Ratnayake	not out	0		
Extras	lb 4, nb 16	20	b 8, lb 4, w 4, nb 6	22
		198	(for 7 wkts)	307

	O	M	R	W	O	M	R	W
de Mel	26.3	5	97	2	13	2	66	—
R.J. Ratnayake	26	5	88	2	23	2	97	1
Ahangama	24	7	52	5	27	6	72	3
Ranatunga	8	5	11	—	16	4	51	1
Jurangpathy					4	—	24	—
Madugalle					1	—	10	—

	O	M	R	W	O	M	R	W
Kapil Dev	19	4	46	2	24	4	74	3
Binny	12	—	49	2				
Chetan Sharma	14	1	40	1	20	4	65	3
Shastri	6	2	28	—	24	5	57	—
Maninder Singh	12.3	4	31	4	34	11	99	—

FALL OF WICKETS
1- 10, 2- 66, 3- 111, 4- 161, 5- 180, 6- 180, 7- 212, 8- 241, 9- 242
1- 74, 2- 178, 3- 206, 4- 211, 5- 289

FALL OF WICKETS
1- 36, 2- 44, 3- 68, 4- 80, 5- 153, 6- 173, 7- 196, 8- 197, 9- 198
1- 5, 2- 8, 3- 34, 4- 250, 5- 250, 6- 266, 7- 267

Umpires: Guneratne & Boultjens

Match drawn

Ranatunga chopped the first ball he received from Chetan Sharma into his stumps and after tea Mendis edged the same bowler to Gavaskar at slip. The Sri Lankan captain had hit 2 sixes and 11 fours and had faced 228 balls in his 318 minutes at the wicket. Mendis and Dias had also become the first Sri Lankans to pass 1000 runs in Test cricket. No country has been better served by its senior players.

Jurangpathy was out fourth ball and Sri Lanka, having lost 4 wickets for 17 runs, were 267 for 7, and, in spite of the heroic stand between Dias and Mendis, they still faced

defeat. Aravinda de Silva, playing with a maturity and sense of responsibility beyond his years, and de Mel survived for 30 minutes until the last twenty overs were due, and, in an atmosphere of great excitement before a capacity crowd of 20,000 they continued to defy the Indian bowlers.

The light began to fade and the overs passed. Forty runs were added and seven overs still remained when bad light brought play to an end, and, amid scenes of great jubilation, Sri Lanka had saved the day and won a Test series for the first time.

There had been some notable performances in the Sri Lankan ranks during the series. With 20 wickets, Rumesh Ratnayake had established a record for a three-match Test series for Sri Lanka, beating the 17 of Somachandra de Silva against Pakistan in 1982. Amal Silva set up a world record for a three-match series with 22 dismissals.

Second One-Day International
SRI LANKA v. INDIA

Reduced from 45 overs to 30 overs because rain had delayed the start, the second one-day international lost another two overs because of India's slow over rate. Sri Lanka began briskly and had scored 21 off 5 overs before Silva was bowled by Kapil Dev. The lively pace was maintained and when Aravinda de Silva was out in the tenth over the score was 54.

LEFT: *Roy Dias – match-saving century in the third Test* v. *India, at Kandy. (Ken Kelly)*

BELOW: *Asgiriya Stadium, Kandy. (Michael King – All Sport)*

Sri Lanka *v.* India – Test Match Averages

SRI LANKA BATTING

	M	Inns	NOs	Runs	HS	Av	100s	50s
L.R.D. Mendis	3	6	1	310	124	62.00	1	3
R.L. Dias	3	6	1	273	106	54.60	1	2
R.S. Madugalle	3	5	1	177	103	44.25	1	1
A. Ranatunga	3	5		185	111	37.00	1	
P.A. de Silva	3	6	1	168	75	33.60		1
S.A.R. Silva	3	6	1	151	111	30.20	1	
S. Wettimuny	3	5		103	34	20.60		
A.L.F. de Mel	3	4	1	26	16	8.66		
F.A. Ahangama	3	3	1	11	11	5.50		
R.J. Ratnayake	3	3	1	9	7	4.50		

Played in one Test: E.A.R. de Silva 1*; S. Weerasinghe 3; R. Jurangpathy 1 & 0.

SRI LANKA BOWLING

	Overs	Mds	Runs	Wkts	Av	Best	5/inns
F.S. Ahangama	133.3	32	348	18	19.33	5/452	1
R.J. Ratnayake	162.5	36	459	20	22.95	6/85	2
A.L.F. de Mel	150.3	28	438	12	36.50	5/64	1
A. Ranatunga	49	20	102	2	51.00	1/8	

Also bowled: E.A.R. de Silva 27-11-38-0; S. Weerasinghe 19-8-36-0; R. Jurangpathy 4-0-24-0; R.S. Madugalle 1-0-10-0.

SRI LANKA CATCHES

22 - S.A.R. Silva (ct 21/st 1); 3 - S. Wettimuny; 2 - A.L.F. de Mel and R.J. Ratnayake; 1 - E.A.R. de Silva, L.R.D. Mendis, A. Ranatunga, F.S. Ahangama, P.A. de Silva, R.S. Madugalle and sub (S.D. Anurasiri)

INDIA BATTING

	M	Inns	NOs	Runs	HS	Av	100s	50s
M.B. Amarnath	2	4	1	216	116*	72.00	1	1
S.M. Gavaskar	3	6		186	52	37.20		2
D.B. Vengsarkar	3	6	1	177	98*	35.40		2
K. Srikkanth	3	6		187	64	31.16		1
L.S. Rajput	2	4		105	61	26.25		1
R.J. Shastri	3	6		157	81	26.16		1
R.N. Kapil Dev	3	6		128	78	21.33		1
Chetan Sharma	3	5	2	57	38	19.00		
M. Azharuddin	3	6		112	43	18.66		
S. Viswanath	3	5		31	20	6.20		
Maninder Singh	2	3	1	3	3	1.50		

Played in one Test: Ghopal Sharma 10* & 1; L. Sivaramakrishnan 18 & 21; R.M.H. Binny 19.

INDIA BOWLING

	Overs	Mds	Runs	Wkts	Av	Best	5/inns
Chetan Sharma	109	12	383	14	27.35	5/118	1
R.N. Kapil Dev	129.4	30	372	11	3.81	3/74	
Maninder Singh	86.3	27	212	6	35.33	4/31	
R.J. Shastri	122.3	31	270	6	45.00	3/74	

Also bowled: R.M.H. Binny 12-0-49-2; Ghopal Sharma 15-6-35-0; M.B. Amarnath 15-2-31-1; L. Sivaramakrishnan 38-5-117-0.

INDIA CATCHES

11 - S. Viswanath; 4 - M. Azharuddin; 3 - S.M. Gavaskar and D.B. Vengsarkar; 2 - Maninder Singh and L. Sivaramakrishnan (one as sub); 1 - K. Srikkanth, R.J. Shastri, L.S. Rajput and R.M.H. Binny

Mendis and Dias were out at the same total, but Madugalle, not renowned for brisk scoring, and Ravi Ratnayeke launched a ferocious assault on the bowling in the closing overs, and they added 73 in under 9 overs.

In spite of losing Srikkanth in the second over, India matched Sri Lanka's early scoring rate and they too were 55 after 10 overs, but thereafter some particularly accurate bowling by Vinothen John and spinner Roger Wijesuriya tied them down and they fell 15 short of their target so that Sri Lanka levelled the series.

Third One-Day International
SRI LANKA *v.* INDIA

The match was reduced to forty overs after rain had delayed the start and was abandoned in the afternoon as the overcast conditions turned to gloom.

India never found run making easy, but a late flourish brought 44 from the last 5 overs. Intent on quick runs in order to beat the weather, Sri Lanka lost Silva to Kapil Dev's fifth ball, and de Silva spooned Chetan Sharma's first ball to mid-wicket. Two more wickets fell just before the abandonment.

Dilip Vengsarkar was named Man of the Match and also won the award as Man of the Series. He gained his third award, one of the two special awards, for his play in the Test matches. The other, not surprisingly, went to record breaker Amal Silva. The Man of the Test series, and the hero of Sri Lanka, was unquestionably Duleep Mendis and he took the award worth Rs 50,000 as well as the President Jayewardene Trophy for his proud team.

The early part of 1986 was to have seen an England 'B' team under the leadership of Mark Nicholas and the management of Peter Lush make a goodwill tour to Bangladesh, Sri Lanka and Zimbabwe. The party was about to board the

Rumesh Ratnayake who took a record 20 wickets in the three-match Test series against India. (Michael King – All Sport)

SECOND ONE-DAY INTERNATIONAL – SRI LANKA v. INDIA
21 September 1985 at Colombo

SRI LANKA							
S.A.R. Silva*	b Kapil Dev						11
P.A. de Silva	c Kapil Dev, b Shastri						24
R.L. Dias	b Ghopal Sharma						27
L.R.D. Mendis†	run out						20
A. Ranatunga	b Binny						7
R.S. Madugalle	not out						50
J.R. Ratnayeke	not out						26
A.L.F. de Mel							
R.J. Ratnayake							
R.G.C.E. Wijesuriya							
V.B. John							
Extras	lb 4, w 1, nb 1						6
(28 overs)	(for 5 wickets)						171

	O	M	R	W
Kapil Dev	5	—	26	1
Chetan Sharma	6	—	49	—
Shastri	6	—	22	1
Binny	5	—	42	1
Ghopal Sharma	6	1	28	1

FALL OF WICKETS
1- 21, 2- 54, 3- 86, 4- 86, 5- 98

INDIA							
R.J. Shastri	st Silva, b Wijesuriya						25
K. Srikkanth	b John						10
M. Azharuddin	c Mendis, b John						26
D.B. Vengsarkar	run out						50
S.M. Gavaskar	not out						36
R.N. Kapil Dev†	not out						6
M.B. Amarnath							
R.M.H. Binny							
S. Viswanath*							
Chetan Sharma							
Ghopal Sharma							
Extras	lb 2, w 2						4
(28 overs)	(for 4 wickets)						157

	O	M	R	W
de Mel	3	—	20	—
John	6	—	26	2
R.J. Ratnayake	6	—	33	—
J.R. Ratnayeke	6	—	34	—
Wijesuriya	5	—	31	1
Ranatunga	2	—	11	—

FALL OF WICKETS
1- 12, 2- 60, 3- 75, 4- 143

Sri Lanka won by 14 runs

plane for Bangladesh when news arrived that the government of that country had cancelled the invitation because of the inclusion in the England party of players who had played cricket in South Africa. Zimbabwe later followed the same course. It seemed that both nations wished the TCCB to force players to sign documents stating their opposition to apartheid. It is probable that players were willing to do this, but such an imposition on a selected side is a violation of individual liberty, the essence of why we are opposed to apartheid itself.

The original breaks with South Africa at international level in cricket were for cricketing reasons. These have long since faded into the background as cricket is used as a shop-window for political posturing, and as the cricketer who may well go to South Africa to coach young players of all races and colours finds himself vilified, the businessmen slip quietly on and off their planes to and from Johannesburg. Apartheid is one of the world's foremost evils, but it will not be ended by hypocrisy.

Thankfully, the Sri Lankan government, firmly opposed to apartheid in word and deed, is prone neither to hypocrisy nor acts of stupid pettiness, and Sri Lankan cricketers and cricket-loving people received the bonus of an extended tour by the England 'B' side so making the 1985–86 season the fullest since Sri Lanka achieved Test status.

The England tour had a very damp start, and the first match, against Sri Lanka Colts had to be rescheduled to begin a day later than intended. The England party was a strong one with, perhaps, two areas where one could find disagreement. The first was in the choice of wicket-keeper where Rhodes of Worcestershire found preference after only one full season in first-class cricket. This seemed hard on players like David East, 'Jack' Russell and Bobby Parks who had proved themselves consistently over the past few years. East had the added claim of having hit centuries against two of the three leading counties in 1985. Rhodes is a very talented young player, but the selectors are not at their best when it comes to wicket-keepers and it seemed that he owed much to the support he had been given by the press. It was hard to follow the reasoning, too, which could select Rhodes on the strength of one season's performance, but ignore Radford and Maru as being 'one-year wonders'.

LEFT: *Three men who handled a difficult situation with tact and calm – Mark Nicholas (captain), Peter Lush (manager) and Norman Gifford (assistant manager). (Michael King – All Sport)*

THIRD ONE-DAY INTERNATIONAL – SRI LANKA v. INDIA
22 September, 1985 at Colombo

INDIA				SRI LANKA			
R.J. Shastri	lbw, b J.R. Ratnayeke		45	S.A.R. Silva*	b Kapil Dev		1
K. Srikkanth	b de Mel		8	P.A. de Silva	c Vengsarkar,		
M. Azharuddin	run out		13		b Chetan Sharma		2
D.B. Vengsarkar	b R.J. Ratnayake		55	R.L. Dias	c Kapil Dev,		
M.B. Amarnath	c Silva, b R.J. Ratnayeke		5		b Chetan Sharma		12
R.N. Kapil Dev†	c Wijesuriya, b Ranatunga		12	L.R.D. Mendis†	not out		14
S.M. Gavaskar	not out		39	R.S. Madugalle	c Viswanath, b Kapil Dev		1
R.M.H. Binny	not out		8	A. Ranatunga	not out		0
S. Viswanath*				J.R. Ratnayeke			
Chetan Sharma				A.L.F. de Mel			
Ghopal Sharma				R.J. Ratnayake			
Extras	b 3, lb 5, w 1		9	R.G.C.E. Wijesuriya			
			—	V.B. John			
(40 overs)	(for 6 wickets)		194	Extras	lb 1, w 1		2
							—
				(9.2 overs)	(for 4 wickets)		32

	O	M	R	W
de Mel	8	—	39	1
John	8	2	22	—
R.J. Ratnayake	7	—	41	2
Ranatunga	6	2	23	1
J.R. Ratnayeke	7	—	38	1
Wijesuriya	4	—	23	—

	O	M	R	W
Kapil Dev	5	—	20	2
Chetan Sharma	4.2	—	11	2

FALL OF WICKETS
1- 25, 2- 55, 3- 84, 4- 102, 5- 135, 6- 173

FALL OF WICKETS
1- 4, 2- 4, 3- 26, 4- 32

Match abandoned

Maru must have pressed his claims hard, for when the selectors came to choose a spinner it was apparent that the cupboard was bare. Marks was not available and the best spinners in the country, Underwood, Acfield and Pocock, were all of the veteran stage. The final choice fell on Nick Cook who had had a miserable time since he last played for England and had left Leicestershire for Northants after a dreadful season in which he could not command a regular place in the county side. He is a pleasant young man and one hoped that the tour would renew his faith and confidence.

12, 13 and 14 January 1986

at P. Savaranamuttu Oval, Colombo

Sri Lanka Colts 247 (A. Ranatunga 120) and 102 for 2 dec
England 'B' 112 (S.D. Anurasiri 5 for 38) and 96 for 3 (C.W.J. Athey 53 not out)

Match drawn

The wet and windy weather continued, and Mark Nicholas invited the opposition to bat when he won the toss. Vonhagt pushed the first ball into the covers for two and the tour had begun at last. Play started 45 minutes late and was disrupted by rain, but the first day produced some drama with Lawrence twice being warned for running on the wicket and being hit for five successive boundaries by Arjuna Ranatunga who shared a third wicket stand of 100 with his brother Dhimikki.

Arjuna ran to his century on the second day at the end of

LEFT: *The victorious captain, Duleep Mendis. He and Dias added a record 216 for Sri Lanka's 4th wicket in the third Test. No country has been better served by its senior players. (Adrian Murrell)*

RIGHT: *Left-arm bowler Don Anurasiri who troubled the England 'B' team in their opening match and later won a Test place in the series against Pakistan. (All Sport)*

which the tourists were in dreadful trouble at 91 for 7. It was left-arm spinner Anurasiri who did most of the damage. Rhodes batted two hours for his 21 not out and was well supported by Lawrence so that the indignity of the follow-on was avoided, but there was further trouble for England 'B' when Nicholas retired with a groin strain which, at first, seemed to be very serious. Athey batted with increasing confidence to prevent further embarrassment.

16, 17 and 18 January 1986

at P. Savaranamuttu Oval, Colombo

Sri Lanka Board President's XI 331 for 5 dec (S. Warnakulasuriya 93, A.P. Gurusinghe 82, S. Wettimuny 57) and 106 for 1 (S.M.S. Kaluperuma 50)
England 'B' 288 (C.L. Smith 116, E.A.R. de Silva 5 for 85)

Match drawn

As the England side fielded throughout a hot first day, the imbalance of their attack became apparent, Cook bowling 27 consecutive overs with no substantial spin support. The President's XI closed the day at 263 for 2, but the following morning Gurusinghe and Warnakulasuriya were out quickly, having added 173 for the third wicket. Warnakulasuriya's form against the Indians and in this match suggested that he could not long be denied a regular Test place.

The tourists' innings was held together by a fine knock by Chris Smith who hit 17 fours and a six in his 116. Asoka de Silva, who had made his Test debut against the Indians, troubled all batsmen with his spin.

Stephen Rhodes appeals for lbw against Gurusinghe, Board President's XI v. England 'B', 16–18 January 1986. Both players had outstanding success in the matches between the touring side and the Sri Lankans. (Michael King – All Sport)

First International
SRI LANKA XI v. ENGLAND 'B'

Anxious to give first-class experience and practice to several players, the Sri Lankan selectors chose two different elevens for the first two international matches, including five players with Test experience in each side.

England 'B' were led by Mark Nicholas who had made a rapid recovery from his groin strain. Neither Cowans nor Lawrence was fit for consideration, and Pringle shared the new ball with Agnew. Nicholas won the toss and the England side batted, but they were soon in difficulties. Moxon was bowled by a beautiful in-swinger, and Ravi Ratnayeke also accounted for Nicholas who shuffled uneasily across his crease. Warnaweera, with his medium pace off cutters, was testing all batsmen and it was no surprise when he accounted for Athey who was bowled as he unwisely attempted to sweep. At lunch, England 'B' were 79 for 3.

Slack and Smith batted sensibly throughout the afternoon and their stand realised 125, ending the first ball after tea when Smith was beaten after a most responsible innings. Barnett dragged a ball on to his stumps and Slack's fine innings, which lasted 290 minutes and contained 13 fours, ended when he was taken at short-leg off Anurasiri's slow left-arm spin. Pringle played some handsome shots until falling to the second new ball, and England 'B' closed the day at 243 for 7.

The second day saw the game swing in favour of the England side. Rhodes, playing straight and forward, gave a gritty display to reach a career best 77 not out. He was given admirable support by the determined Nick Cook, and the pair added 86 runs of great merit before Cook was caught behind, dabbing at a gentle off-break.

ABOVE: *The teams gather for the beginning of the series. England 'B' and the Sri Lankan players. (Michael King – All Sport)*

RIGHT: *An England lapse – D. Ranatunga is missed by Moxon at slip off the bowling of Pringle. (Michael King – All Sport)*

Cook's part in the day was far from over. The England 'B' pace attack was rather savaged by the Sri Lankan openers, but the advent of Cook's slow left-arm changed the course of events. With fielders crowding eagerly around the bat, he floated the ball into the breeze and gained reward. Dhimikki, the elder of the Ranatunga brothers, was taken low at extra cover. Vonhagt popped a catch to silly point and Arjuna was lbw playing a wretched shot. Shortly before the close Samaresekera was also taken at extra cover after batting well, and the day ended with the Sri Lankans on 122 for 4.

The paucity of the England spin attack in support of Cook was never more apparent than on the third day when a chanceless century by the left-handed Gurusinghe took the home side away from danger and nullified Cook's brave, lone effort. Sri Lanka were aided by some poor catching. In all, six catches went down, four of them missed caught and bowled chances, three of them by Cook.

Gurusinghe, a willowy 19-year old, punished anything loose and batted most attractively. His youthful eagerness seemed to symbolise the joy and zest for cricket in his country where so many young players of exciting ability are emerging.

England 'B', leading by 118 on the first innings, lost Moxon before the close, and Rhodes, who had come in as night-watchman, reached his second fifty of the match on the last morning. There was still time for Cook to bring his match haul to ten before the game ended in a draw, and we were left to reflect on what we had felt when the party was first named – 'where have all the spinners gone?'

Special mention should be made of Bill Athey's fielding. He took six catches in the match, five of them at silly point of a highly commendable nature. England had one or two things to be pleased about.

Second International
SRI LANKA XI v. ENGLAND 'B'

Cowans was still unfit for the England side, suffering from strained stomach muscles, and Tremlett was omitted to accommodate Lawrence. Randall was again named as twelfth man even though Slack had a hamstring injury.

Nicholas won the toss and asked Sri Lanka to bat on a wicket which had both bounce and movement. His decision was wrecked, however, when England missed their chances. The most significant was when the fourth ball of Agnew's opening over found the edge of Wettimuny's bat, but Moxon dropped the catch at third slip. Wettimuny went on to reach his first first-class hundred since his innings at Lord's in 1984. He was not dismissed until the second day by which time he had batted 463 minutes, faced 338 balls and hit 17 fours. He had another 'life' when Barnett missed him in the gully, but the Derbyshire captain had been unwell during the first

Success for Nick Cook. Samarasekera is caught by Bill Athey for 5 in the Sri Lankan Xi's second innings of the first match of the series. (Michael King – All Sport)

OPPOSITE LEFT: *Mark Nicholas falls lbw to Ravi Ratnayeke for 11 in the first match of the series. (Michael King – All Sport)*
OPPOSITE RIGHT: *Slack, who later went to the West Indies as replacement for Gatting, is caught behind by de Alwis off the bowling of Ranatunga. Slack made 21, having hit 96 in the first innings. (Michael King – All Sport)*

international and was to retire ill during the course of this one.

The England bowling was generally erratic with Lawrence and Agnew giving a generous sprinkling of wides and no-balls. Three bouncers from Lawrence bounded over the wicket-keeper's head for byes. Sri Lanka closed the first day at 231 for 2, but lost Ranatunga to the first ball of the second over on the second morning when he hit loosely to cover. Kaluperuma was dropped at slip by Athey before he had scored, Lawrence being the unlucky bowler, and he went on to hit 9 fours in his highest first-class score. Mahanama hit 5 fours before being caught at short-leg off Agnew, the best of the England bowlers.

The England openers had an uneasy time against Asoka de Silva's leg-spin, but they came safely to the close at 81 for 0. They completed the first century opening stand of the tour next morning, but it was no surprise when they fell to the

FIRST INTERNATIONAL MATCH – SRI LANKA XI v. ENGLAND 'B'
20, 21, 22 and 23 January 1986 at Sinhalese Sports Club, Maitland Place, Colombo

ENGLAND 'B'

	FIRST INNINGS			SECOND INNINGS	
M.D. Moxon	b Ratnayeke	8	b Amalean		4
W.N. Slack	c Vonhagt, b Anurasiri	96	c de Alwis, b A. Ranatunga		21
M.C.J. Nicholas†	lbw, b Ratnayeke	11			
C.W.J. Athey	b Warnaweera	5	(5) run out		6
C.L. Smith	lbw, b Warnaweera	62	(4) b Warnaweera		2
K.J. Barnett	b Samarasekera	12	not out		16
D.R. Pringle	c de Alwis, b Ratnayeke	27	not out		9
S.J. Rhodes*	not out	77	(3) c A. Ranatunga, b Warnaweera		57
T.M. Tremlett	c Gurusinghe, b Warnaweera	21			
N.G.B. Cook	c de Alwis, b D. Ranatunga	39			
J.P. Agnew	c and b D. Ranatunga	0			
Extras	b 1, lb 3, nb 1	5	lb 5, w 1		6
		363	(for 5 wkts dec)		121

	O	M	R	W	O	M	R	W
J.R. Ratnayeke	22	2	56	3	6	2	11	—
Amalean	17	4	55	—	7	1	22	1
Warnaweera	39	10	97	3	14.3	3	49	2
Anurasiri	34	12	67	1	5	1	12	—
Guneratne	14	2	53	—				
Samarasekera	5	2	20	1				
D. Ranatunga	2.4	—	11	2				
A. Ranatunga					8	1	22	1

FALL OF WICKETS
1- 15, 2- 39, 3- 51, 4- 176, 5- 197, 6- 197, 7- 243, 8- 277, 9- 363
1- 12, 2- 47, 3- 56, 4- 78

SRI LANKA XI

	FIRST INNINGS			SECOND INNINGS	
M.D. Vonhagt	c Athey, b Cook	22	c Tremlett, b Cook		11
D. Ranatunga	c Moxon, b Cook	30	b Cook		26
M.A.R. Samarasekera	c Tremlett, b Cook	32	(4) c Athey, b Cook		5
A. Ranatunga†	lbw, b Cook	0	(3) c Athey, b Cook		0
A.P. Gurusinghe	c Rhodes, b Agnew	111	not out		21
S.D Anurasiri	c Athey, b Cook	8			
R.G. de Alwis*	c Cook, b Tremlett	11			
J.R. Ratnayeke	c Athey, b Agnew	14	(6) not out		42
R.P.W. Guneratne	c Moxon, b Agnew	2			
K.N. Amalean	not out	3			
K.P.J. Warnaweera	c Athey, b Cook	1			
Extras	b 2, lb 5, nb 4	11	b 4, lb 1, nb 1		6
		245	(for 4 wkts)		111

	O	M	R	W	O	M	R	W
Agnew	27	6	77	3	7	2	17	—
Pringle	16	4	40	—	8	2	27	—
Tremlett	22	7	45	1	11	5	15	—
Cook	44.4	20	69	6	17	7	28	4
Smith	2	—	7	—	1	—	4	—
Barnett					3	1	15	—
Athey					1	1	0	—

FALL OF WICKETS
1- 49, 2- 58, 3- 74, 4- 121, 5- 165, 6- 193, 7- 236, 8- 239, 9- 240
1- 31, 2- 31, 3- 41, 4- 53

Umpires: K.T. Francis & P.W. Vidanagamage

Match drawn

SECOND INTERNATIONAL MATCH – SRI LANKA XI v. ENGLAND 'B'
26, 27, 28 and 29 January 1986 at Colombo Cricket Club

SRI LANKA XI

	FIRST INNINGS		SECOND INNINGS	
S. Wettimuny†	b Agnew	138		
A.M. de Silva*	c Rhodes, b Pringle	12	(1) st Rhodes, b Nicholas	39
S. Warnakula-suriya	c Rhodes, b Pringle	22	(4) not out	27
A. Ranatunga	c Smith, b Pringle	52		
R.S. Mahanama	c Moxon, b Agnew	58	not out	32
S.M.S. Kalu-peruma	b Cook	70	(2) c Rhodes, b Agnew	0
H.P. Tillekeratne	c and b Athey	17	(3) c Nicholas, b Cook	17
A.L.F. de Mel	b Athey	11		
E.A.R. de Silva	not out	6		
K.G. Perera	not out	0		
K. Kuruppua-rachchi				
Extras	b 12, lb 16, w 8, nb 6	42	b 4, lb 6, w 1, nb 1	12
	(for 8 wkts dec)	428	(for 3 wkts)	127

ENGLAND 'B'

	FIRST INNINGS	
M.D. Moxon	lbw, b Perera	52
W.N. Slack	c Tillekeratne, b E.A.R. de Silva	50
C.L. Smith	lbw, b de Mel	76
C.W.J. Athey	b Kaluperuma	41
M.C.J. Nicholas†	b Kuruppuarachchi	38
K.J. Barnett	retired ill	51
D.R. Pringle	lbw, b Perera	5
S.J. Rhodes*	c sub, b Perera	10
N.G.B. Cook	not out	14
D.V. Lawrence	b Perera	0
J.P. Agnew	c sub, b E.A.R. de Silva	9
Extras	b 9, lb 9, nb 1	19
		365

	O	M	R	W	O	M	R	W
Agnew	32	12	59	2	4	—	18	1
Lawrence	28	3	114	—	11	3	33	—
Pringle	35	12	72	3				
Nicholas	7	1	28	—	11	4	17	1
Cook	46	13	110	1	5	2	7	1
Athey	5	—	17	2	5	1	22	—
Slack					1	1	0	—
Moxon					5	1	15	—
Smith					3	1	5	—

	O	M	R	W
de Mel	27	7	89	1
Kuruppuarachchi	22	3	77	1
Ranatunga	3	1	10	—
E.A.R. de Silva	46	18	69	2
Perera	38	13	67	4
Kaluperuma	12	3	28	1
Warnakulasuriya	2	—	7	—

FALL OF WICKETS
1- 47, 2- 135, 3- 232, 4- 279, 5- 358, 6- 402, 7- 408, 8- 427
1- 1, 2- 61, 3- 61

FALL OF WICKETS
1- 107, 2- 127, 3- 207, 4- 256, 5- 282, 6- 293, 7- 335, 8- 350, 9- 365

Umpires: D.C. Felsinger & D.C. Perera

Match drawn

spinners. Slack hit 3 fours and Moxon 4 in a 135-minute stay. Chris Smith played a typically sound defensive innings, and it was Nicholas who provided the fireworks with 38 off 56 balls. He hit 8 fours and saw his side safely avoid the follow-on. In hot, sultry conditions, with the wicket giving a little encouragement, the Sri Lankan spinners were below their best, but they were poorly supported in the field where several catches were missed.

England closed the third day at 300 for 6, and the last day brought only the mechanics of a match which had long since been drawn.

Peter Lush, the England manager, had contacted the T.C.C.B. with regard to a reinforcement for the party in the shape of another spinner in view of the fact that the tour had been extended and the wickets encountered in Sri Lanka tended to favour the spinners. The request was refused. It is probable that the T.C.C.B. could not think of anyone to send.

Brendon Kuruppu leaves the field after his match-winning 80 in the first one-day international against England 'B'. (Michael King – All Sport)

First One-Day International
SRI LANKA XI v. ENGLAND 'B'

Sri Lanka had problems before the game with Wettimuny, the designated captain, unable to play through illness. He had missed the closing stages of the second international with influenza and had not recovered sufficiently for this match. Ranatunga and Madugalle, due to play in the following matches, were also unwell.

Sri Lanka were led by de Mel who won the toss and asked

FIRST ONE-DAY INTERNATIONAL – SRI LANKA XI v. ENGLAND 'B'
1 February 1986 at Noratuwa Colombo

ENGLAND 'B'					SRI LANKA XI			
M.D. Moxon	c A.M. de Silva, b Ramanayake		12		D.S.B.P. Kuruppu	b Cook		80
C.L. Smith	c Mahanama, b Ramanayake		7		A.M. de Silva*	lbw, b Pringle		5
D.W. Randall	b Ranasinghe		34		S. Warnakulasuriya	b Cook		21
M.C.J. Nicholas†	c de Mel, b E.A.R. de Silva		38		S.M.S. Kaluperuma	c Rhodes, b Tremlett		11
C.W.J. Athey	c A.M. de Silva, b Ranasinghe		6		R.S. Mahanama	not out		24
D.R. Pringle	c A.M. de Silva, b E.A.R. de Silva		5		S.K. Ranasinghe	c Cowans, b Tremlett		2
S.J. Rhodes*	c Ranasinghe, b Ramanayake		6		A.L.F. de Mel†	lbw, b Agnew		12
T.M. Tremlett	not out		17		H.P. Tillekeratne	not out		1
N.G.B. Cook	c Ranasinghe, b Ramanayake		18		M.A.C.P. Rodrigo			
N.G. Cowans	not out		2		E.A.R. de Silva			
J.P. Agnew					C.P. Ramanayake			
Extras	b 4, lb 8, w 5		17		Extras	lb 7		7
	(45 overs)	(for 8 wickets)	162			(41.3 overs)	(for 6 wickets)	163

	O	M	R	W		O	M	R	W
de Mel	9	—	41	—	Agnew	8	2	18	1
Ramanayake	9	2	36	4	Cowans	5	—	26	—
Rodrigo	9	1	24	—	Pringle	8.3	2	29	1
Ranasinghe	9	2	28	2	Tremlett	8	—	45	2
E.A.R. de Silva	9	2	21	2	Nicholas	3	—	18	—
					Cook	9	2	20	2

FALL OF WICKETS
1- 26, 2- 27, 3- 104, 4- 104, 5- 112, 6- 118, 7- 127, 8- 157

FALL OF WICKETS
1- 32, 2- 87, 3- 118, 4- 126, 5- 145, 6- 161

Sri Lanka XI won by 4 wickets

SECOND ONE-DAY INTERNATIONAL – SRI LANKA XI v. ENGLAND 'B'
2 February 1986 at Kettarama Stadium, Colombo

ENGLAND 'B'			
M.D. Moxon	c and b Perera		29
C.W.J. Athey	c Gurusinghe, b Ranatunga		70
D.W. Randall	run out		4
M.C.J. Nicholas†	c Mahanama, b Perera		1
C.L. Smith	lbw, b Ratnayake		28
D.R. Pringle	c and b Rajadurai		5
S.J. Rhodes*	c Mahanama, b Ratnayake		15
T.M. Tremlett	not out		18
N.G.B. Cook	c Ranatunga, b Samarasekera		0
N.G. Cowans	b Samarasekera		0
J.P. Agnew	not out		2
Extras	b 1, lb 3, nb 2		6
(45 overs)	(for 9 wickets)		178

	O	M	R	W
R.J. Ratnayake	9	1	34	2
Amalean	9	2	24	—
Ranatunga	9	—	35	1
Samarasekera	4	—	22	2
Perera	9	1	34	2
Rajadurai	5	—	25	1

FALL OF WICKETS
1- 59, 2- 65, 3- 82, 4- 120, 5- 132, 6- 155, 7- 164, 8- 165, 9- 170

SRI LANKA XI			
M.D. Vonhagt	c Cook, b Pringle		38
K. de Alwis*	c Pringle, b Cowans		9
P.A. de Silva	c Tremlett, b Pringle		11
A. Ranatunga†	st Rhodes, b Cook		13
A.P. Gurusinghe	c Moxon, b Cook		21
M.A.R. Samarasekera	c Tremlett, b Pringle		26
R.S. Mahanama	not out		39
R.J. Ratnayake	not out		18
K.N. Amalean			
B. Rajadurai			
K.G. Perera			
Extras	lb 4, w 1, nb 2		7
(41.2 overs)	(for 6 wickets)		182

	O	M	R	W
Agnew	8	—	52	—
Cowans	8	—	30	1
Pringle	9	1	35	3
Tremlett	7.2	—	39	—
Cook	9	—	22	2

FALL OF WICKETS
1- 14, 2- 25, 3- 54, 4- 81, 5- 97, 6- 153

Sri Lanka XI won by 4 wickets

England to bat. Moxon and Smith struggled from the start. They both fell to fast-medium bowler Champaka Ramanayake, and it was left to Randall and Nicholas to give the innings both substance and impetus. They added 77 in 21 overs, but the Sri Lankan spinners bowled economically and the England middle order disintegrated. Athey and Pringle were both caught behind, Pringle when he reverse swept, and 5 wickets fell for 23 runs.

Tremlett and Cook played some lusty shots, but the Sri Lankan fielding was excellent and the final total of 162 never looked likely to trouble the home side.

Brendon Kuruppu set the tone when he straight drove Cowans first ball for four. Later he hit him over square-leg for six. He also hit Pringle for six over long-on, and, in all, hit 6 fours in a scintillating innings which occupied 103 balls. By the time Cook bowled him, Sri Lanka were assured of victory and contented themselves with hitting boundaries as England's out-cricket fell apart.

Second One-Day International
SRI LANKA XI v. ENGLAND 'B'

The opening of the Kettarama Stadium, built to celebrate Sri Lanka's attainment of Test status, proved an occasion of total triumph for the Sri Lankans. A crowd of 40,000 excitedly greeted the home side as they moved to a comfortable victory. They were superior in every department of the game and took the one-day series before the third match was played.

Ranatunga won the toss and again England were asked to bat first. Moxon and Athey began with a stand of 59, but the Sri Lankan seam bowling was consistently accurate and the tempo of the innings could never be raised. The home side's fielding was excitingly brilliant, and the England batting spluttered to a rather dismal 178.

This never looked likely to be a score big enough to win the match, but Pringle snatched a couple of wickets and Cook and Tremlett in tandem bowled economically so that half the Sri Lankan side were out for 97. Mahanama and Samarasekera put on 56 in 10 overs, however, and Sri Lanka raced to victory which came when Rumesh Ratnayake hit Tremlett for six over long off in the forty-second over.

Mahanama was named Man of the Match and the reservoir of youthful talent of international calibre in Sri Lanka seemed bottomless.

Third One-Day International
SRI LANKA XI v. ENGLAND 'B'

The England side gained some consolation when they gained a narrow victory in the third and last of the one-day internationals.

There was no indication in the opening stages of the match that England would win. Moxon and Slack began circumspectly and they were out in quick succession. Slack responded slowly to Moxon's call for a leg-bye and was run out, and one run later, Moxon lofted gently to mid-on. Athey was bowled at 32, but Nicholas and Smith, not at his best, added 67 before Smith was caught sweeping. Nicholas hit 6 fours and reached his fifty off 100 balls, but, at 117 for 6, England were still in trouble. Rhodes and Pringle joined in a fine stand which brought 60 in 6.3 overs. Rhodes hit 34 off 39 balls and Pringle made 24 from only 13 deliveries, hitting England's first six of the series. The last 5 overs produced 44

THIRD ONE-DAY INTERNATIONAL – SRI LANKA XI v. ENGLAND 'B'
4 February 1986 at Asgiriya Stadium, Kandy

ENGLAND 'B'					SRI LANKA XI				
M.D. Moxon	c Gurusinghe, b Ratnayeke	7			S.A.R. Silva*	c Moxon, b Smith	53		
W.N. Slack	run out	11			D. Ranatunga	c Rhodes, b Lawrence	5		
C.W.J. Athey	b Ratnayeke	6			P.A. de Silva	c Cook, b Lawrence	0		
M.C.J. Nicholas†	c Silva, b Samarasekera	50			A.P. Gurusinghe	run out	15		
C.L. Smith	c Tillekeratne, Wijesuriya	28			A. Ranatunga†	c Cook, b Tremlett	22		
D.W. Randall	c Silva, b Ramanayake	5			M.A.R. Samarasekera	c Tremlett, b Pringle	29		
S.J. Rhodes*	c Tillekeratne, b John	34			H.P. Tillekeratne	not out	22		
D.R. Pringle	c A. Ranatunga, b Ratnayeke	24			J.R. Ratnayeke	st Rhodes, b Cook	8		
T.M. Tremlett	not out	7			V.B. John	lbw, b Cook	2		
N.G.B. Cook	run out	1			C.P. Ramanayake	run out	5		
D.V. Lawrence	not out	8			R.G.C.E. Wijesuriya	run out	12		
Extras	lb 6, w 4, nb 3	13			Extras	b 1, lb 7, w 4, nb 5	17		
		—					—		
(45 overs)	(for 9 wickets)	194			(45 overs)		190		

	O	M	R	W		O	M	R	W
J.R. Ratnayeke	9	1	41	3	Tremlett	9	—	22	1
John	9	3	42	1	Lawrence	6	—	30	2
Ramanayake	9	1	34	1	Nicholas	9	—	42	—
A. Ranatunga	3	—	16	—	Pringle	9	1	30	1
Samarasekera	6	—	30	1	Cook	9	—	43	2
Wijesuriya	9	—	25	1	Smith	3	1	15	1

FALL OF WICKETS
1- 24, 2- 25, 3- 32, 4- 99, 5- 116, 6- 117, 8- 178, 9- 180

FALL OF WICKETS
1- 24, 2- 24, 3- 54, 4- 96, 5- 139, 6- 139, 7- 158, 8- 160, 9- 173

England 'B' won by 4 runs

---

runs and England took a little more comfort from a final score of 194 than they might have expected earlier.

Amal Silva made 53 off 87 balls, but the rest of the Sri Lankan batsmen failed to find their touch. Lawrence bowled fast and well, and Nicholas employed a spin trio in Cook, Smith and, on this occasion, Tremlett who restricted scoring. The last over was reached with 10 needed, but Pringle bowled admirably and Wijesuriya was run out going for a third run off the last ball from which the Sri Lankans had needed six for victory.

Third International
SRI LANKA XI v. ENGLAND 'B'

One of the saddest events of the English winter was the return home from Sri Lanka of Kim Barnett. A most likeable and hard working young man whose international recognition had been long overdue, Kim Barnett was forced to leave the tour because of a mysterious illness which had troubled him for several weeks and caused him to lose two stone in weight.

The sight of the wicket at the Asgiriya Stadium, damp and bare, caused England to take a most controversial decision and play assistant manager Norman Gifford in their side to the exclusion of Lawrence and Cowans. Peter Lush described the decision as being due to 'absolutely exceptional' circumstances regarding the pitch. One could sympathise with the dilemma facing the tourists. They were keen to try to win the match, but then the purpose of the tour had been to give experience to promising young players like Lawrence who now found himself sitting idle while a 45-year old left-arm spinner played. The problem, of course, was the paucity of spinners with which the selectors were confronted when they selected the side in the first place.

It was Gifford who made the initial breakthrough and who was England's most successful bowler, but the first day honours went to Aravinda de Silva and Gurusinghe, the left-hander. In the most difficult conditions, on a wicket which offered awkward bounce and turn, they added 108 in 134 minutes for the third wicket. Gurusinghe hit 7 fours in his 184-minute stay, and de Silva, surely destined to be one of the very great Test batsmen, hit 15 fours and a six.

Sri Lanka lost wickets early when Ranatunga dribbled the ball on to his own stumps and Silva looped the ball to backward short-leg. Tremlett bowled off-spin to augment the efforts of Cook and Gifford, but England's successes came in the last session of the day when three wickets fell. Gurusinghe was caught at square leg hooking, and Mahanama fell to the last ball of the day, taken at silly point.

Sri Lanka added only 36 the next morning, but England were soon in trouble against the spinners. Athey was the first to go, caught at slip off Weerasinghe's fourth ball, and the leg-spinner was to take two more wickets in his first five overs. Warnaweera, with his brisk off-breaks, also troubled the batsmen, and only stubborn defence by Nicholas saved England from humiliation on a bad wicket. England closed at 144 for 7 and added 16 more runs the following morning.

The second Sri Lankan innings began sensationally. After 8 overs, they were 6 for 5 so that 8 wickets had fallen in the first 85 minutes of the day for 22 runs. Pringle and Agnew struck early, and Gifford caught and bowled both Gurusinghe and Dias in the same over. Undaunted, Roshan Mahanama and Keerthi Ranasinghe put on 100 in as many minutes. Mahanama hit 5 fours and Ranasinghe, with 7 fours, hit 68 off 106 balls. Ratnayeke and John hit out enthusiastically and Dias declared leaving England to make

THIRD INTERNATIONAL MATCH – SRI LANKA XI v. ENGLAND 'B'
6, 7, 8 and 9 February 1986 at Asgiriya, Kandy

SRI LANKA XI

	FIRST INNINGS			SECOND INNINGS	
D. Ranatunga	b Gifford	19		c Rhodes, b Pringle	1
S.A.R. Silva*	c Randall, b Gifford	30		c Gifford, b Agnew	0
P.A. de Silva	lbw, b Cook	81		c Rhodes, b Agnew	0
A.P. Gurusinghe	c Randall, b Agnew	67		c and b Gifford	1
R.L. Dias†	c Athey, b Gifford	20		(6) c and b Gifford	0
R.S. Mahanama	c Athey, b Cook	5		(5) c Nicholas, b Gifford	47
S.K. Ranasinghe	run out	7		run out	68
J.R. Ratnayeke	lbw, b Gifford	0		c Tremlett, b Cook	31
C.D.U.S. Weerasinghe	st Rhodes, b Cook	0		(10) not out	4
V.B. John	run out	25		(9) b Cook	22
K.P.J. Warnaweera	not out	0		not out	3
Extras	b 6, lb 9, nb 2	17		lb 1, nb 2	3
		271		(for 9 wkts dec)	180

ENGLAND 'B'

	FIRST INNINGS			SECOND INNINGS	
W.N. Slack	b Weerasinghe	30		b de Silva	67
C.W.J. Athey	c de Silva, b Weerasinghe	16		c Weerasinghe, b Warnaweera	38
C.L. Smith	c de Silva, b Weerasinghe	20		c Silva, b Warnaweera	18
M.C.J. Nicholas†	b Warnaweera	46		c Gurusinghe, b Warnaweera	1
D.W. Randall	c Ranatunga, b Warnaweera	25		lbw, b Warnaweera	0
S.J. Rhodes*	lbw, b Warnaweera	2		not out	40
D.R. Pringle	st Silva, b Weerasinghe	8		not out	38
T.M. Tremlett	lbw, b Warnaweera	0			
N.G.B. Cook	c Ranatunga, b Warnaweera	0			
N. Gifford	not out	4			
J.P. Agnew	c Silva, b Weerasinghe	1			
Extras	lb 3, w 4, nb 1	8		b 4, lb 7, w 4, nb 4	19
		160		(for 5 wickets)	221

	O	M	R	W	O	M	R	W
Agnew	14	2	43	1	9.2	1	22	2
Pringle	11	2	25	—	7	3	15	1
Cook	39	15	95	3	17	—	72	2
Gifford	36	11	81	4	17	3	47	3
Tremlett	8	3	12	—	6	1	23	—

	O	M	R	W	O	M	R	W
J.R. Ratnayeke	9	1	28	—	5	—	28	—
John	3	1	7	—	5	1	24	—
Warnaweera	35	16	72	5	37	16	53	4
Weerasinghe	30.3	12	49	5	28	10	69	—
P.A. de Silva	2	1	1	—	16	8	16	1
Ranasinghe					6.1	1	20	—

FALL OF WICKETS

1- 42, 2- 72, 3- 180, 4- 222, 5- 235, 6- 235, 7- 236, 8- 261, 9- 271
1- 1, 2- 1, 3- 2, 4- 6, 5- 6, 6- 106, 7- 133, 8- 165, 9- 173

1- 46, 2- 69, 3- 76, 4- 109, 5- 121, 6- 139, 7- 144, 8- 144, 9- 155
1- 60, 2- 105, 3- 113, 4- 113, 5- 150

Umpires: D. Bull Jens & F.R.S. de Mel

Match drawn

292. They were 37 for 0 when bad light ended play.

England batted out the last day to save the game. They were aided by some unimaginative captaincy, and one could have little sympathy for the Sri Lankans who, sadly, resorted to umpire baiting. Smith, Nicholas and Randall fell in the space of 4 overs for 8 runs, but Rhodes, 210 minutes, and Pringle, 110 minutes, held the spinners at bay. Jayananda Warnaweera bowled well, but Weerasinghe was a disappointment after his success in the first innings.

Fourth One-Day International
SRI LANKA XI v. ENGLAND 'B'

The reorganisation of the last part of the England 'B' tour due to disturbances in Radella led to two more one-day internationals being played, and England had the unique distinction of losing a series twice when they were beaten in the first of these.

Nicholas won the toss and asked Sri Lanka to bat on a wicket which promised some early moisture. The seamers made good use of the initial liveliness. Tremlett had the dangerous Kuruppu caught behind and held a good return catch to dismiss Madugalle. In the meantime, Lawrence found the edge of Warnakulasuriya's bat, and Sri Lanka were 10 for 3.

The talented young batsmen, Gurusinghe and Roshan Mahanama halted the England advance and although Gurusinghe left at 54, Mahanama remained undaunted by wickets falling around him and plundered the bowling. The astounding quality of Sri Lankan cricket is the number of young batsmen of outstanding ability who are coming to the fore. Mahanama, at 19, is a player of immense talent. He and Ranasinghe added 76 in 15 overs, and he and Fernando, 35 in 3. Mahanama hit Cook out of the attack and reached a magnificent hundred off 113 deliveries.

England seemed devoid of ideas when Mahanama launched his attack, and they failed to bowl the required 45 overs.

Moxon and Athey were both leg before wicket to Amalean in the sixth over, and Slack saw the ball glance his glove and fly into the wicket-keeper's hands. Devoid of a real strokemaker, England laboured in pursuit of the runs although Smith and Tremlett added 56 in 8 overs, which was the run rate required at the time that they came together.

Smith had come to the wicket in the eleventh over and when the last over started he had strike and was faced with the prospect of hitting 20 runs to win the match. He took 2 off Amalean's first ball, hit the second for 6 and scored 2 off the third, and was run out attempting a second run off the fourth so that Sri Lanka took the honours.

FOURTH ONE-DAY INTERNATIONAL – SRI LANKA XI *v.* ENGLAND 'B'
11 February 1986 at P. Savaranamuttu Oval, Colombo

SRI LANKA XI				ENGLAND 'B'			
D.S.B.P. Kuruppu*	c Rhodes, b Tremlett	1		M.D. Moxon	lbw, b Amalean	13
S. Warnakulasuriya	c Rhodes, b Lawrence	7		W.N. Slack	c Kuruppu, b Ramanayake	11
R.S. Madugalle†	c and b Tremlett	2		C.W.J. Athey	lbw, b Amalean	0
A.P. Gurusinghe	c. Pringle, b Cowans	13		M.C.J. Nicholas†	b Perera	18
R.S. Mahanama	not out	111		C.L. Smith	run out	67
M.A.R.				S.J. Rhodes*	c Kuruppu, b Ranasinghe	13
Samarasekera	c Rhodes, b Cowans	3		D.R. Pringle	lbw, b Ranasinghe	12
S.K. Ranasinghe	c Nicholas, b Pringle	26		T.M. Tremlett	b Ranasinghe	28
T.L. Fernando	c Cowans, b Nicholas	17		D.V. Lawrence	c sub (Tillekeratne),	
C.P. Ramanayake	c Rhodes, b Nicholas	1			b Ranasinghe	0
K.N. Amalean				N.G.B. Cook	not out	0
K.G. Perera				N.G. Cowans	not out	0
Extras	lb 2, w 2	4		Extras	b 2, lb 10, w 3	15
(44 overs)	(for 8 wickets)	185		(44 overs)	(for 9 wickets)	177

	O	M	R	W		O	M	R	W
Tremlett	9	1	29	2	Ramanayake	6	1	14	1
Lawrence	7	—	25	1	Amalean	8	1	38	2
Pringle	9	2	46	1	Fernando	7	—	22	—
Cowans	9	1	39	2	Perera	9	1	20	1
Cook	2	—	10	—	Ranasinghe	9	1	43	4
Nicholas	8	—	34	2	Samarasekera	5	—	28	—

FALL OF WICKETS
1-4, 2-10, 3-10, 4-54, 5-61, 6-137, 7-172, 8-185

FALL OF WICKETS
1-23, 2-23, 3-30, 4-59, 5-90, 6-108, 7-164, 8-164, 9-177

Sri Lanka XI won by 8 runs

Fifth One-Day International
SRI LANKA XI *v.* ENGLAND 'B'

Put in to bat, Sri Lanka lost a wicket without a run on the board when Slack held an excellent running catch to dismiss Kuruppu. Madugalle, Warnakulasuriya and Mahanama, failing for the first time, quickly followed, and Sri Lanka

were 49 for 4. The tall, slender Samarasekera and the short left-handed Tillekeratne then engaged in an exhilarating stand which produced 80 in 13 overs. It was ended when Lawrence, substituting for Randall, held a stunning diving catch at cover to dismiss Samarasekera who had hit 68 off 70 balls, with 3 sixes and 6 fours.

Tillekeratne, 59 off 75 balls, and Keerthi Ranasinghe, 38

FIFTH ONE-DAY INTERNATIONAL – SRI LANKA XI 'B'
13 February 1986 at Nonedescripts C.C., Colombo

SRI LANKA XI				ENGLAND 'B'			
D.S.B.P. Kuruppu*	c Slack, b Agnew	0		M.D. Moxon	st de Silva, b Anurasiri	6
S. Warnakulasuriya	c Rhodes, b Agnew	8		W.N. Slack	not out	122
R.S. Madugalle†	run out	19		C.W.J. Athey	c. Tillekeratne,	
R.S. Mahanama	lbw, b Cowans	6			b Samarasekera	3
M.A.R.				M.C.J. Nicholas†	run out	2
Samarasekera	c sub (Lawrence),			C.L. Smith	not out	60
	b Tremlett	68		D.W. Randall		
H.P. Tillekeratne	not out	59		S.J. Rhodes*		
S.K. Ranasinghe	not out	38		T.M. Tremlett		
J.R. Ratnayeke				N.G.B. Cook		
A.M. de Silva*				J.P. Agnew		
K.N. Amalean				N.G. Cowans		
S.D. Anurasiri				Extras	b 1, lb 5, nb 8	14
Extras	b 1, lb 1, nb 4	6		(43.2 overs)	(for 3 wickets)	207
(45 overs)	(for 5 wickets)	204				

	O	M	R	W		O	M	R	W
Agnew	9	1	44	2	J.R. Ratnayeke	8	—	27	—
Tremlett	9	—	41	1	Amalean	9	—	33	—
Cowans	9	—	34	1	Anurasiri	9	1	30	1
Cook	9	1	22	—	Samarasekera	8	—	41	1
Nicholas	9	—	61	—	Warnakulasuriya	3	—	15	—
					Ranasinghe	6.2	—	55	—

FALL OF WICKETS
1-0, 2-14, 3-27, 4-50, 5-130

FALL OF WICKETS
1-29, 2-49, 3-61

England 'B' won by 7 wickets

off 37, plundered 75 in the last 12 overs and England faced a quite formidable target.

Moxon was caught in bewildered mid-stroke and stumped, and Athey was caught on the leg side. Slack and Nicholas failed to agree and the captain was run out so that England again faced defeat, but Smith joined Slack in a partnership of 146 in 20 overs to gain a fine consolation victory. Smith hit 60 off 60 balls, and Slack made 122 off 135 balls, with 4 sixes and 7 fours. It was his first hundred in any limited-over match and a highly commendable one.

Fourth International
SRI LANKA XI v. ENGLAND 'B'

Put in to bat, England 'B' reached 240 for 3 at the end of the first day and thereby appeared to have made themselves immune from defeat. Athey, beginning to show good form, was adjudged caught behind although only the wicket-keeper, in belligerent mood, appealed. The happiest feature of the day was the batting of Derek Randall who had a miserable tour but was back to his bubbling best. He and Slack added 164 in 219 minutes. The stand was ended when Slack hit to mid wicket and ran suicidally. Randall, tiring, fell to the second new ball.

England consolidated their position on the second day and reached their highest score of the tour, but Sri Lanka produced batting of high quality in reply. After Warnakula-suriya had touched the ball into gully's hands, his first failure in first-class cricket, Madugalle and Samarasekera savaged the bowling.

Samarasekera gave further evidence of the outstanding talent of young Sri Lankan batsmen with some glorious straight driving and an expansive range of shots. He hit a six and 16 fours as he reached a hundred off 130 balls, and Sri Lanka closed the day at 161 for 1.

Madugalle completed his fifty and saw Tremlett deceive Samarasekera with a change of pace. Shortly afterwards the Sri Lankan captain departed himself in most unfortunate fashion. He was struck by a rising ball from Agnew which broke his thumb and gashed his lip.

Mahanama played well but he was one of those to benefit from dropped catches. Rhodes was the main culprit. He had a dreadful day behind the stumps which was sad, for he had had a good tour. Sri Lanka took a first innings lead and declared at their overnight score.

Rumesh Ratnayake was unable to bowl on the last day, having joined Madugalle on the injured list, and England, with Randall again to the fore, gained batting practice as yet another draw loomed.

FOURTH INTERNATIONAL MATCH – SRI LANKA XI v. ENGLAND 'B'
16, 17, 18 and 19 February 1986 at Colombo C.C., Colombo

ENGLAND 'B'

	FIRST INNINGS		SECOND INNINGS	
W.N. Slack	run out	85	c sub, b Perera	33
C.W.J. Athey	c Wickremasinghe,		c Tillekeratne,	
	b Kuruppuarachchi	26	b Samarasekera	37
D.W. Randall	c Wickremasinghe,			
	b Ratnayake	92	not out	60
M.C.J. Nicholas†	lbw, b Fernando	49		
N.G.B. Cook	c Wickremasinghe,			
	b Kuruppuarachchi	10		
C.L. Smith	c Warnakulasuriya,			
	b Kuruppuarachchi	51	(4) c and b Perera	4
S.J. Rhodes*	c Wickremasinge,			
	b Kuruppuarachchi	26	(5) not out	22
T.M. Tremlett	not out	6		
D.V. Lawrence	b Perera	2		
N.G. Cowans	not out	0		
J.P. Agnew				
Extras	b 4, lb 11, nb 7	22	b 5, lb 5, nb 1	11
	(for 8 wkts dec)	369	(for 3 wkts)	167

SRI LANKA XI

	FIRST INNINGS	
S. Warnakulasuriya	c Randall, b Lawrence	4
M.A.R. Samarasekera	b Tremlett	110
R.S. Madugalle†	retired hurt	57
R.S. Mahanama	c Rhodes, b Lawrence	67
H.P. Tillekeratne	c Cook, b Agnew	37
S.K. Ranasinghe	c Rhodes, b Agnew	3
A.G.D. Wickremasinghe*	not out	29
T.L. Fernando	st Rhodes, b Smith	56
K.G. Perera	not out	0
R.J. Ratnayake		
A.K. Kuruppuarachchi		
Extras	b 7, lb 11, w 3, nb 6	27
	(for 6 wkts dec)	390

	O	M	R	W	O	M	R	W
R.J. Ratnayake	20	1	60	1				
Kuruppuarachchi	30	6	85	4	10.4	—	25	—
Fernando	28	6	69	1	8	—	23	—
Samarasekera	8	—	31	—	13	3	24	1
Perera	33	11	73	1	24	4	61	2
Tillekeratne	3	—	8	—	6	3	24	—
Ranasinghe	9	1	28	—				

	O	M	R	W
Agnew	24	4	58	2
Lawrence	20	1	73	2
Tremlett	27	6	85	1
Cowans	24	5	75	—
Cook	28	12	68	—
Smith	3.5	—	13	1

FALL OF WICKETS
1- 42, 2- 206, 3- 233, 4- 273, 5- 281, 6- 354, 7- 359, 8- 364
1- 73, 2- 81, 3- 99

FALL OF WICKETS
1- 8, 2- 182, 3- 276, 4- 298, 5- 304, 6- 390

Umpires: A.L. Felsinger & K.T. Ponnambalm

Match drawn

Fifth International
SRI LANKA XI v. ENGLAND 'B'

Following his success on the 'B' team tour, Wilf Slack was called to West Indies as a replacement for the injured Mike Gatting. His departure allowed a place for Moxon.

Sri Lanka elected to bat when they won the toss, but quickly lost Vonhagt and Ranatunga who was forced to retire hurt and returned later. Cowans and Pringle bowled admirably, and Sri Lanka were only saved from disaster by Dileepa Wickremasinghe who was playing his second first-class match on his own ground. He hit 9 fours in his 87, and Sri Lanka closed at 208 for 6.

Cowans took 3 wickets in 5 overs on the second day and there was hope of England success. Wickremasinghe did not add to his overnight score, and Sri Lanka lost their last 4 wickets for the addition of only 23 runs.

Athey and Moxon began in determined fashion and all went well until Moxon turned a ball from the medium paced Fernando into the hands of Perera, the substitute, who was fielding at short leg. Athey dominated the rest of the day. He and Rhodes added 92 before Rhodes lofted to cover. Athey's

RIGHT: *Ken de Alwis in action. One of several wicket-keepers to gain experience against the English tourists. (Michael King – All Sport)*

FIFTH INTERNATIONAL MATCH – SRI LANKA XI v. ENGLAND 'B'
22, 23, 24 and 25 February 1986 at Galle Stadium, Galle

SRI LANKA XI

	FIRST INNINGS		SECOND INNINGS	
D.M. Vonhagt	b Cowans	0	c Pringle, b Agnew	0
D. Ranatunga	lbw, b Cowans	25	b Cook	15
S. Warnakulasuriya†	c Nicholas, b Pringle	23	lbw, b Agnew	50
M.A.R. Samarasekera	c Rhodes, b Pringle	6	c Pringle, b Cook	8
H.P. Tillekeratne	c Athey, b Cowans	5	not out	105
D.C. Wickremasinghe	lbw, b Cowans	87	lbw, b Lawrence	3
A.M. de Silva*	c Athey, b Pringle	34	lbw, b Lawrence	26
T.L. Fernando	c Lawrence, b Cowans	32	c Nicholas, b Lawrence	9
S.D. Anurasiri	lbw, b Cowans	0	c Randall, b Pringle	1
R.S. Abeysekera	not out	1	b Cook	23
C.P. Ramanayake	c Cook, b Pringle	0	b Randall	25
Extras	b 11, nb 7	18	b 4, lb 2, nb 1	7
		231		**272**

ENGLAND 'B'

	FIRST INNINGS	
M.D. Moxon	c sub, b Fernando	2
C.W.J. Athey	c Warnakulasuriya, b Ramanayake	184
D.W. Randall	c Samarasekera, b Anurasiri	21
M.C.J. Nicholas†	lbw, b Abeysekera	1
S.J. Rhodes*	c sub, b Ramanayake	24
N.G.B. Cook	retired ill	1
C.L. Smith	not out	70
D.R. Pringle	c Anurasiri, b Ramanayake	1
D.V. Lawrence	not out	23
N.G. Cowans		
J.P. Agnew		
Extras	b 4, lb 1, nb 3	8
	(for 6 wkts dec)	**335**

	O	M	R	W	O	M	R	W
Agnew	18	2	44	—	19	3	46	2
Cowans	20	5	50	6	15	3	45	—
Lawrence	17		66	—	23	9	50	3
Pringle	16.5	4	23	4	12	3	30	1
Cook	23	6	37	—	43	16	71	3
Smith					4	1	17	—
Randall					0.4	—	7	1

	O	M	R	W
Ramanayake	35	9	91	3
Fernando	16	1	47	1
Anurasiri	50	10	128	1
Abeysekera	27	6	64	1

FALL OF WICKETS
1- 2, 2- 51, 3- 52, 4- 62, 5- 157, 6- 175, 7- 208, 8- 224, 9- 231
1- 0, 2- 42, 3- 64, 4- 98, 5- 116, 6- 173, 7- 187, 8- 199, 9- 229

FALL OF WICKETS
1- 5, 2- 48, 3- 59, 4- 151, 5- 267, 6- 285

Umpires: H.C. Felsinger & M.D.D.N. Gooneratne

Match drawn

hundred came in the last over of the day, out of 159 for 4.

On the third day, Athey reached a career best 184, a monumental innings which lasted 7¼ hours. Nicholas declared an hour after lunch, and England were in a good position thanks not only to Athey, but to some good stroke-play from Smith.

England's prospects became even brighter when Vonhagt edged the third ball of the innings to Pringle at first slip, and Cook took the wickets of Ranatunga and Samarasekera in quick succession so that Sri Lanka were still 8 runs in arrears at the close.

Hasham Tillekeratne had come to the crease with an hour of the third day remaining and he stayed throughout the final day to become the fourth teenager to record a hundred against the tourists. It was a remarkable feat of application by the young man and gave further emphasis to the wealth of batting talent that is being produced in Sri Lanka.

Agnew took a wicket with the twelfth ball of the day. Three wickets fell after lunch and England still scented victory, but the last two stands of the innings gave Sri Lanka 73 runs and a draw. The one sour event of the day was the angry reaction of Rhodes and Lawrence when an appeal for a catch at the wicket against Tillekeratne was rejected. How quickly young players learn these days. The batsman was on 90 at the time and indicated that he believed that he had not touched the ball.

England had ended the tour without a win, and without a defeat, in the first-class matches. There had been some gains. Slack had surprised many by the quality of his batting although his technique against spin remained in question. Smith reasserted his Test claims and Rhodes, initially, kept wicket well although one still felt that he was most fortunate to have been given the opportunity ahead of some others. His batting was a relevation. The pace men struggled and Cook bowled manfully, but the lack of support spin underlined what was realised at the outset that England are woefully weak in this department.

Sri Lanka used 34 players in the five 'Tests' and revealed a rich vein of talent. For them, the tour was an outstanding success.

For the record, the substitute catches for Sri Lanka were taken by Gurusinghe and Bulankulame in the second match, Maiesh in the fourth, and Perera two in the fifth.

The tour was well conducted and the hosts were kind, generous and well organised. Peter Lush, as tour manager, was an outstanding success, and that England have used him and Tony Brown in the last two years is to their credit and future good.

19, 20 and 21 February 1986

at Kurunegala

Pakistanis 163 for 6 dec and 201 for 3 (Mohsin Khan 101 not out, Rameez Raja 50 not out)
Sri Lankan Colts XI 307 for 7 dec (M.D. Vonhagt 88, D. Bulankulame 53)

Match drawn

Heavy overnight rain prevented any play before lunch on the first day of the Pakistanis' tour. They reached 163 off 55 overs and Imran declared at the end of the first day. Vonhagt

and Bulankulame added 143 for the Colts' second wicket. Skipper Vonhagt hit 10 fours. Sri Lankan Colts were 248 for 5 at the end of the day and batted on the next morning. The tourists were 4 for 2 after 3 overs, but Mohsin Khan and Rameez Raja were in fine form. Mohsin hit 3 sixes and 7 fours in a splendid knock, consolation for a dull draw.

First Test Match
SRI LANKA v. PAKISTAN

Sri Lanka, hit by injuries to Gurusinghe and Madugalle, recalled Amal Silva as wicket-keeper and brought back Asoka de Silva. They gave a first Test cap to Jayananda Warnaweera whose off-spinners and off-cutters had troubled the England 'B' side. Pakistan played their third wicket-keeper of recent months when they included Zulqarnian for his Test debut.

Mendis won the toss and decided to bat. It was a decision that had dire consequences for the home side. Imran Khan took his 250th Test wicket when he dismissed Wettimuny in the opening over, and he and Wasim Akram reduced Sri Lanka to 25 for 3. It was the introduction of the spinners, Tauseef Ahmed and Abdul Qadir which put Pakistan in total dominance. They revelled in the wicket which assisted spin, and the home crowd was bitterly disappointed by some indisciplined batting.

It was only some enterprising hitting from de Mel which took the home side to three figures, but Pakistan themselves were soon in trouble. Mohsin Khan was the first of four lbw victims before the close which came with Pakistan on 58, and Mudassar Nazar 34 not out, the highest score of the day on which 14 wickets had fallen for 167 runs.

The second day saw Mudassar continue courageously. He and Saleem Malik batted throughout the morning session, and when Saleem was eventually caught by Aravinda de Silva off de Mel the pair had added 101. In dismissing Saleem, de Mel became the first Sri Lankan bowler to take 50 wickets in Test cricket.

Mudassar's six hour innings came to an end when he was brilliantly caught by Mendis, diving at short mid-off. Mudassar had faced 238 balls and hit 9 fours. There was more encouragement for Pakistan when Tauseef Ahmed and Wasim Akram put on 39 runs for the last wicket, a lively stand and invaluable in a low scoring match.

Play was ended by bad light with Sri Lanka 7 for 0, and only 12.2 overs were possible on the third day during which time the home side scored 24 runs and lost two wickets. Amal Silva was ill, and Ravi Ratnayeke opened in his place. Imran bowled three successive wides and then bowled Ratnayeke with a straight ball.

Sri Lanka were all out for 101 shortly after lunch on the fourth day as Tauseef Ahmed's off-breaks brought him 6 for 45, his best return in Test cricket. He took full advantage of a turning pitch, and the Sri Lankan batting was again most disappointing.

The day was marred by an incident between Ranatunga and the fielding side. Ranatunga, one of the two batsmen to reach double figures, survived an appeal for a catch at short-leg by Rameez Raja, and the fielders reacted angrily. A verbal barrage directed at Ranatunga by the fielders resulted in Ranatunga complaining to the umpires and leaving the field, followed first by Dias and then by the two umpires. Imran insisted that the anger had been directed at the batsman and not at the umpires, and tempers cooled and the match continued.

Following their recent run of good form and the talent that had become apparent in the matches against the England 'B' side, the result of this first Test was most disappointing to the Sri Lankans who, surprisingly, had been let down by their batsmen. It was certain that young men like Mahanama, Warnakulasuriya and Tillekeratne would very soon find themselves in the Test side.

Hasham Tillekeratne, a young player of immense talent who scored a magnificent 105 not out against England 'B' in their last match of the tour. (Michael King – All Sport)

England 'B' Team in Sri Lanka 1986
First Class Matches

BATTING	v. Sri Lankan Colts (Colombo) 12–14 January 1986		v. Board President's XI (Colombo) 16–18 January 1986	v. Sri Lanka XI (Colombo) 20–23 January 1986		v. Sri Lanka XI (Colombo) 26–29 January 1986		v. Sri Lanka XI (Kandy) 6–9 February 1986		v. Sri Lanka XI (Colombo) 16–19 February 1986		v. Sri Lanka XI (Galle) 22–25 February 1986		M	Inns	NOs	Runs	HS	Av
K.J. Barnett	7	15	11	—	12	16*	51*	—							4	6	2	112	51*	28.00
W. N. Slack	32	7	10	—	96	21	50	—	30	67	85	33			6	10	—	431	96	43.10
C.W.J. Athey	4	53*	41	—	5	6	41	—	16	38	26	37	184	—	7	11	1	451	184	45.10
M.C.J. Nicholas	25	1*			11	—	38	—	46	1	49	—	1	—	6	8	1	172	49	24.57
D.W. Randall	0	1	13	—					25	0	92	60*	21	—	5	8	1	212	92	30.28
D.R. Pringle	1	16*			27	9*	5	—	8	38*			1	—	5	8	3	105	38*	21.00
S.J. Rhodes	21*	—	13	—	77*	57	10	—	2	40*	26	22*	24		7	10	4	292	77*	48.66
T.M. Tremlett	0		0	—	21	—			0	—	6*	—			5	5	1	27	21	6.75
N.G.B. Cook	4	—	0	—	39	—	14*	—	0	—	10	—	1*	—	7	7	2	68	39	13.60
D.V. Lawrence	11	—	27	—			0	—			2	—	23*	—	5	5	1	63	27	15.75
J.P. Agnew	0	—			0	—	9	—	1	—			—	—	6	4	—	10	9	2.50
M.D. Moxon			44	—	8	4	52	—					2	—	4	5	—	110	52	22.00
C.L. Smith			116	—	62	2	76	—	20	18	51	4	70*	—	6	9	1	419	116	52.37
N.G. Cowans			2*	—							0*	—			3	2	2	2	2*	—
N. Gifford									4*	—					1	1	1	4	4*	—
Byes			4		1		9			4	4	5	4							
Leg-byes	5	2	3		3	5	9		3	7	11	5	1							
Wides	2		2			1			4	4										
No-balls		1	2		1		1		1	4	7	1	3							
Total	112	96	288		363	121	365		160	221	369	167	335							
Wickets	10	3	10		10	5	9†		10	5	8	3	6							
Results		D		D		D		D		D		D		D						

Catches 13 – S.J. Rhodes (ct 10/st 3) and C.W.J. Athey   3 – N. Gifford and T.M. Tremlett   †K.J. Barnett retired ill
5 – M. D. Moxon, M.C.J. Nicholas and D.W. Randall   2 – D.R. Pringle
4 – N.G.B. Cook   1 – K.J. Barnett, C.L. Smith and D.V. Lawrence

BOWLING	J.P. Agnew	D.V. Lawrence	D.R. Pringle	T.M. Tremlett	N.G.B. Cook	N.G. Cowans	K.J. Barnett	C.W.J. Athey	C.L. Smith
v. Sri Lankan Colts	21.1–3–57–3	13–2–65–1	24–7–41–3	13–6–14–0	25–10–55–3				
(Colombo) 12–14 January	9–1–17–1	8–2–27–0		8–1–20–1	8.2–3–35–0				
v. Board President's XI		20–1–79–1		23–6–62–0	35.5–14–76–1	19–7–50–1	4–0–17–1	1–0–12–0	2–0–13–0
(Colombo) 16–18 January		5–1–18–0		5–0–26–0	7–3–16–0	5–2–9–0	4–1–20–1		8–4–13–0
v. Sri Lanka XI	27–7–77–3		16–4–40–0	22–7–45–1	44.4–20–69–6				2–0–7–0
(Colombo) 20–23 January	7–2–17–0		8–2–27–0	11–5–15–0	17–7–28–4		3–1–15–0	1–1–0–0	1–0–4–0
v. Sri Lanka XI	32–12–59–2	28–3–114–0	35–12–72–3		48–13–110–1			5–0–17–2	
(Colombo) 26–29 January	4–0–18–1	11–3–33–0			5–2–7–1			5–1–22–0	3–1–5–0
v. Sri Lanka XI	14–2–43–1		11–2–25–0	8–3–12–0	39–15–95–3				
(Kandy) 6–9 February	9.2–1–22–2		7–3–15–1	6–1–23–0	17–0–72–2				
v. Sri Lanka XI	24–4–58–2	20–1–73–2		27–6–85–1	28–12–68–0	24–5–75–0			3.5–0–13–1
(Colombo) 16–19 February	18–2–44–0	17–0–66–0	16.5–4–23–4		23–6–37–0	20–5–50–6			
v. Sri Lanka XI	19–3–46–2	23–9–50–3	12–3–30–1		43–16–71–3	15–3–45–0			4–1–17–0
(Galle) 22–25 February									
	185.3–37–	145–22–	129.5–37–	123–35–	340.5–121–	83–22–	11–2–	12–2–	23.5–6–6
	458–17	525–7	273–12	302–3	739–24	229–7	52–2	51–2	72–1
	av. 26.94	av. 75.00	av. 22.75	av. 100.66	av. 30.79	av. 32.71	av. 26.00	av. 25.50	av. 72.00

a N. Gifford 36–11–81–4   b D.W. Randall 0.4–0–7–1
17–3–47–3

W.N. Slack	M.C.J. Nicholas	M.D. Moxon	Byes	Leg-byes	Wides	No-balls	Total	Wkts
			10	5		17	247	10
			1	2		2	102	2
7-0-15-0			1	6	3	5	331	5
			2	2			106	1
			2	5		4	245	10
			4	1		1	111	4
	7-1-28-0		12	16	8	6	428	8
1-1-0-0	11-4-17-1	5-1-15-0	4	6	1	1	127	3
			6	9		2	271	10
				1		2	180	9a
			7	11	3	6	390	6
			11			7	231	10
			4	2		1	272	10b
8-1	18-5	5-1						
15-0	45-1	15-0						
—	av. 45.00	—						

First One-Day International
SRI LANKA *v.* PAKISTAN

A wet pitch and light rain reduced the first one-day international to 23 overs, and Sri Lanka were given a brisk start. Having reached 68 for 1, however, they lost wickets quickly in the chase for runs, and although de Mel and Mahanama hit well at the close, the final score of 124 was somewhat disappointing and unlikely to give too much trouble to the experienced Pakistan side.

Mudassar and Mohsin gave the visitors a sound start with 66 in 12 overs before Mudassar edged the ball to Ashley de Silva. Mohsin and Javed then added 58 for the second wicket, and Mohsin was caught behind off Rumesh Ratnayake when the scores were level. It was left to Javed to take a single off the third ball of the twenty-second over to win the match.

Mohsin Khan was named Man of the Match for his fluent innings, the foundation of victory.

4, 5 and 6 March 1986

at Galle

Pakistanis 285 for 8 dec (Saleem Malik 106, Qasim Umar 62, Rameez Raja 58)
Sri Lanka Board President's XI 209 for 5
Match drawn

Once again heavy overnight rain delayed the start of one of the tourist's matches, and no play was possible until 30 minutes after lunch. Rizwan and Shoaib fell quickly, but Qasim Umar and Rameez Raja took the score to 115 by the close. Next day, acting captain Saleem Malik was in blistering form. He hit 3 sixes and 7 fours in his century and saw 114 added in as many minutes in the afternoon session before the declaration. The Board President's XI failed to match this and scored barely two runs an over as the match laboured to a draw. On the second day they reached only 52 for 1 in 32 overs.

Second One-Day International
SRI LANKA *v.* PAKISTAN

Put in to bat, Pakistan were restricted to 125 for 8 in 38 overs by some accurate bowling and exciting fielding. Javed and Mudassar alone seemed capable of scoring, and Champaka Ramanayake, on his international debut, had an excellent match. Sadly rain brought the match to an abrupt end and also washed out completely the third international which was to have been played at Colombo the following day.

Fourth One-Day International
SRI LANKA *v.* PAKISTAN

The limited-over series came to a predictably soggy end as rain, which had destroyed the second and third matches, reduced Pakistan's target to 101 in 24 overs, a task they accomplished with ease.

Sent in to bat, Sri Lanka were 25 for 4 after 11 overs, and only reached a respectable score of 160 thanks to a defiant

FIRST TEST MATCH – SRI LANKA v. PAKISTAN
23, 24, 25 and 27 February 1986 at Asgiriya Stadium, Kandy

SRI LANKA

	FIRST INNINGS		SECOND INNINGS	
S. Wettimuny	lbw, b Imran	0	c Rameez, b Wasim	8
S.A.R. Silva*	c Zulqarnian, b Wasim	3	absent ill	—
P.A. de Silva	c Zulqarnian, b Imran	11	b Tauseef	5
R.L. Dias	b Tauseef	11	b Tauseef	26
L.R.D. Mendis†	c Mudassar, b Imran	6	c Mudassar, b Tauseef	4
A. Ranatunga	b Tauseef	18	st Zulqarnian, b Tauseef	33
J.R. Ratnayeke	b Qadir	4	(2) b Imran	7
A.L.F. de Mel	b Tauseef	23	(7) b Tauseef	0
R.J. Ratnayake	c Saleem, b Qadir	4	(8) st Zulqarnian, b Tauseef	4
E.A.R. de Silva	not out	10	(9) not out	4
K.P.J. Warnaweera	c Imran, b Qadir	3	(10) b Imran	0
Extras	lb 7, w 2, nb 7	16	lb 3, w 6, nb 1	10
		109		**101**

	O	M	R	W	O	M	R	W
Imran Khan	9	—	20	3	16	5	29	2
Wasim Akram	8	3	21	1	5	3	5	1
Tauseef Ahmed	13	4	32	3	15	7	45	6
Abdul Qadir	12.4	3	29	3	7	1	19	—

PAKISTAN

	FIRST INNINGS	
Mudassar Nazar	c Mendis, b R.J. Ratnayake	81
Mohsin Khan	lbw, b de Mel	1
Qasim Umar	lbw, b R.J. Ratnayake	11
Javed Miandad	lbw, b E.A.R. de Silva	4
Rameez Raja	lbw, b Warnaweera	3
Saleem Malik	c P.A. de Silva, b de Mel	54
Imran Khan†	c sub, b Ranatunga	7
Abdul Qadir	b R.J. Ratnayake	11
Zulqarnian*	b de Mel	5
Tauseef Ahmed	not out	23
Wasim Akram	run out	19
Extras	b 4, w 7	11
		230

	O	M	R	W
de Mel	17.2	5	50	3
J.R. Ratnayeke	10	1	26	—
R.J. Ratnayake	23	2	57	3
Warnaweera	7.3	2	26	1
E.A.R. de Silva	17	7	37	1
Ranatunga	15.3	6	30	1

FALL OF WICKETS
1-0, 2-14, 3-25, 4-37, 5-44, 6-59, 7-69, 8-78, 9-100
1-14, 2-19, 3-31, 4-43, 5-74, 6-74, 7-80, 8-100, 9-101

FALL OF WICKETS
1-1, 2-28, 3-49, 4-53, 5-154, 6-167, 7-173, 8-181, 9-191

Pakistan won by an innings and 20 runs

FIRST ONE-DAY INTERNATIONAL – SRI LANKA v. PAKISTAN
2 March 1986 at Asgiriya Stadium, Kandy

SRI LANKA				**PAKISTAN**		
A.M. de Silva*	b Zakir Khan	8		Mudassar Nazar	c A.M. de Silva, b Ranasinghe	41
S.K. Ranasinghe	c Abdul Qadir, b Tauseef Ahmed	41		Mohsin Khan	c A.M. de Silva, b R.J. Ratnayake	59
P.A. de Silva	b Imran Khan	21		Javed Miandad	not out	18
A. Ranatunga	c Rameez Raja, b Abdul Qadir	2		Rameez Raja	not out	0
L.R.D. Mendis†	c Wasim Akram, b Abdul Qadir	5		Saleem Malik		
R.L. Dias	c Javed Miandad, b Abdul Qadir	12		Imran Khan†		
R.S. Mahanama	not out	15		Abdul Qadir		
A.L.F. de Mel	not out	16		Zulqarnian*		
R.J. Ratnayake				Taussef Ahmed		
S.D. Anurasiri				Zakir Khan		
K.G. Perera				Wasim Akram		
Extras	lb 3, nb 1	4		Extras	lb 6, nb 1	7
	(23 overs)	(for 6 wickets)	124		(21.3 overs)	(for 2 wickets)	125

	O	M	R	W
Imran Khan	4	—	15	1
Wasim Akram	4	—	34	—
Zakir Khan	5	—	22	1
Tauseef Ahmed	5	—	27	1
Abdul Qadir	5	—	23	3

	O	M	R	W
de Mel	4.3	1	25	—
R.J. Ratnayake	4	—	17	1
Ranasinghe	5	—	31	1
Ranatunga	2	—	12	—
Anurasiri	4	—	19	—
Perera	2	—	15	—

FALL OF WICKETS
1-30, 2-66, 3-71, 4-78, 5-83, 6-101

FALL OF WICKETS
1-66, 2-124

Pakistan won by 8 wickets

SECOND ONE-DAY INTERNATIONAL– SRI LANKA v. PAKISTAN
8 March 1986 at Tyronne Fernando Stadium, Moratuwa

PAKISTAN			
Mudassar Nazar	c Kuruppu, b Ramanayake	29	
Mohsin Khan	c Mahanama, b de Mel	16	
Rameez Raja	c Kuruppu, b Ramanayake	6	
Javed Miandad	c Kuruppu, b Ranasinghe	30	
Saleem Malik	c Mahanama, b Ramanayake	1	
Imran Khan†	c de Silva, b Amalean	20	
Abdul Qadir	run out	1	
Wasim Akram	c Ranasinghe, b Anurasiri	7	
Tauseef Ahmed	not out	0	
Zakir Khan	not out	5	
Zulqarnian*			
Extras	lb 8, w 1, nb 1	10	
(38 overs)	(for 8 wickets)	125	

SRI LANKA
D.S.B.P. Kuruppu*
S.K. Ranasinghe
P.A. de Silva
R.L. Dias
L.R.D. Mendis†
A. Ranatunga
R.S. Mahanama
A.L.F. de Mel
K.N. Amalean
S.D. Anurasiri
C.P. Ramanayake

	O	M	R	W
de Mel	8	1	25	1
Amalean	7	1	15	1
Ramanayake	6	—	25	3
Ranasinghe	9	—	30	1
Anurasiri	8	2	22	1

FALL OF WICKETS
1- 34, 2- 55, 3- 72, 4- 76, 5- 108, 6- 112, 7- 120, 8- 120

Match abandoned as a draw

FOURTH ONE-DAY INTERNATIONAL – SRI LANKA v. PAKISTAN
11 March 1986 at Sinhalese Sports Club, Colombo

SRI LANKA		
D.S.B.P. Kuruppu*	c Zulqarnian, b Zakir Khan	4
S.K. Ranasinghe	c Imran Khan, b Wasim Akram	14
R.L. Dias	c Javed Miandad, b Wasim Akram	1
L.R.D. Mendis†	c Zulqarnian, b Zakir Khan	0
R.S. Mahanama	c Zulqarnian, b Abdul Qadir	22
A. Ranatunga	not out	74
P.A. de Silva	c Saleem Malik, b Abdul Qadir	11
A.L.F. de Mel	b Wasim Akram	13
C.P. Ramanayake	b Wasim Akram	0
S.D. Anurasiri	not out	4
K.N. Amalean		
Extras	b 1, lb 4, w 8, nb 4	17
(38 overs)	(for 8 wickets)	160

PAKISTAN		
Mudassar Nazar	c Kuruppu, b Ranasinghe	35
Mohsin Khan	b Amalean	30
Javed Miandad	not out	22
Rameez Raja	not out	13
Saleem Malik		
Imran Khan†		
Abdul Qadir		
Wasim Akram		
Tauseef Ahmed		
Zakir Khan		
Zulqarnian*		
Extras	lb 2, nb 1	3
(23 overs)	(for 2 wickets)	103

	O	M	R	W
Imran Khan	8	2	22	—
Wasim Akram	9	1	28	4
Zakir Khan	9	—	42	2
Tauseef Ahmed	2	—	10	—
Abdul Qadir	9	—	47	2
Mudassar Nazar	1	—	6	—

	O	M	R	W
de Mel	8	1	22	—
Amalean	7	1	31	1
Ramanayake	3	—	20	—
Ranasinghe	5	—	28	1

FALL OF WICKETS
1- 13, 2- 23, 3- 24, 4- 25, 5- 86, 6- 122, 7- 149, 8- 149

FALL OF WICKETS
1- 65, 2- 72

Pakistan won by 8 wickets

wicket, but the last 5 Pakistan wickets fell for 8 runs, and 132 was the lowest score made against Sri Lanka in 20 Test matches.

Wettimuny and Mahanama, given the added responsibility of opener in his first Test, took Sir Lanka safely to the close at 21 for 0.

Mahanama was run out at 40 and Wettimuny left at 68, but Ranatunga and Aravinda de Silva gave the batting a sense of urgency with 48 quick runs for the fourth wicket. Mendis stayed long enough to see Sri Lanka into the lead, but it was Ranatunga who played the vital role for the home side. In a stay of 247 minutes, he hit 11 fours. Ravi Ratnayeke joined him in adding 80 in 118 minutes for the sixth wicket, Ratnayeke's 38 being his highest score in Test cricket. The stand was decisive in turning the match in favour of Sri Lanka.

Their innings ended early on the third morning, and they soon had Pakistan in trouble again. Kuruppuarachchi, who

LEFT: *Left-arm pace bowler Kuruppuarachchi made a fine Test debut with 7 for 85, a performance that did much to bring Sri Lanka victory in the second Test against Pakistan. He was unable to play in the third Test because of injury. (Michael King – All Sport)*

BELOW: *Guy de Alwis was recalled as Sri Lanka's wicket-keeper and performed admirably in two Test matches against Pakistan. (Michael King – All Sport)*

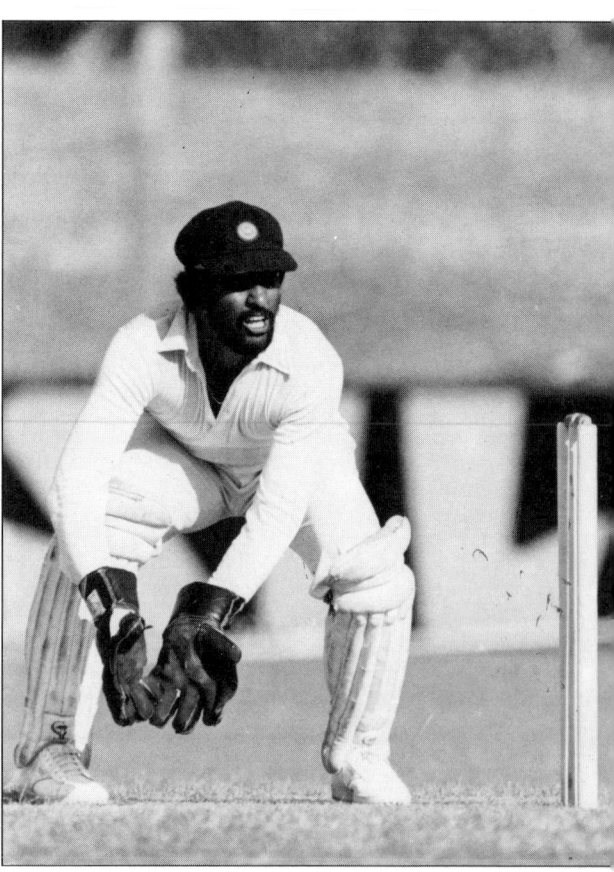

and aggressive innings from Arjuna Ranatunga. He received fine support from Mahanama who enhanced his chances of selection for the Test side.

Mudassar Nazar and Mohsin Khan gave Pakistan a solid start with an opening stand of 65 in 17 overs. After the rain Pakistan needed 56 for 61 balls, and although both openers fell and Rameez Raja survived a difficult chance to Dias off Ranasinghe when 2, they won with few problems.

Second Test Match
SRI LANKA v. PAKISTAN

Sri Lanka gave their side a youthful look for the second Test match, bringing in Mahanama, Anurasiri and Kuruppuarachchi for their Test debuts. They also recalled Guy de Alwis to the Test side in place of Silva.

The medium pace left-arm bowler Kuruppuarachchi, twenty years old, had immediate success when he found the edge of Mudassar's bat with his third ball and de Alwis took the catch. There was further success for Sri Lanka, who had asked Pakistan to bat first when they won the toss, when de Mel trapped Qasim Umar lbw. Five balls later, Javed attempted to hook de Mel, miscued, and was brilliantly caught by the wicket-keeper who ran round to behind backward square-leg, so, after 7 overs, Pakistan were 12 for 3. Mohsin Khan and Rameez Raja added 60 for the fourth wicket, but they fell in quick succession.

Saleem Malik, who batted well when others about him were failing, was aided by Imran in a stand of 46 for the sixth

SECOND TEST MATCH – SRI LANKA v. PAKISTAN
14, 15, 16 and 18 March 1986 at Colombo C.C., Colombo

PAKISTAN

	FIRST INNINGS		SECOND INNINGS	
Mudassar Nazar	c de Alwis, b Kuruppuarachchi	3	lbw, b Kuruppuarachchi	1
Mohsin Khan	lbw, b Kuruppuarachchi	35	c de Alwis, b de Mel	2
Qasim Umar	lbw, b de Mel	3	c de Alwis, b Ratnayeke	52
Javed Miandad	c de Alwis, b de Mel	0	(5) lbw, b Ratnayeke	36
Rameez Raja	lbw, b de Mel	32	(4) c de Alwis, b Ratnayeke	21
Saleem Malik	c Mahanama, b Kuruppuarachchi	42	c Wettimuny, b Ratnayeke	30
Imran Khan†	c Mendis, b Ratnayeke	8	c de Silva, b de Mel	0
Tauseef Ahmed	b Ratnayeke	0	(9) lbw, b Ratnayeke	1
Wasim Akram	c de Mel, b Kuruppuarachchi	0	(8) c Ranatunga, b de Mel	0
Zulqarnian*	c de Silva, b Kuruppuarachchi	1	lbw, b Kuruppuarachchi	5
Mohsin Kamal	not out	1	not out	13
Extras	lb 4, w 1, nb 2	7	b 1, lb 6, nb 4	11
		132		172

	O	M	R	W	O	M	R	W
de Mel	16	6	39	3	16	1	79	3
Kuruppuarachchi	14.5	2	44	5	10.3	1	41	2
J.R. Ratnayeke	17.4	6	29	2	17	3	37	5
Ranatunga	1	—	12	—				
Anurasiri	2	1	4	—	2	—	8	—

SRI LANKA

	FIRST INNINGS		SECOND INNINGS	
S. Wettimuny	c Zulqarnian, b Mudassar	37	c Saleem, b Imran	7
R.S. Mahanama	run out	10	c Zulqarnian, b Imran	8
A.P. Gurusinghe	c Imran, b Wasim Akram	23	not out	9
P.A. de Silva	c sub, b Mohsin Kamal	38	not out	1
A. Ranatunga	c Qasim, b Wasim Akram	77		
L.R.D. Mendis†	c Mohsin Kamal, b Imran	5		
J.R. Ratnayeke	c Imran, b Wasim Akram	38		
R.G. de Alwis*	c Javed, b Mohsin Kamal	10		
A.L.F. de Mel	c Zulqarnian, b Imran	11		
S.D. Anurasiri	c Rameez, b Wasim Akram	4		
A.K. Kuruppuarachchi	not out	0		
Extras	b 7, lb 2, w 4, nb 7	20	b 2, lb 2, w 1, nb 2	7
		273	(for 2 wickets)	32

	O	M	R	W	O	M	R	W
Imran Khan	27	5	79	2	7	2	18	2
Wasim Akram	28.3	9	57	4	6	1	10	—
Mohsin Kamal	14	—	50	2				
Mudassar Nazar	14	2	36	1				
Tauseef Ahmed	11	2	40	—				
Saleem Malik	2	—	2	—				

FALL OF WICKETS
1- 3, 2- 12, 3- 12, 4- 72, 5- 78, 6- 124, 7- 124, 8- 130, 9- 131
1- 6, 2- 6, 3- 72, 4- 93, 5- 131, 6- 136, 7- 136, 8- 145, 9- 154

FALL OF WICKETS
1- 40, 2- 68, 3- 82, 4- 130, 5- 147, 6- 227, 7- 248, 8- 265, 9- 272
1- 10, 2- 31

Sri Lanka won by 8 wickets

had had a magnificent Test debut with 5 for 44 in the first innings, added another scalp when he dismissed the dangerous Mudassar. Mohsin fell to de Mel, but Qasim and Rameez put on 60 and seemed to be negotiating Pakistan to a position of safety. They both fell to Ravi Ratnayeke as did Javed Miandad who reacted badly when given out lbw by umpire Francis. Apparently words were exchanged between Javed and the fieldsmen, and a stone was thrown at Javed as he left the field. He ran into the pavilion brandishing his bat, and the whole episode was a disgrace.

There was some talk of the tour being abandoned, but sense prevailed. It seems that the Pakistani players were angered by abuse aimed at them by spectators and by the standard of umpiring. As Javed has been at the centre of incidents of an unsavoury nature in several of the world's cricketing countries, it is difficult to find sympathy for the tourists.

Once again Pakistan collapsed, losing 5 wickets for 23 runs. Zulqarnian and Mohsin Kamal played a few brave shots on the fourth morning before Kuruppuarachchi took his seventh wicket in his first Test and ended the innings.

Imran took 2 wickets as Sri Lanka searched for 32 runs, the second when the scores were level. Aravinda de Silva hit the winning run and Sri Lanka were victorious in a Test match for the second time. It was a well deserved win.

Third Test Match
SRI LANKA v. PAKISTAN

After Wettimuny had gone for 0, Sri Lanka laboured to 191 for 4 on the opening day. The batsmen were aided by some poor fielding, and throughout the match Pakistan were to drop several vital catches. Gurusinghe and Mahanama put on 67 for Sri Lanka's second wicket, but Gurusinghe was missed at 9 and 27.

Ranatunga and Mendis were in command at the end of the first day, both batsmen having passed 50, but, on the second morning, Imran and Zakir took 5 of the last 6 wickets, and Pakistan's much more efficient out-cricket restricted Sri Lanka to another 90 runs.

Pakistan began disastrously. Mudassar was brilliantly caught behind off de Mel, and 8 runs later, Kaushik Amalean, who was making his Test debut in place of the injured Kuruppuarachchi, took his first wicket when he had Mohsin Khan lbw. Qasim Umar was then caught behind off Ravi Ratnayeke, and Pakistan were 49 for 3. Rameez Raja then came to the wicket and played an innings of great maturity. He halted the slide and, in conjunction with Saleem Malik, took the attack to the opponents. In 11.2 overs, they added 71 for the fifth wicket. Malik fell to Ratnayeke, but Pakistan ended at a healthier 180 for 5. Rameez Raja was

THIRD TEST MATCH – SRI LANKA v. PAKISTAN
22, 23, 24, 26 and 27 March 1986 at P. Saravanamuttu Oval, Colombo

SRI LANKA

	FIRST INNINGS		SECOND INNINGS	
S. Wettimuny	c Rameez, b Wasim Akram	0	c Rameez, b Wasim Akram	14
R.S. Mahanama	c Zulqarnian, b Qadir	41	b Imran	4
A.P. Gurusinghe	c Zulqarnian, b Imran	39	not out	116
A. Ranatunga	c Imran, b Zakir	53	(5) not out	135
P.A. de Silva	c Mohsin Khan, b Zakir	16	(4) c Javed, b Imran	25
L.R.D. Mendis†	c Zulqarnian, b Imran	58		
J.R. Ratnayeke	c Javed, b Zakir	7		
R.G. de Alwis*	b Imran	18		
A.L.F. de Mel	not out	14		
S.D. Anurasiri	b Imran	8		
K.N. Amalean	lbw, b Qadir	2		
Extras	b 7, lb 9, w 6, nb 3	25	b 19, lb 7, w 1, nb 2	29
		281	(for 3 wickets)	323

PAKISTAN

	FIRST INNINGS	
Mudassar Nazar	c de Alwis, b de Mel	8
Mohsin Khan	lbw, b Amalean	12
Qasim Umar	c de Alwis, b Ratnayeke	19
Javed Miandad	lbw, b Amalean	23
Rameez Raja	lbw, b Ratnayeke	122
Saleem Malik	lbw, b Ratnayeke	29
Imran Khan†	c de Alwis, b Ranatunga	33
Abdul Qadir	b Amalean	20
Zulqarnian*	c de Alwis, b Ratnayeke	13
Wasim Akram	run out	11
Zakir Khan	not out	0
Extras	b 10, lb 8, w 1, nb 9	28
		318

	O	M	R	W	O	M	R	W
Imran Khan	32	11	69	4	24	5	56	2
Wasim Akram	22	8	41	1	29	11	72	1
Zakir Khan	24	6	80	3	21	4	70	—
Mudassar Nazar	7	2	19	—	10	2	29	—
Abdul Qadir	23.5	3	56	2	22	5	70	—
Saleem Malik					1	1	0	—

	O	M	R	W
de Mel	27	3	90	1
Amalean	18.1	1	59	3
J.R. Ratnayeke	30	4	116	4
Anurasiri	15	11	9	—
Ranatunga	11	5	26	1

FALL OF WICKETS
1- 12, 2- 79, 3- 109, 4- 149, 5- 202, 6- 218, 7- 251, 8- 260, 9- 272
1- 18, 2- 18, 3- 83

FALL OF WICKETS
1- 24, 2- 32, 3- 49, 4- 87, 5- 158, 6- 234, 7- 279, 8- 305, 9- 318

Match drawn

Sri Lanka v. Pakistan   Test Match Averages

SRI LANKA BATTING

	M	Inns	NOs	Runs	HS	Av	100s	50s
A.P. Gurusinghe	2	4	1	187	116*	93.50	1	
A. Ranatunga	3	5	1	316	135*	79.00	1	1
P.A. de Silva	3	6	1	96	38	19.20		
L.R.D. Mendis	3	4		73	58	18.25		1
A.L.F. de Mel	3	4	1	48	23	16.00		
R.S. Mahanama	2	4		63	41	15.75		
J.R. Ratnayeke	3	4		56	38	14.00		
R.G. de Alwis	2	2		28	18	14.00		
S. Wettimuny	3	6		66	37	11.00		
S.D. Anurasiri	2	2		12	8	6.00		

Played in one Test: K.N. Amalean 2; A.K. Kuruppuarachchi O*; E.A.R. de Silva 10* & 4*; R.L. Dias 11 & 26; R.J. Ratnayake 4 & 4; S.A.R. Silva 3; K.P.J. Warnaweera 3 & 0.

PAKISTAN BATTING

	M	Inns	NOs	Runs	HS	Av	100s	50s
Rameez Raja	3	4		178	122	44.50	1	
Saleem Malik	3	4		155	54	38.75		1
Qasim Umar	3	4		85	52	21.25		1
Mudassar Nazar	3	4		93	81	20.25		1
Javed Miandad	3	4		63	36	15.75		
Abdul Qadir	2	2		31	20	15.50		
Mohsin Khan	3	4		50	35	12.50		
Imran Khan	3	4		48	33	12.00		
Tauseef Ahmed	2	3	1	24	23*	12.00		
Wasim Akram	3	4		30	19	7.50		
Zulqarnian	3	4		24	13	6.00		

Played in one Test: Zakir Khan 0*; Mohsin Kamal 1* & 13*

SRI LANKA BOWLING

	Overs	Mds	Runs	Wkts	Av	Best	5/inns
A.K. Kuruppua-rachchi	25.2	3	85	7	12.14	5/44	1
J.R. Ratnayeke	74.4	12	208	11	18.90	5/37	1
A.L.F. de Mel	76.2	15	258	10	25.80	3/39	
A. Ranatunga	27.3	11	68	2	34.00	1/26	
S.D. Anurasiri	19	12	21	0	—		

Bowled in one innings: R.J. Ratnayake 23 - 2 - 57 - 3; K.N. Amalean 18.1 - 1 - 59 - 3; K.P.J. Warnaweera 7.3 - 2 - 26 - 1; E.A.R. de Silva 17 - 7 - 37 - 1

PAKISTAN BOWLING

	Overs	Mds	Runs	Wkts	Av	Best	5/inns
Tauseef Ahmed	39	13	117	9	13.00	6/45	1
Imran Khan	115	28	271	15	18.06	4/69	
Wasim Akram	98.3	35	206	8	25.75	4/57	
Abdul Qadir	65.3	12	174	5	34.80	3/29	
Zakir Khan	45	10	150	3	50.00	3/80	
Mudassar Nazar	31	6	84	1	84.00	1/36	
Saleem Malik	3	1	2	0	—		

Bowled in one innings: Mohsin Kamal 14 - 0 - 50 - 2

SRI LANKA CATCHES
9 - R.G. de Alwis; 3 - P.A. de Silva; 2 - L.R.D. Mendis and subs; 1 - R.S. Mahanama, S. Wettimuny, A.L.F. de Mel and A. Ranatunga

PAKISTAN CATCHES
10 - Zulqarnian (ct 8/st 2); 4 - Rameez Raja and Imran Khan; 3 - Javed Miandad; 2 - Mudassar Nazar and Saleem Malik; 1 - Mohsin Khan, Qasim Umar, Mohsin Kamal and sub

unbeaten on 73, having hit 10 fours.

He hit 7 more fours on the third day as Pakistan seized control. Rameez reached his maiden Test century and faced 242 deliveries. He had good support from the later batsmen, and Pakistan took a first innings lead of 37. When bad light ended play 20 minutes early the lead had not been wiped out and Wettimuny and Mahanama were back in the pavilion. Wettimuny fended a short pitched delivery into the hands of forward short-leg and Imran knocked back Mahanama's off stump in the next over. Gurusinghe and Aravinda de Silva added 6 runs before the close.

The two young batsmen withstood a hostile attack throughout the morning session on the fourth day, and rain prevented any play in the afternoon. The third wicket stand realised 65 runs in 157 minutes and was ended 45 minutes after tea when de Silva was taken at slip. Play was called off for the day because of bad light almost as soon as de Silva was out.

Gurusinghe and Ranatunga batted throughout the final day and put on 240 for Sri Lanka's fourth wicket, the highest partnership yet recorded for Sri Lanka in Test cricket. Both batsmen reached centuries. Gurusinghe, 19 years old, played a most accomplished innings which was described as the best of the series by Imran Khan. It was Gurusinghe's first Test hundred while Ranatunga hit his second Test century, better by 24 runs than his effort against India.

Both batsmen were aided by some very shoddy fielding. Eight catches were missed on the last day, and Ranatunga had 'lives' at 7, 10, 12, 25 and 26, four of them in the slips, two misses each by Javed and Saleem, and one behind the stumps. Nevertheless, the performance of Ranatunga and Gurusinghe deserves the highest praise and underlines the growing strength of Sri Lankan cricket.

Asia Cup – First Match
SRI LANKA v. PAKISTAN

Sri Lanka's most exciting and exacting season came to an end with the Asia Cup and a triangular tournament of limited-over matches involving Sri Lanka, New Zealand and Pakistan. Unfortunately India withdrew from the Asia Cup which left Sri Lanka, Pakistan and Bangladesh to compete for the trophy.

In the opening match, Mendis won the toss and asked Pakistan to bat. Mudassar began briskly, but he fell to de Mel, and Mohsin Khan and Rameez Raja took the score to 87 without undue worry. Sri Lanka bowled well and fielded well, and the pressure that they exerted on the Pakistani batsmen was rewarded when 5 wickets fell for 32 runs. The tail wagged strongly, but Sri Lanka seemed to have done enough to have made the task of their batsmen a light one.

If Sri Lanka had bowled well, they batted badly. Some wretched, unnecessarily rash shots saw them crumble after a promising start, and Pakistan won with ease.

ASIA CUP MATCH ONE – SRI LANKA v. PAKISTAN
30 March 1986 at P. Savaranamuttu Oval, Colombo

PAKISTAN			
Mudassar Nazar	c de Silva, b de Mel	15
Mohsin Khan	c and b Anurasiri	39
Rameez Raja	c Kuruppu, b Ratnayake	26
Javed Miandad	c Dias, b Anurasiri	9
Qasim Umar	st Kuruppu, b Ratnayake	16
Manzoor Elahi	c Kuruppu, b Ratnayake	6
Imran Khan†	c de Silva, b de Mel	21
Abdul Qadir	c Anurasiri, b Amalean	14
Wasim Akram	c sub, b Ratnayake	24
Zulqarnian*	not out	11
Zakir Khan	b Ratnayake	1
Extras	b 5, lb 7, w 2, nb 1	15
		—
(45 overs)		197

	O	M	R	W
de Mel	9	1	40	2
Amalean	7	1	30	1
R.J. Ratnayake	9	1	32	3
Samarasekera	2	—	19	—
Anurasiri	9	1	27	2
Ranatunga	9	1	37	2

FALL OF WICKETS
1- 18, 2- 87, 3- 87, 4- 108, 5- 118, 6- 119, 7- 141, 8- 179, 9- 187

SRI LANKA			
D.S.B.P. Kuruppu	c and b Abdul Qadir	34
M.A.R. Samarasekera	c Imran Khan, b Zakir Khan	5
A.P. Gurusinghe	c Zulqarnian, b Zakir Khan	8
R.L. Dias	c Javed Miandad, b Zakir Khan	0
A. Ranatunga	c Zulqarnian, b Manzoor Elahi	7
L.R.D. Mendis†	c Zulqarnian, b Imran Khan	0
P.A. de Silva	c Javed Miandad, b Manzoor Elahi	12
R.J. Ratnayake	not out	22
A.L.F. de Mel	c Zulqarnian, b Manzoor Elahi	0
S.D. Anurasiri	c Imran Khan, b Abdul Qadir	5
K.N. Amalean	c Imran Khan, b Abdul Qadir	9
Extras	b 4, lb 3, w 7	14
		—
(33.5 overs)		116

	O	M	R	W
Wasim Akram	6	1	17	—
Zakir Khan	6	—	34	3
Manzoor Elahi	9	1	22	3
Imran Khan	5	1	24	3
Abdul Qadir	7.5	1	24	3

FALL OF WICKETS
1- 24, 2- 32, 3- 32, 4- 52, 5- 53, 6- 67, 7- 83, 8- 94, 9- 105

Umpires: H.D. Bird & D.R. Shepherd

Pakistan won by 81 runs

Gurusinghe hit a maiden Test century at the age of 19 in the final match against Pakistan in Colombo. He and Ranatunga added 240 for Sri Lanka's 4th wicket, the highest partnership recorded for Sri Lanka in Test cricket. (Michael King – All Sport)

Asia Cup – Second Match
PAKISTAN v. BANGLADESH

Bangladesh's first venture into the top echelons of cricket was not a successful one. Imran Khan and Wasim Akram quickly had them struggling, and Wasim went on to take 4 wickets and claim the individual award. Shaheedur Rahman batted bravely, and he and Rafqul Alam added 41 for the 5th wicket, the best stand of the innings.

Mudassar Nasar led the assault on the Bangladesh attack, but Pakistan did not find things all to their liking against accurate bowling and keen fielding.

Had Bangladesh been able to gain invaluable experience against the England 'B' team earlier in the year, they might have given a better account of themselves.

Asia Cup – Third Match
SRI LANKA v. BANGLADESH

Bangladesh were again unlucky in losing the toss and being asked to bat first, but they gave a more spirited display than they had done against Pakistan and survived for their full complement of overs. A third wicket stand of 53 between Minhazul Abedin and Shaheedur Rahman, a batsman of quality, raised hopes of a good score, but survival at the top level has to be achieved before batsmen can adapt to scoring runs quickly.

There was early success for Bangladesh when Kuruppu fell at 8, and after Mahanama and Gurusinghe had added 55, Mahanama and Dias, who had a season well below his best form, were out in quick succession. Gurusinghe and a buoyant Ranatunga scored the last 68 runs in a bustling manner.

Asia Cup – Qualifying Table

	P	W	L	Pts
Pakistan	2	2	—	4
Sri Lanka	2	1	1	2
Bangladesh	2	—	2	0

Mahanama, one of Sri Lanka's brightest young stars, who won his first Test caps against Pakistan. (Michael King – All Sport)

Triangular Tournament – First Match
SRI LANKA v. NEW ZEALAND

The first match in the Triangular Tournament was hampered a little by rain, but New Zealand played impressively to record a comfortable victory. The New Zealand side, without Coney, Hadlee and other leading players, contained a few young men who were contending for places in the party to tour England. One of them, Willie Watson, produced an excellent spell of quick bowling in what was his first international match.

ASIA CUP MATCH TWO – PAKISTAN v. BANGLADESH
31 March 1986 at P. Savaranamuttu Oval, Colombo

BANGLADESH			
Raquibul Hassan	c Zulqarnian, b Zakir Khan	5
Nurul Abedin	c Zulqarnian, b Imran Khan	0
G.A. Hossain†	b Wasim Akram	0
Shaheedur Rahman	c and b Abdul Qadir	37
Minhazul Abedin	c Manzoor Elahi, b Wasim Akram	6
Rafiqul Alam	c Rameez Raja, b Wasim Akram	14
Golam Chowdhury	c Zulqarnian, b Abdul Qadir	14
J.S. Badsha	b Wasim Akram	0
Samiur Rahman	b Imran Khan	8
G.M. Nawsher	not out	1
Hafizur Rahman*	st Zulqarnian, b Abdul Qadir	0
Extras	lb 4, w 4, nb 1	9
(35.3 overs)		94

	O	M	R	W
Wasim Akram	9	2	19	4
Imran Khan	7	3	11	2
Zakir Khan	7	—	27	1
Manzoor Elahi	5	2	18	—
Abdul Qadir	7.3	1	15	3

FALL OF WICKETS
1- 3, 2- 4, 3- 15, 4- 27, 5- 68, 6- 70, 7- 79, 8- 93, 9- 93

PAKISTAN			
Mudassar Nazar	not out	47
Mohsin Khan	lbw, b Badsha	28
Rameez Raja	lbw, b Badsha	0
Javeed Miandad	c Hafizur Rahman, b Hossain	15
Qasim Umar	not out	3
Manzoor Elahi		
Imran Khan†		
Abdul Qadir		
Wasim Akram		
Zulqarnian*		
Zakir Khan		
Extras	lb 4, w 1	5
(32.1 overs)	(for 3 wickets)	98

	O	M	R	W
Nawsher	7	1	32	—
Samiur Rahman	7	1	15	—
Chowdhury	6	—	13	—
Badsha	9	1	23	2
Hossain	3	—	7	1
Hassan	0.1	—	4	—

FALL OF WICKETS
1- 45, 2- 55, 3- 85

Umpires: H.C. Felsinger & P.W. Vidanagamage

Pakistan won by 7 wickets

ASIA CUP MATCH THREE – SRI LANKA v. BANGLADESH
2 April 1986 at Asgiriya Stadium, Kandy

BANGLADESH			
Raquibul Hassan	lbw, b Ranatunga		12
Nurul Abedin	c Mahanama, b Ratnayake		13
G.A. Hossain†	c Kuruppu, b Ranatunga		10
Minhazul Abedin	run out		40
Shaheedur Rahman	c Mendis, b Ratnayake		25
Rafiqul Alam	b Amalean		10
Golam Chowdhury	not out		3
J.S. Badsha	run out		1
Samiur Rahman	c Dias, b Amalean		4
G.M. Nawsher	not out		3
Hafizur Rahman*			
Extras	b 1, lb 4, w 3, nb 2		10
(45 overs)	(for 8 wickets)		131

	O	M	R	W
de Mel	9	1	30	—
Amalean	9	2	15	2
R.J. Ratnayake	9	1	41	2
Ranatunga	9	1	17	2
Anurasiri	9	2	23	—

FALL OF WICKETS
1- 26, 2- 29, 3- 49, 4- 92, 5- 119, 6- 119, 7- 120, 8- 126

SRI LANKA			
D.S.B.P. Kuruppu*	c Samiur, b Nawsher		3
R.S. Mahanama	c Hafizur Rahman, b Chowdhury		25
A.P. Gurusinghe	not out		44
R.L. Dias	c Raqibul Hassan, b Hossain		0
A. Ranatunga	not out		41
L.R.D. Mendis†			
P.A. de Silva			
R.J. Ratnayake			
A.L.F. de Mel			
S.D. Anurasiri			
K.N. Amalean			
Extras	b 3, lb 7, w 9		19
(31.3 overs)	(for 3 wickets)		132

	O	M	R	W
Nawsher	9	—	45	1
Samiur Rahman	3	—	15	—
Badsha	6	—	18	—
Chowdhury	8.3	2	22	1
Hossain	5	—	22	1

FALL OF WICKETS
1- 8, 2- 63, 3- 64

Umpires: H.D. Bird & D.R. Shepherd

Sri Lanka won by 7 wickets

TRIANGULAR TOURNAMENT MATCH ONE – SRI LANKA v. NEW ZEALAND
5 April 1986 at Kettarama Stadium, Colombo

SRI LANKA			
D.S.B.P. Kuruppu*	c McSweeney, b Snedden		23
R.S. Mahanama	lbw, b Snedden		12
A.P. Gurusinghe	c J.J. Crowe, b Watson		14
A. Ranatunga	c McSweeney, b Snedden		23
L.R.D. Mendis†	c Gray, b Bracewell		24
P.A. de Silva	c J.J. Crowe, b Watson		4
S.K. Ranasinghe	c Gray, b Watson		0
R.J. Ratnayake	not out		22
C.P. Ramanayake	run out		0
S.D. Anurasiri	run out		0
K.N. Amalean			
Extras	b 8, lb 5, nb 2		15
(43 overs)	(for 9 wickets)		137

	O	M	R	W
Robertson	8	2	26	—
Watson	9	2	15	3
Gray	9	—	15	—
Snedden	9	1	26	3
Bracewell	8	—	42	1

FALL OF WICKETS
1- 39, 2- 40, 3- 79, 4- 88, 5- 96, 6- 96, 7- 130, 8- 136, 9- 137

NEW ZEALAND			
J.G. Wright†	c and b Ranatunga		24
K.R. Rutherford	c Mahanama, b Ratnayake		34
M.D. Crowe	c Mahanama, b Ranatunga		4
J.J. Crowe	run out		21
T.E. Blain	not out		25
J.G. Bracewell	not out		16
E.J. Gray			
G.K. Robertson			
E.B. McSweeney*			
M.C. Snedden			
W. Watson			
Extras	b 4, lb 8, w 3, nb 1		16
(36.2 overs)	(for 4 wickets)		140

	O	M	R	W
Amalean	7	—	29	—
Ramanayake	3	—	20	—
R.J. Ratnayake	7	1	24	1
Anurasiri	9	1	19	—
Ranatunga	6	—	17	2
Ranasinghe	2	—	7	—
de Silva	2.2	—	12	—

FALL OF WICKETS
1- 62, 2- 71, 3- 72, 4- 110

Umpires: H.D. Bird & D.R. Shepherd

New Zealand won by 6 wickets

ASIA CUP FINAL – SRI LANKA v. PAKISTAN
6 April 1986 at P. Savaranamuttu Oval, Colombo

PAKISTAN			
Mudassar Nazar	b de Mel		2
Mohsin Khan	run out		7
Rameez Raja	c Mahanama, b Amalean		2
Javed Miandad	c Ratnayake, b Amalean		67
Imran Khan†	lbw, b Ratnayake		2
Saleem Malik	c and b Anurasiri		23
Manzoor Elahi	b Amalean		37
Abdul Qadir	c de Mel, b Ratnayake		30
Wasim Akram	c Gurusinghe, b Amalean		6
Zulqarnian*	not out		1
Zakir Khan			
Extras	lb 4, w 8, nb 2		14
(45 overs)	(for 9 wickets)		191

SRI LANKA			
D.S.B.P. Kuruppu*	c Saleem Malik, b Abdul Qadir		30
R.S. Mahanama	c Abdul Qadir, b Manzoor Elahi		21
A.P. Gurusinghe	c Zulqarnian, b Abdul Qadir		4
P.A. de Silva	c sub, b Mudassar Nazar		52
A. Ranatunga	c Mohsin Khan, b Abdul Qadir		57
L.R.D. Mendis†	not out		22
R.L. Dias	not out		0
R.J. Ratnayake			
A.L.F. de Mel			
S.D. Anurasiri			
K.N. Amalean			
Extras	b 1, lb 6, w 2		9
(42.2 overs)	(for 5 wickets)		195

	O	M	R	W
de Mel	9	2	21	1
Amalean	9	1	46	4
R.J. Ratnayake	8	—	50	2
Ranatunga	9	1	27	—
Anurasiri	9	—	24	1
de Silva	1	—	19	—

	O	M	R	W
Wasim Akram	7.2	2	22	—
Zakir Khan	6	—	36	—
Abdul Qadir	9	—	32	3
Manzoor Elahi	9	—	30	1
Saleem Malik	3	—	19	—
Mudassar Nazar	8	—	49	1

FALL OF WICKETS
1- 6, 2- 10, 3- 24, 4- 32, 5- 72, 6- 137, 7- 179, 8- 185, 9- 191

FALL OF WICKETS
1- 40, 2- 59, 3- 64, 4- 161, 5- 191

Umpires: H.D. Bird & D.R. Shepherd

Sri Lanka won by 5 wickets

TRIANGULAR TOURNAMENT MATCH THREE – NEW ZEALAND v. PAKISTAN
7 April 1986 at P. Savaranamuttu Oval, Colombo

NEW ZEALAND			
K.R. Rutherford	c Tauseef Ahmed, b Wasim Akram		9
J.G. Wright†	st Zulqarnian, b Tauseef Ahmed		42
M.D. Crowe	c Manzoor Elahi, b Mohsin Kamal		75
J.J. Crowe	run out		42
B.R. Blair	c Zulqarnian, b Mohsin Kamal		0
G.K. Robertson	c Zulqarnian, b Mohsin Kamal		7
J.G. Bracewell	not out		15
T.E. Blain*	b Mohsin Kamal		0
E.J. Gray	b Wasim Akram		1
M.C. Snedden	not out		2
E.J. Chatfield			
Extras	b 1, lb 14, w 6		21
(42 overs)	(for 8 wickets)		214

PAKISTAN			
Mudassar Nazar	run out		20
Mohsin Khan	c Snedden, b Chatfield		16
Rameez Raja	c Blair, b Gray		25
Javed Miandad†	b Snedden		68
Saleem Malik	run out		32
Manzoor Elahi	c M.D. Crowe, b Snedden		27
Abdul Qadir	not out		11
Wasim Akram	not out		8
Mohsin Kamal			
Zulqarnian*			
Tauseef Ahmed			
Extras	lb 10		10
(40.4 overs)	(for 6 wickets)		217

	O	M	R	W
Wasim Akram	9	2	29	2
Mohsin Kamal	8	—	47	4
Manzoor Elahi	9	—	33	—
Abdul Qadir	9	1	41	—
Tauseef Ahmed	6	—	38	1
Mudassar Nazar	1	—	11	—

	O	M	R	W
Chatfield	9	4	18	1
Robertson	7	—	39	—
Snedden	7.4	—	56	2
M.D. Crowe	3	—	21	—
Bracewell	9	—	41	—
Gray	5	—	32	1

FALL OF WICKETS
1- 16, 2- 102, 3- 181, 4- 182, 5- 194, 6- 202, 7- 202, 8- 211

FALL OF WICKETS
1- 31, 2- 42, 3- 140, 4- 162, 5- 173, 6- 206

Pakistan won by 4 wickets

Sri Lanka, put in to bat, struggled against an accurate attack. The opening partnership realised 39, but the runs occupied 17 overs, and the slowness of the scoring undoubtedly put pressure on the later batsmen. Snedden dismissed both openers and his 3 wickets and economic bowling won him the individual award. As they pressed for runs Sri Lanka collapsed to 96 for 6 and although they recovered somewhat, their total never looked large enough to trouble the New Zealanders. Both Gray and John Bracewell turned the ball sharply and troubled the batsmen.

There was some hope for Sri Lanka when New Zealand, having moved to 62 without loss, lost 3 wickets for 10 runs, but Jeff Crowe and Tony Blain rectified the position, and New Zealand won with 6.4 overs to spare.

Asia Cup Final
SRI LANKA v. PAKISTAN

Once again the side winning the toss asked their opponents to bat first, and with Pakistan reduced to 32 for 4, Mendis's decision was well justified. Javed Miandad came to his side's rescue with a fine innings and received good support from Saleem Malik, Manzoor Elahi and Abdul Qadir so that Sri Lanka faced a target greater than they had expected.

Sri Lanka's batting had disappointed in the closing weeks of the season, but Kuruppu and Mahanama gave them a solid start, and although there was a minor crisis when 3 wickets fell for 64 runs, Aravinda de Silva and Ranatunga put on 97 and assured their side of victory.

This match was also part of the triangular tournament.

Triangular Tournament – Final Match
NEW ZEALAND v. PAKISTAN

A thrilling final match saw Pakistan win with 8 balls to spare and take the Triangular Tournament on a faster scoring rate, each side having won one match. New Zealand were without Willie Watson and Ewen Chatfield returned. Bruce Blair also came into the side, and Tony Blain took over as wicket-keeper.

After the early loss of Rutherford, New Zealand scored at a brisk rate. Wright and Martin Crowe put on 86, and Jeff Crowe showed further evidence that he had recaptured form and confidence with another good knock. The later batsmen sacrificed themselves in the dash for runs.

Mudassar Nazar and Mohsin Khan were out for 42, but Javed Miandad, leading Pakistan in the absence of Imran who had a leg muscle strain, began the assault on the bowling. He hit 5 fours before being bowled by Snedden at 173. Pakistan were falling behind the run rate required until Manzoor Elahi hit Martin Snedden for 2 sixes in the thirty-ninth over. Snedden had his revenge when he had Manzoor Elahi caught at backward square-leg, but Abdul Qadir and Wasim Akram stroked their side to victory.

Triangular Tournament – Final Table				
	P	W	L	Pts	Run Rate
Pakistan	2	1	1	2	4.76
New Zealand	2	1	1	2	4.51
Sri Lanka	2	1	1	2	3.89

FIRST CLASS AVERAGES

BATTING

	M	Inns	NOs	Runs	HS	Av	100s	50s
A.P. Gurusinghe	7	11	3	584	116*	73.00	3	2
S. Warnakulasuriya	6	8	1	441	174*	63.00	1	1
A. Ranatunga	10	16	3	739	135*	56.84	3	3
D.C. Wickremasinghe	3	4	1	170	87	56.66		1
R.S. Madugalle	5	7	1	264	103	44.00	1	2
L.R.D. Mendis	6	10	1	383	124	42.55	1	4
S.M.S. Kaluperuma	3	4		157	70	39.25		2
H.P. Tillekeratne	6	10	4	233	105*	38.83	1	
R.L. Dias	5	10	1	330	106	36.66	1	2
A.M. de Silva	3	6	1	172	39	34.40		
S. Wettimuny	9	14		447	138	31.92	1	2
M.A.R. Samarasekera	5	7		217	110	31.00	1	
R.S. Mahanama	8	15	3	354	67	29.50		2
P.A. de Silva	8	15	2	345	81	26.53		2
S.A.R. Silva	6	11	1	242	111	24.20	1	
D. Ranatunga	5	9		211	44	23.44		
M.D. Vonhagt	4	7		159	88	22.71		1
J.R. Ratnayeke	5	8	1	143	42*	20.42		

(qualification – 100 runs, average 10.00)

BOWLING

	Overs	Mds	Runs	Wks	Av	Best	5/inn
K.P.J. Warnaweera	133	47	297	15	19.80	5/72	1
F.S. Ahangama	180.5	39	507	23	22.04	5/52	1
A.K. Kuruppu-rachchi	120	22	341	15	22.73	5/44	1
J.R. Ratnayeke	116.4	17	331	14	23.64	5/37	1
R.J. Ratnayake	205.5	39	576	24	24.00	6/85	2
S. Weerasinghe	144.3	41	359	13	27.61	5/49	2
S.D. Anurasiri	178.4	56	370	11	33.63	5/38	1
A.L.F. de Mel	253.5	52	785	23	34.13	5/64	1

(qualification – 10 wickets)

LEADING FIELDERS
25 - S.A.R. Silva (ct 23/st 2); 12 - R.G. de Alwis; 8 - P.A. de Silva; 6 - A.G.D. Wickremasinghe (ct 4/st 2); 5 - A.P. Gurusinghe

Without question, the 1985–86 season was the most successful in Sri Lanka's cricket history. Not only were Test victories obtained over India and Pakistan, but the young players who emerged capable of displaying their talents at the highest level excited and encouraged belief that within the next few days Sri Lanka would field one of the strongest Test sides in the world. The prowess of Aravinda de Silva has already been declaimed, but within months of scoring Test centuries against Pakistan, he was joined by Gurusinghe, Mahanama, Warnakulasuriya and Tillekeratne, all of them schoolboys and all of them batsmen of immense talent.

As bowlers, Ahangama, Amalean and Kuruppuarachchi came to the fore. Ahangama had a brilliant start to his Test career and then missed the remainder of the season through injury. Injuries to Rumesh Ratnayake, Madugalle, Tillekeratne and Kuruppuarachchi also handicapped the Sri Lankan selectors at one time or another, but nothing could dispel the optimism that the immediate future of Sri Lankan cricket is very bright indeed.

In Power of Others

The season in Australia.
Sheffield Shield. McDonald's Cup.
Australia *v.* New Zealand.
Benson and Hedges World Series.
Form charts.
Review of the season by Frank Tyson.

Melbourne Cricket Ground. (Philip Tyson)

It was mistakenly believed in some quarters that when peace was declared with the Packer organisation in 1979 all would be well in Australian cricket. The attempt to appease the star players, to encourage 'player power' and to cater for their needs and desires, had led to a blind eye being turned to disciplinary breaches, or, at best, for any transgressions to be dealt with lightly. Many of those who had stayed loyal during the Packer revolution, Yallop, Hughes and Rixon among them, had a right to feel aggrieved at the way that they were treated when the leading players returned.

The rewards offered to the star players, and the sway which they were allowed to influence, showed a short-sighted policy on the part of those who administered the game in Australia, for they chose instant peace at any price in 1979 rather than consider the long term implications of what they were doing. The emphasis on international cricket, at the instigation of the television presenter and his advertisers, reduced the Sheffield Shield to a position of insignificance, so much so that, in 1979–80, Kim Hughes, captain-elect of Western Australia, went through the entire season without representing his state. The six Tests crammed into the pre-Christmas period and the seemingly endless stream of one-day international matches in the post Christmas weeks left little time for reflection on domestic cricket where techniques are honed and character developed.

The one-day internationals offered instant rewards and instant success, and the players, through the short-sighted administrators, were, to transmute Wilde, in danger of knowing the price of everything and the value of nothing. Indeed, the paucity of people with knowledge and experience of the first-class game in administration has led to a state of affairs where it is difficult to determine if there is a policy in Australian cricket at all other than to make as much money as possible while the Sheffield Shield withers into oblivion, the casualty of a false economy.

The standards shown by the Australian side which toured England in 1985 were, at times, lamentable. They were a most pleasant and amiable group of men, but their technique and professional application were, in the main, disastrous. To add to Australian problems, a group of disaffected players had exiled themselves from Australian cricket by going, as a team, to South Africa. Chris Harte traced the events leading to this venture in last year's *Benson and Hedges Cricket Year*, and the price that Australian cricket paid can be seen in that it was robbed of any depth.

There is much ability among young players in the Sheffield Shield, but those players need to serve an apprenticeship, for to throw them too soon into the Test arena would be yet another disaster. Yet how can that apprenticeship be meaningfully spent if the young players of promise are not testing their skills against the mature batsmen and bowlers of proven ability because those more experienced players are competing in round after round of one-day international matches?

The season, 1985–86, offered no respite or chance of rebuilding to Australian cricket which seemed at its lowest point. Test series against New Zealand and India would be followed by the Benson and Hedges World Series, and the Australian party would be off to New Zealand before the completion of either the Sheffield Shield or McDonald's Cup, the fifty-over competition with which the season began.

McDonald's Cup
13 October 1985

at Adelaide

South Australia 199 for 8 (D.F.G. O'Connor 51, B.A. Reid 4 for 40)
Western Australia 200 for 8 (G.R. Marsh 92 not out, S. Wundke 4 for 36)

Western Australia won by 2 wickets

at Brisbane

Queensland 235 for 8 (G.M. Ritchie 74 not out, R.B. Kerr 50, M. Hill 5 for 29)
Tasmania 45 for 0

Match abandoned

In troubled weather the match at Brisbane was abandoned after 11 overs of the second innings. In Adelaide, Western Australia, having slipped from 147 for 5 to 155 for 8, recovered through Marsh, who played splendidly throughout, and Reid to win with 5 balls to spare. Wundke had a fine all round match for the home side.

17, 18, 19 and 20 October 1985

at Adelaide

South Australia 255 (P.R. Sleep 105, K.H. Macleay 4 for 83) and 357 for 4 dec (R.J. Zadow 144, G.A. Bishop 108, D.W. Hookes 82)
Western Australia 337 (T.J. Zoehrer 94 not out, M.R.J. Veletta 87, G.J. Ireland 50, G.C. Small 5 for 89) and 117 for 1 (G.M. Wood 53 not out, G.R. Marsh 50 not out)

Match drawn
Western Australia 4 pts, South Australia 0 pts

18, 19, 20 and 21 October 1985

at Brisbane

Victoria 431 (D.F. Whatmore 109, P.A. Hibbert 65, C.J. McDermott 4 for 116) and 137 for 6
Queensland 539 (A.R. Border 194, G.S. Trimble 90, G.M. Ritchie 86, C.J. McDermott 72, A.I.C. Dodemaide 4 for 151)

Match drawn
Queensland 4 pts, Victoria 0 pts

18, 19 and 20 October 1985

at Townsville

Queensland Combined XI 202 (V.R. Brown 4 for 85) and 68 for 2
New Zealanders 345 for 7 dec (B.A. Edgar 115, T.J. Franklin 94)

Match drawn

The New Zealanders opened their tour with a non first-class match in which Edgar and Franklin put on 189 for the first wicket.

The Sheffield Shield began with two drawn matches. Peter Sleep came out of retirement to hit his sixth first-class hundred, and he lifted what was a generally bleak South Australian first innings. Western Australia were 56 for 3, all three wickets to Warwickshire's Gladstone Small, but Veletta and Ireland added 103, and Tim Zoehrer boosted the latter part of the innings with a hard hit 94 not out. When South Australia batted again Andrew Hilditch, so dreadfully out of form and luck, was caught off Clough at 31. Bob Zadow and Glenn Bishop put on 155 for the second wicket, and Zadow

Glenn Bishop hit 202 for South Australia against the New Zealanders, 26–29 October. It was his maiden double century and his second three-figured innings in successive matches. (David Munden)

and Hookes 159 for the third. Zadow's maiden first-class hundred was a fine innings, and, in all, he batted for 325 minutes, hitting a six and 15 fours. The stand between Hookes and Zadow virtually determined that the match would be drawn.

Dav Whatmore dominated an opening stand of 148 for Victoria in Brisbane, Quinn being his partner and making 46. Victoria batted solidly throughout and reached an impressive 431. Frei, returning to first-class cricket after announcing his retirement, took 2 for 91 in his 38.1 overs. Queensland were 49 for 3 and facing the prospect of following-on, but Border and Ritchie added 167. Allan Border's run of masterly form continued as he reached his highest score for Queensland. His 194 came off 185 balls in 419 minutes and included 4 sixes and 23 fours. He and Trimble put on 168 for the fifth wicket, and McDermott and Frei gave Queensland the first innings points in a ninth wicket stand of 96.

22 and 23 October 1985

at Gold Coast, Cararra

New Zealanders 247 for 5 dec (M.D. Crowe 97 not out, J.F. Reid 79)
Queensland Country XI 160 for 7 (R. Williams 54)
Match drawn

Greg Matthews – Folk hero, player of the season. (George Herringshaw)

25, 26, 27 and 28 October 1985

at Hobart

New South Wales 561 (G.R.J. Matthews 184, S.R. Waugh 107, P.S. Clifford 98, R.L. Brown 4 for 166) and 111 for 1 (M. Taylor 56 not out)
Tasmania 429 (D.C. Boon 196, S.L. Saunders 51, D.R. Gilbert 4 for 108)

Match drawn
New South Wales 4 pts, Tasmania 0 pts

26, 27, 28 and 29 October 1985

at Adelaide

South Australia 278 for 9 dec (D.W. Hookes 106) and 373 for 4 dec (G.A. Bishop 202, P.R. Sleep 133 not out)
New Zealanders 387 for 3 dec (M.D. Crowe 242 not out, J.V. Coney 89) and 209 for 7 (T. May 4 for 67)

Match drawn

The New Zealanders first first-class match of the tour provided two outstanding performances. Martin Crowe's 242 not out, the first double century of his career, was the highest score by a New Zealander in Australia. It was scored in 409 minutes off 364 balls, and included a six and 41 fours. In one over he hit 22 off Don O'Connor. The tourists had lost Wright and Edgar for 15 before Martin Crowe and Coney added a record 245 for the third wicket. In South Australia's first innings, David Hookes had revived his hopes of a recall

Bruce Reid took five wickets in an innings for the first time for Western Australia v. Tasmania, 1–4 November. He was soon to be opening the attack for Australia. (All Sport)

to the Test side with 11 fours and a six in his knock which lasted 207 minutes, but this was overshadowed by Glenn Bishop's maiden double century in the second innings in which he shared a South Australian fourth wicket record stand of 207 with Peter Sleep. It was the second century in as many matches for both batsmen. Bishop, who made such a fine impression when playing in Leicestershire in 1985, is one of the very best of young Australian batsmen and must be close to a place in the national side.

In Hobart, Greg Matthews hit a career best 184 and shared stands of 134 with Peter Clifford and 174 with Steve Waugh who reached a maiden first-class century. Mark Taylor and Mark Waugh, twin brother of all-rounder Steve, made their first-class debuts as New South Wales' opening pair. Taylor hit a fifty in the second innings, but by then the match was doomed to a draw. David Boon, the new captain of Tasmania, batted for over eight hours and held his side's batting together, but Tasmania still fell short of the visitors by 132 runs. Winston Davis, the West Indian pace man, and Hill, another opening bowler, made their debuts for Tasmania. Brian Davison withdrew from the Tasmanian side and announced his retirement from first-class cricket in Australia because of a contract dispute with the Tasmanian Cricket Council.

1, 2, 3 and 4 November 1985

at Perth

Tasmania 102 (D.C. Boon 64) and 169 (B.A. Reid 6 for 54)
Western Australia 278 (M.R.J. Veletta 85)

Western Australia won by an innings and 7 runs
Western Australia 12 pts, Tasmania 0 pts

at Newcastle

New South Wales 232 (M. Taylor 77, M.G. Hughes 5 for 74) and 244 (P.S. Clifford 98, S.P. O'Donnell 5 for 66)
Victoria 308 (J.D. Siddons 76, D.F. Whatmore 72, G.F. Lawson 4 for 82, D.R. Gilbert 4 for 84) and 78 (G.R.J. Matthews 5 for 22)

New South Wales won by 90 runs
New South Wales 8 pts, Victoria 4 pts

at Brisbane

Queensland 407 (B.A. Courtice 112, A.R. Border 102, M.C. Snedden 4 for 88) and 232 for 6 dec (R.B. Phillips 77 not out, S.L. Boock 4 for 83)
New Zealanders 331 for 4 dec (B.A. Edgar 122, J.J. Crowe 79 not out) and 152 for 6

Match drawn

In their last match before the first Test, the New Zealanders suffered a third wicket stand of 162 between Courtice and Border who played his tenth three-figured innings in twenty-three times at the crease since the beginning of the tour of England in May. Snedden had given the tourists a good start with the wickets of Kerr and Wessels, and he later dismissed Ritchie and Trimble in a good spell. Border's 102 occupied only 116 balls, and, in contrast, Edgar played a painstaking innings for New Zealand, his 122 taking 259 balls. Boock bowled well for New Zealand who slumped to 81 for 5 in their second innings before Coney and Snedden assured the draw.

Western Australia gained the first Sheffield Shield outright victory of the season when they beat Tasmania by an innings on the revamped Perth pitch. Only two boundaries were hit on the opening day when the outfield was very spongy. Boon, twice dropped, held the Tasmanian innings together, but their 102 was still their lowest against Western Australia. Tim Zoehrer had three catches and two stumpings and was to take two more catches when Tasmania batted again. A second wicket stand of 91 between Veletta and Marsh put the home state in a good position, and there was consistently sound batting down the order which took Western Australia to a good lead. Read, taking five wickets in an innings for the first time, gave Tasmania early problems in their second innings, and they lost their last 5 wickets for 26 runs.

Merv Hughes returned the best bowling figures by a Victorian bowler for 20 matches, and New South Wales trailed by 76 on the first innings after Siddons had lifted the visitors from the troubled position of 154 for 6. O'Donnell captured five wickets in an innings for the first time and New South Wales lost three wickets in clearing off the arrears. Peter Clifford rallied the home side with his second 98 in three innings, and he was at the wicket for 219 minutes. Lawson, Matthews and Bennett gave valuable support, and Victoria were left to make 169 to win. They lost Quinn and Whatmore with only 1 run scored and never made an effective recovery. Their last 4 wickets fell for 7 runs as Matthews and Holland prospered against flat-footed batsmen.

8, 9, 10 and 11 November 1985

at St Kilda, Melbourne

Tasmania 328 (K. Bradshaw 87, R.D. Woolley 70, S.P. Davis 5 for 73, M.G. Hughes 4 for 81)

Victoria 332 for 6 (J.D. Siddons 74, P.A. Hibbert 62, R.J. Bright 61 not out, M.G. Dimattina 54 not out)

Match drawn
Victoria 4 pts, Tasmania 0 pts

No play on the first day because of rain reduced this match to a contest for first innings points. Tasmania, led by Ray in Boon's absence, batted tediously. Bradshaw and Woolley, who has left the wicket-keeping to Soule while he concentrates on his batting, shared a fourth wicket stand of 138. Five wickets then fell for 44 before Saunders and Brown rallied their side. Victoria lost Whatmore and Jones for 22, but Quinn was stubborn in support of Hibbert, and Siddons played enterprisingly. Dimattina, obviously benefitting from his experience in Zimbabwe, and Bright shared an unbeaten stand of 102 to gain the points.

First Test Match
AUSTRALIA v. NEW ZEALAND

Australia, still smarting from two successive innings defeats in England and from the defections to South Africa, found themselves, again in a humiliating position after the first of the three Tests against New Zealand. The visitors won on Australian soil for the first time and Australia suffered a third successive innings defeat.

Surprisingly, Australia, who omitted O'Donnell of the selected twelve, began the match as favourites. New Zealand, who chose to leave out spinner Boock and give a first Test cap to Vaughan Brown, won the toss and Coney invited Australia to bat in overcast conditions. His decision was rewarded with instant success, but not quite in the way that would have been expected. Wessels opened the scoring with a single off Hadlee, but Hilditch hooked the fifth ball of the match to Chatfield at long leg, the fielder taking a well judged catch above his head. Hilditch's achilles heel was now apparent to all, and his means of dismissal left his Test future in grave doubt.

Wessels and Boon set about righting Australia's position, but they were never happy against some aggressive bowling on a greenish wicket. Hadlee operated off his shorter run, but he still generated considerable pace and two overs before lunch he had Boon caught at second slip, playing back to a sharply rising ball.

New Zealand's great success came with Hadlee's first ball after lunch, a wide half-volley, which Border drove chest high to Edgar at cover. That was in Hadlee's ninth over, and in his eleventh, Ritchie played back, bat away from his body, and Martin Crowe took a fine slip catch.

Kepler Wessels and Wayne Phillips, coming together at 82 for 4, halted further disasters and Australia were 146 for 4 when bad light, and then rain, ended play seven minutes after tea. Wessels, never elegant, but often effective, hit Snedden square on the leg side for six and reached his fifty with a square cut for four off Coney.

Wessels was out in the fifth over of the second morning when he played no stroke to Hadlee's in-swinger. It preluded a total disaster for Australia whose last five wickets fell for 29 runs in less than an hour. Four of these wickets went to Hadlee who bowled with venom and accuracy and was very well supported by his close catchers. Phillips chopped on.

Matthews was comprehensively beaten, and Lawson looped Brown to mid-wicket so giving the off-spinner his first Test wicket but denying Hadlee, who took the catch, all ten wickets.

Hadlee's 9 for 52 was the fourth best bowling return in Test history, bettered only by Laker's two performances at Old Trafford in 1956 and George Lohmann's 9 for 28 against South Africa in 1895. It was bowling of the very highest quality and stood in sharp contrast to the inept display by the Australian bowlers. McDermott, finding no rhythm, was particularly disappointing. Lawson looked a shadow of his former self, and Gilbert was still groping for Test standard. All three frequently overstepped the crease, a sin which Hadlee never committed.

Wright and Edgar began the building of the innings quietly, and at 36, Edgar fell when he failed to take his bat out of the way in time to a rising ball from Gilbert. Reid and Wright, continuing the left-handed partnerships, put on 49 before Wright was lbw to Matthews' quicker ball. Martin Crowe, who took half an hour to get off the mark, and Reid then asserted complete authority as New Zealand moved to 209 before another early close.

On the third morning, John Reid, solid in defence, pugnacious in attack, reached his sixth Test hundred. His presence gives the New Zealand side a stability which it has needed. There is an air of professionalism, of application, about him which permeates the rest of the side.

Martin Crowe revealed the rich vein of high quality batsmanship which has been apparent since he first entered cricket. It was easy to understand why Imran Khan has prophesied that he will be the outstanding batsman of the eighties.

They added a third wicket record 224 before Reid fell to

John Reid, New Zealand centurion and sharer of a record third wicket partnership of 224 with Martin Crowe. (Philip Tyson)

Gilbert. Martin Crowe should have been stumped off Holland when he was 113, and again one pondered on the sanity of using a good batsman as an indifferent wicket-keeper. Crowe eventually played Matthews into his stumps when he had equalled his highest score in Test cricket, 188, which was also the highest score made by a New Zealander against Australia.

All the other batsmen made useful contributions, and Hadlee hit 4 sixes and 4 fours in a whirlwind knock so that Coney was able to declare at the end of third day score of 553 for 7. Martin Crowe's innings lasted for 472 minutes and included 26 fours; Reid batted for six hours and hit 16 fours.

Australia began the fourth day 374 in arrears and with only the faintest hope of avoiding defeat. That faint hope appeared to have evaporated within a few overs. In the fourth over, Wessels played half forward to Hadlee and was caught bat-pad at short square-leg. Unbelievably, Hilditch perished in the same way that he had done in the first innings, and the same way that he had done so often against England. He trudged from the field a sad figure, an end to his Test career, at least temporarily, a certainty. Boon was caught behind and Ritchie easily taken at slip. Phillips attempted to cut and played on, and, shortly after lunch, Australia were 67 for 5, defeat imminent.

That defeat did not come on the fourth day was due to an enterprising stand between Border and Matthews. Border was his customary self, stubborn, unyielding, powerful and belligerent in attack. Matthews, in contrast, was all bubbling excitement. He hit strongly on both sides of the wicket. He reached fifty with a square cut off Brown and swung the same bowler over mid-wicket for six to reach a maiden Test hundred. He celebrated in extrovert fashion, which, though it may have offended some, was testimony to the man's enthusiasm and love of the game. His delight in playing for Australia is infectious, and if the country is to revive its cricket fortunes, the enthusiasm of players like Matthews will be one of the major factors.

Matthews batted 198 minutes for his hundred, and a few minutes later, after 313 minutes at the crease, Border reached his hundred. They had added 197 when Matthews was caught at slip off Hadlee in the third over with the second new ball. Had Matthews been able to survive until the last day, Australia might have dared to hope for escape, but his dismissal effectively meant defeat. By his support of his captain and his effervescent play, he had at least restored some pride to Australian cricket.

The match was over shortly before lunch on the last day when Hadlee bowled Bob Holland so claiming his fifteenth wicket of the match at a cost of 123 runs. Border continued valiantly, his innings lasting for 450 minutes. He hit 2 sixes and 20 fours.

More batsmen need to follow Border's examples in application and technique if the standard of Australian cricket is to reach its former level. Three defeats in a row by an innings is a chastening experience.

For New Zealand, and the record breaking Hadlee whose

FIRST TEST MATCH – AUSTRALIA v. NEW ZEALAND
8, 9, 10, 11 and 12 November 1985 at Brisbane

AUSTRALIA

	FIRST INNINGS			SECOND INNINGS	
K.C. Wessels	lbw, b Hadlee	70	(2) c Brown, b Chatfield	3
A.M.J. Hilditch	c Chatfield, b Hadlee	0	(1) c Chatfield, b Hadlee	12
D.C. Boon	c Coney, b Hadlee	31	c Smith, b Chatfield	1
A.R. Border†	c Edgar, b Hadlee	1	not out	152
G.M. Ritchie	c M. Crowe, b Hadlee	8	c Coney, b Snedden	20
W.B. Phillips*	b Hadlee	34	b Hadlee	2
G.R.J. Matthews	b Hadlee	2	c Coney, b Hadlee	115
G.F. Lawson	c Hadlee, b Brown	8	(9) c Brown, b Chatfield	7
C.J. McDermott	c Coney, b Hadlee	9	(8) c and b Hadlee	5
D.R. Gilbert	not out	0	c Chatfield, b Hadlee	10
R.G. Holland	c Brown, b Hadlee	0	b Hadlee	0
Extras	b 9, lb 5, nb 2	16	lb 3, nb 3	6
		179		**333**

NEW ZEALAND

	FIRST INNINGS	
B.A. Edgar	c Phillips, b Gilbert	17
J.G. Wright	lbw, b Matthews	46
J.F. Reid	c Border, b Gilbert	108
M.D. Crowe	b Matthews	188
J.V. Coney†	c Phillips, b Lawson	22
J.J. Crowe	c Holland, b Matthews	35
V.R. Brown	not out	36
R.J. Hadlee	c Phillips, b McDermott	54
I.D.S. Smith*	not out	2
M.C. Snedden		
E.J. Chatfield		
Extras	b 2, lb 11, nb 32	45
	(for 7 wkts dec)	**553**

	O	M	R	W	O	M	R	W
Hadlee	23.4	4	52	9	28.5	9	71	6
Chatfield	18	6	29	—	32	9	75	3
Snedden	11	1	45	—	19	3	66	1
M.D. Crowe	5	—	14	—	9	2	19	—
Brown	12	5	17	1	25	5	96	—
Coney	7	5	8	—	3	1	3	—

	O	M	R	W
Lawson	36.5	8	96	1
McDermott	31	3	119	1
Gilbert	39	9	102	2
Matthews	31	5	110	3
Holland	22	3	106	—
Wessels	1	—	7	—
Border	0.1	—	0	—

FALL OF WICKETS
1- 1, 2- 70, 3- 72, 4- 82, 5- 148, 6- 150, 7- 159, 8- 175, 9- 179
1- 14, 2- 16, 3- 47, 4- 47, 5- 67, 6- 264, 7- 272, 8- 291, 9- 333

FALL OF WICKETS
1- 36, 2- 85, 3- 309, 4- 362, 5- 427, 6- 471, 7- 549

Umpires: A.R. Crafter & R.A. French

New Zealand won by an innings and 41 runs

return was the best ever by a New Zealander in Test cricket and the eighth best of all time in Test history, no praise can be too high. Theirs was a thoroughly workmanlike approach to the game, dedication coloured by enthusiasm.

15, 16, 17 and 18 November 1985

at Perth

Victoria 111 (C.R. Matthews 5 for 23) and 302 for 7 dec (D.M. Jones 113, M.B. Quinn 62)
Western Australia 94 (S.P. Davis 6 for 19) and 212 for 2 (G.R. Marsh 100 not out, G.M. Wood 82)

Match drawn
Victoria 4 pts, Western Australia 0 pts

at Adelaide

South Australia 290 (R.J. Zadow 52, J.R. Thomson 6 for 72) and 288 for 7 dec (D.W. Hookes 102, A.M.J. Hilditch 59)
Queensland 294 for 5 dec (A.R. Border 88 not out, R.B. Kerr 80) and 285 for 5 (A.R. Border 119, K.C. Wessels 107)

Queensland won by 5 wickets
Queensland 12 pts, South Australia 0 pts

at Sydney

New South Wales 300 (G.R.J. Matthews 111, D.M. Wellham 86, V.R. Brown 4 for 75) and 128 for 6 dec
New Zealanders 120 (R.G. Holland 8 for 33) and 175 for 5 (M.J. Bennett 4 for 56)

Match drawn

Bob Holland captured his hundredth first-class wicket on the Sydney Cricket Ground and returned the best figures ever by an Australian against a New Zealand side so warning the tourists what they could expect in the second Test match. Greg Matthews hit his third century of the season and shared a fourth wicket stand of 180 with skipper Dirk Wellham, and New South Wales were well on top throughout the match. John Wright played well in both innings for New Zealand and helped stave off defeat. He led the side even though Coney was playing.

In Perth, Victoria and Western Australia produced a bizarre match of fluctuating form and fortune. On a slow wicket, left-arm bowler Chris Matthews took a career best 5 for 23 as only Whatmore and Dodemaide reached double figures. Western Australia fared even worse as Simon Davis brought his name to the notice of the selectors with a career best 6 for 19. The batsmen gained the ascendancy in the second innings. Dean Jones showed a welcome return to form, sharing a third wicket stand of 109 with Quinn, but Western Australia batted dourly on the last day to save the match. Wood and Marsh put on 171 for the second wicket. Marsh hit 3 fours in an innings which lasted 410 minutes.

Queensland took full points at Adelaide thanks to consistent batting in the first innings and some fiery bowling by Jeff Thomson. Hilditch, too late to save himself from being dropped from the Test side, and Bishop began South Australia's second innings with a stand of 102, but three wickets fell quickly and it was David Hookes who made a declaration possible with an aggressive century. Queensland

RIGHT: *Simon Davis, Victoria, routed Western Australia at Perth, 15–19 November, and received a call to join the Australian side later in the season. (Philip Tyson)*

were asked to score at 3.5 an over to win the match. They lost Courtice and Kerr for 30, but Border joined Wessels in a stand of 210 which virtually assured the visitors of victory. Wessels needed 229 minutes to reach three figures while Border came to 100 in 172 minutes.

22, 23, 24 and 25 November 1985

at Launceston

South Australia 442 (P.R. Sleep 99, D. Kelly 79, S.D.H. Parkinson 62, R.L. Brown 4 for 159) and 20 for 1
Tasmania 159 (S.D.H. Parkinson 4 for 41) and 299 (R.S. Hyatt 80, A.K. Zesers 4 for 65)

South Australia won by 9 wickets
South Australia 12 pts, Tasmania 0 pts

Consistent batting put South Australia in a strong position. Peter Sleep hit 12 fours and a huge six before being caught behind off Hyatt one short of his century. Sam Parkinson, coming in at number 10, hit a career best as the last two wickets produced 111 runs. Tasmania batted limply in their first innings and failed to save the follow-on. At the second attempt, with Roly Hyatt playing well, they gave a consistent display, but medium pace bowler Andrew Zesers maintained his impressive start to the season and Peter Sleep took 3 wickets to nudge the selectors so that the visitors ran out easy winners.

The Indians, due to play their first match at Canberra, on 27 November, were thwarted by rain. The outfield was waterlogged and the game was abandoned without a ball being bowled, a great blow considering the lack of match practice scheduled before the beginning of the Test series.

Man of the Match Richard Hadlee, 15 for 123, the best ever bowling performance by a New Zealander in Test history.
(Philip Tyson)

Second Test Match
AUSTRALIA v. NEW ZEALAND

Rarely can Australia have faced a Test match with such apprehension as they did the second Test against New Zealand. The defeats in England, and by New Zealand in the first Test, and the defections to the rebel side in South Africa had been followed by Wessels' announcement that he was retiring from Test cricket. He stated that he was not satisfied with the financial terms that he had been offered for the season although it was rumoured that he had been involved in the negotiations which took the Australian party to South Africa. It was now believed that Wessels would revert to his South African nationality, and the implication that some of the Australian side were more interested in the amount of dollars they earned than in playing for their country caused much soul-searching among those close to the game in Australia. It appeared that in standard and commitment the game had reached a low ebb.

The problem that confronted both sides was the Sydney wicket, notorious for its encouragement to spin. Glenn Turner, the master mind behind the New Zealand success, and Jeremy Coney were adamant in their view that spin would decide the match and called off-break bowler John Bracewell from New Zealand to supplement their attack. Australia, without Lawson and omitting McDermott, called up Ray Bright to support Holland and Matthews, and the inclusion of Bright, who has never looked a spinner of Test quality, confirmed for many the paucity of the game in Australia after its recent ravages and retirements. Bright, however, was to provide more than adequate support for Holland during the course of the match.

Border caused a great surprise when he won the toss and asked New Zealand to bat, the general view being that the pitch would play better on the first day than at any other time. Wright and Edgar seemed to confirm this opinion, for the two left-handers were given no problems by Gilbert and O'Donnell, a very moderate opening attack. The complexion of the game changed when Bright was introduced although the change came in somewhat bizarre fashion, Wright hitting a long hop straight to square leg. More significantly, Holland deceived Reid and had him taken at mid-wicket.

Edgar batted for 200 minutes, but his concentration lapsed when, pushing forward at Holland, he was caught bat-pad at silly point. Martin Crowe gave Australia a further boost when he hit the ball to Matthews at mid-off and set off on a suicidal run. His brother Jeff swept at Holland and played on, and Brown was lbw playing back next ball. From 71 for 0, New Zealand had collapsed to 128 for 6, and their innings was in tatters.

Smith played some enterprising shots before sweeping at Bright and skying the ball to slip. Hadlee was lbw on the back foot after one rasping drive, and Coney's innings of infinite patience ended as Edgar's had done. This brought New Zealand to 169 for 9, and seemingly gave Australia the day. Bracewell and Boock hit out, and they had added 48 before the close to make New Zealand's position look far healthier.

With a first-class century to his credit, against England,

RIGHT: *Bob Holland spun Australia to victory, 10 for 174 with his leg-breaks. (George Herringshaw)*

Bracewell is a competent batsman, but Boock has no such pretensions, yet these two took their stand to 124 on the second day with some lively batting against bowling that became increasingly ragged. The stand was ended twenty minutes before lunch, but by then New Zealand seemed to have reached a match-winning position.

Australia were soon in trouble as Kerr, on his Test debut, was lbw playing half forward to Hadlee. Immediately after lunch Boon played back to Hadlee and was also lbw, and Bracewell, introduced into the attack with the score at 42, bowled Border with a beautiful ball that pitched on leg stump and hit the top of the off stump. Phillips went to a ball almost as good, and when Hookes was run out for 0 on his recall to the Test side, Australia were 71 for 5 and again in gloom.

The irrepressible Matthews came to his side's aid once again. Ritchie had looked in solid form and Matthews and he stayed until the close, adding 104.

The stand was increased by another 11 runs on the third morning before, with the fourth ball of his second over, Hadlee had Matthews caught behind off an out-swinger. Ritchie and O'Donnell put on 38 for the seventh wicket before Ritchie, who batted finely, was caught at first slip. Three runs later, the innings was over. The last four wickets fell in 35 deliveries. Hadlee, well supported by Boock, was again the New Zealand hero, his 5 for 65 giving his side a lead of 66 on the first innings.

This lead was consolidated with a splendidly determined opening partnership of 100 by Wright and Edgar. The partnership was ended when Holland took a good catch off his own bowling to dismiss Edgar, the batsman driving at a full toss, and then Matthews caught and bowled Wright in spectacular manner. Martin Crowe was bowled round his legs sweeping, and New Zealand closed at a comfortable 119 for 3.

Holland, ten wickets in the match with his beautifully controlled leg-spin, ably supported by Matthews and Bright, bowled Australia back in to contention on the fourth day. Holland bowled Coney without addition to the overnight score and New Zealand, sparked only by some hard blows from Hadlee, collapsed to 193 all out shortly after lunch. This left Australia a target of 260, which, on a wearing wicket, seemed just about the maximum anyone could hope to attain.

The Australian second innings was interrupted for half an hour by bad light, and Kerr was brilliantly caught by Wright at mid-on when he slashed at a ball from Bracewell soon after the resumption. Rain at tea ended play for the day with Australia 36 for 1, and the odds still in favour of New Zealand.

On the last morning, the Australian batsmen showed a greater sense of application than they had done for several months and helped to restore some faith in the country's cricket. Phillips and Boon batted with patience and determination. They increased the score by 35 runs before rain swept across the ground.

Play was resumed shortly after lunch and the two batsmen took their stand to 100 in 155 minutes. At 132, Phillips swept rashly at Boock and was caught at deep backward square-leg. At tea, Australia were 141 for 2. The rain had aided the home side, the pitch playing better than at any time, but now the threat of a storm was a worry as victory beckoned.

Acceleration was essential. Border was stumped having a slog, and Ritchie chipped Hadlee to square leg. Boon, however, played with great sense and Hookes was quickly into his stride. Boon began to find the boundary, and when the last 20 overs began Australia needed 90 to win. The first four overs yielded 22 runs, and then Boon, after his best innings in Test cricket, swept at Hadlee and was caught at short fine leg.

The New Zealand cricket bore no resemblance to the standard of the first Test and the early part of the second Test, and Matthews and Hookes had no difficulty in keeping the score moving against some untidy bowling and ragged fielding. Matthews hit Hadlee for successive fours, and although he was lbw to the New Zealand pace man with two runs needed, victory was never in doubt for Australia, and they levelled the series with 3.5 overs remaining.

As indicated, the New Zealand out-cricket in the closing stages was disappointing, and Coney's manipulation of spinners left much to be desired in tactical terms.

McDonald's Cup

28 November 1985

at Melbourne

Victoria 209 for 8 (P.W. Young 83, D.F. Whatmore 51)
Tasmania 201 for 7

Victoria won by 8 runs

SECOND TEST MATCH – AUSTRALIA v. NEW ZEALAND
22, 23, 24, 25 and 26 November 1985 at Sydney

NEW ZEALAND

	FIRST INNINGS		SECOND INNINGS	
J.G. Wright	c O'Donnell, b Bright	38	c and b Matthews	43
B.A. Edgar	c Border, b Holland	50	c and b Holland	52
J.F. Reid	c Kerr, b Holland	7	b Matthews	19
M.D. Crowe	run out	8	b Holland	0
J.V. Coney†	c Border, b Holland	8	b Holland	7
J.J. Crowe	b Holland	13	c and b Holland	6
V.R. Brown	lbw, b Holland	0	b Bright	15
I.D.S. Smith*	c Hookes, b Bright	28	c and b Bright	12
R.J. Hadlee	lbw, b Holland	5	lbw, b Gilbert	26
J.G. Bracewell	not out	83	not out	2
S.L. Boock	lbw, b Gilbert	37	c Boon, b Bright	3
Extras	b 6, lb 8, nb 2	16	b 1, lb 4, nb 3	8
		293		193

	O	M	R	W		O	M	R	W
Gilbert	20.3	6	41	1		9	2	22	1
O'Donnell	6	2	13	—		5	4	4	—
Bright	34	12	87	2		17.5	3	39	3
Matthews	17	3	32	—		30	11	55	2
Holland	47	19	106	6		41	16	68	4

AUSTRALIA

	FIRST INNINGS		SECOND INNINGS	
W.B. Phillips*	b Bracewell	31	c Bracewell, b Boock	63
R.B. Kerr	lbw, b Hadlee	7	c Wright, b Bracewell	7
D.C. Boon	lbw, b Hadlee	0	c Reid, b Bracewell	81
A.R. Border†	b Bracewell	20	st Smith, b Bracewell	11
G.M. Ritchie	c J. Crowe, b Hadlee	89	c M. Crowe, b Hadlee	13
D.M. Hookes	run out	0	not out	38
G.R.J. Matthews	c Smith, b Hadlee	50	lbw, b Hadlee	32
S.P. O'Donnell	not out	20	not out	2
R.J. Bright	lbw, b Boock	1		
D.R. Gilbert	c Smith, b Hadlee	0		
R.G. Holland	st Smith, b Boock	0		
Extras	b 5, lb 2, nb 2	9	b 3, lb 9, nb 1	13
		227	(for 6 wickets)	260

	O	M	R	W		O	M	R	W
Hadlee	24	2	65	5		27.1	10	58	2
M.D. Crowe	5	2	15	—		2	1	7	—
Bracewell	25	9	51	2		30	7	91	3
Boock	29.5	14	53	2		22	4	49	1
Brown	13	3	35	—		7	—	28	—
Coney	1		1	—		9	1	15	—

FALL OF WICKETS
1- 71, 2- 92, 3- 109, 4- 112, 5- 128, 6- 128, 7- 161, 8- 166, 9- 169
1- 100, 2- 106, 3- 107, 4- 119, 5- 131, 6- 137, 7- 162, 8- 163, 9- 190

FALL OF WICKETS
1- 19, 2- 22, 3- 48, 4- 71, 5- 71, 6- 186, 7- 224, 8- 225, 9- 226
1- 27, 2- 132, 3- 144, 4- 163, 5- 192, 6- 258

Umpires: M.W. Johnson and B.E. Martin

Australia won by 4 wickets

Victoria clinched a place in the semi-finals with a close victory in the day/night match in Melbourne. King was named Man of the Match for an economic bowling spell and some fine fielding.

29, 30 November, 1 and 2 December 1985

at Brisbane

Western Australia 527 (G.R. Marsh 138, M.R.J. Veletta 130, K.H. Macleay 60)
Queensland 225 for 5 (A.B. Henschell 85 not out)

Match abandoned
Western Australia 2 pts Queensland 2 pts

at Adelaide

South Australia 135 (R.N. Kapil Dev 4 for 24, C. Sharma 4 for 55) and 435 for 8 dec (R.J. Zadow 120, W.M. Darling 107 not out, G.A. Bishop 93, D.F.G. O'Connor 58)
Indians 245 (A.O. Malhotra 67, C. Sharma 67, S.D.H. Parkinson 6 for 56) and 329 for 6 (R.N. Kapil Dev 88, M. Azharuddin 77)

Indians won by 4 wickets

The Indians began their tour well, bowling out South Australia on the first day on a green wicket. The Indian batsmen struggled in their turn, and the tourists were 99 for 7. They were revived by Malhotra and by Chetan Sharma at number 9. The Indian spinners suffered on the third day. Darling, a forgotten man of Australian cricket, hit his ninth first-class hundred, and Bishop and Zadow shared a second wicket stand of 149. The tourists raced to victory on the last day with Kapil Dev and Azharuddin adding 135 for the fifth wicket.

Veletta and Geoff Marsh, both pressing for a Test place, put on 254 for Western Australia's second wicket in Brisbane. The visitors' innings lasted until well into the second day, and Queensland lost Barsby and Wessels to successive deliveries before a run was scored. Rain ended play at tea on the third day and the match was abandoned. Jeff Thomson took his three hundredth wicket for Queensland when he had Wood caught in the covers.

4 December 1985

at Warnambool

Victorian Country XI 116
Indians 175 for 6 (D.B. Vengsarkar 64 not out)

Indians won by 6 wickets

The match continued to give the Indians batting practice.

Third Test Match
AUSTRALIA v. NEW ZEALAND

Once again the bowling of Richard Hadlee undermined the Australian batting and, from the first day, put New Zealand in a position from which victory was possible.

Coney again chose to ask Australia to bat on a wicket which was likely to be more lively at the outset than later. It was Chatfield, injured in net practice when he gashed his leg, who made the initial break-through, Kerr, yet to do himself justice at Test level, sparring outside the off stump. Phillips went the same way and Australia were 74 for 2 at lunch.

Their innings fell apart immediately afterwards. Boon drove at Hadlee and was caught low down at slip. Border

Geoff Lawson, 4 for 79, but defeat for Australia. (George Herringshaw)

pushed forward at the New Zealand pace man and gave Smith his third catch of the innings, and Ritchie was lbw trying to work the nagging Coney to mid-wicket.

The Australian innings was in shreds, and although Hookes hit one huge six and Matthews and McDermott gave their side a boost, the home side only just crept past the two hundred mark as Hadlee captured his twenty-seventh victim in five innings in the series, an astonishing achievement.

Wright and Edgar scored 8 in the last 26 minutes of the day which had belonged entirely to New Zealand. They continued doggedly on the second day. Wright left at 43, and Reid went 12 runs later, but Edgar and Martin Crowe remained solid throughout the rest of the day. They were aided by some sloppy Australian fielding. Edgar, who batted all day and hit one four, was twice dropped at slip while Crowe also had an escape. At the end of a dour day, New Zealand were on 184, Edgar 74, Martin Crowe 70.

The pitch continued to play sluggishly on the third day, and Australia were given an early boost when McDermott dismissed Edgar in the first over. Martin Crowe added only one run in 40 minutes to his overnight score when he played back to McDermott and was lbw. Coney was the third wicket to fall before lunch, caught behind playing forward to

Lawson who bowled better than he had done for a considerable time.

Holland bowled well in the afternoon and dismissed Jeff Crowe and Richard Hadlee. Bracewell again demonstrated his remarkable advance as a batsman. He lifted the score with some good shots, but New Zealand's lead of 96 was a disappointment after the solid foundation of the second day. It became more significant, however, when Kerr was bowled first ball, the fourth of the innings, and Phillips was caught on 28. Boon and Border survived uneasily. Border was almost run out and Boon withstood a unanimous appeal for a bat-pad catch. Australia closed at 38 for 2, and New Zealand scented an historic victory.

It seemed on the fourth day that Australia would negotiate their troubles and deny New Zealand victory. Boon was missed off a straightforward caught and bowled chance by Cairns when he was 19, and several other chances went begging as New Zealand apparently lost their grip on the game. The only success of the morning came when Boon, after a stubborn innings, chopped Hadlee onto his stumps as he attempted to cut shortly before lunch.

Ritchie and Border came through the afternoon unscathed although Smith missed both of them off Bracewell, one a catch and the other a stumping chance. At tea, Australia were 166 for 3. Shortly after tea, Border played outside a ball from Hadlee and was bowled. Then Ritchie hit Coney fiercely to gully where Martin Crowe held on to the only catch of the day. Hookes was bowled by a ball that kept low, and Hadlee trapped Matthews lbw so that, after a disastrous last session, Australia ended the day at 239 for 7, all their recognised batsmen gone.

To make victory a possibility, New Zealand needed to capture the last three Australian wickets quickly on the last morning. They did just that. In half an hour, for the addition of 20 runs, Australia were bowled out, Hadlee taking two more wickets bringing him to 11 for the match and an astonishing 33 wickets for the series.

Wright and Edgar gave the New Zealand innings the solid start that was needed. Matthews bowled well and should have had Wright stumped. In his next over, however, he did have Edgar taken bat-pad at silly mid-off.

Wright and Reid continued to play with great good sense. Wright's fine knock came to an end when he played back to Gilbert and was bowled by a ball that kept low, but at tea, New Zealand were 104 for 2. Reid and Martin Crowe continued the careful progress towards victory, but they were separated when Reid parried at Gilbert. Coney was yorked by the same bowler at 149, and it was left to the Crowe brothers to take New Zealand to a series win over Australia for the first time.

The historic triumph was well deserved. New Zealand had outplayed Australia for nine tenths of the series, and theirs was a victory for team work and team spirit. In Hadlee, they possessed an outstanding bowler, and it is doubtful that any bowler has so dominated a series. In statistics alone, his achievement was remarkable; in the morale boosting effects his bowling had upon his side, the achievement was incalculable.

THIRD TEST MATCH – AUSTRALIA v. NEW ZEALAND
30 November, 1, 2, 3 and 4 December 1985 at Perth

AUSTRALIA

	FIRST INNINGS		SECOND INNINGS	
W.B. Phillips*	c Smith, b Chatfield	37	c Smith, b Chatfield	10
R.B. Kerr	c Smith, b Chatfield	17	b Hadlee	0
D.C. Boon	c Bracewell, b Hadlee	12	b Hadlee	50
A.R. Border†	c Smith, b Hadlee	12	b Hadlee	83
G.M. Ritchie	lbw, b Coney	6	c M. Crowe, b Coney	44
D.W. Hookes	c Bracewell, b Coney	14	b Bracewell	7
G.R.J. Matthews	b Hadlee	34	lbw, b Hadlee	14
G.F. Lawson	c J. Crowe, b Hadlee	11	c J. Crowe, b Hadlee	21
C.J. McDermott	b Chatfield	36	lbw, b Bracewell	11
D.R. Gilbert	not out	12	b Hadlee	3
R.G. Holland	c M. Crowe, b Hadlee	4	not out	0
Extras	lb 6, nb 2	8	b 2, lb 5, nb 9	16
		203		259

	O	M	R	W	O	M	R	W
Hadlee	26.5	6	65	5	39	11	90	6
Cairns	14	1	50	—	26	6	59	—
Chatfield	16	6	33	3	30	9	47	1
Coney	21	11	43	2	8	5	9	1
Bracewell	6	3	6	—	28.5	8	47	2

FALL OF WICKETS
1-38, 2-73, 3-78, 4-85, 5-85, 6-114, 7-131, 8-159, 9-190
1-3, 2-28, 3-109, 4-195, 5-207, 6-214, 7-234, 8-251, 9-255

NEW ZEALAND

	FIRST INNINGS		SECOND INNINGS	
B.A. Edgar	c Hookes, b McDermott	74	(2) c Border, b Matthews	6
J.G. Wright	c Phillips, b Lawson	20	(1) b Gilbert	35
J.F. Reid	b Gilbert	7	c Phillips, b Gilbert	28
M.D. Crowe	lbw, b McDermott	71	not out	42
J.V. Coney†	c Phillips, b Lawson	19	b Gilbert	16
J.J. Crowe	lbw, b Holland	17	not out	2
R.J. Hadlee	c Hookes, b Holland	26		
I.D.S. Smith*	c Matthews, b Lawson	12		
J.G. Bracewell	not out	28		
B.L. Cairns	c Ritchie, b Holland	0		
E.J. Chatfield	c Phillips, b Lawson	3		
Extras	b 1, lb 7, nb 14	22	b 7, lb 7, nb 11	25
		299	(for 4 wickets)	164

	O	M	R	W	O	M	R	W
Lawson	47	12	79	4	21	7	35	—
McDermott	33	9	66	2	13	1	27	—
Gilbert	31	9	75	1	23	5	48	3
Holland	40	12	63	3	8	1	27	—
Matthews	5	3	6	—	9	3	13	1
Hookes	1	—	2	—				

FALL OF WICKETS
1-43, 2-55, 3-184, 4-191, 5-215, 6-253, 7-256, 8-273, 9-276
1-47, 2-77, 3-121, 4-149

Umpires: R.C. Isherwood & P.J. McConnell

New Zealand won by 6 wickets

Australia v. New Zealand – Test Match Averages

AUSTRALIA BATTING

	M	Inns	NOs	Runs	HS	Av	100s	50s
A.R. Border	3	6	1	279	152*	55.80	1	1
G.R.J. Matthews	3	6		247	115	41.16	1	1
G.M. Ritchie	3	6		180	89	30.00		1
W.B. Phillips	3	6		177	63	29.50		1
D.C. Boon	3	6		175	81	29.16		2
D.W. Hookes	2	4	1	59	38*	19.66		
C.J. McDermott	2	4		61	36	15.25		
G.F. Lawson	2	4		47	21	11.75		
D.R. Gilbert	3	5	2	25	12*	8.33		
R.B. Kerr	2	4		31	17	7.75		
R.G. Holland	3	5	1	4	4	1.00		

Played in one Test: S.P. O'Donnell 20 & 2*; R.J. Bright 1; K.C. Wessels 70 & 3; A.M.J. Hilditch 0 & 12

AUSTRALIA BOWLING

	Overs	Mds	Runs	Wkts	Av	Best	5/inn	10/m
R.J. Bright	51.5	15	126	5	25.20	3/39		
R.G. Holland	158	51	370	13	28.46	6/106	1	1
G.R.J. Matthews	92	25	216	6	36.00	3/110		
D.R. Gilbert	122.3	31	288	8	36.00	3/48		
G.F. Lawson	104.5	27	210	5	42.00	4/79		
C.J. McDermott	77	13	212	3	70.66	2/66		

Also bowled: D.W. Hookes 1-0-2-0; A.R. Border 0.1-0-0-0; S.P. O'Donnell 11-6-17-0; K.C. Wessels 1-0-7-0

AUSTRALIA CATCHES

7 - W.B. Phillips; 4 - A.R. Border; 3 - D.W. Hookes and R.G. Holland; 2 - G.R.J. Matthews; 1 - R.B. Kerr, D.C. Boon, G.M. Ritchie, R.J. Bright and S.P. O'Donnell

NEW ZEALAND BATTING

	M	Inns	NOs	Runs	HS	Av	100s	50s
M.D. Crowe	3	5	1	309	188	77.25	1	1
B.A. Edgar	3	5		209	74	41.80		3
J.G. Wright	3	5		182	46	36.40		
J.F. Reid	3	5		169	108	33.80	1	
V.R. Brown	2	3	1	51	36*	25.50		
R.J. Hadlee	3	5		111	54	22.20		1
J.J. Crowe	3	5	1	73	35	18.25		
J.V. Coney	3	5		72	22	14.40		
I.D.S. Smith	3	4	1	54	28	13.50		

Played in two Tests: J.G. Bracewell 28*, 83* & 2*; E.J. Chatfield 3
Played in one Test: B.L. Cairns 0; S.L. Boock 37 & 3; M.C. Snedden did not bat

NEW ZEALAND BOWLING

	Overs	Mds	Runs	Wkts	Av	Best	5/inn	10/m
R.J. Hadlee	169.3	42	401	33	12.15	9/52	5	1
E.J. Chatfield	96.3	30	184	7	26.28	3/33		
J.V. Coney	49	23	79	3	26.33	2/43		
J.G. Bracewell	89.5	27	195	7	27.85	3/91		
S.L. Boock	51.5	18	102	3	34.00	2/53		
V.R. Brown	57	13	176	1	176.00	1/17		
M.D. Crowe	21	5	55	0				

Also bowled: B.L. Cairns 40-7-109-0; M.C. Snedden 30-4-111-1

NEW ZEALAND CATCHES

9 - I.D.S. Smith (ct 7/st 2); 4 - J.V. Coney and M.D. Crowe; 3 - J.J. Crowe, J.G. Bracewell, E.J. Chatfield and V.R. Brown; 1 - B.A. Edgar. J.G. Wright, J.F. Reid and R.J. Hadlee

---

For Australia, a fourth successive series defeat was a bitter blow. Border, a brave leader and the only one available to Australia, offered to resign, but the fault was certainly not his. The reasons for Australia's defeat must be found in the administration of the game in the country within the past six years.

McDonald's Cup

5 December 1985

at Sydney

New South Wales 235 for 5 (D.M. Wellham 62, P.S. Clifford 52)
Western Australia 234 for 7 (G.R. Marsh 73, G.M. Wood 59)

New South Wales won by 1 run

Wellham and Clifford added 87 for New South Wales' third wicket, and Bower and Trevor Chappell hit well at the close. Wood and Marsh put on 113 after Veletta had gone with only a run scored. Gilbert bowled Macleay in the last over and snatched an exciting win for the home side.

6, 7, 8 and 9 December 1985

at Devonport

Tasmania 156 (J.R. Thomson 5 for 76) and 335 (D.J. Buckingham 60, R.E. Soule 53, H. Frei 4 for 71)
Queensland 407 for 9 dec (G.M. Ritchie 89, B.A. Courtice 77, K.C. Wessels 69, R.B. Phillips 56, R.L. Brown 4 for 124) and 85 for 3

Queensland won by 7 wickets
Queensland 12 pts, Tasmania 0 pts

at Melbourne

Victoria 233 (D.M. Jones 83)
India 182 for 7

Match drawn

7, 8, 9 and 10 December 1985

at Sydney

New South Wales 286 (M. Taylor 65, R.J. Bower 63, M.J. Bennett 55 not out, K.H. Macleay 4 for 58) and 157 for 5 dec (D.M. Wellham 55)
Western Australia 187 (G.M. Wood 51, M.J. Bennett 4 for 47) and 105 (M.R.J. Veletta 55, D.R. Gilbert 4 for 16)

New South Wales won by 151 runs
New South Wales 12 pts, Western Australia 0 pts

The Indians seemed destined to have scant practice before the Test series. Their match in Melbourne was ruined by rain.

New South Wales and Queensland maintained their places at the top of the Sheffield Shield table with outright wins. Queensland won in Devonport with half a day to spare. Tasmania were all out in 199 minutes, 43.2 overs, on the first day. Andrew Courtice and Kepler Wessels put on 135 for the Queensland second wicket, and Ritchie played aggressively against an attack hampered by injuries to the two opening bowlers, Mark Hill and Winston Davis. Queensland had bowled 28 no balls in Tasmania's first innings, and they bowled another 39 in the second. The home side was also encouraged by dropped catches, but the issue was never in doubt.

A rain interrupted beginning to the match in Sydney saw New South Wales rally from 56 for 4 thanks to the efforts of Taylor and Bower. Murray Bennett, Greg Dyer and Geoff

Lawson maintained the recovery, and spinners Bennett and Matthews bowled the home side to a first innings lead of 99. Wellham and Matthews attacked the bowling on the third day, and Wellham declared overnight, leaving Western Australia a day in which to make 257. This task was beyond them, and they collapsed on the final afternoon against New South Wales' all Test attack.

McDonald's Cup

11 December 1985

at Melbourne

Victoria 170
Queensland 133 for 3 (T.J. Barsby 52, B.A. Courtice 52)

Queensland won on faster run rate

An opening stand of 109 between Barsby and Courtice put Queensland well ahead of the clock, and they were easy winners when rain ended their innings after 35 overs. Queensland joined Victoria in the semi-finals.

Group A					
	P	W	L	Ab	Pts
Queensland	2	1	—	1	3
Victoria	2	1	1	—	2
Tasmania	2	—	1	1	1

13, 14, 15 and 16 December 1985

at Melbourne

Queensland 288 (G.S. Trimble 75, B.A. Courtice 60, S.P. Davis 6 for 53) and 197 for 2 (B.A. Courtice 111 not out)
Victoria 456 for 9 dec (P.A. Hibbert 137, J.D. Siddons 107, D.F. Whatmore 90)

Match drawn
Victoria 4 pts, Queensland 0 pts

at Sydney

South Australia 175 (W.M. Darling 97, M.J. Bennett 4 for 38, R.G. Holland 4 for 46) and 148
New South Wales 438 for 6 dec (S.R. Waugh 119 not out, M. Taylor 118, S.M. Small 66)

New South Wales won by an innings and 115 runs
New South Wales 12 pts, South Australia 0 pts

New South Wales moved above Queensland at the top of the Shield table when they crushed South Australia in Sydney. Rick Darling, at number six, revived the visitors from the misery of 85 for 7, adding 81 with Harms. Mark Taylor hit a maiden century for New South Wales and shared an opening stand of 143 with Small. Wickets tumbled in the middle of the innings, but Steve Waugh reinforced his claim for a Test place with an aggressive hundred. He also dismissed Bishop for 0 when South Australia batted again, and with Hilditch also falling without a run on the board, the visitors slid quickly to defeat.

Jamie Siddons hit a maiden first-class hundred in Melbourne and added 184 for the fifth wicket with Paul Hibbert who batted for six and a half hours. Victoria took their lead

to 168 before Jones declared. Wessels criticised Jones for the late declaration, but it was unlikely that a result would have been achieved even if the Victoria acting captain had declared earlier. Courtice hit 111 in 409 minutes in the second innings. Victoria owed much to Simon Davis. His fast medium pace troubled Queensland greatly on the first two days and he once again alerted the attention of the Test selectors, anxious to discover quick bowling talent.

First Test Match
AUSTRALIA v. INDIA

Defeat at the hands of the New Zealanders left Australia in a state of perplexity, and, inevitably, changes were made to the side that was to face India, not all of them logical or thoughtful. Gilbert was unable to play through injury, but Lawson and Holland were dropped, Lawson for the first time in his Test career. Marsh, a deserved if belated selection, was brought into the batting line-up, with Boon moving up to the unaccustomed position of opener. Hughes and Reid joined the long list of pace men to have represented Australia in the past two seasons, and Bright was recalled to partner Matthews in the spin department, a decision which could only be construed as defensive.

For their part, India had been badly deprived of match practice and would have wished to have been better prepared for the match. They omitted Sivaramakrishnan who had begun the tour in poor form although he had shown recent improvement. Adelaide Oval, however, promised little for the leg-spinner.

The Australians again began badly. Phillips skied a short ball to mid-on and Marsh was caught at cover point when he mistimed a drive. Border quickly halted any collapse with some positive batting, and he and Boon added 91 in 118 minutes before the Australian captain chopped a ball from Kapil Dev into his stumps.

Ritchie and Boon continued the Australian advance, but Boon should have been caught and bowled by Shastri when he was 83. The escape was no more than he deserved, for he batted with great defiance and determination for all but 25 minutes of the opening day to reach his first hundred in Test cricket. He was taken at third slip when he played back to the second new ball.

Australia closed at 248 for 4. Ritchie was unbeaten on 55 although he was missed by Amarnath at mid-on when he was 16. The Queenslander took full advantage of the escape although he was never at his most fluent. His partnership of 77 with Hookes was laboured, lasting 136 minutes, but by mid-afternoon, Australia had lost only five wickets and were in a good position to build a big score.

Hookes had succumbed to a wild shot against off-spinner Yadav, but it was Kapil Dev who had Matthews lbw to herald an Australian decline. Two balls later, Ritchie, having faced 321 balls in six and a half hours, was caught behind. McDermott was out to the first ball of Kapil Dev's next over, and Reid and Hughes were both caught at slip so that Kapil Dev had finished the innings with 5 wickets in 21 deliveries. His 8 for 106 was the best return by an Indian bowler in a Test on foreign soil.

It was a fine achievement and was given added significance

by the ease with which the Indian openers played the Australian seam attack and the rapidity with which they scored. Runs came at six an over, and Srikkanth reached a thrilling fifty before mishooking McDermott to be caught at mid-wicket shortly before the close.

India were 97 for 1 at the close of the second day with Gavaskar on 39 not out, but he could not resume on the third morning as he was pained by a blow on the arm from a ball by McDermott. India did not enjoy a good day. One and a half sessions were lost to rain and bad light, and the Australian seamers found greater accuracy and more venom than they had done the previous evening. Chetan Sharma batted well, but Vengsarkar struggled, and when play ended early India were 176 for 3, a draw looming.

The draw became inevitable on the third day which ended with India on 391 for 7, Gavaskar, who had returned to bat at the fall of the fifth wicket, on 94 not out. Half an hour's play was lost at the start, but it was a painful crawl for runs. Azharuddin went early, caught behind off Reid who bowled with zest, and Amarnath was caught at short-leg off McDermott, still below his form in England.

Gavaskar completed his thirty-first Test hundred on the last morning. It came off 286 balls and included 10 fours. He and Yadav added 94 for the last wicket, as India recorded their highest score against Australia. Gavaskar passed 9,000 runs in Test cricket, the first man ever to achieve this landmark, and Kapil Dev was named Man of the Match.

The performance of left-arm pace bowler Reid was encouraging for Australia who were in search of comfort.

McDonald's Cup

18 December 1985

at Sydney

South Australia 203 for 8 (W.B. Phillips 66 not out)
New South Wales 204 for 6 (M. Taylor 59)
New South Wales won by 4 wickets

New South Wales won with 13 balls to spare. Steve Waugh was named Man of the Match for his innings of 47 and his 3 for 37 in 10 overs.

Group B		P	W	L	Pts
New South Wales		2	2	—	4
Western Australia		2	1	1	2
South Australia		2	—	2	0

20, 21, 22 and 23 December 1985

at Melbourne

New South Wales 241 (G.F. Lawson 63, R.J. Bright 6 for 74) and 319 for 3 (S.M. Small 123, D.M. Wellham 63)
Victoria 273 for 9 dec (P.A. Hibbert 148, R.J. Bright 69, M.J. Bennett 4 for 71)

Match drawn
Victoria 4 pts, New South Wales 0 pts

FIRST TEST MATCH – AUSTRALIA v. INDIA
13, 14, 15, 16 and 17 December 1985 at Adelaide Oval

AUSTRALIA

	FIRST INNINGS		SECOND INNINGS	
W.B. Phillips*	c Yadav, b Kapil Dev	11		
D.C. Boon	c. Vengsarkar, b Dev	123	(1) not out	11
G.R. Marsh	c Sharma, b Binny	5	(2) not out	2
A.R. Border†	b Kapil Dev	49		
G.M. Ritchie	c Kirmani,			
	b Kapil Dev	128		
D.W. Hookes	b Yadav	34		
G.R.J. Matthews	lbw, b Kapil Dev	18		
R.J. Bright	not out	5		
C.J. McDermott	lbw, b Kapil Dev	0		
B.A. Reid	c Gavaskar, b Dev	2		
M.G. Hughes	c Vengsarkar, b Dev	0		
Extras	lb 4, nb 2	6	lb 3, nb 1	4
		381	(for no wkt)	17

INDIA

	FIRST INNINGS	
S.M. Gavaskar	not out	166
K. Srikkanth	c Ritchie,	
	b McDermott	51
Chetan Sharma	c Phillips, b Reid	54
D.B. Vengsarkar	c Phillips, b Hughes	7
M. Azharuddin	c Phillips, b Reid	17
M.B. Amarnath	c Marsh, b McDermott	37
R.J. Shastri	b Reid	42
R.N. Kapil Dev†	lbw, b Bright	38
R.M.H. Binny	c Phillips,	
	b McDermott	38
S.M.H. Kirmani*	c Boon, b Reid	7
S.N. Yadav	c Hughes, b Hookes	41
Extras	b 2, lb 7, w 1, nb 12	22
		520

	O	M	R	W	O	M	R	W
Kapil Dev	38	6	106	8	3	1	3	—
Binny	24	7	56	1				
Chetan Sharma	19	3	70	—	2	—	9	—
Yadav	27	6	66	1	2	1	2	—
Shastri	38	11	70	—	1	1	0	—
Amarnath	3	—	9	—				

	O	M	R	W
McDermott	48	14	131	3
Hughes	38	6	123	1
Reid	55	22	113	4
Bright	44	15	80	1
Matthews	17	2	60	—
Hookes	2	—	4	1

FALL OF WICKETS
1-19, 2-33, 3-124, 4-241, 5-318, 6-374, 7-375, 8-375, 9-381

FALL OF WICKETS
1-95, 2-131, 3-171, 4-187, 5-247, 6-273, 7-333, 8-409, 9-426

Umpires: A.R. Crafter & S.G. Randell

Match drawn

Kapil Dev, 8 for 106 on a placid wicket. (Philip Tyson)

at Brisbane

Queensland 391 for 8 dec (A.R. Border 118, G.S. Trimble 87 not out, K.C. Wessels 85, G.C. Small 4 for 109) and 162 for 8 dec (G.M. Ritchie 63)
South Australia 251 (W.M. Darling 60 not out) and 192 (D.W. Hookes 72, J.R. Thomson 4 for 29)

Queensland won by 110 runs
Queensland 12 pts, South Australia 0 pts

at Hobart

Tasmania v. Indians

Match abandoned without a ball being bowled

As the Indians suffered further frustration, Queensland regained the leadership of the Sheffield Shield. Border hit 12 fours in his fourth century in five matches for his state. He and Wessels put on 143 for the third wicket. South Australia were in danger of having to follow-on, but Rick Darling and Gladstone Small added 51 for the last wicket to save that indignity. On a wicket that was now assisting the bowlers, Queensland lost 5 for 59, but Ritchie assured the declaration with a stubborn innings. Only Hookes and Sleep offered South Australia any hope of salvation, but Thomson and Trimble, asserting his new authority as an all-rounder, broke through and Queensland swept to a comfortable victory. Kepler Wessels held five catches in the second innings.

In contrast, New South Wales were bundled out on the first day in Melbourne where Ray Bright had his best return

of the season. Victoria fared even worse, losing 6 wickets for 79 runs, but Hibbert, who batted nearly seven hours, and Bright added a record 175 to gain the first innings points. Bad weather determined that the game would be drawn, but Steve Small, the former Tasmanian player, hit his first century for New South Wales. In the first innings, Geoff Lawson hit a career best 63 off 56 deliveries.

Second Test Match
AUSTRALIA v. INDIA

Australia gave a first Test cap to Steve Waugh, the New South Wales all rounder, and brought back Gilbert after injury. Waugh played Essex League cricket in England in 1985, and his team-mate Greg Matthews predicted that he would play for Australia and score more than five thousand runs for his country.

India brought in Laxman Sivaramakrishnan for Chetan Sharma in the hope that the young leg-spinner would find encouragement in the Melbourne wicket and return to form.

Kapil Dev won the toss and asked Australia to bat first on a wicket which, once again, looked to be below Test standard. Shastri was brought into the attack in the seventh over and immediately made the ball turn. It was he who struck the first blow for India when he had Boon lbw playing back to one which kept low. Phillips soon followed, bowled round his legs in attempting to sweep Yadav, and Sivaramak-

rishnan captured the prize wicket of Allan Border who hit a full toss straight back to the bowler.

Sivaramakrishnan was wayward in length and direction, but, like all of the Indian players, he was suffering from a lack of match practice. All the tourists' games had been hit by the weather, and the match against Tasmania had been abandoned without a ball being bowled, a severe blow to the Indians in their preparations for the Test.

The Australians had their problems too in that Ritchie had dropped a log on his foot during Christmas festivities and was unable to play, an accident which gave Waugh his Test chance. The newcomer batted calmly until driving at Sivaramakrishnan and being caught in the gully. Hookes played a fierce innings until driving, head up, at Shastri, and Marsh's patient 30 in 163 minutes came to an end when he was caught at short-leg off bat and pad.

Matthews and Bright provided the best batting of the day, adding 66 sensible runs before Bright was bowled in attempting to cut Shastri. The left-arm spinner also had McDermott caught in the gully so that Australia finished the day tottering on 210 for 8.

Reid went quickly on the second morning when Srikkanth took a splendid diving catch at short-leg, but Greg Matthews batted with great courage and Gilbert played with defiance. They added 46 for the last wicket in 49 minutes and Matthews reached his second Test hundred of the Australian summer.

Gilbert struck a further blow for Australia when he bowled Gavaskar with the score on 15, but Srikkanth was in blistering form. He unleashed a string of gloriously exciting strokes all round the wicket and hit 86 off 89 balls before falling lbw to Gilbert as he played half forward. Mohinder Amarnath also fell before the close, caught behind off Reid, the best of the Australian bowlers. Bad light ended play fifty minutes early, but, at 187 for 3, India were in a very happy position.

India batted methodically on the third day to take their score to 431 for 9. The Australian fielding was poor and their bowling limited. Waugh took two wickets with his medium pace and Reid was again the best of the bowlers, but India moved on remorselessly. The innings was highlighted by Kapil Dev's 55 off 56 deliveries, which took him past 3,000 runs in Test cricket so that he became only the third player in the history of the game, behind Sobers and Botham, to have scored 3,000 runs and taken 200 wickets in Test matches, a magnificent achievement by the Indian captain.

India added 14 runs in twenty minutes on the fourth morning so that Australia trailed by 183 on the first innings. Geoff Marsh formed a new opening partnership with David Boon, Wayne Phillips dropping to number seven, but the score was only 32 when Kapil Dev held a return catch to dismiss Boon. Marsh was caught close to the wicket and Hookes was out first ball so that Australia, 54 for 3, were in deep trouble. Waugh and Border put on 30 and relieved the tension before Waugh was bowled by Shastri.

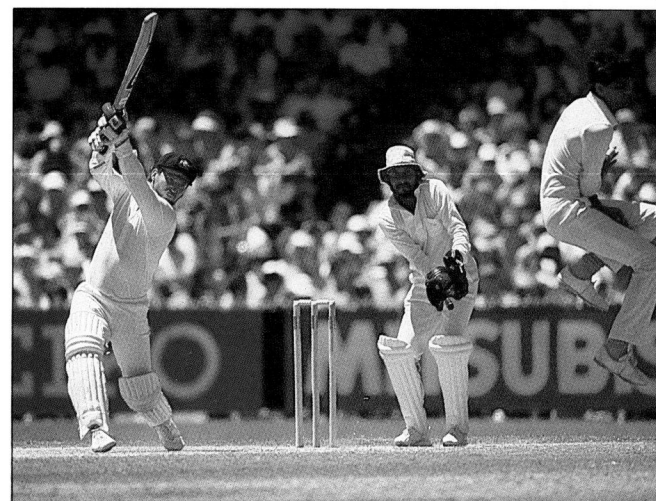

ABOVE: *Allan Border during his magnificent match-saving innings of 163. (All Sport)*

Matthews resisted stubbornly for 71 minutes until he pulled a short ball from Sivaramakrishnan to deep mid-wicket where Azharuddin held a fine running catch. Phillips, who looked to have lost confidence both as batsman and wicket-keeper, was taken at short-leg, but Bright stayed with Border to avoid the innings defeat before he fell to Kapil Dev. McDermott quickly fell to Shastri, but Reid stayed with Border until the close which came with Australia on 228 for 8, Border 98 not out.

Reid turned Yadav to backward short-leg early on the last morning and an Indian victory seemed imminent, but Border protected Gilbert admirably and played some positive shots to frustrate India. He swept and square cut Shastri for boundaries to pass his hundred and continued to bat with authority. Gilbert showed fine qualities of defence and, at lunch, Australia had reached 306 for 9. Border's great innings ended shortly after when he swung at Yadav and was stumped.

The Australian captain's mighty knock had frustrated India, but the visitors still needed only 126 to win in just under four hours, a task that was hardly likely to prove beyond them. Although both Gavaskar and Srikkanth were dismissed, India reached tea at 59 for 2 and victory in the final session appeared a formality. Then the skies darkened and drizzle turned to rain, and no more play was possible. It was a travesty of justice that Australia should have escaped defeat, but Allan Border's heroic innings was as much to blame as the weather, and Kapil Dev still remained without a victory as a Test captain.

Allan Border became the first Australian to reach a thousand runs for the season when he had scored two.

Third Test Match
AUSTRALIA v. INDIA

With the Sydney wicket expected to take spin, Australia recalled Bob Holland to their side while Greg Ritchie returned after injury. India brought back Chetan Sharma in place of Roger Binny.

Kapil Dev won an important toss and India flourished. Australia had a dreadful day in the field, dropping four straight-forward catches, and Srikkanth and Gavaskar prospered. Srikkanth was missed when he was two and took some time to get into his stride, but soon he was lashing the ball to all parts of the field. At one period he moved from 26 to 77 in 47 minutes while Gavaskar remained on 27. A blow on the left foot meant that, for a time, he batted with Sivaramakrishnan as a runner, but he was so consistent in finding the boundary that the runner was scarcely used. In one over, Srikkanth hit Holland for a six and 4 fours, and then took 14 off the next over, from Reid. His 116, a maiden Test hundred, came off 117 balls and included a six and 19 fours. He

---

SECOND TEST MATCH – AUSTRALIA v. INDIA
26, 27, 28, 29 and 30 December 1985 at Melbourne

AUSTRALIA

	FIRST INNINGS		SECOND INNINGS	
W.B. Phillips*	b Yadav	7	(7) c Srikkanth, b Yadav	13
D.C. Boon	lbw, b Shastri	14	c and b Kapil Dev	19
G.R. Marsh	c Siva, b Yadav	30	(1) c Siva, b Shastri	19
A.R. Border†	c and b Siva	11	(3) st Kirmani, b Yadav	163
D.W. Hookes	b Shastri	42	(4) c Srikkanth, b Shastri	0
S.R. Waugh	c Kapil Dev, b Siva	13	(5) b Shastri	5
G.R.J. Matthews	not out	100	(6) c Azharuddin, b Siva	16
R.J. Bright	b Shastri	28	lbw, b Kapil Dev	20
C.J. McDermott	c Kapil Dev, b Shastri	1	c and b Shastri	2
B.A. Reid	c Srikkanth, b Dev	1	c Siva, b Yadav	13
D.R. Gilbert	c Kirmani, b Yadav	4	not out	10
Extras	b 5, lb 6	11	b 11, lb 16, nb 1	28
		262		308

	O	M	R	W	O	M	R	W
Kapil Dev	23	6	38	1	22	7	53	2
Binny	3	—	11	—				
Shastri	37	13	87	4	47	13	92	4
Yadav	27.5	10	64	3	38.5	15	84	3
Sivaramakrishnan	13	2	51	2	13	1	43	1
Amarnath					3	—	9	—

INDIA

	FIRST INNINGS		SECOND INNINGS	
S.M. Gavaskar	b Gilbert	6	b Reid	8
K. Srikkanth	lbw, b Gilbert	86	c Bright, b Reid	38
M.B. Amarnath	c Phillips, b Reid	45	not out	3
D.B. Vengsarkar	c and b Matthews	75	not out	1
M. Azharuddin	b Matthews	37		
R.J. Shastri	c Phillips, b Waugh	49		
R.N. Kapil Dev†	c Hookes, b Reid	55		
R.M.H. Binny	c Matthews, b Reid	0		
S.M.H. Kirmani*	c Phillips, b Waugh	35		
L. Sivarama- krishnan	c Phillips, b Reid	15		
S.N. Yadav	not out	6		
Extras	b 4, lb 15, nb 17	36	b 4, lb 1, nb 4	9
		445	(for 2 wickets)	59

	O	M	R	W	O	M	R	W
McDermott	15	5	52	—	6	1	17	—
Gilbert	22	1	81	2	4	—	9	—
Reid	38.2	11	100	4	8	2	23	2
Bright	31	8	76	—	7	4	5	—
Matthews	31	7	81	2				
Waugh	11	5	36	2				

FALL OF WICKETS
1- 22, 2- 26, 3- 41, 4- 90, 5- 109, 6- 127, 7- 193, 8- 195, 9- 216
1- 32, 2- 54, 3- 54, 4- 84, 5- 126, 6- 161, 7- 202, 8- 205, 9- 231

FALL OF WICKETS
1- 15, 2- 116, 3- 172, 4- 246, 5- 291, 6- 370, 7- 372, 8- 420, 9- 425
1- 39, 2- 57

Umpires: A.R. French & R.C. Isherwood

Match drawn

dominated the opening partnership of 191 and was out when he pulled a ball onto his stumps.

Gavaskar and Amarnath now punished an Australian side that was wilting visibly. The immaculate Gavaskar reached his thirty-second Test hundred off 238 balls in 284 minutes, and by the close, India were a mighty 334 for 1.

Gavaskar and Amarnath took their second wicket stand to 224, an Indian record against Australia, before Gavaskar was bowled round his legs, sweeping at Holland. His innings had lasted 513 minutes and included 19 fours. Amarnath's hundred came in 329 minutes with 6 fours, but he increased his rate of scoring once he had reached three figures and went on to make his highest score in Test cricket.

Kapil Dev and Azharuddin played brisk, enterprising innings, and India reached 600 for 4, their highest score against Australia. Boon and Marsh played out the last 17 minutes and scored 4.

A thunderstorm reduced play on the third day by 75 minutes, and India failed to break through as Boon and Marsh engaged in the highest opening stand by an Australian pair in a Test at Sydney. It was dour batting, but highly commendable in the context of the match. Boon reached his century in the last over of the day, and Australia closed at 169 for 0.

The opening stand reached 217, Australia's first double century opening partnership for 172 Tests and a record against India, before Boon chopped a short ball from Kapil Dev on his stumps. Marsh was denied a well deserved hundred when he was caught at slip off Shastri from a ball that turned sharply. Ritchie was caught at short mid-wicket

David Gilbert just gets home. (All Sport)

and Phillips was taken at short-leg, bat and pad. For a moment it seemed that Australia would crumble, but Border and Matthews reasserted the authority of the bat so that a draw looked inevitable when the home side closed the fourth day at 347 for 4.

THIRD TEST MATCH – AUSTRALIA v. INDIA
2, 3, 4, 5 and 6 January 1986 at Sydney

INDIA

	FIRST INNINGS	
S.M. Gavaskar	b Holland	172
K. Srikkanth	b Reid	116
M.B. Amarnath	c Bright, b Gilbert	138
R.N. Kapil Dev†	b Gilbert	42
D.B. Vengsavkar	not out	37
D.B. Azharuddin	not out	59
R.J. Shastri		
S.M.H. Kirmani*		
L. Sivarama-		
krishnan		
Chetan Sharma		
S.N. Yadav		
Extras	b 5, lb 9, nb 22	36
	(for 4 wkts dec)	600

	O	M	R	W
Gilbert	37	3	135	2
Reid	34	8	89	1
Bright	41	7	121	—
Holland	21	6	113	1
Matthews	29	2	95	—
Waugh	7		33	—

FALL OF WICKETS
1- 191, 2- 415, 3- 485, 4- 510

AUSTRALIA

	FIRST INNINGS		SECOND INNINGS	
D.C. Boon	b Kapil Dev	131	(2) run out	25
G.R. Marsh	c Gavaskar, b Shastri	92	(1) c Azharuddin, b Yadav	28
A.R. Border†	c Sharma, b Shastri	71	(7) c Siva, b Yadav	4
G.M. Ritchie	c Kapil Dev, b Yadav	14	(3) not out	17
W.B. Phillips*	c Srikkanth, b Shastri	14	c Srikkanth, b Shastri	22
G.R.J. Matthews	c Amarnath, b Yadav	40	c Kapil Dev, b Yadav	17
S.R. Waugh	c Siva, b Yadav	8	(4) lbw, b Shastri	0
R.J. Bright	c Kirmani, b Shastri	3	not out	0
B.A. Reid	st Kirmani, b Yadav	4		
D.R. Gilbert	c Azharuddin, b Yadav	1		
R.G. Holland	not out	1		
Extras	lb 14, nb 3	17	b 3, lb 2, nb 1	6
		396	(for 6 wkts)	119

	O	M	R	W	O	M	R	W
Kapil Dev	25	8	65	1	7	3	11	—
Chetan Sharma	13	2	38	—	3	—	11	—
Shastri	57	21	101	4	25	12	36	2
Yadav	62.3	20	99	5	33	22	19	3
Sivaramakrishnan	22	2	79	—	9	—	37	—

FALL OF WICKETS
1- 217, 2- 258, 3- 277, 4- 302, 5- 369, 6- 387, 7- 388, 8- 390, 9- 395
1- 57, 2- 57, 3- 60, 4- 87, 5- 111, 6- 115

Umpires: P.J. McConnell & S.J. Randell

Match drawn

Srikkanth is dropped by Ritchie and goes on to score his first Test hundred. (All Sport)

RIGHT: *Shivlal Yadav whose off-spin nearly brought victory to India (Philip Tyson)*

The final day produced unexpected drama of which there was no hint early on as Border and Matthews added another 22 runs. Then Border was splendidly caught at deep mid-on by Chetan Sharma. Matthews and Waugh took Australia to within 14 of the total required to avoid the follow-on before Waugh was caught at backward short-leg. One run later, Matthews swept carelessly and was caught at square leg, and Australia were tottering. The panic manifested itself in dreadful batting. Bright cut wildly and was caught behind, and Reid swung in insane manner and was stumped. Gilbert drove Yadav to mid-off, and Australia were forced to follow-on.

No praise can be too high for Yadav and Shastri who bowled with immaculate control so beating the batsmen with spin and frustration. Their mammoth efforts were rewarded with four and five wickets respectively.

India still had little hope of victory in spite of Australia's incredible collapse, and Boon and Marsh confirmed this view when they began the second innings much the same way in which they had begun the first. They reached 57 when Boon was run out by Sivaramakrishnan who half stopped a sweep from Marsh and saw Boon come racing down the pitch. Marsh was out next ball, caught at short-leg, and Waugh was lbw three runs later.

Phillips stayed with the defiant Ritchie for an hour before being caught at short-leg, and Australia entered the last twenty overs at 96 for 4. Indian hopes leapt when Yadav, who conceded only 19 runs in 33 overs, dismissed Matthews and Border in quick succession, but Ritchie, who batted nearly three hours for 17, and Bright played out the last seven overs and once again India were thwarted.

Australia v. India – Test Match Averages

AUSTRALIA BATTING

	M	Inns	NOs	Runs	HS	Av	100s	50s
G.M. Ritchie	2	3	1	159	128	79.50	1	
D.C. Boon	3	6	1	323	131	64.60	2	
A.R. Border	3	5		298	163	59.60	1	1
G.R.J. Matthews	3	5	1	191	100*	47.75	1	
G.R. Marsh	3	6	1	176	92	35.20		1
D.W. Hookes	2	3		76	42	25.33		
R.J. Bright	3	5	2	56	28	18.66		
W.B. Phillips	3	5		67	22	13.40		
D.R. Gilbert	2	3	1	15	10*	7.50		
S.R. Waugh	2	4		26	13	6.50		
B.A. Reid	3	4		20	13	5.00		
C.J. McDermott	2	3		3	2	1.00		

Played in one Test: M.G. Hughes 0; R.G. Holland 1*

INDIA BATTING

	M	Inns	NOs	Runs	HS	Av	100s	50s
S.M. Gavaskar	3	4	1	352	172	117.33	2	
M.B. Amarnath	3	4	1	223	138	74.33	1	
K. Srikkanth	3	4		291	116	72.75	1	1
D.B. Vengsarkar	3	4	2	120	75	60.00		1
M. Azharuddin	3	3	1	113	59*	56.50		1
S.N. Yadav	3	2	1	47	41	47.00		
R.J. Shastri	3	2		91	49	45.50		
R.N. Kapil Dev	3	3		135	55	45.00		1
S.M.H. Kirmani	3	2		42	35	21.00		
R.M.H. Binny	2	2		38	38	19.00		

Played in two Tests: L. Sivaramakrishnan 15; Chetan Sharma 54

AUSTRALIA BOWLING

	Overs	Mds	Runs	Wkts	Av	Best	5/inn
B.A. Reid	135.2	43	325	11	29.54	4/100	
S.R. Waugh	18	5	69	2	34.50	2/36	
D.R. Gilbert	63	4	225	4	56.25	2/81	
C.J. McDermott	69	20	200	3	66.66	3/131	
G.R.J. Matthews	77	11	236	2	118.00	2/81	
R.J. Bright	123	34	282	1	282.00	1/80	

Also bowled: R.G. Holland 21-6-113-1; D.W. Hookes 2-0-4-1; M.G. Hughes 38-6-123-1

INDIA BOWLING

	Overs	Mds	Runs	Wkts	Av	Best	5/inn
S.N. Yadav	191.1	74	334	15	22.26	5/99	1
R.N. Kapil Dev	118	31	276	12	23.00	8/106	1
R.J. Shastri	205	71	386	14	27.57	4/87	
R.M.H. Binny	27	7	67	1	67.00	1/56	
L. Sivaramakrishnan	57	5	210	3	70.00	2/51	
M.B. Amarnath	6	0	18	0	—		
Chetan Sharma	37	5	128	0	—		

AUSTRALIA CATCHES

8 - W.B. Phillips; 2 - R.J. Bright and G.R.J. Matthews; 1 - D.W. Hookes, G.M. Ritchie, G.R. Marsh, D.C. Boon and M.G. Hughes

INDIA CATCHES

6 - L. Sivaramakrishnan; 5 - K. Srikkanth, R.N. Kapil Dev and S.M.H. Kirmani (ct 3/st 2); 3 - M. Azharuddin; 2 - S.M. Gavaskar, Chetan Sharma and D.B. Vengsarkar; 1 - R.J. Shastri, S.N. Yadav and M.B. Amarnath

Benson and Hedges World Series

First One-Day International
AUSTRALIA v. NEW ZEALAND

Rain reduced the first match of the series from its scheduled fifty overs to thirty overs an innings and a slow Australian over-rate curtailed the New Zealand innings by another over. It mattered little, for the rain returned during the interval and the match was abandoned.

A spirited innings of 71 from 57 deliveries by Martin Crowe was the highlight of the soggy day. He and Coney added 77 for the fourth wicket after the first three New Zealand wickets had fallen for 50. Edgar and Reid were victims of Simon Davis who was making his international debut. A fast medium bowler, Davis is remembered in England for his fine performances for Durham in the NatWest Trophy.

10, 11, 12 and 13 January 1986

at Perth

New South Wales (C.R. Matthews 5 for 40) and 321 (G. Dyer 68, K.H. Macleay 6 for 93)
Western Australia 450 for 7 dec (W.S. Andrews 139, G.M. Wood 133)

Western Australia won by an innings and 46 runs

at Adelaide

South Australia 313 (D. Kelly 85, R.L. Brown 7 for 80) and 245 for 6 dec (G.A. Bishop 224 not out, R.L. Brown 4 for 103)
Tasmania 343 (D.J. Buckingham 121, R.D. Woolley 94, M. Ray 52) and 260 (E. Harris 118, K. Bradshaw 62, C.L. Harms 4 for 60)

South Australia won by 55 runs
South Australia 8 pts, Tasmania 4 pts

Tasmania took their first points of the season but still lost to South Australia in Adelaide. Andrew Hilditch was left out of the state side and Zadow took over the captaincy. A depleted Tasmanian attack, including debutants Cooley and Dell, was inspired by the lion-hearted Roger Brown who had career bests for an innings and for a match. Wicket-keeper Kelly and Wundke, who was making his debut in first-class cricket, roused South Australia, but Tasmania took the points when Danny Buckingham hit a maiden century and shared a fifth wicket stand of 176 with Roger Woolley. Glen Bishop reached his highest score in first-class cricket when South Australia batted again and carried his bat through the innings. Tasmania looked as if they might get the 316 needed for victory when Harris hit a century on his first-class debut, but they collapsed from 244 for 4 to 260 all out.

New South Wales slipped again when they were shot out in two and a half hours in Perth. Western Australia replied thunderously. They were 91 for 4, but Andrews, with a maiden first-class hundred, and skipper Wood, finding new life at number four, put on 216. New South Wales batted better at the second attempt, but Macleay, the most consistent bowler of the season and desperately unlucky not to be in the Australian side for the one-day internationals, returned a career best and Western Australia romped home by an innings.

Queensland led the table with 42 points, New South Wales had 36, and Western Australia 30. All sides had completed six matches.

Benson and Hedges World Series

Second One-Day International
NEW ZEALAND v. INDIA

The dismissal of John Wright in the fourth over of the day did nothing to impede New Zealand's progress as they moved towards a massive score. Edgar and Martin Crowe added 130 in 26 overs, and Martin Crowe was again in fine form, hitting 76 off 83 balls. The innings never lost its impetus and India were faced with a target of 260, which would mean them reaching the highest total that they had ever made when batting second.

Gavaskar set the tone of the Indian innings when he hit 27 off 17 balls in three overs. For once, Srikkanth was overshadowed, but Amarnath maintained the attack on the bowlers and the second wicket pair added 97 in 18 overs. Srikkanth was needlessly run out when he broke the cardinal rule and ran for a misfield, and Azharuddin, after a promising start, fell the same way. When Boock bowled Amarnath and Vengsarkar fell to Gillespie India had collapsed to 176 for 5 and New Zealand now seemed to have the game in their grasp. Kapil Dev, the best of the Indian bowlers, attacked the bowling from the start of his innings, but also played with control. He had scored only 11, however, when he skied a ball from Boock to backward square leg where Gillespie misjudged the catch. The Indian captain did not offer a second chance and he and Shastri stroked the World Champions to a fine victory with two overs to spare. Not surprisingly, Kapil Dev was named Man of the Match.

Benson and Hedges World Series

Third One-Day International
AUSTRALIA v. INDIA

After the horrors of the Test series the Australians began the Benson and Hedges World Series with a morale-boosting win over India. Border won the toss and put India in, and his decision was abundantly justified when India failed to last for their full quota of overs and were bowled out for 161 which was founded mainly on a ninth wicket partnership of 47 between Chetan Sharma and Kirmani. The Australian seam attack, no spin was used, was accurate and effectively consistent.

The Australian batsmen, however, failed miserably in their efforts to reach the meagre target that their bowlers had created for them, and when Greg Matthews joined Steve Waugh the score was 48 for 5. Pugnacious batting and brisk running between the wickets put the Australians back on course for victory, but Waugh was bowled by Yadav after the pair had put on 79 and Australia still had doubts.

McDermott gave Matthews fine support, and the New South Wales left-hander, quickly becoming a folk hero in Australia, saw his side to victory and took the individual award.

FIRST ONE-DAY INTERNATIONAL – AUSTRALIA v. NEW ZEALAND
9 January 1986 at Melbourne

NEW ZEALAND					AUSTRALIA	
J.G. Wright	run out		5		D.C. Boon	
B.A. Edgar	b Davis		17		G.M. Ritchie	
M.D. Crowe	b Gilbert		71		A.R. Border†	
J.F. Reid	c Phillips, b Davis		7		D.W. Hookes	
J.V. Coney†	c Phillips, b Waugh		24		G.R.J. Matthews	
R.J. Hadlee	b Gilbert		5		W.B. Phillips*	
J.G. Bracewell	c Waugh, b McDermott		13		S.R. Waugh	
B.R. Blair	not out		7		C.J. McDermott	
E.B. McSweeney*	not out		2		S.P. Davis	
E.J. Chatfield					B.A. Reid	
S.L. Boock					D.R. Gilbert	
Extras	lb 5, w 3, nb 2		10			
(29 overs)	(for 7 wickets)		161			

	O	M	R	W
McDermott	6	1	20	1
Davis	6	1	30	2
Reid	6	—	36	—
Matthews	4	—	24	—
Gilbert	5	—	33	2
Waugh	2	—	13	1

FALL OF WICKETS
1- 10, 2- 30, 3- 50, 4- 127, 5- 137, 6- 146, 7- 152

Match abandoned

SECOND ONE-DAY INTERNATIONAL – NEW ZEALAND v. INDIA
11 January 1986 at Brisbane

NEW ZEALAND					INDIA			
B.A. Edgar	b Kapil Dev		75		K. Srikkanth	run out		50
J.G. Wright	c Kirmani, b Binny		2		S.M. Gavaskar	b Chatfield		27
M.D. Crowe	c and b Amarnath		76		M.B. Amarnath	b Boock		61
J.F. Reid	b Shastri		11		M. Azharuddin	run out		13
R.J. Hadlee	c Amarnath, b Yadav		22		D.B. Vengsarkar	c Coney, b Gillespie		9
J.V. Coney†	c Azharuddin, b Yadav		11		R.N. Kapil Dev†	not out		54
B.R. Blair	not out		29		R.J. Shastri	not out		36
E.B. McSweeney*	b Chetan Sharma		6		R.M.H. Binny			
S.R. Gillespie	b Chetan Sharma		7		S.M.H. Kirmani*			
S.L. Boock	run out		0		Chetan Sharma			
E.J. Chatfield	not out		1		S.N. Yadav			
Extras	lb 15, w 1, nb 3		19		Extras	lb 8, w 4, nb 1		13
(50 overs)	(for 9 wickets)		259		(48 overs)	(for 5 wickets)		263

	O	M	R	W			O	M	R	W
Kapil Dev	10	—	28	1		Chatfield	9	2	51	1
Binny	6	1	29	1		Hadlee	10	3	42	—
Chetan Sharma	7	—	43	2		Blair	3	—	27	—
Amarnath	10	1	40	1		Gillespie	9	1	39	1
Yadav	8	—	51	2		Coney	6	—	36	—
Shastri	9	—	53	1		Boock	10	—	55	1
						M.D. Crowe	1	—	5	—

FALL OF WICKETS
1- 12, 2- 142, 3- 171, 4- 196, 5- 209, 6- 223, 7- 238, 8- 254, 9- 256

FALL OF WICKETS
1- 40, 2- 137, 3- 154, 4- 162, 5- 176

India won by 5 wickets

Benson and Hedges World Series

Fourth One-Day International
AUSTRALIA v. NEW ZEALAND

With their second win in three matches, Australia took a three-point lead at the top of the embryo table and re-awakened the faith of their followers. Once again it was the Australian pace attack which made victory possible and David Gilbert took the individual award for his five wickets. It was McDermott and Davis who put the initial stranglehold on the New Zealand batting, however, and it took the visitors 20 overs to raise their scoring rate above two an over. That they reached a total of any proportions was due to skipper Jeremy Coney who hit 58 off 86 deliveries and helped

THIRD ONE-DAY INTERNATIONAL – AUSTRALIA v. INDIA
12 January 1986 at Brisbane

INDIA			
S.M. Gavaskar	b Davis		5
K. Srikkanth	c Matthews, b McDermott		6
M.B. Amarnath	c Phillips, b Gilbert		13
D.B. Vengsarkar	run out		19
M. Azharuddin	b Waugh		35
R.N. Kapil Dev†	run out		16
R.J. Shastri	b Reid		0
R.M.H. Binny	lbw, b Waugh		8
Chetan Sharma	run out		22
S.M.H. Kirmani*	c Matthews, b McDermott		27
S.N. Yadav	not out		0
Extras	lb 6, w 2, nb 2		10
(43 overs)			161

	O	M	R	W
McDermott	9	1	32	2
Davis	7	2	11	1
Gilbert	9	1	42	1
Waugh	10	—	46	2
Reid	8	1	24	1

FALL OF WICKETS
1- 5, 2- 13, 3- 29, 4- 69, 5- 100, 6- 100, 7- 102, 8- 113, 9-160

AUSTRALIA			
W.B. Phillips*	c Amarnath, b Binny		8
D.C. Boon	c Gavaskar, b Binny		14
A.R. Border†	c Kirmani, b Chetan Sharma		16
D.W. Hookes	c Azharuddin, b Binny		5
G.M. Ritchie	c and b Chetan Sharma		1
S.R. Waugh	b Yadav		40
G.R.J. Matthews	not out		46
C.J. McDermott	not out		24
D.R. Gilbert			
B.A. Reid			
S.P. Davis			
Extras	lb 9, w 1		10
(46.2 overs)	(for 6 wickets)		164

	O	M	R	W
Kapil Dev	9.2	1	31	—
Binny	10	2	38	3
Chetan Sharma	6	—	28	2
Shastri	10	1	23	—
Amarnath	3	—	11	—
Yadav	7	1	24	1

FALL OF WICKETS
1- 20, 2- 27, 3- 45, 4- 45, 5- 48, 6- 127

Australia won by 4 wickets

resurrect the score from the depths of 84 for 6.

Batting under floodlights, the Australians found the going almost as hard as the New Zealanders and with the score at 88 for 4, Greg Ritchie was missed at slip by Coney. Ritchie had scored 25 at the time and he went on to make 68 off 92 balls. He and Waugh added 64 in 53 minutes for the fifth wicket and when Ritchie was out only 2 runs were needed for victory.

Benson and Hedges World Series

Fifth One-Day International
AUSTRALIA v. INDIA

The euphoria engendered by Australia's success in the one-day competition attracted a crowd of 52,612 for the encounter with India, but they were disappointed as the home side were totally outplayed by a good team performance.

FOURTH ONE-DAY INTERNATIONAL – AUSTRALIA v. NEW ZEALAND
14 January 1986 at Sydney

NEW ZEALAND			
J.G. Wright	st Phillips, b Matthews		22
B.A. Edgar	c Ritchie, b Davis		0
M.D. Crowe	c Phillips, b Gilbert		9
J.F. Reid	c Phillips, b Waugh		9
J.J. Crowe	c Marsh, b Reid		12
J.V. Coney†	c Boon, b Gilbert		58
J.G. Bracewell	c and b Gilbert		5
R.J. Hadlee	c Phillips, b Gilbert		21
E.B. McSweeney*	b Gilbert		3
S.R. Gillespie	c Matthews, b Davis		1
E.J. Chatfield	not out		4
Extras	lb 2, w 3, nb 3		8
(49.2 overs)			152

	O	M	R	W
McDermott	9	3	21	—
Davis	8.2	3	17	2
Gilbert	10	—	46	5
Matthews	10	1	17	1
Waugh	3	—	12	1
Reid	9	—	37	1

FALL OF WICKETS
1- 1, 2- 19, 3- 42, 4- 44, 5- 68, 6- 84, 7- 140, 8- 144, 9- 147

AUSTRALIA			
D.C. Boon	lbw, b Gillespie		21
G.R. Marsh	c McSweeney, b Chatfield		13
A.R. Border†	st McSweeney, b Bracewell		16
G.M. Ritchie	c McSweeney, b Hadlee		68
W.B. Phillips*	c Coney, b Hadlee		3
S.R. Waugh	not out		19
G.R.J. Matthews	c M.D. Crowe, b Chatfield		1
C.J. McDermott	not out		1
D.R. Gilbert			
B.A. Reid			
S.P. Davis			
Extras	lb 5, w 4, nb 2		11
(45.1 overs)	(for 6 wickets)		153

	O	M	R	W
Hadlee	10	—	42	2
Chatfield	10	3	21	2
Gillespie	7.1	—	30	1
Bracewell	10	2	29	1
Coney	5	—	15	—
M.D. Crowe	3	1	11	—

FALL OF WICKETS
1- 34, 2- 41, 3- 72, 4- 87, 5- 151, 6- 152

Australia won by 4 wickets

Rain reduced the match to 45 overs, but Australia did not quite last the distance. Boon showed some determination early on, but Waugh, named Man of the Match, was the only batsman to master the varied Indian attack.

India, for whom More kept wicket in place of Kirmani who had a groin strain, were given a solid start. Gavaskar blunted the pace attack which had brought Australia victories in their last two matches as he hit 59 off 100 balls. When he was caught behind off Reid there was a ray of hope for Australia, but Amarnath was in impressive form and India won with 28 balls to spare.

16, 17, 18 and 19 January 1986

at Adelaide

New South Wales 239 (M. Taylor 92, G.C. Small 7 for 42) and 535 for 6 (M.D. O'Neill 178 not out, M. Taylor 100, G.C. Dyer 88, S.M. Small 54)
South Australia 435 (D.W. Hookes 243, P.A. Blizzard 4 for 118)
Match drawn
South Australia 4 pts, New South Wales 0 pts

18, 19, 20 and 21 January 1986

at Melbourne

Victoria 295 (A.I.C. Dodemaide 63 not out, M.B. Quinn 53, B. Mulder 6 for 125) and 186 (D.M. Jones 72, C.R. Matthews 4 for 54)
Western Australia 162 (R.J. Bright 5 for 44) and 255 for 6 (G.M. Wood 67 not out, M.R.J. Veletta 55)

Match drawn
Victoria 4 pts, Western Australia 0 pts

Disrupted by international calls and injury to Geoff Lawson, New South Wales slipped again and took nothing but honour from the game in Adelaide. Mark Taylor was almost

Ritchie falls to the Shastri–More combination. (Philip Tyson)

alone in withstanding some fine pace bowling by Gladstone Small who returned the best figures of his career. David Hookes then made the first double century of his career to put South Australia well on top after they had lost 5 for 127. The second New South Wales innings reasserted the champions' pride, however, Mark Taylor hit his second century, and O'Neill and Dyer hit career bests as they shared a sixth wicket stand of 200.

Western Australia struggled dourly in Melbourne after

FIFTH ONE-DAY INTERNATIONAL – AUSTRALIA v. INDIA
16 January 1986 at Melbourne

AUSTRALIA				INDIA			
D.C. Boon	run out		23	K. Srikkanth	run out		22
G.R. Marsh	b Kapil Dev		5	S.M. Gavaskar	c Phillips, b Reid		59
G.R.J. Matthews	run out		11	M.B. Amarnath	not out		58
A.R. Border†	b Binny		0	M. Azharuddin	not out		11
G.M. Ritchie	c More, b Shastri		3	A.O. Malhotra†			
S.R. Waugh	not out		73	R.N. Kapil Dev			
W.B. Phillips*	b Sivaramakrishnan		7	K.S. More*			
C.J. McDermott	c Azharuddin, b Sharma		12	R.M.H. Binny			
D.R. Gilbert	c Sivaramakrishnan, b Sharma		7	Chetan Sharma			
				L. Sivaramakrishnan			
B.A. Reid	c Srikkanth, b Binny		4	R.J. Shastri			
S.P. Davis	run out		6	Extras	lb 5, w 2, nb 5		12
Extras	lb 8, w 1, nb 1		10				
				(40.2 overs)	(for 2 wickets)		162
(44.2 overs)			161				

	O	M	R	W		O	M	R	W
Kapil Dev	8.2	2	25	1	McDermott	8.2	1	29	—
Binny	9	1	39	2	Davis	9	3	16	—
Shastri	9	1	23	1	Reid	9	—	39	1
Chetan Sharma	9	—	29	2	Gilbert	7	—	41	—
Sivaramakrishnan	9	1	37	1	Waugh	3	—	16	—
					Matthews	4	—	16	—

FALL OF WICKETS
1- 18, 2- 31, 3- 31, 4- 40, 5- 50, 6- 80, 7- 100, 8- 128, 9- 141

FALL OF WICKETS
1- 37, 2- 126

India won by 8 wickets

Victoria had led by 133 on the first innings. They needed 320 to win, but Bright bowled 48 overs for 62 runs, Miller, on his debut, 21 for 48, and the match was drawn. Mulder took 5 wickets in an innings for the first time on the opening day.

Benson and Hedges World Series

Sixth One-Day International
NEW ZEALAND v. INDIA

On a wicket which came in for severe criticism, New Zealand beat India with less ease than at one time looked probable, and so only two points separated the three nations after six matches.

Batting was never easy and India struggled against an accurate pace attack which was aided by the pitch. Faced with a meagre 114 target, New Zealand appeared to be cruising to victory at 77 for 2, but Kapil Dev took 3 wickets in 16 balls, and with Chetan Sharma also proving hostile, New Zealand lost 4 wickets for 18 runs. Coney stayed firm and he and McSweeney added a most valuable 16 runs to take their side to the brink of victory. McSweeney fell to Chetan Sharma, but Coney hit Binny to the boundary to give New Zealand victory with ample time, if not too many wickets, to spare.

Benson and Hedges World Series

Seventh One-Day International
AUSTRALIA v. NEW ZEALAND

Australia consolidated their lead at the top of the table with a win which, while comfortable, was punctuated by a few anxious moments. Australia introduced Trimble, the Queensland all-rounder, to international cricket. He replaced David Gilbert who was unfit.

New Zealand began badly and, surprisingly, it was the medium pace of Waugh which discomforted them most. He dismissed Edgar and Martin Crowe in quick succession and New Zealand slumped to 36 for 4. Jeff Crowe batted as well as he had done on the tour to hit 63 and share a fifth wicket stand of 82 with Coney who again showed his tenacity, but the final score of 159 did not look too daunting even on Perth's uncertain wicket.

Boon fell quickly, but Marsh and Border gave the Australian innings a solid foundation with a stand of 52. Border, who took the individual award, continued in resolute style until he was run out, and just as doubts seemed to be creeping into the Australian batting, Wayne Phillips hit 28 off 14 deliveries and took his side to victory with 4.5 overs to spare.

Benson and Hedges World Series

Eighth One-Day International
AUSTRALIA v. INDIA

Geoff Marsh had not been included in the Australian side for the opening matches of the tournament, for it was believed that his style was not suited to the one-day game. He disproved this theory with an innings of 125 from 145 balls which inspired Australia to their highest score in the competition. He and David Boon gave further evidence of their reliability as an opening pair with a stand of 152, and then Marsh and Border added 121 in 67 thrilling minutes. Border's 52 was made off 42 deliveries. The rest of the Australian batsmen perished in the pursuit for quick runs,

---

SIXTH ONE-DAY INTERNATIONAL – NEW ZEALAND v. INDIA
18 January 1986 at Perth

INDIA				NEW ZEALAND			
S.M. Gavaskar	c M.D. Crowe, b Gillespie	9		B.A. Edgar	c Gavaskar, b Binny	13
K. Srikkanth	run out	0		J.G. Wright	c Kapil Dev, b Sharma	13
M.B. Amarnath	c M.D. Crowe, b Snedden	30		M.D. Crowe	c Azharuddin, b Kapil Dev	33
M. Azharuddin	b M.D. Crowe	11		J.F. Reid	c Gavaskar, b Kapil Dev	14
A.O. Malhotra	c Wright, b Hadlee	15		J.J. Crowe	c Gavaskar, b Kapil Dev	0
R.J. Shastri	c McSweeney, b Chatfield	23		J.V. Coney†	not out	19
R.N. Kapil Dev†	c J.J. Crowe, b Hadlee	0		R.J. Hadlee	b Sharma	5
Chetan Sharma	c McSweeney, b Snedden	6		E.B. McSweeney*	c Kapil Dev, b Sharma	5
R.M.H. Binny	c Wright, b Snedden	1		M.C. Snedden	not out	0
K.S. More*	c Snedden, b Chatfield	2		S.J. Gillespie		
L. Sivaramakrishnan	not out	2		E.J. Chatfield		
Extras	lb 6, w 6, nb 2	14		Extras	lb 3, w 2, nb 8	13
		—				—
(44.2 overs)		113		(40.1 overs)	(for 7 wickets)	115

	O	M	R	W		O	M	R	W
Chatfield	9.2	4	9	2	Kapil Dev	10	4	26	3
Hadlee	8	1	16	2	Binny	8.1	—	25	1
Gillespie	10	2	20	1	Chetan Sharma	8	—	26	3
Snedden	8	2	23	3	Amarnath	2	—	8	—
M.D. Crowe	4	—	20	1	Shastri	10	2	17	—
Coney	5	—	19	—	Sivaramakrishnan	2	—	10	—

FALL OF WICKETS
1- 0, 2- 23, 3- 60, 4- 93, 5- 93, 6- 104, 7- 106, 8- 108, 9- 113

FALL OF WICKETS
1- 28, 2- 31, 3- 77, 4- 83, 5- 86, 6- 95, 7- 111

New Zealand won by 3 wickets

SEVENTH ONE-DAY INTERNATIONAL – AUSTRALIA v. NEW ZEALAND
19 January 1986 at Perth

NEW ZEALAND			
B.A. Edgar	c Border, b Waugh		10
J.G. Wright	b Davis		9
M.D. Crowe	c Boon, b Waugh		1
J.F. Reid	b Reid		11
J.J. Crowe	run out		63
J.V. Coney†	c Marsh, b Matthews		33
R.J. Hadlee	not out		15
R.J. McSweeney†	not out		0
M.C. Snedden			
S.J. Gillespie			
E.J. Chatfield			
Extras	b 2, lb 10, w 2, nb 3		17
			—
(50 overs)	(for 6 wickets)		159

	O	M	R	W
McDermott	10	1	20	—
Davis	10	3	13	1
Waugh	10	3	28	2
Reid	10	1	36	1
Trimble	4	—	32	—
Matthews	6	—	18	1

FALL OF WICKETS
1- 12, 2- 13, 3- 32, 4- 36, 5- 118, 6- 156

AUSTRALIA			
D.C. Boon	c Coney, b Hadlee		6
G.R. Marsh	c McSweeney,		
	b M.D. Crowe		20
A.R. Border†	run out		58
G.M. Ritchie	c M.D. Crowe, b Coney		5
S.R. Waugh	c J.J. Crowe, b Chatfield		23
G.R.J. Matthews	c M.D. Crowe, b Hadlee		7
W.B. Phillips*	not out		28
G.S. Trimble	not out		0
C.J. McDermott			
B.A. Reid			
S.P. Davis			
Extras	lb 10, w 3, nb 1		14
			—
(45.1 overs)	(for 6 wickets)		161

	O	M	R	W
Chatfield	10	—	39	1
Hadlee	9.1	1	35	2
Gillespie	8	2	23	—
Snedden	6	—	20	—
M.D. Crowe	8.1	1	16	1
Coney	4	1	18	1

FALL OF WICKETS
1- 9, 2- 61, 3- 78, 4- 117, 5- 131, 6- 144

Australia won by 4 wickets

EIGHTH ONE-DAY INTERNATIONAL – AUSTRALIA v. INDIA
21 January 1986 at Sydney

AUSTRALIA			
G.R. Marsh	c Azharuddin, b Sharma		125
D.C. Boon	c Amarnath, b Shastri		83
A.R. Border†	c Srikkanth, b Sharma		52
W.B. Phillips*	c Kapil Dev, b Sharma		7
G.M. Ritchie	run out		1
S.R. Waugh	not out		6
C.J. McDermott	run out		2
G.R.J. Matthews	not out		1
B.A. Reid			
D.R. Gilbert			
S.P. Davis			
Extras	lb 9, w 2, nb 4		15
			—
(50 overs)	(for 6 wickets)		292

	O	M	R	W
Kapil Dev	10	—	68	—
Binny	7	—	48	—
Chetan Sharma	9	—	61	3
Amarnath	10	—	36	—
Shastri	10	—	42	1
Sivaramakrishnan	4	—	28	—

FALL OF WICKETS
1- 152, 2- 273, 3- 282, 4- 283, 5- 283, 6- 286

INDIA			
K. Srikkanth	c Border, b Davis		20
S.M. Gavaskar	not out		92
M.B. Amarnath	c Matthews, b Gilbert		16
A.O. Malhotra	c Matthews, b Gilbert		5
R.N. Kapil Dev†	c McDermott, b Matthews		28
M. Azharuddin	not out		17
R.J. Shastri			
R.M.H. Binny			
K.S. More*			
Chetan Smarma			
L. Sivaramakrishnan			
Extras	lb 8, w 2, nb 4		14
			—
(50 overs)	(for 4 wickets)		192

	O	M	R	W
McDermott	9	—	27	—
Davis	7	—	30	1
Reid	10	—	28	—
Gilbert	10	—	36	2
Matthews	10	—	49	1
Waugh	3	—	10	—
Marsh	1	—	4	—

FALL OF WICKETS
1- 31, 2- 74, 3- 93, 4- 158

Australia won by 100 runs

but the final total was formidable. It was the Indian pace bowlers who suffered most.

India never approached the required run rate. Gavaskar batted throughout the fifty overs to reach his highest one-day score, but his innings had echoes of his forgettable knock in the World Cup against England at Lord's, in June, 1975.

Not surprisingly, Marsh was named Man of the Match.

Benson and Hedges World Series

**Ninth One-Day International
NEW ZEALAND v. INDIA**

New Zealand won what was probably the most exciting game of the competition by 5 wickets with one ball to spare. Coney elected to field when he won the toss and New Zealand had

LEFT: *Steve Waugh cuts the ball for four. (Philip Tyson)*

who put on 49 in less than 16 overs before Wright, the dominant partner, was brilliantly stumped by More. Edgar gave Martin Crowe fine support in a second wicket stand of 63, and it was Martin Crowe who then took on the role of anchor man. He and Reid, who was in brisk mood, put on 64, and there was a useful knock from Jeff Crowe who shared a stand of 50 with Coney. Jeff Crowe was out in the penultimate over with 4 runs still needed for victory, and it was left to Hadlee to make the winning shot off the fifth ball of the last over.

22 January 1986

at Manuka Oval
Prime Minister's XI 48 for 0
v. New Zealanders

Match abandoned

An unfortunate injury to Bishop put him out of the South Australian side and marred the match which was ended abruptly by rain.

24, 25, 26 and 27 January 1986

at Brisbane
Queensland 389 (C.B. Smart 133, R.B. Kerr 84, M.R. Whitney 4 for 73, M. Waugh 4 for 130) and 105 for 3 (R.B. Kerr 50 not out)
New South Wales 487 (M.D. O'Neill 147, D.M. Wellham 72, R.G. Holland 53)

Match drawn
New South Wales 4 pts, Queensland 0 pts

at Hobart
Western Australia 553 for 7 dec (P. Gonnella 134, R.W. Gartrell

quick reward with the wickets of both openers. India were rallied by Mohinder Amarnath who played steadily and shared stands of 82 with Vengsarkar for the third wicket and 67 with Kapil Dev for the fifth.

It still seemed that India would fall short of a testing score, but Chetan Sharma hit lustily at the close and Hadlee's last over yielded 16 runs.

New Zealand were given a fine start by Wright and Edgar

NINTH ONE-DAY INTERNATIONAL – NEW ZEALAND v. INDIA
23 January 1986 at Melbourne

INDIA					NEW ZEALAND			
K. Srikkanth	c and b Chatfield		9		J.G. Wright	st More, b Amarnath		39
R.J. Shastri	lbw, b Hadlee		6		B.A. Edgar	c Vengsarkar, b Shastri		30
M.B. Amarnath	c and b Bracewell		74		M.D. Crowe	c Shastri, b Kapil Dev		67
D.B. Vengsarkar	b Bracewell		43		J.F Reid	run out		35
M. Azharuddin	run out		12		J.J. Crowe	b Kapil Dev		30
R.N. Kapil Dev†	c Bracewell, b Chatfield		47		J.V. Coney†	not out		27
A.O. Malhotra	c Wright, b Chatfield		7		R.J. Hadlee	not out		1
Chetan Sharma	not out		20		J.G. Bracewell			
R.M.H. Binny	b Chatfield		11		E.B. McSweeney*			
K.S. More*	not out		1		S.L. Boock			
S.N. Yadav					E.J. Chatfield			
Extras	b 2, lb 3, w 3		8		Extras	b 1, lb 7, w 2		10
(50 overs)	(for 8 wickets)		238		(49.5 overs)	(for 5 wickets)		239

	O	M	R	W		O	M	R	W
Hadlee	10	1	52	1	Kapil Dev	10	1	36	2
Chatfield	10	2	28	4	Binny	5.5	1	31	—
Coney	7	—	36	—	Chetan Sharma	10	—	57	—
Bracewell	10	—	53	2	Amarnath	5	—	26	1
Boock	8	—	51	—	Shastri	10	—	30	1
M.D. Crowe	5	—	13	—	Yadav	9	—	51	—

FALL OF WICKETS
1- 15, 2- 16, 3- 98, 4- 115, 5- 182, 6- 205, 7- 205, 8- 220

FALL OF WICKETS
1- 49, 2- 112, 3- 176, 4- 185, 5- 235

New Zealand won by 5 wickets

104, G.M. Wood 102, T. Moody 94) and 129 for 5 dec (T. Moody 59)
Tasmania 407 for 8 dec (R.D. Woolley 124 not out, K. Bradshaw 112, D. Buckingham 57, C.R. Matthews 4 for 116) and 171 for 5 (D. Buckingham 52 not out)

Match drawn
Western Australia 4 pts, Tasmania 0 pts

25, 26, 27 and 28 January 1986

at Melbourne

Victoria 345 (D.F. Whatmore 127, R.J. Bright 67 not out, A.K. Zesers 6 for 73) and 261 for 5 dec (D.M. Jones 91, M.B. Quinn 54, D.F. Whatmore 50)
South Australia 250 (A. Watson 97, P.R. Sleep 52) and 189 for 3 (A.M.J. Hilditch 84 not out, A. Watson 59)

Match drawn
Victoria 4 pts, South Australia 0 pts

28 January 1986

at Adelaide

Australian Country XI 181 for 6 (J. Hogg 59, S. Scudders 55)
Indians 182 for 5

Indians won by 5 wickets

The top of the table clash produced a high-scoring game with honours tilting in favour of New South Wales. Smart's maiden first-class hundred and consistent batting by the tail-enders took Queensland to a good score, but Small and

Taylor began with a century stand and O'Neill hit his second hundred in as many matches, having acquired the taste for three figures. Bob Holland hit a whirlwind maiden fifty at the close, and the match always looked as if it would be drawn once the visitors had taken the first innings points.

There was more high scoring in Hobart where Tasmania put up another brave show, but once again emerged point-less. Veletta and Moody began with a stand of 133 against an attack still lacking Davis and Hill. Gonnella followed with a maiden first-class hundred, and Wood and Gartrell then added 229. Gartrell's maiden century was a spectacular affair. His innings lasted only 91 balls. Tasmania lost 4 for 88 in reply, but Bradshaw and Buckingham righted things, and Woolley had fine support from the tail-enders so that Ray was able to declare once the follow-on had been avoided. Hard hitting by Western Australia could not conjure a win after that.

Ray Bright played his hundredth first-class for Victoria and celebrated breezily when Dav Whatmore's fine work looked likely to be wasted. Zesers again bowled impressively for South Australia who never looked likely to claim the points in spite of Watson's effort. Jones batted brightly as Victoria pressed for maximum points, but Andrew Hilditch, in a welcome return to form on his reinstatement in the side, played a stubborn rearguard innings, and South Australia forced a draw.

The Indian manager, Venkataraghavan, played in the one-day game against the Australian Country XI which the tourists won with 7.1 overs to spare.

Marsh plays on to Kapil Dev. Marsh hit the only century of the tournament. (Philip Tyson)

Benson and Hedges World Series

Tenth One-Day International
NEW ZEALAND v. INDIA

Following a lean spell, India moved back into second place in the table with a convincing win over New Zealand. The initial hero for India was Roger Binny who bowled an immaculate spell and so frustrated the batsmen that, in a desperate attempt to force the pace, New Zealand descended to 65 for 5. That they were able to set India a target that had any meaning was due entirely to the fine hitting of Richard Hadlee who scored 71 of the last 107 runs and completely dominated an invaluable last wicket stand of 28 with Chatfield.

India seemed to have a far from easy task when Shastri, Srikkanth and Amarnath were all out with only 36 scored. Gillespie bowled particularly well and finished with four wickets, but it was the economic bowling of Chatfield, who conceded only 13 runs in 10 overs, that threatened India most.

They were roused by Azharuddin. He showed a return to his best form and had fine support from Vengsarkar and Malhotra so that India cantered to victory with 4 overs to spare.

Benson and Hedges World Series

Eleventh One-Day International
AUSTRALIA v. INDIA

Australia ensured themselves of a place in the final with a convincing win over India. Batting first, Australia gave a solid performance and owed much to a fifth wicket stand of 92 between Waugh and Matthews. Waugh was, perhaps, thrown into the international arena too soon, but he is a player of immense potential and a rapid learner, and he quickly gave evidence that he would serve Australia well. Phillips, the lost man of the Australian season, played some enterprising shots and India were set a daunting task.

It became more daunting when 4 wickets fell for 75, but Gavaskar and Shastri added 97 to give their side hope, but Reid's bowling turned the match in favour of the home team and he took the individual award for his five wickets.

Benson and Hedges World Series

Twelfth One-Day International
AUSTRALIA v. NEW ZEALAND

In an attempt to give their middle order more substance, New Zealand dropped John Wright to number 4 and played John Bracewell as Bruce Edgar's opening partner. The move was not successful, Bracewell falling to the second ball of the match. It was left to the usual opening pair, Edgar and Wright, to give the innings its foundation with a third wicket partnership of 120. They fell in quick succession, but there were useful contributions from all the middle order in a strong batting line-up and New Zealand reached an impressive 276.

Australia began disastrously. Marsh, Waugh, Trimble and Matthews were out with only 20 scored, and, in spite of some lusty blows from Phillips, the home side never recovered. They were dismissed for 70, the second lowest score in the competition, a performance which brought an apology from skipper Allan Border to the 25,000 crowd after the match.

New Zealand's victory moved them into second place and virtually made certain that the final game, between New Zealand and India in Launceston, would decide who played Australia in the final.

TENTH ONE-DAY INTERNATIONAL – NEW ZEALAND v. INDIA
25 January 1986 at Adelaide

NEW ZEALAND					INDIA				
J.G. Wright	c More, b Binny		7		R.J. Shastri	lbw, b Hadlee		2	
B.A. Edgar	c Vengsarkar, b Binny		2		K. Srikkanth	c Coney, Gillespie		16	
M.D. Crowe	c More, b Shastri		28		M.B. Amarnath	c McSweeney, b Gillespie		5	
J.F. Reid	c Vengsarkar, b Kulkarni		9		D.B. Vengsarkar	c M.D. Crowe, b Gillespie		32	
J.J. Crowe	c Malhotra, b Kulkarni		7		M. Azharuddin	not out		69	
J.V. Coney†	c and b Shastri		4		A.O. Malhotra	c Reid, b Gillespie		33	
R.J. Hadlee	b Kapil Dev		71		R.N. Kapil Dev†	not out		6	
J.G. Bracewell	c Kapil Dev, b Amarnath		20		Chetan Sharma				
E.B. McSweeney*	b Chetan Sharma		5		R.M.H. Binny				
S.R. Gillespie	b Kapil Dev		4		K.S. More*				
E.J. Chatfield	not out		4		R.R. Kulkarni				
Extras	lb 4, w 5, nb 2		11		Extras	b 1, lb 4, w 6		11	
	(49.2 overs)		172			(46 overs)	(for 5 wickets)	174	

	O	M	R	W		O	M	R	W
Kapil Dev	9.2	3	24	2	Hadlee	10	3	28	1
Binny	7	1	13	2	Chatfield	10	5	13	—
Chetan Sharma	10	—	46	1	Gillespie	10	3	30	4
Kulkarni	9	1	28	2	M.D. Crowe	4	—	25	—
Shastri	10	1	36	2	Coney	5	—	29	—
Amarnath	4	—	21	1	Bracewell	7	—	44	—

FALL OF WICKETS
1- 12, 2- 13, 3- 37, 4- 57, 5- 58, 6- 65, 7- 119, 8- 130, 9-
144

FALL OF WICKETS
1- 2, 2- 25, 3- 36, 4- 85, 5- 158

India won by 5 wickets

ELEVENTH ONE-DAY INTERNATIONAL – AUSTRALIA v. INDIA
26 January 1986 at Adelaide

AUSTRALIA				INDIA			
D.C. Boon	c Kulkarni, b Ghai		27	K. Srikkanth	lbw, b McDermott		10
G.R. Marsh	c Vengsarkar,			S.M. Gavaskar	c Phillips, b Reid		77
	b Chetan Sharma		25	M.B. Amarnath	c Phillips, b McDermott		0
A.R. Border†	c Kapil Dev, b Shastri		9	D.B. Vengsarkar	c Border, b Reid		17
G.M. Ritchie	run out		28	M. Azharuddin	c Border, b Reid		2
S.R. Waugh	c Kapil Dev,			R.J. Shastri	c Border, b McDermott		55
	b Chetan Sharma		81	R.N. Kapil†	c Phillips, b Reid		25
G.R.J. Matthews	c More, b Chetan Sharma		44	Chetan Sharma	c McDermott, b Reid		13
W.B. Phillips*	not out		23	R.R. Kulkarni	not out		5
C.J. McDermott	b Kapil Dev		1	R.S. Ghai	run out		1
D.R. Gilbert	run out		1	K.S. More*	run out		0
B.A. Reid	not out		1	Extras	b 6, lb 7, w 3, nb 5		21
S.P. Davis							——
Extras	lb 12, w 7, nb 3		22	(45.3 overs)			226
(50 overs)	(for 8 wickets)		262				

	O	M	R	W		O	M	R	W
Kapil Dev	10	2	50	1	McDermott	8	1	20	3
Kulkarni	10	1	53	—	Davis	7.3	—	38	—
Ghai	10	1	54	1	Gilbert	10	1	50	—
Shastri	10	1	33	1	Reid	10	—	53	5
Chetan Sharma	10	—	60	3	Waugh	5	—	26	—
					Matthews	5	—	26	—

FALL OF WICKETS
1- 50, 2- 60, 3- 69, 4- 134, 5- 226, 6- 250, 7- 255, 8- 257

FALL OF WICKETS
1- 26, 2- 26, 3- 40, 4- 75, 5- 172, 6- 182, 7- 218, 8- 218, 9- 220

Australia won by 36 runs

TWELFTH ONE-DAY INTERNATIONAL – AUSTRALIA v. NEW ZEALAND
27 January 1986 at Adelaide

NEW ZEALAND				AUSTRALIA			
J.G. Bracewell	c Border, b McDermott		0	G.R. Marsh	c Coney, b Hadlee		0
B.A. Edgar	c Border, b Reid		61	D.C. Boon	c McSweeney, b Hadlee		10
M.D. Crowe	c Border, b Reid		26	S.R. Waugh	c Coney, b Chatfield		3
J.G. Wright	c Gilbert, b McDermott		61	G.S. Trimble	c Coney, b Hadlee		4
R.J. Hadlee	c McDermott, b Davis		24	G.R.J. Matthews	lbw, b Gillespie		4
J.V. Coney†	c Phillips, b Reid		40	A.R. Border†	c Gillespie, b Chatfield		9
J.J. Crowe	not out		24	W.B. Phillips*	c Chatfield, b Bracewell		22
B.R. Blair	b Davis		21	C.J. McDermott	c Wright, b Gillespie		1
E.B. McSweeney*	not out		4	D.R. Gilbert	c and b Bracewell		8
S.R. Gillespie				B.A. Reid	lbw, b Blair		1
E.J. Chatfield				S.P. Davis	not out		0
Extras	lb 9, w 5, nb 1		15	Extras	lb 3, w 1, nb 4		8
(50 overs)	(for 7 wickets)		276	(26.3 overs)			70

	O	M	R	W		O	M	R	W
McDermott	10	1	70	2	Hadlee	5	1	14	3
Davis	10	—	46	2	Chatfield	7	2	9	2
Reid	10	1	41	3	Gillespie	5	—	21	2
Matthews	10	—	49	—	M.D. Crowe	4	—	13	—
Gilbert	10	—	61	—	Bracewell	3.3	1	3	2
					Blair	2	—	7	1

FALL OF WICKETS
1- 0, 2- 37, 3- 157, 4- 160, 5- 224, 6- 226, 7- 272

FALL OF WICKETS
1- 0, 2- 10, 3- 15, 4- 20, 5- 31, 6- 47, 7- 55, 8- 68, 9- 70

New Zealand won by 206 runs

Benson and Hedges World Series

Thirteenth One-Day International
AUSTRALIA v. NEW ZEALAND

Australia gained quick revenge for the thrashing they had received at New Zealand hands in Adelaide when, prompted by a sound innings from Man of the Match Boon and a hat-trick by Reid, they swept to victory in Sydney by 99 runs.

Boon and Marsh gave Australia a solid start, and Dean Jones, restored to the national side, hit a brisk 53 so that Australia reached a commendable 239. It was not a score beyond New Zealand's reach, but Bracewell again went before a run was scored, and, in spite of Hadlee's spirited 30 towards the end, the innings never really gained momentum.

Bruce Reid dismissed Blair with the last ball of his eighth over and then had McSweeney caught with the first ball of his ninth. He bowled Gillespie first ball to complete a hat-trick, and Australia were left easy winners, still unaware of the identity of their opponents in the final.

At 6 feet 8 inches tall, aggressive and eager to learn, Reid represented Australia's find of the summer and had made a quick rise to international status.

Benson and Hedges World Series

**Fourteenth One-Day International
AUSTRALIA v. INDIA**

Australia were given a firm foundation by Boon and Marsh, the only batsman to hit a century in the entire tournament, but only Jones of the later batsmen gave the innings the impetus that was needed. Kapil Dev both contained and destroyed.

THIRTEENTH ONE-DAY INTERNATIONAL – AUSTRALIA v. NEW ZEALAND
29 January 1986 at Sydney

AUSTRALIA			
D.C. Boon	b Gillespie	64
G.R. Marsh	b Bracewell	37
A.R. Border†	run out	29
D.M. Jones	lbw, b Hadlee	53
S.R. Waugh	run out	17
G.R.J. Matthews	c Wright, b Chatfield	10
W.B. Phillips*	b Hadlee	3
C.J. McDermott	not out	6
D.R. Gilbert	not out	6
B.A. Reid		
S.P. Davis		
Extras	b 1, lb 8, w 5	14
(50 overs)	(for 7 wickets)	239

	O	M	R	W
Hadlee	10	1	36	2
Chatfield	10	1	48	1
Gillespie	10	—	48	1
Bracewell	10	1	43	1
M.D. Crowe	1	—	11	—
Coney	9	—	44	—

FALL OF WICKETS
1- 98, 2- 124, 3- 147, 4- 185, 5- 217, 6- 224, 7- 225

NEW ZEALAND			
J.G. Bracewell	b McDermott	0
B.A. Edgar	c Phillips, b Davis	18
M.D. Crowe	b McDermott	9
J.G. Wright	c Waugh, b Matthews	24
J.V. Coney†	b Gilbert	25
J.J. Crowe	b Davis	19
R.J. Hadlee	not out	30
B.R. Blair	c Marsh, b Reid	3
E.B. McSweeney*	c Border, b Reid	1
S.R. Gillespie	b Reid	0
E.J. Chatfield	b Davis	0
Extras	lb 7, w 2, nb 2	11
(42.4 overs)		140

	O	M	R	W
McDermott	7	1	28	2
Davis	9.4	2	25	3
Reid	9	2	29	3
Matthews	10	—	27	1
Gilbert	7	—	24	1

FALL OF WICKETS
1- 0, 2- 14, 3- 38, 4- 77, 5- 91, 6- 122, 7- 133, 8- 137, 9- 137

Australia won by 99 runs

FOURTEENTH ONE-DAY INTERNATIONAL – AUSTRALIA v. INDIA
31 January 1986 at Melbourne

AUSTRALIA			
D.C. Boon	c Kapil Dev, b Shastri	76
G.R. Marsh	c Gavaskar, b Shastri	74
A.R. Border†	c Malhotra, b Kapil Dev	18
D.M. Jones	b Kapil Dev	33
W.B. Phillips*	run out	8
S.R. Waugh	b Kapil Dev	3
D.M. Wellham	not out	12
C.J. McDermott	lbw, b Kapil Dev	0
D.R. Gilbert	not out	7
B.A. Reid		
S.P. Davis		
Extras	lb 3, w 1	4
(50 overs)	(for 7 wickets)	235

	O	M	R	W
Kapil Dev	9	—	30	4
Binny	6	1	24	—
Shastri	10	—	43	2
Sivaramakrishnan	8	—	52	—
Azharuddin	10	—	54	—
Chetan Sharma	7	—	29	—

FALL OF WICKETS
1- 146, 2- 161, 3- 194, 4- 212, 5- 212, 6- 224, 7- 224

INDIA			
S.M. Gavaskar	b Gilbert	72
K. Srikkanth	c Jones, b Davis	27
A.O. Malhotra	c Davis, b Gilbert	14
D.B. Vengsarkar	not out	77
R.N. Kapil Dev†	c Wellham, b Davis	23
Chetan Sharma	not out	6
M. Azharuddin		
R.J. Shastri		
R.M.H. Binny		
K.S. More*		
L. Sivaramakrishnan		
Extras	lb 14, w 3, nb 2	19
(48.5 overs)	(for 4 wickets)	238

	O	M	R	W
McDermott	9.5	—	55	—
Reid	9	—	34	—
Gilbert	10	—	43	2
Davis	10	2	40	2
Waugh	6	—	34	—
Border	4	—	18	—

FALL OF WICKETS
1- 46, 2- 79, 3- 181, 4- 230

India won by 6 wickets

RIGHT: *Srikkanth is caught and bowled by Chatfield. (Philip Tyson)*

With Gavaskar rivalling Srikkanth in the eagerness to play shots, India began briskly, and when Vengsarkar joined Gavaskar the game moved decidedly in India's favour. Kapil Dev provided the necessary whirlwind burst and although he fell to Davis, India sped to victory with 7 balls remaining.

Benson and Hedges World Series

Fifteenth One-Day International
NEW ZEALAND v. INDIA

India qualified for the final of the competition when they beat New Zealand with some ease in a rain-interrupted game at Launceston.

New Zealand began well enough, Hadlee dismissing Gavaskar with only 1 run scored. Srikkanth and the ever-dependable Amarnath, returned after injury, added 51, but both fell in quick succession and with Azharuddin failing, New Zealand were in the better position. Shastri gave Malhotra good support, but there was a middle-order collapse and, at 127 for 7, India's prospects looked bleak.

Chetan Sharma played a fine rallying innings which was to earn him the individual award, and he was very well supported by Roger Binny in a stand of 53 so that New Zealand's target looked far bigger than expected. They were disturbed by interruptions for rain which reduced their goal to 190 in 45 overs, but the innings never achieved any rhythm or direction and they fell well short.

Final Table

	P	W	L	NR	Pts	Run rate
Australia	10	6	3	1	13	4.27
India	10	5	5	—	10	4.24
New Zealand	10	3	6	1	7	4.31

(In accordance with ACB ruling, run rates do not include the abandoned match)

FIFTEENTH ONE-DAY INTERNATIONAL – NEW ZEALAND v. INDIA
2 February 1986 at Launceston

INDIA			
S.M. Gavaskar	c McSweeney, b Hadlee	1
K. Srikkanth	lbw, b Snedden	22
M.B. Amarnath	c McSweeney, b Gillespie	24
A.O. Malhotra	c Snedden, b Gillespie	39
M. Azharuddin	c McSweeney, b M.D. Crowe	3
R.J. Shastri	b Snedden	23
R.N. Kapil Dev†	lbw, b Gillespie	2
Chetan Sharma	not out	38
R.M.H. Binny	lbw, b Hadlee	24
R.R. Kulkarni	c Gillespie, b Chatfield	9
K.S. More*	not out	1
Extras	lb 7, w 7, nb 2	16
(48 overs)	(for 9 wickets)	202

	O	M	R	W
Hadlee	10	5	17	2
Chatfield	9	—	43	1
Gillespie	9	—	54	3
Snedden	10	—	46	2
M.D. Crowe	10	2	35	1

FALL OF WICKETS
1- 1, 2- 52, 3- 56, 4- 64, 5- 119, 6- 127, 7- 127, 8- 180, 9-199

NEW ZEALAND			
J.J. Crowe	c Kulkarni, b Binny	3
B.A. Edgar	c More, b Shastri	26
M.D. Crowe	c and b Binny	10
J.F. Reid	b Kulkarni	37
J.V. Coney†	c Shastri, b Kapil Dev	37
R.J. Hadlee	c Azharuddin, b Chetan Sharma	5
B.R. Blair	c Srikkanth, b Binny	19
E.B. McSweeney*	b Kapil Dev	0
M.C. Snedden	c Binny, b Kapil Dev	1
S.R. Gillespie	not out	15
E.J. Chatfield	not out	0
Extras	lb 8, w 7	15
(45 overs)	(for 9 wickets)	168

	O	M	R	W
Kapil Dev	9	1	26	3
Binny	9	1	26	3
Chetan Sharma	9	1	35	1
Shastri	9	—	33	1
Kulkarni	9	—	40	1

FALL OF WICKETS
1- 7, 2- 27, 3- 48, 4- 102, 5- 113, 6- 135, 7- 135, 8- 147, 9-163

India won by 21 runs

31 January, 1, 2 and 3 February 1986

at Brisbane

Queensland 365 (K.C. Wessels 167, R.B. Phillips 71, W.W. Davis 7 for 128) and 109 for 4
Tasmania 194 (R.E. Soule 51 not out, G.S. Trimble 5 for 50) and 278 (R.J. Bennett 110, D.J. Buckingham 62)

Queensland won by 6 wickets
Queensland 12 pts, Tasmania 0 pts

Queensland were 89 for 5 before Wessels and Ray Phillips put on 180. Wessels passed 5,000 first-class runs for Queensland who were given a boost when Tazelaar, in his second match for the state, and Thomson added 56 for the last wicket. Davis and Brown shared the wickets for Tasmania, Davis returning his best figures for the islanders. Trimble took 5 wickets in an innings for the first time and Tasmania were forced to follow-on. They were 73 for 4 in their second innings, but Buckingham and Bennett, who reached his maiden first-class century, added 123. Buckingham and Hyatt added another 68, but Tasmania's last 5 wickets fell for 14 runs, and Queensland had a chance of victory. They grabbed the chance by scoring at six an over. Phillips held 8 catches in the match.

With each side having two matches to play, Queensland led the Sheffield Shield table with 54 points. New South Wales were second with 40. Western Australia had 34, Victoria 28 and South Australia 24.

Benson and Hedges World Series

First Final
AUSTRALIA v. INDIA

Put in to bat on a pitch which gave the bowlers some assistance, Australia were restricted to 170 in an innings which was reduced to 44 overs by a thunderstorm. Boon was badly dropped by Gavaskar at slip before he had scored. The former Indian captain damaged a hand and had to leave the field. Boon and Marsh went on to give another impressive opening partnership which was ended when Marsh drove Azharuddin, bowling gentle medium pace, to mid-on. Wellham was bowled trying to run a good length ball to third man, and Border was magnificently caught at deep mid-wicket. Jones played some useful shots, and Zoehrer, named for the side to go to New Zealand and playing his first international match, gave useful support.

India started badly. Srikkanth, out of touch, was bowled in the second over, and Shastri was caught behind playing back. Amarnath was well caught, low at extra cover, and when Azharuddin was bowled by an off-break which went between bat and pad, India were 52 for 4. Vengsarkar began badly, but he was showing some elegant form when he played a wild shot and skied to cover. Kapil Dev played an even worse shot, attempting to hit the first ball he received for six and being bowled. Border effected some good control and India slipped noiselessly to defeat.

Benson and Hedges World Series

Second Final
AUSTRALIA v. INDIA

Australia duly won the Benson and Hedges World Series when they beat India with ease in the second final match at Melbourne. It was some small consolation for what had been a wretched year for Australian cricket.

A crowd of 72,192 saw Border win the toss and ask India to bat first on a pitch that was moist at the outset and allowed the Australian bowlers to obtain both bounce and movement. Gavaskar and Srikkanth began sedately and looked to

BENSON AND HEDGES WORLD SERIES FIRST FINAL – AUSTRALIA v. INDIA
5 February 1986 at Sydney

AUSTRALIA				INDIA			
D.C. Boon	c Malhotra, b Shastri	50		R.J. Shastri	c Zoehrer, b Davis	8
G.R. Marsh	c Chetan Sharma, b Azharuddin	36		K. Srikkanth	b Davis	0
D.M. Wellham	b Amarnath	6		M.B. Amarnath	c Marsh, b Matthews	13
A.R. Border†	c Azharuddin, b Shastri	12		D.B. Vengsarkar	c Jones, b Waugh	45
D.M. Jones	not out	30		M. Azharuddin	b Matthews	1
S.R. Waugh	b Azharuddin	1		S.M. Gavaskar	c Jones, b Border	32
G.R.J. Matthews	run out	7		R.N. Kapil Dev†	b Matthews	0
T.J. Zoehrer*	b Kapil Dev	11		A.O. Malhotra	c and b Border	12
C.J. McDermott	run out	0		Chetan Sharma	not out	19
B.A. Reid	not out	4		R.M.H. Binny	b Border	16
S.P. Davis				K.S. More*	b Davis	2
Extras	b 1, lb 6, w 2, nb 4	13		Extras	b 2, lb 6, w 2, nb 1	11
	(44 overs) (for 8 wickets)	170			(43.4 overs)	159

	O	M	R	W		O	M	R	W
Kapil Dev	9	2	21	1	McDermott	5	—	26	—
Binny	7	—	30	—	Davis	7.4	3	10	3
Chetan Sharma	5	—	34	—	Reid	9	2	34	—
Amarnath	5	—	21	1	Matthews	9	—	27	3
Shastri	9	—	31	2	Waugh	8	1	31	1
Azharuddin	9	—	26	2	Border	5	—	23	3

FALL OF WICKETS
1- 69, 2- 86, 3- 110, 4- 118, 5- 122, 6- 135, 7- 164, 8- 164

FALL OF WICKETS
1- 4, 2- 11, 3- 40, 4- 52, 5- 82, 7- 112, 8- 126, 9- 149

Australia won by 11 runs

BENSON AND HEDGES WORLD SERIES SECOND FINAL – AUSTRALIA v. INDIA
9 February 1986 at Melbourne

INDIA			
S.M. Gavaskar	c Border, b Davis	11
K. Srikkanth	c and b Matthews	37
M.B. Amarnath	handled ball	15
D.B. Vengsarkar	b Matthews	41
R.N. Kapil Dev†	c Zoehrer, b Reid	1
M. Azharuddin	run out	14
R.J. Shastri	run out	49
Chetan Sharma	run out	0
R.M.H. Binny	c and b Reid	4
K.S. More*	run out	1
S.N. Yadav	not out	1
Extras	lb 7, w 4, nb 2	13
	(50 overs)	187

AUSTRALIA			
D.C. Boon	run out	44
G.R. Marsh	lbw, b Kapil Dev	9
D.M. Wellham	c Azharuddin, b Kapil Dev	43
A.R. Border†	not out	65
D.M. Jones	not out	19
S.R. Waugh		
G.R.J. Matthews		
T.J. Zoehrer*		
C.J. McDermott		
B.A. Reid		
S.P. Davis		
Extras	b 1, lb 2, w 5	8
	(47.2 overs) (for 3 wickets)	188

	O	M	R	W
McDermott	10	—	35	—
Davis	10	1	23	1
Reid	10	—	37	2
Matthews	10	1	37	2
Border	7	—	33	—
Waugh	3	—	15	—

	O	M	R	W
Kapil Dev	9	1	26	2
Binny	2	—	13	—
Chetan Sharma	8.2	—	42	—
Azharuddin	8	—	37	—
Yadav	10	—	27	—
Shastri	10	—	40	—

FALL OF WICKETS
1-34, 2-66, 3-70, 4-71, 5-108, 6-151, 7-151, 8-163, 9-168

FALL OF WICKETS
1-31, 2-77, 3-144

Australia won by 7 wickets

Benson and Hedges World Series – Averages

AUSTRALIA BATTING

	M	Inns	NOs	Runs	HS	Av	100s	50s
D.M. Jones	4	4	2	135	53	67.50		1
D.C. Boon	12	11		418	83	38.00		4
S.R. Waugh	12	10	3	266	81	38.00		2
G.R. Marsh	10	10		344	125	34.40	1	1
D.M. Wellham	3	3	1	61	43	30.50		
A.R. Border	12	11	1	284	65*	28.40		3
G.R.J. Matthews	11	9	2	131	46*	18.71		
G.M. Ritchie	7	6		106	68	17.66		1
W.B. Phillips	10	9	2	109	28	15.57		
D.R. Gilbert	9	5	2	29	8	9.66		
C.J. McDermott	12	9	3	47	24*	7.83		
S.P. Davis	12	2	1	6	6	6.00		
B.A. Reid	12	4	2	10	4*	5.00		
G.S. Trimble	2	2	1	4	4	2.00		

Played in two matches: D.W. Hookes 5; T.J. Zoehrer 11

INDIA BATTING

	M	Inns	NOs	Runs	HS	Av	100s	50s
S.M. Gavaskar	10	10	1	385	92*	42.77		4
D.B. Vengsarkar	8	8	1	283	77*	40.42		1
Chetan Sharma	12	8	4	124	38*	31.00		
M.B. Amarnath	11	11	1	309	74	30.90		3
R.J. Shastri	12	9	1	202	55	25.25		1
M. Azharuddin	12	11	3	188	69*	23.50		1
R.N. Kapil Dev	12	11	2	202	54*	22.44		1
K. Srikkanth	12	12		219	50	18.25		1
A.O. Malhotra	8	7		125	39	17.85		
R.R. Kulkarni	3	2	1	14	9	14.00		
R.M.H. Binny	11	6		64	24	10.66		
K.S. More	10	6	2	7	2	1.75		

Played in four matches: L. Sivaramakrishnan 2*; S.N. Yadav 0* & 1*
Played in two matches: S.M.H. Kirmani 27
Played in one match: R.S. Ghai 1

AUSTRALIA BOWLING

	Overs	Mds	Runs	Wkts	Av	Best	5/inn
S.P. Davis	102.1	20	299	18	16.61	3/10	
A.R. Border	16	—	74	3	24.66	3/23	
B.A. Reid	109	7	428	17	25.17	5/53	1
D.R. Gilbert	78	2	376	13	28.92	5/46	1
G.R.J. Matthews	78	2	290	9	32.22	3/27	
S.R. Waugh	53	4	231	7	33.00	2/28	
C.J. McDermott	101.1	10	383	10	38.30	3/20	

Also bowled: G.S. Trimble 4-0-32-0; G.R. Marsh 1-0-4-0

INDIA BOWLING

	Overs	Mds	Runs	Wkts	Av	Best	5/inn
R.N. Kapil Dev	113	17	391	20	19.55	4/30	
R.M.H. Binny	77	1	490	17	28.82	3/26	
R.J. Shastri	116	6	404	12	33.66	2/31	
R.R. Kulkarni	28	2	121	3	40.33	2/28	
M.B. Amarnath	39	1	163	4	40.75	1/21	
S.N. Yadav	34	1	153	3	51.00	2/51	
M. Azharuddin	27	—	117	2	58.00	2/26	
L. Sivarama-krishnan	23	1	127	1	127.00	1/37	

Also bowled: R.S. Ghai 10-1-54-1

AUSTRALIA CATCHES
13 - W.B. Phillips (ct 12/st 1); 11 - A.R. Border; 6 - G.R.J. Matthews; 4 - G.R. Marsh; 3 - C.J. McDermott and D.M. Jones; 2 - D.C. Boon, S.R. Waugh, D.R. Gilbert and T.J. Zoehrer; 1 - G.M. Ritchie, S.P. Davis, B.A. Reid and D.M. Wellham

INDIA CATCHES
8 - M. Azharuddin; 7 - R.N. Kapil Dev; 6 - K.S. More (ct 5/st 1); 5 - S.M. Gavaskar; 4 - M.B. Amarnath & D.B. Vengsarkar; 3 - K. Srikkanth, R.J. Shastri & A.O. Malhotra; 2 - R.M.H. Binny, Chetan Sharma, S.M.H. Kirmani & R.R. Kulkarni; 1 - L. Sivaramakrishnan

have negotiated the early problems when Gavaskar fended a short ball from Davis to Border at short-leg. Srikkanth advanced down the wicket to drive Matthews with great power only for the bowler to change direction and complete a remarkable low catch. Four runs later, Amarnath played half forward to Matthews, hit the ball hard into the ground and, as it bounced back towards the stumps, brushed it away with his hand. He turned and walked away without looking at the umpire, the first batsman to be out 'handled ball' in limited over cricket. Kapil Dev again failed, but Vengsarkar batted well amid the carnage of run outs as quick runs were sought, and Shastri gave the end of the innings necessary substance. Nevertheless, the total of 187 looked unlikely to worry the Australians.

Marsh was lbw playing half forward, but Boon, Wellham and Border blunted the threat of the spinners with skilful batting, and Australia won with plenty to spare in both overs and wickets.

The ebullient Matthews crowned his memorable season by being named as Man of the Series.

NEW ZEALAND BATTING

	M	Inns	NOs	Runs	HS	Av	100s	50s
J.V. Coney	10	10	2	278	58	34.75		1
M.D. Crowe	10	10		330	76	33.00		3
R.J. Hadlee	10	10	3	199	71	28.42		1
B.R. Blair	5	5	2	79	29*	26.33		1
B.A. Edgar	10	10		252	75	25.20		2
J.J. Crowe	8	8	1	158	63	22.57		1
J.G. Wright	9	9		182	61	20.22		1
J.F. Reid	8	8		133	37	16.62		
E.J. Chatfield	10	5	4	9	4*	9.00		
J.G. Bracewell	6	5		38	20	7.60		
S.R. Gillespie	8	5	1	27	15*	6.75		
E.B. McSweeney	10	9	3	26	6	4.33		
M.C. Snedden	3	2	1	1	1	1.00		

Played in three matches: S.L. Boock 0

NEW ZEALAND BOWLING

	Overs	Mds	Runs	Wkts	Av	Best	5/inn
M.C. Snedden	24	2	89	5	17.80	3/23	
E.J. Chatfield	84.2	19	261	14	18.64	4/28	
R.J. Hadlee	82.1	16	282	15	18.80	3/14	
S.R. Gillespie	68.1	8	265	13	20.38	4/30	
J.G. Bracewell	40.3	4	172	6	28.66	2/3	
B.R. Blair	5	—	34	1	34.00	1/7	
M.D. Crowe	40	4	149	3	49.66	1/16	
S.L. Boock	18	—	106	1	106.00	1/55	
J.V. Coney	41	1	197	1	197.00	1/18	

NEW ZEALAND CATCHES

11 - E.B. McSweeney (ct 10/st 1); 7 - J.V. Coney; 6 - M.D. Crowe; 5 - J.G. Wright; 3 - J.G. Bracewell; 2 - E.J. Chatfield, J.J. Crowe, S.R. Gillespie & M.C. Snedden; 1 - J.F. Reid

McDonald's Cup

Semi-Finals

15 February 1986

at Sydney

New South Wales 191 for 9 (P.S. Clifford 73)
Victoria 194 for 6 (P.W. Young 97 not out)

Victoria won by 4 wickets

16 February 1986

at Brisbane

Queensland 212 (R.B. Kerr 74, T.J. Barsby 55 not out)
Western Australia 214 for 3 (M.R.J. Veletta 105 not out)
Western Australia won by 7 wickets

The least fancied sides won their way to the final in excellent fashion, and in each case, the winning side was indebted to a fine individual performance. In Sydney, where Jackson and Dodemaide bowled impressively for Victoria, New South Wales struggled to find their touch, and it was only a good knock from Peter Clifford which took them close to the two hundred. Whitney captured both openers, Whatmore and Ephraims, cheaply, but Dean Jones and Peter Young turned the course of the game, and Young's fine innings won him the individual award.

Queensland batted solidly in the middle order after Courtice had been run out at 7, but Porter and Macleay exerted the strictest economy and the home side were all out with 8 balls of their 50 overs unused. Veletta dominated an opening stand of 107 with Moody and batted magnificently as Western Australia rushed to victory with 6 overs to spare.

21, 22, 23 and 24 February 1986

at Adelaide

South Australia 303 for 8 dec (D.J. Kelly 82, D.W. Hookes 62) and 211 (D. Hickey 7 for 81)
Victoria 250 (A.I.C. Dodemaide 80, A.K. Zesers 4 for 46) and 268 for 2 (M.B. Quinn 103, D.F. Whatmore 84, D.M. Jones 57 not out)
Victoria won by 8 wickets
Victoria 8 pts, South Australia 4 pts

at Perth

Western Australia 322 (G.M. Wood 121) and 195 for 2 (M.R.J. Veletta 78 not out, P. Gonnella 61)
Queensland 319 (A.B. Henschell 110, T.J. Barsby 67, T. Breman 6 for 76)
Match drawn
Western Australia 4 pts, Queensland 0 pts

at Sydney

Tasmania 210 (E. Harris 57) and 107 (R.G. Holland 5 for 25)
New South Wales 364 (S.M. Small 118, G.C. Dyer 59, M.J. Bennett 57 not out, M. Ray 5 for 79, W.W. Davis 4 for 105)
New South Wales won by an innings and 47 runs
New South Wales 12 pts, Tasmania 0 pts

Tasmania's wretched form continued as they went down by an innings in Sydney. New South Wales' win took them to within two points of Queensland who gained nothing from the game in Perth where there was no play on the first day. This was the first time for 31 years that a full day's play had been lost in Perth. Wood continued his impressive form as a number 4, and he also gave further indication of his value as skipper to the young and rapidly improving Western Australian side. Breman took five wickets in an innings for the first time and Queensland were saved from total disaster by Henschell and Barsby who added 145 for the sixth wicket. Cox made his first-class debut as Western Australia's wicket-keeper.

There were two debutants at Sydney, Cruse of Tasmania and P. Taylor of New South Wales. Ray returned a career best bowling performance for Tasmania, but the home side was always on top except for a middle order slump after Small and M. Taylor had begun their innings with a stand of 96. The last 4 wickets produced 149 runs. At their second attempt, Tasmania collapsed to Bob Holland's leg-spin.

Hickey had the best bowling performance of his career at Adelaide and, with 10 wickets in the match, turned probable defeat into victory. South Australia were 151 for 6, but Kelly and Plummer, on his debut, added 108, and Hookes was able to declare. Zesers and Parkinson bowled South Australia to a first innings lead of 53, but then Hickey struck. Whatmore and Quinn made light of Victoria's task of scoring 265 to win when they launched their side on the way to the target with a stand of 139. Jones then joined Quinn in a second wicket stand of 122 which ended when Quinn was run out having just completed his maiden first-class hundred. Dimattina, most unlucky not to have claimed the wicket-keeping spot in the national side, took 9 catches in the match, 6 of them off Hickey in the second innings.

28 February, 1, 2 and 3 March 1986

at Devonport

Tasmania 241 (M.G. Hughes 5 for 53, S.P. O'Donnell 4 for 52) and 115 (D. Hickey 5 for 52, M.G. Hughes 4 for 23)
Victoria 326 for 6 dec (P.A. Hibbert 124, D.M. Jones 70, J.D. Siddons 57) and 31 for 1

Victoria won by 9 wickets
Victoria 12 pts, Tasmania 0 pts

Macleay and Zoehrer, later to become Australia's wicket-keeper, appeal for lbw against Hibbert, Western Australia v. Victoria, at Melbourne. (Philip Tyson)

at Sydney

Queensland 339 (R.B. Kerr 102, K.C. Wessels 93, T.J. Barsby 56 not out, R.G. Holland 5 for 92) and 96 for 3
New South Wales 440 (M.D. O'Neill 117, M. Taylor 89, R.J. Bower 57)

Match drawn
New South Wales 4 pts, Queensland 0 pts

at Perth

South Australia 432 (P.R. Sleep 139, J. Pyke 77) and 181 for 8 dec (G.A. Bishop 50)
Western Australia 433 for 6 dec (M.R.J. Veletta 107, R. Gartrell 92, W.S. Andrews 82) and 128 for 8 (G.M. Wood 64 not out, J. Pyke 4 for 27, G.C. Small 4 for 47)

Match drawn
Western Australia 4 pts, South Australia 0 pts

A second wicket stand of 167 between Wessels and Kerr was followed by the loss of 7 wickets for 61 runs, and Queensland must have been a little disappointed in their final total of 339. New South Wales lost M. Taylor and Wellham for 48, but stands of 99, 92 and 99 followed, and, with O'Neill hitting his third hundred of the season, the home side took first innings points and so climbed above Queensland in the table to gain home advantage for the Sheffield Shield Final. Sri Lankan born Malcolm Francke, the 44-year old leg-spinner, again bowled tidily for Queensland. He had been recalled for the match against New South Wales at the end of January, having been absent from the state side for six years.

Victoria finished on a high note and clambered above Western Australia into third spot after the second successive victory under Dean Jones's captaincy. Jones himself took over as wicket-keeper after Dimattina had injured a finger

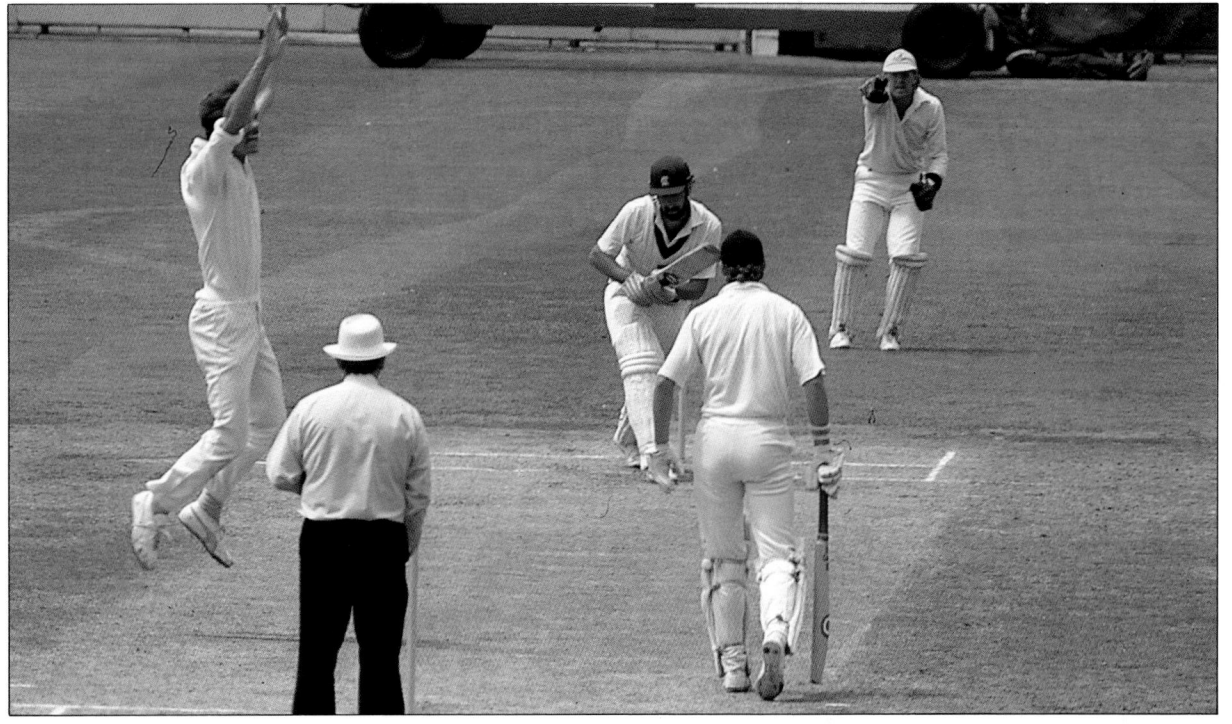

and took 3 catches. Simon O'Donnell happily reappeared after his injury and gathered something from his disappointing season as he joined with Hughes and Hickey in demoralising Tasmania. Hibbert again showed his worth and Tasmania's miserable year came to an end with Bradshaw and Cooley both having a 'pair', Cooley's second in as many matches, and Hyatt being forced to retire hurt.

South Australia gave a first-class debut to Pyke, and he had a fine all-round match. Sleep hit his third century of the summer, but Veletta's hundred and a sparkling stand of 167 with Gartrell, followed by an unbeaten stand of 95 between Andrews and Breman gave Western Australia the first innings points. South Australia batted briskly in an effort to obtain a result, and, in scoring 28 before he was stumped, David Hookes just passed a thousand runs for the season. Led by Wood, the home side made a bold effort to score 181 in 31 overs that were needed for victory, but they slumped and it was the visitors who nearly snatched a win.

Sheffield Shield – Final Table

	P	W	L	D	1st inns lead	Pts
New South Wales	10	4	1	5	6	56
Queensland	10	4	—	6	5	54
Victoria	10	2	1	7	8	48
Western Australia	10	2	1	7	6	42
South Australia	10	2	4	4	3	28
Tasmania	10	—	7	3	1	4

(Western Australia & Queensland 2 points each for match in which first innings lead not decided)

McDonald's Cup Final
VICTORIA v. WESTERN AUSTRALIA

The final of the McDonald's Cup was scheduled for 9 March, but the first game was abandoned because of rain after 26.2 overs. Western Australia had scored 129 for 2 in that time, with Veletta on 67 not out.

A new game was started the following day, and the sides were unchanged from those originally selected.

With Hickey very much the pace bowler in form, Western Australia were reduced to 37 for 5, and the young quick bowler's performance in capturing the first five wickets was to earn him the individual award. Andrews and Cox, an impressive understudy for Zoehrer, salvaged the visitors' hopes with a stand of 80 which exposed Victoria's Achilles heel, the lack of a fifth bowler of substance. Jones used himself and Parker to bowl 8 overs between them, but they conceded 53 runs, a decisive weakness in a low scoring match.

It was Jones who broke the sixth wicket stand when he bowled Cox, and the last 3 wickets fell as batsmen scampered for suicidal runs. Victoria's task of scoring 168 at 4.2 an over did not look too daunting.

They were given a solid start by Whatmore and Ephraims, but Matthews bowled tightly, and Porter, a forgotten man since the World Cup of 1979, effectively stifled the middle order as they pressed for runs. Wood handled his resources well and thwarted any attempt that Victoria made to reach the required run rate. Siddons and Dodemaide gave brief hope to the home side, but the issue was never really in doubt, and Western Australia were comfortable winners in a final in which the bowlers used the conditions to good advantage.

McDONALD'S CUP FINAL – VICTORIA v. WESTERN AUSTRALIA
10 March 1986 at Melbourne

WESTERN AUSTRALIA			
T. Moody	c Dodemaide, b Hickey	14
M.R.J. Veletta	c Jones, b Hickey	0
P. Gonnella	c Siddons, b Hickey	8
G.M. Wood†	c Ephraims, b Hickey	0
R. Gartrell	c Whatmore, b Hickey	1
W.S. Andrews	c Siddons, b Hughes	71
M. Cox*	b Jones	38
T. Breman	run out	10
K.H. MacLeay	not out	11
G.D. Porter	run out	0
C.R. Matthews	run out	1
Extras	lb 6, w 5, nb 2	13
(38 overs)		167

	O	M	R	W
Hickey	8	2	26	5
O'Donnell	8	—	41	—
Parker	4	—	30	—
Hughes	7	1	24	1
Dodemaide	7	3	17	—
Jones	4	—	23	1

FALL OF WICKETS
1- 2, 2- 18, 3- 18, 4- 19, 5- 37, 6- 117, 7- 140, 8- 164, 9- 165

VICTORIA			
D.F. Whatmore	c Wood, b Porter	34
M. Ephraims	c MacLeay, b Matthews	21
D.M. Jones†	c Veletta, b Breman	0
P.W. Young	run out	17
J.D. Siddons	b Porter	22
S.P. O'Donnell	c Wood, b Moody	2
A.I.C. Dodemaide	c Gartrell, b MacLeay	25
G. Parker	c Cox, b Porter	0
M.G. Dimattina*	c and b Moody	3
M.G. Hughes	not out	9
D. Hickey	run out	2
Extras	b 2, lb 7, w 3, nb 1	13
(36.5 overs)		148

	O	M	R	W
Matthews	8	2	16	1
Porter	8	—	28	3
Moody	8	1	35	2
MacLeay	5.5	—	30	1
Breman	7	1	30	1

FALL OF WICKETS
1- 34, 2- 38, 3- 78, 4- 82, 5- 106, 6- 108, 7- 108, 8- 111, 9- 143

Western Australia won by 19 runs

Sheffield Shield Final
NEW SOUTH WALES v. QUEENSLAND

The Australian season ended with an exciting Sheffield Shield Final which marked the close of Jeff Thomson's great career. The fast bowler had announced that this was to be his last first-class match, but there was to be no fairy tale ending. Thomson bowled the penultimate over of the game, but he was unable to break through, and the draw enabled New South Wales to retain the title. Both sides were without leading players who were with the Australian party in New Zealand.

Courtice, who had not enjoyed a good season, and Kerr had seemed to negotiate the new ball when Courtice fell to first change bowler Bower. Kerr and Wessels set about restoring the foundations of the innings in determined fashion. They added 107 before Kerr was caught off Whitney, and the fast bowler, who is best remembered for having been drafted into the Australian side in England in 1981, struck two more quick blows when he dismissed both Smart and Barsby without scoring. At 148 for 4, Queensland were in peril. Trimble stayed with Wessels until the end of the day when the Queensland acting captain had reached 103 and his side 208 for 4.

Trimble and Wessels extended their stand to 179 the next day, and Wessels passed a thousand runs for the season before becoming another Whitney victim. Trimble chose the occasion to reach his maiden first-class century, and with Henschell making a good contribution, Queensland reached an impressive 436, a total which had looked highly improbable mid way through the first day.

Helped by a spray of no-balls, New South Wales closed at 58 for 1, and night-watchman Bennett stayed until the score reached 95, but a mid-order collapse saw the reigning champions slip to 149 for 6. Dyer and Waugh then played the role that Trimble and Wessels had played for Queensland, and they were together at the close with New South Wales 246. Mark Waugh went early on the third morning, but Dyer guarded the tail well and the home side scrambled to 294, a deficit of 142.

Queensland needed quick runs in order to give their bowlers ample time in which to dismiss the opposition. In effect, New South Wales were given 431 minutes, 112 overs, in which to make 276. They began well enough, but 4 wickets fell in quick succession, and the balance tipped in favour of Queensland. Wellham and Mark Waugh appeared to be righting the situation when 2 more wickets fell within the space of a few balls. Still New South Wales pressed for victory, but the loss of Taylor ended their hopes, and a draw satisfied honour although it once again deprived Queensland of the Shield.

Allan Border was named as Sheffield Shield player of the

SHEFFIELD SHIELD FINAL – NEW SOUTH WALES v. QUEENSLAND
14, 15, 17 and 18 March 1986 at Sydney Cricket Ground

QUEENSLAND

	FIRST INNINGS		SECOND INNINGS	
B.A. Courtice	c Dyer, b Bower	8	(2) st Dyer, b Bennett	22
R.B. Kerr	c M. Taylor, b Whitney	64	(1) st Dyer, b Bennett	34
K.C. Wessels†	c Dyer, b Whitney	166	c Small, b P. Taylor	29
C.B. Smart	c M. Taylor, b Whitney	0	(5) b P. Taylor	2
T.J. Barsby	c Dyer, b Whitney	0	(7) c M. Taylor, b P. Taylor	10
G.S. Trimble	b Waugh	112	(4) run out	0
A.B. Henschell	not out	44	(6) not out	20
R.B. Phillips*	c M. Taylor, b P. Taylor	5	c Bower, b P. Taylor	6
H. Frei	c Small, b Whitney	1	not out	1
J.R. Thomson	c Dyer, b Whitney	0		
D. Tazelaar	not out	3		
Extras	b 6, lb 8, w 1, nb 18	33	lb 2, w 3, nb 4	9
	(for 9 wkts dec)	436	(for 7 wkts dec)	133

	O	M	R	W	O	M	R	W
Whitney	34	7	65	6	10	4	14	—
Waugh	27	4	71	1	5	—	25	—
Bower	7	1	28	1				
Holland	39	9	92	—	5	—	25	—
Bennett	27	5	65	—	13	—	36	2
P. Taylor	25	3	78	1	13	1	31	4
O'Neill	6	1	23	—				

NEW SOUTH WALES

	FIRST INNINGS		SECOND INNINGS	
S.M. Small	c Courtice, b Frei	39	c Kerr, b Wessels	50
M. Taylor	c Phillips, b Tazelaar	41	c Phillips, b Frei	30
M.J. Bennett	c Phillips, b Tazelaar	11	(9) not out	2
D.M. Wellham†	lbw, b Henschell	7	(3) run out	80
R.J. Bower	c Tazelaar, b Frei	3	(4) c Phillips, b Tazelaar	12
M.D. O'Neill	b Henschell	20	(5) c Phillips, b Henschell	1
M. Waugh	c Phillips, b Thomson	41	(6) c Smart, b Wessels	24
G.C. Dyer*	not out	88	(7) run out	0
P. Taylor	c Smart, b Thomson	0	(8) lbw, b Tazelaar	42
R.G. Holland	lbw, b Thomson	5	not out	0
M.R. Whitney	c Smart, b Tazelaar	0		
Extras	b 4, lb 4, w 1, nb 30	39	b 3, lb 3, w 2, nb 9	17
		294	(for 8 wickets)	258

	O	M	R	W	O	M	R	W
Thomson	29	3	91	3	19	5	41	—
Frei	37	7	87	2	26	8	71	1
Tazelaar	22	4	48	3	20	6	57	2
Henschell	19	2	48	2	29	13	45	1
Trimble	2	—	12	—	2	—	12	—
Wessels					16	5	26	2

FALL OF WICKETS
1- 34, 2- 141, 3- 148, 4- 148, 5- 327, 6- 412, 7- 424, 8- 426, 9- 427
1- 62, 2- 71, 3- 71, 4- 85, 5- 106, 6- 122, 7- 131

FALL OF WICKETS
1- 53, 2- 95, 3- 112, 4- 116, 5- 124, 6- 149, 7- 248, 8- 251, 9- 264
1- 64, 2- 97, 3- 115, 4- 116, 5- 182, 6- 184, 7- 254, 8- 254

Match drawn

year although, great batsman that the Australian captain is, it was hard to justify the award as he had not played in the competition since 23 December. Simon Davis and Mike Veletta finished joint second on points, but most people's real hero of the Shield, Roger Brown, the Tasmanian lion-hearted toiler, was in third place.

Esso scholarships, a summer's cricket in England, were awarded to Keith Bradshaw of Tasmania who was to go to Sussex, Mark Waugh of New South Wales to M.C.C., Glenn Trimble of Queensland to Essex, and Dennis Hickey, Victoria's exciting paceman, to Glamorgan. Their progress will be noted with care. It had not been a good year for Australian cricket, and the talents of these four young men, and several others, will be very much needed in the next few years.

First-Class Averages

BATTING

	M	Inns	NOs	Runs	HS	Av	100s	50s
M.D. O'Neill	6	9	2	588	178*	84.00	3	
A.R. Border	11	19	2	1247	194	73.35	6	3
G.M. Wood	10	15	3	741	133	61.75	3	5
P.A. Hibbert	10	16	3	695	148	53.46	3	2
G.R.J. Matthews	11	19	2	890	184	52.35	4	1
R. Gartrell	4	8	2	313	104	52.16	1	1
G.R. Marsh	8	14	3	563	138	51.18	2	2
D.C. Boon	9	17	1	818	196	51.12	3	3
M. Taylor	12	20	1	937	118	49.31	2	5
K.C. Wessels	13	22	1	1030	167	49.00	3	4
C.L. Harms	4	6	3	145	43*	48.33		
G.A. Bishop	11	21	1	965	224*	48.25	3	2
D.W. Hookes	12	22	1	1001	243	47.66	3	3
M.R.J. Veletta	10	16	1	715	130	47.66	2	6
A.B. Henschell	11	17	7	460	110	46.00	1	1
P.R. Sleep	12	22	4	793	139	44.05	3	2
G.M. Ritchie	11	20	3	738	128	43.41	1	4
S.M. Small	9	14		605	123	43.21	2	3
D.J. Buckingham	10	18	1	687	121	40.41	1	4
W.S. Andrews	10	14	2	482	139	40.16	1	1
D.F. Whatmore	11	18	1	676	127	39.76	2	4
P. Gonnella	5	9		354	134	39.33	1	
G.S. Trimble	11	19	3	606	112	37.87	1	3
S.R. Waugh	7	12	2	378	119*	37.80	2	
D.M. Jones	11	17	1	603	113	37.68	1	5
A. Watson	5	9		335	97	37.22		2
B.A. Courtice	12	20	3	614	112	36.11	2	2
S. Wundke	2	4		144	42	36.00		
E. Harris	5	10		348	118	34.80	1	1
J.D. Siddons	11	16		540	107	33.75	1	3
T. Moody	5	9		302	94	33.55		2
G.C. Dyer	12	17	2	503	88*	33.53		4
M.J. Bennett	12	18	9	300	57*	33.33		2
A.I.C. Dodemaide	10	15	4	361	80	32.81		2
R.B. Kerr	12	20	1	609	102	32.05	1	4
W.M. Darling	8	14	3	350	107*	31.81	1	2
D.J. Kelly	8	13		410	85	31.53		3
R.D. Woolley	10	18	2	490	124	30.62	1	2
P.S. Clifford	8	13		396	98	30.46		2
R.J. Bright	12	17	4	392	69	30.15		3
T.J. Barsby	6	9	2	209	67	29.85		2
M.B. Quinn	11	18		535	103	29.72	1	3
D.M. Wellham	12	19		562	86	29.57		4
R.J. Zadow	11	20	1	540	144	28.42	2	1
T. Breman	5	8	3	139	45*	27.80		
R.J. Bower	8	13		294	63	26.72		2
R.B. Phillips	12	15	3	320	77*	26.66		3
K.H. MacLeay	10	10	3	186	60	26.57		1
M.G. Dimattina	11	14	5	239	54*	26.55		1
T.J. Zoehrer	8	10	1	233	94*	25.88		1
W.B. Phillips	10	18	1	431	63	25.35		1
K.R. Bradshaw	10	18		450	112	25.00	1	2
R.J. Bennett	5	10		249	110	24.90	1	
G.F. Lawson	7	9		210	63	23.33		1
R.E. Soule	10	17	4	293	53	22.53		2
S.L. Saunders	5	8	1	151	51	21.57		1
C.B. Smart	5	9		190	133	21.11	1	
J.R. Thomson	12	9	4	105	24	21.00		
D.F.G. O'Connor	5	8	1	141	58	20.14		1
R.S. Hyatt	8	14	2	236	80	19.66		1
S.D.H. Parkinson	8	10	4	118	62	19.66		1
M. Ray	10	18		342	52	19.00		1
A.M.J. Hilditch	11	22	2	369	84*	18.45		2
G.J. Ireland	6	7		129	50	18.42		1
P.W. Young	5	7		124	37	17.71		
M. Waugh	7	11		167	41	15.18		
A.K. Zesers	12	17	4	182	32	14.00		
H. Frei	12	12	3	122	43	13.55		
C.J. McDermott	7	12		149	72	12.41		1
R.L. Brown	10	17	4	160	31	12.30		
M.G. Hughes	11	11	1	120	47	12.00		
G.C. Small	10	15	2	144	33	11.07		

(qualification – 100 runs, average 10.00)

BOWLING

	Overs	Mds	Runs	Wkts	Av	Best	10/m	5/inn
S.P. O'Donnell	126.5	37	281	14	20.07	5/52		2
D. Hickey	115.2	23	363	17	21.35	7/81	1	2
M.R. Whitney	195.3	43	483	22	21.95	6/65		1
S.P. Davis	241.1	74	550	25	22.00	6/19		3
T. Breman	147	38	382	17	22.47	6/76		1
C.R. Matthews	283.2	62	757	31	24.41	5/23		2
G.F. Lawson	248.5	65	513	21	24.42	4/79		
K.H. MacLeay	378.4	100	913	35	26.08	6/93		1
G.S. Trimble	263.2	59	759	29	26.17	5/50		1
M.J. Bennett	446.1	144	877	32	27.40	4/38		
D.R. Gilbert	290.3	63	794	28	28.35	4/16		
B.A. Reid	369.1	101	875	30	29.16	6/54		1
P.A. Blizzard	120	24	322	11	29.27	4/118		
M.G. Hughes	390	77	1125	37	30.40	5/53		2
G.C. Small	415.4	74	1244	39	31.89	7/42		2
G.R.J. Matthews	279.4	82	639	20	31.95	5/22		
M. Waugh	124.4	26	352	11	32.00	4/130		
D. Tazelaar	134	22	418	13	32.15	3/48		
R.G. Holland	661.4	214	1555	48	32.29	8/33	1	4
A.K. Zesers	563.3	169	1309	40	32.72	6/73		1
J.R. Thomson	372.3	49	1385	42	32.97	6/72		1
R.L. Brown	384.2	62	1365	41	33.29	7/80	1	1
S.D.H. Parkinson	261.3	52	913	27	33.81	6/56		1
W.W. Davis	287.5	70	768	22	34.90	7/128	1	1
R.J. Bright	499.5	171	1024	27	37.92	6/74		2
H. Frei	449.4	104	1216	32	38.00	4/71		
B. Mulder	214	64	590	15	39.33	6/125		1
C.J. McDermott	309.4	64	867	22	39.40	4/116		
M. Ray	230.2	62	585	14	41.78	5/79		1
T.B.A. May	246.5	56	670	15	44.66	4/67		
A.B. Henschell	305.2	84	774	16	48.37	2/26		
A.I.C. Dodemaide	336.2	92	888	18	49.33	4/151		
P.R. Sleep	289.2	61	943	17	55.47	3/71		

LEADING WICKET-KEEPERS
41 - R.B. Phillips; 38 - G.C. Dyer (ct 31/st 7); 36 - M.G. Dimattina (ct 34/st 2); 26 - T.J. Zoehrer (ct 22/st 4); 24 - W.B. Phillips; 23 - R.E. Soule; 17 - D.J. Kelly (ct 16/st 1)

LEADING FIELDERS
19 - D.W. Hookes; 17 - D.F. Whatmore; 15 - M. Taylor; 13 - K.C. Wessels; 11 - R.B. Kerr, G.A. Bishop and W.S. Andrews; 10 - M.R.J. Veletta and J.D. Siddons

THE SHEFFIELD SHIELD SEASON
1985/86
by Frank Tyson

In 13th-century England, the fanatical Flagellant sect beat themselves to appease the divine anger which they thought occasioned the Black Death. Seven hundred years later, Australian cricket punished itself in similar fashion to assuage the international wrath caused by its former skipper, Kim Hughes, leading a 'rebel' tour to the ostracised South Africa. The revolt of 14 individual players against its government's and the Australian Cricket Board's concurrence with the Gleneagles Agreement was made public in the *Australian* and *Adelaide Advertiser* newspapers of 13 April 1985. On 30 July, Mr D. L. Richards, the Executive Director of the A.C.B., announced that litigation between the Board and the 'rebels' about contractual agreements had been averted by a compromise between the 'legal eagles' of the A.C.B. and the South African Cricket Union – as a result of which, by mutual consent, the defectors would be banned from Australian first-class cricket for 3 years.

'Good riddance to "dead wood" and "has beens"', cried the zealots from the roof tops. More objective observers, however, were quick to realise that Australian cricket could not replace the ability and experience of Kim Hughes, Graham Yallop, John Dyson, Rodney Hogg, Terry Alderman, Carl Rackemann, Steve Rixon, John Maguire, Tom Hogan, Greg Shipperd and Rod McCurdy in a few short weeks. The dual effect of the A.C.B.'s masochistic act of self-denial was to rob the Australian Test team of its reserve strength and greatly reduce the depth of experience in Sheffield Shield ranks until 1987. The ban also produced two divergent reactions amongst state selectors: in some instances the knee-jerk response was to promote youthful ability, often prematurely, and, in more conservative councils, the decision was to fall back on tried-and-true old timers.

Thus the defection of New South Wales openers, Steve Smith and John Dyson, to the Cape, gave the young left-handed duet of Steve Small and Mark Taylor a regular chance to prove themselves. 'Keeper Rixon made way for Greg Dyer, who, within the space of months, had provided such proof of his potential that he earned a place in the Australian team to tour India in August 1986. New South Wales was fortunate – not only in its replacements for its South African truants – but also because its skipper, Dirk Wellham and spinner, Murray Bennett, who were originally contracted to the S.A.C.U., were lured back into the official fold at the last moment.

Queensland's loss of spearhead bowlers Rackemann and Maguire, compelled the state selectors to stick to the 'old faithfuls', Harry Frei and Jeff Thomson, to back up the young enthusiasm of Craig McDermott; at one stage in 1985/86 the northern state's bowling resources were so thin that it recalled the 44-year old leg-spinner, Malcolm Francke to the colours. In Victoria, Rodney Hogg, Mick Taylor and Graham Yallop's South African safari provided batsmen Jamie Siddons, Paul Young and pace bowler Dennis Hickey with extended trials in their state's first eleven. In Perth, Shipperd and Hughes' batting places went to Peter Gonnella, Gartrell and Tom Moody, whilst Wayne Andrew's spin substituted for that of Tom Hogan. The left-handed pace

pair of Bruce Reid and Chris Matthews more than made up for the loss of Terry Alderman. South Australia imported Warwickshire's West Indian speedster, Gladstone Small, to make good Rod McCurdy's loss and supported Small with the experienced left-handed medium-pacer, Sam Parkinson. The gap left in the middle-order batting by Michael Haysman's trip to the high veldt was filled by the re-emergence from retirement of the former Test all-rounder, Peter Sleep. Tasmania missed the many-faceted talents of Peter Faulkner, whose absence meant that more bowling responsibility devolved upon the shoulders of the island's professional recruit, West Indian Winston Davis, and Roger Brown. A substitute for Faulkner's batting was unearthed in opener, Errol Harris; but the Apple Island's season was not helped by the inability of the Tasmanian Cricket Council and Gloucestershire's resident Taswegian, Brian Davison, to agree on financial terms. Davison insisted upon a professional engagement and, when this was not forthcoming, chose to devote himself to his business interests rather than Tasmanian cricket.

By and large, most of the raw recruits and old regulars enjoyed their moments of glory in 1985/86. But there was no avoiding the observable fact that the South African defections left wounds which rendered the Sheffield Shield more anaemic. These wounds will take time to heal and the loss of a significant amount of Australia's playing life-blood tem-

Kepler Wessels – a century in the Sheffield Shield Final, but no victory. (George Herringshaw)

porarily lowered the country's international status. The timing of the South African defections could not have come at a worse time for Australian domestic cricket. In 1986, summit meetings between all sectors of the cricket community were convened in every state to discuss what can be done to revive spectator interest in the almost moribund Sheffield Shield competition; the loss of 14 top-class players to Dr Ali Bacher, Joe Pamensky and the S.A.C.U. will have done little to foster optimism about those councils finding any solutions.

New South Wales won its 39th Sheffield Shield premiership on 18 March 1986 – but only on a technicality. Queensland came within 2 wickets of victory in a drawn final, bereft of current Test players because of the concurrent Australian tour of New Zealand. If the match had been played to a conclusion, the northern state must surely have won its first Sheffield Shield. But by the quirk of a system, which insists on a deciding game but does not provide for it being played to a finish – and which then awards the trophy to the team which headed the premiership ladder at the end of the season – in spite of it losing on the first innings in the final – New South Wales became Sheffield Shield champs for the third time in four years!

Odd though this decision-making process is, Queensland itself, was once again largely responsible for its own defeat. It surrendered its chance of a home-ground advantage in the final by squandering an excellent start of 1/218 in its penultimate game, Wellham's team, thereby losing 4 vital first innings points and yielding up its leading position in the Shield table by 2 points. In the end, that loss cost the Brisbane side the trophy; but Wessels' men could still have salvaged their honour, had they not twice surrendered the initiative in the deciding game.

Batting first and far too slowly, Queensland occupied the crease until 4.30 p.m. on the second day. Acting skipper Wessels' amassed 166, passed the 1000-run mark for the season, and, abetted by Glenn Trimble's maiden Shield century and Robbie Kerr's 64, advanced his team's cause to 9/436. Queensland's bowlers made amends for their batsmen's tardiness by reducing New South Wales to a tottering first-innings total of 6/149. But once more they were unable to capitalize on their advantage and a seventh-wicket stand of 99 between 'keeper Dyer and Mark Waugh saved the home team from following on. Queensland's imaginative declaration at 7/133 in its second innings set New South Wales the feasible task of scoring 276 in 103 overs. At 6/254 the Sydneysiders were poised for victory; but when Wellham was run out for 80 and all-rounder, Peter Taylor, was LBW for 42, it was all that New South Wales could do to cling to the ropes at 8/258, save the round, and gain the referee's decision on points. A propos of referees, an ironic epilogue to the match was provided by Kepler Wessels who, speaking on behalf of the runners-up on television after the game, thanked the match referee, A.C.B. chairman, Fred Bennett, for enabling him to play most of the summer with his Queensland team-mates by offering him such disadvantageous terms to represent Australia that he refused them!

In the game which really decided the destination of the Shield in 1985/86 – the fixture between the two finalists in Sydney in late February – Kerr notched 102 and Wessels 93 in a Queensland total of 339 which should have been much

greater. Holland's leg-spin and Mark Waugh's medium-pace caused the Brisbane side to lose its last 9 wickets for 119; a first-innings collapse which opened the way for Mark O'Neill to barnstorm his way to his third hundred in as many games, and, helped by identical scores of 89 from Taylor and Bower, boost the New South Wales total to 440, thereby gaining the 4 points which took it into the lead in the table.

Mark O'Neill's late season form was one of the reasons behind New South Wales' finishing kick in the race for the premiership. The national averages placed him second only to Allan Border and gave honourable mentions to openers Mark Taylor and Steve Small. Taylor topped the Shield aggregates with 919 runs, whilst Small acquired his 705-run tally at the steady rate of 50.35 runs per innings. All-rounder, Matthews scored a big century in the first game of the season against Tasmania and apparently acquired a taste for 'tons' – scoring 2 more in Tests and 1 in the state game against the New Zealand tourists. Enterprising number 4 batsman, Peter Clifford slapped 2 fast 98s off the Tasmanian and Victorian attacks in the opening matches of the summer, but lost form dramatically after Christmas and eventually surrendered his place in the team to O'Neill. In the spin department, there was no combination in the land to compare with Holland, Bennett, Matthews and, towards the end of the season, off-spinner Peter Taylor and 'leggie' O'Neill. Maintaining the supply of new ball bowlers was, however, a continual thorn in the side of the New South Wales selectors. When he was not in the Test side, Lawson was injured; and Lawson's stressed fractures of the back caused the national panel to make increased demands upon Dave Gilbert's time after the Third Test against New Zealand in Perth. Phil Blizzard's left-handed medium-pace was not the complete answer to these losses, manfully though the former Taswegian strove. Nor did it help when Australia claimed the change-bowling skills of the gifted all-rounder, Steve Waugh. Fortunately for New South Wales, and with perfect timing, former Test bowler, Michael Whitney, announced that he had fully recovered from the leg injury which had sidelined him for over a season. This Messianic deliverance and Mark Waugh's enthusiastic speed sustained New South Wales until the end of the season.

The Sydneysiders travelled south to Van Deimen's Land for the first skirmish of the season, and experienced no difficulty in collecting 4 points. Matthews' career-best of 184, Steve Waugh's maiden century and Clifford's 98 – 52 of them in boundaries – were too much for the locals. New South Wales amassed 561 and although Tasmanian skipper, David Boon, played a lone hand for eight hours and 196 runs, his heroism could not avert a 132 run deficit on the first innings.

Victoria's visit to Newcastle provided one of the most crucial contests of the season. Footscray speedster, Merv Hughes, who was later to win his Australian cap in the Adelaide Test against India, restricted the home team's total to 232 with figures of 5/74: the best analysis from a Victorian bowler for 20 matches. The experience of former Test player, Whatmore produced 72 for the visitors and this score, together with 76 from the young country batsman, Jamie Siddons, put Victoria in command of the match, 76 runs ahead on the first innings. When medium-pacer, O'Donnell, showed a glimpse of the form which gained him a place in the 1985 touring team to England and took 5/66 to dismiss New South Wales a second time for only 244, the game seemed as good as over. With ample time at its disposal, Victoria needed only 169 runs for its first outright victory of the year. But the southern state had apparently forgotten how to win. It was bundled out in its second innings for 78 – its lowest score against New South Wales since 1926/27 – and consequently lost by 90 runs. The 8 points which Ray Bright's southerners literally handed to New South Wales on a plate could have placed Victoria at the head of the Sheffield Shield table when the final accounting was done. The loss of those points would certainly have deprived Wellham's men of their ultimate triumph.

The combination of the spinning S.C.G. pitch and the home team's plethora of slow bowlers won a maximum 24 points for New South Wales from its next two encounters against Western and South Australia. Graeme Wood's Perth team never had a chance from the moment that Wellham won the toss and batted. New South Wales' first-innings gambit of 286 was founded on half-centuries from the bats of Mark Taylor, Bower and Bennett and – on a deteriorating pitch – was a winning score. The young 'Sandgropers' had no answer to the finger spin of Bennett and Matthews and were headed on the first innings by 99. Wellham's 55 and Matthews' 49 extended the New South Welsh advantage to 256 on the third evening – at which stage the home side closed with 5 wickets down. Scoring 257 runs on a last day Sydney pitch was like reaching for the moon or striving for 500 runs under normal circumstances. Young Mike Valetta showed a capacity to combat the spinning ball which probably earned him a berth in the Aussie touring team to the Happy Hunting Ground of spin bowlers – India – at the end of the season. His 55 constituted more than half of his side's paltry second innings total of 105. Valetta's heroics were in vain and Western Australia lost by 151 runs – succumbing strangely enough in its second innings, not to the wiles of Holland, Matthews and Bennett, but rather to the speed of Gilbert and Lawson!

New South Wales' humiliation of South Australia by an innings and 115 runs was *fons et origo* attributable to the latter side's twin frailties of not being able to play spin and not possessing any effective spinners itself. In its first innings, the Adelaide team were in desperate straits at 4/39, when ex-Test batsman, Rick Darling, recently called in from the cold by the selectors, came to the crease. With superb timing, he compiled an innovative 97 which eventually inflated the South Australia total to 175 and denied spinners, Bob Holland and Murray Bennett, figures which would have bordered on the incredible. As it was, Holland appropriated 4/46 and Bennett 4/38. All speculation about the outcome of the game ended when Small and Taylor opened the New South Welsh bank account with a deposit of 143. Taylor received interest on his century and went on to 118, merging with Steve Waugh's 119 not out to hoist the home assets to 6/438 declared. Awakening to the pointless nature of the struggle, the visitors capitulated a second time for 148 in the face of a joint 6-wicket performance from Geoff Lawson and Murray Bennett.

Christmas was not a time of receiving gifts for Wellham's New South Welshmen. A month went by without a point coming their way. In Melbourne, in a game of vacillating fortunes, the home bowlers won and lost the initiative, before redressing the balance of fortunes with their batting. Skipper

Andrew Zesers, 40 wickets for South Australia. One of Australia's hopes for the future. (Philip Tyson)

Ray Bright spun the foundations from beneath the feet of the New South Welsh batsmen with a personal analysis of 6/79; but, after having undermined the opposition to the tune of 7/140, Victoria encountered a granite stratum in Geoff Lawson who scored 63 to elevate his team's total to an unexpected 241. When Victoria, in its first innings, sagged to 6/79, the odds favoured 'The Light Blues', but in the end, experience told. Veteran Hibbert persevered, and, abetted by Bright, registered a record 175 for seventh wicket partnerships against the traditional enemy. 'Dasher' Hibbert who once notched a boundary-less century against a touring Indian side, reached 148, to take the Victorian total to 9/273 and deny Wellham a point.

Going West did not bring the young men of Sydney the fame and fortune which American journalist, John Soule, once promised his countrymen. Rather, it invoked the disaster which attended almost every team which batted first on the freshly-laid Perth wicket in 1985/86. Local left-arm speedster, Chris Matthews, whipped out five New South Welsh batsmen in the space of 10 deliveries and the visitors found themselves back in the pavilion for a paltry 83. With the pitch improving, the home skipper and ex-Test opener, Graeme Wood, dropped himself down the order. He and Wayne Andrews then proceeded to rub salt in Wellham's open wounds with a 5th wicket partnership of 215. Andrews' maiden hundred and Wood's 133 enabled the home team to declare at 7/450 – 367 ahead. With little stomach for a fight on a pitch which they did not trust, the visiting batsmen always struggled and finally capitulated for 321, with English-born medium-pacer and former Australian repre-

Farewell to a great bowler. Jeff Thomson played his last game for Queensland in the Sheffield Shield Final. (Adrian Murrell)

sentative, Ken Macleay complementing his first-innings figures of 3/25 with a hard-earned return of 6/93.

Warwickshire paceman, Gladstone Small and South Australian skipper, David Hookes, were the main architects of the Sydney team's first-innings rout when it visited Adelaide. Small's 7/42 return shot the visitors out for 239 on the opening day, setting the stage for Hookes' one-man blitzkrieg of 243 off 254 balls. 164 of his runs came in boundaries as the home side took a vice-like grip on the game with a first-innings total of 435. Thereafter, it was merely a question of New South Wales attempting to stave off defeat – which it did in style with a second-innings score of 6/535. Taylor notched a century, as did Mark O'Neill, as he and 'keeper Dyer added 200 for the 6th wicket amidst South Australian frustration, which degenerated into on-field anger, as Wellham steadfastly refused to declare.

Three first-innings losses in three games was not the ideal confidence booster for New South Wales' highest hurdle in the competition: the away match against its closest and most able rival, Queensland. From the outset of the game, rain dictated that the struggle would only produce 4 first-innings points. But they were vital points, and the two teams haggled bitterly over them. Queensland's Chris Smart laboured seven hours over his first Shield hundred as his side ground its way to an unimpressive 389 in 527 minutes. Returning to the Sydney team, Whitney bowled with persistence and economy, conceding only 73 runs in 30 overs and taking 4 wickets in the process. O'Neill's 147 subsequently underlined the inadequacy of the Queensland total, as the Habour City team scorched its way to 487. Forty-four-year-old Sri Lankan leg-spinner, Malcolm Francke, marked his return to the Queensland side with a marathon 45 overs which yielded him

the laudable figures of 2/132. The match was also notable for the fact that it saw Jeff Thomson claim his 345th Shield victim, making him the second most prolific wicket-taker in 94 years of Shield cricket – albeit 68 victims behind the immortal Clarrie Grimmett.

Tasmania's journey north to Sydney in mid-February was hardly necessary. Determined to milk the remaining games of every available point and gain the home-ground advantage for the final, New South Wales made short shrift of the competition's Cinderella side. Wellham's men won by an innings and 47 in three days. Bundled out for 210 in the space of 345 minutes by Bennett's orthodox spin, the Apple Island struck back through its own left-arm spinner, Mark Ray, to put the home team on the rack at 5/150. Only Small's second century of the summer and dogged 50s from Dyer and Bennett enabled the home team to establish a lead of 154. With the wicket crumbling, this advantage was enough to win the game. 'Dutchy' Holland's leg-spinning wiles proved too much for the island batsmen, five of whom succumbed to the Newcastle slow bowler for 25, as their side collapsed for 107. The same Sydney Cricket Ground, seven days later, saw New South Wales gain 4 points against Queensland and, move to the head of the Shield ladder and, by virtue of drawing the Final, win the trophy.

Queensland in 1985/86 – as in 1984/85 – was the bridesmaid of the Sheffield Shield, and not the blushing bride. In the latter year, however, it was understandable that its maiden success in the competition eluded the northern team. Two of its fast strike-force and its leading all-rounder fell victims to the Australian 'Rebel' team in South Africa. Its captain, Border, and three of his leading henchmen were regularly claimed by the Test selectors, who, towards the end of the season, also appropriated all-rounder, Glenn Trimble. Thus for most of the summer, Queensland was represented by a side, more than half of whom were, in status, second eleven players. The situation could easily have been worse, if former Australian opener and surrogate Queensland skipper, Kepler Wessels, had reached a financial accord with the Australian Cricket Board and turned out for his adopted country rather than for his adopted state. In the light of such depredations of its regular players, the Brisbane team performed remarkably well to reach the final of the competition.

Queensland, with its advantages of fine weather and good playing surfaces early in the season, prepared well for the 1985/86 Shield and were rewarded by a flying start. Brisbane's first southern visitor, Victoria, recorded its highest score in that city for many years: 431 – with the experienced players, Whatmore and Hibbert, contributing 109 and 65 respectively. But with Allan Border in his most punishing mood, Victoria's total was not enough. The Queensland skipper's 194, complemented by 90 from Trimble, 86 from Ritchie and a career-best of 72 from McDermott, sent the 'Gabba scoreboard clicking around to 539. Indeed, Victoria only narrowly averted an innings defeat, losing 6/137 in its second innings and being only 29 runs ahead when time expired.

Queensland owed its first outright victory and 16 points to the generosity of South Australian captain, David Hookes. Batting supinely on a good Adelaide pitch, the home side yielded to Jeff Thomson's pace to be all out for 290. In reply Border expeditiously accumulated 88 out and Kerr 80, before the former declared Queensland's innings closed 4 runs in the lead. Border thus encouraged South Australia to set his side a goal which could produce the full quota of points for either team. Hookes took up the challenge personally, lambasting a lightning 102 and declaring at 7/288. Hookes miscalculated, for his closure meant that Queensland's victory march did not have to rise above 3.5 runs per over to bring home the bacon. Border and Wessels made it look easy, each registering a hundred and adding 210 for the 3rd wicket.

When Perth came to Brisbane, it brought rain and lots of runs. Opener Valetta scored his third first-class century, Geoff Marsh 130 and Jeff Thomson took his 300th Shield wicket, when Western Australia batted first to amass 527. Losing Barsby and Wessels to successive deliveries without a run on the board, Queensland began its reply in disastrous fashion. But with the help of an undefeated 85 from Brett Henschell, it had recovered to 5/225 at tea on the third day when the rains came and stayed for two days.

'The Banana Benders' moved to the head of the Shield table when they travelled to Devonport and picked up 12 points at Tasmania's expense. Apart from Boon himself, no batsman had an answer to Jeff Thomson's pace when the home side batted first. The blond speedster overthrew five Taswegians at a cost of 76 as the locals were dismissed for 156. Courtice and Wessels added 135 for the 2nd wicket when the visitors batted and, after Ritchie had contributed 89 and Phillips 56, Border was able to declare 251 runs ahead with 9 wickets down. Boon's team made a better fist of its second batting attempt, although dropped catches and an epidemic of no-balls contributed greatly to its 335-run revival. Buckingham compiled 60, 'keeper Soule 53 and Bradshaw and Ray 49 and Queensland were asked to score 85 for victory: a mere formality – but one which, it turned out, cost the wickets of Border, Trimble and Ritchie.

It was early December before Queensland failed to gain a point from a match. Melbourne was the venue; and the pin-point accuracy of Victorian medium-pacer, 'Sniffer' Davis was the cause of the northerners' discomfiture. Davis nagged his way through the defences of six opponents at a thrifty cost of 53 runs. Trimble resisted for 75 runs and Andrew Courtice chipped in with 60; but neither of these innings could prevent Queensland from being dismissed for an inadequate 288. The insufficiency of that total lay revealed when Paul Hibbert occupied the crease for 6 $\frac{1}{2}$ hours for 137 and Jamie Siddons experienced the 293-minute delight of scoring a century in first-class company for the first time. Together, Hibbert and Siddons added 184 for the 5th wicket and with Whatmore notching 90, Victorian skipper Bright declared belatedly, 168 runs ahead. The remaining 409 minutes of the game produced nothing more than spectator boredom and an undefeated innings of 111 for Courtice.

Determined to make amends for its lapse from grace, Queenland entertained South Australia in its state capital a few days before Christmas. The Adelaide side was apparently overcome by the spirit of the festive season, for it made a present of 12 points to its host, with a simple gesture – bad batting. A 143-run partnership between the two left-handers, Border and Wessels, permitted the home team to close its first innings at 8/391. Trimble, McDermott, Thomson and Frei soon had the visitors in all sorts of bother and at 9/200, South

Australia had still not saved the follow-on. This was only averted by a last-ditch, 51-run partnership between fast bowler, Gladstone Small and Rick Darling, who top-scored for his side with 60 not out. In a flurry of strokes, Queensland raced to 8/162 to stretch its lead to 302, before unleashing Thomson on the unfortunate South Australian batsmen a second time. Hookes held the fates at bay for 72 runs and Sleep scored 49 not out, but Thomson's 4/29 finally won a match which was totally flawed by controversy and Hookes' 'whinging' to the A.C.B. referee.

New South Wales had the better of the drawn game in Brisbane, but Queensland's eighth match of the season saw it defeat Tasmania by 6 wickets and draw 14 points clear of Wellham's challengers in the Shield table. The 'Gabba pitch provided early life for Tasmania's West Indian paceman, Winston Davis, when the home side took first strike. Within minutes, Kerr, Courtice, Richie, Smart and Trimble were all back in the pavilion with only 89 runs on the board. But skipper Wessels held firm and at the end of the first day was undefeated on 161. His 180-run association with 'keeper Phillips turned the tide and enabled Queensland to reach the respectability of 365. Tasmania did not posses a batsman of Wessels' stoic determination and, in consequence, were bundled out for 194, Soule doing best with 51 not out and Glenn Trimble collecting 5 wickets with his medium-pace seamers. Following on, the Apple Islanders found a saviour in their number three batsman, Richard Bennett, who registered his first, dogged Shield century in 6 $\frac{1}{2}$ hours. He was still at the crease when the first ball of the last day was bowled, with the visitors 90 runs ahead and only five batsmen out. Without rhyme or reason, the residual batting disintegrated against Frei and Thomson, leaving Queensland almost all day in which to score 109 for victory. Wessels sealed the fate of the match which he had dominated with an exemplary 45, before being caught behind off Davis.

Unseasonal rain in normally sunny Perth washed out the first day of Queensland's clash with Western Australia. The loss of the initial three sessions condemned the contest to a draw and denied the home team its last slim chance of winning a place in the Shield final. Whilst it failed in its quest for maximum points, the Perth team did have the satisfaction of winning on the first innings – by the slender margin of 3 runs! At one stage of the game, it seemed that Wood's young men would provide one of the major upsets of the tournament. Their skipper's 121 steered them to a sound first innings total of 322 – after which medium-pacers Todd Breman, Macleay and Matthews mowed down their first five opponents for 99. It was at this apposite moment that all-rounder, Brett Henschell, made his first 100 in three seasons and helped Trevor Barsby to add 145 for the 6th wicket in the brisk time of 117 minutes. Breman, however, had the last laugh, picking up 4 of the last 5 wickets to fall, to finish with the figures of 6/76 and win 4 points for his side. Those points would have been as precious as rubies to Queensland, since in its ensuring encounter with New South Wales in Sydney, it lost its top billing in the Shield – and subsequently the Shield itself – by a brace of points.

After persisting with its policy of encouraging youthful promise for three seasons, Victoria in 1985/86 succeeded in refuting Oscar Wilde's wicked little epigram about youth being wasted on the young. Opener Michael Quinn and

New South Wales 1985–86
First Class Matches

BATTING

Columns (each match shows 1st and 2nd innings):
1. v. Tasmania (Hobart) 25–28 October 1985
2. v. Victoria (Newcastle) 1–4 November 1985
3. v. New Zealanders (Sydney) 15–18 Nov. 1985
4. v. Western Australia (Sydney) 7–10 Dec. 1985
5. v. South Australia (Sydney) 13–16 Dec. 1985
6. v. Victoria (Melbourne) 20–23 Dec. 1985
7. v. Western Australia (Perth) 10–13 January 1986
8. v. South Australia (Adelaide) 16–19 January 1986
9. v. Queensland (Brisbane) 24–27 January 1986
10. v. Tasmania (Sydney) 21–24 February 1986
11. v. Queensland (Sydney) 28 Feb.–3 Mar. 1986

Batting	Tas (Hobart)	Vic (Newcastle)	NZ (Sydney)	WA (Sydney)	SA (Sydney)	Vic (Melbourne)	WA (Perth)	SA (Adelaide)	Qld (Brisbane)	Tas (Sydney)	Qld (Sydney)
M. Taylor	12 56*	77 7	29 5	65 10	118 —	46 40	12 23	92 100	41 —	44 —	89 —
M. Waugh	13 28	0 4	17 0						12 —	1 —	27 —
D.M. Wellham	14 —	15 22	86 0	11 55	41 —	5 63	28 14	0 41	72 —	4 —	4 —
P.S. Clifford	98 —	29 98	6 40	16 22			0 35	29 17	6 —	0 —	
G.R.J. Matthews	184 —	35 28	111 32*	0 49		13 —					
S.R. Waugh	107 —	15 11	21 6		119* —	32 41*					
G.C. Dyer	35 —	14 2	1 41	22 3*	— —	7 —	7 68	26 88	23 —	59 —	19 —
G.F. Lawson	23 —	23 30		24 —		63 —					
M.J. Bennett	20* 20*	1 26*	17 1*	55* —	15 —	1 —	2* 12	12 14*	20 —	57* —	14 —
D.R. Gilbert	22 —	16* 0	0 —	0 —							
R.G. Holland	10 —	0 6	0* —	16 —	— —	2 —	1 2	17 —	53 —	15 —	19 —
P.A. Blizzard			4 —			18* —	0 12	12* —	24 —		
S.M. Small				4 4	66 —	25 123	3 48	3 54	46 —	118 —	22 —
R.J. Bower				63 3*	10 —	18 40*	4 43	4 30		7 —	57 —
W.J.S. Seabrook					8 —						
M.D. O'Neill					38* —		24 39	24 178*	147 —		117 —
M.R. Whitney							0 0*	4 —	10* —	19 —	0* —
P. Taylor									19 —	19 —	43 —
Byes	4 1	1	2 2	4	5	2 4		1 1	2	3	3
Leg-byes	7	4 3	5	4	14	5 6	10	9 3	6	4	11
Wides		2	1 1		1	4		1	2	4	1
No-Balls	12 4	1 6	1 1	6 7	3	2	2 13	4 26		14	15
Total	561 111	232 244	300 128	286 157	438	241 319	83 321	239 535	487	364	440
Wickets	10 1	10 10	10 6	10 5	6	10 3	10 10	10 6	10	10	10
Results	D	W	D	W	W	D	L	D	D	W	D
Points	4	8	—	12	12	0	0	0	4	12	4

Catches:
38 – G.C. Dyer (ct 31/st 7)
15 – M. Taylor
9 – S.M. Small
6 – M.J. Bennett and R.G. Holland
5 – M. Waugh, P. Taylor and R.J. Bower
4 – S.R. Waugh, D.M. Wellham, D.R. Gilbert and M.D. O'Neill
2 – P.S. Clifford, P.A. Blizzard and subs.
1 – G.F. Lawson and G.R.J. Matthews

BOWLING

Match	G.F. Lawson	D.R. Gilbert	M.J. Bennett	R.G. Holland	G.R.J. Matthews	S.R. Waugh	M. Waugh	P.A. Blizzard	M.D. O'Neill
v. Tasmania (Hobart) 25–28 October 1985	37–12–85–3	32–6–108–4	29–10–48–0	41–11–119–2	24–11–39–1	5–0–22–0			
v. Victoria (Newcastle) 1–4 November 1985	32.4–4–82–4 / 8–3–7–2	26–4–84–4 / 6–2–12–1	18–5–40–1	15–2–51–0 / 15–9–17–2	8–2–20–0 / 15.5–9–22–5	14–5–25–1 / 5–0–17–0	1–1–0–0		
v. New Zealanders (Sydney) 15–18 November 1985			14–11–12–1 / 7–1–19–0	22–7–36–0 / 28–10–56–4	25–10–33–8 / 31–7–77–1	5–1–21–0 / 8–6–4–0		6–2–17–1 / 4–1–12–0	
v. Western Australia (Sydney) 7–10 December 1985	12–2–31–0 / 7.2–1–11–3	10–1–30–2 / 10–3–16–4	33–12–47–4 / 15–6–19–0	34–16–52–1 / 19–5–34–2	6.5–3–14–3 / 13–7–15–1				
v. South Australia (Sydney) 13–16 December 1985	6–1–18–0 / 15–6–20–3		23.5–12–38–4 / 25.5–13–32–3	33–17–46–4 / 26–8–39–2		5–1–12–0 / 5–2–15–1			17–2–55–2 / 9–3–32–0
v. Victoria (Melbourne) 20–28 December 1985	26–9–49–1		26.4–6–71–4	11–3–31–0	25–7–52–2	16–5–30–0	15–3–30–1		
v. Western Australia (Perth) 10–13 January 1986			32–8–85–3	30–8–107–0				31–7–72–3	12–2–34–1
v. South Australia (Adelaide) 16–19 January 1986			16.4–2–75–1	33–11–91–2				32–4–118–4	9–2–22–0
v. Queensland (Brisbane) 24–27 January 1986			27–12–50–0 / 22–9–24–1	26–8–62–0 / 10–3–11–0			33–5–130–4 / 8–1–18–0	24–7–49–2 / 8–0–24–0	4–2–4–0 / 10–7–10–1
v. Tasmania (Sydney) 21–24 February 1986			24.1–7–53–2 / 19–9–23–2	23–6–42–0 / 12.4–6–25–5			15–5–31–2 / 7–3–15–0		7–1–22–0
v. Queensland (Sydney) 28 February–3 March 1986			37–6–77–0 / 7–5–2–0	43–15–92–5 / 11–3–20–0			18.4–3–49–3 / 10–4–13–1		7–3–15–0
v. Queensland (Sydney) 14–18 March 1986			27–5–65–0 / 13–0–36–2	39–9–92–0 / 5–0–25–0			27–4–71–1 / 5–0–25–0		6–1–23–0
Totals	144–38–303–16 av. 18.93	105–28–281–16 av. 17.56	446.1–144–877–32 av. 27.40	482.4–157–1072–34 av. 31.52	105.4–46–187–12 av. 15.58	50–13–121–2 av. 60.50	124.4–26–352–11 av. 32.00	120–24–322–11 av. 29.27	81–23–217–3 av. 72.33

v. Queensland (Sydney) 14–18 March 1986		M	Inns	NOs	Runs	HS	Av
41	30	12	20	1	937	118	49.31
41	24	7	11	—	167	41	15.18
7	80	12	19	—	562	89	29.57
		8	13	—	396	98	30.46
		5	8	1	452	184	64.57
		5	8	2	352	119*	58.66
88*	0	12	17	2	503	88*	33.53
		5	5	—	163	63	32.60
11	2*	12	18	9	300	57*	33.33
		4	5	1	38	22	9.50
5	0*	12	14	2	146	53	12.16
		5	6	2	70	24	17.50
39	50	9	14	—	605	123	43.21
3	12	8	13	2	294	63	26.72
		1	1	—	8	8	8.00
20	1	6	9	2	588	178*	84.00
0	—	6	7	3	33	19	8.25
0	42						
294	258						
10	8						
D							
—							

M.R. Whitney	R.J. Bower	P. Taylor	Byes	Leg-byes	Wides	No-balls	Total	Wkts
				8	3	15	429	10
				6		8	308	10
				3		1	78	10
			1			1	120	10
			6	1			175	5
			5	8	3	3	187	10
			7	3			105	10
				6			175	10
			4	6		1	148	10
			2	8		4	273	9
22–3–84–0	10–2–55–1		10	3	2	15	450	7
33–7–110–2	1–0–16–0		1	2		4	435	10
30.3–5–73–4			6	15		7	389	10
6–2–7–0			1	4		3	105	3
18–4–40–3		20–4–42–2		2	2	4	210	10
8–3–12–3	1–0–1–0	8–1–24–0	6	1			107	10
23–5–63–2	6–1–13–0	11–5–27–0		3		4	339	10
11–3–15–2		8–0–22–0		2		5	96	3
34–7–65–6	7–1–28–1	25–3–78–1	6	8	1	18	436	9
10–4–14–0		13–1–31–4		2		3	133	7
195.3–43–	25–4–	85–14–						
483–22	113–2	224–7						
av. 21.95	av. 56.50	av. 32.00						

middle-order batsman, Jamie Siddons rewarded the selectors' faith in them by recording their maiden 100s. The southern state's fast attack acquired a sharp cutting edge; Merv Hughes' speedy inswingers yielded him 33 wickets at 29.09 and won him a Test cap against India, whilst the accuracy of Simon Davis' medium-pace earned him top place in the national averages and a berth in the Australian World Series Cup team. As a bonus, the Melbourne side unearthed a promising speedster in the person of Dennis Hickey: a 20-year-old, whose genuine pace and ability to make the ball rise from just short of a length surprised 15 Tasmanian and South Australian batsmen in only two games. Throughout the season Tony Dodemaide showed that his experiences in England as an Esso Scholarship holder and in Zimbabwe with the Australian Under 25 side had benefited his batting – but his medium-pace bowling fell below expectations. In spite of the prolonged absence of its Test star, Simon O'Donnell, because of injury or national commitments, Victoria enjoyed its most successful summer since 1980/81, winning two games outright and only being headed twice on the first innings in 10 matches. The state's two outright victories exactly doubled the number of its conclusive wins in the last four years. The leadership of the side fell to Bright and, when he was absent on international duty, the irrepressibly impatient Dean Jones. Jones responded well to the demands of leadership, providing his men with an excellent example and scoring 4 half-centuries in the last four games. Ironically, however – in the light of the state selectors' bias towards youth – Victoria owed a great debt of gratitude to the steady reliability of their elder statesmen, former Test men, Dav Whatmore and Paul Hibbert, who between them notched 5 hundreds in the course of the season.

For Bright's bright young men, the worst came first. They were outscored by Border's side in Brisbane and lost outright to New South Wales in Newcastle. Their initial home fixture took place at the St Kilda Cricket Ground, to give the M.C.G. time to recover from its annual football battering – and it produced 4 points. After rain obliterated the first day, the visiting Taswegians batted in leisurely fashion for 328 runs and 571 minutes against the sustained accuracy of Davis and Hughes, who between them accounted for all but one of the 10 wickets to fall. Much of the substance of the islanders' innings came from a 138-run stand for the 4th wicket between Woolley and Bradshaw. Tasmania missed its chance of winning the points by muffing 5 catches and allowing Bright and Dimattina to compile 102 for an unbroken 7th wicket partnership.

Like most of the teams visiting Perth, Victoria were baffled, bewildered and bowled out on their first day on the new W.A.C.A. pitch. Whatmore and Dodemaide alone reached double figures as Chris Matthews' left-handed pace reaped him a personal reward of 5/27 and demolished his batting opposition for 111. But Western Australia was hoist on its own petard when Simon Davis outshone Matthews to take 6/19 and give his team a first-innings lead of 17. The wicket improved, Jones notched 113, Michael Quinn 62 and Bright was able to close the Victorian innings at 7/302. The declaration proved to be an exercise in futility. Taking advantage of the now placid batting surface, Wood compiled a patient 82 and Geoff Marsh indulged in 410 minutes of batting practice to record a round 100 and see his side safely

Queensland 1985–86
First Class Matches

BATTING

BATTING	v. Victoria (Brisbane) 18–21 October 1985		v. New Zealanders (Brisbane) 1–4 November 1985		v. South Australia (Adelaide) 15–18 Nov. 1985		v. Western Australia (Launceston) 22–25 Nov. 1985		v. Tasmania (Devonport) 6–9 December 1985		v. Victoria (Melbourne) 13–16 Dec. 1985		v. South Australia (Brisbane) 20–23 Dec. 1985		v. New South Wales (Brisbane) 24–27 January 1986		v. Tasmania (Brisbane) 31 Jan.–3 Feb. 1986		v. Western Australia (Perth) 21–24 February 1986		v. New South Wales (Sydney) 28 Feb.–3 Mar. 1986	
R.B. Kerr	0	—	20	39	80	4			27	—			19	6	84	50*	12	9	28	—	102	—
B.A. Courtice	4	—	112	21*	36	4	48	—	77	—	60	111*	0	11	10	23	3	0	9	—	20	35*
K.C. Wessels	32	—	25	42	1	107	0	—	69	20*	15	24	85	3	20	13	167	45	1	—	93	—
A.R. Border	194	—	102	—	88*	119			8	11			118	30								
G.M. Ritchie	86	—	7	18	16	24*			89	49			24	63			0	23*				
G.S. Trimble	90	—	49	26	24	4	41	—	2	1	75	41*	87*	10			9	12*	4	—	19	0
A.B. Henschell	7	—	24	0	40*	16*	85*	—	3	1*	5	—	12	21*	14	—			110	—	15	43
R.B. Phillips	1	—	30	77*	—	—	24*	—	56	—	0	—	23	3	1	—	71	—	5	—	11	7*
C.J. McDermott	72	—	4	1	—	—							6	2								
H. Frei	43	—	7	—					14	—	9	—	4*	6*	19	—	4	—	13	—	1	—
J.R. Thomson	2*	—	11*	—					17*	—	13*	—			14	—	24	—	10	—	14	—
T.J. Barsby							0	—			31	9			30	6*			67	—	56*	—
A. Brown							12	—														
P.W. Twible									18*	—	39	—										
M.G. Maranta											4	—										
N. Jelich											30	—										
C.B. Smart															133	5	7	7	32	—	0	4
M. Francke															22	—	2	—			1	—
D. Tazelaar															14*	—	29*	—	10*	—		
Byes			3						2		7		5	4	6	1	5					
Leg-byes	3		4	1	7	6	3		9	3	5	3	4	2	15	4	6	3	10		3	2
Wides	1												2	1					19			
No-Balls	4		12	4	2	1	12		16		2	2	2	1	7	3	31	5	1		4	5
Total	539		407	323	294	285	225		407	85	288	197	391	162	389	105	365	109	319		339	96
Wickets	10		10	6	5	5	5		9	3	10	2	8	8	10	3	10	4	10		10	3
Results	D		D		W		D		W		D		W		D		W		D		D	
Points	4		—		12		2		12		0		12		0		12		0		0	

Catches

41 – R.B. Phillips	7 – C.B. Smart, A.B. Henschell and B.A. Courtice	4 – D. Tazelaar and T.J. Barsby
13 – K.C. Wessels	6 – G.S. Trimble and H. Frei	2 – C.J. McDermott, M.G. Maranta and subs.
10 – R.B. Kerr	5 – G.M. Ritchie and A.R. Border	1 – J.R. Thomson and P.W. Twible

BOWLING

	C.J. McDermott	H. Frei	J.R. Thomson	A.B. Henschell	A.R. Border	K.C. Wessels	G.S. Trimble	M. Francke	P.W. Twible
v. Victoria (Brisbane) 18–21 October 1985	37–8–116–4	38.1–9–91–2	30–2–137–3	37–8–57–1	4–2–11–0	8–1–18–0			
	15–4–41–3	10–3–31–2	13–3–28–1	14–5–24–0					
v. New Zealanders (Brisbane) 1–4 November 1985	21–2–54–1	28–7–72–0	20–2–74–0	11–0–65–0		2–1–14–1	18–4–48–2		
	9–0–36–1	6–2–14–2		18–4–55–1			15–3–30–2		
v. South Australia (Adelaide) 15–18 November 1985	29–3–71–1	17–5–42–1	24.1–8–72–6	16–4–40–0			13–1–63–2		
	15–5–35–2	23–5–92–1	10–1–50–3	27–5–89–1			3–0–13–0		
v. Western Australia (Brisbane) 29 Nov.-2 Dec. 1985		34–10–91–3	23–3–103–2	33–8–97–2			21–7–59–1		26–5–70–0
v. Tasmania (Devonport) 6–9 December 1985		9–2–24–2	17–2–76–5				12.2–4–38–2		5–1–16–0
		27.1–8–71–4	32–5–122–2	14–2–32–0	3–0–13–0		19–3–61–3		13–5–27–0
v. Victoria (Melbourne) 13–16 December 1985		30–5–80–1	22–2–78–2	4–0–16–0			27–2–99–2		35.2–5–82–2
v. South Australia (Brisbane) 20–23 December 1985	18.4–4–47–2	15–2–58–1	19–3–61–2	22–14–36–2			19–9–41–3		
	19–5–55–2	6–2–14–1	13.2–2–29–4	9–2–39–1			13–2–47–2		
v. New South Wales (Brisbane) 24–27 January 1986		33–7–110–0	25–1–116–2	12.2–6–36–2		5–4–3–0		45–7–132–2	
v. Tasmania (Brisbane) 31 Jan.-3 Feb. 1986		17–2–38–1					22–5–50–5	13–3–31–2	
		15.3–6–24–3	26–2–109–3				21–4–32–2	18–4–36–0	
v. West Australia (Perth) 21–24 February 1986		25.5–2–84–3	12–0–83–2	15–4–41–2		10–2–29–1	9–1–43–1		
		16–1–47–0	6–0–23–1	5–4–1–0		15–3–44–0	7–2–16–0		
v. New South Wales (Sydney) 28 Feb.-3 March 1986		36–11–75–2	32–5–92–1	20–3–53–1		12–4–25–2	40–12–95–2	32.3–8–86–2	
v. New South Wales (Sydney) 14–18 March 1986		37–7–87–2	29–3–91–3	19–2–48–2			2–0–12–0		
		26–8–71–1	19–5–41–0	29–13–45–1		16–5–26–2	2–0–12–0		
	163.4–31–	449.4–104–	372.3–49–	305.2–84–	7–2–	75–24–	263.2–59–	108.3–22–	79.2–16–
	455–16	1216–32	1385–42	774–16	24–0	165–6	759–29	285–6	195–2
	av. 28.43	*av.* 38.00	*av.* 32.97	*av.* 48.37	—	*av.* 27.50	*av.* 26.17	*av.* 47.50	*av.* 97.50

a B.A. Courtice 3–1–11–0, G.M. Ritchie 1–0–3–0   b N. Jelich 1–0–4–0

v. New South Wales (Sydney) 14–18 March 1986		M	Inns	NOs	Runs	HS	Av
64	34	10	16	1	578	102	38.53
8	22	12	20	3	614	112	36.11
166	29	12	20	1	957	167	50.36
		5	8	1	670	194	95.71
		6	11	2	399	89	44.33
112	0	11	19	3	606	112	37.87
44*	20*	11	17	7	460	110	46.00
5	6	12	15	3	320	77*	26.66
		3	5	—	85	72	17.00
1	1*	12	12	3	122	43	13.55
0	—	12	9	4	105	24	21.00
0	10	6	9	2	209	67	29.85
		1	1	—	12	12	12.00
		3	2	1	57	39	57.00
		2	1	—	4	4	4.00
		1	1	—	30	30	30.00
0	2	5	9	—	190	133	21.11
		3	3	—	25	22	8.33
3*	—	4	4	4	56	29*	—
6							
8	2						
1	3						
18	4						
436	133						
10	7						
D	—						

M.G. Maranta	A. Brown	D. Tazelaar	Byes	Leg-byes	Wides	No-balls	Total	Wkts
				1	1	32	431	10
			12	1		3	137	6
				4	1	30	331	4
				3			152	6a
			1	1	1	18	290	10
			2	7		13	288	7
18–3–69–0	10.1–0–34–2			4	1	16	527	10
				2		28	156	10
				9		39	335	10
25–2–78–0			5	12		6	456	9b
			1	7	1	11	251	10
			5	3		5	192	10
		24–2–84–3		6	1	26	487	10
		16–1–73–2		2		12	194	10
		22–5–55–2	6	10	4	28	278	10
		8–0–40–0		2	2	19	322	10
		22–4–61–1		3	3	14	195	2
			3	11		15	440	10
		22–4–48–3	4	4	1	30	294	10
		20–6–57–2	3	3	2	9	258	8
43–5–	10.1–0–	134–22–						
147–0	34–2	418–13						
—	av. 17.00	av. 32.15						

into harbour at 2/212.

Before girding up for its return fixture with Western Australia in Melbourne, Victoria showed itself to be more than a match for the eventual Shield finalists by taking 4 points off both teams at the M.C.G. It then added to its growing tally by completing a first-innings double over its Perth visitors. Afforded a longer recuperation period after the football season in 1985, the M.C.G. pitch had more bounce in the following summer. But the leopard had not completely changed its spots and the Melbourne surface was still sympathetic to spin. Western Australia's young off-spinner, Brett Mulder, revealed this characteristic by making the early breakthrough when the home side batted first. Fortunately for Bright's team, Mulder was unable to maintain his accuracy and opener Quinn and the improving Dodemaide stuck to their guns, each scoring half-centuries to raise the Victorian total to 295. Mulder's figures of 6/125 were overshadowed when the visitors took strike; the orthodox left-handed spin of the home skipper reaped a far more economical harvest of 5/44 and won his side a first-innings lead of 133. Batting a second time, Victoria only improved on Western Australia's 162-run effort by 24. But even this moderate total posed Wood the problem of notching 320 to win on a pitch which was now unconducive to stroke play. He chose to ignore the challenge and the Western Australian innings meandered pointlessly along to 6/255 before the match ended amidst mutual accusations of unenterprising captaincy.

The same lack of leadership initiative characterized the following game in Melbourne when the home side batted first against South Australia. To celebrate his record 100th appearance for Victoria –a feat of endurance which outstripped Bill Lawry's 99 games – Bright scored 67 not out to reinforce Dav Whatmore's previous 127. Together they lifted Victoria's total to 345 in the face of an accurate 6-wicket performance from Australia's Under 19 medium-pacer, Andrew Zesers. The Adelaide side's 251-run riposte owed much of its substance to the 30-year-old opener, Andrew Watson, who, making his third representative appearance, compiled a sound 97. The visitors' fortunes were assisted by 53 from the bat of Sleep and the fact that fast bowler, Merv Hughes, was removed from the Victorian attack after repeatedly running on the pitch. Inspired by a two-hour innings of 91 from Dean Jones and fifties from the ever reliable Whatmore and Quinn, the locals declared their second innings at 5/261, asking the usually daring Hookes to demand 356 runs from his batsman on the last day. The South Australian skipper turned a deaf ear to the request and for the second time in a fortnight, Melbourne spectators were insulted by the sight of a team's unenterprising occupation of the crease. When the umpires mercifully called 'time', Australian opener Andrew Hilditch had batted all day for 89 not out and South Australia were virtually motionless on 3/189.

The memory of Hookes' media condemnation of Bright's declaration in Melbourne still lingered and rankled in the minds of the Victorian players when they travelled west for the return fixture against South Australia. Particularly fired-up was tyro fast bowler, Dennis Hickey, returning to the Melbourne side after a foot injury sustained during a McDonald's Cup match. Hickey was given an opportunity to display his prowess on the first day of the game. His

South Australia 1985–86
First Class Matches

BATTING

Match column key (each match shows two innings, 1 and 2):
- **WA** = v. Western Australia (Adelaide) 17–20 October 1985
- **NZ** = v. New Zealanders (Adelaide) 26–29 October 1985
- **QA** = v. Queensland (Adelaide) 15–18 Nov. 1985
- **TL** = v. Tasmania (Launceston) 22–25 Nov. 1985
- **In** = v. Indians (Adelaide) 29 Nov.–2 Dec. 1985
- **NS** = v. New South Wales (Sydney) 13–16 Dec. 1985
- **QB** = v. Queensland (Brisbane) 20–23 Dec. 1985
- **TA** = v. Tasmania (Adelaide) 10–13 January 1986
- **NA** = v. New South Wales (Adelaide) 16–19 January 1986
- **VM** = v. Victoria (Melbourne) 25–28 January 1986
- **VA** = v. Victoria (Adelaide) 21–24 February 1986

Batsman	WA 1	WA 2	NZ 1	NZ 2	QA 1	QA 2	TL 1	TL 2	In 1	In 2	NS 1	NS 2	QB 1	QB 2	TA 1	TA 2	NA 1	NA 2	VM 1	VM 2	VA 1	VA 2
A.M.J. Hilditch	1	7	7	1	46	59	29	7*	17	0	12	0	12	3					15	84*	16	12
G.A. Bishop	4	108	11	202	19	44	37	0	14	93	18	0	14	9	45	224*	29	—			0	8
R.J. Zadow	8	144	26	0	52	7*	21	—	11	120	2	46	40	1	25	8	0	—	2	8	0	19
D.W. Hookes	40	82	106	14	47	102							7	72			243	—	23	9	62	11
P.R. Sleep	105	11*	12	133*	9	21	99	—	22	19	6	19	18	49*	3	13	4	—	52	10*	16	33
D.F.G. O'Connor	5	—	11	12*			31	—	20	58	0	4										
W.B. Phillips	26	1*	44	—	46	23			2	0	3	0	33	14								
T.B.A. May	3	—	42*		17	6*	10	—	2	0	3	0	5	10								
A.K. Zesers	31*	—	9	—	2	—	22	—	9	25	3*	—	5	0	0	—	27*	—	0	—	12*	32
G.C. Small	16	—	0	—	7	0					0	9	33	12	12	—	14	—	12	—	6*	22
I.R. Carmichael	1	—	—	—	8*	—																
W.M. Darling					16	4	18	8*	0	107*	97	3	60*	6	7	4	7		13			
D.J. Kelly							79	—	16	2	3	27			85	14	42		4		82	12
S.D.H. Parkinson							62	—	0	4*			4	3	0	—	36		2*	—		0*
P. Gladigan							10*	—	12*	—												
C.L. Harms													25	29*	43*	5*	23	—	20			
A. Watson															30	22	3	—	97	59	44	15
S. Wundke															42	39						
N. Plummer																					49	42
J. Pyke																						
Byes			1		1	2	1		2			4	1	5	2	9	1		2	8		1
Leg-byes	11		2	2	1	7	8	2	8	2	6	6	7	3	6	1	2		1	8	15	2
Wides	2		1	1	1		3	1	1				1		1		2					1
No-Balls	2	4	6	8	18	13	12	2	1	5		1	11	5	11	6	4		8	3	1	1
Total	255	357	278	373	290	288	442	20	135	435	175	148	251	192	313	345	435		251	189	303	211
Wickets	10	4	9	4	10	7	10	1	10	8	10	10	10	10	10	6	10		10	3	8	10
Result	D		D		L		W		L		L		L		W		D		D		L	
Points	0		—		0		12		—		0		0		8		4		0		4	

Catches
- 17 – D.J. Kelly (ct 16/st 1)
- 15 – D.W. Hookes
- 11 – G.A. Bishop
- 9 – W.B. Phillips
- 7 – A.M.J. Hilditch
- 5 – R.J. Zadow, A.K. Zesers, P.R. Sleep, S.D.H. Parkinson and A. Watson

BOWLING

(Each cell shows both innings as *innings 1 / innings 2*.)

Match	G.C. Small	I.R. Carmichael	A.K. Zesers	T.B.A. May	P.R. Sleep	D.F.G. O'Connor	D.W. Hookes	P. Gladigan	S.D.H. Parkinson
v. Western Australia (Adelaide) 17–20 October 1985	29–7–89–5 / 6–0–30–1	25–8–68–1 / 10–2–25–0	26–4–71–2 / 6–1–12–0	20–2–61–1 / 9–2–14–0	14.2–1–43–1 / 12–4–29–0				
v. New Zealanders (Adelaide) 26–29 October 1985	19–6–49–2 / 6–2–13–0	24–7–79–0 / 7–2–15–0	25–8–69–0 / 7–3–16–0	31–10–96–0 / 23–6–67–4	9–2–40–0 / 13–2–49–2	2–0–30–0	9–4–22–0 / 5–0–43–1		
v. Queensland (Adelaide) 15–18 November 1985	32–7–77–2 / 10–0–32–1	14–6–46–0 / 21–2–75–0	31–10–67–3 / 16–1–56–2	17–4–48–0 / 25.5–3–86–2	8–0–49–0		7–0–30–0		
v. Tasmania (Launceston) 22–25 November 1985			26–17–28–2 / 45–17–65–2	26–10–42–2 / 24–6–58–2	6.4–3–6–2 / 32–10–71–3			13–2–35–0 / 20–6–40–0	24–9–41–4 / 15–5–42–1
v. Indians (Adelaide) 29 Nov.–2 Dec. 1985			27–6–65–1 / 27.2–5–80–2	4–0–16–0 / 18–2–70–2	15–4–42–1 / 21–2–63–0			20–3–56–2 / 5.4–0–24–0	21.2–3–56–6 / 17–1–84–1
v. New South Wales (Sydney) 13–16 December 1985	37–7–90–1		23–5–64–1	41–11–86–2	41–9–110–1				
v. Queensland (Brisbane) 20–23 December 1985	31–4–109–4 / 16–2–55–3		21–8–64–1 / 21–5–43–3	8–0–26–0	11–2–49–1		14–2–49–0 / 9–2–17–0		21–3–85–2 / 13–2–41–2
v. Tasmania (Adelaide) 10–13 January 1986	29–8–76–1 / 18–2–65–1		28.1–9–77–3 / 14–4–40–2		10–3–26–0 / 21–6–76–2				24–4–86–3 / 4–2–12–0
v. New South Wales (Adelaide) 16–19 January 1986	22.4–4–42–7 / 31–5–113–1		21–4–51–2 / 41–13–78–0		33–7–109–2		2–0–3–1 / 5–0–22–0		17–4–48–0 / 24–2–105–2
v. Victoria (Melbourne) 25–28 January 1986	22–4–54–0 / 18–0–85–2		38–13–73–6 / 23–6–75–1		14.2–2–67–2 / 14–1–39–0		4–0–14–0		14–2–64–1 / 13.1–2–48–1
v. Victoria (Adelaide) 21–24 February 1986	24–3–87–2 / 15–1–54–0		34–13–46–4 / 22–7–44–0		9–2–33–0 / 4–0–42–0		1–0–10–0 / 4–0–20–1	7–1–33–0	20–7–50–3 / 7–1–33–0
v. Western Australia (Perth) 28 Feb.–3 March 1986	34–10–77–2 / 16–2–47–4		39–10–112–1 / 2–0–13–0		4–1–0–0 / 1–1–0–0		1–0–4–0 / 1–0–16–0		25–5–96–1 / 2–0–22–0
Totals	415.4–74–1244–39 av. 31.89	101–27–308–1 av. 308.00	563.3–169–1309–40 av. 32.72	246.5–56–670–15 av. 44.66	289.2–61–943–17 av. 55.47	2–0–30–0 —	62–8–250–3 av. 83.33	58.4–11–155–2 av. 77.50	261.3–52–913–27 av. 33.81

a R.J. Zadow 1–0–6–0, A. Watson 1–0–2–0   b J. Pyke 24–6–84–2, 9–3–27–4

v. Western Australia (Perth) 28 Feb.–3 Mar. 1986		M	Inns	NOs	Runs	HS	Av
1	28	10	20	2	357	84*	19.83
36	50	11	21	1	965	224*	48.25
		11	20	1	540	144	28.42
20	28	8	15	—	866	243	57.73
139	0	12	22	4	793	139	44.05
		5	8	1	141	58	20.14
		4	7	1	187	46	31.16
		7	11	2	98	42*	10.88
5	0	12	17	4	182	32	14.00
0	1*	10	15	2	144	33	11.07
		3	2	1	9	8*	9.00
39	5	8	14	3	350	107*	31.81
7*	—	8	13	—	410	85	31.53
		8	10	4	118	62	19.66
		2	2	2	22	12*	—
		4	6	3	145	43*	48.33
39	26	5	9	—	335	97	37.22
35	28	2	4	—	144	42	36.00
		1	2	—	91	49	45.50
77	8*	1	2	1	85	77	85.00
4	1						
14	3						
2	1						
14	2						
432	181						
10	8						
D							
0							

* – D.F.G. O'Connor and subs
‡ – G.C. Small, C.L. Harms, T.B.A. May and S. Wunde
† – J. Pyke

C.L. Harms	S. Wundke	N. Plummer	Byes	Leg-byes	Wides	No-balls	Total	Wkts
			3	2	1	9	337	10
			4	3	1	2	117	1
				2		3	387	3
			2	4			209	7
				7		2	294	5
				6		1	285	5
			2	5		4	159	10
			16	7		4	299	10
			3	7	1	2	245	10
			4	4	1		329	6
27.3–8–69–0			5	14	1	3	438	6
			5	4	2	2	391	8
			4	2	1		162	8
22–5–49–3	4–1–12–0		6	11	2		343	10
28.2–10–60–4			5	2	1	1	260	10
26–5–85–0			1	9	2	4	239	10
27–2–103–1			2	3	4	4	535	6
20–2–62–1			4	7		1	345	10
			5	9	1	1	261	5
		17–3–48–1	3	6	2	2	250	10
		14.2–0–53–0	11	12		1	268	2a
			5	13	1	2	433	6b
			1	2			128	8
150.5–32–	4–1–	31.2–3–						
428–9	12–0	101–1						
av. 47.55	—	av. 101.00						

spiteful bounce and inward movement made initial inroads into the home team's batting, but he was unable to prevent a recovery which was led by 'keeper Kelly's 82, Hookes' 62, sustained by 49 from Plummer and resulted in a South Australian total of 8/303 declared. At 5/68 Victoria's reply was foundering, and it was only a spirited ninth-wicket partnership of 67 between Dodemaide and paceman Hughes which restricted Victoria's first-innings deficit to 53. It was at this juncture that Hickey decided the outcome of the game with a paralysing burst of speed which yielded him 7/81 and toppled the home side for 211. It was a magnificent exhibition of fast bowling – abetted by Dimattina's 6 catches behind the stumps – and might have had even more disastrous consequences for the home side, who were at one stage on the canvas at 7/115. The lesson of Hickey's youthful enthusiasm was not lost on opener Quinn; he rose to the occasion with his maiden shield century and, backed by veteran Whatmore's 84 and Jones' unbeaten 57, steered his side to its first outright victory of the season.

Having learned to win, and realising that a position in the Shield final was still a remote possibility, Victoria carried on in Devonport where it left off in Adelaide. When Tasmania batted first, Hughes, taking a leaf out of Hickey's Adelaide text book, snatched 5/53 with his inslanting speed. O'Donnell, returning to the side after a nagging leg injury, complemented Hughes perfectly with a return of 4/52 and Tasmania found itself back in the pavilion with only 241 on the board. Hibbert's third century of the season, allied to Jones' 70 and 57 from the dimunutive Siddons put Victoria in a commanding position at 6/326 declared. By this stage of the contest, Ray's batsmen were totally dispirited and put up only token resistance in their second innings. In the space of 152 minutes they were dismissed a second time for 115 – Hickey blasting his triumphant way to 5/52 and Hughes taking his wicket tally for the game to 9 with an analysis of 4/23. Needing only 31 for victory, the 'Dark Blues' comfortably doubled their aggregate of outright wins in four seasons in the space of two matches. The Australian cricket world was left to ponder on Victoria's developing potential, its emergent batting brigade and the zest of its three-pronged fast spearhead.

Western Australia began the 1985/86 season 'behind the eight ball'. Age and circumstances had robbed the state of virtually all its experienced players in the space of three short years. Although the Lillees, Marshes, Aldermans, Yardleys, Hogans, Lairds, Hughes and Shipperds are not easily replacable commodities, the Perth selectors have performed miracles in the past two seasons to produce youthful talent out of the hat. A testimony to their judgement is embodied in their discovery of gifted batsmen like Valetta, McPhee, Marsh, Gonnella and Gartrell – bowlers of the calibre of Reid and Matthews – and a keeper like Zoehrer. But in 1985/86, the W.A.C.A. nabobs had to pit the inexperience of their young tyros against hardened competitors on the minefield of a home pitch which was only laid two months before the beginning of the season. It was a hard and sudden education for youngsters brought up on the pluperfection of the Perth wickets of yesteryear. It was a short course in survival tactics which would have tested an inured English country batsman. By and large, the young men of the West emerged from their ordeal with a great deal of credit. Playing half of their games

Tasmania 1985–86
First Class Matches

BATTING

BATTING	v New South Wales (Hobart) 25–28 October 1985		v Western Australia (Perth) 1–4 November 1986		v Victoria (Melbourne) 8–11 Nov. 1985		v South Australia (Launceston) 22–25 Nov. 1985		v Queensland (Devonport) 6–9 December 1985		v Indians (Hobart) 20–23 Dec. 1985		v South Australia (Adelaide) 10–13 January 1986		v Western Australia (Hobart) 24–27 January 1986		v Queensland (Brisbane) 31 Jan.–3 Feb. 1986		v New South Wales (Sydney) 21–24 February 1986		v Victoria (Devonport) 28 Feb.–3 Mar. 1986	
M. Ray	7	—	0	27	25	—	49	47	1	49			52	10	0	13	0	1	8	9	44	0
G.W. Goodman	14	—	0	9	38	—	4	10														
D.C. Boon	196	—	64	0					44	16												
K.R. Bradshaw	26	—	7	8	87	—	8	37	1	49			11	62	112	22	7	10	0	3	0	0
R.D. Woolley	16	—	5	40	70	—	22	10	14	0			94	16	124*	22*	10	0	11	15	0	17
D.J. Buckingham	41	—	0	45	17	—	0	22	21	60			121	15	57	52*	43	62	36	10	49	36
S.L. Saunders	51	—	11	8	41*	—	13	14	0	13												
R.E. Soule	15	—	2	9	4	—	35*	31*	15	53			3	0	1	—	51*	0	13	9*	25	27
R.L. Brown	27	—	1	0	31	—	1	10	5	9			0*	1*	17*	—	12	1	27*	10	3	5
W.W. Davis	9	—	8	6	0	—	0	1	21	8							10	0	1	7	0*	11*
M. Hill	1*	—	0*	0*	0	—	4	10	4*	3*												
R.S. Hyatt					3	—	12	80	0	27			5	14	7	—	7	33*	9	0	38	1*
E. Harris													11	118	31	21	2	5	57	37	49	17
R.J. Bennett													23	15	2	21	31	110	24	0	22	1
C. Dell													4	0								
T. Cooley													0	0	—	—					0	0
B. Cruse																			16	0		
M.P. Tame															32	3	7	4				
Byes				11			2	16					6	5	8	10	2	6			6	3
Leg-byes	8		2	2	6		5	7	2	9			11	2	2	3	10		2	1	7	
Wides	3		2	1	1								2	1					4	2		
No-Balls	15		3	5			4	4	28	39			1		14	4	12	28	4		1	
Total	429		102	169	328		159	299	156	335			343	260	407	171	194	278	210	107	231	115
Wickets	10		10	10	10		10	10	10	10			10	10	8	5	10	10	10	10	10	9†
Results	D		L		D		L		L		Ab		L		D		L		L		L	
Points	0		0		0		0		0		—		4		0		0		0		0	

Catches:
23 – R.E. Soule
8 – R.D. Woolley
7 – D.J. Buckingham
6 – M. Ray and K.R. Bradshaw
5 – R.S. Hyatt
4 – R.J. Bennett
3 – R.L. Brown, S.L. Saunders and W.W. Davis
2 – E. Harris, M. Hill and Subs
1 – D.C. Boon, C. Dell, T. Cooley and B. Cruse

† R.S. Hyatt, retired hurt

BOWLING

BOWLING	W.W. Davis	M. Hill	R.L. Brown	M. Ray	S.L. Saunders	K.R. Bradshaw	R.S. Hyatt	R.D. Woolley	D.J. Buckingham
v. New South Wales (Hobart) 25–28 October 1985	38–9–129–3 / 12–9–9–0	32–9–94–0 / 12–2–44–1	35–2–166–4 / 6–1–17–0	35.5–6–102–2 / 5–3–3–0	10–1–59–1 / 12–0–37–0				
v. Western Australia (Perth) 1–4 November 1985	36–11–64–2	25–9–54–2	22.4–5–49–3	33–10–80–3	7–2–16–0	3–1–4–0			
v. Victoria (Melbourne) 8–11 November 1985	43–14–101–0	30–3–88–2	37–10–105–3	18–9–26–1	1–0–4–0				
v. South Australia (Launceston) 22–25 November 1985	43–12–126–2 / 2–0–3–1	20–5–52–1 / 2–0–11–0	39–10–159–4	17.3–3–36–1	4–0–26–0		15–6–34–1	0.4–0–4–0	
v. Queensland (Devonport) 6–9 December 1985	14.2–5–31–0	4–1–12–0	47.4–16–124–4 / 6–0–31–0	13–3–31–0	4–1–30–0	27–5–85–2 / 7–1–40–2	17–7–54–3	9–0–29–0	2–0–9–1
v. Indians (Hobart) 20–23 December 1985									
v. South Australia (Adelaide) 10–13 January 1986			29.3–5–80–7 / 21–2–103–4	17–5–44–1 / 6–2–33–0		9–5–10–0 / 6–0–24–0	13–1–44–0 / 28–5–77–2		
v. Western Australia (Hobart) 24–27 January 1986			37–2–152–3 / 7–0–24–0	21–3–69–0		9–0–38–1	21–6–77–0		
v. Queensland (Brisbane) 31 Jan.–3 Feb. 1986	37.3–5–128–7 / 8–0–41–3		30–3–124–3 / 7–2–34–1	13–4–25–0		11–1–36–0 / 1–0–12–0			
v. New South Wales (Sydney) 21–24 February 1986	41–2–105–4		22.4–2–79–1	35–12–79–5		1–0–4–0	19–2–54–0		
v. Victoria (Devonport) 28 Feb.–3 March 1986	13–3–31–0		31.3–2–102–4 / 5–0–16–0	16–2–57–1		6–0–32–1	9–1–29–0		
	287.5–70–768–22 av. 34.90	125–29–355–6 av. 59.16	384.2–62–1365–41 av. 33.29	230.2–62–585–14 av. 41.78	38–4–172–1 av. 172.00	80–13–285–6 av. 47.50	122–28–369–6 av. 61.50	9.4–0–33–0 av. —	2–0–9–1 av. 9.00

a D.C. Boon 0.4–0–2–0   b E. Harris 0.3–0–3–1   c R.E. Soule 1.4–0–11–0   d B. Cruse 13–2–36–0

M	Inns	NOs	Runs	HS	Av
10	18	—	342	52	19.00
4	6	—	75	38	12.50
3	5	—	320	196	64.00
10	18	—	450	112	25.00
10	18	2	490	124*	30.62
10	18	1	687	121	40.41
5	8	1	151	51	21.57
10	17	4	293	53	22.53
10	17	4	160	31	12.30
8	14	2	82	21	6.83
5	8	5	22	10	7.33
8	14	2	236	80	19.66
5	10	—	348	118	34.80
5	10	—	249	110	24.90
1	2	—	4	4	4.00
3	4	—	0	0	0.00
1	2	—	16	16	8.00
2	4	—	46	32	11.50

T. Cooley	C. Dell	M. P. Tame	Byes	Leg-byes	Wides	No-balls	Total	Wkts
			4	7		12	561	10
			1		2	4	111	1
			3	8	1	13	278	10
			2	6	2	12	332	6
			1	8	3	12	442	10
				2	1	2	20	1
			2	9		16	407	9
						3	85	3a
								Ab
24–5–87–2	6–1–40–0		2	6	2	11	313	10
12–0–83–0	1–0–15–0		9	1		6	345	6
19–2–78–0		35–4–127–2	2	10	1	11	553	7
4–0–33–3		8–0–67–0		2		5	129	5b
		19–5–46–0		6		31	365	10
		1–0–3–0	5	3		5	109	4c
			3	4		14	364	10d
10–0–69–0				6	2	10	326	6
4.5–1–15–1							31	1
73.5–8–	7–1–	63–9–						
365–6	55–0	243–2						
av. 60.83	—	av. 121.50						

on the Perth wicket as they did, it would have been nothing short of a miracle if they had won the Sheffield Shield. But Western Australia came close enough to graduating to the final to convince many sage observers that it is a team of the future. Such a conclusion was evidenced by its innings victory over the eventual 'champs', New South Wales, in Perth in January and its tenacious triumph over the same proven combination in the final of the McDonald's Cup.

The backbone of the Perth side's batting was its young 'veteran' captain, former Test opener, Graeme Wood, whose consistency in the opening position and middle-order, won him third place in the national averages with 741 runs at 61.75. Not far behind Wood was the former national Under-19 skipper, Mike Valetta, whose 715 runs included 2 centuries and 6 fifties and whose composure on difficult pitches undoubtedly earned him a berth in the Australian touring team to India. Before the end of the summer, Geoff Marsh's powerful front-foot play and monolithic concentration had partnered him with David Boon in one of Australia's most successful opening combinations in many a moon. Peter Gonnella, Rob Gartrell and Wayne Andrews all vindicated the selectors' faith in them by scoring centuries in the course of the season, whilst Tim Zoehrer occasionally reinforced his competency behind the stumps with some timely innings. On the bowling front, the left-handed speed of the two beanpoles, Bruce Reid and Chris Matthews, quickly made them one of the most feared combinations in Sheffield Shield cricket. Reid's unerring middle-and-off line won his side's home game against Tasmania and eventually brought him the just recognition of the national selectors. Matthews' figures of 7/133 against New South Wales and 5/103 against Victoria more than suggest that a similar reward is just around the corner for this immensely tall paceman.

Western Australia's bowlers opened their 1985/86 Shield campaign in Adelaide on 17 October in brisk businesslike fashion. Expatriate Tasmanian quick bowler Clough and medium-pacer Macleay immediately struck an effective line and length, disposing of Hilditch, Bishop, Zadow, Hookes and O'Connor for only 92. But Peter Sleep proved obdurate and showed that his voluntary fallow year of 1984/85 had not blunted his batting skills; his 105 was his sixth 100 in the upper echelons of the game and put some starch into a South Australian innings which eventually struggled to 255. Warwickshire's opening bowler, Gladstone Small surprised Wood and Marsh with his nip off the pitch and was eventually rewarded by the figures of 5/89 in his first outing in Shield cricket. But Valetta held his ground, gleaning 87 runs and adding 103 in harness with Ireland for the fourth wicket. Zoehrer clinched matters, coming to the wicket at 204 and extending Western Australia's first-innings advantage to 82 with an unbeaten 94. Bob Zadow lingered 325 minutes over his maiden 100 when the home batsmen took advantage of their second opportunity at the crease; his 144, Bishop's 108 and Hookes' 82 were the cornerstones of South Australia's declaration at 4/357. 'Too late, too late', commented Wood, as he and Marsh played out time, helping themselves to half-centuries en route.

Western Australia received its first ration of 12 points from Tasmania, who succumbed by an innings and 7 runs in Perth. The first day of the first match played on the relaid W.A.C.A. Oval set the pattern for the remainder of the games staged on

Victoria 1985–86
First Class Matches

BATTING	v Queensland 18–21 October 1985	v New South Wales (Newcastle) 1–4 November 1985	v Tasmania (Melbourne) 8–11 Nov. 1985	v Western Australia (Perth) 15–18 Nov. 1985	v Indians (Melbourne) 6–9 December 1985	v Queensland (Melbourne) 13–16 Dec. 1985	v New South Wales (Melbourne) 20–23 Dec. 1985	v Western Australia (Melbourne) 18–21 January 1986	v South Australia (Melbourne) 25–28 January 1986	v South Australia (Adelaide) 21–24 February 1986	v Tasmania (Devonport) 28 Feb.–3 Mar. 1986
M.B. Quinn	46 19	5 1	38 —	3 62	31 —	12 —	3 —	53 14	33 54	29 103	24 5
D.F. Whatmore	109 7	72 0	6 —	29 22	19 —	90 —	6 —	21 5	127 50	2 84	4 23*
D.M. Jones	16 6	19 9	8 —	0 113	83 —	9 —	12 —	37 72	1 91	0 57*	70 —
P.A. Hibbert	65 31*	14 21	62 —	9 19		137 —	148 —	10 18	32 5*	0 0*	124 —
J.D. Siddons	33 17	76 5	74 —	7 7	12 —	107 —	1 —	45 17	2 36	44 —	57 —
M.G. Dimattina	46 15*	48 7	54* —	2 2*	19 —	23* —	2* —	5 2	4 —	10 —	
P.W. Young	11 20				29 —	8 —	9 —	10 37			
A.O.C. Dodemaide	32 6	0 11	7 —	27 33*		31 —	5 —	63* 5*	48 9	80 —	4* —
R.J. Bright	38 —	39 16	61* —	6 3	10 —		69 —	26 —	0 67*		
M.G. Hughes	1 —	8 0		9* —	23 —		4 —	9 0	19 —	47 —	
S.P. Davis	0* —	3* 0*		3 —	0* —	2 —					
S.P. O'Donnell		10 4		6 22							25
R.C.A. McCarthy			—								
G. Parker					2 —					15 —	
D. Hickey					0 —					8*	
D.A. Emerson						14 —					
C. Miller								0 9	0 —		
P. Jackson									0 —	2 —	0*
Byes		12	2	1	1	5	2	7 1	4 5	3 11	
Leg-byes	1 1	6 3	6	3 6	1	12	8	5 3	7 9	6 12	6
Wides	1		2					1 1		1 2	2
No-balls	32 3	8 1	12	6 12	2	6	4	4 3	1 1	2 1	10 3
Total	431 137	308 78	332	111 302	233	456	273	295 186	345 261	250 268	326 31
Wickets	10 6	10 10	6	10 7	10	9	9	10 10	10 5	10 2	6 1
Results	D	L	D	D	D	D	D	D	D	W	W
Points	0	4	4	4	—	4	4	4	4	8	12

Catches: 36 – M.G. Dimattina (ct 34/st 2)
17 – D.F. Whatmore
10 – J.D. Siddons
9 – A.I.C. Dodemaide
7 – D.M. Jones
6 – P.A. Hibbert
3 – S.P. O'Donnell, R.C.A. McCarty and subs
2 – S.P. Davis and M.B. Quinn
1 – R.J. Bright, G. Parker, P.W. Young, C. Miller, P. Jackson and D. Hickey

BOWLING	A.I.C. Dodemaide	M.G. Hughes	S.P. Davis	R.J. Bright	J.D. Siddons	P. Jackson	P.A. Hibbert	S.P. O'Donnell	D.M. Jones
v. Queensland (Brisbane) 18–21 October 1985	34.2–7–151–4	34–4–116–3	25–4–106–1	26–3–127–1	4–0–25–0		1–1–0–0		
v. New South Wales (Newcastle) 1–4 November 1985	12–5–21–1	24–4–74–5	12–0–48–1	13–5–31–0				15.5–3–53–2	
	11–4–36–1	25–4–90–1	14–5–32–2	11–4–17–0				24.2–5–66–5	
v. Tasmania (Melbourne) 8–11 November 1985	21–5–48–0	29.5–6–81–4	33–11–73–5	31–14–61–1					
v. Western Australia (Perth) 15–18 November 1985			17–4–36–2	15.4–4–19–6				20–7–33–2	
v. Indians (Melbourne) 6–9 December 1985	11–1–28–0	25–4–78–1	18–3–29–0	22–10–22–0	2–0–5–0		6–0–10–0	24–6–29–1	
		26–12–42–3	18–5–24–1	15–6–17–1	7–1–25–0				
v. Queensland (Melbourne) 13–16 December 1985	34–7–101–2		34.5–14–53–6				5–2–14–0		10–2–30–1
	28–10–48–2		32–19–46–0		4–1–11–0		9–3–12–0		9–2–19–0
v. New South Wales (Melbourne) 20–23 December 1985	15–3–45–0	16–3–50–1	24.4–7–64–3	36–12–74–6					2–1–1–0
	27–5–76–1	16–1–70–1	14–2–56–0	26–6–56–1					9–1–33–0
v. Western Australia (Melbourne) 18–21 January 1986	21–7–52–2	14–4–39–1		30–12–44–5				2–0–9–0	2–0–8–0
	22–4–58–1	23–5–69–1		48–20–62–3					2–1–5–0
v. South Australia (Melbourne) 25–28 January 1986	12–3–29–0	12.1–2–34–2		42–18–73–3		29.5–9–51–2			
	12–3–33–0	10–1–29–0		25–12–32–0		19–8–36–0			
v. South Australia (Adelaide) 21–24 February 1986	24–8–68–2	19–3–54–1		19–4–48–1		12–5–19–0			5–0–17–0
	27–15–37–1	28–7–64–1							
v. Tasmania (Devonport) 28 Feb.–3 March 1986	23–5–48–1	23–6–53–5				4–1–10–0		23.4–7–52–4	
	2–0–9–0	10–1–23–4						8–3–31–0	
	336.2–92– 888–18 av. 49.33	352–71– 1002–36 av. 27.83	241.1–74– 550–25 av. 22.00	325–122– 616–21 av. 29.33	18–2– 70–0 —	83.5–27– 164–3 av. 54.66	23–6– 45–0 —	115.5–31– 264–14 av. 18.85	39–7– 113–1 av. 113.00

a P.W. Young 1–0–11–0
b R.C.A. McCarthy 24–3–59–0
c P.W. Young 6–2–11–0
d M.B. Quinn 2–0–5–0, D.F. Whatmore 1–0–4–0
e C. Miller 8–1–19–2, 21–5–48–1
f C. Miller 16–3–61–2

M	Inns	NOs	Runs	HS	Av
11	18	—	535	103	29.72
11	18	1	676	127	39.76
11	17	1	603	113	37.68
10	16	3	695	148	53.46
11	16	—	540	107	33.75
11	14	5	239	54*	26.55
5	7	—	124	37	17.71
10	15	4	361	80	32.81
8	11	2	335	69	37.22
10	10	1	120	47	13.33
7	6	4	8	3*	4.00
3	5	—	67	25	13.40
1					—
2	2	—	17	15	8.50
4	2	1	8	8*	8.00
1	1	—	14	14	14.00
2	3	—	9	9	3.00
3	3	1	2	2	1.00

D. Hickey	G. Parker	D. Emerson	Byes	Leg-byes	Wides	No-balls	Total	Wkts
			3	1		4	539	10a
			1	4	1	1	232	10
				3	1	6	244	10
			6	1		5	328	10b
				6		2	94	10
			6	5		8	212	2
18–4–52–1	7–3–15–1		4	3		3	182	7
8–3–17–1		16–3–68–0		5		2	288	10
		17–4–40–0	7	3		2	197	2c
			2	5	4		241	10
			4	6		2	319	3d
						5	162	10e
			3	6		6	255	6
			2	1		8	251	10f
			8	8		3	189	3g
27–4–93–3	2–0–8–0			15		1	303	8
28.5–10–81–7	4–0–7–1		1	2	1	1	211	10
20–1–68–0				3	7	1	241	10
13.3–1–52–5						1	115	9h
115.2–23–	13–3–	33–7–						
363–17	30–2	108–0						
av. 21.35	av. 15.00	—						

C. Miller 19–8–39–1, M.G. Dimattina 1–0–4–1
R.S. Hyatt retired hurt

the ground in 1985/86. Handicapped by a slow, low-bouncing wicket and an outfield which was so sluggish that it needed almost herculean strength for the batsmen to find the boundary, Tasmania were dismissed by Macleay and Bush for 102, with wicketkeeper Zoehrer contributing 5 catches. If Boon had not been dropped twice in scoring 64, his team would not have reached three figures. Valetta's subsequent 85 in over six hours told the full, long story of the difficulty of the pitch and the slowness of the outfield. His innings was a marathon of application and, allied to 46 from Marsh and 38 from Zoehrer, hoisted the Western Australian score to 278. On such a wicket survival for a long period of time was out of the question against the lofty and accurate Reid, who delivered the ball from a height of almost 2 metres – with a complete lack of bounce! Buckingham scored a plucky 45 and Woolley 40 as their side went under for the third and last time for 169, with Reid's 32 overs yielding him 6/54.

The next three games against Victoria, Queensland and New South Wales took the wind of victory out of Western Australia's sails. Gaining only 2 points from the trio of matches, the Perth side drifted off the course which it had set itself for the Sheffield Shield. Its next tack brought it back into the breeze as it took maximum points off Wellham's New South Welshmen in Perth; but it lost way again by going down on the first innings to Victoria in Melbourne. Hobart and the return encounter with Tasmania presented the best opportunity of getting back into position for line honours. But the Perth-Hobart race was a grave disappointment to Wood and his men, who benefited by only 4 points when they expected 12. The Hobart pitch was a batsman's paradise and produced 5 centuries and over 1200 runs in four days. The visitors began with 7/553 declared. The tall, bespectacled left-handed Gonnella top-scored with 134, receiving substantial support from Gartrell's 104, Wood's 102, Moody's 94 and Valetta's 53. It was rapid-fire batting. The whole innings only occupied 542 minutes and Gartrell ripped off his 100 on the second day in only 90 minutes! For Gonnella and Gartrell it was their initiation into the apparently not-so-exclusive 'Ton Club'. But if Western Australia believed that, after its mammoth first innings total, maximum points were a 'cert', it was in for a shock, Woolley, suffering from a viral infection, epitomized the gameness of the Taswegians. He occupied the crease for 238 balls and, taking advantage of the Western Australian laxness in the field, helped himself to 124 not out. Bradshaw's 112 was a good guide to the nature of the wicket, whilst Buckingham's 57 was as noble as his namesake. After saving the follow-on, Tasmania declared at 8/407, opening the door for a Western Australian closure which could have afforded both teams an opportunity to gain 12 points. The home team, however, deemed the final demand of 276 on the last day, too hard an impost and the match degenerated into a draw with Tasmania 5/171 in its second innings.

Its 3-run triumph over Queensland in Perth meant that Western Australia, in the course of the season, had taken more points off the runners-up in the Sheffield Shield than it had conceded and was on an equal footing with the eventual champions. Illusions of a last minute graduation to the Shield final still tantalized Western Australian imaginations, as their side prepared to leap its last South Australian hurdle on the W.A.C.A. ground. This ultimate trial proved to

Western Australia 1985–86
First Class Matches

BATTING (each cell shows 1st and 2nd innings)

BATTING	v. South Australia (Adelaide) 17–20 Oct 1985	v. Tasmania (Perth) 1–4 Nov 1985	v. Victoria (Perth) 15–18 Nov 1985	v. Queensland (Brisbane) 29 Nov–2 Dec 1985	v. New South Wales (Sydney) 7–10 Dec 1985	v. New South Wales (Perth) 10–13 Jan 1986	v. Victoria (Melbourne) 18–21 Jan 1986	v. Tasmania (Hobart) 24–27 Jan 1986	v. Queensland (Perth) 21–24 Feb 1986	v. South Australia (Perth) 28 Feb–3 Mar 1986
G.M. Wood	10 53*	10 —	14 82	13 —	51 12	133 —	0 67*	102 —	121 —	9 64*
M.R.J. Veletta	87 —	85 —	0 7	130 —	5 55	16 —	26 55	53 9	0 78*	107 2
G.R. Marsh	11 50*	46 —	2 100*	138 —	35 5					
M.W. McPhee	18 4	23 —	0 4*	10 —	0 3					
G.J. Ireland	50 —	6	19 —	39	9 5	1 —				
W.S. Andrews	29 —	20 —	12 —	41 —	30 0	139 —	11 22	31* 11	43 —	82* 11
K.H. MacLeay	3 —	23 —	10 —	60 —	14 2	41* —	10* —	— —	21* —	— 2
T.J. Zoehrer	94* —	38 —	15 —	24 —	5 1	39 —	4 13	0		
G.E. Bush	3 —	1 —	5 —	4 —	4 0					
B.A. Reid	16 —	1 —	3* —	23* —	11* 9					
P.M. Clough	1 —	0* —								
C.R. Matthews			6 —	24 —		—	11		0	— 1*
B. Mulder					4 3*		0 —	— —		
P. Gonnella						10 —	0 49	134 36	27 61	0 37
T. Moody						19 —	29 14	94 59	39 0	46 2
T. Breman						22* —	20 13*	11 6	22 —	45* 0
P. Capes							— —			
R. Gartrell							46 7	104 1*	24 36*	92 3
M. Cox									2 —	31 3
G.D. Porter									0 —	
Byes	3 4	3	— 6	—	5 7	10	3 2			5 1
Leg-byes	2 3	8	6 5	4	8 3	3	6 10	2 —	2 3	13 2
Wides	1 1	1	— —	1	3 —	2		1 —	2 —	3 1
No-balls	9 2	13	2 8	16	3 —	15	5 6	11 5	19 14	2 —
Total	337 117	278	94 212	527	187 105	450	162 255	553 129	322 195	433 128
Wickets	10 1	10	10 2	10	10 10	7	10 6	7 5	10 2	6 8
Results	D	W	D	D	L	W	D	D	D	D
Points	4	12	0	2	0	12	0	4	4	4

Catches

26	T.J. Zoehrer (ct 22/st 4)
11	W.S. Andrews
10	M.R.J. Veletta
7	M. Cox (ct 6/st 1)
6	P. Gonnella
5	G.M. Wood and G.J. Ireland
4	B. Mulder, G.E. Bush and K.H. MacLeay
3	C.R. Matthews
2	G.R. Marsh, T. Breman, B.A. Reid and subs (ct 1/st 2)
1	T. Moody, R. Gartrell and M.W. McPhee

BOWLING

Match	B.A. Reid	K.H. MacLeay	P.M. Clough	G.E. Bush	W.S. Andrews	C.R. Matthews	B. Mulder	P. Capes	T. Breman
v. South Australia (Adelaide) 17–20 October 1985 (1st)	31.4–8–71–2	30–8–83–4	25–4–71–3	12–4–19–1	2–2–0–0				
(2nd)	24.4–7–90–1	17–3–68–0	22–6–75–1	28–3–104–2	5–1–20–0				
v. Tasmania (Perth) 1–4 November 1985 (1st)	21–12–15–0	16–8–22–3	9–4–15–0	27.4–7–31–3	12–1–17–2				
(2nd)	32–8–54–6	14.3–3–31–1	12–2–22–1	27–3–31–0	14–6–18–1				
v. Victoria (Perth) 15–18 November 1985 (1st)	19.1–4–41–3	18–5–43–2				21–8–23–5			
(2nd)	40–7–113–2	27–11–35–2		19–5–40–0	12–3–24–0	31–4–84–2			
v. Queensland (Brisbane) 29 Nov.–2 Dec. 1985	26–8–59–1	20–5–44–3		22–7–57–0	4–2–4–0	24–7–58–1			
v. New South Wales (Sydney) 7–10 December 1985 (1st)	26.2–3–74–2	23–5–58–4		38–9–92–2	8–5–9–0		26–7–49–1		
(2nd)	13–1–33–2	7–0–30–1		10–2–47–1	3–1–5–1		7–0–38–0		
v. New South Wales (Perth) 10–13 January 1986 (1st)		14–5–25–3				8.5–0–40–5		10–6–14–1	4–1–4–0
(2nd)		38.1–10–93–6				35–7–93–2		12–0–53–0	21–9–47–2
v. Victoria (Melbourne) 18–21 January 1986 (1st)		18–6–38–0			15–3–32–1	23–7–49–1	39–10–125–6		12–2–39–1
(2nd)		22–5–50–3			6–0–15–0	23.5–5–54–4	15–5–35–2		6–0–28–0
v. Tasmania (Hobart) 24–27 January 1986 (1st)		31–7–83–0			10–2–24–1	36.2–9–116–4	47–14–129–1		28–10–45–1
(2nd)		6–0–24–0				11–0–34–1	23–5–55–2		18–4–43–2
v. Queensland (Perth) 21–24 February 1986		31–7–90–2			6–0–30–0	25–8–75–2			21–2–76–6
v. South Australia (Perth) 28 Feb.–3 March 1986 (1st)		39–9–72–1				36.2–5–112–2	47–21–112–3		29–9–74–3
(2nd)		7–3–24–0			8–3–33–2	8–2–19–2	10–2–47–0		8–1–26–2
Totals	233.5–58–550–19 av. 28.94	378.4–100–913–35 av. 26.08	68–16–183–5 av. 36.60	183.4–40–421–9 av. 46.77	105–29–231–8 av. 28.87	283.2–62–757–31 av. 24.41	214–64–590–15 av. 39.33	22–6–67–1 av. 67.00	147–38–382–17 av. 22.47

a G.M. Wood 0.1–0–1–0

M	Inns	NOs	Runs	HS	Av
10	15	3	741	133	61.75
10	16	1	715	130	47.66
5	8	2	387	138	64.50
5	8	1	62	23	8.85
6	7	—	129	50	18.42
10	14	2	482	139	40.16
10	10	3	186	60	26.57
8	10	1	233	94*	25.88
5	6	—	17	5	2.83
5	6	3	63	23*	21.00
2	2	1	1	1	1.00
7	5	1	42	24	10.50
4	3	1	7	4	3.50
5	9	—	354	134	39.33
5	9	—	302	94	33.55
5	8	3	139	45*	27.80
1					—
4	8	2	313	104	52.16
2	3	—	36	31	12.00
1	1	—	0	0	0.00

T. Moody	G.D. Porter	M.R.J. Veletta	Byes	Leg-byes	Wides	No-balls	Total	Wkts
				11	2	2	255	10
				4			357	4
					2	2	102	10
			11	2	1	3	169	10
			1	3		6	111	10
				6	1	12	302	7
				3		12	225	5
				4		6	286	10
			4	7			157	5
					2		83	10
9–2–24–0			1	10	1	13	321	10
				7	5	4	295	10
			1	3		3	186	10
			8	2		14	407	8
1–0–1–0		1–0–1–0	10	3		4	171	5
	17–5–38–0		10		1	19	319	10
19–5–44–1			4	14	2	14	432	10
9–3–27–1			1	3	1	2	181	8a
38–10–	17–5–	1–0–						
96–2	38–0	1–0						
av. 48.00	—	—						

Western Australian cricket followers that their cricket was on the threshold of a phoenix-like revival. Batting first, South Australia accumulated a daunting 432-run total, with Sleep, batting number three at his own request, contributing 139 and debutant, Australian Under 19 Indian tourist, Jamie Pyke, 77. Was Western Australia downhearted? Not a bit! Its answer was swift and positive: 6/433 declared with Valetta registering his third 100 of the season and adding a joint 167 for the fourth wicket with Gartrell, who followed his breath-taking display in Hobart with another 92 in 201 minutes. The Perth team finally needed 181 runs for victory-prestissimo: but it could do little against the accuracy of Gladstone Small and Pyke, who each claimed four victims, to have Wood's side with its back to the wall when the final bell sounded with the scoreboard showing 8/128. Wood himself remained undefeated on 64, and one could sense that he was promising himself that, next year, his youthful protégés would return, like General MacArthur, with a vengeance.

March 1986 at the Adelaide Oval was a far cry from the halcyon days of 1981/82 when South Australia last won the Sheffield Shield. Everything went wrong for skipper Hookes and, in consequence, his team plummeted to the second last position in the championship ladder. The Adelaide side's only victories came against the bottom team, Tasmania – although it did pick up 4 consolation first-innings points against the eventual champions, New South Wales in Sydney. The brave declarations which characterized Hookes' charismatic leadership in previous years completely misfired in 1985/86. Queensland exploited his erratic gambling instincts to collect 12 points in mid-November, whilst teams like Victoria were unwilling to afford South Australia even the sniff of an unlikely victory which Hookes's own dynamic batting could transform into an easy win.

On the personnel front, batsman Haysman and fast bowler McCurdy fell victims to the lure of the krugerrand, whilst left-handed medium-pacer, Carmichael, who, as recently as 1983/84, captured 41 Shield wickets, disappeared into limbo. The S.A.C.A. selectors conjured up one bowling replacement in the person of English county speedster, Gladstone Small, who toiled manfully to reward his employers with 37 wickets. It was incongruous to think that, in the previous season, because of Victoria's Yorkshire philosophy of only fielding home-grown players, Small had only played in junior cricket in Melbourne. Australia's Under 19 Australian medium-pacer, Andrew Zesers, added cubits to his reputation for accuracy by equalling Small's statistical achievement – but, by and large, bowling talent was thin on the ground in Adelaide in 1985/86. So much so that the South Australian selectors were compelled to recall the veteran left-handed swing bowler, Sam Parkinson, to the colours. The Kensington Club captain-coach had played a vital role in South Australia's 1981/82 Shield triumph – and he did not let the 'Croweaters' down in 1985/86, taking 20 wickets at an average cost of 38.65.

South Australia's batting problems were exacerbated by Andrew Hilditch's complete loss of form. His fall from grace was so abrupt that, after opening the innings for his country against New Zealand in Brisbane in November, Hilditch was jettisoned for South Australia's clash with Tasmania in early January – for the 30-year-old Andrew Watson! Hilditch's erstwhile opening partner and Australia's Under 25 representative in Zimbabwe, Glenn Bishop, began the season in his most belligerent mood, despoiling the Tasmanian attack to the tune of 224 runs, helping himself to 108 against Western Australia and plundering 202 off the touring Indian bowlers. But he, too, lost his touch and ended the season batting down the order at number five and only collecting a moderate aggregate of 645. Peter Sleep's re-emergence into first-class cricket provided the South Australian batting with stability, 3 centuries and 2 fifties – whilst wicketkeeper Kelly showed a sense of responsibility, batting at number 7; but Hookes's brilliance was exasperatingly ephemeral. The Australian selectors made him vice-captain of the national side, but were eventually disillusioned by a man who, in one innings, could savage 243 runs off the strong New South Wales attack, and at other times look so inept. The disillusionment of Greg Chappell and his co-selectors was shared by the South Australian administration who, at the end of the summer, replaced Hookes as state coach with the more cerebral mentor, John Inverarity.

Defeated on the first innings by Western Australia and by Queensland outright, South Australia had to wait until its visit to Launceston to pick up its first points of the season at the expense of Tasmania. Its opening total of 442 was founded on Sleep – who missed his third 100 in three matches by only a single – Kelly's 79 and Parkinson's 62. Parkinson followed up his unexpected batting success with 4/41 as the home resistance crumbled for 159. Batting a second time, the Apple Islanders did better, reaching 299, with all-rounder, Roly Hyatt registering a career-best of 80 and opener Mark Ray supplementing his earlier 49-run resistance with another stubborn knock of 47. The fates were against the home side, for, no sooner had South Australia knocked off the 20 runs needed for victory for the loss of 1 wicket than steady relentless rain set in.

Two months elapsed before Tasmania visited Adelaide and gave Hookes' men their next cause for celebration. Successive outright losses to New South Wales and Queensland had sapped South Australian enthusiasm and this time the visitors extended the home side, taking first-innings points and coming within 55 runs of complete success. South Australia's first knock was a collective effort, with Kelly contributing 85 and Bishop, Harms and all-rounder Stephen Wundke – well known in English league circles – 40s to the overall result of 313. Roger Brown, Tasmania's medium-paced representative on the Australian Under 25 tour of Zimbabwe, reflected the new determination in Tasmanian ranks, sticking to his task to be rewarded with figures of 7/80: an analysis which he complemented with second innings figures of 4/103. Following Brown's example, the visiting batsman demanded a 343-run tribute from the bowling of Parkinson, Small, Zesers, Harms, Sleep and Wundke; part of Buckingham's 121 and Woolley's 94 produced a fifth wicket partnership of 175 and set Tasmanian feet firmly on the path towards first-innings points. The wind of the game's fortunes, however, swung to the opposite quarter when Bishop strode to the crease for a second time. Twenty-eight times the ball crunched into the boundary as the South Australian opener stormed to his second double hundred of the season

and acting-skipper, Bob Zadow felt confident enough to declare at 6/345. For a while the batsmen from across Bass Strait looked capable of reaching their victory target of 316. Twenty-two-year-old opener Errol Harris gave Tasmania and his own first-class career a splendid start with an innings of 118; but the later batting could not cope with the wiles of spinners Harms and Sleep and the nagging perseverance of Zesers and – disappointingly – even failed to save the game – but only by 4 balls!

This saga of South Australian success ended amidst great excitement on 13 January 1986. The rest of the season's story was one of unmitigated defeat and despair: not another point came the way of the Adelaide side in the next six weeks as it lost on the first innings to New South Wales, Victoria and Western Australia and succumbed yet again to Victoria – this time outright by 8 wickets.

But if the end of the South Australian story was unhappy, it was not the black tragedy written into the 1985/86 record books by Tasmania. The Apple Islanders' first innings win over South Australia was the only sunny moment in their stormy year. A great deal of their misery was of their own making. An amicable contractual agreement with Gloucestershire's Zimbabwean Taswegian, Brian Davison, would have greatly enriched their team in batting depth, experience and professional 'nous'. Nor was Dame Fortune kind to the Cinderella state. Having to settle for one, instead of its permissable two overseas players, it was reduced to dependence on local stock when, in the last game before Christmas aginst Queensland, its West Indian Test paceman, Winston Davis broke down and was sidelined until the next Queensland game almost two months later. To make matters worse, West Australian recruit, Mark Hill, a distinctly slippery fast bowling prospect was also injured in the same match and took no further part in the season's activities. Young pacemen Troy Cooley and Chris Dell were pressed into service but bristled with inexperience, throwing more than a fair share of responsibility on the workhorse of the Tasmanian attack, Roger Brown. Brown toiled like a Trojan and was justly rewarded with 40 wickets – just two less than the leading wicket-taker in the Shield competition, Queensland's Jeff Thomson. Roger Woolley – perhaps unwisely deposed as skipper in favour of David Boon – who for most of the summer was an absentee captain, gave unselfish service. Not only did he stand down from the wicketkeeping position to give Australian Under 19 representative, Richard Soule, his opportunity behind the stumps, but he also batted with great heart in times of crisis and, on one occasion, sickness. His 500-run aggregate was bettered in Tasmanian ranks only by Danny Buckingham, who accumulated 1 century and 4 fifties in an aggregate of 687 and averaged 40.41. There is a great deal of ability in Taswegian cricket and better times are undoubtedly around the corner for the sport in the Apple Isle. But future prospects are cold comfort for a side which finished the season as wooden spoonists of the domestic competition of a nation, which, on the Test evidence of 1985/86, must rank below the West Indies, England, New Zealand and India in international ratings.

Age Of Gold

The season in New Zealand.
Shell Cup and Shell Trophy.
New Zealand *v*. Australia
Test series and One-Day
International series

Age of gold. Jeremy Coney discusses tactics as New Zealand prepare to beat Australia.
(Ross Setford)

When the selectors met to choose the New Zealand party to go to Australia for a three-match Test series they decided that the Test career of Geoff Howarth was at an end. It was not unexpected that he would be replaced as captain. He was approaching his thirty-fifth birthday and his form had declined in recent years. He had suffered sadly at Surrey where he had been named as captain and had then been unable to find a place in the team because Gray had been imported to take the place of the injured Clarke. At the end of the 1985 season, Surrey announced that Howarth was being released, and he passed from the English county scene in silence. His Test career should not be allowed to end in the same way. Here was a captain whose international career should be remembered with a 'bang' rather than a 'whimper'.

His Test career was spread over ten years and he was captain of New Zealand for the last five of them, save for the tour of Pakistan in 1984 when he was unable to make the trip. He first led New Zealand in 1980 when West Indies were the visitors. New Zealand took the first Test in dramatic fashion and outplayed the West Indies in the two remaining, drawn Tests. It was an achievement which no other Test captain has since equalled, and it heralded the greatest period in New Zealand's cricket history.

Howarth brought to New Zealand cricket a professionalism that was never tainted by sharp practice nor by an

Geoff Howarth. His leadership was always one of quiet dignity and intelligent authority. New Zealand owes him much. (Tony Edenden)

antagonism born of a sense that cricket is a crusade in which one can rectify past wrongs. Howarth's leadership was always one of quiet dignity and intelligent authority. His reward was victory over England for the first time in a series and the first Test win in England.

He has never received the praise or the publicity of an extrovert intelligence, like Brearley, but his achievement has been at least as great. New Zealand owes him much, and the world Test arena will be a lesser place without him.

Howarth continued to lead Northern Districts in a season which was compacted into three distinct sections; the Shell Cup, the Shell Trophy and the visit of the Australians.

For the first time the Shell Cup, the one-day competition, preceded the Shell Trophy, having previously been interspersed with it, and was scheduled to be completed in nine days.

Shell Cup

27 December 1985

at Ashburton
Auckland 136
Canterbury 136 for 9 (A.J. Hunt 5 for 27)
Canterbury (2 pts) won on losing fewer wickets

at New Plymouth
Central Districts 120
Otago 123 for 6 (P.J. Visser 5 for 20)
Otago (2 pts) won by 4 wickets

at Tauranga
Wellington 161 for 9 (K. Treiber 4 for 28)
Northern Districts 153 (B.L. Cairns 60, P.J. W. Allott 4 for 12)
Wellington (2 pts) won by 8 runs

The first round of matches produced some exciting cricket. Last wicket pair Hart and Tracy nudged Canterbury to victory at Ashburton, levelling the scores off the last ball. John Reid, with 46, was the leading batsman in the match where the surprise was the bowling of Alan Hunt who had previously bowled only three overs in the competition. Hunt captured 5 for 27 in 9 overs with his off-breaks.

Tight bowling by Boock, Cushen and McKechnie stifled Central Districts at New Plymouth, and Otago won with 4 overs to spare.

At Tauranga, Wellington lost Vance and Coney for 12, and the only real substance of the innings came in a fifth wicket stand of 50 between Jones and McSweeney. Allott, Maguiness and Larsen bowled Wellington into a winning position as Northern collapsed to 90 for 7, but Lance Cairns, soon to announce his retirement, hit a whirlwind, characteristic 60, totally dominating a stand of 56 with Child. He was finally bowled by Allott, and Wellington scraped home.

29 December 1985

at Alexandra
Otago 188 for 6 (K.R. Rutherford 74)
Auckland 189 for 4 (J.F. Reid 99 not out)
Auckland (2 pts) won by 5 wickets

RIGHT: *Paul Allott – an outstanding season for Wellington.*
(Adrian Murrell)

at Christchurch

Northern Districts 174 for 6 (B.R. Blair 52)
Canterbury 176 for 2 (J.G. Wright 77, P.E. McEwan 59 not out)

Canterbury (2 pts) won by 8 wickets

at Wellington

Central Districts 89
Wellington 90 for 1

Wellington (2 pts) won by 9 wickets

Canterbury and Wellington finished the second round of matches as the two sides with maximum points. The all-round efficiency of the Wellington attack was too much for Central Districts who reached 44 with only Blain out while Canterbury inflicted an equally crushing defeat on Northern Districts. Facing a target of 175, Wright and Nathu began with a stand of 75, and Wright and McEwan added 92 for the second wicket. Canterbury won with 11.5 overs to spare.

Auckland won with 3.2 overs to spare at Alexandra. Rutherford and Burns put on 81 for Otago's 3rd wicket, but John Reid's masterly display took Auckland to victory. Reid and Hunt put on 84 for the third wicket.

31 December 1985

at Wellington

Wellington 217 for 6 (B.A. Edgar 84)
Canterbury 197 (J.G. Wright 102)

Wellington (2 pts) won by 20 runs

at Alexandra

Northern Districts 181
Otago 182 for 6 (R.N. Hoskin 56)

Otago (2 pts) won by 4 wickets

at Auckland

Auckland 261 for 7 (J.F. Reid 118)
Central Districts 213 (C.J. Smith 55)

Auckland (2 pts) won by 48 runs

Wellington beat Canterbury in a splendid top of table clash. Justin Boyle and Bruce Edgar, who has a remarkable record in this competition, gave the home side a fine start with a stand of 81, and although Vance went quickly, Wellington reached a very strong position when Edgar and Coney put on 98. There was some good hitting by Jones, and Wellington became the first side in the season to pass 200. Wright was in majestic form for Canterbury and was the dominant partner in an opening stand of 93. The middle order could contribute only 3 runs between 4 batsmen, but Kennedy and Hadlee gave Wright good support as runs came quickly. Hadlee fell to Maguiness who also bowled Tracy. Hart was run out in the scamper for runs and Wright went the same as he attempted to keep the bowling, the last two wickets falling without addition.

Otago's win with one over to spare brought them level with Canterbury, and Auckland, inspired by another splendid innings from John Reid, also moved to 4 points.

2 January 1986

at Nelson

Canterbury 152 (P.E. McEwan 68)
Central Districts 100 (R.J. Hadlee 4 for 19)

Canterbury (2 pts) won by 52 runs

at Wellington

Otago 193 for 6
Wellington 139

Otago (2 pts) won by 54 runs

at Auckland

Auckland 202 for 7 (J.G. Bracewll 56)
Northern Districts 184 (B.L. Cairns 52, G.B. Troup 4 for 51)

Auckland (2 pts) won by 8 runs

The fourth round of matches ended with four teams level on 6 points although Canterbury's average was inferior to Wellington and Auckland. Hadlee, who was to be leading wicket-taker in the tournament, bowled Canterbury to a

Auckland 1986
First Class Matches

BATTING

BATTING	v. Canterbury (Christchurch) 6–8 Jan 1986		v. Otago (Dunedin) 10–12 Jan 1986		v. Central Districts (Auckland) 14–16 Jan 1986		v. Wellington (Auckland) 18–20 Jan 1986		v. Northern Districts (Tauranga) 25–27 Jan 1986		v. Canterbury (Auckland) 29–31 Jan 1986		v. Central Districts (New Plymouth) 2–4 Feb 1986		v. Northern Districts (Auckland) 6–8 Feb 1986		M	Inns	NOs	Runs	HS	Av
T.J. Franklin	176	—	16	5	0	9	60	18*	64	26	51	0	69	8	10	80	8	15	1	592	176	42.28
P.A. Horne	32	—	4	—			19	17*	3	25	1	62			0	116	6	10	1	279	116	31.00
M.J. Greatbatch	7	—	24	19*	119*	88*	4	—	20	0	12	15*	2	6			7	12	4	316	119*	39.50
D.N. Patel	174	—	10	11*	29	7	89	—	34	23	2	10	22	10	11	37	8	14	1	469	174	36.07
D.G. Scott	50*	—	52	4	79	26			7	9	27	37	13	3			6	11	1	307	79	30.70
A.J. Hunt	8	—	18	—	—	25	20	—					23	79*	0	13*	6	8	2	186	79*	31.00
P.N. Webb	1*	—	49	—	42*	22	63	—	16	10*	84	10*	24	115	5	0*	8	13	5	441	115	55.12
P.J. Kelly	—	—	12	—	—	15	20	—	0	1	84	—	33	34*	93	—	8	9	1	292	93	36.50
B.J. Barrett	—	—	0*	—	—	—											3	1	1	0	0*	
G.B. Troup	—	—	12	—	—	20*	7	—	1	12	8*		8	—	29*	—	8	8	3	97	29*	19.40
W. Watson	—	—	0	—	—	—	4*	—			—	—	0*	—			6	3	2	4	4*	4.00
D. Morrison					—	—	0*	—	0*	0	5*	—	5	17			5	6	3	27	17	9.00
B. Bradley							6	—	—	10	—	—					3	2	—	16	10	8.00
R. Reid									23*	0			22	25			2	4	1	70	25	23.33
J.F. Reid															26	26	1	2	—	52	26	26.00
J.G. Bracewell															54	0	1	2	—	54	54	27.00
M.C. Snedden															20	—	1	1	—	20	20	20.00
S.R. Gillespie															1	3	1	2	—	4	3	2.00
Byes	1		1			2	4	4	1	2	10	10			4							
Leg-byes	3		4	1		2	10	7	2	2	8	2	5	12	5	7						
Wides	1				2	1	2						1									
No-balls	1		3		5	3			1	2	1		1	1		1						
Total	454		205	40	278	228	305	42	173	120	292	146	228	310	258	283						
Wickets	5		10	2	3	6	9†	0	8	10	7	4	10	7	10	6						
Results	W		D		W		D		L		W		L		W							
Points	16		0		16		0		4		16		0		16							

Catches
23 – P.J. Kelly (ct 22/st 1)
11 – P.N. Webb
10 – T.J. Franklin
9 – M.J. Greatbatch
4 – D.G. Scott, P.A. Horne and A.J. Hunt
3 – G.B. Troup
2 – J.G. Bracewell
1 – D.N. Patel, S.R. Gillespie, M. Bradley and sub

† D.M. Morrison retired hurt

BOWLING

BOWLING	G.B. Troup	W. Watson	D.N. Patel	B.J. Barrett	A.J. Hunt	D.G. Scott	D. Morrison	P.N. Webb	M. Bradley
v. Canterbury (Christchurch) 6–8 January	10–2–29–1	7–2–16–0	31–8–76–4	12–1–54–3	21–7–54–2				
	10–2–26–0	16–2–44–3	34–11–62–4	11.3–2–43–2	3–0–7–1				
v. Otago (Dunedin) 10–12 January	23–9–43–5	12–3–36–0	29–7–74–1	15.5–3–51–4		9–2–21–0			
v. Central Districts (Auckland) 14–16 January	22–7–41–3	16–4–52–0	27–9–54–1	20–6–38–1	10–4–19–0		20–2–68–3		
	9–3–20–1	6–2–15–0	16.1–5–52–3	5–0–24–0	13–2–45–2		13–4–24–0	8–1–34–2	
v. Wellington (Auckland) 18–20 January	29–5–62–1	26–2–78–3	27–9–72–1		5–1–15–0		32–7–89–2		25–5–55–3
v. Northern Districts (Tauranga) 25–27 January	18.1–6–43–5		15–1–46–2			3–1–5–0	3–0–19–0		11–1–37–3
	13–6–18–1		29–6–53–2				8.5–2–28–1		18–4–39–2
v. Canterbury (Auckland) 29–31 January	11.2–7–11–2	8–0–16–1	31–11–47–4				4–1–5–1		7–3–15–2
	17.2–6–41–4	4–1–14–1	31–13–41–5				6–2–8–0		9–2–24–0
v. Central Districts (New Plymouth) 2–4 February	11–6–17–0	5–0–20–0	40–15–69–0		14–2–50–0	20–7–44–2	10–5–19–0		
	11–2–46–1	12–0–62–0	15–1–58–0		3–0–13–0	16–0–61–1	8–0–35–1		
v. Northern Districts (Auckland) 6–8 February	13–4–41–2		17–4–38–2						
	12–6–18–1		13–5–14–0		2–0–11–0				
	209.5–71–	112–16–	355.1–105–	64.2–12–	71–16–	48–10–	104.5–28–	8–1–	70–15–
	456–27	353–8	756–29	210–10	214–5	131–3	295–8	34–2	170–10
	av. 16.88	av. 44.12	av. 26.06	av. 21.00	av. 42.80	av. 43.66	av. 36.87	av. 17.00	av. 17.00

a T.J. Franklin 6–1–21–1, R. Reid 3–0–9–0   b M.J. Greatbatch 3–0–2–0

comfortable win at Nelson. He and Thiele, 3 for 22, reduced Central to 32 for 6, and they never recovered.

Wellington, given a good start by Edgar, collapsed from 100 for 4 to 139 all out against Mallender and McKechnie. In a rain affected match at Auckland, Northern's target was reduced to 192 in 36 overs, and they died bravely after another thundering effort from Cairns. John Bracewell, used as opener, shared a second wicket stand of 108 with John Reid, and this gave Auckland's innings the necessary substance.

4 January 1986

at Oamaru

Canterbury 208 for 7 (J.G. Wright 68, S.L. Boock 4 for 16)
Otago 127
Canterbury (2 pts) won by 81 runs

at Gisborne

Northern Districts 248 for 7 (L.M. Crocker 74, R. Mawhinney 50)
Central Districts 225 (B.R. Blair 4 for 58)
Northern Districts (2 pts) won by 23 runs

at Auckland

Match abandoned
Auckland 1 pt, Wellington 1 pt

Rain prevented a ball being bowled in Auckland so that Canterbury, somewhat fortuitously, became holders of the Shell Cup when they beat Otago. Again it was John Wright who held together the Canterbury batting. He and McEwan put on 84 for the second wicket, and there was a late, valuable burst of 56 from Stead and Hart. This came after Stephen Boock had finished his remarkable spell of 4 for 16 in 10 overs. Wright was one of his four victims. Hadlee and Tracy strangled the Otago innings at the outset, and Hadlee and McEwan brought it to an abrupt close.

Crocker and Mawhinney began Northern's innings with a

John Wright played splendidly for Canterbury in the Shell Cup before departing for Australia. (Alan Cozzi)

stand of 107, and there were useful contributions throughout. Central batted vigorously in their turn, but quick wickets from Bruce Blair in the middle of the innings gave the game to Northern.

Shell Cup – Final Table

	P	W	L	D	Pts
Canterbury	5	4	1	—	8
Auckland	5	3	1	1	7
Wellington	5	3	1	1	7
Otago	5	3	2	—	6
Northern Districts	5	1	4	—	2
Central Districts	5	—	5	—	0

Shell Trophy

6, 7 and 8 January 1986

at Fitzherbert Park, Palmerston North

Otago 216 (K.R. Rutherford 126, G.K. Robertson 4 for 67) and 263 for 9 dec (R.N. Hoskin 75, K.R. Rutherford 67, D.A. Stirling 5 for 91)
Central Districts 100 (J.A.J. Cushen 6 for 34) and 120 (B.J. McKechnie 4 for 38)
Otago won by 259 runs
Otago 16 pts, Central Districts 0 pts

S.R. Gillespie	M.C. Snedden	J.G. Bracewell	Byes	Leg-byes	Wides	No-balls	Total	Wkts
			2	4		4	235	10
			3			8	185	10
			5	13		2	243	10
				5		18	277	9
			6	8		2	228	9
			1	11	1	11	383	10
				3		4	153	10
			1	4		4	143	10
			10	5	3		109	10
			1	5	1	3	134	10
			1	4		4	254	3a
			5	3		1	285	4b
13-3-33-1	15-3-40-0	27-9-43-4	1	3		2	199	10
15-7-15-3	19-2-47-3	26-7-86-3	5	8		1	204	10
28-10-	34-5-	53-16-						
48-4	87-3	129-7						
av. 12.00	av. 29.00	av. 18.42						

at Lancaster Park, Christchurch

Auckland 454 for 5 dec (T.J. Franklin 176, D.N. Patel 174, D.G. Scott 50 not out)
Canterbury 235 (R.T. Latham 64, D.N. Patel 4 for 76) and 185 (D.N. Patel 4 for 62)

Auckland won by an innings and 34 runs
Auckland 16 pts, Canterbury 0 pts

at Harry Barker Reserve, Gisborne

Northern Districts 199 (C.M. Kuggeleijn 58, S.J. Maguiness 4 for 32) and 208 (D.J. White 67, P.J.W. Allott 5 for 56)
Wellington 318 (G.R. Larsen 92, T.D. Ritchie 60) and 90 for 6

Wellington won by 4 wickets
Wellington 16 pts, Northern Districts 0 pts

Canterbury 1986
First Class Matches

BATTING	v. Auckland (Christchurch) 6–8 January 1986	v. Northern Districts (Christchurch) 10–12 January 1986	v. Wellington (Lower Hutt) 14–16 January 1986	v. Otago (Christchurch) 18–20 January 1986	v. Central Districts (Levin) 25–27 January 1986	v. Auckland (Auckland) 29–31 January 1986	v. Wellington (Auckland) 2–4 February 1986	v. Otago (Dunedin) 6–8 February 1986	M	Inns	NOs	Runs	HS	Av
A.P. Nathu	8 5	9 —	38 44	29 10	26 153	14 8	42 8	0 23*	8	15	1	417	153	29.78
P.G. Kennedy	22 14	10 —	15 9	2 5	10 20		19 81	53	7	12	—	260	81	21.66
P.E. McEwan	22 34	118 —	30 12	27 63	0 4	13 4	17 4	70	8	14	—	418	118	29.85
V.R. Brown	11 30	134 —	10 1	10 6	17 5	17 4	12 11	1	8	14	—	269	134	19.21
R.T. Latham	64 9	66* —	25 18	26 40	0 16	5 13	13 47	81	8	14	1	423	81	32.53
D.W. Stead	46 31*	8 —	52 22	14 11	6 42	24* 37	2 18	0	8	14	2	313	52	26.08
D.J. Hartshorn	38 15	0 —	32 2	47* 32	6 32				5	9	1	204	47*	25.50
A.W. Hart	0 12	1 —	44 1	1 9	0 10*	1 11*	0 15	17*	8	14	3	122	44	11.09
G.K. MacDonald	9 0			14 2*		0 0			3	6	1	25	14	5.00
C.H. Thiele	4 17	9* —	10* 8*		0* 6	0 3	12* 0		6	11	5	69	17	11.50
S.R. Tracy	1* 7	—	4 0	1 6	0 0	1 7			6	10	1	27	7	3.00
S.R. McNally		13 —	16 0	17 29	0 6	16 1	0 22	3	7	12	—	123	29	10.25
D.J. Boyle						0 36	9 68	149 5*	3	6	1	267	149	53.40
S. Roberts							0 1*	1*	2	2	1	1	1*	1.00
A.J. Hintz								1*	1	1	1	1	1*	—
Byes	2 3	1	5 10	2 4	2	10 1	13 2							
Leg-byes	4	12	12 6	8 4	1	5 5	3	10 14						
Wides		4			1	4	3 1	1						
No-balls	4 8	2	4	6 7	19	3 3	3 10							
Total	235 185	387	297 133	205 228	68 317	109 134	133 302	401 28						
Wickets	10 10	8	10 10	10 10	10 10	10 10	10 10	8 0						
Results	L	D	L	L	D	L	L	D						
Points	0	4	4	0	0	0	0	0						

Catches 18 – A.W. Hart (ct 16/st 2) 4 – D.W. Stead 2 – P.E. McEwan
6 – D.J. Hartshorn and A.P. Nathu 3 – G.K. MacDonald, C.H. Thiele, 1 – D.J. Boyle and S.R. McNally
5 – R.T. Latham and P.G. Kennedy V.R. Brown and subs

BOWLING	C.H. Thiele	S.R. Tracy	R.T. Latham	V.R. Brown	D.W. Stead	G.K. MacDonald	D.J. Hartshorn	S.R. McNally	P.E. McEwan
v. Auckland (Christchurch) 6–8 January	32.3–7–103–3	17–1–86–0	3–1–13–0	25–1–76–1	12–1–43–0	21–4–74–0	21–8–55–0		
v. Northern Districts (Christchurch) 10–12 January	20–3–87–0 / 3.4–1–10–1	15.5–1–70–4 / 5–0–15–0	7–1–40–0	1–0–3–0	6–3–20–0		22–3–70–2	29–1–97–4 / 3–1–13–0	
v. Wellington (Lower Hutt) 14–16 January	26.5–7–74–4 / 15–2–49–1	14–0–51–1		23–8–63–1 / 22–9–53–6	1–0–12–0		3–1–9–0	18–4–39–4 / 29–13–65–3	13–3–49–0 / 4–1–5–0
v. Otago (Christchurch) 18–20 January		16–1–69–0 / 5–1–33–0		21.2–7–41–3 / 10.1–6–16–1		15–2–38–0 / 8–4–21–1	12–3–41–1	21–3–83–3 / 2–2–0–0	18–3–70–2
v. Central Districts (Levin) 25–27 January	19–3–67–2 / 7–0–22–1	14.5–2–24–2 / 11–4–19–5		7.4–0–36–1	18–5–54–1 / 3–1–6–0			22–5–86–0	
v. Auckland (Auckland) 29–31 January	22–7–49–2	16–3–64–1 / 4–1–15–0		30–12–46–4 / 24–7–59–2	9–2–30–0 / 17–9–35–2	8–1–29–0 / 9–2–25–0		13–6–27–0	8–3–29–0
v. Wellington (Christchurch) 2–4 February	20–4–59–3			3–0–19–0 / 11–5–21–4	7–3–19–0 / 16–6–37–2			14–2–57–2	4–1–16–0
v. Otago (Dunedin) 6–8 February	19–4–42–2			32–15–54–0	28–3–92–1			17–4–42–1 / 27–6–83–0	10–6–10–1
	185–38– 562–19 av. 29.57	120.5–17– 466–13 av. 35.84	10–2– 53–0 av. —	210.1–70– 487–20 av. 24.35	117–33– 348–6 av. 58.00	61–13– 187–1 av. 187.00	58–15– 175–3 av. 58.33	195–47– 592–17 av. 34.82	57–17– 179–3 av. 59.66

a A.W. Hart 1–0–1–0

The Shell Trophy began with the leading New Zealand players absent, engaged in the one-day series in Australia which was to occupy them for most of the duration of the Trophy. Their absence was to give opportunities to several young players, and some older ones, but as the young New Zealand side was also to tour Australia in the early months of the year, David Hartshorn, Grant Bradburn, Brian Barrett, Fred Beyeler and Kim Hancock were also to miss several matches. Barrett, the Auckland pace bowler, has been engaged by Worcestershire.

Three English county players, Allott, Patel and Mallender were to appear regularly in the competition although Allott was hampered by injury. It was Patel who stole the headlines in the opening round of matches.

It had not been Auckland's policy to include their coaches in their Shell Trophy sides, but the fact that five regular members of the team were with the New Zealand party in Australia prompted the selectors to break with this rule. Patel hit 174 off 202 deliveries and 'gave one of the most fluent and polished displays seen in Christchurch for many years'. He and Trevor Franklin added 278 for the third wicket, and with Scott scoring briskly, Auckland moved to a position of strength. Although Latham and Stead put on 100 for Canterbury's fifth wicket, the home side never looked like saving the follow-on. Patel's off-spin brought him 8 wickets to complete a fine all round match and Barrett bowled well as Auckland moved to an emphatic victory.

Ken Rutherford, shaking off the traumas of the West Indian tour six months earlier, dominated Otago's innings at Palmerston North. His 126 was full of fine shots, and skipper Warren Lees was next highest scorer with 22. Central Districts were routed by veteran John Cushen, and Otago built on their first innings lead of 116 with some more sparkling batting. Central crashed again to Otago's medium pacers, and Brian McKechnie, on yet another return to first-class cricket, nagged away with particular accuracy as the visitors won with ease.

Northern Districts, although dismissed for 199, had the

ABOVE: *Trevor Franklin shared a third wicket stand of 278 for Auckland against Canterbury at Christchurch, 6 January. Franklin was to score 592 runs in the season and earn a place in the party to England. (Adrian Murrell)*

BELOW: *Dipak Patel, 174 off 202 deliveries for Auckland against Canterbury, 6 January, 'one of the most fluent and polished displays seen in Christchurch for many years'. (David Munden)*

S. Roberts	A.P. Nathu	A.J. Hintz	Byes	Leg-byes	Wides	No-balls	Total	Wkts
			1	3		1	454	5
				16	1	1	383	10
							58	1
				2		2	278	10
			6	3	1	1	222	10
			9	9		1	360	10
			2	2			74	2
			7	8			282	6
			2	2			51	6
			10	8			292	7
			10	2			146	4
16.3–1–77–5				11	1	3	242	10
18–3–67–2	10–2–28–1			9	2		262	9
22–5–60–1	6–1–9–0	21–3–75–2	9	10	3	3	403	5a
56.3–9–	16–3–	21–3–						
204–3	37–1	75–2						
av. 25.50	av. 37.00	av. 37.50						

Central Districts 1986
First Class Matches

BATTING

BATTING	v. Otago (Palmerston N.) 6–8 Jan		v. Wellington (Wellington) 10–12 Jan		v. Auckland (Auckland) 14–16 Jan		v. Northern Districts (Hamilton) 18–20 Jan		v. Canterbury (Levin) 25–27 Jan		v. Otago (Oamaru) 29–31 Jan		v. Auckland (New Plymouth) 2–4 Feb		v. Wellington (Hastings) 6–8 Feb		v. Australians (New Plymouth) 8–10 Mar		M	Inns	NOs	Runs	HS	Av
R.T. Hart	0	5	207	—	56	15	5	3	48	26	1*	14							6	11	1	380	207	38.00
C.J. Smith	39	2	101	—	41	70	25	103	2	1	22	1	89	80	29	18	13	38	9	17	—	674	103	39.64
P.S. Briasco	14	7	42	—	39	18	15	2	3	8*	109	12	91	79	6	60	1	29	9	17	1	535	109	33.43
R.E. Hayward	8	23	35	—	49	9	1	25	69*	0	10	43	—	0	12	58			8	14	1	342	69*	26.30
I.D.S. Smith	1	19	0	—					81	4	84	8	—	23*	10	20	23*	—	7	11	2	273	84	30.33
D. Guthardt	16	10	13	—	17	2													3	5	—	58	17	11.60
D.A. Stirling	12	33	3*	—	36	35	7	26	29*	0	51*	0	—	—	21*	37	6	10	9	15	4	306	51*	27.81
G.K. Robertson	5	0	—	—	3	50*	35	66*	—	—	—	99*	—	—	0	0	33*	—	9	10	4	291	99*	48.50
S.W. Duff	1	15*	—	—			45	2	—	—	—	51	14*	17	11	7*	71	2*	7	11	4	236	71	33.71
T. Murphy	0	0	—	—	0*	1													3	4	1	1	1	0.33
P.J. Visser	0*	0	—	—	0*	0*	0	0	—	—	—	0	—	—	1	—	—	—	9	8	3	1	1	0.20
G. Walton			—	—	7	11	0*	10			—	36							4	5	1	64	36	16.00
T.E. Blain					6	1	6	70	33	5	63	31	35*	77*	8	18	30	15	7	14	2	389	77*	33.16
R. Glover							8	0									28	—	2	3	—	36	28	12.00
S. Robertson									2	3*			16	—	35	11	2	2*	4	7	2	71	35	14.20
K.W. Martin															14	—			1	1	—	14	14	14.00
M.D. Crowe																	97	42	1	2	—	139	97	69.50
Byes			8				6	1	5	7	2				4	5	1	4						
Leg-byes	1	2	23		5	8	3	8	2	3	4	1	3	5	4	3	1							
Wides		1	1						2									1						
No-balls	3	3			18	2			1		1	1	4	1	1		5	5						
Total	100	120	433	—	277	228	148	318	282	51	344	300	254	285	153	233	313	149						
Wickets	10	10	6	—	9	9	10	10	6	6	5	10	3	4	10	8	8	5						
Results	L		D		L		L		D		L		W		D		D							
Points	0		2		0		0		4		4		16		0		—							

Catches
18 – I.D.S. Smith (ct 15/st 3)
8 – T.E. Blain (ct 7/st 1)
7 – S.W. Duff
6 – P.J. Visser and P.S. Briasco
5 – R.E. Hayward and S. Robertson
4 – D.A. Stirling and D. Guthardt
3 – G.K. Robertson and subs
2 – R. Glover
1 – G. Walton, C.T. Smith, R.T. Hart and M.D. Crowe

BOWLING

Match	G.K. Robertson	T. Murphy	P.J. Visser	D.A. Stirling	S.W. Duff	P.S. Briasco	R.E. Hayward	G. Walton	K.W. Martin
v. Otago (Palmerston North) 6–8 January	15.2–1–67–4 / 19–4–68–0	20–8–39–2 / 12–4–15–2	20–5–47–3 / 23–6–67–1	6–0–28–0 / 21–2–91–5	7–1–14–0	4–2–11–1 / 2–0–12–0	1–1–0–0		
v. Wellington (Wellington) 10–12 January	21–1–55–0	11–2–33–1	20–4–60–2	15–2–56–0		3–1–12–0		24–8–48–0	
v. Auckland (Auckland) 14–16 January	15–3–34–1 / 8.5–1–48–0	16–3–58–0 / 6–0–26–1	21–4–55–0 / 3–0–11–1	20–7–55–2 / 11–1–50–0		3–0–9–0 / 5–0–24–0		19–7–65–0 / 14–1–57–1	
v. Northern Districts (Hamilton) 18–20 January	14–2–51–0		28–8–82–2 / 7–1–18–0	12–2–49–0 / 0.4–0–6–0	44–7–111–4 / 6–0–11–1	11–6–19–0	6–4–7–0	35–8–97–0	
v. Canterbury (Levin) 25–27 January	5–1–15–4 / 21–1–76–4		11.4–5–28–6 / 31–6–89–2		7–2–22–0 / 25–5–75–4	24–6–64–0 / 2–0–7–0	2–0–6–0		
v. Otago (Oamaru) 29–31 January	12–1–60–0 / 9–0–55–0		19–5–56–2 / 16.1–2–77–1		10–1–62–1 / 2–0–15–0	14.5–7–36–6 / 24–2–119–4		17–0–81–1 / 18–1–71–1	
v. Auckland (New Plymouth) 2–4 February	15.4–3–47–5 / 25–7–68–4		22–7–51–1 / 20–9–44–1	13–2–49–1 / 12.2–1–52–1	12–3–39–1 / 23–6–48–0	1–0–4–0	2–1–1–0		11–2–37–2 / 21–6–81–1
v. Wellington (Hastings) 6–8 February	18–4–39–3 / 19–2–57–2		15–2–35–1 / 17–5–46–1	17–2–46–4 / 18–2–69–2	4–3–2–0 / 4–2–5–0				13–3–52–1 / 20–4–65–0
v. (New Plymouth) 8–10 March	20.5–2–70–4 / 16–2–66–0		14–0–69–1 / 11–3–66–1	14–1–91–3 / 13–2–56–3	21–5–68–1 / 34.3–11–87–4	3–1–19–1			
Totals	245.4–35–876–31 av. 28.25	65–17–171–6 av. 28.50	298.5–72–901–26 av. 34.65	217–32–872–26 av. 33.53	218.2–53–604–21 av. 28.76	34–10–117–2 av. 58.50	11–6–14–0 av. —	127–25–419–3 av. 139.66	65–15–235–4 av. 58.75

a B.A. Reid absent ill

better of the game at Gisborne until Tim Ritchie and Gavin Larsen came together and revived Wellington from 114 for 6 to 251 before they were parted. Larsen hit 16 fours and a six in his career best knock. Northern batted doggedly in the second innings and Wellington lost wickets as they chased 90 for victory at more than 4 an over.

10, 11 and 12 January 1986

at Basin Reserve, Wellington

Central Districts 433 for 6 dec (R.T. Hart 207, C.J. Smith 101)
Wellington 280 for 4 (J.G. Boyle 70, R.H. Vance 66, T.D. Ritchie 58 not out, A.H. Jones 54 not out)

Match drawn
Wellington 2 pts, Central Districts 2 pts

at Lancaster Park, Christchurch

Northern Districts 383 (L.M. Crocker 105, B.G. Cooper 83, C.M. Kuggeleijn 73, S.R. Tracy 4 for 70, S.R. McNally 4 for 97) and 58 for 1
Canterbury 387 for 8 dec (V.R. Brown 134, P.E. McEwan 118, R.T. Latham 66 not out)

Match drawn
Canterbury 4 pts, Northern Districts 0 pts

at Carisbrook, Dunedin

Auckland 205 (D.G. Scott 52, J.A.J. Cushen 4 for 51, N.A. Mallender 4 for 68) and 40 for 2
Otago 243 (G.B. Troup 5 for 43, B.J. Barrett 4 for 51)

Match drawn
Otago 4 pts, Auckland 0 pts

The second round of Trophy matches was hindered by the weather. At Basin Reserve, first innings points could not be decided, but the game produced remarkable individual performances. Ron Hart established a record for Central Districts when he hit 207 in 468 minutes. He hit 25 fours and shared an opening partnership of 250 with the slightly built, but immensely promising John Smith. Hart then added 124

M.D. Crowe	Byes	Leg-byes	Wides	No-balls	Total	Wkts
	3			13	216	10
	7	3			263	9
	10	6		4	280	4
		2	2	5	278	3
	2	10	1	3	228	6
	3	12	1	3	431	6
			1	2	36	1
		2	1		68	10
			4	19	317	10
	4	4		8	303	10
	3	2			342	6
		5	1	1	228	10
		12		1	310	7
		5		3	179	10
		7		1	249	5
1–0–6–0	2	3	2	4	309	9a
	9	2	1	4	305	10
1–0–6–0						

Brian Barrett, a pace bowler of great potential who made an impressive debut for Auckland in the opening matches of the Shell Trophy. (Sporting Pictures UK Ltd)

with Scott Briasco for the second wicket. Allott had to retire from the Wellington attack after bowling 8 overs. He had a pinched back nerve. Boyle and Vance put on 139 for Wellington's second wicket.

Northern Districts were 44 for 3 at Christchurch, but Crocker and Cooper added 125, and some bright batting by the tail, including a last wicket stand of 64 between Carrington, a maiden fifty, and Hancock saw them to a formidable total. Canterbury were 48 for 2 in reply, but Paul McEwan and Vaughan Brown, who reached a career best 134, put on a record 190, and Canterbury took first innings points.

Otago's bright and determined approach gave them the points at Dunedin, but they owed much to their last three batsmen, Wilson, Mallender and Cushen. Earlier Derek Scott had shown some exciting, flowing strokes in his second fifty of the season.

14, 15 and 16 January 1986

at Eden Park, Auckland

Central Districts 277 for 9 dec (R.T. Hart 56) and 228 for 9 dec (C.J. Smith 70)
Auckland 278 for 3 dec (M.J. Greatbatch 119 not out, D.G. Scott 79) and 228 for 6 (M.J. Greatbatch 88 not out)

Auckland won by 4 wickets
Auckland 16 pts, Central Districts 0 pts

Northern Districts 1986
First Class Matches

BATTING

BATTING	v. Wellington (Gisborne) 6–8 Jan		v. Canterbury (Christchurch) 10–12 Jan		v. Otago (Alexandra) 14–16 Jan		v. Central Districts (Hamilton) 18–20 Jan		v. Auckland (Tauranga) 25–27 Jan		v. Wellington (Wellington) 29–31 Jan		v. Otago (Hamilton) 2–4 Feb		v. Auckland (Auckland) 6–8 Feb		v. Australians (Hamilton) 16–18 Feb		M	Inns	NOs	Runs	HS	Av
L.M. Crocker	18	29	105	38*	7	21	16	11*	23	20	3	37	0	67	39	12	30	23	9	18	2	499	105	31.18
R. Mawhinney	19	30	1	20	37	48	75	10	9	5	110	3	7	45	22	2	26*	0	9	18	1	469	110	27.58
D.J. White	43	67	11	—	9	1	209	12*	7	9	15	47	4	41*	20	22	53	8	9	17	2	578	209	38.53
G.P. Howarth	16	18	0	—	—	—	—	—	—	—	5	79	4	—	25	15	—	6	6	9	—	168	79	18.66
B.G. Cooper	6	10	83	—	49	6	29	—	15	10	6	31	—	—	—	—	—	—	6	10	—	245	83	24.50
C.M. Kuggeleijn	58	3	73	—	74	3	27*	—	26	35*	47	2	26	—	44	1	—	5	9	14	2	424	74	35.33
B.A. Young	17	0	4	—	0	16	2*	—	3	14*	8	1*	30*	—	21*	23	—	31	9	14	5	170	31	18.88
G. Bradburn	4	17	19	—	16	0	—	—	6*	—									5	6	1	62	19	12.40
S.J. Scott	11	18	6	—	20	32	—	—	28	—	0	6	10	—	10	10	—	17	9	12	—	168	32	14.00
S.M. Carrington	1*	10	53	—	0	10	—	—	0	—	0	—	0	—	1	15	—	1*	9	11	2	91	53	10.11
K.B. Hancock	0	0*	10*	—	0*	0*													3	5	4	10	10*	10.00
G.W. McKenzie					21	30	49	—	7	20			17	25*					4	7	1	169	49	28.16
M.J. Child							5	—	22	21	1	37	0		2	66*	0		6	9	1	154	66*	19.25
K. Treiber											0*		0		0	21		8	4	5	1	29	21	7.25
B.R. Blair															9	3	51*	46	2	4	1	109	51*	36.33
Byes	1				4		3			1	2	7		4	1	5		8						
Leg-byes	3	3	16		11	8	12	1	3	4	5	12	1		3	8	3	8						
Wides	2	1	1				1	2	7		1													
No-balls			2	1	9		3		4	4	9	6	4		2	1	4	6						
Total	199	208	383	58	257	175	431	36	153	143	212	268	103	182	199	204	167	167						
Wickets	10	10	10	1	10	10	6	1	10	6	10	8	10	2	10	10	2	10						
Results	L		D		L		W		W		D		W		L		L							
Points	0		0		0		16		12		4		16		0		—							

Catches 24 – B.A. Young (ct 21/st 3)
11 – C.M. Kuggeleijn
7 – R. Mawhinney
6 – D.J. White and L.M. Crocker
5 – G.W. McKenzie
4 – S.J. Scott and G. Bradburn
3 – G.P. Howarth and M.J. Child
2 – K.B. Hancock, B.G. Cooper, B.R. Blair, K. Treiber and subs
1 – S.M. Carrington

BOWLING

	S.M. Carrington	K.B. Hancock	S.J. Scott	G. Bradburn	D.J. White	C.M. Kuggeleijn	D.G. Cooper	R. Mawhinney	M.J. Child
v. Wellington (Gisborne) 6–8 January	23–4–63–3	24–2–107–3	28.5–9–68–2	28–13–43–2	4–0–18–0	2–1–4–0			
	7–0–23–1	7–1–37–3	4–2–6–1	2–0–12–0		1.1–0–5–0			
v. Canterbury (Christchurch) 10–12 January	24–3–102–0	21–3–99–1	29–6–78–2	23–7–80–3		4–1–15–0			
v. Otago (Alexandra) 14–16 January	13–4–28–2	7–1–31–0	29.4–8–61–0	21–4–62–0	4–0–10–0	29–8–62–2			
	8–0–34–0		6–2–14–0	10–0–40–0	4–0–29–0	5–0–14–0	6.5–0–34–0	1–0–5–0	
v. Central Districts (Hamilton) 18–20 January	14–2–38–4		13–4–15–0	16.4–3–38–3					21–5–56–2
	30.5–6–118–3		19–7–35–1	23–6–57–1	1–0–4–0	7–3–17–0			28–7–69–4
v. Auckland (Tauranga) 25–27 January	11–0–23–1		14–6–40–2	22–6–53–4		12–4–12–0			15–5–42–0
	15–7–29–2		5–0–18–1	18.1–4–40–4					9–2–30–2
v. Wellington (Wellington) 29–31 January	20–1–59–3		16–0–43–0			*			10.3–0–26–4
	20–2–78–2		15–5–33–3			9–2–35–0			12–3–34–0
v. Otago (Hamilton) 2–4 February	14–5–21–1		16–1–37–1						
	15–3–49–1		13.4–3–42–4			2–0–12–0			15–2–34–2
v. Auckland (Auckland) 6–8 February	21–3–54–1		25–8–77–4			7–4–19–1			16.3–5–49–3
	9–3–30–0		22–3–85–2			25–3–70–2			18–2–50–0
v. Australians (Hamilton) 16–18 February	6–1–18–0		11–3–45–1			7–1–41–0			5–2–25–0
	9–2–25–1		4–0–24–0			3–0–14–0		1–1–0–0	11–1–23–1
	259.5–46–	59–7–	271.1–67–	163.5–43–	13–0–	113.1–27–	6.5–0–	2–1–	161–34–
	792–25	274–7	721–24	425–17	61–0	320–5	34–0	5–0	438–18
	av. 31.68	av. 39.14	av. 30.04	av. 25.00	—	av. 64.00	—	—	av. 24.33

a L.M. Crocker 0.4–0–3–0

RIGHT: *Evan Gray, Wellington, who took a career best 8 for 37 against Canterbury, 16 January, and finished the season with 545 runs and 34 wickets, the outstanding all-rounder in New Zealand cricket. (Mark Leech)*

at Molyneux Park, Alexandra

Northern Districts 257 (C.M. Kuggeleijn 74) and 175
Otago 261 for 4 dec (K.R. Rutherford 105, R.N. Hoskin 55 not out) and 174 for 0 (K.R. Rutherford 105 not out, S.J. McCullum 65 not out)

Otago won by 10 wickets
Otago 16 pts, Northern Districts 0 pts

at Lower Hutt Recreation Ground

Wellington 278 (R.H. Vance 114, S.R. McNally 4 for 39, C.H. Thiele 4 for 74) and 222 (J.G. Boyle 56, V.R. Brown 6 for 53)
Canterbury 297 (D.W. Stead 52, E.J. Gray 6 for 114) and 133 (E.J. Gray 8 for 37)

Wellington won by 70 runs
Wellington 12 pts, Canterbury 4 pts

Otago, Auckland and Wellington surged ahead of the rest of the field after the third round of Shell Trophy matches. Wellington were held together by Bob Vance in their first innings, and in spite of the skipper's knock and some fine bowling by Evan Gray, they still conceded first innings points to some consistent and determined Canterbury batting. Wellington lost their way after a bright start to their second innings, and Canterbury, needing 204 for victory, looked set for a win. The wicket had offered help to the bowlers throughout, however, and now Evan Gray exploited the conditions magnificently, returning a career best 8 for 37 and bowling his side to a comfortable win.

Mark Greatbatch hit a maiden century at Auckland and shared a second wicket stand of 160 with the enterprising Derek Scott. Needing to make 228 in 100 minutes plus 20 overs, Auckland, again indebted to Greatbatch, won the match with one ball to spare.

G.W. McKenzie	K. Treiber	B.R. Blair	Byes	Leg-byes	Wides	No-balls	Total	Wkts
			2	13	3		318	10
			4	3	3		90	6
			1	12	4	2	387	8
			2	5	5	1	261	4
			1	3			174	0
			1				148	10
2-0-10-0			5	3	2	1	318	10
			1	2		2	173	8
			2	1		1	120	10
	14-2-42-2		6	6	3	5	182	10
	15-3-46-0		9	15		1	250	6
	20.1-7-42-7			2		2	102	10
	16-5-38-2		1	4	2	5	180	10
	15-4-50-0		4	5			258	10
	1-0-5-0	8-1-36-0		7		1	283	6
	5-2-7-0	1-0-9-0	4	4			153	1
	23-5-92-4		1			2	182	6a
2-0-	109.1-28-	9-1-						
10-0	322-15	45-0						
—	*av. 21.46*	—						

Auckland's win left them in second place to Otago whose thrilling cricket had earned them top of the table spot. Rutherford and McCullum added 143 for the second wicket, and Lees declared as soon as Otago had claimed first innings points. Lindsay and Walker then spun out Northern, but Otago barely had time to make the 172 needed for victory. In just over 40 overs, however, 144 minutes, Rutherford and McCullum reached the target, and Rutherford hit his second, exciting hundred of the match.

18, 19 and 20 January 1986

at Eden Park, Auckland

Auckland 305 (D.N. Patel 89, P.N. Webb 63, T.J. Franklin 60) and 42 for 0
Wellington 383 (A.H. Jones 99, E.J. Gray 67)

Match drawn
Wellington 4 pts, Auckland 0 pts

at Lancaster Park, Christchurch

Canterbury 205 (N.A. Mallender 4 for 68) and 228 (P.E. McEwan 63, J.A.J. Cushen 5 for 54)
Otago 360 (D.J. Walker 106, K.J. Burns 93) and 74 for 2

Otago won by 8 wickets
Otago 16 pts, Canterbury 0 pts

at Seddon Park, Hamilton

Central Districts 148 (S.M. Carrington 4 for 38) and 318 (C.J. Smith 103, T.E. Blain 70, G.K. Robertson 66 not out, M.J. Child 4 for 69)
Northern Districts 431 for 6 dec (D.J. White 209, R. Mawhinney 75, S.W. Duff 4 for 111) and 36 for 1

Northern Districts won by 9 wickets
Northern Districts 16 pts, Central Districts 0 pts

Otago 1986
First Class Matches

BATTING	v. Central Districts (Palmerston N.) 6–8 January 1986		v. Auckland (Dunedin) 10–12 January 1986		v. Northern Districts (Alexandra) 14–16 January 1986		v. Canterbury (Christchurch) 18–20 January 1986		v. Wellington (Wellington) 25–27 January 1986		v. Central Districts (Oamaru) 29–31 January 1986		v. Northern Districts (Hamilton) 2–4 February 1986		v. Canterbury (Dunedin) 6–8 February 1986		M	Inns	NOs	Runs	HS	Av
S.J. McCullum	0	9	33	—	42	65*	40	21	94	—	77	38	2	29	134	—	8	13	1	584	134	48.66
K.R. Rutherford	126	67	10	—	105	105*	11	35	0	—	42	70	12	12	44	—	8	13	1	639	122	53.25
R.N. Hoskin	13	75	46	—	55*		24	6*	5	—	24	111	19	0	23	—	8	12	2	401	111	40.10
K.J. Burns	14	0	47	—	24		93	8*	10	—	43	16	7	6	29	—	8	12	1	297	93	27.00
D.J. Walker	5	30	6	—	12*		106		89	—	6	3	2	6	76*	—	8	11	2	341	106	37.88
T.J. Wilson	3	15	26*	—	—		31			—	9	22	1	0			6	8	1	107	31	15.28
B.J. McKechnie	0	1	4	—	—		9		4	—	35	—	24	7		—	8	8		84	35	10.50
W.K. Lees	22	6	13	—	—		11		9	—	1	12*	2	62*	13*	—	8	10	3	151	62*	21.57
J.K. Lindsay	17*	21	10	—	10		13		34	—	29	65*	10	21	59	—	8	11	2	289	65*	32.11
N.A. Mallender	0	23*	16	—	—		0		52*	—	20	—	19	19		—	8	8	2	149	52*	24.87
J.A.J. Cushen	0	6*	12	—	—		3*		9*	—	1*	—	0*	6		—	8	8	5	37	12	12.33
K.B.K. Ibadulla									5	—							1	1		5	5	5.00
S.L. Boock																—	1	—				—
Byes	3	7	5		2	1	9	2	5		4	3		1	9							
Leg-byes		3	13		5	3	9	2	4		4	2	2	4	10							
Wides					5									2	3							
No-balls	13		2		1		1				8		2	5	3							
Total	216	263	243		261	174	360	74	320		303	342	102	180	403							
Wickets	10	9	10		4	0	10	2	9		10	6	10	10	5							
Results		W		D		W		W		D		W		L		D						
Points		16		0		16		16		2		12		0		4						

Catches 25 – W.K. Lees (ct 24/st 1) 6 – D.J. Walker 3 – S.J. McCullum
8 – K.R. Rutherford 5 – R.N. Hoskin 2 – J.A.J. Cushen, T.J. Wilson,
7 – K.J. Burns and J.K. Lindsay 4 – B.J. McKechnie and N.A. Mallender

BOWLING	N.A. Mallender	J.A.J. Cushen	B.J. McKechnie	T.J. Wilson	J.K. Lindsay	D.J. Walker	K.B.K. Ibadulla	K.R. Rutherford	S.L. Boock
v. Central Districts	14–2–36–3	26–11–34–6	15–10–19–1	4–2–6–0	2–1–4–0				
(Palmerston North) 6–8 January	11–5–14–1	15–5–28–2	18.2–6–38–4		14–5–38–3				
v. Auckland (Dunedin)	25.5–6–68–4	29–13–51–4	11–3–21–0	13–2–50–1		6–2–10–0			
10–12 January	7–2–20–1	7–2–17–1	1–0–2–0						
v. Northern Districts	20–3–59–3	27–13–46–1	23–11–27–1	21.1–6–43–3	22–7–67–2				
(Alexandra) 14–16 January	7–2–16–0	17–8–24–1	10–3–18–2	6–2–12–1	18–5–55–3	9–2–42–3			
v. Canterbury (Christchurch)	21–3–68–4	20–10–43–1	18–7–40–0	13–1–42–3	4.3–2–2–0				
18–20 January	14–2–45–1	23.3–7–54–5	10–3–26–0	4–0–28–0	18–4–67–3				
v. Wellington (Wellington)	6–1–16–1	27–9–40–1	7–3–15–0		32–6–128–2		24–5–64–1		
25–27 January									
v. Central Districts	22–7–37–0	31–4–90–2	19–5–53–0	6–0–21–0	31–6–115–3	6–0–25–0			
(Oamaru) 29–31 January	20–2–67–1	38–14–100–2	17.5–4–42–3		24–6–87–3				
v. Northern Districts	16.2–2–31–4	25–13–38–2	17–6–33–3						
(Hamilton) 2–4 February	11–2–22–0	5–0–16–0	5–2–15–0		17–3–53–1			7.2–2–25–0	
v. Canterbury (Dunedin)	32–9–98–1	37–11–85–2	43–14–108–3		3–0–20–0			6–2–17–0	36–13–57–1
6–8 February		7–1–14–0			2–0–11–0				
	227.1–48–	349.3–128–	215.1–75–	72.1–15–	187.3–45–	21–4–	24–5–	13.2–4–	36–13–
	597–24	711–31	458–17	217–8	647–20	77–3	64–1	42–0	57–1
	av. 24.87	av. 22.93	av. 26.94	av. 27.12	av. 32.35	av. 25.66	av. 64.00	—	av. 57.00

Ken Rutherford hit a century in each innings for Otago against Northern Districts at Alexandra, 14 to 16 January. (Mark Leech)

R.N. Hoskin	Byes	Leg-byes	Wides	No-balls	Total	Wkts
		1		3	100	10
		2	1	3	120	10
	1	4		3	205	10
		1			40	2
	4	11		9	257	10
		8			175	10
	2	8	1	6	205	10
	4	4		7	228	10
	1	4		2	268	5
		3		1	344	5
		4		1	300	10
		1		4	103	10
	4				182	2
	2	14		10	401	8
					28	0
4–2–3–0						
4–2–						
3–0						
—						

Auckland and Wellington fought out a determined draw at Eden Park where the wicket was a little spiteful. Jones, Gray and the numbers ten and eleven, Milne and Aberhart, were the batsmen responsible for giving Wellington the points, for they lost their eighth wicket at 284.

While these two were drawing, Otago were moving into an 18-point lead in the Trophy with another exciting performance at Christchurch. Facing 205, Otago were 89 for 4 when Derek Walker joined Kevin Burns. They added 170, and runs came at 4 an over. The competent and varied Otago attack took wickets regularly and a target of 74 in ample time presented no problems for the batsmen so that Otago reached the half way stage of the competition with the Trophy almost in their grasp.

Central Districts collapsed to 68 for 7 on the first day at Hamilton and in spite of a brave stand by Robertson and Duff, they never effectively recovered. A stunning double century from White who shared a second wicket stand of 199 with Mawhinney put Northern in an unassailable position, and Central were beaten although John Smith hit his second century of the season in a courageous second innings fight back.

25, 26 and 27 January 1986

at the Domain, Tauranga

Auckland 173 for 8 dec (T.J. Franklin 64, G. Bradburn 4 for 53) and 120 (G. Bradburn 4 for 40)
Northern Districts 153 (G.B. Troup 5 for 43) and 143 for 6

Northern Districts won by 4 wickets
Northern Districts 12 pts, Auckland 4 pts

at the Domain, Levin

Central Districts 282 for 6 dec (I.D.S. Smith 91, R.E. Hayward 69 not out) and 51 for 6 (S.R. Tracy 5 for 19)
Canterbury 68 (P.J. Visser 6 for 28, G.K. Robertson 4 for 15) and 317 (A.P. Nathu 153, D.A. Stirling 4 for 75, G.K. Robertson 4 for 76)

Match drawn
Central Districts 4 pts, Canterbury 0 pts

at Basin Reserve, Wellington

Otago 320 for 9 dec (S.J. McCullum 94, D.J. Walker 89, N.A. Mallender 52 not out, P.J.W. Allott 5 for 79)
Wellington 268 for 5 (E.J. Gray 128 not out, R.H. Vance 59)

Match drawn
Wellington 2 pts, Otago 2 pts

The top of the table clash at Basin Reserve was ruined by rain, but it still produced some fine cricket. McCullum and Walker put on 126 for Otago's fourth wicket. Mallender struck some ferocious blows at the close, and Evan Gray, enjoying a season of all round glory, hit a career best 128 not out.

Auckland failed to capitalise on the shared points at Wellington. On a dreadful wicket at Tauranga, their batsmen failed to reproduce their known form. They lacked the necessary application and although leading by 20 runs on the first innings, Auckland succumbed to a great fight by Northern. Acting skipper Chris Kuggeleijn showed the resource that was needed to lead his side from 76 for 5 past the 144 mark that was the victory target.

An astounding match at Levin ended in a draw. Hayward and Ian Smith added 130 for Central's sixth wicket, and

Wellington 1986
First Class Matches

BATTING

BATTING	v. Northern Districts (Gisborne) 6–8 January 1986		v. Central Districts (Wellington) 10–12 January 1986		v. Canterbury (Lower Hutt) 14–16 January 1986		v. Auckland (Auckland) 18–20 January 1986		v. Otago (Wellington) 25–27 January 1986		v. Northern Districts (Wellington) 29–31 January 1986		v. Canterbury (Christchurch) 2–4 February 1986		v. Central Districts (Hastings) 6–8 February 1986		M	Inns	NOs	Runs	HS	Av
J.G. Boyle	9	14	70	—	3	56	32	—	12	—	19	4	1	26	5	1	8	13	—	252	70	19.38
R.W. Ormiston	21	7	7	—	31	33	6	—	5	—	52	0	24	8	34	29	8	13	—	257	52	19.76
R.H. Vance	48	8	66	—	114	47	5	—	59	—	7	84	14	16	4	16	8	13	—	488	114	37.53
J.D. Milne	12	—	—	—	0	2	36	—	—	—	13	—	6	23			7	7	—	92	36	13.14
E.J. Gray	11	26	5	—	44	5	67*	—	128*	—	0	71	2	53	24	109	8	13	2	545	128*	49.54
A.H. Jones	8	23*	54*	—	10	33	99	—	26	—	10	5	17	1*			7	11	3	286	99	35.75
T.D. Ritchie	60	0	58*	—	41	2	31	—	31	—	37*	41*	30	27	13	49	8	13	3	420	60	42.00
G.R. Larsen	92	0	—	—	2	0	48	—	0*	—	1	20*	9	40	16*	1*	8	12	4	229	92	28.62
P.J.W. Allott	12	2*	—	—			4	—	—	—	8	—	66*	42	0	—	7	7	2	135	66*	27.00
S.J. Maguiness	18	—	—	—	19*	3							54	1	27	—	5	6	1	122	54	24.40
F. Beyeler	8*	—	—	—	6	30											3	3	1	44	30	22.00
W.M. Aberhart					4	0*	26	—									2	3	1	30	26	15.00
D. Molony							5	—	—	—	12	—	4	14*			4	4	1	35	14*	11.66
A.A. Griffiths									—	—							1					
G.N. Cederwall											3	0					1	2	—	3	3	1.50
R. Verry													16	16			1	2	—	32	16	16.00
E.B. McSweeney													32	20*			1	2	1	52	32	52.00
E.J. Chatfield															0	—	1	1	—	0	0	0.00
Byes	2	4	10		6	1	1				6	9										
Leg-byes	13	3	6		2	3	11		4		6	15	11	9	5	7						
Wides	3	3					1		1		3				1	2						
No-balls			4		2	1	11		2		5	1	3		3	1						
Total	318	90	280		278	222	383		268		182	250	242	262	179	249						
Wickets	10	6	4		10	10	10		5		10	6	10	9	10	6						
Results	W		D		W		D		D		D		W		D							
Points	16		2		12		4		2		0		16		4							

Catches
21 – J.D. Milne (ct 20/st 1)
8 – E.J. Gray and R.W. Ormiston
6 – S.J. Maguiness and E.B. McSweeney
5 – R.H. Vance
4 – T.D. Ritchie and G.R. Larsen
3 – P.J.W. Allott, J.G. Boyle and A.H. Jones
2 – F. Beyeler
1 – D. Molony and R. Verry

BOWLING

BOWLING	F. Beyeler	P.J.W. Allott	E.J. Gray	S.J. Maguiness	A.H. Jones	G.R. Larsen	W.M. Aberhart	D. Molony	T.D. Ritchie
v. Northern Districts (Gisborne) 6–8 January	22-6-48-2	24-10-46-3	26-11-69-1	22.2-11-32-4					
	22-6-45-2	18.3-7-56-5	32-17-60-1	14-3-25-1	10-4-19-1				
v. Central Districts (Wellington) 10–12 January	33-7-88-1	8-1-16-0	32-11-62-1	52.3-14-127-2	6-2-23-0	30-8-86-1			
v. Canterbury (Wellington) 14–16 January	10-4-30-0		50-19-114-6	14-6-22-0	12.1-3-26-2	27-11-46-2	14-3-42-0		
	3-0-8-0		26.1-12-37-8	2-0-5-0	10-5-23-0	14-2-34-2	2-0-10-0		
v. Auckland (Auckland) 18–20 January		36.1-17-57-2	28-6-65-2			28-7-47-2	19-6-50-1	26-6-75-2	
		4-1-4-0					4-0-17-0		2-1-2-0
v. Otago (Wellington) 25–27 January		37-9-79-5	32-7-95-2		5-1-12-0	8-0-29-0		14.2-0-39-1	
v. Northern Districts (Wellington) 29–31 January		26-9-40-5	7-2-18-0		2-1-6-0	21-9-43-1		17-4-40-1	
		32-10-59-4	10-2-32-1			36-12-65-1		6-0-41-0	
v. Canterbury (Christchurch) 2–4 February		3-0-11-0	5-5-0-3	21-10-29-2		11.2-1-28-1		18-2-62-3	
			30.3-11-60-2	34-9-70-3		24.3-5-59-1		20-3-69-3	
v. Central Districts (Hastings) 6–8 February		27-12-46-3	23-11-37-4	17-6-29-1		1-1-0-0			
		15-4-46-3	28.4-5-99-3	11-5-32-1					
	90-23-219-5	230.4-80-460-30	330.2-119-748-34	187.5-64-371-14	45.1-16-109-3	200.5-56-437-11	39-9-119-1	101.2-15-326-10	2-1-2-0
	av. 43.80	av. 15.33	av. 22.00	av. 26.50	av. 36.33	av. 39.72	av. 119.00	av. 32.60	—

a D. Morrison retired hurt
b R.W. Ormiston 3-0-10-0
c E.J. Chatfield 35.5-18-36-2
d E.J. Chatfield 16-5-33-0
R. Verry 5-1-14-0

Gary Robertson who returned match figures of 8 for 91 for Central Districts in the drawn game with Canterbury, 25 to 27 January. (Ross Setford)

Gary Troup bowled well for Auckland throughout the season and earned a recall to the Test side. (Ross Setford)

R.H. Vance	A.A. Griffiths	G.N. Cederwall	Byes	Leg-byes	Wides	No-balls	Total	Wkts
			1	3	2		199	10
				3	1	2	208	10
			8	23	1		433	6
			5	12		4	297	10
			10	6			133	10
			4	7	2		305	9a
2–0–13–0			4	2		1	42	0
	19–3–57–0		5	4			320	9
		20.3–1–58–3	2	5	1	9	212	10
		8–0–52–1	7	12		6	268	8
				3	1	3	133	10
7–4–11–1			13	10	1	3	302	10b
				5	1		153	10c
2–0–5–0				4			233	8d
11–4–	19–3–	28.3–1–						
29–1	57–0	110–4						
av. 29.00	—	av. 27.50						

Canterbury lost their last 8 wickets for 6 runs as Visser and Robertson tore them apart. Nathu then hit a career best, and Central, in search of 104 to win, slipped to 51 for 6 in 21 overs as Sean Tracy returned a career best bowling performance.

29, 30 and 31 January 1986

at Eden Park, Auckland

Auckland 292 for 7 dec (P.N. Webb 84, P.J. Kelly 84, T.J. Franklin 51, V.R. Brown 4 for 46) and 146 for 4 dec (P.A. Horne 62)
Canterbury 109 (D.N. Patel 4 for 47) and 134 (D.N. Patel 5 for 41, G.B. Troup 4 for 41)

Auckland won by 195 runs
Auckland 16 pts, Canterbury 0 pts

at Basin Reserve, Wellington

Northern Districts 212 (R. Mawhinney 110, P.J.W. Allott 5 for 40) and 268 for 8 dec (G.P. Howarth 79, P.J.W. Allott 4 for 59)
Wellington 182 (R.W. Ormiston 52, M.J. Child 4 for 26) and 250 for 6 (R.H. Vance 84, E.J. Gray 71)
Match drawn
Northern Districts 4 pts, Wellington 0 pts

at Centennial Park, Oamaru

Central Districts 344 for 5 dec (P.S. Briasco 109, I.D.S. Smith 84, T.E. Blain 63, D.A. Stirling 52 not out) and 300 (G.K. Robertson 99 not out, S.W. Duff 51)
Otago 303 (S.J. McCullum 77, S.W. Duff 6 for 36) and 342 for 6 (R.N. Hoskin 111, K.R. Rutherford 70, J.K. Lindsay 65 not out, S.W. Duff 4 for 119).

Otago won by 4 wickets
Otago 12 pts, Central District 4 pts

Regaining their batting form, Auckland moved to a competent and comfortable win over Canterbury. A sixth wicket stand of 160 by the consistent Peter Webb and wicket-keeper Kelly made it possible for Webb to declare, and Patel and promising off-spinner Martin Bradley bowled Auckland to a commanding lead. When Canterbury batted a second time, following Webb's second declaration, they succumbed to the pace of Troup and the spin of Patel, who had match figures of 9 for 88.

Mawhinney played a fine innings to hold Northern Districts together at Basin Reserve, and the visitors took an unexpected lead. Howarth made a challenging declaration, but although Vance and Gray shared a sparkling stand of 155 for the third wicket, Wellington fell well short of their target.

The match at Oamaru provided one of the most sensational wins in the history of the tournament and saw Otago put one hand on the Trophy. Central Districts reached a good position on the first day although Hart was forced to retire hurt. Briasco's hundred and hard hitting by Blain, Smith and Stirling meant that Otago would have to score quickly to stay in the game. Rutherford and McCullum gave them a brisk start, but the rest 'batted like millionaires on a spree to concede a first innings deficit of 41 runs'. The loss of these points could have cost them the title in view of what happened later, and Stu Duff returned the best figures of his brief career with his left-arm spin. The game seemed to be heading for a tame draw when Central were bowled out on the last afternoon, leaving Otago 182 minutes and 20 overs in which to make 342 to win, a seemingly impossible task. Rutherford and McCullum, as so often in the season, got their side off to a flying start with a stand of 108 in better than even time. Both fell to Duff who also captured Burns and Walker so that, at tea, on 149 for 4, all hope seemed gone for Otago. Wilson fell at 176, but Richard Hoskin and John Lindsay, an invaluable all rounder, engaged in a magnificent partnership which produced 147 runs in 87 minutes. Hoskin was caught off Visser, but Otago won with ample time to spare, having hit 342 runs in 69.1 overs, so taking a 14-point lead over Auckland with two matches remaining.

2, 3 and 4 February 1986

at Seddon Park, Hamilton

Otago 102 (K. Treiber 7 for 42) and 180 (W.K. Lees 62 not out, S.J. Scott 4 for 42)
Northern Districts 103 (N.A. Mallender 4 for 31) and 182 for 2 (L.M. Crocker 67)

Northern Districts won by 8 wickets
Northern Districts 16 pts, Otago 0 pts

at Pukekura Park, New Plymouth

Auckland 228 (T.J. Franklin 69, G.K. Robertson 5 for 47) and 310 for 7 dec (P.N. Webb 115, A.J. Hunt 79 not out, G.K. Robertson 4 for 68)
Central Districts 254 for 3 dec (P.S. Briasco 91, C.J. Smith 89) and 285 for 4 (C.J. Smith 80, P.S. Briasco 79, T.E. Blain 77 not out)

Central Districts won by 6 wickets
Central Districts 16 pts, Auckland 0 pts

at Lancaster Park, Christchurch

Wellington 242 (P.J.W. Allott 66 not out, S.J. Maguiness 54, S. Roberts 5 for 77) and 262 for 9 dec (E.J. Gray 53)
Canterbury 133 and 302 (P.G. Kennedy 81, D.G. Boyle 68)

Wellington won by 69 runs
Wellington 16 pts, Canterbury 0 pts

Put in to bat on a damp pitch at Seddon Park, Otago were bowled out for 102 as Karl Treiber recorded by far the best performance of his career. Northern Districts struggled in their turn against the pace of Mallender, Cushen and McKechnie. They were 79 for 7, but Young and Scott added 24 to take them into the lead at which point they lost their last three wickets. Otago did not bat well enough in their second innings to gain advantage from the opportunity that their bowlers had given them, and it was only skipper Lees who played with the usual confidence and aggression. Crocker and Mawhinney began the bid for victory by Northern with a stand of 108, and the rest was simple.

With Otago having suffered their first defeat of the season, Auckland had the chance to take the lead in the Trophy, but, on a good wicket at Pukekura Park, they batted well below form. John Smith and Scott Briasco demonstrated the quality of the pitch in an opening stand of 172, but Auckland stumbled for a second time against Visser and Robertson. Webb revived hopes with a fine hundred and he and Hunt put on 108 for the seventh wicket so that a declaration was possible. The wicket was still first rate, however, and John Smith and Briasco shared the second century opening partnership of the match, 148. The exciting young batsman Blain then stroked Central to victory, and Auckland still trailed Otago by 14 points.

Wellington moved level with them with a good team performance against Canterbury. Wellington's batsman struggled against pace bowler Stu Roberts who took 5 for 77 on his debut until Allott and Maguiness added 96 for the ninth wicket. Allott had to retire from bowling after 3 overs, but Molony, Larsen and Maguiness still troubled Canterbury, and Gray took 3 middle order wickets in 5 overs without conceding a run. Wellington batted more consistently in their second innings, but Canterbury made a bold bid for victory. They lost Nathu and McEwan for 32, but David Boyle and Kennedy put on 143, and the tail wagged well if in vain.

6, 7 and 8 February 1986

at Eden Park, Auckland

Auckland 258 (P.J. Kelly 93, J.G. Bracewell 54, S.G. Scott 4 for 77) and 283 for 6 dec (P.A. Horne 116, T.J. Franklin 80)
Northern Districts 199 (J.G. Bracewell 4 for 43) and 204 (M.J. Child 66 not out)

Auckland won by 138 runs
Auckland 16 pts, Northern Districts 0 pts

at Nelson Park, Hastings

Wellington 179 (D.A. Stirling 4 for 46) and 249 for 6 dec (E.J. Gray 109)
Central Districts 153 (E.J. Gray 4 for 37) and 223 for 8 (P.S. Briasco 60, R.E. Hayward 58)

Match drawn
Wellington 4 pts, Central Districts 0 pts

at Carisbrook, Dunedin

Canterbury 401 for 8 dec (D.J. Boyle 149, R.T. Latham 81, P.E. McEwan 70, P.G. Kennedy 53) and 28 for 0
Otago 403 for 5 dec (S.J. McCullum 134, D.J. Walker 76 not out, J.K. Lindsay 59)

Match drawn
Otago 4 pts, Canterbury 0 pts

Otago needed just the four points for first innings lead in their last game to win the Shell Trophy. Successive stands of 105, 140 and 77 for the second, third and fourth wickets took Canterbury to a mammoth score, and it seemed that Otago would be hard pressed after David Boyle's career best. Rutherford and McCullum, in a stand of 98, gave Otago their customary good start, but McCullum, having reached a career best, and Burns were out in quick succession and at 251 for 4, Otago's position looked uncertain. Derek Walker, only 17 runs in his previous four innings, and John Lindsay, whose value as an all rounder increased match by match, then added 116 in 135 minutes and took Otago to within 35 runs of the Shell Trophy. It was appropriate that Warren Lees, a positive, zestful captain, should join Walker in the final flurry which gained the four points.

Auckland had done all that they could in beating Northern Districts at Eden Park. John Bracewell took 7 for 129 in his only Shell Trophy game of the season, and Phillip Horne hit a maiden first-class hundred as he and Trevor Franklin began Auckland's second innings with a stand of 197.

Evan Gray, the outstanding all rounder of the season, hit his second century of the year in the drawn game with Central Districts.

Warren Lees whose inspiring captaincy played a decisive part in Otago winning the Shell Trophy. (Patrick Eagar)

A crowd of 20,000 saw the Australians begin their tour with a victory in a fifty-over game against Auckland. Boon and Marsh began the Australian run chase with a stand of 93, and Ritchie and Waugh stroked them to their target with 2.2 overs to spare.

Shell Trophy – Final Table						
(1985 positions in brackets)					*1st inns*	
	P	*W*	*L*	*D*	*Lead*	*Pts*
Otago (4)	8	4	1	3	5	70
Auckland (3)	8	4	2	2	5	68
Wellington (1)	8	3	—	5	4	56
Northern Districts (6)	8	3	3	2	3	48
Central Districts (6)	8	1	4	3	3	26
Canterbury (2)	8	—	5	3	2	8

15 February 1986

at Eden Park, Auckland

Auckland 250 for 7 (T.J. Franklin 79, J.J. Crowe 66)
Australians 252 for 4 (G.R. Marsh 78, G.M. Ritchie 66 not out, D.C. Boon 57)

Australians won by 6 wickets

16, 17 and 18 February 1986

at Seddon Park, Hamilton

Northern Districts 167 for 2 dec (D.J. White 53, B.R. Blair 51 not out) and 167 (R.J. Bright 5 for 42, B.A. Reid 4 for 25)
Australians 153 for 1 dec (G.R.J. Matthews 57 not out) and 182 for 6 (A.R. Border 77, K. Treiber 4 for 92)

Australians won by 4 wickets

The Australians gained a boost for morale on the eve of the first Test when they scored 182 in under 3 hours in difficult conditions to beat Northern Districts. The match was marred by rain and Border and Howarth kept the game alive with two declarations. Ray Bright used the conditions to advantage, and Bruce Reid gave further indication of his rapid advance since reaching international level. David White, who hit the season's highest score, 209, scored a good fifty in the first innings, and one had to reflect that although he has been playing first-class cricket for six years, he is still only 24. Bruce Blair batted with his usual panache.

First Test Match
NEW ZEALAND v. AUSTRALIA

Australia introduced Tim Zoehrer and Simon Davis to Test cricket. Both had played in the Benson and Hedges World Series as had Stuart Gillespie who earned his first cap for New Zealand.

Coney won the toss and asked Australia to bat. This was the fourteenth Test in succession between the two countries in which the winner of the toss had elected to field. On this occasion there seemed to be little justification for Coney's decision as Boon and Marsh continued their fruitful liaison in a disciplined and authoritative manner against some wayward bowling. The openers put on 104, but New Zealand went some way to nullifying this start when they captured 4 wickets for 62 runs, among them was Allan Border who was lbw to Hadlee.

This wicket was Richard Hadlee's three hundredth in Test cricket. This remarkable bowler had gone from 200 to 300 wickets in just 17 Tests. He was playing his sixty-first Test match.

The best part of the Australian innings was the fifth wicket stand between Greg Ritchie and Greg Matthews which produced a record 213 runs. Ritchie was at his very best, majestic in his command of the bowling and array of strokes. Matthews balanced Ritchie's regal authority with a bubblingly extrovert innings which brought him his third Test century in 7 Tests. He was missed on 97, but his effervescent play deservedly took him to his highest score in Test cricket.

Not for the first time Australia collapsed following this fine stand, and their last 5 wickets fell for 31 in 41 minutes.

Captains in conflict. Jeremy Coney steers New Zealand to safety. Allan Border is at slip. Coney ended on 101 not out. (Ross Setford)

FIRST TEST MATCH – NEW ZEALAND v. AUSTRALIA
21, 22, 23, 24 and 25 February 1986 at Basin Reserve, Wellington

AUSTRALIA

FIRST INNINGS		
D.C. Boon	c Smith, b Troup	70
G.R. Marsh	c Coney, b Chatfield	43
W.B. Phillips	b Gillespie	32
A.R. Border†	lbw, b Hadlee	13
G.M. Ritchie	b Troup	92
G.R.J. Matthews	c Rutherford, b Coney	130
S.R. Waugh	c Smith, b Coney	11
T.J. Zoehrer*	c sub (J.G. Bracewell), b Coney	18
C.J. McDermott	b Hadlee	2
B.A. Reid	not out	0
S.P. Davis	c and b Hadlee	0
Extras	b 2, lb 9, w 4, nb 9	24
		435

	O	M	R	W
Hadlee	37.1	5	116	3
Chatfield	36	10	96	1
Troup	28	6	86	2
Gillespie	27	2	79	1
Coney	18	7	47	3

FALL OF WICKETS
1- 104, 2- 143, 3- 166, 4- 166, 5- 379, 6- 414, 7- 418, 8- 435, 9- 435

NEW ZEALAND

FIRST INNINGS		
T.J. Franklin	c Border, b McDermott	0
B.A. Edgar	c Waugh, b Matthews	38
J.F. Reid	c Phillips, b Reid	32
S.R. Gillespie	c Border, b Reid	28
M.D. Crowe	b Matthews	19
K.R. Rutherford	c sub (Bright), b Reid	65
J.V. Coney†	not out	101
R.J. Hadlee	not out	72
I.D.S. Smith*		
G.B. Troup		
E.J. Chatfield		
Extras	b 2, lb 6, w 1, nb 15	24
	(for 6 wickets)	379

	O	M	R	W
McDermott	25.3	5	80	1
Davis	25	4	70	—
Reid	31	6	104	3
Matthews	37	10	107	2
Border	4	3	1	—
Waugh	4	1	9	—

FALL OF WICKETS
1- 0, 2- 57, 3- 94, 4- 115, 5- 138, 6- 247

Umpires: F.R. Goodall & S.J. Woodward

Match drawn

A great moment in New Zealand cricket history, Allan Border is lbw to Richard Hadlee for 13. It was Hadlee's 300th wicket in Test cricket. (Ross Setford)

Trevor Franklin, playing because John Wright had a back injury, was out in McDermott's opening over, but John Reid and Bruce Edgar batted solidly until Reid fell shortly before the close of the second day. Gillespie came in as night watchman and was to stay for nearly two hours in all and play a significant part in thwarting the Australians.

When Greg Matthews bowled Martin Crowe, the fifth wicket to fall, at 138, New Zealand were in some trouble, but Ken Rutherford played a quite delightful innings, hitting 11 fours, strong and handsome shots. He had earned his recall to the side at the expense of Jeff Crowe after some excellent batting in the Shell Trophy, but he still had the weight of dreadful failure in the West Indies hanging about his neck when he came to the wicket, no easy weight for a 20-year old to carry. His response to the situation was to bat exquisitely and share a record sixth wicket stand of 109 for New Zealand against Australia.

Coney, sound and determined, was joined by the eager Hadlee after Rutherford had fallen to Reid. They took the score to 311 for 6 by the close and on the fourth morning added a further 68 before rain ended the match. Coney's hundred was his first as New Zealand's captain and his third in Test cricket. The Hadlee – Coney stand of 132 was a seventh wicket record for New Zealand against Australia.

Second Test Match
NEW ZEALAND v. AUSTRALIA

The Australian side showed two changes for the second Test as Bright and Gilbert replaced Davis and McDermott. The New Zealand side also showed two changes as Wright and John Bracewell returned for Franklin and Gillespie.

Once again Coney asked Australia to bat first and this time his decision seemed a wise one as the visitors slumped to 74 for 5 against the fire of Hadlee and the ever faithful support of the steady Chatfield. Inevitably it was Border who roused Australia and he had fine support from Waugh. They added 177, and useful innings from Zoehrer, Bright and Gilbert lifted Australia to an unexpected 364.

Zoehrer's contribution was not at an end. Two fine catches accounted for Wright and Reid, and with Edgar falling lbw to Bruce Reid, New Zealand finished the second day on a precarious 48 for 3. It became 48 for 4 early the next morning when Rutherford was out, but Martin Crowe and the unquenchable Coney set about correcting matters. Crowe was hit in the face by a Reid bouncer and forced to retire and have eight stitches in his jaw, but he returned at 191 for 6 to continue his innings and reach a courageous century.

Rain restricted play to 94 minutes on the fourth day, and the game seemed to be heading for a dull draw when Australia underwent the type of collapse for which she was becoming renowned, and shortly after lunch on the last day, they were 130 for 6. Border then scored his second century of the match, his eighteenth in Test cricket, and Australia were once more saved by their valiant captain, one of the great left-handers of Test history.

6 March 1986

at Trafalgar Park, Nelson

Australians 276 for 7 (G.R.J. Matthews 66)
Nelson 194 for 9 (G.N. Edwards 55)
Australians won by 82 runs

The tourists completed a comfortable victory in a relaxed 50-over match. Jock Edwards, the former Test player, delighted the home crowd with a bright innings.

8, 9 and 10 March 1986

at New Plymouth

Australians 309 (D.C. Boon 109, T.J. Zoehrer 71, G.K. Robertson 4 for 70) and 305 (G.R. Marsh 101, G.M. Ritchie 80, S. Duff 4 for 87)
Central Districts 313 for 8 dec (M.D. Crowe 97, S. Duff 71) and 149 for 5
Match drawn

Marsh was out for 0, but Boon hit 20 fours in an aggressive display and was ably supported by Tim Zoehrer. In reply, Central Districts were 22 for 3, but Martin Crowe and Tony Blain added 103, and Duff batted finely for the home side to

LEFT: *Jeremy Coney lashes out during his innings of 98. Greg Matthews is the fielder. Coney had an outstanding series, averaging 146 from three innings and leading his side to victory over Australia for the second time within five months. (Ross Setford)*

Captain courageous. Allan Border – a century in each innings. (George Herringshaw)

take the lead. Marsh hit the second century of the match and shared century stands with Wayne Phillips and Greg Ritchie as the game moved to a draw.

Third Test Match
NEW ZEALAND v. AUSTRALIA

New Zealand gave a first Test cap to Gary Robertson who had represented his country in one-day international matches in 1981 and 1984. McDermott returned to the Australian side in place of Gilbert.

Allan Border chose to bat when he won the toss. It was a wise decision, if out of fashion with recent practice, and it was shown to be justified when Marsh and Phillips established a new Australian second wicket record against New Zealand with a stand of 167. Marsh faced 224 deliveries, batted for 245 minutes and hit 12 fours in his first Test century. He became Richard Hadlee's three hundred and thirteenth Test victim when he slashed wildly, and uncharacteristically, and was taken at slip.

Australia dominated the first day until the last half hour when New Zealand captured three quick wickets, including the coveted one of Border, so that the day ended with the visitors on 227 for 4.

The second day was a portent of what was to come. Matthews remained motionless on 1 for almost 75 minutes and then became one of John Bracewell's four victims. The off-spinner restricted Australia's last 6 wickets to another 87

SECOND TEST MATCH – NEW ZEALAND v. AUSTRALIA
28 February, 1, 2, 3 and 4 March 1986 at Lancaster Park, Christchurch

AUSTRALIA

	FIRST INNINGS			SECOND INNINGS	
G.R. Marsh	b Hadlee	28	(2) lbw, b Bracewell	15
D.C. Boon	c Coney, b Hadlee	26	(1) c Coney, b Troup	6
W.B. Phillips	c Smith, b Chatfield	1	b Hadlee	25
A.R. Border†	b Chatfield	140	not out	114
G.M. Ritchie	lbw, b Hadlee	4	c Smith, b Bracewell	11
G.R.J. Matthews	c Smith, b Hadlee	6	c sub (J.J. Crowe), b Hadlee	3
S.R. Waugh	lbw, b Hadlee	74	c Smith, b Bracewell	1
T.J. Zoehrer*	c Coney, b Hadlee	30	c Rutherford, b Bracewell	13
R.J. Bright	c Smith, b Bracewell	21	not out	21
D.R. Gilbert	b Hadlee	15		
B.A. Reid	not out	1		
Extras	b 1, lb 9, nb 8	18	lb 6, w 1, nb 3	10
		364	(for 7 wkts dec)	**219**

	O	M	R	W	O	M	R	W
Hadlee	44.4	8	116	7	25	4	47	2
Troup	34	4	104	—	15	—	50	1
Chatfield	36	13	56	2	17	6	29	—
Bracewell	27	9	46	1	33	12	77	4
Coney	9	—	28	—	3	1	10	—
M.D. Crowe	2	1	4	—				
Reid					1	1	0	—

FALL OF WICKETS
1- 57, 2- 58, 3- 58, 4- 64, 5- 74, 6- 251, 7- 319, 8- 334, 9- 358
1- 15, 2- 32, 3- 76, 4- 120, 5- 129, 6- 130, 7- 167

NEW ZEALAND

	FIRST INNINGS			SECOND INNINGS	
J.G. Wright	c Zoehrer, b Gilbert	10	(2) not out	4
B.A. Edgar	lbw, b Reid	8	(1) c and b Matthews	9
J.F. Reid	c Zoehrer, b Waugh	2	not out	0
M.D. Crowe	c Waugh, b Reid	137		
K.R. Rutherford	lbw, b Gilbert	0		
J.V. Coney†	c Reid, b Waugh	98		
R.J. Hadlee	c Zoehrer, b Reid	0		
I.D.S. Smith*	b Waugh	22		
J.G. Bracewell	c Marsh, b Reid	20		
G.B. Troup	lbw, b Waugh	10		
E.J. Chatfield	not out	2		
Extras	b 6, lb 8, nb 16	30	nb 3	3
		339	(for 1 wicket)	**16**

	O	M	R	W	O	M	R	W
Gilbert	26	4	106	2	7	4	9	—
Reid	34.3	8	90	4	4	—	7	—
Waugh	23	6	56	4				
Bright	18	6	51	—				
Matthews	6	1	22	—	3	3	0	1

FALL OF WICKETS
1- 17, 2- 29, 3- 29, 4- 48, 5- 124, 6- 190, 7- 263, 8- 311, 9- 331

Umpires: F.R. Goodall & B.L. Aldridge

Match drawn

ABOVE: *Man of the Match. John Bracewell, all fire and passion, on his way to bowling New Zealand to victory. (Ross Setford)*

runs, a great disappointment, but New Zealand ended the day in some trouble.

Wright and Edgar gave them a solid start, but the advent of Greg Matthews and Ray Bright turned the match in favour of Australia. Edgar was lbw when he played back to a ball which spun sharply, Rutherford was bowled by an off-break and Crowe suffered the same fate as Edgar.

New Zealand, 75 for 3, began the third day with some trepidation, and when Wright and Reid fell in quick succession it seemed that Australia had taken a firm grip on the game. Once more it was Jeremy Coney who raised New Zealand. He and Hadlee scored brisk runs to end all fears of the follow-on, and Coney, batting with fluency and author-ity, guided Smith, Bracewell and Robertson through stands which realised 80 runs and brought New Zealand in sight of the Australian score.

Coney's splendidly determined innings ended 7 short of what would have been a most deserved century, with the score at 250, and New Zealand eventually found themselves 56 runs in arrears.

Richard Hadlee gave his side a tremendous boost when he had Marsh lbw with the first ball of the second Australian innings, and Chatfield had Phillips taken at second slip so

that the visitors closed the day on 32 for 2, their early authority eroded.

Night-watchman Zoehrer became Chatfield's second victim early on the fourth day, and the medium pacer also accounted for Greg Ritchie, but the day belonged to John Bracewell. The off spinner demoralised Australia with his finest performance in Test cricket. He beat and bowled Border as he did three other batsmen and generally de-moralised the Australians who, Boon apart, were totally unable to cope with him. For Boon no praise can be too high. He stood firm as all around him crumbled and he carried his bat for 58 out of 103 in 60 gruelling overs.

The New Zealand bowlers had turned the game com-pletely in favour of their side, but, on a wicket that was giving the spinners assistance, the task of scoring 160 should have been no simple one. Reid bowled Edgar at 1, and Australian hopes revived, but by the end of the day, Wright and Rutherford, his confidence completely restored by his suc-cess in this series, had taken the score to 85, and they were unruffled.

Both batsmen reached patient fifties on the last morning, and although Wright fell to Matthews, Martin Crowe joined Rutherford in bringing the match and the series to New Zealand. Matthews and Bright bowled accurately, but neither of them has the ability to spin the ball nor the craft that is needed at the highest level.

John Bracewell was named Man of the Match, but to Jeremy Coney, Man of the Series, went the final plaudits for having led his side twice to series victories over Australia within the space of a few months.

BELOW: *'Whence all but he had fled'. David Boon steadfast among the debris. (Adrian Murrell)*

THIRD TEST MATCH – NEW ZEALAND v. AUSTRALIA
13, 14, 15, 16 and 17 March 1986 at Eden Park, Auckland

AUSTRALIA

	FIRST INNINGS		SECOND INNINGS	
D.C. Boon	c Coney, b Hadlee	16	(2) not out	58
G.R. Marsh	c Coney, b Hadlee	118	(1) lbw, b Hadlee	0
W.B. Phillips	c Smith, b Bracewell	62	c Bracewell, b Chatfield	15
A.R. Border†	c Smith, b Chatfield	17	(5) b Bracewell	6
T.J. Zoehrer*	c Coney, b Robertson	9	(4) lbw, b Chatfield	1
G.M. Ritchie	c Smith, b Chatfield	56	lbw, b Chatfield	1
G.R.J. Matthews	b Bracewell	5	st Smith, b Bracewell	4
S.R. Waugh	c Reid, b Bracewell	1	b Bracewell	0
R.J. Bright	c Smith, b Hadlee	5	b Bracewell	0
C.J. McDermott	lbw, b Bracewell	9	b Bracewell	6
B.A. Reid	not out	0	c Hadlee, b Bracewell	8
Extras	b 2, lb 11, nb 3	16	lb 4	4
		314		103

	O	M	R	W	O	M	R	W
Hadlee	31	12	60	3	20	6	48	1
Robertson	24	6	91	1				
Chatfield	29	10	54	2	18	9	19	3
M.D. Crowe	3	2	4	—				
Bracewell	43.3	19	74	4	22	8	32	6
Coney	5	—	18	—				

FALL OF WICKETS
1- 25, 2- 193, 3- 225, 4- 225, 5- 278, 6- 293, 7- 294, 8- 301, 9- 309
1- 0, 2- 28, 3- 35, 4- 59, 5- 62, 6- 62, 7- 71, 8- 71, 9- 71

NEW ZEALAND

	FIRST INNINGS		SECOND INNINGS	
J.G. Wright	c Zoehrer, b McDermott	56	c Boon, b Matthews	59
B.A. Edgar	lbw, b Matthews	24	b Reid	1
K.R. Rutherford	b Matthews	0	not out	50
M.D. Crowe	lbw, b Matthews	0	not out	23
J.F. Reid	c Phillips, b Bright	16		
J.V. Coney†	c Border, b McDermott	93		
R.J. Hadlee	b Reid	33		
I.D.S. Smith*	b Waugh	3		
J.G. Bracewell	c Boon, b Bright	4		
G.K. Robertson	st Zoehrer, b Matthews	12		
E.J. Chatfield	not out	1		
Extras	b 7, lb 8, nb 1	16	b 18, lb 4, nb 5	27
		258	(for 2 wickets)	160

	O	M	R	W	O	M	R	W
McDermott	17	2	47	2	14	3	29	—
Reid	19	2	63	1	12.4	2	30	1
Matthews	34	15	61	4	31	18	46	1
Bright	22	4	60	2	23	12	29	—
Waugh	5	1	12	1	4	1	4	—

FALL OF WICKETS
1- 73, 2- 73, 3- 73, 4- 103, 5- 107, 6- 170, 7- 184, 8- 203, 9- 250
1- 6, 2- 106

Umpires: S.J. Woodward & R. McHarg

New Zealand won by 8 wickets

New Zealand v. Australia – Test Match Averages

NEW ZEALAND BATTING

	M	Inns	NOs	Runs	HS	Av	100s	50s
J.V. Coney	3	3	1	292	101*	146.00	1	2
M.D. Crowe	3	4	1	179	137	59.66	1	
R.J. Hadlee	3	3	3	105	72*	52.50		1
J.G. Wright	2	4	1	129	59	43.00		2
K.R. Rutherford	3	4	1	115	65	38.33		2
J.F. Reid	3	4	1	50	32	16.66		
B.A. Edgar	3	5		80	38	16.00		
I.D.S. Smith	3	2		25	22	12.50		
J.G. Bracewell	2	2		24	20	12.00		

Played in three Tests: E.J. Chatfield 2* & 1*.
Played in two Tests: G.B. Troup 10
Played in one Test: T.J. Franklin 0, S.R. Gillespie 28, G.K. Robertson 12

AUSTRALIA BATTING

	M	Inns	NOs	Runs	HS	Av	100s	50s
A.R. Border	3	5	1	290	140	72.50	2	
D.C. Boon	3	5	1	176	70	44.00		2
G.R. Marsh	3	5		204	118	40.80	1	
G.M. Ritchie	3	5		164	92	32.80		2
G.R.J. Matthews	3	5		148	130	29.60	1	
W.B. Phillips	3	5		135	62	27.00		1
S.R. Waugh	3	5		87	74	17.40		1
R.J. Bright	2	4	1	47	21*	15.66		
T.J. Zoehrer	3	5		71	30	14.20		
B.A. Reid	3	4	3	9	8	9.00		
C.J. McDermott	2	3		17	9	5.66		

Played in one Test: S.P. Davis 0; D.R. Gilbert 15

NEW ZEALAND BOWLING

	Overs	Mds	Runs	Wkts	Av	Best	5/inn	10/m
J.G. Bracewell	125.3	48	229	15	15.26	6/32	1	1
R.J. Hadlee	157.5	35	387	16	24.18	7/116		1
E.J. Chatfield	136	48	254	8	31.75	3/19		
J.V. Coney	35	8	103	3	34.33	3/47		
G.B. Troup	77	10	240	3	80.00	2/86		
M.D. Crowe	5	3	8	—	—			

Bowled in one innings: G.K. Robertson 24 - 6 - 91 - 1; S.R. Gillespie 27 - 2 - 79 - 1; J.F. Reid 1 - 1 - 0 - 0

AUSTRALIA BOWLING

	Overs	Mds	Runs	Wkts	Av	Best	5/inn	10/m
S.R. Waugh	36	9	81	5	16.20	4/56		
G.R.J. Matthews	111	47	236	8	29.50	4/61		
B.A. Reid	100.3	18	294	9	32.66	4/90		
C.J. McDermott	56.3	10	156	3	52.00	2/47		
D.R. Gilbert	33	8	115	2	57.50	2/106		
R.J. Bright	63	22	140	2	70.00	2/60		

Bowled in one innings: S.P. Davis 25 - 4 - 70 - 0; A.R. Border 4 - 3 - 1 - 0

NEW ZEALAND CATCHES

12 - I.D.S. Smith (ct 11/st 1); 7 - J.V. Coney; 2 - K.R. Rutherford, R.J. Hadlee and subs (J.G. Bracewell and J.J. Crowe); 1 - J.F. Reid and J.G. Bracewell

AUSTRALIA CATCHES

5 - T.J. Zoehrer (ct 4/st 1); 3 - A.R. Border; 2 - W.B. Phillips, D.C. Boon and S.R. Waugh; 1 - G.R. Marsh, G.R.J. Matthews, B.A. Reid and sub (R.J. Bright)

Geoff Marsh. Boon and Border promised a fighting performance, but no batsman was able to play the big innings that was needed, and New Zealand were always in a winning position.

Third One-Day International
NEW ZEALAND v. AUSTRALIA

Displaying a spirit and tenacity which had been lacking in their earlier matches, Australia won a thrilling victory in the third limited-over match.

Once more New Zealand were given a fine start by Edgar and Rutherford, but the later batsmen failed to build on the good beginning and the final score was lower than had been hoped for. Nevertheless, it seemed ample for victory as Australia lost Boon, Border and Ritchie for 56. Marsh and Waugh brightened the position, but at 142 for 5 with only 11 overs remaining, Australia looked set for defeat.

It was at this point that Wayne Phillips joined Steve Waugh. Waugh hit 3 fours in reaching fifty off 73 balls, but it was Phillips, with 9 boundaries and 53 off 32 deliveries, who brought Australia close to victory.

Phillips fell to the first ball of the last over when 2 runs were needed, and Waugh was run out next ball, but McDermott kept his head and hit the runs to bring Australia a heartening win.

Fourth One-Day International
NEW ZEALAND v. AUSTRALIA

Australia batted first for the first time in the four-match series and, thanks to a stand of 100 for the fifth wicket between Ritchie and Matthews, reached 231 in the 45 overs to which their innings had been reduced. The visitors had

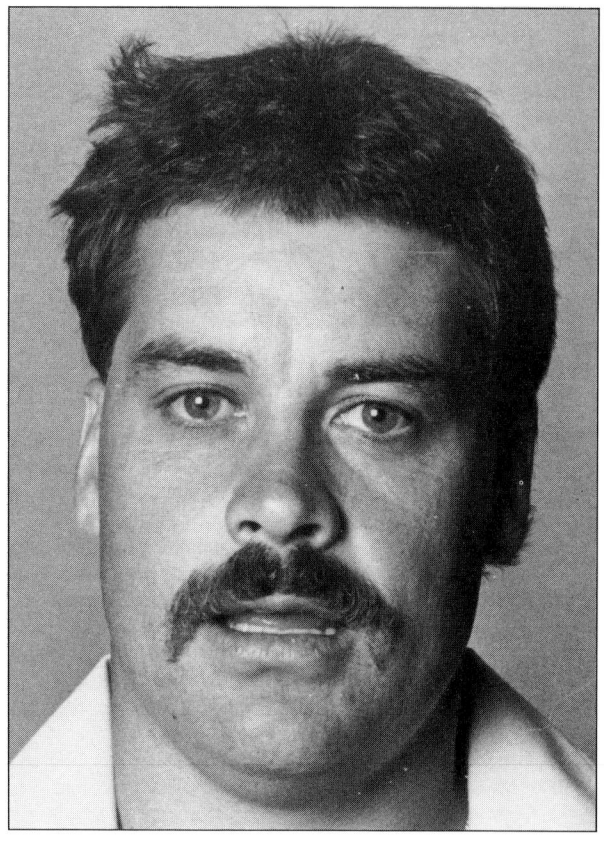

Bruce Blair – one-day specialist, but no Test place. (Ross Setford)

FOURTH ONE-DAY INTERNATIONAL – NEW ZEALAND v. AUSTRALIA
29 March 1986 at Eden Park, Auckland

AUSTRALIA			
D.C. Boon	b Bracewell		40
G.R. Marsh	run out		19
A.R. Border†	run out		21
G.M. Ritchie	b Gray		53
S.R. Waugh	run out		1
G.R.J. Matthews	b Chatfield		54
W.B. Phillips*	c Blain, b Chatfield		10
R.J. Bright	b Hadlee		6
C.J. McDermott	not out		12
B.A. Reid	b Hadlee		1
S.P. Davis	run out		0
Extras	b 1, lb 12, nb 1		14
(44.5 overs)			231

	O	M	R	W
Hadlee	8.5	—	35	2
Chatfield	9	—	37	2
Gillespie	8	1	55	—
M.D. Crowe	2	—	15	—
Bracewell	9	—	31	1
Gray	8	—	45	1

FALL OF WICKETS
1- 25, 2- 86, 3- 87, 4- 96, 5- 196, 6- 209, 7- 209, 8- 229, 9- 231

NEW ZEALAND			
K.R. Rutherford	run out		12
B.A. Edgar	c Boon, b Reid		22
M.D. Crowe	c Border, b Matthews		14
J.V. Coney†	run out		11
R.J. Hadlee	c Matthews, b Davis		40
B.R. Blair	c Boon, b Matthews		11
T.E. Blain*	c and b Matthews		7
E.J. Gray	c Phillips, b Reid		7
J.G. Bracewell	c Matthews, b Waugh		20
S.R. Gillespie	not out		18
E.J. Chatfield	not out		7
Extras	b 1, lb 16, nb 1		18
(45 overs)	(for 9 wickets)		187

	O	M	R	W
McDermott	9	1	23	—
Davis	8	2	28	1
Reid	9	1	30	2
Matthews	9	1	33	3
Waugh	9	1	45	1
Boon	1	—	11	—

FALL OF WICKETS
1- 32, 2- 53, 3- 59, 4- 77, 5- 78, 6- 100, 7- 112, 8- 149, 9- 161

Australia won by 44 runs

begun well, but faltered badly in the pursuit of quick runs as Marsh, Border and Waugh were all run out. The decline from 86 for 1 to 96 for 4 was all too familiar to Australian supporters, and the stand by Ritchie and Matthews was as sensible as it was enterprising and morale-lifting.

Greg Matthews' part in the match was by no means finished. New Zealand did not make their usual good start, but just as a recovery seemed likely, Matthews entered the attack to dispose of Martin Crowe. He also accounted for both Blair and Blain as well as catching Bracewell and Hadlee. The catch to dismiss Hadlee was taken on the boundary, and the umpires rejected the appeal, but Hadlee drew generous applause when he walked as the fielder indicated a fair catch.

Not surprisingly, Matthews was named Man of the Match.

The win gave Australia some consolation for their dismal year and their defeats at the hands of New Zealand in the two Test series. The defeat mattered little to New Zealand who reached the end of a highly successful season in high spirits. Two fine wins over Australia had been achieved and young players, like Rutherford and Blain, were emerging who promised to reach the highest level. The tour to England was eagerly anticipated, but first a party, for which neither Hadlee nor Coney was available, was to tour Sri Lanka and Sharjah and compete in one-day tournaments. There would also be matches in Hong Kong. The thirteen selected would gain a chance to further their claims for inclusion in the side to tour England.

J.G. Wright (captain), T.E. Blain, B.R. Blair, E.B. McSweeney, E.J. Gray, J.J. Crowe, M.D. Crowe, J.G. Bracewell, E.J. Chatfield, G.K. Robertson, K.R. Rutherford, M.C. Snedden and W. Watson were the players selected.

First-Class Averages

BATTING	M	Inns	NOs	Runs	HS	Av	100s	50s
J.V. Coney	3	3	1	292	101*	146.00	1	2
M.D. Crowe	4	6	1	318	137	63.60	1	1
P.N. Webb	8	13	5	441	115	55.12		
D.J. Boyle	3	6	1	267	149	53.40	1	1
R.J. Hadlee	3	3	1	105	72*	52.50		1
K.R. Rutherford	11	17	2	754	126	50.26	3	4
E.J. Gray	8	13	2	545	128*	49.54	2	3
S.J. McCullum	8	13	1	584	134	48.66	1	3
G.K. Robertson	10	11	4	303	99*	43.28		3
J.G. Wright	2	4	1	129	59	43.00		2
T.D. Ritchie	8	13	3	420	60	42.00		2
R.N. Hoskin	8	12	2	401	111	40.10	1	2
C.J. Smith	9	17		674	103	39.64	2	3
M.J. Greatbatch	7	12	4	316	119*	39.50	1	1
T.J. Franklin	9	16	1	592	176	39.46	1	5
D.J. White	9	17	2	578	209	38.53	1	2
R.T. Hart	6	11	1	380	207	38.00	1	1
D.J. Walker	8	11	2	341	106	37.88	1	2
R.H. Vance	8	13		488	114	37.53	1	3
P.J. Kelly	8	9	1	292	93	36.50		2
B.R. Blair	2	4	1	109	51*	36.33		1
D.N. Patel	8	14	1	469	174	36.07	1	1
A.H. Jones	7	11	3	286	99	35.75		2
C.M. Kuggeleijn	9	14	2	424	74	35.33		3
S.W. Duff	7	11	4	236	71	33.71		2
P.S. Briasco	9	17	1	535	109	33.43	1	3
T.E. Blain	7	14	2	398	77*	33.16		3
R.T. Latham	8	14	1	423	81	32.53		3

	M	Inns	NOs	Runs	HS	Av	100s	50s
J.K. Lindsay	8	11	2	289	65*	32.11		2
L.M. Crocker	9	18	2	499	105	31.18	1	1
P.A. Horne	6	10	1	279	116	31.00	1	1
A.J. Hunt	6	8	2	186	79*	31.00		1
D.G. Scott	6	11	1	307	79	30.70		3
P.E. McEwan	8	14		418	118	29.85	1	2
A.P. Nathu	8	15	1	417	153	29.78	1	
G.R. Larsen	8	12	4	229	92	28.62		1
G.W. McKenzie	4	7	1	169	49	28.16		
D.A. Stirling	9	15	4	306	51*	27.81		1
R. Mawhinney	9	18	1	469	110	27.58	1	1
I.D.S. Smith	10	13	2	298	84	27.09		2
K.J. Burns	8	12	1	297	93	27.00		1
P.J.W. Allott	7	7	2	135	66*	27.00		1
R.E. Hayward	8	14	1	342	69*	26.30		2
D.W. Stead	8	14	2	313	52	26.08		1
D.J. Hartshorn	5	9	1	204	47*	25.50		
N.A. Mallender	8	8	2	149	52*	24.83		1
B.G. Cooper	6	10		245	83	24.50		1
S.J. Maguiness	5	6	1	122	54	24.40		1
P.G. Kennedy	7	12		260	81	21.66		2
W.K. Lees	8	10	3	151	62*	21.57		1
R.W. Ormiston	8	13		257	52	19.76		1
J.G. Boyle	8	13		252	70	19.38		2
M.J. Child	6	9	1	154	66*	19.25		1
V.R. Brown	8	14		269	134	19.21	1	
B.A. Young	9	14	5	170	31	18.88		
G.P. Howarth	6	9		168	79	18.66		1
G.B. Troup	10	8	3	107	29*	17.83		
T.J. Wilson	6	8	1	107	31	15.28		
S.J. Scott	9	12		168	32	14.00		
A.W. Hart	8	14	3	122	44	11.09		
S.R. McNally	7	12		123	29	10.25		

(Qualification – 100 runs, average 10.00)

BOWLING	Overs	Mds	Runs	Wkts	Av	Best	10/m	5/inn
P.J.W. Allott	230.4	80	460	30	15.33	5/40		3
J.G. Bracewell	178.3	64	358	22	16.27	6/32	1	1
M. Bradley	70	15	170	10	17.00	3/37		
B.J. Barrett	64.2	12	210	10	21.00	4/51		
K. Treiber	109.1	28	322	15	21.46	7/42		1
E.J. Gray	330.2	119	748	34	22.00	8/37	1	2
J.A.J. Cushen	349.3	128	711	31	22.93	6/34		2
G.B. Troup	286.5	81	696	30	23.20	5/43		2
R.J. Hadlee	157.5	35	387	16	24.18	7/116		1
M.J. Child	161	34	438	18	24.33	4/26		
V.R. Brown	210.1	70	487	20	24.35	6/53		1
N.A. Mallender	227.1	48	597	24	24.87	4/31		
G. Bradburn	163.5	43	425	17	25.00	4/40		
D.N. Patel	355.1	105	756	29	26.06	5/41		1
S.J. Maguiness	187.5	64	371	14	26.50	4/32		
B.J. McKechnie	215.1	75	458	17	26.94	4/38		
S.W. Duff	218.2	53	604	21	28.76	6/36	1	1
C.H. Thiele	185	38	562	19	29.57	4/74		
S.J. Scott	271.1	67	721	24	30.04	4/42		
G.K. Robertson	269.4	41	967	32	30.21	5/47		1
S.M. Carrington	259.5	46	792	25	31.68	4/38		
E.J. Chatfield	197.5	71	323	10	32.30	3/19		
J.K. Lindsay	187.3	45	647	20	32.35	3/38		
D. Molony	101.2	15	326	10	32.60	3/62		
D.A. Stirling	217	32	872	26	33.53	5/91		1
P.J. Visser	298.5	72	901	26	34.65	6/28		1
S.R. McNally	195	47	592	17	34.82	4/39		
S.R. Tracy	120.5	17	466	13	35.84	5/19		1
G.R. Larsen	200.5	56	437	11	39.72	2/34		

(Qualification – 10 wickets)

LEADING FIELDERS
30 - I.D.S. Smith (ct 26/st 4); 25 - W.K. Lees (ct 24/st 1); 24 - B.A. Young (ct 21/st 3); 23 - P.J. Kelly (ct 22/st 1); 21 - J.D. Milne (ct 20/st 1); 18 - A.W. Hart (ct 16/st 2); 11 - P.N. Webb and C.M. Kuggeleijn; 10 - T.J. Franklin and K.R. Rutherford;

tral Districts who replaced the injured Ian Smith in the one-day internationals at home, and immediately made the strongest impression.

But before finishing a description of the summer Border deserves more mention.

He is among the finest modern batsmen, a strong and confident striker of the ball and he scored 569 runs, with three centuries, during the six Tests. He never quite won the battle against Hadlee, but it was pertinent that Border had other battles to fight.

Cricket in Australia is a high-profile sport, drawing yards of newspaper space, hours of television and radio exposure. As captain of a youngish side Border was freely available to the media whenever appropriate and his early remarks had a strong ring of confidence. Border enjoys playing cricket, I suspect he enjoys the glamour of captaincy, but I wonder whether he is totally enamoured of the glare of publicity.

By the end of the Gabba Test Border seemed almost distraught at the end-of-match interview. All his castles had tumbled down around him. He certainly did not enjoy being the first Australian captain to lose to New Zealand at home.

He was, naturally, much chirpier after the win in Sydney, but the WACA loss seemed to open up old wounds. Frequently Border expressed himself as completely baffled that what he regarded as a good Australian side should be so comprehensively out-played by a side that many Australians did not regard among the top cricketing nations.

By the time Australia had lost the Test series in New Zealand and were 0–2 in the one-day internationals Border seemed to have had quite enough of trying to carry his erratic side into any more battles. In a quite astonishing interview he wondered whether he wanted to carry on playing, and wondered aloud at the motivation of many of his own players.

It was a sobering sight, watching a very fine player and a gentleman baring his soul in this manner. The next day Border made light of his outburst, and even suggested that it had been delivered with tongue in cheek. If such was the case Border is a better actor than he is a batsman.

One of the bizarre aspects of the summer was public reaction to Matthews, the pop-age cricketer with the burning ambition to succeed, and perhaps with the talent to do just that. Matthews in Australia was the darling of the crowds and of television. He was bouncy, brash and sometimes brilliant. He breathed life into the dullest day. Matthews also had the charming habit of signing youngsters' autographs, no matter how long the queue of little lads stretched.

New Zealanders, who had seen Matthews and his exotic habits during telecasts of the one-day matches in Australia, for some reason took an instant dislike to the engaging young man. He was sometimes booed, mocked in the posters which are a modern drudge of the game. He still signed autographs but so much of the spark had gone out of his cricket that he was not a success in New Zealand.

On the home front it seemed as if New Zealand had at last found the right mix for its domestic matches. The Shell Cup one-day matches were played together over the Christmas–New Year holiday period, with all the leading players involved between their trips to Australia.

The public interest was high, so was the standard of play and on the last day four teams, Auckland, Wellington (playing each other at Auckland), Canterbury and Otago (playing at Oamaru) were level on points. Unfortunately rain washed out the match at Auckland, Canterbury won at Oamaru and thus won the one-day trophy.

The three-day Shell Trophy took up the rest of January and early February, with the New Zealand players available for the last two series of matches. Auckland started at a great pace, but slowly and steadily the unsung Otago side worked their way through the field. Going into the last match Auckland threw out a challenge, but Otago had to score over 400 to head Canterbury and take the trophy, which they did most ably.

They had piles of runs from Rutherford and Stuart McCullum at the top of the batting, and everyone else chipped in with solid scores, and an agreeably fast scoring rate. The bowling leant heavily on Neil Mallender and the long-serving John Cushen.

But perhaps the most significant aspect of Otago's win was the overall control exercised by Gren Alabaster, the chairman of selectors. Alabaster, a batsman and off-spin bowler, had only a brief New Zealand career in 1973–74, without playing a Test. However he was a keen student of the game and its players, a strong captain of the field, and a man with a flair for leadership.

For many years another man from the deep south, Frank Cameron, had been chairman of selectors and the strong hand behind the New Zealand team. Cameron was a fine medium-fast bowler for New Zealand, and it was a steady selection policy which has given New Zealand such a stable side over the last five or six years.

Cameron is stepping down from his post this year, handing some of the organisation of the side to Glenn Turner, the great batsman, who has been the cricket manager since October.

However, there is the interesting prospect that Alabaster will be moved on to the national selection panel later this year, perhaps going straight into the chairman's position. In this way the Cameron influence may well continue for Alabaster is not a man given to swift and unreasonable change. If so, it will be a coup for Otago. They are not the most fashionable side in the country, but with Cameron, Turner and perhaps Alabaster Otago show that they are not short on cricketing nous.

It may not be long, either, before there is a change at the top of the administration. Bob Vance, the forthright chairman of the New Zealand Cricket Council for the last few years, has had health problems and may step down within the next year or two. His likely successor is Sir Alan Wright, manager of the New Zealand side to England in 1983.

If Vance is to pull out in the near future he may have left a useful legacy. Very much at Vance's insistence, and with the financial support of Shell Oil, the NZCC have engaged Dennis Lillee, the famous Australian bowler, to make annual visits to New Zealand to coach promising young fast bowlers. Lillee has been delighted both with the invitation, and the youthful talent he has started to mould.

The hope is that he will find a budding Richard Hadlee or two among the youngsters – and judging on last summer's performance, and the prospect that Hadlee's big-match days are running out, the sooner Lillee finds someone to fill Hadlee's big boots the better.

Sport that Wrinkled Care Derides

The season in India.
Duleep Trophy, Irani Cup.
Ranji Trophy. Averages.

Syed Kirmani—one of the greatest of wicket-keepers whose Test career is close to its end. (Adrian Murrell)

A season of quiet domesticity such as some might envy was promised for India in 1985–86. Once again, most of it would be contested without the leading players who were engaged initially in Sri Lanka, a tour which did not conflict with the Indian season, and later in Australia, a tour which, with three Test matches and twelve one-day internationals played from November until February, most positively did deny the national squad the opportunity of playing in the domestic competition.

The touring party returned from their unsuccessful venture in Sri Lanka in time to participate in the Duleep Trophy which began in miserable fashion, the preliminary match at Vijayawada being abandoned without a ball being bowled because of rain on all four days.

Duleep Trophy

Preliminary Round

5, 6, 7 and 8 October 1985

at Vijayawada
Central Zone v. East Zone
Match abandoned. East Zone won on toss of a coin

Semi-Finals

11, 12, 13 and 14 October 1985

at Trivandrum

West Zone 575 for 7 dec (L.S. Rajput 221, D.B. Vengsarkar 110, S.M. Gavaskar 72, B. Mistry 58, R.J. Shastri 55, Maninder Singh 5 for 145) and 52 for 1
North Zone 519 (M.B. Amarnath 136, A.O. Malhotra 116, Yashpal Sharma 76, S.C. Khanna 52, R.J. Shastri 8 for 145)

Match drawn
West Zone won on first innings

at Secunderabad

South Zone 293 for 7 dec (S.M.H. Kirmani 61 not out, K.A. Qayyum 60)
East Zone 229

Match drawn
South Zone won on first innings

On a docile pitch at Trivandrum, Shastri had no hesitation in batting first when he won the toss. Gaekwad fell early, bowled by off-spinner Talwar for 21. Rajput was in a rather stodgy mood, but he was obviously intent on impressing the selectors that he should retain his place as India's opener and he and Gavaskar, batting number three, put on 156 for the second wicket before Gavaskar, who became the leading run-scorer in the history of the competition when he passed Wadekar's record of 1545 runs, was bowled by Maninder Singh. It was the North's last success of the day which ended with the West Zone on 258 for 2. Rajput and Vengsarkar took their stand to 205 before Vengsarkar was stumped off Maninder. Rajput batted 630 minutes for his 221, a dour effort, but one to commend him to the selectors with the tour to Australia looming. Shastri and Mistry continued to

pillage the North's attack and Shastri declared early on the third morning at a daunting 575 for 7.

North Zone batsmen responded magnificently. Khanna and Navjot Singh Sidhu put on a brisk 95, and then Amarnath and Malhotra shared a scintillating stand of 200 at a run a minute after Sidhu had retired hurt. North Zone began the last day needing 280 for the lead with 9 wickets in hand, but the honours went to Shastri who dismissed both centurions and then brought off a splendid caught and bowled to account for Kapil Dev after the North's captain had added 71 with Yashpal Sharma. Shastri, leading the West for the first time, completed a triumphant day when he thwarted the North's brave attempt to win and finished with his best figures in the competition. Shastri is a remarkably talented cricketer, still only 24 years old, and one feels that the best of him has yet to be seen at international level.

In contrast, two days were lost to rain at Secunderabad and batsmen struggled. South Zone reached 253 for 6 on the first day, and the score was boosted by Kirmani's brisk knock which enabled Srikkanth to declare. Both East Zone openers, Dubey and skipper Arun Lal, were out with only 2 scored, both caught by Kirmani, and although Bora and Mitra played steadily, wickets fell at regular intervals. The main threat to the South was a last wicket stand of 63 between Harmohan Praharaj and Randhir Singh who played out 19 of the last 20 overs before Arshad Ayub bowled Praharaj.

Duleep Trophy Final
WEST ZONE v. SOUTH ZONE

Srikkanth won the toss and elected to bat. It seemed an unwise decision when 4 wickets fell for 36, three of them to spin. Roger Binny and Ranjit Khanwilkar changed the complexion of the match with an authoritative and exciting stand. Binny hit 18 fours and was out to a smart piece of fielding by substitute Pandit who ran him out from silly point. Khanwilkar was out in the last over of the day. Anxious to complete his hundred, he mishooked and wicket-keeper More took a running catch.

South Zone collapsed the next morning. Rajput played poorly and Gaekwad was quickly caught behind, but Gavaskar and Vengsarkar played cricket of the highest quality in a stand of 142. Vengsarkar also shared a stand of 126 with Sandeep Patil who was as exciting as ever and with Shastri playing a good knock, West Zone took complete control.

Like Azharuddin, another hero of the previous season, Sivaramakrishnan experienced a lean time, and it was apparent that he had lost confidence. Gavaskar dealt with him most severely. Azharuddin seemed right out of luck and form. Srikkanth reached a patient hundred, which must have impressed the selectors, but on a wicket which was now assisting the spinners, South Zone's chances of avoiding defeat had evaporated, and only 11 overs were needed to finish the match on the final day.

Apart from Gavaskar, Vengsarkar and the other run-makers, Shivlal Yadav had an impressive game and did much to regain his place as India's premier off-spinner.

DULEEP TROPHY FINAL – WEST ZONE v. SOUTH ZONE
17, 18, 19, 20 and 21 October 1985 at Bangalore

SOUTH ZONE

	FIRST INNINGS		SECOND INNINGS	
K. Srikkanth†	c Patil, b Sandhu	4	c Rajput, b Patel	120
C.S. Suresh Kumar	lbw, b Patel	13	b Kulkarni	8
M. Azharuddin	c Gavaskar, b Patel	6	b Kulkarni	1
R. Madhavan	b Shastri	3	c Sandhu, b Shastri	19
R.M.H. Binny	run out	115	lbw, b Patel	15
R.D. Khanwilkar	c More, b Kulkarni	98	run out	1
S.M.H. Kirmani*	c and b Kulkarni	6	lbw, b Patel	22
L. Sivarama-krishnan	lbw, b Shastri	10	run out	2
B. Arun	c and b Patel	29	b Patel	4
S.N. Yadav	not out	7	not out	19
A.R.B. Bhat	c Mistry, b Patel	0	c Gavaskar, b Shastri	13
Extras	b 3, lb 3, nb 8	14	b 1, lb 6, nb 5	12
		305		236

WEST ZONE

	FIRST INNINGS		SECOND INNINGS	
A.D. Gaekwad	c Kirmani, b Binny	6		
L.S. Rajput	c Khanwilkar, b Madhavan	25	not out	31
S.M. Gavaskar	lbw, b Yadav	119	(1) c Siva, b Yadav	44
D.B. Vengsarkar	c Azharuddin, b Yadav	147		
S.M. Patil	b Arun	65		
R.J. Shastri†	not out	55		
B. Mistry	c Khanwilkar, b Yadav	7		
K.S. More†	c Arun, b Yadav	6	(3) not out	9
B.S. Sandhu	c Arun, b Bhat	6		
A. Patel	c sub (Jaisimha), b Yadav	0		
R.R. Kulkarni	lbw, b Yadav	0		
Extras	b 4, lb 7, nb 6	17	b 4, nb 1	5
		453	(for 1 wicket)	89

	O	M	R	W	O	M	R	W
Sandhu	12	2	45	1	7	1	27	—
Kulkarni	19	1	73	2	10	1	19	2
Shastri	38	16	66	2	25.2	5	75	2
Patel	33.5	8	86	4	36	3	95	4
Mistry	3	1	9	—	8	2	13	—
Gaekwad	3	—	9	—				
Patil	4	—	11	—				

	O	M	R	W	O	M	R	W
Binny	10	3	15	1				
Arun	20	2	78	1	3	1	9	—
Bhat	43	13	90	1	4	1	11	—
Khanwilkar	9	2	23	—				
Sivaramakrishnan	24	3	92	—	3	—	26	—
Yadav	51	10	109	6	9	3	18	1
Madhavan	15	3	33	1	4	1	15	—
Srikkanth	1	—	2	—				
Azharuddin					1	—	2	—
Suresh Kumar					1	—	4	—

FALL OF WICKETS
1- 4, 2- 29, 3- 36, 4- 36, 5- 242, 6- 259, 7- 259, 8- 281, 9- 305
1- 40, 2- 43, 3- 79, 4- 116, 5- 118, 6- 177, 7- 184, 8- 198, 9- 205

FALL OF WICKETS
1- 15, 2- 84, 3- 226, 4- 352, 5- 398, 6- 414, 7- 429, 8- 444, 9- 445
1- 78

Umpires: P.G. Pandit & R.S. Rathore

West Zone won by 9 wickets

Irani Trophy

The Irani Cup, often the curtain raiser to the Indian season, found itself as a postscript to the Duleep Trophy. The match died on the fourth of the five days when Shastri contented himself with allowing his side to sit on their first innings lead rather than press for an outright win. It was a sad and distressing end to the match.

Shastri won the toss and batted first. Their innings revolved entirely around two fine stands. Shastri and Pandit added 162 for the seventh wicket, and Pandit and Kulkarni put on 135 for the ninth. Both Pandit and Shastri hit maiden centuries in the Irani Cup, and Raju Kulkarni made a ferocious career best.

Azharuddin, looking far above the rest of the select side, showed a welcome return to form, but Sivaramakrishnan again had a dreadful match. The match was soiled when Bombay batted a second time. After dismissing Vengsarkar, Kapil Dev took himself off and chose not to bowl again. Shastri responded by not declaring his innings closed and the match died.

The Indian press were quick to condemn the attitudes in this game and their points should be noted. 'It is the attitude of Test players to domestic cricket which will sound its death knell. If a team, a champion at that, is not prepared to bowl out a side, how can those players expect to do so in Test matches against higher opposition?' 'Unless Indian bowlers at all levels get used to the idea of bowling out sides in 30-hour matches, how can India's lacklustre record in Test cricket be improved?'

It is interesting to note that, for the first four days, while the match was alive, the attendance was high. Thereafter the public, like the players, lost interest.

Ranji Trophy

Three new sides were admitted to the Ranji Trophy for the 1985–86 season, a welcome broadening of the competition although none of the new teams appeared strong enough to make an impact on the tournament. Himachal Pradesh brought the North Zone to six teams while the South was also increased to six by the advent of Goa. The East Zone gained necessary impetus with the admission of Tripura.

IRANI CUP – BOMBAY (RANJI TROPHY CHAMPIONS) *v.* REST OF INDIA
24, 25, 26, 27 and 28 October 1985 at Nagpur

BOMBAY

	FIRST INNINGS		SECOND INNINGS	
L.S. Rajput	run out	50	b Sivaramakrishnan	20
G.A.H.M. Parkar	lbw, b Ghai	30	lbw, b Prabhakar	11
S.S. Hattangadi	lbw, b Ghai	6	c sub (Mudkavi), b Siva	85
D.B. Vengsarkar	c Viswanath, b Dev	4	c Viswanath, b Dev	83
S.M. Patil	lbw, b Ghai	7	c Dev, b Azharuddin	78
S.V. Manjrekar	c Viswanath, b Dev	9	lbw, b Sharma	12
R.J. Shastri†	c sub (Mudkavi), b Ghai	112	run out	68
C.S. Pandit*	lbw, b Ghai	123	c Dev, b Shastri	1
B.S. Sandhu	c Viswanath, b Prabhakar	4	c Azharuddin, b Shastri	14
R.R. Kulkarni	lbw, b Ghai	97	not out	9
K.D. Mokashi	not out	0	c sub (Mudkavi), b Siva	0
Extras	lb 11, nb 11	22	b 7, lb 6, nb 6	19
	penalty runs	8		
		472		400

	O	M	R	W	O	M	R	W
Kapil Dev	35	6	70	2	9	3	34	1
Prabhakar	31	6	101	1	6	—	14	1
Ghai	37.5	6	130	6	12	1	54	—
Sivaramakrishnan	16	—	92	—	30.1	—	132	3
Maninder Singh	3	1	13	—				
Ghopal Sharma	18	—	47	—	26	—	83	1
Azharuddin					8	—	35	1
Padam Shastri					10	—	35	2

REST OF INDIA

	FIRST INNINGS		SECOND INNINGS	
Padam Shastri	c Pandit, b Sandhu	15	c Pandit, b Kulkarni	44
M. Prabhakar	lbw, b Kulkarni	0	lbw, b Rajput	74
M. Azharuddin	not out	100	b Mokashi	49
K.P. Bhaskar Pillai	c Pandit, b Kulkarni	0	not out	103
A.O. Malhotra	lbw, b Shastri	52	retired hurt	25
L. Sivaramakrishnan	lbw, b Shastri	5	c Hattangadi, b Mokashi	10
R.N. Kapil Dev†	b Shastri	70	(10) not out	11
S. Viswanath*	c Hattangadi, b Shastri	3	(7) c Parkar, b Mokashi	16
Ghopal Sharma	c Patil, b Sandhu	21	(8) lbw, b Mokashi	0
R.S. Ghai	lbw, b Kulkarni	8	(9) c Rajput, b Patil	0
Maninder Singh	not out	0		
Extras	b 2, lb 10, w 1, nb 1	14	b 2, lb 6, nb 2	10
	penalty runs	24		
	(for 9 wkts dec)	312	(for 7 wkts)	342

	O	M	R	W	O	M	R	W
Sandhu	16.1	7	61	2	20	6	62	—
Kulkarni	28	6	93	3	18	8	57	1
Shastri	30	12	68	4	5	3	2	—
Mokashi	13	—	45	—	36	3	101	4
Manjrekar	2	—	9	—	6	1	15	—
Patil					13	1	43	1
Rajput					15	2	48	1
Hattangadi					1	1	0	—
Parkar					3	1	6	—

FALL OF WICKETS

1- 55, 2- 71, 3- 76, 4- 83, 5- 99, 6- 137, 7- 299, 8- 319, 9- 454
1- 14, 2- 60, 3- 130, 4- 239, 5- 266, 6- 362, 7- 365, 8- 390, 9- 392

1- 4, 2- 23, 3- 24, 4- 92, 5- 106, 6- 230, 7- 236, 8- 270, 9- 287
1- 74, 2- 154, 3- 184, 4- 295, 5- 321, 6- 323, 7- 324

Umpires: B. Ganguly & M.G. Subramaniam

Match drawn

Central Zone

17, 18 and 19 November 1985

at Indore

Uttar Pradesh 453 for 5 dec (Yusuf Ali Khan 139, S. Chaturvedi 122, R. Sapru 60, R.B. Kala 51 not out) and 151 for 3 (S.S. Khandkar 53)
Madhya Pradesh 464 for 9 dec (Sanjeeva Rao 79, M. Sahni 58, M. Hasan 50, Mazhar Ali 4 for 120)

Match drawn
Uttar Pradesh 9 pts, Madhya Pradesh 5 pts

at Jodhpur

Rajasthan 218 (B. Thakre 5 for 44) and 115 (V. Gawate 4 for 30, S. Takle 4 for 39)
Vidarbha 140 (P. Sunderam 10 for 78) and 184 (V. Gawate 50 not out, P. Sunderam 6 for 76)

Rajasthan won by 9 runs
Rajasthan 27 pts, Vidarbha 11 pts

India's major competition could not have wished for a more sensational start to its fifty-second season. On the matting at Jodhpur, Rajasthan, having won the toss, reached 218, thanks to 20 penalty runs and 39 extras. In all, 80 penalty runs were conceded in the match as the over rate fell five short of the required number in each innings. Pradeep Sunderam opened the bowling for Rajasthan and in his second over he had Vidarbha skipper Telang lbw for 0. In his next over he caught and bowled Hingnikar and had Hedaoo caught. Takle and Phadkar were bowled for 0, and Gawate was caught and bowled, also without scoring so that Vidarbha slumped to 8 for 6. Sahasrabuddhe hit lustily, but he was bowled by the bespectacled right-arm fast medium bowler for 45. Debutant Thakre was caught off the last ball of Sunderam's twenty-second over, and the Rajasthan medium pacer, son of Gundibail, the former Test player, had become only the second bowler in the history of the Ranji Trophy to take all ten wickets in an innings. His 22 overs included 5 maidens. Rajasthan made only 77 with the bat in their second innings so that Vidarbha needed 194 to win. They were soon in trouble to Sunderam who had both openers caught for 1. He also ended middle order resistance, but Gawate and Wasu, in a brave last wicket stand, almost brought victory with some powerful hitting. The innings was ended when Wasu was stumped off Vyas's tenth ball of the match.

Pradeep Sunderam who established a Ranji Trophy record by taking all ten wickets for Rajasthan against Vidarbha and returning match figures of 16 for 154.

Sunderam's 6 for 76 gave him match figures of 16 for 154, the best return in the history of the Ranji Trophy.

The bat dominated at Indore where Chaturvedi and Yusuf Ali Khan shared a second wicket stand of 216 for Uttar Pradesh, and Sapru then joined Yasuf Ali Khan in a stand of 126. Madhya Pradesh batted consistently in reply and inevitably the match was drawn.

23, 24 and 25 November 1985

at Jaipur
Railways 203 (R. Jadhav 59) and 115 (S. Vyas 6 for 43, S. Mudkavi 4 for 42)
Rajasthan 298 for 9 dec (Padam Shastri 59, A. Mudkavi 50 not out) and 21 for 0

Rajasthan won by 10 wickets
Rajasthan 26 pts, Railways 5 pts

at Nagpur
Vidarbha 302 for 8 dec (S. Takle 66, V. Gawate 61, P. Hingnikar 51, N. Hirwani 4 for 90) and 292 (S. Phadkar 127, P.P. Pandit 53, D. Nilosey 4 for 93)
Madhya Pradesh 214 (S. Lahore 53, S. Takle 4 for 45, V. Gawate 4 for 80) and 330 for 8 (M. Sahni 123, Sanjeeva Rao 72, U. Gani 5 for 115)

Match drawn
Vidarbha 13 pts, Madhya Pradesh 10 pts

Rajasthan's second victory in their first two matches virtually determined that they would reach the final stages of the competition. Railways won the toss and batted first, but collapsed from 138 for 4 to 203 all out, and consistent batting saw Rajasthan to a worthwhile lead. It was not the pace of Sunderam, but the spin of skipper Vyas which proved to be Rajasthan's match winner this time. He was ably supported by S. Mudkavi, and Rajasthan moved to a comfortable victory.

Hingnikar and Telang began Vidarbha's innings with a stand of 103 after they had been put in to bat at Nagpur. Five wickets then fell for 23 runs, but Gawate and Takle rallied the side and a declaration was possible. The same pair starred as bowlers when Vidarbha took a first innings lead of 88. Phadkar and P.P. Pandit, who was making his debut, put on 127 for Vidarbha's fifth wicket when they batted again, and Madhya Pradesh were left to make 381 to win. They lost Ansari for 1, but Sanjeeva Rao and Sahni raised hopes with a stand of 155. Debutant Gani gnawed away at the middle order with his spin, but Nilosey and Satokar staved off defeat.

14, 15 and 16 December 1985

at Gwalior
Madhya Pradesh 158 (C.P. Singh 54, H. Joshi 4 for 38) and 241 (M. Hasan 68, I. Rajkumar 4 for 62, H. Joshi 4 for 83)
Railways 283 (P. Karkera 59, N. Hirwani 7 for 64) and 66 for 4

Match drawn
Railways 8 pts, Madhya Pradesh 6 pts

at Meerut
Vidarbha 135 (R.P. Singh 4 for 33) and 49 for 2 dec
Uttar Pradesh 38 for 0 dec and 30 for 0

Match drawn
Uttar Pradesh 5 pts, Vidarbha 0 pts

Some rather laborious batting by Madhya Pradesh and Railways doomed the game at Gwalior to a draw. Railways eventually needed to make 117 in 11 overs to win, a task beyond them.

There was no play possible on the first day at Meerut as the pitch was waterlogged. Hans asked Vidarbha to bat and he was among the bowlers to reap a reward, but in spite of some brave declarations, Uttar Pradesh had no chance to snatch the victory that they needed.

20, 21 and 22 December 1985

at Agra
Railways 202 (P. Karkera 55, Ghopal Sharma 6 for 64) and 194 (R.S. Hans 6 for 66, Ghopal Sharma 4 for 69)
Uttar Pradesh 192 (H. Joshi 5 for 54) and 205 for 1 (S.S. Khandkar 121 not out, S. Chaturvedi 63)

Uttar Pradesh won by 9 wickets
Uttar Pradesh 26 pts, Railways 6 pts

at Bhinmal
Rajasthan 100 (N. Hirwani 5 for 33, S. Jain 4 for 17) and 168 (N. Hirwani 6 for 98)
Madhya Pradesh 202 (C.P. Singh 68) and 67 for 6

Madhya Pradesh won by 4 wickets
Madhya Pradesh 24 pts, Rajasthan 7 pts

Uttar Pradesh reasserted their authority of the zone with a splendid victory at Agra. Put in to bat, Railways batted inconsistently, the substance of their innings coming in a seventh wicket stand of 75 between Ved Raj and Joshi. Ghopal Sharma, omitted from the national squad, bowled well in conjunction with Hans. It was a stand of 78 between Kala and Mahur that lifted Uttar Pradesh who had slipped to 105 for 6, but they still trailed on the first innings. The combined spin of Ghopal Sharma and Hans troubled Railways a second time, but on a wicket which still assisted the bowlers, Uttar Pradesh faced a difficult task in their second innings. Khandkar and Chaturvedi resorted to belligerence, and a blistering opening partnership of 161 at nearly five an over set up a magnificent victory.

Rajasthan's run of success was brought to an abrupt end by Madhya Pradesh. Hirwani and Jain monopolised the bowling and took 18 wickets between them. C.P. Singh and Sanjeeva Rao gave Madhya Pradesh a good start with a partnership of 74, but, on a difficult wicket, they had a struggle for victory against Vyas and S. Mudkavi.

27, 28 and 29 December 1985

at Yavatmal

Railways 154 (B. Thakre 4 for 41) and 422 for 9 dec (A. Burrows 193, H. Wasu 4 for 92)
Vidarbha 460 (P. Hingnikar 100, S. Hedaoo 95, R. Pankule 76)

Match drawn
Vidarbha 8 pts, Railways 7 pts

at Allahbad

Uttar Pradesh 219 for 8 dec (S. Anand 58, P. Sunderam 6 for 94) and 258 for 2 dec (S.S. Khandkar 131 not out, Yusuf Ali Khan 61)
Rajasthan 169 (K.K. Sharma 7 for 63) and 161 (R.P. Singh 6 for 75, K.K. Sharma 4 for 50)

Uttar Pradesh won by 147 runs
Uttar Pradesh 30 pts, Rajasthan 7 pts

With neither Railways nor Vidarbha able to win a place in the knock-out round of the competition, interest centred on individual performances. Put in to bat on the matting at Yavatmal, Railways were shot out in their first innings and amassed 422 for 9 in their second thanks to a mighty innings from opener Burrows who shared a third wicket stand of 108 with Fernandes who was making his debut in the tournament. Vidarbha lost Agasti at 9, but Hingnikar and Pankule added 134 and they passed 300 before the fourth wicket fell.

Uttar Pradesh began their last game, against Rajasthan, the leaders of the zone, 5 points behind Madhya Pradesh. They were put in to bat and could manage only two batting points in their first innings as Sunderam produced another fine performance. The Uttar Pradesh opening bowlers, R.P. Singh and K.K. Sharma bowled 16 overs each before a change was made, and by that time, 9 wickets were down and Uttar Pradesh had qualified for the play offs. Khandkar and Chaturvedi began the second innings with a stand of 85, and Yusuf Ali Khan then joined Khandkar to add 158. Uttar Pradesh scored their runs at five an over, they had reached 180 for 1 after 40 overs, and so gave their bowlers every opportunity to win the match, which the medium pacers did with another impressive performance.

Central Zone

	P	W	L	D	Pts
Uttar Pradesh	4	2	—	2	70
Rajasthan	4	2	2	—	67
Madhya Pradesh	4	1	—	3	45
Vidarbha	4	—	1	3	32
Railways	4	—	2	2	

West Zone

23, 24 and 25 November 1985

at Pune

Baroda 293 (A.D. Gaekwad 69, G. Tilakraj 66, R. Parikh 62) and 179 for 9 dec (Azim Khan 5 for 17)
Maharashtra 325 (M.D. Gunjal 89, R. Poonawala 61, D.V. Pardeshi 4 for 82) and 35 for 0

Match drawn
Maharashtra 10 pts, Baroda 7 pts

at Surat

Gujarat 290 (S. Amarnath 89, P. Desai 70) and 82 (S.M. Patil 6 for 20)
Bombay 301 for 4 dec (S.S. Hattangadi 141 not out, S.M. Patil 59, L.S. Rajput 54) and 72 for 1

Bombay won by 9 wickets
Bombay 28 pts, Gujarat 4 pts

Maharashtra asked Baroda to bat first in Pune, but Gaekwad and Parikh thwarted them with an opening stand of 116. Conditions always favoured the batsmen. Maharashtra were consistent and a fine spell of 5 for 17 in 11 overs from Azim Khan gave them some hope, but there was insufficient time remaining when Gaekwad declared.

Bombay, depleted by Test calls, asked Gujarat to bat first on the matting at Surat, but they were held up by Desai and Amarnath who shared a fourth wicket partnership of 126. The Bombay batsmen were in fine form and scored at a brisk rate. Rajput and Hattangadi began with a stand of 122, and skipper Sandeep Patil was in his belligerent mood. He declared as soon as his side passed 300 and then produced a career best performance with his medium pace as Gujarat were shot out for 82. Patil's figures were 11.5 overs, 6 maidens, 6 for 20. Bombay raced to victory in under 16 overs.

21, 22 and 23 December 1985

at Baroda

Gujarat 305 (S. Talati 82, A. Saheba 51, S. Amarnath 50) and 214 for 9 dec (S. Talati 81, T. Arothe 6 for 57)
Baroda 234 (A.D. Gaekwad 71, H. Patel 4 for 71, N. Patel 4 for 75) and 142 for 4 (G. Tilakraj 59 not out)

Match drawn
Gujarat 13 pts, Baroda 8 pts

at Bombay

Saurashtra 308 for 4 dec (A. Pandya 110 not out, B. Jadeja 76, S. Keshwala 56, K. Chauhan 52) and 316 for 4 dec (K. Chauhan 143, S. Keshwala 80 not out)
Bombay 322 for 3 dec (J. Sanghani 80, S.S. Hattangadi 76, C.S. Pandit 65 not out, S.M. Patil 60 not out) and 102 for 5

Match drawn
Saurashtra 10 pts, Bombay 7 pts

Batsmen dominated both matches, and a result never looked likely in either. There were centuries for Pandya and Chauhan in Bombay, and Pandya shared stands of 107 and 103 with Jadeja and Keshwala for the third and fourth wickets. Keshwala shared a fourth wicket stand of 132 with Chauhan in the second innings. Consistently aggressive batting by Bombay brought excitement and Patil played another blistering knock.

28, 29 and 30 December 1985

at Baroda

Bombay 340 for 5 dec (S.M. Patil 111, J. Sanghani 67, L.S. Rajput 52) and 182 for 2 dec (A. Sippy 112 not out)
Baroda 321 (M. Narula 73, G. Tilakraj 53) and 106 for 5

Match drawn
Bombay 12 pts, Baroda 5 pts

at Pune

Saurashtra 213 and 233 (R. Badiyani 60, N. Oza 56, Azim Khan 4 for 34)
Maharashtra 403 for 4 dec (R. Poonawala 111, V. Khedkar 110, S. Kalyani 95, M.D. Gunjal 64) and 44 for 3

OPPOSITE: *Sandeep Patil. With both bat and ball, he had an outstanding season for Bombay and led them with intelligence and flair for the early part of the year. (Alan Cozzi)*

Maharashtra won by 7 wickets
Maharashtra 25 pts, Saurashtra 5 pts

With draws predominant in the West Zone, Maharashtra's fine win over Saurashtra, qualifiers in 1984–85, was a significant result and gave them every chance of reaching the final stages of the competition. They gave first-class debuts to two players, Khedkar and Kher, and both made their mark. Kher took a wicket with the first ball he bowled in the Ranji Trophy, his victim being Badiyani, but Saurashtra recovered somewhat after that shock and reached 213 with consistent application. Poonawala and Khedkar began Maharashtra's reply with a stand of 166, which was dominated by Poonawala, and Khedkar then shared a partnership of 135 with Kalyani. The opening batsman reached 110 on his debut before being lbw to Doshi. In their second innings, Saurashtra collapsed from 200 for 3 to 233 all out, and Maharashtra ran to victory in 9 overs.

In Baroda, the bat again ruled. Patil and Sippy hit sparkling hundreds, and Baroda ground their way to safety.

4, 5 and 6 January 1986

at Bombay

Maharashtra 289 (M.D. Gunjal 125, Azim Khan 64, P. Kasliwal 5 for 91) and 381 for 7 dec (S. Jadhav 93, S. Kalyani 54)
Bombay 300 for 4 dec (C.S. Pandit 130 not out, S.M. Patil 66, S.V. Manjrekar 51 not out) and 55 for 0

Match drawn
Bombay 9 pts, Maharashtra 8 pts

at Rajkot

Saurashtra 288 (B. Jadeja 65) and 232 for 5 dec (R. Badiyani 108 not out, S. Keshwala 50)
Gujarat 274 (A. Saheba 52, B. Mistry 52, B. Radia 5 for 61) and 137 for 3

Match drawn
Saurashtra 12 pts, Gujarat 10 pts

The clash between the zone's leading contenders, Maharashtra and Bombay, ended, predictably, in a draw. On the opening day, Maharashtra were in deep trouble at 44 for 5, but Milind Gunjal hit the fifth century of his career and put on 146 with Azim Khan to lift the visitors to an impressive score. Bombay's innings followed a similar pattern. They were 57 for 3 when Pandit joined Patil in a stand of 102. Pandit reached the fourth hundred of his career, and he and Manjrekar shared an unfinished partnership of 141. There was no collapse by Maharashtra in their second innings, and they batted consistently to ensure a draw.

The match at Rajkot was evenly balanced and also ended in a draw with neither side displaying the necessary bite to win the match.

18, 19 and 20 January 1986

at Bulsar

Gujarat 225 (A. Saheba 86, P. Desai 60 not out, Azim Khan 5 for 54) and 194 (B.K. Patel 53, Azim Khan 4 for 48)
Maharashtra 357 for 6 dec (V. Khedkar 127, S. Kalyani 86, M.D. Gunjal 54) and 66 for 1

Maharashtra won by 9 wickets
Maharashtra 26 pts, Gujarat 5 pts

at Gandhidham
Saurashtra 308 for 5 dec (A. Pandya 138, S. Keshwala 51, D.V. Pardeshi 4 for 66) and 204 for 1 (B. Pujara 103 not out, B. Jadeja 78 not out)
Baroda 483 for 6 dec (R. Parikh 123, A.D. Gaekwad 108, M. Narula 100 not out, S.S. Hazare 65)

Match drawn
Saurashtra 7 pts, Baroda 5 pts

With Bombay having finished their programme on 56 points and confident of a place in the last stages of the Trophy, interest centred on who would win the other qualifying place, and Maharashtra won in fine style at Bulsar to clinch the West Zone title. They always had the better of Gujarat and having dismissed their opponents for 225, they took the lead with only one wicket down as Khedkar, with his second century in three matches, and Kalyani put on 175 at 4 runs an over. Gujarat offered stubborn resistance in their second innings, but Azim Khan, Gudge and Jadhav gnawed away at them, and Maharashtra raced to a jubilant victory.

Saurashtra and Baroda produced a rather tedious draw on the matting at Gandhidham. Pandya and Keshwala were enterprising enough in adding 142 for the fourth wicket, and Pujara and Jadeja put on 185 for the Saurashtra second wicket in the second innings at 4 an over, but by then some dull batting by Baroda whose centuries failed to increase the tempo had killed the game.

West Zone					
	P	*W*	*L*	*D*	*Pts*
Maharashtra	4	2	—	2	69
Bombay	4	1	—	3	56
Saurashtra	4	—	1	3	34
Gujarat	4	—	2	2	32
Baroda	4	—	—	4	25

South Zone

30 November, 1 and 2 December 1985

at Vasco
Goa 188 (A. Varma 4 for 60) and 153 (N. Raote 72, S. Santosh 5 for 43)
Kerala 196 and 148 for 4 (K. Jayaraman 54 not out)

Kerala won by 6 wickets
Kerala 26 pts, Goa 9 pts

Kerala, bottom of the South Zone in 1984–85, welcomed new-comers Goa with a consistent display which brought them a comfortable victory.

7, 8 and 9 December 1985

at Bhadravati
Goa 322 (N. Phadte 156, A.R.B. Bhat 4 for 90) and 136 (M. Desai 57, H. Surendra 4 for 19, A.R.B. Bhat 4 for 46)
Karnataka 335 for 6 dec (M.R. Srinivasa Prasad 106, R. Khanwilkar 88, G.R. Viswanath 69, S. Pednekar 4 for 69) and 124 for 4 (M.R. Srinivasa Prasad 51)

Karnataka won by 6 wickets
Karnataka 25 pts, Goa 7 pts

Goa surprised Karnataka with a confident performance on the matting at Bhadravati. Led by a sound innings from Phadte, who hit their maiden century in the Ranji Trophy, they reached a good total. Karnataka replied in exciting fashion. They lost Sadanand Viswanath for 0, but Srinivasa Prasad and Khanwilkar put on 181, and the final total of 335 for 6 was made in only 58.3 overs. Goa could not find their first innings form when they batted again, and Bhat and Surendra put Karnataka in a position from which victory became a formality.

14, 15 and 16 December 1985

at Madras
Tamil Nadu 260 for 7 dec (M. Gautam 56, V. Sivaramakrishnan 50, T.S. Mahadevan 4 for 102)
Kerala 80 (S. Vasudevan 6 for 27) and 82 (M. Gautam 4 for 16, S. Vasudevan 4 for 36)

Tamil Nadu won by an innings and 98 runs
Tamil Nadu 31 pts, Kerala 3 pts

Tamil Nadu asserted their authority in the South with an emphatic victory over Kerala in a match in which bowlers generally had the upper hand. Tamil Nadu lost both openers for 24, but batted sensibly to reach 260. The spin of Vasudevan perplexed Kerala into submission and they lost their last 9 wickets for 31 runs. Following on, they fared no better against the combined wiles of Gautam and Vasudevan.

21, 22 and 23 December 1985

at Bellary
Kerala 316 (S. Santosh 79, K. Jayaram 59, S. Ramesh 59, Jeshwant 4 for 56) and 330 (Thomas Mathew 111, S. Rajesh 65, S. Ramesh 64, P.K. Rathod 4 for 84)
Karnataka 251 (R.D. Khanwilkar 64, G.R. Viswanath 50, A. Verma 5 for 82) and 177 for 3 (S. Viswanath 59, M.R. Srinivasa Prasad 51)

Match drawn
Karnataka 10 pts, Kerala 9 pts

at Vizianagram
Andhra 593 for 9 dec (M.F. Rehman 141, Jugal Kishore 110, B. Ramamurthy 100 not out, K.V.S.D. Kamaraju 83, D. Meher Baba 61, S. Vasudevan 4 for 137) and 176 for 7 (D. Meher Baba 61, M. Gautam 4 for 47)
Tamil Nadu 321 for 4 dec (P.C. Prakash 125 not out, V. Sivaramakrishnan 86, A. Jabbar 51 not out)

Match drawn
Andhra 9 pts, Tamil Nadu 9 pts

The decline in the powers of Karnataka was revealed when Kerala had the better of the drawn match at Bellary, their batsmen giving a consistently good account of themselves.

Runs flowed profusely at Vizianagram where Andhra, put in to bat, reached the highest score that they have ever recorded in the Ranji Trophy. They were 126 for 4 when Kamaraju joined Rehman, who was making his debut in the competition, in a stand of 129, but this was bettered by Ramamurthy and Jugal Kishore who established an association record for the eighth wicket with a stand of 202. Tamil Nadu batted in usual competent fashion in reply, and the game ebbed to a draw, Ramamurthy having delayed his declaration until well into the second day as Andhra built their massive score.

28, 29 and 30 December 1985

at Dharwad

Tamil Nadu 218 (P.C. Prakash 107 not out, J. Abhiram 4 for 42) and 292 (Robin Singh 62, H. Surendra 5 for 111)
Karnataka 279 (M.R. Srinivasa Prasad 64, S. Vasudevan 6 for 57) and 24 for 2

Match drawn
Karnataka 10 pts, Tamil Nadu 8 pts

at Sirpur Kagaznagar

Andhra 283 (L.K. Adisheshu 88, Jugal Kishore 59, M.V. Narasimha Rao 6 for 112) and 461 for 9 dec (M.F. Rehman 81, D. Meher Baba 71, Chamundeswaranath 63, K.B. Ramamurthy 51 retired, Hari Mohan 4 for 106)
Hyderabad 300 for 5 dec (Abdul Azeem 93, M.V. Narasimha Rao 78 not out, V. Mohan Raj 71) and 64 for 3

Match drawn
Andhra 8 pts, Hyderabad 8 pts

The South Zone remained the most open of tournaments as Hyderabad played their first match and drew on the matting at Sirpur Kagaznagar where Andhra's batsmen once again enjoyed themselves. Mohammed Rehman gave further account of his prowess when he shared a second wicket stand of 132 with Chamundeswaranath in the second innings. Narasimha Rao was as dependable as ever for Hyderabad and gave a fine all round performance.

Tamil Nadu elected to bat at Dharwad and were reduced to 47 for 6 by Abhiram and Khanwilkar. Prakash played nobly to revive them, and Vasudevan's spin kept them in contention. A dour second innings in which Surendra sent down 44.2 overs determined the match would be drawn and took Tamil Nadu to the head of the table, 3 points clear of Karnataka, but as the year ended, all sides had a chance of qualifying for the final stages of the Trophy.

4, 5 and 6 January 1986

at Cuddapah

Goa 150 (S. Mahadevan 79, Jugal Kishore 4 for 43) and 121 (Jugal Kishore 5 for 49)
Andhra 350 (D. Meher Baba 134 not out, L.K. Adisheshu 63, S. Mahadevan 4 for 82)

Andhra won by an innings & 79 runs
Andhra 32 pts, Goa 5 pts

at Tellicherry

Kerala 178 (M.V. Narasimha Rao 5 for 44) and 115 (R. Yadav 7 for 58)
Hyderabad 384 (V. Mohan Raj 80, Ehtheshamuddin 58, Abdul Azeem 56, T.S. Mahadevan 8 for 108)

Hyderabad won by an innings and 91 runs
Hyderabad 32 pts, Kerala 6 pts

Goa suffered their third defeat in as many matches as Andhra took maximum points at Cuddapah. There was compensation for the losers in the fine all round performance of S. Mahadevan, but they were no match for the bowling of Jugal Kishore and an excellent century by Meher Baba.

Kerala were also crushed as Hyderabad took maximum points on the matting at Tellicherry. Narasimha Rao again spun the ball to great purpose, and, in the second innings, Rajesh Yadav's medium pace caused havoc among the Kerala batsmen. Hyderabad batted solidly throughout their innings. Opener Mohan Raj was forced to retire hurt after scoring 2, but he returned to share a seventh wicket partnership of 109 with Yadav. Kerala produced their own hero in defeat. T.S. Mahadevan's 8 for 108 was a career best performance and the second best in the history of the association.

Goa dropped out of contention after this defeat, but only 9 points separated Andhra at the top of the table from Hyderabad in fifth place, and Hyderabad had a game in hand.

11, 12 and 13 January 1986

at Madras

Tamil Nadu 226 for 7 (V. Sivaramakrishnan 84, R. Madhavan 79)
v. Hyderabad

Match abandoned
Hyderabad 3 pts, Tamil Nadu 2 pts

at Visakhapatnam

Andhra 334 (G.A. Pratap Kumar 79 not out, K.V.S.D. Kamaraju 55, K.B. Ramamurthy 54, Jeswant 4 for 64) and 162 for 6 dec (K.B. Ramamurthy 50 not out, Jeswant 4 for 60)
Karnataka 214 and 61 for 2

Match drawn
Andhra 8 pts, Karnataka 7 pts

No play after tea on the first day ruined the vital match at Madras and severely affected the chances of both sides in qualifying for the final stages.

Andhra again showed their remarkable batting strength in depth when Pratap Kumar and Krishna Mohan put on 105 for the ninth wicket. Karnataka batted doggedly and a draw always seemed probable on a wicket where stroke play was never easy.

17, 18 and 19 January 1986

at Hyderabad

Karnataka 449 for 8 dec (G.R. Viswanath 160 not out, C. Saldanha 91, Jeswant 60, R.D. Khanwilkar 55) and 224 for 9 (R.D. Khanwilkar 70, B.P. Patel 54 not out, Kanwlajit Singh 5 for 39)
Hyderabad 309 for 7 dec (V. Jaisimha 80 not out, Arun Paul 71, Ehteshamuddin 59, V. Mohan Raj 54)

Match drawn
Karnataka 9 pts, Hyderabad 8 pts

18, 19 and 20 January 1986

at Madras

Tamil Nadu 328 (V. Sivaramakrishnan 110, S. Mahadevan 5 for 98)
Goa 108 (R. Misra 4 for 11, S. Vasudevan 4 for 35) and 110 (R. Venkatesh 5 for 16)

Tamil Nadu won by an innings and 110 runs
Tamil Nadu 32 pts, Goa 4 pts

at Tellicherry

Andhra 250 (K.V.S.D. Kamaraju 68) and 263 for 8 dec (K.V.S.D. Kamaraju 108, M.S. Kumar 57 not out)
Kerala 215 (K. Jayaram 73, Jugal Kishore Ghia 7 for 74) and 161 (M.F. Rehman 4 for 11)

Andhra won by 137 runs
Andhra 29 pts, Kerala 8 pts

The South Zone championship continued to be the closest of contests to the very end. Tamil Nadu completed their programme with a maximum point win over Goa which left them with 82 points. Goa were handicapped by an injury to Pednekar who did not bat in the second innings, but they could never cope adequately with the Tamil Nadu bowling after Sivaramakrishnan had helped the home side to a useful total.

Karnataka also completed their programme, but failed to qualify for the final stages of the competition after their draw at Hyderabad. Gundappa Viswanath hit his fifteenth Ranji Trophy century, the forty-fourth of his career, and led his side to a large score, but the home side replied with some bright batting which ensured that the match would be drawn. The draw left Hyderabad needing the maximum 32 points from their last game to overtake Tamil Nadu and clinch second spot in the table. First place went to Andhra who completed a workmanlike win on the matting at Tellicherry.

Put in to bat, they struggled fitfully and were only roused by an eighth wicket stand of 91 between Kamaraju and Pratap Kumar. Kerala started badly against Jugal Kishore Ghia, but Jayaram produced some worthy resistance from the middle order which kept them in the match.

Once again it was Kamaraju who asserted Andhra's authority, this time sharing a partnership of 147 for the 4th wicket with Kumar. Kerala never looked like nearing their target of 299 and were beaten with time to spare.

25, 26 and 27 January 1986

at Margao

Goa 194 (Hari Mohan 4 for 56) and 220 (S. Kangralkar 69, C. Ashok 50 not out, R. Yadav 4 for 68)
Hyderabad 501 for 5 dec (Abdul Azeem 136, V. Mohan Raj 113, A. Paul 72, K.A. Qayyum 65 not out, V. Jaisimha 63)

Hyderabad won by an innings and 87 runs
Hyderabad 30 pts, Goa 3 pts

Hyderabad failed by two points to qualify for the knock-out section of the Ranji Trophy. Having bowled out Goa, who elected to bat on winning the toss, they amassed 501, but failed to take more than 5 wickets in 40 overs in the second innings and so gathered only 2 second innings bowling points. Abdul Azeem and Mohan Raj put on 249 for Hyderabad's first wicket, and skipper Jaisimha and Qayyum added 112 brisk runs for the 5th wicket, but it was the stubborn batting of Goa's captain, Kangralkar, which thwarted Hyderabad at the last.

South Zone Final Table					
	P	*W*	*L*	*D*	*Pts*
Andhra	5	2	—	3	86
Tamil Nadu	5	2	—	3	82
Hyderabad	5	2	—	3	81
Karnataka	5	1	—	4	61
Kerala	5	1	3	1	52
Goa	5	—	5	—	28

North Zone

15, 16 and 17 September 1985

at Srinagar

Jammu and Kashmir 83 (M. Prabhakar 4 for 42) and 212 (Zahoor Bhatt 77)
Delhi 406 for 5 dec (S.C. Khanna 155, Bhaskar Pillai 101 not out)

Delhi won by an innings and 111 runs
Delhi 30 pts, Jammu and Kashmir 4 pts

The North Zone competition began with a predictable result. Valson and Prabhakar routed Jammu and Kashmir after Madan Lal had put them in. Khanna was in belligerent mood for Delhi and completely dominated a third wicket stand of 150 with Kirti Azad, who scored 39. Bhaskar Pillai and A. Sharma then added 101 for the 5th wicket and Madan Lal declared with Pillai had reached his century. Jammu and

LEFT: *Surinder Khanna, 155 for Delhi against Jammu and Kashmir, 16 September, 1985. (Adrian Murrell)*

Kashmir lost 5 for 52, but Chowdhary and Zahoor Bhatt gave some respectability before the spin of Shukla and Kirti Azad brought the innings to its close.

20, 21 and 22 September 1985

at Srinagar

Jammu and Kashmir 279 (Akhtar Aijaz 121, Harjinder Singh 6 for 72) and 91 (Umesh Kumar 4 for 5)
Punjab 306 for 6 dec (D. Chopra 81 not out, N.S. Sidhu 65, M.I. Singh 54, Kulwant Singh 51) and 66 for 2

Punjab won by 8 wickets
Punjab 27 pts, Jammu and Kashmir 6 pts

Akhtar Aijaz hit the first century for Jammu for two seasons in spite of some good bowling by medium pacer Harjinder Singh, and with Punjab at 170 for 5, it even looked as if Jammu might take a first innings lead. Chopra and M.I. Singh added 102, however, and the home side collapsed in their second innings to the combined spin of Chopra and Umesh Kumar. Harjinder Singh had match figures of 9 for 105.

30 September, 1 and 2 October 1985

at Srinagar

Himachal Pradesh 112 (Idris Gundroo 4 for 31) and 197 (N. Khanday 5 for 64)
Jammu and Kashmir 375 for 9 dec (Akhtar Aijaz 100, Ravi Pandit 87, Khalid Drabu 62, S. Chowdhary 54)

Jammu and Kashmir won by an innings and 66 runs
Jammu and Kashmir 30 pts, Himachal Pradesh 3 pts

A second century in as many matches by Akhtar Aijaz, the Jammu and Kashmir skipper, who shared an opening partnership of 153 with Ravi Pandit was the foundation of the home side's victory. Himachal Pradesh batted uncertainly against the medium pace bowlers in both innings and their big defeat raised questions as to whether they should have been granted first-class status, for Jammu and Kashmir, so long the Cinderellas of Indian cricket, found themselves in the unexpected splendour of top place in the table, having played three matches before Haryana and Services had begun their programmes. Chowdhary and Drabu put on 109 for Jammu and Kashmir's fifth wicket.

4, 5 and 6 October 1985

at Srinagar

Haryana 243 (R. Dogra 57, D. Pandit 4 for 44) and 198 for 6 (R. Chadha 71 not out)
Jammu and Kashmir 138 (Chetan Sharma 4 for 46, S. Talwar 4 for 56)

Match drawn
Haryana 10 pts, Jammu and Kashmir 7 pts

Bad weather marred Jammu's fourth match, but Haryana, 39 for 4 in their first innings, were surprised by the improvement in the opposition and failed to dominate as expected.

8, 9 and 10 October 1985

at Srinagar

Services 264 (A. Jha 74, Bhaskar Ghosh 72, Ravi Pandit 4 for 34)
Jammu and Kashmir 45 for 3

Match drawn
Jammu and Kashmir 4 pts, Services 4 pts

Jammu and Kashmir's last match was ruined by rain. Jha and Gohil raised Services from 174 for 7 to 249, and Jha took all three Jammu wickets that fell. With one victory and two draws in their five matches, Jammu and Kashmir finished with 51 points, their best season for many years.

2, 3 and 4 November 1985

at Chandigarh

Haryana 307 (S. Talwar 79, R.K. Verma 4 for 92)
Services 104 (S. Talwar 7 for 44) and 142 (S. Talwar 4 for 60)

Haryana won by an innings and 61 runs
Haryana 28 pts, Services 4 pts

at Jallandar

Punjab 356 (N.S. Sidhu 85, Balkar Singh 82, Amarjeet Kaypee 53) and 16 for 0
Delhi 322 for 4 dec (M. Prabhakar 104, R. Lamba 80, Kirti Azad 75 not out)

Match drawn
Delhi 4 pts, Punjab 3 pts

Haryana asserted their authority in the North Zone with a convincing win over Services. Jha and Verma bowled well, and Haryana slumped to 179 for 8, but Sarkar Talwar and Arya put on 108 and transformed the match. Talwar's part in the game was by no means over. He destroyed Services in the first innings, and, combining with the spin of Sharanjit, he routed them for a second time to return match figures of 11 for 104.

Punjab batted dourly in Jallandar, Navjot Singh and Balkar Singh putting on 148 for the first wicket. Prabhakar and Lamba opened Delhi's innings with a partnership of 171, Prabhakar hitting the second century of his career.

7, 8 and 9 November 1985

at Jallandar

Himachal Pradesh 89 (D. Chopra 5 for 43) and 182 (M.I. Singh 6 for 61, D. Chopra 4 for 53)
Punjab 425 for 5 dec (Yashpal Sharma 129 not out, Amarjeet Kaypee 86, Y. Dutta 59, D. Chopra 51)

Punjab won by an innings and 154 runs
Punjab 32 pts, Himachal Pradesh 3 pts

at Delhi

Haryana 225 (R. Jolly 100, M. Prabhakar 4 for 56) 202
Delhi 400 for 5 dec (R. Lamba 110, Kirti Azad 82, Bhaskar Pillai 81 not out, S.C. Khanna 55) and 31 for 0

Delhi won by 10 wickets
Delhi 26 pts, Haryana 5 pts

Delhi moved majestically into the lead in the North Zone with an emphatic win over rivals Haryana. Coming in at number 8, Jolly hit 100 out of 155 and took Haryana to a better total than had seemed possible. Delhi responded by scoring runs at 4 an over. Lamba and Khanna began with a stand of 95, and Kirti Azad joined Lamba in a third wicket stand of 156. After his lean time in the previous season Lamba showed a welcome return to confidence and aggressive form. Haryana batted consistently in their second innings, but no one stayed long enough to threaten Delhi's superiority.

Punjab maintained their challenge by trouncing Himachal

Manoj Prabhakar batted with supreme confidence for Delhi throughout the season and earned his place in the party to tour England. (Patrick Eagar)

Pradesh. Deepak Chopra played a captain's part with a fine all-round performance. He took 9 for 96 with his slow left-arm spin and hit a brisk fifty in an innings which was dominated by Yashpal Sharma who lashed the bowling in an unfinished sixth wicket partnership of 147 with Kulwant Singh.

12, 13 and 14 November 1985

at Delhi

Himachal Pradesh 265 (V. Sen 76, Inderjit Singh 74) and 195 (V. Sen 62, Inderjit Singh 62, K.K. Gohil 5 for 54)
Services 487 for 9 dec (K. Srikant 157, R. Das 111, K.M. Roshan 69)

Services won by an innings and 27 runs
Services 31 pts, Himachal Pradesh 7 pts

at Faridabad

Punjab 172 (Yashpal Sharma 70, R.N. Kapil Dev 4 for 44, Chetan Sharma 4 for 65) and 165
Haryana 250 (R. Chadha 63) and 88 for 1

Haryana won by 9 wickets
Haryana 25 pts, Punjab 6 pts

Sharing a fourth wicket partnership of 100 and hitting the first fifties scored for Himachal Pradesh in the competition,

skipper Sen and Inderjit Singh gave their side some hope, but these were dashed when Srikant and Das opened Services' innings with a stand of 254. Facing a mammoth task to try to save the game, Himachal Pradesh were once again indebted to Sen and Inderjit Singh for their courage.

Faced by India's Test attack, Haryana crumpled on a doubtful wicket at Faridabad. They were 46 for 5 and were roused only by Yashpal Sharma's fine knock. Batting with consistent application after losing their first 4 wickets for 51, Haryana took a useful lead, and when Punjab succumbed to spin at their second attempt Haryana moved quickly to victory and became firm favourites to join Delhi in the final stages of the competition.

17, 18 and 19 November 1985

at Rothak

Himachal Pradesh 144 (S. Talwar 6 for 40) and 171 (Darshan Singh 50, Sharanjit Singh 6 for 79, S. Talwar 4 for 65)
Haryana 453 for 6 dec (R. Chadha 156, R. Jolly 82)

Haryana won by an innings and 138 runs
Haryana 30 pts, Himachal Pradesh 2 pts

Sarkar Talwar took 10 wickets in a match for the second time in four matches as Haryana crushed Himachal Pradesh. Himachal offered little resistance, and their bowlers were savaged by Chadha and Jolly who put on 193 for the fifth wicket.

25, 26 and 27 November 1985

at Delhi

Himachal Pradesh 164 (Harish Kumar 66, U.S. Madan Lal 4 for 49) and 112 (S. Valson 6 for 40)
Delhi 441 for 5 dec (Kirti Azad 215, Bhaskar Pillai 140)

Delhi won by an innings and 165 runs
Delhi 32 pts, Himachal Pradesh 2 pts

Himachal Pradesh's programme came to an end with yet another innings defeat as this time they felt the full might of Delhi crush them. The outstanding feature of Delhi's batting, after they had been 59 for 3, was Kirti Azad's innings of 215, the highest score of his career. He and Bhaskar Pillai, enjoying a wonderful season, put on 318 for the fourth wicket at 5 runs an over. This constituted a record for Delhi, and it was the fifth highest fourth wicket stand in the history of the Ranji Trophy. When they batted again, 277 runs in arrears, Himachal Pradesh fell to Valson, the medium pacer, who was in the World Cup party of 1983, but did not play in a match.

30 November, 1 and 2 December 1985

at Patiala

Punjab 287 (R. Kalsi 87, Balkar Singh 75, Bhaskar Ghosh 6 for 56) and 192 for 4 dec (Y. Dutta 67, Amarjeet Kaypee 54 not out)
Services 181 and 126 for 3 (R. Das 57 not out)

Match drawn
Services 8 pts, Punjab 7 pts

Kalsi, on his debut in the Ranji Trophy, hit 87 before becoming one of Ghosh's six victims. He and Balkar Singh put on 170 for the second wicket, and Kaypee and Dutta put on 118 for the fourth wicket in Punjab's second innings. Services batted very dourly and a draw became inevitable.

10, 11 and 12 December 1985

at Delhi

Delhi 350 for 4 dec (Gursharan Singh 114 not out, Kirti Azad 114, S.C. Khanna 54) and 87 for 4
Services 107

Match drawn
Delhi 8 pts, Services 3 pts

Rain interrupted the last game of the season in the North Zone, but Kirti Azad hit his second century in succession and shared another big partnership. This time, he and Gursharan Singh put on 201 for the third wicket.

North Zone Final Table					
	P	*W*	*L*	*D*	*Pts*
Delhi	5	3	—	2	100
Haryana	5	3	1	1	98
Punjab	5	2	1	2	75
Jammu and Kashmir	5	1	2	2	51
Services	5	1	1	3	50
Himachal Pradesh	5	—	5	—	17

East Zone

28, 29 and 30 December 1985

at Balasore

Orissa 419 for 4 dec (A. Jayaprakash 142, S. Mitra 103 not out, A. Bharadwaj 71, K. Dubey 51)
Assam 203 and 181 (R. Bora 85, S. Mitra 5 for 16)

Orissa won by an innings and 35 runs
Orissa 30 pts, Assam 6 pts

at Calcutta

Bengal 408 for 6 dec (P. Roy 177, J. Arun Lal 113, A. Deb Burman 4 for 124)
Tripura 101 (G. Shome, jnr 4 for 46) and 86

Bengal won by an innings and 221 runs
Bengal 32 pts, Tripura 1 pt

Orissa began their season in most convincing fashion. Jayaprakash and Bharadwaj added 134 after 3 wickets had fallen for 121, and then Jayaprakash and Mitra, both of whom reached fine hundreds, were unseparated as they put on 164. Mitra was in belligerent mood, and he was to have a decisive influence on the match with his bowling. Assam followed-on 216 in arrears, but, having lost 3 for 30, they were rejuvenated by Das and Bora with a stand of 108. Mitra then joined the attack and in 10.5 overs took 5 for 16.

Tripura's venture into the Ranji Trophy had an unhappy baptism when they were crushed by Bengal for whom Prabnob Roy and skipper Arun Lal shared a 2nd wicket stand of 209. Tripura's batsmen offered limp resistance against a varied attack. Tripura's single point came from taking 4 wickets inside 90 overs.

4, 5 and 6 January 1986

at Talcher

Orissa 365 for 6 dec (S. Das 124, A. Jayaprakash 66, D. Mahanti 64, K. Dubey 54)

Tripura 182 (S. Paul 100, H. Praharaj 4 for 28) and 164 (S. Mitra 5 for 60, B.D. Mohanty 4 for 35)

Orissa won by an innings and 19 runs
Orissa 31 pts, Tripura 3 pts

at Ranchi

Assam 141 (S. Dutta 65, A. Kumat 4 for 31, M.R. Bhalla 4 for 32) and 228 (S. Dutta 68, R. Bora 59, A. Kumar 5 for 47)
Bihar 453 for 5 dec (B.S. Gosai 195, R. Deora 145, H. Gidwani 60, H. Barroah 4 for 114)

Bihar won by an innings and 84 runs
Bihar 29 pts, Assam 3 pts

Orissa gained their second innings victory in as many matches, a win based on consistent and aggressive batting. Dubey and Das started with a partnership of 150, and there were worthwhile contributions from all batsmen. Tripura were 39 for 4, but Paul, who came in at number three, batted most courageously and sensibly to reach a fine hundred. He could not save his side from having to follow on, however, and Mitra and Mohanty bowled Orissa to a comfortable victory.

Assam suffered their second innings defeat. They were overwhelmed by some mighty batting. Deora and Godwani put on 111 after Das had been lbw at 2, and Deora and Gosai added 259 for the 3rd wicket, a record for Bihar. Bihar averaged $4\frac{1}{2}$ runs an over throughout their innings.

9, 10 and 11 January 1986

at Calcutta

Assam 402 for 6 dec (R. Bora 107, S. Dutta 71, Amal Das 73, S. Uzir 54 not out) and 121
Bengal 274 for 8 dec (R. Dani 69 not out, J. Arun Lal 50) and 284 for 6 (J. Arun Lal 91)

Bengal won by 4 wickets
Bengal 28 pts, Assam 9 pts

at Ranchi

Bihar 320 (R. Deora 75, H. Gidwani 62, S. Saba Karim 57, A. Das 6 for 76)
Tripura 92 (V. Venkatram 5 for 17) and 88 (V. Venkatram 4 for 38)

Bihar won by an innings and 140 runs
Bihar 32 pts, Tripura 4 pts

A remarkable game in Calcutta saw Bengal the ultimate winners although they had trailed by 128 on the first innings. Arun Lal asked Assam to bat first when he won the toss and must have regretted his decision as Dutta and Das added 117 for the second wicket, Bora and Barroah 127 for the fifth, and Assam sailed past 400. With their captain setting an example, Bengal scored briskly and Arun Lal declared when still in arrears. His thinking was right in that Assam collapsed against a varied attack. Assam's over-rate was dreadfully slow. They conceded 36 penalty runs in the first innings and they were to concede another 32 in the second innings as Bengal, inspired by a brilliant innings by Arun Lal, scored at more than 8 an over to record a memorable victory.

Bihar notched their second innings victory when a consistently good batting performance was followed by bowling which was far too good for the East Zone newcomers. Venkatram had match figures of 9 for 55 in 30.3 overs.

15, 16 and 17 January 1986

at Rourkela
Bengal 152 for 2 dec (J. Arun Lal 63 not out) and 13 for 0
Orissa 250 for 6 dec (K. Dubey 56)
Match drawn
Orissa 3 pts, Bengal 3 pts

at Nowgong
Tripura 79 (Naba Konwar 4 for 18, H. Barua 4 for 29) and 155 (T. Dey Roy 57, Naba Konwar 4 for 68)
Assam 196 (G. Hazaeika 50, S. Das Gupta 5 for 51) and 39 for 4
Assam won by 6 wickets
Assam 23 pts, Tripura 6 pts

Rain ruined the key match between Bengal and Orissa. To make up for lost time, Bengal, again inspired by Arun Lal, hit 136 in 24 overs and claimed 16 penalty runs. Orissa batted sedately in comparison after Dubey and Das had given them a good start with a stand of 109.

There was no play on the second day at Nowgong, but Assam still found time to win the bottom of the table fixture. Tripura failed limply to the medium pacers, but their bowlers gave them some hope, and they batted with more confidence at the second attempt. Assam's race for victory was against time. They scored the runs that they needed in 7.3 overs, three batsmen being run out in the scurry for runs. It was a sad comment on this first-class fixture that K. Venkatraman was the only umpire available and a local umpire stood at square-leg throughout the match.

23, 24 and 25 January 1986

at Ranchi
Bihar 532 for 5 dec (A. Dayal 174, B.D. Gosai 111 not out, R. Deora 104, H. Gidwani 57 not out) and 155 (P. Nandy 5 for 24)
Bengal 393 for 8 dec (P. Nandy 105, A. Mitra 91, A. Bhattacharjee 71 not out, M. Das 55) and 155 for 7
Match drawn
Bihar 12 pts, Bengal 10 pts

With two matches remaining in the East Zone, the two qualifying places rested between Bihar, Bengal and Orissa. With 61 points to their credit and matches against both rivals, Bihar were clear favourites to gain one of the places. They could not have wished for a better start than was given them by Rajesh Deora and Amikar Dayal in the match against Bengal. Venkatram had chosen to bat when he won the toss, and Deora and Dayal responded with a stand of 257 before Deora was run out. Dayal, making his debut in the Ranji Trophy, went on to reach 174 before falling to Shome. Gosai flayed a tired attack, and Gidwani, having been forced to retire hurt early in his innings, returned to complete his fifty. Bengal replied spiritedly, and Mitra and Nandy put on 173 for the fourth wicket. Bhattacharjee hit well, and Arun Lal was able to declare and keep the game alive. Bihar slumped in their second innings, but Bengal had no time left to attempt more than brisk runs and batting points. Three points were achieved as they reached 155 in 17 overs. They were to prove decisive.

29, 30 and 31 January 1986

at Baripada
Bihar 451 (R. Deora 70, H. Gidwani 68, S.S. Karim 59, S. Roy 56, A. Dayal 54) and 11 for 0
Orissa 245 (D. Mahanty 70, Avinash Kumar 4 for 62) and 213 (Avinash Kumar 7 for 83)
Bihar won by 10 wickets
Bihar 28 pts, Orissa 8 pts

An opening stand of 107 between Deora and Dayal gave Bihar's innings a firm foundation, and the batting was consistent throughout. In reply, Orissa lost 4 for 83, and they never really recovered so that the follow-on became inevitable. It was the spin of Avinash Kumar which unsettled them and he returned the best match figures of his career as Bihar swept to a ten-wicket victory and the East Zone Championship. Orissa gained 8 points from the match and so failed by 2 points to win a place in the play-offs.

East Zone Final Table					
	P	W	L	D	Pts
Bihar	4	3	—	1	101
Bengal	4	2	—	2	73
Orissa	4	2	1	1	72
Assam	4	1	3	—	41
Tripura	4	—	4	—	14

Pre-Quarter Finals

7, 8, 9 and 10 February 1986

at Pune
Maharashtra 585 (B. Joglekar 177, M.D. Gunjal 176, R. Poonawala 84) and 278 for 4 (V. Khedkar 68, S. Jadhav 62 not out, P.R. Pradhan 50, J. Arun Lal 4 for 79)
Bengal 373 (A. Mitra 106, J. Arun Lal 58)
Match drawn
Maharashtra qualified for quarter-finals on first innings lead

at Kanpur
Tamil Nadu 508 (Ravi Mishra 75, P.C. Prakash 70, S. Vasudevan 65, W.V. Raman 58, Ghopal Sharma 4 for 125)
Uttar Pradesh 149 for 1 (S. Chaturvedi 74 not out, Yusuf Ali Khan 56 not out)
Match drawn
Tamil Nadu won on toss of a coin

After Tamil Nadu had reached 508 with an even batting display highlighted by an eighth wicket stand of 110 between Mishra and Vasudevan, Uttar Pradesh lost Khandkar at 5, but Chaturvedi and Yusuf Ali Khan had added 144 when rain brought the match to an end. Sadly, it was the toss of a coin that decided who would advance in the competition.

At Pune, the decision was reached in a more satisfactory manner although one not totally satisfying. Batting first, Maharashtra reached 107 for 3 when Gunjal and Jogelkar came together. They added 284 and took Maharashtra to a position of dominance which they were never likely to relinquish.

Quarter-Finals

14, 15, 16 and 17 February 1986

at Madras

Tamil Nadu 233 (S.M. Patil 4 for 54) and 212 for 5 (P.C. Prakash 79, Robin Singh 73 not out)
Bombay 380 (L.S. Rajput 95, G.A.H.M. Parkar 53, A. Jabbar 4 for 63)

Match drawn
Bombay qualified for semi-finals on first innings lead

at Pune

Delhi 604 (R. Lamba 231, M. Prabhakar 119, S. C. Khanna 93, S.C. Gudge 4 for 214) and 160 for 4 dec (R. Lamba 62)
Maharashtra 352 (M.D. Gunjal 104, V. Khedkar 95, S. Kalyani 71, Kirti Azad 4 for 42) and 64 for 3

Match drawn
Delhi qualified for semi-finals on first innings lead

at Jamshedpur

Haryana 270 (V. Venkatram 5 for 99) and 385 (D. Sharma 93, R. Jolly 50, V. Venkatram 5 for 83)
Bihar 268 (U. Das 53, Chetan Sharma 4 for 83)

Match drawn
Haryana qualified for semi-finals on first innings lead

at Jaipur

Andhra 185 (D. Meher Baba 76) and 227 for 4 (K.V.S.D. Kamaraju 110 not out, D. Meher Baba 60)
Rajasthan 431 (Dalbir Singh 109, Padam Shastri 69, Parminder Singh 58, S. Mudkavi 52, Jugal Kishore Ghia 4 for 123)

Match drawn
Rajasthan qualified for semi-finals on first innings lead

Raman Lamba hit 231 for Delhi against Maharashtra in the quarter-final of the Ranji Trophy. This was the highest score ever made for Delhi in the competition. Lamba's prolific scoring earned him a place in the side to tour England. (Sporting Pictures (UK) Ltd)

Each of the quarter-final matches was decided by the side leading on the first innings going through to the semi-finals. Once again Bombay proved that they were the side for the big occasion. Having been ousted from the leading position in the West Zone by Maharashtra and without four of their leading players, they faced Tamil Nadu, strengthened by the return of Laxman Sivaramakrishnan and Srikkanth, with some trepidation. They were splendidly led by Sandeep Patil who opened the bowling in the absence of Raju Kulkarni and took 4 for 54 in 30 overs. He took the first three wickets to fall, including the important one of Srikkanth, and more than anyone was responsible for restricting Tamil Nadu to 233. Bombay batted solidly in reply. Rajput defended well and played some fine shots off the front foot before being bowled round his legs by Sivaramakrishnan. He and Hattangadi put on 75 for the first wicket, and Parkar made a valuable late contribution as Bombay ground their way into the semi-final.

The match at Pune was most one-sided. Delhi gained a great advantage by winning the toss and batting first on a placid wicket. Raman Lamba and Surinder Khanna began as skipper Madan Lal would have desired. They had put on 191 before Khanna fell to Gudge. Lamba went on to reach 231, the highest score made for Delhi in the Ranji Trophy, bettering a record that had stood for 28 years. He played soundly, without risks, but never lost the opportunity to score. Manoj Prabhakar hit his second century of the season and Delhi reached 604 and were assured of a place in the

semi-finals. Maharashtra batted bravely in their turn, but in spite of Gunjal's particularly fine innings, Delhi were never threatened.

The most absorbing quarter-final tussle was the match at Jamshedpur between Bihar and Haryana. The Bihar bowlers operated splendidly on the first day and restricted Haryana to 243 for 9. They were less successful on the second morning when Chetan Sharma and Sarkar Talwar extended their last wicket stand to 53 so that Haryana closed at 270. Bihar were soon in trouble when Chetan Sharma had Rajesh Deora lbw for 1. Dayal again displayed his rich promise, but he was run out for 47, and Bihar slipped to 142 for 6. It seemed that Haryana would easily take the vital first innings lead, but skipper Venkatram and Uijal Das put on 75 and the game was in the balance. There followed another fine stand for the ninth wicket when Avinash Kumar and Randhir Singh added 46 and took Bihar to within 4 of the Haryana total. Kuldip joined Randhir in tense circumstances, but only 2 were added before Kuldip was run out. The second Haryana innings had little significance as they dug in, unwilling to relinquish the advantage that their bowlers had gained.

The greatest sympathy went to Andhra who had done so well to win the South Zone Ghulam Ahmed Trophy ahead of more fancied associations. They failed to do themselves justice and were bowled out for a paltry 185. The first four Rajasthan batsmen all passed fifty, and centurion Dalbir Singh and Padam Shastri, who had not enjoyed the success of the previous season, put on 141 for the second wicket.

Semi-Finals

15, 16, 17 and 18 March 1986

at Bombay

Haryana 423 (R. Chadha 159 not out, K.D. Mokashi 6 for 140) and 252 (A.O. Malhotra 63, R.J. Shastri 5 for 65)
Bombay 296 (R.J. Shastri 65, A. Sippy 61, C.S. Pandit 57, G.A.H.M. Parkar 51, Sarkar Talwar 6 for 103, R.N. Kapil Dev 4 for 47) and 229 (C.S. Pandit 99 not out)

Haryana won by 150 runs

at Kota

Delhi 192 (Ratan Singh 5 for 72) and 358 (Kirti Azad 118, R. Lamba 110, U.S. Madan Lal 56, Suresh Shastri 7 for 94)
Rajasthan 169 (S. Mudkavi 88, Kirti Azad 4 for 59) and 177 (Suresh Shastri 52, Kirti Azad 4 for 50, Maninder Singh 4 for 57)

Delhi won by 204 runs

Haryana pulled off the surprise of the season with a convincing win over Bombay which put them into the final of the Ranji Trophy. Bombay were without Patil, but they welcomed back Ravi Shastri, who led the side, Vengsarkar and Raju Kulkarni. Shastri won the toss and asked Haryana to bat. Bombay had immediate success when Kulkarni bowled Ashwini Kumar for 3, but thereafter, with Chadha holding the side together in splendid manner, Haryana batted consistently and reached an impressive 423. In reply, Bombay started wretchedly as Kapil Dev dismissed Rajput, Hattangadi and Vengsarkar with only 22 scored. Sippy and Parkar added 105, and there were good contributions from Shastri and Pandit, but Bombay trailed by 127 on the first innings as the magnificent Talwar seduced batsmen to destruction. Shastri and Mokashi gave Bombay hope with some fine bowling, but, in search of 380 to win, they again started disastrously as they lost their first 4 wickets, 3 of them to Kapil Dev, for 59. Pandit played a most heroic innings, but was denied his hundred when Mokashi, who had stayed with him while 34 were scored, was caught, and so the champions passed from the competition.

At Kota, Delhi, after a tense first day, ran out comfortable winners against Rajasthan. Madan Lal chose to bat when he won the toss, but Lamba, Khanna and A. Sharma were dismissed by Suresh Shastri with only 30 scored. Kirti Azad and Mohinder Amarnath put on 78, but nobody stayed long after that and Delhi were out for 192, a score which must have disappointed. Rajasthan's reply was perplexed by Maninder Singh and Kirti Azad, slow left-arm and off-break, and they slumped to 94 for 7. They were rallied by Jain and S. Mudkavi, and the last 3 wickets added 75. Enjoying an unexpected first innings advantage, Delhi grasped the chance

C.S. Pandit, the most exciting batsman of the Indian season. (Mark Leech)

Maninder Singh bowled Delhi to a victory in the Ranji Trophy with a magnificent 8 for 54 in the second innings. (George Herringshaw)

to build a big lead. Lamba and Khanna began with a stand of 107. It was dominated by Raman Lamba who was gloriously aggressive. Another century stand, 120 for the fifth wicket between Kirti Azad and Madan Lal, took Delhi to a position of total command. Like Lamba, Kirti Azad had enjoyed an outstanding season, but unlike Lamba, he was not chosen for the side to tour England and could consider himself a little unfortunate. Mention should again be made of Suresh Shastri who bowled magnificently, taking 7 for 94 in 40.2 overs. It was of no avail as Rajasthan collapsed again before Maninder and Kirti Azad.

Ranji Trophy Final
DELHI v. HARYANA

After being runners-up for the past two seasons, Delhi won the Ranji Trophy for the first time since 1982 and for the fourth time in their history. Their victory was an overwhelming one. Four of their batsmen hit centuries and Maninder Singh, the left-arm spinner, returned match figures of 11 for 120 in an outstanding performance.

Kapil Dev had no hesitation in batting first when he won the toss, and Haryana began well enough, but although several batsmen promised much, none played the big innings

Mohinder Amarnath who hit 194 in the Ranji Trophy Final. It was his best score in the competition. (Adrian Murrell)

RANJI TROPHY FINAL – DELHI v. HARYANA
28, 29, 30 and 31 March, 1 April 1986 at Delhi

HARYANA

	FIRST INNINGS		SECOND INNINGS	
Ashwini Kumar	c Shashikant, b Azad	74	c Shashikant, b Maninder	12
D. Sharma	c Lamba, b Madan Lal	26	b Maninder	36
Aman Kumar	c Prabhakar, b Maninder	32	c Madan Lal, b Prabhakar	7
A.O. Malhotra	c Pillai, b Azad	34	(6) b Maninder	98
R. Chadha	c Sharma, b Maninder	17	st Shashikant, b Maninder	2
R. Jolly	c Shukla, b Maninder	9	lbw, b Maninder	16
R.N. Kapil Dev†	c Prabhakar, b Azad	2	b Maninder	25
Salim Ahmed*	run out	55	(4) lbw, b Maninder	1
Chetan Sharma	c Shashikant, b Prabhakar	18	c Azad, b Maninder	0
Sharanjit Singh	not out	4	absent injured	—
Sarkar Talwar	b Prabhakar	0	(10) not out	0
Extras	lb 5, nb 12	17	b 4, lb 2, nb 6	12
		288		**209**

DELHI

	FIRST INNINGS	
R. Lamba	c Sharanjit, b C. Sharma	25
S.C. Khanna	lbw, b C. Sharma	5
M. Prabhakar	run out	113
Kirti Azad	c Aman Kumar, b Talwar	107
M.B. Amarnath	c D. Sharma, b Talwar	194
K. Bhaskar Pillai	c Salim Ahmed, b Kapil Dev	2
U.S. Madan Lal†	c D. Sharma, b Talwar	14
A. Sharma	c D. Sharma, b Jolly	110
R. Shukla	lbw, b Talwar	15
Maninder Singh	not out	14
Shashikant*	b D. Sharma	7
Extras	b 5, lb 7, w 5, nb 15	32
		638

	O	M	R	W	O	M	R	W
Madan Lal	14	1	55	1	7	1	13	—
Prabhakar	14.5	1	54	2	10	2	25	1
Maninder Singh	41	15	66	3	33.1	17	54	8
Kirti Azad	32	9	90	3	22	2	83	—
Shukla	6	1	15	—	6	—	20	—
A. Sharma	2	1	3	—	1	—	8	—

	O	M	R	W
Chetan Sharma	25	3	101	2
Kapil Dev	38.3	8	148	1
Sarkar Talwar	58	4	194	4
Sharanjit Singh	20.3	6	58	—
D. Sharma	31.2	3	90	1
Jolly	9	1	23	1
Malhotra	4	—	12	—

FALL OF WICKETS
1- 68, 2- 123, 3- 159, 4- 180, 5- 203, 6- 205, 7- 207, 8- 268, 9- 268
1- 28, 2- 40, 3- 46, 4- 52, 5- 106, 6- 140, 7- 204, 8- 204, 9- 209

FALL OF WICKETS
1- 9, 2- 47, 3- 230, 4- 299, 5- 311, 6- 363, 7- 565, 8- 604, 9- 629

Umpires: S. Banerjee & V.K. Ramaswamy

Delhi won by an innings and 141 runs

that was needed to provide the backbone for a match-winning score. In contrast, Delhi began badly, but Prabhakar and Kirti Azad confirmed their wonderful seasons with a stand of 183, both reaching centuries. When Bhaskar Pillai and Madan Lal failed to make notable contributions Haryana had hopes of restricting Delhi's lead, but Mohinder Amarnath was at his purposeful, elegant best, and he found a splendid partner in Sharma. Together they added 202 for the seventh wicket, the second highest stand ever made for Delhi for this wicket. It took the game out of Haryana's reach.

On a wicket that was now offering some encouragement to spin, Maninder Singh revealed his immense development as a bowler in recent months, and the Haryana batsmen floundered. The exception was Malhotra who played heroically to embarrass selectors who had given him scant opportunity in Australia and then omitted him from the side to tour England. His effort was in vain, and Delhi swept to victory and the Trophy.

First-Class Averages

BATTING

	M	Inns	NOs	Runs	HS	Av	100s	50s
C.S. Pandit (Bombay)	7	11	5	570	130*	95.00	2	3
M.B. Amarnath (Delhi)	3	4		374	194	93.50	2	
Kirti Azad (Delhi)	9	11	1	858	215	85.80	4	2
M.D. Gunjal (Maharashtra)	6	8		677	176	84.62	3	3
B.D. Gosai Singh (Bihar)	5	6	1	402	195	80.40	2	
S.M. Gavaskar (West Zone)	2	3		235	119	78.33	1	1
A. Sippy (Bombay)	5	6	3	226	112*	75.33	1	1
A. Dayal (Bihar)	3	5	1	300	174	75.00	1	1
S.S. Khandkar (Uttar P.)	5	9	4	374	131*	74.80	2	1
Yashpal Sharma (Punjab)	5	6	1	366	129*	73.20	1	2
M. Prabhakar (Delhi)	9	10	3	502	119	71.71	3	1
R.J. Shastri (Bombay)	4	6	1	358	112	71.60	1	4
A. Mitra (Bengal)	6	9	4	351	106	70.20	1	1
P.C. Prakash (Tamil Nadu)	7	9	2	484	125*	69.14	2	2
R. Lamba (Delhi)	7	11	1	691	231	69.10	3	2
S. Chaturvedi (Uttar P.)	5	8	2	414	122	69.00	1	2
Bhaskar Pillai (Delhi)	9	13	5	544	140	68.00	3	1
R. Deora (Bihar)	5	7	1	408	145	68.00	2	2
V. Mohan Raj (Hyderabad)	6	5		330	113	66.00	1	3
Abdul Azeem (Hyderabad)	5	5		317	136	63.40	1	2
Ehteshamuddin (Hyderabad)	5	3	1	126	59	63.00		1
J. Arun Lal (Bengal)	6	8	1	427	113	61.00	1	4
G.R. Viswanath (Karn.)	5	9	3	362	160*	60.33	1	2
D.B. Vengsarkar (Bombay)	4	6		358	147	59.66	2	1
S. Keshwala (Saurashtra)	4	7	1	355	80*	59.16		4
H. Gidwani (Bihar)	5	6	1	295	69	59.00		4
Yusuf Ali Khan (Uttar P.)	5	7	2	294	139	58.80	1	2
A. Jayaprakash (Orissa)	4	5	1	228	142*	57.00	1	1
S. Das (Orissa)	4	4		228	124	57.00	1	
D. Meher Baba (Andhra)	6	11	1	557	134*	55.70	1	5
V. Khedkar (Maharashtra)	5	8		444	127	55.50	2	2
K.V.S.D. Kamaraju (Andh.)	6	11	1	552	110*	55.20	2	3
Arun Paul (Hyderabad)	4	3		160	72	53.33		2
V. Sivaramakrishnan (T.N.)	7	9	1	425	110	53.12	1	3
R. Chadha (Haryana)	8	13	2	581	159*	52.81	2	2
K. Srikkanth (Tamil Nadu)	3	4		211	120	52.75	1	
K.B. Ramamurthy (Andhra)	6	10	4	315	100*	52.50	1	3
P. Roy (Bengal)	5	8	1	367	177	52.42	1	
R. Poonawala (Maharashtra)	6	11	2	471	111	52.33	1	2
S.S. Hattangadi (Bombay)	7	13	4	473	141*	52.25	1	2
M. Narula (Baroda)	4	7	2	260	100*	52.00	1	1
R.B. Kala (Uttar Pradesh)	5	4	2	104	51*	52.00		1
S.M. Patil (Bombay)	8	10	1	462	111	51.33	1	5
J. Sanghani (Bombay)	3	4		202	80	50.50		2
A. Burrows (Railways)	3	5		251	193	50.20	1	
A.O. Malhotra (Haryana)	7	12	1	549	116	49.90	1	3
Chetan Sharma (Haryana)	6	10	5	248	72*	49.60		1
M.R. Srinivasa Prasad (K)	4	7		344	106	49.14	1	3
K.A. Qayyum (Hyderabad)	5	5	1	196	65*	49.00		2
A. Pandya (Saurashtra)	4	7	1	294	138	49.00	2	
B. Joglekar (Maharashtra)	7	5	1	195	177	48.75	1	
L.S. Rajput (Bombay)	9	16	2	670	221	47.85	1	4
Dalbir Singh (Rajasthan)	2	3		143	109	47.66	1	
R. Sapru (Uttar Pradesh)	5	6	3	143	60	47.66		1
S. Mitra (Orissa)	4	5	1	190	103*	47.50	1	
Robin Singh (Tamil Nadu)	6	6	2	190	73*	47.50		2
R. Das (Services)	5	7	1	285	111	47.50	1	1
K. Chauhan (Saurashtra)	4	7		330	143	47.14	1	1
R.M.H. Binny (South Z.)	2	3		140	115	46.66	1	
V. Jaisimha (Hyderabad)	4	5	1	181	80*	45.25		2
M. Azharuddin (South Z.)	3	5	1	179	100*	44.75	1	
M. Gautam (Tamil Nadu)	5	4	1	134	56	44.66		1
Amarjeet Kaypee (Punjab)	4	6	1	219	86	43.80		3
R.D. Khanwilkar (Karnat.)	7	12	1	477	98	43.36		5
B. Jadeja (Saurashtra)	4	8	1	302	78*	43.14		3
A.D. Gaekwad (Baroda)	6	9		388	108	43.11	1	2
Sunit Dutta (Assam)	4	7		301	71	43.00		3
S. Kalyani (Maharashtra)	6	9		387	95	43.00		4
Akhtar Aijaz (Jammu & K)	5	7		300	121	42.85	2	
U.S. Madan Lal (Delhi)	9	10	4	255	56	42.50		1
S.V. Manjrekar (Bombay)	6	7	2	212	51*	42.40		1
S.C. Khanna (Delhi)	9	11		464	155	42.18	1	4
R. Bora (Assam)	5	11	1	417	107	41.70	1	2
C.P. Singh (Madhya P.)	3	5		206	68	41.20		2
S. Talati (Gujarat)	4	8		327	82	40.87		2
K. Shrikant (Services)	5	7		285	157	40.71	1	
P. Nandy (Bengal)	3	3		121	105	40.33	1	
G. Tank (Railways)	4	7	4	120	46	40.00		
Azim Khan (Maharashtra)	6	7	2	200	64	40.00		1
B. Pujara (Saurashtra)	4	5	2	120	103*	40.00	1	
A. Jabbar (Tamil Nadu)	7	8	2	239	51*	39.83		1
V. Gawate (Vidarbha)	4	6	2	159	61	39.75		2
D. Chopra (Punjab)	4	5	1	157	81*	39.25		2
R.R. Kulkarni (Bombay)	4	5	1	157	97	39.25		1
N. Oza (Saurashtra)	4	7	3	156	56	39.00		1
R.N. Kapil Dev (Haryana)	5	9	2	273	70	39.00		1
R. Parikh (Baroda)	4	7		271	123	38.71	1	1
S. Phadkar (Vidarbha)	4	6		230	127	38.33	1	
G. Tilak Raj (Baroda)	4	7	1	230	66	38.33		3
A. Saheba (Gujarat)	4	8		303	86	37.87		3

Player	M	I	NO	Runs	HS	Avge	100	50
S. Jadhav (Maharashtra)	6	10	4	226	93	37.66		2
A. Sharma (Delhi)	6	5		187	110	37.40	1	
R. Jolly (Haryana)	8	13		486	100	37.38	1	2
G.A.H.M. Parkar (Bombay)	4	7	1	223	53	37.16		2
R. Badyani (Saurashtra)	4	8	1	260	108*	37.14	1	1
S. Roy (Bihar)	3	4		146	56	36.50		1
W.V. Raman (Tamil Nadu)	3	4		109	58	36.33		1
Y. Dutta (Punjab)	4	7	1	218	67	36.33		2
Kulwant Singh (Punjab)	4	6	2	144	51	36.00		1
P. Desai (Gujarat)	4	7	1	214	70	35.66		2
Satya Dev (Haryana)	5	7	1	213	49	35.50		
B.P. Patel (Karnataka)	5	8	3	176	54*	35.20		1
D. Mahanti (Orissa)	5	6		211	70	35.16		2
K. Dubey (Orissa)	5	6		210	56	35.00		3
C. Saldanha (Karnataka)	5	8	2	210	91	35.00		1
Gursharan Singh (Delhi)	6	7	1	208	114*	34.66	1	
Balkar Singh (Punjab)	4	7	1	207	82	34.50		2
A. Bharadwaj (Orissa)	4	5	1	134	71	33.50		1
T.C. Suresh (Kerala)	3	6	3	100	32	33.33		
Sanjeeva Rao (Madhya P.)	4	7		233	79	33.28		2
N. Phadte (Assam)	4	8		261	156	32.62	1	
S. Amarnath (Gujarat)	4	8	1	228	89	32.57		2
S. Mudkavi (Rajasthan)	6	10		325	88	32.50		2
P. Hingnikar (Vidarbha)	3	5		162	100	32.40	1	1
S.C. Gudge (Maharashtra)	6	8	4	128	39	32.00		
D. Sharma (Haryana)	7	12		383	93	31.91		1
S.S. Karim (Bihar)	6	7		222	59	31.71		2
M.F. Rehman (Andhra)	6	11		348	141	31.63	1	1
S. Santosh (Kerala)	5	10		316	79	31.60		1
G.A. Pratap Kumar (And.)	6	10	3	221	79*	31.57		1
S. Vasudevan (Tamil Nadu)	6	4		126	65	31.50		1
N.S. Sidhu (Punjab)	6	9		277	85	30.77		2
M. Arya (Haryana)	4	5	1	121	39	30.25		
K. Jayraman (Kerala)	5	10	1	269	73	29.88		3
Ravi Pandit (Jammu & K.)	5	7	1	179	87	29.83		1
P.P. Pradhan (Maharashtra)	6	9	2	208	50	29.71		1
S. Chowdhary (Jammu & K.)	5	6		178	54	29.66		1
M.V. Narasimha Rao (Hyd.)	4	5	1	118	78*	29.50		1
A. Bhattacharjee (Bengal)	6	7	2	144	71*	28.80		1
R. Jadhav (Railways)	3	5		143	59	28.60		1
M. Sahni (Madhya Pradesh)	4	7		199	123	28.42	1	1
P. Karkera (Railways)	4	8		223	59	27.87		2
C. Ashok (Goa)	5	10	3	194	50*	27.71		1
S. Hedaoo (Vidarbha)	4	7	1	166	95	27.66		1
S. Ramesh (Kerala)	5	9	1	219	64	27.37		2
M. Hasan (Madhya Pradesh)	4	7	1	163	68	27.16		2
Ghopal Sharma (Uttar P.)	6	5	1	108	46	27.00		
Thomas Mathew (Kerala)	5	10		267	111	26.70	1	
Ashwini Kumar (Haryana)	8	14	1	345	74	26.53		1
S.S. Hazare (Baroda)	4	7	1	159	65	26.50		1
K.M. Roshan (Services)	4	5		132	69	26.40		1
Jugal Kishore Ghia (And.)	6	11	1	261	110	26.10	1	1
M.S. Kumar (Andhra)	4	6	1	127	57*	25.40		1
Darshan Singh (Himachal)	5	10		252	50	25.20		1
Inderjit Singh (Himachal)	5	10		250	74	25.00		2
D.V. Pardeshi (Baroda)	4	4		100	42	25.00		
L.K. Adisherhu (Andhra)	6	11		275	88	25.00		2
P. Banerjee (Railways)	4	8	2	148	57	24.66		1
K.K. Gohil (Services)	5	6	1	120	33	24.00		
A. Laghate (Madhya P.)	4	7		165	48	23.57		
B. Reddy (Tamil Nadu)	7	7	1	141	45	23.50		
B. Arun (Tamil Nadu)	8	10	2	183	38	22.87		
Bhaskar Ghosh (Services)	5	7		160	72	22.85		1
V. Sen (Madhya Pradesh)	5	10		225	76	22.50		2
H. Praharaj (Orissa)	5	6	1	112	43	22.40		
Padam Shastri (Rajasthan)	7	13	1	267	69	22.25		2
R. Talwar (Madhya P.)	3	5		110	28	22.00		
S. Paul (Tripura)	4	8		175	100	21.87	1	
S. Rajesh (Kerala)	4	8		175	65	21.87		1
S. Viswanath (Karnataka)	6	10		218	59	21.80		1
A. Jha (Services)	5	6		107	74	21.40		1
S. Kangralkar (Goa)	5	10		207	69	20.70		1
R. Misra (Tamil Nadu)	4	5		101	65	20.20		1
G. Shome, jnr (Bengal)	6	7	1	120	38	20.00		
B. Mistry (Gujarat)	6	11	2	178	58	19.77		2
J. Abhiram (Karnataka)	5	8	2	118	38	19.66		
Amal Dais (Assam)	4	7		137	73	19.57		1
Ved Raj (Railways)	4	8		152	47	19.00		
V.S. Prasad (Andhra)	6	9	1	151	39	18.87		
S. Mahadevan (Goa)	5	10		188	79	18.80		1
T. Deb Roy (Tripura)	4	8		147	57	18.37		1
D. Nilosey (Madhya P.)	4	7	1	110	40	18.33		
G. Hazarika (Assam)	4	8	1	128	50	18.28		1
Sarkar Tarwar (Haryana)	9	12	3	163	79	18.11		1
A. Asawa (Rajasthan)	6	10	1	163	47*	18.11		
A. Nandi (Railways)	4	7	1	108	36	18.00		
Aman Kumar (Haryana)	8	13		233	43	17.92		
A. Mudkavi (Rajasthan)	6	10	1	157	50*	17.44		1
R. Madhavan (Tamil Nadu)	7	9		156	79	17.33		1
Salim Ahmed (Haryana)	8	13		220	55	16.92		1
R. Krishna Mohan (Andhra)	6	9	1	135	37	16.87		
V. Telang (Vidarbha)	4	7	1	101	48	16.83		
R. Dogra (Haryana)	4	7		114	57	16.28		1
S. Uzir (Assam)	4	8	1	114	54*	16.28		1
Parminder Singh (Rajast.)	6	10		158	58	15.80		1
S. Kaushik (Rajasthan)	4	7		108	39	15.42		
S. Vyas (Rajasthan)	6	10		146	43	14.60		
A. Deb Burman (Tripura)	4	8		106	34	13.25		
R. Dutta (Madhya Pradesh)	5	10		126	46	12.60		
S. Pednekar (Goa)	5	10		122	44	12.20		

(Qualification 100 runs, average 10.00)

BOWLING

	Overs	Mds	Runs	Wkts	Av	Best	10/m	5/in
S. Jain (Madhya Pradesh)	82.3	38	145	12	12.08	4/17		
S. Vasudevan (Tamil Nadu)	177.1	40	406	29	14.00	6/27	1	2
S. Mitra (Orissa)	75.3	16	216	14	15.42	5/16		2
S. Valson (Delhi)	98	24	314	20	15.70	6/40		1
S. Vyas (Rajasthan)	122.5	27	324	19	17.05	6/43		1
M.R. Bhalla (Bihar)	69.1	13	171	10	17.10	4/32		
S. Shastri (Rajasthan)	93.2	27	224	13	17.23	7/94	1	1
Azim Khan (Maharashtra)	190.1	45	455	26	17.50	5/17		2
Maninder Singh (Delhi)	325.5	102	691	39	17.71	8/54	1	2
N. Venkatram (Bihar)	140.5	31	428	23	18.60	5/17	1	3

Player	O	M	R	W	Avge	Best		
P. Sunderam (Rajasthan)	137	25	486	26	18.69	10/78	1	3
N. Hirwani (Madhya P.)	169.3	38	478	24	19.91	7/64	1	3
S.M. Patil (Bombay)	141	34	359	18	19.94	6/20		1
M.I. Singh (Punjab)	112.2	19	260	13	20.00	6/61		1
A. Kumar (Bihar)	214.1	48	578	28	20.64	7/83	1	2
S. Takle (Vidarbha)	96.4	11	319	15	21.26	4/39		
D. Chopra (Punjab)	152.5	42	368	17	21.64	5/43		1
H. Praharaj (Orissa)	93	34	217	10	21.70	4/28		
T.S. Mahadevan (Kerala)	117	12	397	18	22.05	8/108		1
T. Arothe (Baroda)	57.5	3	222	10	22.20	6/57		1
H. Joshi (Railways)	167.2	38	387	17	22.76	5/54		1
Sharanjit Singh (Haryana)	162.1	24	481	21	22.90	6/79	1	1
Jeshwant (Karnataka)	106.2	19	322	14	23.00	4/56		
H. Baroah (Assam)	89.1	16	323	14	23.07	4/29		
B. Thakre (Vidarbha)	77	11	301	13	23.15	5/44		1
R.P. Singh (Uttar Pradesh)	103.2	14	417	18	23.16	6/75		1
S. Santosh (Kerala)	123.3	20	394	17	23.17	5/43		1
S. Pednekar (Goa)	88.1	6	351	15	23.40	4/69		
R. Yadav (Hyderabad)	124	13	476	20	23.80	7/58	1	1
Jugal Kishore Ghia (And.)	223	47	572	24	23.83	7/74		2
R.J. Shastri (Bombay)	230.2	66	501	21	23.85	8/145		2
V.P. Raju (Hyderabad)	108	19	313	13	24.07	3/6		
K.K. Sharma (Uttar P.)	76.2	8	339	14	24.21	7/63	1	1
Kirti Azad (Delhi)	178.4	28	512	21	24.38	4/42		
T. Raj Kumar (Railways)	80.5	8	318	13	24.46	4/62		
U.S. Madan Lal (Delhi)	173	31	515	21	24.52	4/49		
V. Gawate (Vidarbha)	82.4	6	297	12	24.75	4/30		
R.S. Hans (Uttar Pradesh)	155.3	45	298	12	24.83	6/66		1
S. Mudkavi (Rajasthan)	146.2	41	348	14	24.85	4/42		
S. Talwar (Haryana)	417.2	57	1147	46	24.93	7/44	2	3
M. Gautam (Tamil Nadu)	83	9	250	10	25.00	4/16		
N. Kanday (Jammu & K.)	108.2	10	450	18	25.00	5/64		1
A. Jha (Services)	110.1	10	410	16	25.62	3/24		
M. Prabhakar (Delhi)	151.5	23	521	20	26.05	4/42		
Umesh Kumar (Punjab)	167	44	345	13	26.53	4/5		
P.K. Rathod (Karnataka)	200.1	67	401	15	26.73	4/84		
Ravi Pandit (Jammu & K.)	84.4	11	349	13	26.84	4/34		
Ghopal Sharma (Uttar P.)	205.3	35	498	18	27.66	6/64	1	1
M.V. Narasimha Rao (Hyd.)	157.4	20	529	19	27.84	6/112		2
S. Jadhav (Maharashtra)	153.4	27	423	15	28.20	3/40		
A.R.B. Bhat (Karnataka)	166.4	50	370	13	28.46	4/46		
R.N. Kapil Dev (Haryana)	166.3	37	456	16	28.50	4/44		
R.K. Varma (Services)	70.4	9	285	10	28.50	4/92		
K.B. Ramamurthy (Andhra)	99.1	14	315	11	28.63	3/32		
D. Sharma (Haryana)	122.5	29	300	10	30.00	3/12		
A. Varma (Kerala)	117.5	13	465	15	31.00	5/82		1
D. Meher Baba (Andhra)	125.1	22	341	11	31.00	3/63		
Chetan Sharma (Haryana)	161.3	30	499	16	31.18	4/46		
G. Shom, jnr (Bengal)	173.4	29	599	19	31.52	4/46		
A. Bhattarcharjee (Bengal)	213.3	42	574	18	31.88	3/17		
Nabar Kanwar (Assam)	128.2	21	418	13	32.15	4/18		
Randhir Singh (Bihar)	145.3	24	584	18	32.44	3/44		
D.V. Pardeshi (Baroda)	162.1	45	392	12	32.66	4/66		
Kanwaljit Singh (Hyderab.)	144.2	18	436	13	33.53	5/39		1
H. Surendra (Karnataka)	190.4	25	578	17	34.00	5/111		1
Hari Mohan (Hyderabad)	112.2	15	409	12	34.08	4/56		
K.K. Gohil (Services)	121.5	24	342	10	34.20	5/54		1
B. Mistry (Gujarat)	115	22	354	10	35.40	3/47		
S. Mahadevan (Goa)	137	20	444	12	37.00	5/98		1
N. Patel (Gujarat)	122.5	17	412	11	37.45	4/75		
K.D. Mokashi (Bombay)	336	63	987	26	37.96	6/140	1	
S. Ramesh (Kerala)	108	13	392	10	39.20	2/36		
S.C. Gudge (Maharashtra)	228.5	35	709	18	39.38	4/214		
P. Kasliwal (Bombay)	146	18	564	14	40.28	5/91		1
B. Arun (Tamil Nadu)	122.5	9	532	12	44.33	3/142		
V.V. Oak (Maharashtra)	143.1	21	563	12	46.91	3/63		

(Qualification - 10 wickets)

LEADING FIELDERS

20 - S.C. Khanna (Delhi) (ct 18/st 2); 19 - Salim Ahmed (Haryana) (ct 12/st 7); 18 - Ehteshamuddin (Hyderabad) (ct 15/st 3) and C.S. Pandit (Bombay) (ct 16/st 2); 17 - S. Chaturvedi (Uttar Pradesh); 16 - M. Das (Bengal) (ct 12/st 4); 15 - S. Viswanath (Karnataka) (ct 13/st 2) and A. Sharma (Punjab) (ct 10/st 5); 14 - R. Krishna Mohan (Andhra) (ct 11/st 3) and S. Kaushik (Rajasthan) (ct 8/st 6); 12 - S.S. Karim (Bihar) (ct 6/st 6), A. Mudkavi (Rajasthan) and S. Kalyani (Maharashtra) (ct 10/st 1); 11 - A. Panicker (Kerala) (ct 10/st 1) and Bhaskar Pillai (Delhi) (ct 10/st 1); 10 - S.M. Patil (Bombay), R. Das (Services) (ct 7/st 3), D. Sharma (Haryana), P. Hingnikar (Vidarbha) (ct 8/st 2) and M. Satokar (Madhya Pradesh) (ct 9/st 1)

Solitary Way

The Season in South Africa.
Castle Currie Cup. Castle Bowl.
Nissan Shield. Benson and Hedges Trophy.
The Australian party under Kim Hughes.

The statistics in the South African section are based on
scores provided by official statistician Peter Sichel, and
wides and no-balls are not debited to the bowlers.

Cape Town.
(Adrian Murrell)

The South African season was again illuminated by a 'rebel' tour. The arrival of a strong Australian party under Kim Hughes focussed the attention of the cricket world on the republic and roused the passions concerning the debate on sport and politics.

The South African cricket authorities entice touring teams to their country because they are concerned for the future of the game there. They believe that in their efforts to bring about multi-racial cricket in South Africa they have met the demands which the rest of the cricketing world made of them, but that those efforts have been ignored and they remain isolated. They feel that they are left with no option but to seek their own means of maintaining the standards of the game and staging international competition in the country. Others deem that the presence of a national side in South Africa implies toleration of the policies of the South African government and condones apartheid and all that is associated with it. Certainly, at a time when they were facing the most serious opposition and the greatest threat to the fabric of their system, the South African government was happy to welcome the Australian tourists, but then it is difficult to find a country anywhere in the world where politicians do not exploit the prowess of their sportsmen. The Los Angeles Olympic Games was a prime example, and many political commentators have pointed to the benefit which Mr Harold Wilson gained from England's victory in the World Cup in 1966. Perhaps in England we will be able to be proud that politics have no place in sport when the facilities and opportunities for cricket at a London or Liverpool comprehensive school are comparable to those at Millfield or Winchester. In the mean time, in South Africa, there will be cricketers, some of them committed, some naive, some greedy, some indifferent and some disillusioned, who will be caught in the vice of political argument as the South African cricket authorities strive to keep the game alive and healthy in their country by whatever means are available to them.

3, 4 and 5 October 1985

at Oude Libertas, Stellenbosch

South African Defence Force 177 (O. Henry 4 for 44) and 148 (A. Watts 4 for 54)
Boland 160 and 166 for 8 (L.P. Jacobs 52, M.C. Smit 52, C.J. van Heerden 4 for 45)

Boland won by 2 wickets

A low scoring match provided a thrilling start to the season. Needing 166 to win, Boland lost Spilhaus and Joubert without scoring. From 5 for 2, they progressed to 31 for 3, but Jacobs and Smit then added 61 to give hope of success. When 3 wickets fell for 7 runs in mid-innings Boland looked doomed, but Watts and Justus, coming together at 153 for 8, won the match.

Nissan Shield

12 October 1985

at Oude Libertas Stellenbosch

Natal 200 for 7 (R.M. Bentley 104)
Boland 161

Natal won by 39 runs

at East London

Western Province 222 for 9 (P.H. Rayner 86, P.N. Kirsten 72)
Border 164 for 9 (M.B. Minnaar 5 for 33)

Western Province won by 58 runs

There were no surprises in the first matches to be played in South Africa's premier limited-over competition, the 55-over Nissan Shield. Rob Bentley became the first centurion of the season, and Paul Rayner and Peter Kirsten shared a 2nd wicket stand of 149 for Western Province at East London.

Benson and Hedges Trophy

16 October 1985

at Technicon Ground, Pretoria

Northern Transvaal 219 for 7
Western Province 220 for 7 (P.N. Kirsten 52)

Western Province (2 pts) won by 3 wickets

The floodlit tournament, 45 overs, began with a win for Western Province.

Nissan Shield

19 October 1985

at Kimberley

Transvaal 247 for 8 (M. Yachad 74, H.R. Fotheringham 50)
Griqualand West 173 for 7 (A.D. Methven 61 not out)

Transvaal won by 74 runs

at Bloemfontein

Orange Free State 211 for 6
Northern Transvaal 214 for 6 (N.T. Day 78 not out, L.J. Barnard 50)

Northern Transvaal won by 4 wickets

at Durban

Eastern Province 220 for 6 (P.G. Amm 72, D.J. Richardson 56)
Natal 221 for 7 (C.L. King 69, M.B. Logan 63)

Natal won by 3 wickets

23 October

at Port Elizabeth

Natal 216 for 7 (M.B. Logan 88)
Eastern Province 93 (R.K. McGlashan 4 for 19)

Natal won by 123 runs

Again the Nissan Shield produced no surprises, and the four favoured teams entered the semi-final. Brian Whitfield and Mark Logan put on 101 for Natal's first wicket at Durban, but Collis King, who had had a poor season in 1984–85, took the batting prize with some fine hitting. Natal overwhelmed Eastern Province in the second leg in Port Elizabeth.

Castle Currie Cup

25, 26 and 27 October 1985

at St George's Park, Port Elizabeth

Border 203 (M.K. van Vuuren 4 for 28) and 169 for 6

Eastern Province 311 for 7 dec (R.L.S. Armitage 71 not out, P.G. Amm 60)

Match drawn
Eastern Province 3 pts, Border 3 pts

at Ramblers Ground, Bloemfontein

Western Province 402 for 8 dec (K.S. McEwan 142, S.T. Jefferies 51 not out, L. Seeff 51)
Orange Free State 196 (J.J. Strydom 53, S.T. Jefferies 4 for 38) and 182 (P.N. Kirsten 6 for 48)

Western Province won by an innings and 24 runs
Western Province 21 pts, Orange Free State 4 pts

26, 27 and 28 October 1985

at Kingsmead, Durban

Natal 203 (R.M. Bentley 85, B.J. Whitfield 51, R.C. Ontong 5 for 33, C.D. Mitchley 4 for 57) and 292 (G.S. Cowley 75, M.B. Logan 60, M.D. Clare 4 for 70, R.C. Ontong 4 for 106)
Northern Transvaal 295 (N.T. Day 88) and 137 for 5 (L.J. Barnard 56)

Match drawn
Northern Transvaal 8 pts, Natal 4 pts

Castle Bowl

25, 26 and 27 October 1985

at De Beers Country Club, Kimberley

Griqualand West 360 for 9 dec (C.W. Symcox 100 not out, A.D. Methven 62, K.G. Bauermeister 4 for 92)
Eastern Province 'B' 173 (K.G. Bauermeister 55) and 186 (D.G. Emslie 69, B.E. van der Vyver 5 for 56)

Griqualand West won by an innings and 1 run
Griqualand West 21 pts, Eastern Province 'B' 4 pts

25, 26 and 28 October 1985

at Berea Park, Pretoria

Natal 'B' 348 (C.M. Lister-James 88 not out, M.J. Pearse 74, A.C. Hudson 62, J.C. van Duyker 4 for 89, E. duP. Klopper 4 for 108) and 165 for 8 dec (A.C. Hudson 71, F. de Villers 5 for 33)
Northern Transvaal 'B' 246 (C.P.L. de Lange 104) and 128 (J.A. O'Donoghue 5 for 39)

Natal 'B' won by 139 runs
Natal 'B' 19 pts, Northern Transvaal 'B' 6 pts

The two major competitions began with some fine individual performances. Ken McEwan, having retired from county cricket in England, showed that his appetite for runs in his native country had not diminished when he hit the season's first first-class century. He and the most promising Cullinan shared a fourth wicket stand of 124, and Jefferies' hard hitting saw Western Province past 400. Orange Free State, captained by Chris Broad, were soon in trouble against le Roux and Jefferies, and when they followed-on and showed signs of resistance Peter Kirsten was employed with his off-breaks and returned what were by far the best figures of his career.

Border, admitted to the Currie Cup for 1985–86, held out for a draw against Eastern Province for whom Robbie Armitage and Tim Shaw added an unbeaten 117. Sadly for Border, they had lost the services of Rodney Ontong who had moved to Northern Transvaal and who, in conjunction

Ken McEwan enjoyed his finest season in his native country and helped Western Province to break Transvaal's hold on the Currie Cup. (Tony Edenden)

with another newcomer, Cyril Mitchely from Transvaal, bowled his new province to a commanding position against Natal. Another player to have transferred his allegiance, Gavin Cowley, the former Eastern Province captain, played well for Natal in the second innings, and Northern Transvaal were left two hours in which to make 201 to win. They lost du Preez for 1, and then there was a 22-minute interruption for rain which ended hopes of victory. The Natal bowling was opened by Ian Pont of Essex and Graham Dilley of Kent.

In the Castle Bowl, Griqualand West, with Laurie Potter and Gordon Parsons in their side, trounced Eastern Province 'B'. It was Symcox at number 7, however, who turned the match in the home side's favour with a fine hundred.

There was an equally good innings by Cornelius de Lange at Pretoria, but he could not save his side from defeat.

Benson and Hedges Trophy

30 October 1985

at Green Point, Cape Town

Match abandoned due to high winds
Western Province 1 pt, Impalas 1 pt

Nissan Shield – Semi-Finals – First Leg

2 November

at Durban

Natal 240 for 7 (M.B. Logan 87, C.L. King 50)
Western Province 231 (P.N. Kirsten 52, A.P. Kuiper 50, T.J. Packer 5 for 32, G.R. Dilley 4 for 47)

Natal won by 9 runs

at Pretoria

Northern Transvaal 167
Transvaal 168 for 2 (S.J. Cook 66 not out, R.G. Pollock 59 not out)

Transvaal won by 8 wickets

Collis King hit 50 in 62 minutes, and Graham Dilley and Trevor Packer bowled Natal to an exciting victory in Durban while in Pretoria, Graeme Pollock hit a six and 8 fours as he lashed 59 not out in 73 minutes and Transvaal won with 6.5 overs to spare.

Benson and Hedges Trophy

6 November 1985

at Wanderers, Johannesburg

Northern Transvaal 219 for 7 (K.D. Verdoorn 60)
Transvaal 220 for 4 (R.G. Pollock 61 not out, S.J. Cook 50)

Transvaal (2 pts) won by 6 wickets

8 November 1985

at St George's Park, Port Elizabeth

Eastern Province 105 for 6
v. **Natal**

Match abandoned
Eastern Province 1 pt, Natal 1 pt

Castle Currie Cup

8, 9 and 11 November 1985

at Berea Park, Pretoria

Northern Transvaal 343 for 7 dec (N.T. Day 117, V.F. du Preez 51) and 219 for 5 dec (L.J. Barnard 93)
Border 253 (A.L. Wilmot 78, S.F.A. Bacchus 70, C.D. Mitchley 5 for 26) and 313 for 8 (G.L. Hayes 92)

Border won by 2 wickets
Border 16 pts, Northern Transvaal 9 pts

at Wanderers, Johannesburg

Transvaal 358 for 7 dec (H.R. Fotheringham 110, R.G. Pollock 50)
Orange Free State 148 (H.A. Page 4 for 28, A.J. Kourie 4 for 36) and 122 (H.A. Page 4 for 48)

Transvaal won by an innings and 88 runs
Transvaal 19 pts, Orange Free State 2 pts

In their second match in the top company Border obtained a remarkable victory against the previous year's Currie Cup runners-up, Northern Transvaal. Noel Day hit a six and 20 fours in his 4-hour innings and with Cyril Mitchley's medium pace again proving effective, Northern Transvaal took a first innings lead of 90. It would have been greater but for the

Rodney Ontong moved to Northern Transvaal and produced some fine all-round cricket. (Mark Leech)

efforts of Faoud Bacchus and veteran Lorrie Wilmot. Lee Barnard hit a brisk 93 for the home side and declared when he was dismissed, leaving Border 295 minutes in which to make 310. Minnaar was out for 1, and 6 wickets fell for 148 as well as Wilmot being forced to retire hurt. Greg Hayes, at number 7, found a good partner in Ballantyne and they added 72. Wilmot then returned to share a stand of 70 with Hayes, and when Hayes's splendid innings ended, caught behind off Ontong, it was Wilmot who steered Border to a famous victory.

In Johannesburg, the might of Transvaal was too great for Orange Free State. Henry Fotheringham hit a fine century, emphasising his right to a place in the national side, and the bowling quartet of Clarke, Radford, Page and Kourie, a most formidable attack, twice dismissed the visitors for under 150.

Benson and Hedges Trophy

13 November 1985

at St George's Park, Port Elizabeth

Transvaal 220 for 9 (M. Yachad 75)
Impalas 180 for 9

Transvaal (2 pts) won by 40 runs

Castle Currie Cup

15, 16 and 17 November 1985

at Kingsmead, Durban

Natal 338 (C.L. King 154) and 173 (C.J.P.G. van Zyl 5 for 54)
Orange Free State 308 for 6 dec (B.C. Broad 101 not out, R.J. East 59, J.J. Strydom 56) and 120 for 6

Match drawn
Natal 10 pts, Orange Free State 8 pts

15, 16 and 18 November 1985

at Berea Park, Pretoria

Northern Transvaal 299 (A.M. Ferreira 105, E.O. Simons 5 for 52) and 242 for 5 dec (R.F. Pienaar 79, A. Geringer 67 not out)
Western Province 272 (A.G. Elgar 66) and 99 for 1

Match drawn
Northern Transvaal 8 pts, Western Province 7 pts

Castle Bowl

15, 16 and 18 November 1985

at Oude Libertas, Stellenbosch

Boland 343 for 9 dec (O. Henry 118, S. Nackerdein 81) and 159 for 6 dec
Natal 'B' 204 (D.A. Scott 94, P. Anker 5 for 48, O. Henry 5 for 95) and 151 (P. Anker 5 for 34)

Boland won by 148 runs
Boland 19 pts, Natal 'B' 5 pts

Openers Vernon du Preez and Roy Pienaar, formerly of Western Province, put on 79, but Northern Transvaal slumped to 133 for 7 at Berea Park. Anton Ferreira then hit 105 in 158 minutes to lift the home side to unexpected prosperity. Eric Simons troubled his old province consistently and not even Ferreira could take liberties with his medium pace. A rather uneven batting display brought Western Province to within 27 runs of Northern Transvaal's score, but the visitors showed no enthusiasm for their eventual target of 270 in under three hours.

A splendid all-round performance by Omar Henry and some excellent off-break bowling from Pienaar Anker gave Boland victory in the Castle Bowl game in Stellenbosch. Henry came in at 154 for 5 and he freely as he dominated the later stages of the innings. He then joined forces with Anker to dismiss the visitors for 204, and Anker was again in destructive form as Natal slipped quietly to defeat.

The Natal senior team were indebted to a blistering innings from Collis King for their big score in Durban. They were 67 for 4 when King came to the wicket and he hit a six and 19 fours in his knock which lasted 238 minutes. Orange Free State were 142 for 5 in reply, but skipper Chris Broad, at number 5, hit a fine hundred and shared stands of 87 with Robbie East and an unbeaten 79 with Alan Beukes. Cornelius van Zyl, pressing for a place in the national squad, had Natal in trouble in their second innings, but with both sides beset by injury problems, a draw always looked likely.

Benson and Hedges Trophy

20 November 1985

at Technicon Ground, Pretoria

Northern Transvaal 253 for 4 (K.D. Verdoorn 113, R.F. Pienaar 58)
Impalas 215 (N.P. Minnaar 64)

Northern Transvaal (2 pts) won by 38 runs

Brave batting from Minnaar, Jones and Henry failed to save Impalas against Northern Transvaal for whom Kevin Verdoorn gave a sparkling display.

Castle Bowl

21, 22 and 23 November 1985

at R.J.E. Burt Oval, Constantia

Natal 'B' 253 (K.D. Dawson 53) and 151 (C.M. Lister-James 54 not out, D. Norman 6 for 56)
Western Province 'B' 201 for 8 dec (G.J. Turner 69 not out, M.R. Hobson 5 for 56) and 207 for 7

Western Province 'B' won by 3 wickets
Western Province 'B' 14 pts, Natal 'B' 5 pts

22, 23 and 24 November 1985

at Wanderers, Johannesburg

Eastern Province 'B' 223 (M.B. Billson 53, G.N. McNab 4 for 29) and 311 for 7 (M.J.P. Ford 96, D.G. Emslie 82, K.G. Bauermeister 61 not out)
Transvaal 'B' 460 for 5 dec (M.S. Venter 225 not out, B.M. McMillan 129, B. Roberts 53)

Match drawn
Transvaal 'B' 8 pts, Eastern Province 'B' 3 pts

Western Province 'B' came from behind to gain a hard earned victory at Constantia. They were given a great boost in their search for the 204 that they needed for victory when Elgar and Wingreen began their second innings with a stand of 80, but the real hero was David Norman whose right-arm medium pace earned him match figures of 9 for 131, including a career best 6 for 56 in the second innings.

There was another career best at Wanderers where Mark Venter and McMillan put on 318 for the Transvaal 'B' fourth wicket, a record for any wicket for the Castle Bowl side. Venter reached the first double century of his career, but the match, saturated with runs, was drawn.

Castle Currie Cup

22, 23 and 24 November 1985

at St George's Park, Port Elizabeth

Transvaal 298 for 9 dec (M. Yachad 90, C.E.B. Rice 73 H.R. Fotheringham 56, T.G. Shaw 4 for 98) and 207 for 2 dec (H.R. Fotheringham 114 not out, R.G. Pollock 52 not out)
Eastern Province 277 (P.G. Amm 55, K.J. Kerr 4 for 101) and 211 for 6 (P.G. Amm 65, M. Michau 50 not out)

Match drawn
Transvaal 9 pts, Eastern Province 7 pts

23, 24 and 25 November 1985

at Kingsmead, Durban

Western Province 314 for 7 dec (K.S. McEwan 101, G.S. le Roux 57 not out, G.R. Dilley 4 for 73) and 235 for 4 dec (K.S McEwan 82 not out, P.N. Kirsten 52)
Transvaal 260 (C.L. King 69, G.S. le Roux 4 for 45) and 182 (G.S. le Roux 5 for 54)

Western Province won by 107 runs
Western Province 20 pts, Natal 7 pts

The first indications of a shift in power in South African cricket came in these matches. Two magnificent innings by Fotheringham were not enough to bring the reigning champions victory over Eastern Province who batted with great determination against the vaunted Transvaal attack in both innings. Indeed, searching for 229 in three hours, the home side came close to victory with Michau and Rushmere making a brave effort at the close. Fotheringham, a six and 14 fours, and Pollock had shared an unbeaten stand of 127 for Transvaal's third wicket.

While Transvaal were failing to win Western Province were claiming another decisive victory and taking a commanding lead in the league table. They lost Rayner, Seeff and Kirsten for 30, but Ken McEwan hit his second hundred of the season, the sixty-fourth of his career, and with some good support from Darryl Cullinan and some lusty blows from Garth le Roux, the visitors passed 300. Natal batted doggedly in reply, but they trailed by 54 on the first innings. Again Western Province had early lapses, but Kirsten and McEwan played entertaining cricket, and Kuiper shared an unbeaten stand of 117 with McEwan before the declaration. A good all-round attack, spearheaded by le Roux who dismissed Whitfield without a run scored, took Western Province to victory.

22, 23 and 25 November 1985

at Ramblers, Bloemfontein

Australians 345 for 8 dec (J. Dyson 141) and 301 for 5 dec (M.D. Taylor 102 not out, G.N. Yallop 62, J. Dyson 52)
Orange Free State 319 (B.C. Broad 88, A.P. Beukes 51, R.J. McCurdy 4 for 85) and 76 for 1

Match drawn

The Australian tour began with one-day matches against country district sides, but the first three-day encounter saw them give an encouraging batting display at Bloemfontein. Dyson gave the tour a good start when he made a patient 141 from 259 deliveries. Yallop, Hughes briefly, and Taylor all showed more aggression as the Australians closed the day at 334 for 6. Dyson was out without adding to his overnight score, and Hughes declared. McCurdy showed lively pace and Rackemann took 2 wickets in 3 balls to leave the state side at 34 for 3, but Broad played with great application and took his side close to the tourists' score. The tail-enders relished Hohns's spin and he was hit for 6 sixes. Taylor hit a brisk century in the second innings, but the match ended in a tame draw.

27 November 1985

at Technicon Ground, Pretoria

Northern Transvaal 211 for 9 (A.M. Ferreira 61, A. Geringer 50)
Australians 204 (K.J. Hughes 72)

Northern Transvaal won by 7 runs

Put in to bat in the day/night match, Northern Transvaal slumped to 26 for 3 against Hogg and McCurdy, but lusty hitting from the middle order took them to a commendable score from their 50 overs. The Australians were frustrated by the home side's accurate bowling and well organised field so that four batsmen were run out, three in an over by Ferreira, and, in spite of Hughes's good innings, they were beaten with 4 balls remaining.

Castle Bowl

28, 29 and 30 November 1985

at Uitenhage C.C., Uitenhage

Western Province 'B' 241 (I.M. Wingreen 103) and 163 for 7 dec (B. de K. Robey 4 for 73)
Eastern Province 'B' 148 (D.B. Rundle 4 for 40, B.A. Matthews 4 for 50) and 259 for 6 (D.G. Emslie 111 not out, P.A. Tullis 64 not out)

Eastern Province 'B' won by 4 wickets
Eastern Province 'B' 15 pts, Western Province 'B' 8 pts

29, 30 November and 1 December 1985

at Kingsmead, Durban

Griqualand West 128 (A.D. Hall 5 for 22) and 210 (P.J. R. Steyn 63, J.A. O'Donoghue 5 for 51)
Natal 'B' 191 (G.W. Symmonds 4 for 50) and 150 for 3 (A.C. Hudson 70)

LEFT: *Kim Hughes, leader of the 'rebel' Australians. (Adrian Murrell)*

Natal 'B' won by 5 wickets
Natal 'B' 16 pts, Griqualand West 5 pts

29, 30 November and 2 December 1985

at Pietersburg

Northern Transvaal 'B' 372 for 6 dec (P.L. Symcox 107) and 106 (W.H. van Wyk 7 for 55)
Transvaal 'B' 344 for 8 dec (C.R. Norris 101, R.W. Adair 63, L.H. Vorster 50) and 120 for 5 (G.L. Ackermann 4 for 51)

Match drawn
Northern Transvaal 'B' 7 pts, Transvaal 'B' 7 pts

Ivan Wingreen's century put Western Province 'B' in a good position at Uitenhage. Matthews, Martin and van der Merwe bowled the visitors to a first innings lead of 93, and During's declaration left Eastern Province 'B' to make 257 at $3\frac{1}{2}$ an over. Ford retired hurt without a run scored, and Daniell and Keevey went with only 12 on the board. Callaghan helped Emslie to bring about a slight recovery, but at 121 for 6, defeat looked highly probable. Tullis then joined his skipper in an exciting stand which brought a fine victory. David Emslie reached the first century of his career, and wicket-keeper Tullis hit his career best 64 not out.

In a low scoring match at Kingsmead, Hudson and Mellor provided the basis of Natal's win with an opening stand of 78 in the second innings. There was more impressive bowling by O'Donoghue.

At Pietersburg, centuries by Symcox and Norris were overshadowed by van Wyk's unchanged spell of 14.1 overs which brought him a career best 7 for 55.

Carl Rackemann. In pace and stamina he was the most impressive of the Australian bowlers. (Adrian Murrell)

Castle Currie Cup

29 and 30 December 1985

at Newlands, Cape Town

Western Province 266 (P.N. Kirsten 51, W.K. Watson 6 for 47)
Eastern Province 91 (S.T. Jefferies 5 for 30) and 156

Western Province won by an innings and 19 runs
Western Province 19 pts, Eastern Province 5 pts

29, 30 November, and 1 December 1985

at Wanderers, Johannesburg

Northern Transvaal 222 (K.D. Verdoorn 74, N.V. Radford 5 for 52) and 128 for 5
Transvaal 243 (R.G. Pollock 78, M.D. Clare 5 for 70)

Match drawn
Northern Transvaal 7 pts, Transvaal 6 pts

at Jan Smuts Ground, East London

Border 81 (E.J. Hodkinson 4 for 26) and 225 for 9 (V.G. Cresswell 50, R.K. McGlashan 4 for 72)
Natal 287 for 7 dec (R.M. Bentley 134 not out, N.P. Daniels 53)

Match drawn
Natal 7 pts, Border 3 pts

Western Province overwhelmed Eastern Province in two days at Newlands and consolidated their position at the top of the table. Watson, the former Notts player, bowled impressively as did David Capel, but Jefferies and le Roux tore Eastern Province apart and the visiting batsmen offered little resistance.

Transvaal again failed to win, and they were handicapped by injury to Sylvester Clarke. They had Northern Transvaal struggling at 96 for 5, but Verdoorn played well and Ferreira also batted usefully.

Border batted woefully in East London, their 81 occupying 47.2 overs. Thanks to Bentley, Natal took a commanding lead, but Border, who had been put in to bat in difficult conditions, batted with greater sense of purpose and saved the match.

29, 30 November, and 2 December 1985

at Berea Park, Pretoria

President's XI 150 (T.R. Madsen 54) and 126 (J.N. Maguire 5 for 58)
Australians 186 (K.J. Hughes 73) and 91 for 5

Australians won by 5 wickets

Electing to bat on a wicket which always aided the bowlers, the President's XI were bowled out by the Australian pace men. Terry Madsen was the only batsman to offer serious resistance and the Natal wicket-keeper created a further good impression when he held two fine catches off Page and van Zyl to send back Dyson and Smith with only 10 scored. Hughes and Shipperd put on 103 for the third wicket and this proved to be a match-winning stand. The Australians took a lead of 36, and they had the President's XI limping at 67 for 5 by the end of the second day. Cullinan from whom so much was anticipated was bowled by Alderman for 0. The visitors won on the last afternoon, but not before they had had many moments of apprehension.

4 December 1985

at Wanderers, Johannesburg

Transvaal 269 for 3 (H.R. Fotheringham 72, S.J. Cook 60, R.G. Pollock 59 not out)
Australians 211 for 6 (S.B. Smith 93)

Transvaal won by 58 runs

Cook and Fotheringham negotiated a difficult start to put on 139 for the first wicket. Pollock then hit 59 from 46 balls, and Transvaal reached a score that the Australians could not hope to match.

Nissan Shield – Semi-Finals – Second Leg

7 December 1985

at Newlands, Cape Town

Natal 235 for 8 (R.M. Bentley 65, D. Bestall 57 not out, E.O. Simons 5 for 45)
Western Province 239 for 6 (A.G. Elgar 84, K.S. McEwan 76)

Western Province won by 4 wickets

at Wanderers, Johannesburg

Northern Transvaal 227 (R.F. Pienaar 102)
Transvaal 229 for 2 (S.J. Cook 82, K.A. McKenzie 76 not out)

Transvaal won by 8 wickets

Alan Elgar and Kenny McEwan added 135 for Western Province's third wicket against Natal and made possible an exciting win which came with 4 balls to spare. The victory meant that the sides would have to meet in a deciding match in Durban. Meanwhile Transvaal took their customary place in the final with an emphatic win over Northern Transvaal in spite of Roy Pineaar's century.

6, 7 and 8 December 1985

at Jan Smuts Ground, East London

Border 168 (J.N. Maguire 5 for 62, C.G. Rackemann 4 for 51)
Australians 236 for 8 (J. Dyson 62, M.D. Taylor 54)

Match drawn

Rain washed out play on the last day of a match in which the Australian pace men had again impressed.

Benson and Hedges Trophy

11 December 1985

at Green Point, Cape Town

Western Province 243 for 8 (P.H. Rayner 65, A.G. Elgar 59, K.S. McEwan 54)
Natal 219 (M.B. Logan 74, D. Norman 4 for 56)

Western Province (2 pts) won by 24 runs

Western Province, leading in the Currie Cup, took a clear lead at the top of the Benson and Hedges Trophy league when they produced some more entertaining batting at Green Point.

11 December 1985

at St George's Park, Port Elizabeth

Australians 222 for 7 (J. Dyson 78, G.N. Yallop 50)
Eastern Province 217 for 9 (D.J. Richardson 61)

Australians won by 5 runs

13, 14 and 15 December 1985

at St George's Park, Port Elizabeth

Australians 382 for 9 dec (M.D. Haysman 125 not out, K.J. Hughes 72, T.G. Hogan 63, T.G. Shaw 4 for 116) and 101 for 1 dec (J. Dyson 71 not out)
Eastern Province 235 (R.L.S. Armitage 98 not out, M. Michau 53, T.G. Hogan 8 for 86) and 250 for 8 (D.J. Richardson 64, R.M. Hogg 4 for 70)

Eastern Province won by 2 wickets

Having won an exciting 50-over match at Port Elizabeth, the Australians suffered a surprise defeat on the same ground in the first-class match. Haysman and Hogan put on 116 for the tourists' seventh wicket and lifted their side to a formidable score. Eastern Province lost their first 3 wickets for 28 runs, but Michau and Armitage put on 106. Nevertheless, Hogan's spin demoralised the remaining batsmen and he returned career best figures of 8 for 86. With Dyson again in good form, the Australians scored briskly and Hughes declared. Amm and Birrell gave their side a good start, but Hogg undermined the middle order, and 8 wickets went down for 219. Determined batting by Rushmere and Rayment saw the home side to a surprise victory.

Castle Bowl

12, 13 and 14 December 1985

at Cape Town C.C., Plumstead

Western Province 'B' 137 (S. van Rooyen 4 for 50) and 174 (O. Henry 5 for 67)
Boland 148 (S.A. Jones 65) and 122 (W.M. van der Merwe 5 for 35)

Western Province 'B' won by 41 runs
Western Province 'B' 15 pts, Boland 5 pts

13, 14 and 15 December 1985

at Wanderers, Johannesburg

Transvaal 'B' 276 (B. McBride 58, G.E. McMillan 56, L.H. Vorster 51, P. McLaren 5 for 68) and 184 for 4 dec (B. Roberts 79)
Griqualand West 182 (P. Botha 4 for 28) and 173 for 9 (P.R.J. Steyn 54)

Match drawn
Transvaal 'B' 9 pts, Griqualand West 3 pts

Western Province 'B' surprisingly beat Boland who had been impressive in their opening match of the season. Having dismissed the home side for 137, Boland collapsed alarmingly to 48 for 7, but they were rescued by skipper Stephen Jones and Watts who added 67. Set to make 164 to win, Boland again collapsed before van der Merwe. They were 72

Brian McMillan of Transvaal, one of South Africa's most promising young players. (Ken Kelly)

for 6, but this time there was no effective recovery.

In Johannesburg, Griqualand West, having won the toss and asked Transvaal 'B' to bat, found themselves facing defeat when their ninth wicket went down at 171, but Parsons and Symonds held out and earned a draw.

Castle Currie Cup

13, 14 and 15 December 1985

at Jan Smuts Ground, East London

Border 130 (H.A. Page 5 for 31, A.J. Kourie 4 for 51) and 369 (S.F.A. Bacchus 95, G.L. Hayes 65 not out, A.L. Wilmot 65, E.N. Trotman 63)
Transvaal 403 for 6 dec (R.G. Pollock 113, C.E.B. Rice 80, A.J. Kourie 54 not out) and 100 for 2

Transvaal won by 8 wickets
Transvaal 21 pts, Border 2 pts

Transvaal gave notice that they would not relinquish the Currie Cup easily and, as expected, they beat Border with some ease although the newcomers, trailing by 273 on the first innings, batted bravely at the second attempt and forced the champions to bat again. Even without Clarke, the Transvaal attack was formidable and Page's 5 for 31 came off 12 overs. Transvaal took the lead for the loss of only 3 wickets, and Pollock, in majestic form, and Rice shared a stand of 186 for the fourth wicket which put the visitors in total command. Border lost Minnaar and Cresswell with 43 on the board, but Bacchus and Trotman, the two West

Indians, added 102, and some impressive and courageous late order batting took Border to 369. It could not stop Transvaal's win, but it showed Border's determination to become accepted in the top class.

17, 18 and 19 December 1985

at Oude Libertas, Stellenbosch

Boland 271 (S.A. Jones 132, O. Henry 50) and 159 for 6 (N.M. Lambrechts 52 not out)
Australians 456 for 9 dec (K.J. Hughes 116, S.B. Smith 112, T.V. Hohns 90, P. Anker 4 for 126)

Match drawn

Shortly after lunch Boland, who had decided to bat when they won the toss, were 66 for 5, but skipper Stephen Jones hit a career best 132 and turned the course of the match. He faced only 148 balls and hit 4 sixes and 14 fours in a furious assault on the Australian bowling. Australians, 25 for 0 at the close, were bolstered on the second day by a second wicket stand of 209 between Steve Smith and Kim Hughes. Later Trevor Hohns hit mightily, but Boland avoided an innings defeat with some defiant batting.

Castle Currie Cup

19, 20 and 21 December 1985

at Wanderers, Johannesburg

Transvaal 196 (R.V. Jennings 50 not out, G.R. Dilley 7 for 63) and 195 for 4 (S.J. Cook 82)
Natal 200 for 8 dec (D. Bestall 69 not out)

Match drawn
Natal 7 pts, Transvaal 5 pts

at Berea Park, Pretoria

Eastern Province 319 (R.L.S. Armitage 56, C.D. Mitchley 5 for 73, M.D. Clare 4 for 112) and 230 for 7 dec (P.G. Amm 82)
Northern Transvaal 241 (A.M. Ferreira 95) and 260 for 8 (N.T. Day 62, L.J. Barnard 54)

Match drawn
Eastern Province 9 pts, Northern Transvaal 6 pts

Castle Bowl

19, 20 and 21 December 1985

at Union Ground, Port Elizabeth

Northern Transvaal 'B' 279 (M.J.R. Rindel 115) and 201 (K.G. Bauermeister 4 for 45)
Eastern Province 'B' 201 (J.C. van Duyker 4 for 58) and 283 for 4 (I.K. Daniell 113, A. Snyman 92)

Eastern Province 'B' won by 6 wickets
Eastern Province 'B' 17 pts, Northern Transvaal 'B' 9 pts

Put in to bat, Transvaal struggled on a dubious wicket which Graham Dilley exploited to the full to return the best performance of his career. Natal fared worse than the home side and were 91 for 7 against Page, Radford and 'Spook' Hanley who was making a welcome return in the absence of Clarke. Skipper Bestall found a good partner in Chris Lister-James, however, and the pair added 89. Bestall declared as soon as Natal had taken the lead, but there was no second innings collapse by Transvaal who were held together by Jim Cook.

An even batting performance took Eastern Province to 319 after they had lost opener Birrell for 0. Northern Transvaal struggled painfully in reply and were 82 for 6. A violent 95 in under 2½ hours by Anton Ferreira rallied them. The Warwickshire all-rounder hit a six and 14 fours and dominated a stand of 113 with Rodney Ontong. Eventually asked to make 309 in 4 hours, 10 minutes, Northern Transvaal made a bold bid, but they lost 3 wickets for 13 runs and were thankful to Ontong and de Villiers for holding out.

Their 'B' side was less successful in the Bowl match where Eastern Province 'B' came from behind to win a fine victory. Asked to make 280 at more than 4 an over, Eastern were given a splendid start by Snyman who played only twice in the season. Ian Daniell then took over with a fierce attack on the bowling which brought him the highest score of his career and victory to his side. Michael Rindel had dominated the first day with his maiden century in first-class cricket.

21 December 1985

at Newlands, Cape Town

Australians 260 for 4 wickets (J. Dyson 126 not out, K.J. Hughes 61)
Western Province 212 for 9 (P.N. Kirsten 96, R.M. Hogg 4 for 36)

Australians won by 48 runs

23 December 1985

at Kingsmead, Durban

Australians 234 for 6 (G.N. Yallop 63, S.B. Smith 61)
Natal 206 (J.N. Maguire 4 for 42)

Australians won by 28 runs

Two wins on the eve of the first international match gave the Australian tourists some heart. Dyson, the most consistent and impressive of the Australian batsmen, gave further reason to wonder why he was not selected for the side that toured England in 1985, and, in the second match, Yallop, batting with a runner after pulling a hamstring, played well to put his side in a strong position.

The South African selectors named Hugh Page as the only newcomer in their side for the first match. The Transvaal pace bowler had well deserved his selection. Rodney Ontong stated that he was not available for selection as the T.C.C.B. had informed him that if he played, he would lose his English residential qualification.

Castle Bowl

26, 27 and 28 December 1985

at Oude Libertas, Stellenbosch

Boland 407 for 8 dec (S. Nackerdien 122, S.A. Jones 85, N.M. Lambrechts 84, G. Vermeulen 58) and 37 for 2
Transvaal 'B' 133 (O. Henry 5 for 46) and 307 (B. McBride 66 not out, B. Roberts 65, L.H. Vorster 52)

Boland won by 8 wickets
Boland 17 pts, Transvaal 'B' 2 pts

Boland gained a decisive win over Transvaal 'B', the holders of the Castle Bowl, and strengthened their position at the top of the table. They had lost 2 wickets for 15 runs, but Vermeulen and Nackerdien improved matters considerably. Salieg Nackerdien went on to reach a maiden first-class century, and some aggression from Lambrechts and Jones, enjoying a magnificent season, took Boland to a position of complete authority. With Omar Henry again in good form with the ball, Boland forced the visitors to follow-on, but some dogged batting avoided an innings defeat. Henry brought his match figures to 8 for 160, and he bowled 53.2 overs in the second innings to take 3 for 114.

First International Match
SOUTH AFRICAN XI *v.* AUSTRALIAN XI

Clive Rice won the toss and decided to bat, and his decision seemed perfectly justified as Cook and Fotheringham began the match with a stand of 124 which took South Africa into the afternoon with serenity. A change in the fortunes of the match was brought about by Rodney Hogg who, in a furious spell after lunch, took 3 for 5 in 17 deliveries. Fotheringham was caught behind by Rixon who also accounted for Peter Kirsten, and throughout the season Rixon was to win the highest praise from all the critics. He had not been too well treated by Australian Test selectors over the years, yet it is

hard to believe that Australia have had anyone his equal since Marsh's retirement.

Pollock came in to a rapturous reception, but almost immediately he lost his partner Cook who was lbw to Hogg after grafting hard for 131 balls. Rackemann was generating much pace in a sustained spell, and he had McEwan caught by Rixon. Four wickets had fallen for 24 runs, but Pollock and Rice avoided further trouble, and play ended shortly after tea, at 182 for 4, when storm clouds threatened.

The Australians had been hit by injuries when Yallop, Smith, McCurdy and Alderman were all unavailable for selection, but they continued to have the better of the match when Hogg dismissed Rice and Kourie early on the second morning. Rackemann accounted for le Roux after he had figured in a valuable stand with Pollock, but the great left-hander was now in total command.

It would be foolish to suggest that Pollock, nearing his forty-second birthday, retains all the greatness that made him the oustanding Test batsman since the war with an international average second only to Don Bradman, but the elegance and authority have not been diminished by time. He reached 50 off 116 deliveries, and in the next 41 minutes, off another 54 balls, he reached 108. It was the sixty-second first-class hundred of his career, and it contained 13 fours. One of the greatest sadnesses in cricket to have come since South

Africa have been excluded from the Test arena is that there are those in their twenties who love the game who have never seen Pollock bat.

He brought up the 300 with a glorious cover drive off Rackemann, and then chopped Maguire to third man for his century. He was dismissed when Hughes took a fine diving catch in the covers off Rackemann.

Jennings and Jefferies made excellent late contributions, and South Africa reached a total which seemingly put them in an impregnable position. Their grip on the game strengthened when Jefferies, after an erratic opening spell, returned to dismiss Dyson and Haysman so that the Australians closed at 72 for 2.

They consolidated with a consistent batting performance on the third day which took them to within 34 runs of South Africa's big total. The innings was held together by Mick Taylor who did not offer a chance in his stay during which he faced 176 balls and hit a six and 14 fours. The South African bowling was generally wayward, and Taylor and Hogan put on 79 in 14 overs for the seventh wicket when the second new ball was taken.

The Australian innings did not end until the final morning so that a draw seemed inevitable, but Hogg and Rackemann were again in fine form. Hogg took 2 for 1 in his first 20 balls, and Rackemann 3 for 19 as he bowled unchanged for 11 overs. He displayed remarkable stamina throughout the tour. In 20 overs, South Africa were 30 for 5.

Taylor missed Kourie shortly after lunch, and it was he who stayed with Fotheringham to add 100 and bring the

OPPOSITE: *Graeme Pollock, now at the veteran stage, but a batsman who still delights with every stroke. (Adrian Murrell)*

FIRST INTERNATIONAL MATCH – SOUTH AFRICAN XI v AUSTRALIAN XI
26, 27, 28 and 29 December 1985 at Kingsmead, Durban

SOUTH AFRICAN XI

	FIRST INNINGS		SECOND INNINGS	
S.J. Cook	lbw, b Hogg	52	c Haysman, b Hogg	2
H.R. Fotheringham	c Rixon, b Hogg	70	(6) not out	100
P.N. Kirsten	c Rixon, b Hogg	2	(2) c Rixon, b Hogg	5
R.G. Pollock	c Hughes, b Rackemann	108	b Rackemann	6
K.S. McEwan	c Rixon, b Rackemann	4	(3) c Haysman, b Rackemann	5
C.E.B. Rice†	c Dyson, b Hogg	11	c Hogan, b Rackemann	9
A.J. Kourie	c Haysman, b Hogg	1	run out	44
G.S. le Roux	c Rixon, b Rackemann	9	c Haysman, b Hogan	28
R.V. Jennings*	c Rixon, b Rackemann	46		
S.T. Jefferies	not out	43		
H.A. Page	c Hogan, b Rackemann	10		
Extras	b 11, lb 17, w 5, nb 4	37	b 3, nb 1	4
		393	(for 7 wkts dec)	203

	O	M	R	W	O	M	R	W
Hogg	32	13	83	5	13	6	25	2
Rackemann	42.1	6	112	5	15	4	28	3
Hogan	16	4	62	—	14.4	1	77	1
Maguire	24	2	78	—	9	1	22	—
Hohns	5	2	21	—	8	1	38	—
Haysman					4	1	9	—

AUSTRALIAN XI

	FIRST INNINGS		SECOND INNINGS	
J. Dyson	c Jennings, b Jefferies	29	c Cook, b Page	4
G. Shipperd	b Kourie	59	lbw, b le Roux	6
M.D. Haysman	lbw, b Jefferies	0	not out	3
K.J. Hughes†	c Pollock, b Page	38	not out	17
M.D. Taylor	c Jennings, b Jefferies	109		
T.V. Hohns	c Kourie, b Rice	10		
S.J. Rixon*	c Rice, b Jefferies	20		
T.G. Hogan	c Rice, B Kirsten	53		
J.N. Maguire	c Kirsten, b Page	10		
C.G. Rackemann	c Jennings, b le Roux	8		
R.M. Hogg	not out	12		
Extras	lb 5, w 3, nb 3	11	lb 1, nb 1	2
		359	(for 2 wickets)	32

	O	M	R	W	O	M	R	W
le Roux	24	1	74	1	6	2	23	1
Jefferies	34	10	100	4				
Page	25.3	6	82	2	5	2	7	1
Rice	8	1	20	1				
Kourie	27	6	72	1				
Kirsten	1	1	0	1				

FALL OF WICKETS
1- 124, 2- 130, 3- 133, 4- 148, 5- 184, 6- 186, 7- 237, 8- 327, 9- 359
1- 2, 2- 7, 3- 16, 4- 23, 5- 30, 6- 130, 7- 203

FALL OF WICKETS
1- 51, 2- 51, 3- 115, 4- 160, 5- 185, 6- 236, 7- 315, 8- 331, 9- 343
1- 4, 2- 12

Umpires: D.H. Bezuidenhout & O.R. Schoof

Match drawn

South African innings back to sanity. Fotheringham had not intended to bat because of badly bruised ligaments in his right hand, but his century saved South Africa from embarrassment.

Rice made a token declaration, and the game was brought to an end 16 overs early. It had, however, indicated that the two sides could engage in an entertaining series and that the Australian side seemed to have a bit more mettle in it than the one that had toured England earlier in the year.

Second International Match
SOUTH AFRICAN XI v. AUSTRALIAN XI

South Africa were forced to make one change for the second international match which spanned the New Year festival. McEwan had a virus infection, and he was replaced by McKenzie. The selection of McKenzie, who was to play well in the series, highlighted the problem that confronted South Africa. The Transvaal batsman is 37 years old and, in being called into the national side, he was joining a side of which the majority were veterans. Since South Africa's exclusion from Test cricket younger players have been deprived of an overseas tour which would enable them to develop in skill and temperament. The problem remains for South African cricket, for players like van Zyl, Page, Cullinan, Amm, Rushmere and Norman are desperately in need of wider

experience if they are to succeed Pollock, Rice, Kirsten and the rest. The chances of a tour, for political reasons, are nil, which is why Ali Bacher and the rest strive to give some form of international cricket to the country and keep the game alive.

The Australians made two changes. Yallop and McCurdy came in for Hohns and Maguire.

Clive Rice again won the toss and a large crowd saw South Africa reach 293 for 5 on the opening day. The sun shone, and the happenings in the townships could be forgotten although not by the rest of the world. Cook made an accomplished 91 and shared a second wicket stand of 132 with Peter Kirsten who batted delightfully, but the day again belonged to Graeme Pollock who, from 124 balls, made 79 with a six and 10 fours. Hogan maintained an admirable line and length for 30 overs and was most economical until Pollock got into his stride. The left-hander was out 7 minutes before the close when he was bowled by Hogg.

The lower order batsmen batted with verve on the second day as the pace men shared the bowling. Reared in the modern school, Kim Hughes is not a great believer in slow bowling.

Faced with a daunting 430, the Australians lost Shipperd and Haysman to Jefferies, but Hughes and the reliable Dyson added 105. Hughes fell to Kirsten whose off-spinners, like a good wine, are improving with age and Australia closed at 135 for 3.

SECOND INTERNATIONAL MATCH – SOUTH AFRICAN XI v. AUSTRALIAN XI
1, 2, 3 and 4 January 1986 at Newlands, Cape Town

SOUTH AFRICAN XI

	FIRST INNINGS		SECOND INNINGS	
S.J. Cook	lbw, b McCurdy	91	c Rixon, b Rackemann	70
H.R. Fotheringham	c Rixon, b Rackemann	10	b Rackemann	31
P.N. Kirsten	b Rackemann	72	c Haysman, b Rackemann	20
R.G. Pollock	b Hogg	79	c Dyson, b McCurdy	3
C.E.B. Rice†	c Haysman, b McCurdy	21	not out	27
K.A. McKenzie	lbw, b Hogg	20	(7) not out	18
A.J. Kourie	c Rixon, b Rackemann	8		
G.S. le Roux	c Dyson, b McCurdy	45	(6) c Haysman, b Rackemann	15
R.V. Jennings*	c Dyson b McCurdy	9		
S.T. Jefferies	c Hughes, b Rackemann	22		
H.T. Page	not out	33		
Extras	b 5, lb 8, nb 7	20	lb 15, nb 3	18
		430	(for 5 wkts dec)	202

	O	M	R	W	O	M	R	W
Hogg	29	6	85	2	14	2	43	—
Rackemann	37.2	3	117	4	26	1	105	4
McCurdy	30	2	127	4	12	2	36	1
Hogan	30	6	81					

FALL OF WICKETS
1- 37, 2- 169, 3- 204, 4- 287, 5- 287, 6- 308, 7- 352, 8- 367, 9- 387
1- 86, 2- 121, 3- 128, 4- 156, 5- 176

AUSTRALIAN XI

	FIRST INNINGS		SECOND INNINGS	
J. Dyson	c Jennings, b Kirsten	95	c Jennings, b Page	33
G. Shipperd	b Jefferies	17	lbw, b le Roux	8
M.D. Haysman	b Jefferies	4	lbw, b Rice	33
K.J. Hughes†	b Kirsten	53	not out	97
R.M. Hogg	c Jennings, b Page	0		
M.D. Taylor	c and b Kirsten	22	(5) c McKenzie, b Kourie	17
G.N. Yallop	b le Roux	51	(6) not out	24
S.J. Rixon*	b le Roux	11		
T.G. Hogan	lbw, b le Roux	28		
R.J. McCurdy	not out	4		
C.G. Rackemann	b le Roux	2		
Extras	lb 10, nb 7	17	lb 10, w 1, nb 1	12
		304	(for 4 wickets)	224

	O	M	R	W	O	M	R	W
le Roux	20.3	4	51	4	13	3	23	1
Jefferies	19	3	57	2	13	5	30	—
Page	16	3	39	1	11	2	41	1
Kourie	16	3	58	—	23	7	54	1
Rice	10	3	21	—	13	3	30	1
Kirsten	17	3	61	3	17	4	34	—

FALL OF WICKETS
1- 25, 2- 30, 3- 135, 4- 142, 5- 171, 6- 230, 7- 225, 8- 260, 9- 302
1- 31, 2- 54, 3- 106, 4- 185

Umpires: D.D. Schoof & D.A. Sansom

Match drawn

In fact, Kirsten was more effective than Kourie and captured two more important wickets when he had Dyson caught behind and held a stinging return catch to dismiss Taylor. Dyson batted with his usual determination, and his dismissal was a blow to the Australians who suffered a severe reverse when le Roux bowled Yallop and Rixon in the same over. Hogan and Rackemann also fell to the quick bowler, and the visitors only narrowly averted the follow-on.

By the close, South Africa had extended their lead to 264 for the loss of Fotheringham, Kirsten and Pollock.

The last day promised an excitement which never materialised. Rice batted on for just under an hour and declared, leaving the Australians to make 329 in 95 overs. Nine balls after lunch Dyson was out, and it looked as though South Africa, having dismissed both openers, could snatch victory. Hughes took command, however, and when he and Yallop were together with 20 overs remaining, 131 runs were needed for victory on a wicket that was still true. To most people's surprise, Hughes scorned the challenge. He scored only 5 runs in 15 overs after which he left the field. He was 3 runs short of his century, and his side had accepted a draw when a victory should have been attempted.

6, 7 and 8 January 1986

at St George's Park, Port Elizabeth

South African Universities 219 for 9 dec (T.G. Shaw 66) and 237 for 5 dec (R.F. Pienaar 82)
Australians 220 (B.A. Matthews 4 for 43) and 203 for 9 (M.D. Taylor 70, P.A. Rayment 6 for 62)

Match drawn

An exciting match saw a talented universities side almost snatch victory.

Benson and Hedges Trophy

10 January 1986

at Kingsmead, Durban

Natal 137
Transvaal 104 for 3

Transvaal (2 pts) won on faster scoring rate

Rain restricted the match, but Jim Cook's 47 not out coupled with Radford's bowling brought Transvaal victory.

Castle Currie Cup

10 and 11 January 1986

at Newlands, Cape Town

Western Province 388 for 7 dec (G.S. le Roux 86, P.N. Kirsten 83, A.G. Elgar 81, E.N. Trotman 4 for 94)
Border 115 (G.S. le Roux 4 for 42) and 252 (V.G. Cresswell 51, M.B. Minnaar 4 for 61)

Western Province won by an innings and 21 runs
Western Province 20 pts, Border 2 pts

10, 11 and 13 January 1986

at Ramblers, Bloemfontein

Orange Free State 212 (D.P. le Roux 92) and 198 (T.G. Shaw 7 for 79)
Eastern Province 194 (M.W. Rushmere 78, A.A. Donald 5 for 46) and 220) for 9 (A.V. Birrell 59, D.J. Richardson 50)

Eastern Province won by 1 wicket
Eastern Province 15 pts, Orange Free State 7 pts

A career best 86 by Garth le Roux who hit 4 sixes lifted Western Province to a daunting score after Elgar and Kirsten had put on 153 for the second wicket. Border twice collapsed against the varied home attack, and Western Province scored their second innings victory inside two days. It put them in a position in the Currie Cup where their only real concern was who was to meet them in the final.

In Bloemfontein, Orange Free State, with Darryl le Roux in fine form, reached 150 for 2, and then lost their last 8 wickets for 62 runs. Eastern Province's innings was shaped in the opposite way. They were 53 for 5 and 94 for 6, and their last 3 wickets added 78 runs, 41 of them for the last wicket by Watson and van Vuuren. Tim Shaw returned a career best 7 for 79 in 36 overs to lift Eastern Province's hopes further, and his nagging left-arm spin allied to his useful batting which he had demonstrated when playing for South African Universities against the Australians a few days earlier made many feel that he deserved consideration for the national side. Needing 217 to win, Eastern Province were given a fine start, Birrell and Richardson adding 94 for the 2nd wicket, and they reached 184 for 4, but 5 wickets fell for 19 runs. Rayment joined Watson with 14 runs needed from the last wicket, and he took control to hit 13 not out and win the match.

Neil Burns made his first-class debut for Western Province 'B' against Griqualand West, 10–12 January, 1986. He held the catch behind the wicket which won his side the game by 3 runs. (Adrian Murrell).

Rod McCurdy, full of fire and energy. (Adrian Murrell)

Castle Bowl

10, 11 and 12 January 1986

at De Beers Country Club, Kimberley

Western Province 'B' 252 for 9 dec (G.J. Turner 58, D. Norman 56) and 177 (G.W. Symonds 4 for 57)
Griqualand West 251 (P.J.R. Steyn 53, G.J. Parsons 52, B.A. Matthews 4 for 47) and 175 (L. Potter 57, B.A. Matthews 4 for 32)

Western Province 'B' won by 3 runs
Western Province 'B' 17 pts, Griqualand West 8 pts

10, 11 and 13 January 1986

at Albany Sports Club Ground, Grahamstown

Eastern Province 'B' 189 (D.J. Capel 54, O. Henry 4 for 46) and 278 (I.K. Daniell 116, D.J. Capel 60, I.W. Callen 4 for 71)
Boland 211 (S.A. Jones 53) and 256 (C. Spilhaus 82, S. Nackerdien 60, A.L. Hobson 4 for 39)

Match tied
Boland 12 pts, Eastern Province 'B' 11 pts

Two wonderfully exciting matches began the second half of the season in the Castle Bowl. In Kimberley, Western Province 'B' recovered from the depths of 80 for 6 to reach 252 thanks largely to a violent 56 from Norman and a more careful innings from skipper During. The home side were boosted by a late 50 from Gordon Parsons which meant that only 1 run separated the teams at the end of the first innings. Parsons played a big part in dismissing the visitors for 177 when they batted again, taking 3 for 20 after being unsuccessful in his first spell as the last 4 wickets fell for 14 runs. Griqualand West needed 179 to win, and at 152 for 4, they looked to be heading for a comfortable win. Matthews and Norman returned to the attack, and 5 wickets went down for 14 runs. Symonds joined McLaren for the last wicket, and they nudged the score nearer to the target. Then Matthews found the edge of Symond's bat and Neil Burns, the Essex second team wicket-keeper who was making his first-class debut, held the catch that gave Western Province 'B' victory.

The match at Grahamstown provided an even more sensational finish. With Henry and Jones again to the fore, Boland led by 22 on the first innings, but Ian Daniell's second century of the season which bettered his previous effort and won him promotion to the Currie Cup side swung the game in favour of the home side. Needing 257 to win at well over 3 an over, Boland were given a splendid start. Spilhaus and Vermeulen put on 57 for the first wicket, and Spilhaus and Nackerdien took the score to 172 before they were separated so that victory seemed within easy reach. At 209 for 2, Boland were cruising to a win, but Tony Hobson's leg spin changed matters. Eight wickets fell for 30 runs, and when Coetzee joined Anker Boland were still 18 short of their target. They played with great sense and, never afraid to hit the loose ball, they nudged nearer to a win. With the scores level, Coetzee was run out in going for the run which would have meant victory, and the match was tied.

10, 11 and 13 January 1986

at Berea Park, Pretoria

Australians 229 (M.D. Taylor 66, C.D. Mitchley 4 for 57) and 326 for 2 dec (P.I. Faulkner 109, M.D. Taylor 101 not out, G. Shipperd 79)
Northern Transvaal 190 (C.D. Mitchley 58, R.J. McCurdy 5 for 85) and 340 (R.C. Ontong 85, K.D. Verdoorn 58)
Australians won by 25 runs

A solid first innings batting performance by the Australians was followed by some devastating bowling which reduced Northern Transvaal to 26 for 6 inside an hour. McCurdy, whom many believed to be the fastest bowler in South Africa, had Vernon du Preez caught off the first ball of the innings, and Terry Alderman, striving to prove his fitness, was also in fine form. Verdoorn and Ferreira staged a recovery, and on the second morning, the home side went from 91 for 7 to 190 all out. Shipperd and Faulkner, who had had few opportunities on the tour, began the tourists' second innings with a stand of 161, and Taylor, enjoying a splendid tour, joined Faulkner in a stand of 87. Alderman and Hogg sent back both openers with only 8 scored when the home side batted again, but with McCurdy unable to bowl with a hamstring injury, the Australians struggled to capture the remaining wickets, and Northern Transvaal got closer to victory than had been expected.

Nissan Shield – Semi Final – Third Leg

14 January 1986

at Kingsmead, Durban

Natal 204 for 8 (R.M. Bentley 73)
Western Province 207 for 4 (D.J. Cullinan 57 not out)
Western Province won by 6 wickets

Western Province's season of success continued when they qualified to meet Transvaal in the final of the Nissan Shield.

Third International Match
SOUTH AFRICAN XI v. AUSTRALIAN XI

South Africa included Cornelius van Zyl in their side while the Australians brought in Smith, Faulkner and Alderman for their first matches of the series.

Put in to bat on a lively match, South Africa were soon in trouble when Hogg trimmed Cook's bails, but Australia soon suffered a grave mishap when Hogg was forced to retire from bowling for the rest of the match. He had bowled only 4 overs when he pulled a hamstring, and this placed great strain on Alderman and Rackemann who had to bowl long spells. They responded magnificently, but South Africa were able to hold out to 184 for 8 when rain ended play an hour early. Had Australia not been restricted to three bowlers, it is doubtful that the South African innings would have lasted as late as tea time.

Rixon, who had taken a splendid catch to account for

Steve Smith, the Australian batsman. He impressed all with his temperament and technique, but he was troubled by injury. (Adrian Murrell)

Pollock on the opening day, brought his number of catches to six for the innings when he held van Zyl off Rackemann to end a last wicket stand which had raised the score to 211. South Africa owed much to Kevin McKenzie who had played an attractive innings with some delightful shots off the front foot. The Australian hero was undoubtedly Carl Rackemann, unquestionably Man of the Series, who took a career best 8 for 84 and underlined how valuable he would have been to Border's side in England.

Steve Smith gave the visitors a sparkling start with an aggressive century. He and Greg Shipperd put on 114 in 152 minutes against an attack which looked a little mundane. At tea, the Australians were 156 for 1, in total command, but van Zyl, who maintained an admirable line and length, dismissed Smith and Hughes with successive deliveries, and he also had Yallop caught behind off the last ball of the day which came with Australia on 214 for 5.

Inspired by captain Clive Rice, South Africa climbed back into contention on the third day. Shipperd's dour innings was brought to an end by le Roux, and Rice had Faulkner caught before dismissing Rackemann and Hogg with successive deliveries.

Delighted to be trailing by only 56 runs on the first innings, South Africa moved to 192 for 3 by the close. Rackemann had been forced to retire with heat exhaustion, and Australia were reduced to two bowlers, Alderman and Faulkner, a

THIRD INTERNATIONAL MATCH – SOUTH AFRICAN XI v. AUSTRALIAN XI
16, 17, 18, 20 and 21 January 1986 at Wanderers, Johannesburg

SOUTH AFRICAN XI

	FIRST INNINGS		SECOND INNINGS	
S.J. Cook	b Hogg	5	lbw, b Alderman	21
H.R. Fotheringham	lbw, b Alderman	19	c Rixon, b Rackemann	5
P.N. Kirsten	c Rixon, b Rackemann	12	b Faulkner	10
P.N. Pollock	c Rixon, b Rackemann	19	not out	65
C.E.B. Rice†	c Faulkner, b Rackemann	9	c Rixon, b Rackemann	50
K.A. McKenzie	c Rixon, b Rackemann	72	b Alderman	110
A.J. Kourie	c Rixon, b Rackemann	14	lbw, b Alderman	0
G.S. le Roux	c Alderman, b Rackemann	23	c Rixon, b Rackemann	18
R.V. Jennings*	c Rixon, b Rackemann	0	run out	0
H.A. Page	not out	14	lbw, b Alderman	2
C.J.P.G. van Zyl	c Rixon, b Rackemann	13	c Rixon, b Alderman	2
Extras	b 2, lb 8, nb 1	11	lb 17, w 2, nb 3	22
		211		**305**

AUSTRALIAN XI

	FIRST INNINGS		SECOND INNINGS	
S.B. Smith	c Pollock, b van Zyl	116	c Jennings, b van Zyl	14
J. Dyson	c Rice, b Page	9	not out	18
G. Shipperd	b le Roux	44	b le Roux	3
K.J. Hughes†	lbw, b van Zyl	0	c Jennings, b le Roux	0
M.D. Taylor	c Jennings, b Page	21	lbw, b le Roux	0
G.N. Yallop	c Jennings, b van Zyl	20	b Rice	6
P.I. Faulkner	c McKenzie, b Rice	25	c Fotheringham, b Rice	7
S.J. Rixon*	lbw, b van Zyl	3	b Page	2
C.G. Rackemann	lbw, b Rice	8	b Rice	2
T.M. Alderman	not out	3	c Jennings, b Page	1
R.M. Hogg	b Rice	0	c Jennings, b Page	0
Extras	lb 13, w 1, nb 4	18	b 2, lb 5, nb 1	8
		267		**61**

SOUTH AFRICAN XI bowling (Australian bowlers)

	O	M	R	W	O	M	R	W
Hogg	4	3	3	1				
Alderman	28	6	67	1	37	6	112	4
Rackemann	26.4	3	84	8	30	6	106	4
Faulkner	13	4	46	—	19	—	65	1

	O	M	R	W	O	M	R	W
le Roux	25	6	65	1	7	2	11	3
van Zyl	27	4	82	4	8	3	15	1
Page	26	8	37	2	7.4	—	19	3
Rice	24	8	42	3	6	2	8	3
Kourie	4	—	23	—				

FALL OF WICKETS
1-12, 2-31, 3-51, 4-69, 5-155, 6-166, 7-166, 8-166, 9-191
1-25, 2-31, 3-80, 4-204, 5-207, 6-242, 7-242, 8-258, 9-274

FALL OF WICKETS
1-45, 2-159, 3-159, 4-192, 5-214, 6-230, 7-237, 8-263, 9-267
1-24, 2-29, 3-29, 4-29, 5-36, 6-48, 7-53, 8-60, 9-61

Umpires: O.R. Schoof & D.D. Schoof

South African XI won by 188 runs

South African XI v. Australian XI – Averages

SOUTH AFRICAN BATTING

	M	Inns	NOs	Runs	HS	Av	100s	50s
K.A. McKenzie	2	4	1	220	110	73.33	1	1
R.G. Pollock	3	6	1	280	108	56.00	1	2
H.R. Fotheringham	3	6	1	235	100*	47.00	1	1
S.J. Cook	3	6		241	91	40.16		3
H.A. Page	3	4	2	59	33*	29.50		
C.E.B. Rice	3	6	1	127	50	25.40		1
G.S. le Roux	3	6		138	45	23.00		
P.N. Kirsten	3	6		121	72	20.16		1
R.V. Jennings	3	4		55	46	13.75		
A.J. Kourie	3	5		67	44	13.40		

Played in two matches: S.T. Jefferies 43* & 22
Played in one match: K.S. McEwan 4 & 5; C.J.P.G. van Zyl 13 & 2

AUSTRALIAN BATTING

	M	Inns	NOs	Runs	HS	Av	100s	50s
K.J. Hughes	3	6	2	105	97*	51.25		2
J. Dyson	3	6	1	188	95	37.60		1
M.D. Taylor	3	5		169	109	33.80	1	
G.N. Yallop	2	4	1	101	51	33.66		1
G. Shipperd	3	6		137	59	22.83		1
M.D. Haysman	2	4	1	40	33	13.33		
S.J. Rixon	3	4		36	20	9.00		
C.G. Rackemann	3	4		20	8	5.00		
R.M. Hogg	3	4	1	12	12*	4.00		

Played in two matches: T.G. Hogan 53 & 28
Played in one match: T.V. Hohns 10; J.N. Maguire 10; R.J. McCurdy 4*; Smith 116 & 14; P.I. Faulkner 25 & 7; T.M. Alderman 3* & 1

SOUTH AFRICAN BOWLING

	Overs	Mds	Runs	Wkts	Av	Best	10/m	5/inn
C.E.B. Rice	61	17	121	8	15.12	3/8		
C.J.P.G. van Zyl	35	7	97	5	19.40	4/82		
G.S. le Roux	95.3	18	247	11	22.45	4/51		
H.A. Page	91.1	21	225	10	22.50	3/19		
P.N. Kirsten	35	8	95	4	23.75	3/61		
S.T. Jefferies	66	18	187	6	31.16	4/100		
A.J. Kourie	70	16	207	2	103.50	1/54		

AUSTRALIAN BOWLING

	Overs	Mds	Runs	Wkts	Av	Best	10/m	5/inn
C.G. Rackemann	177.1	23	552	28	19.71	8/84	1	2
R.M. Hogg	92	30	239	10	23.90	5/83		1
R.J. McCurdy	42	4	163	5	32.60	4/127		
T.M. Alderman	65	12	179	5	35.80	4/112		
P.I. Faulkner	32	4	111	1	111.00	1/65		
T.G. Hogan	60.4	11	220	1	220.00	1/77		
T.V. Hohns	13	3	59	0	—			
J.N. Maguire	33	3	100	0	—			

Bowled in one innings: M.D. Haysman 4 - 1 - 9 - 0

SOUTH AFRICAN CATCHES
13 - R.V. Jennings; 3 - C.E.B. Rice; 2 - P.N. Kirsten, R.G. Pollock and K.A. McKenzie; 1 - S.J. Cook, H.R. Fotheringham and A.J. Kourie

AUSTRALIAN CATCHES
19 - S.J. Rixon; 7 - M.D. Haysman; 4 - J. Dyson; 2 - K.J. Hughes and T.G. Hogan; 1 - P.I. Faulkner and T.M. Alderman

state of affairs of which the South African batsmen took full advantage over the last session. In fairness to South Africa, it should be mentioned that they too suffered a serious mishap when Pollock, on 51, had to retire hurt with a broken bone in his right hand.

The fourth day was mutilated by rain, and South Africa entered the last day with a lead of 217 and 2 wickets standing. They lost van Zyl in the second over of the last day which brought back Pollock, against doctor's orders, and he bravely remained for 11 overs while Kevin McKenzie reached his maiden century for his country. He hit a six and 10 fours, and his dismissal left the Australians $5\frac{1}{4}$ hours in which to mke 250 to win. Rixon's ten catches in the match equalled the South African record.

There was no sign of any problems for the batsmen as Smith and Dyson began in workmanlike fashion. In the eighth over, van Zyl found the outside edge of Smith's bat and Jennings took the catch. The standard of wicket-keeping in the series was refreshingly high, and one must consider that this important aspect of the game is being devalued in other parts of the world.

At 29, Shipperd lost his off-stump to le Roux, and next ball Hughes was caught behind, out first ball for the second time in the match. Taylor pushed forward tentatively at his first delivery and was lbw to give le Roux the hat-trick and leave the Australian innings in shreds.

Clive Rice brought himself on to bowl after lunch and with his first ball he bowled Yallop so giving him a hat-trick which had begun when he dismissed Rackemann and Hogg with the last two balls of the first innings. He took two more wickets and Page picked up three so that the Australians were all out in 28.4 overs, and Dyson had carried his bat for 18.

The win was a great triumph for Rice and his men. It had been a match of fluctuating fortunes and heroic deeds, and, uniquely, of two hat tricks.

The reactions in South Africa were, naturally, ones of pleasure, but there was an article in *South African Cricketer* which argued that the public were deceived if they thought that they had been watching Test cricket, and that South African lovers of the game had to face the fact that the world would not play with the sporting representatives of their country until South Africa changed its society. Both statements are true, but they should not detract from the fact that the series had given much enjoyment, produced some fine cricket and stimulated interest in the game in the republic

Benson and Hedges Trophy

22 January 1986

at St George's Park, Port Elizabeth

Eastern Province 214 (M. Michau 58, H.A. Page 4 for 34)
Transvaal 171

Eastern Province (2 pts) won by 43 runs

A surprise win for Eastern Province kept alive their hopes of qualifying for the semi-finals.

RIGHT: *Haysman, the young Australian batsman who has also played for Leicestershire, impressed all with his fine fielding. (Adrian Murrell)*

Castle Bowl

23, 24 and 25 January 1986

at Berea Park, Pretoria

Boland 180 (A. Watts 57) and 224 (F. de Villiers 4 for 48)
Northern Transvaal 'B' 147 (I.W. Callen 5 for 59) and 249 (F.L. Symcox 64, O. Henry 7 for 82)

Boland won by 8 runs
Boland 16 pts, Northern Transvaal 'B' 5 pts

Another close game ended in victory for Boland which put them firmly at the top of the Castle Bowl log. Ian Callen, the former Australian Test bowler, took 5 for 59 to give them a first innings lead of 33, and a solid second innings batting performance meant that they left the home side to make 258 to win. Northern Transvaal 'B' lost 6 wickets for 142, but the last 4 wickets added 107, Symcox and Ackermann sharing a defiant seventh wicket stand of 62. It was Omar Henry's slow left-arm which brought Boland victory as he continued his memorably successful season with the ball.

First One-Day International
SOUTH AFRICAN XI v. AUSTRALIAN XI

For the first match in the six-game series, the South African selectors gave international baptism to Rob Bentley (Natal), Roy Pienaar (Northern Transvaal) and Eric Simons (Western Province). South Africa disappointed after their victory in the international series. Dyson and Smith, who won the batting prize, gave Australia a solid start, but Rice bowled a splendidly containing and attacking spell which won him the

bowling award. Having restricted their opponents to 197, South Africa could never get into their stride with the bat and slipped limply to defeat.

Michael Haysman, who had thrilled crowds everywhere with his energetic fielding, was awarded the fielding prize in this day/night match.

Second One-Day International
SOUTH AFRICAN XI v. AUSTRALIAN XI

Recovering from 42 for 4 to 221 in their 50 overs, South Africa owed everything to Henry Fotheringham and Clive Rice who played some wonderful cricket in their stand of 130. Rice, who was to win 4 awards in the six matches, won

FIRST ONE-DAY INTERNATIONAL – SOUTH AFRICAN XI v. AUSTRALIAN XI
24 January 1986 at Wanderers, Johannesburg

AUSTRALIAN XI

J. Dyson	c Jennings, b le Roux	57
S.B. Smith	c Rice, b le Roux	56
K.J. Hughes†	b Rice	21
M.D. Taylor	not out	29
M.D. Haysman	lbw, b Rice	16
T.G. Hogan	c and b Rice	0
P.I. Faulkner	not out	3
G. Shipperd*		
R.M. Hogg		
T.M. Alderman		
C.G. Rackemann		
Extras		15
(50 overs)	(for 5 wickets)	197

	O	M	R	W
le Roux	10	—	33	2
van Zyl	10	1	35	—
Simons	10	2	37	—
Page	10	—	53	—
Rice	10	—	29	3

FALL OF WICKETS
1- 116, 2- 125, 3- 145, 4- 189, 5- 189

SOUTH AFRICAN XI

S.J. Cook	c Shipperd, b Rackemann	2
H.R. Fotheringham	c Haysman, b Hogg	33
R.M. Bentley	c and b Hogan	35
K.A. McKenzie	run out	24
C.E.B. Rice†	lbw, b Hogan	2
R.F. Pienaar	c Shipperd, b Rackemann	2
G.S. le Roux	b Faulkner	11
R.V. Jennings*	run out	1
H.A. Page	b Hogg	5
E.O. Simons	not out	13
C.J.P.G. van Zyl	b Hogan	3
Extras		20
(47.5 overs)		151

	O	M	R	W
Rackemann	10	2	23	2
Alderman	10	1	24	—
Hogg	8	1	28	2
Faulkner	10	—	32	1
Hogan	9.5	—	25	3

FALL OF WICKETS
1- 2, 2- 78, 3- 80, 4- 82, 5- 93, 6- 113, 7- 114, 8- 125, 9- 144

Australian XI won by 46 runs

SECOND ONE-DAY INTERNATIONAL – SOUTH AFRICAN XI v. AUSTRALIAN XI
26 January 1986 at Kingsmead, Durban

SOUTH AFRICAN XI

S.J. Cook	lbw, b Alderman	10
R.F. Pienaar	c Rixon, b Alderman	6
R.M. Bentley	c Rixon, b Hogg	1
H.R. Fotheringham	c Hogan, b Rackemann	71
K.A. McKenzie	b Hogan	10
C.E.B. Rice†	c Rixon, b Alderman	91
G.S. le Roux	not out	24
R.V. Jennings*		
E.O. Simons		
H.A. Page		
C.J.P.G. van Zyl		
Extras		8
(50 overs)	(for 6 wickets)	221

	O	M	R	W
Rackemann	10	1	43	1
Alderman	10	3	29	3
Hogan	10	—	55	1
Hogg	10	2	32	1
Faulkner	10	—	57	—

FALL OF WICKETS
1- 16, 2- 21, 3- 21, 4- 42, 5- 172, 6- 221

AUSTRALIAN XI

S.B. Smith	c Rice, b Page	70
J. Dyson	c sub, b Page	41
M.D. Haysman	c le Roux, b Rice	37
K.J. Hughes†	run out	15
M.D. Taylor	lbw, b le Roux	22
P.I. Faulkner	c Pienaar, b le Roux	15
T.G. Hogan	not out	1
S.J. Rixon*	not out	9
R.M. Hogg		
T.M. Alderman		
C.G. Rackemann		
Extras		14
(49.3 overs)	(for 6 wickets)	224

	O	M	R	W
le Roux	10	1	41	2
van Zyl	10	—	29	—
Page	10	1	33	2
Simons	9	—	66	—
Rice	9.3	1	34	1
Bentley	1	—	9	—

FALL OF WICKETS
1- 94, 2- 155, 3- 172, 4- 181, 5- 213, 6- 213, 6- 213

Australian XI won by 4 wickets

the batting prize, but his effort was still not enough to give his side victory. Smith and Dyson again gave their team a fine start, and the momentum was maintained so that Australia won the match with 3 balls to spare.

Third One-Day International
SOUTH AFRICAN XI v. AUSTRALIAN XI

South Africa, needing to win in Port Elizabeth to stay in the series, brought in Lee Barnard (Northern Transvaal) and Tim Shaw (Eastern Province) for their first representative games in place of Pienaar and Simons who had disappointing games at Durban. Surprisingly, they still failed to recall McEwan, now fit again, and Kirsten.

Cook was soon hitting the ball well, but Bentley, Barnard and Fotheringham fell quickly and when Cook became Maguire's second victim South Africa were 66 for 4. Once more Clive Rice came to the rescue, shared a stand of 113 with McKenzie and steered his side to 223 in their 50 overs.

Without Smith, Australia made a poor start. Yallop and Haysman went without scoring, and Dyson, having played with his customary soundness, became le Roux's third victim. Hughes and Taylor offered resistance, and McCurdy and Rackemann hit some fierce blows at the end, but le Roux's bowling had put South Africa in an impregnable position long before this.

Benson and Hedges Trophy

29 January 1986

at Jan Smuts Ground, Pietermaritzburg

Impalas 94 (H.F. Dammann 5 for 37)
Natal 98 for 3

Natal (2 pts) won by 7 wickets

Fourth One-Day International
SOUTH AFRICAN XI v. AUSTRALIAN XI

Kirsten and McEwan returned to the South African side and were to play an important part in an enthralling match which saw South Africa level the series. For the fourth time in as many matches, the game was watched by a capacity crowd.

Rice won the toss and decided to bat. His side began well on an easy paced pitch, but neither Cook nor Fotheringham could build on their promising start. McEwan and Kirsten added 46, but they too fell as they attempted to force the pace. Rice and McKenzie added 65, and le Roux hit 15 runs in one over from Rackemann, but 234 looked a total short of what had been expected. Seven batsmen had played well, but not one of them had stayed long enough to make the big score that was needed.

In reply, Dyson and Shipperd seemed to have set Australia on the path to victory with an opening stand of 63, and Hughes and Taylor came together to add 92 in 20 overs for the third wicket. At 173 for 2, the visitors were cruising to victory, for 61 were needed in 10 overs with 8 wickets standing so that risks could be afforded.

Hughes reached a delightful fifty with a six, but le Roux returned to have him caught behind. This signalled a collapse, and a mixture of panic and inefficiency saw Australia slip to defeat by 24 runs.

Castle Currie Cup

31 January, 1 and 3 February 1986

at Jan Smuts Ground, East London

Border 479 for 5 dec (S.F.A. Bacchus 134, A.L. Wilmot 108 not out, E.N. Trotman 74, G.L. Long 73)
Orange Free State 363 for 8 (J.J. Strydom 100 not out, R.J. East 76, B.C. Broad 65, I. Foulkes 4 for 99)

THIRD ONE-DAY INTERNATIONAL – SOUTH AFRICAN XI v. AUSTRALIAN XI
28 January 1986 at St George's Park, Port Elizabeth

SOUTH AFRICAN XI

S.J. Cook	c Taylor, b Maguire	45
R.M. Bentley	c Rixon, b Alderman	7
L.J. Barnard	b Alderman	1
H.R. Fotheringham	lbw, b Maguire	7
K.A. McKenzie	c Haysman, b McCurdy	62
C.E.B. Rice†	not out	78
G.S. le Roux	c Taylor, b Rackemann	6
T.G. Shaw	b Rackemann	1
R.V. Jennings*	c Rixon, b Rackemann	0
H.A. Page	c Taylor, b McCurdy	1
C.J.P.G. van Zyl	not out	0
Extras		15
(50 overs)	(for 9 wickets)	223

	O	M	R	W
Rackemann	10	2	41	3
Alderman	10	3	28	2
McCurdy	10	—	40	2
Faulkner	10	1	49	—
Maguire	10	—	53	2

FALL OF WICKETS
1- 41, 2- 43, 3- 66, 4- 66, 5- 179, 6- 189, 7- 196, 8- 196, 9- 205

AUSTRALIAN XI

G.N. Yallop	c Jennings, b le Roux	0
J. Dyson	c Jennings, b le Roux	7
M.D. Haysman	c Jennings, b le Roux	0
K.J. Hughes†	c Page, b Shaw	31
M.D. Taylor	b Rice	43
P.I. Faulkner	run out	5
S.J. Rixon*	b Rice	0
J.N. Maguire	b Rice	7
R.J. McCurdy	c Shaw, b le Roux	32
C.G. Rackemann	not out	15
T.M. Alderman	c Rice, b le Roux	3
Extras		8
(40.1 overs)		151

	O	M	R	W
le Roux	8.1	2	13	5
van Zyl	8	—	33	—
Page	7	—	21	—
Shaw	10	—	53	1
Rice	7	—	25	3

FALL OF WICKETS
1- 0, 2- 6, 3- 39, 4- 71, 5- 77, 6- 78, 7- 99, 8- 104, 9- 141

South African XI won by 72 runs

Garth le Roux, South Africa's opening bowler and hard-hitting batsman. (Adrian Murrell)

Match drawn
Border 10 pts, Orange Free State 5 pts

Castle Bowl

1, 2 and 3 February 1986

at R.J.E. Burt Oval, Constantia

Western Province 'B' 186 and 138 (J.C. van Duyker 4 for 31)
Northern Transvaal 'B' 136 and 69 (J. During 5 for 20)

Western Province 'B' won by 119 runs
Western Province 'B' 16 pts, Northern Transvaal 'B' 5 pts

The Currie Cup game between the newcomers was saturated with runs and ended in stalemate. Trotman and Wilmot added 118 for Border's fifth wicket, and Orange Free State, 35 for 3, were rescued by East and Broad who put on 120.

In contrast, no batsman reached fifty in the Castle Bowl match in Constantia where Western Province 'B' maintained their challenge on Boland at the top of the table. The oustanding performance came from skipper John During who hit 27 not out and 17 and had match figures of 8 for 53 with his medium pace, including a career best 5 for 20 in the second innings.

Fifth One-Day International
SOUTH AFRICAN XI v. AUSTRALIAN XI

South Africa gave national recognition to Anton Ferreira, and he won the bowling prize for a spell that was both threatening and economical. He dismissed both openers after they had threatened to build a big score and cut down Hughes when he too promised to put Australia in a dominant position. In fact, the Australians could never establish a pace to their innings, and South Africa, again inspired by Rice, moved to a comfortable win and a 3–2 lead in the series.

FOURTH ONE-DAY INTERNATIONAL – SOUTH AFRICAN XI v. AUSTRALIAN XI
30 January 1986 at Newlands, Cape Town

SOUTH AFRICAN XI

S.J. Cook	b Alderman	30
H.R. Fotheringham	lbw, b McCurdy	22
P.N. Kirsten	b Maguire	26
K.S. McEwan	c Shipperd, b Hogan	22
C.E.B. Rice†	c Shipperd, b Rackemann	44
K.A. McKenzie	b Maguire	34
G.S. le Roux	b Alderman	32
T.G. Shaw	c Dyson, b Rackemann	3
R.V. Jennings*	not out	7
H.A. Page	c Taylor, b Alderman	0
C.J.P.G. van Zyl	not out	0
Extras		14
(50 overs)	(for 9 wickets)	234

	O	M	R	W
Rackemann	10	—	60	2
Alderman	10	1	33	3
McCurdy	10	1	49	1
Hogan	10	1	40	1
Maguire	10	—	40	2

FALL OF WICKETS
1- 44, 2- 58, 3- 104, 4- 104, 5- 169, 6- 214, 7- 226, 8- 228, 9- 233

AUSTRALIAN XI

J. Dyson	c McKenzie, b Rice	33
G. Shipperd*	c and b Shaw	35
K.J. Hughes†	c Jennings, b le Roux	60
M.D. Taylor	b Rice	36
M.D. Haysman	run out	15
T.V. Hohns	c Cook, b Rice	8
T.G. Hogan	b Rice	5
J.N. Maguire	not out	3
R.J. McCurdy	run out	1
C.G. Rackemann	run out	0
T.M. Alderman	b le Roux	0
Extras		14
(49 overs)		210

	O	M	R	W
le Roux	10	—	34	2
van Zyl	8	1	27	—
Page	10	—	40	—
Shaw	8	—	40	1
Rice	10	—	45	4
Kirsten	3	—	13	—

FALL OF WICKETS
1- 63, 2- 81, 3- 173, 4- 179, 5- 195, 6- 206, 7- 207, 8- 209, 9- 210

South African XI won by 24 runs

FIFTH ONE-DAY INTERNATIONAL – SOUTH AFRICAN XI *v.* AUSTRALIAN XI
1 February 1986 at Wanderers, Johannesburg

AUSTRALIAN XI

S.B. Smith	c Cook, b Ferreira	20
J. Dyson	lbw, b Ferreira	32
K.J. Hughes†	c le Roux, b Ferreira	25
M.D. Taylor	c Jennings, b le Roux	11
G.N. Yallop	run out	42
G. Shipperd*	c Jennings, b Page	17
T.G. Hogan	b Page	0
J.N. Maguire	not out	21
R.J. McCurdy	not out	7
R.M. Hogg		
T.M. Alderman		
Extras	lb 9, w 1	10
(49 overs)	(for 7 wickets)	185

	O	M	R	W
le Roux	10	2	40	1
van Zyl	10	2	29	—
Page	10	—	38	2
Ferreira	10	1	31	3
Rice	9	—	38	—

FALL OF WICKETS
1- 36, 2- 76, 3- 85, 4- 105, 5- 139, 6- 139, 7- 165

SOUTH AFRICAN XI

S.J. Cook	c Shipperd, b Alderman	12
H.R. Fotheringham	c Shipperd, b Maguire	43
P.N. Kirsten	c sub, b Maguire	24
K.S. McEwan	b Hogan	22
C.E.B. Rice†	not out	34
K.A. McKenzie	c Hughes, b Dyson	28
G.S. le Roux	not out	6
K.V. Jennings*		
A.M. Ferreira		
H.A. Page		
C.J.P.G. van Zyl		
Extras	lb 13, w 2, nb 5	20
(39.4 overs)	(for 5 wickets)	189

	O	M	R	W
Hogg	10	2	30	—
Alderman	5	—	21	1
McCurdy	10	—	44	—
Maguire	10	—	56	2
Hogan	4	—	18	1
Dyson	0.4	—	7	1

FALL OF WICKETS
1- 15, 2- 85, 3- 93, 4- 140, 5- 183

South African XI won by 5 wickets

---

3 February 1986

at de Beers Country Club, Kimberley

Australians 219 for 9 (M.D. Taylor 50)
Griqualand West 221 for 4 (L. Potter 120, F.W. Swarbrook 65)

Griqualand West won by 4 wickets

Swashbuckling innings by two English county players saw Griqualand West to a surprisingly easy victory with 3 overs to spare.

Sixth One-Day International
SOUTH AFRICAN XI *v.* AUSTRALIAN XI

South Africa took the series by 4 matches to 2 after losing the first two matches, a remarkable performance. The tourists were again well served by John Dyson who still looked to be the most reliable Australian born opener in the world, and their 272 from 50 overs, by far the highest score of the series, seemed to have assured them of victory. Clive Rice had other ideas, however. South Africa were 69 for 3 when he came to the wicket. He dominated a stand of 105 with Jim Cook and scored 99 with Kevin McKenzie which took his side to success with 10 balls to spare. In the later part of his innings he was handicapped by a foot injury, received when he was hit on the foot by a ball from Rackemann, and this injury was to hamper him for the rest of the season. He was named as Man of the Series and took the batting prize for the fourth time in 6 matches. Many believed that this great all-rounder was playing better than at any time in his career.

So the Australian tour, part one, came to an end. The tourists had been enthusiastically received by the crowds, but

Clive Rice – South Africa's Player of the Year. (Tony Edenden)

SIXTH ONE-DAY INTERNATIONAL – SOUTH AFRICAN XI v. AUSTRALIAN XI
5 February 1986 at Berea Park, Pretoria

AUSTRALIAN XI

S.B. Smith	c McEwan, b Ferreira	29
J. Dyson	c Kirsten, b le Roux	115
K.J. Hughes†	c McEwan, b Ferreira	46
M.D. Taylor	c Cook, b van Zyl	49
G.N. Yallop	b Rice	14
T.G. Hogan	b Rice	1
J.N. Maguire	not out	1
R.J. McCurdy	not out	0
G. Shipperd*		
C.G. Rackemann		
T.M. Alderman		
Extras	lb 13, w 3, nb 1	17
(50 overs)	(for 6 wickets)	272

	O	M	R	W
le Roux	10	1	55	1
van Zyl	10	1	57	1
Page	10	—	38	—
Ferreira	10	2	55	2
Rice	10	—	54	2

FALL OF WICKETS
1- 67, 2- 160, 3- 232, 4- 270, 5- 271, 6- 272

SOUTH AFRICAN XI

S.J. Cook	lbw, b Rackemann	76
H.R. Fotheringham	c Shipperd, b Rackemann	13
P.N. Kirsten	b McCurdy	23
K.S. McEwan	run out	1
C.E.B. Rice†	not out	95
K.A. McKenzie	not out	57
A.M. Ferreira		
G.S. le Roux		
R.V. Jennings*		
H.A. Page		
C.J.P.G. van Zyl		
Extras	lb 5, w 1, nb 2	8
(48.2 overs)	(for 4 wickets)	273

	O	M	R	W
Rackemann	10	1	52	2
Alderman	10	1	34	—
McCurdy	9.2	—	54	1
Hogan	10	1	59	—
Maguire	9	—	69	—

FALL OF WICKETS
1- 19, 2- 63, 3- 69, 4- 174

South African XI won by 6 wickets

---

they had suffered severely from injuries. In their final match against a provincial side, versus Griqualand West, they had to coax Graham McKenzie out of retirement to fill a gap. McKenzie, aged 44, performed creditably, but the Australians, and their manager Bruce Francis, will need to look to the problem of fitness before the 1986–87 tour.

Castle Currie Cup

7, 8 and 9 February 1986

at St George's Park, Port Elizabeth

Eastern Province 167 (R.K. McGlashan 5 for 53) and 274 (M.W. Rushmere 128, G.R. Dilley 4 for 32, R.M. Bentley 4 for 37)
Natal 454 for 7 dec (B.J. Whitfield 140, C.L. King 77, R.M. Bentley 76, M.B. Logan 72, D. Bestall 65 not out)

Natal won by an innings and 13 runs
Natal 17 pts, Eastern Province 0 pts

7, 8 and 10 February 1986

at Ramblers Ground, Bloemfontein

Northern Transvaal 272 (R.F. Pienaar 90, N.T. Day 62, A.M. Green 4 for 59) and 206 (A.A. Donald 5 for 43)
Orange Free State 324 (A.M. Green 104, B.C. Broad 56, W.F. Morris 4 for 76) and 148 (W.F. Morris 6 for 66)

Northern Transvaal won by 8 runs
Northern Transvaal 19 pts, Orange Free State 10 pts

8, 9 and 10 February 1986

at Newlands, Cape Town

Transvaal 364 (S.J. Cook 124, B.M. McMillan 85, H.A. Page 51, G.S. le Roux 4 for 52) and 188 for 4 dec
Western Province 223 (K.S. McEwan 56) and 153 for 4

Match drawn
Transvaal 7 pts, Western Province 4 pts

The last round of matches in the Currie Cup provided some excellent performances, and Northern Transvaal's victory over Orange Free State lifted them into the semi-final.

Northern Transvaal's win was an exciting one. Alan Green's best bowling performance with his medium pace was followed by a fine century which gave Orange Free State a first innings lead of 52. The combined seam bowling of Donald, van Zyl and Green gave Orange Free State further advantage as the visitors were bowled out for 206 so that Broad's men needed only 157 to win. They passed the hundred for the loss of 5 wickets, and victory seemed in their grasp, but off-spin from Rodney Ontong and Willie Morris brought down the last 5 wickets for 38 runs so that Northern Transvaal snatched victory by 8 runs and a place in the semi-final above Natal and Eastern Province who had come pointless from their last game. Morris, 10 for 140 in the match, had career best bowling figures of 6 for 66 in the second innings.

A brave century by Mark Rushmere, the highest score of his career, failed to save Eastern Province at Port Elizabeth where Natal, sparked by an opening stand of 144 between Whitfield and Logan, ran to a massive score.

Western Province, already assured of a place in the final as the undisputed league winners, disappointed their supporters at Newlands who had expected them to beat Transvaal who were without Rice with a broken toe, Pollock with a broken bone in his hand and McKenzie with a groin strain. Western Province lacked the services of Jefferies who had missed the one-day internationals with a broken toe. It seemed that Western Province missed Jefferies more than Transvaal missed their star performers, for Cook, acting captain, led his side to a formidable score after they had lost their first 2 wickets for 37. Most impressive was Brian McMillan who hit an exciting 85 on his first team debut. Western Province batted indifferently, but a draw always looked likely.

Castle Currie Cup – Final Table

	P	W	L	D	Pts
Western Province	6	4	—	2	91
Transvaal	6	2	—	4	67
Northern Transvaal	6	1	1	4	57
Natal	6	1	1	4	52
Eastern Province	6	1	2	3	39
Border	6	1	2	3	36
Orange Free State	6	—	4	2	36

Transvaal at home to Northern Transvaal, the winner to meet Western Province, in Cape Town, for the Currie Cup.

Castle Bowl

7, 8 and 9 February 1986

at Jan Smuts Ground, Pietermaritzburg

Natal 'B' 367 (C. Lowe 64, A.C. Hudson 58, J.A. O'Donoghue 53, A.L. Hobson 7 for 114) and 204 for 5 dec
Eastern Province 'B' 279 (J.W. Furstenburg 122, J.A. O'Donoghue 5 for 102) and 292 (T.B. Reid 87, D.G. Emslie 69)

Match tied
Natal 'B' 13 pts, Eastern Province 'B' 13 pts

at Wanderers, Johannesburg

Transvaal 'B' 248 (J.J. Kerr 74, G.E. McMillan 59, B.A. Matthews 5 for 32) and 193 for 3 dec (C.R. Norris 101 not out, K.J. Rule 61 not out)
Western Province 'B' 126 for 7 dec and 3 for 1

Match drawn
Transvaal 'B' 6 pts, Western Province 'B' 4 pts

Eastern Province 'B' engaged in their second tied match of the season, an amazing game on the Jan Smuts Ground. Natal 'B''s last 3 wickets produced 113 runs, O'Donoghue and Lowe being the only batsmen to counter effectively the leg-spin of Tony Hobson who returned the best bowling performance of his career. O'Donoghue then bowled well, and his spin troubled all batsmen except Furstenberg, the left-handed opener, who held the innings together in his first match of the season. Natal 'B' scored briskly in their second innings and Mellor declared. Set to make 293, Eastern Province 'B' lost Furstenberg at 19 and Keevey at 107, but Reid and Emslie gave the challenge some substance. The visitors reached 268 for the loss of only 6 wickets, but 2 wickets fell at that score and the odds moved in favour of Natal 'B'. When the last pair came together 7 were needed and time was running out. Six were scored and Dakin was run out as he went for what would have been the winning run.

Rain ruined the game at Wanderers and with it any hope Western Province 'B' had of depriving Boland of the title. Norris and Rule shared an unbeaten fourth wicket stand of 147, and there was some impressive left-arm pace bowling from Brett Matthews.

Benson and Hedges Trophy

12 February 1986

at Technicon Ground, Pretoria

Northern Transvaal 211 for 9 (R.F. Pienaar 58)
Eastern Province 202

Northern Transvaal (2 pts) won by 9 runs

Castle Bowl

13, 14 and 15 February 1986

at de Beers Country Club, Kimberley

Griqualand West 282 (F.W. Swarbrook 104 not out, G.J. Parsons 50, G.L. Ackermann 5 for 48) and 206 for 7 dec (L. Potter 70, J.C. van Duyker 4 for 71)
Northern Transvaal 'B' 190 (P.L. Symcox 51) and 154 for 6 (P.L. Symcox 52)

Match drawn
Northern Transvaal 'B' 8 pts, Griqualand West 6 pts

The most notable thing about the match at Kimberley was the performance of Fred Swarbrook who opened the innings and carried his bat for 104. When the ninth wicket fell Griqualand West were 228 for 9, but McLaren stayed with Swarbrook while 54 runs were scored and the left-hander reached his hundred. Fred Swarbrook's career began in 1967 when, at the age of 16 years, 6 months, he was the youngest player ever to appear for Derbyshire. Nineteen years, and more than 4000 runs and 400 wickets later, he had reached his maiden first-class century.

Castle Currie Cup – Semi-Final

14, 15, 16 and 17 February 1986

at Wanderers, Johannesburg

Transvaal 319 (B.M. McMillan 80, M.S. Ventre 63) and 320 for 9 dec (K.A. McKenzie 84, H.R. Fotheringham 64, B.M. McMillan 53, S.J. Cook 51, I.F.N. Weidemann 4 for 60)
Northern Transvaal 218 (R.F. Pienaar 74, N.V. Radford 5 for 57) and 144 (K.D. Verdoorn 55, R.C. Ontong 50, S.T. Clarke 6 for 19)

Transvaal won by 277 runs

As expected, Transvaal qualified to meet Western Province in the Currie Cup final. Transvaal were still without Pollock and Rice, but although they lost Yachad at 8 and Cook at 54, they were never in danger of defeat. There were more impressive batting displays by Brian McMillan, and Sylvester Clarke whom many had thought to be past his best after two knee operations inside twelve months took 6 for 19 in 11 overs in the second innings to maintain his reputation as being the most feared bowler in South Africa.

Nissan Shield Final
WESTERN PROVINCE v. TRANSVAAL

The might of Transvaal was asserted once again as they paced their innings to perfection to reach the target of 231 with an over to spare. It was the fourth year in succession that Transvaal had won the trophy, and the seventh time that

Australians in South Africa 1985–86
First Class Matches

BATTING

BATTING	v. Orange Free State (Bloemfontein) 22–25 Nov. 1985		v. President's XI (Pretoria) 29 Nov.–2 Dec. 1985		v. Border (East London) 6–8 December 1985		v. Eastern Province (Port Elizabeth) 13–15 Dec. 1985		v. Boland (Stellenbosch) 17–19 Dec. 1985		First International (Durban) 26–29 Dec. 1985		Second International (Cape Town) 1–4 January 1986		v. S.A. Universities (Port Elizabeth) 6–8 January 1986		v. Northern Transvaal (Pretoria) 10–13 January 1986		Third International (Johannesburg) 16–21 January 1986	
J. Dyson	141	52	0	28	62	—	5	71*			29	4	95	33	29	1			9	18*
S.B. Smith	47	—	6	17	29	—	40	13	112	—			51	24*	15	20			116	14
G.N. Yallop	35	62			6		7	—	26	—									20	6
K.J. Hughes	17	3	73	16			72	—	116	—	38	17*	53	97*	1	22	33	27*	0	0
M.D. Haysman	14	7	4	4	39	—	125*	—	41	—	0	3*	4	33	40	12				
M.D. Taylor	42	102*	1	19*	54	—			1	—	109	—	22	17	43	70	66	101*	21	0
T.V. Hohns	14	46			23	—			90	—	10	—			2	6	15	—		
S.J. Rixon	17*	21*	5	5*	0	—	28	—			20	—	11	—			14	—	3	2
R.J. McCurdy	1	—					17	—					4*	—			14	—		
C.G. Rackemann	—	—	11	—	—	—	0	—	1*	—	8	—	2	—					8	2
T.M. Alderman	—	—	0	—					1*	—					19	0*	0*	—	3*	1
G. Shipperd			37	0			6	14*	16	—	59	6	17	8	14	48	46	79	44	3
J.N. Maguire			20	—	0*	—			2*	—	10	—			10	2*	8	—		
R.M. Hogg			9*	—					—	—	12*	—	0	—			13	—	0	0
T.G. Hogan					2	—	63	—	4	—	53	—	28	—			12	7	—	
P.I. Faulkner					9*	—			32	—					31*	6	7	109	25	7
Byes	2	1			8				5							1		1		2
Leg-byes	5	5	7	1			5	1	8		5	1	10	10	11	2	2	3	13	5
Wides							3				3			1	1	1	1		1	
No-balls	10	2	13	1	4		11	2	2		3	1	7	1	4		3	6	4	1
Total	345	301	186	91	236		382	101	456		359	32	304	224	220	203	229	326	267	61
Wickets	8	5	10	5	8		9	1	9		10	2	10	4	10	9	10	2	10	10
Results	D		W		D		L		D		D		D		D		W		L	

Catches
36 – S.J. Rixon (ct 34/st 2)
12 – M.D. Haysman
10 – T.G. Hogan
9 – G. Shipperd (ct 8/st 1)
7 – K.J. Hughes
6 – T.M. Alderman and J. Dyson
4 – M.D. Taylor
3 – G.N. Yallop
2 – S.B. Smith
1 – P.I. Faulkner, J.N. Maguire, C.G. Rackemann and T.V. Hohns

BOWLING

BOWLING	R.J. McCurdy	T.M. Alderman	C.G. Rackemann	T.V. Hohns	M.D. Haysman	R.M. Hogg	J.N. Maguire	T.G. Hogan	P.I. Faulkner
v. Orange Free State (Bloemfontein) 22–25 Nov. 1985	24–2–85–4	13–3–40–0	19–3–70–3	29.5–5–114–3					
	6–1–15–0	11–2–43–1	4–0–16–0		2–2–0–0				
v. President's XI (Pretoria) 29 Nov.–2 Dec. 1985		10.5–2–23–3	10–1–37–1				13–2–44–3	15–4–41–3	
		14–3–37–2					10–0–26–2	14.2–1–58–5	
v. Border (East London) 6–8 December 1985			11–0–51–4				18–3–62–5	2.2–0–6–1	14–3–41–0
v. Eastern Province (Port Elizabeth) 13–15 December 1985	4–0–15–0		25.4–7–59–2		5–1–21–0		11–1–40–0	40–12–86–8	
			9.4–0–64–1				23–3–70–4	22–0–107–1	
v. Boland (Stellenbosch) 17–19 December 1985		12–3–12–2		25–8–69–3	1–1–0–0		26–2–95–1	22–7–64–2	9.4–2–19–2
		9–1–22–0		18–5–42–0			14–5–20–2	22–9–34–2	8–1–28–1
First International (Durban) 26–29 December 1985			42–6–112–5	5–2–21–0	4–1–9–0	32–13–83–5	24–2–78–0	16–4–62–0	
			15–4–28–3	8–1–38–0		13–6–25–2	9–1–22–0	14.4–1–77–1	
Second International (Cape Town) 1–4 January 1986	30–2–127–4		37.2–3–117–4			29–6–85–2		30–6–81–0	
	12–2–36–1		26–1–105–4			14–2–43–0			
v. South African Universities (Port Elizabeth) 6–8 Jan. 1986		19–5–24–2		19–3–52–2	10–0–54–0		21.1–4–36–2	14–3–38–0	17–4–45–3
		17–7–33–2		12–0–59–1			16–4–38–1		14–2–40–1
v. Northern Transvaal (Pretoria) 10–13 January 1986	16–1–85–5	14–4–36–3				6–1–25–1	3–0–13–0	1–1–0–0	3–0–11–1
	4–0–11–0	17–6–40–3				17–2–71–1	23–5–81–1	22–8–63–1	9.2–1–39–2
Third International (Johannesburg) 16–21 Jan. 1986		28–6–67–1	26.4–3–84–8				4–3–3–1	13–4–46–0	
		37–6–112–4	30–6–106–4					19–0–65–1	
	96–8–374–14 av. 26.71	201.5–48–489–23 av. 21.26	256.3–34–849–39 av. 21.76	116.5–24–395–9 av. 39.22	22–5–84–0	172–39–515–21 av. 24.52	183.3–51–544–20 av. 27.20	206–51–618–16 av. 38.62	107–17–334–11 av. 30.36

	M	Inns	NOs	Runs	HS	Av
	8	15	2	577	141	44.38
	6	9	—	394	116	43.77
	7	11	1	272	62	27.20
	9	16	3	585	116	45.00
	8	13	2	326	125*	29.63
	9	15	3	668	109	55.66
	6	8	—	206	90	25.75
	8	11	3	126	28	15.75
	4	4	1	36	17	12.00
	7	6	—	31	11	5.16
	6	7	4	24	19	8.00
	8	15	1	397	79	28.35
	6	7	3	52	20	13.00
	6	6	2	34	13	8.50
	7	7	—	169	63	24.14
	5	8	2	226	109	37.66

G.N. Yallop

1-1-0-0

Byes	Leg-byes	Wides	No-balls	Total	Wkts
2	1	1	6	319	10
	1		1	76	1
	3		2	150	10
	3		2	126	10
	2		6	168	10
5	5		4	235	10
.2	6	1		250	8
1	6	2	4	271	10
1	12			159	6
11	17	5	4	393	10
3			1	203	7
5	8		7	430	10
	15		3	202	5
1	9	2	12	219	9
	4		9	237	5
	16		4	190	10
16	7	8	4	340	10
2	8		1	211	10
	17	2	3	305	10

1-1-
0-0
—

Clive Rice had led them to victory in the competition.

The Western Province batsmen could never dominate the impressive Transvaal attack although Kirsten and McEwan promised to do so when they came together after two wickets had gone for 30. Kirsten swung at a full toss from Kourie when he was just getting into his stride, and McEwan, who had played delightfully, was needlessly run out as he attempted to force the pace. Kuiper and le Roux played some aggressive shots, but 230 was unlikely to prove too awesome a target for Transvaal.

Cook and Fotheringham began in their customary accomplished style and although Pollock, returning after injury, fell to Kirsten, Rice and McMillan took Transvaal to victory with some effortless batting. Rice was still troubled by injury, but it did not hamper the fluency of his stroke play while McMillan, who won the fielding prize, gave further evidence of his oustanding quality as a player.

Western Province badly missed Steve Jefferies, but had some consolation in that Brett Matthews was given the bowling prize.

Henry Fotheringham won the individual award for batting, but four of the first five Transvaal batsmen must have run him close.

Benson and Hedges Trophy

26 February 1986

at St George's Park, Port Elizabeth

Eastern Province 219 for 7 (I.K. Daniell 59)
Impalas 94 (P.A. Rayment 4 for 14, T.G. Shaw 4 for 33)

Eastern Province (2 pts) won by 125 runs

28 February 1986

at Green Point, Cape Town

Eastern Province 211 for 7 (D.J. Richardson 68, A.P. Kuiper 4 for 33)
Western Province 216 for 5 (K.S. McEwan 101, A.P. Kuiper 60 not out)

Western Province (2 pts) won by 5 wickets

A glorious century from Ken McEwan assured Western Province of a home tie in the semi-finals.

Castle Bowl

1, 2 and 3 March 1986

at Jan Smuts Ground, Pietermaritzburg

Transvaal 'B' 321 for 6 dec (C.R. Norris 126 not out, L.P. Vorster 70) and 215 for 6 (L.P. Vorster 95, M. Yachad 71)
Natal 'B' 254 (M.J. Pearse 90, M.D. Mellor 51) and 132 for 5

Match drawn
Transvaal 'B' 7 pts, Natal 'B' 5 pts

6, 7 and 8 March 1986

at Oude Libertas, Stellenbosch

Boland 262 (S.A. Jones 58, O. Henry 50, L. Potter 4 for 52) and 45 for 1
Griqualand West 116 and 190

Boland won by 9 wickets
Boland 19 pts, Griqualand West 5 pts

NISSAN SHIELD FINAL – WESTERN PROVINCE v. TRANSVAAL
22 February 1986 at Wanderers, Johannesburg

WESTERN PROVINCE

P.H. Rayner	b Clarke	0
A.G. Elgar	c Jennings, b McMillan	6
P.N. Kirsten	b Kourie	44
K.S. McEwan	run out	66
D.J. Cullinan	lbw, b Kourie	16
A.P. Kuiper†	not out	47
G.S. le Roux	run out	28
E.O. Simons		
J. During		
R.J. Ryall*		
B.A. Matthews		
Extras	b 1, lb 10, w 10, nb 2	23
(55 overs)	(for 6 wickets)	230

	O	M	R	W
Clarke	11	1	34	1
Radford	11	2	44	—
Page	11	1	39	—
McMillan	11	—	50	1
Kourie	11	2	40	2

FALL OF WICKETS
1- 0, 2- 30, 3- 90, 4- 125, 5- 172

TRANSVAAL

S.J. Cook	b le Roux	39
H.R. Fotheringham	c le Roux, b Simons	71
B.M. McMillan	not out	39
R.G. Pollock	c Elgar, b Kirsten	13
C.E.B. Rice†	not out	59
K.A. McKenzie		
K.A. Kourie		
R.V. Jennings*		
H.A. Page		
N.V. Radford		
S.T. Clarke		
Extras	lb 4, w 8, nb 1	13
(49 overs)	(for 3 wickets)	234

	O	M	R	W
Matthews	11	3	25	—
Simons	7	1	34	1
During	8	—	40	—
le Roux	11	—	41	1
Kirsten	11	—	49	1
Kuiper	6	1	32	—

FALL OF WICKETS
1- 109, 2- 118, 3- 140

Umpires: D.A. Sansom & D.H. Bezuidenhout

Transvaal won by 7 wickets

CURRIE CUP FINAL – WESTERN PROVINCE v. TRANSVAAL
7, 8, 9 and 10 March 1986 at Newlands, Cape Town

WESTERN PROVINCE

	FIRST INNINGS		SECOND INNINGS	
A.G. Elgar	c Jennings, b Radford	65	b Radford	5
L. Seeff	c Fotheringham, b Clarke	44	c Kourie, b Page	9
P.N. Kirsten	c Jennings, b Radford	66	c Jennings, b Radford	1
K.S. McEwan	c Jennings, b Page	28	b Clarke	1
D.J. Cullinan	b Page	56	c Jennings, b Page	12
A.P. Kuiper†	c McKenzie, b Radford	48	not out	20
G.J. Turner	not out	26	c Jennings, b Page	1
G.S. le Roux	not out	6	c McKenzie, b Kourie	3
S.T. Jefferies			c McKenzie, b Clarke	1
R.J. Ryall*			not out	17
B.A. Matthews				
Extras	b 4, lb 15, w 5, nb 5	29	b 4, lb 3, nb 3	10
	(for 6 wkts dec)	368	(for 8 wkts)	80

	O	M	R	W	O	M	R	W
Clarke	24	7	74	1	13	7	16	2
Radford	25	2	96	3	14	4	15	2
Kourie	21	6	56	—	11	5	21	1
Page	18	3	74	2	11	6	18	3
McMillan	12	3	39	—				

FALL OF WICKETS
1- 123, 2- 123, 3- 192, 4- 233, 5- 298, 6- 356
1- 5, 2- 7, 3- 8, 4- 26, 5- 29, 6- 31, 7- 48, 8- 49

TRANSVAAL

	FIRST INNINGS		SECOND INNINGS	
S.J. Cook	c Ryall, b Matthews	23	c Ryall, b Jefferies	102
H.R. Fotheringham	c Seeff, b Kuiper	59	lbw, b le Roux	0
B.M. McMillan	c Kuiper, b Matthews	4	c Ryall, b le Roux	34
R.G. Pollock	c Matthews, b le Roux	32	c Ryall, b Matthews	26
C.E.B. Rice†	b Matthews	1	c Ryall, b Matthews	0
K.A. McKenzie	c Ryall, b Jefferies	7	c Seeff, b Matthews	0
A.J. Kourie	lbw, b le Roux	46	c Seeff, b le Roux	82
R.V. Jennings*	lbw, b Jefferies	1	c Kuiper, b Jefferies	6
H.A. Page	c Ryall, b Jefferies	16	c Cullinan, b Jefferies	7
N.V. Radford	b Jefferies	10	(11) not out	13
S.T. Clarke	not out	0	(10) b Jefferies	15
Extras	lb 6, w 3, nb 4	13	b 3, lb 3, w 4, nb 3	13
		212		298

	O	M	R	W	O	M	R	W
le Roux	19	3	72	2	24	3	67	3
Jefferies	19.2	5	50	5	33	4	90	4
Kuiper	12	1	30	1	7	1	20	—
Matthews	22	8	47	2	26	6	66	3
Kirsten					17	2	42	—

FALL OF WICKETS
1- 41, 2- 54, 3- 117, 4- 122, 5- 126, 6- 144, 7- 155, 8- 194, 9- 212
1- 1, 2- 82, 3- 142, 4- 142, 5- 142, 6- 222, 7- 236, 8- 252, 9- 270

Umpires: O.R. Schoof & D.H. Bezuidenhout

Match drawn

Western Province won the Currie Cup on league position

Transvaal 'B''s fall from grace was completed in the last match of their season when failure to beat Natal 'B' left them nestling at the bottom of the table with Northern Transvaal 'B'. There were compensations. Norris hit the highest score of his career, his third century of the season, and Vorster played the two best innings of his career.

At Stellenbosch Boland gave a champions display in their final match with Omar Henry and Stephen Jones appropriately rescuing them from a worrying 85 for 4. Griqualand West lost their first 4 wickets for 17 runs and never truly recovered against the eager Boland side.

Castle Bowl – Final Table

	P	W	L	D	Tied	Pts
Boland	6	4	1	—	1	88
Western Province 'B'	6	4	1	1	—	74
Eastern Province 'B'	6	2	1	1	2	63
Natal 'B'	6	2	2	1	1	63
Griqualand West	6	1	3	2	—	48
Transvaal 'B'	6	—	1	5	—	40
Northern Transvaal 'B'	6	—	4	2	—	40

Castle Currie Cup Final
WESTERN PROVINCE v. TRANSVAAL

Both sides were at full strength and Western Province took advantage of first use of an easy paced wicket with a consistently impressive batting display which took them to 368 for 6 in 100 overs. They were given a splendid start by Alan Elgar and Lawrie Seef – who both fell at the same total, but any hint of collapse was quickly averted by Kirsten who played what was probably his best innings of the summer.

McEwan shone all too briefly, but entertaining batting from Cullinan and Kuiper took the home side to an impressive position.

Transvaal, winners of the Currie Cup for the past three seasons, were given a competent start by Cook and Fotheringham, but McMillan, Rice and McKenzie, three batsmen of whom much was expected, all failed, and with no batsman playing an innings of substance, Transvaal were forced to follow-on. This was an unexpected indignity for the reigning champions and worse was to follow as Henry Fotheringham was lbw without scoring.

Five wickets fell before the arrears were cleared, and Jim Cook's fine innings, his second century of the season against Transvaal's greatest rivals, came to an end when he was caught behind off Jefferies at 222. The return of Jefferies had much strengthened the Western Province attack as his 9 wickets in the match indicated, and there was more good bowling from left-arm pace man Brett Matthews, a happy recruit for Western Province.

Alan Kourie now stood alone between Transvaal and defeat and he responded admirably to steer his side to a position where they could at least escape humiliation.

Western Province needed 143 to win, a simple task it seemed, and the Currie Cup for which they had worked so hard throughout the season was in their grasp. The run rate required was little more than 3 an over, and with Clarke

again troubled by a knee injury, the Western Province batsmen appeared to have few problems.

The start was horrendous for the home side. Elgar was bowled by Radford at 5, and Kirsten and McEwan, the two leading batsmen in the side, went at 7 and 8. Seeff and Cullinan appeared to have righted matters, but another 3 wickets fell as 5 runs were scored. When the last 20 overs began Western Province were 49 for 8, and it was as if the Currie Cup was about to be dashed from their lips.

Skipper Adrian Kuiper and wicket-keeper Richie Ryall, a close rival to Jennings as the best in the republic, held out defiantly, and Western Province took the Cup by virtue of having won the league. It was a thrilling climax although not the type of climax that had been envisaged earlier on the last day, nor indeed at any time after the first half day.

Benson and Hedges Trophy

12 March 1986

at Kingsmead, Durban

Northern Transvaal 201 for 6 (K.D. Verdoorn 57, A.M. Ferreira 50)
Natal 189 (T.R. Madsen 54)
Northern Transvaal (2 pts) won by 12 runs

14 March 1986

at Wanderers, Johannesburg

Western Province 158 for 2 (A.G. Elgar 63, L. Seeff 54)
Transvaal 46 for 1
Match abandoned
Western Province 1 pt, Transvaal 1 pt

Benson and Hedges Trophy – Semi-Finals

19 March 1986

at St George's Park, Port Elizabeth

Eastern Provide 159 (G.S. le Roux 4 for 25)
Western Province 161 for 5
Western Province won by 5 wickets

21 March 1986

at Wanderers, Johannesburg

Transvaal 152
Northern Transvaal 153 for 5 (R.F. Pienaar 65)
Northern Transvaal won by 5 wickets

Benson and Hedges Trophy – Log

	P	W	L	Ab	Pts
Western Province	5	3	—	2	8
Transvaal	5	3	1	1	7
Northern Transvaal	5	3	2	—	6
Eastern Province	5	2	2	1	5
Natal	5	1	3	1	3
Impalas	5	—	4	1	1

Benson and Hedges Trophy Final
WESTERN PROVINCE v. NORTHERN TRANSVAAL

Transvaal's dominance in South African cricket was broken when Western Province took the Currie Cup, and their hold was broken totally when Northern Transvaal surprisingly beat them in the semi-final of the Benson and Hedges Trophy.

The final itself was a splendid match. Ken McEwan, the outstanding batsman of the season, played another delightful innings full of grace and power. He led Western Province to a formidable total, and when Northern Transvaal lost their four front line batsmen, three of them to the ever improving Matthews, for 89 it seemed that the Cape side would stroll to victory. Courageous knocks from Day, Ferreira, Ontong and Mitchley bolstered the closing stages of the innings, and Northern Transvaal came closer to their target than any had dreamed possible.

For Western Province, the victory sealed a season of triumph.

It had been a good season for South African cricket. The Australian opposition had allowed several young players to display their talents at a level higher than the Currie Cup, and on the purely domestic front the sharing of honours and the breaking of the Transvaal monopoly had reawakened an interest which was in danger of becoming dormant.

First-Class Averages

BATTING

	M	Inns	NOs	Runs	HS	Av	100s	50s
C.R. Norris	6	11	4	477	126*	68.14	3	
K.S. McEwan	7	11	2	510	142	56.66	2	2
C.L. King	5	7		374	154	53.42	1	2
B.M. McMillan	5	9	1	419	129	52.37	1	3
M.W. Rushmere	8	15	4	570	128	51.81	1	1
R.G. Pollock	9	15	2	671	113*	51.61	2	5
R.M. Bentley	6	9	1	407	134*	50.87	1	2
B. McBride	7	8	3	234	66*	46.80		2
H.R. Fotheringham	11	20	2	841	114*	46.72	3	4
A.L. Wilmot	7	12	2	448	108*	44.80	1	1
S.J. Cook	11	20	1	840	124	44.21	2	5
K.A. McKenzie	9	14	2	511	110*	42.58	1	2
M.S. Venter	7	12	1	459	225*	41.72	1	1
S.F.A. Bacchus	7	12		494	134	41.16	1	2
L.P. Vorster	6	11	1	404	95*	40.40		5
A.G. Elgar	7	11		438	81	39.81		3
A.P. Kuiper	7	9	2	273	55*	39.00		1
D. Bestall	4	6	2	155	69*	38.75		2
A.M. Ferreira	8	14	1	499	105	38.38	1	1
B.C. Broad	7	12	1	416	101*	37.81	1	3
S.A. Jones	8	14		518	132	37.00	1	4
P.G. Amm	7	13		475	82	36.53		4
C.M. Lister-James	6	10	2	292	88*	36.50		2
T.G. Shaw	7	11	4	249	66	35.57		1
G.E. McMillan	5	8	3	174	59	34.80		2
A.V.N. Snyman	2	4		139	92	34.75		1
A.M. Green	5	9	1	275	104	34.37	1	
R.F. Pienaar	8	16		546	90	34.12		4
B. Roberts	6	11	1	339	79	33.90		3
I.K. Daniell	6	12		398	116	33.16	2	
G. Vermeulen	4	8	2	197	58	32.83		1
S.T. Jefferies	8	8	3	164	51*	32.80		1
D.J. Callaghan	5	9	1	262	44*	32.75		
A.C. Hudson	6	12		388	71	32.33		4
J.J. Strydom	7	13	3	323	100*	32.30	1	2
P.L. Symcox	5	10		322	107	32.20	1	3
D.G. Emslie	7	14	1	418	111*	32.15	1	3
L.J.E. Coetzee	6	12	4	252	75*	31.50		1
J. During	7	13	7	189	37*	31.50		
N.T. Day	8	16	1	471	117	31.40	1	3
R.C. Ontong	8	15	4	343	85	31.18		2
A.J. Kourie	10	14	2	374	82	31.16		2
B.J. Whitfield	6	9		280	140	31.11	1	1
M.J. Pearse	6	11		335	90	30.45		2
P.N. Kirsten	10	18	1	516	83	30.35		5
R.L.S. Armitage	7	13	1	354	98*	29.50		3

BENSON AND HEDGES TROPHY FINAL – WESTERN PROVINCE v. NORTHERN TRANSVAAL
26 March 1986 at Wanderers, Johannesburg

WESTERN PROVINCE

A.G. Elgar	b Mitchley	29
L. Seeff	lbw, b Ontong	21
P.N. Kirsten	b Ackermann	39
K.S. McEwan	not out	102
D.J. Cullinan	b Ackermann	33
A.P. Kuiper†	not out	20
G.S. le Roux		
S.T. Jefferies		
R.J. Ryall*		
D. Norman		
B.A. Matthews		
Extras	b 8, lb 12, w 1	21
(45 overs)	(for 4 wickets)	265

	O	M	R	W
Mitchley	9	1	42	1
Weideman	8	1	43	—
Ontong	7	1	33	1
Morris	8	1	40	—
Pienaar	8	—	50	—
Ackermann	5	—	36	2

FALL OF WICKETS
1-47, 2-72, 3-143, 4-194

NORTHERN TRANSVAAL

K.D. Verdoorn	b Matthews	29
R.F. Pienaar	b Matthews	35
P.L. Symcox	b Matthews	7
L.J. Barnard†	b Kirsten	9
N.T. Day*	c Kirsten, b Kuiper	47
A.M. Ferreira	b le Roux	26
R.C. Ontong	b le Roux	62
I.F.N. Weideman	lbw, b Kuiper	0
C.D. Mitchley	c and b le Roux	20
W.F. Morris	not out	1
G.L. Ackermann		
Extras	lb 7, w 5, nb 5	17
(45 overs)	(for 9 wickets)	253

	O	M	R	W
le Roux	9	—	32	3
Jefferies	6	—	37	—
Kirsten	9	—	44	1
Matthews	9	1	26	3
Kuiper	9	—	67	2
Norman	3	—	30	—

FALL OF WICKETS
1-55, 2-72, 3-85, 4-89, 5-134, 6-134, 7-229, 8-244, 9-253

Umpires: D.H. Bezuidenhout & D.A. Sansom
Western Province won by 12 runs

	M	I	NO	Runs	HS	Av	100	50
P.A. Tullis	6	10	4	175	64*	29.16		1
S. Nackerdien	9	18	2	466	122	29.12	1	2
M.J.R. Rindel	6	12		349	115	29.08	1	
G.L. Hayes	7	12	3	260	92	28.88		2
K.D. Verdoorn	8	15	1	400	74	28.57		3
L.J. Barnard	8	16		456	93	28.50		3
M. Michau	7	13	1	339	53	28.25		2
M.B. Logan	7	10		281	72	28.10		2
E.N. Trotman	7	12		337	74	28.08		2
A.D. Methven	5	9		250	62	27.77		1
G.S. le Roux	10	14	2	333	86	27.75		2
G.J. Turner	7	14	3	305	69*	27.72		2
C.E.B. Rice	9	14	2	331	80	27.58		3
D.A. Scott	6	11	2	247	44	27.44		1
L. Potter	6	11		301	70	27.36		2
T.B. Reid	6	11		299	87	27.18		1
N.M. Lambrechts	7	12	1	298	84	27.09		2
G.S. Cowley	6	9	1	216	75	27.00		1
R.J. East	7	12		317	76	26.41		2
I.M. Wingreen	6	12	1	283	103	25.72	1	
M.D. Mellor	6	12		308	51	25.66		1
D.P. le Roux	6	11	1	255	92	25.50		1
P.R. Steyn	5	10		254	63	25.40		3
C.P.L. de Lange	6	12		304	104	25.33	1	
D.J. Cullinan	8	13	1	299	56	24.91		1
M. Yachad	8	15		362	90	24.13		2
P.P.H. Trimborn	5	9	3	143	37	23.83		
A.P. Beukes	7	12	2	238	51	23.80		1
A. Watts	7	10	2	189	57	23.62		1
F.W. Swarbrook	6	11	1	234	104*	23.40	1	
M.J.P. Ford	5	10	1	206	96	22.88		1
L. Seeff	7	12	1	249	51	22.63		1
A. Geringer	8	16	2	314	67*	22.42		1
K.D. Dawson	6	12		269	53	22.41		1
N.P. Daniells	5	8		178	53	22.25		1
D. Norman	5	7	2	111	56	22.20		1
V.G. Cresswell	6	10		221	51	22.10		2
M.W. Pfaff	3	5		110	48	22.00		
G.L. Long	5	8	1	151	73	21.57		1
L.J. Ketts	8	14	2	256	117	21.33	1	
G.J. Parsons	6	11	1	211	52	21.10		2
D.B. Rundle	4	8		168	49	21.00		
M.P. Minnaar	7	12		250	48	20.83		
R.V. Jennings	11	14	4	208	50*	20.80		1
D.J. Richardson	7	13		270	64	20.76		2
M.C. Smit	4	8	1	141	52	20.14		1
D.J. Capel	5	9		180	60	20.00		2
D.J. Ferrant	5	10	2	154	43	19.25		
L.M. Phillips	6	11		219	47	19.09		
H.A. Page	11	13	3	188	51	18.80		1
I.L. Howell	7	11	1	188	36	18.80		
C.J. van Heerden	7	14	1	240	46	18.46		
S.D. Bruce	4	6		110	44	18.33		
O. Henry	9	14		256	50	18.28		2
C.W. Symcox	5	9	1	144	100*	18.00	1	
C. Spilhaus	8	16		281	82	17.56		1
K.G. Bauermeister	6	11	1	174	61*	17.40		2
B.E. van der Vyver	6	11	2	156	33*	17.33		
T.N. Lazard	6	12		203	43	16.91		
A. da Costa	4	8		133	47	16.62		
A.V. Birrell	6	11	1	162	59	16.20		1
V.F. du Preez	8	16		259	51	16.18		1
J.A. O'Donoghue	7	10	1	145	53	16.11		1
R.B.C. Ranger	6	9	1	128	30	16.00		
P.H. Rayner	5	8		127	34	15.87		
L.W. Griesel	4	7		108	42	15.42		
T.R. Madsen	5	8		122	54	15.25		1
W.K. Watson	7	10	3	105	36	15.00		
W. Kirsh	4	8		118	43	14.75		
R.A. le Roux	4	8		113	41	14.12		
G.L. Ackermann	5	9	1	109	43	13.62		
C.J.P.G. van Zyl	9	15	2	175	36	13.46		
C.D. Mitchley	8	12	2	134	58	13.40		1
W.M. van der Merwee	5	9		116	30	12.88		
P.A. Rayment	7	12	3	113	41	12.55		

(Qualification – 100 runs, average 10.00) (J.W. Furstenburg 122 & 13)

BOWLING

	Overs	Mds	Runs	Wkts	Av	Best	10/m	5/inn
C.E.B. Rice	101	31	206	14	14.71	3/8		
B.A. Matthews	303.4	77	626	42	14.90	5/32		1
F. de Villiers	106	15	277	18	15.38	5/33		1
I.W. Callen	112.5	27	279	17	16.41	5/59		1
J. During	166.4	41	346	21	16.47	5/20		1
G.R. Dilley	206.4	57	486	29	16.75	7/63		1
E.O. Simons	190	40	474	28	16.92	5/52		1
W.M. van der Merwee	133.4	25	324	19	17.05	5/35		1
W.F. Morris	68.4	12	223	13	17.15	6/66		1
N.V. Radford	213.5	37	627	35	17.91	5/52		2
O. Henry	344	116	809	45	17.97	7/82	1	4
G.S. le Roux	334.3	66	884	49	18.04	5/54		1
P. Anker	308.1	105	562	31	18.12	5/34	1	2
H.A. Page	317.2	70	847	46	18.41	5/31		1
S.A. Jones	92.2	24	186	10	18.60	2/14		
G.E. McMillan	161	45	317	17	18.64	3/33		
D. Norman	145.1	22	450	23	19.56	6/56		1
G.W. Symonds	106	23	298	15	19.86	4/50		
C.J.P.G. van Zyl	311.4	77	696	34	20.47	5/54		1
W.H. van Wyk	116.1	23	311	15	20.73	7/55		1
M.D. Mellor	184.1	62	385	18	21.38	3/35		
G.L. Ackermann	147.3	16	506	23	22.00	5/48		1
B. McNab	167.5	53	354	16	22.12	4/29		
C.M. Lister-James	112	26	271	12	22.58	3/85		
P. McLaren	126.3	18	386	17	22.70	5/68		1
A. Watts	131	26	341	15	22.73	4/54		
S.T. Jefferies	293.4	72	810	35	23.14	5/30		2
C.D. Mitchley	238.5	43	695	30	23.16	5/26		2
B.E. van der Vyver	159	44	397	17	23.35	5/56		1
P.L. Symcox	105.1	30	236	10	23.60	3/19		
A.A. Donald	175.2	28	504	21	24.00	5/43		2
G.J. Parsons	200.5	37	530	22	24.09	3/20		
M.R. Hobson	122.4	20	343	14	24.50	5/56		1
J.C. van Duyker	231.4	44	645	26	24.80	4/31		
M.K. van Vuuren	161	38	411	16	25.68	4/28		
G. Dakin	118	20	336	13	25.84	3/52		
A.L. Hobson	146	24	469	18	26.05	7/114		1
S.T. Clarke	193	50	474	18	26.33	6/19		1
J.A. O'Donoghue	232	53	711	26	27.34	5/39		3
B.P. Martin	120.2	34	276	10	27.60	4/40		
W.K. Watson	186.3	40	497	18	27.61	6/47		1
S. van Rooyen	141	37	387	14	27.64	4/50		
E.J. Hopkinson	131.2	33	313	11	28.45	4/26		
R.K. McGlashan	161	49	461	16	28.81	5/53		1
M.D. Clare	201.2	34	647	22	29.40	5/70		1
E. du Klopper	101.1	14	300	10	30.00	4/108		
C.J. van Heerden	142	23	516	17	30.35	4/45		
R.C. Ontong	274.5	69	773	25	30.92	5/33		1
T.G. Shaw	336	85	869	28	31.03	7/79	1	1
K.G. Bauermeister	151.2	19	505	16	31.56	4/45		
P.N. Kirsten	140.3	35	380	12	31.66	6/48		1
M.B. Minnaar	270.1	79	591	18	32.83	4/61		
J.J. Hooper	131.1	26	376	11	34.18	2/45		
A.J. Kourie	318.5	85	805	23	35.00	4/36		
K.J. Kerr	213	47	635	18	35.27	4/101		
A.P. Beukes	224.1	47	642	18	35.66	3/32		
B. de K. Robey	174	41	511	14	36.50	4/73		
P.A. Rayment	136.5	28	444	12	37.00	4/62		
E.N. Trotman	162	28	474	12	39.50	4/94		
I.L. Howell	243	70	581	13	44.69	3/77		
R.L.S. Armitage	177.3	34	542	12	45.16	2/34		

(Qualification – 10 wickets)

LEADING FIELDERS

41 - R.V. Jennings; 29 - N.T. Day (ct 27/st 2); 27 - R.J. Ryall; 25 - R.J. East (ct 24/st 1); 24 - L.J. Kets (ct 15/st 9); 23 - B. McBride; 21 - P.P.H. Trimborn (ct 20/st 1) and L.M. Phillips (ct 20:st 1); 20 - L.J. Barnard; 19 - C. Fost (ct 17/st 2); 18 - K.J. Kerr; 17 - D.J. Richardson (ct 14/st 3); 16 - T.R. Madsen (ct 14/st 2); 14 - L. Potter; 13 - A. da Costa and V.G. Cresswell (ct 10/st 3); 12 - P.A. Tullis (ct 11/st 1) and O. Henry; 10 - C.E.B. Rice, C. Spilhaus and S.A. Jones

Hovering Dreams

The season in Zimbabwe
Young Australian tour
The tour by New South Wales, Sheffield Shield Champions

Dave Houghton, the Zimbabwe captain, who took his 100th first-class catch during the season. (David Munden)

The Zimbabwe side had returned from the tour of England with mixed feelings, for the weather had been so appalling as to make the conditions in which games were played unnatural and often depressing. Nevertheless, the tour had been a significant success, even though it was apparent from the start that the Zimbabwe attack, without Rawson, unavailable owing to business commitments, and Curran, performing splendidly for Gloucestershire, would struggle against first-class opposition.

The team enjoyed an unbeaten run in the limited-over matches, and several players made great advances as cricketers. Graeme Hick matured into an attacking batsman who excited the approval of the sternest judges and moved into a place in the Worcestershire side with ease. Equally vital for Zimbabwe was the development of Ian Butchart into a genuine all-rounder. He was the oustanding bowler of the tour, a fine fielder and an aggressive number nine batsman with the temperament to excel in a crisis. He is a man of courage and determination. Grant Paterson was another to make great progress, as an opening batsman, while Laurence de Grandhomme made the most of his opportunities with gritty batting and useful off-spinners. The details of the tour, inadvertently omitted in last year's annual, are appended in this year's book.

Zimbabwe in England 1985
First Class Matches

BATTING

BATTING	v. Oxford University (Oxford) 8–11 June 1985		v. Glamorgan (Swansea) 19–21 June 1985		v. Warwickshire (Edgbaston) 22–25 June 1985		v. Minor Counties (Cleethorpes) 29 June–1 July 1985		v. Surrey (The Oval) 17–19 July 1985		v. Gloucestershire (Bristol) 20–23 July 1985		M	Inns	NOs	Runs	HS	Av
R.D. Brown	4	—			23	5	2	23	27	—	27	2	5	8	—	113	27	14.12
G.A. Paterson	5	—	69	—	10	24	15	26	43	—	36	92	6	9	—	320	92	35.55
G.A. Hick	230	—	192	—	4	65	19	38	10	—	1	39	6	9	—	598	230	66.44
A.J. Pycroft	24	—	0	—	21	46*	44	110*					4	6	2	245	110*	61.25
D.L. Houghton	104	—	24	—	35	30*	17	2	19	—	0	—	6	8	1	231	104	33.00
A.C. Waller	12	—			56*	1							2	3	1	69	56*	34.50
L.L. de Grandhomme	32*	—	10	—			59	0	48	—	8	—	5	6	1	157	59	31.40
I.P. Butchart	3	—	4	—	18		5	82	4	—	18	0*	6	8	1	134	82	19.14
A.J. Traicos	0	—	16	—			6*		8	—	27*	—	6	5	2	57	27*	19.00
M.P. Jarvis	6	—	3	—					1*	—			4	3	1	10	6	5.00
K.G. Duers	1	—									0	—	3	2	—	1	1	0.50
K.G. Walton			1	—			15	1			20	20*	3	5	1	57	20*	14.25
A.H. Omarshah			1	—	5*	26			7		16	40	4	6	1	95	40	19.00
D.H. Streak			26*	—			17	—	29				3	3	1	72	29	36.00
E.A. Brandes							8	3*	19	—	0	—	3	4	1	30	19	10.00
Byes	9		5		1	9	2	4	4			1						
Leg-byes	4		6		3	6	3	4	4		3	11						
Wides	2				1				2	2								
No-balls	4		7				1	2				1						
Total	440		364		159	231	214	293	226		156	205						
Wickets	10		10		5	6	10	7	10		10	4						
Results	D		D		D		D		D		L							

Catches
7 – A.J. Traicos
6 – G.A. Hick
3 – D.L. Houghton
2 – A.J. Pycroft, A.C. Waller, L.L. de Grandhomme and K.G. Walton
1 – D.H. Streak, I.P. Butchart, A.H. Omarshah, R.D. Brown and M.P. Jarvis

BOWLING

BOWLING	M.P. Jarvis	K.G. Duers	A.J. Traicos	I.P. Butchart	G.A. Hick	L.L. de Grandhomme	D.H. Streak	A.H. Omarshah	E.A. Brandes
v. Oxford University (Oxford) 8–11 June	12–2–23–0	20–7–63–0	29–13–52–2	16–6–51–3	21–7–55–2	1–0–1–0			
	14–3–37–3	7–3–16–1	11–5–15–0	12–1–51–1	8–0–23–0				
v. Glamorgan (Swansea) 19–21 June	18–3–58–1		20.4–6–45–2	24–6–65–5	4–0–14–0		9–3–27–2		
	13–0–52–1		16–5–39–1	15–5–32–1	6–1–20–1	9–4–26–0		6–2–13–0	
v. Warwickshire (Edgbaston) 22–25 June	21–4–80–1	19–2–62–0	18–3–44–0	18–5–58–1	9–0–30–0			6–1–23–0	
	7–0–35–0		7–0–41–1	14–2–60–2					
v. Minor Counties (Cleethorpes) 29 June–1 July			23–8–39–0	21–6–46–3	10–1–49–0	27–5–79–3	3–0–13–0		12.4–0–46–2
v. Surrey (The Oval) 17–19 July	16–0–71–1		14–3–49–0	17–5–58–3	1–0–2–0	9–0–42–1	3.3–0–11–0	12–3–52–0	7–0–45–0
	9–1–36–1		9–1–33–2	8–1–32–0	7–0–23–0		5–1–18–1	4–1–18–0	13–1–53–0
v. Gloucestershire (Bristol) 20–23 July		6–1–19–0	4–3–1–0	9–3–26–1					7–1–16–1
		14–0–75–3	15.3–1–81–0	13–2–68–0	5–0–20–0				8–1–30–0
	110–13–392–10	66–13–235–4	167.1–48–439–8	167–42–547–20	71–9–236–3	46–9–148–4	20.3–4–69–3	28–7–106–0	47.4–3–190–3
	av. 39.20	av. 58.75	av. 54.87	av. 27.35	av. 78.66	av. 37.00	av. 23.00	—	av. 63.33

The Zimbabwe Cricket Authorities, among the most energetic and competent in the world, arranged an exciting programme for 1985–86, bringing strong Australian and English sides to test the strength of Zimbabwe cricket. Unfortunately, politics clouded cricketing issues and the invitation to the England 'B' team was withdrawn, a sad and blinkered decision, and one for which cricketers themselves were not responsible.

The first Young Australian side which had visited Zimbabwe, in 1983, had contained players, Boon, Ritchie, Wellham, Wayne Phillips, Bennett, McCurdy and Whitney, who were soon to gain international experience at a high level, and the side that was sent from Australia in 1985 was equally strong, but, as manager Des Rundle pointed out, the opposition that Zimbabwe provided was stronger and richer in experience in spite of the retirements of Fletcher, Heron and Hogg. Indeed, the Australian side included Reid, Davis, Gilbert and Waugh, all of whom were to become regular members of the national side within a few months of the end of the tour of Zimbabwe.

Before the start of the Zimbabwe season it was announced that David Houghton would succeed Andy Pycroft as captain of the Zimbabwe side. It came as no real surprise, for Pycroft had struggled to find his batting form while he led the team, and it seemed to be a position he did not relish.

---

18 September 1985

at Harare South Country Club

Young Australians 270 for 4 (D.M. Jones 87 not out, P.S. Clifford 70, B.A. Courtice 69)
Zimbabwe Country Districts 158
Young Australians won by 112 runs

The Young Australians made an encouraging start to their tour with an easy win in a fifty over match against a Country Districts side which included Paterson, Brown, Waller, Brent and Butchart. Jones and Clifford, two batsmen who were unlucky not to have been selected for the tour of England, shared a third wicket stand of 132.

First International
ZIMBABWE v. YOUNG AUSTRALIA

The tourists' batting was wrecked by Peter Rawson on the opening day. He bowled at a fiery pace and received admirable support from Kevin Curran who, with Hick, had arrived from England only hours before the match. Dodemaide's tenacity was the redeeming feature of the Australian innings.

Zimbabwe lost Paterson and Omarshah quickly, but closed at 65 for 2. The following day Hick scored an impressive century, his first first-class hundred in his own country. He reached his hundred off 135 balls and, in all, batted for 208 minutes and hit 21 fours. He gave ample evidence of his range of strokes and the maturity that his batting has acquired since gaining experience in England. Curran and the hard-hitting Butchart added 69 for the eighth wicket and Zimbabwe took a substantial lead.

Kerr and Courtice negotiated the final hour, but Kerr fell early on the last day, the Monday. Zimbabwe anticipated victory, but too many chances were missed and both Jones and Dodemaide batted well.

Young Australian Bruce Reid walks away after his stumps have been spread-eagled by Kevin Curran. (Bob Nixon)

Bishop is bowled by Curran in the second innings of the first international. (Bob Nixon)

Byes	Leg-byes	Wides	No-balls	Total	Wkts
6	11		1	262	7
2	5		1	149	5
4	1		2	214	10
4	1		1	187	4
2	9			308	2
3				139	5
5	16	3	1	293	8
2	11	1		343	5
2	5	1		220	4
		3		65	2
18	7		1	299	3

FIRST INTERNATIONAL – ZIMBABWE v. YOUNG AUSTRALIA
20, 21 and 23 September 1985 at Harare Sports Club

YOUNG AUSTRALIA

	FIRST INNINGS		SECOND INNINGS	
B.A. Courtice	c Butchart, b Rawson	2	lbw, b Rawson	29
R.B. Kerr†	c Butchart, b Curran	6	lbw, b Curran	26
D.M. Jones	c and b Butchart	20	b Traicos	70
P.S. Clifford	c Houghton, b Rawson	9	b Traicos	29
G.A. Bishop	c Houghton, b Rawson	32	b Curran	15
S.L. Saunders	b Butchart	19	lbw, b Rawson	29
A.I.C. Dodemaide	c Hick, b Rawson	41	not out	36
M.G. Dimattina*	lbw, b Traicos	5	lbw, b Rawson	14
B.A. Reid	c Houghton, b Rawson	14	b Traicos	0
D.R. Gilbert	c Hick, b Curran	14	c Omarshah, b Curran	4
R.L. Brown	not out	4	not out	0
Extras	lb 5, w 2, nb 2	9	b 9, lb 7, w 2, nb 2	20
		175	(for 9 wickets)	272

	O	M	R	W	O	M	R	W
Rawson	27.5	11	56	5	33	9	65	3
Curran	19	6	58	2	23	7	61	3
Butchart	15	3	45	2	8	2	29	—
Traicos	9	3	11	1	36	12	78	3
Omarshah					8	4	19	—
Hick					5	3	4	—

FALL OF WICKETS
1- 4, 2- 18, 3- 36, 4- 41, 5- 78, 6- 98, 7- 112, 8- 137, 9- 164
1- 43, 2- 72, 3- 136, 4- 173, 5- 175, 6- 210, 7- 241, 8- 242, 9- 248

ZIMBABWE

	FIRST INNINGS	
R.D. Brown	c and b Brown	22
G.A. Paterson	b Gilbert	8
A.H. Omarshah	c Gilbert, b Brown	3
A.J. Pycroft	c Saunders, b Gilbert	37
G.A. Hick	lbw, b Brown	127
D.L. Houghton*†	c Kerr, b Reid	35
A.C. Waller	lbw, b Reid	0
K.M. Curran	not out	49
I.P. Butchart	c Dodemaide, b Reid	38
P.W.E. Rawson	c Kerr, b Reid	1
A.J. Traicos	c Dimattina, b Dodemaide	7
Extras	b 6, lb 4, w 2, nb 6	18
		345

	O	M	R	W
Gilbert	30	3	97	2
Brown	22.2	4	90	3
Reid	26.4	5	91	4
Dodemaide	22.4	6	53	1
Saunders	2	1	4	—

FALL OF WICKETS
1- 13, 2- 16, 3- 69, 4- 115, 5- 208, 6- 210, 7- 253, 8- 322, 9- 328

Umpires: D.B. Arnott & I.D. Robinson

Match drawn

FIRST ONE-DAY INTERNATIONAL – ZIMBABWE v. YOUNG AUSTRALIA
22 September 1985 at Harare Sports Club

YOUNG AUSTRALIA

B.A. Courtice	c Traicos, b Butchart	32
R.B. Kerr†	run out	63
D.M. Jones	c Houghton, b Butchart	62
P.S. Clifford	c Waller, b Traicos	4
G.A. Bishop	c Rawson, b Traicos	4
S.R. Waugh	c Waller, b Hick	26
A.I.C. Dodemaide	not out	18
M.G. Dimattina*	run out	3
B.A. Reid	not out	15
D.R. Gilbert		
S.P. Davis		
Extras	lb 5, w 2	7
(50 overs)	(for 7 wickets)	234

	O	M	R	W
Rawson	10	1	25	—
Curran	10	1	47	—
Butchart	10	—	52	2
Traicos	10	—	37	2
Hick	10	—	68	1

FALL OF WICKETS
1- 76, 2- 115, 3- 130, 4- 145, 5- 195, 6- 195, 7- 200

ZIMBABWE

R.D. Brown	c Dimattina, b Waugh	27
G.A. Paterson	c Davis, b Dodemaide	73
G.A. Hick	c Dimattina, b Waugh	1
A.J. Pycroft	b Reid	19
D.L. Houghton*†	c Dimattina, b Dodemaide	20
A.C. Waller	c Dimattina, b Reid	6
K.M. Curran	not out	21
A.H. Omarshah	c Bishop, b Davis	6
I.P. Butchart	not out	43
P.W.E. Rawson		
A.J. Traicos		
Extras	lb 11, w 3, nb 8	22
(47.4 overs)	(for 7 wickets)	238

	O	M	R	W
Gilbert	9	1	65	—
Davis	8.4	2	36	1
Dodemaide	10	1	41	2
Waugh	10	—	46	2
Reid	10	—	39	2

FALL OF WICKETS
1- 49, 2- 53, 3- 93, 4- 141, 5- 158, 6- 160, 7- 186

Umpires: R. Jackson & K. Kanjee

Zimbabwe won by 3 wickets

First One-Day International
ZIMBABWE v. YOUNG AUSTRALIA

Australia were without Brown, the medium pacer, who had been forced to retire after bowling two balls of his twenty-third over on the Saturday.

The visitors began well, and Courtice, Kerr and Jones played with such panache that even a slump in the middle order could not weaken the Australian advance too much. Zimbabwe were faced with a reasonably stiff task in having to make 235 at 4.7 an over.

Grant Paterson batted splendidly, but the middle order batsmen failed to maintain the required run rate. With five overs left, Zimbabwe needed to score at more than 8 runs an over and had only three wickets standing. Iain Butcher had just come to the crease and he responded to the situation with a ferocious assault on the bowling. Hitting cleanly, he took 3 sixes and a four in five balls off Gilbert, and then went down the other end to hit Simon Davis for two successive sixes to win the match. His 43 came off only 15 balls, a tremendously powerful effort from a fine cricketer who never resorts to slogging in his quest for quick runs.

25 September 1985

at Mutare Sports Club

Zimbabwe 'B' 186 (C.A.T. Hodgson 92, J.F. Brent 53, S.P. Davis 5 for 15)
Young Australians 190 for 1 (G.A. Bishop 129 not out)
Young Australians won by 9 wickets

Glen Bishop hit the only Australian century of the tour in the match at Mutare which the tourists dominated from start to finish.

Robbie Kerr is caught Rawson, bowled Curran 8 in the second one-day international which Zimbabwe won by 1 wicket. (Bob Nixon)

Peter Clifford becomes another Traicos victim. (Bob Nixon)

Second One-Day International
ZIMBABWE v. YOUNG AUSTRALIA

Dean Jones was again the pick of the Australian batsmen who, in a solid display, reached a good total against some tight bowling, especially by Butchart, and some excellent fielding.

The home side's batting disappointed. Hick, Houghton, Curran and Omarshah failed while the other batsmen failed to prosper after starting well. When Traicos, last man in, joined Rawson, Zimbabwe were 38 short of their target and had less than five overs remaining so that the Australians seemed set to level the series. Traicos defended admirably while Rawson, as Butchart had done six days earlier, attacked the bowling. He hit 45 off 22 balls and snatched victory for Zimbabwe with one ball to spare.

SECOND ONE-DAY INTERNATIONAL – ZIMBABWE v. YOUNG AUSTRALIA
28 September 1985 at Bulawayo Athletic Club

YOUNG AUSTRALIA

B.A. Courtice	st Houghton, b Omarshah	23
R.B. Kerr†	c Rawson, b Curran	8
D.M. Jones	c Hick, b Butchart	55
P.S. Clifford	c Paterson, b Butchart	6
G.A. Bishop	c Omarshah, b Butchart	43
S.R. Waugh	c Houghton, b Rawson	42
A.I.C. Dodemaide	c Omarshah, b Butchart	22
B.A. Reid	c Hick, b Butchart	13
M.G. Dimattina*	not out	0
D.R. Gilbert	not out	0
S.P. Davis		
Extras	lb 7, w 1	8
(50 overs)	(for 8 wickets)	220

	O	M	R	W
Rawson	10	3	45	1
Curran	10	4	30	1
Traicos	10	1	27	—
Omarshah	8	—	34	1
Butchart	9	—	56	5
Hick	3	—	21	—

FALL OF WICKETS
1- 18, 2- 61, 3- 93, 4- 96, 5- 155, 6- 194, 7- 212, 8- 218

ZIMBABWE

R.D. Brown	run out	21
G.A. Paterson	c Kerr, b Dodemaide	33
G.A. Hick	c Courtice, b Dodemaide	0
A.J. Pycroft	run out	30
D.L. Houghton*†	c Dimattina, b Dodemaide	7
A.C. Waller	run out	38
K.M. Curran	c Dimattina, b Reid	9
A.H. Omarshah	c Clifford, b Dodemaide	1
I.P. Butchart	c Kerr, b Davis	19
P.W.E. Rawson	not out	45
A.J. Traicos	not out	6
Extras	lb 9, w 1, nb 2	12
(49.5 overs)	(for 9 wickets)	221

	O	M	R	W
Gilbert	10	2	47	—
Davis	9.5	1	52	1
Waugh	10	—	46	1
Dodemaide	10	2	28	4
Reid	10	—	39	1

FALL OF WICKETS
1- 46, 2- 57, 3- 57, 4- 71, 5- 118, 6- 141, 7- 148, 8- 152, 9- 183

Umpires: K. Oddie & I.D. Robinson

Zimbabwe won by 1 wicket

THIRD ONE-DAY INTERNATIONAL – ZIMBABWE v. YOUNG AUSTRALIA
29 September 1985 at Bulawayo Athletic Club

YOUNG AUSTRALIA

B.A. Courtice	st Houghton, Omarshah	33
P.S. Clifford	c Paterson, b Curran	15
R.B. Kerr†	c Houghton, b Curran	0
D.M. Jones	c Waller, b Rawson	4
G.A. Bishop	c Houghton, b Curran	3
S.R. Waugh	c Houghton, b Butchart	1
A.I.C. Dodemaide	c Omarshah, b Traicos	36
M.G. Dimattina*	c sub (Hodgson), b Omarshah	3
B.A. Reid	not out	6
D.R. Gilbert	c and b Traicos	4
S.P. Davis	c Brown, b Butchart	1
Extras	lb 2, w 4, nb 1	7
(44.5 overs)		113

	O	M	R	W
Rawson	7	2	17	1
Curran	10	1	30	3
Butchart	7.5	1	15	2
Omarshah	10	—	29	2
Traicos	10	2	20	2

FALL OF WICKETS
1- 21, 2- 27, 3- 32, 4- 36, 5- 40, 6- 84, 7- 88, 8- 103, 9- 112

ZIMBABWE

R.D. Brown	c Dimattina, b Dodemaide	10
G.A. Paterson	not out	65
G.A. Hick	b Reid	7
A.J. Pycroft	not out	24
D.L. Houghton*†		
A.C. Waller		
K.M. Curran		
A.H. Omarshah		
I.P. Butchart		
P.W.E. Rawson		
A.J. Traicos		
Extras	lb 2, w 4, nb 2	8
(29.1 overs)	(for 2 wickets)	114

	O	M	R	W
Gilbert	6.1	1	29	—
Davis	3	—	9	—
Dodemaide	9	—	33	1
Reid	8	1	26	1
Waugh	3	—	15	—

FALL OF WICKETS
1- 29, 2- 40

Umpires: K. Oddie & I.D. Robinson

Zimbabwe won by 8 wickets

ABOVE: *Steve Waugh is caught by Houghton off the effervescent Butchart for 42. Courtice is the non-striking batsman. Oddie is the umpire. (Bob Nixon)*

LEFT: *Grant Paterson, a fine innings in the third one-day international. (David Munden)*

Third One-Day International
ZIMBABWE v. YOUNG AUSTRALIA

Zimbabwe took the series when they overwhelmed the Australians in Bulawayo. Curran broke what had promised to be a useful opening stand, and dismissed Kerr and the promising Bishop in quick succession. The Young Australians never recovered from these blows and had it not been for Dodemaide's determination, they would not have reached a hundred.

Led by Paterson, Zimbabwe raced to an easy victory in spite of the failure of Hick for whom Bulawayo remains a city in which he has yet to make a substantial score.

Second International
ZIMBABWE v. YOUNG AUSTRALIA

Until half-way through the first day the match went entirely in favour of Zimbabwe. Put in to bat, the Young Australians struggled. Jones again promised much, but was caught just as he looked set for a big score, and, at 147 for 7, the visitors seemed doomed. Curran had run out the reliable Dodemaide from cover and with only Saunders and the tail remaining, a score of 200 looked out of the question.

Three times in one over Saunders snicked Curran short of the slips, but no chances were given and Australia, with Saunders content to score in singles and Dimattina mixing stern defence with belligerent attack, moved to a position of respectability. Dimattina reached a maiden first-class fifty,

RIGHT: *Graeme Hick hits Waugh high over the top during his mighty innings of 154. Hick was destined to be the outstanding batsman of 1986. (Bob Nixon)*

and Kerr declared in time to give Zimbabwe a few hostile overs.

Gilbert was soon bowling at fiery pace, and he had Paterson taken at short-leg off a ball which reared menacingly. Resuming at 6 for 1, Zimbabwe suffered dreadfully at the hands of Gilbert who, in a sustained spell of top class fast bowling, caused the ball to cut and lift viciously from just short of a length. The home batsmen were unable to cope with such deliveries, and it was not until Gilbert was rested that Butchart and Waller took the score past the hundred, and it was only when the last pair were together that the follow-on was avoided.

Kerr, who failed to find his form on the tour, struggled

LEFT: *Peter Rawson who took his 100th first-class wicket during the season. (Ken Kelly)*

to invite them to the 'greatest show on turf' in 1985, for they might well have shaken up that rather jaded occasion.

What Zimbabwe cricket needs is more experience at the first-class level. The leading batsmen, Hick apart, are not building big innings, and the bowlers are more geared to the one-day game.

The Australians, like many before them, must have been surprised by the strength of the opposition, and they returned home chastened and wiser in spite of their success in 'Gilbert's match'. They created a good impression as sportsmen even if Dodemaide and Gilbert were the only ones who really enhanced their reputations.

The cancellation of the tour by the England 'B' party because some of the members of that party had played in South Africa disappointed many of the followers of the game in Zimbabwe and was a severe blow to Zimbabwe's preparations for the I.C.C. Trophy. To compensate for the absence of the England party there were visits from the Irish national side, a young side without five of its top players including Dermot Monteith, and from New South Wales, Sheffield Shield winners. The Irish team played mainly against district, schools and invitation teams, but finished their tour with a three-day game against Zimbabwe Cricket Union President's XI. This match was made memorable by Graeme Hick who hit 2 sixes and 34 fours in an innings which lasted for 394 minutes.

16, 17 and 18 January 1986

at Harare Sports Club

Ireland 211 (D.G. Dennison 84, M.A. Masood 53, C.J. Cox 6 for 65) and 239 (M.A. Masood 81, T.J.T. Patterson 67)

Zimbabwe Cricket Union President's XI 517 for 9 dec (G.A. Hick 309, A. Viljoen 58)

Zimbabwe Cricket Union President's XI won by an innings and 67 runs

The remainder of the season was an anti-climax. The disappointment over the cancellation of the England 'B' tour, a cancellation which did nothing to damage the political structure in South Africa, but hurt cricket in Zimbabwe and elsewhere, was apparent to all. India promised to send a 'B' team as replacement, but after weeks of procrastination they backed down. That Zimbabwe received visitors at all was due to the efforts of Bob Radford, executive director of the New South Wales Cricket Association, who responded to a telephone call from Harare by arranging the visit of the state side within three days.

The New South Wales side was well below strength, with only Bob Holland and Mark Whitney having had Test experience, and the Zimbabwe team and public seemed to respond apathetically. The selectors dropped key players from important matches in order to give youngsters a chance, and, denied a settled policy, the Zimbabwe side was lack-lustre in both the first-class and limited-over series. New South Wales impressed as a side. They were admirably led by Greg Dyer, who won admiration as captain, wicket-keeper, batsman and as a man, and they were a determined and disciplined professional unit. They played well as a side, fielded magnificently and indicated high potential.

Zimbabwe performed spasmodically, and they received a severe blow on the eve of the tour when it was announced that the government had declared Kevin Curran ineligible to represent Zimbabwe. Dual citizenship was abolished in December, 1985, and government policy is that only Zimbabwe citizens, with Zimbabwe passports, should be allowed to represent Zimbabwe at any sport. Curran chose to retain his Irish passport, as to surrender it would have cost him his professional career with Gloucestershire. Negotiations were carried out between the cricket union and the government on the clause in the regulations which allowed a person to retain dual citizenship for up to three years if the change in his status adversely affected his career, but to no avail. The absence of Curran gave Eddo Brandes his opportunity to play for Zimbabwe, and he bowled well, but Curran was sadly missed. The Zimbabwe government did not do well by their cricketers in 1986.

First Limited-Over Match
22 March 1986

at Harare Sports Club

New South Wales 232 for 7 (P.S. Clifford 55)
Zimbabwe 234 for 6 (D.L. Houghton 68, A.C. Waller 57 not out)

Zimbabwe won by 4 wickets

Quickly acclimatising to the conditions, New South Wales gave a good account of themselves, batting soundly after losing 3 quick wickets to slip to 65 for 4. Peter Clifford, making his second tour of Zimbabwe in six months, was top scorer. Zimbabwe struggled to 77 for 4 before Dave Houghton and Andy Waller rescued them with a stand of 72. At 170 for 6, Zimbabwe were still behind the required run rate, but Iain Butchart joined Waller in an aggressive stand which brought victory with an over to spare.

Second Limited-Over Match
23 March 1986

at Harare Sports Club

Zimbabwe 220 (P.W.E. Rawson 53, A.J. Pycroft 52, M. Waugh 4 for 52)
New South Wales 224 for 8 (T. Bayliss 57, M.A. Taylor 50)
New South Wales won by 2 wickets

The New South Wales victory, which came with 4 balls to spare, ended Zimbabwe's run of success in limited-over matches. They had won 19 consecutive one-day games before this defeat. New South Wales had given indication in the first match that they would test the home side, and this proved to be the case as Waugh and Whitney caused early problems. Zimbabwe's run rate was slow, and they were rescued in the middle-order by Pycroft and Rawson whose 1000 runs in the National League had earned him promotion from number 10 to number 8. In contrast, New South Wales began briskly, but slipped to 132 for 6 and looked to be heading for defeat. Two of the least experienced players, Trevor Bayliss and Peter Taylor, rallied their side with a fine stand of 68, and this took New South Wales to the brink of victory and ended Zimbabwe's marvellous run. The blame for defeat rested mainly with the batsmen who failed to build a score substantial enough to give a chance of victory.

26 March 1986

at Mutare

Zimbabwe Cricket Union President's XI *v.* New South Wales

Match abandoned

28, 29 and 31 March 1986

at Harare Sports Club

Zimbabwe 307 (A.J. Pycroft 90, R.G. Holland 4 for 95) and 189 for 8 dec (D.L. Houghton 66, A.J. Pycroft 61, P. Taylor 5 for 39)
New South Wales 214 for 8 dec (G.C. Dyer 85, P.W.E. Rawson 5 for 92) and 166 for 5 (M. Waugh 51 not out)

Match drawn

The match at Mutare was abandoned because of rain and so several young players were deprived of needed experience. For the first of the three-day matches Zimbabwe were without Curran, ineligible, and Paterson who was injured. They were replaced by Gary Wallace, reappearing in first-class cricket after an absence of four years, and Eddo Brandes. Ali Omarshah, back to open the innings, fell to his customary weakness outside the off stump without scoring. Brown played solidly, however, and Pycroft was in magnificent form, but some tight bowling restricted Zimbabwe to 287 for 8 by the close.

Brandes bowled at a lively pace on the second morning, and Rawson, improving after an indifferent start, troubled the visiting batsmen so that, at 166 for 6, New South Wales

were in danger of having to follow-on. They were saved that indignity by skipper Greg Dyer who played a fine aggressive innings before being caught at cover, Hick's third fine catch of the innings. At this point, Dyer declared, and Zimbabwe lost 3 quick wickets, closing at 59 for 3.

The home side failed to score quickly on the last morning, and Houghton's declaration left the tourists to make 283 at more than 5 an over. Inevitably, the game drifted to a draw.

The highlights of the match for Zimbabwe were that Rawson took his hundredth first-class wicket and Houghton his hundredth first-class catch.

Third Limited-Over Match
30 March 1986

at Harare Sports Club

New South Wales 224 for 9 (M.A. Taylor 73)
Zimbabwe 226 for 8 (G.A. Hick 77, A.C. Waller 52)
Zimbabwe won by 2 wickets

A most thrilling game ended with victory for Zimbabwe with two balls to spare. An uneven New South Wales batting display was lifted by M. Taylor and Bower, with a third wicket stand of 77, and by Whitney and Tucker who put on an unbeaten, and invaluable, 26 for the last wicket. Returning to the place of opener, Houghton was caught off Whitney for 0, but Hick and Paterson engaged in a glorious partnership of 92. There followed another fine innings by Waller, and Zimbabwe looked set for victory until Hick fell to a rash shot which sparked a middle-order decline. By the time Iain Butchart came to the wicket, nearly 8 runs an over were required over the last 7 overs. When Mark Waugh began the last over 11 runs were needed. Butchart hit the first ball to the boundary, but, rather unwisely, ran a leg-bye off the second. Jarvis swung wildly at the third and a single was scampered. Butchart put the fourth ball into the crowd to bring victory to Zimbabwe.

Fourth Limited-Over Match
2 April 1986

at Bulawayo Athletic Club

New South Wales 186 (M. Waugh 61)
Zimbabwe 125 (R.P. Done 5 for 21)
New South Wales won by 61 runs

Torn between the desire to win the series and to give young players experience, the Zimbabwe selectors plumped for the latter and paid the price. Paterson, Wallace and Traicos were left out, and batsman Albert Viljoen, pace bowler David Brain and left-arm spinner Chris Cox were included. None of the three newcomers met with success and Zimbabwe were well beaten even though New South Wales, put in to bat on a pitch that had been over-watered, had the worst of the conditions. Waugh played splendidly, but after Hick and Waller had added 47 for Zimbabwe's 2nd wicket, the home side collapsed against Done who having hit 31 at number 10, completed a good all-round match.

4, 5 and 7 April 1986

at Harare Sports Club

New South Wales 314 for 6 dec (M.D. O'Neill 132, M. Waugh 83) and 155 for 5 dec (M.D. O'Neill 55 not out)

The cricketers of Pakistan once again faced an exhausting season. Three domestic competitions were supplemented by a Test and one-day series against Sri Lanka and a one-day international series against West Indies. The national side also had to engage in tournaments in Sharjah, twice, and Sri Lanka where both a Test series and the Asia Cup were contested as well as a three-nation tournament.

The three domestic competitions involved more first-class matches than in any other country with the exception of England; thirty-one matches were scheduled for the Patron's Trophy, sixty-six for the Quaid-e-Azam Trophy and ten in the PACO Pentagular tournament. It is interesting to note that Imran Khan, one of the world's four leading all-rounders and Pakistan's captain, did not appear in any of the domestic competitions.

The season began with the visit of the Sri Lankan party fresh from their first Test triumph, the series win over India.

11 October 1985

at Pindi Club, Rawalpindi
Board President's XI 101
Sri Lankans 104 for 3

Rain reduced this match to one day, and a limited-over game was played which the visitors won by 7 wickets.

First One-Day International
PAKISTAN v. SRI LANKA

Put in to bat on a damp wicket, Sri Lanka were routed by a good all round Pakistan attack. The visitors never recovered from losing both openers for 'ducks'. Silva and Dias followed while the score reached 50, and the only substantial stand was one of 36 for the 8th wicket between de Mel and Rumesh Ratnayake.

When Pakistan batted the pitch had dried and Mudassar and Shoaib ended any hopes of Sri Lanka forcing their way back into the game with an opening stand of 113.

Mudassar fell to de Mel, and Rameez Raja was bowled by slow left-armer Wijesuriya, but Pakistan moved easily to victory with 7.1 overs to spare.

First Test Match
PAKISTAN v. SRI LANKA

The decision by Javed Miandad, the Pakistan captain, and Hanif Mohammad, the chairman of selectors, to play the match on the old wicket rather than a newly-laid one was the main reason that the game was doomed to a draw. Javed believed that the new wicket was uneven and could be dangerous, but the old wicket was notorious for producing huge scores and blunting the efforts of all bowlers.

It was no surprise when Mendis elected to bat on winning the toss, but they must have been very disappointed to lose Silva and Madugalle before lunch, with only 40 scored. Wettimuny and Dias restored Sri Lanka's fortunes with a stand of 85, but both fell in quick succession. Imran, bowling quick and well, had Mendis lbw before the close which came at a miserable 180 for 5 off 77 overs, a slowness of scoring which virtually ended Sri Lanka's chances of winning the match. Pakistan were handicapped when Wasim Akram had to leave the field for a time with a suspected ankle injury.

Sri Lanka recovered to a position of safety on the second day, 363 for 7, thanks mainly to a stand of 121 for the sixth wicket, a Sri Lankan record against Pakistan, between Ranatunga and de Silva. Both batsmen were in good form, but they were aided by some poor Pakistani fielding, four catches being dropped during the day.

Once more the Sri Lankan run rate had been appallingly slow, but on the third day there was a greater sense of

---

FIRST ONE-DAY INTERNATIONAL – PAKISTAN v. SRI LANKA
13 October 1985 at Peshawar

SRI LANKA				PAKISTAN			
P.A. de Silva	c Ashraf, b Imran	0		Mudassar Nazar	lbw, b de Mel	40
R.S. Madugalle	b Zakir	0		Shoaib Mohammad	not out	72
S.A.R. Silva*	b Tahir	25		Rameez Raja	b Wijesuriya	7
R.L. Dias	b Mudassar	5		Javed Miandad†	not out	8
L.R.D. Mendis†	b Abdul Qadir	23		Zaheer Abbas		
A. Ranatunga	lbw, b Abdul Qadir	11		Saleem Malik		
J.R. Ratnayeke	b Mudassar	0		Imran Khan		
A.L.F. de Mel	run out	36		Ashraf Ali*		
R.J. Ratnayake	b Tahir	19		Abdul Qadir		
R.G.C.E. Wijesuriya	lbw, b Imran	0		Tahir Naqqash		
V.B. John	not out	3		Zakir Khan		
	b 4, lb 4, w 9, nb 6	23			b 4, lb 3, w 7, nb 6	20
	(39.2 overs)	145			(32.5 overs) (for 2 wickets)	147

	O	M	R	W		O	M	R	W
Imran Khan	8	—	22	1	de Mel	8	2	27	1
Zakir Khan	8	2	21	1	John	5	—	28	—
Mudassar Nazar	8	—	31	2	R.J. Ratnayake	5	—	22	—
Tahir Naqqash	7.2	—	34	2	Wijesuriya	6	1	18	1
Abdul Qadir	8	—	34	2	J.R. Ratnayeke	4.5	—	33	—
					Ranatunga	4	—	12	—

FALL OF WICKETS
1- 2, 2- 11, 3- 35, 4- 50, 5- 66, 6- 69, 7- 90, 8- 126, 9- 133

FALL OF WICKETS
1- 113, 2- 138

Pakistan won by 8 wickets

urgency. Aravinda de Silva hit Imran for six to reach a maiden Test century on the day after his twentieth birthday. He was finally caught behind off Imran, but by then he had batted for 510 minutes and hit 3 sixes and 17 fours. By the close, Pakistan were 86 for 0 and the game was dying.

There was a spark of excitement on the fourth morning when Rumesh Ratnayake dismissed Shoaib in the first over of the day. He also had Mudassar lbw in the first over after lunch, but from then on the bat dominated. Javed and Qasim established a 3rd wicket record against Sri Lanka with a stand of 397 which was not ended until after tea on the last day when, following the dismissal of Qasim, the captains agreed to close the match.

Second One-Day International
PAKISTAN v. SRI LANKA

With the ground packed with more spectators than it could safely hold, a tragedy occured when a branch of a tree from which some of the crowd were watching broke. One man was killed and eight others were injured in the accident.

Pakistan were struggling somewhat until a blistering 5th wicket partnership between Zaheer Abbas and Saleem Malik realised 116 runs and set Sri Lanka a target of $5\frac{1}{2}$ runs an over.

RIGHT: *Qasim Umar, 206, and a record partnership with Javed Miandad in the first Test against Sri Lanka at Faisalabad. (David Munden)*

FIRST TEST MATCH – PAKISTAN v. SRI LANKA
16, 17, 18, 20 and 21 October 1985 at Faisalabad

SRI LANKA

	FIRST INNINGS	
S. Wettimuny	lbw, b Qadir	52
S.A.R. Silva*	c Shoaib, b Imran	17
R.S. Madugalle	b Mudassar	5
R.L. Dias	c Ashraf, b Jalaluddin	48
L.R.D. Mendis†	lbw, b Imran	15
A. Ranatunga	c Shoaib, b Qadir	79
P.A. de Silva	c Ashraf, b Imran	122
J.R. Ratnayeke	run out	34
A.L.F. de Mel	c Ashraf, b Wasim	17
R.J. Ratnayake	lbw, b Qadir	56
R.G.C.E. Wijesuriya	not out	7
	b 4, lb 12, w 2, nb 9	27
		479

	O	M	R	W
Imran Khan	49	15	112	3
Wasim Akram	42.3	12	97	1
Jalaluddin	39	10	89	1
Mudassar Nazar	13.3	3	29	1
Abdul Qadir	53.3	16	132	3
Shoaib Mohammad	2	1	4	—

FALL OF WICKETS
1- 23, 2- 40, 3- 125, 4- 129, 5- 165, 6- 286, 7- 352, 8- 391, 9- 443

PAKISTAN

	FIRST INNINGS	
Mudassar Nazar	lbw, b R.J. Ratnayake	78
Shoaib Moham- mad	c Silva, b R.J. Ratnayake	33
Qasim Umar	b J.R. Ratnayeke	206
Javed Miandad†	not out	203
Zaheer Abbas		
Saleem Malik		
Imran Khan		
Ashraf Ali*		
Abdul Qadir		
Wasim Akram		
Jalaluddin		
	b 6, lb 7, w 1, nb 11	35
	(for 3 wickets)	555

	O	M	R	W
de Mel	27	3	107	—
R.J. Ratnayake	32	4	93	2
J.R. Ratnayeke	29	5	117	1
Wijesuriya	44	12	102	—
Ranatunga	18	1	74	—
Madugalle	7	1	18	—
de Silva	5	—	21	—

FALL OF WICKETS
1- 86, 2- 158, 3- 555

Umpires: Mahboob Shah & Khizar Hayat

Match drawn

SECOND ONE-DAY INTERNATIONAL – PAKISTAN v. SRI LANKA
23 October 1985 at Gujranwala

PAKISTAN				SRI LANKA			
Mudassar Nazar	c Silva, b R.J. Ratnayake		11	S.A.R. Silva	c Saleem Yousuf,		
Shoaib Mohammad	c Madugalle, b de Mel		4		b Abdul Qadir		19
Rameez Raja	b Wijesuriya		45	P.A. de Silva	run out		86
Javed Miandad†	c Silva, b R.J. Ratnayake		10	R.S. Madugalle	c Javed, b Abdul Qadir		7
Zaheer Abbas	c de Silva, b R.J. Ratnayake		61	R.L. Dias	c Tahir, b Imran		45
Saleem Malik	not out		72	L.R.D. Mendis†	run out		4
Imran Khan	not out		1	A. Ranatunga	not out		17
Tahir Naqqash				A.L.F. de Mel	b Tahir		7
Saleem Yousuf*				R.J. Ratnayake	run out		9
Abdul Qadir				J.R. Ratnayeke	not out		0
Zakir Khan				R.G.C.E. Wijesuriya			
	lb 7, w 11, nb 2		20	V.B. John			
			—		lb 10, w 4, nb 3		17
(40 overs)	(for 5 wickets)		224				—
				(40 overs)	(for 7 wickets)		209

	O	M	R	W		O	M	R	W
de Mel	6	—	41	1	Imran Khan	8	—	47	1
John	8	1	17	—	Zakir Khan	3	—	23	—
R.J. Ratnayake	8	—	51	3	Abdul Qadir	8	—	25	2
J.R. Ratnayeke	6	—	44	—	Mudassar Nazar	8	—	39	—
Wijesuriya	8	—	40	1	Shoaib Mohammad	6	—	30	—
Ranatunga	4	—	24	—	Tahir Naqqash	7	—	35	1

FALL OF WICKETS
1- 6, 2- 49, 3- 68, 4- 106, 5- 222

FALL OF WICKETS
1- 53, 2- 65, 3- 161, 4- 163, 5- 169, 6- 185, 7- 209

Pakistan won by 15 runs

While Aravinda de Silva was batting Sri Lanka always had a chance of victory. He had been named Man of the Match in the first Test and won the individual award again with a fine knock which included 4 sixes, two of them off Imran Khan. He and Dias gave Sri Lanka hope with a brisk stand of 96, but they went in quick succession and the challenge faded.

Third One-Day International
PAKISTAN v. SRI LANKA

A crowd of more than 40,000 people saw Pakistan clinch the one-day series with a five wicket victory. The match was reduced to 38 overs a side in order to finish early enough for Moslem Friday prayer meetings.

THIRD ONE-DAY INTERNATIONAL – PAKISTAN v. SRI LANKA
25 October 1985 at Lahore

SRI LANKA			SRI LANKA			
S.A.R Silvia*	lbw, b Tahir	19	PAKISTAN	Mudassar Nazar	run out	16
P.A. de Silva	lbw, b Imran	0		Shoaib Mohammad	b de Mel	14
R.S. Madugalle	c Imran, b Mudassar	73		Rameez Raja	c de Mel, b R.J. Ratnayake	56
A. Ranatunga	b Tahir	39		Javed Miandad†	not out	91
R.L. Dias	c Saleem Malik,			Zaheer Abbas	b Ranatunga	21
	b Mudassar	9		Saleem Malik	c de Mel, b R.J. Ratnayake	13
L.R.D. Mendis†	not out	25		Imran Khan	not out	2
A.L.F. de Mel	c Saleem Yousuf, b Tahir	2		Saleem Yousuf*		
R.J. Ratnayake	c Zahir, b Mohsin Kamal	26		Tahir Naqqash		
R.G.C.E. Wijesuriya	not out	6		Abdul Qadir		
F.S. Ahangama				Mohsin Kamal		
V.B. John					b 1, lb 5, w 6, nb 6	18
	b 4, lb 16, w 8, nb 1	29				—
		—		(36.3 overs)	(for 5 wickets)	231
(38 overs)	(for 7 wickets)	228				

	O	M	R	W		O	M	R	W
Imran Khan	7	1	33	1	de Mel	7	—	38	1
Mohsin Kamal	6	1	18	1	John	8	—	45	—
Abdul Qadir	8	—	26	—	R.J. Ratnayake	6.3	—	50	2
Tahir Naqqash	8	—	58	3	Ahangama	3	—	23	—
Mudassar Nazar	6	—	41	2	Wijesuriya	8	—	46	—
Saleem Malik	2	—	22	—	Ranatunga	4	—	23	1
Shoaib Mohammad	1	—	10	—					

FALL OF WICKETS
1- 2, 2- 42, 3- 135, 4- 151, 5- 165, 6- 174, 7- 211

FALL OF WICKETS
1- 27, 2- 53, 3- 130, 4- 188, 5- 206

Pakistan won by 5 wickets

Sri Lanka batted first and began uncertainly, but Madugalle batted splendidly and dominated a 3rd wicket stand of 83 with Ranatunga. Wickets then fell regularly, but Mendis and Rumesh Ratnayake bolstered the innings and Pakistan were left a target of 229 at more than six an over.

Mudassar and Shoaib failed to establish themselves, but Rameez Raja and Javed added 77 at the required rate and Pakistan were always on course for victory after their stand. Javed took total command and brought his side a win with nine balls to spare. He was named Man of the Match.

Second Test Match
PAKISTAN v. SRI LANKA

The first Test match to be played in the northern town of Sialkot close to the Indian border ended in triumph for Pakistan, but there was much incident and controversy on the way.

Sri Lanka struggled from the start on a lively wicket. Wettimuny and Silva began firmly enough, but Silva fell to change bowler Mudassar and Madugalle went to Mohsin Kamal without addition to the score. Dias was also struck on the wrist by a ball from Mohsin and was taken to hospital where an X-ray revealed that the wrist was not broken. He returned to the crease at the fall of the 7th wicket.

The back of the Sri Lankan innings was broken by Imran who, in a post lunch spell, captured three wickets for 3 runs in two overs. Wettimuny, who had batted with much assurance in difficult circumstances, was caught behind, and Aravinda de Silva quickly followed. De Silva shaped to play Imran down the leg side, but dislodged a bail as he moved back. In the same over Ravi Ratnayeke was also caught behind to leave Sri Lanka floundering at 101 for 6.

Ranatunga offered brave resistance, but Dias, badly bruised, could not regain his touch and Sri Lanka were all out twenty minutes before the close. Pakistan had scored 4 when bad light ended play early.

By lunch time on the second day, Pakistan had reached 93 for 2 and were in a position of total dominance. The wicket, which never played easily and always offered the pace men some help, was at its most encouraging for the batsmen early in the morning and Mudassar and Mohsin Khan made the most of it in a sparkling opening stand. Mohsin fell to Rumesh Ratnayake and Qasim went quickly, the first of Ravi Ratnayeke's eight victims.

Controversy flared in the afternoon when Rumesh Ratnayake passed the outside of Javed's bat with a fiercely lifting ball. There was a mighty appeal from all the Sri Lankan players close to the wicket as Silva caught the ball. Umpire Javed Akhtar ruled not out, and the visitors reacted angrily. Three times the umpires had to suspend play and complain to

---

SECOND TEST MATCH – PAKISTAN v. SRI LANKA
27, 28, 29 and 31 October 1985 at Sialkot

SRI LANKA

Batsman	FIRST INNINGS		SECOND INNINGS	
S. Wettimuny	c Saleem Yousuf, b Imran	45	lbw, b Imran	0
S.A.R. Silva*	c Qasim, b Mudassar	12	c Wasim, b Mudassar	35
R.S. Madugalle	c Saleem Yousuf, b Kamal	0	c Javed, b Kamal	65
R.L. Dias	c Qasim, b Mohsin Kamal	21	lbw, b Mudassar	7
L.R.D. Mendis†	c Mudassar, b Kamal	20	c Saleem Yousuf, b Wasim	3
A. Ranatunga	not out	25	c Malik, b Imran	29
P.A. de Silva	hit wkt, b Imran	2	c Saleem Yousuf, b Wasim	8
J.R. Ratnayeke	c Saleem Yousuf, b Imran	0	not out	16
A.L.F. de Mel	lbw, b Wasim	1	b Imran	0
R.J. Ratnayake	b Imran	1	c sub, b Imran	2
R.G.C.E. Wijesuriya	lbw, b Wasim	8	lbw, b Imran	0
	b 6, lb 2, w 3, nb 11	22	b 9, lb 10, nb 16	35
		157		200

	O	M	R	W	O	M	R	W
Imran Khan	19	3	55	4	18.3	5	40	5
Wasim Akram	14.2	4	38	2	19	4	74	2
Mohsin Kamal	17	3	50	3	12	2	38	1
Mudassar Nazar	6	1	6	1	11.5	1	28	2
Abdul Qadir					1.1	—	1	—

PAKISTAN

Batsman	FIRST INNINGS		SECOND INNINGS	
Mudassar Nazar	c Silva, b R.J. Ratnayake	78	not out	24
Mohsin Khan	lbw, b R.J. Ratnayake	50	run out	44
Qasim Umar	c Wijesuriya, b J.R. Ratnayeke	1	c Ranatunga, b de Mel	3
Javed Miandad†	lbw, b J.R. Ratnayeke	40		
Zaheer Abbas	lbw, b J.R. Ratnayeke	4		
Saleem Malik	lbw, b J.R. Ratnayeke	22		
Imran Khan	c sub, b J.R. Ratnayeke	6	(4) not out	13
Saleem Yousuf*	lbw, b J.R. Ratnayeke	23		
Abdul Qadir	c Silva, b J.R. Ratnayeke	10		
Wasim Akram	c Silva, b J.R. Ratnayeke	4		
Mohsin Kamal	not out	4		
	b 5, lb 3, w 1, nb 8	17	b 4, lb 4, nb 8	16
		259	for 2 wkts	100

	O	M	R	W	O	M	R	W
de Mel	15	3	63	—	10	1	43	1
R.J. Ratnayake	18	2	77	2	6	—	24	—
J.R. Ratnayeke	23.2	5	83	8	7.4	1	25	—
Ranatunga	3	—	18	—				
Wijesuriya	4	1	10	—				

FALL OF WICKETS
1- 41, 2- 41, 3- 81, 4- 99, 5- 101, 7- 110, 8- 130, 9- 131
1- 0, 2- 98, 3- 111, 4- 121, 5- 147, 6- 163, 7- 188, 8- 188, 9- 200

FALL OF WICKETS
1- 88, 2- 93, 3- 181, 4- 185, 5- 209, 6- 216, 7- 216, 8- 245, 9- 252
1- 76, 2- 82

Umpires: Javed Akhtar & Mian Aslam

Pakistan won by 8 wickets

Ravi Ratnayeke who established a Sri Lankan record for Test cricket when he took 8 for 83 in the second Test in Sialkot. (Michael King)

Zaheer Abbas. A great batsman says goodbye to Test cricket. (Tony Edenden)

Mendis about the behaviour of his side who continued to remonstrate bitterly. At one point Javed, who had scored 11 when the incident happened, and Ranatunga had to be separated by other players as their argument became more heated.

This incident tended to overshadow the performance of medium pace bowler Ravi Ratnayeke who returned figures of 8 for 83, a career best and the best achieved by a Sri Lankan in Test cricket, beating Rumesh Ratnayake's month old record. Ratnayeke moved the ball appreciably and his inswinger proved particularly devastating. It was an outstanding performance, but it could not prevent Pakistan from taking a first innings lead of 102. They had scored their runs at four an over and so made victory a distinct probability.

The third day was one of fluctuating fortune, but at the end of it, Pakistan were in sight of victory. Imran dismissed Wettimuny in the first over of the day, but Silva and Madugalle then played admirably in a stand of 98 which took Sri Lanka safely into the afternoon. It was Mudassar who again displayed his usefulness as a medium pace swing bowler who broke the stand when he had Silva caught. Mudassar then had Dias lbw, and with Mendis also falling before tea, Sri Lanka were stumbling again at 142 for 4.

Ranjan Madugalle, who batted 271 minutes and hit 9 fours, was caught at slip shortly after tea with the score on 147. It was Imran who put Pakistan in total command. He had no success since his first over of the day, but in his 18th over he had Ranatunga taken by Saleem Malik. At the same total, 188, he bowled de Mel, and in his next over, he had

Rumesh Ratnayake caught by substitute Rameez Raja at forward short leg. He ended a spell of 4 for 3 when he had Wijesuriya leg before. Imran's 5 for 40 was the 17th time he had taken five or more wickets in a Test innings and it left Pakistan with a simple task.

Mudassar and Mohsin ended any lingering hopes of a miracle that Sri Lanka may have cherished with an opening stand of 76. Mohsin Khan was run out and Qasim fell six runs later, but Saleem Yousuf hit Ravi Ratnayeke for four shortly before lunch to bring victory, a victory which was greeted with a crescendo of firecrackers.

At the end of the match Javed Miandad announced that he was to give up the captaincy after the current series in order to concentrate on his batting, and, not surprisingly, Imran, re-established as a national hero, was named as his successor. Zaheer Abbas also announced that he was retiring from Test cricket although he would still be available for one-day internationals.

The consolation for Sri Lanka was that Ravi Ratnayeke, with his record-breaking haul in Pakistan's first innings, was named Man of the Match.

Fourth One-Day International
PAKISTAN v. SRI LANKA

Pakistan completed a clean sweep of the one-day internationals with their fourth win in four matches. Put in to bat, Pakistan reached only a moderate score and owed most to a steady innings by Javed Miandad who was ably supported by the enthusiastic young Rameez Raja. Play was suspended for twenty-five minutes after Madugalle had been hit on the head by a stone thrown from the crowd. The Sri Lankans insisted on assurance as to their safety before they would return to the field.

Aravinda de Silva began in lively enough fashion, but once he had fallen, the innings disintegrated limply and only skipper Mendis offered any sort of resistance.

Third Test Match
PAKISTAN v. SRI LANKA

There was some disappointment for Pakistan on the eve of the Test when it was announced that Zaheer Abbas had withdrawn from the match. This was to have been Zaheer's last Test, and it was sad that this great batsman who had brought so much charm to the international scene should be denied a suitable farewell. Zaheer hit more than five thousand Test runs, including 12 centuries. His place was taken by Rameez Raja.

Sri Lanka dropped Amal Silva who, a few weeks earlier, had been the hero of the series against India, and gave a first Test cap to Asanka Gurusinghe.

Mendis won the toss and seemed to have no hesitation in batting first. Sri Lanka began quietly, but, in his second spell, Wasim Akram bowled Wettimuny and had Madugalle lbw within the space of ten deliveries. At lunch, Sri Lanka were 56 for 2. The afternoon brought total disaster.

Imran had Roy Dias caught behind and then Abdul Qadir

tormented with his leg-spin. He found that the pitch gave him some assistance and the Sri Lankan batsmen groped painfully as he flighted the ball intelligently and bewildered with his spin. For the ninth time in a Test innings, he took five or more wickets, and Sri Lanka were all out seven minutes before the scheduled close. Among his victims he numbered top-scorer Ravi Ratnayeke, the make-shift opener. The only other Sri Lankan batsman to offer substantial resistance was Rumesh Ratnayake who came in at 125 for 8 and was mainly responsible for the score reaching 162.

If it seemed that Sri Lanka had forfeited any hope of victory, Asantha de Mel had other ideas, for, on the second morning, he took four wickets in 28 balls to reduce Pakistan to 68 for 4 at lunch. Mohsin Khan was the first to go, edging to the wicket-keeper, and Qasim Umar followed when he touched to Ranatunga at slip. Mudassar also went caught behind and when Saleem Malik was bowled Pakistan were in dire straits.

Javed Miandad and Rameez Raja engaged in an afternoon stand of 85 which swayed the game back in favour of Pakistan, and Imran Khan then arrived to play an enterprising innings. He excited the crowd as he dominated a sixth wicket partnership of 75 in 71 minutes with Rameez Raja. Pakistan ended the day with a lead of 132 in spite of de Mel's career best performance.

They added only one run on the third morning before the innings ended, but Sri Lanka were once again quickly in trouble. Imran Khan, who was leading the side in the absence of Javed who had injured a thumb, dismissed Ratnayeke with the last ball of his fourth over and had Wettimuny caught behind with the final ball of his next over. Aravinda

---

FOURTH ONE-DAY INTERNATIONAL – PAKISTAN v. SRI LANKA
3 November 1985 at Hyderabad

PAKISTAN				SRI LANKA			
Mudassar Nazar	c and b Wijesuriya	29		P.A. de Silva	c Mohsin Khan,		
Mohsin Khan	lbw, b John	6			b Mohsin Kamal	19	
Rameez Raja	lbw, b J.R. Ratnayeke	45		J.R. Ratnayeke	c Saleem Yousuf,		
Javed Miandad†	c sub, b J.R. Ratnayeke	56			b Mohsin Kamal	8	
Zaheer Abbas	c Gurusinghe,			R.S. Madugalle	c Tahir, b Mudassar	9	
	b J.R. Ratnayeke	26		R.L. Dias	b Mudassar	13	
Saleem Malik	c Mendis, b Wijesuriya	16		L.R.D. Mendis†	st Saleem Yousuf,		
Saleem Yousuf*	b R.J. Ratnayeke	0			b Abdul Qadir	46	
Abdul Qadir	not out	20		A. Ranatunga	c Tahir, b Tauseef	1	
Tahir Naqqash	not out	7		A.P. Gurusinghe*	run out	0	
Tauseef Ahmed				A.L.F. de Mel	c sub, b Zaheer	0	
Mohsin Kamal				R.J. Ratnayake	c Mohsin Kamal, b Zaheer	2	
	b 4, lb 7	11		R.G.C.E. Wijesuriya	not out	12	
				V.B. John	c Saleem Malik,		
	(39 overs)	(for 7 wickets)	216		b Abdul Qadir	7	
					lb 7, w 1, nb 2	10	
					(37.2 overs)	127	

	O	M	R	W		O	M	R	W
John	8	1	34	1	Mohsin Kamal	4	—	26	2
de Mel	8	1	42	—	Tahir Naqqash	3	—	12	—
R.J. Ratnayake	8	—	45	1	Mudassar Nazar	8	—	23	2
Wijesuriya	5	—	25	2	Tauseef Ahmed	8	2	20	1
J.R. Ratnayeke	6	—	34	3	Abdul Qadir	7.2	2	13	2
Ranatunga	4	—	25	—	Zaheer Abbas	7	—	26	2

FALL OF WICKETS
1- 12, 2- 81, 3- 91, 4- 127, 5- 163, 6- 168, 7- 195

FALL OF WICKETS
1- 20, 2- 34, 3- 41, 4- 69, 5- 80, 6- 83, 7- 87, 8- 91, 9- 112

Pakistan won by 89 runs

THIRD TEST MATCH – PAKISTAN v. SRI LANKA
7, 8, 9 and 11 November 1985 at Karachi

SRI LANKA

	FIRST INNINGS			SECOND INNINGS	
S. Wettimuny	b Wasim Akram	17	c Yousuf, b Imran	10
J. R. Ratnayeke	b Abdul Qadir	36	c Yousuf, b Imran	3
R.S. Madugalle	lbw, b Wasim Akram	0	(8) b Tauseef	5
R.L. Dias	c Yousuf, b Imran	7	c Malik, b Qadir	4
L.R.D. Mendis†	c Javed, b Qadir	15	(7) b Imran	2
A. Ranatunga	c Javed, b Tauseef	12	(5) c Yousuf, b Akram	25
P.A. de Silva	c and b Qadir	13	(3) c Yousuf, b Tauseef	105
A.P. Gurusinghe*	lbw, b Imran	17	(6) c Yousuf, b Tauseef	12
A.L.F. de Mel	st Yousuf, b Qadir	3	lbw, b Tauseef	18
R.J. Ratnayake	not out	21	c Umar, b Tauseef	22
R.G.C.E. Wijesuriya	lbw, b Qadir	2	not out	2
	b 5, lb 10, w 1, nb 3	19	b 5, lb 11, nb 6	22
		162		**230**

PAKISTAN

	FIRST INNINGS			SECOND INNINGS	
Mudassar Nazar	c Gurusinghe, b de Mel	16	not out	57
Mohsin Khan	c Gurusinghe, b de Mel	13	not out	36
Qasim Umar	c Ranatunga, b de Mel	8		
Javed Miandad†	lbw, b de Mel	63		
Saleem Malik	b de Mel	4		
Rameez Raja	c and b de Mel	52		
Imran Khan	c R.J. Ratnayake, b J.R. Ratnayake	63		
Saleem Yousuf*	lbw, b R.J. Ratnayake	27		
Abdul Qadir	c Wettimuny, b Wijesuriya	19		
Tauseef Ahmed	b R.J. Ratnayake	1		
Wasim Akram	not out	5		
	b 13, lb 8, w 2, nb 1	24	b 1, lb 3, nb 1	5
		295	(for no wkt)	**98**

	O	M	R	W	O	M	R	W
Imran Khan	20	9	36	2	14.1	5	28	3
Wasim Akram	14	7	17	2	14	4	24	1
Tauseef Ahmed	22	10	50	1	23.2	8	54	5
Abdul Qadir	20.5	5	44	5	25.5	4	102	1
Mudassar Nazar					3	—	6	—

	O	M	R	W	O	M	R	W
de Mel	22	1	109	6	3	—	28	—
R.J. Ratnayake	15	2	48	2	4	—	33	—
J.R. Ratnayeke	15	4	48	1	6	1	24	—
Wijesuriya	22	5	68	1	3.4	2	9	—
Ranatunga	1	—	1	—				

FALL OF WICKETS
1- 27, 2- 28, 3- 60, 4- 89, 5- 90, 6- 106, 7- 122, 8- 125, 9- 151
1- 14, 2- 15, 3- 57, 4- 104, 5- 132, 6- 139, 7- 157, 8- 191, 9- 221

FALL OF WICKETS
1- 27, 2- 43, 3- 60, 4- 68, 5- 153, 6- 228, 7- 259, 8- 288, 9- 290

Umpires: Mahboob Shah & Khizar Hayat

Pakistan won by 10 wickets

Pakistan v. Sri Lanka Test Match Averages

PAKISTAN BATTING

	M	Inns	NOs	Runs	HS	Av	100s	50s
Javed Miandad	3	3	1	306	203*	153.00	1	1
Mudassar Nazar	3	5	2	253	78	84.33		3
Qasim Umar	3	4		218	206	54.50	1	
Mohsin Khan	2	4		143	50	47.66		1
Imran Khan	3	2		69	63	34.50		1
Saleem Yousuf	2	3	1	63	27	31.50		
Abdul Qadir	3	2		29	19	14.50		
Saleem Malik	3	2		26	22	13.00		
Wasim Akram	3	2	1	9	5*	9.00		

Played in two Tests: Zaheer Abbas 4
Played in one Test: Mohsin Kamal 4*, Shoaib Mohammad 33, Rameez Raja 52, Tauseef Ahmed 1, Ashraf Ali and Jalaluddin did not bat

SRI LANKA BATTING

	M	Inns	NOs	Runs	HS	Av	100s	50s
P.A. de Silva	3	5		250	122	50.00	2	
A. Ranatunga	3	5	1	170	79	42.50		1
R.J. Ratnayake	3	5	1	102	56	25.50		1
S. Wettimuny	3	5		124	52	24.80		1
J.R. Ratnayeke	3	5	1	89	36	22.25		
S.A.R. Silva	2	3		64	35	21.33		
R.L. Dias	3	5		87	48	17.40		
R.S. Madugalle	3	5		75	65	15.00		1
L.R.D. Mendis	3	5		55	20	11.00		
A.L.F. de Mel	3	5		39	18	7.80		
R.G.C.E. Wijesuriya	3	5	2	19	8	6.33		

Played in one Test: A.P. Gurusinghe 17 & 12

PAKISTAN BOWLING

	Overs	Mds	Runs	Wkts	Av	Best	5/inns
Imran Khan	120.4	37	271	17	15.94	5/40	1
Mudassar Nazar	34.2	5	69	4	17.25	2/28	
Tauseef Ahmed	45.2	18	104	6	17.33	5/54	1
Mohsin Kamal	29	5	88	4	22.00	3/50	
Abdul Qadir	101.2	25	279	9	31.00	5/44	1
Wasim Akram	103.5	31	250	8	31.25	2/17	
Jalaluddin	39	10	89	1	89.00	1/89	

Also bowled: Shoaib Mohammad 2-1-4-0

SRI LANKA BOWLING

	Overs	Mds	Runs	Wkts	Av	Best	5/inns
J.R. Ratnayeke	81	20	297	10	29.70	8/83	1
R.J. Ratnayake	75	8	275	6	45.83	2/48	
A.L.F. de Mel	77	8	350	7	50.00	6/109	1
R.G.C.E. Wijesuriya	73.4	20	189	1	189.00	1/68	
A. Ranatunga	22	1	93	0	—	—	

Also bowled: R.S. Madugalle 7-1-18-0; P.A. de Silva 5-0-21-0

PAKISTAN CATCHES
12 - Saleem Yousuf (ct 11/st 1); 3 - Javed Miandad, Ashraf Ali and Qasim Umar; 2 - Saleem Malik and Shoaib Mohammad; 1 - Mudassar Nazar, Abdul Qadir, Wasim Akram and sub (Rameez Raja)

SRI LANKA CATCHES
4 -S.A.R. Silva; 2 - A.P. Gurusinghe and A. Ranatunga; 1 - S. Wettimuny, A.L.F. de Mel, R.J. Ratnayake, R.G.C.E. Wijesuriya and sub

ABOVE: *Aravinda de Silva hit two centuries for Sri Lanka in the Test series against Pakistan. A young batsman of immense talent. (Patrick Eagar)*

RIGHT: *Tauseef Ahmed established himself at home and abroad as Pakistan's leading off-spinner. (Adrian Murrell)*

de Silva responded with some exciting shots, and at lunch Sri Lanka were 52 for 2.

There was a delay of twenty minutes in the afternoon due to crowd trouble, but Sri Lanka lost three more wickets in the session, and, never happy against the mixture of pace and spin, they crumpled to 137 for 5. There was no effective recovery in the final session when Imran bowled Mendis and off-spinner Tauseef captured two cheap wickets. Imran had been forced to leave the field before the close with a suspected thigh injury. Mudassar became the third player to lead Pakistan during the match.

Sri Lanka's one bright light was the batting of Aravinda de Silva. He reached his second Test hundred with a majestic pull to mid-wicket off Abdul Qadir. It was the sixteenth four of a fine innings which had lasted for 265 minutes. Barely twenty years old, de Silva is unquestionably destined to be one of the world's great Test batsmen.

Sri Lanka finished the third day with a lead of 83 and only two wickets in hand. They added 14 on the fourth morning in 26 minutes. Aravinda de Silva was caught behind as he attempted to pull. His innings had lasted 249 minutes and he was named as Man of the Match and Sri Lanka's Man of the Series. Tauseef Ahmed captured both wickets that fell to finish with 5 for 54.

It took Mudassar and Mohsin only 74 minutes in which to score the runs that Pakistan needed for victory, a victory that was accomplished with $3\frac{1}{2}$ hours and a day to spare. Javed Miandad, the triumphant captain, was named as Pakistan's Man of the Series.

B.C.C.P. Patron's Trophy

The Trophy was again contested by seventeen teams. The match between Sukkur and Quetta in Group A was not played, each side received 9 points.

Group A

14 and 15 November 1985

at National Stadium, Karachi

Sukkur 117 (Jalal-ud-Din 5 for 32) and 79 (Iqbal Sikander 6 for 29, Ijaz Faqih 4 for 14)
Karachi Whites 322 for 5 (Moin-ul-Atiq 177 not out, Asif Mujtaba 50)

Karachi Whites won by an innings and 126 runs
Karachi Whites 18 pts, Sukkur 3 pts

Karachi Whites, far superior to any other side in the group, overwhelmed Sukkur in two days. Moin-ul-Atiq opened the innings and shared a third wicket stand of 102 with Asif Mujtaba and a fifth wicket stand of 101 with Sajid Riaz.

19, 20 and 21 November 1985

at Niaz Stadium, Hyderabad

Hyderabad 282 (Nadeem Jamal 149, Rasheed Ghanchi 52, Mohammad Younus 5 for 87) and 172 (Javed Ali 4 for 59)
Sukkur 209 for 8 (Israr Ahmed 108) and 142 (Anwar Iqbal 6 for 43)

Hyderabad won by 103 runs
Hyderabad 18 pts, Sukkur 6 pts

at National Stadium, Karachi

Quetta 115 (Iqbal Qasim 4 for 15) and 124 (Shahid Mahboob 76, Iqbal Sikander 6 for 36)
Karachi Whites 289 for 4 (Asif Mujtaba 131 not out, Ijaz Faqih 112)

Karachi Whites won by an innings and 50 runs
Karachi Whites 18 pts, Quetta 2 pts

Karachi Whites won in two days and were well served by Asif Mujtaba and Ijaz Faqih who added 237 for the fourth wicket, the second best stand for any wicket in the competition during the season. Hyderabad, the only side likely to challenge the Whites in Group A, recovered from 121 for 7 against Sukkur, Nadeem and Rasheed Ghanchi adding 144 for the eighth wicket.

24, 25 and 26 November 1985

at National Stadium, Karachi

Quetta 326 for 6 (Raees Ahmed 102 not out, Imran Khan 66, Rashid Raza 56) and 218 for 5 dec. (Tehsin Ahmed 102 not out)
Hyderabad 185 (Ghulam Ali 64, Tehsin Ahmed 5 for 54) and 264 for 7 (Nadeem Jamal 120)

Match drawn
Quetta 10 pts, Hyderabad 4 pts

Rashid and Imran, not to be confused with the Pakistan captain, put on 119 for Quetta's first wicket.

3 and 4 December 1985

at Niaz Stadium, Hyderabad

Hyderabad 128 and 100 (Iqbal Sikander 6 for 35)
Karachi Whites 298 for 6 (Ijaz Faqih 89, Asif Mujtaba 77)

Karachi Whites won by an innings and 70 runs
Karachi Whites 18 pts, Hyderabad 3 pts

Karachi Whites completed a clean sweep in Group A when they took maximum points with an innings victory inside two days. Iqbal Sikander had match figures of 9 for 80, the best performance by a Karachi Whites bowler during the tournament.

Group A Final Table						
	P	W	L	D	Ab	Pts
Karachi Whites	3	3	–	–	–	54
Hyderabad	3	1	1	1	–	25
Quetta	3	–	1	1	1	21
Sukkur	3	–	2	–	1	18

Group B

8, 9 and 10 November 1985

at Bahawal Stadium, Bahawalpur

Karachi Blues 207 (Mohammad Altaf 5 for 61) and 243 for 8 dec (Rizwan-uz-Zaman 80, Nasir Shah 54, Mohammad Altaf 4 for 52)
Bahawalpur 158 (Rizwan-uz-Zaman 5 for 16) and 159 (Rizwan-uz-Zaman 5 for 27)

Karachi Blues won by 133 runs
Karachi Blues 16 pts, Bahawalpur 5 pts

at Qasim Bagh Stadium, Multan

Multan 229 (Rizwan Sattar 62, Sajjad Akbar 5 for 71, Ghaafar Kazmi 4 for 47) and 161 (Sajjad Akbar 4 for 26, Ghaffar Kazmi 4 for 63)
Lahore City Blues 282 for 9 (Tanvir Ahmed 109, Shahid Butt 4 for 68) and 111 for 2 (Tanvir Ahmed 50)

Lahore City Blues won by 8 wickets
Lahore City Blues 18 pts, Multan 7 pts

The two most favoured teams in the group began with impressive wins.

13, 14 and 15 November 1985

at Bahawal Stadium, Bahawalpur

Bahawalpur 118 and 185 (Rashid Shera 163, Abdur Rahim 61, Sajjad Akbar 4 for 42)
Lahore City Blues 238 (Saadat Ali 56, Mohammad Altaf 6 for 63) and 66 for 1

Lahore City Blues won by 9 wickets
Lahore City Blues 17 pts, Bahawalpur 4 pts

at Montgomery Biscuit Factory, Sahiwal

Karachi Blues 223 (Nadeem Moosa 71, Rashid Khan 67 not out, Manzoor Elahi 4 for 52) and 299 for 8 dec (Rizwan-uz-Zaman 81, Zulfiqar Ali 4 for 85)
Multan 164 (Javed Ilyas 52, Azeem Hafeez 4 for 63) and 193 (Zahoor Elahi 50, Azeem Hafeez 5 for 90)

Karachi Blues won by 165 runs
Karachi Blues 16 pts, Multan 5 pts

The Karachi and Lahore sides overcame inferior opposition and so ensured that they would decide the semi-final place between themselves. Karachi Blues were 91 for 6 on the opening day, but Nadeem and Rashid added 98.

18, 19 and 20 November, 1986

at Bahawal Stadium, Bahawalpur

Multan 139 (Mohammad Zahid 5 for 27) and 389 for 7 dec (Manzoor Elahi 129, Rizwan Sattar 109, Mohammad Zahid 5 for 131)
Bagawalpur 226 (Qasim Shera 89) and 225 for 6 (Qasim Shera 88, Jahangir Alvi 50)

Match drawn
Bahawalpur 9 pts, Multan 4 pts

at Qaddafi Stadium, Lahore

Karachi Blues 291 for 3 (Zahid Ahmed 125 not out, Rizwan-uz-Zaman 113 not out) and 295 for 4 (Rizwan-uz-Zaman 175, Nasir Shah 65 not out)
Lahore City Blues 242 (Shafiq Ahmed 72, Ashraf Ali 65, Rashid Khan 5 for 59)

Karachi Blues 10 pts, Lahore City Blues 5 pts

The drawn match in Lahore supplied Karachi Blues with sufficient points to top the table. They were indebted to Rizwan-uz-Zaman, their captain, and Zahid Ahmed who shared an unbeaten fourth wicket stand of 227. Rizwan, in mighty form, completed his second century of the match and shared in two century partnerships in the second innings.

In the other match, the highlights were a stand of 180 between Manzoor and Rizwan Sattar for Multan's fifth wicket and the second innings and the wicket-keeping of Tahir Pirzada of Bahawalpur who took five catches in the first innings and made three stumpings in the second. The only other wicket-keeper in the competition to take eight dismissals was Anil Dalpat for Karachi Whites against Quetta.

Group B Final Table

	P	W	L	D	Pts
Karachi Blues	3	2	–	1	42
Lahore City Blues	3	2	–	1	40
Bahawalpur	3	–	2	1	18
Multan	3	–	2	1	16

Group C
29, 30 and 31 October 1985

at LCCA Ground, Lahore

Lahore City Whites 260 for 6 (Mohammad Ishaq 119) and 195 for 2 (Mansoor Rana 71 not out, Shahid Anwar 56)
Sargodha 212 (Arshad Pervez 107 not out, Ghayyur Qureshi 5 for 41)

Match drawn
Lahore City Whites 10 pts, Sargodha 5 pts

at Municipal Stadium, Gujranwala

Gujranwala 76 (Tanvir Shaukat 6 for 47) and 84
Faisalabad 254 for 9 (Mohammad Ashraf 83, Tahir Mahmood 5 for 62)

Faisalabad won by an innings and 94 runs
Faisalabad 18 pts, Gujranwala 4 pts

Faisalabad swamped Gujranwala in two days while Lahore City Whites were defied by Arshad Pervez, who rallied his side from 98 for 5, and the rain.

3, 5 and 6 November 1985

at Sargodha Stadium

Lahore Division 176 (Aziz-ur-Rehman 7 for 67) and 176 (Altaf Shah 55)
Sargodha 133 (Shahid Tanvir 6 for 44) and 214 for 4 (Arshad Pervez 61 not out)

Sargodha won by 6 wickets
Sargodha 14 pts, Lahore Division 5 pts

at LCCA Ground, Lahore

Gujranwala 225 (Farhat Masood 59, Ijaz Ahmed 52) and 215 (Tahir Mahmood 81, Ghayyur Qureshi 6 for 44)
Lahore City Whites 321 for 7 dec (Ali Zia 100, Mazhar Hussain 87, Imtiaz Bashir 4 for 78) and 123 for 1 (Shahid Anwar 54 not out)

Lahore City Whites won by 9 wickets
Lahore City Whites 18 pts, Gujranwala 7 pts

Zulqarnian whose wicket-keeping for Lahore City Whites in the Patron's Trophy was outstanding. His form earned him a place in the national side. (Adrian Murrell)

Arshad Pervez inspired his side to a fine win after they had trailed on the first innings in their match with Lahore Division while Ali Zia gave indication of his all-round qualities as Lahore City Whites asserted their authority against Gujranwala.

9, 10 and 11 November 1985

at Iqbal Stadium, Faisalabad

Faisalabad 137 (Shahid Tanvir 4 for 34) and 349 for 5 dec (Shakir Javed 164, Anwar Awais 75)
Lahore Division 228 for 8 (Shahid Tanvir 68, Maqsood Raza 58, Humayun Farkhan 5 for 90) and 169 (Sarfraz Azeem 77 not out)

Faisalabad won by 89 runs
Faisalabad 14 pts, Lahore Division 7 pts

at Sargodha Stadium

Gujranwala 120 (Aziz-ur-Rehman 4 for 30) and 378 for 8 dec (Ijaz Ahmed 131, Farhat Masood 80, Nadeem Ahsan 50 not out)
Sargodha 127 (Arshad Pervez 50, Farhat Masood 5 for 43) and 145 for 4 (Azhar Sultan 61)

Match drawn
Sargodha 6 pts, Gujranwala 4 pts

Faisalabad maintained their strong challenge with a splendid recovery which saw them snatch victory after trailing by 91 runs on the first innings. They owed much to Shakir Javed

Ali Zia accomplished one of the most remarkable all-round feats in the history of cricket when he took 8 for 60 and scored 229 not out for Lahore City Whites against Faisalabad, 14–16 November, 1985. (Adrian Murrell)

who batted excitingly and shared a third wicket stand of 172 with Anwar Awais.

14, 15 and 16 November 1985

at LCCA Ground, Lahore

Faisalabad 203 (Mohammad Ashraf 51, Ali Zia 8 for 60) and 267 for 6 (Anwar Awais 57, Shakir Javed 55)
Lahore City Whites 383 for 4 (Ali Zia 229 not out, Shahid Anwar 76)

Match drawn
Lahore City Whites 10 pts, Faisalabad 4 pts

at Jinnah Stadium, Sialkot

Lahore Division 136 (Farhat Masood 6 for 37) and 108 (Farhat Masood 4 for 19)
Gujranwala 285 for 8 (Sajid Bashir 123, Saif-ur-Rehman 5 for 78)

Gujranwala won by an innings and 41 runs
Gujranwala 18 pts, Lahore Division 4 pts

While Gujranwala were winning inside two days and condemning Lahore Division to the wooden spoon Lahore City Whites were drawing with Faisalabad in a game which virtually assured them of a place in the semi-final. All else in the game was dwarfed by the performance of Ali Zia who took a career best 8 for 60 with his leg-breaks and followed this by hitting the highest score of his career. His performances also represented the best batting and bowling

achievements of the Pakistan season. In the second innings he took 3 for 29 in 22 overs as Faisalabad laboured to save the game, scoring at barely two runs an over.

19, 20 and 21 November 1985

at Sargodha Stadium

Sargodha 161 (Tanvir Afzal 4 for 49) and 221 (Arshad Pervez 56, Tanvir Afzal 5 for 92)
Faisalabad 280 for 9 (Shakir Javed 79, Anwar Awais 61) and 106 for 5 (Aziz-ur-Rehman 4 for 26)

Faisalabad won by 5 wickets
Faisalabad 18 pts, Sargodha 5 pts

at LCCA Ground, Lahore

Lahore City Whites 375 for 5 dec (Mansoor Rana 140, Naved Anjum 101 not out)
Lahore Division 131 (Maqsood Raza 57, Naeem Taj 7 for 42) and 180 (Shahid Tanvir 100, Tahir Shah 5 for 33)

Lahore City Whites won by an innings and 64 runs
Lahore City Whites 18 pts, Lahore Division 3 pts

Victory on the second day confirmed Lahore City Whites as winners of Group C so that Faisalabad's maximum-point victory the following day was of no avail.

Group C Final Table					
	P	*W*	*L*	*D*	*Pts*
Lahore City Whites	4	2	–	2	56
Faisalabad	4	3	–	1	54
Gujranwala	4	1	2	1	33
Sargodha	4	1	1	2	30
Lahore Division	4	–	4	–	19

Group D
29 and 30 October 1985

at Pindi Club, Rawalpindi

Rawalpindi 354 for 2 (Masood Anwar 202 not out, Raja Afaq 116 not out)
Hazara 114 and 65 (Sabih Azhar 6 for 29)

Rawalpindi won by an innings and 175 runs
Rawalpindi 18 pts, Hazara 1 pt

at Shahi Bagh Stadium, Peshawar

Dera Ismail Khan 87 and 84 (Farrukh Zaman 4 for 15)
Peshawar 285 for 2 (Ibrar-ul-Haq 138, Aamer Mirza 82)

Peshawar won by an innings and 114 runs
Peshawar 18 pts, Dera Ismail Khan 1 pt

Peshawar and Rawalpindi demonstrated the gap between them and the other two sides by winning in two days. Aamer and Ibrar put on 192 for Peshawar's first wicket while Masood Anwar and Raja Afaq engaged in the competition's best stand of the season, an unbeaten 268 for Rawalpindi's third wicket.

3 and 5 November 1985

at Pindi Club, Rawalpindi

Dera Ismail Khan 131 (Sajid Hussain 7 for 65) and 107 (Sajid

Hussain 4 for 22, Sabih Azhar 4 for 30)
Rawalpindi 284 for 3 (Tariq Javed 80, Masood Anwar 78, Azmat Jalil 62)

Rawalpindi won by an innings and 46 runs
Rawalpindi 18 pts, Dera Ismail Khan 2 pts

at Shahi Bagh Stadium, Peshawar

Peshawar 302 for 4 (Ibrar-ul-Haq 112 not out, Aamer Mirza 72, Abdur Rahim 55)
Hazara 103 (Khawar Nadeem 53, Khurshid Akhtar 4 for 16, Mohammad Saleem 4 for 37) and 121 (Farrukh Zaman 6 for 32)

Peshawar won by an innings and 73 runs
Peshawar 18 pts, Hazara 2 pts

The chasm between the two top sides and the two bottom sides was again evident as Rawalpindi and Peshawar once more gained innings victories inside two days. Aamer and Abdur added 112 for Peshawar's second wicket, and Aamer and Ibrar 118 for their fourth.

9, 10 and 11 November 1985

at POF Oval, Wah Cantt

Dera Ismail Khan 214 (Sardar Badshah 65)
Hazara 221 for 8 (Rizwan Bokhari 70)

Match drawn
Hazara 8 pts, Dera Ismail Khan 6 pts

at Shahi Bagh Stadium, Peshawar

Peshawar 135 (Aamer Mirza 55, Raja Afaq 4 for 33) and 131 for 8
Rawalpindi 112 (Khurshid Akhtar 4 for 38)

Match drawn
Peshawar 6 pts, Rawalpindi 4 pts

Rain mutilated both matches so that Peshawar qualified for the semi-finals by virtue of taking six points from the final match in which there was a shortened first day and a barren second day. In the other game, play was abandoned at tea on the last day.

Group D Final Table					
	P	*W*	*L*	*D*	*Pts*
Peshawar	3	2	–	1	42
Rawalpindi	3	2	–	1	40
Hazara	3	–	2	1	11
Dera Ismail Khan	3	–	2	1	9

Semi-Finals
23, 24, 25 and 26 November 1985

at LCCA Ground, Lahore

Lahore City Whites 454 for 8 (Wasim Raja 129, Mansoor Rana 98, Tahir Shah 90, Zahid Ahmed 5 for 94) and 239 (Ali Zia 87)
Karachi Blues 263 for 9 (Rizwan-uz-Zaman 93, Shaukat Mirza 75, Akram Raza 5 for 90) and 164 (Rizwan-uz-Zaman 72, Tahir Shah 4 for 26)

Lahore City Whites won by 266 runs

9, 10 and 11 December 1985

at National Stadium, Karachi

Veteran left-hander Wasim Raja hit 129 for Lahore City Whites in the Patron's Trophy semi-final against Karachi Blues. (Adrian Murrell)

Peshawar 171 (Ijaz Faqih 5 for 55) and 202 (Farrukh Zaman 54)
Karachi Whites 315 for 3 (Mansoor Akhtar 101 not out, Sajid Ali 82, Moin-ul-Atiq 66) and 59 for 0

Karachi Whites won by 10 wickets

Lahore City Whites took such a grip on the game with Karachi Blues in the first innings that it was unlikely after the second day that they would be deprived of a place in the final. They lost their first 4 wickets for 125, but Mansoor Rana and Wasim Raja put on 227 for the fifth wicket and Lahore moved to a commanding position. Wasim Raja was playing his first significant innings of the season, having batted himself low down in the earlier matches. The magnificent Rizwan gave further notice that he was ready for a recall to the national side in a second wicket stand of 172 with Shaukat, but Karachi Blues could never match the Lahore City Whites scoring rate of 5.3 an over and closed 191 behind on the first innings. It was too great a deficit, and Lahore City Whites moved to an easy win.

The other semi-final was decided with a day to spare. An opening stand of 134 by Moin and Sajid Ali was followed by an unfinished fourth wicket stand of 129 between Mansoor Akhtar and Sajid Riaz so that Karachi Whites led by 144 on the first innings, too much for Peshawar.

Final

The final of the B.C.C.P. Patron's Trophy was ruined by rain. There was no play on the first two days and play started late on the third. Ali Zia bowled his leg-breaks to good effect, but Mansoor Akhtar hit the only fifty of the shortened match. Lahore City Whites lost wickets at regular intervals, a mid-innings spell by slow left-arm spinner Iqbal Qasim proving decisive. Jalal-ud-Din returned to take the last two wickets, and Karachi Whites took the trophy on their first innings lead.

In between the semi-finals and final of the B.C.C.P. Patron's Trophy Pakistan played a five-match limited-over international series with West Indies who had flown from the tournament in Sharjah.

First One-Day International
PAKISTAN v. WEST INDIES

Mudassar Nazar provided the backbone of the Pakistan innings with an accomplished innings of 77, and Imran Khan injected vigour into the closing overs, but the total of 218 never looked likely to trouble the West Indies in the first of the five-match series.

Richardson fell quickly, but Haynes and Logie added 97 for the second wicket before Haynes went to Wasim Akram. Viv Richards came in to play a devastating innings. He hit 80 in 39 minutes, with 4 sixes and 10 fours.

So severe was Richards' assault on the bowling that Imran Khan, who had not intended to bowl because of a hamstring injury, was forced into his full quota of overs, at a much reduced pace, after Abdul Qadir had been hit for 24 in one over and Tauseef Ahmed for 16 in another.

The stand of 119 at a blistering pace between Logie and Richards put the match beyond doubt. Not surprisingly, the West Indies captain was named Man of the Match.

Second One-Day International
PAKISTAN v. WEST INDIES

Pakistan levelled the series with a hard earned victory at Lahore, Abdul Qadir gaining revenge for his mauling at Gujranwala with a 4 for 17 spell which won him the individual award.

A crowd of 30,000 saw West Indies begin carefully after Imran Khan had asked them to bat first. Haynes and Richardson put on 45 for the first wicket, and although three wickets fell for 25 runs, it seemed West Indies would reach a big score when Richards began to play with customary aggression.

He was not as ruthless as he had been in the first match, but he passed fifty and looked in threatening mood until bowled by Mudassar, a most valuable cricketer. Mudassar also accounted for Harper, but it was Abdul Qadir's four-wicket spell which restricted West Indies to 173 and ended their innings with 3.4 overs remaining of their quota.

Accurate bowling and enthusiastic fielding gave Pakistan a hard time, but Mohsin played with admirable calm. Javed Miandad batted with élan, and Imran and Saleem Malik scored the last 49 runs at an easy pace to bring victory with 9 balls to spare.

Third One-Day International
PAKISTAN v. WEST INDIES

The brooding might of Viv Richards erupted once more into an innings which placed West Indies in a commanding position and won him the individual award. He chose to bat first on a grassless pitch and saw Haynes and Richardson give his side a solid start. Richards came to the wicket with the score at 100 for 2 and hit 66 out of 92 off 38 balls. He hit 4 mighty sixes and 5 fours, and the Pakistan attack which had contained West Indies quite well in the early stages began to falter.

Needing to score at five runs an over, Pakistan never looked like approaching the target. Rameez Raja played some crisp shots and there was late bravery from Abdul Qadir, but Holding, at medium pace, was in destructive mood, and with Marshall finding his best line and pace of the tour, Pakistan wilted disappointingly.

Fourth One-Day International
PAKISTAN v. WEST INDIES

Pakistan drew level in the series when they beat West Indies by five wickets with five balls to spare in spite of being without Mudassar and Mohsin who were ill.

West Indies were given a good start by Richardson and Haynes, but the quick dismissal of Logie, and the decisive

LEFT: *Zakir Khan won a place in the Pakistani side for the one-day international series against West Indies. (Adrian Murrell)*

B.C.C.P. PATRON'S TROPHY FINAL – LAHORE CITY WHITES v. KARACHI WHITES
15, 16, 17, 18 and 19 December 1985 at Qaddafi Stadium, Lahore

KARACHI WHITES

	FIRST INNINGS		SECOND INNINGS	
Shoaib Moham-				
mad	lbw, b Ali Zia	39	c Zulqarnian, b Ali Zia	17
Moin-ul-Atiq	c and b Mohsin	4	not out	31
Mansoor Akhtar	c Zulqarnian,		(4) not out	4
	b Waheed	59		
Sajid Ali	lbw, b Wasim	2	(3) c Rana, b Waheed	12
Asif Mujtaba	b Ali Zia	5		
Ijaz Faqih	c Zulqarnian,			
	b Waheed	16		
Iqbal Sikander	lbw, b Ali Zia	7		
Anil Dalpat*	c Ali Zia, b Mohsin	5		
Iqbal Qasim†	c Waheed, b Ali Zia	5		
Saleem Jaffer	c Tahir, b Waseem	22		
Jalal-ud-Din	not out	2		
	b 1, lb 5, w 1, nb 9	16	b 1, nb 3	4
		182	(for 2 wickets)	68

	O	M	R	W	O	M	R	W
Wasim Akram	23.1	3	58	2	5	—	20	—
Mohsin Kamal	19	1	67	2	2	—	11	—
Waheed Niazi	11	6	14	2	3	1	10	1
Ali Zia	16	2	37	4	4	2	15	1
Saleem Malik					2	—	3	—
Akram Raza					3	2	2	—
Aamer Sohail					3	1	6	—

FALL OF WICKETS
1- 8, 2- 87, 3- 93, 4- 110, 5- 133, 6- 139, 7- 150, 8- 150, 9- 160
1- 29, 2- 48

LAHORE CITY WHITES

	FIRST INNINGS	
Tahir Shah	c Anil, b Saleem	17
Aamer Sohail	c and b Iqbal Qasim	49
Rameez Raja†	c Shoaib, b Jalal	5
Saleem Malik	st Anil,	
	b Iqbal Qasim	17
Ali Zia	st Anil,	
	b Iqbal Qasim	2
Mansoor Rana	lbw,	
	b Mansoor Akhtar	19
Akram Raza	lbw, b Iqbal Qasim	7
Zulqarnian*	not out	28
Wasim Akram	c Anil, b Saleem	5
Mohsin Kamal	c Sajid, b Jalal	5
Waheed Niazi	lbw, b Jalal	5
	lb 3	3
		162

	O	M	R	W
Jalal-ud-Din	14.5	3	44	3
Saleem Jaffer	19	4	61	2
Mansoor Akhtar	11	4	17	1
Iqbal Qasim	7	1	26	4
Ijaz Faqih	3	—	11	—

FALL OF WICKETS
1- 25, 2- 30, 3- 61, 4- 63, 5- 106, 6- 110, 7- 125, 8- 133, 9- 142

Umpires: Javed Akhtar & Tariq Ata

Match drawn. Karachi Whites won Trophy on first innings lead.

FIRST ONE-DAY INTERNATIONAL – PAKISTAN v. WEST INDIES
27 November 1985 at Gujranwala

PAKISTAN

Mudassar Nazar	c Walsh, b Holding	77
Mohsin Khan	c Dujon, b Walsh	17
Rameez Raja	b Harper	17
Javed Miandad	lbw, b Harper	22
Imran Khan†	c Harper, b Holding	45
Saleem Malik	not out	11
Saleem Yousuf*	not out	0
Abdul Qadir		
Wasim Akram		
Mohsin Kamal		
Tauseef Ahmed		
	b 3, lb 13, w 8, nb 5	29
	(40 overs) (for 5 wickets)	218

	O	M	R	W
Marshall	8	—	47	—
Garner	6	1	24	—
Walsh	8	—	39	1
Holding	8	1	39	2
Harper	8	2	37	2
Richards	2	—	16	—

FALL OF WICKETS
1- 29, 2- 74, 3- 113, 4- 169, 5- 218

WEST INDIES

D.L. Haynes	c sub, b Wasim Akram	39
R.B. Richardson	lbw, b Mohsin Kamal	5
A.L. Logie	not out	78
I.V.A. Richards†	not out	80
P.J. Dujon*		
M.D. Marshall		
R.A. Harper		
H.A. Gomes		
M.A. Holding		
C.A. Walsh		
J. Garner		
	b 1, lb 8, w 13	22
	(35.3 overs) (for 2 wickets)	224

	O	M	R	W
Wasim Akram	6	1	31	1
Mohsin Kamal	5.3	1	34	1
Abdul Qadir	6	1	39	—
Mudassar Nazar	5	—	31	—
Tauseef Ahmed	5	1	46	—
Imran Khan	8	—	34	—

FALL OF WICKETS
1- 8, 2- 105

West Indies won by 8 wickets

SECOND ONE-DAY INTERNATIONAL – PAKISTAN v. WEST INDIES
29 November 1985 at Lahore

WEST INDIES			
D.L. Haynes	b Zakir Khan	26	
R.B. Richardson	c Rameez Raja,		
	b Wasim Akram	22	
A.L. Logie	b Zakir Khan	9	
I.V.A. Richards†	b Mudassar Nazar	53	
H.A. Gomes	b Adbul Qadir	23	
P.J. Dujon*	b Abdul Qadir	4	
R.A. Harper	c Saleem Malik,		
	b Mudassar	5	
M.D. Marshall	b Wasim Akram	1	
M.A. Holding	st Saleem Yousuf, b Qadir	0	
A.H. Gray	not out	7	
C.A. Walsh	c Wasim Akram,		
	b Abdul Qadir	7	
	b 3, lb 7, w 4, nb 2	16	
(36.2 overs)		173	

PAKISTAN			
Mudassar Nazar	c Walsh, b Gray	15	
Mohsin Khan	lbw, b Gray	43	
Rameez Raja	c and b Holding	12	
Javed Miandad	b Harper	41	
Imran Khan†	not out	22	
Saleem Malik	not out	26	
Saleem Yousuf*			
Abdul Qadir			
Wasim Akram			
Zakir Khan			
	b 1, lb 8, w 2, nb 5	16	
(38.3 overs)	(for 4 wickets)	175	

	O	M	R	W
Imran Khan	5	1	25	—
Wasim Akram	5	—	24	2
Zakir Khan	8	—	31	2
Mohsin Kamal	8	—	40	—
Abdul Qadir	5.2	—	17	4
Mudassar Nazar	5	—	26	2

	O	M	R	W
Marshall	7.3	—	38	—
Gray	8	—	36	2
Walsh	8	—	32	—
Holding	7	1	33	1
Harper	8	—	27	1

FALL OF WICKETS
1- 54, 2- 61, 3- 70, 4- 129, 5- 143, 6- 151, 7- 156, 8- 156,
9- 164

FALL OF WICKETS
1- 23, 2- 47, 3- 124, 4- 126

Pakistan won by 6 wickets

wicket, Richards caught behind off Shoaib Mohammad, a surprise bowler, frustrated them in their attempts to build quickly on that foundation. They batted indifferently although Richie Richardson played well in by far his best innings of the series.

Shoaib and Qasim gave Pakistan the launching that the innings required, and Shoaib, whose all round performance won him the Man of the Match award, added 84 with Javed for the second wicket.

Imran, Saleem Malik and Rameez Raja fell in quick

THIRD ONE-DAY INTERNATIONAL – PAKISTAN v. WEST INDIES
2 December 1985 at Peshawar

WEST INDIES			
D.L. Haynes	c Mohsin Kamal, b Imran	60	
R.B. Richardson	st Saleem Yousuf,		
	b Tauseef	27	
H.A. Gomes	run out	15	
I.V.A. Richards†	c Mohsin Khan, b Imran	66	
A.L. Logie	lbw, b Imran Khan	0	
P.J. Dujon*	not out	9	
R.A. Harper	not out	0	
M.D. Marshall			
M.A. Holding			
J. Garner			
C.A. Walsh			
	b 4, lb 13, w 3, nb 4	24	
(40 overs)	(for 5 wickets)	201	

PAKISTAN			
Mudassar Nazar	c and b Holding	19	
Mohsin Khan	c Harper, b Marshall	6	
Rameez Raja	run out	38	
Javed Miandad	c Gomes, b Holding	2	
Imran Khan†	b Harper	8	
Saleem Malik	b Walsh	7	
Abdul Qadir	b Marshall	37	
Saleem Yousuf*	b Holding	8	
Wasim Akram	b Holding	9	
Mohsin Kamal	b Marsall	5	
Tauseef Ahmed	not out	3	
	b 3, lb 9, w 3, nb 4	19	
(39.3 overs)		161	

	O	M	R	W
Imran Khan	7	—	39	3
Wasim Akram	6	—	24	—
Tauseef Ahmed	8	1	24	1
Moshin Kamal	8	—	31	—
Abdul Qadir	6	1	42	—
Mudassar Nazar	5	—	24	—

	O	M	R	W
Marshall	8	1	36	3
Garner	8	1	22	—
Walsh	8	—	36	1
Holding	7.3	—	17	4
Harper	8	1	38	1

FALL OF WICKETS
1- 70, 2- 100, 3- 169, 4- 170, 5- 192

FALL OF WICKETS
1- 15, 2- 37, 3- 47, 4- 65, 5- 80, 6- 106, 7- 138, 8- 142,
9- 149

West Indies won by 40 runs

FOURTH ONE-DAY INTERNATIONAL – PAKISTAN v. WEST INDIES
4 December 1985 at Rawalpindi

WEST INDIES			
D.L. Haynes	run out		23
R.B. Richardson	not out		92
A.L. Logie	c sub, b Tauseef Ahmed		0
I.V.A. Richards†	c Zulqarnian, b Shoaib		21
H.A. Gomes	run out		1
P.J. Dujon*	run out		12
R.A. Harper	lbw, b Abdul Qadir		10
M.D. Marshall	c Zulqarnian, b Wasim Akram		20
M.A. Holding	c Imran Khan, b Wasim Akram		2
J. Garner	not out		1
C.A. Walsh			
	b 4, lb 10, w 1, nb 2		17
(40 overs)	(for 8 wickets)		199

PAKISTAN			
Shoaib Mohammad	c Walsh, b Garner		53
Qasim Umar	lbw, b Walsh		27
Javed Miandad	not out		67
Saleem Malik	c Haynes, b Harper		14
Imran Khan†	run out		8
Rameez Raja	c and b Richards		3
Abdul Qadir	not out		0
Tauseef Ahmed			
Wasim Akram			
Mohsin Kamal			
Zulqarnian*			
	b 9, lb 15, nb 7		31
(39.1 overs)	(for 5 wickets)		203

	O	M	R	W
Imran Khan	6	—	33	—
Wasim Akram	6	—	41	2
Tauseef Ahmed	6	2	12	1
Mohsin Kamal	6	—	44	—
Shoaib Mohammad	8	—	30	1
Abdul Qadir	8	2	25	1

	O	M	R	W
Marshall	8	2	27	—
Garner	8	1	33	1
Walsh	8	—	43	1
Harper	8	—	41	1
Richards	2	—	6	1
Holding	5.1	—	29	—

FALL OF WICKETS
1- 57, 2- 57, 3- 99, 4- 100, 5- 124, 6- 136, 7- 166, 8- 198

FALL OF WICKETS
1- 57, 2- 141, 3- 171, 4- 184, 5- 195

Pakistan won by 5 wickets

succession while only 24 runs were scored, but a Pakistan victory never seemed in doubt, and Javed led the side home with five balls remaining.

Fifth One-Day International
PAKISTAN v. WEST INDIES

West Indies took the series by 3–2 when they won the final match with ease, but a crowd disturbance and pitch invasion when Pakistan were 87 for 4 ruined the match and caused it to be reduced to 38 overs.

Pakistan were put in to bat and never recovered from an atrocious start. Gray bowled particularly well at the outset although it was Marshall, with the wickets of Mohsin Khan and Rameez Raja, who was named as Man of the Match. The only significant stand in the Pakistan innings was for the fifth wicket between Mohsin Khan and Javed Miandad. It realised 71.

The visitors were never likely to be worried in their bid for victory as there was no need to hurry. Abdul Qadir and Imran Khan bowled tight spells, but Richards quickly ended any speculation as to the result with 40 of the last 51 runs, victory comming with 23 balls to spare.

Quaid-e-Azam Trophy

Yet again the Quaid-e-Azam Trophy, Pakistan's premier competition, was restructured, and the 1985–6 championship was contested by a hotchpotch of teams. Only five departmental teams qualified directly to the twelve-team championship. Others, even those who had taken part in the previous season, were relegated to a non-first-class qualify-

ing competition. The winners of this tournament, ADBP, joined the five other departmental sides in the Quaid-e-Azam championship, and Lahore and Karachi, as the major city organisations, were placed directly in the championship round. The four remaining sides were combined zonal teams.

Zone A was drawn from Hyderabad, Sukkur and Quetta. Zone B took players from Bahawalpur, Multan and Lahore Division. Zone C's cricketers were from Gujranwala, Sargodha and Faisalabad while Zone D comprised players from Rawalpindi, Peshawar and Dera Ismail Khan. The Board's intention was to give the tournament universal participation and allow players from all parts of the country to take part in the premier championship, but the system proved to be an unhappy one. Zone A, torn by internal wranglings, were dreadfully weak and used forty players although the Board had said that no more than 25 players should be used by any one team.

Leading teams like Pakistan International Airlines, National Bank and Muslim Commercial Bank could find no place in the Trophy Championship under the new system, and Karachi immediately employed the services of players who would normally have appeared for these sides. Not surprisingly, Karachi dominated the competition.

8, 9, 10 and 11 January 1986

at National Stadium, Karachi

Zone A 127 (Ijaz Faqih 4 for 24) and 242 (Raj Hans 71, Ijaz Faqih 5 for 67, Hasan Askari 4 for 46)
Karachi 374 for 1 (Moin-ul-Atiq 203 not out, Zafar Ahmed 113 not out)

Karachi won by an innings and 5 runs
Karachi 18 pts, Zone A 1 pt

FIFTH ONE-DAY INTERNATIONAL – PAKISTAN v. WEST INDIES
6 December 1985 at Karachi

PAKISTAN			
Mohsin Khan	c Richardson, b Marshall		54
Shoaib Mohammad	c Richardson, b Gray		1
Rameez Raja	c Dujon, b Marshall		0
Saleem Malik	run out		7
Imran Khan†	run out		19
Javed Miandad	b Holding		28
Abdul Qadir	not out		5
Wasim Akram	b Holding		0
Zulqarnian*	not out		4
	lb 4, w 4, nb 1		9
(38 overs)	(for 7 wickets)		127

WEST INDIES			
D.L. Haynes	c Mohsin Khan, b Mohsin Kamal		39
R.B. Richardson	lbw, b Wasim Akram		13
H.A. Gomes	not out		20
I.V.A. Richards†	not out		40
A.L. Logie			
P.J. Dujon*			
M.D. Marshall			
R.A. Harper			
M.A. Harper			
C.A. Walsh			
A.H. Gray			
	b 1, lb 5, w 7, nb 3		16
(34.1 overs)	(for 2 wickets)		128

	O	M	R	W
Marshall	8	1	25	2
Gray	6	4	14	1
Walsh	8	—	20	—
Holding	8	—	35	2
Harper	6	—	20	—
Richards	2	—	9	—

	O	M	R	W
Wasim Akram	8	—	25	1
Mohsin Kamal	7	1	47	1
Abdul Qadir	8	2	19	—
Imran Khan	8	2	19	—
Tauseef Ahmed	3.1	—	12	—

FALL OF WICKETS
1- 2, 2- 3, 3- 14, 4- 45, 5- 116, 6- 117, 7- 119

FALL OF WICKETS
1- 26, 2- 77

West Indies won by 8 wickets

---

at Niaz Stadium, Hyderabad

HBFC 227 (Ijaz Ahmed 54, Mian Fayyaz 5 for 70) and 266 (Raees Ahmed 67, Tariq Alam 50, Mian Fayyaz 4 for 69) **PACO** 247 (Raees Ahmed 4 for 99) and 195 for 5 (Ijaz Ahmed 113 not out)

Match drawn
PACO 9 pts, HBFC 7 pts

at Bahawal Stadium, Bahawalpur

Habib Bank 317 (Arshad Pervez 119, Bilal Rana 5 for 100) and 108 (Shakeel Shah 6 for 51, Bilal Rana 4 for 30)
Zone B 201 (Rizwan Sattar 66, Abdur Raqeeb 5 for 69) and 226 for 5 (Farooq Shera 95)

Zone B won by 5 wickets
Zone B 16 pts, Habib Bank 8 pts

at LCCA Ground, Lahore

Lahore 305 for 7 (Sajjad Akbar 81, Wasim Ali 63, Akram Raza 53) and 243 (Shahid Anwar 100, Aamer Wasim 4 for 48)
Zone C 229 (Saadat Gul 65, Haroon Rashid 5 for 78) and 111

Lahore won by 208 runs
Lahore 18 pts, Zone C 7 pts

at Pindi Club, Rawalpindi

Railways 258 for 8 (Abdus Sami 65, Sajid Hussain 5 for 72) and 235 (Sajid Hussain 5 for 94)
Zone D 170 (Mohammad Arif snr 55 not out, Mohammad Nazir 6 for 41, Nadeem Ghauri 4 for 93) and 87 (Nadeem Ghauri 5 for 28, Mohammad Nazir 5 for 32)

Railways won by 236 runs
Railways 18 pts, Zone D 5 pts

The gulf between teams in the competition was clearly exposed in the opening matches. It took Karachi only two and a half days to beat Zone A. Ijaz Faqih mesmerised batsmen with his off-breaks, and, after Basit Ali and Moin-

ul-Atiq had put on 109 for Karachi's first wicket, Moin-ul-Atiq and Zafar Ahmed combined in an unbeaten stand of 265. Moin-ul-Atiq reached the first double century of his career.

Zone B also won with a day to spare in spite of trailing by 116 runs on the first innings. Shakeel Shah returned career best bowling figures when Habib Bank batted again, and Farooq Shera, the Zone B captain, dominated a fifth wicket stand of 124 which took his side to victory. Azhar Abbas gave good support.

Railways were the third side to win in three days, and, inevitably, owed much to skipper Mohammad Nazir who was ably supported by Nadeem. HBFC and PACO played the only draw in the first round of matches, but there were sensations at the LCCA Ground in Lahore. Haroon Rashid bowled the home side to a first innings lead of 76, and Lahore reached 243 for 7 in the second innings when Aamer Wasim dismissed Haroon, Naeem Taj and Ghayyur Qureshi with successive deliveries to perform the hat-trick. All three batsmen were lbw. Zone C, needing 320 to win, lost 5 wickets for 27 runs and never looked likely to avoid defeat.

13, 14, 15 and 16 January 1986

at National Stadium, Karachi

Karachi 252 for 6 (Basit Ali 101, Ijaz Faqih 59) and 292 for 5 dec (Rizwan-uz-Zaman 149)
HBFC 214 for 9 (Sagheer Abbas 116 not out, Ijaz Faqih 5 for 72) and 137 for 8 (Iqbal Sikander 5 for 70)

Match drawn
Karachi 10 pts, HBFC 5 pts

at Niaz Stadium, Hyderabad

Zone A 194 (Shahid Mahboob 5 for 79, Mian Fayyaz 4 for 50) and 138 (Mian Fayyaz 6 for 37)

PACO 378 for 9 (Ijaz Ahmed 182, Siddiq Patni 50)

PACO won by an innings and 46 runs
PACO 18 pts, Zone A 5 pts

at Jinnah Stadium, Sialkot

Zone C 103 (Saleem Jaffer 6 for 50, Ali Zia 4 for 18) and 127 (Saleem Jaffer 6 for 50)
United Bank 286 (Saadat Ali 84, Naved Anjum 63, Tanvir Afzal 5 for 38)

United Bank won by an innings and 56 runs
United Bank 18 pts, Zone C 4 pts

at LCCA Ground, Lahore

ADBP 329 for 8 (Tanvir Ahmed 84, Atif Rauf 71, Ghaffar Kazmi 65) and 192 (Manzoor Elahi 50, Afzaal Butt 4 for 39)
Lahore 267 (Ameer Akbar 60, Shahid Anwar 56, Ghaffar Kazmi 5 for 92, Raja Afaq 4 for 64) and 255 for 3 (Shahid Anwar 89, Rameez Raja 59 not out)

Lahore won by 7 wickets
Lahore 18 pts, ADBP 8 pts

Having lost their first three wickets for 44, Karachi were restricted to 252 in their 85 overs at the National Stadium. Ijaz Faqih exploited the conditions well to give his side a 38-run lead on the first innings which was soon extended by Rizwan's exciting knock. Set to make 331 to win in 75 overs, HBFC laboured painfully and were happy to escape with a draw.

Ijaz Ahmed, formerly of National Bank, and Mian Fayyaz were the leading players as PACO routed Zone A, and Zone C, also beaten in three days, were savaged by Saleem Jaffer who had match figures of 12 for 100, twice producing a career best.

Lahore recovered splendidly to beat ADBP. Shahid Anwar and Aamer Sohail led the charge with an opening stand of 114 in the second innings.

18, 19, 20 and 21 January 1986

at National Stadium, Karachi

Habib Bank 166 (Sultan Rana 53, Shahid Mahboob 7 for 84) and 492 (Agha Zahid 147, Saleem Malik 67, Anwar Miandad 66, Arshad Pervez 53, Mian Fayyaz 4 for 145)
PACO 377 for 6 (Umar Rasheed 112, Ijaz Ahmed 102, Moin Mumtaz 58 not out) and 79 for 2 (Ijaz Ahmed 54)

Match drawn
PACO 10 pts, Habib Bank 4 pts

at Bahawal Stadium, Bahawalpur

Zone B 216 (Farooq Shera 63, Kazim Mehdi 5 for 46) and 161 (Zahoor Elahi 58, Kazim Mehdi 5 for 49)
HBFC 225 (Tahir Rasheed 55, Rafat Alam 53, Bilal Rana 5 for 79) and 155 for 6

HBFC won by 4 wickets
HBFC 17 pts, Zone B 6 pts

at Iqbal Stadium, Faisalabad

Railways 302 for 9 (Shahid Saeed 129 not out, Musleh-ud-Din 81, Wasim Haider 4 for 45) and 323 (Shahid Pervez 88, Aamer Wasim 6 for 121)
Zone C 269 (Wasim Haider 61, Shakir Javed 60, Nadeem Gahuri 4 for 104) and 208 for 9 (Mohammad Nawaz 65, Mohammad 57, Mohammad Nazir 5 for 58)

Match drawn
Railways 10 pts, Zone C 8 pts

at LCCA Ground, Lahore

United Bank 188 (Afzaal Butt 4 for 68) and 379 for 9 dec (Shafiq Ahmed 109, Saadat Ali 106, Ashraf Ali 57 not out, Naved Anjum 51)
Lahore 226 for 6 (Akram Raza 76) and 147

United Bank won by 194 runs
United Bank 14 pts, Lahore 7 pts

at Pindi Club, Rawalpindi

ADBP 177 (Maqsood Kundi 74 not out, Ghaffar Kazmi 58, Sajid Hussain 4 for 51) and 390 for 9 dec (Aamer 113, Mansoor Rana 50, Atif Rauf 50, Nazir Javed 5 for 73)
Zone D 233 (Mohammad Riaz 70, Raja Afaq 5 for 80, Ghaffar Kazmi 5 for 99) and 276 for 9 (Mohammad Riaz 78, Tariq Javed 50, Khatib Rizwan 5 for 104)

Match drawn
Zone D 9 pts, ADBP 5 pts

For the second time in three matches, Aamer Wasim performed the hat-trick. In the Railways first innings, 6 wickets fell for 123. Musleh-ud-Din then launched a violent assault on the bowling, and he and Shahid Saeed put on 105. Shahid carried his bat, and Railways reached 302. They led by 33 on the first innings and moved to 167 for 4 in their second innings. At this point, Aamer Wasim had Ijaz Ahmed caught, Iqbal Saeed lbw and Pervez Shah caught behind off successive deliveries. Mohammad Nazir and Shahid Pervez later added 95 for the ninth wicket, and in the end Zone C narrowly avoided defeat.

Having bowled out Habib Bank on the opening day, PACO seemed well set for victory when Ijaz Ahmed and Umar Rasheed put on 205 for the third wicket. Habib rallied strongly, however, and skipper Agha Zahid batted into the last day and the game was saved. HBFC owned much to Kazim Mehdi as they gained a tight win over Zone B while ADBP rallied well in an exciting draw with Zone D for whom last pair Mohammad Arif senior and Faridoon Khan put on 60 and remained undefeated to save the game.

United Bank recovered splendidly to beat Lahore, all their bowlers exploiting a wearing wicket well on the last day.

23, 24, 25 and 26 January 1986

at National Stadium, Karachi

PACO 111 (Ijaz Faqih 6 for 20) and 260 (Umar Rasheed 72, Khalid Alvi 64, Ijaz Faqih 4 for 73, Iqbal Qasim 4 for 85)
Karachi 297 for 2 (Rizwan-uz-Zaman 140, Moin-ul-Atiq 111 not out) and 79 for 3

Karachi won by 7 wickets
Karachi 18 pts, PACO 1 pt

at Pindi Club, Rawalpindi

Match abandoned
Lahore 9 pts, Zone D 9 pts

at Niaz Stadium, Hyderabad

Zone A 92 (Abdur Raqeeb 6 for 23) and 128 (Raj Hans 56, Abdur Raqeeb 5 for 49, Anwar Miandad 4 for 22)
Habib Bank 309 for 4 (Arshad Pervez 90, Anwar Miandad 62, Agha Zahid 60)

Habib Bank won by an innings and 89 runs
Habib Bank 18 pts, Zone A 2 pts

at Iqbal Stadium, Faisalabad

Zone C 320 for 5 (Mansoor Khan 109 not out, Shakir Javed 55)

and 141 (Khatib Rizwan 4 for 21, Zakir Khan 4 for 60)
ADBP 331 for 8 (Ghaffar Kazmi 67, Mansoor Rana 50) and 132 for 2 (Masood Anwar 72 not out)

ADBP won by 8 wickets
ADBP 17 pts, Zone C 8 pts

Karachi continued their progress to the championship title by outplaying PACO. Ijaz Faqih and Rizwan-uz-Zaman were again in fine form as victory was achieved in three days. Zone A again suffered defeat in three days, but ADBP came from behind to beat Zone C. They were 225 for 7, but late hitting gave them a first innings lead. Rain delayed the start on the first day.

28, 29, 30 and 31 January 1986

at National Stadium, Karachi

Zone B 117 (Iqbal Qasim 7 for 39) and 102 (Iqbal Sikander 5 for 20, Ijaz Faqih 5 for 53)
Karachi 286 for 3 (Rizwan-uz-Zaman 154 not out, Basit Ali 70, Zafar Ahmed 51 not out)

Karachi won by an innings and 67 runs
Karachi 18 pts, Zone B 2 pts

at Bahawal Stadium, Bahawalpur

Zone A 80 (Kazim Mehdi 6 for 13) and 65 (Rafat Alam 5 for 24)
HBFC 258 (Tahir Rasheed 81 not out, Habib Baloch 5 for 74)

HBFC won by an innings and 113 runs
HBFC 18 pts, Zone A 4 pts

at Qaddafi Stadium, Lahore

ABDP 227 (Mansoor Rana 82, Mansoor Elahi 65, Sikhander Bakht 5 for 49) and 357 for 7 dec (Atif Rauf 102 not out, Mansoor Rana 72, Tanvir Ahmed 50)
United Bank 260 (Saadat Ali 82, Ashraf Ali 52) and 60 for 1

Match drawn
United Bank 10 pts, ADBP 7 pts

at LCCA Ground, Lahore

Railways 267 for 9 (Babar Altaf 51) and 218 (Talat Mirza 93)
Lahore 180 for 9 (Mohammad Nazir 5 for 65) and 267 for 9 (Akram Rana 60, Shahid Anwar 51, Mohammad Nazir 6 for 96)

Match drawn
Railways 10 pts, Lahore 5 pts

at Shahi Baugh Stadium, Peshawar

Zone D 215 (Tariq Javed 85, Ghulam Abbas 7 for 42) and 302 (Aamer Mirza 82, Shahid Javed 51, Aamer Wasim 5 for 118)
Zone C 183 (Mohammad Riaz 5 for 58) and 121 (Mohammad Riaz 6 for 56)

Zone D won by 213 runs
Zone D 16 pts, Zone C 5 pts

Karachi beat Zone B by mid-afternoon on the second day to emphasise their dominance of the competition. Veteran spinners Iqbal Qasim, Ejaz Faqih and Iqbal Sikander were too much for the Zone side who were bowled out in 38.1 and 39.1 overs.

HBFC also won in under two days, but the dreadfully weak Zone A side had some consolation when Habib Baloch performed the hat-trick, bowling Shaukat Mirza and Ijaz Ahmed and having Tariq Alam lbw. HBFC slipped to 89 for 7, but some fine hitting from wicket-keeper Tahir Rasheed restored them.

ADBP's second innings batting ensured a draw in Lahore while at the LCCA Ground in the same city, Lahore were saved by last pair Afzaal Butt and Haroon Rashid who shared an unbeaten stand of 52. Zone D swamped Zone C in Peshawar.

2, 3, 4 and 5 February 1986

at National Stadium, Karachi

Karachi 92 (Saleem Malik 5 for 19) and 429 (Zafar Ahmed 117 not out, Asif Mujtaba 99, Rizwan-uz-Zaman 66, Anil Dalpat 61, Abdul Qadir 5 for 178)
Habib Bank 203 (Ijaz Faqih 4 for 81) and 286 for 8 (Saleem Malik 71, Arshad Pervez 59, Ijaz Faqih 6 for 106)

Match drawn
Habib Bank 8 pts, Karachi 4 pts

at Bahawal Stadium, Bahawalpur

Zone A 111 (Qasim Shera 6 for 50, Mohammad Altaf 4 for 32) and 140 (Qasim Shera 6 for 54)
Zone B 193 and 62 for 1

Zone B won by 9 wickets
Zone B 15 pts, Zone A 4 pts

at Iqbal Stadium, Faisalabad

Railways 301 for 7 (Shahid Saeed 95, Abid Sarwar 64, Talat Mirza 50, Khatib Rizwan 4 for 83) and 218 (Abid Sarwar 54, Ghaffar Kazmi 4 for 52)
ADBP 155 (Aamer Malik 76, Mohammad Nazir 4 for 17) and 122 (Mohammad Nazir 4 for 22)

Railways won by 242 runs
Railways 18 pts, ADBP 5 pts

at Pindi Club, Rawalpindi

Zone D 206 (Mohammad Riaz 67, Saleem Jaffer 5 for 52) and 160 (Tauseef Ahmed 6 for 59)
United Bank 199 (Nasir Valika 77 not out, Mohammad Riaz 8 for 66) and 169 for 6 (Saadat Ali 80)

United Bank won by 4 wickets
United Bank 15 pts, Zone D 6 pts

Karachi were shocked by Habib Bank who, by the end of the first day, led by 23 runs with 7 wickets in hand. Four quick wickets on the second morning gave Karachi some hope, but they lost 3 wickets before clearing the first innings arrears. Asif and Zafar rallied them splendidly, and ultimately Habib Bank were set the daunting task of making 319 to win and had most of the last day in which to get the runs. They scored at close on four an over, but eventually were thankful for a draw.

Zone A were once more routed in less than two days, and Railways won convincingly in Faisalabad. Shahid shared stands of 93 with Talat and 104 with Abid Sarwar to set them on their way. Career best bowling by Riaz could not save Zone D from defeat at Rawalpindi, the home of Riaz's former side.

7, 8, 9 and 10 February 1986

at Bahawal Stadium, Bahawalpur

Zone B 322 for 5 (Farooq Shera 123 not out, Zahoor Elahi 74) and 142 (Shahid Mahboob 7 for 63)
PACO 321 for 9 (Umar Rasheed 77, Siddiq Patni 57) and 157 for 8 (Tahir Mahmood 61 not out, Shakeel Shah 5 for 64)

PACO won by 2 wickets
PACO 17 pts, Zone B 8 pts

at Iqbal Stadium, Faisalabad

Railways 228 (Hammad Butt 69, Shahid Pervez 57, Sikhander Bakht 5 for 41) and 157 for 4
United Bank 237 (Saadat Ali 72, Nasir Valika 51, Nadeem Ghauri 5 for 85)

Match drawn
United Bank 9 pts, Railways 7 pts

at LCCA Ground, Lahore

HBFC 266 for 5 (Munir-ul-Haq 134 not out) and 153 for 1 (Noor-ul-Qamar 70, Saleem Taj 56 not out)
Habib Bank 282 for 6 (Anwar Miandad 67, Sultan Rana 54, Azhar Khan 77 not out)

Match drawn
Habib Bank 9 pts, HBFC 7 pts

There was no play on the last day in Faisalabad or Lahore due to rain, but PACO won an exciting game in Bahawalpur, Tahir Mahmood and Masood Anwar bringing victory in an unbeaten ninth wicket stand of 34.

13, 14, 15 and 16 February 1986

at National Stadium, Karachi

Railways 240 (Abdus Sami 68, Iqbal Sikander 4 for 39) and 317 (Abid Sarwar 142, Shahid Saeed 61, Ijaz Faqih 6 for 79)
Karachi 282 for 6 (Zafar Ali 54, Moin-ul-Atiq 54, Ijaz Faqih 53 not out, Zafar Ahmed 52) and 123 for 5

Match drawn
Karachi 10 pts, Railways 6 pts

at Bahawal Stadium, Bahawalpur

United Bank 360 for 5 (Shafiq Ahmed 124, Nasir Valika 100 not out, Saadat Ali 60, Habib Baloch 4 for 141)
Zone A 49 (Saleem Jaffer 6 for 20) and 35 (Shahid Aziz 5 for 6)

United Bank won by an innings and 276 runs
United Bank 18 pts, Zone A 3 pts

at Jinnah Stadium, Sialkot

Match abandoned
Zone C 9 pts, HBFC 9 pts

at LCCA Ground, Lahore

Matched abandoned
Lahore 9 pts, Habib Bank 9 pts

at Pindi Club, Rawalpindi

Match abandoned
Zone D 9 pts, PACO 9 pts

Widespread rain caused the abandonment of three matches and the loss of the first day in Bahawalpur. This did not prevent United Bank from winning in two days, however, as the miserable Zone A batting twice failed to muster fifty. Shafiq and Nasir added 133 for the Bank's fourth wicket. Karachi's failure to beat Railways meant that United Bank headed them in the table.

19, 20, 21 and 22 February 1986

at National Stadium, Karachi

ADBP 200 (Masood Anwar 82, Iqbal Sikander 4 for 54, Iqbal

Qasim 4 for 78) and 180 (Ijaz Faqih 5 for 59)
Karachi 349 for 2 (Moin-ul-Atiq 161, Sajid Ali 157 not out)

Karachi won by an innings and 14 runs
Karachi 18 pts, ADBP 3 pts

at Bahawal Stadium, Bahawalpur

United Bank 283 (Ali Zia 133, Mohammad Altaf 4 for 50) and 269 for 8 dec (Shafiq Ahmed 76, Ashraf Ali 53 not out, Qasim Shera 5 for 90)
Zone B 158 (Qasim Shera 58, Sikhander Bakht 4 for 43) and 167 (Shahid Aziz 6 for 44)

United Bank won by 227 runs
United Bank 18 pts, Zone B 5 pts

at Niaz Stadium, Hyderabad

Railways 374 for 9 (Abid Sarwar 122, Hammad Butt 56, Shahid Pervez 59 not out)
Zone A 91 (Nadeem Ghauri 5 for 42, Mohammad Nazir 4 for 24) and 81 (Nadeem Ghauri 7 for 38)

Railways won by an innings and 202 runs
Railways 18 pts, Zone A 4 pts

at LCCA Ground, Lahore

Lahore 301 for 4 (Shahid Anwar 163 not out, Wasim Ali 50 not out) and 72 for 1
PACO 279 for 7 (Moin Mumtaz 51, Akram Raza 7 for 82)

Match drawn
Lahore 10 pts, PACO 6 pts

at Pindi Club, Rawalpindi

Zone D 161 (Raees Ahmed 4 for 31, Ali Ahmed 4 for 68) and 254 for 7 dec (Mujahid Hameed 89, Shahid Javed 59 not out)
HBFC 148 (Mohammad Riaz 6 for 64) and 99 for 5

Match drawn
Zone D 7 pts, HBFC 4 pts

at Iqbal Stadium, Faisalabad

Zone C 197 (Anwar Awais 53) and 180 (Waheed Niazi 5 for 73)
Habib Bank 267 for 9 (Arshad Pervez 96, Naeem Khan 4 for 45, Wassim Haider 4 for 83) and 111 for 3

Habib Bank won by 7 wickets
Habib Bank 18 pts, Zone C 5 pts

There was no play on the first day at Rawalpindi where run getting was never easy, and rain also brought the game in Lahore to an abrupt close. Yet again Zone A failed to take their match beyond the second day as their batsmen once more wilted. Railways' victory helped them to maintain their challenge at the top of the championship table. Habib Bank gained a welcome second win of the season, beating Zone C comfortably, while both the leading sides had decisive victories.

The United Bank bowlers always had the better of Zone B after Ali Zia had prompted his side with a challenging innings. In Karachi, it was the batsmen who dominated once ADBP had fallen to the spin of Iqbal Qasim and Iqbal Sikander. Moin-ul-Atiq and Sajid Ali began Karachi's innings with a stand of 248, the best opening stand of the season, after which ADBP were a beaten side.

25, 26, 27 and 28 February 1986

at National Stadium, Karachi

United Bank 241 for 9 (Shafiq Ahmed 72, Ijaz Faqih 5 for 93) and

293 (Ashraf Ali 62 not out, Ali Zia 59, Rashid Khan 4 for 54)
Karachi 268 for 9 (Asif Mujtaba 69 not out, Ali Zia 4 for 62) and 269 for 4 (Sajid Khan 73, Ijaz Faqih 79 not out, Asif Mujtaba 51)

Karachi won by 6 wickets
Karachi 18 pts, United Bank 7 pts

at Niaz Stadium, Hyderabad

Zone A 116 (Ghaffar Kazmi 7 for 55) and 234 (Iqbal Malik 53)
ADBP 345 for 3 (Masood Anwar 166, Aamer Malik 105, Mansoor Rana 60 not out) and 9 for 0

ADBP won by 10 wickets
ADBP 18 pts, Zone A 2 pts

at Bahawal Stadium, Bahawalpur

Zone B 139 (Shahid Tanvir 71, Mohammad Nazir 4 for 46) and 232 (Bilal Rana 117, Sibtain Haider 6 for 38)
Railways 319 (Abdus Sami 100, Shahid Saeed 70, Mohammad Altaf 4 for 87) and 53 for 1

Railways won by 9 wickets
Railways 18 pts, Zone B 4 pts

at Iqbal Stadium, Faisalabad

Zone C 268 for 6 (Shakir Javed 105 not out, Saadat Gul 50 not out) and 305 (Mohammad Ashraf 108, Wasim Haider 54 not out, Masood Anwar 5 for 73)
PACO 289 for 9 (Yahya Toor 59, Moin Mumtaz 50, Aamer Wasim 4 for 94) and 286 for 8 (Moin Mumtaz 71, Siddiq Patni 62, Tahir Mahmood 52)

PACO won by 2 wickets
PACO 17 pts, Zone C 8 pts

at LCCA Ground, Lahore

HBFC 253 (Saleem Taj 52, Sajjad Akbar 6 for 67) and 341 (Tariq Alam 107, Tahir Rasheed 75, Munir-ul-Haq 64, Akram Raza 4 for 81)
Lahore 251 for 9 (Amer Akbar 72, Kazim Mehdi 5 for 82) and 228 for 1 (Shahid Anwar 101 not out, Aamer Sohail 86)

Match drawn
HBFC 10 pts, Lahore 8 pts

at Pindi Club, Rawalpindi

Habib Bank 166 (Mohammad Riaz 7 for 74) and 160 (Arshad Pervez 60 not out, Mohammad 8 for 70)
Zone D 277 for 4 (Tariq Javed 154 not out) and 50 for 2

Zone D won by 8 wickets
Zone D 18 pts, Habib Bank 3 pts

Karachi won the vital game with United Bank in fine style. They ended the first day at 28 for 2, and they slipped to 44 for 3 early on the second morning, but by close of play that evening they had taken a first innings lead of 27 and captured two United Bank second innings wickets for 71. The Bank side batted throughout the third day, however, and although they were all out within five minutes of the start of the last day, Karachi faced a stiff task in scoring 267 to win. Sajid Khan and Sajid Ali gave them a bristling start with a stand of 103, and runs continued to flow at 3.8 an over to give Karachi a most impressive victory.

Aamer Malik and Masood Anwar put on 227 for ADBP's first wicket in the win over Zone A which was achieved in three days while Abdus Sami and Shahid Saeed put on 191 for the first wicket as Railways beat Zone B also in three days. At one time in their second innings Zone B were 3 for 5.

PACO scored at 4 an over to win excitingly against Zone C, and Habib Bank won with a day to spare.

3, 4, 5 and 6 March 1986

at National Stadium, Karachi

Zone C 165 (Sajid Bashir 52, Ijaz Faqih 4 for 41) and 184 (Sajid Bashir 69, Iqbal Qasim 5 for 48, Ijaz Faqih 4 for 59)
Karachi 371 for 4 (Sajid Ali 113, Zafar Ahmed 104 not out)
Karachi won by an innings and 24 runs

Karachi 18 pts, Zone C 3 pts

at Pindi Club, Rawalpindi

Zone B 82 (Mohammad Riaz 6 for 32) and 446 (Farooq Shera 135, Abdur Rahim 132, Bilal Rana 73, Mohammad Riaz 4 for 165)
Zone D 252 for 8 (Tariq Javed 111 not out) and 259 (Mohammad Arif jnr 54, Shahid Javed 52)

Zone B won by 17 runs
Zone B 14 pts, Zone D 8 pts

at Iqbal Stadium, Faisalabad

United Bank 316 for 6 (Saadat Ali 140, Nasir Valika 76 not out) and 194 (Ashraf Ali 72 not out, Nasir Valika 66, Shahid Mahboob 4 for 46)
PACO 277 for 7 (Yahya Toor 61 not out, Nadeem Ahsan 55 not out, Umar Rasheed 51, Shahid Butt 4 for 91) and 237 for 7 (Umar Rasheed 92, Shahid Butt 4 for 63)

PACO won by 3 wickets
PACO 17 pts, United Bank 8 pts

at Sargodha Stadium

Railways 303 (Babar Altaf 80, Ajmal Hussain 60, Talat Mirza 51, Abdur Raqeeb 4 for 69) and 193 (Abdur Raqeeb 5 for 80)
Habib Bank 169 (Mohammad Nazir 5 for 51, Nadeem Ghauri 4 for 75) and 135 (Arshad Pervez 57, Mohammad Nazir 5 for 34, Nadeem Ghauri 5 for 72)

Railways won by 192 runs
Railways 18 pts, Habib Bank 5 pts

at Qaddafi Stadium, Lahore

HBFC 272 for 6 (Tahir Rasheed 102 not out, Tariq Alam 100) and 226 (Shaukat Mirza 74, Ghaffar Kazmi 4 for 57
ADBP 237 (Manzoor Elahi 63, Ali Ahmed 7 for 70) and 162 for 6 (Aamer Malik 68 not out, Ali Ahmed 4 for 78)

Match drawn
HBFC 10 pts, ADBP 6 pts

at LCCA Ground, Lahore

Zone A 147 (Asim Butt 4 for 21, Sajjad Akbar 4 for 29) and 184 (Mansoor Khan 71, Afzaal Butt 4 for 73)
Lahore 433 (Aamer Sohail 101, Mohammad Jamil 101, Shahid Anwar 74, Sajjad Akbar 68, Afzal Chaudri 5 for 118)

Lahore won by an innings and 102 runs
Lahore 18 pts, Zone A 4 pts

In the previous match Mohammad Riaz had returned figures of 15 for 144, the best of the season, and he continued in this vein when Zone D met Zone B, being instrumental in bowling out Zone B for 82 on the opening day in Rawalpindi. Zone D took a first innings lead of 170, and Zone B lost three wickets in clearing the arrears, but stands of 130 between Abdur and Farooq and 132 between Abdur and Bilal turned the course of the match. Zone D needed 277 to win and began the last day on 52 for 3. They reached 199 for 6, but 4 wickets fell for 41 runs and Zone B achieved a remarkable victory.

It took Karachi only three days to beat Zone C and consolidate their position at the top. A second innings collapse, they were 19 for 6 at one time, cost United Bank the game against PACO, and they dropped out of contention. Railways maintained their challenge as veteran off-spinner Mohammad Nazir took 10 Habib wickets. HBFC recovered from 88 for 5 on the first day when Tahir and Tariq added 170, but the match was drawn. Shahid Anwar and Aamer Sohail put on 177 for Lahore's first wicket as Zone A, inevitably, lost by an innings inside three days.

8, 9 and 10 March 1986

at Gymkhana Ground, Karachi

Zone D 110 (Ijaz Faqih 6 for 49) and 243 (Shahid Javed 65, Mujahid Hameed 64, Iqbal Qasim 6 for 73)
Karachi 262 (Zafar Ahmed 62, Shakeel Ahmed 4 for 43) and 94 for 4

Karachi won by 6 wickets
Karachi 18 pts, Zone D 4 pts

By winning in three days with maximum points, Karachi moved into an almost impregnable position at the top of the championship table.

9, 10, 11 and 12 March 1986

at Iqbal Stadium, Faisalabad

Railways 194 (Shahid Saeed 52) and 313 for 9 dec (Shahid Saaed 136)
PACO 214 for 7 (Yahya Toor 61, Nadeem Ghauri 5 for 103) and 128 (Tahir Mahmood 53, Nadeem Ghauri 7 for 69)

Railways won by 165 runs
Railways 15 pts, PACO 6 pts

at Jinnah Stadium, Sialkot

Zone A 156 (Shahid Nazir 4 for 31) and 261 (Hameed-ul-Haq 81, Raj Hans 52, Tariq Mahmood 8 for 69)
Zone C 442 for 8 (Sajid Bashir 109, Abdul Waheed 100, Khawar Malik 59, Wasim Haider 56)

Zone C won by an innings and 25 runs
Zone C 18 pts, Zone A 5 pts

at Qaddafi Stadium, Lahore

HBFC 100 (Sikhander Bakht 5 for 40, Ehtesham-ud-Din 4 for 58) and 208 (Mohammad Javed 88, Ehtesham-ud-Din 4 for 68)
United Bank 72 (Mohinder Kumar 5 for 36) and 206 (Ali Ahmed 7 for 80)

HBFC won by 30 runs
HBFC 14 pts, United Bank 4 pts

at LCCA Ground, Lahore

Lahore 165 and 309 (Akram Raza 59, Tahir Shah 55, Sajjad Akbar 53 not out)
Zone B 292 for 9 (Farooq Shera 100 not out, Abdur Rahim 86, Sajjad Akbar 4 for 80) and 135 (Bilal Rana 51 not out, Tahir Shah 5 for 47)

Lahore won by 47 runs
Lahore 15 pts, Zone B 8 pts

Railways won comfortably in Faisalabad, but their failure in the first innings cost them three points and handicapped them in their effort to overtake Karachi. The game in Sialkot

did not begin until 3.00 pm because of a dispute over the composition of the Zone A side. Eventually, Zone C, with Abdul Waheed and Khawar Malik adding 167 for the second wicket, won by an innings. It was Zone A's tenth consecutive defeat. In spite of good bowling by their veteran seam bowlers Sikhander and Ehtesham-ud-Din, United Bank lost a well fought contest with HBFC, and Lahore recovered bravely to beat Zone B after being 111 for 4 in their second innings, still 16 runs short of avoiding an innings defeat.

15, 16, 17 and 18 March 1986

at Bahawal Stadium, Bahawalpur

PACO 189 (Moin Mumtaz 50) and 180 (Tahir Mahmood 58, Raja Afaq 4 for 40)
ADBP 155 (Mian Fayyaz 5 for 42) and 216 for 4 (Ghaffar Kazmi 96 not out, Tanvir Ahmed 66)

ADBP won by 6 wickets
ADBP 15 pts, PACO 5 pts

at Sargodha Stadium

Match abandoned
Railways 9 pts, HBFC 9 pts

at Shahi Bagh Stadium, Peshawar

Zone D w.o. *v.* **Zone A** who failed to arrive for the match

Zone D 14 pts, Zone A 0 pts

The abandonment of Railways' last game left Karachi as champions.

17, 18, 19 and 20 March 1986

at Qaddafi Stadium, Lahore

United Bank 177 (Liaqat Ali 7 for 42) and 383 (Nasir Valika 75, Mansoor Akhtar 65, Saadat Ali 51, Agha Zahid 4 for 65)
Habib Bank 108 (Sikhander Bakht 6 for 54) and 86 for 3

Match drawn
United Bank 6 pts, Habib Bank 4 pts

at LCCA Ground, Lahore

Lahore 134 and 155 (Asif Mujtaba 4 for 39, Ijaz Faqih 4 for 44)
Karachi 110 (Akram Rana 6 for 29) and 97 (Sajjad Akbar 7 for 40)

Lahore won by 82 runs
Lahore 14 pts, Karachi 4 pts

Rain curtailed play between United Bank and Habib Bank, and Karachi, defeated for the first time in the season, faced an interruption of another kind. Rain shortened play on the first day, and there was no play on the second when it was discovered that the pitch had been vandalised. The champions succumbed on a wearing wicket on the last day, but there was consolation for when Ijaz had Sohail Fazal caught he claimed his 100th wicket of the season so equalling Abdul Qadir's feat of being the only bowler outside England to have taken 100 wickets in a domestic season.

21, 22 and 23 March 1986

at Bahawal Stadium, Bahawalpur

Zone B 116 (Ghaffar Kazmi 4 for 11) and 206 (Ghaffar Kazmi 6 for 75)
ADBP 327 (Manzoor Elahi 115, Qasim Shera 5 for 105)

ADBP won by an innings and 5 runs
ADBP 18 pts, Zone B 4 pts

ABOVE: *Mohammad Nazir bowled 783.2 overs of off-spin for Railways, took 88 wickets and led them to second place in the Quaid-e-Azam Trophy. (Adrian Murrell)*

BELOW: *Iqbal Qasim's left-arm spin played a decisive part in Karachi winning the Quaid-e-Azam Trophy. (Patrick Eagar)*

ADBP, who won in three days, were lifted by a sixth wicket stand of 105 between Atif Rauf and Manzoor Elahi after 5 wickets had fallen for 94.

27, 28, 29 and 30 March 1986

at Jinnah Stadium, Sialkot
Match abandoned
Zone C 9 pts, Zone B 9 pts

at National Stadium, Karachi
Habib Bank 249 for 9 (Arshad Pervez 101, Raja Afaq 5 for 88) and 315 for 8 (Anwar Miandad 88, Zaheer Ahmed 55, Raja Afaq 5 for 125)
ADBP 252 for 9 (Atif Rauf 55, Masood Anwar 51)
Match drawn
ADBP 10 pts, Habib Bank 7 pts

The Quaid-e-Azam Trophy ended with Arshad Pervez, a great fighter for lost causes, hitting a fine and valiant century.

Quaid-e-Azam Championship Trophy					
	P	W	L	D/Ab	Pts
Karachi	11	7	1	3	154
Railways	11	6	–	5	147
Lahore	11	5	1	5	131
United Bank	11	5	3	3	127
PACO	11	4	3	4	118
ADBP	11	4	3	4	112
HBFC	11	3	–	8	110
Zone D	11	3	4	4	105
Habib Bank	11	2	3	6	93
Zone B	11	3	7	1	91
Zone C	11	1	7	3	84
Zone A	11	–	11	–	34

PACO Pentagular Tournament

As in previous seasons, the top five teams in the Quaid-e-Azam Trophy competed in the PACO Pentagular Championship.

22, 23, 24 and 25 March 1986

at Qaddafi Stadium, Lahore
Railways 132 (Saleem Jaffer 6 for 64) and 148 (Saleem Jaffer 5 for 69)
United Bank 284 (Ashraf Ali 63, Sibtain Haider 4 for 107)
United Bank won by an innings and 4 runs
United Bank 18 pts, Railways 4 pts

at LCCA Ground, Lahore
Karachi 193 (Sajid Khan 93, Sajjad Akbar 7 for 50) and 309 (Basit Ali 98, Sajid Ali 86, Zafar Ali 51)
Lahore 287 for 8 (Mohammad Jamil 96, Wasim Ali 60, Ijaz Faqih 6 for 103) and 144 for 5
Match drawn
Lahore 10 pts, Karachi 5 pts

United Bank beat Railways inside three days after winning the toss and asking the opposition to bat first. Karachi chose to bat on winning the toss, but they fared badly, escaping defeat through an improved batting performance in the second innings.

27, 28, 29 and 30 March 1986

at LCCA Ground, Lahore

Lahore 187 (Shahid Anwar 60, Mohammad Nazir 5 for 47, Nadeem Ghauri 5 for 92) and 141 (Mohammad Nazir 6 for 62, Nadeem Ghauri 4 for 54)
Railways 169 (Sajjad Akbar 6 for 53) and 152 (Hammad Butt 66 not out, Akram Raza 4 for 38)

Lahore won by 7 runs
Lahore 15 pts, Railways 5 pts

at Qaddafi Stadium, Lahore

United Bank 285 (Mansoor Akhtar 80, Naved Anjum 59, Jalal-ud-Din 5 for 80, Barkatullah 4 for 59) and 276 (Nasir Valika 60 not out)
Karachi 216 (Asif Mujtaba 79, Zafar Ahmed 50, Naved Anjum 4 for 42) and 279 (Basit Ali 81, Anil Dalpat 56, Saleem Jaffer 4 for 61)

United Bank won by 66 runs
United Bank 18 pts, Karachi 6 pts

With their second maximum point win, United Bank asserted the leading place in the competition although PACO were yet to play a match. Karachi, weakened and tired, would have lost more heavily had Asif Mujtaba and Zafar Ahmed not added 117 for their fifth wicket in the first innings. In a match dominated by spinners at the LCCA Ground, Lahore won excitingly after Railways had reached 149 for 8, only 11 short of victory, on the third afternoon.

1, 2, 3 and 4 April 1986

at Qaddafi Stadium, Lahore

PACO 299 (Ijaz Ahmed 117, Tahir Mahmood 57, Nadeem Moosa 4 for 34) and 92 for 2
Karachi 148 (Shahid Mahboob 7 for 74) and 239 (Masood Anwar 6 for 55)

PACO won by 8 wickets
PACO 18 pts, Karachi 4 pts

at LCCA Ground, Lahore

United Bank 241 (Sajjad Akbar 5 for 76, Akram Raza 4 for 67) and 363 for 8 dec (Ali Zia 89, Saadat Ali 85, Nasir Valika 57 not out, Akram Raza 5 for 104)
Lahore 250 for 6 (Tahir Shah 86, Aamer Malik 74) and 355 for 6 (Aamer Malik 101, Ameer Akbar 82)

Lahore won by 4 wickets
Lahore 18 pts, United Bank 6 pts

PACO entered the tournament with a win in three days over Karachi who were forced to follow-on. PACO recovered after being put in and losing both openers with only 4 scored. A fifth wicket stand of 123 between Ijaz Ahmed and Tahir Mahmood gave substance to PACO's innings.

United Bank's run came to an end when they were beaten by Lahore who accepted the challenge to score 355 with panache. Ameer Akbar gave the innings its early impetus, and Man of the Match Aamer Malik hit a sparkling century to make victory possible.

6, 7, 8 and 9 April 1986

at Qaddafi Stadium, Lahore

Railways 230 (Shahid Saaed 81, Haseeb-ul-Hasan 5 for 75) and 274 (Shahid Saaed 109, Raza Khan 5 for 76)
Karachi 155 and 196 for 9 (Sibtain Haider 4 for 52)

Match drawn
Railways 9 pts, Karachi 5 pts

at LCCA Ground, Lahore

United Bank 274 for 6 (Mansoor Akhtar 78, Saadat Ali 69, Masood Anwar 6 for 97) and 270 (Shafiq Ahmed 72, Ali Zia 51, Masood Anwar 4 for 73)
PACO 283 (Umar Tasheed 82, Moin Mumtaz 52, Shahid Aziz 5 for 112) and 262 for 7 (Ijaz Ahmed 93, Tahir Mahmood 57, Shahid Aziz 6 for 101)

PACO won by 3 wickets
PACO 17 pts, United Bank 8 pts

Rain interrupted the game between Railways and Karachi, and Karachi were saved from defeat by the stubborn defence of last pair Nadeem Moosa and Raza Khan.

PACO achieved a good win over United Bank. Inspired by Ijaz Ahmed, they scored at more than 3 runs an over on the last day. In spite of fine bowling performances by Shahid Aziz and Masood Anwar, Ijaz was named Man of the Match.

11, 12, 13 and 14 April 1986

at Qaddafi Stadium, Lahore

Railways 139 (Masood Anwat 4 for 19, Shahid Mahboob 4 for 72) and 255 (Shahid Saaed 90)
PACO 282 for 8 (Shahid Mahboob 100 not out, Mohammad Nazir 4 for 102) and 114 for 3

PACO won by 7 wickets
PACO 18 pts, Railways 4 pts

A fine all round performance by skipper Shahid Mahboob who bowled his medium pace to fine effect and then hit the second century of his career set up PACO's third win in the tournament. He returned match figures of 7 for 171 and made his hundred out of 148.

16, 17, 18 and 19 April 1986

at Qaddafi Stadium, Lahore

Lahore 221 for 9 (Shahid Mahboob 6 for 109) and 323 for 5 dec (Aamer Malik 122, Mansoor Rana 116, Masood Anwar 4 for 112)
PACO 218 for 6 dec (Umar Rasheed 61 not out, Ijaz Ahmed 53, Sajjad Akbar 4 for 75) and 17 for 1

Match drawn
Lahore 7 pts, PACO 6 pts

The season came to a tired and apathetic end as the captains agreed to call off the match before lunch time on the last day. More attention seemed to be focussed on Sharjah than on PACO winning a national title for the first time. Some individual landmarks were reached in the game. Sajjad Akbar, the off-spinner, took his 31st wicket to become the leading wicket-taker in the tournament. Ijaz Ahmed finished short of 1500 runs, but he was still the leading run-scorer in the country. Aamer Malik and Mansoor Rana put on 212 for Lahore's third wicket in the second innings.

PACO Pentagular Cup – Final Table					
	P	W	L	D	Pts
PACO	4	3	–	1	59
Lahore	4	2	–	2	50
United Bank	4	2	2	–	50
Railways	4	–	3	1	22
Karachi	4	–	2	2	20

Individual Awards

Man of the Tournament	Shahid Mahboob (PACO)
Batting	Ijaz Ahmed (PACO)
Bowling	Sajjad Akbar (Lahore)
Wicket-Keeping	Ashraf Ali (United Bank)
Fielding	Moin Mumtaz (PACO)

First Class Averages

BATTING

	M	Inns	Nos	Runs	HS	Av	100s	50s
Rizwan-uz-Zaman (K)	8	15	2	1198	175	92.15	5	5
Javed Miandad (Pak/HB)	5	5	1	337	203*	84.25	1	1
Moin-ul-Atiq (K)	12	17	5	972	203*	81.00	4	2
Nasir Valika (UB)	12	21	8	865	100*	66.53	1	7
Asif Mujtaba (K)	16	22	6	869	131*	54.31	1	6
Arshad Pervez (Sg/HB)	14	24	3	1113	119	53.00	3	9
Tahir Rasheed (HBFC)	7	11	2	443	102*	49.22	1	3
Shahid Saeed (Rly)	14	27	2	1210	136	48.40	3	6
Zafar Ahmed (K)	15	23	5	864	117*	48.00	3	4
Ijaz Ahmed (G/PACO)	18	33	1	1476	182	46.12	5	4
Ali Zia (LC/UB)	17	26	2	1091	229*	45.45	3	4
Masood Anwar (Rp/ADBP)	14	22	2	903	202*	45.15	2	4
Saadat Ali (LC/UB)	17	29	1	1210	140	43.21	2	9
Shahid Anwar (LC/L)	18	33	3	1279	163*	42.63	3	8
Tariq Javed (Rp/ZD)	11	19	2	718	154*	42.23	2	3
Shakir Javed (F/ZC)	9	18	2	673	164	42.06	2	4
Aamer Malik (LC/ADBP/L)	14	24	1	938	122	40.78	4	3
Mansoor Rana (LC/ADBP/L)	19	31	3	1124	140	40.14	2	7
Umar Rasheed (PACO)	14	25	4	841	112	40.04	1	6
Ashraf Ali (Pak/LC/UB)	16	24	7	677	72*	39.82		7
Tariq Alam (HBFC)	9	16	3	514	107	39.53	2	1
Farooq Shera (B/ZB)	11	21	3	709	135	39.38	3	2
Aamer Sohail (LC/L)	14	22	3	727	101	38.26	1	1
Yahya Toor (PACO)	14	20	7	490	61*	37.69		3
Shafiq Ahmed (LC/UB)	18	28	0	1028	124	36.71	2	4
Sajid Ali (K)	14	23	1	786	157*	35.72	2	2
Shahid Javed (ZD)	7	14	2	426	65	35.50		4
Manzoor Elahi (M/ADBP)	13	21	0	740	129	35.23	2	3
Ijaz Faqih (K)	18	21	4	589	112	34.64	1	4
Wasim Ali (L)	9	14	4	345	63	34.50		3
Wasim Haider (F/ZC)	11	20	5	511	61	34.06		3
Sajid Bashir (G/ZC)	8	14	0	475	123	33.92	2	2
Mujahid Hameed (Rp/ZD)	7	11	0	347	89	31.54		2
Mudassar Nazar (Pak/UB)	7	12	2	314	78	31.40		3
Anwar Miandad (JB)	10	18	2	501	88	31.31		4

Anil Dalpat (Karachi) headed the wicket-keeper's list for the season with 67 dismissals. (Adrian Murrell)

	M	Inns	Nos	Runs	HS	Av	100s	50s
Tahir Mahmood (G/PACO)	17	27	3	746	81	31.08		7
Saadat Gul (F/ZU)	8	13	2	340	65	30.90		2
Mohammad Riaz (LC/ZD)	8	15	0	463	78	30.86		3
Qasim Shera (B/ZB)	8	15	1	431	89	30.78		3
Basit Ali (K)	11	18	0	551	101	30.61	1	3
Aamer Mirza (Ps/ZD)	10	18	1	520	82	30.58		4
Atif Rauf (ADBP)	11	17	2	446	102*	29.73	1	2
Ghaffar Kazmi (LC/ADBP)	13	20	2	533	96*	29.61		4
Mohammad Jamil (L)	8	14	1	385	101	29.61	1	1
Raja Afaq (Rp/ADBP)	12	14	3	317	116*	28.81	1	
Mansoor Akhtar (K/UB)	18	29	3	743	101*	28.57	1	4
Ameer Akbar (LC/L)	14	24	2	624	82	28.36		3
Nadeem Jamal (Hyd/ZA)	10	20	0	566	149	28.30	2	
Hammad Butt (Rly)	14	26	2	676	69	28.16		3
Mohammad Ashraf (F/ZC)	13	24	1	647	108	28.13	1	3
Tahir Shah (LC/L)	13	20	1	532	90	28.00		3
Bilal Rana (M/ZB)	12	22	4	503	117	27.94	1	2
Moin Mumtaz (K/PACO)	15	25	2	640	71	27.82		6
Shahid Tanvir (LD/ZB)	11	21	0	581	100	27.66	1	2
Sajjad Akbar (LC/L)	16	21	3	496	81	27.55		3
Abid Sarwar (Rly)	12	23	0	633	142	27.52	2	2
Sajid Khan (K)	9	17	0	466	93	27.41		2

Anwar Awais (F/ZC)	8	15	0	411	75	27.40		4
Naved Anjum (LC/UB)	17	27	1	692	101*	26.61	1	3
Akram Raza (LC/L)	14	21	3	475	76	26.38		4
Shahid Pervez (Rly)	13	23	4	497	88	26.15		3
Tanvir Ahmed (LC/ADBP)	13	23	1	569	109	25.86	1	4
Musleh-ud-Din (Rly)	7	14	2	309	81	25.75		1
Mansoor Khan (ZC)	8	15	1	359	109*	25.64	1	
Agha Zahid (HB)	10	18	0	460	147	25.55	1	1
Abdur Rahim (B/ZB)	11	22	1	534	132	25.42	1	2
Munir-ul-Haq (K/HBFC)	8	15	2	320	134*	24.61	1	1
Sultan Rana (HB)	9	15	2	318	54	24.46	2	
Shaukat Mirza (K/HBFC)	13	24	1	558	75	24.26		2
Raees Ahmed (Q/HBFC)	10	17	1	386	102*	24.12	1	1
Abdus Sami (Rly)	13	24	1	584	100	23.82	1	2
Zahoor Elahi (M/ZB)	11	22	0	511	74	23.22		4
Talat Mirza (Rly)	13	25	1	556	93	23.16		3
Maqsood Kundi (Ps/ADBP)	15	22	8	316	74*	22.57		1
Siddiq Patni (PACO)	10	17	0	377	62	22.17		3
Shahid Mahboob (Q/PACO)	16	26	2	518	100*	21.58	1	1
Khalid Alvi (PACO)	14	26	3	494	64	21.47		1
Raj Hans (Q/ZA)	9	18	0	346	71	19.22		3
Babar Altaf (Rly)	12	22	0	420	80	19.09		2
Tehsin Javed (HB)	9	17	0	311	48	18.29		
Azhar Abbas (B/ZB)	10	19	2	304	33	17.88		
Mohammad Nazir (Rly)	14	25	2	390	49	16.95		
Bilal Ahmed (F/ZC)	11	21	0	350	47	16.66		

BOWLING

	Overs	Mdns	Runs	Wkts	Av	Best	10/m	5/inn
Sikander Bakht (UB)	189.5	36	581	41	14.17	6/54		4
Mohammad Nazir (Rly)	783.2	274	1269	88	14.42	6/41	4	9
Farrukh Zaman (Ps/ZD)	91.3	19	233	15	14.86	6/32	1	
Sabih Azhar (Rp/ADBP)	119	37	330	21	15.71	6/29		1
Imran Khan (Pak)	120.4	37	271	17	15.94	5/40	1	
Iqbal Sikander (K)	342.5	70	1038	65	15.96	6/29		5
Ijaz Faqih (K)	743	160	1719	107	16.06	6/20	2	11
Iqbal Qasim (K)	453.3	117	1024	62	16.51	7/39		3
Sajjad Akbar (LC/L)	687.1	168	1626	96	16.93	7/40	1	6
Asim Butt (LC/L)	95.3	15	257	15	17.13	4/21		
Mohammad Riaz (LC/ZD)	402	89	1049	61	17.19	8/66	4	7
Sajid Hussain (Rp/ZD)	264.4	56	745	42	17.73	7/65	2	3
Aziz-ur-Rehman (Sg/ZC)	182.1	41	484	27	17.92	7/67		1
Ali Ahmed (HBFC)	241	34	723	39	18.53	7/70	1	2
Farhat Masood (G/ZC)	127	23	393	21	18.71	6/37	1	2
Tahir Shah (LC/L)	98.3	21	319	17	18.76	5/33		2
Naeem Taj (LC/L)	133	38	301	16	18.81	7/42		1
Tauseef Ahmed (Pak/UB)	216.1	68	511	27	18.92	6/59		2
Saleem Jaffer (K/UB)	452	85	1539	80	19.23	6/20	2	6

Nadeem Ghauri (Rly)	727.5	198	1678	87	19.28	7/38	2	8
Shahid Aziz (UB)	209.4	37	650	33	19.69	6/44	1	4
Raja Afaq (RP/ADBP)	373.2	82	955	48	19.89	5/80	1	3
Akram Raza (LC/L)	494.2	112	1179	58	20.32	7/82		4
Qasim Shera (B/ZB)	203.1	28	762	37	20.59	6/50	1	4
Nasir Javed (Rp/ZD)	144.3	14	388	18	21.55	5/73		1
Ali Zia (LC/UB)	335.2	73	902	41	22.00	8/60	1	1
Rashid Khan (K)	173.4	33	511	23	22.21	5/59		1
Kazim Mehdi (HBFC)	289.1	74	758	34	22.29	6/13	1	4
Barkatullah (K)	90.3	9	361	16	22.56	4/59		
Abdur Raqeeb (HB)	386.1	92	1071	47	22.78	6/23	1	4
Ghaffar Kazmi (LC/ADBP)	512.5	79	1490	65	22.92	7/55	2	4
Mohammad Altaf (B/ZB)	397.1	62	1217	53	22.96	6/63		4
Sibtain Haider (LC/Rly)	149	24	535	23	23.26	6/38		1
Mohammad Zahid (B/ZB)	112.3	16	377	16	23.56	5/27	1	2
Shakeel Shah (LD/ZB)	191.3	29	715	30	23.83	6/51		2
Masood Anwar (PACO)	535.4	122	1328	55	24.14	6/55	1	3
Agha Zahid (HB)	177	33	467	19	24.57	4/65		
Tanvir Shaukat (F/ZC)	118.2	12	486	19	25.57	6/47		1
Khatib Rizwan (ADBP)	313.1	70	772	30	25.73	5/104		1
Bilal Rana (M/ZB)	336.5	62	964	37	26.05	5/79		2
Ghayyur Qureshi (LC/L)	228.4	53	725	27	26.85	6/44		2

Sikhander Bakht topped the bowling averages with 41 wickets for United Bank. (Adrian Murrell)

Asif Faridi (Rp/ADBP)	150	22	490	18	27.22	3/62		
Afzaal Butt (LC/L)	236.1	41	767	28	27.39	4/39		
Shahid Mahboob (Q/PACO)	592.2	66	2088	72	29.00	7/63	1	5
Abdul Qadir (Pak/HB)	174.2	34	499	17	29.35	5/44		2
Jalal-ud-Din (K)	200.5	41	676	23	29.39	5/32		2
Wasim Haider (F/ZC)	199	21	743	25	29.72	4/45		
Shahid Tanvir (LD/ZB)	249.3	31	754	25	30.16	6/44		1
Raees Ahmed (Q/HBFC)	159.5	31	492	16	30.75	7/42		1
Shahid Butt (M/UB)	298.1	56	902	29	31.10	5/54		1
Mohinder Kumar (HBFC)	580	155	1347	43	31.32	4/63		
Tanvir Afzal (F/ZC)	139.1	23	472	15	31.46	5/36		1
Azeem Hafeez (K)	375	33	1139	36	31.63	5/38		2
Aamer Wasim (ZC)	124.4	21	494	15	32.93	5/90		1
Mian Fayyaz (PACO)	341.5	49	1124	34	33.05	6/121		2
Waheed Niazi (LC/HB/L)	594.3	134	1502	45	33.37	6/37	1	3
Habib Baloch (Q/ZA)	186.1	30	671	20	33.55	5/73		1
	173	16	745	22	33.86	5/74		1
R. Ghulam Abbas (Sg/ZC)	248.5	56	652	19	34.31	7/42		1
Manzoor Elahi (M/ADBP)	243.1	32	900	26	34.61	4/52		
Tahir Mahmood (G/PACO)	208	20	738	21	35.14	5/62		1
Haroon Rasheed (L)	161	16	574	15	38.26	5/78		1

LEADING FIELDERS

20 - Iqbal Qasim and Ijaz Ahmed; 19 - Mohammad Altaf and Mansoor Rana; 17 - Arshad Pervez and Masood Anwar; 16 - Abdus Sami and Zafar Ali; 15 - Mohammad Arif senior, Yahya Toor, Ali Zia and Saadat Ali

LEADING WICKET-KEEPERS

67 - Anil Dalpat (ct 39/st 28); 62 - Ashraf Ali (ct 53/st 9); 46 - Maqsood Kundi (ct 39/st 7); 35 - Babar Altaf (ct 26/st 9); 25 - Zaheer Ahmed (ct 16/st 9); 23 - Tahir Rasheed (ct 21/st 2) and Bilal Ahmed (ct 15/st 8); 22 - Zulqarnian (ct 19/st 3) and Nadeem Ahsan (ct 21/st 1); 21 - Saleem Yousuf (ct 19/st 2) and Tahir Pizzada (ct 17/st 4)

Abbreviations of team names used: ADBP – Agricultural Development Bank of Pakistan; B – Bahawalpur; DIK – Dera Ismail Khan; F – Faisalabad; G – Gujranwala; HB – Habib Bank; Hz – Hazara; HBFC – House Building Finance Corporation; Hyd – Hyderabad; K – Karachi; L – Lahore; LC – Lahore City; LD – Lahore Division; M – Multan; Pak – Pakistan (in Tests); PACO – Pakistan Automobile Corporations; Ps – Peshawar; Q – Quetta; Rly – Railways; Rp – Rawalpindi; Sg – Sargodha; Sk – Sukkur; UB – United Bank; ZA – Zone A; ZB – Zone B; ZC – Zone C; ZD – Zone D

Fresh Woods and Pastures New

The Three Nations Tournament
and Australasian Cup in Sharjah

Javed Miandad – the hero of Pakistan and Sharjah. A six off the last ball of the match to win the Australasian Cup. (Tony Edenden)

The advance of cricket in the United Arab Emirates in the past few years has been phenomenal. Cricket was started in Kuwait and Bahrain in the 1930s, but it did not take root in the United Arab Emirates until shortly after the Second World War. Now, mainly through the enthusiasm of the many Indian, Pakistani and Sri Lankan expatriates, there are more than eighty clubs in the U.A.E. Thanks to the efforts of an Arab cricketer and enthusiast, Abdul Rehman Bukhatir, Sharjah has moved ahead of all other clubs in the Gulf. For more than four years it has boasted two grass cricket fields, one of which is the magnificent Sharjah Stadium where international competitions have been staged in recent years, the matches being played in front of capacity crowds for the richest prizes that have ever been offered for the game.

In 1985–86, Abdul Rehman Bukhatir masterminded two limited-over competitions, a three nations tournament between India, West Indies and Pakistan in November, 1985, and the Australasian Cup which involved India, Pakistan, Sri Lanka, Australia and New Zealand in April, 1986. Sadly, England, Australia and New Zealand have yet to gauge the importance and significance of the Sharjah tournaments, and they have tended to field sides which have not been representative of their full strength. This is a short-sighted policy for Sharjah could become one of the most important centres of international cricket within the next few years, and the energy, intelligence and generous sponsorship which have propelled the game forward in the U.A.E. in recent years may even propel the area towards staging the World Cup in the not too distant future.

Three Nations Tournament – Match One
PAKISTAN v. WEST INDIES

Electing to bat first, Pakistan gave an impressive performance even if their final total was not too daunting. Mohsin Khan and Mudassar Nazar, one of the most established and reliable opening partnerships in the world, began solidly with a stand of 50. Qasim again failed to do himself justice in a limited over international, providing Gray with his first wicket in international cricket, but Rameez Raja, appreciating the need to keep the score moving, scampered between the wickets and hurried the score along.

The stand of 84 between Rameez and Mohsin tended to expose the West Indies' complacency in the field. Catches were missed and the ground fielding was slipshod. Rameez was finally caught and bowled by Garner, but it was the big man's only success. He suffered the indignity of being hit for 3 sixes in an over by Imran, to the delight of the capacity crowd, and earlier, Javed had hit Marshall for three successive fours.

Mohsin continued on his elegant way to the end which came at 196, leaving West Indies to score at 4.37 an over. They could not have begun worse, Haynes being bowled in the first over. Gomes and Richardson added 72 careful runs before Gomes was caught behind. This brought Richards to the crease and he began in careless manner. He touched the second ball he received to wicket-keeper Saleem Yousuf who dropped a straight-forward chance. It was a crucial miss. Richards seemed galvanised into action by his lapse. He and Richardson unleased a series of thrilling shots.

By the time Saleem Yousuf had made amends by catching

Richards off Imran, the batsman had scored 51, and West Indies were only 13 short of victory with two overs remaining. Richardson unleashed the final attack and West Indies clinched victory with five balls to spare. It was a fine win, but Pakistan had performed well and but for one missed chance, they might well have been victors.

Three Nations Tournament – Match Two
PAKISTAN v. INDIA

In spite of the fact that Imran Khan was forced to withdraw from the attack, Pakistan beat India with considerable ease in the second match of the competition. Pakistan were put in to bat and had an early upset when Mohsin Khan was run out. Mudassar and Rameez were soon into their stride, however, and a bustling stand realised exactly 100 before Mudassar fell to the leg spin of Sivaramakrishnan.

Javed Miandad maintained the impetus with an inventive innings, but the Pakistan total looked far from unbeatable. It took on greater proportions when Srikkanth was caught behind in the ninth over and the out of form Azharuddin followed two overs later.

Laxman Sivaramakrishnan, the Indian leg-spinner, still struggling for form. (Sporting Pictures UK Ltd)

THREE NATIONS TOURNAMENT – PAKISTAN v. WEST INDIES
15 November 1985 at Sharjah

PAKISTAN					WEST INDIES			
Mudassar Nazar	c Logie, b Holding			18	D.L. Haynes	b Wasim Akram		0
Mohsin Khan	not out			86	R.B. Richardson	not out		99
Qasim Umar	c Richards, b Gray			2	H.A. Gomes	c Saleem Yousuf,		
Rameez Raja	c and b Garner			35		b Mudassar		32
Javed Miandad	b Marshall			16	I.V.A. Richards†	c Saleem Yousuf, b Imran		51
Imran Khan†	not out			25	A.L. Logie	not out		6
Saleem Malik					P.J. Dujon*			
Saleem Yousuf*					M.D. Marshall			
Abdul Qadir					R.A. Harper			
Wasim Akram					J. Garner			
Tauseef Ahmed					M.A. Holding			
Extras	b 1, lb 6, w 4, nb 3			14	A.H. Gray			
				—	Extras	lb 8, nb 3		11
(45 overs)	(for 4 wickets)			196				—
					(44.1 overs)	(for 3 wickets)		199

	O	M	R	W		O	M	R	W
Garner	9	1	59	1	Wasim Akram	8.1	1	40	1
Gray	8	1	32	1	Imran Khan	9	—	41	1
Holding	5	—	17	1	Mudassar Nazar	9	—	32	1
Marshall	8	1	30	1	Tauseef Ahmed	9	1	38	—
Harper	9	2	26	—	Abdul Qadir	9	—	40	—
Richards	6	—	25	—					

FALL OF WICKETS
1- 50, 2- 58, 3- 142, 4- 161

FALL OF WICKETS
1- 0, 2- 72, 3- 177

West Indies won by 7 wickets

Gavaskar batted solidly, but the Pakistan attack was keen and accurate, with Tauseef giving further evidence of his advance as an accurate off-spinner. Mudassar confirmed his status as an all-rounder with a decisive spell which won him the individual award, and India slipped quietly to defeat.

Pakistan's victory in this second match kept alive their hopes in the competition which had seemed to vanish after they had been beaten by West Indies, for should India beat West Indies in the final match, the tournament would be decided on run aggregate.

THREE NATIONS TOURNAMENT – PAKISTAN v. INDIA
17 November 1985 at Sharjah

PAKISTAN					INDIA			
Mudassar Nazar	c Vengsarkar,				S.M. Gavaskar	st Saleem Yousuf,		
	b Sivaramakrishnan			67		b Tauseef		63
Mohsin Khan	run out			2	K. Srikkanth	c Saleem Yousuf,		
Rameez Raja	c Gavaskar, b Binny			66		b Mohsin Kamal		4
Javed Miandad	not out			37	M. Azharuddin	lbw, b Wasim Akram		3
Imran Khan†	run out			9	D.B. Vengsarkar	c Saleem Malik,		
Saleem Malik	not out			12		b Tauseef Ahmed		27
Saleem Yousuf*					R.J. Shastri	run out		12
Abdul Qadir					R.N. Kapil Dev†	lbw, b Tauseef Ahmed		0
Mohsin Kamal					M.B. Amarnath	b Mudassar Nazar		11
Wasim Akram					R.M.H. Binny	c Tauseef Ahmed,		
Tauseef Ahmed						b Mohsin Kamal		11
Extras	lb 8, w 1, nb 1			10	Chetan Sharma	b Mudassar Nazar		1
				—	S.M.H. Kirmani*	not out		5
(45 overs)	(for 4 wickets)			203	L. Sivaramakrishnan	run out		1
					Extras	b 2, lb 9, w 4, nb 2		17
								—
					(40.4 overs)			155

	O	M	R	W		O	M	R	W
Kapil Dev	7	1	26	—	Wasim Akram	7.4	2	15	1
Binny	9	1	36	1	Mohsin Kamal	7	—	27	2
Chetan Sharma	7	1	40	—	Mudassar Nazar	9	—	43	2
Shastri	9	1	26	—	Imran Khan	1.1	—	3	—
Sivaramakrishnan	9	—	40	1	Abdul Qadir	6.5	—	26	—
Amarnath	4	—	27	—	Tauseef Ahmed	9	2	30	3

FALL OF WICKETS
1- 18, 2- 118, 3- 169, 4- 185

FALL OF WICKETS
1- 9, 2- 28, 3- 84, 4- 115, 5- 118, 6- 129, 7- 135, 8- 139, 9- 151

Pakistan won by 48 runs

Three Nations Tournament – Match Three
INDIA *v.* WEST INDIES

West Indies, not unexpectedly, won the Three Nations Tournament when they beat India with some ease in the final match. They were deserving winners, but Pakistan, in second place, ran them much closer than statistics reveal.

India never recovered from the early onslaught of Joel Garner who more than made amends for his poor showing in the previous match. He sent back Amarnath, Srikkanth and Vengsarkar while only 26 were scored, and he had so contained the batsmen that Gavaskar scored only three runs in the first fifteen overs.

Gavaskar's caution was necessary if a complete collapse was to be avoided, but by the time he and Azharuddin added 99, India were well behind a reasonable rate of scoring. It was Garner's ability to make the ball lift steeply on the line of the off stump that disconcerted the earlier batsmen, but Gavaskar, Azharuddin and the powerful Kapil Dev at least ensured that West Indies would have to score at four an over.

Such a feat was well within the capabilities of the West Indian batsmen. Haynes and Richardson bustled away from the start, and Richie Richardson's second outstanding innings of the week stamped him unquestionably as the Man of the Tournament, an honour which brought him three thousand dollars and a new car. He was the dominant partner in an opening stand of 114. Gomes went cheaply, and the Indian spinners exerted a temporary halt to the scoring, but the West Indies always looked to be winners.

Viv Richards came to the wicket to end matters with a cascade of shots. The winning runs came with a six off Ghai.

It was a highly satisfactory competition with some fine cricket, and the wicket showing every sign of providing batsmen with an opportunity to play their shots.

ABOVE: *Joel Garner. His speed and accuracy denied India in the Three Nations Tournament. (Adrian Murrell)*

RIGHT: *Richie Richardson, the outstanding player of the Three Nations Tournament. (Adrian Murrell)*

THREE NATIONS TOURNAMENT – INDIA v. WEST INDIES
22 November 1985 at Sharjah

INDIA				WEST INDIES			
S.M. Gavaskar	not out		76	D.L. Haynes	not out		72
K. Srikkanth	b Garner		6	R.B. Richardson	b Ghai		72
M.B. Amarnath	c Richards, b Garner		0	H.A. Gomes	b Kapil Dev		10
D.B. Vengsarkar	c Garner, b Holding		6	I.V.A. Richards†	not out		24
M. Azharuddin	run out		35	A.L. Logie			
R.N. Kapil Dev†	not out		28	P.J. Dujon*			
R.J. Shastri				R.A. Harper			
R.M.H. Binny				M.D. Marshall			
S.M.H. Kirmani*				J. Garner			
R.S. Ghai				C.A. Walsh			
L. Sivaramakrishnan				M.A. Holding			
Extras	lb 17, w 4, nb 8		29	Extras	lb 8		8
(45 overs)	(for 4 wickets)		180	(41.3 overs)	(for 2 wickets)		186

	O	M	R	W		O	M	R	W
Marshall	9	2	35	—	Kapil Dev	8	1	29	1
Garner	9	4	11	2	Binny	7	—	36	—
Walsh	9	1	37	—	Ghai	8.3	—	54	1
Holding	9	3	28	1	Shastri	9	1	27	—
Harper	9	—	52	—	Sivaramakrishnan	9	—	32	—

FALL OF WICKETS
1- 10, 2- 11, 3- 26, 4- 125

FALL OF WICKETS
1- 114, 2- 147

West Indies won by 8 wickets

AUSTRALASIAN CUP – INDIA v. NEW ZEALAND
10 April 1986 at Sharjah

NEW ZEALAND				INDIA			
K.R. Rutherford	b Maninder Singh		12	S.M. Gavaskar	c McSweeney, b Chatfield		0
M.C. Snedden	c Patil, b Maninder Singh		26	K. Srikkanth	c Blair, b Chatfield		11
M.D. Crowe	lbw, b Madan Lal		1	M. Azharuddin	c and b Chatfield		6
J.J. Crowe†	not out		36	S.M. Patil	b M.D. Crowe		7
T.E. Blain	c Patil, b Maninder Singh		0	R.J. Shastri	st McSweeney, b Gray		25
B.R. Blair	run out		0	Kirti Azad	b Bracewell		30
J.G. Bracewell	b Shastri		25	R.N. Kapil Dev†	c Blain, b Snedden		9
E.J. Gray	b Shastri		2	C.S. Pandit*	not out		33
G.K. Robertson	b Kirti Azad		0	U.S. Madan Lal	not out		8
E.B. McSweeney*	not out		18	R.M.H. Binny			
E.J. Chatfield				Maninder Singh			
Extras	lb 12		12	Extras	lb 5		5
(44 overs)	(for 8 wickets)		132	(41.1 overs)	(for 7 wickets)		134

	O	M	R	W		O	M	R	W
Kapil Dev	6	3	7	—	Chatfield	9	5	14	3
Binny	5	—	12	—	Robertson	4	—	13	—
Madan Lal	7	1	12	—	M.D. Crowe	5	1	16	1
Maninder Singh	9	—	23	3	Snedden	7	1	24	1
Shastri	9	—	25	2	Bracewell	9	1	34	1
Kirti Azad	8	—	41	1	Gray	7.4	1	28	1

FALL OF WICKETS
1- 37, 2- 42, 3- 48, 4- 48, 5- 48, 6- 81, 7- 95, 8- 96

FALL OF WICKETS
1- 0, 2- 8, 3- 19, 4- 25, 5- 81, 6- 81, 7- 116

India won by 3 wickets

Final Table

	P	W	L	Runs	Pts
West Indies	2	2	—	385	4
Pakistan	2	1	1	399	2
India	2	—	2	335	0

Australasian Cup – Match One
INDIA v. NEW ZEALAND

A weak New Zealand side, without Coney and Hadlee who had expressed a wish not to be considered for the trip, was further weakened by injury so that skipper John Wright was unable to play and Martin Snedden acted as substitute opener. Snedden, in fact, did well, and New Zealand got off to a reasonable, if slow, start. Their troubles began when

AUSTRALASIAN CUP – PAKISTAN v. AUSTRALIA
11 April 1986 at Sharjah

AUSTRALIA			
D.C. Boon	c Mohsin Khan, b Tauseef Ahmed		44
G.R. Marsh	c Mudassar Nazar, b Abdul Qadir		26
D.M. Jones	lbw, b Tauseef Ahmed		8
G.M. Ritchie	not out		60
S.R. Waugh	c Zulqarnian, b Wasim Akram		26
G.R.J. Matthews	c Javed Miandad, b Mohsin Kamal		20
C.J. McDermott	run out		1
T.J. Zoehrer*	run out		5
S.P. Davis			
B.A. Reid			
R.J. Bright†			
Extras	b 1, lb 10, w 1		12
(50 overs)	(for 7 wickets)		202

	O	M	R	W
Wasim Akram	10	—	38	1
Mohsin Kamal	10	—	51	1
Manzoor Elahi	10	—	58	—
Tauseef Ahmed	10	1	19	2
Abdul Qadir	10	—	26	1

FALL OF WICKETS
1- 63, 2- 79, 3- 90, 4- 140, 5- 195, 6- 197, 7- 202

PAKISTAN			
Mudassar Nazar	b Reid		95
Mohsin Khan	lbw, b Bright		46
Rameez Raja	not out		56
Manzoor Elahi	not out		2
Javed Miandad†			
Saleem Malik			
Zulqarnian†			
Wasim Akram			
Mohsin Kamal			
Tauseef Ahmed			
Abdul Qadir			
Extras	lb 5, w 2		7
(49.1 overs)	(for 2 wickets)		206

	O	M	R	W
McDermott	10	2	29	—
Davis	8	2	28	—
Reid	9.1	—	51	1
Waugh	6	1	25	—
Bright	10	1	28	1
Matthews	6	—	40	—

FALL OF WICKETS
1- 80, 2- 195

Pakistan won by 8 wickets

Mudassar Nazar displayed fine all-round talents in both Sharjah tournaments. (Adrian Murrell)

Maninder Singh joined the attack, for the left-arm spinner dismissed both openers, and New Zealand lost 5 wickets for 11 runs. Jeff Crowe, leading the side, played sensibly, and he and John Bracewell added 33. There was also some lively batting from McSweeney and he helped Jeff Crowe in an unbeaten ninth wicket stand of 36.

Facing a meagre target of 133, India started dreadfully when Gavaskar was caught behind without a run scored, and Azharuddin and Patil followed in quick succession. When Srikkanth fell to Chatfield, four men had gone for 25, and had New Zealand not dropped two early catches, the position would have been much worse.

Shastri and Kirti Azad revived India with a stand of 56, but they fell at the same total and it was left to Pandit on his international debut to bring India to a victory which was much harder than they had expected.

Australasian Cup – Match Two
PAKISTAN v. AUSTRALIA

Australia won the toss and elected to bat against a Pakistani attack handicapped by the absence of the injured Imran. Boon and Marsh gave their side a fine start, and Ritchie played well so that it was only the advent of the Pakistani spinners that curtailed the scoring.

The wicket was perfect, however, and Pakistan made light of the task of scoring the 203 that they needed for victory. Mudassar Nazar and Mohsin Khan put on 80 for the first wicket, and Mudassar went on to hit 95 off 140 deliveries, including 5 fours, before being bowled by Reid when Pakistan were only 8 short of victory.

AUSTRALASIAN CUP – INDIA v. SRI LANKA
13 April 1986 at Sharjah

SRI LANKA				INDIA			
P.A. de Silva	c Maninder Singh, b Sharma	5		S.M. Gavaskar	c de Silva, b de Mel	71
A.P. Gurusinghe	b Kirti Azad	68		K. Srikkanth	st de Alwis, b Anurasiri	59
R.L. Dias	b Maninder Singh	9		M. Azharuddin	b de Mel	30
L.R.D. Mendis†	c Azharuddin, b Madan Lal	32		S.M. Patil	b de Mel	10
A. Ranatunga	run out	28		Kirti Azad	c Gurusinghe, b Anurasiri	1
R.G. de Alwis*	run out	19		R.N. Kapil Dev†	c Dias, b Anurasiri	3
A.L.F. de Mel	not out	15		R.J. Shastri	not out	21
R.S. Mahanama	c Patil, b Sharma	9		C.S. Pandit*	run out	2
R.J. Ratnayake	c Kirti Azad, b Sharma	1		U.S. Madan Lal	not out	1
J.R. Ratnayeke	run out	3		Maninder Singh		
S.D. Anurasiri	not out	2		Chetan Sharma		
Extras	b 1, lb 12, nb 1	14		Extras	b 1, lb 6, nb 1	8
(50 overs)	(for 9 wickets)	205		(49.1 overs)	(for 7 wickets)	206

	O	M	R	W		O	M	R	W
Kapil Dev	10	1	39	—	de Mel	10	—	40	3
Chetan Sharma	9	1	35	3	R.J. Ratnayake	9.1	1	36	—
Madan Lal	8	—	40	1	Anurasiri	10	—	40	3
Maninder Singh	10	2	19	1	J.R. Ratnayeke	10	—	38	—
Shastri	8	—	40	—	de Silva	3	—	9	—
Kirti Azad	5	—	20	1	Ranatunga	7	—	36	—

FALL OF WICKETS
1- 8, 2- 20, 3- 58, 4- 129, 5- 135, 6- 165, 7- 188, 8- 195, 9- 201

FALL OF WICKETS
1- 93, 2- 165, 3- 170, 4- 171, 5- 175, 6- 191, 7- 194

India won by 3 wickets

Australasian Cup – Semi-Final
INDIA v. SRI LANKA

As winners of the Asia Cup, Sri Lanka had a bye into the semi-final of the Australasian Cup. They began badly, losing Aravinda de Silva, who had enjoyed no luck since his successes in Pakistan, and the out of form Dias for 20. Gurusinghe was slow to get into his stride, but Mendis hit forcefully, and when he was dismissed Ranatunga gave Gurusinghe good support. There were useful contributions from de Alwis and de Mel, and the Sri Lankans reached a better score than had looked probable earlier in their innings.

Srikkanth and Gavaskar gave India a rollicking start, and Azharuddin continued in the same vein as he and Gavaskar added 72, but 4 wickets fell for 10 runs, and eventually India limped home with 3 wickets and 5 balls to spare.

Australasian Cup – Semi-Final
PAKISTAN v. NEW ZEALAND

A depleted and dispirited New Zealand side sank without trace against Pakistan. Put in to bat, they lost the top half of their batting to Wasim Akram and Imran and their middle order to the leg-spin of Abdul Qadir who mesmerised the New Zealand batsmen. In 10 overs, he conceded only 9 runs and took 4 wickets, and the individual award.

Mudassar and Mohsin rapidly took Pakistan to victory.

Australasian Cup – Final
INDIA v. PAKISTAN

The energy, enthusiasm and vision which has brought cricket to Sharjah were rewarded with an Australasian Cup Final which was among the most thrilling, entertaining and dramatic one-day internationals seen anywhere in the world. As 40,000 dollars was the richest prize ever offered for a cricket match, it was right that the game should be so exciting.

Put in to bat, India made a magnificent start with both Srikkanth and Gavaskar quickly into their strokes. Once again, the Pakistani fielding was below what one has come to expect from such a talented side, but nothing should detract from the brilliance of the batting.

Srikkanth hit 75 out of 177 before falling to Abdul Qadir who once again demonstrated that the leg-spinner can be as effective in limited-over cricket as any other type of bowler. Vengsarkar then joined Gavaskar in a stand of 99, and the later batsmen perished in the pursuit of quick runs.

In contrast, Pakistan began in a subdued manner, and the loss of Mudassar, Mohsin and Rameez with only 61 scored, tipped the scales very much in favour of India. Maninder, as well as dismissing the dangerous Rameez, bowled a tight spell for India, and it was only the presence of Javed Miandad that steadied Pakistan.

He was given good support by Saleem Malik, but when he was run out, Pakistan faced a mighty task, and 90 were needed off the last 10 overs.

Javed batted superbly. He never lost concentration nor control, and he launched a violent assault on the accurate Indian bowling, hitting one of his 3 sixes out of the ground. Abdul Qadir played a useful knock, but when the last over began Pakistan were 235 for 8. Wasim Akram was run out and Zulqarnian bowled, but Tauseef saw that Javed had the strike and when the last ball was reached 4 were wanted. Chetan Sharma had bowled admirably in a tense situation, but Javed lashed the last ball into the crowd for six and a memorable victory for Pakistan.

AUSTRALASIAN CUP – PAKISTAN v. NEW ZEALAND
15 April 1986 at Sharjah

NEW ZEALAND				
K.R. Rutherford	c Javed Miandad, b Imran Khan			2
M.C. Snedden	b Wasim Akram			0
M.D. Crowe	c Abdul Qadir, b Wasim Akram			9
J.J. Crowe†	c Zulqarnian, b Wasim Akram			1
E.J. Gray	b Manzoor Elahi			17
B.R. Blair	b Abdul Qadir			9
T.E. Blain	b Abdul Qadir			0
J.G. Bracewell	b Abdul Qadir			0
E.B. McSweeney*	c Wasim Akram, b Abdul Qadir			7
E.J. Chatfield	c sub (Umar), b Manzoor Elahi			2
W. Watson	not out			1
Extras	b 1, lb 5, w 8, nb 2			16
(35.5 overs)				64

	O	M	R	W
Imran Khan	7	2	11	1
Wasim Akram	7	3	10	3
Abdul Qadir	10	4	9	4
Tauseef Ahmed	10	2	20	—
Manzoor Elahi	1.5	—	8	2

FALL OF WICKETS
1- 4, 2- 15, 3- 18, 4- 18, 5- 32, 6- 32, 7- 32, 8- 48, 9- 55

PAKISTAN				
Mudassar Nazar	not out			32
Mohsin Khan	not out			34
Rameez Raja				
Javed Miandad				
Saleem Malik				
Imran Khan†				
Abdul Qadir				
Manzoor Elahi				
Zulqarnian*				
Wasim Akram				
Tauseef Ahmed				0
(22.4 overs)	(for no wicket)			66

	O	M	R	W
Chatfield	3	2	3	—
Watson	7	—	15	—
Gray	8.4	3	22	—
Bracewell	4	—	26	—

Pakistan won by 10 wickets

AUSTRALASIAN CUP FINAL – INDIA v. PAKISTAN
18 April 1986 at Sharjah

INDIA				
K. Srikkanth	c Wasim Akram, b Abdul Qadir			75
S.M. Gavaskar	b Imran Khan			92
D.B. Vengsarkar	b Wasim Akram			50
Kirti Azad	b Wasim Akram			0
R.N. Kapil Dev†	b Imran Khan			8
Chetan Sharma	run out			10
R.J. Shastri	b Wasim Akram			1
C.S. Pandit*	not out			6
M. Azharuddin				
U.S. Madan Lal				
Maninder Singh				
Extras	lb 6, w 2, nb 1			9
(50 overs)	(for 7 wickets)			245

	O	M	R	W
Imran Khan	10	2	40	2
Wasim Akram	10	1	42	3
Manzoor Elahi	5	—	33	—
Mudassar Nazar	5	—	32	—
Abdul Qadir	10	2	49	1
Tauseef Ahmed	10	1	43	—

FALL OF WICKETS
1- 117, 2- 216, 3- 216, 4- 229, 5- 242, 6- 245, 7- 245

PAKISTAN				
Mudassar Nazar	lbw, b Chetan Sharma			5
Mohsin Khan	b Madan Lal			36
Rameez Raja	b Maninder Singh			10
Javed Miandad	not out			116
Saleem Malik	run out			21
Imran Khan†	b Madan Lal			7
Manzoor Elahi	c Shastri, b Chetan Sharma			4
Abdul Qadir	c sub, b Kapil Dev			34
Wasim Akram	run out			3
Zulqarnian*	b Chetan Sharma			0
Tauseef Ahmed	not out			1
Extras	lb 11			11
(50 overs)	(for 9 wickets)			248

	O	M	R	W
Kapil Dev	10	1	45	1
Chetan Sharma	10	—	51	3
Madan Lal	10	—	53	2
Maninder Singh	10	—	36	1
Shastri	8	—	38	—
Azharuddin	2	—	14	—

FALL OF WICKETS
1- 9, 2- 39, 3- 61, 4- 110, 5- 181, 6- 209, 7- 215, 8- 236, 9- 241

Pakistan won by 1 wicket

SHARJAH 1986
by Tony Lewis

Whenever I am in Sharjah for the cricket, I smile and think of happy days at the Scarborough Festival. You will already think that I have a touch of the sun. It is true that I play golf on the desert dunes at the Sharjah Wanderers golf course: not a blade of grass, blinding images in dazzling sun and Sylvia Sims beckoning in her tropical army uniform, transported from the unforgettable movie *Ice Cold in Alex* ... but I do mean Scarborough.

Sharjah is a festival because all the matches, perhaps five or six in ten days, are played on the same ground. All of the teams, and there were five contesting the Austral-Asia cup in the April competition, stay at the same Continental Hotel. This means that they play hard all day and yet have the chance to meet in a friendly environment when they are not practising or playing.

There is a relaxed social programme, which is optional, but can take you into the homes of friends locally, or the Wanderers Club, to Dubai or just on to a sun-chair on the beach. When the cricket is there Sharjah becomes a cricket town as Scarborough does. You can buy your Festival

Wasim Akram bowling for Pakistan. (All-Sport/Adrian Murrell)

kippers in Scarborough: in Sharjah, full page newspaper advertisements have cricket themes like Abdul Qadir appealing, an umpire standing with the finger of justice aloft, both photographed behind two motor cars and a giant caption which reads TOYOTA UMPIRES, they stand for what's right in automotive engineering.

The perfect Sharjah competition ends with an India versus Pakistan final. That is because three-quarters of a million Asians work in the Emirate and this is their big chance to see their heroes at close quarters. They cannot all manage it. Many tickets find themselves fiercely on the black market. Each day involving India or Pakistan is a sell-out.

The Austral-Asia cup included Sri Lanka, New Zealand and Australia. Unfortunately Australia only played one match, lost it and were knocked out of the whole competition. It would be more satisfactory if every side were assured of two games. New Zealand were missing leading players such as Hadlee, Coney, Edgar and Smith. England when they played there went under the temporary leadership of Norman Gifford and with some young players who were unlikely to make a test career. The cricket is played so seriously by the front-line of talent in Pakistan and India and the West Indies, it is not surprising that England, New Zealand and Australia have been a bit of a joke. Uncomfortable for the many exiles of those countries who hike up and down the Gulf to support their men.

Saleem Malik, Pakistan. (All-Sport/Adrian Murrell)

The Sharjah stadium has been extended and there is room for much more if ever required. What was once a deep hole in the desert is now a grassy outfield and a well rolled brown middle, exactly the sight which MCC sides used to meet in Karachi or Bombay. The pitches are kept moist during the week to ensure lasting quality, then, for the final, the sun works its wonder and instead of the ball turning, it comes sweetly on to the bat with decent speed and even bounce.

The Ruler of Sharjah and many Sheikhs support cricket. The VIP enclosure, up on the first tier of the pavilion stand cannot be bettered. Its plush seats attract the fashionable set from Bombay and Karachi – film stars, millionairesses, the Arab businessman in cool dish-dash, guests of the players and of the organisers. In the intervals they pad quietly into a giant air-conditioned lounge backstage, take a cool drink, perhaps some light lunch and watch the cricket on jumbo television sets.

Asif Iqbal, former captain of Pakistan and Kent, has devised the cricket and the man who first conceived the idea of taking cricket to the desert is Abdul Rehmann Bukhathir. To my mind, the appeal is that large sums of money are given to cricketers past and present. This is why all the cricket in Sharjah goes under the name of the Cricketers Benefit Fund

Series. Javed Miandad and Dilip Vengsarkar were the prime beneficiaries in April.

The West Indies won on their only visit there, but usually the titanic struggle between India and Pakistan ends in an India victory. Not that time. Famously, Javed Miandad, wanting four to win, hit a full toss from Chetan Sharma straight out of the ground.

It was probably the most famous blow struck between the two countries, because it was the most watched. My role in Sharjah is to lead the television commentary team. Having described this exciting contest I was rather shocked by the information which came later, that we had been broadcasting to India and Pakistan, 'live'. The estimated viewing was 70 million television sets. Multiply that by twenty-four to a room. . . .!

Oh! There is one serious difference between Sharjah and Scarborough – the cricket in Sharjah is played much more seriously. The fielding of the New Zealanders was outstanding. Tony Blain, the reserve wicket-keeper was brilliant. Sunil Gavaskar always plays well, proving on the turning wickets what a master he is of spin. Imran is star quality. Not many Sharjahs ago he was striking Joel Garner for three sixes in an over. Yet, of all the cricket I have seen there, nothing has

Imran Khan, Pakistan. (All-Sport/Adrian Murrell)

Abdul Qadir, Pakistan. (All-Sport/Adrian Murrell)

surpassed Miandad's century that day when Pakistan won.

I was with some Pakistan friends the night before and was asked which international batsman would I choose to play for my life? I thought of dependability, cussedness in a tight corner, talent, cunning. Above Viv Richards even, I went for Javed Miandad.

He has the warring instincts of the alley cat. He is not distracted by schoolboy strains of loyalty, or noblesse or dignity in the battle. He is hell-bent on self preservation and the demolition of those who threaten to demolish him. His hundred was the best I have ever seen in a one-day match which could not have meant more to either side. India and Pakistan do not play friendlies. There was a sanity about being the neutral observer.

Sharjah will soon be attracting visitors from the participating countries. It has reached the point now that if you have not seen a Sharjah final, you are lacking something in your cricket experience.

Mellowing Year

The English season.
Britannic Assurance County Championship. The Benson and Hedges Cup.
The NatWest Bank Trophy. The John Player Special League.
The Texaco Trophy – England *v.* India, England *v.* New Zealand. The Indian tour.
The New Zealand tour. The Cornhill Test series.
The I.C.C. Trophy. Form Charts for One-Day and First-Class matches.
Review of the season. Book Reviews.
First-class averages. Women's Cricket by Rachael Heyhoe-Flint.

The Oval.
(Michael King)

Cricket in England had a restless close season. Inevitably, Ian Botham stole many of the headlines. He resigned as captain of Somerset and was succeeded by Peter Roebuck, a quiet, studious, reticent man who would not have been everybody's choice. One felt some sympathy for the cheerful and eminently likeable Vic Marks who, in the past few years, has been surrogate captain of Somerset on many occasions and has dealt with a multitude of difficult problems in a tactful and easy way and now finds himself passed over for the captaincy.

Botham's second act was to walk from John O'Groats to Land's End to raise thousands of pounds for leukaemia research. This was a momentous and noble deed, and whatever criticism was to be levelled at Botham in the months to come for some of his other activities, this achievement should never be derided, for it was grand in conception and execution and many in need benefited from the action of Botham and those who walked with him.

Even before the 1985 season had closed the Mound Stand at Lord's was in its first stage of redevelopment, and the famous ground resembled a builder's yard for much of the winter.

There was the usual winter transfer market. Waterton and Potter left Kent who re-signed Terry Alderman. The retirement of Alan Knott and the departure of Waterton for Northants left Marsh as the Kent wicket-keeper. He has a long and distinguished line to follow. Potter, having declined an offer from Gloucestershire, joined Leicestershire, a county he hoped would give him more scope for his batting. Graham Dilley was another who had expressed a desire to leave Kent, but the county stated that he would be kept to his contract. On the brighter side for Kent, Les Ames celebrated his 80th birthday. What a joy it is to be with this man and what a privilege to chat to him about the game that he has never stopped serving, and to which he has brought so much distinction.

Essex's formidable pair. Gooch and Border in consultation, or pensive mood. (Adrian Murrell)

The season's first centurion – Richard Bartlett of Somerset. (Mark Leech)

Disenchanted with the organisation at Sussex, Gehan Mendis left to join Lancashire. John Barclay was reappointed captain of Sussex, and Lancashire began the year with Clive Lloyd as captain, served by several deputies on various occasions.

Hardy, unable to be sure of a regular place in the Hampshire side, joined Somerset, and Keith Tomlins, so long a faithful reserve, left Middlesex for Gloucestershire.

There were rumbles of discontent at Warwickshire, but David Brown remained as cricket manager, and Reg Kirk resigned as Yorkshire chairman. Raman Subba Row succeeded Charles Palmer as chairman of the Test and County Cricket Board. And then the rain arrived which was, of course, the signal for the start of the season.

19, 21 and 22 April

at Cambridge

Leicestershire 254 for 9 dec (I.P. Butcher 58, J.J. Whitaker 57, C.C. Ellison 5 for 82)
Cambridge University 64 for 4

Match drawn

at Oxford

Somerset 236 for 9 dec (R.J. Bartlett 117 not out)
Oxford University 11 for 2

Match drawn

There was no play after the first day of the two opening matches of the season. Peter Roebuck was out to the fifth ball of the match at Oxford where Richard Bartlett, 19 years old, hit 13 fours in his century on his first-class debut. Dropped when 2, the young man who had headed the averages at Taunton School the previous summer, owed much to Dredge, for Somerset were 183 for 9 and Bartlett 78, when the left-hander from Frome came to the wicket. Dredge stayed, and with some particularly fine drives and hooks, Bartlett reached his century. Hardy, Blitz, wicket-keeper from Essex, and Taylor, the pace bowler formerly with Yorkshire and Surrey, were also making their debuts for Somerset.

At Cambridge, there was some solid and consistent Leicestershire batting and a career-best bowling performance by Charles Ellison, younger brother of the England bowler.

23, 24 and 25 April

at Lord's
M.C.C. v. Middlesex
Match abandoned

at Cambridge
Essex 266 for 4 dec (A.R. Border 80) and 191 for 3 dec (P.J. Prichard 77, D.R. Pringle 63 not out)
Cambridge University 109 (D.L. Acfield 5 for 38) and 25 for 5 (J.K. Lever 4 for 12)

Match drawn

at Oxford
Gloucestershire 309 for 6 dec (K.M. Curran 103 not out, P. Bainbridge 66) and 79 for 4 dec
Oxford University 179 for 9 dec (D.A. Thorne 72) and 3 for 0

Match drawn

The season's first big event is the match at Lord's where the old club takes on the Champion County. Sadly, the ground was so waterlogged that not a ball could be bowled and the match was abandoned. Even more sadly, as another cricket season was beginning, we lost two of the greatest of cricketers in the space of twenty-four hours with the deaths of Jim Laker and Bill Edrich. Laker was the greatest off-spinner the game has known, and after his retirement he became a wise commentator and valued adviser. Bill Edrich, a personal friend, had a lust for life that was transmitted to his cricket. He was one who shone torches through our youth, and the world became a lesser place for his passing.

A newer hero, Allan Border, made his Essex debut in the drawn match at Cambridge and, not surprisingly, batted impressively. Just as impressively, John Lever began his 19th season with 9 maiden overs and 2 wickets, and 4 for 12 in 12 overs in the second innings.

At Oxford, Kevin Curran hit a handsome maiden hundred. Here, as at Cambridge, there was rain.

While the rain stopped the cricket one was able to ponder on the generosity of sponsors. Texaco's John Ambler and Sue Ville welcomed cricket in their usual warm and friendly manner, and one felt how lucky the game is to have such allies. Brittanic Assurance, thankfully, extended their sponsorship of the County Championship until 1989, and once again, advised by Mike Denness, Messrs Williams, Hamilton Shaw and Potter welcomed the season in a concerned and affable manner, announcing that the winners of the 1986 Championship would receive £22,000. A third and interesting sponsorship was announced at Lord's where Seagram Ltd, launching Cricketer's Gin, introduced the monthly award for gentlemanly play, a valuable addition. At county level, Tolly Cobbold extended their sponsorship of Essex for another three years and were joined by H.W. Stone, an Essex firm, whose commitment was also for three years.

If one has taken time out from cricket to dwell a while upon the generosity of sponsors, it is because they have become an integral part of the game, and there are still players who seem blind to how much they owe to the support of these organisations.

26, 27 and 28 April

at Bristol
Glamorgan 226 for 8 dec (Younis Ahmed 94, P. Bainbridge 4 for 85) and 48 for 2
Gloucestershire 83 for 5 dec

Match drawn
Glamorgan 4 pts, Gloucestershire 3 pts

at Leicester
Kent 85 (J.P. Agnew 5 for 27) and 299 (E.A.E. Baptiste 80, G.R. Cowdrey 59, P.A.J. de Freitas 4 for 61)
Leicestershire 242 (R.A. Cobb 74, J.J. Whitaker 57, E.A.E. Baptiste 4 for 58) and 2 for 1

Match drawn
Leicestershire 6 pts, Kent 3 pts

at Trent Bridge
Nottinghamshire 265 (C.E.B. Rice 76, R.T. Robinson 65, R.J. Maru 4 for 71) and 181 for 3 dec (B.C. Broad 68 not out)
Hampshire 241 for 8 dec (R.J. Parks 51 not out, R.A. Smith 50, C.E.B. Rice 4 for 54) and 209 for 1 (C.G. Greenidge 118, V.P. Terry 74 not out)

Hampshire won by 9 wickets
Hampshire 21 pts, Nottinghamshire 5 pts

at Taunton
Yorkshire 323 for 5 dec (K. Sharp 96, M.D. Moxon 73, A.A. Metcalfe 55) and 0 for 0 dec
Somerset 0 for 0 dec and 318 (J.J.E. Hardy 79, P.M. Roebuck 60)

Yorkshire won by 5 runs
Yorkshire 19 pts, Somerset 1 pt

at Hove
Lancashire 431 for 4 dec (G. Fowler 180, N.H. Fairbrother 84, J. Abrahams 73 not out, S.J. O'Shaughnessy 50) and 23 for 1
Sussex 160 (P.J.W. Allott 5 for 32) and 293 (P.W.G. Parker 78, M. Watkinson 5 for 90)

Lancashire won by 9 wickets
Lancashire 24 pts, Sussex 2 pts

at Edgbaston
Warwickshire 271 for 8 dec (P.A. Smith 88) and 250 for 4 (D.L. Amiss 108 not out, B.M. McMillan 64)
Essex 303 for 8 dec (B.R. Hardie 81)

Match drawn
Essex 7 pts, Warwickshire 6 pts

LEFT: *Brian McMillan preferred in the Warwickshire side to Kallicharran and Ferreira. McMillan was played because of his potential as a seam bowler, but he was, in fact, more successful as a batsman during the season. (Ken Kelly)*

OPPOSITE: *The most coveted wicket in county cricket at the beginning of the season. Allan Border falls to Tim Munton, who is congratulated by Gladstone Small and Norman Gifford, Warwickshire v. Essex, 26–28 April. (Ken Kelly)*

at Worcester

Worcestershire 231 (S.J. Rhodes 77 not out, G. Monkhouse 4 for 37) and 254 for 8 dec (G.A. Hick 103, S.T. Clarke 5 for 69)
Surrey 226 (A.J. Stewart 53, A. Needham 52, N.V. Radford 4 for 66) and 228 for 9 (A.R. Butcher 71, P.J. Newport 4 for 58)
Match drawn
Worcestershire 6 pts, Surrey 6 pts

26, 28 and 29 April

at Lord's

Middlesex 306 for 4 dec (C.T. Radley 103 not out, W.N. Slack 96) and 131 for 2 dec (R.O. Butcher 60, G.D. Barlow 52 not out)
Derbyshire 202 (N.G. Cowans 4 for 64)
Match drawn
Middlesex 7 pts, Derbyshire 3 pts

at Cambridge

Northamptonshire 248 for 6 dec (R.J. Boyd-Moss 61, R.J. Bailey 55) and 205 for 7 dec (D.J. Wild 101)
Cambridge University 150 (D.G. Price 60, D.J. Wild 4 for 4) and 129 for 4
Match drawn

The Britannic Assurance County Championship began, almost as by tradition, in cold, damp weather. At Lord's, there were only 33 overs on the first day, but Radley, who had just been offered a three-year contract and a benefit in 1987, showed why Middlesex value him so highly, though he is now at the veteran stage, by hitting the forty-fifth hundred of his career in the first innings of his 23rd season. He shared with Slack a stand of 127 in 43 overs for the 3rd wicket, and it seemed that Middlesex had taken a grip on the match with their pacemen, Cowans and Williams in particular; but missed chances and gritty batting by Morris, Finney and Roberts, used as wicket-keeper for the first time, gave Derbyshire a deserved draw. Miller was taken ill and was unable to bat in the Derbyshire innings.

There was no play on the first day at Taunton or Bristol where Younis Ahmed batted well and Graveney attempted salvation by declaration but was beaten by the weather. At Taunton, however, the forfeiture of two innings contrived a spectacularly exciting finish. Yorkshire batted rather dourly until Kevin Sharp lifted them on the last morning. Somerset were left to make 324 in 75 overs, and, by tea, Felton and Roebuck having given them a fine start and Hardy displaying excellent form, they were 143 for 1 with 35 overs remaining. When the final 20 over mark was reached Somerset needed 90 with 6 wickets standing. Richards had gone, run out when

LEFT: *Graeme Fowler began the season with a magnificent innings of 180 for Lancashire against Sussex and led his side to victory. (George Herringshaw)*

Botham rightly sent him back as he attempted an impossible single, and Marks was handicapped by a blow on the head by a drive from Rose. Wickets tumbled in the pursuit for runs, and with Dredge and Coombs, the last pair, together, 16 were needed from the final over, bowled by Carrick. Dredge swung Carrick's fifth ball for six and attempted to repeat the stroke off the last ball and win the match, but Peter Hartley dived forward at deep mid-wicket to bring off a spectacular catch and give victory to Yorkshire.

The Red Rose won with more ease, less drama, but no less panache at Hove. To the delight of followers of the game, Graeme Fowler, the nightmare of 1985 behind him, scored an impressive 180, and with two other left-handers, Abrahams and Fairbrother, showing good form and Steve O'Shaughnessy making an encouraging start to the season, Lancashire ran to a big score. Disturbed by the pace of Allott and Patterson, Sussex were forced to follow-on 271 runs in arrears. Parker held out for three hours in the second innings, but Watkinson's newly found off-breaks brought the innings to a close and Lancashire moved to a comfortable win.

Rain had the better of the match at Edgbaston where South African Brian McMillan was given the overseas spot in the Warwickshire side ahead of Kallicharran and Ferreira. That energetic all-rounder Paul Smith rescued Warwickshire in the first innings, but Essex took the lead with impressively consistent batting against the new look home attack which, apart from McMillan, included Parsons and Munton from Leicestershire. The highlight of the game was the 97th century of Dennis Amiss's career. He remains the master technician.

Kent were rushed out by Leicestershire's all pace attack on the Saturday, and at 143 for 5 in their second innings, they faced defeat. A stand of 123 in 33 overs between Baptiste and Graham Cowdrey revived them and confirmed the view that the younger Cowdrey is a very fine player.

Another batsman to confirm his authority was Graeme Hick, a player capable of attaining the highest levels of the game. He made possible a declaration that left Surrey to make 260 in 55 overs. Butcher and Clinton began the challenge with 88, but a gradual decline saw Surrey reach the point where the last pair, Monkhouse and skipper Pocock, had to stave off defeat until aided by an early end for bad light.

Hampshire were presented with a surprisingly easy task at Trent Bridge after Notts had recovered well on the first day. Tim Robinson, the traumas of the Caribbean behind him, played reassuringly, and Clive Rice was, as ever, totally professional in application. Nicholas declared 24 runs behind after a rather dour display by his batsmen on a sluggish wicket. The inability of batsmen to achieve any sort of fluency must have prompted Rice to set Hampshire 206 to win in 50 overs. It was a target which was mocked by Gordon Greenidge who, pulling Hadlee for six in the opening over, reached 100 off 88 balls and sparked Hampshire's win with 10 overs to spare. Greenidge made 118 out of 170 that constituted the 1st wicket stand with Terry.

Duncan Wild, Northants, career best with the ball and a century against Cambridge University. (George Herringshaw)

Duncan Wild hit a century and recorded a career best bowling performance at Cambridge where the university held out well for a draw.

30 April, 1 and 2 May

at Chesterfield

Derbyshire 223 (K.J. Barnett 64, J.E. Morris 53, I.V.A. Richards 4 for 36) and 438 for 5 dec (B. Roberts 124 not out, A. Hill 93, J.E. Morris 81, K.J. Barnett 51)
Somerset 309 (J.J.E. Hardy 73, I.T. Botham 61, P.G. Newman 5 for 62)

Match drawn
Somerset 8 pts, Derbyshire 5 pts

at Southampton

Glamorgan 201 (G.C. Holmes 52) and 342 for 7 dec (Younis Ahmed 85, H. Morris 58, R.C. Ontong 52)
Hampshire 308 for 8 dec. (V.P. Terry 80, C.L. Smith 79)

Match drawn
Hampshire 8 pts, Glamorgan 5 pts

at Canterbury

Kent 272 for 7 dec (R.M. Ellison 62 not out) and 250 for 8 dec (C.J. Tavare 105, G.R. Cowdrey 75)
Northamptonshire 250 for 3 dec (G. Cook 109 not out, A.J. Lamb 72)

Match drawn
Northamptonshire 6 pts, Kent 3 pts

at Old Trafford

Lancashire 301 for 9 dec (G. Fowler 72, D.W. Varey 72, C. Maynard 59, P.B. Clift 4 for 87) and 284 for 7 dec (N.H. Fairbrother 64 not out, G. Fowler 56)
Leicestershire 303 for 5 dec (J.J. Whitaker 102 not out, D.I. Gower 76) and 40 for 2

Match drawn
Leicestershire 8 pts, Lancashire 6 pts

at The Oval

Surrey 365 for 7 dec (M.A. Lynch 152, T.E. Jesty 99) and 272 for 6 dec (A.J. Stewart 76, G.S. Clinton 61, C.J. Richards 50 not out, E.E. Hemmings 4 for 95)
Nottinghamshire 327 for 6 dec (R.J. Hadlee 105 not out, J.D. Birch 62) and 152 for 9 (P.I. Pocock 4 for 45)

Match drawn
Nottinghamshire 7 pts, Surrey 6 pts

at Oxford

Middlesex 309 for 5 dec (P.R. Downton 126 not out, W.N. Slack 59) and 109 for 6 dec
Oxford University 122 (A.A.G. Mee 51, J.E. Emburey 4 for 20) and 119 (D.A. Hagan 51)

Middlesex won by 177 runs

at Cambridge

Cambridge University 226 for 9 dec (C.C. Ellison 51 not out) and 104 (G.J. Parsons 5 for 24)
Warwickshire 291 for 6 dec (G.W. Humpage 125, A.I. Kallicharran 121, A.M.G. Scott 4 for 100) and 40 for 1

Warwickshire won by 9 wickets

The second round of matches in the Britannic Assurance County Championship could provide no winner. Somerset looked set for victory at Chesterfield when Derbyshire ended the second day only 38 runs ahead with both openers gone, but Hill and Morris extended their stand to 153 on the last day, and Bruce Roberts hit a career best, batting impressively, ultimately against a motley assortment of bowlers as the game lost all purpose.

Chris Smith and Paul Terry added 142 for Hampshire's 3rd wicket at Southampton, and the home side seemed to be in a strong position, but Marshall was absent with a muscle spasm in his back on the last day and the remainder of the Hampshire bowling resources were inadequate to bowl out Glamorgan. The visitors conducted a stubborn rearguard action. Younis hit 85 off 119 deliveries and John Steele batted 90 minutes for 10 which was comprised of three scoring strokes.

There was disappointing cricket at Old Trafford and at Canterbury. Kent began the last day at 19 for 2 in their second innings, a lead of 41, but in spite of an enterprising century by Tavare who shared a stand of 100 in 42 overs with Graham Cowdrey, the game died on the last day. On the second day, Geoff Cook had reached a determined hundred and Allan Lamb had played a variety of attractive shots.

Lancashire, 87 ahead at the beginning of the last day at Old Trafford, allowed the match with Leicestershire to die as they dragged their second innings to a belated declaration. The pleasant memory of the match was the batting of James Whitaker who had gone in to stop the hat-trick and stayed to score a century, sharing a 5th wicket stand of 180 with David Gower for whom Patterson in Lancashire held no terrors.

Surrey were narrowly thwarted of victory at The Oval. Some exhilarating batting by Lynch and Jesty took them from 50 for 3 to 274 for 4 on the opening day. At 132 for 5, Notts were in some disarray just after lunch on the Thursday, but Hadlee and Birch revived them with a stand of 112. Hadlee, leading Notts in the absence of Rice, completed a cultured and aggressive hundred off 126 balls and declared 38 runs in arrears. Ultimately, Notts were asked to make 311.

After 11 overs they were 31 for 3 and the challenge was at an end. The early damage had been done by Clarke, and it was Pocock who nearly brought victory to Surrey. Hadlee played in complete contrast to the way in which he had played on the previous day and stayed 87 minutes to hit 8 off 75 deliveries. Saxelby was out to the second ball of the last over, but Pick defied Pocock and Notts were saved.

Paul Downton hit a career best as Middlesex beat Oxford University, and at Cambridge, Warwickshire recovered from 17 for 4 as Humpage and Kallicharran put on 224. Both batsmen hit centuries, and Kallicharran's brisk hundred was a reminder as to what Warwickshire was missing by their decision to play McMillan in championship matches. Gordon Parsons turned in his best bowling performance for his new county as Warwickshire moved to a comfortable win.

Benson and Hedges Cup

3 May

at Lord's

Surrey 207 for 7 (A.R. Butcher 65)
Middlesex 208 for 4 (M.W. Gatting 90 not out)

Middlesex (2 pts) won by 6 wickets
(*Gold Award* – M.W. Gatting)

at Slough

Minor Counties 135 for 5
Northamptonshire 138 for 5

Northamptonshire (2 pts) won by 5 wickets
(*Gold Award* – R. Herbert)

at Oxford

Combined Universities 146 (P.A.C. Bail 59, C.A. Connor 4 for 35)
Hampshire 147 for 2 (C.G. Greenidge 83 not out)

Hampshire (2 pts) won by 8 wickets
(*Gold Award* – C.G. Greenidge)

3 and 4 May

at Glasgow (Titwood)

Scotland 109 for 9
Worcestershire 110 for 8

Worcestershire (2 pts) won by 2 wickets
(*Gold Award* – T.S. Curtis)

3 and 5 May

at Chesterfield

Derbyshire 236 for 8 (M.A. Holding 69, K.J. Barnett 52)
Leicestershire 53 for 7

Derbyshire (2 pts) won on faster scoring rate
(*Gold Award* – M.A. Holding)

at Bristol

Somerset 178 (D.V. Lawrence 4 for 36)
Gloucestershire 182 for 2 (P.W. Romaines 79, A.W. Stovold 72 not out)

Gloucestershire (2 pts) won by 8 wickets
(*Gold Award* – D.V. Lawrence)

at Old Trafford

Lancashire 208 for 9 (C.H. Lloyd 101, A. Sidebottom 4 for 24)
Yorkshire 212 for 2 (M.D. Moxon 106 not out, G. Boycott 55)

Yorkshire (2 pts) won by 8 wickets
(*Gold Award* – M.D. Moxon)

at Hove

Essex 277 for 7 (B.R. Hardie 119 not out, G.A. Gooch 73)
Sussex 259 for 6 (Imran Khan 112 not out, A.M. Green 50)

Essex (2 pts) won by 18 runs
(*Gold Award* – Imran Khan)

The first round of matches in the Benson and Hedges Cup began rather soggily, and only three games could be completed on the Saturday. At Lord's, Surrey, put in to bat, got off to a good start with Butcher and Clinton putting on 120. After that the visitors lost their way. They were too anxious, too hasty and only Trevor Jesty, 42 not out, showed the right attitude. Middlesex lost both openers within a run of each other, at 61 and 62, but Gatting and Radley, in their different ways, assured them of victory with a stand of 97.

At Slough, Minor Counties again demonstrated that although they could survive against first-class bowling, they could not score quickly. Plumb and Herbert, both former Essex players, lifted them with an unfinished stand of 60. Herbert bowled his off-breaks to good effect, having Lamb

Tim Curtis, Worcestershire, took the Gold Award against Scotland for nursing his side to a tense victory in the Benson and Hedges Cup match, 3 and 4 May. (Mark Leech)

Brian Hardie crashes the ball to the boundary during his innings of 119 not out for Essex against Sussex, Benson and Hedges Cup, 3 May. (Adrian Murrell)

stumped for 0 and bowling Capel to take his first Gold Award, but Northants won with 15.4 overs to spare. Although they lost Terry and Robin Smith for 58, Hampshire made short work of the Oxbridge side. Greenidge and Turner added an unbeaten 89 and took their side to victory with 25 overs remaining.

On Saturday evening Scotland seemed poised for their first ever Benson and Hedges victory. They had struggled to 109 for 9 on a turning wicket, but when play was brought to a close they had reduced Worcestershire to 57 for 7. Tim Curtis, the opening batsman, was on 22 not out. On the Sunday he lost Radford at 71, bowled by Omar Henry who took 2 for 17 in his 11 overs, but he nursed Illingworth and his side through 39 tense runs more to take the match and the individual award.

David Lawrence won his first Gold Award when he accounted for Felton, Roebuck, Botham and Dredge at Bristol. Stovold and Romaines put the match firmly in Gloucestershire's grasp with an opening stand of 146. There was another fine opening stand at Old Trafford where Moxon and Boycott put on 123. Moxon and Love finished the game with an unbeaten stand of 82. Earlier Clive Lloyd had countered Sidebottom's superb opening spell with a bludgeoning century off 142 balls. He and Abrahams added 94 in 21 overs for the 5th wicket to bring Lancashire to a respectability which was to prove insufficient for victory.

A blistering 69 by Michael Holding lifted Derbyshire at Chesterfield, and then he and Mortensen combined to send back Cobb, Butcher and Potter for 11 on Saturday evening. When the game resumed on Monday Leicestershire fared little better, and the rain came as a merciful release from further punishment and embarrassment.

That the game at Hove passed over until the Monday was as much due to Sussex's dreadfully slow over-rate as to the weather. Their pace men took a terrible hammering at the beginning of the match. Hardie and Gooch began at a furious rate and they put on 139 in 27.3 overs. Hardie batted throughout the innings which closed with Essex on a formidable 277. Sussex, 80 for 1 off 28 overs at the close, were splendidly served by Imran on the Monday. He hit 2 sixes and 8 fours and came close to giving Sussex an improbable victory.

4 May

at Arundel

Indians 217 for 9
Lavinia, Duchess of Norfolk's XI 181 for 5 (T.E. Jesty 74)
Lavinia, Duchess of Norfolk's XI won on faster scoring rate

John Player Special League

at Chelmsford

Essex 284 for 4 (G.A. Gooch 100, B.R. Hardie 95)
Warwickshire 237 for 4 (M. Asif Din 108 not out, B.M. McMillan 78 not out)
Essex (4 pts) won by 47 runs

Gathering clouds at Chelmsford. (Mike King)

at Cardiff

Hampshire 242 for 6 (R.A. Smith 69, C.G. Greenidge 56, M.C.J. Nicholas 52 not out)
Glamorgan 222 for 7 (H. Morris 79)

Hampshire (4 pts) won by 20 runs

at Canterbury

Kent 249 for 6 (C.J. Tavare 88)
Gloucestershire 145 (E.A.E. Baptiste 4 for 35)

Kent (4 pts) won by 104 runs

at Old Trafford

Lancashire 176 (C.H. Lloyd 53, A.C.S. Pigott 5 for 24)
Sussex 178 for 5

Sussex (4 pts) won by 5 wickets

at Leicester

Leicestershire 230 for 5 (L. Potter 105)
Derbyshire 211 for 9 (G. Miller 73 not out, I.S. Anderson 63)

Leicestershire (4 pts) won by 19 runs

at Lord's

Nottinghamshire 237 for 2 (C.E.B. Rice 94 not out, P. Johnson 61 not out)
Middlesex 191

Nottinghamshire (4 pts) won by 46 runs

at Leeds

Somerset 217 for 7 (B.C. Rose 62, P.M. Roebuck 51)
Yorkshire 220 for 5

Yorkshire (4 pts) won by 5 wickets

The first round of matches in the Sunday League saw Gooch and Hardie repeat their performance of the previous day and begin the Essex innings with a stand of 184 in 28 overs. They were almost upstaged by Asif Din and McMillan who established a record for the competition's 5th wicket with a partnership of 185 in 25 overs. Asif Din hit his first century in limited-over cricket, but Essex never looked like losing.

Clive Rice and Paul Johnson took Notts to a dominant position with an unbeaten 3rd wicket stand of 153 at Lord's, and Tony Pigott took 5 wickets at Old Trafford where Sussex won with 3 balls to spare. Yorkshire had a fine competent team performance to crush Somerset, and Kent overwhelmed Gloucestershire with a spirited display.

At Arundel, that loveliest of grounds, the Indians began their tour in chilly and damp conditions. The Duchess's XI won when a shower reduced their target to 178 in 41 overs, but the Indians displayed enough exciting strokes to give a taste of pleasures to come.

6, 7 and 8 May

at Worcester

Worcestershire 230 for 9 dec (G.A. Hick 70) and 56 for 0
Indians 297 (M. Azharuddin 76, R.N. Kapil Dev 51)

Match drawn

ABOVE LEFT: *Asif Din who hit a maiden Sunday League century for Warwickshire, Chelmsford, 4 May. (Ken Kelly)*
BELOW: *The arrival of the Indians. Pandit hits out at Arundel. Bob Taylor is behind the stumps. (Adrian Murrell)*

ABOVE: *Andy Lloyd is run out, Essex v. Warwickshire, Chelmsford, 4 May. David East appeals as he gathers Foster's throw and launches himself at the wicket. (Mike King)*

7, 8 and 9 May

at Chelmsford

Kent 272 for 9 dec (S.G. Hinks 67, M.R. Benson 64, J.K. Lever 4 for 57) and 170 for 9 dec (C.S. Cowdrey 70 not out, J.K. Lever 4 for 69)
Essex 174 (G.A. Gooch 60, G.R. Dilley 5 for 69, T.M. Alderman 4 for 59) and 243 (K.W.R. Fletcher 51, T.M. Alderman 5 for 46)

Kent won by 25 runs
Kent 22 pts, Essex 4 pts

at Old Trafford

Hampshire 251 for 3 (C.G. Greendige 127 not out, C.L. Smith 70)
v. Lancashire

Match drawn
Hampshire 3 pts, Lancashire 1 pt

at Lord's

Leicestershire 259 for 8 (D.I. Gower 83, J.J. Whitaker 60)
v. Middlesex

Match drawn
Middlesex 3 pts, Leicestershire 3 pts

at Northampton

Gloucestershire 301 for 4 dec (C.W.J. Athey 171 not out, P. Bainbridge 55) and 30 for 0
Northamptonshire 503 (R.A. Harper 234, G. Cook 82, A.J. Lamb 50, J.W. Lloyds 4 for 39, G.E. Sainsbury 4 for 146)

Match drawn
Northamptonshire 5 pts, Gloucestershire 5 pts

at Taunton

Somerset 300 for 4 dec (I.V.A. Richards 102, P.M. Roebuck 76, N.A. Felton 55) and 16 for 0 dec
Glamorgan 26 for 2 dec and 230 for 9 (G.C. Holmes 68)

Match drawn
Somerset 4 pts, Glamorgan 1 pt

at The Oval

Warwickshire 174 (B.M. McMillan 58, A.H. Gray 6 for 83) and 89 (A.H. Gray 6 for 30)
Surrey 336 for 5 dec (M.A. Lynch 128 not out, A.J. Stewart 76, G.S. Clinton 60)

Surrey won by an innings and 73 runs
Surrey 24 pts, Warwickshire 3 pts

at Leeds

Sussex 195 (N.J. Lenham 75) and 55 for 1 dec
Yorkshire 0 for 0 dec and 251 for 9 (G.B. Stevenson 58 not out, P. Carrick 51, D.A. Reeve 4 for 82)

Yorkshire won by 1 wicket
Yorkshire 20 pts, Sussex 1 pt

at Oxford

Nottinghamshire 228 for 0 dec (M. Newell 112 not out, D.W. Randall 101 not out) and 211 for 2 dec (P. Johnson 91, D.J.R. Martindale 88)
Oxford University 98 (P.M. Such 5 for 36) and 131 (P.M. Such 4 for 20, R.A. Pick 4 for 26)

Nottinghamshire won by 210 runs

The traditional opening first-class match for the tourists saw the Indians perform creditably in the cold and damp at Worcester where no play was possible on the last day. Worcestershire reached 131 for 2 on the first day, but Prabhakar and Sharma took 3 wickets each as 7 wickets fell

for 98. Hick was most impressive for the county, and on the second day, Azharuddin whose debut in England had been most eagerly awaited did not disappoint, displaying a sound defence coupled with a willingness to play his wide range of shots.

Only 41 minutes play was possible after the first day at Lord's and none at all at Old Trafford where Greenidge and Chris Smith added 167 for Hampshire's 3rd wicket on the first, and only, day.

At Taunton, a reduced first day was followed by a second on which Viv Richards hit 102 off 48 balls. He and Roebuck, who played a more passive role, added 115 in 13 overs for the 3rd wicket. The great West Indian hit 6 sixes and 12 fours on a wicket which gave the bowlers some assistance. The man's achievements have exhausted the superlatives. Both captains attempted to resuscitate the game by making challenging declarations so that Glamorgan were left to make 291. They never looked like reaching the target although they batted bravely. Rain cost Somerset 14 overs, but they were finally thwarted by Davies and Base with a stubborn last wicket stand.

At Northampton, Gloucestershire batted rather dourly and rain fractured the second day when Bill Athey completed his highest score in England. The visitors seemed to hold the advantage at the close with Northants 219 for 5, and when Cook was out on the last morning there seemed a possibility of a close finish. Roger Harper proceeded to dominate the day, hitting a career best 234, a majestic innings which included 12 sixes and 24 fours.

In a thrilling game at Chelmsford, Kent won by 25 runs with 10 overs to spare. Gooch had asked Kent to bat, but Hinks and Benson thwarted Essex with a stand of 121 for the 1st wicket. Lever and Foster bowled the home county back into the match on a wicket which always gave the seam bowlers encouragement. Alderman and Dilley certainly found it encouraging on the second day when Dilley, looking brisker and more purposeful off his shorter run, did the hat-trick. The feat spanned 84 minutes, Fletcher falling at slip on the last ball before lunch and Lilley and East being taken at first and fourth slip after a delay for rain. Chris Cowdrey batted splendidly against the Essex pace attack on the last day and judged his declaration perfectly, setting Essex 269 to win off a minimum of 74 overs. Border and Fletcher gave their side hope as they took the score to 157, but there was a collapse which saw 3 wickets fall for 10 runs. Lilley and East gave Essex another boost, but they fell to Chris Cowdrey in the same over, and the Kent captain's all-round peformance coupled with the exuberance and quality of Alderman's bowling gave the visitors the match.

There was no such closeness at The Oval where Warwickshire gave two wretched batting performances against Tony Gray, the West Indian pace bowler, who was deputizing for Clarke. On the opening day, Warwickshire lost their last 6 wickets for 32 runs, and their bowlers were put to the sword on the second when Clinton and Stewart added 104 for the 2nd wicket and Stewart and Lynch followed this with a stand of 114. Monte Lynch hit his second century in successive matches, and with Gray demolishing Warwickshire for a second time, Surrey won with 38 minutes and 20 overs to spare.

There was no play on the first day at Headingley, and

Azharuddin in England. The Indians at Worcester, 7 May. (Adrian Murrell)

Roger Harper hit a career best 234, 12 sixes and 24 fours, Northants v. Gloucestershire, 7 and 8 May. (George Herringshaw)

Lenham's exemplary technique highlighted the second. Eventually, Yorkshire were asked to make 251 in 58 overs, a task which seemed beyond them once the Sussex seamers had reduced them to 75 for 5. Carrick, missed on 24, hit 51 off 76 balls, and Stevenson, a violent fifty off 36 balls, turned the game in Yorkshire's favour. Stevenson and Jarvis added 32 for the last wicket to give Yorkshire victory with 5 balls to spare and put them top of the embryo Britannic Assurance County Championship.

At Oxford, Randall and Newell put on an unbeaten 228 for Nottinghamshire's 1st wicket in the first innings, and Johnson and Martindale 129 in the second, Johnson hitting 91 of them. Such, Pick and Afford dismissed the undergraduates with some ease.

Colin Cowdrey was named as next President of MCC, and Alan Smith was selected as the new chief executive of the TCCB to take over from Donald Carr who held the post of secretary. The TCCB appointment, the most important in cricket, came to a straight decision between Smith and Peter Lush, and most would have favoured Lush, the energetic and progressive man whose honesty, diplomacy and good humour have been a boon to the game, but Smith has a wide experience of cricket and has served well as an administrator, factors which turned the vote in his favour.

10, 11 and 12 May

at Cheltenham Town C.C.

Indians 322 for 5 dec (D.B. Vengsarkar 74, R.J. Shastri 70 not out, S.M. Patil 57, C.S. Pandit 50 not out) and 135 for 3 dec
Gloucestershire 271 for 5 dec (K.M. Curran 69 not out, P. Bainbridge 58)

Match drawn

The Victoria ground at Cheltenham staged its first county match for 49 years, and the Indians gave a bright batting display on the first day after which the weather was the only winner.

Benson and Hedges Cup

10 May

at Leicester

Leicestershire 192 for 7
Warwickshire 193 for 9 (B.M. McMillan 51)

Warwickshire (2 pts) won by 1 wicket
(Gold Award – B.M. McMillan)

at Northampton

Derbyshire 225 for 3 (A. Hill 90 not out, B. Roberts 86 not out)
Northamptonshire 187

Derbyshire (2 pts) won by 38 runs
(Gold Award – B. Roberts)

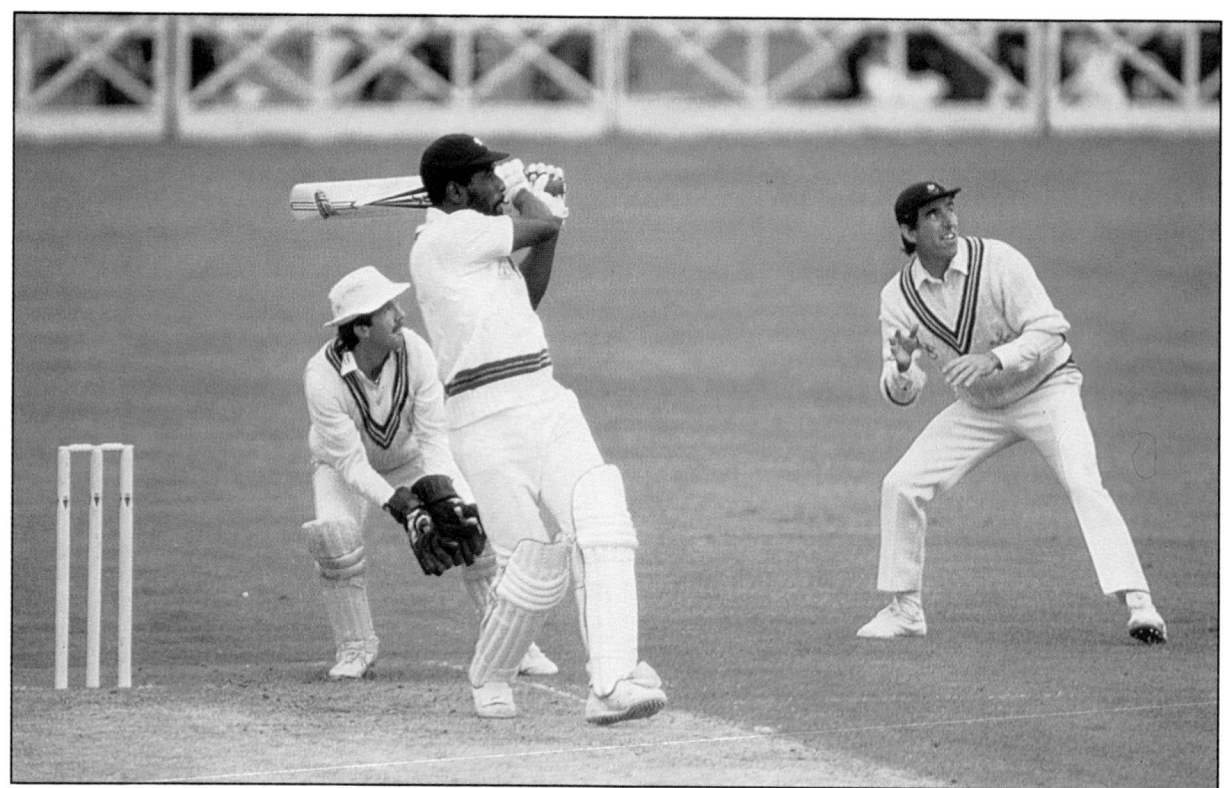

Viv Richards, 102 off 48 balls, Somerset v. Glamorgan, 7 May. He hit 6 sixes and 12 fours. (Adrian Murrell)

10 and 11 May

at Perth

Scotland 156 for 9
Lancashire 153 for 9

Scotland (2 pts) won by 3 runs
(Gold Award – R.G. Swan)

10 and 12 May

at Canterbury

Kent 270 for 6 (C.S. Cowdrey 89 not out, G.R. Cowdrey 65)
Surrey 274 for 6 (T.E. Jesty 94 not out, M.A. Lynch 58)

Surrey (2 pts) won by 4 wickets
(Gold Award – T.E. Jesty)

at Trent Bridge

Nottinghamshire 227 for 6 (D.W. Randall 82 not out, B.C. Broad 70)
Yorkshire 219 for 8

Nottinghamshire (2 pts) won by 8 runs
(Gold Award – D.W. Randall)

At Taunton

Essex 206 (D.R. Pringle 65, C.H. Dredge 4 for 30)
Somerset 194

Essex (2 pts) won by 12 runs
(Gold Award – D.R. Pringle)

at Southampton

Middlesex 230 for 7 (R.O. Butcher 69, M.W. Gatting 57)
Hampshire 27 for 0

Match abandoned

Hampshire 55 for 5
Middlesex 80 for 3 (M.W. Gatting 60 not out)

Middlesex (2 pts) won by 7 wickets
(Gold Award – M.W. Gatting)

12 May

at Swansea

Sussex 98 for 2
Glamorgan 93 for 6

Sussex (2 pts) won by 5 runs

Rain again interfered with the cricket so that only two matches could be completed on the Saturday, and the games at Swansea and Southampton were reduced to 10-over slogs late on the Monday afternoon. Hampshire had held the edge in the first game at Southampton, but Gatting played a violent innings to give Middlesex the replay.

Surrey made a remarkable recovery to beat Kent at Canterbury. On the Saturday, the Cowdrey brothers had put on 127 in 16 overs for the 5th wicket after Kent had blundered to 107 for 4 in 35 overs. Dilley and Ellison restricted Surrey to 74 for the loss of Butcher, Clinton and Richards in 25 overs before the early close. On the Monday, however, Jesty and Lynch took the score to 180 before Lynch fell to Dilley. They had added 108 in 16 overs. Stewart hit 3 fours in 14 balls, and when Doughty joined Jesty 72 were

Sidebottom fails to collect the ball, and Gold Award winner Derek Randall gets home, Notts v. Yorkshire, at Trent Bridge, Benson and Hedges Cup, 10 May. (David Munden)

needed from 12 overs. Doughty contributed 30 in a partnership of 70, and Jesty took the Gold Award for his magnificent 94 not out off 81 balls.

Essex, too, recovered well to beat Somerset. They were 118 for 7 when the veteran Turner joined Pringle to put on 71 in 11 overs. Garner and Dredge had caused Essex great discomfort early on, but Pringle hit Garner for 3 successive fours to reach his fifty. When Somerset batted Turner dismissed Roebuck, Hardy and Bartlett, and Pringle accounted for Richards and Marks. Resuming on the Monday at 72 for 6, Somerset batted bravely, but once Foster had bowled Botham, the odds were always in favour of Essex.

Derbyshire continued to impress with Hill and Roberts sharing an unbeaten stand of 155. The opening attack of Mortensen and Holding then limited Northants who never effectively recovered from the depths of 49 for 5. The only other game to be completed on the Saturday was at Leicester where, for the 10th time in the history of the competition, the match was decided on the last ball. Leicestershire had hit only 8 boundaries as they struggled to 192 for 7 in their 55 overs. It appeared an easy task for Warwickshire, but they lost 6 wickets in the last 20 overs, the last of them with the scores level; but Gifford snatched the winning single off the last delivery.

An injury to Boycott, who had to retire hurt, did not help the Yorkshire cause. Randall had held the Notts innings together on the Saturday, and Yorkshire, who had won all their previous matches of the season, reached the last 2 overs of the match 26 short of victory. Peter Hartley and Jarvis, the last pair, were hitting the ball sweetly, and when Rice bowled the last over only 13 were needed and the game was in the balance, but the Notts' skipper, the most astute in the game, conceded only 4 runs.

The outstanding performance of the round was by Scotland who, in their 26th match in the competition, notched their first victory. Put in to bat, Scotland reached 156 on a difficult wicket by means of several useful contributions. Lancashire lost Fowler in the 3rd over, but Mendis and Abrahams put on 60 for the 2nd wicket and appeared to have steered the county to a comfortable position, but collapse followed and in spite of a late flurry from Simmons and Allott, Scotland snatched victory by 3 runs. Richard Swan, the Scottish captain, who made 31 and handled his side admirably, was given the Gold Award.

John Player Special League

11 May

---

at Derby

Sussex 163 for 6 (Imran Khan 55)
Derbyshire 164 for 2 (K.J. Barnett 74 not out, J.E. Morris 66 not out)

Derbyshire (4 pts) won by 8 wickets

at Swansea

Leicestershire 132 for 6
Glamorgan 135 for 4

Glamorgan (4 pts) won by 6 wickets

at Southampton

Hampshire 158 for 8
Northamptonshire 154 for 8 (M.C.J. Nicholas 4 for 41)

Hampshire (4 pts) won by 4 runs

at Trent Bridge

Warwickshire 236 for 6 (G.W. Humpage 86, T.A. Lloyd 58, C.E.B. Rice 4 for 49)
Nottinghamshire 188 (J.D. Birch 66)

Warwickshire (4 pts) won by 48 runs

at Taunton

Middlesex 196 for 7 (C.T. Radley 78 not out, P.R. Downton 50)
Somerset 197 for 4 (P.M. Roebuck 68)

Somerset (4 pts) won by 6 wickets

at The Oval

Surrey 206 for 7 (G.S. Clinton 92 not out)
Yorkshire 210 for 4 (D.L. Bairstow 83 not out, A.A. Metcalfe 74 not out)

Yorkshire (4 pts) won by 6 wickets

at Worcester

Worcestershire 191 for 6
Kent 193 for 4 (C.S. Cowdrey 50 not out, C.J. Tavare 50)

Kent (4 pts) won by 6 wickets

The outstanding feature of the Sunday League games was the performance of Ian Botham at Taunton. Somerset had been given a good start by Roebuck and Wyatt who, sadly, was taken to hospital with a broken arm after being hit by a ball from Daniel. When the same bowler bowled the last over Somerset needed 15 to win. Harden took 3 off the 3rd delivery and Botham hit 2 sixes in the last three balls to win the match. Elsewhere Barnett and Morris shared an unbeaten 3rd wicket stand of 132 which won the match against Sussex at Derby, and Bairstow, coming in at The Oval at 80 for 4, hit 83 in 12 overs, sharing a stand of 130 with Metcalfe and winning the match with 3 overs to spare.

Benson and Hedges Cup

13 May

at Chelmsford

Essex 271 for 7 (D.R. Pringle 56 not out, P.J. Prichard 52, G.A. Gooch 51)
Gloucestershire 254 for 9 (C.W.J. Athey 78)

Essex (2 pts) won by 17 runs
(Gold Award – N.A. Foster)

at Northampton

Northamptonshire 226 for 5 (A.J. Lamb 106)
Leicestershire 203 (N.A. Mallender 5 for 53)

Northamptonshire (2 pts) won by 23 runs
(Gold Award – A.J. Lamb)

at Trent Bridge

Scotland 166 for 6 (I.L. Philip 73)
Nottinghamshire 170 for 2 (R.T. Robinson 76 not out)

Nottinghamshire (2 pts) won by 8 wickets
(Gold Award – I.L. Philip)

at Taunton

Somerset 258 for 7 (I.T. Botham 126 not out)

Glamorgan 183 (R.C. Ontong 56, H. Morris 51, N.S. Taylor 5 for 51)

Somerset (2 pts) won by 75 runs
(Gold Award – I.T. Botham)

at The Oval

Surrey 239 for 7 (T.E. Jesty 71 not out, A.R. Butcher 59, T.M. Tremlett 4 for 30)
Hampshire 240 for 7 (C.L. Smith 67, C.G. Greenidge 58)

Hampshire (2 pts) won by 3 wickets
(Gold Award – T.M. Tremlett)

at Worcester

Worcestershire 231 for 8 (D.N. Patel 76, P.A. Neale 52)
Lancashire 231 for 8 (G. Fowler 76)

Lancashire (2 pts) won on faster scoring rate over first 30 overs
(Gold Award – P.J.W. Allott)

at Walsall

Warwickshire 184 (D.L. Amiss 73)
Minor Counties 137

Warwickshire (2 pts) won by 47 runs
(Gold Award – D.L. Amiss)

at Cambridge

Combined Universities 81
Kent 84 for 2

Kent (2 pts) won by 8 wickets
(Gold Award – R.M. Ellison)

Trevor Jesty punishes his old county. He hit 71 not out for Surrey v. Hampshire at The Oval, 13 May. Bobby Parks is the wicket-keeper. (Adrian Murrell)

Put in to bat at Chelmsford, Essex enjoyed some wayward bowling by Walsh, in particular, and initially by Lawrence, so that they gave an aggressively even batting display which took them past 250 for the 14th time in the Benson and Hedges Cup, a record. In reply, Romaines, Athey and Curran batted with spirit, but Gloucestershire never looked likely to prevent Essex from qualifying for the quarter-finals.

At the other end, the Combined Universities of Oxford and Cambridge were bowled out for 81, the 7th time that they have failed to reach a hundred in the competition, an unenviable record and one which emphasises the need to look urgently at the quality of players available at Exeter, Durham, Birmingham, Manchester and the other consistently strong members of the UAU.

Allan Lamb hit his second century in the Benson and Hedges Cup and shared a record stand for the competition's 5th wicket of 160 with Capel. Mallender bowled with sparkle and Leicestershire's defeat put them out of the tournament, the fourth year in succession in which the holders have failed to reach the quarter-finals.

Notts beat Scotland with 10.2 overs to spare and enhanced their chances of reaching the last eight, but Philip's 73, which equalled Russell's record not out innings for Scotland in the competition, won him the Gold Award. Warwickshire claimed a grim victory over Minor Counties in difficult

Surrey's hopes dwindle. Lynch is run out by Nicholas. Surrey v. Hampshire, Benson and Hedges Cup, The Oval, 13 May. (Mark Leech)

conditions at Walsall. They were 63 for 5 and were resurrected by Amiss and Paul Smith. Steve Malone, formerly of Essex, Hampshire and Glamorgan, bowled a good, brisk spell for Minor Counties which brought him 3 for 26 in 10.4 overs.

Tim Tremlett took the Gold Award for the first time with his 4 for 30 in 11 overs at The Oval. He also shared an unbeaten 8th wicket stand of 27 with Cowley which brought Hampshire victory with 4 balls to spare, but Hampshire's failure to bowl out Surrey put pressure on them in their effort to reach the last stages of the competition from the strongest group.

Ian Botham hit his first century in the Benson and Hedges Cup. He started cautiously and then reached his fifty with a six. He repeated the shot immediately and reached his second fifty off 21 balls. He and Gard added 95 in 10 overs at the close, and Botham's innings contained 8 sixes and 10 fours. He followed this with 2 for 10 in 8 overs and gave the adjudicator little problem in deciding to whom the Gold Award should go.

The most sensational events were at New Road. Allott bowled a good quota for Lancashire, dismissing both openers, and later Newport, for 30 runs. He then found himself in a match-winning situation with the bat. Neale's calculations had gone astray a little as the excitement grew and he was forced to entrust the last over to Hick with Lancashire needing 10 for victory and 4 wickets standing. With his second ball, Hick had Simmons caught in the deep and then had Fairbrother brilliantly caught on the

Alan Butcher during his innings of 140 for Surrey against the Indians, The Oval, 15 May. (Adrian Murrell)

boundary's edge by substitute Weston off his fourth ball. Allott was left to face the last two deliveries. He hit the first for four and, having checked, hit the last for two to bring the scores level, but giving victory to Lancashire who had scored more quickly over the first 30 overs of their innings than Worcestershire had done. It was the seventh occasion in the history of the Benson and Hedges Cup that a match had ended with the scores level, but it was the first time that the match had actually been 'tied'.

15 May

at The Oval

Surrey 230 for 8 (A.R. Butcher 140)
Indians 231 for 5 (S.M. Gavaskar 81, M. Azharuddin 55, D.B. Vengsarkar 51 not out)

Indians won by 5 wickets

In spite of a fine hundred by Butcher and the loss of 4 wickets in 4 overs for 10 runs, the tourists gained a splendid victory at The Oval, pacing their innings beautifully and winning with 15 balls to spare. Gavaskar was majestic, Azharuddin again impressive and Vengsarkar hit 51 off 34 balls when crisis threatened.

Benson and Hedges Cup

15 May

at Chelmsford

Glamorgan 205 for 9 (R.C. Ontong 58 not out)
Essex 206 for 4 (D.R. Pringle 54 not out, K.W.R. Fletcher 51 not out)

Essex (2 pts) won by 6 wickets
(Gold Award – K.W.R. Fletcher)

at Southampton

Kent 250 for 5 (M.R. Taylor 67, M.R. Benson 65, G.R. Cowdrey 60 not out)
Hampshire 189 for 9 (D.L. Underwood 4 for 26)

Kent (2 pts) won by 63 runs
(Gold Award – G.R. Cowdrey)

at Lord's

Combined Universities 209 for 8 (C.D.M. Tooley 62)
Middlesex 210 for 2 (C.T. Radley 62 not out, W.N. Slack 52)

Middlesex (2 pts) won by 8 wickets
(Gold Award – C.D.M. Tooley)

at Worcester

Nottinghamshire 218 for 7
Worcestershire 219 for 2 (G.A. Hick 103 not out, D.M. Smith 81 not out)

Worcestershire (2 pts) won by 8 wickets
(Gold Award – G.A. Hick)

at Leeds

Yorkshire 317 for 5 (K. Sharp 105, M.D. Moxon 83)
Scotland 150 (W.A. Donald 52, P.J. Hartley 5 for 43)

Yorkshire (2 pts) won by 167 runs
(Gold Award – P.J. Hartley)

15 and 16 May

at Edgbaston

Northamptonshire 283 for 5 (R.J. Bailey 86, R.J. Boyd-Moss 58)
Warwickshire 127 for 7 (M. Asif Din 52 not out, D.J. Capel 4 for 29)

Northamptonshire (2 pts) won by 156 runs
(Gold Award – R.J. Bailey)

16 May

at Derby

Minor Counties 138 for 8
Derbyshire 140 for 3 (K.J. Barnett 62)

Derbyshire (2 pts) won by 7 wickets
(Gold Award – K.J. Barnett)

at Bristol

Gloucestershire 134
Sussex 136 for 3

Sussex (2 pts) won by 7 wickets
(Gold Award – A.N. Jones)

Both Northamptonshire and Yorkshire reached their highest scores in the Benson and Hedges Cup and gained overwhelming victories although at Headingley, it was a bowler, Peter Hartley, who took the Gold Award for some impressive bowling on a batsman's paradise.

Essex completed a clean sweep of Group C as Fletcher and Pringle had an unbeaten stand of 108 to beat Glamorgan. Sussex clawed their way back into contention in this group by beating Gloucestershire at soggy Bristol. Adrian Jones took 3 for 14 in 7 overs to gain the Gold Award.

Middlesex and Derbyshire consolidated their places as group leaders with easy wins over weaker opposition although the Westcliff captain, Reuben Herbert, again bowled impressively for Minor Counties and Oxford's Chris Tooley took the Gold Award for a good innings at Lord's.

Zimbabwe's Graeme Hick gave an awesome display of his prodigious talent by scattering the Notts attack to the winds at New Road. He and David Smith shared an unbeaten 3rd wicket stand of 190. It was a mightily impressive performance, and Hick, a week before his 20th birthday, hit 12 fours as Worcestershire won with 17 balls to spare.

The most significant win came at Southampton where Kent produced a splendid team effort to beat Hampshire and give themselves a chance of qualifying for the quarter-finals. Benson and Taylor took them from 38 for 2 to 148 before being parted, but 3 wickets then fell for 14 runs before

Graham Cowdrey, in a sparkling performance, put on 88 with Baptiste. Hampshire lost Greenidge and Robin Smith for 37 and could never recover against the gnawing accuracy of Derek Underwood.

Off the field, it was announced that Javed Miandad had resigned from Glamorgan. Javed had failed to return to his county at the required time, preferring instead to be fêted in his own land following his winning performance in the Australasia Cup in Sharjah. Javed is one of the very great Test cricketers, unfortunately he has not seemed amenable to the disciplines and demands of a county club, and it is to be regretted.

17, 18 and 19 May

at Southampton

Indians 297 for 6 dec (R.N. Kapil Dev 115 not out, R.M.H. Binny 64) and 132 for 5 dec (M. Azharuddin 55 not out)

Minor Counties 1986
Benson and Hedges Cup

BATTING	v. Northamptonshire (Slough) 3 May 1986	v. Warwickshire (Walsall) 13 May 1986	v. Derbyshire (Derby) 16 May 1986	v. Leicestershire (Leicester) 19 May 1986	Runs
S.R. Atkinson	4				4
N. Priestley	2	10	14	37	63
P.A. Todd	32	44	4	0	80
G.R.J. Roope	17	8	26	8	59
N.A. Riddell	0	20	12	74	106
S.G. Plumb	37*	9	20	16	82
R. Herbert	26*	6	4	6	42
K.A. Arnold	—				—
J.S. Hitchmough	—	1		5	6
W.G. Merry	—	3	5*	1*	9
D. Surridge	—		—		—
A. Patel		15	35		50
A.J. Webster		4	4	5	13
S.J. Malone		1*	1*	0	2
N.A. Fell				12	12
Byes	1				
Leg-byes	14	11	8	4	
Wides	2	5	5	1	
No-balls					
Total	135	137	138	169	
Wickets	5	10	8	10	
Results	L	L	L	L	
Points	0	0	0	0	

Catches 2 – N. Priestley (ct 1/st 1), S.G. Plumb and G.R.J. Roope
1 – D. Surridge and R. Herbert

BOWLING	W.G. Merry	D. Surridge	K.A. Arnold	R. Herbert	J.S. Hitchmough	S.G. Plumb	S.J. Malone	A.J. Webster
v. Northamptonshire (Slough) 3 May	5–0–23–0	5–1–25–0	7–0–16–2	11–3–30–2	5–2–13–0	6.2–4–19–0		
v. Warwickshire (Walsall) 13 May	8–1–25–0			8–2–25–0	11–3–41–2	7–1–20–1	10.4–1–26–3	10–2–31–2
v. Derbyshire (Derby) 16 May	7–2–17–0	9–1–30–0		10–1–26–3			6–0–21–0	8–0–43–0
v. Leicestershire (Leicester) 19 May	10–1–37–2			11–0–55–0	3–0–22–0	10–0–38–0	10–0–48–1	11–1–66–0
Wickets	2	0	2	5	2	1	4	2

Hampshire 151 for 1 dec (V.P. Terry 65 not out) and 227 for 6 (C.G. Greenidge 86, V.P. Terry 57)

Match drawn

A blank first day was followed by some enterprising cricket. Kapil Dev and Roger Binny added 158 in 30 overs, Nicholas made a sporting declaration and Kapil Dev asked Hampshire to make 279 at more than 7 an over. The challenge was accepted, but after Greenidge was dismissed the task looked formidable. Greenidge and Terry began with a stand of 124.

John Player Special League

18 May

at Leek C.C.

Derbyshire 132
Warwickshire 133 for 5

Warwickshire (4 pts) won by 5 wickets

at Swindon

Gloucestershire 126 for 7
Essex 130 for 1 (B.R. Hardie 71 not out)

Essex (4 pts) won by 9 wickets

at Leicester

Lancashire 141 for 8 (J. Abrahams 55, W.K.R. Benjamin 4 for 19)
Leicestershire 142 for 1 (L. Potter 63 not out, N.E. Briers 52)

Leicestershire (4 pts) won by 9 wickets

at Lord's

Kent 177
Middlesex 170 (E.A.E. Baptiste 4 for 25)

Kent (4 pts) won by 7 runs

at Trent Bridge

Nottinghamshire 198 for 8 (R.T. Robinson 55, A.N. Jones 7 for 41)
Sussex 203 for 9 (I.J. Gould 63)

Sussex (4 pts) won by 1 wicket

at The Oval

Surrey 161 for 7 (G.S. Clinton 66)
Glamorgan 149

Surrey (4 pts) won by 12 runs

at Leeds

Worcestershire 163 for 9 (P.W. Jarvis 4 for 13)
Yorkshire 164 for 5 (K. Sharp 59)

Yorkshire (4 pts) won by 5 wickets

	Byes	Leg-byes	Wides	No-balls	Total	Wkts
	8	4	5	1	138	5
		16	3		184	10
		3	5		140	3
		12	11	3	278	3

Adrian Jones established a Sussex Sunday League record when he took 7 for 41 against Notts at Trent Bridge, 18 May. (George Herringshaw)

Yorkshire and Kent took joint first place in the embryo Sunday League with wins over Middlesex and Worcestershire respectively. Essex remained unbeaten after accounting for Gloucestershire in a 25-over match at Swindon where Gooch and Hardie continued their opening success with a stand of 80. Potter and Briers began Leicestershire's innings with a stand of 124 which helped to overwhelm Lancashire who were rather poor. Glamorgan lost their way at The Oval against a tight spell by Needham, and on their venture into

Staffordshire, Derbyshire had Warwickshire at 15 for 3, but fell to the combined onslaught of Humpage, McMillan and Asif Din. Three Derbyshire middle-order batsmen failed to score as the last 7 wickets went down for 40 runs. At Trent Bridge, Adrian Jones recorded one of the five best bowling performances in the history of the competition after Broad and Robinson had begun with a stand of 89. Chasing 199, Sussex were 181 for 9 when Jones came in. He hit 17 not out. Twelve of these runs came off the last over and 5 off the last ball when, with the scores level, he pushed a single which was overthrown to the boundary.

17, 19 and 20 May

at Northampton

Northamptonshire 244 (G. Cook 81, J.H. Childs 5 for 97)
Essex 23 for 2

Match drawn
Essex 4 pts, Northamptonshire 2 pts

No play was possible on the first or last days, but on the one day when it did not rain John Childs returned his best figures for Essex with his slow left-arm spin bowling. This most likeable young man had had few opportunities since joining Essex from Gloucestershire.

Benson and Hedges Cup

17 and 19 May

at Canterbury

Middlesex 258 for 8 (M.W. Gatting 62, P.R. Downton 53 not out)
Kent 124 (M.R. Benson 57 not out)

Middlesex (2 pts) won by 134 runs
(Gold Award – M.W. Gatting)

Combined Universities 1986
Benson and Hedges Cup

BATTING	v. Hampshire (Oxford) 3 May 1986	v. Kent (Cambridge) 13 May 1986	v. Middlesex (Lord's) 15 May 1986	v. Surrey (The Oval) 19 May 1986	Runs
P.A.C. Bail	59	3	30	40	132
C.D.M. Tooley	15	8	62	1	86
G.J. Toogood	3	5			8
D.J. Fell	10	3	44	4	61
D.A. Thorne	2	1	36*	14	53
D.G. Price	30	13	0	25	68
R.S. Rutnagur	2	32	1	6*	41
A.K. Golding	4	0	0	31*	35
A.D. Brown	7	5*	2	10*	24
J.E. Davidson	0*				0
A.M.G. Scott	0	2	—	—	2
C.C. Ellison		1	1*	—	2
D.A. Hagan			10	11	21
Byes			3	4	
Leg-byes	10	4	14	5	
Wides	4	3	1	3	
No-balls		1	5	7	
Total	146	81	209	161	
Wickets	10	10	8	6	
Results	L	L	L	L	
Points	0	0	0	0	

Catches 1 – A.D. Brown (st 1), A.K. Golding and A.M.G. Scott

BOWLING	J.E. Davidson	A.M.G. Scott	G.J. Toogood	A.K. Golding	D.A. Thorne	C.C. Ellison	R.S. Rutnagur	P.A. Bail	C.D.M. Tooley
v. Hampshire (Oxford) 3 May	4-0-12-0	11-1-44-1	8-1-50-1	4-0-28-0	3-0-9-0				
v. Kent (Cambridge) 13 May		4-0-16-0	6-3-14-0	5.3-1-20-1	6-1-13-0	3-0-8-0	5-2-8-1		
v. Middlesex (Lord's) 15 May		8-1-36-0		10-0-71-0	6.3-0-36-0	8-1-30-0	11-2-31-2		
v. Surrey (The Oval) 19 May		9.1-3-26-1		11-1-48-0	5-0-15-0	8-0-45-0		4-0-20-1	1-0-6-0
Wickets	0	2	1	1	0	0	3	1	0

at Liverpool

Nottinghamshire 263 for 7 (C.E.B. Rice 71, R.T. Robinson 58)
Lancashire 243 for 8 (C.H. Lloyd 67, R.J. Hadlee 4 for 35)

Nottinghamshire (2 pts) won by 20 runs
(Gold Award – R.J. Hadlee)

19 May

at Swansea

Gloucestershire 196 for 7
Glamorgan 151

Gloucestershire (2 pts) won by 45 runs
(Gold Award – I.R. Payne)

at Leicester

Leicestershire 278 for 3 (L. Potter 112, I.P. Butcher 103 not out)
Minor Counties 169 (N.A. Riddell 74, W.K.R. Benjamin 5 for 17)

Leicestershire (2 pts) won by 109 runs
(Gold Award – L. Potter)

at The Oval

Combined Universities 161 for 6
Surrey 162 for 2 (M.A. Lynch 68 not out, A.J. Stewart 63 not out)

Surrey (2 pts) won by 8 wickets
(Gold Award – A.J. Stewart)

at Hove

Sussex 218 for 9 (N.J. Lenham 82)
Somerset 176 (G.V. Palmer 53, A.N. Jones 4 for 32)

Sussex (2 pts) won by 42 runs
(Gold Award – N.J. Lenham)

at Edgbaston

Warwickshire 213 for 9 (B.M. McMillan 76, D.L. Amiss 59)
Derbyshire 215 for 7 (A. Hill 51)

Derbyshire (2 pts) won by 3 wickets
(Gold Award – B.M. McMillan)

at Leeds

Worcestershire 213 for 9 (D.B. d'Oliveira 66)
Yorkshire 169

Worcestershire (2 pts) won by 44 runs
(Gold Award – D.B. d'Oliveira)

	Byes	Leg-byes	Wides	No-balls	Total	Wkts
		4			147	2
		5	1		84	2
		6	2	1	210	2
	1	1	3	3	162	2

Benson and Hedges Cup – Group Tables

Group A					
	P	*W*	*L*	*Pts*	*Striking Rate*
Derbyshire	4	4	—	8	31.82
Northants	4	3	1	6	52.64
Warwickshire	4	2	2	4	44.58
Leicestershire	4	1	3	2	40.43
Minor Counties	4	—	4	2	49.30

Group B					
	P	*W*	*L*	*Pts*	*Striking Rate*
Worcestershire	4	3	1	6	37.76
Nottinghamshire	4	3	1	6	54.29
Yorkshire	4	2	2	4	36.29
Lancashire	4	1	3	2	49.84
Scotland	4	1	3	2	51.12

Group C					
	P	*W*	*L*	*Pts*	*Striking Rate*
Essex	4	4	—	8	38.64
Sussex	4	3	1	6	29.48
Gloucestershire	4	2	2	4	38.06
Somerset	4	1	3	2	41.25
Glamorgan	4	—	4	—	51.60

Group D					
	P	*W*	*L*	*Pts*	*Striking Rate*
Middlesex	4	4	—	8	32.53
Kent	4	2	2	4	36.69
Hampshire	4	2	2	4	41.24
Surrey	4	2	2	4	56.82
Combined Universities	4	—	4	—	105.87

The last round of matches in the zonal part of the Benson and Hedges Cup saw Worcestershire beat Yorkshire at Headingley in what was a straight contest for a place in the quarter-finals. The other qualifiers from Group B were Nottinghamshire who were 171 for 5 off 44 overs when play was abandoned on the Saturday, Paul Allott having frustrated them. The last 11 overs on the Monday, with Hadlee and Birch in full flow, produced another 92 runs, and when Fowler and Abrahams were dismissed with only 9 scored the game passed out of Lancashire's reach.

South African all-rounder McMillan won his second Gold Award in four matches, but Derbyshire, with good contributions from Anderson, Roberts and Miller supporting Hill, passed into the quarter-finals. Derbyshire's victory came with only one ball to spare as Miller and Finney added the last 32 runs in an 8th wicket stand.

Kent took 8 Middlesex wickets on the Saturday to clinch their quarter-final place on striking rate. Jarvis, given a rare outing, bowled well, and there was some fine catching,

inspired by skipper Chris Cowdrey. Kent collapsed miserably on the Monday, but Mark Benson carried his bat through the innings.

Gloucestershire and Leicestershire won lost causes, but Potter and Butcher put on 196 for Leicestershire's 1st wicket and the county reached the highest score ever made against the Minor Counties in the competition. Benjamin's bowling performance was also the best registered against them. Potter, like Alec Stewart and Neil Lenham, who played splendidly in Sussex's important victory over Somerset, won his first Gold Award.

Sport Aid Match

20 May

at Edgbaston
West Indies 78 for 1
v. **Rest of the World**
Match abandoned

Rain restricted this worthy game to 13.3 overs during which Greenidge was caught by Kapil Dev off Botham 11, Richardson batted excitingly for 39 and Clive Lloyd made 21. Generous sponsorship from Colegate, Grocery World and others helped to stage this match which drew a capacity crowd, and large sums of money were raised for famine relief.

On the eve of this match, Ian Botham was withdrawn from the England party to play in the Texaco Trophy matches against India and, later, after a disciplinary hearing, he was banned from first-class cricket until the end of July. In a front page statement in a Sunday newspaper, Botham had admitted to taking drugs in the past. The statement was made to bring to an end an astronomically expensive libel action that he had brought against the newspaper concerned. He was

Neil Lenham, a young batsman of immense potential, who won his first Benson and Hedges Gold Award for Sussex against Somerset, 19 May. (Mark Leech)

BELOW: *The teams pose for the Sport Aid match, West Indies v. Rest of the World, Edgbaston, 20 May. (Ken Kelly)*

suspended from first-class cricket because it was considered that he had brought the game into disrepute and had lied to the TCCB. There were those who believed that these misdemeanours should have been ignored, and happily there was a saner majority with the interests of the future of the game at heart who believed that the TCCB had been reasonable in both their judgement and their punishment. No one disputes Botham's wonderful abilities as a cricketer and as an entertainer, nor can one ignore the man's vitality and infectious enthusiasm, but he has not always chosen his advisers wisely. His vision has often been blurred, and on more than one occasion he has supposed a 'bush' a 'bear'. There are those who would cast him in the role of some peasant leader struggling against authority, but this would be a gross distortion of his true posture. He has won fame, fortune and an ardent following among young people, but the responsibilities that come with such adulation have not always been met. The TCCB is the corporate voice of the seventeen counties. Their judgement is not infallible, but their voice should be heeded, for it is the voice of cricket. Ian Botham is a very great cricketer. What we now looked to was that he should become an equally great man.

21, 22 and 23 May

at Canterbury

Kent 378 for.6 (M.R. Benson 128, N.R. Taylor 64, C.J. Tavare 58)
v. **Indians**

Match abandoned

at Chelmsford

Essex 295 (B.R. Hardie 110, P.J. Prichard 82, P.W. Jarvis 6 for 78) and 34 for 0 dec
Yorkshire 51 for 0 dec and 252 (P.J. Hartley 87 not out, A.A. Metcalfe 57, D.R. Pringle 7 for 46)

Essex won by 26 runs
Essex 19 pts, Yorkshire 4 pts

at Lord's

Glamorgan 159 (M.P. Maynard 57, W.W. Daniel 4 for 34)
Middlesex 81 for 4

Match drawn
Middlesex 4 pts, Glamorgan 2 pts

at Trent Bridge

Leicester 312 for 9 dec (D.I. Gower 82, J.J. Whitaker 76, P.A.J. de Freitas 55, R.J. Hadlee 5 for 41) and 0 for 0 dec
Nottinghamshire 0 for 0 dec and 315 for 5 (R.T. Robinson 104, C.E.B. Rice 86)

Nottinghamshire won by 5 wickets
Nottinghamshire 20 pts, Leicestershire 4 pts

at Taunton

Somerset 348 (R.J. Harden 81, V.J. Marks 65, I.T. Botham 61, C.A. Walsh 4 for 72) and 0 for 0 dec
Gloucestershire 19 for 0 dec and 211 (C.W.J. Athey 75, J. Garner 4 for 35)

Somerset won by 118 runs
Somerset 20 pts, Gloucestershire 3 pts

A capacity crowd is disappointed in spite of the efforts of groundsman Rob Franklin who received the Man of the Match award for his endeavours. (Ken Kelly)

at Hove

Surrey 365 (G.S. Clinton 98, M.A. Lynch 59, A.R. Butcher 50)
Sussex 38 for 2

Match drawn
Sussex 4 pts, Surrey 4 pts

at Edgbaston

Warwickshire 165 and 231 for 7 dec (T.A. Lloyd 64, P.A. Smith 51, B.M. McMillan 50 not out)
Northamptonshire 124 for 3 dec (R.J. Bailey 83) and 232 for 7 (R.A. Harper 59 not out, A.J. Lamb 52, N. Gifford 4 for 78)

Match drawn
Northamptonshire 4 pts, Warwickshire 2 pts

at Worcester

Lancashire 279 (N.H. Fairbrother 54, N.V. Radford 5 for 77) and 43 for 1 dec
Worcestershire 0 for 0 dec and 319 (D.B. d'Oliveira 89, S.J. Rhodes 61, D.J. Makinson 4 for 80)

Lancashire won by 3 runs
Lancashire 19 pts, Worcestershire 4 pts

at Cambridge

Hampshire 244 for 4 dec (V.P. Terry 70, D.R. Turner 69 not out, R.A. Smith 58) and 91 for 5 dec (J.E. Davidson 5 for 35)
Cambridge University 129 (R.J. Maru 5 for 38) and 98 for 8

Match drawn

Eighty minutes play at Canterbury was all that was possible on Wednesday, 21 May. Benson hit a century and Kent batted throughout the second day, earning a satirical rebuke from Gavaskar who was not playing. There was no play on the third day. Play was possible only on the second day at Lord's and Hove. At Lord's, Keith Brown held three catches in 7 balls off Daniel and Glamorgan despaired at 25 for 5. Matthew Maynard then batted very well to revive the Welshmen, and Middlesex struggled in their turn against Thomas and Moseley.

Clinton hit 14 fours and batted for 217 minutes to provide the backbone to Surrey's enterprising 365 in 101 overs against Sussex who lost Lenham and Parker to Clarke before the match came to its premature close.

Northants enjoyed a good start against Warwickshire at Edgbaston, for, having dismissed the home side for 165, they romped to 124 in 24.5 overs, Geoff Cook declaring when Bailey's sparkling innings came to a close. Poor Robin Dyer collected his second 'duck' of the day, but on the last day, Lloyd and Smith took their stand to 119 and eventually Gifford asked Northants to make 273 in 52 overs. The visitors began well, but Gifford thwarted them with some good control which accounted for Geoff Cook, Lamb, Capel and Ripley and left Harper without the necessary support to maintain the challenge.

David Gower and John Whitaker added 137 for Leicestershire's 4th wicket after Hadlee had threatened to demolish the visitors at Trent Bridge. Each side forfeited an innings and Notts were left to make 313 in 92 overs. Broad fell at 14 and Randall at 73, but Rice and Robinson paced the innings finely and 100 were needed from the last 20 overs. Their stand had realised 147 when Robinson, having hit his first century of the season, was run out by de Freitas. Rice and Johnson were also dismissed, but Birch hit lustily so that Notts won with 7 balls to spare.

A championship best 81 by Richard Harden and enterprising knocks from emergency opener Marks and from Ian Botham took Somerset to maximum batting points and gave them a platform for victory. The home county forfeited their second innings, and Gloucestershire had to make 330 in a minimum of 90 overs for victory. Garner had Stovold taken at slip off the third ball of the innings, and in spite of suggestions of aggression by Romaines and Athey, Gloucestershire never looked likely to combat the bowling of Garner, Dredge and Taylor, and the match was over with 27 overs remaining.

Jim Davidson, the University seam bowler, returned a career best in Hampshire's second innings at Fenner's where Cambridge held on narrowly for a draw.

Hardie and Prichard, who had to retire hurt for 90 minutes after being hit on the arm, batted admirably on a Chelmsford wicket which always gave hope to the bowler. Yorkshire, looking a little lax in the field, did not make the most of the conditions excepting Paul Jarvis who bowled well, keeping the ball up to the bat and accounting for Hardie, Prichard,

Peter Hartley – impressive bowling and heroics with the bat for Yorkshire against Essex at the end of May. (George Herringshaw)

Border, Fletcher, Lilley and Acfield, an impressive haul. Last day sacrifices and mathematics meant that Yorkshire had to score 279 in 70 overs to win. Ravaged by Derek Pringle, they slipped to 120 for 8 and Essex were on the point of victory. Remarkably, Peter Hartley and Paul Jarvis added 124 in 20 overs. Both batsmen reached career best scores, Jarvis hit a six and 6 fours and Hartley hit 12 fours in his 95-ball innings. Pringle returned to dismiss Jarvis and Fletcher and give Essex their first championship win of the season.

Lancashire went to the top of the Britannic Assurance County Championship with a most dramatic win at Worcester. They encountered early problems against Radford, but sturdy play by the later batsmen took them to 279. Forfeiture and romp began the last day, and Worcestershire were left needing 323 from 87 overs. Undeterred by the loss of 3 wickets for 69, Worcestershire maintained their challenge. D'Oliveira gave the early impetus, but he fell to Watkinson who had changed to off-spin, and the home side were 189 for 6 with 32 overs remaining. Rhodes hit excitingly and made 61 off 91 balls before being caught off Makinson. Radford fell two balls later, and Worcestershire were 24 short of of victory with their last pair together. Illingworth and Inchmore pushed and scurried, and when Allott began the last over only 5 were needed, but, on the second ball, Fairbrother hit the stumps with a direct throw as Illingworth backed up, and Lancashire were victors by 3 runs.

24, 25 and 26 May

at Derby

Nottinghamshire 279 (C.E.B. Rice 120, G. Miller 4 for 88) and 235 for 6 dec (P. Johnson 71)
Derbyshire 151 (R.J. Finney 54, R.J. Hadlee 6 for 31) and 248 for 9 (J.E. Morris 89, C. Marples 50 not out, J.A. Afford 5 for 71)

Match drawn
Nottinghamshire 7 pts, Derbyshire 5 pts

24, 26 and 27 May

at Cardiff

Glamorgan 314 for 7 dec (R.C. Ontong 78, H. Morris 67, J.G. Thomas 50 not out, V.J. Marks 6 for 112) and 243 (J. Derrick 61 not out, V.J. Marks 8 for 100)
Somerset 359 (I.V.A. Richards 136) and 111 for 6 (R.C. Ontong 4 for 10)

Match drawn
Glamorgan 6 pts, Somerset 6 pts

at Bournemouth

Gloucestershire 296 for 7 dec (A.W. Stovold 65, K.M. Curran 62, P.W. Romaines 52) and 150 for 6 dec (M.D. Marshall 6 for 51)
Hampshire 190 (C.A. Walsh 5 for 68) and 110 (C.A. Walsh 6 for 26)

Gloucestershire won by 146 runs
Gloucestershire 22 pts, Hampshire 2 pts

at Lord's

Middlesex 342 for 9 dec (G.D. Barlow 107, A.J.T. Miller 73, R.O. Butcher 50) and 70 (Imran Khan 8 for 34)
Sussex 300 for 5 dec (P.W.G. Parker 107, A.M. Green 88, Imran Khan 60) and 113 for 3

Sussex won by 7 wickets
Sussex 22 pts, Middlesex 6 pts

at Northampton

Northamptonshire 273 (D.J. Capel 111, R.J. Bailey 88, P.A.J. de Freitas 5 for 54, J.P. Agnew 4 for 81) and 318 for 5 (R.J. Bailey 106, D.J. Capel 60 not out, R.A. Boyd-Moss 53)
Leicestershire 371 (N.E. Briers 83, P. Whitticase 57, R.A. Harper 5 for 84)

Match drawn
Northamptonshire 5 pts, Leicestershire 5 pts

at Edgbaston

Worcestershire 360 for 8 dec (D.M. Smith 102, P.A. Neale 84 not out, G.A. Hick 62) and 146 (G.A. Hick 53, G.C. Small 5 for 35, N. Gifford 4 for 34)
Warwickshire 301 for 5 dec (P.A. Smith 119, T.A. Lloyd 70) and 134 (D.N. Patel 4 for 37)

Worcestershire won by 71 runs
Worcestershire 22 pts, Warwickshire 7 pts

at Leeds

Lancashire 296 (C. Maynard 132 not out, P.J.W. Allott 65, P.W. Jarvis 5 for 86) and 268 for 7 dec (G.D. Mendis 62, P. Carrick 4 for 114)
Yorkshire 314 (P. Carrick 50, P.J.W. Allott 4 for 68) and 90 for 1

Match drawn
Yorkshire 8 pts, Lancashire 7 pts

The top of the table struggle between Lancashire and Yorkshire ended as dourly as its eight immediate predecessors. On the opening day, Lancashire were in chaotic

Chris Maynard, a maiden century for Lancashire in the Roses Match, 24–26 May. (Sporting Pictures UK Ltd)

retreat at 47 for 5, Jarvis and Sidebottom being the pursuers, but Watkinson and Maynard added 84 in 28 overs. More impressively, Maynard and Allott put on 134 in 38 overs for the 8th wicket. The wicket-keeper reached the first century of his career, and with Yorkshire 7 for the loss of Moxon by the close, Lancashire were on top. Consistent batting from the middle order and a good rearguard action revived them on the Monday, and the Lancashire batting and lack of penetration in both attacks determined a draw from that point on.

Derbyshire surprisingly forced a draw with Nottinghamshire after looking well beaten for most of the match. A century from Clive Rice and some excellent pace bowling from Richard Hadlee gave Notts a first innings lead of 128. Rice was able to declare his second innings and leave his bowlers the best part of a day in which to bowl out the home side. Victory for Notts seemed a formality when Derbyshire were 26 for 6, but Morris and Finney added 121 in 43 overs of defiance. Both fell to Afford, but neither he nor Hemmings could provide the ultimate penetration and although Hadlee repeatedly beat the bat in the closing stages, Marples and Mortensen survived.

Richards enlivened the game at Cardiff with a sparkling hundred which took Somerset to a first innings lead over Glamorgan who had batted with some sparkle themselves on the Saturday. Vic Marks ended with the best match figures of his career when he added 8 for 100 on the last day to his 6 for

ABOVE: *Vic Marks, 14 wickets at Cardiff but no victory for Somerset. (George Herringshaw)*

112 on the first. This left Somerset a target of 199 in 27 overs. Botham and Richards opened in violent fashion, but Ontong took 4 wickets for 1 run in 7 balls, and Somerset were thankful to draw.

Mark Nicholas won the toss and asked Gloucestershire to bat first at Bournemouth on a green wicket. His delight was short-lived, for Stovold and Romaines put on 106 for the 1st wicket, and eventually Gloucestershire batted out the day in solid fashion that gave no hint of delight. On the Monday, Walsh and Payne exploited the pitch far better than the home bowlers had done, and in spite of Marshall's fine bowling in the second innings, Hampshire were left to make 257 in 62 overs. Terry and Chris Smith began with a stand of 57, but thereafter, Walsh, Lawrence and Payne dominated, and Gloucestershire gained their first championship win of the season.

On the first day at Lord's, Middlesex looked well placed. Barlow and Miller opened the match with a stand of 194 after Gould had put Middlesex in. There was some faltering against the unvaried attack of seven fast or medium paced bowlers, but the reigning champions ended the day strongly. An obdurate century from Parker, who shared stands of 158 with Green and 107 with Imran, allowed Sussex to declare 42 runs behind, and the Pakistan captain dismissed Barlow and the night-watchman before the close. On the last morning, Imran produced some outstanding fast bowling on a lively, but never lethal, wicket. He took a career best 8 for 34 as Middlesex were routed for 70 and Sussex moved to a comfortable win. Imran bowled unchanged in the innings, his 14.3 overs containing 4 maidens.

Two young players of great promise, Bailey and Capel, batted finely in both innings at Northampon in what was otherwise a meaningless draw. Capel's 111 in the first innings was his career best score.

Another to hit a career best was Paul Smith of Warwickshire who reached a maiden century on the second day at Edgbaston. With David Smith challenging for an England place and Hick and Neale in fine form, Worcestershire reached 360 for 8 in 94 overs on the first day and captured the wicket of the luckless Robin Dyer, run out for 0, before the close. On the second day, Lloyd and Smith extended their stand to 110 and the ebullient, though increasingly more controlled, Smith reached his century and brought Warwickshire to a position of near parity. The final day showed a complete contrast to what had gone before. Seventeen wickets fell as Worcestershire, resuming at 103 for 3, disintegrated to 146 all out against Gifford and Small, and Warwickshire, needing only 206 for victory, slid to 26 for 5 and were all out for 134. Spinners Patel and Illingworth were Warwickshire's main destroyers, but as the nature of the pitch had not changed drastically, the slaughter of the last day remained something of a mystery.

John Player Special League
25 May

at Cardiff
Glamorgan 216 for 4 (H. Morris 57, G.C. Holmes 55)

LEFT: *Imran Khan, Sussex, devastated Middlesex with bat and ball at Lord's, 24–27 May. (Mark Leech)*

Somerset 217 for 7

Somerset (4 pts) won by 3 wickets

at Canterbury

Kent 187 for 9 (E.A.E. Baptiste 52)
Surrey 187 for 9 (A.R. Butcher 64, E.A.E. Baptiste 4 for 22)

Match tied
Kent 2 pts, Surrey 2 pts

at Northampton

Northamptonshire 202 for 7 (R.J. Bailey 89, D.J. Capel 54)
Leicestershire 155 for 8

Northamptonshire (2 pts) won by 47 runs

at Hove

Sussex 221 for 5 (P.W.G. Parker 78, A.M. Green 58)
Gloucestershire 107 (D.A. Reeve 4 for 22)

Sussex (4 pts) won by 114 runs

at Edgbaston

Warwickshire 174 for 7 (A.I. Kallicharran 101)
Worcestershire 175 for 6 (D.M. Smith 64 not out)

Worcestershire (4 pts) won by 4 wickets

at Sheffield

Essex 162 for 9
Yorkshire 164 for 8 (N.A. Foster 4 for 38)

Yorkshire (4 pts) won by 2 wickets

ABOVE: *Monkhouse, stumped Richards for 10 as Kent and Surrey tie in the Sunday League game at Canterbury, 25 May. (Tom Morris)*
BELOW: *David East appeals and Bairstow is lbw, but Yorkshire won the Sunday League game on the last ball of the match, 25 May. (George Herringshaw)*

Kent lost their place at the head of the Sunday League table when they tied with Surrey at Canterbury. Surrey, without Lynch who was omitted for disciplinary reasons, set off in search of 188 to win in good shape, Butcher and Needham playing well, but the last ball arrived with the scores level and Feltham was run out as he attempted to scramble the necessary run. Meanwhile, Yorkshire went clear top of the League and ended Essex's run of 16 consecutive victories in one-day matches in sensational manner. Bolstered by Keith Pont and Turner, Essex reached 162, and this score looked enough for victory when Yorkshire were reduced to 102 for 8 in 32 overs. Sidebottom and Jarvis then combined in an heroic stand which meant that 12 were needed off the last over and eventually 6 off the last ball which Sidebottom flailed over long-on for the winning runs. Kallicharran showed Warwickshire how much they needed him, but still finished on the losing side, and Bailey and Capel impressed with a 3rd wicket stand of 113 at Northampton. Green and Parker put on 112 for Sussex's 1st wicket at Hove, and Botham hit well as Somerset won with 5 balls to spare at Cardiff.

Texaco Trophy

First Texaco One-Day International
ENGLAND v. INDIA

Athey, who had been called in to the England party as replacement for Botham, was named as twelfth man and Edmonds was the other unlucky player from the thirteen.

Gower, who had been appointed captain for the Texaco Trophy matches and for the first Test and so was under another period of probation, lost the toss and England had

Gooch pulls Chetan Sharma in the first match at The Oval. (Adrian Murrell)

Fowler is run out by Pandit. (Mark Leech)

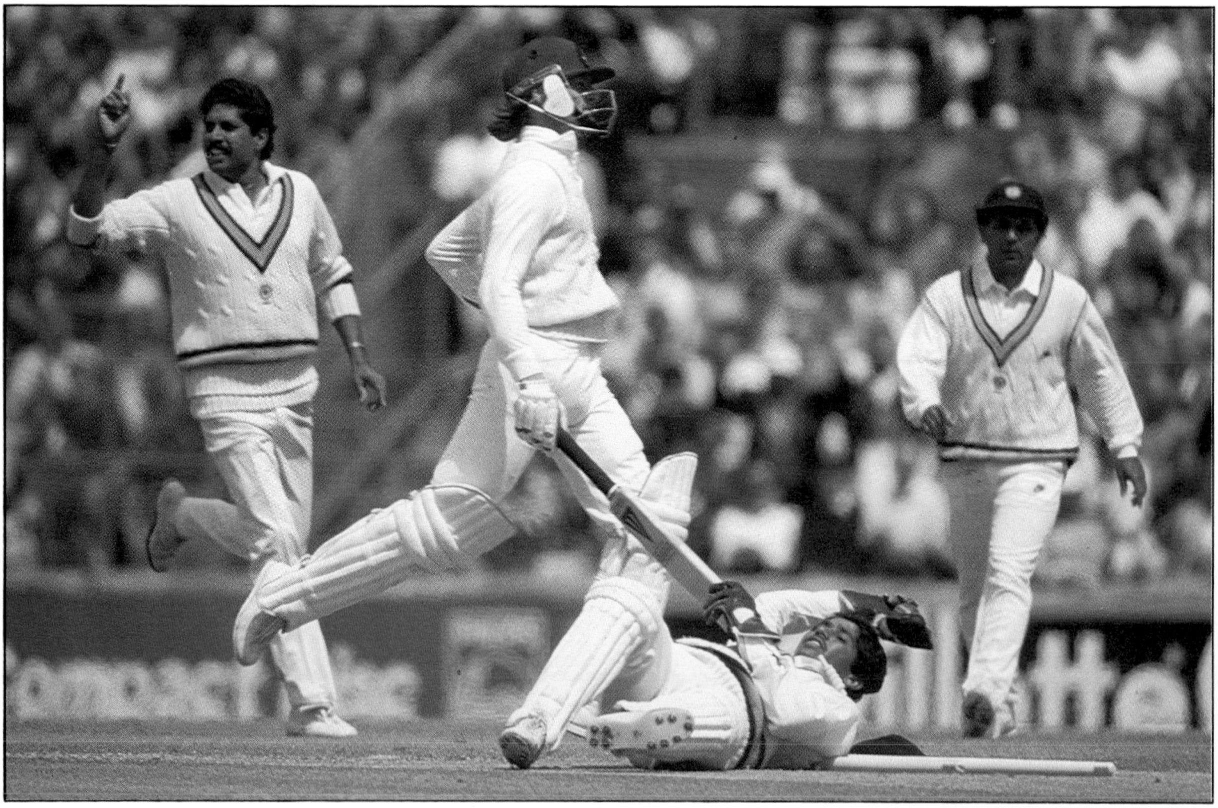

to bat first. This did not seem to be a daunting task as the pitch appeared to hold no terrors. Gooch and Fowler, a late replacement for Slack, began well enough, but Fowler, after his horrendous season in 1985, was naturally tentative and became bogged down. In 21 overs, they had put on 54 and a period of stagnation threatened. Gooch tried to break loose and pulled Chetan Sharma to square-leg where Azharuddin juggled momentarily before taking a straightforward catch.

Maninder Singh had already threatened menace with a tantalising opening over in which Fowler had been missed at slip, India's one error of the day, but it was the Sikh who accounted for Fowler from the field. Shastri bowled the 23rd over and Fowler cut him to Maninder who misfielded, but quickly recovered. Fowler, coming back for a second run, watched the fielder and not his partner Gatting, who must also take blame for what occurred. The batsmen collided and Fowler was run out as Pandit sprawled into the stumps. Gower was out first ball, lofting gently to mid-wicket, and Lamb confronted the spin of Shastri and Maninder as if it were an unknown alphabet. He played Maninder towards mid-wicket and was placidly caught at mid-off.

England were ill at ease and although Gatting and Pringle took them past the hundred, they suggested neither permanence nor the ability to accelerate. Gatting swatted Shastri to extra-cover, and the two left-arm spinners had vanquished the vaunted England middle-order. Pringle made them in singles, but Downton cut Binny to Azharuddin, and Binny himself took a splendid low down return catch to account for Ellison. Pringle finally hooked high to give Azharuddin his third catch, and Pandit whose

ABOVE: *Fowler nibbles at a ball outside the off stump bowled by Chetan Sharma. (Adrian Murrell)*
BELOW: *Ellison is magnificently caught and bowled by Binny. (Adrian Murrell)*

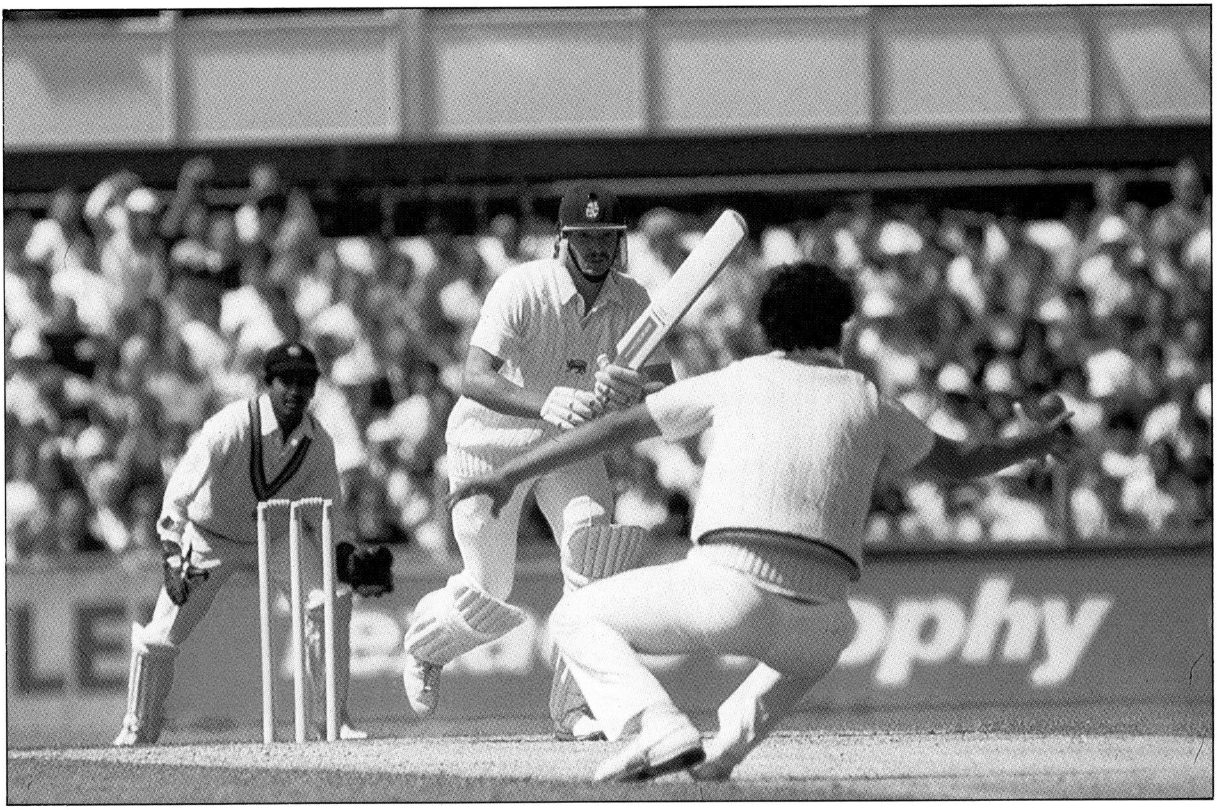

OPPOSITE LEFT: *Dilley drops a simple return catch offered by Gavaskar. (Adrian Murrell)*

OPPOSITE RIGHT: *Man of the Match Azharuddin. (Mark Leech)*

enthusiasm could not conceal imperfections in his wicket-keeping took a simple chance to dismiss Dilley. Emburey pushed a few with Taylor, and England ended on a miserable 162.

Dilley made a romantic return to international cricket when he had Srikkanth caught behind off a very good first ball. He might also have caught and bowled Gavaskar a little later, but from then on the Indian batsmen dominated. Azharuddin, in particular, playing strongly off the back foot, gave a most impressive display. Here is a batsman of such class as to conjure visions of a future studded with diamonds of great wealth. He had arrived in England as the man who had scored centuries in each of his first three Test matches, but had done little since. Now he emerged as no passing wonder, but as a batsman of such variety and technical accomplishment as to place him on the very highest level in the history of the game. To bat with Gavaskar and not to suffer in comparison is in itself praise enough.

Azharuddin and Gavaskar also gave the England batsmen a lesson in how to run between the wickets which had been an apparent weakness in the West Indies, and India won with 7.4 overs and 9 wickets to spare.

OPPOSITE: *Pandit leaps in appeal, but Pringle survives. Maninder Singh is the bowler. (Adrian Murrell)*

Second Texaco One-Day International
ENGLAND v. INDIA

Edmonds for Taylor was the only change in either side for the second match of the series. This time Gower won the toss and it was India who batted first. Srikkanth played a maiden from Dilley, and then Gavaskar, having driven Ellison's first ball majestically for 4, was caught at slip off the last ball of the second over. Srikkanth was soon hitting the ball powerfully, but Azharuddin could not find his touch and he was eventually brilliantly caught by Gower. The batsman, in his frustration, lashed Edmonds over mid-on, but Gower, reeling backwards, held the ball right-handed high above his head.

Vengsarkar suggested contemptuous ease, but he lost Srikkanth who, having hit 5 fours and faced 93 balls, was caught in the deep off Emburey. Vengsarkar himself became too contemptuous and was bowled by Emburey when, in dodging about to unsettle the bowler, he succeeded only in unbalancing himself.

India lunched at 130 for 4, but Patil was bowled by the first ball after the interval. This brought Kapil Dev and Shastri together in a thrilling stand which realised 104 in 16 overs. The Indian captain should have been stumped off Emburey when he was 23, and this cost England dear, for India scored 90 from the last 10 overs. Kapil's 51 came off 45 balls and Shastri's 62 off 72, and England were left staggering on the ropes at the end of their spree which, while aggressive, was never profane in the manner of accomplishment.

England started badly. In the 7th over, Gooch was adjudged lbw to a ball which flicked his pad and went

---

FIRST TEXACO ONE-DAY INTERNATIONAL – ENGLAND v. INDIA
24 May 1986 at The Oval

ENGLAND				INDIA			
G.A. Gooch	c Azharuddin, b Sharma	30		K. Srikkanth	c Downton, b Dilley	0
G. Fowler	run out	20		S.M. Gavaskar	not out	65
M.W. Gatting	c Kapil Dev, b Shastri	27		M. Azharuddin	not out	83
D.I. Gower†	c Kapil Dev, b Shastri	0		D.B. Vengsarkar		
A.J. Lamb	c Kapil Dev, b Maninder Singh	0		S.M. Patil		
D.R. Pringle	c Azharuddin, b Sharma	28		R.J. Shastri		
P.R. Downton*	c Azharuddin, b Binny	4		R.N. Kapil Dev†		
R.M. Ellison	c and b Binny	10		C.S. Pandit*		
J.E. Emburey	run out	20		Chetan Sharma		
G.R. Dilley	c Pandit, b Sharma	6		R.M.H. Binny		
L.B. Taylor	not out	1		Maninder Singh		
Extras	b 1, lb 10, w 3, nb 2	16		Extras	lb 9, w 4, nb 2	15
	(55 overs)	162			(47.2 overs) (for 1 wicket)	163

	O	M	R	W		O	M	R	W
Kapil Dev	11	1	32	—	Dilley	11	—	53	1
Binny	11	2	38	2	Taylor	7	1	30	—
Chetan Sharma	11	2	25	3	Pringle	8.2	4	20	—
Maninder Singh	11	1	31	1	Ellison	10	1	36	—
Shastri	11	—	25	2	Emburey	11	2	15	—

FALL OF WICKETS
1- 54, 2- 67, 3- 67, 4- 70, 5- 102, 6- 115, 7- 131, 8- 138, 9-151

FALL OF WICKETS
1- 0

Umpires: D.R. Shepherd & A.G.T. Whitehead

Man of the Match: M. Azharuddin

India won by 9 wickets

LEFT: *Srikkanth in glory. (Adrian Murrell)*

through to the wicket-keeper, and three overs later, Binny made another of his marvellous sprawling caught and bowled efforts to get rid of Fowler. Gower and Lamb then had the double mission of redeeming themselves and their side. They did so. In 24 overs they added 115, and their partnership was broken in the unluckiest way. Gower drove at Chetan Sharma who stuck out his foot to deflect the ball on to the stumps with Lamb out of his ground.

When Gower's high-class innings came to an end after 94 balls England still needed 98 for victory, but Gatting and Pringle rose to the occasion in fine style to add 85 in 14 overs before Gatting was run out. Pringle has never batted better for England and it was he who nursed the side to victory when 27 were needed from the last 4 overs. He lashed Sharma for his 3rd four in 52 balls and England were home with 7 deliveries to spare.

Gower was named Man of the Match and England's Man of the Series, which suggests that Texaco need to look more closely at their selection of adjudicators or was the panel not counting the first match. Shastri was India's Man of the Series.

India rightly took the Texaco Trophy on the faster scoring rate over the two games, and they left one with the sneaking impression that they were a better batting side, better fielding side and ran better between the wickets than England, and that their bowling had been grossly underrated and could well prove too much for England in the coming Tests.

The Texaco weather once again was perfection, and the organisation, hospitality and public relations exemplary.

LEFT: *Kapil Dev drives with tremendous power at Old Trafford. (Adrian Murrell)*

BELOW: *Allan Lamb at his best as England win the second Texaco Trophy match. (Adrian Murrell)*

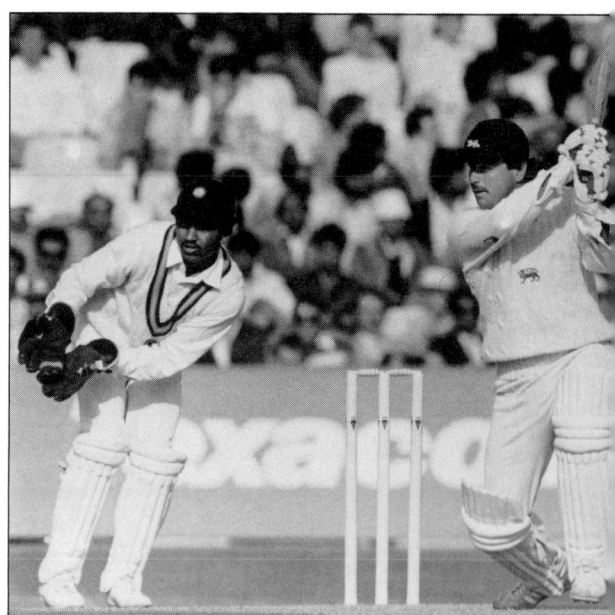

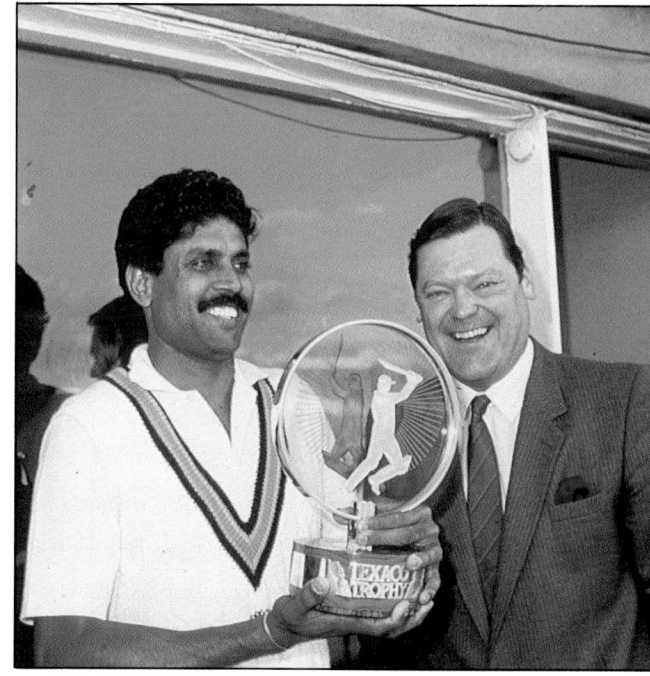

ABOVE: *To the victor the spoils. Kapil Dev receives the Texaco Trophy. (Adrian Murrell)*

LEFT: *David Gower, Man of the Match, in violent mood. (Adrian Murrell)*

SECOND TEXACO ONE-DAY INTERNATIONAL – ENGLAND v. INDIA
26 May 1986 at Old Trafford, Manchester

INDIA			
K. Srikkanth	c Fowler, b Emburey	67
S.M. Gavaskar	c Gooch, b Ellison	4
M. Azharuddin	c Gower, b Edmonds	7
D.B. Vengsarkar	b Emburey	29
S.M. Patil	b Dilley	12
R.J. Shastri	not out	62
R.N. Kapil Dev†	c Downton, b Dilley	51
C. Sharma	not out	8
C.S. Pandit*		
R.M. H. Binny		
Maninder Singh		
Extras	b 5, lb 4, w 2, nb 3	14
(55 overs)	(for 6 wickets)	254

	O	M	R	W
Dilley	11	2	46	2
Ellison	11	—	55	1
Pringle	11	—	49	—
Edmonds	11	1	49	1
Emburey	11	1	46	2

FALL OF WICKETS
1-4, 2-49, 3-109, 4-117, 5-130, 6-234

ENGLAND			
G.A. Gooch	lbw, b Kapil Dev	10
G. Fowler	c and b Binny	10
D.I. Gower†	b Binny	81
A.J. Lamb	run out	45
M.W. Gatting	run out	39
D.R. Pringle	not out	49
P.R. Downton*	not out	4
P.H. Edmonds		
J.E. Emburey		
R.M. Ellison		
G.R. Dilley		
Extras	lb 13, w 5	18
(53.5 overs)	(for 5 wickets)	256

	O	M	R	W
Kapil Dev	10	—	41	1
Binny	10	1	47	2
Sharma	9.5	—	49	—
Shastri	11	—	37	—
Maninder Singh	11	—	55	—
Azharuddin	2	—	14	—

FALL OF WICKETS
1-18, 2-27, 3-142, 4-157, 5-242

Umpires: H.D. Bird & D.J. Constant

Man of the Match: D.I. Gower

England won by 5 wickets

Benson and Hedges Cup

Quarter Finals

28 May

at Derby

Derbyshire 238 for 6 (J.E. Morris 65)
Kent 242 for 6 (C.S. Cowdrey 63 not out)

Kent won by 4 wickets
Gold Award – C.S. Cowdrey

28 and 29 May

at Chelmsford

Essex 195 for 9 (C.E.B. Rice 5 for 48)
Nottinghamshire 196 for 7 (R.J. Hadlee 60 not out, C.E.B. Rice 50)

Nottinghamshire won by 3 wickets
Gold Award – C.E.B. Rice

at Worcester

Northamptonshire 233 for 8 (A.J. Lamb 71, R.A. Harper 56)
Worcestershire 234 for 2 (G.A. Hick 103 not out, D.M. Smith 90 not out)

Worcestershire won by 8 wickets
Gold Award – G.A. Hick

at Lord's

Middlesex 256 for 5 (R.O. Butcher 65)
Sussex 172

Middlesex won by 84 runs
Gold Award – R.O. Butcher

ABOVE: *Allan Border – a maiden century for Essex against Derbyshire at Derby, 31 May. (Ken Kelly)*
LEFT: *Chris Cowdrey. A splendid all-round performance won the Kent captain the Gold Award at Derby. (George Herringshaw)*

The weather was less kind to the Benson and Hedges Cup than it had been to the Texaco Trophy, and only the game at Derby was completed in one day.

Derbyshire must have been bitterly disappointed by their defeat at the hands of Kent, for they had seemed to have done enough to be in a winning position until the Cowdrey brothers came together. The home side had started slowly with only 18 runs coming from the first 12 overs in which Barnett had fallen to Ellison. They accelerated impressively, however, and owed much to Morris who again shone brightly as a young batsman of much talent. He hit 3 sixes in his 63. He and Roberts transformed the Derbyshire innings with a stand of 91 in 14 overs, and some lusty blows from Miller and Warner took Derbyshire to a score that had, earlier in the innings, seemed very remote. The wicket was certainly more favourable to Kent than it had been to Derbyshire, but Mortensen, newly capped, and Finney, who removed both Hinks and the dangerous Tavare, exerted restraint on the batting, and when tea arrived Derbyshire were the better placed. Newman had Taylor caught at cover after a stand of 71 in 17 overs with Chris Cowdrey, but Kent needed 103 from their last 14 overs. It was now that Barnett erred. Warner bowled 9.4 wretched overs from which 79 runs were plundered, and although Barnett had 8 possible bowlers

ABOVE: *Keith Fletcher (Essex) grimaces with pain after being hit by a ball from Richard Hadlee (Notts) who looks on in sympathy with Bruce French, Benson and Hedges Quarter Final at Chelmsford. (Adrian Murrell)*

in his side, if one includes himself and Roberts who was keeping wicket, Warner continued to suffer. The Cowdrey brothers set up the victory, and Ellison provided the final flourish with his skipper after Baptiste had gone cheaply. The last 49 runs were made from 5 overs as Kent won with 8 balls to spare.

An even batting display took Middlesex to a position of authority at Lord's where Sussex made an inept reply as Cowans dismissed both openers and Gould at a personal cost of 27 runs. Dermot Reeve was awarded his county cap for Sussex.

There were three county caps awarded at Worcester where the recipients were Hick, Weston and Illingworth. Weston bowled his 11 overs for 23 runs and captured the wicket of Geoff Cook, caught by Hick. Harper, who survived a stumping chance and a missed catch in front of the sight screen, and Lamb revived Northamptonshire with a stand of 120, but Worcestershire always looked the better side. Such an opinion seemed doubtful early on the second day when d'Oliveira was out and the home county needed 182 in 34 overs. Hick now joined Smith and in a masterful display of powerful driving took his side to victory with 16 balls to spare. His century came off 88 deliveries and he hit 2 sixes and 8 fours. The 49th over produced 13 runs and the 50th, in

which Hick reached his hundred, 10. This meant that 3 runs were needed from 3 overs, but only two balls were needed. Hick, anxious to play Test cricket, withdrew from the Zimbabwe side in order to hasten his qualification to play for England. It was a sad blow to his native country, but he had established himself as the most exciting young batsman in county cricket.

Essex did reasonably well to reach 195 on an uneven wicket at Chelmsford, but in spite of Keith Pont's lusty blows and Pringle, given a hero's welcome, batting intelligently, no batsman could build the large innings that was required to take the favourites to a dominant total. They seemed well on top, however, when Robinson and Randall were held at slip and Broad was well caught down the leg side to see Notts end the day in gloom at 39 for 3. On the resumption, Rice, who had bowled admirably, swinging the ball and keeping a full length, played the innings that was needed for his side, and Johnson gave good early support. Birch also batted well when Johnson was caught at slip off Pringle, and although Rice, badly missed at backward square leg, was one of Gooch's three victims, Hadlee hit straight and clean, and Notts looked winners from the moment he came to the wicket. He on drove Foster for 6, pulled Turner over the midwicket boundary and finished the match by driving Lever over mid-off for another 6. It was powerful stuff and Essex were in tatters.

BELOW: *Graeme Hick – Gold Award winner at Worcester. (Ken Kelly)*

Clive Rice led by example and took Notts into the semi-final with an outstanding all-round performance against Essex at Chelmsford. (Adrian Murrell)

28 May

at Downpatrick

Indians 57 for 3
v. Ireland

Match abandoned
Only 18 overs were possible

29 May

at Downpatrick

Indians 210 for 7 (S.M. Patil 61)
Ireland 201 for 6

Indians won by 9 runs

31 May, 1 and 2 June

at Northampton

Indians 301 for 5 dec (M.B. Amarnath 101, M. Azharuddin 100 not out)
Northamptonshire 118 (R.N. Kapil Dev 5 for 35) and 239 for 4 (R.J. Boyd-Moss 79, D.J. Capel 67 not out)

Match drawn

31 May, 2 and 3 June

at Derby

Essex 300 for 7 dec (A.R. Border 110, N.A. Foster 53 not out, K.W.R. Fletcher 53) and 0 for 0 dec.
Derbyshire 44 for 0 dec and 140 (J.K. Lever 5 for 32, J.H. Childs 4 for 36)

Essex won by 116 runs
Essex 20 pts, Derbyshire 3 pts

at Southampton

Nottinghamshire 162 (M.D. Marshall 5 for 38)
Hampshire 80 for 5

Match drawn
Hampshire 4 pts, Nottinghamshire 3 pts

at Tunbridge Wells

Kent 208 for 2 (S.G. Hinks 86, C.J. Tavare 75 not out)
v. Worcestershire

Match drawn
Kent 2 pts, Worcestershire 0 pts

at Old Trafford

Warwickshire 301 for 5 dec (G.W. Humpage 130, M. Asif Din 69, D.J. Makinson 4 for 69) and 120 for 4 dec
Lancashire 152 for 4 dec (M.R. Chadwick 61) and 265 for 8 (C. Maynard 64)

Match drawn
Warwickshire 5 pts, Lancashire 3 pts

at Leicester

Leicestershire 239 (N.E. Briers 81, R.A. Cobb 66) and 149 for 0 dec (L. Potter 81 not out, R.A. Cobb 68 not out)
Gloucestershire 153 for 6 dec and 236 for 4 (A.W. Stovold 61, C.W.J. Athey 61, K.M. Curran 52)

Gloucestershire won by 6 wickets
Gloucestershire 21 pts, Leicestershire 4 pts

at The Oval

Surrey 109 (S.P. Hughes 7 for 35)
Middlesex 162 for 6 (A.J.T. Miller 62)

Match drawn
Middlesex 5 pts, Surrey 2 pts

at Horsham

Sussex v. Somerset

Match abandoned
No points

On Saturday, 31 May, only 8 balls were possible at Northampton, but Gareth Smith, on the occasion of his first-class debut, had Gavaskar caught behind with his second delivery. The following day, Amarnath reached a century before lunch with a six and 17 fours, and Azharuddin, after an uncertain start, reached his century with 13 fours. Northants were then devastated by Kapil Dev who had a spell of 4 wickets in 8 balls without conceding a run.

There were 57 overs on the opening day at Old Trafford, 23 at Leicester and none elsewhere. Warwickshire brought back Kallicharran, for their batting had needed him most urgently, but it was Humpage who put them in a good position on the Monday. Lancashire saved the follow-on and declared, and Gifford's declaration left the home side to make 270 to win. Some fine hitting from Chadwick, Fairbrother

Maynard and Simmons took them to within 15 of the target with one over remaining, but only 10 were scored and the match was drawn.

There was a positive finish at Leicester where Gloucestershire also declared in arrears and Stovold and Romaines served the home county 21 overs of gentle bowling so that a target could be set which was acceptable to both sides. In fact, the target turned out to be 236 in 47 overs. Gloucestershire lost Romaines with a damaged finger, but Athey and Stovold hit 85 in 21 overs, and with Kevin Curran supplying another belligerent knock and David Lawrence hitting 26 violent runs, Gloucestershire won with 9 balls to spare.

Little could be salvaged from the matches at Tunbridge Wells, Southampton or The Oval, but Simon Hughes, ably supported by some fine close catching, did return the best bowling figures of his career as he routed Surrey.

Essex were cheered by Allan Border's first century for the club. It was an admirable innings, for, with Hardie, he added 117 and revived Essex from the depths of 15 for 2. He then shared a stand of 68 with Fletcher, and Foster hit gleefully to take Essex to maximum batting points. The forfeiture of Essex's second innings set Derbyshire a target of 257 in 270 minutes, but they soon lost their way and settled for defence. Anderson batted 30 overs for 25, and Hill 31 for 31, but both fell to the incomparable Lever, and with Childs again bowling his left-arm spin to good effect, Essex won with more than 13 overs remaining.

John Player Special League

1 June

at Derby

Derbyshire 108 for 7 (B. Roberts 53 not out, N.A. Foster 5 for 17)
Essex 111 for 2 (G.A. Gooch 50 not out)

Essex (4 pts) won by 8 wickets

at Southampton

Hampshire 197 for 5 (R.A. Smith 82 not out)
Nottinghamshire 200 for 3 (B.C. Broad 94, R.T. Robinson 67)

Nottinghamshire (4 pts) won by 7 wickets

at Old Trafford

Warwickshire 87 for 3
Lancashire 76 for 5

Warwickshire (4 pts) won by 11 runs

at Leicester

Gloucestershire 132 for 7
Leicestershire 150 for 1 (N.E. Briers 60 not out, D.I. Gower 51 not out)

Leicestershire (4 pts) won on faster scoring rate

at The Oval

Surrey 187 for 5
Middlesex 188 for 7

Middlesex (4 pts) won by 3 wickets

at Horsham

Sussex 108 for 9
Somerset 111 for 2

Somerset (4 pts) won by 8 wickets

ABOVE: *Kane and Abel? Peter Roebuck, the new Somerset captain, in conversation with one of Somerset's most noted supporters, Jeffrey Archer. (Adrian Murrell)*

Trevor Gard is badly injured in the Sunday League match at Horsham, 1 June. (Adrian Murrell)

Only at Southampton and The Oval were there uninterrupted 40-over matches. Lancashire failed to reach their target in a 10-over slog at Old Trafford, Somerset won with 4.5 of their 25 overs left at Horsham and Essex, Gooch and Pringle adding an unbeaten 72, beat Derbyshire with 4 of their 30 overs unused. Briers and Gower shared an unfinished stand of 100 as Leicestershire beat the rain and Gloucestershire. Hampshire were well contained, especially by Cooper, until Robin Smith played as well as he had done all season, but Robinson and Broad began Nottinghamshire's reply with a stand of 159. The run-rate needed increased, however, and when Nicholas dismissed Broad and Johnson with successive deliveries there were problems, but Rice and Hadlee struck some fine blows and victory came with 3 balls to spare.

Viv Richards in unaccustomed role. He takes over behind the stumps for Somerset following Gard's injury. (Adrian Murrell)

1 June

at Dublin

Yorkshire 222 for 6 (J.D. Love 76, D.L. Bairstow 71)
Ireland 101 (P.W. Jarvis 4 for 3)

Yorkshire won by 121 runs

2 June

at Dublin

Yorkshire 207 for 6 (K. Sharp 52)
Ireland 152 for 6

Yorkshire won by 55 runs

4, 5 and 6 June

at Swansea

Essex 366 (A.R. Border 150, C. Gladwin 73, K.W.R. Fletcher 67, E.A. Moseley 4 for 70)

Glamorgan 160 (J.K. Lever 6 for 57) and 133 (J.H. Childs 7 for 51)

Essex won by an innings and 73 runs
Essex 24 pts, Glamorgan 3 pts

at Bristol

Gloucestershire 352 (K.M. Curran 92, J.W. Lloyds 78, G.J. Parsons 5 for 75) and 262 for 4 dec (C.W.J. Athey 98, A.W. Stovold 64)
Warwickshire 300 for 4 dec (A.I. Kallicharran 132 not out, G.W. Humpage 75, T.A. Lloyd 56) and 249 for 8 (D.L. Amiss 104, A.I. Kallicharran 76)

Match drawn
Warwickshire 8 pts, Gloucestershire 5 pts

at Tunbridge Wells

Sussex 246 (P.W.G. Parker 79, I.J. Gould 60 not out, T.M. Alderman 6 for 70) and 173 for 5 dec (D.L. Underwood 4 for 59)
Kent 178 for 6 dec (S.A. Marsh 52 not out) and 77 for 2

Match drawn
Kent 5 pts, Sussex 4 pts

at Hinckley

Surrey 254 (G.S. Clinton 73, A.J. Stewart 56, P.A.J. de Freitas 4 for 67, P.B. Clift 4 for 70) and 164 (W.K.R. Benjamin 5 for 41, J.P. Agnew 4 for 61)
Leicestershire 288 (P.A.J. de Freitas 63, W.K.R. Benjamin 52 not out, R.J. Doughty 4 for 52, A.H. Gray 4 for 92) and 131 for 4 (J.J. Whitaker 88 not out)

Leicestershire won by 6 wickets
Leicestershire 23 pts, Surrey 7 pts

at Trent Bridge

Somerset 459 for 4 dec (P.M. Roebuck 221 not out, R.J. Harden 77, N.A. Felton 51) and 185 for 4 dec (I.V.A. Richards 65)
Nottinghamshire 350 for 5 dec (R.J. Hadlee 129 not out, J.D. Birch 79 not out, B.C. Broad 52, P. Johnson 51) and 157 for 2 (C.E.B. Rice 87 not out, M. Newell 51 not out)

Match drawn
Somerset 6 pts, Nottinghamshire 5 pts

at Worcester

Middlesex 244 (J.D. Carr 84 not out, N.V. Radford 5 for 80) and 176 (A.P. Pridgeon 6 for 52)
Worcestershire 421 for 6 dec (P.A. Neale 118 not out, D.N. Patel 108, G.A. Hick 70)

Worcestershire won by an innings and 1 run
Worcestershire 24 pts, Middlesex 3 pts

at Sheffield

Derbyshire 398 (A. Hill 172, M. Jean-Jacques 73, S.J. Dennis 4 for 89) and 140 for 2 dec (A. Hill 76 not out, J.E. Morris 53 not out)
Yorkshire 259 for 7 dec (K. Sharp 74, A.A. Metcalfe 67, M.A. Holding 4 for 70) and 180 (G. Boycott 69, M.A. Holding 5 for 28)

Derbyshire won by 99 runs
Derbyshire 22 pts, Yorkshire 7 pts

at Oxford

Oxford University 96 (B.P. Patterson 6 for 31) and 285 (D.A. Hagan 88)
Lancashire 320 for 4 dec (J. Abrahams 117, G.D. Mendis 98, N.H. Fairbrother 59 not out) and 63 for 1

Lancashire won by 9 wickets

An emphatic win over Glamorgan which was achieved after only 34 deliveries on the last morning took Essex to the top of the Britannic Assurance County Championship. They had lost Hardie and Prichard early on the opening day, but Allan Border hit his second century of the week and shared stands of 125 with Gladwin, making his first appearance of the season, and 137 with Fletcher. Hopkins was caught behind off Lever before the close, and Glamorgan lost 17 wickets on the second day. Lever wrecked their first innings and John Childs, totally rehabilitated, spun them out in the second. Childs had match figures of 10 for 98 which, like his 7 for 51 in the second innings, represented his best performance for Essex.

Put in to bat at Trent Bridge, Somerset batted into the second day, Roebuck facing 426 balls for his career best 221 not out which spanned more than 8 hours. Notts replied with an innings of contrast, Hadlee reaching 105 off 101 deliveries. Richards and Rice enlivened the last day of a game which, for the most part, was played in bitterly cold weather.

Wretched weather ruined Tunbridge Wells week although Terry Alderman again showed his immense worth to Kent. Sussex were handicapped by an injury to Garth le Roux who broke a finger.

A 5th wicket stand of 182 in 44 overs between Curran and Lloyds took Gloucestershire to a position of strength at Bristol, but on the second day Alvin Kallicharran hit the 80th century of his career and brought Warwickshire back into contention. He and Humpage added 169 for the 4th wicket. Graveney asked Warwickshire to make 315 in 4 hours on the last afternoon, and although David Lawrence removed both openers, Kallicharran and Amiss put on 154 and set their side on the path to victory. Kallicharran was bowled by Graveney, and Amiss sliced the same bowler to cover point shortly after reaching the 98th century of his fine career. In the end, Warwickshire were battling for survival.

Peter Willey, back in the Leicestershire side after his operation and captain in the absence of Gower, asked Surrey to bat first at Hinckley and seemed to have been embarrassed when Faulkner, Clinton and Stewart all scored well so that 150 was passed with only 2 wickets down. Paddy Clift took 4 wickets in a spell which saw Surrey collapse from 185 for 3 to 215 for 9. Pocock and Needham brought the 4th batting point, and Gray and Doughty restricted Leicestershire on the second day. The home side were 173 for 7 until Benjamin, enjoying a splendid season with the bat, joined de Freitas in a stand of 95 in 17 overs. Both batsmen recorded career best scores. Winston Benjamin then took 5 championship wickets in an innings for the first time, and Whitaker played very well to take Leicestershire to their first championship win of the season with 4 overs to spare.

Hit by Test calls, Middlesex were overwhelmed by an enthusiastic Worcestershire side. Carr revived the visitors after they had plummeted to 99 for 5, but Worcestershire ravaged the Middlesex bowling on the second day. Hick hit another blistering 70, and Neale and Patel put on 195, both reaching fine hundreds. On the last day, hopes of Middlesex resistance were ended by Paul Pridgeon who returned his best figures for 10 years. Carr, with 40 not out, was again the top scorer for the losers.

Patrick Patterson returned to Caribbean form for Lancashire as they swamped Oxford University. Gehan Mendis hit his best score for his new county and shared a 2nd wicket stand of 169 with John Abrahams.

For only the second time in 27 years Derbyshire beat Yorkshire. Recovering from a poor start, Derbyshire reached 290 for 9 by the end of the first day. The not out batsmen were Alan Hill and Martin Jean-Jacques, the first in his benefit year, the second making his first-class debut. On the second morning, they extended their stand to 132, a Derbyshire record for the last wicket. Hill reached the highest score of his career, and Jean-Jacques hit a six and 5 fours. He then proceeded to bowl Geoff Boycott with his 5th ball. After Bairstow had declared 139 runs in arrears Hill and Morris scored briskly against generous bowling, and Barnett set Yorkshire a target of 280 in 81 overs. Mortensen quickly accounted for Moxon, and Jean-Jacques for Metcalfe and Sharp, but it was Michael Holding who brought Derbyshire victory with a spell of 5 for 9 in 23 balls.

6 June

at Northampton

Zimbabwe 249 for 6 (A.C. Waller 60)
Northamptonshire 253 for 3 (D.J. Capel 73 not out, R.A. Harper 69 not out, R.J. Bailey 57)

Northamptonshire won by 7 wickets

Deprived of their two leading players, Curran and Hick, who had chosen to further his career in England and hopefully to qualify for the England Test side, Zimbabwe still showed great batting strength and confirmed their position as favourites for the ICC Trophy.

First Cornhill Test Match
ENGLAND v. INDIA

Dilley and Pringle returned to Test duty for England while Robinson retained his place against strong challenges. India gave a first Test cap to Kiran More. Greg Thomas was the unlucky player from England's selected twelve.

Kapil Dev won the toss and in keeping with an increasingly more popular custom asked England to bat. His decision almost had immediate reward, for Robinson must have been perilously close to being lbw to the fifth ball of the match to which he offered no stroke. He was even closer to being run out when Gooch suggested a run and then sent his partner back. Had Kapil Dev hit the wicket with his throw, Robinson would have been out by yards.

The Nottinghamshire opener did not suggest confidence, and Gooch was struggling with his technique. His balance seemed to have deserted him and his front foot was not always getting to the pitch of the ball. He battled gamely and played an innings which, if remote from his usual style and character, was invaluable to his side.

At 66, Robinson was caught at silly mid-off shortly after Maninder Singh had joined the attack. The left-arm spinner bowled with admirable control, intelligence and variety. Warmly received, Gower drove his first ball through the covers for 4, a stroke of lazy majesty. England lunched at 81 for 1 unaware of the terrors in store.

It was Chetan Sharma, the much underrated fast medium bowler, who wrecked England in the early afternoon. Gower attempted to swing him to leg and was caught behind on the off side. Gatting was bowled between bat and pad second

Gooch hits a six during his celebratory hundred in the first Test at Lord's. (Ken Kelly)

Chetan Sharma – five wickets in a Test innings for the first time. (Ken Kelly)

ball, and Lamb, thrusting his bat forward and leaving his feet behind, was taken at short leg. In 11 balls, Chetan Sharma had taken 3 for 6, and England were 98 for 4.

Pringle now played an innings of great maturity and responsibility. With his Essex captain he added 147, a stand which not only revived England but took them to a position of some strength. Chetan Sharma returned to bowl Gooch just before the close. Gooch batted for just under six hours and hit a six and 12 fours. England closed the first day at 245 for 5.

They were all out shortly after lunch on a bitterly cold second day which was fractured by rain. Emburey cut at Kapil Dev and was caught in the gully. Pringle's highest innings in a Test ended when he was beaten by Binny, and Downton became Chetan Sharma's fifth victim on the stroke of lunch. Like Pringle, Chetan Sharma recorded his best Test performance. Ellison was splendidly taken at slip by Kapil Dev, an energetic and encouraging leader, and Dilley was caught by More who had a most impressive debut behind the stumps.

Srikkanth was athletically caught at slip after his usual rollicking start, and some dour batting in the evening took India to 83 for 1 off 51 overs by the close.

On the Saturday the sun shone and the Indian batting flowered. Gavaskar was caught at third slip early on, but Amarnath and Vengsarkar were quickly on the attack, and it took an economic spell from Emburey to quieten Amarnath who took 14 from one over by Dilley. Amarnath fell to Edmonds, lofting to mid-on, but Azharuddin revelled in the conditions, and he and Vengsarkar threatened a partnership of class and longevity which was ended only when Azharuddin drove the ball back at Dilley and was well caught low down.

India now lost their way. Pringle bowled with admirable control and enough movement to raise some doubts while Dilley produced some explosive deliveries and some rank

RIGHT: *Centurion and Man of the Match, Dilip Vengsarkar. It was his third Test match century at Lord's. (Adrian Murrell)*

bad ones. Five wickets for 32 runs, and India still trailed. More then showed a composure, confidence and willingness to hit the bad ball which confirmed his position as a most worthy successor to Kirmani, but when he was lbw to Pringle India led by only 9 runs and Vengsarkar was 95 not out.

Maninder Singh, defending sensibly and once hitting over the top, straight for 4, stayed while 38 runs were added to give India a strong psychological advantage. Moreover, Dilip Vengsarkar became the first overseas batsman to complete three Test hundreds at Lord's. His innings was not only of the greatest value to his side, but it was one of charm and elegance, ever suggesting authority tinged with beauty. He was at the wicket for 248 minutes, facing 241 deliveries and hitting 16 fours. He was particularly delightful in his driving on the on side.

England, 8 for 0 on Saturday evening, were torn apart on the Monday by Kapil Dev and technical deficiencies were magnified for all to see. Robinson was caught at gully when Kapil Dev reared a ball at him from a length. Next over the Indian captain cut a ball back at Gooch to have him lbw, and Gower fell in the same manner so that England had lost their first three batsmen and still not cleared the arrears. In 19 balls, Kapil Dev had taken 3 for 1, and India scented a famous victory.

The gap between Gatting's bat and pad was exposed by Chetan Sharma who nearly bowled him off an inside edge, but Gatting and Lamb counter-attacked to add 50 in 11 overs. England lunched at 89 for 3. Gatting and Lamb fell within quick succession in the afternoon. Lamb, making room, tried to cut Shastri, an unwise shot, and was very well caught behind while Gatting again fell to Chetan Sharma,

FIRST CORNHILL TEST MATCH – ENGLAND v. INDIA
5, 6, 7, 9 and 10 June 1986 at Lord's

ENGLAND

	FIRST INNINGS		SECOND INNINGS	
G.A. Gooch	b Sharma	114	lbw, b Kapil Dev	8
R.T. Robinson	c Azharuddin, b Maninder	35	c Amarnath, b Kapil Dev	11
D.I. Gower†	c More, b Sharma	18	lbw, b Kapil Dev	8
M.W. Gatting	b Sharma	0	b Sharma	40
A.J. Lamb	c Srikkanth, b Sharma	6	c More, b Shastri	39
D.R. Pringle	b Binny	63	c More, b Kapil Dev	6
J.E. Emburey	c Amarnath, b Kapil Dev	7	(9) c and b Maninder	1
P.R. Downton*	lbw, b Sharma	5	(7) c Shastri, b Maninder	29
R.M. Ellison	c Kapil Dev, b Binny	12	(8) c More, b Binny	19
G.R. Dilley	c More, b Binny	4	not out	2
P.H. Edmonds	not out	7	c Binny, b Maninder	7
Extras	lb 15, w 1, nb 7	23	lb 6, w 1, nb 3	10
		294		180

	O	M	R	W	O	M	R	W
Kapil Dev	31	8	67	1	22	7	52	4
Binny	18.2	4	55	3	15	3	44	1
Sharma	32	10	64	5	17	4	48	1
Maninder Singh	30	15	45	1	20.4	12	9	3
Amarnath	7	1	18	—	2	2	0	—
Shastri	10	3	30	—	20	8	21	1

FALL OF WICKETS
1- 66, 2- 92, 3- 92, 4- 98, 5- 245, 6- 264, 7- 269, 8- 271, 9- 287
1- 18, 2- 23, 3- 35, 4- 108, 5- 113, 6- 121, 7- 164, 8- 170, 9- 170

INDIA

	FIRST INNINGS		SECOND INNINGS	
S.M. Gavaskar	c Emburey, b Dilley	34	c Downton, b Dilley	22
K. Srikkanth	c Gatting, b Dilley	20	c Gooch, b Dilley	0
M.B. Amarnath	c Pringle, b Edmonds	69	lbw, b Pringle	8
D.B. Vengsarkar	not out	126	b Edmonds	33
M. Azharuddin	c and b Dilley	33	run out	14
R.J. Shastri	c Edmonds, b Dilley	1	not out	20
R.M.H. Binny	lbw, b Pringle	9		
R.N. Kapil Dev†	c Lamb, b Ellison	1	(7) not out	23
Chetan Sharma	b Pringle	2		
K. More*	lbw, b Pringle	25		
Maninder Singh	c Lamb, b Emburey	6		
Extras	lb 5, w 1, nb 9	15	b 1, lb 9, w 1, nb 5	16
		341	(for 5 wickets)	136

	O	M	R	W	O	M	R	W
Dilley	34	7	146	4	10	3	28	2
Ellison	29	11	63	1	6	—	17	—
Emburey	27	13	28	1				
Edmonds	22	7	41	1	11	2	51	1
Pringle	25	7	58	3	15	5	30	1

FALL OF WICKETS
1- 31, 2- 90, 3- 161, 4- 232, 5- 238, 6- 252, 7- 253, 8- 264, 9- 303
1- 10, 2- 31, 3- 76, 4- 78, 5- 110

Umpires: K.E. Palmer & D.R. Shepherd

India won by 5 wickets

14, 15 and 16 June

at Leicester

Leicestershire 269 (W.K.R. Benjamin 95 not out, C. Sharma 4 for 89) and 244 for 3 dec (R.A. Cobb 80, L. Potter 65)
Indians 272 for 8 dec (M. Azharuddin 142, D.B. Vengsarkar 60, P.B. Clift 4 for 54) and 145 for 4 (K. Srikkanth 90)

Match drawn

at Hove

Sussex 379 for 5 dec (A.M. Green 132, P.W.G. Parker 109, C.M. Wells 69) and 153 for 2 dec
Cambridge University 283 for 3 dec (D.J. Fell 114, D.W. Browne 61 not out) and 97 for 5

Match drawn

14, 16 and 17 June

at Ilford

Hampshire 260 (R.A. Smith 87, R.J. Parks 68, N.A. Foster 5 for 64, D.R. Pringle 5 for 65) and 135 (N.A. Foster 4 for 36)
Essex 198 (A.R. Border 71, C.A. Connor 4 for 54) and 185 (A.R. Border 54, M.D. Marshall 4 for 26)

Hampshire won by 12 runs
Hampshire 23 pts, Essex 5 pts

at Gloucester

Gloucestershire 182 (D.E. Malcolm 5 for 42) and 332 (J.W. Lloyds 111, R.C. Russell 63, D.E. Malcolm 4 for 91)
Derbyshire 313 (K.J. Barnett 95, I.S. Anderson 62, J.E. Morris 56, C.A. Walsh 4 for 84) and 53 for 0

Match drawn
Derbyshire 6 pts, Gloucestershire 2 pts

at Old Trafford

Lancashire 367 for 4 dec (N.H. Fairbrother 131, J. Abrahams 100 not out, G.D. Mendis 66) and 170 for 2 dec (J. Abrahams 73 not out)

Worcestershire 253 (D.N. Patel 94) and 146 for 4

Match drawn
Lancashire 7 pts, Worcestershire 4 pts

at Lord's

Yorkshire 276 (G. Boycott 69, S.N. Hartley 56, P.H. Edmonds 4 for 71) and 153 (N.G. Cowans 4 for 49)
Middlesex 173 (P.W. Jarvis 4 for 45) and 187 (P.W. Jarvis 6 for 47)

Yorkshire won by 69 runs
Yorkshire 22 pts, Middlesex 3 pts

at Northampton

Warwickshire 266 for 8 dec (G.J. Parsons 58 not out) and 230 for 6 dec (P.A. Smith 83, D.L. Amiss 62)
Northamptonshire 202 for 2 dec (A.J. Lamb 79 not out, R.J. Boyd-Moss 66 not out) and 177 (N. Gifford 6 for 27)

Warwickshire won by 117 runs
Warwickshire 17 pts, Northamptonshire 5 pts

at Trent Bridge

Nottinghamshire 294 (J.D. Birch 67 not out, R.T. Robinson 52, A.H. Gray 4 for 59)
Surrey 95 (R.J. Hadlee 4 for 39) and 192 (T.E. Jesty 55, R.J. Hadlee 6 for 33)

Nottinghamshire won by an innings and 7 runs
Nottinghamshire 23 pts, Surrey 4 pts

at Bath

Somerset 433 for 6 dec (I.V.A. Richards 128, B.C. Rose 107 not out, V.J. Marks 68, R.J. Harden 51, T.M. Alderman 4 for 122)
Kent 226 (M.R. Benson 55, J. Garner 4 for 29) and 183 (J. Garner 5 for 56)

Somerset won by an innings and 24 runs
Somerset 24 pts, Kent 4 pts

at Oxford

Oxford University 171 (C.D.M. Tooley 60, D.J. Hickey 5 for 57) and 174
Glamorgan 371 for 5 dec (M.P. Maynard 148, G.C. Holmes 93)

Glamorgan won by an innings and 26 runs

Nottinghamshire whose last 4 wickets produced 100 runs on the Saturday, beat Surrey inside two days. Surrey, 38 for 3 at the close of the first day, were shot out twice on the Monday with Richard Hadlee exploiting a doubtful wicket to take 10 for 72. The win put Nottinghamshire in third place in the Britannic Assurance County Championship table.

Yorkshire moved into second place by beating Middlesex at Lord's for the first time in 11 years. Yorkshire batted rather tediously on the first day, but Middlesex showed the uncertainty of the wicket by surrendering a first innings advantage of 103 to the visitors. In the context of the match it was decisive as could be seen when Yorkshire struggled for the second time in the match. Needing 257 in 90 overs, Middlesex made a useful start, but Jarvis dismissed both Slack and Gatting and maintaining the basic virtues he returned match figures of 11 for 92, emphasising his great talent and taking Yorkshire to a comfortable victory.

LEFT: *Paul Jarvis, 10 for 92 as Yorkshire beat Middlesex at Lord's, 14–17 June. (Simon Miles)*

Essex stayed at the top of the table in spite of losing to Hampshire in a splendid game at Ilford. Electing to bat, Hampshire wilted to 49 for 4 against Foster and Pringle, and even though they were rallied by Robin Smith and David Turner, they were 130 for 7. It was Bobby Parks who lifted them to a third batting point with his best championship score. He is a charming man and an eager cricketer who deserves more praise than he has been given, for he is among the very best of wicket-keepers. He was to catch East off Connor who also sent back Prichard, newly and deservedly capped, while Maru, more significantly, bowled Gooch. On the Monday, 19 wickets fell. Border played a fine innings on a wearing wicket, and Gladwin and Childs gave sensible support, but Essex finished a vital 62 runs behind. Foster, in rich form, broke the back of the Hampshire second innings so that 7 wickets were down for 69, but Cowley and Parks, once again, revived the visitors. Needing 198 to win, Essex lost Gooch and Prichard for 27 before the close. Stubborn resistance from the middle order, Border, Pringle and Lilley, gave Essex hope of victory, but they slipped from 156 for 5 to 159 for 8. Foster then hit powerfully until, having hit one massive six, he attempted another and was caught by Robin Smith off Maru to the delight of the Hampshire players.

Like Hampshire, Somerset celebrated their second victory of the season. They shattered the Kent attack on the opening day with some gloriously positive batting. Richards and Harden added 158 in 37 overs for the 4th wicket, and the great West Indian hit 128 off 138 deliveries. Brian Rose and Vic Marks were equally dominant and shared a 6th wicket stand of 167 in 46 overs, Rose reaching his first century for three seasons. Kent could not match this form and in spite of brave efforts from Benson, Tavare, Chris Cowdrey and Marsh, they succumbed twice to Garner, Marks and Coombs.

Warwickshire gained their first championship win of the season after a dreadfully tedious first innings batting display which saw them reach only 187 for 7 in 100 overs. To their credit, Northants batted in complete contrast. Boyd-Moss and Allan Lamb shared an unbeaten 3rd wicket stand of 137, and Harper declared at 202 after 63 overs. A more positive approach by Warwickshire in their second innings enabled Gifford to declare and set the home side a target of 295. They never looked like getting it as Gifford exploited a wearing pitch to the full after Small had made early inroads.

A side to suffer from their inability to force the pace was Derbyshire for whom Malcolm returned career best bowling figures. Barnett gave his side a fine start with 95 out of an opening stand of 145, but Morris apart, none followed his exciting lead. Nevertheless, Derbyshire seemed set for victory when Gloucestershire lost 5 second innings wickets before clearing the arrears. Jeremy Lloyds and 'Jack' Russell then added 127 and saved the game. Both batted admirably, and Lloyds reached the 7th century of his career.

A stand of 243 between Fairbrother and Abrahams was the highlight of the game at Old Trafford, and Maynard hit his second century of the season for Glamorgan who gained a welcome victory in the Parks. Holmes and Maynard put on 234 for the 4th wicket.

After Neil Lenham had been forced to retire hurt without scoring, Green and Parker took the score to 199 at Hove before being separated. Fell hit a century for Cambridge, but

the match was also drawn. The home side recovered excitingly from 146 for 8 through Benjamin's powerful hitting which brought him a career best. India replied with some lovely batting, Azharuddin completing a fine hundred. Sadly, Leicestershire denied the spirit of the game and allowed the match to die.

John Player Special League

15 June

at Ilford
Essex 256 for 5 (A.R. Border 75, K.W.R. Fletcher 62)
Hampshire 257 for 4 (C.L. Smith 75 not out, M.C.J. Nicholas 53 not out)

Hampshire (4 pts) won by 6 wickets

at Gloucester
Gloucestershire 163 for 7 (C.W.J. Athey 56)
Derbyshire 166 for 5

Derbyshire (4 pts) won by 5 wickets

at Old Trafford
Lancashire 249 for 4 (G. Fowler 107, C.H. Lloyd 64)
Worcestershire 210 for 8 (G.A. Hick 68)

Lancashire (4 pts) won by 39 runs

at Lord's
Yorkshire 210 (K. Sharp 52, J.E. Emburey 4 for 52)
Middlesex 214 for 1 (W.N. Slack 101 not out, A.J.T. Miller 69)

Middlesex (4 pts) won by 9 wickets

at Northampton
Warwickshire 132 for 8
Northamptonshire 133 for 3

Northamptonshire (4 pts) won by 7 wickets

at Trent Bridge
Surrey 193 for 9 (M.A. Lynch 78)
Nottinghamshire 194 for 7 (R.T. Robinson 60)

Nottinghamshire (4 pts) won by 3 wickets

at Bath
Somerset 244 for 6 (P.M. Roebuck 75, B.C. Rose 66)
Kent 141 (G.V. Palmer 4 for 28)

Somerset (4 pts) won by 103 runs

Somerset, with Roebuck hitting 75 off 90 balls and Rose 66 off 65, trounced Kent to go level at the top of the table with Essex and Yorkshire, both of whom lost. Essex reached a formidable total at Ilford, but Hampshire won in remarkable fashion. They were 153 for 4, needing 104 off the last 10 overs, when Nicholas joined Chris Smith. The Hampshire skipper hit 53 off 28 balls, 3 sixes and 3 fours, and saw his side home with 9 balls to spare. Slack and Miller put on 148 for Middlesex's 1st wicket against Yorkshire to assure victory after Emburey had taken four wickets for 11 runs in his final over, the first 7 having cost 41. Fowler and Clive Lloyd put on 101 for the 2nd wicket in Lancashire's victory over

Worcestershire, Notts won a tight game with one ball to spare, and Northants and Derbyshire won more comfortably.

I.C.C. Trophy

16 June

at Sutton Coldfield C.C.
Kenya 82
Zimbabwe 85 for 3
Zimbabwe (2 pts) won by 7 wickets

at Old Edwardians C.C.
Denmark 274 for 7 (S. Mikkelsen 60, O.H. Mortensen 59 not out, S. Henriksen 50)
East Africa 161
Denmark (2 pts) won by 113 runs

at Solihull C.C.
United States 88 (P.J. Bakker 5 for 20)
Holland 89 for 0
Holland (2 pts) won by 10 wickets

at Walsall C.C.
Canada 356 for 5 (P. Prashad 164 not out, D. Singh 65)
Papua New Guinea 267 for 9 (K. Au 67, T. Vai 51, F. Waiteh 4 for 37, D. Etwaroo 4 for 64)
Canada (2 pts) won by 89 runs

at Aldridge C.C.
Israel 86 (T. Burgess 4 for 10)
Bermuda 87 for 1 (W. Reid 63 not out)
Bermuda (2 pts) won by 9 wickets

at Banbury C.C.
Gibraltar 185 for 7 (T. Buzaglo 88)
Fiji 187 for 4 (E. Vaksusa 55)
Fiji (2 pts) won by 6 wickets

The most delightful and most hospitable Midland grounds again provided the settings for the third round of ICC Trophy matches. Traditional strengths came to the fore as Zimbabwe, Denmark, with Ole Mortensen hitting violently, Holland, with Hampshire's Bakker in fine form, and Bermuda won with ease.

18 June

at Fordhouse C.C.
Zimbabwe 357 for 7 (P.W. Rawson 125, G.C. Wallace 77)
Argentina 150
Zimbabwe (2 pts) won by 207 runs

at Moseley Ashfield
Malaysia 239 (A. Stevens 68, Y. Imran 64 not out, J.S. Badshah 4 for 39)
Bangladesh 182 (R. Alam 51, D. John 5 for 40)
Malaysia (2 pts) won by 57 runs

at Halesowen C.C.
Hong Kong 261 for 7 (N. Stearns 86, S. Myles 82)
Canada 265 for 6 (P. Prashad 76, F. Kirmani 51)
Canada (2 pts) won by 4 wickets

at Cannock & Rugeley C.C.
Papua New Guinea 455 for 9 (B. Harry 127, C. Amini 97, A. Leka 69, R. Ila 60 not out, G. De'Ath 5 for 88)
Gibraltar 86 (W. Maha 5 for 12, G. Ravu 4 for 16)
Papua New Guinea (2 pts) won by 369 runs

at Old Silhillians C.C.
Holland 425 for 4 (S. Atkinson 162, R. Lifman 110, R. Gomes 64 not out, S. Lubbers 50)
Israel 158 (D. Moss 62, S. Pearlman 51, R. Elfernik 6 for 21)
Holland (2 pts) won by 267 runs

at Stratford-on-Avon C.C.
Bermuda 224 for 9 (R. Hill 58, A.R. Manders 56)
United States 225 for 7
United States (2 pts) won by 3 wickets

Papua New Guinea established a new record for the competition by scoring 455 off their 60 overs. Babina Harry, at 19 the youngest player on their side, hit a fine century. Holland also reached a massive total. Steve Atkinson, formerly of Durham, and Rob Lifmann shared an opening stand of 251. Prashad continued his heavy scoring for Canada, but Bangladesh and Bermuda were both beaten, so providing the major shocks of the competition.

18, 19 and 20 June

at Ilford
Essex 242 (P.J. Prichard 68, K.W.R. Fletcher 52, N.A. Foster 51 not out, A.C.S. Pigott 5 for 57) and 229 for 5 dec (A.R. Border 96 not out, P.J. Prichard 55)
Sussex 112 (T.D. Topley 5 for 52) and 290 (I.J. Gould 68, D.A. Reeve 51, T.D. Topley 4 for 68, J.H. Childs 4 for 84)
Essex won by 69 runs
Essex 22 pts, Sussex 4 pts

at Swansea
Warwickshire 301 (D.L. Amiss 110, G.W. Humpage 55, J.G. Thomas 4 for 89) and 290 for 3 dec (A.I. Kallicharran 102 not out, T.A. Lloyd 51)
Glamorgan 186 (R.C. Ontong 50) and 121 (K.J. Kerr 5 for 47)
Warwickshire won by 284 runs
Warwickshire 24 pts, Glamorgan 5 pts

at Gloucester
Kent 238 (G.R. Cowdrey 61, C.S. Cowdrey 51, P. Bainbridge 5 for 49) and 113 (C.A. Walsh 4 for 29)
Gloucestershire 125 (T.M. Alderman 6 for 49) and 227 for 6 (A.J. Wright 87, T.M. Alderman 4 for 86)
Gloucestershire won by 4 wickets
Gloucestershire 20 pts, Kent 6 pts

at Basingstoke
Hampshire 410 for 5 dec (R.A. Smith 101, C.G. Greenidge 97, M.D. Marshall 51 not out, M.C.J. Nicholas 50)
Surrey 144 (C.J. Richards 56 not out, M.D. Marshall 4 for 26) and 64 (T.M. Tremlett 4 for 14)
Hampshire won by an innings and 193 runs
Hampshire 24 pts, Surrey 2 pts

at Trent Bridge
Nottinghamshire 192 (N.G. Cowans 4 for 22) and 346 for 4 dec (C.E.B. Rice 156 not out, R.T. Robinson 67, J.D. Birch 54 not out)

Middlesex 135 (J.D. Carr 57, E.E. Hemmings 4 for 12) and 277 (C.T. Radley 58, P.R. Downton 53)

Nottinghamshire won by 126 runs
Nottinghamshire 21 pts, Middlesex 4 pts

at Bath

Northamptonshire 355 for 6 dec (D.J. Capel 103 not out, D.J. Wild 85, R.J. Bailey 69) and 195 (G. Cook 70, G.V. Palmer 4 for 77)
Somerset 228 (I.V.A. Richards 59, J.J.E. Hardy 50) and 241 for 8 (P.M. Roebuck 62, J.J.E. Hardy 50)

Match drawn
Northamptonshire 8 pts, Somerset 4 pts

at Worcester

Yorkshire 405 (A.A. Metcalfe 108, G. Boycott 76, P. Carrick 50 not out) and 196 for 4 dec (M.D. Moxon 82)
Worcestershire 300 for 2 dec (T.S. Curtis 122 not out, D.M. Smith 82) and 248 for 7 (G.A. Hick 60)

Match drawn
Worcestershire 6 pts, Yorkshire 4 pts

Ashley Metcalfe drives on the off side during his innings of 108 for Yorkshire against Worcestershire, 18 June. Rhodes is the wicket-keeper. Metcalfe and Rhodes were young players who had outstanding seasons. (Simon Bruty)

Kevin Sharp is bowled by Phil Newport who is thankful. Yorkshire v. Worcestershire, 18 June. (Simon Bruty)

For the second time in a week Surrey were defeated in two days. Greenidge and Terry began Hampshire's innings with a partnership of 142, and Nicholas declared at the end of 100 overs. Surrey were 21 for 0 at the close of the first day, but gave two wretched performances on the second day, losing 20 wickets while 172 runs were scored. All but one wicket fell to the seam bowlers. The win moved Hampshire into third place in the Britannic Assurance County Championship. It followed their success over Essex, the leaders, who beat Sussex in an extraordinary game at Ilford.

Weakened by injury and Test calls, Essex reached 242 in an innings of fits and starts. Prichard, newly capped, and Fletcher put on 98 for the fourth wicket, and Foster hit fiercely towards the close. Left 14 overs to bat before the end of the day, Sussex lost 6 wickets for 16 runs. As Paul Parker indicated later, the collapse had nothing to do with the wicket; it was simply a bizarre occurence. Imran and Alikhan delayed Essex the following day, but Don Topley finished with career best bowling figures. Border then played a most thrilling innings, hitting 5 sixes in his 110-minute innings before the declaration. Sussex lost both openers for 11 before the close, but they battled tenaciously on the last day. Gould and Alikhan provided the major resistance in late afternoon and there were only 16 balls of the match remaining when East caught Bredin off Acfield.

For Middlesex nothing would go right, and, having bowled Notts out for 192 on the opening day, they still lost by 126 runs. Twenty wickets fell on the first day, but on the second, Rice, sharing century stands with Robinson and Birch, played an innings of great authority and took his side to a point where a declaration left Middlesex the task of scoring 404 to win. The reigning champions batted with greater resilience than they had done in the first innings, but defeat was inevitable.

Gloucestershire moved into fifth place with a fine win over Kent. The Cowdrey brothers added 75 for Kent's fifth wicket, but acting captain Phil Bainbridge took 3 wickets in an over to restore the home side's advantage. It was short-lived, for Terry Alderman exploited a pitch of uneven bounce to reduce Gloucestershire to 76 for 8, the threat of having to follow on looming. Lloyds steered them out of danger, but

Worcester in summer. (David Munden)

they still trailed by 113 on the first innings. Walsh encouraged the home side into positive thinking with aggressive bowling and he was ably supported. Gloucestershire were still faced with a difficult target of 227 to win after 19 wickets had fallen for 212 runs on the second day, but Wright and Stovold began with a solid partnership of 75, and with Wright continuing in determined fashion on the last morning, an excellent victory was achieved.

Warwickshire gained their second championship win of the season when they outplayed Glamorgan at Swansea. Amiss hit the 99th hundred of his career on the opening day which ended with Glamorgan on 72 for 5, and the visitors in total command. Ontong and Steele showed the necessary application to avoid the follow on, but Kallicharran played another forceful innings, and Glamorgan wilted against Gifford and Kerr, the young off-spinner, who took 5 for 47 in what was only his third championship match.

Exhilarating batting by Northamptonshire's younger players, Bailey, Wild and Capel, took the county to a strong position at Bath. Capel and Wild added 105 in 38 overs. Somerset lost Roebuck and Felton for 7, but Marks and Davis, in both innings, saved the home side, first from the follow on and then from defeat after they had been asked to make 323 to win, a task which they had attempted bravely.

Phil Neale asked Yorkshire to bat first at New Road, but saw Boycott and Metcalfe put on 181 after Pridgeon had bowled Moxon at 3. Yorkshire batted into the second day, but Worcestershire responded challengingly, reaching 300 in 82.2 overs. Tim Curtis and David Smith put on 167 in 45 overs. Curtis reached his first century of the season. Ultimately, Bairstow asked Worcestershire to make 302 in 53 overs. The home side reached the last 20 overs with Hick in

full flow and 116 runs needed, but he was caught behind off Neil Hartley, and Newport and Patel were left to fight a rearguard action.

Second Cornhill Test Match
ENGLAND v. INDIA

England had a new captain, Mike Gatting, and showed five changes from the side which lost at Lord's. Slack came in as Gooch's opening partner; French, capped for the first time, replaced Downton; Edmonds and Ellison were omitted in favour of Athey and the veteran John Lever; while Chris Smith came as a late replacement for the injured Gower. India were forced to make two changes as both Amarnath and Chetan Sharma were injured. They were replaced by Pandit, winning his first cap, and Madan Lal, who was called from the Central Lancashire League. It was argued that Madan Lal, like Lever, had the experience and the technical ability to enjoy the favours that the Headingley pitch tended to offer bowlers of medium pace.

Kapil Dev won the toss and India batted first although Kapil Dev might have hesitated before making his decision. A pattern was established on the first morning that was to recur throughout the match in that the England bowlers began the day poorly. Understandably, Gatting was nervous, but his bowlers could not have enjoyed his fidgeting which manifested itself in constant field changes. Lever could not settle, and after 4 overs, India were 26 for 0. Lever, bowling with no third man, suffered in that area. From England's point of view, things could only improve, and in the forty minutes before lunch, two wickets fell. Srikkanth, with his inborn desire for self-destruction, drove Pringle carelessly to mid-on, and the same bowler had Gavaskar caught behind. The great man speculated unnecessarily

ABOVE: *Back to Test cricket. John Lever opening the England bowling at Headingley. (Ken Kelly)*

ABOVE: *Srikkanth in aggressive vein against Pringle. Test debutant Bruce French looks on. (Adrian Murrell)*

RIGHT: *Vengsarkar the magnificent on his way to his second century in successive Tests. (Ken Kelly)*

outside the off stump, and French took his first catch in Test cricket. Shastri drove Emburey over long on for six and India lunched at 92 for 2.

Gatting relied mainly on pace, and at 128, Dilley had a deserved wicket when Shastri was caught at first slip. Azharuddin, not at his best in this match, pushed forward to Gooch and was lbw, but Vengsarkar and Pandit threatened to take the game out of England's reach. They took the score past 200 in brisk fashion before Lever slanted a ball across Vengsarkar and had him caught behind although one felt that the batsman could well have ignored the delivery. The next ball Lever brought back to Kapil Dev and had the Indian captain lbw. At 211, the perky Pandit edged Pringle to first slip, and two runs later, Binny prodded to short leg. England were back in the match.

India closed at 235 for 8, and the following morning, again encouraged by some untidy bowling, they added 37 invaluable runs, More demonstrating his incalculable worth as a number ten. The value of the innings played by More and Madan Lal was quickly emphasised when England crashed to 14 for 3. Madan Lal and More, contemptuous of the new ball, had added 64 for the ninth wicket, and India looked set for many more until Maninder fell in an extraordinary manner. He edged to Gooch at slip who was moving the wrong way. The fielder managed to knock the ball towards French who got a glove underneath it and scooped it up. Gooch then flicked the ball up with his boot to complete a remarkable catch.

In the second over of the England innings, Slack was bowled off his pads by a ball which came back at him. In the seventh, Gooch was opened up by a fearsome delivery from

RIGHT: *Slack is caught at slip by Gavaskar off Binny and England slide towards defeat. (Adrian Murrell)*

Jubilant return to Test cricket. Madan Lal bowls Wilf Slack for 0. (Adrian Murrell)

Kapil Dev and looped the ball to gully. The next over saw Smith bowled between bat and pad by a ball from Madan Lal which came back prodigiously. The experienced medium pacer had earned his recall.

When care and discretion were needed Gatting chased a wide ball from Binny and was caught behind. England lunched in tatters at 41 for 4. The first ball of the afternoon accounted for Lamb who drove Binny to cover where Pandit took a good tumbling catch. In the circumstances, it was a most injudicious stroke. Pringle never settled, and he was splendidly caught at short-leg off a firm hit. Kapil Dev held Emburey at slip first ball so that French, in his first Test,

Kiran More clips the ball to leg. More proved to be an excellent wicket-keeper and most useful batsman throughout the series. (Adrian Murrell)

came in to survive the hat-trick. He negotiated two overs before he was bowled by Binny who had taken 3 for 3 in 6 deliveries. He finished with 5 for 40, his best bowling in Test cricket.

Athey and Dilley showed some character, and the follow-on was avoided, but England were dismissed for 102, one run more than the lowest total that they have ever made against India. By the end of the second day, with the help of the crowd and some good bowling by Lever, they had fought their way back into the game.

French, who had an excellent first Test behind the stumps, gave England heart with a magnificent leg side catch to account for Gavaskar, and by the time Azharuddin, clearly unsettled by the hysteria of the 'Mexican wave' which was sweeping the ground, was lbw, India were 35 for 4. Pandit and Vengsarkar, undeterred by crowd and moving ball, doubled the score, but Pandit played across a ball from Pringle and India closed at 70 for 5.

The Saturday belonged entirely to India. The sun shone. The England bowlers were erratic. India prospered. More gave Vengsarkar studied support. Kapil Dev hit a riotous 31 off 23 balls which gave India impetus and convinced all that they were about to win the series. Madan Lal looked technically more competent than the top order England batsmen, and Binny, an awesome number ten, emphasised his all-round quality with an excellent knock which included hooking a Dilley bouncer high over square leg for six.

Meanwhile, Dilip Vengsarkar had shown a temperament and technical efficiency which no one else on either side had matched. He adopted the method that the pitch demanded with its help to movement off the seam by playing on the front foot with bat and pad together. It was exemplary craftsmanship and brought him his second century in successive Tests. He scored 163 runs for once out in the match on a wicket where English batsmen failed, and these were 'English conditions'.

The demons of the wicket which had appeared quiescent while Vengsarkar was batting reasserted themselves when England went in. Gooch pushed forward and was held gently at short square leg. It was a delivery to which Gooch should

ABOVE: *Gatting is caught behind off Roger Binny who took 5 wickets in a Test innings for the first time. (Adrian Murrell)*

RIGHT: *Gooch clutches the ball at the end of his acrobatic double act with French to catch Maninder Singh. (Adrian Murrell)*

SECOND CORNHILL TEST MATCH – ENGLAND v. INDIA
19, 20, 21 and 23 June 1986 at Headingley, Leeds

INDIA

	FIRST INNINGS		SECOND INNINGS	
S.M. Gavaskar	c French, b Pringle	35	c French, b Lever	1
K. Srikkanth	c Emburey, b Pringle	31	b Dilley	8
R.J. Shastri	c Pringle, b Dilley	32	lbw, b Lever	3
D.B. Vengsarkar	c French, b Lever	61	not out	102
M. Azharuddin	lbw, b Gooch	15	lbw, b Lever	2
C.S. Pandit	c Emburey, b Pringle	23	b Pringle	17
R.N. Kapil Dev†	lbw, b Lever	0	(8) c Gatting, b Lever	31
R.M.H. Binny	c Slack, b Emburey	6	(10) lbw, b Pringle	26
U.S. Madan Lal	c Gooch, b Dilley	20	run out	22
K.S. More*	not out	36	(7) c Slack, b Pringle	16
Maninder Singh	c Gooch, b Dilley	3	c Gatting, b Pringle	1
	lb 5, nb 5	10	b 4, lb 4	8
		—		—
		272		237

ENGLAND

	FIRST INNINGS		SECOND INNINGS	
G.A. Gooch	c Binny, b Kapil Dev	8	c Srikkanth, b Kapil Dev	5
W.N. Slack	b Madan Lal	0	c Gavaskar, b Binny	19
C.L. Smith	b Madan Lal	6	c More, b Shastri	28
A.J. Lamb	c Pandit, b Binny	10	c More, b Binny	10
M.W. Gatting†	c More, b Binny	13	not out	31
C.W.J. Athey	c More, b Madan Lal	32	c More, b Maninder	8
D.R. Pringle	c Srikkanth, b Binny	8	(8) lbw, b Maninder	8
J.E. Emburey	c Kapil Dev, b Binny	0	(9) c Azharuddin, b Kapil Dev	1
B.N. French*	b Binny	8	(10) c Vengsarkar, b Maninder	5
G.R. Dilley	b Shastri	10	(11) run out	2
J.K. Lever	not out	0	(7) c More, b Maninder	0
	b 1, lb 2, w 4	7	lb 9, nb 2	11
		102		128

	O	M	R	W		O	M	R	W
Dilley	24.2	7	54	3		17	2	71	1
Lever	30	4	102	2		23	5	64	4
Pringle	27	6	47	3		22.3	6	73	4
Emburey	17	4	45	1		7	3	9	—
Gooch	6	—	19	1		7	2	12	—

	O	M	R	W		O	M	R	W
Kapil Dev	18	7	36	1		19.2	7	24	2
Madan Lal	11.1	3	18	3		9.4	2	30	—
Binny	13	1	40	5		8	1	18	2
Maninder Singh						16.3	6	26	4
Shastri	3	1	5	1		10	3	21	1

FALL OF WICKETS
1- 64, 2- 75, 3- 128, 4- 163, 5- 203, 6- 203, 7- 211, 8- 213, 9- 267
1- 9, 2- 9, 3- 29, 4- 35, 5- 70, 6- 102, 7- 137, 8- 173, 9- 233

FALL OF WICKETS
1- 4, 2- 14, 3- 14, 4- 38, 5- 41, 6- 63, 7- 63, 8- 72, 9- 100
1- 12, 2- 46, 3- 63, 4- 77, 5- 90, 6- 90, 7- 101, 8- 104, 9- 109

Umpires: J. Birkenshaw & D.J. Constant

India won by 279 runs

*Night-watchman Lever is out first ball and India rejoice.
(Adrian Murrell)*

*Dilley is run out. More and Maninder turn for the pavilion.
India take the series. (Adrian Murrell)*

have gone back, for it was well short of a length. Slack drove
wildly and was taken at slip. Smith's suggestion of permanence was an illusion. Shastri pitched a ball on middle
stump which turned to take the outside edge of Smith's bat.
Lamb received a violently lifting outswinger, and Athey
provided the admirable More with another victim as Maninder and Shastri joyfully took control. Nightwatchman Lever
was out first ball, and at 90 for 6, England had Sunday in
which to contemplate the possibility of rain as their only
salvation.

It never came. By 12.15 on Monday morning, the match
was over. India won by 279 which, in the conditions, was a
huge margin. Pringle and French were bemused by Maninder who had grown in stature minute by minute during the
series. Emburey edged Kapil Dev to slip, and Dilley was run
out. Gatting threw the bat, but it mattered not. Kapil Dev
was forced to leave the field with a back injury before the end,
but he had played a crucial part in this victory, for he had
insisted his side played happy cricket. They had done so, and
they had outplayed England in every department of the
game.

I.C.C Trophy

20 June

at Kidderminster C.C.

Denmark 146 (E.A. Brandes 4 for 21)
Zimbabwe 148 for 2 (G.A. Paterson 86 not out)
Zimbabwe (2 pts) won by 8 wickets

at Coventry and North Warwick C.C.

Bangladesh 162 (S. Lakha 4 for 31)
East Africa 166 for 4 (B. Bouri 66 not out, F. Gool 53 not out)
East Africa (2 pts) won by 6 wickets)

at Himley

Malaysia 154 (A. Stevens 66)
Kenya 158 for 5

Kenya (2 pts) won by 5 wickets

at Blossomfield C.C.

Fiji 251 (C. Brown 57)
United States 252 for 5 (N. Lashkari 104 not out, K. Khan 73)

United States (2 pts) won by 5 wickets

at Swindon

Gibraltar 46 (D. Abrahams 5 for 9)
Canada 48 for 0

Canada (2 pts) won by 10 wickets

at Worcester City C.C.

Papua New Guinea 377 for 6 (B. Harry 162, W. Maha 52)
Israel 100 (C. Amini 5 for 19)

Papua New Guinea (2 pts) won by 277 runs

at Wroxeter and Uppingham C.C.

Holland 327 for 7 (S. Atkinson 107, R. Gomes 101)
Hong Kong 157 for 9

Holland (2 pts) won by 170 runs

Gibraltar were dismissed in 25.4 overs for 46, the lowest score ever made in the competition. It took the Canadians only 23 balls in which to knock off the runs. Zimbabwe and Holland confirmed their position as favourites to win their respective groups.

21, 22 and 23 June

at Chesterfield

Derbyshire 198 (A. Hill 71, C.A. Walsh 7 for 62) and 310 for 8 (K.J. Barnett 114, I.S. Anderson 93, D.V. Lawrence 4 for 84)
Gloucestershire 334 (A.W. Stovold 118, M.A. Holding 4 for 76, J.P. Taylor 4 for 81)

Match drawn
Gloucestershire 8 pts, Derbyshire 5 pts

21, 23 and 24 June

at Swansea

Lancashire 475 for 8 dec (J. Abrahams 189 not out, G.D. Mendis 100, C. Maynard 60)
Glamorgan 230 for 4 (Younis Ahmed 68, H. Morris 54, D.B. Pauline 53)

Match drawn
Lancashire 5 pts, Glamorgan 4 pts

at Southampton

Hampshire 214 (C.G. Greenidge 53, D.L. Underwood 4 for 30) and 143 (T.M. Alderman 6 for 56)
Kent 189 (M.R. Benson 90, N.G. Cowley 5 for 17) and 172 for 5 (M.R. Benson 97 not out)

Kent won by 5 wickets
Kent 21 pts, Hampshire 6 pts

at Lord's

Middlesex 208 (R.O. Butcher 86, K.R. Pont 4 for 63, T.D. Topley 4 for 33)
Essex 130 (N.G. Cowans 5 for 61, W.W. Daniel 4 for 27) and 179 for 5 (A.R. Border 59 not out)

Essex won by 5 wickets
Essex 20 pts, Middlesex 6 pts

at Luton

Northamptonshire 385 for 4 (R.J. Bailey 200 not out, R.J. Boyd-Moss 67) and 193 for 7 dec (R.J. Boyd-Moss 58)
Yorkshire 314 for 6 dec (A.A. Metcalfe 151, D.L. Bairstow 88) and 240 for 8 (G. Boycott 68, P.J. Hartley 54)

Match drawn
Northamptonshire 6 pts, Yorkshire 5 pts

at Edgbaston

Warwickshire 322 for 8 dec (T.A. Lloyd 70, A.M. Ferreira 68, M. Asif Din 61, D.L. Amiss 54) and 142 for 5 dec (G.W. Humpage 56)
Leicestershire 218 (J.J. Whitaker 90, R.A. Cobb 78, G.C. Small 4 for 41) and 150 for 4 (L. Potter 68)

Match drawn
Warwickshire 7 pts, Leicestershire 3 pts

at Worcester

Sussex 250 for 9 dec (P.W.G. Parker 125, N.V. Radford 7 for 94) and 158 for 6 dec
Worcestershire 148 (D.A. Reeve 5 for 32) and 102 for 1

Match drawn
Sussex 7 pts, Worcestershire 4 pts

at Cambridge

Surrey 375 for 8 dec (A.R. Butcher 157)
Cambridge University 223 and 160 for 7 (A.R. Butcher 4 for 25)

Match drawn

With Nottinghamshire idle, Essex extended their lead at the top of the Britannic Assurance County Championship to 33 points by beating Middlesex in most praiseworthy fashion. Put in to bat, Middlesex were 66 for 5 before Mike Roseberry, making his debut, joined Roland Butcher in a stand of 82. On a wicket that encouraged the seam bowlers, Essex surrendered a first innings lead of 78, but came back strongly to bowl out Middlesex for 97. Neil Foster led the assault on the Middlesex batting which was painfully inadequate for the conditions and for the quality of the opposition. Essex sought victory aggressively. Prichard was in violent mood until brilliantly caught in the gully by Edmonds, and Border and Lilley both played with panache to take the leaders to a surprisingly easy victory. The debit for Essex was that Fletcher sustained a broken finger.

Hampshire disappointed after recent successes. Put in to bat, they were given a splendid start by Greenidge and Terry who put on 103, but they then lost 5 wickets for 26 runs. Nevertheless, they gained two batting points and Nigel Cowley bowled them to a first innings lead of 25 after Benson's fine knock had threatened to take the match out of Hampshire's reach. Kent lost their last 5 wickets for 8 runs. For the third time in four championship matches, Terry Alderman took six wickets in an innings as Hampshire were bowled out for 143, leaving Kent to make 169 to win. Again Benson stood firm, but at 104 for 5, the match was in the balance. Ellison arrived to give Benson positive support, and Kent won by 5 wickets.

There was no play on the last day at Swansea where Gehan Mendis hit his first century for Lancashire and John Abrahams gave further evidence of his confident form. Neal Radford took a career best against Sussex at Worcester, but

John Abrahams hit 189 not out for Lancashire against Glamorgan at Swansea and enjoyed a fine season. (George Herringshaw)

Don Topley had match figures of 8 for 100 as Essex gained a fine victory over Middlesex at Lord's 21–23 June. Topley's success as understudy for players on Test duty played a great part in another splendid season for Essex. (Mark Leech)

The New Zealanders arrive. Cricket at Arundel, 22 June. (Adrian Murrell)

rain and a lack of adventure doomed the game to a draw.

The match at Chesterfield was also drawn after Courtenay Walsh and Andy Stovold had put Gloucestershire in a commanding position. Kim Barnett and Iain Anderson began Derbyshire's second innings with a partnership of 189 and assured a draw. Leicestershire settled for a draw at Edgbaston, but Yorkshire and Northants kept interest alive to the end at Luton. On the first day, Robert Bailey reached the first double century of his career, but Ashley Metcalfe led Yorkshire's positive reply on the friendliest of wickets. Set to make 265 to win, Yorkshire reached the last 20 overs at 124 for 2. Boycott was soon caught behind off Capel, and the visitors slumped to 161 for 6. Peter Hartley maintained the challenge with a hard hit 54, but the spin of Nick Cook and Roger Harper thwarted Yorkshire at the last.

22 June

---

at Arundel

New Zealanders 255 for 6 dec (T.J. Franklin 74, M.D. Crowe 70)
Lavinia, Duchess of Norfolk's XI 184 for 6 (T.E. Jesty 68 not out)

Match drawn

John Player Special League

at Swansea

Lancashire 147
Glamorgan 152 for 5 (J.A. Hopkins 65, Younis Ahmed 50)

Glamorgan (4 pts) won by 5 wickets

Chris Broad hit 100 not out for Notts against Somerset at Bath, 22 June. (George Herringshaw)

at Basingstoke

Kent 149 for 9
Hampshire 150 for 6

Hampshire (4 pts) won by 4 wickets

at Lord's

Essex 217 for 6 (P.J. Prichard 97)
Middlesex 89 for 2

*Match abandoned
Essex 2 pts, Middlesex 2 pts*

at Luton

Yorkshire 220 (K. Sharp 94)
Northamptonshire 199 for 3 (W. Larkins 92)

Northamptonshire (4 pts) won on faster scoring rate

at Bath

Nottinghamshire 241 for 7 (B.C. Broad 100 not out, C.E.B. Rice 68)
Somerset 209 (R.J. Harden 71, I.V.A. Richards 64, C.E.B. Rice 4 for 33)

Nottinghamshire (4 pts) won by 32 runs

at Egbaston

Warwickshire 192 for 5 (A.I. Kallicharran 78 not out, D.L. Amiss 59)
Leicestershire 132 (G.C. Small 4 for 26)

Warwickshire (4 pts) won on faster scoring rate

at Worcester

Sussex 163 for 7 (Imran Khan 72)
Worcestershire 164 for 5 (D.M. Smith 60, G.A. Hick 59)

Worcestershire (4 pts) won by 5 wickets

The New Zealanders entertained on a grey day at Arundel, and in the Sunday League, Hampshire and Northants drew closer to Essex who were behind on run rate when the game at Lord's was abandoned. Larkins and Sharp batted well at Luton where Arnold Sidebottom sustained a broken finger. Notts, without Cooper and Birch who had been hurt in a car crash, owed much to Broad and Rice who put on 126 for the second wicket.

I.C.C. Trophy

23 June

at Egerton Park C.C.

Malaysia 89 (E.A. Brandes 4 for 12, P.W.E. Rawson 4 for 21)
Zimbabwe 90 for 2

Zimbabwe (2 pts) won by 8 wickets

at Stourbridge C.C.

East Africa 261 for 8
Argentina 167 (A. Kumar 6 for 26)

East Africa (2 pts) won by 94 runs

at Leamington C.C.

Hong Kong 144 (C. Collins 53)
United States 148 for 5

United States (2 pts) won by 5 wickets

Robert Bailey – a young batsman of exceptional talent – hit the first double century of his career for Northants against Yorkshire at Luton. (Adrian Murrell)

at Taunton

Somerset 128 (S.N. Yadav 6 for 30) and 213 for 5 (N.A. Felton 104)
Indians 389 for 8 dec (S.M. Gavaskar 136 not out, R. Lamba 69, R.J. Shastri 64)

Match drawn

28 and 30 June, 1 July

at Bristol

Gloucestershire 185 (A.J. Wright 56) and 284 for 8 dec (J.W. Lloyds 74, K.M. Curran 67)
Surrey 158 (A.J. Stewart 65 not out, C.A. Walsh 6 for 41) and 215 (A.J. Stewart 52, C.A. Walsh 5 for 72, J.W. Lloyds 4 for 60)

Gloucestershire won by 96 runs
Gloucestershire 21 pts., Surrey 5 pts

Coney leaps out of the way as Andy Miller square cuts during his 56 for Middlesex against New Zealand at Lord's. (Adrian Murrell)

LEFT: *Jim Love caught at silly mid-off, Yorkshire v. Warwickshire, 28–30 June. (Simon Bruty)*

at Maidstone

Glamorgan 277 (H. Morris 92, D.B. Pauline 55, M.P. Maynard 52, T.M. Alderman 5 for 57) and 264 for 6 dec (H. Morris 128 not out)
Kent 282 (C.J. Tavare 93, S.A. Marsh 55) and 143 for 6 (N.R. Taylor 82 not out)

Match drawn
Kent 7 pts., Glamorgan 7 pts.

at Liverpool

Lancashire 94 and 270 for 4 (G. Fowler 88 not out, N.H. Fairbrother 52)
Derbyshire 465 for 9 dec (J.E. Morris 153, B. Roberts 87, C. Marples 57, D.J. Makinson 4 for 105)

Match drawn
Derbyshire 8 pts, Lancashire 2 pts

at Leicester

Leicestershire 376 for 4 dec (J.J. Whitaker 200 not out, P. Willey 119) and 204 for 5 dec (D.I. Gower 80 not out)
Nottinghamshire 247 (P. Johnson 80, R.A. Pick 55, P.A.J. de Freitas 5 for 73) and 58 (W.K.R. Benjamin 6 for 33)

Leicestershire won by 275 runs
Leicestershire 24 pts, Nottinghamshire 3 pts

at Hastings

Sussex 283 for 9 dec (Imran Khan 59, A.M. Green 55) and 173 for 3 dec (Imran Khan 62 not out, P.W.G. Parker 54)
Northamptonshire 136 (C.M. Wells 4 for 23) and 321 for 9 (A.J. Lamb 157, R.J. Bailey 57, D.J. Capel 54, C.M. Wells 4 for 72

Northamptonshire won by 1 wicket
Northamptonshire 19 pts, Sussex 7 pts

John Morris enjoyed splendid mid-season form for Derbyshire and was awarded his county cap. (David Munden)

ABOVE: *Winston Benjamin destroyed Notts in the second innings at Leicester, 1 July. Benjamin had an excellent season as pace bowler and hard-hitting batsman for Leicestershire. (George Herringshaw)*

RIGHT: *James Whitaker hit 200 not out for Leicestershire against Notts, 28 June–1 July. Whitaker was the leading young batsman in the country until he suffered broken fingers. (David Munden)*

at Worcester

Hampshire 158 (P.J. Newport 5 for 52) and 156 (C.L. Smith 66, P.J. Newport 6 for 48)
Worcestershire 204 (M.D. Marshall 4 for 70) and 112 for 4 (M.D. Marshall 4 for 29)

Worcestershire won by 6 wickets
Worcestershire 22 pts, Hampshire 3 pts

Nottinghamshire were humiliated by Leicestershire, and Gloucestershire moved into second place in the Championship table. Peter Willey and James Whitaker, one of the most consistently exciting batsmen in the country, shared a fourth wicket stand of 244 on the opening day, and Whitaker reached the first double century of his career. He caught Broad off Agnew before the close to complete a memorable day. Nightwatchman Pick and Johnson saved Notts from having to follow-on on the Monday, but Gower was able to declare early on the last day and set the visitors a target of 334. This was never likely to be easy especially as Robinson was unable to bat, but the abject surrender in under 23 overs by the Notts side was inexcusable. Benjamin and Agnew bowled unchanged, and the Antiguan returned his best figures for the county.

Gloucestershire obtained their first win at Bristol since 1982 and owed much to Walsh. Eighteen wickets fell on the first day, and eventually the home side took a first innings lead of 27. This seemed of no account when three Gloucestershire second innings wickets fell to the Surrey pace bowlers for 37 runs, but Lloyds and Curran joined in the decisive stand of the match, adding 132. More useful runs followed from Athey and Russell so that Surrey were left to make 312 in 87 overs. At tea, they were 156 for 4 and a draw looked likely, but Walsh, although not aided by the pitch as he had

been on the first day, took 5 wickets in 61 balls, and Gloucestershire went to 18 points behind Essex in the table.

Hampshire's challenge faltered again. Phil Newport returned best bowling figures for innings and match to put Worcestershire in a strong position, and sensible application saw them to victory in spite of Marshall's bursts of speed. Hampshire were handicapped by the absence of the injured Maru. Newport, Smith and Patel played valuable innings for the home county during the match.

Hugh Morris played two innings of great character for Glamorgan at Maidstone. Here is a young batsman of technique and temperament, and his second innings century was his career best performance. He and Pauline began the match with Glamorgan's highest first wicket partnership of the season, 104, but Kent struck back with the magnificently consistent Alderman. In the end, Kent were indebted to Neil Taylor for salvation just as they were indebted to Tavare and Marsh for resuscitating them in the first innings.

The elegant and energetic John Morris, newly capped, hit a career best for Derbyshire at Aigburth, and the visitors took a monumental lead of 371 on the first innings after Lancashire's first day disaster. Durable batting, however, saw the home side bat through the last day and lose only 4 wickets.

Once again Yorkshire were pleased to rest on the developing batting talents of Peter Hartley to save them from defeat. McMillan and Lloyd, pleasingly, hit centuries in a match which saw Warwickshire bat rather slowly in their first innings when McMillan and Amiss added 159 for the third wicket. Sharp's excellent hundred, his second of the summer, kept Yorkshire in touch, but, asked to make 287 in 50 overs, they slumped in their second innings and were 56 for 7 when Peter Hartley came to the wicket. He battled through 27

Miller is caught behind by the splendid Marsh off the bowling of Chris Cowdrey. (Patrick Eagar)

Andy Miller drives square on the off-side. Miller played a solid innings at the start of the match. (Patrick Eagar)

consistently taking the rising ball high on his body and runs were not coming easily. The first boundary came in the sixth over when Miller edged Baptiste through the slips. Baptiste bowled quickly, wildly and rather widely.

The first 10 overs brought 28 runs, and Chris Cowdrey made a double change. He took over from Dilley himself at the Pavilion End while Ellison replaced Baptiste at the Nursery End. Twice in Chris Cowdrey's first over, Gatting cut the ball high over Graham Cowdrey's head, both shots were close to being caught. Gatting played another risky shot when he slashed Ellison past Tavare at slip in the 18th over.

BELOW: *Clive Radley reaches fifty and acknowledges the applause of the crowd. (Patrick Eagar)*

Ellison was by far the most impressive of the Kent bowlers, and he dismissed Gatting and Butcher with successive deliveries in the 20th over. Both batsmen were splendidly caught behind the wicket by Marsh who had an outstanding game. His wicket-keeping was alert and active, and he gave a vibrance to the fielding side which was a delight to watch. He has quickly established himself as a worthy successor to Knott, Evans, Ames, Hubble and the rest.

After the fall of Gatting and Butcher Middlesex went into a quiet period. The remaining 14 overs until lunch produced only another 23 runs, and in the 31st over, Miller became the third batsman to be caught at the wicket. Radley moved down the wicket to smother Underwood, and at lunch he was 8 not out and Middlesex were 89 for 4 from 34 overs.

Chris Cowdrey conceded 10 runs in the first over after the break, and Middlesex now began the necessary acceleration. Cowdrey changed the bowling frequently, and in the 42nd over, Downton was lbw to Ellison. Radley's fifty came in the 48th over, and Kent's problems revolved mostly around Baptiste who was unable to maintain either line or length and suffered in consequence. Emburey collected runs briskly, but Radley's fine innings came to an end when he was run out in the 50th over. It was a remarkable piece of work by Marsh that accounted for Radley, the wicket-keeper throwing to the bowler's end.

Radley batted with his usual sense and composure. He had hit Underwood over the top and run him down to third man for four when the spinner threatened to dampen the Kent innings, and he had followed these shots with a cover drive and a pull over mid-wicket off the same bowler.

Baptiste bowled Emburey, and Hughes and Edmonds plundered well to take Middlesex just short of 200, a score which left the game wide open, but if the Kent batting could

John Emburey lies on the ground after his magnificent slip catch to dismiss Chris Cowdrey. (Patrick Eagar)

Graham Cowdrey turns a ball to leg during his heroic innings of 58 off 70 balls. (Patrick Eagar)

LEFT: *Courtney Walsh took a career best 9 for 72 as Gloucestershire beat Somerset by an innings, 19–21 July. Walsh was the first bowler in the season to reach 100 wickets, and he was the most significant reason for Gloucestershire's success in 1986. (David Munden)*

at Southend

Essex 273 for 6 (G.A. Gooch 94, A.W. Lilley 52)
Worcestershire 230 (T.S. Curtis 82)

Essex (4 pts) won by 43 runs

at Neath

Glamorgan 188 for 6 (G.C. Holmes 65 not out, H. Morris 51)
Northamptonshire 138 (A.J. Lamb 66, G.C. Holmes 4 for 27)

Glamorgan (4 pts) won by 50 runs

at Bristol

Somerset 213 for 7 (I.V.A. Richards 52)
Gloucestershire 217 for 2 (P. Bainbridge 106 not out, K.M. Curran 66 not out)

Gloucestershire (4 pts) won by 8 wickets

at Portsmouth

Warwickshire 152
Hampshire 154 for 4 (R.A. Smith 58 not out)

Hampshire (4 pts) won by 6 wickets

at Canterbury

Lancashire 251 for 5 (G. Fowler 112, G.D. Mendis 66)
Kent 214 (M.R. Benson 63)

Lancashire (4 pts) won by 37 runs

at Leicester

Sussex 204 for 6 (C.M. Wells 68, P.W.G. Parker 55)
Leicestershire 176 for 8 (P. Bowler 55)

Sussex (4 pts) won by 46 runs

Northants were beaten by Glamorgan so that Hampshire's victory over Warwickshire took them level at the top of the table. Essex maintained their challenge with some splendid hitting from Gooch, Lilley and Stephenson, but the news broke that Allan Border would not be returning in 1987 and would, in fact, end his brief career with the county in mid-August. Bainbridge and Curran took Gloucestershire to victory with a third wicket stand of 158, and Fowler and Mendis put on 177 for Lancashire's first wicket against Kent. John Emburey had his nose broken by a ball from Warner, an injury which cost him his place in the England side for the first Test.

19, 20 and 21 July

at Dublin

M.C.C 399 for 7 dec (M. Waugh 239 not out) and 205 for 2 dec (M. Waugh 101 not out, B. Hassan 61)
Ireland 326 for 9 dec (D. Dennison 85, S. Warke 68, M. Halliday 62 not out, C.R. Trembath 6 for 93) and 231 for 8 (J. Garth 64)

Match drawn

23, 24 and 25 July

at Portsmouth

Hampshire 184 (M.C.J. Nicholas 55, M.A. Holding 5 for 89) and 254 for 2 dec (C.G. Greenidge 144 not out, R.J. Parks 80)

the highest score of his career and reached 1000 runs for the season. Most people believed he had assured himself of a place in the side to go to Australia.

John Player Special League

20 July

at Derby

Middlesex 161 for 8
Derbyshire 164 for 3 (K.J. Barnett 85 not out, B. Roberts 55)

Derbyshire (4 pts) won by 7 wickets

Stuart Turner, the Essex all-rounder, receives a commemorative record of his 300 wickets in the John Player Special League from Les Hatton of the Association of Cricket Statisticians, Southend, 20 July. Turner who also scored more than 2000 runs in the Sunday League announced his retirement at the end of the season. He will be greatly missed. (John Barker)

Derbyshire 216 (B.J.M. Maher 69, T.M. Tremlett 5 for 46) and 217 (J.E. Morris 78, M.D. Marshall 4 for 54)

Hampshire won by 5 runs
Hampshire 21 pts, Derbyshire 6 pts

at Southport

Nottinghamshire 350 for 8 dec (R.T. Robinson 97, B.C. Broad 51)
Lancashire 182 (C. Maynard 59, E.E. Hemmings 5 for 70) and 301 for 7 (C.H. Lloyd 75, G.D. Mendis 69, M. Watkinson 58 not out)

Match drawn
Nottinghamshire 8 pts, Lancashire 4 pts

at Leicester

Glamorgan 183 (M.P. Maynard 50, P.A.J. de Freitas 4 for 44) and 150 for 5 dec
Leicestershire 47 for 1 dec and 273 (T.J. Boon 80, R.A. Cobb 77, J.G. Thomas 4 for 83, R.C. Ontong 4 for 88)

Glamorgan won by 13 runs
Glamorgan 17 pts, Leicestershire 4 pts

at The Oval

Essex 250 (A.R. Border 52, A.H. Gray 4 for 50) and 276 for 7 (A.R. Border 138)
Surrey 448 for 5 dec (T.E. Jesty 221, M.A. Lynch 85, A.J. Stewart 67)

Match drawn
Surrey 8 pts, Essex 5 pts

at Hove

Worcestershire 280 for 6 dec (T.S. Curtis 62, D.M. Smith 63, D.B. d'Oliveira 62) and 213 for 5 dec (G.A. Hick 100)
Sussex 203 (R.I. Alikhan 67, A.M. Green 60, R.K. Illingworth 4 for 54) and 292 for 5 (P.W.G. Parker 97, R.I. Alikhan 56)

Sussex won by 5 wickets
Sussex 20 pts, Worcestershire 7 pts

at Scarborough

Yorkshire 341 for 7 dec (A.A. Metcalfe 123, P.E. Robinson 104 not out) and 206 for 2 dec (P.E. Robinson 91, S.N. Hartley 51 not out)

Ashley Metcalfe reached a thousand runs for the season, 23–25 July, and confirmed his promise as one of the best opening batsmen in England. (Ken Kelly)

ABOVE: *H.M. The Queen meets the two teams. (Adrian Murrell)*

BELOW: *Martyn Moxon clips the ball to leg during Test debut innings of 74. (Adrian Murrell)*

RIGHT: *Martin Crowe on the way to a century. (Adrian Murrell)*

replaced by Bob Taylor whose appearance seemed to cause more comment and debate than the match itself. On the Saturday, Bobby Parks of Hampshire appeared, and this was a heartening sight, for he looked in his proper place in an England side.

Martin Crowe and Edgar took their stand to 210. Edgar played with the grittiness which makes him so valuable a member of the New Zealand side, and Martin Crowe suggested that he was a class above any other batsman, excepting Gower, who was playing in the match, and certainly only Vengsarkar could approach him in this English summer. His 106 contained 11 fours, and if one criticises him, it is becuase he played tiredly when he had completed his inspiring hundred instead of consolidating his position and setting his sights on 150 or 200. Edgar was caught at slip off a Gooch outswinger so that both batsmen had fallen within 3 runs of each other.

Jeff Crowe was taken high, one handed at slip, a reflex catch by Gatting, but Coney threatened to tear England apart with a series of rasping shots. He had hit 6 fours when he pulled a wretched long hop from Radford into the hands of Gooch at square leg. It was a good catch, but it was a dreadful way to throw away a valuable wicket, and Coney knew it.

Gray was unluckily out. He drove Edmonds into the ground, but the umpire, Harold Bird, declared that the ball had ricocheted from Moxon's toe to Gower at silly mid-off. Edmonds was rather fortunate to get this wicket, but he well deserved to pass 100 Test wickets in this innings. He was providing the personality for which English cricket was in desperate search, and he bowled Hadlee who, unwisely, had abnegated his natural attacking game. Edmonds was still not finished, for he flung himself to his right to hold a wonderful gully catch to get rid of Smith. New Zealand closed at 342 for 9 and Watson was lbw to Dilley without addition on the Monday morning. A lead of 35 was valuable, but one could not help but feel that New Zealand had let slip a position of strength. Willey did not field on the Saturday, and Prichard of Essex substituted.

The Monday was a wretched day, ruined by the weather and by umpires who seemed unwilling that the game should be played. Only 48 overs were bowled although there seemed no good reason why at least another 20 were not managed. The paying customer is still, it appears, the last person to be considered. Moxon was lbw to a ball that kept low, and Athey, having been missed at short leg and badly dropped at the wicket, was bowled sweeping. Gower advanced down the wicket, but Gray turned a ball massively from the rough outside the left-hander's off stump and bowled him. All were amazed. England closed at 110 for 3, Gooch 64 not out, but it was a day to be forgotten.

Gatting took us back to the fifties with his pad play on the last morning and then lost his head and his wicket when he hit Gray to mid-on. Gooch batted with immense control and growing strength to save the match for England and reach his

ABOVE: *Hadlee strikes again. Moxon lbw for 5. (Adrian Murrell)*

RIGHT: *Gooch during his majestic innings of 183. His second Test century of the season at Lord's. (Adrian Murrell)*

*Dennis Amiss reaches his hundredth hundred – LEFT: He hits a boundary off John Abrahams to move into the nineties.
CENTRE: He plays a late cut off the bowling of Abrahams to reach his century of centuries. Fowler is the substitute
wicket-keeper wearing a helmet. RIGHT: He receives congratulations from Abrahams, Humpage and Fowler. (Ken Kelly)*

the challenge. Twenty runs were needed from the last two overs, and 2 sixes helped bring this down to six off the last over. Peter Hartley was caught off the first ball, Bairstow run out off the second and Shaw run out off the final ball going for a second run which would have given victory.

John Player Special League

27 July

at Ebbw Vale

Glamorgan 223 for 6 (H. Morris 100)
Derbyshire 219 for 9 (J. Derrick 4 for 48)

Glamorgan (4 pts) won by 4 runs

at Southampton

Hampshire 276 for 3 (V.P. Terry 142, C.G. Greenidge 73)
Leicestershire 184 for 7

Hampshire (4 pts) won on faster scoring rate

at Northampton

Northamptonshire 228 for 4 (R.A. Harper 57 not out, R.J. Bailey 52)
Kent 128

Northamptonshire (4 pts) won by 100 runs

at Taunton

Lancashire 211 for 6 (J. Abrahams 103 not out)
Somerset 212 for 2 (P.M. Roebuck 75 not out, I.V.A. Richards 62)

Somerset (4 pts) won by 8 wickets

at Guildford

Sussex 214 for 9 (A.M. Green 69, M.A. Feltham 4 for 35)

Surrey 203 for 9 (G.S. Clinton 56)

Sussex (4 pts) won by 11 runs

at Hereford

Worcestershire 233 for 6 (T.S. Curtis 73)
Gloucestershire 230 (R.C. Russell 108)

Worcestershire (4 pts) won by 3 runs

at Hull

Yorkshire 255 for 6 (J.D. Love 104 not out, P.E. Robinson 64)
Nottinghamshire 153 (C.E.B. Rice 53)

Yorkshire (4 pts) won by 102 runs

Terry and Greenidge put on 163 for Hampshire's first wicket, and the victory over Leicestershire put them clear at the top of the table with Northants who had an easy win over Kent. 'Jack' Russell opened the batting and scored his first century for Gloucestershire, but still finished on the losing side. Notts lost ground by being defeated at Hull. The Yorkshire hero was Jim Love who hit 104 off as many balls with 2 sixes and 7 fours.

NatWest Bank Trophy – Quarter Finals

30 July

at The Oval

Surrey 204 for 9 (D.J. Thomas 65, R.J. Hadlee 5 for 17)
Nottinghamshire 158 (R.J. Hadlee 55)

Surrey won by 46 runs
(Man of the Match – R.J. Hadlee)

Dennis Amiss stands in front of the scoreboard at Edgbaston which records his historic achievement, Warwickshire v. Lancashire, 29 July. (Ken Kelly)

ABOVE: 'Jack' Russell hit his first century for Gloucestershire in the Sunday League game at Hereford, yet still finished on the losing side. Russell's quietly efficient wicket-keeping was a feature of Gloucestershire's play throughout the season. (Simon Bruty)

BELOW: David Thomas revived Surrey when all seemed lost in the NatWest Trophy quarter-final at The Oval. (Adrian Murrell)

Ian Gould. His inspiration and enthusiasm took Sussex into the semi-final of the NatWest Trophy. (George Herringshaw)

30 and 31 July

at Leeds

Sussex 213 for 7 (I.J. Gould 88)
Yorkshire 125 (P. Carrick 54, G.S. le Roux 4 for 17, A.N. Jones 4 for 26)

Sussex won by 88 runs
(Man of the Match – I.J. Gould)

31 July

at Worcester

Warwickshire 136 for 8
Worcestershire 137 for 2 (D.M. Smith 62, T.S. Curtis 51 not out)

Worcestershire won by 8 wickets
(Man of the Match – D.M. Smith

31 July and 1 August

at Leicester

Leicestershire 223 for 8 (P.A.J. de Freitas 69, P.J.W. Allott 4 for 28, A.N. Hayhurst 4 for 40)
Lancashire 226 for 4 (N.H. Fairbrother 93 not out, S.J. O'Shaughnessy 53 not out)

Lancashire won by 6 wickets
(Man of the Match – N.H. Fairbrother)

Rain interrupted the quarter-finals of the NatWest Trophy, but Surrey still managed to win on the scheduled day. A magnificent spell by Richard Hadlee put Notts in the strongest of positions, for Surrey were struggling at 72 for 5. It was Thomas who revived them with some powerful hitting, and it was he and Clarke who achieved the initial breakthroughs. Pocock bowled an economical spell, and Notts plumbed the depths of 70 for 6. There was an heroic knock from Hadlee, but Notts were well beaten.

Sussex decided to bat first at Headingley and lost Green and Parker for 32 in the 15 overs bowled on the first day. Skipper Ian Gould justified his decision with a rumbustuous 88 on the second day, and the Sussex seam attack made short work of Yorkshire who were all out in 38.3 overs. They were 42 for 6 before Phil Carrick played a spirited knock.

Worcestershire took only 39.3 overs to reach their target after Warwickshire's painful 60 overs.

Chasing 227, Lancashire were in trouble at 28 for 3, but Abrahams and Fairbrother put on 105, and Steve O'Shaughnessy joined Fairbrother to see the visitors home with 6.3 overs to spare.

30, 31 July and 1 August

at Northampton

Northamptonshire 300 for 6 dec (R.J. Bailey 95, R.G. Williams 93)
New Zealanders 246 for 5 (J.G. Bracewell 100 not out)

Match drawn

John Bracewell reached the second century of his career at a run a minute in this rain-ruined match.

31 July

at Jesmond

Rest of World XI 300 for 6 (C.G. Greenidge 114, A.R. Border 79 not out)
England 268 (A.J. Lamb 106)

Rest of World XI won by 32 runs

1 August

at Jesmond

Rest of World XI 276 (C.G. Greenidge 76, A.R. Border 61, J.K. Lever 4 for 57)
England XI 277 for 7 (I.T. Botham 94, R.A. Harper 4 for 38)

England XI won by 3 wickets

These matches marked the return of Ian Botham. In the second, he took 3 wickets and then hit 94 off 57 balls with 6 sixes and 10 fours.

It was announced that Peter Lush, manager, and Micky Stewart, assistant manager, would be in charge of the side to Australia, sound choices. Sadly, Graham Barlow announced that he had been forced to retire from first-class cricket through injury. Pat Pocock, another good man, stated that he was to retire at the end of the season.

2, 3 and 4 August

at Derby

Derbyshire 366 (B.J.M. Maher 126, G. Miller 51, A.E. Warner 50, D.A. Stirling 4 for 95)
New Zealanders 266 for 5 dec (B.A. Edgar 110 not out, M.D. Crowe 51)

Match drawn

Chris Broad is stumped by Jack Richards off the bowling of Pat Pocock, NatWest quarter-final at The Oval, 30 July. (Tom Morris)

2, 4 and 5 August

at Cheltenham

Gloucestershire 201 and 184 (K.D James 5 for 34, M.D. Marshall 4 for 44)
Hampshire 270 (C.L. Smith 72 not out, T.M. Tremlett 52, C.A. Walsh 6 for 90) and 98 (C.A. Walsh 6 for 34, D.V. Lawrence 4 for 64)

Gloucestershire won by 17 runs
Gloucestershire 22 pts, Hampshire 7 pts

at Canterbury

Kent 329 for 8 dec (C.S. Cowdrey 60, S.A. Marsh 52 not out) and 87 (P.A.J. de Freitas 6 for 21)
Leicestershire 199 (P.A.J. de Freitas 106, T.M. Alderman 8 for 70) and 212 (P. Willey 104, T.M. Alderman 6 for 74)

Kent won by 5 runs
Kent 24 pts, Leicestershire 4 pts

at Old Trafford

Lancashire 170 (G.D. Mendis 54, P.W. Jarvis 4 for 36) and 251 for 6 (N.H Fairbrother 116 not out, J. Abrahams 80)
Yorkshire 399 for 7 dec (A.A. Metcalfe 151, M.D. Moxon 147, A.N. Hayhurst 4 for 69)

Match drawn
Yorkshire 8 pts, Lancashire 1 pt

at Lord's

Middlesex 447 (M.W. Gatting 158, P.R. Downton 50, C.T. Radley 50)
Northamptonshire 159 (W.W. Daniel 4 for 50) and 245 (A.J. Lamb 117, W.W. Daniel 4 for 55)

ABOVE: *Bernard Maher hit a maiden century for Derbyshire against the New Zealanders, 2 August, and won back his place as the county wicket-keeper. (Tony Edenden)*

LEFT: *Botham's back. He returned to first-class cricket with an innings of 104 not out off 66 balls at Weston-super-Mare, 4 August. (Adrian Murrell)*

Middlesex won by an innings and 43 runs
Middlesex 24 pts, Northamptonshire 2 pts

at Weston-super-Mare

Worcestershire 379 for 4 dec (D.M. Smith 165 not out, P.A. Neale 70, T.S. Curtis 64) and 247 for 2 dec (D.B. d'Oliveira 91, T.S. Curtis 74)
Somerset 286 for 4 dec (I.T. Botham 104 not out, P.M. Roebuck 68, N.A. Felton 52 not out) and 341 for 5 (P.M. Roebuck 147 not out, V.J. Marks 71 not out, B.C. Rose 56)

Somerset won by 5 wickets
Somerset 20 pts, Worcestershire 5 pts

at Eastbourne

Sussex 346 (C.M. Wells 106, N.J. Lenham 68, N.A. Foster 5 for 84) and 272 for 6 dec (G.S. le Roux 72 not out, C.M. Wells 59, R.I. Alikhan 59)
Essex 300 for 6 dec (B.R. Hardie 80, K.W.R. Fletcher 57 not out) and 303 for 7 (A.R. Border 108 not out, G.A. Gooch 78, P.J. Prichard 60)

Match drawn
Essex 8 pts, Sussex 6 pts

An amazing win over Hampshire put Gloucestershire 54 points clear at the top of the Britannic Assurance County Championship, the title seemingly within their grasp. The opening day had left the game very much in the balance. Marshall, Connor, Tremlett and James had bowled Gloucestershire out for 201, but the visitors had closed at 127 for 5. On the Monday, an heroic performance by Chris Smith, who broke a finger, and Tim Tremlett took Hampshire to a 69-run lead. Smith, batting one-handed, and Tremlett put on 112 for the ninth wicket. A championship best performance by the enthusiastic Kevan James left Hampshire with what appeared to be the simple task of scoring 116 for victory. Walsh and Lawrence bowled with fire and fervour. The Gloucestershire fielding was magnificent, and a succession of stunning catches were held in the close to the wicket positions. Hampshire, 39 without loss and 63 for 2, collapsed against a side eager for success, and Cheltenham pulsated with excitement. Walsh returned match figures of 12 for 124 to take his total of wickets to 95.

Nearest challengers Essex, with two games in hand, failed bravely at Eastbourne. Lenham and Colin Wells revived Sussex on the opening day with a stand of 170 after 3 wickets had fallen for 39. Essex claimed their four batting points and declared, and ultimately they were asked to make 319 in 49 overs, a very demanding task. Gooch and Prichard put on 115 in 21 overs for the second wicket, and Border hit a six and 11 fours in his 108 not out which came off only 86 balls, but Essex fell 16 runs short of their target.

Weston-super-Mare marked the return of Ian Botham to first-class cricket. He claimed the wicket of Curtis on the opening day as David Smith stole the limelight with a most aggressive innings. The Monday, however, belonged to Botham. He hit 104 not out off 66 balls, with 7 sixes and 10 fours. The man is irrepressible. Set to make 341 in 78 overs, Somerset were led to victory by Peter Roebuck who batted with masterly control. He and Vic Marks shared an unbeaten stand of 133 for the sixth wicket.

Mike Gatting played his best championship innings of the season at Lord's where Middlesex won their first championship match of the season in spite of Allan Lamb's fine innings, a nudge to the Test selectors that he had refound his form.

Martyn Moxon and Ashley Metcalfe put on 282 for Yorkshire's first wicket in the Roses Match, but Abrahams and Fairbrother batted solidly on the last day and saved the game for Lancashire.

The match at Canterbury saw two remarkable individual performances. Kent made a spirited recovery on the opening day through Chris Cowdrey and Marsh, and by the close Leicestershire were 21 for 3. This soon became 43 for 7 on the Monday, but Phillip de Freitas hit a pugnacious maiden first-class century and shared a stand of 149 with Whitticase. Nevertheless, Kent's first innings lead was 130. This was due almost entirely to some outstanding seam bowling by Terry Alderman who took 8 for 70. The home side then proceeded to bat with a mixture of insanity and indiscretion, the one consistent factor being the inability of anybody to play straight. De Freitas followed his century with six wickets, but by the close Leicestershire were struggling again at 39 for 3, all three wickets to Alderman. The last day turned into a mighty struggle between Willey and Alderman. An eighth wicket stand between Willey and Agnew realised 57, but it

was broken by Underwood who had Willey taken as he mis-pulled a ball. Taylor and Agnew added 16 before Taylor fell to Dilley, and, inevitably, it was Alderman who had Ferris lbw to win the match for Kent by 5 runs. Alderman had match figures of 14 for 144, a testimony to his unrelenting accuracy. It was an outstanding display by one of the world's great seam bowlers who never forgets the basic virtues.

The tourists' match at Derby was a dull affair, but Maher, recently recalled as opening batsman rather than wicket-keeper, hit a maiden first-class hundred.

John Player Special League

3 August

at Cheltenham

Match abandoned
Gloucestershire 2 pts, Hampshire 2 pts

at Canterbury

Match abandoned
Kent 2 pts, Leicestershire 2 pts

at Old Trafford

Lancashire 184 for 5 (G. Fowler 71)
Yorkshire 41 for 1

David Smith cracks the ball through the off-side in his aggressive innings of 165 not out for Worcestershire against Somerset at Weston-super-Mare, 2 August (Adrian Murrell)

Allan Lamb hits Emburey for 4 during his valiant innings of 117, but he could not prevent Middlesex from gaining their first championship win of the season, 4 August. (Mark Leech)

Terry Alderman bowled magnificently for Kent throughout the season and took 14 wickets in the match against Leicestershire at Canterbury when Kent won by 5 runs, 2–5 August. (Tom Morris)

Match abandoned
Lancashire 2 pts, Yorkshire 2 pts

at Lord's

Match abandoned
Middlesex 2 pts, Northamptonshire 2 pts

at Trent Bridge

Match abandoned
Nottinghamshire 2 pts, Glamorgan 2 pts

at Weston-super-Mare

Worcestershire 147 for 8
Somerset 125 for 6

Somerset (4 pts) won on faster scoring rate

at Eastbourne

Essex 138 for 7
Sussex 99 for 5

Essex (4 pts) won by 39 runs

at Edgbaston

Match abandoned
Warwickshire 2 pts, Surrey 2 pts

In one of only two matches to be completed, Essex beat Sussex in a 20-over game and moved to within 4 points of the leaders Northants and Hampshire. Gooch and Prichard put on 76 for the first wicket for Essex in 10 overs.

Ken Higgs – 5 for 22 on his return to first-class cricket at the age of 49, Leicestershire v. Yorkshire, 6–8 August. (Mark Leech)

6, 7 and 8 August

at Chelmsford

Essex 382 for 8 dec (K.W.R. Fletcher 91, A. W. Lilley 87, J.P. Stephenson 54, J.F. Sykes 4 for 102)
Middlesex 116 (N.A. Foster 5 for 51) and 174 (W. N. Slack 92, N. A. Foster 4 for 56, J.H. Childs 4 for 64)

Essex won by an innings and 92 runs
Essex 24 pts, Middlesex 3 pts

at Cheltenham

Gloucestershire 345 (P. Bainbridge 105, A.W. Stovold 81, K.E. Cooper 5 for 102) and 249 for 5 dec (K.M. Curran 117 not out, A. W. Stovold 74 not out)
Nottinghamshire 300 for 3 dec (R.T. Robinson 108, B.C. Broad 105)

Match drawn
Nottinghamshire 7 pts, Gloucestershire 5 pts

at Canterbury

Hampshire 234 (N.G. Cowley 78 not out, C.S. Cowdrey 5 for 69) and 181 for 5 (R.A. Smith 55 not out)
Kent 431 for 8 dec (S.G. Hinks 131, M.R. Benson 94)

Match drawn
Kent 8 pts, Hampshire 4 pts

at Leicester

Yorkshire 216 (A.A. Metcalfe 60, K. Higgs 5 for 22, P.A.J. de Freitas 4 for 94) and 256 for 7 dec (P.E. Robinson 71, D.L. Bairstow 52 not out)
Leicestershire 235 for 9 dec (J.J. Whitaker 100 not out) and 239 for 3 (J.J. Whitaker 82 not out, T.J. Boon 78 not out)

Championship aspirations. David Graveney directs affairs at Cheltenham, Gloucestershire v. Notts, 6–8 August. (Simon Bruty)

Tim Robinson crashes the ball through the off side during his century for Notts against Gloucestershire. (Simon Bruty)

Leicestershire won by 7 wickets
Leicestershire 22 pts, Yorkshire 6 pts

at Northampton

Northamptonshire 441 for 3 dec (R.J. Boyd-Moss 148 not out, G. Cook 120, W. Larkins 86, A.J. Lamb 56)
Glamorgan 282 (M.P. Maynard 77, J. Derrick 76, R.A. Harper 4 for 83) and 138 for 3 (J.A. Hopkins 54, H. Morris 52)

Match drawn
Northamptonshire 6 pts, Glamorgan 2 pts

at Weston-super-Mare

Warwickshire 302 for 4 dec (P.A. Smith 87, A.J. Moles 66, D.L. Amiss 53) and 239 for 2 dec (A.J. Moles 102, P.A. Smith 78)
Somerset 186 for 1 dec (B.C. Rose 76 not out, I.V.A. Richards 74 not out) and 232 for 3 (I.V.A. Richards 115, B.C. Rose 96 not out)

Match drawn
Warwickshire 4 pts, Somerset 2 pts

at The Oval

Lancashire 192 (S.T. Clarke 4 for 51, M.A. Feltham 4 for 47) and 292 for 4 dec. (J. Abrahams 81 not out, G. Fowler 68, N.H. Fairbrother 55)
Surrey 190 (M.A. Lynch 72, J. Simmons 4 for 21) and 295 for 8 (T.E. Jesty 71, A.J. Stewart 69)

Surrey won by 2 wickets
Surrey 22 pts, Lancashire 5 pts

at Eastbourne

Derbyshire 351 for 7 dec (A. Hill 130 not out, R. Sharma 64 not out) and 169 for 3 dec (B.J.M. Maher 77 not out)

Sussex 205 for 2 dec (P.W.G. Parker 100 not out, R.I. Alikhan 64) and 319 for 7 (I.J. Gould 78 not out, N.J. Lenham 77, R.I. Alikhan 72, C.M. Wells 50)

Sussex won by 3 wickets
Sussex 21 pts, Derbyshire 3 pts

Just as it seemed that Gloucestershire were disappearing out of sight in the race for the county championship their run of five successive victories was brought to an end. Put in to bat by Notts, they batted stutteringly and, hampered by interruptions for rain, they owed much to Bainbridge and Stovold who put on 148 for the third wicket. Robinson and Broad replied emphatically for Notts with an opening stand of 221 after which Gloucestershire, 58 for 5 in the second innings, were content to let the game dwindle to a draw. Kevin Curran and Andy Stovold added an unbeaten 191.

Meanwhile Essex were closing the gap as they swept aside Middlesex with contemptuous ease. Their formidable first innings was based on an exhilarating fifth wicket stand of 167 between Alan Lilley and Keith Fletcher. Middlesex were then routed by Lever, Foster and Childs, and in spite of Slack's defiance, they were beaten early on the last day.

Hampshire's challenge faltered again when they were thankful to draw at Canterbury. Chris Cowdrey had a spell of 3 for 0 in ten balls on the first day, and Hinks, who hit a career best 131, and Benson shared Kent's highest opening partnership for 13 years when they put on 191.

Leicestershire, hit by injury, recalled Ken Higgs, five months short of his 50th birthday. He showed younger players how it used to be done by taking 5 for 22. He shared the glory with de Freitas, however, who was awarded his

The end of Robinson's innings. Russell takes a spectacular catch, 7 August. (Simon Bruty)

county cap and with Whitaker who, returning after injury, hit 100 not out in the first innings and 82 off 84 deliveries in the second as he and Boon put on 137 and won the game with 14 balls to spare.

Northants indulged themselves against the weakened Glamorgan attack. Cook and Larkins put on 151 for the first wicket, and Cook and Boyd-Moss 130 for the second. The third wicket produced a stand of 139 between Boyd-Moss and Lamb, but although Glamorgan could not match the Northants' rate of scoring, they had little difficulty in avoiding defeat.

On a placid wicket at Weston-super-Mare, the highlights were a maiden first-class hundred for Andy Moles who shared two century opening partnerships with Paul Smith, and 115 off 94 balls with 5 sixes and 11 fours by Viv Richards.

Surrey beat Lancashire with 7 balls to spare, Stewart and Jesty adding 138 in 23 overs, and Sussex beat Derbyshire with 11 balls to spare at Eastbourne. Put in to bat, Derbyshire moved to 351 after a rain-marred first day. Alan Hill,

who hit a typically stubborn 130, and Sharma shared an unbeaten stand of 135 for the seventh wicket. Sussex raced to two batting points and declared, and they were eventually asked to make 316 in 66 overs. Green and Parker, who batted so well in the first innings, were out for 31, but Alikhan and Lenham added 112, and Colin Wells and Ian Gould led the final assault which brought the target within range. The Derbyshire cause was not advanced by missed chances.

Second Cornhill Test Match
ENGLAND v. NEW ZEALAND

In the fortnightly search for a fast bowler, England brought in Gladstone Small for his first Test match and Greg Thomas for his first Test match in England. Thomas replaced the original choice, Dilley, who was unfit. Emburey returned in place of Willey who was twelfth man. New Zealand included an extra pace bowler, Derek Stirling, at the expense of a batsman, Rutherford.

Jeremy Coney won the toss and asked England to bat first on a day that was mainly cloudy and very windy. Gooch, with his decision as to whether or not he would tour Australia hanging over English cricket like the Sword of Damocles, assaulted Hadlee from the start. He hit 18 off 18 balls, all the runs scored for the first wicket, before attempting to drive Hadlee on the on-side. He was surprised by the pace of Hadlee's delivery and was lbw playing across the line. Athey began soundly, but Moxon was bowled through the gate and England were 43 for 2.

By lunch, Athey and Gower, showing that effortless grace which makes him the most attractive of batsmen, had taken the score to 102, and the England batting had one of its rare shafts of light of the summer. They extended their stand to 83 before Athey fell to a ball from Watson which cut back at him. He had completed his first fifty in Test cricket and had batted with pleasing assurance if not total confidence.

Gower did not look like being out until, playing no shot at

LEFT: *Gower falls lbw to Gray for 71. (Adrian Murrell)*

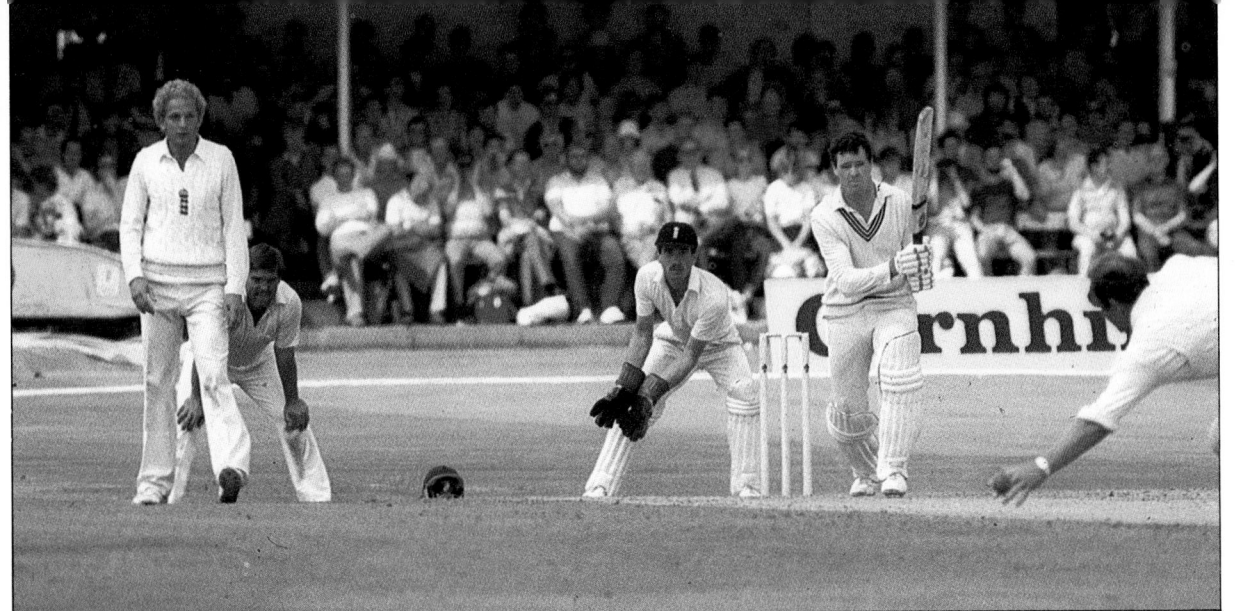

a ball from Gray, he was lbw to a ball which turned violently out of the rough outside the left-hander's off stump. Shortly after Hadlee claimed his third wicket of the innings when, with some sense of inevitability, he bowled Gatting through the gate. The England captain played an embarrassing shot after offering solid defence at the beginning of his innings.

Rain brought an early tea, and a refreshed Hadlee demolished Emburey and Edmonds in one over shortly after the resumption. Both fell to catches behind off balls that rose sharply and moved away late. It was beautiful bowling and it took Hadlee into third place in the list of wicket-takers in Test cricket, only Lillee and Botham lay ahead of him. It also meant that he had taken five wickets in a Test innings for the 27th time, a record. He should have had Pringle caught at slip, but Bracewell dropped a straight-forward chance. Pringle was out when he hooked Stirling to Watson, and one felt that the failure was more one of confidence than of technique. The Essex all-rounder seemed frightened to hit

BELOW: *Small captures his first Test wicket. Jeff Crowe walks away as the England players gather round the Warwickshire bowler. (Adrian Murrell)*

John Bracewell drives past bowler Edmonds for four on his way to his first Test century, a match-winning innings for New Zealand. (Ken Kelly)

Gower is caught by Jeff Crowe off Bracewell, and England face defeat. (Adrian Murrell)

the ball in his old manner. Thomas played some spirited shots before becoming Hadlee's sixth victim, the ball moving back at him sharply, and when bad light brought play to an early close England were 240 for 9 and New Zealand well satisfied.

If New Zealand had a failing, it was certainly in their slip fielding. Small enjoyed two 'lives' on the second morning, and French played some robust shots so that the last England wicket realised 16 runs. Thomas was fast, but wild; Small suggested pace and movement. A yorker accounted for Edgar, but Wright and Jeff Crowe played firmly, and it was well into the afternoon before England gained another success. John Wright seemed in total command. He had taken 12 off an over from Small when he played lazily and flicked the ball into the hands of square-leg. In this next over Small had Jeff Crowe splendidly caught by the diving French.

Coney and Martin Crowe played with authority. Coney was dropped by Gooch at slip, but neither batsman appeared to be in trouble. Then disaster struck. In the last over before tea Martin Crowe called from a rather unwise short single. Coney hesitated and was run out. Straight after the interval Martin Crowe turned Emburey gently into the hands of backward short leg. New Zealand were 144 for 5 and in some trouble. Gray and Hadlee showed no sign of this trouble as they dealt comfortably with all that was bowled for the rest of the day. Gray concentrated on defence; Hadlee hit whatever was available to hit. The man who had troubled England with the ball, now defied them with the bat. New Zealand closed on 211 for 5, Hadlee 53, Gray 14, the game evenly balanced.

By the end of the third day, New Zealand had taken command of the game. The Gray-Hadlee stand moved to 95 before Hadlee, having been dropped by Gooch at slip, was caught by the same player high above his head at second slip. New Zealand still trailed by 17 runs, but any hope England had of pressing their advantage was quickly dispelled by Bracewell who hit with vigour. At lunch, he and Gray had

taken their side to a 22-run lead.

Gray's first Test fifty arrived, and he was caught at silly mid-off almost immediately. He had batted with unflinching resolution, curbing his natural flair in the needs of the occasion. He had faced 238 balls in his 301 minutes at the crease, and, as much as anybody, he had made a New Zealand victory possible. Smith did not stay long, but Stirling swung the bat happily. This was a distressing resistance for England, and they fell apart in the field. There was no apparent leadership and no evidence of pre-thought as field placings became haphazard affairs, tediously arranged and ill-conceived.

When Stirling was bowled by Small Bracewell was on 96 and New Zealand led by 135. Watson defended bravely, but Bracewell thought nothing of personal achievement, gathering what singles were offered even if they deprived him of the bowling. He reached a marvellously brave century and then skied Emburey to deep square leg. England had been in the field for 11 hours, and it was 5.20 on the third day. Bracewell's day had not ended. He bowled one over in which he had Gooch caught bat-pad at silly point. The batsman was not happy with the decision, and on Saturday evening, 31 for 1, England were thoroughly miserable.

The sun which had shone on New Zealand disappeared on the fourth day when, in the 75 minutes play that were possible, England lost Moxon and Athey as the score moved on to 64. Moxon drove rashly, and Athey tried to turn a ball to leg although, like Gooch, he seemed to think he was the victim of a conspiracy.

England had a day in which to save the match. New Zealand lost Edgar with a cut hand and dropped Edmonds at slip. Martin Crowe was the culprit. The night-watchman, who had performed nobly, had added only 2 to his score when he fell to a ball from Hadlee which came back at him sharply. Gatting hit Hadlee for 4 and then pushed forward at Gray and was caught behind. Smith had joined the record-breakers with more dismissals in Test matches than any other New Zealand keeper.

Gower was playing sensibly. He had passed 6,000 runs in Test cricket when he received a ball from Bracewell which turned and took the shoulder of the bat for Jeff Crowe to take a simple catch at slip.

Pringle, with resolute defence, and Emburey, in more aggressive vein, added 74, and for England there was a glimmer of hope. New Zealand remained calm, most ably led by Coney who changed his bowlers with intelligence and marshalled his men shrewdly. Stirling reared a ball at Pringle who did his best to play it down, but it looped towards gully where Gray ran to take a good catch. The second new ball accounted for Emburey, well taken at slip, and Thomas. After a couple of fine shots Small offered no stroke and Hadlee had taken 10 wickets in the match.

There were slight stammers from New Zealand when Jeff Crowe fell to a good ball and John Wright to a straight one at which he played no stroke, but there was no nonsense from Martin Crowe and Coney, and the Kiwis won their second Test match in England. It was most thoroughly deserved.

LEFT: *The end of England and ten wickets in a match for Hadlee. Small is lbw without offering a stroke. (Ken Kelly)*

9, 11 and 12 August

at Buxton

Lancashire 173 (A.E. Warner 4 for 38) and 178 for 2 dec (G. Fowler 86, G.D. Mendis 65)
Derbyshire 72 for 1 dec and 179 for 7 (B.J.M. Maher 51, A. Hill 51)

Match drawn
Derbyshire 4 pts, Lancashire 1 pt

at Cheltenham

Middlesex 349 (K.R. Brown 66, J.D. Carr 66, C.A. Walsh 5 for 95, D.V. Lawrence 4 for 112) and 68 for 1 dec
Gloucestershire 61 for 3 dec and 252 (J.W. Lloyds 94, S.P. Hughes 4 for 40)

Middlesex won by 104 runs
Middlesex 20 pts, Gloucestershire 2 pts

at Southampton

Hampshire 320 for 6 dec (D.R. Turner 79, C.G. Greenidge 78, T.M. Tremlett 59) and 242 for 2 dec (R.A. Smith 128 not out, C.G. Greenidge 79)
Sussex 302 for 4 dec (Imran Khan 104, P.W.G. Parker 83, C.M. Wells 56 not out) and 209 for 8

Match drawn
Sussex 6 pts, Hampshire 5 pts

at Leicester

Essex 216 (B.R. Hardie 53) and 159 for 3 dec (A.W. Lilley 63)
Leicestershire 55 for 2 dec and 190 (P. Whitticase 55 not out, N.A. Foster 5 for 84)

Essex won by 130 runs
Essex 18 pts, Leicestershire 4 pts

at Wellingborough

Somerset 210 (V.J. Marks 76 not out) and 195 for 6 dec (R.J. Harden 53 not out, D.J. Capel 5 for 61)
Northamptonshire 185 for 5 dec (A.J. Lamb 83, W. Larkins 59) and 80 for 2

Match drawn
Northamptonshire 5 pts, Somerset 4 pts

at The Oval

Worcestershire 381 for 5 dec (D.N. Patel 132 not out, S.J. Rhodes 67 not out, T.S. Curtis 51) and 123 for 1 (T.S. Curtis 64 not out)
Surrey 500 for 9 dec (T.E. Jesty 179, M.A. Lynch 77, C.J. Richards 60, P.J. Newport 4 for 136)

Match drawn
Surrey 6 pts, Worcestershire 6 pts

at Edgbaston

Warwickshire 326 for 5 dec (B.M. McMillan 106, G.W. Humpage 59, P.A. Smith 55) and 57 for 0 dec
Kent 23 for 0 dec and 299 for 8 (M.R. Benson 82, N.R. Taylor 81, T.A. Munton 4 for 60)

Match drawn
Warwickshire 4 pts, Kent 2 pts

at Leeds

Glamorgan 134 (S.J. Dennis 4 for 26) and 212 for 3 (M.P. Maynard 85 not out)

SECOND CORNHILL TEST MATCH – ENGLAND *v.* NEW ZEALAND
7, 8, 9, 11 and 12 August 1986 at Trent Bridge, Nottingham

ENGLAND

	FIRST INNINGS		SECOND INNINGS	
G.A. Gooch	lbw, b Hadlee	18	c Coney, b Bracewell	17
M.D. Moxon	b Hadlee	9	c Smith, b Hadlee	23
C.W.J. Athey	lbw, b Watson	55	(4) c Smith, b Bracewell	6
D.I. Gower	lbw, b Gray	71	(5) c J. Crowe, b Bracewell	26
M.W. Gatting†	b Hadlee	17	(6) c Smith, b Gray	4
D.R. Pringle	c Watson, b Stirling	21	(7) c Gray, b Stirling	9
J.E. Emburey	c Smith, b Hadlee	8	(8) c M. Crowe, b Hadlee	75
P.H. Edmonds	c Smith, b Hadlee	0	(3) lbw, b Hadlee	20
J.G. Thomas	b Hadlee	28	c Gray, b Stirling	10
B.N. French*	c Coney, b Watson	21	not out	12
G.C. Small	not out	2	lbw, b Hadlee	12
	b 1, lb 3, nb 2	6	b 4, lb 9, w 1, nb 2	16
		256		230

NEW ZEALAND

	FIRST INNINGS		SECOND INNINGS	
B.A. Edgar	lbw, b Thomas	8		
J.G. Wright	c Athey, b Small	58	(1) b Emburey	7
J.J. Crowe	c French, b Small	23	(2) lbw, b Small	2
M.D. Crowe	c Edmonds, b Emburey	28	(3) not out	44
J.V. Coney†	run out	24	(4) not out	20
E.J. Gray	c Athey, b Edmonds	50		
R.J. Hadlee	c Gooch, b Thomas	68		
J.G. Bracewell	c Moxon, b Emburey	110		
I.D.S. Smith*	lbw, b Edmonds	2		
D.A. Stirling	b Small	26		
W. Watson	not out	8		
	lb 4, w 2, nb 2	8	nb 1	1
		413	(for 2 wickets)	74

	O	M	R	W	O	M	R	W		O	M	R	W	O	M	R	W
Hadlee	32	7	80	6	33.1	15	60	4	Small	38	12	88	3	8	3	10	1
Stirling	17	3	62	1	18	5	48	2	Thomas	39	5	124	2	4	—	16	—
Gray	13	4	30	1	24	9	55	1	Pringle	20	1	58	—	2	—	16	—
Watson	16.5	6	51	2	9	3	25	—	Edmonds	28	11	52	2	4	1	16	—
Coney	7	1	18	—					Emburey	42.5	17	87	2	6	1	15	1
Bracewell	4	1	11	—	11	5	29	3	Gooch	2	2	0	—				
									Gower					0.0	—	1	—

FALL OF WICKETS
1- 18, 2- 43, 3- 126, 4- 170, 5- 176, 6- 191, 7- 191, 8- 205, 9- 240
1- 23, 2- 47, 3- 63, 4- 87, 5- 98, 6- 104, 7- 178, 8- 203, 9- 203

FALL OF WICKETS
1- 39, 2- 85, 3- 92, 4- 142, 5- 144, 6- 239, 7- 318, 8- 326, 9- 391
1- 5, 2- 19

Umpires: D.J. Constant & K.E. Palmer

New Zealand won by 8 wickets

Yorkshire 310 for 7 dec (A.A. Metcalfe 149, J.D. Love 88, S.J. Base 4 for 74)

Match drawn
Yorkshire 8 pts, Glamorgan 3 pts

Gloucestershire ended a miserable week at Cheltenham with their second defeat of the season and their once seemingly impregnable lead cut to 19 points over Essex who had two games in hand. Middlesex, put in to bat, moved evenly if uninspiringly into the second day. Gloucestershire's one consolation was that Walsh became the first bowler in the country to reach 100 wickets. He reached the mark on 11 August, the earliest date that the peformance had been achieved for 15 years. Rain marred the game, and some jostling left the home side to make a formidable 357. They lost Wright and Tomlins for 13, and although Lloyds batted bravely at the close, they never looked like winning. Lloyds hit 2 sixes and 12 fours before falling to a Roland Butcher leg-break as the game ended in drizzle and gloom.

Essex, on the other hand, snatched victory from nothing. Bowled out for 216 on the first day after electing to bat, they suffered a blank day on the Monday, but profited from Leicestershire's generous declaration and occasional bowling on the last morning. Leicestershire were finally asked to score 321 in 80 overs on a rather lively pitch. The odds seemed very much in favour of Essex, and the home side were never remotely in the hunt as Foster, Topley and Childs found little opposition.

There was no play on the second day at Buxton, Wellingborough and Edgbaston, but agreed declarations could bring no result on the last day. Hampshire were thwarted at Southampton by Reeve and Alan Wells who held out for the last 8 overs. Consistent batting had taken Hampshire to a good position on the Saturday, but Imran Khan and Paul Parker added 147 for Sussex's third wicket on the Monday to balance the game. A second wicket stand of 185 between Greenidge and Robin Smith who passed 1,000 runs for the season enabled Nicholas to ask Sussex to make 261 in 60 overs. Once Maru had superbly caught and bowled Parker the Sussex challenge faded. Hampshire were handicapped by injuries, particularly the one sustained by Tremlett who was forced to retire hurt after being hit on the hand on the Saturday.

Ashley Metcalfe celebrated the award of his county cap with his fifth championship century of the summer in the rain-ruined game at Headingley, and there was high scoring at The Oval where the Worcestershire attack became depleted through illness and injury. Patel and Rhodes shared an unbeaten sixth wicket stand of 191 in 37 overs. For Surrey, Jesty shared stands of 193 with Lynch and 129 with Richards.

John Player Special League

10 August

at Buxton

Lancashire 149 for 6 (N.H. Fairbrother 52 not out)
Derbyshire 155 for 7 (B. Roberts 60 not out)

Derbyshire (4 pts) won by 3 wickets

at Cheltenham

Match abandoned
Gloucestershire 2 pts, Middlesex 2 pts

at Bournemouth

Hampshire 221 for 6 (R.A. Smith 57 not out, G.S. le Roux 4 for 40)
Sussex 199 for 3 (P.W.G. Parker 92, A.P. Wells 63)

Sussex (4 pts) won on faster scoring rate

at Leicester

Essex 151 for 3 (B.R. Hardie 79)
Leicestershire 127 for 8

Essex (4 pts) won by 24 runs

at Wellingborough

Somerset 272 for 5 (I.T. Botham 175 not out)
Northamptonshire 54 for 1

Match abandoned
Northamptonshire 2 pts, Somerset 2 pts

at The Oval

Worcestershire 189 for 6
Surrey 191 for 6 (G.S. Clinton 59)

Surrey (4 pts) won by 4 wickets

at Edgbaston

Kent 74 for 2 (S.G. Hinks 50)
v. Warwickshire

Match abandoned
Kent 2 pts, Warwickshire 2 pts

at Scarborough

Yorkshire 200 for 6
Glamorgan 181 (S.D. Fletcher 4 for 32)

Yorkshire (4 pts) won by 19 runs

Parker and Alan Wells put on 147 for the first Sussex wicket and set their side on the path to victory over Hampshire who thereby lost their spot at the top of the table. Essex drew level with them with some astonishingly quick scoring in an 18-over game at Leicester. Northamptonshire went top by virtue of their abandoned match against Somerset. The new leaders could count themselves rather fortunate in that they faced a target of 273 in 39 overs when the game was called off. They were the victims of an amazing innings by Ian Botham who established a record for the competition by hitting 13 sixes. He also hit 12 fours, and his 175 not out came off only 122 balls. He forfeited the record score in the Sunday League because only 39 overs were bowled, so much time having been lost retrieving the ball after his massive hits. He had certainly come in from the cold.

13, 14 and 15 August

at Edgbaston

New Zealanders 218 for 9 dec (J.G. Wright 59, J.J. Crowe 58, D.J. Capel 4 for 61) and 291 for 6 dec (K.R. Rutherford 104, M.D. Crowe 61)
TCCB XI 268 for 6 dec (R.J. Bailey 68, A.A. Metcalfe 58) and 121 for 1 (A.A. Metcalfe 71 not out)

Match drawn

This was an extra match fitted into the tourists' programme and gave a good opportunity for several young players to display their talents. None did better than Ashley Metcalfe with two good innings.

NatWest Bank Trophy – Semi-Finals

13 August

at The Oval

Lancashire 229 (C.H. Lloyd 65, S.J. O'Shaughnessy 62, S.T. Clarke 4 for 21)
Surrey 225 (T.E. Jesty 112)

Lancashire won by 4 runs
(Man of the Match – T.E. Jesty)

13, 14 and 15 August

at Worcester

Worcestershire 125
Sussex 126 for 5

Sussex won by 5 wickets
(Man of the Match – Imran Khan)

Bad weather dragged the semi-final at Worcester into the third morning. Only 32 balls were possible on the first day when Worcestershire, having been put in, reached 20 for 0 in damp conditions. Play could not begin until 2.30 on the second day. At tea, after 33 overs, Worcestershire were 82 for 2 and looking forward to a substantial innings. D'Oliveira had stupidly run himself out, and Curtis had lofted a gentle catch off Colin Wells, but Smith and Hick were at the crease, and the home side was optimistic. The optimism quickly vanished after tea when Imran Khan destroyed the middle order with a fine spell of pace bowling. The last 8 wickets fell for 43 runs in 20 overs. Hick played on to Imran, Neale was lbw and Patel caught behind. Imran had fine support from Jones, Pigott and le Roux, and Sussex were left with a simple task. It seemed less simple when Radford captured the

RIGHT: *Patel is caught off Imran Khan and Worcestershire are on the verge of collapse. NatWest Trophy semi-final. (Adrian Murrell)*

BELOW: *A helicopter helps in the drying up process at Worcester where the NatWest Trophy semi-final went into the third day. (Adrian Murrell)*

Trevor Jesty played the innings of the season in the NatWest semi-final at The Oval, but still finished on the losing side. (Simon Bruty)

wickets of Green and Parker before the close and had Imran caught at slip in the first over of the third day to make it 31 for 3, but Alikhan, fortuitously, and Colin Wells, more positively, survived and added 72 which assured Sussex of a place in the final.

At The Oval, the match was completed on the Wednesday as scheduled. Pocock asked Lancashire to bat first when he won the toss, and a torrid first over from Sylvester Clarke showed the reason. It produced a single to Mendis who was then caught off Bicknell's first delivery, Clarke taking a good catch in the gully. Worse was to come for Lancashire when Fowler, fending away a rising ball from Clarke, was caught

Rehan Alikhan, a dangerous, but effective innings for Sussex in their victory over Worcestershire in the NatWest Bank Trophy semi-final. (Adrian Murrell)

John Hopkins – a miserable season lightened by a century for Glamorgan against the New Zealanders. (Mark Leech)

one-handed by Richards diving to his right down the leg side. It was unquestionably one of the finest wicket-keeping catches one has ever seen. Abrahams was the batsman in form, but he missed an inswinger from Feltham, and Lancashire were 28 for 3 in 15 overs. Bicknell and Clarke had bowled at a very lively pace, and Clive Lloyd was left floundering time and again by his fellow West Indian, but the great batsman is he who survives when things are not going well, and Lloyd still has the mark of greatness on him. Fairbrother suggested quality if not permanence, and in the 25th over he fell to Thomas. Lancashire were 59 for 4 and in deep trouble, but the pace of Bicknell and Clarke could not be sustained. Bicknell had tired, and Clarke was being held back for the final burst. Thomas, Feltham and Pocock presented fewer problems. Lloyd found a partner of character in Steve O'Shaughnessy, not always well used by his county during the season, but a player of infinite courage and determination. The pair added 99 in 21 overs. It was the decisive stand of the match. Lloyd was caught behind cutting at Pocock. Hayhurst fell in a similar manner off the bowling of Butcher who bowled 7 tidy overs. Maynard gave a violent interlude, but any hopes that Lancashire had of a large total were blighted by the return of Clarke who had O'Shaughnessy taken at slip and Allott caught at extra cover before bowling Simmons with the third ball of the 59th over.

Allott redeemed himself when he had Butcher caught at long leg off a most unwise and unnecessary hook and Clinton caught at slip. Stewart was lbw to Watkinson, and Surrey were 30 for 3. Lynch and Jesty rectified the situation somewhat until Lynch insanely ran himself out although credit should be give to O'Shaughnessy's throw. Jesty was

now driving handsomely, but nobody else seemed capable of establishing an innings. The Lancashire out cricket was splendid, and Lloyd manipulated his limited bowling resources admirably. At 173 for 7, the game was tilting in favour of Lancashire, but Clarke hit fiercely and the 200 was passed. Then Clarke hit rashly and was caught at square-leg. When Pocock was bowled by Allott Surrey were 24 short of victory with only Bicknell left to support the magnificent Jesty who, having pulled a leg muscle, had been batting with a runner since reaching 76. There were conversations between all three Surrey players, and Bicknell impressed as much with his solid defence as he had done earlier with his fast bowling. Jesty reached an outstanding century. His driving was majestic, a glimpse at a dimly remembered golden age. When Hayhurst began the penultimate over Surrey needed 7 to win, and Jesty was taking strike. He hit the first ball for 2 and off the fifth ball he attempted a massive lofted on drive. It was, perhaps, his only injudicious stroke, but it looked like a winning hit until Fowler making ground round the boundary held the catch at long-on as he rolled over and over. It was a pulsating climax to a memorable match.

16, 17 and 18 August

at Swansea

New Zealand 378 for 5 dec (J.J. Crowe 159, J.V. Coney 140 not out) and 71 for 3
Glamorgan 303 for 5 dec (J.A. Hopkins 142, G.C. Holmes 74)

Match drawn

16, 18 and 19 August

at Chesterfield

Yorkshire 177 (M.A. Holding 5 for 46) and 162 for 2 dec (P.E. Robinson 70 not out)
Derbyshire 68 for 0 dec and 244 for 7 (A.E. Warner 64, G. Miller 51 not out, P.J. Hartley 4 for 57)

Match drawn
Derbyshire 4 pts, Yorkshire 1 pt

at Colchester

Northamptonshire 302 (A.J. Lamb 81, R.J. Bailey 63, N.A. Foster 5 for 83) and 181 (J.H. Childs 8 for 61)
Essex 337 (G.A. Gooch 87, P.J. Prichard 72, B.R. Hardie 66, N.A. Mallender 5 for 110, N.G.B. Cook 4 for 76) and 44 (N.G.B. Cook 5 for 14, N.A. Mallender 4 for 22)

Northamptonshire won by 102 runs
Northamptonshire 24 pts, Essex 8 pts

at Lord's

Middlesex 155 and 226 for 3 (A.J.T. Miller 111 not out, J.D. Carr 56)
Hampshire 158 for 7 dec and 129 for 3 (C.G. Greenidge 70 not out)

Match drawn
Hampshire 5 pts, Middlesex 4 pts

at Trent Bridge

Lancashire 324 for 8 dec (G.D. Mendis 108, N.H. Fairbrother 97, G. Fowler 57) and 42 for 1 dec
Nottinghamshire 72 for 2 dec and 295 for 3 (P. Johnson 120 not out, B.C. Broad 66, M. Newell 61)

Nottinghamshire won by 7 wickets
Nottinghamshire 17 pts, Lancashire 3 pts

at Taunton

Surrey 427 for 9 dec (G.S. Clinton 117, A.J. Stewart 78, C.J. Richards 70 not out) and 0 for 0 dec
Somerset 83 for 9 dec and 166 (S.T. Clarke 5 for 31)

Surrey won by 178 runs
Surrey 20 pts, Somerset 4 pts

at Hove

Kent 191 (A.C.S. Pigott 4 for 32) and 145 (A.C.S. Pigott 5 for 50)
Sussex 252 (C.M. Wells 82, G.R. Dilley 5 for 101, R.M. Ellison 4 for 53) and 85 for 4 (P.W.G. Parker 51 not out)

Sussex won by 6 wickets
Sussex 23 pts, Kent 5 pts

at Nuneaton

Warwickshire 381 for 9 dec (A.J. Moles 100, J.W. Lloyds 5 for 124) and 102 for 0 dec (P.A. Smith 70 not out)
Gloucestershire 115 for 2 dec (P.W. Romaines 67 not out) and 205 (K.M. Curran 57)

Warwickshire won by 163 runs
Warwickshire 20 pts, Gloucestershire 3 pts

at Worcester

Leicestershire 209 (T.J. Boon 63, P.J. Newport 5 for 76) and 114 (P.J. Newport 4 for 30)
Worcestershire 128 for 2 dec and 199 for 6 (D.M. Smith 76)

Worcestershire won by 4 wickets
Worcestershire 20 pts, Leicestershire 4 pts

The struggle for the Britannic Assurance County Championship became more intense than ever as both the leading counties lost. Gloucestershire were never in the hunt at Nuneaton where Moles hit the second century of his career before becoming one of Lloyds' victims. There was dependable batting from Warwickshire right down the order, and they ended the first day in total command. Rain ruined the second day, and Graveney declared at the start of play on the Tuesday. Gifford was able to ask Gloucestershire to make 369 in five hours, a massive task which they never looked likely to accomplish in spite of Curran's 57 off 62 balls.

Essex cut the Gloucestershire lead to 14 points, but they looked set to go top of the table until an extraordinary collapse on the last afternoon. Northants were pulled back after Lamb had threatened to tear the Essex bowling apart, and Gooch, violently, Prichard and Hardie took Essex to a valuable first innings lead. The left-arm spin of the admirable John Childs then put Northants in a position of desolation, and left Essex with only 147 needed to win and take the lead in the title race. A mixture of indiscretion, nerves and good bowling saw them collapse to 44 all out, the lowest score of the season, and Northants gain an improbable victory. Gooch was the only batsman to reach double figures. Border, in his last game for Essex, got an inside edge from Nick Cook and diverted the ball onto his stumps. In $4\frac{1}{2}$ hours on the last day, 19 wickets fell for 189 runs.

Surrey moved closer in third place with a fine victory at Taunton. Sparked by a second wicket stand of 114 between Clinton and Stewart, they raced to 427 in 96.1 overs on the first day. There was no play on the second day, but the forfeiture of an innings after Somerset had been offered brisk runs left the home county to score 345 in 95 overs. The wicket was good, but Somerset batted badly. They lost their first 4

Andy Miller hit his first championship century for Middlesex against Hampshire, Lord's, 16–18 August. (George Herringshaw)

wickets for 38 runs, three of them to Sylvester Clarke, and never recovered.

Miller scored his first championship century in the game at Lord's, but the sides could conjure nothing from the rain-hit match. Derbyshire, asked to make 272 in 70 overs at Chesterfield, fell 28 runs short in spite of Warner's 64 off 58 balls. Derbyshire made a bad start in the chase as Peter Hartley claimed four of the first five wickets.

The bowling of Tony Pigott gave Sussex command over Kent at Hove where a two-day victory looked possible at one time. Eventually, acting skipper Paul Parker nursed his side through a fraught hour on the last morning.

Mendis and Fowler put on 116 for Lancashire's first wicket at Trent Bridge, and Neil Fairbrother took them to a position of strength with another excitingly impressive knock. Rain spoiled the second day, and Simmons left Notts 89 overs in which to score 295 on the last day. It was a generous declaration, and Notts, led by Paul Johnson, who hit a sparkling 120 not out and reached 1000 runs for the season for the first time, the youngest Notts player to achieve this feat, won with 13.5 overs to spare.

Only 11 overs were possible at Worcester on the second day, but the sole concession that the teams made to the weather was that Neale declared while still 81 runs behind on the first innings. His bowlers then performed admirably on an unpredictable wicket, and Phil Newport, enjoying his best season, finished with match figures of 9 for 106. Needing to score 196 in 53 overs, Worcestershire never found the task easy, but Hick provided some flair, and David Smith hit imperiously to reach 50 off 84 balls. He and Patel added 78 before Smith was out with only 22 runs needed. Victory was achieved with 3 overs to spare.

There was no play on the last day at Swansea where Jeff Crowe, with his first century in England, and Jeremy Coney added 218 for New Zealand's fourth wicket. On the second day, John Hopkins ended his miserable season with a fine century, sharing a third wicket stand of 180 with Holmes.

John Player Special League

17 August

at Chesterfield

Yorkshire 132 for 9
Derbyshire 135 for 0 (K.J. Barnett 72 not out)

Derbyshire (4 pts) won by 10 wickets

at Colchester

Essex 234 for 5 (B.R. Hardie 109)
Northamptonshire 202 for 9 (R.J. Bailey 63)

Essex (4 pts) won by 32 runs

at Lord's

Hampshire 195 for 5 (R.A. Smith 65)
Middlesex 200 for 2 (W.N. Slack 75)

Middlesex (4 pts) won by 8 wickets

at Trent Bridge

Nottinghamshire 237 for 5 (D.W. Randall 88, C.E.B. Rice 70)
Lancashire 211 (N.H. Fairbrother 79, C.E.B. Rice 4 for 25)

Nottinghamshire (4 pts) won by 26 runs

at Taunton

Surrey 198 for 5 (G.S. Clinton 70, A.R. Butcher 50)
v. Somerset

Match abandoned
Somerset 2 pts, Surrey 2 pts

at Hove

Sussex 181 for 5 (I.J. Gould 65 not out)
Kent 182 for 9 (Imran Khan 4 for 31)

Kent (4 pts) won by 1 wicket

at Edgbaston

Warwickshire 284 for 5 (A.J. Moles 85, A.I. Kallicharran 71, D.L. Amiss 60)
Gloucestershire 238 for 7 (C.W.J. Athey 64)

Warwickshire (4 pts) won by 46 runs

at Worcester

Worcestershire 162 for 8 (P.A.J. de Freitas 4 for 20)
Leicestershire 150 for 8

Worcestershire (4 pts) won by 12 runs

Essex went to the top of the Sunday League by beating Northants. In spite of Brian Hardie's fine century—he shared an opening stand of 104 with Gooch—it seemed that Essex may not have scored quite enough runs at Colchester although they were aided by some bizarre Northants fielding which conceded 7 overthrows off the last two balls of the innings. Northants lost Larkins to a fine catch at long leg by Lever, and they could never reach the required run rate. Bailey made 63 rather slowly before skying to Border who, on his last Sunday appearance for Essex, had Mallender stumped off the last ball of the last over. Surprisingly, Hampshire lost to Middlesex, Radley and Slack putting on 115 for the first wicket. Kent won with 4 balls and 1 wicket to spare, and Derbyshire routed Yorkshire, winning with 11.5 overs remaining.

20, 21 and 22 August

at Chesterfield

Derbyshire 378 for 9 dec (A.E. Warner 91, J.E. Morris 62, A. Hill 56) and 39 for 1
Leicestershire 293 (J.J. Whitaker 175, R.J. Finney 7 for 54)

Match drawn
Derbyshire 8 pts, Leicestershire 6 pts

at Colchester

Essex 311 (D.E. East 82, P.J. Prichard 65, C.A. Walsh 6 for 83) and 172 for 5 dec (D.E. East 100 not out, D.A. Graveney 4 for 73)
Gloucestershire 183 (J.W. Lloyds 52, J.H. Childs 8 for 58) and 139 for 9 (P. Bainbridge 53 not out, D.R. Pringle 4 for 27)

Match drawn
Essex 8 pts, Gloucestershire 5 pts

at Bournemouth

Hampshire 237 (V.P. Terry 74, P.J. Newport 5 for 74) and 91 for 4 dec
Worcestershire 120 (R.J. Maru 4 for 33) and 160 for 5 (G.A. Hick 81)

Match drawn
Hampshire 6 pts, Worcestershire 4 pts

at Dartford

Kent 379 for 8 dec (M.R. Benson 123, N.R. Taylor 88) and 214 for 5 dec (N.R. Taylor 65, D.G. Aslett 57)
Surrey 300 for 5 dec (M.A. Lynch 119 not out, A.J. Stewart 61) and 245 for 8 (A.J. Stewart 105)

Match drawn
Kent 6 pts, Surrey 6 pts

at Lytham

Lancashire 192 (J. Abrahams 99) and 149 for 9 dec (M.R. Chadwick 50, R.C. Ontong 4 for 44, P.D. North 4 for 49)
Glamorgan 164 for 8 dec (I. Folley 4 for 42) and 156 for 8 (J. Simmons 7 for 79)

Match drawn
Glamorgan 5 pts, Lancashire 4 pts

at Northampton

Nottinghamshire 328 (B.C. Broad 92, C.D. Fraser-Darling 61, R.A. Harper 4 for 50) and 118 for 2 dec (M. Newell 53 not out)
Northamptonshire 179 for 8 dec (R.J. Bailey 98, C.D. Fraser-Darling 5 for 84) and 49 for 0

Match drawn
Nottinghamshire 5 pts, Northamptonshire 4 pts

at Taunton

Somerset 333 (V.J. Marks 110, R.J. Harden 108, A.C.S. Pigott 5 for 81)
Sussex 66 for 1

Match drawn
Somerset 3 pts, Sussex 1 pt

at Leeds

Middlesex 252 (W.N. Slack 105 not out, S.J. Dennis 5 for 71, S.D. Fletcher 5 for 90)
Yorkshire 216 for 8 dec (J.D. Love 65 not out, S.P. Hughes 4 for 92)

Match drawn
Yorkshire 6 pts, Middlesex 6 pts

The clash between the two top sides in the championship went very much in favour of Essex, but in the end, they were denied victory by some dogged batting, Bainbridge playing heroically and without blemish to score 53 not out in 4 hours. Fletcher had chosen to bat first when he won the toss, and although Stephenson went early, David East and Paul Prichard batted with great panache to take the score from 53 to 134 before Walsh returned to have East lbw, Prichard taken at slip by Lloyds who held three catches and catch and bowl Hardie in fine fashion. Lilley and Fletcher revived Essex, and Foster's aggression brought the maximum batting points. Childs captured two wickets before the close, and Essex ended the day happily. They were even happier on the second day even though it was curtailed by 32 overs. John Childs produced another magnificent spell of bowling to finish with 8 for 58, his second eight-wicket haul of the week. He is a dedicated and intelligent bowler who has worked hard to establish himself, and he must now rank close to

Two players who had an outstanding match combine. Keith Tomlins is caught by centurion David East off the bowling of John Childs, Essex v. Gloucestershire, 20–22 August. (Simon Bruty)

ABOVE: *David East strikes again. He stumps Bainbridge off Childs. (Simon Bruty)*

ABOVE: *Keith Medlycott – impressive spin bowling for Surrey. (Tom Morris)*

Hero of the hour. John Childs dismisses David Graveney, caught at silly mid-off by Keith Fletcher. (Simon Bruty)

Edmonds and Emburey among English spinners. It was particularly sweet for him to do well against the county who had rejected him two years earlier. David East batted excitingly on the last morning, hitting 4 sixes and 9 fours as he reached his first hundred of the season off 167 balls. No wicket-keeper in England has greater potential as a batsman, nor keeps to a more varied attack. Asked to make 301 in 86 overs, Gloucestershire could bat only for survival. Romaines played 51 balls without scoring before being taken by Fletcher at silly mid-off off the bowling of Childs who was to finish with match figures of 11 for 95. Straight after lunch Tomlins glanced Pringle to backward short leg, but Bainbridge and Stovold then dug in. Mid way through the afternoon, however, Pringle had Stovold and Curran lbw, and Acfield accounted for left-handers Lloyds and Russell. Pringle claimed Alleyne in between these wickets so that when Russel was out 10 minutes and 20 overs remained for Essex to capture 3 wickets. Rain reduced the time to 16.4

overs, and with 11 overs to go, Walsh was outwitted by Childs and stumped. Four overs later, Graveney was brilliantly caught at short leg by Hardie, but Bainbridge and a straight-batting Lawrence held out so that Essex remained 11 points behind Gloucestershire.

All other matches, affected by the weather were drawn. Some splendid batting by Benson and Taylor, who put on 212 for the first wicket, set Kent off on a high note at Dartford, but Lynch and Stewart kept Surrey well in the match on the second day. Rain marred the last day after Surrey had been asked to make 294 in 57 overs, and Tavare and Benson shared the new ball to keep the game alive, Surrey scoring at 10 an over. Stewart hit a rapid century, but in the fever, the visitors began to lose wickets and finished 49 runs short of their target, having scored 245 in 35 overs.

There was no play on the last day at Headingley or Taunton where Marks and Harden added 187 for Somerset's 5th wicket.

Alan Warner hit a career best 91 for 90 balls to take Derbyshire to four batting points against Leicestershire, but Leicestershire declined to sustain the contest on the last day after rain had hindered progress in the match and settled for bonus points only. Whitaker gave another impressive display, and under lowering skies, Roger Finney returned the best bowling figures of his career.

Hampshire held the upper-hand at Bournemouth but were thwarted by the weather while David Fraser-Darling, deputising for Richard Hadlee, returned best performances with bat and ball in the sodden game at Northampton.

A low-scoring, rain-affected game at Lytham was dominated by the spinners. Lancashire were saved from humiliation on the opening day by the resourceful Abrahams, and Jack Simmons nearly brought his side victory on the last day with his best spell of the season.

Jack Simmons – Flat Jack – 7 for 79 for Lancashire against Glamorgan. (Adrian Murrell)

ABOVE: *Manager and selector. Mickey Stewart, named as England's assistant manager for the tour to Australia, talks to selector Fred Titmus. (Adrian Murrell)*

Third Cornhill Test Match
ENGLAND v. NEW ZEALAND

With Ian Smith injured, New Zealand gave a first Test cap to Tony Blain, and Chatfield returned to the exclusion of Watson. Ian Botham returned to Test cricket, and Allan Lamb was recalled so that Athey moved up to become Gooch's fifth opening partner in the six Test matches of the summer.

Gatting won the toss and with victory the only way by which England could avoid their first home series defeat by New Zealand, he elected to field. Dilley and Small opened the bowling when play began 35 minutes late. They were tidy without being too menacing, and the score after 10 overs was 17. At this point, to great acclaim, Botham, the prodigal son, was brought into the attack. His first ball was just short of a good length and swung away. Edgar, as if magnetised, steered it into the hands of Gooch at second slip. This wicket brought Botham level with Dennis Lillee on 355 Test wickets.

Jeff Crowe edged the next ball to third slip where Emburey, diving to his left, missed a difficult, low chance. The last ball of Botham's second over came back sharply at Jeff Crowe and he was adjudged lbw. The Somerset all-rounder had now become the leading wicket-taker in Test cricket. The king had returned from exile and reclaimed his kingdom.

Half an hour after lunch, Martin Crowe hit laxly across the line at a well pitched up ball from Dilley, and New Zealand were 59 for 3. Wright had played with sense and sound technique while these three wickets fell, and he remained solid till the close. Coney chose to attack. He made 38 off 41 deliveries with some glorious shots. He off-drove Small for a marvellous six, and had relished hooking Botham. He attempted the shot again at a ball from Botham which came through to him slower than expected and skied it to second

John Wright disturbs the England fielders Gatting, Athey and French on his way to a fine century. (Adrian Murrell)

slip. Gray should have been caught by Edmonds at mid-off when he drove wildly at Emburey, but Edmonds missed the easiest of chances, and when rain ended play 35 minutes after tea New Zealand were 142 for 4.

Fifty-eight overs only had been possible on the first day, and only one more was bowled on the second when New Zealand advanced to 257 for 8. Botham failed to take another wicket and missed Wright at slip off Emburey. By then Gray had been yorked by Dilley after another useful knock, and Hadlee had fallen to a dubious catch behind.

Bracewell was taken at short leg, having survived an appeal for a catch there a few moments earlier.

Wright reached a splendidly determined century. It was an innings of great value to his side in that he stood firm when there were signs of the house crumbling and he defied England for long enough, 344 balls, to make it exceedingly difficult for them to win the match. Blain played some authoritative and pleasant shots until he was becalmed before the final shower and closure.

New Zealand added another 30 runs on the Saturday morning, and Dilley took the last two wickets to give him four for the innings.

Again England did not start well. Hadlee beat Athey as he edged across the line, and he had Gooch very well caught by Stirling, running in from long leg to take the mis-hook. Chatfield moved one back through Lamb's hesitant shot, and England were 62 for 3. Now came England's best batting of the summer. Gower was in glorious mood. He refused to let Gray exploit the rough outside his off-stump and was brutal to anything pitched short. There is poetry in the man's batting. It is measured. It scans. There is liquidity of movement.

Gatting's innings had not the same qualities. He is essentially one who breathes defiance and ruggedness. He is strong and belligerent rather than aesthetically pleasing, but he is a tenacious fighter, and that is a quality that demands the highest respect. The fourth wicket pair scored at 4 an over, and England were prospering at 281 for 3 when play ended.

There was little more than an hour's cricket on the fourth day, and in 15 overs, England scored 107 runs for the loss of Gower and Gatting. Their stand ended when Gower chopped on to Chatfield who also bowled Gatting. The England captain was missed by Edgar off Gray early in the day, but he completed his sixth Test hundred, a fine, fighting effort, and the fourth wicket stand was worth 223.

We were then treated to an innings of excitement and power by Botham who hit 59 off 36 balls and took 24 off one over from Stirling. He hit 2 sixes and 8 fours in a stunning display although he should have been caught when he sent the ball spiralling into the air. Blain was unable to judge the catch and the ball fell to earth as he groped vainly.

Sadly this was to be the end of events. Gatting declared on the last morning when it was apparent that rain would delay and hinder play. One over was bowled, in two spells of three balls, and New Zealand scored 7 runs. Then there was more gesticulating, and the game was abandoned.

So England had ended one of the worst seasons in their cricket history on a higher note than they had attained all summer, but New Zealand had taken a series in England for the first time, and deservedly so. There was a sense of total commitment in the New Zealand side, a corporate spirit that generated a supportive attitude among the players. They were entertaining to watch, for they breathed honest endeavour and belief in each other, and they played the game with a freshness which suggested trust and respect.

OPPOSITE: INSET, *Botham equals Lillee's world record number of Test wickets as Edgar steers the ball to Gooch at slip and walks away. (Adrian Murrell)* MAIN PICTURE, *Jeff Crowe is lbw and Botham is the leading wicket-taker in Test history. (Adrian Murrell)*

Gower in full flow at The Oval. (Adrian Murrell)

Gatting – a pugnacious and courageous innings in the third Test. (Adrian Murrell)

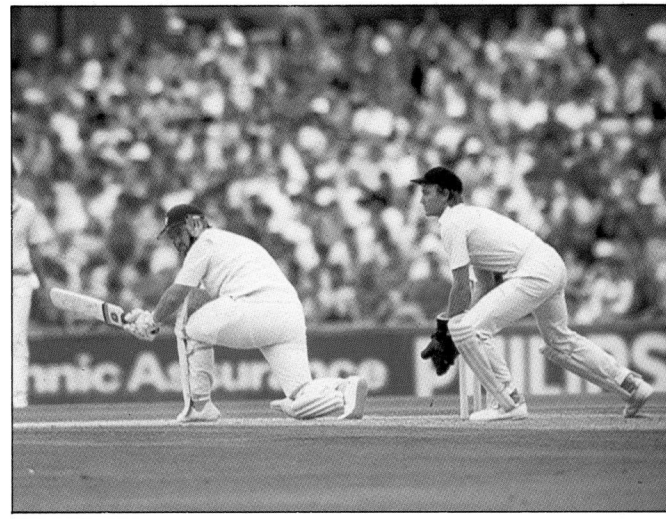

THIRD CORNHILL TEST MATCH – ENGLAND v. NEW ZEALAND
21, 22, 23, 25 and 26 August 1986 at The Oval

NEW ZEALAND

	FIRST INNINGS			SECOND INNINGS	
J.G. Wright	b Edmonds	119		not out	7
B.A. Edgar	c Gooch, b Botham	1		not out	0
J.J. Crowe	lbw, b Botham	8			
M.D. Crowe	lbw, b Dilley	13			
J.V. Coney†	c Gooch, b Botham	38			
E.J. Gray	b Dilley	30			
R.J. Hadlee	c French, b Edmonds	6			
J.G. Bracewell	c Athey, b Emburey	3			
T.E. Blain*	c Gooch, b Dilley	37			
D.A. Stirling	not out	18			
E.J. Chatfield	c French, b Dilley	5			
	b 1, w 1, nb 7	9			0
		287		(for no wicket)	**7**

ENGLAND

	FIRST INNINGS	
G.A. Gooch	c Stirling, b Hadlee	32
C.W.J. Athey	lbw, b Hadlee	17
D.I. Gower	b Chatfield	131
A.J. Lamb	b Chatfield	0
M.W. Gatting†	b Chatfield	121
I.T. Botham	not out	59
J.E. Emburey	not out	9
P.H. Edmonds		
G.R. Dilley		
B.N. French*		
G.C. Small		
	lb 9, w 5, nb 5	19
	(for 5 wkts, dec)	**388**

	O	M	R	W		O	M	R	W
Dilley	28.2	4	92	4					
Small	18	5	36	—					
Botham	25	4	75	3	1	—	7	—
Emburey	31	15	39	1					
Edmonds	22	10	29	2					
Gooch	4	1	15	—					

	O	M	R	W
Hadlee	23.5	6	92	2
Stirling	9	—	71	—
Chatfield	21	7	73	3
Gray	21	4	74	—
Bracewell	11	1	51	—
Coney	5	—	18	—

FALL OF WICKETS
1- 17, 2- 31, 3- 59, 4- 106, 5- 175, 6- 192, 7- 197, 8- 251, 9- 280

FALL OF WICKETS
1- 36, 2- 62, 3- 62, 4- 285, 5- 326

Umpires: H.D. Bird & D.R. Shepherd

Match drawn

CORNHILL TEST MATCH AVERAGES – ENGLAND v. NEW ZEALAND

ENGLAND BATTING

	M	Inns	NOs	Runs	HS	Av	100s	50s
D.I. Gower	3	5		293	131	58.60	1	2
G.A. Gooch	3	5		268	183	53.60	1	
J.E. Emburey	2	3	1	92	75	46.00		1
M.W. Gatting	3	5		170	121	34.00	1	
B.N. French	3	3	2	33	21	33.00		
M.D. Moxon	2	4		111	74	27.75		1
C.W.J. Athey	3	5		138	55	27.60		1
G.R. Dilley	2	1		17	17	17.00		
G.C. Small	2	2	1	14	12	14.00		
P.H. Edmonds	3	4	1	35	20	11.66		

Played in one Test: P. Willey 44 & 42; N.A. Foster 8; N.V. Radford 12*; D.R. Pringle 21 & 9; J.G. Thomas 28 & 10; A.J. Lamb 0; I.T. Botham 59*

NEW ZEALAND BATTING

	M	Inns	Nos	Runs	HS	Av	100s	50
M.D. Crowe	3	5	2	202	106	67.33	1	
J.G. Bracewell	3	3	1	114	110	57.00	1	
J.V. Coney	3	4		133	51	44.33		1
D.A. Stirling	2	2	1	44	26	44.00		
J.G. Wright	3	6	1	191	119	38.20	1	
R.J. Hadlee	3	3		93	68	31.00		1
E.J. Gray	3	3		91	50	30.33		1
B.A. Edgar	3	5	1	92	83	23.00		1
J.J. Crowe	3	4		51	23	12.75		
I.D.S. Smith	2	2		20	18	10.00		
W. Watson	2	2	1	9	8*	9.00		

Played in one Test: K.R. Rutherford 0 & 24*; T.E. Blain 37; E.J. Chatfield 5

ENGLAND BOWLING

	Overs	Mds	Runs	Wkts	Av	Best
G.R. Dilley	69.3	16	179	9	19.88	4/82
P.H. Edmonds	101	32	212	8	26.50	4/97
I.T. Botham	26	4	82	3	27.33	3/75
G.C. Small	64	20	134	4	33.50	3/88
J.E. Emburey	79.5	33	141	4	35.25	2/87
G.A. Gooch	19	9	38	1	38.00	1/23
N.A. Foster	28	7	69	1	69.00	1/13
J.G. Thomas	43	5	140	2	70.00	2/124
D.I. Gower	1	—	2	—	—	
D.R. Pringle	22	1	74	—	—	

Bowled in one innings: N.V. Radford 25-4-71-1

NEW ZEALAND BOWLING

	Overs	Mds	Runs	Wkts	Av	Best	10/m	5/inn
R.J. Hadlee	153.5	42	390	19	20.52	6/80	1	2
J.G. Bracewell	75.4	22	213	6	35.50	3/29		
W. Watson	72.5	18	196	4	49.00	2/51		
E.J. Gray	117	40	271	5	54.20	3/83		
D.A. Stirling	44	8	181	3	60.33	2/48		
J.V. Coney	16	1	48	—	—			
M.D. Crowe	12	1	51	—	—			

Bowled in one innings: K.R. Rutherford 3-0-8-0; E.J. Chatfield 21-7-73-3

ENGLAND CATCHES
6 - G.A. Gooch; 3 - C.W.J. Athey, D.I. Gower, B.N. French and P.H. Edmonds; 2 - M.W. Gatting; 1 - M.D. Moxon

NEW ZEALAND CATCHES
7 - I.D.S. Smith; 4 - M.D. Crowe; 2 - J.V. Coney, J.J. Crowe, E.J. Gray and W. Watson; 1 - D.A. Stirling

23, 25 and 26 August

at Chelmsford

Essex 222
Surrey 166 for 7 (G.S. Clinton 55, J.H. Childs 4 for 62)

Match drawn
Essex 5 pts, Surrey 5 pts

at Cardiff

Glamorgan 157 for 7 (J. Derrick 52)
v. **Kent**

Match drawn
Kent 3 pts, Glamorgan 1 pt

at Bournemouth

Yorkshire 212
Hampshire 58 for 4

Match drawn
Hampshire 4 pts, Yorkshire 3 pts

at Old Trafford

Gloucestershire 354 for 8 dec (P. Bainbridge 98, J.W. Lloyds 76 not out, K.P. Tomlins 59)
Lancashire 93 for 1 (G.D. Mendis 61 not out)

Match drawn
Gloucestershire 4 pts, Lancashire 2 pts

at Leicester

Leicestershire 367 for 9 dec (R.A. Cobb 91, W.K.R. Benjamin 57 not out, J.J. Whitaker 51, N.G.B. Cook 4 for 69)
v. **Northamptonshire**

Match drawn
Leicestershire 3 pts, Northamptonshire 2 pts

at Trent Bridge

Derbyshire 275 (K.J. Barnett 77, E.E. Hemmings 5 for 107)
Nottinghamshire 78 for 1

Match drawn
Nottinghamshire 3 pts, Derbyshire 3 pts

at Hove

Middlesex 284 for 6 (R.O. Butcher 69, K.R. Brown 60, A.C.S. Pigott 4 for 91)
v. **Sussex**

Match drawn
Middlesex 3 pts, Sussex 2 pts

at Worcester

Warwickshire 215 for 7
v. **Worcestershire**

Match drawn
Worcestershire 3 pts, Warwickshire 2 pts

Not a ball was bowled on the last day of any of the Britannic Assurance County Championship matches, and in no game were two innings completed. A second wicket stand of 155 between Tomlins and the ever reliable Bainbridge set Gloucestershire on the way to a big score at Old Trafford, but Mendis thwarted them on the second day before the rain.

At Chelmsford, on a wicket criticised by Pat Pocock, Essex chose to bat first and reached 111 for 2 with Prichard and Hardie in full flow, but the Surrey spinners then captured 3 wickets for 3 runs. Pringle brought about a recovery and played well until he was run out. He played the ball back to Pocock and dozed out of his crease while the bowler threw

the wicket down. Lever sensibly took Essex to two batting points, and on the second day, before rain ended the match, Childs spun Essex to three bowling points which brought them one point closer to Gloucestershire.

At Bournemouth, Malcolm Marshall took three Yorkshire wickets to pass 1000 in first-class cricket.

John Player Special League

24 August

at Chelmsford

Essex 163 for 8
Surrey 167 for 9 (A.J. Stewart 59)

Surrey (4 pts) won by 1 wicket

at Bournemouth

Yorkshire 196 for 7 (J.D. Love 55)
Hampshire 197 for 3 (C.G. Greenidge 125 not out)

Hampshire (4 pts) won by 7 wickets

at Old Trafford

Northamptonshire 195 for 5 (R.J. Bailey 75)
Lancashire 196 for 5 (C.H. Lloyd 85)

Lancashire (4 pts) won by 5 wickets

at Trent Bridge

Nottinghamshire 233 for 2 (B.C. Broad 104 not out, C.E.B. Rice 64)
Derbyshire 210 for 9

Nottinghamshire (4 pts) won by 23 runs

at Hove

Sussex 208 for 6 (P.W.G. Parker 74)
Middlesex 107 (A.N. Jones 4 for 30)

Sussex (4 pts) won by 101 runs

at Edgbaston

Warwickshire 88
Somerset 90 for 4

Somerset (4 pts) won by 6 wickets

at Worcester

Worcestershire 227 for 2 (T.S. Curtis 102, G.A. Hick 68 not out)
Glamorgan 164 for 8 (R.K. Illingworth 4 for 25)

Worcestershire (4 pts) won by 63 runs

Essex lost the advantage that they had gained the previous week when they were surprisingly beaten at home by Surrey. In a low-scoring match, it seemed that Essex, well served by Foster with the bat, would win when the 8th Surrey wicket fell at 133, 31 short of victory, in the 36th over. Anthony Gray, however, hit 24 off 13 balls, including 4 off the last ball of the match when the scores were level. Northants, savaged by Clive Lloyd, lost more ground, but Hampshire, with Greenidge hitting 125 in 36.1 overs, moved level on points at the top with a game in hand of Essex and Notts. Broad and Rice put on 118 for Notts's 2nd wicket, and Broad and Randall 102 for the 3rd. Chris Broad reached his second Sunday League century of the season. More significantly, Somerset announced that Garner and Richards would not be offered new contracts at the end of the season and that they were offering a contract to Martin Crowe. The decision

New Zealand Touring Team, 1986
First Class Matches

BATTING

BATTING	Comb. Univ. 1	2	Middlesex 1	2	Essex 1	2	Sussex 1	2	Minor C. 1	2	Warwick 1	2	Notts 1	2	1st Test 1	2	Northants 1	2	Derby 1	2	2nd Test 1	2
B.A. Edgar	75	—	27	0	51	41	14*	56*			43	0	5	48*	83	0	27	—	110*	—	8	—
J.G. Wright	40	—	13	40	96	—			65	—	66	16			0	0	48	—	2	—	58	7
K.R. Rutherford	91*	—	4	23	63	—	6	2			14	52*	33	45	0	24*	5	—	29	—		
J.J. Crowe	13	—			21*	6	41	31	69	—		65*	75	6	18	—	4	—	5	—	23	2
J.V. Coney	56*	—			93	10		36*	30	22	56	—	45		51		21	—	42	—	24	20*
T.J. Franklin	—	96	5	0			20	23	20	—			7	—								
E.J. Gray	—	56*	6	53*				14	108	—			10	—	11	—	17*	—	5*	—	50	—
T.E. Blain						24	34	12*	0	—							17*	—				
J.G. Bracewell			16	—				30*	36	—					1*	—	100*	—			110	—
D.A. Stirling			6	—					18	13*			20	—							26	—
W. Watson			4*	—			10	—	7*	—							1	—			8*	—
M.D. Crowe			2	78	100*	—			26	—	86*	—	80	56*	106	11*			51	—	28	44*
I.D.S. Smith			48	24*			4	—	7	—			46*	—	18	—					2	—
B.J. Barrett							0	—	3*	5*												
E.J. Chatfield							0*	—														
R.J. Hadlee															19	—					68	—
Byes			2	6			7		2						2	4			7			
Leg-byes	6	9	3	2	16	7	4	1	8		2	2	5		5	9	4		6		7	4
Wides	1	2	2		3				1						3	6	1				2	
No-Balls	6		3		6		2	1	1		4	1			15	2			8		2	1
Total	288	163	232	239	353	165	201	148	334		271	136	326	165	342	41	246		266		413	73
Wickets	3	1	10	6	3	4	9†	4	8		4	2	8	2	10	2	5		5		10	2
Results	W		D		W		D		W		D		D		D		D		D		W	

Match headings (left to right):
- v. Combined Univ. (Cambridge) 25–27 June
- v. Middlesex (Lord's) 28–30 June
- v. Essex (Chelmsford) 2–4 July
- v. Sussex (Hove) 5–7 July
- v. Minor Counties (Lakenham) 9–11 July
- v. Warwickshire (Edgbaston) 12–14 July
- v. Nottinghamshire (Trent Bridge) 19–21 July
- First Test Match (Lord's) 24–29 July
- v. Northamptonshire (Northampton) 30 July–1 August
- v. Derbyshire (Derby) 2–4 August
- Second Test Match (Trent Bridge) 7–12 August

Catches

22 – T.E. Blain (ct 19/st 3)	10 – M.D. Crowe	5 – B.A. Edgar and T.J. Franklin
19 – I.D.S. Smith (ct 17/st 2)	9 – E.J. Gray	4 – D.A. Stirling and J.G. Wright
11 – J.J. Crowe	7 – J.V. Coney and K.R. Rutherford	3 – W. Watson and E.J. Chatfield

BOWLING

Match	D.A. Stirling	W. Watson	E.J. Gray	J.G. Bracewell	M.D. Crowe	J.V. Coney	B.J. Barrett	E.J. Chatfield	R.J. Hadlee	K. Rutherford
v. Combined Universities (Cambridge) 25–27 June	18-3-71-1	15.2-5-31-4	19-8-19-1	30-17-22-4						
	10-2-29-1	5-1-24-1	25-12-36-2	35.2-18-55-6						
v. Middlesex (Lord's) 28–30 June	31-6-98-5	25-3-76-0	20-3-82-1	41.5-4-144-4	6-1-14-0	4-0-14-0				
v. Essex (Chelmsford) 2–4 July	11-0-50-1		21-6-55-1	38-10-110-5			6-3-24-0	10.4-0-54-3		
	4-0-27-0		32-16-61-7	29-11-62-1				14.5-1-45-2		
v. Sussex (Hove) 5–7 July		8-1-23-0						9-0-43-0	8-2-9-1	
		9-2-24-1		4-2-9-0				6-1-35-0	13-3-27-2	
v. Minor Counties (Lakenham) 9–11 July	15-1-82-3	12-2-28-1	27-9-54-5					12-1-22-0	14-6-20-1	
	6-0-32-0	3-1-7-1	15.4-2-52-4					12-4-32-3	7-0-15-1	
v. Warwickshire (Edgbaston) 12–14 July		14-4-59-0	14-1-65-0	23-5-57-2	9-1-37-1	11-3-32-2		24.4-6-64-0		
		7-1-30-2	26-11-49-2	32-15-56-2	10-2-38-1			12-2-21-1		
v. Nottinghamshire (Trent Bridge) 19–21 July	17-2-68-2	23-6-38-2	19.4-5-51-5					24-4-63-1		
	12-2-34-1	13-3-33-3	19-3-82-1			4-1-17-0	6-1-14-2	8-2-25-0		
First Test Match (Lord's) 24–29 July		30-7-70-2	13-9-29-0	26-8-65-1	8-1-38-0	4-0-12-0			37.5-11-80-6	
		17-2-50-0	46-14-83-3	23.4-7-57-2	4-0-13-0				27-3-78-1	3-0-8-0
v. Northamptonshire (Northampton) 30 July–1 Aug	17-1-76-2	18-4-66-1	14-3-45-1	14-2-48-0				15-2-62-2		
v. Derbyshire (Derby) 2–4 August	26-7-95-4	28-4-100-1	30-14-43-1			5-2-10-0	15-6-29-1	16.2-2-71-2		
Second Test Match (Trent Bridge) 7–12 August	17-3-62-1		13-4-30-1	4-1-11-0		7-1-18-0			32-7-80-6	
	18-5-48-2	9-3-25-0	24-9-55-1	11-5-29-3					33.1-15-60-4	
v. TCCB XI (Edgbaston) 13–15 August		17-1-58-2		23.4-4-57-2			16-1-85-1	23-8-53-1		
		4-0-20-0		7-2-13-0			6-0-37-1	9-1-34-0		
v. Glamorgan (Swansea) 16–18 August	11-0-51-1		18-5-61-1	23-2-86-1		3.5-0-23-0	5-4-1-0	8-0-36-0	22-4-38-2	
Third Test Match (The Oval) 21–26 August	9-0-71-0		21-4-74-0	11-1-51-0		5-0-18-0			21-7-73-3	23.5-6-92-2
v. D.B. Close's XI (Scarborough) 31 Aug–2 Sept	15-1-56-3	14-2-57-2	11-3-36-0	16.3-6-51-4				19-5-52-1		
	18-2-75-1	20-1-93-1	10-2-25-0	18-2-59-0		12-5-32-2		19-3-51-0		1-0-9-0
Total	255-35-1025-28 av. 36.60	308.1-59-969-26 av. 37.03	438.2-143-1087-37 av. 29.37	411-122-1042-37 av. 28.16	49.5-8-190-2 av. 95.00	75-23-194-7 av. 27.71	157.5-18-610-15 av. 40.66	191.4-47-457-13 av. 35.15	153.5-42-390-19 av. 20.52	5-0-25-0 av. —

a. B.N. French retired hurt

v. TCCB XI (Edgbaston) 13-15 August		v. Glamorgan (Swansea) 16-19 August		Third Test Match (The Oval) 21-26 August		v. D.B. Close's XI (Scarborough) 31 Aug.–2 Sept.		M	Inns	NOs	Runs	HS	Av
				1	0*	1	—	12	19	5	590	110*	42.14
59	2	6	24	119	7*		—	12	19	1	668	119	37.11
2	104	10	24		317	—		12	19	3	848	317	53.00
58	18	159	2	8	—			13	19	2	624	159	36.70
		140*	4*	38	—	0	—	13	17	5	688	140*	57.33
11	0				45	—		7	10	—	227	96	22.70
	19	—	30	—	88	—		13	13	4	467	108	51.88
29	16		37	—	3	—		9	9	2	172	37	24.57
8	41*	9*	3	—	32*	—		12	11	6	386	110	77.20
		—	18*	—	15*	—		11	7	3	116	26	29.00
0	—				—	—		12	6	3	30	10	10.00
4	61	28	8*	13	—	1	—	12	18	6	783	106	65.25
31	35*	—						9	9	3	215	48	35.83
0*	—	—						8	4	3	8	5*	8.00
				5	—	—	—	7	2	1	5	5	5.00
				6				3	3	—	93	68	31.00
4			1										
7	6	5	5			15							
		1	4	1									
9	4	1		7		2							
218	291	378	71	287	7	519							
9	6	5	3	10	0	7							
D		D		D		D							

2 – J.G. Bracewell and subs
1 – B.J. Barrett
† B.A. Edgar retired hurt

	T.J. Franklin	I.D.S. Smith	B.A. Edgar	Byes	Leg-byes	Wides	No-balls	Total	Wkts
				10	5		8	158	10
				4	6	1	5	154	10
				1	7		10	436	10
				2	12		4	307	10
				6	6		2	207	10
						1		75	1
							2	95	3
				3			16	209	10
				1	2	1	1	141	10
				4	12		2	330	5
				9	7		4	210	9
				4	3	1	2	227	10
				8	6		2	219	7
				6	7		7	307	9a
						6	1	295	6
					3	1	11	300	6
3–0				1	4		1	366	10
				1	3		2	256	10
				4	9	1	2	230	10
	1–0–5–0					10	12	268	6
		2–0–8–0		1				121	1
				7			13	303	5
				9		5	5	388	5
				5			5	257	10
			1–0–2–0	1	11		17	358	5
	1–0–5–0	2–0–8–0	1–0–2–0						
	—	—	—						

Gordon Greenidge, 222, 27 August, the beginning of a remarkable run. (Adrian Murrell)

caused protest and debate, and there was a threat from Ian Botham that he would join another county, but those close to the events would suggest that Somerset's action was wise and in the best interests of the county and of the game.

27, 28 and 29 August

at Swansea

Surrey 210 for 6 dec (A.R. Butcher 69)
Glamorgan 117 for 4 (A.L. Jones 50)

Match drawn
No points

at Leicester

Leicestershire 292 (P. Willey 168 not out, O.H. Mortensen 4 for 61) and 262 for 6 (J.J. Whitaker 106 not out, G. Miller 4 for 114
Derbyshire 336 (J.E. Morris 118, K.J. Barnett 96, P.A.J. de Freitas 4 for 92)

Match drawn
Derbyshire 8 pts, Leicestershire 7 pts

at Lord's

Middlesex 432 for 8 dec (P.R. Downton 84, W.N. Slack 83, C.T. Radley 71, R.O. Butcher 53)
Lancashire 71 and 204 (G. Fowler 70, N.G. Cowans 4 for 36)

Middlesex won by an innings and 157 runs
Middlesex 24 pts, Lancashire 2 pts

Derbyshire C.C.C.
Limited-Over Matches – 1986

BATTING

BATTING	v Leicestershire (Chesterfield) 3 & 5 May (B.&H.)	v Leicestershire (Leicester) 4 May (J.P.)	v Northamptonshire (Northampton) 10 May (B.&H.)	v Sussex (Derby) 11 May (J.P.)	v Minor Counties (Derby) 16 May (B.&H.)	v Warwickshire (Leek) 18 May (J.P.)	v Warwickshire (Edgbaston) 19 May (B.&H.)	v Kent (Derby) 28 May (B.&H.)	v Essex (Derby) 1 June (J.P.)	v Surrey (The Oval) 8 June (J.P.)	v Gloucestershire (Gloucester) 15 June (J.P.)	v Cornwall (Derby) 25 June (N.W.)	v Kent (Derby) 6 July (J.P.)	v Surrey (Derby) 9 July (N.W.)	v Northamptonshire (Finedon) 13 July (J.P.)	v Middlesex (Derby) 20 July (J.P.)	v Glamorgan (Ebbw Vale) 27 July (J.P.)	v Lancashire (Buxton) 10 August (J.P.)
K.J. Barnett	52	6	7	74*	62	23	12	8	5	92	8	26	71	47	46	85*	45	12
I.S. Anderson	0	63	25	11	26	11	42	24	2	25	30	134	2	0		—	19*	
A. Hill	24	6	90*	4	16*	43	51	29	2	14	34	153	5	16	1	2		6
J.E. Morris	13	11	1	66*	6	13	5	65	13	1	38	12*	52	0	11	—	24	5
B. Roberts	5	11	86*	—	22*	8	35	43	53*	44	29	2*	18	12	0	55	12	60*
G. Miller	32	73*	—	—	—	0	25*	29*	11	0	7*	—	22*	32*	9	—	26	
M.A. Holding	69	1	—	—	—	0	2	4	4	14	2*	—		0		—	1	27
P.G. Newman	7	23	—	—	—			1										
R.J. Finney	7*	1	—	—	—	16	12*	—	13*	2*	—							—
P.E. Russell	6*	1	—	—	—					—	—							
O.H. Mortensen	—	1*	—	—	—	1							—		11	3*	—	0*
A.E. Warner						3*	—	17*					1*	6	5		9	2
R. Sharma						0	2				0*		27	9	3		5	7*
J.P. Taylor										—	—	—						
M. Jean-Jacques													—		16	1		
D.E. Malcolm													—			16		
C. Marples															42	1	10	2
B.J.M. Maher																11*	45	21
Byes	1	2	4			1		2			5		2	4	1			1
Leg-byes	10	9	8	7	3	7	18	6	1	7	12	5	8	8	3	3	14	6
Wides		2	4	2	5	4	9	6	3		30		3	4		6	6	4
No-balls	10	1				2	2	5			1	3	3	2		1	3	2
Total	236	221	225	164	140	132	215	238	108	199	166	365	214	167	145	164	219	155
Wickets	8	9	3	2	3	10	7	6	7	7	5	3	6	10	10	3	9	7
Results	W	L	W	W	W	L	W	L	L	W	W	W	L	L	L	L	W	W
Points	2	0	2	4	2	0	2	—	0	4	4	—	0	—	0	0	4	4

Catches

14 – B. Roberts (ct 13/st 1)
10 – M.A. Holding
9 – J.E. Morris
8 – K.J. Barnett
7 – G. Miller
6 – I.S. Anderson and R. Sharma
5 – B.J.M. Maher

4 – R.J. Finney
3 – P.G. Newman and A.E. Warner
2 – O.H. Mortensen
1 – P.E. Russell, J.P. Taylor, A. Hill, D.E. Malcolm, C. Marples and M. Jean-Jacques

BOWLING

BOWLING	M.A. Holding	O.H. Mortensen	G. Miller	P.G. Newman	R.J. Finney	P.E. Russell	A.E. Warner	R. Sharma	J.P. Taylor
(B.&H.) v. Leics (Chesterfield) 3 & 5 May	7–1–13–2	6–1–17–3	4–1–13–2			3–0–8–0			
(J.P.) v. Leicestershire (Leicester) 4 May	8–0–43–0	8–0–31–1	8–0–43–1	7–0–38–3	4–0–35–0		5–0–22–0		
(B.&H.) v. Northants. (Northampton) 10 May	9–4–25–2	11–2–30–2	11–1–34–1	8.2–1–28–1	7–0–29–0		4–0–18–1		
(J.P.) v. Sussex (Derby) 11 May	8–1–37–3	8–0–37–1	8–1–16–0	4–0–14–0	8–1–20–2		4–0–26–0		
(B.&H.) v. Minor Counties (Derby) 16 May	11–1–25–0	11–3–16–2	11–2–39–2	11–0–27–2	8–4–19–0		3–1–4–1		
(J.P.) v. Warwickshire (Leek) 18 May	8–2–18–0	8–0–32–2	8–1–22–0		7–2–20–1		6–0–15–1	2–0–11–0	
(B.&H.) v. Warwickshire (Edgbaston) 19 May	11–1–40–2	11–1–34–2	11–4–29–0			11–1–34–1	11–0–67–3		
(B.&H.) v. Kent (Derby) 28 May	10–2–33–1	11–2–36–0	3–0–17–0	9–0–41–2	11–2–26–2		9.4–0–79–1		
(J.P.) v. Essex (Derby) 1 June	8–2–29–2	8–1–29–0			5–1–20–0	5–0–25–0			
(J.P.) v. Surrey (The Oval) 8 June	8–1–19–2	8–0–42–2	8–0–33–1			5–0–30–1		7–0–39–1	4–0–30–0
(J.P.) v. Gloucestershire (Gloucester) 15 June	8–2–38–1		8–0–31–0			8–0–25–0	8–1–27–2	3–0–15–0	5–0–14–3
(N.W.) v. Cornwall (Derby) 25 June	6–2–8–0				6–2–13–1	6–0–25–1	9–2–20–0	12–3–29–4	
(J.P.) v. Kent (Derby) 6 July			8–2–26–2	8–0–39–0			6–0–38–3	2–0–25–0	
(N.W.) v. Surrey (Derby) 9 July	12–2–24–1	10–1–47–1	12–2–30–2				5–0–49–0	8–1–23–0	
(J.P.) v. Northants. (Finedon) 13 July		8–1–33–0	4–0–20–1				8–0–55–2	4–0–24–0	
(J.P.) v. Middlesex (Derby) 20 July	8–1–22–1	8–0–33–1	8–1–22–2				8–0–36–2		
(J.P.) v. Glamorgan (Ebbw Vale) 27 July	8–1–34–2	8–0–35–0					8–0–43–2		8–1–35–0
(J.P.) v. Lancashire (Buxton) 10 Aug.	8–1–30–2					8–0–23–2	8–0–32–2		8–1–24–0
(J.P.) v. Yorkshire (Chesterfield) 17 Aug.	8–1–16–3	8–4–18–3	8–1–18–0		8–1–40–1		8–0–37–1		
(J.P.) v. Notts. (Trent Bridge) 24 Aug.	8–0–49–0	8–0–43–0	8–0–46–0		8–0–42–2		8–0–42–0		
(J.P.) v. Hampshire (Heanor) 31 Aug.	8–2–29–3	8–0–53–0	2–0–26–0		8–0–51–1		8–0–59–1		
(J.P.) v. Worcestershire (Worcester) 7 Sept.	8–0–35–0	8–1–14–2			6–1–13–1		8–0–59–1	4–0–30–0	
(J.P.) v. Somerset (Taunton) 14 Sept.	7–0–36–0	8–0–39–0			8–0–40–3		8–0–51–1		
Wickets	29	24	12	9	18	1	23	5	3

a K.J. Barnett 11.1–3–34–3   A. Hill 3–0–13–0

v. Yorkshire (Chesterfield) 17 August (J.P.)	v. Nottinghamshire (Trent Bridge) 24 August (J.P.)	v. Hampshire (Heanor) 31 August (J.P.)	v. Worcestershire (Worcester) 7 September (J.P.)	v. Somerset (Taunton) 14 September (J.P.)	Runs
72*	37	6	78	40	914
					414
47*	36	17	29	50	675
—	41	6	2	10	395
—	15	6	21	40*	577
—	21	1			278
—	15	3	5	14	161
					31
—	14	2	24*	—	91
					7
—	0*	1*	1*	—	18
—	4	68	2	27*	144
—	12*	37	10	—	112
					—
			0	—	17
					16
					55
—	4	21	4	14	120
			6	1	
5	9	11	12	8	
3	1			2	
8	1	5	5	1	
135	210	184	199	207	
0	9	10	9	5	
W	L	L	W	L	
4	0	0	4	0	

M. Jean-Jacques	D.E. Malcolm	B. Roberts	Byes	Leg-byes	Wides	No-balls	Total	Wkts
				2		2	53	7
				18	2		230	5
			8	15	5	3	187	10
				13	6	1	163	6
				8	5		138	8
			6	9	9	2	133	5
			3	6	12	5	213	9
				10	2	3	242	6
			1	7	4	2	111	2
				5	7		198	8
			5	8	6		163	7
5–1–14–1			1	4	9	3	161	10a
8–0–42–1	8–0–47–1		5	3	4	5	225	7
12–0–43–3			7	6	7	1	229	7
8–0–53–0	8–0–40–2		1	16	8	1	242	6
		8–0–39–1	1	8	2		161	8
		8–0–61–1	1	14	4		223	6
				12	3	4	149	6
			3	4	3		132	9
				11	1	2	233	2
		6–0–28–1		11	4	2	257	6
6–0–36–3				11	8		198	9
8–0–39–1				6	6	4	211	7
9	3	3						

English Counties Form Charts

The statistics of all limited-over cricket matches follow in pages 402 to 441. The games covered are:

John Player League (J.P.)   Tilcon Trophy (T.T.)
Benson and Hedges (B.&H.)   Asda Trophy (Asda)
National Westminster Bank Trophy (N.W.)

Once again averages are not produced as it is felt that they have little relevance in limited-over cricket where batsmen often sacrifice wickets for quick runs and bowlers are ordered to contain rather than capture wickets.
In the batting tables a blank indicates that a batsman did not *play* in a game, a dash (—) that he did not *bat*.

at Northampton

Hampshire 338 for 2 dec (C.G. Greenidge 222, V.P. Terry 55) and 0 for 0 dec
Northamptonshire 0 for 0 dec and 169 (M.D. Marshall 4 for 41, R.J. Maru 4 for 47)

Hampshire won by 169 runs
Hampshire 20 pts, Northamptonshire 0 pts

at Trent Bridge

Nottinghamshire 240 (R.J. Hadlee 88, R.T. Robinson 52, T.M. Alderman 5 for 84) and 241 for 1 dec (R.T. Robinson 159 not out)
Kent 140 (S.A. Marsh 61, J.A. Afford 4 for 22) and 209 (J.A. Afford 6 for 81, E.E. Hemmings 4 for 59)

Nottinghamshire won by 132 runs
Notinghamshire 22 pts, Kent 4 pts

at Taunton

Essex 129 (D.E. East 58 not out, N.S. Taylor 4 for 40) and 343 for 7 dec (B.R. Hardie 113 not out)
Somerset 200 (I.T. Botham 67, I.V.A. Richards 53, J.H. Childs 4 for 27) and 263 (I.V.A. Richards 94, V.J. Marks 56)

Essex won by 9 runs
Essex 20 pts, Somerset 6 pts

at Edgbaston

Warwickshire 282 for 2 dec (A.I. Kallicharran 103 not out, A.J. Moles 91, P.A. Smith 55) and 0 for 0 dec
Yorkshire 0 for 0 dec and 228 (P.J. Hartley 80, D.L. Bairstow 57)

Warwickshire won by 54 runs
Warwickshire 19 pts, Yorkshire 0 pts

at Bristol

Gloucestershire 209 for 9 dec (C.W.J. Athey 73, D.N. Patel 5 for 88) and 110 for 3
Worcestershire 300 for 4 dec (D.B. d'Oliveira 146 not out, G.A. Hick 85)

Match drawn
Worcestershire 8 pts, Gloucestershire 3 pts

In a match brought forward from 13 September, Gloucestershire suffered badly, and the fact that they took only 3 points from the drawn game virtually ended their chances of the championship. Put in to bat, they struggled against the Worcestershire spinners on a damp pitch. Only Athey commanded the necessary technique to deal with the situation. The first day was shortened by the rain, and the second day was restricted to 50 overs by it. On the last morning,

Essex C.C.C.
Limited-Over Matches – 1986

BATTING

BATTING	v. Sussex (Hove) 3 & 5 May (B.&H.)	v. Warwickshire (Chelmsford) 4 May (J.P.)	v. Somerset (Taunton) 10 & 12 May (B.&H.)	v. Gloucestershire (Chelmsford) 13 May (B.&H.)	v. Glamorgan (Chelmsford) 15 May (B.&H.)	v. Gloucestershire (Swindon) 18 May (J.P.)	v. Yorkshire (Sheffield) 25 May (J.P.)	v. Nottinghamshire (Chelmsford) 28 & 29 May (B.&H.)	v. Derbyshire (Derby) 1 June (J.P.)	v. Nottinghamshire (Chelmsford) 8 June (J.P.)	v. Hampshire (Ilford) 15 June (J.P.)	v. Middlesex (Lord's) 22 June (J.P.)	v. Northumberland (Jesmond) 25 June (N.W.)	v. Lancashire (Old Trafford) 6 July (J.P.)	v. Warwickshire (Edgbaston) 9 July (N.W.)	v. Somerset (Chelmsford) 13 July (J.P.)	v. Worcestershire (Southend) 20 July (J.P.)	v. Sussex (Eastbourne) 3 August (J.P.)
G.A. Gooch	73	100	16	51	30	43		25	50*		39		44		48	52	94	43
B.R. Hardie	119*	95	13	4	25	71*	7	2	5	29						3	41	13*
A.R. Border	11	40	7	31	17	12*	4	15	10	58	75	29	23	5	6	40	17	2
D.R. Pringle	7	16*	65	56*	54*	—		35	32*	—	0		22		33	64*	5	11
K.W.R. Fletcher	8	4	5	42	51*		18	37	—	12	62	11						8
P.J. Prichard	15	6*	3	52	18	—	29	16	—	23	15	97	10	103*	2	69	0	40
A.W. Lilley	15	—	18			—	18		—	7	5*	11	113	23	5	6*	52	
D.E. East	1	—	9	7		—	5	16*	—	10	—	8*	28	2*	0	—	1*	
S. Turner	—	—	41	0		—	24	2	—				—					
N.A. Foster	—	—	8	4*		—	2	0	—	9	—	6*	6		20	—	—	1
J.K. Lever	—	—	0*	—		—	5*	2*	—	0	—		1*	—	7		—	—
T.D. Topley				—		—			—	0*	—							
D.L. Acfield							2									4*	—	
K.R. Pont							34	24		26*	24*	3	20	14	0	—		
C. Gladwin													28	10	2			
J.H. Childs														—				
J.P. Stephenson															45	55	35*	13
N.D. Burns																		—
Nasser Hussain																		
Byes			1		1			1	1	1	4	1	1			1	2	
Leg-byes	9	16	16	14	4	2	10	12	7	7	21	19	14	13	7	14	14	5
Wides	12	4	2	8	3	2	3	5	4	7	9	3	5	4	4	4	11	1
No-balls	7	3	2	2	3		1	3	2	1	2	1	1	1			1	1
Total	277	284	206	271	206	130	162	195	111	190	256	217	298	212	191	253	273	138
Wickets	7	4	10	7	4	1	10	9	2	8	5	6	9	5	10	4	6	7
Results	W	W	W	W	W	W	L	L	W	W	L	Ab.	W	L	L	W	W	W
Points	2	4	2	2	2	4	0	—	4	4	0	2	—	0	—	4	4	4

Catches

29 – D.E. East (ct 26/st 3)
14 – G.A. Gooch
8 – A.R. Border
7 – J.K. Lever
6 – N.A. Foster
5 – D.R. Pringle and K.W.R. Fletcher

4 – B.R. Hardie and J.P. Stephenson
3 – S. Turner
2 – P.J. Prichard, A.W. Lilley, D.L. Acfield and Nasser Hussain
1 – C. Gladwin, N.D. Burns and T.D. Topley

BOWLING

BOWLING	J.K. Lever	N.A. Foster	G.A. Gooch	D.R. Pringle	S. Turner	A.W. Lilley	T.D. Topley	D.L. Acfield	K.R. Pont
(B.&H.) v. Sussex (Hove) 3 & 5 May	11–2–44–2	11–0–70–1	11–1–48–0	11–2–47–2	11–2–42–0				
(J.P.) v. Warwickshire (Chelmsford) 4 May	7–0–37–0	8–0–30–1	8–0–47–2	8–0–55–0	8–0–52–0	1–0–1–0			
(B.& H.) v. Somerset (Taunton) 10 & 12 May	10–2–20–2	11–1–40–1	11–1–39–0	11–0–42–3	11–2–43–3				
(B.&H.) v. Gloucestershire (Chelmsford) 13 May	11–1–44–2	11–1–42–3		11–0–57–0	11–0–61–2		11–1–40–0		
(B.&H.) v. Glamorgan (Chelmsford) 15 May	11–2–38–3	11–1–33–2		11–0–50–0	11–3–38–1		11–2–34–2		
(J.P.) v. Gloucestershire (Swindon) 18 May	5–1–30–1	5–0–29–1		5–0–23–1	5–0–19–1			5–1–18–1	
(J.P.) v. Yorkshire (Sheffield) 25 May	8–1–25–0	8–1–38–4			8–1–36–1			8–0–36–1	8–0–27–2
(B.&H.) v. Notts. (Chelmsford) 28 & 29 May	10–1–40–1	11–1–58–2		11–3–26–3	10–1–25–1	9–2–37–0			
(J.P.) v. Derbyshire (Derby) 1 June	8–2–30–1	8–3–17–5	4–0–8–1	6–0–30–0				4–0–22–0	
(J.P.) v. Notts. (Chelmsford) 8 June	8–0–40–0	8–1–43–3					8–0–26–2	8–0–34–1	8–0–25–1
(J.P.) v. Hampshire (Ilford) 15 June	7.3–0–57–0	8–1–49–1	8–0–38–1	7–0–51–1					7–0–44–1
(J.P.) v. Middlesex (Lord's) 22 June		3–0–13–0					5–0–24–0	4–0–22–1	5–0–21–1
(N.W.) v. Northumberland (Jesmond) 25 June	10–4–26–0	12–2–30–2	12–3–43–1	9–2–36–1			7–1–27–0	8–1–35–0	
(J.P.) v. Lancashire (Old Trafford) 6 July	8–0–37–0				8–0–54–0		8–0–51–0	8–1–29–1	8–1–36–1
(N.W.) v. Warwickshire (Edgbaston) 9 July	11–0–69–0	12–1–31–3	12–2–31–3	10.5–0–47–3			10–0–46–1	4–0–20–0	
(J.P.) v. Somerset (Chelmsford) 13 July	7–0–21–5	8–1–33–2	8–0–35–0		6.4–0–31–1			7–0–63–1	1–0–24–0
(J.P.) v. Worcestershire (Southend) 20 July	8–0–47–1	8–0–41–3	8–0–36–2	7–0–38–3			8–0–46–0		
(J.P.) v. Sussex (Eastbourne) 3 August	4–0–19–1	4–0–16–1	4–0–22–0	4–0–17–0			4–0–19–2		
(J.P.) v. Leicestershire (Leicester) 10 August		4–0–21–2				4–0–32–0	3–0–23–1	3–0–25–2	
(J.P.) v. Northamptonshire (Colchester) 17 Aug.	7–0–35–0	8–0–52–2	8–0–40–3				8–0–29–0		
(J.P.) v. Surrey (Chelmsford) 24 August	8–1–33–3	8–0–28–1		8–1–33–0			8–2–22–2	8–1–39–1	
(J.P.) v. Kent (Folkestone) 31 August	8–0–42–1	8–2–22–0	8–1–27–2	8–0–30–2				8–0–39–1	
(Asda) v. Hampshire (Scarborough) 5 Sept.			10–0–60–2	10–1–62–2	10–6–18–1		10–1–36–3		
(J.P.) v. Glamorgan (Chelmsford) 14 Sept.	8–2–21–2	8–0–28–1	8–0–28–3	8–0–26–1			8–0–24–2		
Wickets	25	41	23	24	9	0	14	11	6

	v. Leicestershire (Leicester) 10 August (J.P.)	v. Northamptonshire (Colchester) 17 August (J.P.)	v. Surrey (Chelmsford) 24 August (J.P.)	v. Kent (Folkestone) 31 August (J.P.)	v. Hampshire (Scarborough) 5 September (Asda)	v. Glamorgan (Chelmsford) 14 September (J.P.)	Runs
		45		1	21	61	836
	79	109	8	72	28	38	761
	13	25					440
		20	15	6	11	8*	460
	25*	7*	3	18		8*	319
	27	7*	19	22	1	5	579
	—	2	9	12	8	—	304
	—	—	23	7			117
					8		75
	—	—	38	8*		—	102
		—	0*	1*		—	16
	—	—	8*		3	—	11
	—	—		—			6
							145
			28	5	59		132
					1*		1
							148
	—				9		9
					1		1
		2	1		1	4	
	2	11	7	9	5	2	
	4	5	1	7		1	
	1	1	3	1	7	11	
	151	234	163	169	163	138	
	3	5	8	8	10	3	
	W	W	L	W	L	W	
	4	4	0	4	—	4	

John Childs bowled his left-arm spin to devastating effect, and he could be considered the outstanding bowling success of the season, contributing greatly to the triumph of Essex. (Mark Leech)

A.R. Border	J.H. Childs	Byes	Leg-byes	Wides	No-balls	Total	Wkts
			8		1	259	6
			15	2		237	4
			10	8	1	194	10
			10	10	4	254	9
			12	3	3	205	9
		2	5		2	126	7
			2	3		164	8
			10	8	1	196	7
			1	3		108	7
		4	7	2		179	8
			18	4	1	257	4
			9	8		89	2
2–0–11–0			11	4		219	5
		1	6	3	2	214	2
			11	6		255	10
		4	7	6		218	10
		1	21	2		230	10
		1	5	4		99	5
4–0–21–2		2	3	1		127	8
1–0–5–1			5	4		202	9
			12	3		167	9
		2	6	3		168	7
	10–0–54–1	4	16	4	1	250	9
			9	7	1	136	10
3	1						

d'Oliveira and Hick took their third wicket stand to 157, and d'Oliveira reached the highest score of his career, some consolation for a disappointing season. After that, all that Gloucestershire could do was to listen hopefully to news from Taunton.

Initially, the news was good for them. Essex chose to bat first on a damp pitch which encouraged the Somerset seamers and were bowled out shortly after lunch for 129. They were 57 for 7 before David East, in fine form, and John Lever put on 52 in 10 overs. East hit 2 sixes and 7 fours in his 58 which was made off 63 balls. Richards and Botham threatened to put the game out of Essex's reach with some vigorous stroke-play, but Childs took four wickets before the close, and on the second day the Somerset lead was restricted to 71. Some determined batting, rich in character and concentration, took Essex to 343 in the second innings by lunch on the last day. Hardie was the rock on which the innings was founded, batting for six hours for his second championship century of the summer, although it was an impressive team effort with East again batting flamboyantly. Set to make 273 in 68 overs, Somerset appeared to be cruising to success as first Richards and then Botham launched violent attacks on the Essex seamers. Richards hit 94 off 94 balls and shared a stand of 88 in 17 overs with Marks before being caught at mid-on by the flying Hardie. Botham hit 41 off 29 balls before being caught at long on. Botham had been unwell, suffering from flu symptoms, but he showed a total

Glamorgan C.C.C.
Limited-Over Matches – 1986

BATTING

BATTING	v. Hampshire (Cardiff) 4 May (J.P.)	v. Leicestershire (Swansea) 11 May (J.P.)	v. Sussex (Swansea) 12 May (B.&H.)	v. Somerset (Taunton) 13 May (J.P.)	v. Essex (Chelmsford) 15 May (B.&H.)	v. Surrey (The Oval) 18 May (J.P.)	v. Gloucestershire (Swansea) 19 May (B.&H.)	v. Somerset (Cardiff) 25 May (J.P.)	v. Warwickshire (Edgbaston) 8 June (J.P.)	v. Lancashire (Swansea) 22 June (J.P.)	v. Staffordshire (Stone) 25 June (N.W.)	v. Kent (Maidstone) 29 June (J.P.)	v. Gloucestershire (Cardiff) 6 July (J.P.)	v. Sussex (Hove) 9 July (N.W.)	v. Sussex (Hove) 13 July (J.P.)	v. Northamptonshire (Neath) 20 July (J.P.)	v. Derbyshire (Ebbw Vale) 27 July (J.P.)	v. Nottinghamshire (Trent Bridge) 3 August (J.P.)
J.A. Hopkins	8	26	26	5	31	12	23	49	10	65	5	31	89	47	4	15	34	
H. Morris	79	38	7*	51	21	44	0	57	97*	5	48	39	5	27	2	51	100	
Younis Ahmed	16							16	18	50	2	6				31	15	
G.C. Holmes	12	27*	29	30	0	4	0	55	19	0	13	25	54	45	11	65*	18	
R.C. Ontong	19	3*	9	56	58*	23	22	18*	24	1*	54*	25	23*	32	35	17	17	
M.P. Maynard	14	4	0		0	12		—	—	9	9	4	31	7	18	0	18	
J.G. Thomas	24	—	0	0	9	16	4	6*	21*	6*	19	2	2	1	20	4	0	
T. Davies	16*	—	—	11	2	3	9	—	—	—	30*	5	1*	16	1	3*	3*	
J. Derrick	17*	—	—	5	8	6*	8	—	—	—	26	—			23	12	14*	
S.J. Base	—	—	4		1	4*		—						2				
J.F. Steele	—	—		6*	2*	11					1*				0	12		
D.B. Pauline		22		—	4	15	4	31	—									
A.L. Jones				2	0	16		32										
E.A. Moseley			9*		25						4							
I. Smith								6										
D.J. Hickey													0	—		0*	2*	
P.A. Cottey																—	—	
S.R. Barwick																		
S.L. Watkin																		
M.L. Roberts																		
Byes	8		3			1		5	1		5		1	1		1	1	
Leg-byes	7	10	6	9	12	7	9	6	7	11	8	8	13	15	7	14	14	
Wides	2	5	1	1	3	5	2	4	2	1	5	1	1	8	3	5	4	
No-balls			1	1	3		1			4	3	2	2	8		1		
Total	222	135	93	183	205	149	151	216	199	152	205	175	222	240	153	188	223	
Wickets	7	4	6	10	9	10	10	4	4	5	7	10	5	10	10	6	6	
Results	L	W	L	L	L	L	L	L	W	W	W	L	W	L	L	W	W	Ab.
Points	0	4	0	0	0	0	0	0	4	4	—	0	4	—	0	4	4	2

Catches

18 – T. Davies (ct 15/st 3)	3 – D.J. Hickey
12 – H. Morris	2 – M.P. Maynard, G.C. Holmes,
9 – J.F. Steele	A.L. Jones, J.A. Hopkins
6 – R.C. Ontong	and S.J. Base
5 – J.G. Thomas	1 – E.A. Moseley, M.L. Roberts
4 – J. Derrick	and P.A. Cottey

BOWLING

BOWLING	J.G. Thomas	S.J. Base	R.C. Ontong	J.F. Steele	J. Derrick	G.C. Holmes	S.L. Watkin	E.A. Moseley	I. Smith
(J.P.) v. Hampshire (Cardiff) 4 May	7-0-47-1	4-0-33-1	8-0-36-1	8-0-35-1	8-0-53-0	5-0-31-2			
(J.P.) v. Leicestershire (Swansea) 11 May	7-1-25-1	5-0-19-0	8-1-26-1	5-0-17-1	8-1-19-1	7-0-20-2			
(B.&H.) v. Sussex (Swansea) 12 May	2-0-11-0		1-0-11-0			2-0-21-0	2-0-10-1	2-0-18-0	
(B.&H.) v. Somerset (Taunton) 13 May	11-2-42-2	8-1-70-0	11-0-38-1	11-2-41-1	6-0-17-1	8-0-45-0			
(B.&H.) v. Essex (Chelmsford) 15 May	9-1-36-0			11-1-43-0	11-2-37-3	5-1-12-0	6-0-24-1	10-2-49-0	
(J.P.) v. Surrey (The Oval) 18 May	7-1-24-1	8-0-31-3	8-0-28-2	8-0-26-0		5-0-25-0	4-0-22-0		
(B.&H.) v. Gloucestershire (Swansea) 19 May	11-3-44-1	11-0-34-2	11-5-20-0			11-0-34-2	4-0-22-1		7-0-32-0
(J.P.) v. Somerset (Cardiff) 25 May	6-1-26-0	4-0-15-1	8-0-52-1			8-0-46-1	7.1-0-40-1		
(J.P.) v. Warwickshire (Edgbaston) 8 June	8-0-43-2	4-0-24-0	8-1-21-1	8-0-41-0		8-0-32-3	4-0-20-0		
(J.P.) v. Lancashire (Swansea) 22 June	7-1-28-1		8-0-24-2	5-0-28-1		8-0-42-0	4-0-10-0		
(N.W.) v. Staffordshire (Stone) 25 June	9-2-29-0		12-3-50-3	4-1-8-2	5.3-0-21-2	12-3-21-3		7-1-12-0	
(J.P.) v. Kent (Maidstone) 29 June	8-0-51-2		8-0-42-1	4-0-30-0		8-0-53-0	5-0-36-1		
(J.P.) v. Gloucestershire (Cardiff) 6 July	8-0-32-1		8-0-28-4	8-0-29-2		4-0-32-1	4-0-17-0		
(N.W.) v. Sussex (Hove) 9 July	12-1-45-0	12-0-49-2	8-0-44-0	7-0-24-1			12-1-39-0		
(J.P.) v. Sussex (Hove) 13 July	8-2-19-3		8-1-46-1	8-0-36-0		4-0-23-2	7-0-39-1		
(J.P.) v. Northamptonshire (Neath) 20 July	6-2-14-1		8-1-16-1			4-0-23-1	4.4-0-27-4		
(J.P.) v. Derbyshire (Ebbw Vale) 27 July	8-0-40-1		8-0-40-0			8-0-48-4	2-0-16-0		
(J.P.) v. Notts. (Trent Bridge) 3 August									
(J.P.) v. Yorkshire (Scarborough) 10 Aug.			8-0-36-1	8-0-28-2	7-0-31-0	7-0-57-2			
(J.P.) v. Worcestershire (Worcester) 24 Aug.	8-0-50-1		8-0-32-0	8-0-44-1	5-0-33-0				
(J.P.) v. Middlesex (Cardiff) 7 Sept.	5-0-23-0		8-0-23-0			6-0-32-0		4-0-22-0	
(J.P.) v. Essex (Chelmsford) 14 September	8-0-27-0		8-1-33-1			2.1-0-13-0	8-0-37-1		
Wickets	19	9	21	15	18	19	1	0	0

a. D.B. Pauline 1-0-18-0

v. Yorkshire (Scarborough) 10 August (J.P.)	v. Worcestershire (Worcester) 24 August (J.P.)	v. Middlesex (Cardiff) 7 September (J.P.)	v. Essex (Chelmsford) 14 September (J.P.)	Runs
36	10	31	20	577
18	0	21	31	741
				154
37	21	9	8	482
19	24	12	8	499
24	22	13	28	213
	5	7	8	154
7	0			107
23	9	10		161
				11
1	30*			63
				76
				50
				38
		3*	0	9
0	—			2
2		2	1	5
2*	29*	1*	2	34
		—	7	7
			6*	6
4		5	—	
8	7	10	9	
	7	6	7	
		2	1	
181	164	132	136	
10	8	8	10	
L	L	L	L	
0	0	0	0	

Younis Ahmed	D.J. Hickey	S.R. Barwick	Byes	Leg-byes	Wides	No-balls	Total	Wkts
			3	4	4	1	242	6
			4	2	6		132	6
			4	5	3		98	2a
			3	2	7		258	7
			1	4	3	3	206	4
			3	2	5		161	7
			4	6	9	4	196	7
6–0–28–2			1	9	7		217	7
			3	7	5		191	9
	5.4–1–5–2		8	4	2		147	10
			3	1	1		144	10
	7–0–41–4		1	15	6	3	269	9
	7.5–1–33–2			6	1		177	10
	9–0–64–1		4		3	5	269	8
	5–0–11–0			7	2	1	181	8
	5–0–26–1	8–0–31–0		1	5	6	138	10
	6–0–24–1	8–0–37–2		14	6	3	219	9 Ab.
	5–1–20–0	5–1–10–0	2	16	4		200	6
	7–0–44–0	4–0–16–0		8	3	3	227	2
		6.3–1–30–0		3	1	2	133	1
		6–0–22–1	4	2	1	11	138	3
	2	11	3					

Andy Afford, 10 wickets as Notts beat Kent, 27–29 August. A rapidly maturing spin bowler. (George Herringshaw)

disregard for his own health or the well being of the bowlers in his brief, but excellent knock. Somerset required 20 from 18 overs to win with 5 wickets standing. At this point Botham was out. Gard was lbw one run later, and Pringle captured another wicket when he bowled Marks who had played finely. Harman was run out in a mix up with Dredge, but the last pair batted for 10 minutes before Childs had Taylor lbw. The Essex players erupted in joy. They had achieved a memorable triumph and they led the championship table by 7 points. Somerset had lost 5 wickets for 10 runs in 40 minutes, but Essex had never lost concentration, nor belief in their own ability to win a game which others would have surrendered long before.

Third-place Surrey suffered the worst of fates when rain reduced play to the final day, and they were unable to gain a point. Nottinghamshire became the most realistic of challengers to Essex when they swamped Kent. They had batted indifferently at the start, losing their first 5 wickets for 86 before being rescued by Birch and Hadlee. Kent closed on 24 for 3, and only Marsh offered real resistance on the second day. Broad and Robinson began Notts' second innings with a stand of 116, and Robinson made his highest score of the season before Rice declared. There was little to stop spinners Hemmings and Afford on the last day, and Afford, the young left-arm bowler, took a career best 6 for 81 to finish with 10 for 103 in the match.

A double century by Gorden Greenidge who shared a record opening partnership of 250 for Hampshire with Paul Terry after a blank first day made possible the victory over Northants. Innings were forfeited, and Marshall and Maru backed up Greenidge's knock with some impressive bowling.

There were no such fireworks at Leicester where Willey, Morris, Barnett and the unquenchable Whitaker played commendable cricket but could not shape a result.

Middlesex overwhelmed a rather limp Lancashire side.

Gloucestershire C.C.C.
Limited-Over Matches – 1986

BATTING

BATTING	v. Somerset (Bristol) 3 & 5 May (B.&H.)	v. Kent (Canterbury) 4 May (J.P.)	v. Essex (Chelmsford) 13 May (B.&H.)	v. Sussex (Bristol) 16 May (B.&H.)	v. Essex (Swindon) 18 May (J.P.)	v. Glamorgan (Swansea) 19 May (B.&H.)	v. Sussex (Hove) 25 May (J.P.)	v. Leicestershire (Leicester) 1 June (J.P.)	v. Yorkshire (Leeds) 8 June (J.P.)	v. Leicestershire (Harrogate) 12 June (T.T.)	v. Derbyshire (Gloucester) 15 June (J.P.)	v. Berkshire (Reading) 25 June (N.W.)	v. Surrey (Bristol) 29 June (J.P.)	v. Glamorgan (Cardiff) 6 July (J.P.)	v. Leicestershire (Bristol) 9 July (N.W.)	v. Nottinghamshire (Trent Bridge) 13 July (J.P.)	v. Somerset (Bristol) 20 July (J.P.)	v. Worcestershire (Hereford) 27 July (J.P.)
A.W. Stovold	72*		0	3		4	35			29		58	26	33	11	0		
P.W. Romaines	79	6	42	24	33	36	19	6										22
C.W.J. Athey	8	2	78	2	10	35		40	74	0	56	4	15	2	24	17	106*	9
P. Bainbridge	9*	32	9	9	37	10	7			22	0	14	12					
K.M. Curran	—	14	47	37	0	16	2	29	24		38	38	52	6	21	71*	66*	1
J.W. Lloyds	—	45*		6	1	3	0		6		4	1	1	9				
I.R. Payne	—	0	0	19*	9	40	1	2	0	17	12*	23		0	12	—		1
D.A. Graveney	—	5	35*	11	25*	20*	8	0*			11*	1*	31	0*				
R.C. Russell	—	4	11	0	—	1	7*		14	1*	3	21	9	39		—	6	108
D.V. Lawrence	—	0	5	4	16*	4*	4	21*			0	3	0					
C.A. Walsh	—	0	2*	8	—	—	0	—	—	1	1	25*	0	35	1	0*	—	
K.P. Tomlins	17	1						26	22*	6	30	11	38	8	45	—		8
G.E. Sainsbury			4					1			1		0*	7*		—		0
A.J. Wright								6	12	2	51		0			43		11
G. Bradburn									9									
D.A. Burrows												0*						1*
M.W. Alleyne																1	—	46
P.H. Twizell																	—	4
Byes	6	2			2	4	1	1		4	5	4					1	4
Leg-byes	5	9	10	9	2	6	7	4	20	3	8	7	10	6	15	10	10	9
Wides	1	7	10	3		9	4	3	4	5	6	9	3	1	1	2	2	6
No-balls	2	2	4	6	5	4	5	5	4	1		1	2		2			2
Total	182	145	254	134	126	196	107	152	200	124	163	249	157	177	177	169	217	230
Wickets	2	10	9	10	7	7	10	7	6	10	7	9	9	9	10	5	2	10
Results	W	L	L	L	L	W	L	L	W	L	W	L	L	L	L	L	W	L
Points	2	0	0	0	0	2	0	0	4	—	0	—	0	0	—	0	4	0

Catches

17 – R.C. Russell (ct 10/st 7)
11 – C.W.J. Athey
5 – K.M. Curran, J.W. Lloyds, K.P. Tomlins and P. Bainbridge
4 – A.W. Stovold and D.A. Graveney
3 – D.V. Lawrence, I.R. Payne and G.E. Sainsbury
2 – A.J. Wright and D.A. Burrows
1 – P.W. Romaines, C.A. Walsh, M.W. Alleyne and sub.

BOWLING

BOWLING	D.V. Lawrence	C.A. Walsh	I.R. Payne	P. Bainbridge	D.A. Graveney	J.W. Lloyds	C.W.J. Athey	G.E. Sainsbury	K.P. Tomlins
(B.&H.) v. Somerset (Bristol) 3 & 5 May	11–1–36–4	11–0–38–0	11–2–38–2	8.1–0–35–1	11–1–18–1	2–0–6–0			
(J.P.) v. Kent (Canterbury) 4 May	8–0–55–1	8–0–56–2	8–0–38–0	6–0–37–0	8–0–42–2			2–0–11–1	
(B.&H.) v. Essex (Chelmsford) 13 May	11–1–57–3	11–0–65–2	11–2–57–0	11–1–25–2	7–0–29–0			4–0–24–0	
(B.&H.) v. Sussex (Bristol) 16 May	9–0–41–0	9–1–40–1	2.3–0–15–0			7–1–22–1		3.2–1–14–1	
(J.P.) v. Essex (Swindon) 18 May	5–1–19–0	4.4–0–19–0	2–0–13–0	2–0–16–0	2–0–15–0	3–0–19–1		5–1–27–0	
(B.&H.) v. Glamorgan (Swansea) 19 May	4–0–20–0	9–4–19–1	11–2–22–3	10–3–39–1	6–1–21–0		10.2–1–21–3		
(J.P.) v. Sussex (Hove) 25 May	6–0–36–0	8–0–49–2		8–0–37–0	4–0–25–1	6–1–30–1		8–1–32–0	
(J.P.) v. Leicestershire (Leicester) 1 June	8–0–41–0	8–1–29–0	3–0–18–1	6–0–18–0		3–0–18–0		4–0–15–0	
(J.P.) v. Yorkshire (Leeds) 8 June		5.1–1–13–2	8–0–19–1	6–1–17–2		3–0–19–2		8–1–23–3	5–0–30–0
(T.T.) v. Leicestershire (Harrogate) 12 June		7.4–0–28–1	10–0–33–0	11–3–38–6				8–2–24–1	6–1–18–0
(J.P.) v. Derbyshire (Gloucester) 15 June		7.2–1–29–3	6–0–33–0	7–0–21–0		7–0–18–0	7–0–26–1	7–0–22–1	
(N.W.) v. Berkshire (Reading) 25 June	8–0–36–4	7–0–30–2			11–2–24–2	11.3–3–35–2			
(J.P.) v. Surrey (Bristol) 29 June	4–0–25–0	8–0–30–0		5–0–34–0	2–0–13–0	6–0–27–1		8–0–28–1	
(J.P.) v. Glamorgan (Cardiff) 6 July		8–0–33–2	7–0–34–0	6–0–35–0	8–0–49–1	3–0–17–0		8–0–40–0	
(N.W.) v. Leicestershire (Bristol) 9 & 10 July	8–0–27–0	12–2–21–1	12–3–35–0	11–2–45–2	11–4–15–1		1.1–0–14–0		1–0–10–0
(J.P.) v. Notts. (Trent Bridge) 13 July		8–0–35–2	8–1–20–1	8–0–40–2	5–0–30–0	3–0–24–0		8–0–26–1	
(J.P.) v. Somerset (Bristol) 20 July		8–1–36–1	8–0–48–0	8–1–38–3	4–0–22–0			7–0–41–0	
(J.P.) v. Worcestershire (Hereford) 27 July			8–0–39–0	8–0–53–1				8–0–48–2	
(J.P.) v. Hampshire (Cheltenham) 3 August									
(J.P.) v. Middlesex (Cheltenham) 10 August									
(J.P.) v. Warwickshire (Edgbaston) 17 August		7–0–46–1	7–0–63–1	4–0–26–0	8–0–49–0			6–0–38–1	
(J.P.) v. Northants. (M'ton-in-Marsh) 31 Aug.		8–2–31–0		8–0–29–2				8–0–32–2	
(J.P.) v. Lancashire (Bristol) 7 September		8–0–60–1	8–0–31–0	8–0–25–1	5–0–23–1			7–0–24–3	
Wickets	12	23	9	25	11	9	1	16	0

a G. Bradburn 6–0–33–1

v. Hampshire (Cheltenham) 3 August (J.P.)	v. Middlesex (Cheltenham) 10 August (J.P.)	v. Warwickshire (Edgbaston) 17 August (J.P.)	v. Northamptonshire (Moreton-in-Marsh) 31 August (J.P.)	v. Lancashire (Bristol) 7 September (J.P.)	Runs
					271
	33	21	—		321
	64	0	73		510
	3	71	27*		460
	49	24	—		535
	4	25	—		105
	5				141
	3*	6*	—		156
	43	0	94*		361
					57
		1	—		74
	22*	11*			245
	—	—	—		13
					125
					9
					1
					47
					4
	—	—			4

			4		
	9	5	3		
	3	2			
			2		
	238	170	199		
	7	7	1		
Ab.	Ab.	L	L	W	
2	2	0	0	4	

D.A. Burrows	K.M. Curran	P.H. Twizell	Leg-byes	Wides	No-balls	Total	Wkts	Byes
			2	5	1	15	178	10
			3	7	5	2	249	6
				14	8	2	271	7
			3	1	3	8	136	3
				2	2		130	1
				9	2	1	151	10
				12		1	221	4
			4	7	2	2	150	1
				11	5		132	10
5–2–19–0				4	9		197	10a
			5	12		1	166	5
				4	4	10	129	10
				4	4		161	2
			1	13	1	2	222	5
			4	8	4	2	179	4
				6	5		181	6
		5–0–20–1	1	7	2		213	7
8–0–38–1		8–0–47–2		8	5	1	233	6
								Ab.
								Ab.
		8–0–55–2	5	2	3		284	5
	8–0–36–1	8–0–46–1		8	5		182	6
	4–0–23–0		1	9	5	1	196	8
1	1	6						

ABOVE: *Andy Moles, Warwickshire, a dedicated young cricketer, who formed a highly successful opening partnership with ... Paul Smith, BELOW. (Ken Kelly)*

Miller and Slack gave Middlesex a solid start with a stand of 114, and thereafter nearly all the batsmen made useful contributions to take the home side to a big score. In contrast, Lancashire wilted against a varied attack, and although Mendis, Fowler and Abrahams showed more spirit in the second innings, the last 9 wickets went down for 63 runs.

Rain marred play at Edgbaston, and some friendly bowling helped Alvin Kallicharran to his fifth hundred of the season. This was followed by the forfeiture of innings which left Yorkshire to make 283 in 56 overs. At 65 for 5, the cause was lost, but Bairstow and Peter Hartley played with pluck. It seemed that Yorkshire might save the game, but Paul Smith had Shaw lbw with the first ball of the last over.

Hampshire C.C.C.
Limited-Over Matches – 1986

BATTING

BATTING	v. Combined Univ. (Oxford) 3 May (B.&H.)	v. Glamorgan (Cardiff) 4 May (J.P.)	v. Middlesex (Southampton) 10 May (B.&H.)	v. Northamptonshire (Southampton) 11 May (J.P.)	v. Middlesex (Southampton) 12 May (B.&H.)	v. Surrey (The Oval) 13 May (B.&H.)	v. Kent (Southampton) 15 May (B.&H.)	v. Nottinghamshire (Southampton) 1 June (J.P.)	v. Essex (Ilford) 15 June (J.P.)	v. Kent (Basingstoke) 22 June (J.P.)	v. Hertfordshire (Southampton) 25 June (N.W.)	v. Worcestershire (Worcester) 29 June (J.P.)	v. Somerset (Taunton) 6 July (J.P.)	v. Worcestershire (Southampton) 9 July (N.W.)	v. Warwickshire (Portsmouth) 20 July (J.P.)	v. Leicestershire (Southampton) 27 July (J.P.)	v. Gloucestershire (Cheltenham) 3 August (J.P.)	v. Sussex (Bournemouth) 10 August (J.P.)
C.G. Greenidge	83*	56		12	1	58	6	16	20	41	18					73		43
V.P. Terry	20	6		32	31	32	41	14	17	42	1	78*	5	8	8	142		15
R.A. Smith	0	69		0	37	20	4	82*	32	23*	18	—	46*	39	58*	31		57*
D.R. Turner	40*	5		2	0*	21	1	40	37	12		22	40*	17				23
C.L. Smith	—	24		31	—	67	21	0	75*			25				1	4	—
M.C.J. Nicholas	—	52*		41	3	1	7	28	53*	1	17	62*	1		29	1	13*	34
N.G. Cowley	—	4*		18		21*	5	1*	—	16	4				8			29
T.M. Tremlett	—	—		4*		7*	36*	—	—			—				28*		
R.J. Parks	—	—		4*			16	—	—			—				6		—
C.A. Connor	—	—		—		4*		—	—			—				5		—
P.J. Bakker	—																	
M.D. Marshall		14		4	2	2	33	—		4	15*		—		32	39*	2*	
K.D. James								0*	17*			—			19	34		0
R.J. Scott																		
R.J. Maru																		
Byes		3			1	2	1					1						2
Leg-byes	4	4		7	1	5	8	2	18	8	3	19	5	8	4	8		11
Wides		4		3	1	3	4	12	4	3	5		5	6	5	2		7
No-balls		1			1			2	1			2	2	6	1	5		
Total	147	242		158	77	240	187	197	257	150	124	183	104	212	154	276		221
Wickets	2	6		8	5	7	9	5	4	6	6	1	2	10	4	3		6
Results	W	W	Ab.	W	L	W	L	L	W	W	W	W	W	W	L	W	W	Ab.	L
Points	2	4	—	4	0	2	0	0	4	4	—	4	4	—	4	4	2	0

Catches

32 – R.J. Parks (ct 25/st 7)	5 – T.M. Tremlett and C.A. Connor
12 – R.A. Smith	4 – C.L. Smith and N.G. Cowley
10 – V.P. Terry	3 – M.D. Marshall
8 – C.G. Greenidge and M.C.J. Nicholas	1 – R.J. Maru, D.R. Turner and sub.
6 – K.D. James	

BOWLING

BOWLING	C.A. Connor	P.J. Bakker	T.M. Tremlett	M.C.J. Nicholas	N.G. Cowley	M.D. Marshall	K.D. James	R.J. Maru	C.L. Smith
(B.&H.) v. Comb. Univ. (Oxford) 3 May	9.5–0–35–4	11–5–19–2	11–0–35–1	10–2–20–2	11–2–27–1				
(J.P.) v. Glamorgan (Cardiff) 4 May	8–0–31–0		8–0–53–3	8–0–56–1	8–0–32–2	8–0–35–1			
(B.&H.) v. Middlesex (Southampton) 10 May	11–0–78–1		11–2–29–0	11–0–47–1	11–2–36–2	11–2–27–2			
(J.P.) v. Northants (Southampton) 11 May	8–1–29–0		8–0–24–2	8–0–41–4	8–1–28–0	8–2–27–0			
(B.&H.) v. Middlesex (Southampton) 12 May	2–0–13–2		2–0–20–0	2–0–26–0	1–0–13–0	2–0–8–0			
(B.&H.) v. Surrey (The Oval) 13 May	11–1–43–0		11–0–30–4	11–0–74–0	11–0–50–1	11–1–34–1			
(B.&H.) v. Kent (Southampton) 15 May	11–0–51–1		11–0–51–1	11–0–43–1	11–0–69–1	11–4–25–1			
(J.P.) v. Notts (Southampton) 1 June	8–0–42–0		8–0–24–0	8–0–49–2	7.3–0–55–1	8–0–28–0			
(J.P.) v. Essex (Ilford) 15 June	8–0–51–0		8–0–33–1	8–0–62–1	7–2–55–0	8–1–30–2			
(J.P.) v. Kent (Basingstoke) 22 June	8–1–18–1		8–0–28–3	5–0–21–1	3–0–12–2	8–0–44–0	8–1–17–2		
(N.W.) v. Hertfordshire (Southampton) 25 June	11.3–2–23–2		12–1–29–2	4–1–9–0	12–3–19–3	12–4–12–1	7–1–19–2		
(J.P.) v. Worcestershire (Worcester) 29 June	8–0–54–3		8–0–31–0		8–0–33–3	8–0–24–1	8–1–30–0		
(J.P.) v. Somerset (Taunton) 6 July	6–0–13–1		7–0–18–4		6–0–18–0	7–1–20–1	8–0–24–4		
(N.W.) v. Worcestershire (Southampton) 9 July	12–2–30–2		10–1–48–0	4–0–28–0	12–0–36–0	12–1–50–1	10–0–72–1		
(J.P.) v. Warwickshire (Portsmouth) 20 July	6–0–23–2		7.5–0–16–3	5–0–25–1	2–0–12–0	8–0–29–2	7–0–41–2		
(J.P.) v. Leicestershire (Southampton) 27 July	8–0–76–1		8–0–44–3		1–0–9–0	8–0–27–2	2–0–26–0		
(J.P.) v. Gloucestershire (Cheltenham) 3 Aug.									
(J.P.) v. Sussex (Bournemouth) 10 August	8–0–32–0	7–0–46–2			8–0–58–1	8–0–34–0	4–1–20–0		
(J.P.) v. Middlesex (Lord's) 17 August	7–0–38–0		8–0–46–0		8–0–40–1	8–0–42–0	8–0–30–1		
(J.P.) v. Yorkshire (Bournemouth) 24 August	8–1–29–2		8–0–44–2		8–0–57–1	8–0–28–1	8–1–26–0		
(J.P.) v. Derbyshire (Heanor) 31 August	6.5–0–25–4		4–0–35–0		8–1–48–3	8–0–33–1	6–1–23–4		
(Asda) v. Yorkshire (Scarborough) 4 Sept.	10–3–34–2		10–0–43–1		10–1–38–0	10–2–40–0	10–1–55–2		
(Asda) v. Essex (Scarborough) 5 Sept.	7–1–40–1			1–0–6–0	10–3–25–3	4–0–16–2	8–1–17–1	10–0–45–1	2.1–0–8–2
(J.P.) v. Surrey (The Oval) 7 September	8–0–21–2		8–0–34–3		8–1–28–0	8–0–27–2	8–0–32–0		
(J.P.) v. Lancashire (Southampton) 14 Sept.	6–0–20–1	6–0–20–0	6–1–38–2		6–0–30–2		6–1–23–4		
Wickets	32	4	35	14	27	21	20	1	2

v. Middlesex (Lord's) 17 August (J.P.)	v. Yorkshire (Bournemouth) 24 August (J.P.)	v. Derbyshire (Heanor) 31 August (J.P.)	v. Yorkshire (Scarborough) 4 September (Asda)	v. Essex (Scarborough) 5 September (Asda)	Surrey (The Oval) 7 September (J.P.)	v. Lancashire (Southampton) 14 September (J.P.)	Runs
13	125*	51	41	27	16	27	727
26	21	1	0	61	2	63*	666
65	11	95	57	24	21	39	828
							260
	1*	73	33	31	16	—	402
41	20	6	10	12	0	5*	437
23	—	5*	30	9	0	—	173
3*	—	4*	7*		4	—	93
—	—	—	—	32	10*	—	68
—	—	—	—	0*	—	—	9
							—
—	—	5	10*	2	1		165
—	—	—	20	17	54*	—	161
8*							8
				10*			10
	2		1	4	6		
8	15	11	10	16	5	10	
5		4	2	4	11	3	
3	2	2	4	1	3	1	
195	197	257	225	250	149	148	
5	3	6	7	9	8	2	
L	W	W	W	W	W	W	
0	4	4	—	—	4	4	

Byes	Leg-byes	Wides	No-balls	Total	Wkts
	10	4		146	10
8	7	2		222	7
	13	5	2	230	7
	5	8		154	8
		2		80	3
	8	12	1	239	7
	11	2		250	5
	2	6		200	3
4	21	9	2	256	5
4	5	6	2	149	9
4	7	12	2	122	10
4	6	2		182	8
4	6	3	1	103	10
	14	3	8	278	5
	6	2		152	10
	2	1	1	184	7
					Ab.
4	5	3		199	3
	4	6		200	2
	12	4	2	196	7
	11		5	184	10
	12	2	4	222	5
1	5		7	163	10
	4		7	146	8
3	10	4		144	9

30, 31 August, 1 September

at Hove

Sussex 182 (A.P. Wells 63) and 430 for 8 dec (A.P. Wells 150 not out, P.W.G. Parker 111, A.C.S. Pigott 80)
Nottinghamshire 312 for 4 dec (B.C. Broad 116, P. Johnson 65) and 4 for 0

Match drawn
Nottinghamshire 8 pts, Sussex 2 pts

30 August, 1 and 2 September

at Derby

Derbyshire 209 (K.J. Barnett 96, M.D. Marshall 5 for 49) and 222 for 4 dec (A. Hill 119 not out)
Hampshire 176 for 2 dec (C.G. Greenidge 103, C.L. Smith 54 not out) and 257 for 1 (C.G. Greenidge 180 not out)

Hampshire won by 9 wickets
Hampshire 21 pts, Derbyshire 2 pts

at Folkestone

Essex 280 (D.R. Pringle 97, G.A. Gooch 74, C.S. Cowdrey 4 for 24, D.L. Underwood 4 for 96) and 127 for 3 dec (J.P. Stephenson 71 not out)
Kent 224 (C.S. Cowdrey 60, D.L. Acfield 4 for 50) and 160 (J.H. Childs 7 for 58)

Essex won by 23 runs
Essex 22 pts, Kent 6 pts

at Leicester

Leicestershire 293 (T.J. Boon 83, P. Whitticase 67 not out, I.T. Botham 6 for 125) and 70 for 1
Somerset 113 (W.K.R. Benjamin 5 for 45) and 416 (N.A. Felton 110, I.T. Botham 74, P.M. Roebuck 72, R.J. Harden 63, L.B. Taylor 4 for 106)

Match drawn
Leicestershire 7 pts, Somerset 4 pts

at Edgbaston

Middlesex 319 (M.W. Gatting 56, W.N. Slack 51) and 231 for 6 dec (M.W. Gatting 50 not out)
Warwickshire 300 for 5 dec (G.W. Humpage 81, A.I. Kallicharran 73, M. Asif Din 62 not out) and 150 (P.A. Smith 79, J.E. Emburey 5 for 51, P.H. Edmonds 4 for 67)

Middlesex won by 100 runs
Middlesex 22 pts, Warwickshire 8 pts

1, 2 and 3 September

at Scarborough

D.B. Close's XI 257 (G. Boycott 81, J.G. Bracewell 4 for 51) and 358 for 5 (Javed Miandad 102 not out, Sadiq Mohammad 77, M.A. Harper 55)
New Zealanders 519 for 7 dec (K.R. Rutherford 317, E.J. Gray 88)

Match drawn

The New Zealanders ended their tour in enterprising style at Scarborough. Having bowled out Close's XI for 257 on the Saturday, they gave an exhilarating display on the Sunday in the individual performance of Rutherford who hit the highest score made by a New Zealander abroad. In 230 minutes, off 245 balls, he hit 317 with 8 sixes and 45 fours. Of the 417 runs scored while he was at the wicket (he came in at 15 for 1) he scored all but 100. Estwick had dismissed Martin Crowe and Jeremy Coney with successive deliveries when

Kent C.C.C.
Limited-Over Matches – 1986

BATTING

BATTING	v. Gloucestershire (Canterbury) 4 May (J.P.)	v. Surrey (Canterbury) 10 & 12 May (B.&H.)	v. Worcestershire (Canterbury) 11 May (J.P.)	v. Combined Univ. (Cambridge) 13 May (B.&H.)	v. Hampshire (Southampton) 15 May (B.&H.)	v. Middlesex (Canterbury) 17 & 19 May (B.&H.)	v. Middlesex (Lord's) 18 May (J.P.)	v. Surrey (Canterbury) 25 May (J.P.)	v. Derbyshire (Derby) 28 May (B.&H.)	v. Worcestershire (Worcester) 11 June (B.&H.)	v. Somerset (Bath) 15 June (J.P.)	v. Hampshire (Basingstoke) 22 June (J.P.)	v. Scotland (Edinburgh) 25 June (N.W.)	v. Glamorgan (Maidstone) 29 June (J.P.)	v. Derbyshire (Derby) 6 July (J.P.)	v. Nottinghamshire (Trent Bridge) 9 July (N.W.)	v. Middlesex (Lord's) 12 July (B.&H.)	v. Lancashire (Canterbury) 20 July (J.P.)
M.R. Benson	37	28	3	35	65	57*	25	11	12	22	6	14	18	0		32	1	63
S.G. Hinks	26	9	1	25	2	10	46	37	41	41	8			99	10	44	13	45
C.J. Tavare	88	35	50	18*	11	0	4	18	1	68	30	1	48*		38	0	3	10
E.A.E. Baptiste	5	3	—	—	25*	4	16	52	1	21	1	4	—	13	6	4	20	2
C.S. Cowdrey	9	89*	50*		7	3	45	10	63*	12	14	45	62*	59	31	1	19	18
G.R. Cowdrey	48	65	47*		60*	13	10	21	34	2	14	10	—	38	6	22	58	4
R.M. Ellison	16*	6*	—	—		3			34*	2	1			15*	9	29	5	
N.R. Taylor	3*	23	28	0*	67	5	9	16	41	68	36	28	26	28	75*	21	19	32
S.A. Marsh	—	—	—	—	—	15	6	6	—	3*	22*	3		4	8	1	14*	8
G.R. Dilley	—	—	—	—	—									2	1*	14*	4*	1
D.L. Underwood	—	—	—	—	—	0	2	6*	—	1*	2	1*	—	1*	—	2*	—	2*
C. Penn				—			1	2			4							
K.B.S. Jarvis						0	0*	1*	—	0	0*		0*					
D.G. Aslett												22	—	0	18			
C.S. Dale																		
S.C. Goldsmith																		
Byes	3	2				2	1	4				4			1	5	5	5
Leg-byes	7	6	12	5	11	3	8	3	10	7	4	5	2	15	3	5	9	8
Wides	5	4	2	1	2	8	1		2	4	2	6	10	6	4	1	8	8
No-balls	2					1	3		3	1	1	2		3	5			3
Total	249	270	193	84	250	124	177	187	242	252	141	149	166	269	225	161	197	214
Wickets	6	6	4	2	5	10	10	9	6	8	10	9	2	9	7	9	8	10
Results	W	L	W	W	W	L	W	Tie	W	W	L	L	W	W	W	L	L	L
Points	4	0	4	2	2	0	4	2	—	—	0	0	—	4	4	—	—	0

Catches

26 – S.A. Marsh	3 – M.R. Benson, N.R. Taylor,
15 – C.J. Tavare	G.R. Cowdrey, C.S. Cowdrey,
7 – S.G. Hinks and	C. Penn and D.G. Aslett
E.A.E. Baptiste	2 – R.M. Ellison
4 – D.L. Underwood	1 – K.B.S. Jarvis and G.R. Dilley

BOWLING

BOWLING	G.R. Dilley	R.M. Ellison	C.S. Cowdrey	E.A.E. Baptiste	D.L. Underwood	S.G. Hinks	C. Penn	K.B.S. Jarvis	G.R. Cowdrey
(J.P.) v. Gloucestershire (Canterbury) 4 May	6.5–1–18–2	6–2–16–2	8–0–43–1	8–0–35–4	8–1–22–1				
(B.&H.) v. Surrey (Canterbury) 10 & 12 May	11–1–41–3	10.5–1–48–1	7–0–44–0	10–0–54–1	8–0–50–0	7–0–29–1			
(J.P.) v. Worcestershire (Canterbury) 11 May	8–0–35–0	8–0–45–2	8–0–43–2	8–0–30–0	8–2–23–2				
(B.&H.) v. Comb. Univ. (C'bridge) 13 May	6–1–16–2	11–6–11–3			6–1–20–1	7–5–7–2		8–2–23–2	
(B.&H.) v. Hampshire (Southampton) 15 May	11–0–40–1	11–2–39–2	11–1–54–0	11–2–19–2	11–2–26–4				
(B.&H.) v. Middx (Canterbury) 17 & 19 May		11–2–27–1	11–0–49–0	10–0–56–2	7–0–39–0	5–0–15–1		11–0–54–3	
(J.P.) v. Middlesex (Lord's) 18 May			8–0–26–1	7.5–0–25–4	6–0–30–0	2–0–10–1		8–0–33–1	8–0–30–1
(J.P.) v. Surrey (Canterbury) 25 May			8–0–42–2	8–0–22–4	4–0–27–0	4–0–14–0		8–0–33–1	8–1–39–0
(B.&H.) v. Derbyshire (Derby) 28 May	11–1–52–0	11–1–44–1	9–0–49–2	11–0–38–2	11–2–37–0	2–0–10–0			
(B.&H.) v. Worcestershire (Worcester) 11 June		11–3–49–2	11–0–40–0	11–1–56–1	11–1–56–1			11–4–28–1	
(J.P.) v. Somerset (Bath) 15 June		8–0–51–2	8–0–41–1	8–0–70–1	8–0–32–2			8–0–36–0	
(J.P.) v. Hampshire (Basingstoke) 22 June			7–0–42–1	7.3–0–29–1	8–3–5–3		8–0–37–0	7–1–29–0	
(N.W.) v. Scotland (Edinburgh) 25 June	9.5–0–29–5		2–0–12–0	6–0–16–0	12–5–17–0			9–1–27–1	11–2–30–1
(J.P.) v. Glamorgan (Maidstone) 29 June	6–0–23–1		4–0–18–1		6–0–44–0	7.2–0–43–5		8–0–39–3	
(J.P.) v. Derbyshire (Derby) 6 July	8–0–35–1	8–0–37–1	8–0–43–3	8–0–40–0	8–0–49–1				
(N.W.) v. Notts. (Trent Bridge) 9 July	5–0–15–0	10.4–2–46–2	7–0–31–0	12–3–46–2	7–1–19–0				
(B.&H.) v. Middlesex (Lord's) 12 July	11–2–19–1	11–2–27–3	11–0–48–1	11–0–61–1	11–4–36–0				
(J.P.) v. Lancashire (Canterbury) 20 July	8–0–46–1	8–0–34–0	5–0–35–0	8–0–55–2	8–0–47–0	3–0–24–0			
(J.P.) v. Northants (Northampton) 27 July		8–0–36–0	8–1–32–2	8–0–49–1	8–0–45–0			8–0–57–0	
(J.P.) v. Leicestershire (Canterbury) 3 Aug.									
(J.P.) v. Warwickshire (Edgbaston) 10 Aug.									
(J.P.) v. Sussex (Hove) 17 August		8–1–40–0	8–0–22–2	8–1–44–0	8–0–33–0			8–1–23–2	
(J.P.) v. Essex (Folkestone) 31 August	8–0–24–0	8–0–39–3	8–0–37–0	8–0–43–4	8–0–17–1				
(J.P.) v. Notts. (Canterbury) 7 Sept.	8–1–20–2	5.4–1–17–2	8–0–37–2	6–0–21–1	8–3–18–3				
(J.P.) v. Yorkshire (Canterbury) 14 Sept.									
Wickets	19	27	21	34	25	3	6	9	1

Alan Wells hit a career best 150 not out for Sussex against Notts at Hove. He saved the game and was awarded his county cap. (Mark Leech)

v. Northamptonshire (Northampton) 27 July (J.P.)	v. Leicestershire (Canterbury) 3 August (J.P.)	v. Warwickshire (Edgbaston) 10 August (J.P.)	v. Sussex (Hove) 17 August (J.P.)	v. Essex (Folkestone) 31 August (J.P.)	v. Nottinghamshire (Canterbury) 7 September (J.P.)	v. Yorkshire (Canterbury) 14 September (J.P.)	Runs
23	17		42	3			514
5	50	22		7			541
11	5*	8	50	63*			560
9	—	44	9	—			239
0	—	14	10	6			567
1	0*	13	12	25*			503
15	—	33*	0	—			168
45			26				596
10		6	0*	—			106
							22
2		0*	—	—			19
			0				7
3*							4
		31	8*	3			82
			—				—
		6					6
			2				
3	1	3	6	6			
1	1	1	3	8			
	1	1		2			
128	74	182	168	123			
10	2	9	7	4			
L	Ab.	Ab.	W	L	W	Ab.	
0	2	2	4	0	4	2	

N. R. Taylor	Byes	Leg-byes	Wides	No-balls	Total	Wkts
	2	9	7	2	145	10
		8	4	4	274	6
	2	13	3		191	6
		4	3	1	81	10
	1	8	4		187	9
	1	17	7	1	258	8
	4	12	2	1	170	10
		10	2	1	187	9
	2	6	6	5	238	6
	2	10	5	1	241	7
		14	10	1	244	6
		8	3		150	6
9–3–19–0	1	14	4	3	165	10
		8	1	2	175	10
	2	8	3	3	214	6
		5	2	5	162	4
		8	11	4	199	7
		10	7	1	251	5
	1	8	4	2	228	4
						Ab.
						Ab.
		19	5		181	5
		9	7	1	169	8
	1	8	4		122	10
						Ab.
0						

Gray joined Rutherford in a record 5th wicket partnership of 319 in 154 minutes. Rutherford completed his century before lunch, moved from 101 to 300 between lunch and tea, and his third hundred came in 33 minutes. Boycott scored 81 and 21 in what was rumoured to be his last match.

In more serious vein, Nottinghamshire's championship hopes received a setback when they failed to force home their advantage against Sussex. Another fine innings from Chris Broad gave Notts a first innings lead of 130, but Alan Wells and Tony Pigott shared a fierce 8th wicket stand of 109, and Paul Parker batted elegantly to thwart Rice's men. Alan Wells reached his first century of the season, the highest of his career, and was awarded his county cap.

Derbyshire, hit by injuries to Mortensen, Sharma and Warner, gave a ragged display against Hampshire and were well beaten. Barnett dominated their first innings which fell away after his dismissal at 147 for 2. Greenidge raced to a hundred, and Nicholas declared in arrears to compensate for time lost to rain. Derbyshire dawdled, but offerings from the Smith brothers increased the run rate and helped Alan Hill to a not out century. Barnett generously gave Hampshire 59 overs in which to score 256. Against a depleted attack and some poor fielding, they needed only 52.1 overs as Greenidge hit 3 sixes and 20 fours and reached 180 off 168 balls, his second century of the match.

Botham bowled a long and successful spell at Leicester, but Somerset were forced to follow on. Felton and Roebuck started their second innings with a partnership of 198, and the match was saved. Emburey and Edmonds spun Middlesex to their fourth win of the season as Warwickshire lost their last 6 wickets in half an hour for 19 runs at Edgbaston.

Lancashire C.C.C.
Limited-Over Matches – 1986

BATTING

Player	v. Yorkshire (Old Trafford) 3 & 5 May (B.&H.)	v. Sussex (Old Trafford) 4 May (J.P.)	v. Scotland (Perth) 11 May (B.&H.)	v. Worcestershire (Worcester) 13 May (B.&H.)	v. Nottinghamshire (Liverpool) 17 & 19 May (B.&H.)	v. Leicestershire (Leicester) 18 May (J.P.)	v. Warwickshire (Old Trafford) 1 June (J.P.)	v. Middlesex (Old Trafford) 8 June (J.P.)	v. Worcestershire (Old Trafford) 15 June (J.P.)	v. Glamorgan (Swansea) 22 June (J.P.)	v. Cumberland (Old Trafford) 25 June (N.W.)	v. Essex (Old Trafford) 6 July (J.P.)	v. Somerset (Taunton) 9 July (N.W.)	v. Kent (Canterbury) 20 July (J.P.)	v. Somerset (Taunton) 27 July (J.P.)	v. Leicestershire (Leicester) 31 July & 1 Aug. (N.W.)	v. Yorkshire (Old Trafford) 3 August (J.P.)	v. Derbyshire (Buxton) 10 August (J.P.)
G. Fowler	7	25	1	76	2	2	17	40	107	19	8	20	17	112	0	12	71	17
G.D. Mendis	0	13	30	21	35	7	—	23	31	3	25	48	72	66	3	2	18	2
S.J. O'Shaughnessy	8	9	9		14					34		1		6	53*	—		
C.H. Lloyd	101	53			67	10	30*	4	64	27	57*	91*	36	35	7	6	2	22
N.H. Fairbrother	23	17	12	47	33	0	12	38*	11	14	—	43*	7	2	39	93*	20	52*
J. Abrahams	39	2	31	20	0	55	—	8	—	6	67*	—	52	—	103*	34	41*	3
C. Maynard	9	8	7	14	22	2	3	49*	12*	6	—	—	5	4*	8	—	—	13*
M. Watkinson	0	3	16	7	19	2*	—	—	13*	9	—	—	12	3*	34*	—	3*	—
J. Simmons	10*	15	16*	7	7*	—	—	—	—	0	—	—	—	—	—	—	—	—
D.J. Makinson	—	0*		0*		0	—	—	—	0*	—	—	8*	—	—	—	—	—
P.J.W. Allott	2	20	13	6*	23*	10*	4	—	—	15	—	—	4	11	—	—	8	—
D.P. Hughes			4	1														17
B.P. Patterson			3*															
A.N. Hayhurst					34	1			—				1		—			
I. Folley													1		—			
J. Stanworth																	—	
I.D. Austin																		4
S. Henriksen																		
D.W. Varey																		
A.J. Murphy																		
Byes			3	4	1						9	1	1					
Leg-byes	3	6	3	19	9	10	4	8	8	8	8	6	8	4	10	6	18	12
Wides	2	2	5	4	8	7	2	4	2	4	5	3	7	4	16	3	3	
No-balls	4	3		5	3	2	3		1	2			2	1	1	1	5	4
Total	208	176	153	231	243	141	76	174	249	147	179	214	221	251	211	226	184	149
Wickets	9	10	9	8	8	8	5	4	4	10	2	2	10	5	6	4	5	6
Results	L	L	L	W	L	L	L	W	W	L	W	W	W	W	L	W	Ab.	L
Points	0	0	0	0	0	0	0	4	4	0	—	4	4	4	4	0	2	0

Catches

16 – C. Maynard (ct 13/st 3)	4 – J. Stanworth	2 – J. Simmons, D.J. Makinson,
8 – G. Fowler and C.H. Lloyd	3 – P.J.W. Allott, J. Abrahams and	G.D. Mendis, A.N. Hayhurst and sub.
7 – N.H. Fairbrother	S.J. O'Shaughnessy	1 – I. Folley, D.P. Hughes and B.P. Patterson
6 – M. Watkinson		

BOWLING

	M. Watkinson	P.J.W. Allott	S.J. O'Shaughnessy	D.J. Makinson	J. Simmons	J. Abrahams	B.P. Patterson	D.P. Hughes	A.N. Hayhurst
(B.&H.) v. Yorkshire (Old Trafford) 3 & 5 May	11–0–50–0	10–1–31–1	9–1–47–0	6–0–16–0	11–0–38–1	4–1–15–0			
(J.P.) v. Sussex (Old Trafford) 4 May	8–1–31–0	7.3–1–27–1	8–1–33–1	8–0–39–0	8–1–33–3				
(B.&H.) v. Scotland (Perth) 11 May	11–3–25–1	10–2–24–3	2–0–9–0			7–2–17–0	5–0–11–1	9–2–31–3	11–1–24–1
(B.&H.) v. Worcestershire (Worcester) 13 May	6–0–42–0	11–3–30–3			11–3–36–3	10–2–31–0	6–0–30–0	11–1–43–0	
(B.&H.) v. Notts. (Liverpool) 17 & 19 May	10–0–50–0	11–2–53–3	5–0–39–0		9–0–37–1	11–3–33–2	9–1–39–0		
(J.P.) v. Leicestershire (Leicester) 18 May	7–0–25–1	5–0–9–0			6.5–0–41–0	8–0–25–0			8–0–33–0
(J.P.) v. Warwickshire (Old Trafford) 1 June	2–0–26–0	2–0–11–0			2–0–10–0	2–0–17–2			2–0–17–1
(J.P.) v. Middlesex (Old Trafford) 8 June	8–0–19–2	8–0–22–2			8–1–36–0	8–0–34–3			8–0–39–0
(J.P.) v. Worcs. (Old Trafford) 15 June	8–0–34–2	8–0–44–1			8–0–43–0	8–0–38–3			8–0–42–1
(J.P.) v. Glamorgan (Swansea) 22 June	6–1–12–1	8–1–26–1	6–1–28–1	8–0–32–0	8–0–37–0	2–1–6–1			
(N.W.) v. Cumberland (Old Trafford) 25 June	11–0–29–0	12–2–32–1	6–1–22–1	7–1–30–0		12–3–26–2			
(J.P.) v. Essex (Old Trafford) 6 July	8–1–34–1	8–1–35–0		6–0–39–1	8–1–38–1	8–1–40–1			
(N.W.) v. Somerset (Taunton) 9 July	12–0–44–3	12–1–40–1	12–2–47–1	12–2–49–2					
(J.P.) v. Kent (Canterbury) 20 July	5–0–27–0	7–1–19–2	8–0–43–2	6.3–0–44–2		2–0–11–2			
(J.P.) v. Somerset (Taunton) 27 July	7.2–0–34–0	8–0–25–1	8–0–43–0	7–0–39–0	8–0–59–1				
(N.W.) v. Leics. (Leicester) 30 July & 1 Aug.	10–0–40–0	12–3–28–4	10–0–59–0		12–6–18–0	4–0–23–0			12–1–40–4
(J.P.) v. Yorkshire (Old Trafford) 3 August	6–0–18–0	6–1–18–1							
(J.P.) v. Derbyshire (Buxton) 10 August				8–2–22–0	7.4–2–41–2	8–1–24–1		4–0–29–0	
(N.W.) v. Surrey (The Oval) 13 August	11–1–37–2	12–3–47–3	12–0–48–1		12–3–32–2				11.5–0–52–1
(J.P.) v. Notts. (Trent Bridge) 17 August	8–0–34–1		8–0–55–0	8–0–41–0	8–1–53–0				8–1–38–1
(J.P.) v. Northants. (Old Trafford) 24 Aug.	6–0–28–0		8–0–35–0	2–0–17–0	8–0–54–1	8–1–31–0			8–0–20–0
(J.P.) v. Surrey (Old Trafford) 31 August	8–1–39–1		8–3–20–2	8–0–33–2	8–0–38–2				8–0–40–1
(N.W.) v. Sussex (Lord's) 6 September	11.2–0–40–0	11–3–34–1	6–0–52–0		12–2–31–1	3–0–15–0			12–2–38–1
(J.P.) v. Glos. (Bristol) 7 September	7–0–31–0		7–0–46–1	7–0–44–0	8–0–30–0	4–0–22–0			5–0–23–0
(J.P.) v. Hampshire (Southampton) 14 Sept.	4.4–0–25–1		3–0–20–0	3–0–10–0	3–0–20–0				6–0–30–0
Wickets	16	33	11	13	22	8	3	1	10

a N.H. Fairbrother 3–0–16–0   b A.J. Murphy 6–0–33–1

v. Surrey (The Oval) 13 August (N.W.)	v. Nottinghamshire (Trent Bridge) 17 August (J.P.)	v. Northamptonshire (Old Trafford) 24 August (J.P.)	v. Surrey (Old Trafford) 31 August (J.P.)	v. Sussex (Lord's) 6 September (N.W.)	v. Gloucestershire (Bristol) 7 September (J.P.)	v. Hampshire (Southampton) 14 September (J.P.)	Runs
0	10	46	23	24	17		673
1	1	22	4	17	39	7	490
62	33	22	23	4	30	51	359
65	43	85	26	0	2		833
18	79		25	63	19	15	682
15	0	11	45	20	49	11	653
22	10	5*	24*	14	1	5	243
2*	4*	—	4*	15*	10	2	158
9	0	—		6*	—	3*	73
	2	—			12*	9	31
0		0*	—	—			116
							22
							3
3	10	—	—	49	1*	19	117
							1
							—
							4
				3			3
				2*			2
1	1	1		1	1	3	
18	14	3	6	17	9	10	
9	4	1	3	6	5	4	
4			2	6	1		
229	211	196	185	242	196	144	
10	10	5	6	8	8	9	
W	L	W	W	L	L	L	
—	0	4	4	—	0	0	

I. Folley	S. Hendriksen	I.D. Austin	Byes	Leg-byes	Wides	No-balls	Total	Wkts
				15	1	1	212	2
			3	12		1	178	5
			8	7	2	2	156	9
			1	18		9	231	8
				12	6	8	263	7
			2	7		2	142	1
				6	2		87	3
			2	18	3	1	170	7
				9	6	1	210	8
				11	1	4	152	5
12–1–32–1				7	8	2	178	5
2–0–13–0				13	4	1	212	5
12–1–34–2				4	4	5	218	9
8–0–57–2			5	8	8	3	214	10
				12	5		212	2
			1	5	13	5	223	8
				5			41	1
	4–0–7–0	8–1–25–0	1	6	4	2	155	7
				9	6	4	225	10
			1	15	6	2	237	5
				10	2		195	5
				14			184	8
				17	6		243	3a
				3		2	199	1
				10	3	1	148	2b
5	0	0						

ABOVE: *Stephenson hits out and Aslett grimaces. Marsh is the wicket-keeper, Essex v. Kent, Folkestone, 30 August. (Simon Bruty)*

Gooch is bowled. Ellison celebrates. Kent v. Essex, Folkestone. (Simon Bruty)

Most eyes were focussed on Folkestone, however, where Essex gained another remarkable victory and virtually assured themselves of the Britannic Assurance County Championship. On a slow wicket they laboured somewhat on the Saturday in spite of Gooch's brisk beginning, and it was left to Pringle to hit lustily on the Monday and take them to 280. Kent found progress equally slow, and when bad light ended play early on the second day they had scored only 177 for 7 from 86 overs. Chris Cowdrey alone played the spinners with any confidence, but he was in no mood for generosity and Essex had to spin out the last three wickets on the last morning. There was now a sense of urgency in the batting as Stephenson and Hardie, shrugging off the early loss of Gooch and Prichard, went for quick runs. Chris Cowdrey seemed to think that Gooch should have declared earlier, but

Leicestershire C.C.C.
Limited-Over Matches – 1986

BATTING

BATTING	v. Derbyshire (Chesterfield) 3 & 5 May (B.&H.)	v. Derbyshire (Leicester) 4 May (J.P.)	v. Warwickshire (Leicester) 10 May (B.&H.)	v. Glamorgan (Swansea) 11 May (J.P.)	v. Northamptonshire (Northampton) 13 May (B.&H.)	v. Lancashire (Leicester) 18 May (J.P.)	v. Minor Counties (Leicester) 19 May (B.&H.)	v. Northamptonshire (Northampton) 25 May (J.P.)	v. Gloucestershire (Leicester) 1 June (J.P.)	v. Gloucestershire (Harrogate) 12 June (T.T.)	v. Warwickshire (Harrogate) 13 June (T.T.)	v. Warwickshire (Edgbaston) 22 June (J.P.)	v. Ireland (Leicester) 25 June (N.W.)	v. Nottinghamshire (Leicester) 29 June (J.P.)	v. Yorkshire (Middlesbrough) 6 July (J.P.)	v. Gloucestershire (Bristol) 9 & 10 July (N.W.)	v. Middlesex (Leicester) 13 July (J.P.)	v. Sussex (Leicester) 20 July (J.P.)
I.P. Butcher	0	—		8*	12		103*	18	—	21	2	43						0
R.A. Cobb	4		22							11	0		26			23		
L. Potter	5	105	6	7	28	63*	112		24	13	31	26	11	63	51	24	52	17
D.I. Gower	11	28	36	15	42	16*	1		51*				121*	2		1	43*	0
J.J. Whitaker	2	17	12	10	30		17	6		38	41	12	25	3				
N.E. Briers	8	26	7	36	37	52		32	60*									
P.B. Clift	7	13*	25*	6	0			7							7			10
P.A.J. de Freitas	8*		3*		11			1		18	0		6*		13	0	0*	13
L.B. Taylor													0			0*		
W.K.R. Benjamin	4*	7*		19*	0		19*	12		12	1	0	5	3*		13		
J.P. Agnew				2							0	17*	0				2	
T.J. Boon		14	43	19	10		13			35	1	3		31*	19	10*	7	49*
P. Whitticase		13		19*						7*	45*	2			7			
J.C. Balderstone								47								29	66	
M. Blackett								3*										
P. Gill								2*										
P. Willey										22	28	25	101	59	7	37*	23	15
L. Tennant										7								2*
P. Bowler														12	4	4	6*	55
G.J.F. Ferris																		
G.A. Harris																		
Byes			1	4		2		4	4			2		1			4	
Leg-byes	2	18	14	2	8	7	12	8	7	4		1	4	12	11	8	5	5
Wides			2	4	6	4		11	2	2	9		2	10	1	5	4	7
No-balls	2		6			4		2	3		2			4		1		2
Total	53	230	192	132	203	142	278	155	150	197	172	132	305	191	155	179	138	176
Wickets	7	5	7	6	10	1	3	8	1	10	8	10	5	6	10	4	3	8
Results	L	W	L	L	L	W	W	L	W	W	W	L	W	L	L	W	W	L
Points	0	4	0	0	0	4	2	0	2			0		0	0		4	0

Catches
25 – P. Whitticase (ct 23/st 2)
12 – L. Potter
9 – P. Willey
8 – I.P. Butcher
7 – D.I. Gower
5 – W.K.R. Benjamin
4 – T.J. Boon
3 – J.C. Balderstone, L.B. Taylor and P.A.J. de Freitas
2 – J.J. Whitaker
1 – N.E. Briers, P. Gill, R.A. Cobb, P. Bowler and L. Tennant

BOWLING

BOWLING	J.P. Agnew	W.K.R. Benjamin	L.B. Taylor	P.A.J. de Freitas	P.B. Clift	N.E. Briers	L. Potter	L. Tennant	P. Willey
(B.&H.) v. Derbyshire (Chesterfield) 3 & 5 May	11-1-54-2	11-1-45-3	11-0-33-1	11-3-34-1	11-0-59-1				
(J.P.) v. Derbyshire (Leicester) 4 May		8-1-28-2	8-0-41-1	7-0-41-2	6-0-34-1	5-0-32-1	6-0-24-1		
(B.&H.) v. Warwickshire (Leicester) 10 May		11-2-42-2	11-0-23-3	11-2-28-3	7-0-31-0	7-0-26-1	8-0-32-0		
(J.P.) v. Glamorgan (Swansea) 11 May		7-0-33-2		6.1-0-18-0	8-1-20-1	8-1-35-1			
(B.&H.) v. Northants. (Northampton) 13 May	11-2-42-1	10-3-23-1		11-0-46-1	11-2-43-2	5-0-23-0	7-2-33-0		
(J.P.) v. Lancashire (Leicester) 18 May		8-1-19-4		8-0-35-1	8-2-18-1	4-0-23-0	4-0-12-0		
(B.&H.) v. Minor Counties (Leicester) 19 May		9.4-2-17-5	8-3-15-1	7-1-15-0	11-3-14-2	5-0-34-0	10-0-70-2		
(J.P.) v. Northants. (Northampton) 25 May	8-0-22-2	8-1-39-3			8-1-31-1	8-0-55-1	8-0-48-0		
(J.P.) v. Gloucestershire (Leicester) 1 June	6-0-24-1			8-0-35-2	6-1-18-2	8-0-33-1	4-0-13-0		
(T.T.) v. Gloucestershire (Harrogate) 12 June	5-1-11-0	5-1-11-2			9-0-39-1		4-0-15-2	8-1-25-1	10.5-3-16-4
(T.T.) v. Warwickshire (Harrogate) 13 June	11-3-20-3	7-1-11-1			6.5-1-18-1		2-1-7-0	11-1-30-2	11-3-15-3
(J.P.) v. Warwickshire (Edgbaston) 22 June	6-0-41-1	6-0-39-0			5-0-28-2				6-0-39-0
(N.W.) v. Ireland (Leicester) 25 June	6-2-12-0	11-0-23-0	10-1-28-1	7-2-18-1			12-2-28-1		12-3-19-1
(J.P.) v. Nottinghamshire (Leicester) 29 June	7.1-0-28-1	8-1-38-1	7-0-47-0	6-0-28-0			2-0-15-0		6-0-32-0
(J.P.) v. Yorkshire (Middlesbrough) 6 July	8-0-23-2	7-0-19-2	4-0-21-0	4.5-0-21-1		5-0-30-0			8-1-29-0
(N.W.) v. Gloucestershire (Bristol) 9 & 10 July		10-2-28-3	12-2-44-2	9.4-3-24-2			11-2-39-2		12-1-27-0
(J.P.) v. Middlesex (Leicester) 13 July	8-0-35-1	8-1-22-2	8-0-26-0	7-1-17-1					2-0-8-0
(J.P.) v. Sussex (Leicester) 20 July		7.1-0-42-0		8-0-54-0		8-0-44-2	0.5-0-13-0	8-1-21-2	8-0-39-1
(J.P.) v. Hampshire (Southampton) 27 July			8-0-64-1	8-0-68-1			8-0-56-1	8-0-42-0	
(N.W.) v. Lancs. (Leicester) 31 July & 1 Aug.	11-5-30-1		9-1-35-2	10-1-50-0			2-1-7-0		12-1-46-1
(J.P.) v. Kent (Canterbury) 3 August									
(J.P.) v. Essex (Leicester) 10 Aug.		4-0-32-0	4-0-36-0	4-0-25-1				3-0-25-0	3-0-31-0
(J.P.) v. Worcestershire (Worcester) 17 August		8-0-45-0	8-1-27-1	8-2-20-4					8-0-33-2
(J.P.) v. Somerset (Leicester) 31 August		8-0-32-0	6-0-29-0	6.2-0-31-3				8-1-25-3	8-0-37-4
(J.P.) v. Surrey (The Oval) 14 Sept.		8-0-20-1	7-1-27-1	8-2-15-3				6-0-32-1	6.3-0-21-1
Wickets	15	34	18	35	15	2	9	9	17

a D.I. Gower 0.3-0-4-0 b G.A. Harris 8-2-27-1

Kent v. *Essex at Folkestone. Exit Dilley, stumped East, bowled Acfield. (Simon Bruty)*

Batting:

v. Hampshire (Southampton) 27 July (J.P.)	v. Lancashire (Leicester) (N.W.) 31 July & 1 Aug.	v. Kent (Canterbury) 3 August (J.P.)	v. Essex (Leicester) 10 August (J.P.)	v. Worcestershire (Worcester) 17 August (J.P.)	v. Somerset (Leicester) 31 August (J.P.)	v. Surrey (The Oval) 14 September (J.P.)	Runs
31							238
—	8	10*				1*	105
28	1	36	16	30		4	753
	13		5				385
		1	7	73		16	310
							258
							75
32	69	1	20	8*		15	218
0	6*	2*	14*				22
		18	10	2*		4	139
	5*						26
35	19	17	19	0		39	383
4*	32	0	29*	4		19	181
14	45						201
				17			20
							5
	1	33	10	51		0	412
	—		—			—	9
34		3	9	19		18	164
2*	—						2
			—				—
	1	2		4			
2	5	3	3	8	3		
1	13	1	6	1			
1	5		2		4		
184	223		127	150	217	123	
7	8		8	8	7	8	
L	L	Ab.	L	L	W	L	
0	—	2	0	0	4	0	

Bowling:

T.J. Boon	J.J. Whitaker	G.J.F. Ferris	Byes	Leg-byes	Wides	No-balls	Total	Wkts
			1	10		10	236	8
			2	9	2	1	211	9
				11	3	7	193	9
				10	5		135	4
				16	12	1	226	5
				10	7	2	141	8
				4	1		169	10
				7	5		202	7
			1	4	3	5	152	7
			4	3	5	1	124	10
				3	7		104	10
				4	1	2	192	5
1–0–2–0	1–1–0–0			8	11	7	138	4
				7	3	1	195	3
				13	1	2	156	5
				15	1		177	10
			1	8	4	2	137	9
				9	5	1	222	6
		8–0–38–0		8	2	5	276	3
		9–0–49–0		5	16	5	226	4a Ab.
				2	3	1	151	3
			4	6	2	3	162	8b
			6	1	5	3	161	10
0	0	0						

a target of 184 in a minimum of 47 overs looked eminently fair, for the sun at last began to shine and the outfield quickened. At tea, Kent were 46 for 0, but the second ball after tea saw Taylor brilliantly caught by Fletcher diving forward at slip. Three overs later, Tavare was taken at backward short leg off Acfield. At this point John Childs took over. Benson made room to cut and was bowled. The younger Cowdrey fell to a ball which turned across him, and Chris Cowdrey was bowled by a straight one. Ellison was lbw, and in the second over of the last twenty, Kent were 92 for 6. Aslett and Marsh began to hit well and added 35 before Aslett was stumped, East's fourth stumping of the match. Dilley helped Marsh to maintain the challenge, and at 150 for 7 with 6 overs remaining, Kent had every chance of victory. Dilley then mishit Childs to mid-on, and the left-arm spinner dismissed Underwood in his next over. Marsh had batted splendidly, but when he went down the wicket to Acfield and missed he was beautifully stumped on the leg side by East, and Essex were victors with 20 balls to spare. After an uncertain start on a difficult wicket David East kept splendidly, asserting his claim for a place in the side to tour to Australia. For John Childs, the game was another personal triumph. Since the beginning of August he had taken 54 wickets.

John Player Special League

31 August

at Heanor

Hampshire 257 for 6 (R.A. Smith 95, C.L. Smith 73, C.G. Greenidge 51)
Derbyshire 184 (A.E. Warner 68, C.A. Connor 4 for 25)

Hampshire (4 pts) won by 73 runs

at Moreton-in-Marsh

Northamptonshire 182 for 6
Gloucestershire 170 for 7 (P. Bainbridge 71)

Northamptonshire (4 pts) won by 12 runs

at Folkestone

Kent 168 for 7 (C.J. Tavare 50)
Essex 169 for 9 (B.R. Hardie 72, E.A.E. Baptiste 4 for 43)

Essex (4 pts) won by 1 wicket

Middlesex C.C.C.
Limited-Over Matches – 1986

BATTING

BATTING	v. Surrey (Lord's) 3 May (B.&H.)	v. Nottinghamshire (Lord's) 4 May (J.P.)	v. Hampshire (Southampton) 10 & 12 May (B.&H.)	v. Somerset (Taunton) 11 May (J.P.)	v. Hampshire (Southampton) 12 May (B.&H.)	v. Combined Univ. (Lord's) 15 May (B.&H.)	v. Kent (Canterbury) 17 & 19 May (B.&H.)	v. Kent (Lord's) 18 May (J.P.)	v. Sussex (Lord's) 28 & 29 May (B.&H.)	v. Surrey (The Oval) 1 June (J.P.)	v. Lancashire (Old Trafford) 8 June (J.P.)	v. Nottinghamshire (Lord's) 11 & 12 June (B.&H.)	v. Yorkshire (Lord's) 15 June (J.P.)	v. Essex (Lord's) 22 June (J.P.)	v. Northamptonshire (Northampton) 25 June (N.W.)	v. Warwickshire (Lord's) 6 July (J.P.)	v. Yorkshire (Leeds) 9 & 10 July (N.W.)	v. Kent (Lord's) 12 July (B.&H.)
G.D. Barlow	30	45	27	18		48	1		14	15								
W.N. Slack	28	2	10	5	5	52	21	2	24		50	65	101*		18	9	27	0
M.W. Gatting	90*	0	57	15	60*	39*	62	43	42	12		3	36*		118*		8	25
C.T. Radley	34	36	8	78*	7	62*	48	5	48*		14	36*	—	8*	67	38	29	54
R.O. Butcher	5	1	69	0	0	—	22	12	65	21	11	36	—	11	10*	12	30	0
P.R. Downton	13*	11	2	50	6*	—	53*	39	32	46		3	—			41	31	13
J.E. Emburey	—	49	31	0	—	—	8	2	9*	33		15*					7	28
P.H. Edmonds			1*			9			2*								0	15*
N.F. Williams		6	5*				8											
N.G. Cowans							0*	0									1	
W.W. Daniel		4						1*									1*	
J.D. Carr		4						41								7*		
A.R.C. Fraser		5*		9*				2		2*								
S.P. Hughes				13				4		8*	8						3	4*
A.J.T. Miller										37	37	27	69	30*	35	23	34	37
G.D. Rose										4	16		4*				3	
C.P. Metson													4*					
A.G.C. Fraser												—	—					
G.K. Brown													4					
M.A. Roseberry															23		22	
J.F. Sykes																		—
N.R.C. MacLaurin																		
K.R. Brown																		
Byes	1	2					1	4	2	1	2							
Leg-byes	4	23	13	5		6	17	12	10	12	18	8	8	9	10	7	10	8
Wides	3		5	2	2	2	7	2	6	7	3			8	4	5	2	11
No-balls		3	2	1		1	1	1	4		1					1	2	4
Total	208	191	230	196	80	210	258	170	256	188	170	193	214	89	262	168	185	199
Wickets	4	10	7	7	3	2	8	10	5	7	7	5	1	2	3	7	10	7
Results	W	L	Ab.	L	W	W	W	L	W	W	L	W	W	Ab.	W	Tie	L	W
Points	2	0		0	2	2	2	0	2	4	0	2	4			2		2

Catches   17 – P.R. Downton (ct 15/st 2)   7 – C.T. Radley   5 – M.W. Gatting and P.H. Edmonds   3 – J.D. Carr, N.G. Cowans   2 – W.N. Slack and
12 – J.E. Emburey   6 – A.J.T. Miller   4 – G.D. Rose   and R.O. Butcher   C.P. Metson

BOWLING

BOWLING	N.G. Cowans	W.W. Daniel	N.F. Williams	J.E. Emburey	M.W. Gatting	P.H. Edmunds	J.D. Carr	A.R.C. Fraser	S.P. Hughes
(B.&H.) v. Surrey (Lord's) 3 May	11–2–30–2	11–0–36–0	11–2–46–1	11–2–35–2	9–2–36–2	2–0–12–0			
(J.P.) v. Nottinghamshire (Lord's) 4 May		8–1–37–0	8–0–28–0	8–0–58–0	5–0–43–1		3–0–21–0	8–0–45–1	
(B.&H.) v. Hampshire (Southampton) 10 May									
(J.P.) v. Somerset (Taunton) 11 May	8–1–18–0	8–0–56–2		8–0–49–1				8–0–33–1	8–0–30–0
(B.&H.) v. Hampshire (Southampton) 12 May	2–0–8–1	2–0–18–0	1–0–5–0	2–0–10–0			2–0–24–1		1–0–10–0
(B.&H.) v. Comb. Univ. (Lord's) 15 May	11–2–27–0	11–0–43–2	10–1–37–1	10–0–43–2		1–0–10–0	11–4–32–1		
(B.&H.) v. Kent (Canterbury) 17 & 19 May	11–2–26–3	10–1–38–3	8–0–20–1	11–3–22–2			2.4–0–13–1		
(J.P.) v. Kent (Lord's) 18 May	8–0–39–0	7.1–0–20–3		7–2–29–3				8–0–41–2	8–0–39–2
(B.&H.) v. Sussex (Lord's) 28 & 29 May	11–3–27–3	9–0–41–1		9–0–31–0			11–0–52–3		8–1–15–1
(J.P.) v. Surrey (The Oval) 1 June		8–0–36–0		8–2–42–1			8–1–29–0		8–0–33–3
(J.P.) v. Lancashire (Old Trafford) 8 June		7.5–2–34–0						8–1–43–1	8–0–33–1
(B.&H.) v. Notts. (Lord's) 11 & 12 June		11–1–36–2		11–2–22–4	3–0–22–0	11–2–30–0		11–1–36–1	8–0–36–1
(J.P.) v. Yorkshire (Lord's) 15 June				8–0–52–4		8–0–43–2		8–0–30–1	8–0–51–2
(J.P.) v. Essex (Lord's) 22 June	8–0–42–2	8–1–28–1				8–0–36–2			8–0–56–1
(N.W.) v. Northants. (Northampton) 25 June	8–0–35–0	12–2–33–4		12–0–43–2	2–0–6–0	12–0–62–0			12–1–52–3
(J.P.) v. Warwickshire (Lord's) 6 July							6–1–22–1		7–0–38–2
(N.W.) v. Yorkshire (Leeds) 9 & 10 July	10–4–24–4	12–1–40–2		12–1–35–1	3–1–9–0	12–1–36–0			11–0–39–2
(B.&H.) v. Kent (Lord's) 12 July	9–2–18–2	11–1–43–1		11–5–16–0	4–0–18–0	11–1–58–3			9–2–35–2
(J.P.) v. Leicester (Leicester) 13 July	8–0–30–1			8–2–11–0		8–0–37–1			8–1–31–1
(J.P.) v. Derbyshire (Derby) 20 July	8–0–28–1					8–1–25–0	7–0–32–0		4–0–24–0
(J.P.) v. Northamptonshire (Lord's) 3 Aug.									
(J.P.) v. Gloucestershire (Cheltenham) 10 Aug.									
(J.P.) v. Hampshire (Lord's) 17 August	8–1–39–2			8–1–23–2	6–0–39–0	8–0–28–1	2–0–18–0		8–0–40–0
(J.P.) v. Sussex (Hove) 24 August	8–0–35–2								8–0–48–1
(J.P.) v. Worcestershire (Lord's) 31 August	8–1–22–0			8–0–52–1		2–0–13–0			8–0–25–2
(J.P.) v. Glamorgan (Cardiff) 7 September	6–1–21–0			8–1–25–3	8–0–18–0		3–0–10–2		7–0–18–1
Wickets	23	21	3	28	3	15	3	7	25

a J.F. Sykes 8–0–27–1   b R.O. Butcher 0.4–0–1–0   c J.F. Sykes 8–0–49–3   d J.F. Sykes 6–0–28–1   e J.F. Sykes 8–1–25–0

v. Leicestershire (Leicester) 13 July (J.P.)	v. Derbyshire (Derby) 20 July (J.P.)	v. Northamptonshire (Lord's) 3 August (J.P.)	v. Gloucestershire (Cheltenham) 10 August (J.P.)	v. Hampshire (Lord's) 17 August (J.P.)	v. Sussex (Hove) 24 August (J.P.)	v. Worcestershire (Lord's) 31 August (J.P.)	v. Glamorgan (Cardiff) 7 September (J.P.)	Runs
								198
	24			75		52	7	577
				—		16	—	626
8	30			47	5	21	75*	758
14				42*	2	12	—	375
20	40			—	5	28*	—	433
2	0*			—		44*	—	228
8	14*			—				49
								19
0*	4*			—	13	—	—	18
								6
38	12			26*	13	0	45*	186
								18
1	7			—	1	—	—	49
20	14			—	46			409
11*	2				0	—		36
								4
					2*			2
								4
								45
					6	—	—	6
0	3							3
					6			6
137	161			200	107	185	133	
9	8			2	10	5	1	
L	L	Ab.	Ab.	W	L	W	W	
0	0	2	2	4	0	4	4	

1 – S.P. Hughes, N.F. Williams, M.A. Roseberry, J.F. Sykes and sub.

A.G.C. Fraser	G.D. Rose	W.N. Slack	Byes	Leg-byes	Wides	No-balls	Total	Wkts
			1	11	3	5	207	7
			1	4	1	6	237	2
								Ab.
				11	8	2	197	4
			1	1	1		77	5
			3	14	1	5	209	8
			2	3	8		124	10
			1	8	1	3	177	10
				6	6	2	172	10
8-0-32-1			1	14	1	4	187	5
8-0-25-1	8-1-31-0			8	4		174	4
				7	10	7	189	8
	8-1-22-0			12	3	2	210	10
	8-1-35-0		1	19	3	1	217	6
		2-0-14-0	4	10	3		259	10
5-0-19-1	6-0-22-0	8-0-29-1	1	10	2		168	8a
			2	20	4	1	205	9
				9	8		197	8
	4-0-24-0			5	2		138	3b
	8-0-31-2	4-0-21-0		3	6	1	164	3
								Ab.
								Ab.
			8	5	3		195	5
8-1-36-0	8-1-27-0			13	2		208	6c
	8-0-35-0			8	2		183	6d
			5	10	6	2	132	8e
3	2	1						

at Leicester
Leicestershire 217 for 7 (J.J. Whitaker 73, P. Willey 51)
Somerset 161 (N.A. Felton 59, P. Willey 4 for 37)
Leicestershire (4 pts) won by 56 runs

at Old Trafford
Surrey 184 for 8 (C.J. Richards 52)
Lancashire 185 for 6
Lancashire (4 pts) won by 4 wickets

at Lord's
Worcestershire 183 for 6
Middlesex 185 for 5 (W.N. Slack 52)
Middlesex (4 pts) won by 5 wickets

at Leeds
Warwickshire 162 for 5
Yorkshire 162 for 8
Warwickshire 2 pts, Yorkshire 2 pts

Hampshire tightened their grip on the Sunday League by trouncing Derbyshire. They remained equal with Essex at the top of the table, but Essex, last ball winners at Folkestone, had played a game more. Northants' faint hopes were kept alive with their victory over Gloucestershire who were rallied by Bainbridge and Lloyds after a poor start. Willey had a good all-round game for Leicestershire where it was announced that David Gower would not play again in the season as he was in need of a rest. Yorkshire suffered three run outs as they tied with Warwickshire.

30 August

at The Hague
New Zealanders 238 for 8 (J.J. Crowe 116)
Holland 173 for 7
New Zealanders won by 65 runs

Ken Rutherford hit 317 off 245 balls, with 8 sixes and 45 fours in the New Zealanders' last match of the tour, at Scarborough. A most remarkable innings. (Adrian Murrell)

Northamptonshire C.C.C.
Limited-Over Matches – 1986

BATTING

Columns (left→right):
1. v. Minor Counties (Slough) 3 May (B.&H.)
2. v. Derbyshire (Northampton) 10 May (B.&H.)
3. v. Hampshire (Southampton) 11 May (J.P.)
4. v. Leicestershire (Northampton) 13 May (B.&H.)
5. v. Warwickshire (Edgbaston) 15 May (B.&H.)
6. v. Leicestershire (Northampton) 25 May (J.P.)
7. v. Worcestershire (Worcester) 28 & 29 May (B.&H.)
8. v. Worcestershire Northampton 8 June (J.P.)
9. v. Warwickshire (Northampton) 15 June (J.P.)
10. v. Yorkshire (Luton) 22 June (J.P.)
11. v. Middlesex (Northampton) 25 June (N.W.)
12. v. Sussex (Hastings) 29 June (J.P.)
13. v. Surrey (Tring) 6 July (J.P.)
14. v. Derbyshire (Finedon) 13 July (J.P.)
15. v. Glamorgan (Neath) 20 July (J.P.)
16. v. Kent (Northampton) 27 July (J.P.)
17. v. Middlesex (Lord's) 3 August (J.P.)
18. v. Somerset (Wellingborough) 10 August (J.P.)

	1	2	3	4	5	6	7	8	9	10	11	12	13	14	15	16	17	18
G. Cook	14	1	12	19	37	4	30	4		—	57		4*	8*	2	15*		—
R.J. Bailey	38	17	11	0	86	89	6	118*	31	13	34	14	58	34	16	52		1
R.J. Boyd-Moss	32*	0	0	24	58	12	31	14	37*	28		0	86	20	0			
A.J. Lamb	0	4	0	106	39		71		22		80	7	56	97	66	17		14*
R.A. Harper	16	23	37	4	19	4	56	25*	26*	20*	1	43	24*	4	3	57*		—
D.J. Capel	3	22	38	43*	8*	54	8	61	—	32*	13	49	16	47	13	41		—
D.J. Wild	17*	38	0	1*	1*	0	—	—	—		0	19	6	6	8			—
D. Ripley	—	26	36*	—	—	7*	0											
N.A. Mallender		3	1*	—	—		1*				0					2		
N.G.B. Cook	—	19	6	—	—	4*	14*	—	—		13	0*				5		—
A. Walker	—	3*	—	—	—	—	—				3*				9*			—
M.R. Gouldstone							4											
R.G. Williams						12			—	9								
S.N.V. Waterton										—		1		13*		2		—
W. Larkins											92	40	26				31	38*
Byes	8	8		1		1		4			4		3	1		1		
Leg-byes	4	15	5	16	18	7	13	5	3	8	10	5	16	1	8			1
Wides	5	5	8	12	13	5		1		5	3	9	6	8	5	4		1
No-balls	1	3		1	3		2		1	1		2		1	6	2		1
Total	138	187	154	226	283	202	233	228	133	199	259	188	264	242	138	228		54
Wickets	5	10	8	5	5	7	8	3	3	3	10	7	5	6	10	4		1
Results	W	L	L	W	W	W	L	W	W	W	L	W	W	W	L	W	Ab.	Ab.
Points	2	0	0	2	2	4	—	4	4	4		4	4	4	0	4	2	2

Catches

- 16 – R.A. Harper
- 11 – S.N.V. Waterton (ct 7/st 4)
- 7 – D. Ripley
- 6 – D.J. Capel, R.J. Bailey, N.G.B. Cook, A.J. Lamb and N.A. Mallender
- 5 – G. Cook and A. Walker
- 4 – R.J. Boyd-Moss
- 3 – D.J. Wild
- 2 – W. Larkins

BOWLING

	N.A. Mallender	D.J. Capel	A. Walker	R.A. Harper	N.G.B. Cook	D.J. Wild	R.J. Bailey	R.G. Williams	R.J. Boyd-Moss
(B.&H.) v. Minor Counties (Slough) 3 May	7-2-10-1	11-2-20-0	8-0-32-0	11-5-17-1	11-7-18-1	7-0-23-1			
(B.&H.) v. Derbyshire (Northampton) 10 May	9-1-26-0	8-2-16-1	11-1-53-0	11-3-33-1	11-0-47-0	5-0-38-1			
(J.P.) v. Hampshire (Southampton) 11 May	8-0-42-3	8-0-24-1	8-0-44-2	8-1-21-0	8-1-20-1				
(B.&H.) v. Leicestershire (Northampton) 13 May	10.3-0-53-5	5-1-16-0	6-0-31-0		11-1-22-2	11-0-33-0	11-1-40-3		
(B.&H.) v. Warks. (Edgbaston) 15 & 16 May	8-2-19-2	11-2-29-4	8-1-29-1	10-5-18-0	4-0-10-0		11-2-16-0	3-3-0-0	
(J.P.) v. Leicestershire (Northampton) 25 May	5-1-13-0	4-0-21-0	7-0-29-2	8-0-18-3	8-1-34-0			8-0-28-1	
(B.&H.) v. Worcs. (Worcester) 28 & 29 May	9.2-1-40-0	10-3-35-0	11-1-52-1	11-2-42-0	11-0-57-1				
(J.P.) v. Worcestershire (Northampton) 8 June	6.3-1-31-1	4-0-23-1	8-1-38-3	8-0-42-1	8-0-32-3	5-0-24-0			
(J.P.) v. Warwickshire (Northampton) 15 June	6-0-25-0	5-0-19-1	7-1-21-2	8-1-18-2	8-0-26-0	6-0-21-2			
(J.P.) v. Yorkshire (Luton) 22 June	6.3-1-29-1	5-0-27-1	7-0-42-0	8-0-36-1	5-0-32-1	7-0-42-2			
(N.W.) v. Middlesex (Northampton) 25 June	12-0-44-1	12-1-29-1	11-1-53-0	11-0-56-1	6-0-38-0	7-0-32-0			
(J.P.) v. Sussex (Hastings) 29 June	5-0-13-0	7-1-21-1	6-0-17-1	8-0-17-4	8-0-23-3	1-0-4-1			
(J.P.) v. Surrey (Tring) 6 July	6-1-14-2	5-0-24-0	7-0-35-2	8-0-44-2	8-0-33-3	6-0-31-0			
(J.P.) v. Derbyshire (Finedon) 13 July	4-0-21-0	3-0-27-0	5-0-18-1	8-1-25-1	8-0-32-2	7.1-2-7-5			1-0-11-0
(J.P.) v. Glamorgan (Neath) 20 July	5-1-15-0	8-0-17-1	7-0-37-0	8-0-41-0	8-0-37-1	4-0-26-2			
(J.P.) v. Kent (Northampton) 27 July	5-0-13-1	8-0-28-3	6.1-0-15-3	4-0-15-1	8-0-40-2	4-0-14-0			
(J.P.) v. Middlesex (Lord's) 3 August									
(J.P.) v. Somerset (Wellingborough) 10 Aug.	7-0-48-1	8-1-31-2	8-0-64-1	5-0-39-0	3-0-27-1	8-0-57-0			
(J.P.) v. Essex (Colchester) 17 August	6-0-28-1	5-0-25-0	7-0-55-0	8-1-40-0	8-0-30-1			6-0-43-1	
(J.P.) v. Lancashire (Old Trafford) 24 Aug.	7.5-0-63-2	8-1-17-0	7-0-57-1	8-1-23-0	8-0-32-2				
(J.P.) v. Glos. (Moreton-in-Marsh) 31 Aug.	6-1-17-1	6-0-23-1	8-1-38-0	8-0-35-1	8-1-20-1			4-0-28-2	
(J.P.) v. Notts. (Trent Bridge) 14 Sept.	8-0-28-2	8-0-44-0	7.3-0-36-1	8-0-35-0	5-0-24-0	1-0-6-0			
Wickets	24	18	21	21	23	20	0	1	0

v. Essex Colchester) 17 August (J.P.)	v. Lancashire (Old Trafford) 24 August (J.P.)	v. Gloucestershire (Moreton-in-Marsh) 31 August (J.P.)	v. Nottinghamshire (Trent Bridge) 14 September (J.P.)	Runs
5	11	14*	7	244
63	75	36	30	822
18		18*	11	389
	18	43		640
26	36*	28	11	463
33	8	4	27	520
1	35*	7	13	152
	—		1	70
1	—	—	1*	9
11*	—	13*	2	87
—	—	—	—	15
				4
				21
28				44
7	0	6	46	286
				6
5	10	8	10	
4	2	5	9	
202	195	182	174	
9	5	6	9	
L	L	W	L	
0	0	0	0	

Byes	Leg-byes	Wides	No-balls	Total	Wkts
1	14	2		135	5
4	8	4		225	3
	7	3		158	8
	8	4		203	10
	6	3		127	7
4	8	2		155	8
	8	2	1	234	2
	9	2		199	10
1	1	2		132	8
12		2		220	9
	10	4		262	3
	5			100	10
	14	3		195	9
1	3	4		145	10
1	14	5	1	188	6
	3	1		128	10
					Ab.
	6	6	1	272	5
2	11	5	1	234	5
1	3	1		196	5
	9	7	1	170	7
1	4	1		178	3

Asda Cricket Challenge

3 September

at Scarborough

Essex beat Lancashire on the toss of a coin

4 September

Yorkshire 222 for 5 (K. Sharp 52, P.E. Robinson 50 not out)
Hampshire 225 for 7 (R.A. Smith 57)

Hampshire won by 3 wickets

Final

5 September

Hampshire 250 for 9 (V.P. Terry 61)
Essex 163 (C. Gladwin 59)

Hampshire won by 87 runs

3, 4 and 5 September

at Derby

Northamptonshire 421 (A.J. Lamb 159, R.J. Bailey 114, M. Jean-Jacques 4 for 99)
Derbyshire 267 (A. Hill 55, B.J.M. Maher 50, D.J. Capel 7 for 86) and 312 for 6 dec (K.J. Barnett 143, J.E. Morris 127)

Match drawn
Northamptonshire 7 pts, Derbyshire 6 pts

at Cardiff

Nottinghamshire 121 (R.C. Ontong 5 for 26) and 270 (B.N. French 58, B.C. Broad 56, R.C. Ontong 8 for 101)
Glamorgan 219 (J.G. Thomas 70, R.C. Ontong 60, J.A. Afford 5 for 80) and 148 (E.E. Hemmings 6 for 45, J.A. Afford 4 for 71)

Nottinghamshire won by 24 runs
Nottinghamshire 20 pts, Glamorgan 6 pts

Rodney Ontong. A fine all-round performance for Glamorgan against Notts at Cardiff, but still on the losing side. (Adrian Murrell)

Nottinghamshire C.C.C.
Limited-Over Matches – 1986

BATTING

	v. Middlesex (Lord's) 4 May (J.P.)	v. Yorkshire (Trent Bridge) 10 & 12 May (B.&H.)	v. Warwickshire (Trent Bridge) 11 May (J.P.)	v. Scotland (Trent Bridge) 13 May (B.&H.)	v. Worcestershire (Worcester) 15 May (B.&H.)	v. Lancashire (Liverpool) 17 & 19 May (B.&H.)	v. Sussex (Trent Bridge) 18 May (J.P.)	v. Essex (Chelmsford) 28 & 29 May (B.&H.)	v. Hampshire (Southampton) 1 June (J.P.)	v. Essex (Chelmsford) 8 June (J.P.)	v. Middlesex (Lord's) 11 & 12 June (B.&H.)	v. Surrey (Trent Bridge) 15 June (J.P.)	v. Somerset (Bath) 22 June (J.P.)	v. Devon (Exmouth) 25 June (N.W.)	v. Leicestershire (Leicester) 29 June (J.P.)	v. Worcestershire (Worcester) 6 July (J.P.)	v. Kent (Trent Bridge) 9 July (J.P.)	v. Gloucestershire (Trent Bridge) 13 July (J.P.)
B.C. Broad	28	70	17	10	40	2	46	7	94	33	42	44	100*	32	60	63	73	38
R.T. Robinson	42	19	7	76*	29	58	55	2	67		2	60	9	9	—		49	24
C.E.B. Rice	94*	9	11	27*	44	71	23	50	27*	15	0	35	68	15	16*	7	15*	40
P. Johnson	61*	2	1		18	19	10	22	0	34	0	1	0	4	90	6	0	54
J.D. Birch	—	15	66	—	19*	48*	4	20	—	3	28*	5						
D.W. Randall	—	82*	33	44	12	0	12	6	—	33	65	26	4	53	9	67*	5*	
R.J. Hadlee	—	16	9	—	16	37	2	61*	4*	24	1	8	30	20	9*	34*	6	
B.N. French	—	1*	12		7	2	14*	7		14	1	1*		46	—		2*	2*
E.E. Hemmings	—							2*	—	1*	26*		—	4*	—	—	—	—
R.A. Pick	—	—	6		3*	—	5	—		1	0	1*	12*	9*				
K.E. Cooper	—	—	5		—	—	1*											
K. Saxelby		—	4*										—	—	—			
P.M. Such					—													
J.A. Afford								—										
K.P. Evans										8*				1	10		—	3
D.J.R. Martindale														4				
M.K. Bore																		
R.J. Evans																	—	11
C.W. Scott																	—	
C.D. Fraser-Darling																		
Byes	1	1	5		1					4		1	1					
Leg-byes	4	10	9	9	22	12	16	10	2	7	7	9	10	6	7	5	5	6
Wides	1	2	3	4	6	6	9	8	6	2	10	3	2	2	3	4	2	3
No-balls	6				1	8	1	1			7			2	1	4	5	
Total	237	227	188	170	218	263	198	196	200	179	189	194	241	212	195	190	162	181
Wickets	2	6	10	2	7	7	8	7	3	8	8	7	7	8	3	3	4	6
Results	W	W	L	W	L	L	L	W	W	L	L	W	W	W	W	W	W	W
Points	4	2	0	2	0	2	0	—	4	0	0	—	4	4	—	4	—	4

Catches
21 – B.N. French (ct 18/st 3)
11 – C.E.B. Rice
8 – P. Johnson
7 – D.W. Randall
6 – B.C. Broad
5 – R.T. Robinson and R.J. Hadlee
4 – C.W. Scott (ct 3/st 1)
3 – K. Saxelby, R.A. Pick and J.D. Birch
2 – E.E. Hemmings, K.E. Cooper and subs.
1 – C.D. Fraser-Darling

BOWLING

	R.J. Hadlee	K.E. Cooper	C.E.B. Rice	R.A. Pick	E.E. Hemmings	K. Saxelby	P.M. Such	J.A. Afford	K.P. Evans
(J.P.) v. Middlesex (Lord's) 4 May	7–0–29–0	8–3–12–2	6.4–0–32–2	8–0–37–3	8–0–56–3				
(B.&H.) v. Yorks. (Trent Bridge) 10 & 12 May	11–2–32–1	11–2–28–1	11–0–45–2	11–0–43–1		11–0–61–1			
(J.P.) v. Warwickshire (Trent Bridge) 11 May	8–0–43–0	8–1–21–0	8–1–49–4	8–0–55–1		8–0–55–0			
(B.&H.) v. Scotland (Trent Bridge) 13 May	11–2–30–1	11–3–22–1	11–1–29–0	11–1–41–3	11–3–24–0				
(B.&H.) v. Worcestershire (Worcester) 15 May	9.1–5–22–2	11–2–35–0	10–0–55–0	11–2–41–0				11–0–58–0	
(B.&H.) v. Lancs. (Liverpool) 17 & 19 May	11–0–53–4	11–2–25–1	11–0–52–0	11–0–60–2				11–0–43–1	
(J.P.) v. Sussex (Trent Bridge) 18 May	8–0–40–0	8–0–25–1	8–0–58–3	8–0–40–3				8–1–27–1	
(B.&H.) v. Essex (Chelmsford) 28 & 29 May	11–1–30–2	11–2–34–0	11–0–48–5	11–0–27–2	11–4–43–0				
(J.P.) v. Hampshire (Southampton) 1 June	8–0–31–1	8–0–19–0	8–0–55–2	8–0–44–1	8–0–46–1				
(J.P.) v. Essex (Chelmsford) 8 June	8–1–25–1	8–0–40–1	5–0–22–0	6–0–43–2	8–1–26–3				5–0–26–0
(B.&H.) v. Middlesex (Lord's) 11 & 12 June	11–3–27–1	11–4–22–1	10.2–0–58–1	10–1–44–0	11–2–34–0				
(J.P.) v. Surrey (Trent Bridge) 15 June	8–1–37–2	8–1–34–1	8–0–34–1	8–0–44–2	8–0–41–3				
(J.P.) v. Somerset (Bath) 22 June	8–0–38–3		7–0–33–4	6.3–0–28–2	1–0–14–0				8–0–56–1
(N.W.) v. Devon (Exmouth) 25 June	9–3–10–2		10–2–19–0	11–1–23–2	12–2–27–2	12–2–36–2			6–0–23–0
(J.P.) v. Leicestershire (Leicester) 29 June	8–1–24–2		8–0–34–1	6–0–44–0	8–1–29–1	8–0–40–1			2–0–8–1
(J.P.) v. Worcestershire (Worcester) 6 July	8–2–22–0		8–0–33–4	8–0–38–0	8–0–34–1	2–0–14–1			6–0–35–1
(N.W.) v. Kent (Trent Bridge) 9 July	9–2–17–3		11–0–35–0	12–5–15–1	9–2–25–0	7–0–29–1			12–2–30–4
(J.P.) v. Gloucestershire (Trent Br.) 13 July		8–1–17–0	7–2–25–1	7–0–40–1	3–0–19–0	8–1–36–1			7–1–22–1
(J.P.) v. Yorkshire (Hull) 27 July		8–1–16–2	6–0–50–0	8–0–55–1	4–0–26–0	6–0–53–1			
(N.W.) v. Surrey (The Oval) 30 July	12–4–17–5	12–3–48–1	9–2–29–1	10–0–58–1	12–4–28–0				5–2–11–1
(J.P.) v. Glamorgan (Trent Bridge) 3 Aug.									
(J.P.) v. Lancashire (Trent Bridge) 17 Aug.			7.3–1–25–4		8–0–54–0	8–0–37–3			8–0–48–0
(J.P.) v. Derbyshire (Trent Bridge) 24 Aug.			8–0–42–3	8–0–32–1	8–0–43–2	8–0–49–1			
(J.P.) v. Kent (Canterbury) 7 September	8–2–31–0		6–1–14–1	7.1–0–29–0		8–1–25–2			
(J.P.) v. Northants. (Trent Bridge) 14 Sept.	8–0–24–1	8–4–16–0	8–0–33–4	5–0–24–0		8–0–34–2			
Wickets	31	12	43	30	16	15	1	1	9

Kevin Kerr, the Warwickshire off-break bowler. Kerr met with considerable success in his first season and showed the ability to spin the ball venomously, but his future with Warwickshire is in doubt. (Ken Kelly)

v. Yorkshire (Hull) 27 July (J.P.)	v. Surrey (The Oval) 30 July (N.W.)	v. Glamorgan (Trent Bridge) 3 August (J.P.)	v. Lancashire (Trent Bridge) 17 August (J.P.)	v. Derbyshire (Trent Bridge) 24 August (J.P.)	v. Kent (Canterbury) 7 September (J.P.)	v. Northamptonshire (Trent Bridge) 14 September (J.P.)	Runs
4	34		15	104*	30	25	1011
0	0		9	2	2	20	541
53	1		70	64	10	38*	803
2	18		10	—	7	79	438
12			20*	—			240
	5		88	49*	12	10*	615
	54				31	—	362
	12		—		4		125
14	3*		—	—	2		52
24	7		—		7	—	75
0	0					—	6
6*			—		1*	—	11
							—
							—
	1		—				23
							4
							11
10				—			10
9			1*	—	3	—	13
	4		1		1	1	
10	11		15	11	8	4	
6	1		6	1	4	1	
3	7		2	2			
153	158		237	233	122	178	
10	10		5	2	10	3	
L	L	Ab.	W	W	L	W	
0	—	2	4	4	0	4	

M.K. Bore	C.D. Fraser-Darling	Byes	Leg-byes	Wides	No-balls	Total	Wkts
		2	23		3	191	10
			10	1		219	8
			13	3		236	6
			20	3	1	166	6
		8			2	219	2
		1	9	8	3	243	8
			13	4	5	203	9
		1	12	5	3	195	9
			2	12	2	197	5
		1	7	7	1	190	8
			8			193	5
		6		6		193	5
6-0-30-0			10	6	1	209	10
		6	9	4	2	153	8
			12	1		191	6
		1	10		1	187	7
		5	5	1		161	9
			10	2	2	169	5
	8-0-45-1		10	4	1	255	6
			13	3		204	Ab.
	8-0-32-2	1	14	4		211	10
	8-1-35-2		9	1	1	210	9
	6-1-18-1		6	8	2	123	4
	3-0-27-1	6	10	9		174	9
0	7						

at Folkestone

Warwickshire 267 (A.J. Moles 82, D.L. Amiss 73, E.A.E. Baptiste 4 for 53) and 65 (D.L. Underwood 7 for 11)
Kent 362 (C.S. Cowdrey 100, S.A. Marsh 70, D.G. Aslett 63, N. Gifford 5 for 96)

Kent won by an innings and 30 runs
Kent 22 pts, Warwickshire 4 pts

at The Oval

Gloucestershire 297 (C.W.J. Athey 76, R.C. Russell 71, J.W. Lloyds 66) and 269 for 4 dec (K.M. Curran 103 not out, A.W. Stovold 55, K.P. Tomlins 53 not out)
Surrey 256 (C.J. Richards 115, M.A. Feltham 76, C.A. Walsh 5 for 61) and 191 for 6 (A.J. Stewart 86 not out, C.A. Walsh 4 for 67)

Match drawn
Surrey 7 pts, Gloucestershire 7 pts

at Worcester

Worcestershire 345 for 5 dec (T.S. Curtis 153, D.M. Smith 52)
Somerset 127 (N.V. Radford 9 for 70) and 209 (J.J.E. Hardy 67, D.N. Patel 4 for 56)

Worcestershire won by an innings and 9 runs
Worcestershire 24 pts, Somerset 2 pts

Nottinghamshire, the only county with a chance of overtaking Essex in the race for the Britannic Assurance County Championship, had a wretched first day at Cardiff. Rice won the toss and elected to bat, but Thomas had Broad lbw in the opening over, and in spite of some defiance from Robinson, Notts were all out before lunch. Glamorgan slipped to 78 for

Somerset C.C.C.
Limited-Over Matches – 1986

BATTING

BATTING	v. Gloucestershire (Bristol) 3 & 5 May (B.&H.)	v. Yorkshire (Leeds) 4 May (J.P.)	v. Essex (Taunton) 10 May (B.&H.)	v. Middlesex (Taunton) 11 May (J.P.)	v. Glamorgan (Taunton) 13 May (B.&H.)	v. Sussex (Hove) 19 May (B.&H.)	v. Glamorgan (Cardiff) 25 May (J.P.)	v. Sussex (Horsham) 1 June (J.P.)	v. Kent (Bath) 15 June (J.P.)	v. Nottinghamshire (Bath) 22 June (J.P.)	v. Dorset (Taunton) 25 June (N.W.)	v. Hampshire (Taunton) 6 July (J.P.)	v. Lancashire (Taunton) 9 July (N.W.)	v. Essex (Chelmsford) 13 July (J.P.)	v. Gloucestershire (Bristol) 20 July (J.P.)	v. Lancashire (Taunton) 27 July (J.P.)	v. Worcestershire (Weston-s-Mare) 3 August (J.P.)	v. Northamptonshire (Wellingborough) 10 August (J.P.)
N.A. Felton	0	0*	3								59*	0	14	96	19	—	13	35
P.M. Roebuck	11	51	26	68	1	13	48	21	75	0	41	25	0	1		75*	—	9
J.J.E. Hardy	14	7	8	3	25	11	—	40	12	19	0		53	8				
I.V.A. Richards	29	24	22	19	20	14	1	42*	2	64	6*	0	50	29	52	62	10	21
I.T. Botham	24	45*	41	28*	126*	6	48										3	175*
B.C. Rose	49	62						—	66	25		21	43*	9		30	15	7
V.J. Marks	11	10	0	5	32	24	13	15	7	18	—	0	8	32	30	—	32*	—
M.R. Davis	7												6	0*	—	0*		
J. Garner	0	1	14*	—	—	6*	—	—	5*	0		2*	8	23	23			3*
C.H. Dredge	6	—	25	—	0*	3	28*	—	—	0		17	8	3	7*			
T. Gard	4*	—	27	—	14	34	2	—				19	3	0	—			—
M.S. Turner		1					22*											
R.J. Bartlett				0		4												
J.G. Wyatt				48*											38			
R.J. Harden				5*	24	0	37	19*	17	71	—	3	17	1	26	28*	12	9
N.S. Taylor		9				1	—			0			2	1*	1*			
G.V. Palmer						53	1		7*	1*	1						33	—
R.J. Blitz											1							
J.C.M. Atkinson											—							
P.A.C. Bail																		
Byes	2				3	5	1				2	4		4	1			
Leg-byes	5	11	10	11	2	2	9	6	14	10	3	6	4	7	7	12	4	6
Wides	1	5	8	8	7	1	7	6	10	6	1	3	4		2	5	3	6
No-balls	15		1	2		3			2	1	1	4	1	5	6			1
Total	178	217	194	197	258	176	217	111	244	209	135	103	218	218	213	212	125	272
Wickets	10	7	10	4	7	10	7	2	6	10	2	10	9	10	7	2	6	5
Results	L	L	L	W	W	L	W	W	W	L	W	L	L	L	L	W	W	Ab.
Points	0	0	0	4	2	0	4	4	4	0	—	0	—	0	0	4	4	2

Catches

16 – T. Gard (ct 13/st 3)
10 – I.V.A. Richards
8 – R.J. Harden
7 – C.H. Dredge
6 – J.J.E. Hardy
5 – N.A. Felton

4 – I.T. Botham and N.S. Taylor
3 – J. Garner, V.J. Marks, P.M. Roebuck and subs.
2 – M.S. Turner
1 – G.V. Palmer, R.J. Blitz, B.C. Rose and M.R. Davis

BOWLING

BOWLING	J. Garner	I.V.A. Richards	M.S. Turner	V.J. Marks	C.H. Dredge	M.R. Davis	I.T. Botham	N.S. Taylor	G.V. Palmer
(B.&H.) v. Gloucestershire (Bristol) 3 & 5 May	11–5–16–0	11–2–28–0		10–1–37–0	10.2–2–35–1	11–0–55–1			
(J.P.) v. Yorkshire (Leeds) 4 May	7.4–2–25–0	8–0–28–1	8–0–68–1	8–0–48–0	7–0–38–3				
(B.&H.) v. Essex (Taunton) 10 & 12 May	11–0–48–1	6–2–19–0		9–2–22–1	11–0–30–4		11–0–53–3	7–1–17–0	
(J.P.) v. Middlesex (Taunton) 11 May	8–1–17–0	1–0–10–0	7–0–63–2	8–1–31–3	8–0–31–0		8–0–39–2		
(B.&H.) v. Glamorgan (Taunton) 13 May	9–2–19–1				11–0–38–0	11–2–56–2	8–3–10–2	10.5–0–51–5	
(B.&H.) v. Sussex (Hove) 19 May	11–2–34–2				11–1–36–2	10–1–34–1	9–3–44–2	8–0–43–0	6–1–20–2
(J.P.) v. Glamorgan (Cardiff) 25 May	8–1–47–0	2–0–13–0		6–0–32–0	5–0–27–0		6–0–26–0	8–0–38–2	5–0–22–1
(J.P.) v. Sussex (Horsham) 1 June	5–0–8–1			5–0–19–1	5–0–31–3			5–0–14–0	5–0–24–2
(J.P.) v. Kent (Bath) 15 June	4–1–7–1	2–0–14–0		5.4–0–46–1	5–0–14–0			8–1–28–2	6–0–28–4
(J.P.) v. Nottinghamshire (Bath) 22 June	8–1–33–2	5–0–27–2		7–0–49–0	8–0–41–0			8–0–42–3	4–0–38–0
(N.W.) v. Dorset (Taunton) 25 June	9–0–36–4	12–3–22–2		12–5–15–0	6–1–16–1			9.1–2–21–2	
(J.P.) v. Hampshire (Taunton) 6 July	8–2–21–2	6.1–0–19–0		4–0–12–0	4–0–13–0			6–0–34–0	
(N.W.) v. Lancashire (Taunton) 9 July	12–3–23–2	12–0–40–1		12–0–60–1	12–1–46–2			12–1–47–3	
(J.P.) v. Essex (Chelmsford) 13 July	8–0–43–1	5–0–49–0		3–0–20–0	8–0–49–0	8–0–41–1		8–0–36–2	
(J.P.) v. Gloucestershire (Bristol) 20 July	8–0–30–1	7–0–45–0		3–0–24–0	8–0–37–1	5–0–21–0		6.5–0–49–0	
(J.P.) v. Lancashire (Taunton) 27 July	8–0–29–0	3–0–29–0	7–0–45–1	6–0–30–1			8–0–35–2	8–0–37–2	
(J.P.) v. Worcs. (Weston-super-Mare) 3 Aug.		5–0–25–2		3–0–21–0		5–0–26–1	4–0–18–2	4–0–30–1	3–0–20–1
(J.P.) v. Northants. (Wellingborough) 10 Aug.		7–1–21–1					1–0–8–0		2–0–16–0
(J.P.) v. Surrey (Taunton) 17 Aug.	6–1–23–1	5–0–21–0			8–0–33–1		6–0–48–1	8–0–41–2	3–0–29–0
(J.P.) v. Warwickshire (Edgbaston) 24 August	6.1–1–14–2	8–1–19–2			5–1–18–2	4–0–16–2		7–2–18–2	
(J.P.) v. Leicestershire (Leicester) 31 Aug.	8–2–30–2				8–0–36–0	7.5–0–56–1	8–0–44–1	8–0–39–3	
(J.P.) v. Derbyshire (Taunton) 14 Sept.	8–1–27–1	8–0–21–1			8–0–39–1	8–1–35–1		8–0–60–1	4–0–16–0
Wickets	24	12	4	14	19	8	14	29	10

v. Surrey (Taunton) 17 August (J.P.)	v. Warwickshire (Edgbaston) 24 August (J.P.)	v. Leicestershire (Leicester) 31 August (J.P.)	v. Derbyshire (Taunton) 14 September (J.P.)	Runs
—	43*	59	3	344
—	1	31		497
		1	12	213
—	1		55	523
—		0	32	528
—	0	4		331
—	31*		23*	289
		—	1*	14
—	—	11	13	109
		8	14*	119
—	—	3	—	106
				23
				4
				86
—	10	0	25	304
—	—	28	—	42
				95
				1
				—
			18	18

		6		
3	1	6	
	5	6	
1	3	4	

	90	161	211	
	4	10	7	
Ab.	W	L	W	
2	4	0	4	

Derek Underwood – an amazing 7 for 11 in 35.5 overs for Kent v. Warwickshire at Folkestone. (Tom Morris)

5, but Greg Thomas joined Rodney Ontong in a stand of 124. Andy Afford, rapidly improving with his left-arm spin, took five wickets, but Glamorgan led by 98 on the first innings. This deficit was wiped out by Broad and Robinson, the most consistent opening pair in the country, who put on 114 before Robinson was taken at silly point off Ontong. The off-spinner accounted for Newell and Johnson in his next over, and then captured the wickets of Broad and Rice to reduce Notts to 138 for 5. Ontong's five wickets had come in a spell of 24 balls at a personal cost of 6 runs. He claimed two more victims, Hadlee and Birch, and Glamorgan looked set for victory, but French, with useful aid from Pick and Hemmings, breathed hope into the Notts cause, and Glamorgan were left to make 171 to win on the last day. Morris and Hopkins began with a stand of 50, and the score was 84 before the third wicket fell. The wily Hemmings and the impressive youngster, Afford, then took over and spun Notts to a fine victory, so keeping alive faint hopes of the championship.

Second place Gloucestershire shared the spoils with Surrey. The batsmen were generally on top, and Richards, one of two fine wicket-keepers on view, hit a splendid century after Surrey had fallen to 5 for 3 and 40 for 4, with Clinton retired hurt. Russell, the Gloucestershire keeper, considered by many to be the best in England, had helped in the reduction of Surrey to 5 for 3 by taking a hat-trick of catches although not all three were off the same bowler. In achieving this record, Russell equalled the performance of Dawkes, the only other first-class wicket-keeper to do the hat-trick. Earlier, Russell had hit his highest score of the season. A result never looked possible when bad light interrupted, but there was time for Walsh to bring his season's total to 118 wickets and Alec Stewart to give further indication of his stature.

J.C.M. Atkinson	R.J. Harden	Byes	Leg-byes	Wides	No-balls	Total	Wkts
		6	5	1	2	182	2
			13	4		220	5
		1	16	2	2	206	10
			5	2	1	196	7
			9	1	1	183	10
		1	6		3	218	9
		5	6	4		216	4
			12	2		108	9
			4	2	1	141	10
		1	10	2		241	7
6–2–16–1			6	4	7	132	10
			5	5	2	104	2
		1	4		1	221	10
		1	14	4		253	4
		1	10	2		217	2
			6	4	1	211	6
			7	5	1	147	8
			1			54	1
			3	6		198	5
			3	3	1	88	10
	0.1–0–0–0	4	8	1		217	7
		1	8	2	1	207	5
1	0						

Lamb and Bailey put on 217 in 38 overs for the fourth wicket and led Northants to a massive score at Derby. The home side batted grimly in reply, and David Capel's seven wickets helped Northants to enforce the follow-on. At the second attempt Derbyshire showed more enterprise, and Barnett and Morris shared a third wicket stand of 221 in 57 overs.

Somerset, ravaged by internal wranglings over the non-renewal of the Richards and Garner contracts, were beaten in two days at Worcester. Tim Curtis hit a career best on the first day when Botham bowled a two-hour spell. Botham had again displayed his masterly lack of tact and timing by announcing to the BBC that he would leave Somerset if the present regime continued in power, presumably the regime that had stood by him in troubled times. Neal Radford, whom none expected to be on the plane to Australia, produced career best bowling figures, and the best of the season, as Somerset capitulated. The visitors followed-on and slumped a second time to a variety of bowlers of whom Patel was the most successful.

Chris Cowdrey and the exciting Steve Marsh shared a stand of 104 that lifted Kent to a first innings lead of 95 over Warwickshire. Cowdrey reached his first hundred of the season, and Marsh the highest score of his career. Marsh took six dismissals in Warwickshire's first innings to equal the Kent record which is shared by all their distinguished line of wicket-keepers. Derek Underwood then produced his best spell of the season and the most remarkable figures of the season by any bowler when he bowled 35.5 overs, 29 of them maidens, and took 7 for 11.

NatWest Bank Trophy Final
SUSSEX v. LANCASHIRE

Ian Gould's decision to ask Lancashire to bat first when he won the toss brought no immediate success to Sussex. The opening round of the match was very much in favour of Lancashire as Mendis and Fowler suggested that there was menace in neither the pitch nor the bowling. The first ten overs produced 33 runs, and the only hint of danger was when Fowler, as is his custom, flirted with balls outside the off-stump. Jones was brought into the attack, but he could find no rhythm, and 13 runs came from the 12th over of the innings. When Fowler crashed the first ball of the next over for four the fifty was raised, but Lancashire jubilation was short-lived as Fowler chased a wide delivery and was caught behind low down.

Dermot Reeve emphasised Sussex's determination to take a hold on the game by producing a spell of bowling which was quick, eager and accurate. In the 18th over he trapped Mendis lbw, and he accounted for Clive Lloyd in the same manner four balls later. Lloyd had received an emotional reception as he made yet another anticipated last appearance at Lord's, but Reeve showed no sign of sentiment in his treatment of the Lancashire captain.

Abrahams and Fairbrother hinted at a Lancashire revival, with Abrahams playing particularly well until he cut Reeve straight into the hands of second slip on the first ball of the 28th over.

Clive Lloyd, lbw for 0 to Man of the Match Dermot Reeve. (All-Sport)

FIELDING POSITIONS N°2

EXTRA COVER

Over the years, we've taken up some interesting positions ourselves.

In 328 years of banking, we've achieved quite a bit and after only seven years' major involvement in cricket, our record is already impressive.

In 1981 we introduced the NatWest Trophy, one of the country's most sought after limited overs trophies.

Each season the competition attracts over 100,000 spectators to cricket grounds.

And we're active off the field, too. Together with the National Cricket Association we've produced a first-class series of coaching films.

We lend our support to the Under 13's Ken Barrington Cup.

And the National Cricket Association Proficiency Award Scheme also gets our backing.

Right now our relationship with cricket couldn't be sunnier. Nor our position clearer.

The Lancashire heroes confer – Fairbrother and Hayhurst. (All-Sport)

Rehan Alikhan is bowled by Allott. (All-Sport)

Paul Parker. His innings was one of the gems of the season. (All-Sport)

Lunch was taken five overs later with the score at 99 for 4, and in the first over after lunch, O'Shaughnessy, a fighting cricketer, but one who was to have an unhappy match, was beaten and bowled by the lively Reeve. Reeve was to be named Man of the Match, a just reward for a fine spell which broke the back of the Lancashire innings.

Of Fairbrother much had been expected, but Hayhurst was a revelation. He displayed no sign of nervousness or tension as he drove powerfully and outscored his partner. He straight drove le Roux majestically for four to bring up the 150 in the 46th over. The next 50 runs came in 8 overs, and for the first time the Sussex fielding showed signs of panic. Alikhan looked awkward, and even the incomparable Parker slipped as he attempted a run out. Gould was magnificent. He cajoled and urged his fielders and bowlers into greater efforts, and in discipline and enthusiasm his leadership was exemplary.

Hayhurst's fine innings came to an end in the 55th over when he tried to run the ball down to the third man area and was caught behind. It was a sad end to a positive knock. Fairbrother was out in the next over, and Maynard, after some typically lusty blows, followed 7 balls later. Watkinson and Simmons played boldly, and Watkinson hit Pigott into the Nursery End stand for a splendid six in the last over so that Lancashire reached 242, a highly respectable score, and one far greater than expected. They were much indebted to Fairbrother and Hayhurst who had added 103 in 21 overs at

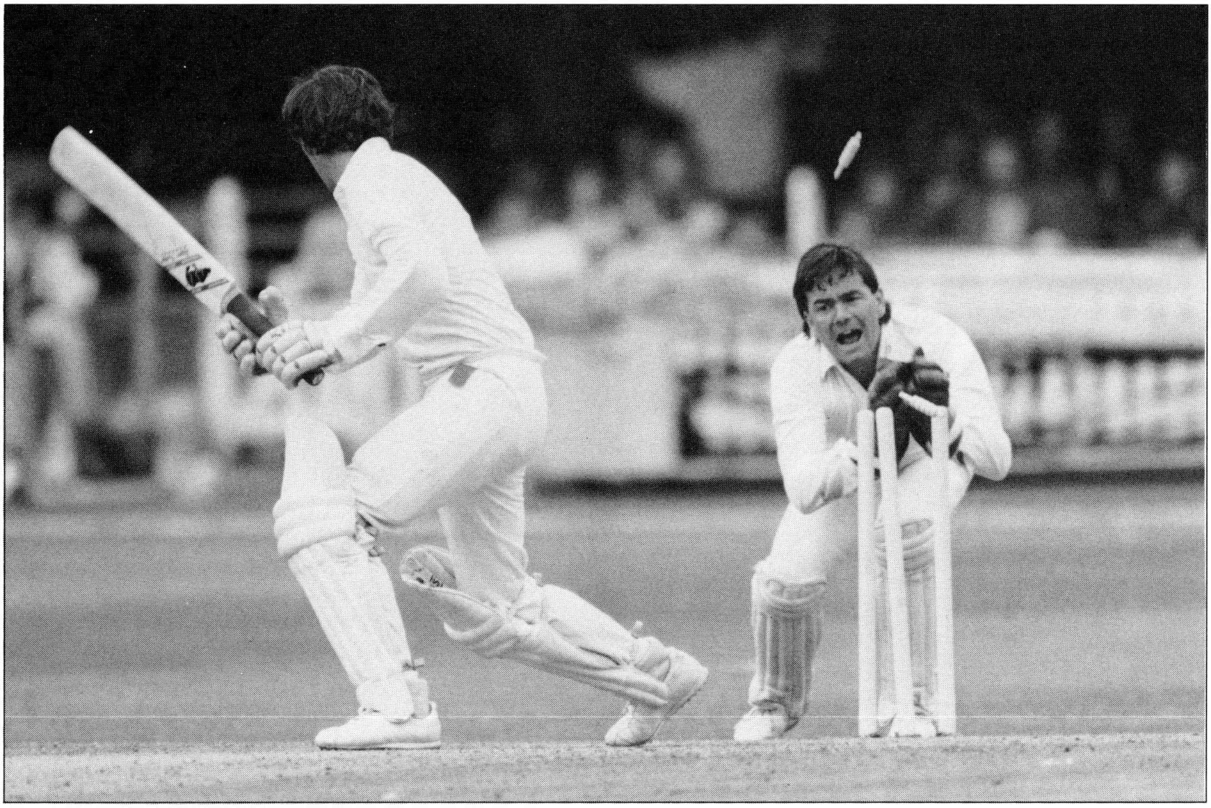

Green is stumped by Maynard off Simmons. (All-Sport)

BELOW: *Worried men – Lancashire meet. (All-Sport)*

a time when all seemed lost.

The Sussex innings began quietly, and it was no surprise when Alikhan, looking out of his depth on this occasion, was comprehensively bowled in the 10th over. This brought Parker to the wicket to join Green and to give us some of the finest batting seen at Lord's in the past decade in any form of cricket. Parker instilled an urgency into the play. His running between the wickets was quite splendid, and one hoped that the Test side was watching to see how runs could be taken. He stood, straight and still, bat only raised as the bowler's arm came over, and drove with rapture and delight through the off-side. This was beauty, a rare treat in the days of waving bats and clouts to leg.

Green caught the mood and gave him admirable support. O'Shaughnessy suffered badly, and when Simmons was brought on to stem the flow of runs Parker hit him bravely into the pavilion for six. He had seized the game for Sussex. The Lancashire attack was weak, and the fielding, Lloyd included, creaked painfully. Green reached his 50 in the 32nd over with a lovely off-drive. The 100 had been reached early in the same over, and at tea, after 35 overs, with Parker having reached his 50 with an exquisite cover drive, Sussex were 117 for 1.

Parker was in full flow after the interval, scoring 27 of the 34 runs which came from the next five overs. At 156, after a stand of 137 in 33 overs, Green moved well down the wicket to Simmons, missed and was stumped. Seven overs later, just as he seemed set for a century, Parker hooked the persevering Hayhurst to Abrahams. It was sad to see him leave for he had given us one of the gems of the summer, indeed one of the gems of many a summer.

Sussex needed 53 off the last 10 overs when Parker was out, but Imran and Colin Wells showed no sign of concern. Imran

National Westminster Bank Trophy 1986

The County winning the Trophy will receive a prize of £19,000, the losing Finalist £9,500, the losing Semi-finalists £4,500 each and the losing Quarter-finalists £2,250 each.

MARYLEBONE CRICKET CLUB

NatWest Bank Trophy Final

20p   LANCASHIRE v. SUSSEX   20p

at Lord's Ground, †Saturday, September 6th, 1986

LANCASHIRE		
1 G. Fowler	c Gould b C. Wells	24
2 G. D. Mendis	l b w b Reeve	17
3 J. Abrahams	c Pigott b Reeve	20
‡4 C. H. Lloyd	l b w b Reeve	0
5 N. H. Fairbrother	b Pigott	63
6 S. J. O'Shaughnessy	b Reeve	4
7 A. N. Hayhurst	c Gould b Imran	49
*8 C. Maynard	c Gould b Imran	14
9 M. Watkinson	not out	15
10 J. Simmons	not out	6
11 P. J. W. Allott		
B 1, l-b 17, w 6, n-b 6,		30
	Total...	242

FALL OF THE WICKETS

1.. 50 2...56 3...56 4...85 5...100 6.. 203 7...205 8...217 9... 10...

Bowling Analysis	O.	M.	R.	W.	Wd.	N-b
Imran	12	2	43	2	1	...
le Roux	9	0	43	0	1	3
Jones	3	0	25	0	1	1
C. Wells	12	3	34	1	1	1
Reeve	12	4	20	4	1	...
Pigott	12	1	59	1	1	1
....	...	...	...	...	...	...

SUSSEX		
1 A. M. Green	st Maynard b Simmons	62
2 R. I. Alikhan	b Allott	6
3 P. W. G. Parker	c Abrahams b Hayhurst	85
4 Imran Khan	not out	50
5 C. M. Wells	not out	17
6 A. P. Wells		
‡*7 I. J. Gould		
8 G. S. le Roux		
9 D. A. Reeve		
10 A. C. S. Pigott		
11 A. N. Jones		
B , l-b 17, w 6, n-b ,		23
	Total...	243

FALL OF THE WICKETS

1...19 2...156 3...190 4... 5... 6... 7... 8... 9... 10...

Bowling Analysis	O.	M.	R.	.W.	Wd.	N-b
Watkinson	11.2	0	40	0	2	...
Allott	11	3	34	1	...	...
O'Shaughnessy	6	0	52	0	2	...
Hayhurst	12	2	38	1	2	...
Simmons	12	2	31	1	...	...
Abrahams	3	0	15	0	...	...
Fairbrother	3	0	16	0	...	...

Any alterations to teams will be announced over the public address system

RULES—1 The Match will consist of one innings per side and each innings is limited to 60 overs.
2 No one bowler may bowl more than 12 overs in an innings.
3 Hours of play: 10.30 a.m. to 7.10 p.m. In certain circumstances the Umpires may order extra time.

Luncheon Interval 12.45 p.m.—1.25 p.m.   Tea Interval will be 20 minutes and will normally be taken at 4.30 p.m.

‡ Captain   * Wicket-keeper

Umpires—H. D. Bird & K. E. Palmer   Scorers—E. Solomon, L. V. Chandler & W. Davies

†This match is intended to be completed in one day, but three days have been allocated in case of weather interference

Sussex won the toss and elected to field

Sussex won by 7 wickets

Total runs scored at end of each over:

First Innings	1	2	3	4	5	6	7	8	9	10	11	12	13	14	15	16	17	18	19	20
	21	22	23	24	25	26	27	28	29	30	31	32	33	34	35	36	37	38	39	40
	41	42	43	44	45	46	47	48	49	50	51	52	53	54	55	56	57	58	59	60

Second Innings	1	2	3	4	5	6	7	8	9	10	11	12	13	14	15	16	17	18	19	20
	21	22	23	24	25	26	27	28	29	30	31	32	33	34	35	36	37	38	39	40
	41	42	43	44	45	46	47	48	49	50	51	52	53	54	55	56	57	58	59	60

Neil Fairbrother in defiant form. (All-Sport)

took everything that was going. He swept impressively and fruitfully and moved relentlessly towards the target. The last 5 overs began with 25 needed. Colin Wells had been patient as Imran reached a fifty that was totally professional in accomplishment. Eight were needed from two overs, but only two balls were necessary as Colin Wells hit Watkinson into the Tavern for six and turned the next ball to leg for two. It was a brave end to a good match, and the gathering gloom, the presentations and an emptying Lord's marked the end of summer.

John Player Special League

7 September

at Cardiff

Glamorgan 132 for 8
Middlesex 133 for 1 (C.T. Radley 75 not out)

Middlesex (4 pts) won by 9 wickets

at Bristol

Lancashire 196 for 8
Gloucestershire 199 for 1 (R.C. Russell 94 not out, C.W.J. Athey 73)

Gloucestershire (4 pts) won by 9 wickets

at Canterbury

Nottinghamshire 122
Kent 123 for 4 (C.J. Tavare 63 not out)

Kent (4 pts) won by 6 wickets

at The Oval

Hampshire 149 for 8 (K.D. James 54 not out)
Surrey 146 for 8

Hampshire (4 pts) won by 3 runs

at Hove

Yorkshire 182 for 7 (P.E. Robinson 76 not out)
Sussex 185 for 3 (P.W.G. Parker 89 not out, A.P. Wells 50)

Sussex (4 pts) won by 7 wickets

at Worcester

Worcestershire 198 for 9 (G.A. Hick 53)
Derbyshire 199 for 9 (K.J. Barnett 78, S.M. McEwan 4 for 35)

Derbyshire (4 pts) won by 1 wicket

Hampshire became the last champions of the John Player League when Tony Gray failed to hit the last ball of the match for the six which would have given Surrey victory at The Oval. It was a sun-lit day, but a rather desolate setting for the climax of a competition, many of the seats in the famous old ground being empty. Hampshire found runs hard to make, but Kevan James hit a brave 54 off 78 balls to give them some hope. That hope was increased when Surrey found runs equally difficult, but they were boosted by Falkner and Thomas. Indeed, Thomas, dropped by Connor, hit 17 off one over to give Surrey a glimpse of victory, but he swung wildly at the first two balls of the final over, bowled by Connor, and was caught by James off the third. Gray found the task of scoring 9 from the last three balls just beyond him. Notts' hopes of the title faded when they were bowled out cheaply at Canterbury and thwarted by Tavare after capturing the first 4 Kent wickets for 45. Gloucestershire won nobly, but still finished bottom. Athey and Russell shared an opening stand of 142, and Russell made his second impressive score in four matches as an opener. Lancashire, the losers for the second time in the week-end, dismissed coach Peter Lever and manager Jack Bond. Ole Mortensen scored a single off the last ball to give Derbyshire victory at Worcester, but Finney and Barnett were the main heroes.

10, 11 and 12 September

at Old Trafford

Lancashire 171 (N.H. Fairbrother 65, V.J. Marks 4 for 41) and 445 for 6 dec (N.H. Fairbrother 115 not out, J. Abrahams 92, D.W. Varey 83, C. Maynard 66)
Somerset 408 (I.T. Botham 139, P.A.C. Bail 55, M. Watkinson 4 for 59) and 182 (J. Simmons 5 for 53)

Lancashire won by 26 runs
Lancashire 21 pts, Somerset 8 pts

at Trent Bridge

Nottinghamshire 267 (B.C. Broad 120, J.K. Lever 5 for 87, N.A. Foster 4 for 77) and 184 for 8 dec (R.T. Robinson 64, R.J. Hadlee 55 not out, D.R. Pringle 4 for 47)
Essex 139 (R.J. Hadlee 6 for 51) and 232 for 6

Match drawn
Nottinghamshire 7 pts, Essex 4 pts

at Hove

Hampshire 385 for 7 dec (C.G. Greenidge 126, N.G. Cowley 65 not out) and 245 for 2 dec (C.L. Smith 114 not out, R.A. Smith 87 not out)

Surrey C.C.C.
Limited-Over Matches – 1986

BATTING

BATTING	v. Middlesex (Lord's) 3 May (B.&H.)	v. Kent (Canterbury) 10 & 12 May (B.&H.)	v. Yorkshire (The Oval) 11 May (J.P.)	v. Hampshire (The Oval) 13 May (B.&H.)	v. Indians (The Oval) 15 May	v. Glamorgan (The Oval) 18 May (J.P.)	v. Combined Univ. (The Oval) 19 May (B.&H.)	v. Kent (Canterbury) 25 May (J.P.)	v. Middlesex (The Oval) 1 June (J.P.)	v. Derbyshire (The Oval) 8 June (J.P.)	v. Nottinghamshire (Trent Bridge) 15 June (J.P.)	v. Cheshire (Birkenhead) 25 June (N.W.)	v. Gloucestershire (Bristol) 29 June (J.P.)	v. Northamptonshire (Tring) 6 July (J.P.)	v. Derbyshire (Derby) 9 July (N.W.)	v. Sussex (Guildford) 27 July (J.P.)	v. Nottinghamshire (The Oval) 30 July (N.W.)	v. Warwickshire (Edgbaston) 3 August (J.P.)
A.R. Butcher	65	1	1	59	140	5	1	64	47		2	38	13	21				
G.S. Clinton	47	13	92*			66	22	9	32	55	21	49	67*		18	56	10	
A.J. Stewart	5	15	28	25	9	31	63*	16	0	18	17	31	17	40	16	0	5	
M.A. Lynch	5	58	10	22		0	68*		12	45	78	29	14	4	20	34	26	
T.E. Jesty	42*	94*	11	71*	30	26	—		3	40*	5	4	7			9	21	
C.J. Richards	13	45	32	10	3	8	—	23*	15*	35	22	23*	55*	14	53*	13	10	
R.J. Doughty	10	30	14	13		1	—		0	—	1		—	22		36		
M.A. Feltham	0*		0*	6*	0*	4*		3	—	1	1		—		37			
G. Monkhouse	—	2*	5		8	—		2	—	3	24*			19*	18	1*	17	
S.T. Clarke	0	—		4	2	—		—		7*				15	13*	9*	23	
P.I. Pocock		—	—	—		—		—		1*	2*	—	1*			1*	9*	
A. Needham				8		10*	—	49	21				5	4		20	13	
N.J. Falkner					6										36	0		
D.M. Ward				24				5		17			—	17				
A.H. Gray						—			—	6	3		—					
M.P. Bicknell												0*	1			13	2*	
D.J. Thomas																0	65	
K.T. Medlycott																	0	
C.K. Bullen																		
Byes	1				1	3	1		1			6	1			7		
Leg-byes	11	8	8	8	1	2	1	10	14	5		5	4	14	6	7	13	
Wides	3	4	4	12	1	5	3	2	1	7	6		2	4	3	7	3	
No-balls	5	4	1	1	5		3	1	4			2				1	1	
Total	207	274	206	239	230	161	162	187	187	198	193	198	161	195	229	203	204	
Wickets	7	6	7	7	8	7	2	9	5	8	9	9	2	9	7	9	9	
Results	L	W	L	L	L	W	W	Tie	L	L	L	W	W	L	W	L	W	Ab.
Points	0	2	0	0		4	2	2	0	0	0	—	4	0	—	0	—	2

Catches

27 – C.J. Richards (ct 21/st 6)
14 – M.A. Lynch
9 – A.J. Stewart
6 – S.T. Clarke, A.R. Butcher, M.P. Bicknell and C.K. Bullen
5 – A. Needham
4 – G. Monkhouse
3 – N.J. Falkner, D.M. Ward and T.E. Jesty
2 – P.I. Pocock, M.A. Feltham, R.J. Doughty, G.S. Clinton and A.H. Gray
1 – K.T. Medlycott, D.J. Thomas and sub

BOWLING

BOWLING	S.T. Clarke	R.J. Doughty	M.A. Feltham	G. Monkhouse	P.I. Pocock	T.E. Jesty	A.H. Gray	A. Needham	A.R. Butcher
(B.&H.) v. Middlesex (Lord's) 3 May	11–2–15–1	11–2–40–0	10.3–0–54–0	11–2–35–2	4–0–29–0	6–0–30–1			
(B.&H.) v. Kent (Canterbury) 10 May	11–0–35–2	8–1–62–0	11–3–47–1	11–2–37–1	9–1–41–1	5–0–40–0			
(J.P.) v. Yorkshire (The Oval) 11 May	6–0–13–1	8–0–25–0	5–0–50–0	6–0–48–0	4–0–37–1	8–0–28–2			
(B.&H.) v. Hampshire (The Oval) 13 May	11–1–36–0	8–0–46–2	10.2–0–59–0	11–1–46–1	11–2–37–2	3–0–9–0			
v. Indians (The Oval) 15 May	9–0–33–1		9.3–0–62–2	9–0–46–0	10–0–30–0		10–0–52–0		
(J.P.) v. Glamorgan (The Oval) 18 May	7.1–0–18–1	4–0–21–1	6–1–32–0	8–1–21–2		3–0–21–0		8–2–13–2	3–0–15–1
(B.&H.) v. Comb. Univ. (The Oval) 19 May		6–1–18–1			10–1–41–2	11–5–16–1	11–1–33–0	10–3–21–0	7–2–23–2
(J.P.) v. Kent (Canterbury) 25 May	8–0–41–3	8–0–29–1		8–0–42–2	8–0–23–1			8–0–45–1	
(J.P.) v. Middlesex (The Oval) 1 June	8–0–28–0	8–0–29–1		8–1–37–2	7.1–0–45–0			8–0–46–3	
(J.P.) v. Derbyshire (The Oval) 8 June	7–1–32–1			7–0–39–0	7–1–50–2	8–0–30–2	1–0–14–0		
(J.P.) v. Notts. (Trent Bridge) 15 June		8–0–38–0			8–0–31–1	8–0–36–1	8–0–35–3	7–0–42–1	0·5–0–2–1
(N.W.) v. Cheshire (Birkenhead) 25 June				10–3–27–2	9.4–3–24–1		12–3–23–3	4–1–12–1	12–3–27–1
(J.P.) v. Gloucestershire (Bristol) 29 June		5–1–13–1	6–0–36–2		4–0–23–0		8–1–24–2	8–1–24–3	
(J.P.) v. Northamptonshire (Tring) 6 July	8–1–44–0	6–0–30–0		8–0–48–3	4–0–39–1		8–0–51–1		
(N.W.) v. Derbyshire (Derby) 9 July	9–3–19–0			11.5–1–55–2	12–5–24–2			12–2–32–4	
(J.P.) v. Sussex (Guildford) 27 July	8–0–35–2	8–1–38–1	6–0–35–4		8–0–31–1				
(N.W.) v. Notts. (The Oval) 30 July	10–6–7–2			8.5–0–34–3	12–3–21–2				
(J.P.) v. Warwickshire (Edgbaston) 3 August									
(J.P.) v. Worcestershire (The Oval) 10 August		8–1–41–0		8–0–39–1				8–0–31–2	
(N.W.) v. Lancashire (The Oval) 13 August	11.3–4–21–4			12–0–51–2	9–0–43–1				7–0–30–1
(J.P.) v. Somerset (Taunton) 17 August									
(J.P.) v. Essex (Chelmsford) 24 August			8–0–51–1		8–0–30–2			8–0–24–3	8–0–32–0
(J.P.) v. Lancashire (Old Trafford) 31 Aug.		8–0–29–1			5–1–30–0		8–0–39–2	8–0–31–0	4.3–0–10–0
(J.P.) v. Hampshire (The Oval) 7 Sept.							8–1–37–2	4–0–16–0	4–0–12–2
(J.P.) v. Leicestershire (The Oval) 14 Sept.				6–0–30–0		1–0–2–0	8–0–21–4		
Wickets	18	9	19	21	17	3	21	16	8

a K.T. Medlycott 2–0–21–0   b M.A. Lynch 1–0–5–0

v. Worcestershire (The Oval) 10 August (J.P.)	v. Lancashire (The Oval) 13 August (N.W.)	v. Somerset (Taunton) 17 August (J.P.)	v. Essex (Chelmsford) 24 August (J.P.)	v. Lancashire (Old Trafford) 31 August (J.P.)	v. Hampshire (The Oval) 7 September (J.P.)	v. Leicestershire (The Oval) 14 September (J.P.)	Runs
24	6	50	8	25	44		614
59	11	70	16	0	6	18	737
1	7	1	59	7		1	412
4	15	15	8	23	0	29	519
31	112		13	26		0	545
13	9	47*	4	52	10	30	539
9*	—		7	15*			148
—	12					11*	75
			11				110
	19	—					92
	2		2*	—			17
				—	1	5	
						31	73
		1			3	10	77
			24*	20*	2*	5	60
	1*				—	—	17
37*	12	5*		1	34	4	158
							0
—			0		0*	1*	1
						1	
7	9	3	12	14	4	8	
5	6	6	3			6	
1	4				7		
191	225	198	167	184	146	124	
6	10	5	9	8	8	8	
W	L	Ab.	W	L	L	W	
4	—	2	4	0	0	4	

M.P. Bicknell	D.J. Thomas	C.K. Bullen	Byes	Leg-byes	Wides	No-balls	Total	Wkts
			1	4	3		208	4
			2	6	4		270	6
			1	8	3	1	210	4
			2	5	3	1	240	7
				8	4	5	231	5
			1	7	5		149	10
			4	5	3	7	161	6
			4	3			187	9
			1	2	7		188	7
8-0-27-0				7			199	7
			1	9	3		194	7
8-1-36-2			1	9	3	2	159	10
6-0-27-1				10	3	2	157	9
6-0-44-0			3	5	6		264	5
9-2-25-1			4	8	4	2	167	10
	8-0-42-0		3	9	3	3	214	9a
10-2-19-1	10-0-57-2		4	11	1	7	158	10b Ab.
	8-0-45-2	8-0-26-1		7	1	3	189	6
10-1-25-1	9-2-40-1		1	18	9	4	229	10 Ab.
		8-1-18-2	1	7	1	3	163	8
	6-1-40-2			6	3	2	185	6
8-1-19-2	8-1-41-1	8-1-13-0	6	5	11	3	149	8
7-0-21-1	7-1-22-1	8-2-24-1		3		4	123	8
9	9	4						

Sussex 350 for 7 dec (A.M. Green 114, A.C.S. Pigott 75 not out, P.W.G. Parker 51) and 243 for 8 (R.J. Maru 4 for 71)

Match drawn
Sussex 7 pts, Hampshire 6 pts

at Worcester

Glamorgan 399 for 7 dec (H. Morris 114, G.C. Holmes 107) and 206 for 3 dec (J.A. Hopkins 93)
Worcestershire 304 for 5 dec (D.M. Smith 100, G.A. Hick 61, T.S. Curtis 50) and 302 for 3 (G.A. Hick 107, D.M. Smith 67, P.A. Neale 60 not out)

Worcestershire won by 7 wickets
Worcestershire 21 pts, Glamorgan 6 pts

at Scarborough

Yorkshire 352 for 7 dec (J.D. Love 109, G. Boycott 61)
Northamptonshire 197 (C. Shaw 5 for 38) and 422 for 8 dec (D. Ripley 134 not out, D.J. Wild 74)

Match drawn
Yorkshire 7 pts, Northamptonshire 3 pts

At 3.49 pm on Wednesday, 10 September, David East dived low to his right to hold an outside edge from Bruce French off the bowling of Graham Gooch. The catch brought Nottinghamshire to 207 for 7, gave Essex their third bowling point and assured them of the Britannic Assurance County Championship. It was a confirmation of what had seemed inevitable since the remarkable victories at Taunton and Folkestone. Gooch had put Notts in to bat when he won the toss, but Chris Broad, rejoicing in his selection as a member of the party to go to Australia, batted splendidly. He was sound in defence and strong in attack, and he showed a

Chris Broad hooks Foster to the boundary during his century for Notts in the vital championship match against Essex, 10–12 September. (David Munden)

Sussex C.C.C.
Limited-Over Matches – 1986

BATTING

	v. Essex (Hove) 3 & 5 May (B.&H.)	v. Lancashire (Old Trafford) 4 May (J.P.)	v. Derbyshire (Derby) 11 May (J.P.)	v. Glamorgan (Swansea) 12 May (B.&H.)	v. Gloucestershire (Bristol) 16 May (B.&H.)	v. Notts. (Trent Bridge) 18 May (J.P.)	v. Somerset (Hove) 19 May (B.&H.)	v. Gloucestershire (Hove) 25 May (J.P.)	v. Middlesex (Lord's) 28 & 29 May (B.&H.)	v. Somerset (Horsham) 1 June (J.P.)	v. Worcestershire (Worcester) 22 June (J.P.)	v. Suffolk (Hove) 25 June (N.W.)	v. Northamptonshire (Hastings) 29 June (J.P.)	v. Glamorgan (Hove) 9 July (N.W.)	v. Glamorgan (Hove) 13 July (J.P.)	v. Leicestershire (Leicester) 20 July (J.P.)	v. Surrey (Guildford) 27 July (J.P.)	v. Yorkshire (Leeds) 30 & 31 July (N.W.)
A.M. Green	50	15	22	—	32	36	13	58	33	11	8	22	10	102	4	0	69	5
J.R.T. Barclay	9	—				6*	—	3*	15									
P.W.G. Parker	20	35	22	13	9	22	9	78	9	25	2	40*	33	21	12	55	8	3
Imran Khan	112*	27	55	48*	20*	15	25	9	47	2	72	28		54	3	0	13	23
A.P. Wells	17	26*	23	—	—	2	21	0		0	3*		17	21	52	38	21	4
I.J. Gould	16	17	2	25	—	63	8	11	0	16	39	—	5	20	7	16	30	88
G.S. le Roux	3	24	5	—	—	1	7	41*	6	1							4	39*
D.A. Reeve	—	—	2*	—	—	8	21*	—	6	1	4		5	1	9	3*	2	1*
A.C.S. Pigott	—	—	—	—	—	0	21	—	2	18*		6*		5*		10*		1*
A.N. Jones						17*	1*	—	20	1*	6*		—			—	9*	
C.M. Wells	23*	18*			27*	11	0	11*	26	4	19	—	4	28	61	68	34	20
C.P. Phillipson		—	12*	—							1	2		6		5	27*	5
N.J. Lenham					33		82		6					6				
A.M. Babington											—		—	0	4*		—	
D.K. Standing											—		1*	4	0*	8*	—	
R.I. Alikhan													0	10	0*			14
M.P. Speight																		
Byes		3		4	3		1				8			4			3	
Leg-byes	8	12	13	5	1	13	6	12	6	12	7	2	5		7	9	9	10
Wides			6	3	3	4			6	2	2	3		3	2	5	3	6
No-balls	1	1	1		8	5	3	1	2		5			5	1	1	3	
Total	259	178	163	98	136	203	218	221	172	108	163	109	100	269	181	222	214	213
Wickets	6	5	6	2	3	9	9	5	10	9	7	3	10	8	8	6	9	7
Results	L	W	L	W	W	W	W	W	L	L	L	W	L	W	W	W	W	—
Points	0	4	0	2	2	4	2	4	—	0	0	—	0	—	4	4	4	—

Catches

- 35 – I.J. Gould
- 7 – A.C.S. Pigott, P.W.G. Parker and C.M. Wells
- 6 – A.M. Green, J.R.T. Barclay and Imran Khan
- 5 – G.S. le Roux, D.A. Reeve and A.P. Wells
- 4 – C.P. Phillipson
- 3 – subs.
- 2 – N.J. Lenham, A.N. Jones, A.M. Babington and D.K. Standing
- 1 – R.I. Alikhan and M.P. Speight

BOWLING

	G.S. le Roux	Imran Khan	D.A. Reeve	C.M. Wells	A.C.S. Pigott	A.N. Jones	J.R.T. Barclay	A.P. Wells	A.M. Babington
(B.&H.) v. Essex (Hove) 3 & 5 May	10-0-50-0	11-0-46-2	10-0-54-0	2-0-15-0	11-0-53-1	11-0-50-2			
(J.P.) v. Lancashire (Old Trafford) 4 May	8-1-30-2	7-0-43-0		8-1-30-0	7.4-0-24-5	8-0-43-2			
(J.P.) v. Derbyshire (Derby) 11 May	7-0-27-1	8-1-16-0	6-0-32-0		6.3-0-34-0	8-1-28-1	2-0-20-0		
(B.&H.) v. Glamorgan (Swansea) 12 May	2-0-13-3	2-0-10-1	2-0-15-0		2-0-23-0	2-0-23-1			
(B.&H.) v. Gloucestershire (Bristol) 16 May	6.1-0-14-1	11-0-37-2		11-2-36-2	11-5-24-2	7-3-14-3			
(J.P.) v. Notts. (Trent Bridge) 18 May	7-0-20-0	5-0-24-0		8-0-35-1	5-0-21-0	8-0-41-0	7-0-41-7		
(B.&H.) v. Somerset (Hove) 19 May	11-1-34-1	11-2-36-0	11-3-32-2	1-0-2-0	9-2-33-3	8-0-32-4			
(J.P.) v. Gloucestershire (Hove) 25 May	4-0-14-0	4-1-13-0	7.2-1-22-4		8-1-20-3	8-1-30-2			
(B.&H.) v. Middlesex (Lord's) 28 & 29 May	11-2-55-0	11-2-24-0	11-0-54-2			11-0-59-2	11-0-52-0		
(J.P.) v. Somerset (Horsham) 1 June	3-1-4-0	5-0-23-0	2-0-8-0		5-0-37-0	5-0-29-2		0.1-0-4-0	
(J.P.) v. Worcestershire (Worcester) 22 June		8-0-32-0	8-0-33-0	4-0-22-1		8-1-31-2			3-0-23-0
(N.W.) v. Suffolk (Hove) 25 June		12-1-27-3	12-7-8-2	3-1-7-0			7-0-25-0		3-0-9-2
(J.P.) v. Northamptonshire (Hastings) 29 June			7-0-41-1	8-0-33-1	8-2-27-2				8-0-39-1
(N.W.) v. Glamorgan (Hove) 9 July		11-2-16-3	12-0-53-1	12-0-35-2					10-0-45-2
(J.P.) v. Glamorgan (Hove) 13 July		7-1-22-1		7-0-39-1	8-0-26-2	8-0-44-2	7.4-2-15-3		
(J.P.) v. Leicestershire (Leicester) 20 July		7-2-13-1		8-0-51-1	8-1-22-3			1-0-7-1	8-2-38-0
(J.P.) v. Surrey (Guildford) 27 July	8-0-36-2	7-0-31-2	5-0-39-1	3-0-24-1	4-0-22-0	8-0-44-1			
(N.W.) v. Yorkshire (Leeds) 30 & 31 July	10.3-2-17-4	6-0-16-0	4-0-24-1	8-0-27-0	2-0-12-0	8-2-26-4			
(J.P.) v. Essex (Eastbourne) 3 August	2-0-16-0	4-0-28-0	3-0-19-3	3-0-26-0	4-0-22-2	4-0-22-1			
(J.P.) v. Hampshire (Bournemouth) 10 Aug.	8-0-40-4	8-1-37-1	8-0-54-1	8-0-37-0					
(N.W.) v. Worcs. (Worcester) 13–15 Aug.	12-1-31-1	12-2-26-3	5-2-7-0	12-3-24-1	2-2-0-1	8-1-23-2			
(J.P.) v. Kent (Hove) 17 August	8-0-39-0	8-3-31-4	8-0-44-3	2-0-12-0	5.2-0-23-1				
(J.P.) v. Middlesex (Hove) 24 August	7-2-12-2	4-1-11-0	5-0-28-1		5.2-0-23-3	8-0-30-4			
(N.W.) v. Lancashire (Lord's) 6 September	9-0-43-0	12-2-43-2	12-4-20-4	12-3-34-1	12-1-59-1	3-0-25-0			
(J.P.) v. Yorkshire (Hove) 7 September	8-0-33-2		8-0-48-0	8-0-13-1	8-0-40-2	8-1-42-1			
(J.P.) v. Warwickshire (Edgbaston) 14 Sept.	6-0-16-0	8-0-45-3	6-1-20-0	7-0-29-2	8-0-49-3	5-0-19-0			
Wickets	23	28	29	17	32	43	0	1	5

v. Essex (Eastbourne) 3 August (J.P.)	v. Hampshire (Bournemouth) 10 August (J.P.)	v. Worcestershire (Worcester) (N.W.) 13–15 August	v. Kent (Hove) 17 August (J.P.)	v. Middlesex (Hove) 24 August (J.P.)	v. Lancashire (Lord's) 6 September (N.W.)	v. Yorkshire (Hove) 7 September (J.P.)	v. Warwickshire (Edgbaston) 14 September (J.P.)	Runs
—	—	11		43	62	4	3	613
								33
7	92	2	18	74	85	89*	51	834
9	19	4	3	31	50*		89	758
7	63	3	30	9	—	50	11	418
5	2*	1*	65*		—	0*		436
6	—	—	16	3	—	—	12*	168
—	—	—	—	3*	—	—	—	66
—	—	—	—	—	—	—	13	70
—	—	—	—	—	—	—	—	54
33*	11*	45*	1		17*	23	10	494
22*	—		24*	23		—	16*	137
						—	7*	134
								4
								13
		41			6			71
						—	—	
1	4	3						
5	5	7	19	13	17	8	2	
4	3	2	5	2	6	7	5	
		7				4	4	
99	199	126	181	208	243	185	216	
5	3	5	5	6	3	3	6	
L	W	W	L	W	W	W	W	
0	4	—	0	4	—	4	4	

D.K. Standing	A.M. Green	N.J. Lenham	Byes	Leg-byes	Wides	No-balls	Total	Wkts
				9	12	7	277	7
				6	2	3	176	10
				7	2		164	2
			3	6	1	1	93	6
				9	3	6	134	10
				16	9	1	198	8
			5	2	1		176	10
			1	7	4	5	107	10
			2	10	6	4	256	5
				6	6	2	111	2
4.1–1–16–1				7	3		164	5
12–3–27–2			2	3	9	1	108	10
8–0–35–1	1–0–7–0			6	9	2	188	7
5–0–27–0		9–0–48–1	1	15	8	8	240	10
				7	3		153	10
8–0–40–1				5	7		176	8
				7		1	203	9
				3	4	2	125	10
				5	1	1	138	7
		8–0–40–0	2	11	7		221	6
				14	4	5	125	10
				3	1	1	182	9
				3	3		107	10
			1	17	6	6	242	8
			1	5	8		182	7
			4	19	6			
5	0	1						

Newell is bowled by Foster and Essex move another wicket closer to the title, Notts v. Essex, 10 September. (David Munden)

pleasing power in his driving on the off-side. Lever and Foster worked their way through the Notts batting, however, and they were ably supported by East behind the stumps, by Pringle at slip and by Fletcher who took a fine catch running from gully to third man. Gooch began in thunderous mood and 36 runs came in the first four overs of the Essex innings. He was out in the seventh with the score at 50. They closed at 92 for 2, and next day, no doubt having celebrated well, they collapsed to Hadlee and Rice and were all out for 139. After an opening partnership of 63 Notts themselves lost their way, and Neil Foster reached 100 wickets for the season, an outstanding achievement for an England pace bowler in the nineteen-eighties. Eventually, Essex were asked to make 313 in 84 overs. At 97 for 5, they looked likely to be beaten, but Fletcher, Lilley and East saved them.

At the other end of the table, Glamorgan were condemned to the wooden spoon when they lost to Worcestershire. Morris and Holmes put on 168 for Glamorgan's third wicket on the opening day. Both reached excellent hundreds, for Morris it was the first as Glamorgan's captain. The home side kept in touch through a century from Smith, and Hopkins then hit well as Glamorgan pressed for quick runs. Morris left Worcestershire 52 overs in which to make 302 to win. Curtis retired hurt, but d'Oliveira and Smith saw the score to 83 in 10 overs before d'Oliveira was out for 49. Smith hit 67, and when the last 20 overs were reached 131 runs were needed with 8 wickets in hand. Hick reached his sixth century

Warwickshire C.C.C.
Limited-Over Matches – 1986

BATTING

BATTING	v. Essex (Chelmsford) 4 May (J.P.)	v. Leicestershire (Leicester) 10 May (B.&H.)	v. Nottinghamshire (Trent Bridge) 11 May (J.P.)	v. Minor Counties (Walsall) 13 May (B.&H.)	v. Northamptonshire (Edgbaston) 15 & 16 May (B.&H.)	v. Derbyshire (Leek) 18 May (J.P.)	v. Derbyshire (Edgbaston) 19 May (B.&H.)	v. Worcestershire (Edgbaston) 25 May (J.P.)	v. Lancashire (Old Trafford) 1 June (J.P.)	v. Glamorgan (Edgbaston) 8 June (J.P.)	v. Leicestershire (Harrogate) 13 June (T.T.)	v. Northamptonshire (Northampton) 15 June (J.P.)	v. Leicestershire (Edgbaston) 22 June (J.P.)	v. Durham (Edgbaston) 25 June (N.W.)	v. Middlesex (Lord's) 6 July (J.P.)	v. Essex (Edgbaston) 9 July (N.W.)	v. Hampshire (Portsmouth) 20 July (J.P.)	v. Worcestershire (Worcester) 31 July (N.W.)
T.A. Lloyd	8	22	58	2	0	1	1	2	—	74	1	13	12	4	61	44		
D.L. Amiss	0	13	40	73	6	4	59	42	11*	36		44	59	77	6	10	30	0
G.W. Humpage	23	21	86	9	8	25	16	2	9	11		12	1	7	9	70	7	2
G.J. Lord	3		1*		6	0												
B.M. McMillan	78*	51	1	4	39	37*	76								9	10	8	
M. Asif Din	108*	14	14	9	52*	33	4	5	8	10	11	24*	4	7	11	38*	16	10
P.A. Smith	—	26	14	35	4	1*	18	1	28*	18	2	13		79	12	26	4	4
G.J. Parsons	—	9	6*	20	3	—	11*	1*	—	2	0	1		2	23	6	9*	7
G.C. Small	—	2		5*			2	—		0		1		7*	0		23	3*
T.A. Munton	—	0*	—	0*	—					29	—						3	
N. Gifford	—	1*	—	2							0*					0	2	
R.I.H.B. Dyer		13									0	1						
A.R.K. Pierson		—	11					0			5*							
A.I. Kallicharran									101	23	13	6	5	78*	99			39
A.J. Moles									7	—	10*	0		2*			18	14
K.J. Kerr									1*	2					3	5*	13	
A.M. Ferreira											23	10	29	32*				27*
G.A. Tedstone											13							
S. Monkhouse											9							
D.A. Thorne															12	21	24	21
Byes						6	3			6	3		1		1			
Leg-byes	15	11	13	16	6	9	6	4		7	3	1	4	7	10	11	6	3
Wides	2	3	3	3	3	9	12	6	2	5	7	2	1		2	6	2	5
No-balls		7				2	5	2							2			1
Total	237	193	236	184	127	133	213	174	87	191	104	132	192	317	168	255	152	136
Wickets	4	9	6	10	7	5	9	7	3	9	10	8	5	8	8	10	10	8
Results	L	W	W	W	L	W	L	L	W	L	L	L	W	W	Tie	W	L	L
Points	0	2	4	2	0	4	0	0	4	0	—	0	4	—	2	—	0	—

Catches

21 – G.W. Humpage (ct 20/st 1)
6 – T.A. Lloyd
5 – B.M. McMillan, G.J. Parsons and P.A. Smith
4 – G.C. Small
3 – G.J. Lord, N. Gifford, D.L. Amiss, A.J. Moles, A.I. Kallicharran and A.M. Ferreira
2 – M. Asif Din and T.A. Munton
1 – A.R.K. Pierson and G.A. Tedstone

BOWLING

BOWLING	B.M. McMillan	G.C. Small	T.A. Munton	P.A. Smith	G.J. Parsons	N. Gifford	A.R.K. Pierson	T.A. Lloyd	A.J. Moles
(J.P.) v. Essex (Chelmsford) 4 May	8–0–56–1	8–0–30–1	8–0–43–0	1–0–21–0	8–0–67–2	7–0–51–0			
(B.&H.) v. Leicestershire (Leicester) 10 May	11–1–43–0	11–1–40–2	11–1–20–1			11–0–46–1	11–2–28–1		
(J.P.) v. Notts. (Trent Bridge) 11 May	6.3–1–23–3			8–1–31–2	8–0–33–2	7–0–26–2	7–0–48–1		
(B.&H.) v. Minor Counties (Walsall) 13 May	9–1–12–2			10–0–25–2		10·4–1–36–3	9–0–28–1	11–3–25–1	
(B.&H.) v. Northants. (Edgbaston) 15 May	11–2–51–3	11–0–61–0	10–2–57–1			10–0–41–1	11–2–34–0		2–0–20–0
(J.P.) v. Derbyshire (Leek) 18 May	8–2–22–3	7–1–20–0	8–0–34–2			8–0–33–1	7.4–1–15–2		
(B.&H.) v. Derbyshire (Edgbaston) 19 May	11–0–55–1	10.5–1–36–2				11–1–47–2	11–3–26–0	11–1–33–1	
(J.P.) v. Worcestershire (Edgbaston) 25 May		8–1–33–1				7–0–41–2	7.2–0–34–0	1–0–10–0	8–0–25–1
(J.P.) v. Lancashire (Old Trafford) 1 June		2–0–13–1	2–0–20–1			2–0–12–1	2–0–13–1		2–0–14–0
(J.B.) v. Glamorgan (Edgbaston) 8 June		8–1–44–0			8–0–35–2	8–0–39–0	8–0–34–0		
(T.T.) v. Leicestershire (Harrogate) 13 June			7–3–19–3			11–1–46–0	11–6–10–1		
(J.P.) v. Northants. (Northampton) 15 June		6–1–25–0			6–0–21–1	6–2–13–1	8–0–26–0	8–1–30–0	
(J.P.) v. Leicestershire (Edgbaston) 22 June		6–0–26–4		5–0–27–2	5–0–24–0				3–0–37–0
(N.W.) v. Durham (Edgbaston) 25 June		6–1–17–0		12–1–28–2	6–2–14–1			6–0–43–1	
(J.P.) v. Middlesex (Lord's) 6 July	8–0–38–0	8–1–20–1			8–1–20–2	5–0–32–2			
(N.W.) v. Essex (Edgbaston) 9 July	11.4–1–54–3	8–0–36–2			12–4–34–1	8–1–29–2			
(J.P.) v. Hampshire (Portsmouth) 20 July	5.5–0–38–0	6–1–16–2	6–0–24–1	2–0–10–0	8–0–22–0				1–0–11–0
(N.W.) v. Worcestershire (Worcester) 31 July		10–4–26–1			5–0–29–0	8–2–21–0			6–0–27–0
(J.P.) v. Surrey (Edgbaston) 3 August				2–0–11–0	3–0–16–0	5–0–17–1			
(J.P.) v. Kent (Edgbaston) 10 August									
(J.P.) v. Gloucestershire (Edgbaston) 17 Aug.		8–0–36–1	8–0–54–1	5–0–23–0		8–0–40–3			
(J.P.) v. Somerset (Edgbaston) 24 August			3–2–10–0	2–0–6–1	6–1–11–3	5–1–21–0			
(J.P.) v. Yorkshire (Leeds) 31 August		8–1–8–2	8–1–19–1	8–0–41–0		8–1–33–1			2–0–20–0
(J.P.) v. Sussex (Edgbaston) 14 September		8–1–46–2	6–0–47–0	6–0–28–1		8–1–37–1			
Wickets	16	22	17	7	23	18	3	1	1

a G. Monkhouse 9–1–33–2   b D.A. Thorne 3–0–19–0   c D.A. Thorne 7–0–29–0   d D.A. Thorne 1–0–4–0   e D.A. Thorne 4–0–18–1

v. Surrey (Edgbaston) 3 August (J.P.)	v. Kent (Edgbaston) 10 August (J.P.)	v. Gloucestershire (Edgbaston) 17 August (J.P.)	v. Somerset (Edgbaston) 24 August (J.P.)	v. Yorkshire (Leeds) 31 August (J.P.)	v. Sussex (Edgbaston) 14 September (J.P.)	Runs
						303
		60	2	7	34	613
—		3	13	43*	0	377
						10
						313
—		40*	4	0	25	447
—		7	6	17	10	329
—			1			101
—			—		5	48
—			2*	—	5*	39
—			1	—	—	6
						14
						16
—		71	8	36	44	523
—		85	15	3	2	156
—			1	—		25
—		8*	28	32*	28	217
						13
						9
—					19*	97
		5		2	4	
		2	3	20	19	
		3	3	1	6	
			1	1		
		284	88	162	201	
		5	10	5	8	
Ab.	Ab.	W	L	Tie	L	
2	2	4	0	2	0	

K.J. Kerr	Asif Din	A.M. Ferreira	Byes	Leg-byes	Wides	No-balls	Total	Wkts
				16	4	3	284	4
			1	14	4	6	192	7
			5	9	3		188	10
				11	5		137	10
			1	18	13	3	283	5
			1	7	4	2	132	10
				18	9	2	215	7
8–2–22–2			3	7	2		175	6
				4	2	3	76	5
8–0–39–1			1	7	2		199	4
	6–1–21–0	11–0–41–2		2		4	172	8a
	2–0–11–1		4	3		1	133	3
		2–0–17–2		1	2		132	10
12–2–32–2	1.1–0–5–1	10–2–28–3	1	14	2	3	182	10
8–1–23–1				7	5	1	168	7b
12–1–42–1				7	4		191	10
				4	5	1	154	4c
		9.3–0–24–1	1	5	3	4	137	2d Ab.
5–0–29–0		0.2–0–0–1	1	1			74	2
3–0–20–0	1–0–7–0	7–0–49–2		9	3		238	7
8–1–23–0	1.3–0–12–0	2–0–4–0	3				90	4
		8–0–32–1		9	2	1	162	8
		8–0–38–0		2	5	4	216	6
7	2	12						

Neil Foster passed 100 wickets in the season, a magnificent achievement by an England pace bowler. (Adrian Murrell)

of the season and passed two thousand runs in the process. He is an exciting talent. Neale gave fine support, and victory came with 3 balls to spare.

Geoff Boycott reappeared for Yorkshire in what many thought would be his last game of first-class cricket. He was run out for 61 and failed to reach a thousand runs as Northants saved the game by batting throughout the last day after being made to follow-on. Jim Love, once an England prospect, hit his first century of the season, and Chris Shaw took a career best 5 for 38. David Ripley, a fine young wicket-keeper, hit the first century of his career.

There were runs galore at Hove. Greenidge hit his fourth championship hundred in succession, and, after Green had again impressed for Sussex, the Smith brothers added 180 in 44 overs of sparkling batting. Marshall dismissed Green and Parker for 0 in his second over, but Sussex maintained their challenge to score 281 in three and a half hours. They failed and nearly died bravely after Pigott had played some handsome strokes for the second time in the match. They were 181 for 8, but le Roux and Reeve could not be separated and continued to hit hard.

Sad Somerset routed Lancashire on the opening day at Old Trafford and were then lifted by a piece of Botham brilliance which produced 139 off 79 balls. It was his fastest hundred of the season. He hit 9 sixes and 17 fours. He got off the mark with a single, and his next four scoring strokes were all sixes off Folley. He took 20 in one over from Murphy. Somerset

Worcestershire C.C.C.
Limited-Over Matches – 1986

BATTING

	v. Scotland (Glasgow) 3 & 4 May (B.&H.)	v. Kent (Canterbury) 11 May (J.P.)	v. Lancashire (Worcester) 13 May (B.&H.)	v. Nottinghamshire (Worcester) 15 May (B.&H.)	v. Yorkshire (Leeds) 18 May (J.P.)	v. Yorkshire (Leeds) 19 May (B.&H.)	v. Warwickshire (Edgbaston) 25 May (J.P.)	v. Northamptonshire (Worcester) 28 & 29 May (B.&H.)	v. Northamptonshire (Northampton) 8 June (J.P.)	v. Kent (Worcester) 11 June (B.&H.)	v. Lancashire (Old Trafford) 15 June (J.P.)	v. Sussex (Worcester) 22 June (J.P.)	v. Oxfordshire (Worcester) 25 June (N.W.)	v. Hampshire (Worcester) 29 June (J.P.)	v. Nottinghamshire (Worcester) 6 July (J.P.)	v. Hampshire (Southampton) 9 July (N.W.)	v. Essex (Southend) 20 July (J.P.)	v. Gloucestershire (Hereford) 27 July (J.P.)
T.S. Curtis	40*	4	3		11							1	14	48	10	94	82	73
D.B. D'Oliveira	8	11	6	22	29	66	17	15	41	18	44	12*	99	11	59	50	21	22
G.A. Hick	0	17	32	103*	45	35	3	103*	14	72	68	59	27	30	33	9	47	0
D.N. Patel	2	41	76	—		6	8	—	0	1	9	3	20	34	29	31*		48
P.A. Neale	0	49*	52	—	6	28	8	—	1	53	14	16	42	4	7	36	0	29
M.J. Weston	11	22	0	3	4	42	47	15	18	23	18	0*	44*	9	30*		3	13*
S.J. Rhodes	3	28	0	—	30*	3	12	—	46	4	4	—	11*	18	4	32*	15	17
P.J. Newport	5		15		1						9			12	3		1	17*
N.V. Radford	11	1*	3*		0	2	4*		11	29*				2*	0*		5*	
R.K. Illingworth	17*	—			5*			3		14*				2*	0*		10	
A.P. Pridgeon	—	—				1*			0*									
J.D. Inchmore			2*		3	11			2	18*	5*							3
D.M. Smith			14	81*	8	1	64*	90*	52	5	9	60	17				1	19
S.M. McEwan																		—
Byes	1	2	1	8	11	1	3			2			4	4	1		1	
Leg-byes	4	13	18		12	7	7	8	9	10	9	7	6	6	10	14	21	8
Wides	7	3			2	1	2	2	2	5	6	3	8	2			3	5
No-balls	1		9	2	1	4		1		1	1	3			1	8		1
Total	110	191	231	219	163	213	175	234	199	241	210	164	292	182	187	278	230	233
Wickets	8	6	8	2	9	9	6	2	10	7	8	5	6	8	7	5	10	6
Results	W	L	L	W	L	W	W	W	L	L	L	W	W	L	L	L	W	W
Points	2	0	0	2	0	2	4	—	0		0	4		0		0	0	4

Catches 30 – S.J. Rhodes (ct 20/st 10)
13 – P.A. Neale
9 – G.A. Hick
8 – N.V. Radford
6 – D.N. Patel
5 – M.J. Weston
4 – D.B. D'Oliveira
3 – R.K. Illingworth and T.S. Curtis
2 – D.M. Smith, A.P. Pridgeon, J.D. Inchmore and P.J. Newport
1 – S.M. McEwan and sub.

BOWLING

	N.V. Radford	P.J. Newport	A.P. Pridgeon	R.K. Illingworth	D.N. Patel	G.A. Hick	D.B. d'Oliveira	M.J. Weston	J.D. Inchmore
(B.&H.) v. Scotland (Glasgow) 3 & 4 May	7-1-16-0	4-0-9-0	6-2-9-1	11-1-22-1	11-4-12-2	8-1-22-1	8-2-12-3		
(J.P.) v. Kent (Canterbury) 11 May	7-0-42-2		8-0-31-1	6-1-30-0	4-0-26-0			4-0-17-0	8-0-35-0
(B.&H.) v. Lancashire (Worcester) 13 May	11-2-36-1	11-0-39-1	10-3-38-1		8-0-30-1	4-0-25-2			11-0-40-2
(B.&H.) v. Notts. (Worcester) 15 May	11-2-35-0	11-0-43-0		11-1-49-2				11-1-35-2	11-2-33-2
(J.P.) v. Yorkshire (Leeds) 18 May	8-1-30-2	5-0-26-0			8-1-18-2	2-0-17-0		4.1-0-20-1	8-0-43-0
(B.&H.) v. Yorkshire (Leeds) 19 May	9-2-28-1			11-0-57-3	11-3-21-1	8-1-24-0		1-0-1-0	9-1-23-1
(J.P.) v. Warwickshire (Edgbaston) 25 May	8-0-32-1		5-0-8-0		8-1-32-2	7-0-34-3		8-0-37-1	4-0-27-0
(B.&H.) v. Northants. (Worcester) 28 & 29 May	11-0-58-2		11-0-43-2	6-0-33-0	5-0-22-0			11-3-23-1	11-2-40-1
(J.P.) v. Northants. (Northampton) 8 June	8-0-47-1		8-1-34-0	6-0-38-0	2-0-27-0			8-0-34-1	8-0-43-1
(B.&H.) v. Kent (Worcester) 11 June	11-0-62-2		8-1-42-0	3-0-23-0	11-1-32-1			11-1-37-1	11-1-49-2
(J.P.) v. Lancashire (Old Trafford) 15 June		8-0-32-1	8-0-60-2	4-0-28-0	8-0-48-1			4-0-30-0	8-0-43-0
(J.P.) v. Sussex (Worcester) 22 June		8-0-42-1	8-1-27-3		8-1-41-0			8-1-23-0	8-1-23-3
(N.W.) v. Oxfordshire (Worcester) 25 June	10-1-28-0		8-1-15-0		7-4-8-1	7-1-21-1	8-1-24-1	9-1-20-0	9-1-19-0
(J.P.) v. Hampshire (Worcester) 29 June	8-1-26-0		8-0-42-0		1-0-13-0			8-1-33-1	
(J.P.) v. Notts. (Worcester) 6 July		6-0-31-0	6.2-0-29-0	6-1-38-3	8-0-31-0			4-0-22-0	8-0-34-0
(N.W.) v. Hampshire (Southampton) 9 July	9-1-43-2	12-0-62-3		11.1-1-28-2		12-4-31-0			9-1-40-2
(J.P.) v. Essex (Southend) 20 July	8-0-38-2	8-0-64-0			8-1-49-2			8-0-66-1	8-0-40-1
(J.P.) v. Gloucestershire (Hereford) 27 July		8-0-52-2	8-0-23-3	7.5-0-32-2	8-0-62-1				
(N.W.) v. Warwickshire (Worcester) 31 July	12-1-23-3	12-3-19-1	12-0-28-0			12-2-36-3			12-1-27-1
(J.P.) v. Somerset (Weston-super-Mare) 2 Aug.	5-0-36-1		4.3-0-39-1	5-0-25-1					
(J.P.) v. Surrey (The Oval) 10 August	7.3-1-43-0	2-0-18-0	8-0-36-3	8-0-34-0	8-1-28-2				5-0-25-1
(N.W.) v. Sussex 13–15 August	12-3-20-3	12-2-33-0	12-4-23-1	12-4-23-1	5-0-24-0	3-0-4-0			
(J.P.) v. Leicestershire (Worcester) 17 Aug.				8-1-21-1		8-0-30-1		8-1-28-2	8-1-33-3
(J.P.) v. Glamorgan (Worcester) 24 August			4-0-16-0	8-0-31-0	8-0-25-4	4-0-23-1		8-1-24-2	
(J.P.) v. Middlesex (Lord's) 31 August	8-1-24-2			7.2-0-45-0	2-1-10-1		8-0-36-1	8-0-29-1	
(J.P.) v. Derbyshire (Worcester) 7 Sept.	8-0-33-1			8-1-32-2	6-0-24-1			3-0-22-0	8-0-35-0
Wickets	26	9	23	24	17	6	4	14	20

Batting

	v. Warwickshire (Worcester) 31 July (N.W.)	v. Somerset (Weston-s-Mare) 2 August (J.P.)	v. Surrey (The Oval) 10 August (J.P.)	v. Sussex (Worcester) (N.W.) 13–15 August	v. Leicestershire (Worcester)	v. Glamorgan (Worcester) 17 August (J.P.)	v. Middlesex (Lord's) 24 August (J.P.)	v. Derbyshire (Worcester) 31 August (J.P.)	7 September (J.P.)	Runs
	51*	39		22	20	102	5	47		666
	11	23	11	21	33	—	0	13		663
	0*	4	27	1	3	68*	36	53		889
	—	31	31	6	31	1*	40*	9		457
	—	15	25*	1	10	—	46	0		442
					4	—	0	1		307
	—	12*	45	3	8	42	22	1		360
	—		3	15						81
	—	1	4*	0			24*	37*		134
	—	1	—	8	9*	—	—	11		80
	—			4*						5
	—	—		2*				1		47
	62	1	32	21	27					564
		7*		—	—	—		6*		13

	1				4			
	5	7	7	14	6	8	8	11
	3	5	1	4	2	3	2	8
	4	1	3	5	3	3		
Total	137	147	189	125	162	227	183	198
Wkts	2	8	6	10	8	2	6	9
	W	L	L	L	W	W	L	L
	—	0	0	—	4	4	0	0

Bowling / Extras

D.M. Smith	S.J. Rhodes	S.M. McEwan	Leg-byes	Wides	No-balls	Total	Wkts	Byes
			4	3	7	109	9	1
			12	2		193	4	
			4	19	4	231	8	5
			1	22	6	218	7	1
			10	3	6	164	5	
			4	11	2	169	10	10
			4	6	2	174	7	
			1	13	2	233	8	
			5	1		228	3	
			7	4	1	252	8	
			8	2	1	249		
			7	2		163	7	
1–0–5–0	1–0–1–0		7	2		148	3	
			19			183	1	
			5	4	4	190	3	
			8	6	6	212	10	
			2	14	11	273	6	1
		8–0–48–1	4	9	6	230	10	
			3	5	1	136	8	
		5–1–21–2	4	3		125	6	
			7	5	1	191	6	
1–1–0–1			3	7	2	126	5	7
		8–1–35–0	3	6	2	150	8	
		8–0–38–1	7	7		164	8	
		6–0–32–0	3	6		165	5	3
		7–0–35–4	6	12		199	9	5
1	**0**	**8**						

led by 237 on the first innings, but Lancashire batted with determination. Varey and Abrahams added 117 for the second wicket, and Fairbrother played a delightful innings of 115, and Maynard hit fiercely. Somerset were asked to make 209 in 35 minutes plus 20 overs. With 17 overs remaining, they were 59 for 3. Botham fell almost immediately, and they collapsed before Jack Simmons, being bowled out with 7 balls remaining. It was an astounding victory for Lancashire, and a defeat which emphasised the plight of Somerset.

John Player Special League

14 September

at Chelmsford

Glamorgan 136
Essex 138 for 3 (G.A. Gooch 61)

Essex (4 pts) won by 7 wickets

at Southampton

Lancashire 144 for 9 (S.J. O'Shaughnessy 51, K.D. James 4 for 23)
Hampshire 148 for 2 (V.P. Terry 63 not out)

Hampshire (4 pts) won by 8 wickets

at Canterbury

Match abandoned
Kent 2 pts, Yorkshire 2 pts

at Trent Bridge

Northamptonshire 174 for 9 (C.E.B. Rice 4 for 33)
Nottinghamshire 178 for 3 (P. Johnson 79)

Nottinghamshire (4 pts) won by 7 wickets

David Ripley, the Northamptonshire wicket-keeper, who hit a maiden century against Yorkshire, 12 September. (David Munden)

Yorkshire C.C.C.
Limited-Over Matches – 1986

BATTING

BATTING	v. Lancashire (Old Trafford) 3 & 5 May (B.&H.)	v. Somerset (Leeds) 4 May (J.P.)	v. Nottinghamshire (Trent Bridge) 10 May (B.&H.)	v. Surrey (The Oval) 11 May (J.P.)	v. Scotland (Leeds) 15 May (B.&H.)	v. Worcestershire (Leeds) 18 May (J.P.)	v. Worcestershire (Leeds) 19 May (B.&H.)	v. Essex (Sheffield) 25 May (J.P.)	v. Gloucestershire (Leeds) 8 June (J.P.)	v. Middlesex (Lord's) 15 June (J.P.)	v. Northamptonshire (Luton) 22 June (J.P.)	v. Cambridgeshire (Leeds) 25 June (N.W.)	v. Leicestershire (Middlesbrough) 6 July (J.P.)	v. Middlesex (Leeds) 9 & 10 July (N.W.)	v. Nottinghamshire (Hull) 27 July (J.P.)	v. Sussex (Leeds) 30 & 31 July (N.W.)	v. Lancashire (Old Trafford) 3 August (J.P.)	v. Glamorgan (Scarborough) 10 August (J.P.)
M.D. Moxon	106*	28	40	11	83	12	2	43		48		75		65		6	17*	
G. Boycott	55		27*									31						
K. Sharp	0	49	14	9	105*	59	17	4	2	52	94	33*	1	2			—	10
J.D. Love	34*	44	15	13	25	36	25	30	20		11	8*	5		104*	12	—	10
S.N. Hartley	—	24	13	7	0	8	28	2	11	15	46		57	24	3	0	15*	30
D.L. Bairstow	—	12*	31	83*	22	—	6	4	12	34	7		2*	8	14	3		23
P. Carrick	—	—	10	—	—	4*	14	0	4	0	25	—	4*	0	16	54	—	39*
A. Sidebottom	—	—	13	—	—	18*	35*	2	1	0*		1						
P.J. Hartley	—	—	29*	—	—	—	0	5	1	0	4	—			1*	23	—	
G.B. Stevenson	—	0*	10	—	27*	22*	21		4									
P.W. Jarvis	—	—	6*	—	—	—	0	27*	0*	0	10	—	—	9*	—	10		
A.A. Metcalfe		46		74*	31	4	11		19	13	9	23	3	0	35	6	4	46
S.D. Fletcher				—										1*		2*		
P.E. Robinson								9	41	29	0		68	66	64	0		4
S.J. Dennis											1*	0*				3		—
R.J. Blakey														2		0		—
C. Shaw																		
D. Byas																		10
C.S. Pickles																		16*
Byes			1				4				12	2		2				2
Leg-byes	15	13	10	8	14	10	11	2	11	12		2	13	20	10	3	5	16
Wides	1	4	1	3	7	3	2	3	5	3		2	3	1	4	4	4	4
No-balls	1		1		3	6	10			2			2	1	1	2		
Total	212	220	219	210	317	164	169	164	132	210	220	177	156	205	255	125	41	200
Wickets	2	5	8	4	5	5	10	8	10	10	9	3	5	9	6	10	1	6
Results	W	W	L	W	W	W	L	W	L	L	L	W	W	W	W	L	Ab.	W
Points	2	4	0	4	2	4	0	4	0	0	0	—	4	—	4	—	2	4

Catches

14 – D.L. Bairstow (ct 13/st 1)
9 – J.D. Love
6 – A. Sidebottom, K. Sharp, P.J. Hartley and P. Carrick
4 – S.N. Hartley

3 – M.D. Moxon, S.D. Fletcher, P.W. Jarvis, P.E. Robinson, R.J. Blakey and A.A. Metcalfe
2 – S.J. Dennis
1 – G.B. Stevenson, C. Shaw and sub.

BOWLING

BOWLING	A. Sidebottom	G.B. Stevenson	P.J. Hartley	P.W. Jarvis	P. Carrick	S.D. Fletcher	S.N. Hartley	S.J. Dennis	J.D. Love
(B.&H.) v. Lancs. (Old Trafford) 3 & 5 May	11-6-24-4	11-0-58-3	11-0-55-0	11-1-32-1	11-1-36-1				
(J.P.) v. Somerset (Leeds) 4 May	8-0-28-1	8-0-46-1	8-0-34-2	8-1-50-0	8-1-48-3				
(B.&H.) v. Notts. (Trent Bridge) 10 & 12 May	11-1-48-2	11-1-42-1	11-0-49-2	11-4-30-0	11-0-47-1				
(J.P.) v. Surrey (The Oval) 11 May	8-0-47-3			6-0-34-2		8-0-32-1	2-0-20-0		
(B.&H.) v. Scotland (Leeds) 15 May	8-0-44-0	7-0-19-2	11-0-43-5	11-1-24-1	3.4-0-14-2				
(J.P.) v. Worcestershire (Leeds) 18 May	8-0-40-0	8-1-31-1	8-1-20-1		8-4-13-4	8-0-36-2			
(B.&H.) v. Worcestershire (Leeds) 19 May	10-1-36-3	7-1-29-0	8-1-38-1		11-0-34-1	11-1-38-2	8-0-30-1		
(J.P.) v. Essex (Sheffield) 25 May	8-0-33-2		8-0-15-1		8-0-38-2	8-0-48-2	8-2-18-2		
(J.P.) v. Gloucestershire (Leeds) 8 June	8-0-36-3		8-0-40-2		8-1-27-0	8-0-45-0	8-0-32-1		
(J.P.) v. Middlesex (Lord's) 15 June	5.3-0-29-0		4-0-24-0		8-0-53-0	8-0-36-0	7-0-37-1	5-0-27-0	
(N.W.) v. Northamptonshire (Luton) 22 June			8-0-47-3		6.4-0-45-0	3-0-20-0	4-0-19-0	7-0-29-0	5-0-31-0
(N.W.) v. Cambridgeshire (Leeds) 25 June			12-1-49-3		12-4-19-0	12-8-7-2	12-1-53-3	12-3-39-0	
(J.P.) v. Leics. (Middlesbrough) 6 July	8-0-27-1				7.1-0-21-0	8-1-32-4	8-1-29-0		
(N.W.) v. Middlesex (Leeds) 9 & 10 July	12-0-31-1				10.3-2-32-3	12-4-40-3	11-0-38-1		
(J.P.) v. Nottinghamshire (Hull) 27 July			8-1-33-1	5-0-21-3	8-1-27-3		8-0-37-2		
(N.W.) v. Sussex (Leeds) 30 & 31 July			12-3-47-3	12-1-41-0	12-5-22-0	12-3-37-1			
(J.P.) v. Lancashire (Old Trafford) 8 Aug.			8-0-49-2	8-1-38-0	8-0-19-1	8-0-33-1			
(J.P.) v. Glamorgan (Scarborough) 10 Aug.					8-0-29-1	7.4-0-32-4		8-0-27-2	
(J.P.) v. Derbyshire (Chesterfield) 17 Aug.			8-0-24-0			6-0-22-0		8-0-42-0	
(J.P.) v. Hampshire (Bournemouth) 24 Aug.			8-0-44-0		5-0-20-1	8-0-52-0		7.1-1-41-0	
(J.P.) v. Warwickshire (Leeds) 31 August	8-0-27-1			8-0-28-2	8-0-21-1	8-1-36-0		8-0-28-1	
(Asda) v. Hampshire (Scarborough) 4 Sept.	10-0-40-3				9-2-35-0	10-1-39-2		10-1-43-1	
(J.P.) v. Sussex (Hove) 7 September	7-0-25-1				4.1-0-36-0	8-0-45-0	1-0-12-0	8-0-30-1	
(J.P.) v. Kent (Canterbury) 14 September									
Wickets	25	8	28	17	30	18	3	5	0

v. Derbyshire (Chesterfield) 17 August (J.P.)	v. Hampshire (Bournemouth) 24 August (J.P.)	v. Warwickshire (Leeds) 31 August (J.P.)	v. Hampshire (Scarborough) 4 September (Asda)	v. Sussex (Hove) 7 September (J.P.)	v. Kent (Canterbury) 14 September (J.P.)	Runs
10			21	8		575
						82
	30	5	52	23		551
10	55	48	14	22		541
13	14	5		4		319
5	7	7	10			290
36	2	4	13*	23		248
			3*	—	0	73
35	14*					112
						84
		0				62
1	45	40	44	2		456
2*	—	—	—	—		5
5	8	36	50*	76*		456
1	3*	2*	—	10*		17
						3
4*	—		—	—		6
						10
						16
3				1		
	12	9	12	5		
4	4	2	2	8		
3	2	1	4			
132	196	162	222	182		
9	7	8	5	7		
L	L	Tie	L	L	Ab.	
0	0	2	—	0	2	

C. Shaw	C.S. Pickles	Byes	Leg-byes	Wides	No-balls	Total	Wkts
			3	2	4	208	9
			11	5		217	7
		1	10	2		227	6
			8	4	1	206	7
		1	5	2	1	150	10
		11	12	2	1	163	9
		1	7	1	4	213	9
			10	3	1	162	10
			20	4	4	200	6
			8			214	1
			8	5	1	199	3
			9	10	2	176	8
8–0–35–2			11			155	10
12–2–34–2			10	2	2	185	10
4.3–0–19–1		6	10		3	153	10
12–2–56–2			10	6		213	7
8–0–27–0			18	3		184	5
8–0–30–1	8–0–51–1	4	8			181	10
6.1–1–42–0			5	3	8	135	0
8–1–23–0		2	15		2	197	3
		2	20	1	1	162	5
9.3–0–57–1		1	10	2	4	225	7
8–0–29–0			8	7	4	185	3
							Ab.
9	1						

at Taunton

Derbyshire 207 for 5 (A. Hill 50)
Somerset 211 for 7 (I.V.A. Richards 55)

Somerset (4 pts) won by 3 wickets

at The Oval

Leicestershire 123 for 8 (A.H. Gray 4 for 21)
Surrey 124 for 8

Surrey (4 pts) won by 2 wickets

at Edgbaston

Sussex 216 for 6 (Imran Khan 89, P.W.G. Parker 51)
Warwickshire 201 for 8

Sussex (4 pts) won by 15 runs

The last day of the John Player League saw Essex clinch second place with a comfortable win over Glamorgan, rich in spirit, but lacking in technique. Hampshire confirmed their superiority with victory over Lancashire, and there was another good performance from Kevan James, such an asset in limited-over cricket. Notts beat Northants to secure third place, and they owed much to Clive Rice, an outstanding captain, who took four wickets and brought his season's total to 34 so equalling Bob Clapp's Sunday League record.

At Taunton, there was more concern for demonstration on the Richards-Garner-Botham issue than there was for the cricket. Once again radio and television had provided Botham with ample opportunity to voice ill-judged opinions and attack those who had been steadfast to him when he needed it most. Radio now offered much time to Tim

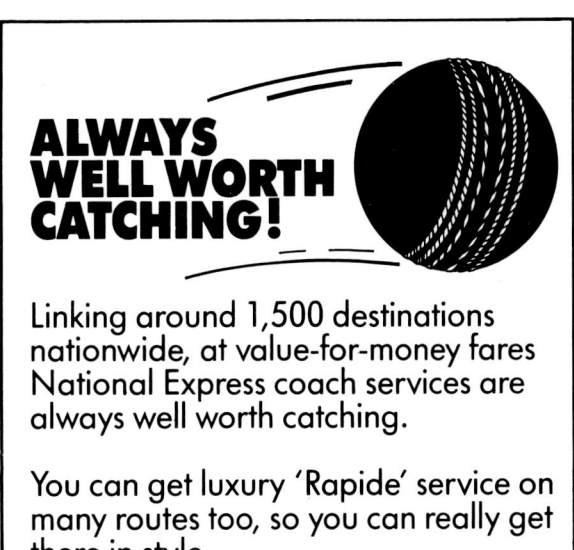

Derbyshire C.C.C. — First-Class Matches – Batting, 1986

Batsman	v. Middlesex (Lord's) 26–29 April		v. Somerset (Chesterfield) 30 April–2 May		v. Nottinghamshire (Derby) 24–26 May		v. Essex (Derby) 31 May–3 June		v. Yorkshire (Sheffield) 4–6 June		v. Surrey (The Oval) 7–10 June		v. Gloucestershire (Gloucester) 14–17 June		v. Gloucestershire (Chesterfield) 21–23 June		v. Lancashire (Liverpool) 28 June–1 July		v. Worcestershire (Derby) 2–4 July		v. Kent (Derby) 5–8 July		v. Warwickshire (Edgbaston) 16–18 July		v. Middlesex (Derby) 19–22 July		v. Hampshire (Portsmouth) 23–25 July	
K.J. Barnett	23	—	64	51	3	1	26*	20	19	0	0	4	95	—	14	114	49	—	0	62	4	40	77	3	19	16	4	16
I.S. Anderson	4	—	3	12	0	6	16*	25	3	5	48	26	62	—	1	93	6	—	25	20	6	26	30	18	9	42	7	4
A. Hill	19	—	17	93	7	3	—	31	172*	76*	4	0	26	—	71	13	11	—	14	59	12	17			45	45	43	24
J.E. Morris	44	—	53	81	1	81	—	0	24	53*	0	62	56	—	0	5	153	—	36	54	16	191	13	50*	28	9	25	78
B. Roberts	28	—	40	124*	42	0	—	17	11	—	43	10	9	—	4	2	87	—	3	16	0	6	3	—	22	55	6	10
G. Miller	—				21	2			19	—	5	16	2	—			22		65	10	0	8	9	—	8	20	0	22
P.G. Newman	34	—	3	25*											22	—	0*		0*	—								
R.J. Finney	13	—	25*	—	54	45	—	29*					4	4	0	41*	0											
M.A. Holding	17	—	5	—					11	—	21	5			9	1			18	5	36*	13			19	31	26	5
A.E. Warner	5	—	0	—	4	39							4	—	10*	0			57*	52	3	53	28*	—	5*	23*	2	11
O.H. Mortensen	2*	—	2	—	10*	2*			9	—	5*	0													0	0*	0*	0*
R. Sharma			7	24			—	1	16	—			14	—					40	—			71	—				
J.G. Wright					3	7	—	4																				
C. Marples			0	50*					12	—	15	7	24	24*	12	14	57		21	0	13	19	45	—	13	6	18	34
C.F.B.P. Rudd							—	1																				
L.J. Wood							—	5																				
M. Jean-Jacques									73	—	12	1*							7	21*	21	0	34	—				
J.P. Taylor													0	—	6	3*			0	—								
D.E. Malcolm													0*	29*			—						1	—				
B.J.M. Maher																									31	52*	69	3
A.M. Brown																												
Byes				6		1							5	1	11		8	11	9					8		4	1	2	1	1
Leg-byes	3		1	14	6	10	1	7	9	4	15		6	3	6	3	8		11	5		4	16	10	6	16	9	3
Wides	1			2		1					1				3	1			1	2	1	2			1	1	1	
No-balls	9		3	6				1	20	2	1	2	4		14	9	22			2	4	9	15	5	1	13	6	6
Total	202		223	438	151	248	44	140	398	140	179	138	313	53	198	310	465		260	314	117	391	374	140	177	290	216	217
Wickets	9†		10	5	10	9	0	10	10	2	10	10	10	0	10	8	9		10	9	10	10	10	2	10	9	10	10
Results	D		D		D		L		W		L		D		D		D		D		W		D		W		L	
Points	3		5		5		3		22		5		6		5		8		5		20		4		21		6	

Catches

23 – C. Marples (ct 31/st 4)	13 – B. Roberts (ct 12/st 1)	7 – M.A. Holding
24 – K.J. Barnett	12 – G. Miller	6 – I.S. Anderson and A.E. Warner
23 – B.J.M. Maher	10 – A. Hill	2 – R.J. Finney, subs and
14 – R. Sharma	8 – J.E. Morris	D.E. Malcolm

English Counties Form Charts

The statistics of all first-class matches are given on pages 442 to 509. The games covered are:

Britannic Assurance County Championship.
Matches against touring and representative sides.

In the batting table a blank indicates that a batsman did not *play* in a game, a dash (—) that he did not *bat*. A dash (—) is placed in the batting averages if a player had 2 innings or less, and in the bowling figures if no wicket was taken.

John Player Special League Final Table

	P	W	L	Nr	T	Pts
Hampshire (3)	16	12	3	1	0	50
Essex (1)	16	11	4	1	0	46
Notts (12)	16	10	5	1	0	42
Sussex (2)	16	10	6	0	0	40
Northants (5)	16	9	5	2	0	40
Kent (10)	16	7	5	3	1	36
Somerset (10)	16	8	6	2	0	36
Yorkshire (6)	16	7	6	2	1	34
Derbyshire (4)	16	7	9	0	0	28
Middlesex (12)	16	5	7	3	1	28
Warwickshire (6)	16	5	7	2	2	28
Glamorgan (14)	16	6	9	1	0	26
Lancashire (14)	16	6	9	1	0	26
Surrey (17)	16	5	8	2	1	26
Leicestershire (6)	16	5	10	1	0	22
Worcestershire (16)	16	5	11	0	0	20
Gloucestershire (6)	16	3	11	2	0	16

1985 positions in brackets

M. Jean-Jacques

Batting, bowling and averages

	v. Glamorgan (Abergavenny) 26–29 July	v. New Zealanders (Derby) 2–4 August	v. Sussex (Eastbourne) 6–8 August	v. Lancashire (Buxton) 9–12 August	v. Yorkshire (Chesterfield) 16–19 August	v. Leicestershire (Chesterfield) 20–22 August	v. Nottinghamshire (Trent Bridge) 23–26 August	v. Leicestershire (Leicester) 27–29 August	v. Hampshire (Derby) 30 Aug–2 Sept.	v. Northamptonshire (Derby) 3–5 September	v. Somerset (Taunton) 13–16 September	M	Inns	NOs	Runs	H/S	Av
	84* 93	18 —	39 10	11 20	34* 3	1 15	77 —	96 —	98 9	13 143	14 —	25	43	3	1502	143	37.55
	1 0		130* 35	27* 51	— 23	56 8*	15 —	12 —	5 119*	55 6	45 —	13	23	1	449	93	20.40
	23 4	49 —	31 26	— 15	— 42	62 —	15 —	118 —	15 26	3 127	34* —	24	40	6	1438	172*	42.29
	0 31	1 —	9 19*	— 25*	— 2	15 —	37 —	23 —	3 11	40 8	10 —	25	39	3	1703	191	47.30
	0 26	51 —	40 —		— 51*	30 —	6 —	0 —	0 39*			25	37	3	772	124*	22.70
		2 —		— 1*			23* —	13 —	19 —	4 —		20	27	2	512	65	20.48
16-0-55-2			— 0		— 18	34* —			21 —		0 —	3	4	2	62	34	31.00
12-0-38-2	8* 27	50 —	7 —	— 0	— 64	91 —	12 —	8 —	8 —	6 5	19 —	17	17	5	277	54	23.08
	— —				— 7*	31* —		3 —	4 —			14	20	2	295	36*	16.38
	0 3*		64* —				29 —	38 —	0* —	4 0*	3* —	20	28	6	593	91	26.95
												16	17	9	69	31*	8.62
	12 32*	24 —	11 —	— 3								15	17	6	321	71	29.18
												2	3	—	14	7	4.66
							2 —					15	24	3	466	57	22.19
								8 —		29* —	0 —	1	1	—	1	1	1.00
												2	2	—	7	5	3.50
		9 —										9	12	3	208	73	23.11
		7 —					0 —	0* —	0* —			4	5	2	18	9*	6.00
	8 29	126 —	8 77*	31* 51	14* 19	22 6*	31 —	14 —	43 7	50 0	49 —	9	7	4	37	29*	12.33
		23 —								21 9*		14	24	5	752	126	39.57
												2	3	1	53	23	26.50

Bowling and match results:

	Glamorgan	New Zealanders	Sussex	Lancashire	Yorkshire	Leicestershire	Nottinghamshire	Leicestershire	Hampshire	Northamptonshire	Somerset
18-4-71-1 / 5-2-6-0	5	1	1	3	4 5	2	9		7	5	1
19-1-77-8 / 11-2-48-2	5 10	4	4 1	3 1	7 5	14 1	19	2	1 10	6 8	6
			6		2	5 1				10 1	
	2 2	1	1 1	7	9 5	15 6		9	6 1	5	3
9-1-25-1 / 6-0-18-0	143 262	366	351 169	72 179	68 244	378 39	275	336	209 222	267 312	184
	7 7	10	7 3	1 7	0 7	9 1	10	10	9‡ 4	10 6	7
	W	D	L	D	D	D	D	D	L	D	W
	20		3	4	4	8	3	8	2	6	12

1 – P.G. Newman, J.G. Wright, J.P. Taylor, A.M. Brown, O.H. Mortensen and M. Jean-Jacques
†G. Miller absent ill   ‡R. Sharma retired hurt

Left-margin bowling totals: 18-1-70-0, 11-1-48-0, 11-2-44-2, 23-2-99-4, 11-2-44-2, 159-16-599-22, av. 27.22

Hudson's proposals to take over Lancashire and buy the Somerset trio. The dignity that may have been left was taken away when the trio made a balcony appearance for their supporters. The other eight members of the victorious Somerset side did not appear.

13, 15 and 16 September

at Chelmsford

Glamorgan 107 for 6 dec (N.A. Foster 4 for 51) and 193 for 2 dec (J.A. Hopkins 79, H. Morris 62)
Essex 0 for 0 dec and 188 (A.W. Lilley 62, J.G. Thomas 4 for 60)

Glamorgan won by 112 runs
Glamorgan 16 pts, Essex 2 pts

at Southampton

Hampshire v. Lancashire

Match abandoned
No points

at Canterbury

Middlesex 101 for 1
v. Kent

Match drawn
No points

at Trent Bridge

Nottinghamshire 145 and 313 for 8 dec (B.C. Broad 112, E.E. Hemmings 54 not out, R.A. Harper 4 for 71)
Northamptonshire 216 (J.A. Afford 4 for 43) and 186 for 9 (J.A. Afford 4 for 55)

Match drawn
Northamptonshire 6 pts, Nottinghamshire 4 pts

at Taunton

Somerset 182 (J.J.E. Hardy 52)
Derbyshire 184 for 7

Derbyshire won by 3 wickets
Derbyshire 12 pts, Somerset 0 pts

at The Oval

Surrey 270 for 4 dec (A.J. Stewart 81, T.E. Jesty 56, C.J. Richards 54 not out) and 0 for 0
Leicestershire 0 for 0 dec and 180 (P. Willey 76)

Surrey won by 90 runs
Surrey 19 pts, Leicestershire 1 pt

Essex C.C.C First-Class Matches – Bowling, 1986	J.K. Lever	D.R. Pringle	T.D. Topley	D.L. Acfield	J.H. Childs	N.A. Foster	G.A. Gooch	A.R. Border	K.R. Pont
v. Cambridge University (Cambridge) 23–25 April	9–9–0–2 12–6–12–4	17.5–7–26–2 4–4–0–0	5–2–7–0 11.3–2–10–0	27–14–38–5	23–13–31–1 3–3–0–1				
v. Warwickshire (Edgbaston) 26–28 April	28.1–13–71–3 13–1–56–1	20–6–40–2 9–0–30–0		9–2–27–0 10–3–27–0		24–6–81–1 15–2–75–2	22–6–46–2 13–1–47–1	4–0–12–0	
v. Kent (Chelmsford) 7–9 May	29–10–57–4 26–6–69–4	24–8–76–1 14.5–7–19–2		14–5–23–0		27–6–69–3 27–7–81–3	21–9–41–0		
v. Northamptonshire (Northampton) 17–20 May	8–3–10–0	19–4–39–2		22–4–54–3	45.3–15–97–5	10–3–32–0			
v. Yorkshire (Chelmsford) 21–23 May	6–2–16–0 20–4–74–2	3–2–7–0 17.5–6–46–7		3–1–8–0 10–1–60–0		6–2–19–0 17–4–60–1	3–2–4–0		
v. Derbyshire (Derby) 31 May–3 June	7–2–13–0 17–9–32–5	3–1–10–0		3–1–4–0 9.2–3–14–1	4–1–7–0 22–10–36–4	5–2–19–0 17–6–41–0			
v. Glamorgan (Swansea) 4–6 June	28.5–10–57–6 3–0–17–0			10–2–29–0 25–8–46–2	13–2–47–3 28.4–10–51–7	12–3–19–1 2–0–2–0		3–0–8–1	
v. Nottinghamshire (Chelmsford) 7–10 June	21–1–107–2 10–4–29–1			14–2–34–1 8–1–27–1	18–4–62–2 29–8–93–3	23–3–85–5 27.2–5–69–5			
v. Hampshire (Ilford) 14–17 June	20–4–66–0 7–1–28–1	26–8–65–5 8–2–27–2		11–1–25–0 12–4–28–2	8–1–27–0 1.5–0–11–1	26.2–8–64–5 16–3–36–4	2–1–8–0		
v. Sussex (Ilford) 18–20 June			21–4–52–5 25–5–68–4	1.3–0–1–1 23.4–4–60–1	13–6–13–2 40–14–84–4	19–2–44–1 31–7–63–1			
v. Middlesex (Lord's) 21–24 June			24–4–67–4 14.1–5–33–4	2–0–6–0		19.3–5–66–2 15–2–57–6			23–6–63–4
v. New Zealanders (Chelmsford) 2–4 July			21–2–69–1 5–3–7–0	26–10–54–0 21–5–55–3	24–6–74–1 23.4–4–66–1			3–1–8–0 2–0–12–0	4–1–7–0
v. Lancashire (Old Trafford) 5–8 July	26.1–9–41–3		29–8–67–1		25–9–47–3				5.5–1–9–0
v. Leicestershire (Southend) 16–18 July	33–8–86–2		32–7–120–5	15–7–21–2	6–1–17–1				3–0–13–0
v. Worcestershire (Southend) 19–22 July	25–2–110–3 16–2–55–4	12–2–49–1 14–4–31–1			9–1–30–0 3–1–2–0	32.3–7–93–6 24–5–64–5	14–2–40–0		
v. Surrey (The Oval) 23–25 July	25–1–124–1		26–3–140–2					9–1–28–0	
v. Sussex (Eastbourne) 2–5 August	23–2–116–1 16–4–47–1	19–3–67–1 19–4–57–3			11–4–34–2 7–3–10–0	27.4–3–84–5 27–5–99–2	13–6–33–1	5–1–52–0	
v. Middlesex (Chelmsford) 6–8 August	12–4–35–3 14–2–40–1			9–2–9–1	14–5–24–2 27.1–8–64–4	17.2–2–51–5 20–4–56–4			
v. Leicestershire (Leicester) 9–12 August	7–1–20–0		5–1–10–1 18–3–69–3		1–0–4–0 13.5–6–36–2	10–6–21–1 22–3–84–5			
v. Northamptonshire (Colchester) 16–19 August	14–2–53–0 4–0–11–0	21–3–64–2 14–4–36–2		3–2–4–1 9–0–36–0	24–5–75–1 30.2–9–61–8	23.1–7–83–5 8–0–27–0	8–3–16–1		
v. Gloucestershire (Colchester) 20–22 August	6–2–19–0 5–2–14–0	12–2–32–0 12–4–27–4		4–0–9–0 32–12–54–2	22–6–58–8 41–21–37–3	12.3–3–53–2 1–1–0–0			
v. Surrey (Chelmsford) 23–26 August	10–4–19–0	4–1–10–0		21–5–39–1	26–9–62–4	12–3–27–1			
v. Somerset (Taunton) 27–29 August	21–7–59–1 18–2–104–2	4–0–23–0 12–1–45–2			8–0–27–4 9.1–2–23–2	26.3–7–62–2 20–4–79–3	4–0–28–1		
v. Kent (Folkestone) 30 August–2 September	8–0–21–0 5–0–12–1	9–5–11–0		25.2–5–50–4 21.4–3–70–2	39–15–65–3 21–9–58–7	24–10–59–3 4–1–13–0			
v. Nottinghamshire (Trent Bridge) 10–12 September	23–5–87–5 9–1–37–1	16–1–64–0 9.3–1–47–4			6–0–15–0	25.1–4–77–4 18.2–0–74–3	12–3–16–1 16.4–0–24–0		
v. Glamorgan (Chelmsford) 13–16 September		14–4–24–0	13–6–25–2		2–1–1–0	21–1–51–4	2–0–2–0 7–1–24–0		
	585.1–145–1824–64 av. 28.50	358–94–972–43 av. 22.60	249.4–55–744–32 av. 23.25	401.3–107–912–33 av. 27.63	642.1–212–1449–89 av. 16.28	715.2–152–2139–100 av. 21.39	137.4–34–329–7 av. 47.00	26–3–120–1 av. 120.00	35.5–8–102–4 av. 25.50

I.L. Pont	S. Turner	D.E. East	J.P. Stephenson	B.R. Hardie	A.W. Lilley	Byes	Leg-byes	Wides	No-balls	Total	Wkts
						3	4			109	10
							3	1		25	5
							6	3	1	271	8
							3			250	4
						2	4	1	1	272	9
							1			170	9
						7	5			244	10
						1				51	0
						4	4			252	10
							1		1	44	0
							7			140	10
							8		1	160	10
						4	5			133	10
						8	3			299	10
						7	8	2		233	10
						4	1	2	1	260	10
						2	3	1	2	135	10
							2			112	10
						9	6	4	5	290	10
							6	2	2	208	10
						3	4			97	10
13–2–49–0	19–6–66–1						16		6	353	3
5–2–11–0						7	7			165	4
18.2–2–68–3						4	4		3	240	10
							7		5	264	10
		0.2–0–1–0								1	0
							1			323	10
							6			158	10
14–0–62–0	21–5–72–1					2	20		5	448	5
							12	3		346	10
			2–0–5–0				2	1	2	272	6
						5	1		1	116	10
						1	4	1		174	10
									4	55	2
							1	3	10	190	10
						1	6			302	10
						7	3			181	10
						2	10			183	10
						4	3		5	139	9
						7	2			166	7
							1			200	10
						4	8		1	263	10
						9	9	1		224	10
						1	6		1	160	10
						2	6	2		267	10
							2		2	184	8
							4	3	2	107	6
					12–0–58–0	18.3–1–104–2	1	6	2		193	2

I.L. Pont	S. Turner	D.E. East	J.P. Stephenson	B.R. Hardie	A.W. Lilley
50.2–6–190–3	40–11–138–2	0.2–0–1–0	2–0–5–0	12–0–58–0	18.3–1–104–2
av. 63.33	av. 69.00	—	—	—	av. 52.00

Glamorgan C.C.C. — First-Class Matches – Batting, 1986

(Each match cell shows 1st innings / 2nd innings scores.)

Player	v Gloucestershire (Bristol) 26–28 April	v Hampshire (Southampton) 30 April–2 May	v Somerset (Taunton) 7–9 May	v Middlesex (Lord's) 21–23 May	v Somerset (Cardiff) 24–27 May	v Essex (Swansea) 4–6 June	v Warwickshire (Edgbaston) 7–10 June	v Oxford University (Oxford) 14–17 June	v Warwickshire (Swansea) 18–20 June	v Lancashire (Swansea) 21–24 June	v Kent (Maidstone) 28 June–1 July	v Sussex (Cardiff) 2–4 July	v Gloucestershire (Cardiff) 5–8 July	v Worcestershire (Neath) 16–18 July
J.A. Hopkins	33 0	5 22	0 14	3 —	43 12	0 6								
A.L. Jones	13 20*	6 —	12* 14	7 —	24 11	24 13								
H. Morris	10 0	34 58	8 20	0 —	67 29	30 16	2 —	10 —	0 20	54 —	92 128*	37 —	98 55	3 1
G.C. Holmes	17 27*	52 29	3* 68	6 —	15 5	14 9	10 —	93 —	20 2	68 —	15 20	105* —	1 23	85 1
Younis Ahmed	94 —	17 85	— 11	1 —	20 22	28 41	48 —		16 35					37 3
R.C. Ontong	0 —	4 52	— 11	19 —	78 14	1 6	14 —		50 3	7* —	0 26	0 —	42 0	38 51
J.F. Steele	18 —	25 10	— 4			4 9		31* —	38 1			15 —	0 13	24* 7
J.G. Thomas	18* —	20 37*	— 31	19 —	50* 32		32 —		11 9*		17 —		0 19	24 6
T. Davies	10 —	13* 2*	— 28*	5* —			13* —		10 0		0 12	22 —	0 22	19* 17*
J. Derrick	1* —	4 15			2* 61*	27 17	42 —	47* —	6 0		8 3*	1* —		6 38
S.J. Base	— —		— 15*	4 —		0	3* 3*		4 —				4 10*	
E.A. Moseley		13 —	— 2	19 —		0 2			4* 0					— 15
M.P. Maynard				57 —	4 3		129 —	148	20 13	36* —	52 12	0 —	61 43	4 1
D.B. Pauline							1 —	20 —	4 31	53 —	55 7	33 —	16 20	13 97
D.J. Hickey							0* —				9* —		2* 0	
P.A. Cottey								6 —					2 0	
S.R. Barwick											4 —			
P.D. North														
M.L. Roberts														
I. Smith														
S.L. Watkin														
M. Cann														
Byes		4			3	4		6	4 2		8 1	9	5 1	2 12
Leg-byes	4	4 24		9	5 1	8 5	2	5	1 1		4 5	6	10 5	5 4
Wides	1	3 3		3	2 4	1		1			6	1	1	5 3
No-balls	8	1 1	3 12	7	1 8	1	3		4	5	6 2	7 8	3 6	3
Total	226 48	201 342	26 230	159	314 243	160 133	300	371	186 121	230	277 264	294	245 217	268 256
Wickets	8 2	10 7	2 9	10	7 10	10 10	9	5	10 10	4	10 6	7	10 10	8 10
Results	D	D	D	D	D	L	D	W	L	D	D	D	L	L
Points	4	5	1	2	6	3	5	—	5	4	7	4	6	2

Catches

- 39 – T. Davies (ct 38/st 1)
- 19 – G.C. Holmes
- 13 – M.P. Maynard
- 10 – J.A. Hopkins
- 9 – J.F. Steele and H. Morris
- 8 – R.C. Ontong
- 7 – J.G. Thomas and A.L. Jones
- 4 – J. Derrick, Younis Ahmed, D.B. Pauline and subs.
- 3 – S.J. Base, S.R. Barwick, D.J. Hickey and M.L. Roberts (ct 2/st 1)

Britannic Assurance County Championship Final Table

	P	W	L	D	Bonus pts Bt	Bonus pts Bl	Pts
Essex (4)	24	10	6	8	51	76	287
Glos (3)	24	9	3	12	50	65	259
Surrey (6)	24	8	6	10	54	66	248
Notts (8)	24	7	2	15	55	80	247
Worcestershire (5)	24	7	5	12	58	72	242
Hampshire (2)	24	7	4	13	54	69	235
Leics (16)	24	5	7	12	55	67	202
Kent (9)	24	5	7	12	42	75	197
Northants (10)	24	5	3	16	53	60	193
Yorkshire (11)	24	4	5	15	62	59	193
Derbyshire (13)	24	5	5	14	42	70	188
Middlesex (1)	24	4	9	11	47	65	176
Warwickshire (15)	24	4	5	15	61	51	176
Sussex (7)	24	4	7	13	46	56	166
Lancashire (14)	24	4	5	15	41	51	156
Somerset (17)	24	3	7	14	52	52	152
Glamorgan (12)	24	2	7	15	39	47	118

1985 positions in brackets

Yorkshire total includes eight points for a drawn match when scores finished level. Derbyshire total includes 12 points for a win in a one innings match.

First-Class Averages

BATTING

	M	Inns	NOs	Runs	HS	Av	100s	50
C.G. Greenidge	20	34	4	2035	222	67.83	8	6
J.J. Whitaker	22	32	9	1526	200*	66.34	5	8
G.A. Hick	24	37	6	2004	227*	64.64	6	11
A.J. Lamb	18	27	4	1359	160*	59.08	4	8
B.M. McMillan	12	21	4	999	136	58.76	3	6
R.J. Bailey	28	43	9	1915	224*	56.32	4	10
A.I. Kallicharran	14	23	5	1005	163*	55.83	4	2
M.W. Gatting	18	23	3	1091	183*	54.55	4	2
G. Boycott	13	20	1	992	135*	52.21	2	8
R.J. Hadlee	17	21	5	813	129*	50.81	2	4
T.S. Curtis	24	40	10	1498	153	49.93	2	10
C.H. Lloyd	7	8	1	347	128	49.57	1	2
A.R. Border	21	32	4	1385	150	49.46	4	9
A.J. Moles	11	18	3	738	102	49.20	2	5
N.H. Fairbrother	22	33	8	1217	131	48.68	3	4
Imran Khan	11	18	3	730	135*	48.66	2	4
C.L. Smith	20	30	8	1061	114*	48.22	2	7
R.T. Robinson	21	34	5	1398	159*	48.20	4	7
I.T. Botham	13	20	2	863	139	47.94	2	5
D.N. Patel	24	30	9	1005	132*	47.85	3	2
P.M. Roebuck	22	35	8	1288	221*	47.70	4	5
A.C.S. Pigott	19	18	6	572	104*	47.66	1	2
J.E. Morris	26	40	3	1739	191	47.00	4	10
A.J. Stewart	15	39	3	1665	166	46.25	3	14
A.M. Ferreira	12	15	6	413	69*	45.88		3

D.J. Hickey

The match-by-match record and the season summary columns (M, Inns, NOs, Runs, H/S, Av) follow. Season-summary figures:

M	Inns	NOs	Runs	H/S	Av
15	26	—	738	142	28.38
12	21	4	429	50	25.23
26	44	2	1522	128*	36.23
26	44	5	1106	107	28.35
15	23	2	845	105*	40.23
24	37	4	744	80*	22.54
12	17	5	282	41*	23.50
21	25	6	485	70	25.52
24	28	13	316	41	21.06
18	24	8	569	78*	35.56
12	11	4	53	15*	7.57
6	8	1	5	19	7.85
22	34	4	1002	148	33.40
12	20	—	455	97	22.75
13	9	5	19	9*	4.75
4	5	1	24	9*	6.00
11	8	2	33	9	5.50
5	5	2	22	17*	7.33
2	1	—	8	8	8.00
3	2	—	0	0	0.00
1					
1	1	1	16	16*	—

Bowling figures (left margin):
21-4-97-0
16.1-3-57-5
21.5-7-49-2
22-2-102-3
19.5-1-87-3
9-1-39-2
19-1-71-0
7-0-19-0
13-1-58-1
10-2-35-1
15-2-89-1
4-1-23-1
4-2-8-0
12-3-30-1
9-1-51-2
4-0-27-0
30-2-122-1
17-0-79-0
23-5-48-1
5-1-11-0
281.5-39-1102-24
av. 45.91

2 – P.A. Cottey
1 – I.L. Smith and M. Cann

	M	Inns	NOs	Runs	HS	Av	100s	50s
A.A. Metcalfe	26	41	1	1803	151	45.07	6	8
C.E.B. Rice	22	31	6	1118	156*	44.72	2	5
P. Willey	18	30	5	1117	172*	44.68	4	3
P.W.G. Parker	25	43	7	1595	125	44.30	6	8
V.J. Marks	25	36	12	1057	110	44.04	1	7
C.W. Scott	10	8	3	220	69*	44.00		1
R.J. Bartlett	6	9	2	307	117*	43.85	1	
K.M. Curran	26	39	8	1353	117*	43.64	4	7
B.C. Rose	14	23	5	784	129	43.55	2	3
I.V.A. Richards	18	28	1	1174	136	43.48	4	5
D.M. Smith	20	28	4	1041	165*	43.37	3	5
J.W. Lloyds	26	39	9	1295	111	43.16	1	8
A. Hill	24	40	6	1438	172*	42.29	3	7
G. Cook	22	30	4	1084	183	41.69	3	3
K. Saxelby	10	8	5	124	34	41.33		
R.A. Smith	25	38	8	1237	128*	41.23	2	8
C.W.J. Athey	19	31	1	1233	171*	41.10	1	7
M. Newell	19	30	9	862	112*	41.04	1	5
W.K.R. Benjamin	20	20	10	404	95*	40.40		3
J. Abrahams	24	38	7	1251	189*	40.35	3	6
C.J. Richards	23	34	9	1006	115	40.24	2	5
Younis Ahmed	15	23	2	845	105*	40.23	1	4
G.D. Mendis	23	37	3	1363	108	40.08	2	10
B.C. Broad	25	42	2	1593	122	39.82	6	7
B.J.M. Maher	14	24	5	752	126	39.57	1	5
D.I. Gower	14	23	2	830	131	39.52	1	6
M.R. Benson	23	39	2	1461	128	39.48	2	7
P. Johnson	26	37	5	1250	128	39.06	3	5
G.D. Barlow	5	6	1	194	107	38.80	1	1

	M	Inns	NOs	Runs	HS	Av	100s	50s
G. Fowler	20	32	2	1163	180	38.76	1	9
T.J. Boon	23	36	10	1003	117	38.57	1	4
G.W. Humpage	26	42	4	1462	130	38.47	3	6
K. Sharp	19	31	6	958	181	38.32	2	5
W.N. Slack	23	35	3	1224	106	38.25	3	7
G.A. Gooch	19	32		1221	69*	38.15	3	5
C.M. Wells	24	38	9	1098	106	37.86	1	7
P.R. Downton	24	29	5	905	126*	37.70	2	5
P.A. Smith	25	44	4	1508	119	37.70	1	13
D.L. Amiss	26	45	6	1450	110	37.17	4	6
N.E. Briers	6	7	1	223	85	37.16		2
K.J. Barnett	26	45	3	1544	143	36.76	2	10
P.A. Neale	25	34	7	987	118*	36.55	1	6
D.R. Turner	10	14	1	472	96	36.30		3
H. Morris	26	44	2	1522	128*	36.23	2	11
R.A. Harper	25	30	4	933	234	35.88	1	2
P.E. Robinson	8	13	2	392	104*	35.63	1	3
J. Derrick	18	24	8	569	78*	35.56		4
C.D. Fraser-Darling	5	4	—	142	61	35.50		1
N.J. Falkner	11	18	2	567	102	35.43	1	2
R.I. Alikhan	18	28	4	843	72	35.12		7
J.D. Love	21	29	5	831	109	34.62	1	4
T.E. Jesty	20	30	1	997	221	34.37	2	4
M.A. Lynch	25	39	3	1234	152	34.27	3	5
J.D. Birch	21	28	7	718	79*	34.19		4
E.A.E. Baptiste	7	8		273	113	34.12	1	1
J.D. Carr	17	26	3	782	84*	34.00		5
P.J. Hartley	15	17	4	441	87*	33.92		4
D.W. Varey	6	10	2	271	83	33.87		2

Glamor
First-Cla
Bowling

v. Glouces
(Bristol
v. Hampsh
30 Apri
v. Somers
(Taunt
v. Middle
(Lord's
v. Somers
(Cardif
v. Essex
(Swans
v. Warwic
(Edgba
v. Oxford
(Oxfor
v. Warwic
(Swan
v. Lancas
(Swan
v. Kent (I
28 Jun
v. Sussex
(Cardif
v. Glouce
(Cardif
v. Worce
(Neath
v. Northa
(Swan
v. Leicest
(Leice
v. Derbys
(Aberg
v. Northa
(North
v. Yorksh
(Leeds
v. New Z
(Swar
v. Lancas
(Lytha
v. Kent (
23–26
v. Surrey
(Swar
v. Nottin
(Cardi
v. Worce
(Worc
v. Essex
13–16

Gloucestershire C.C.C. — First-Class Matches – Batting, 1986

	v Oxford Univ (Oxford) 23–25 Apr	v Glamorgan (Bristol) 26–28 Apr	v Northants (Northampton) 7–9 May	v Indians (Cheltenham) 10–12 May	v Somerset (Taunton) 21–23 May	v Hampshire (Bournemouth) 24–27 May	v Leicester (Leicester) 31 May–3 Jun	v Warwicks (Bristol) 4–6 Jun	v Yorkshire (Harrogate) 7–10 Jun	v Derbyshire (Gloucester) 14–17 Jun	v Kent (Gloucester) 18–20 Jun	v Derbyshire (Chesterfield) 21–23 Jun	v Surrey (Bristol) 28 Jun–1 Jul	v Yorkshire (Bristol) 2–4 Jul
A.W. Stovold	20 11	20 —	2 12*	20 —	7* 0	65 14	24 61	9 64	13* —	41 25	3 40	118 —	16 5	43 0
P.W. Romaines	4 20	10 —	17 18*	23 —	10* 29	52 29	4 4*		59 —	16 19	21 87	15 —	56 4	0 4
A.J. Wright	39 34	4 —				28 13				43 6		39 —		
P. Bainbridge	66 —	11 —	55 —	58	— 13	7 22	23 2*	30 37	75	20 4	15 6	3	11 3	24
K.P. Tomlins	9 11*									26	9 1	14	40 —	
K.M. Curran	103* —	4* —	39* —	69* —	— 18	62 38*	40 52	92 20*	0	43 12	1 23	5	12 67	61 36
J.W. Lloyds	28 0	13* —	6 —	35 —	— 18	48 22	11* 4*	79 33*	39* —	8 111	45* 13*	24	27 74	23 8
I.R. Payne	23* —			30* —	— 2	9* 6	0 —	2 —					4* —	8 9
D.A. Graveney	— 1*	— —	— —		— 0			0	3* —	5 —			3 —	
R.C. Russell	— —	— —	— —		— 17*	1* —	4* —	14 —	0	20 63	13 17	22* —	17 29	26 23
G.E. Sainsbury	— —	— —	— —											1* 14*
C.W.J. Athey		11 —	171* —	23	— 75		35 61	37 98	29	0 46			2 47	4 52
C.A. Walsh		— —	— —		— 17			9* —		0* 15*	10 —	0	12 2*	
D.V. Lawrence		— —	— —		— 0	1 —	— 26	9 —	9	12 10	10 —	6	14* 10	33 13
M.W. Alleyne											2 13*	0		8 0
P.H. Twizell														
Byes	2 1	4		1	8	1	8	5		1 12		1	12	1
Leg-byes	5		10	4	1 7	9 1	3 11	16 4	8	4 4	1 8	30	1 24	8 4
Wides	4	5			1 1	2 1	1	2	1	2 2	1	5	1 1	1
No-balls	6 1	1	1	8	6	11 4	8 7	5	4	1 8	5	17	9 6	6
Total	309 79	83	301 30	271	19 211	296 150	153 236	352 262	257	182 332	125 227	334	185 284	246 173
Wickets	6 4	5	4 0	5	0 10	7 6	6 4	10 4	6	10 9†	10 6	10	9 8	10 10
Results	D	D	D	D	L	W	W	D	D	D	W	D	W	D
Points			3			22	20	5	4	2	20	8	21	6

Catches
56 – R.C. Russell (ct 53/st 3)   20 – D.A. Graveney   12 – P. Bainbridge
29 – K.M. Curran   18 – C.W.J. Athey   9 – A.W. Stovold
21 – J.W. Lloyds   14 – A.J. Wright   7 – I.R. Payne and C.A. Walsh

	M	Inns	NOs	Runs	HS	Av	100s	50s
M. D. Moxon	20	33	4	982	147	33.86	3	3
D.J. Wild	14	21	3	608	101	33.77	1	4
K.W.R. Fletcher	20	28	6	736	91	33.45		6
M.P. Maynard	22	34	4	1002	148	33.40	2	6
C.J. Tavaré	26	42	4	1267	123	33.34	2	6
G.S. Clinton	23	35	4	1027	117	33.12	1	6
R.J. Harden	22	36	3	1093	108	33.12	2	6
A.P. Wells	23	34	7	891	150*	33.00	1	2
M. Asif Din	24	38	14	788	69*	32.83		5
P.J. Prichard	26	44	3	1342	147*	32.73	1	10
P. Whitticase	18	21	4	554	67*	32.58		5
I.J. Gould	20	24	6	586	78*	32.55		4
J.G. Wright	14	22	1	682	119	32.47	1	5
C. Maynard	19	26	5	662	132*	31.52	1	5
A.M. Green	25	46	4	1343	179	31.23	3	3
N.R. Taylor	26	42	5	1151	106	31.10	1	7
A.J.T. Miller	23	35	4	963	11*	31.06	1	5
R.O. Butcher	26	37	4	1016	171	30.78	1	7
S.A. Marsh	26	36	8	857	70	30.60		6
R.J. Boyd-Moss	27	42	3	1192	155	30.56	2	8
M.W. Alleyne	10	16	5	336	116*	30.54	1	1
N.A. Felton	23	37	3	1030	156*	30.29	3	5
D. Ripley	13	15	5	301	134*	30.10	1	
S.J. Rhodes	25	27	10	509	77*	29.94		3
G.S. le Roux	14	16	6	298	72*	29.80		1
J.J.E. Hardy	19	29		863	79	29.75		8
B.R. Hardie	22	35	5	883	113*	29.43	2	4
D.J. Capel	28	36	7	853	111	29.41	2	3
C.T. Radley	25	33	6	792	113*	29.33	2	3
T.M. Tremlett	21	23	12	322	59*	29.27		2
R. Sharma	15	17	6	321	71	29.18		2
C.S. Cowdrey	21	33	3	873	100	29.10	1	5
R.J. Maru	17	10	6	116	23	29.00		
K.P. Tomlins	16	29	5	696	75	29.00		4
D.A. Thorne	14	21	4	490	104*	28.82	1	3
A.W. Stovold	26	43	4	1123	118	28.79	1	7
D.B. d'Oliveira	25	41	3	1094	146*	28.78	1	3
D.J.R. Martindale	3	4		115	88	28.75		1
R.A. Cobb	25	41	3	1092	91	28.73		8
T.C. Middleton	8	14	3	316	68*	28.72		1
J.A. Hopkins	15	26		738	142	28.38	1	3
G.C. Holmes	26	44	5	1106	107	28.35	1	6
T.A. Lloyd	16	28		793	100	28.32	1	6
S.N. Hartley	21	30	2	785	87	28.03		4
V.P. Terry	23	36	4	896	80	28.00		7
D.J. Thomas	9	12	4	222	47*	27.75		
D.J. Fell	9	17	3	388	114	27.71	1	
D.L. Bairstow	24	33	4	796	88	27.44		3
P. Bainbridge	26	43	4	1065	105	27.30	1	7
P.J.W. Allott	17	19	5	382	65	27.28		1
J.P. Stephenson	14	25	1	647	85	26.95		4
A.E. Warner	20	28	6	593	91	26.95		6
R.C. Russell	27	31	9	585	71	26.59		2
W. Larkins	17	29	4	664	86	26.56		2
P.A.C. Bail	11	20		530	174	26.50	1	1
S.J. O'Shaughnessy	10	14	3	291	74	26.45		2
M.A. Feltham	12	14	5	237	76	26.33		1
K.R. Brown	10	16	2	367	66	26.21		2

Batting – match by match

	v. Glamorgan (Cardiff) 5–8 July	v. Sussex (Bristol) 16–18 July	v. Somerset (Bristol) 19–22 July	v. Worcestershire (Worcester) 26–29 July	v. Hampshire (Cheltenham) 2–5 August	v. Nottinghamshire (Cheltenham) 6–8 August	v. Middlesex (Cheltenham) 9–12 August	v. Warwickshire (Nuneaton) 16–19 August	v. Essex (Colchester) 20–22 August	v. Lancashire (Old Trafford) 23–26 August	v. Worcestershire (Bristol) 27–29 August	v. Surrey (The Oval) 3–5 September	M	Inns	NOs	Runs	H/S	Av
	12 9	62 6	6 —	4 5	17 48	81 74*	— 13	— 8	9 23	26 —	12 —	20 55	26	43	4	1123	118	28.79
	55 14	46 0	13 —	3 5	10 0	32 0	0 27	67* 41	22 0	0 —	22 10	0 25	15	27	4	476	67*	20.69
							13 6						15	26	—	603	87	23.19
	24 48	1 5	51 —	10 17*	22 21	105 1	9 34	0* 1	10 53*	98 —	2 1	5 17	26	43	4	1065	105	27.30
	2 18	51 13	3 —	75 23*	10 30	27 37	35* 0	22 0	43 23	59 —	0 46*	16 53*	16	29	5	696	75	29.00
	116 23	0 0	3 —	0 —	25 14	17 117*	— 11	— 57	14 0	38 —	12 —	6 103*	26	39	8	1353	117*	43.64
	35 56*	17 0	29 —	82 —	35 0	3 1	— 94	— 31	52 11	76* —	38 —	66 —	26	39	9	1295	111	43.16
													11	12	4	106	30*	13.25
	1 —	— 10	30*	1* —	7* 2*		— 7	— 0*	0 2		5* —	17* —	22	18	9	94	30*	10.44
	0 —	45* 23*	49 —	9 —	16 9	2 —	0* 27	— 7	9 2	16* —	23 11*	71	26	31	9	585	71	26.59
			13 —										6	3	2	28	14*	28.00
			55 —		42 36			20 36			73 42	76 2	14	22	1	1017	171*	48.42
	6 —	— 0	9 —	16 —	0 3	2 —	— 17*	— 19	5* 4	16 —	3 —	0 —	23	24	6	221	52	12.27
	0 —	— 7*	2 —	0 0	34* —	— 0		— 1	0 1*	0 —	9* —	0 —	23	25	5	198	34*	9.90
	17* 6*	116* 19	21 —	73* —	23 15				7 8	8 —			10	16	5	336	116*	30.54
			0 —										1	1	—	0	0	0·00

Fielding

	Glam	Sussex	Somerset	Worcs	Hants	Notts	Middx	Warwicks	Essex	Lancs	Worcs	Surrey
	4	1 2	16	2	2 1		6		2 4	5	4	6 1
	6 6	7 3	8	15	6 18	14 3	7	4 2	10 3	10	5	10 1
	4	1 4	1	1	2	1		1				3 4
	1	3 2	4	7	7 2	4 1	4 3	2 1		5	2	1 8

Totals / Results

	Glam	Sussex	Somerset	Worcs	Hants	Notts	Middx	Warwicks	Essex	Lancs	Worcs	Surrey
Runs	275 188	350 94	308	300 50	201 184	345 249	61 252	115 205	183 139	354	209 110	297 269
Wkts	10 5	6 9	10	9 2	10 10	10 5	3 10	2 10	10 9	8	9 3	10 4
Result	W	W	W	W	W	D	L	L	D	D	D	D
Points	23	22	24	20	22	5	2	3	5	4	3	7

5 – D.V. Lawrence   1 – K.P. Tomlins   †D.A. Graveney absent injured
4 – P.W. Romaines and M.W. Alleyne
2 – subs

Averages

	M	Inns	NOs	Runs	HS	Av	100s	50s
S.G. Hinks	23	38	2	936	131	26.00	2	2
N.G. Cowley	19	21	7	360	78*	25.71		2
D.A. Reeve	19	21	9	307	51	25.58		1
A.R. Butcher	16	25	—	634	157	25.36	1	3
D.W. Browne	7	13	4	228	61*	25.33		1
I.G. Swallow	9	11	5	152	43*	25.33		
A.L. Jones	13	21	4	429	50	25.23		1
A.W. Lilley	15	26	2	604	87	25.16		3
K.D. James	12	13	2	275	62	25.00		1
J. Simmons	13	17	5	300	61	25.00		1
P.D. Bowler	8	11	1	249	100*	24.90	1	1
J.G. Thomas	22	27	6	523	70	24.90		2
M.A. Roseberry	5	8	1	174	70*	24.85		1
P.B. Clift	15	16	1	370	49	24.66		
C.D.M. Tooley	6	10	1	221	60	24.55		1
P. Carrick	25	33	7	637	51	24.50		3
D.A. Hagan	9	16	1	364	64	24.26		2
S.N.V. Waterton	14	17	4	314	58*	24.15		1
R.M. Ellison	20	29	6	552	62*	24.00		2
M.R. Chadwick	10	18	—	423	61	23.50		2
A.K. Golding	7	11	3	188	47	23.50		
J.F. Steele	12	17	5	282	41*	23.50		
D.W. Randall	14	22	1	493	101*	23.47	1	1
R.J. Parks	25	23	5	420	80	23.33		3
A.J. Wright	15	26	—	603	87	23.19		4
M. Jean-Jacques	9	12	3	208	73	23.11		1
R.J. Finney	17	17	5	277	54	23.08		1
P.A.J. de Freitas	27	30	2	645	106	23.03	1	3
R.G. Williams	5	7	—	161	93	23.00		1
R.J. Doughty	15	19	2	387	48	22.76		
D.B. Pauline	12	20	—	455	97	22.75		3
B. Roberts	25	37	3	772	124*	22.70	1	2
R.C. Ontong	24	37	4	744	80*	22.54		6
D.G. Aslett	17	23	—	517	63	22.47		3
C. Marples	15	24	3	466	57	22.19		2
P.J. Newport	23	17	4	285	68	21.92		1
D.R. Pringle	20	32	4	611	97	21.82		3
N.J. Lenham	18	29	4	544	77	21.76		3
T. Davies	24	28	13	316	41	21.06		
N.V. Salvi	4	7	1	126	36	21.00		
P.W. Romaines	15	27	4	476	67*	20.69		2
G. Miller	20	27	2	512	65	20.48		3
R.J. Blakey	4	7	—	143	46	20.42		
I.S. Anderson	13	23	1	449	93	20.40		2
D.E. East	25	40	4	730	100*	20.27	1	2
G. Monkhouse	10	12	4	162	51	20.25		1
L. Potter	20	30	3	545	81*	20.18		5
B.N. French	20	23	5	361	58	20.05		1
D.M. Ward	4	6	1	100	34	20.00		
N.A. Foster	23	30	7	458	53*	19.91		2
M.J. Kilborn	7	12	1	219	59	19.90		1
M.C.J. Nicholas	24	32	2	564	55	18.80		2
J.C. Balderstone	14	23	1	410	115	18.63	1	
J.E. Emburey	18	22	3	354	75	18.63		1
M. Watkinson	21	25	4	389	58*	18.52		1
P.W. Jarvis	15	17	7	183	47	18.30		
M.S. Ahluwalia	6	11	—	198	36	18.00		
D.K. Standing	17	26	3	412	65	17.91		1

Hampshire C.C.C. — First-Class Matches – Batting, 1986

Player	v. Nottinghamshire (Trent Bridge) 26–28 April		v. Glamorgan (Southampton) 30 April–2 May		v. Lancashire (Old Trafford) 7–9 May		v. Indians (Southampton) 17–19 May		v. Cambridge Univ. (Cambridge) 21–23 May		v. Gloucestershire (Bournemouth) 24–27 May		v. Nottinghamshire (Southampton) 31 May–3 June		v. Somerset (Bournemouth) 7–9 June		v. Essex (Ilford) 14–17 June		v. Surrey (Basingstoke) 18–20 June		v. Kent (Southampton) 21–24 June		v. Worcestershire (Worcester) 28 June–1 July		v. Leicestershire (Leicester) 2–4 July		v. Somerset (Taunton) 5–8 July	
C.G. Greenidge	21	118	0	—	127*	—	33	86					1		148	15	26	11	97		53	49	12	0			1	—
V.P. Terry	14	74*	80	—	2	—	65*	57	70	—	17	31	19		35	23	2	6	44		47	1	8	1	0	11*	1	—
R.A. Smith	50	13*	19	—	21	—	44*	13	58	22*	1	0	6*		0	94	87	3	101		29	0	9	15	14		53	
C.L. Smith	9	—	79	—	70	—		19	32	12	27	26	26		4	103*	15	23					0	66	58*			
M.C.J. Nicholas	23	—	26	—	14*	—		30	2	23	11	2	15		18	1	0	10	50		7	39	24	10	30		37	
M.D. Marshall	35	—	45	—							23	0	1		1	—	9	0	51*		1	0	4	24	6			
N.G. Cowley	4	—	21	—				9	3*	19			8*		1	—	28	3*	6*				18	1	0	5	37	
T.M. Tremlett	5	—	8*	—				4*		1	5	5					31*	14*			13	0	7	2	6*			
R.J. Parks	51*	—	3	—				1*		0	36	6			18	—	68	37			13	0	31	0	12*	14*		11
R.J. Maru	17*	—	0*	—				8*	17	1					21	—	23	7*										
C.A. Connor	—		—								0	4*			7	—	0*	0			0	16	11*	0*				4
S.J.W. Andrew											—	—			2*						7	2						
P.J. Bakker							—	—	3*	3																		
D.R. Turner									69*	—	35	20					22	5	12		5	12			49		23	
K.D. James																							41	14	47		21*	22*
T.C. Middleton																											68*	2*
M.E. O'Connor																												
Byes	3	2	5						3	4	1	5			4	2	11				1				8	4	4	
Leg-byes	5	2	5		10		3	8	4	2	5		1		11	4	1	3	15		2	9	8	13	12	1	9	2
Wides	1		1				1		1								2	1	4								2	
No-balls	3		16		7		5		2		9	3			5		1	2	10		1		3	5	16		2	
Total	241	209	308		251		151	227	244	91	190	110	80		298	245	260	135	401		214	143	158	156	295	30	220	41
Wickets	8	1	8		3		1	6	4	5	10	10	5		10	4	10	10	5		10	10	10	10	7	0	4	2
Results	W		D		D		D		D		L		D		D		W		W		L		L		D		D	
Points	21		8		3						2				4		23		24		6		5		4		6	

Catches

81 – R.J. Parks (ct 73/st 8)	17 – V.P. Terry	7 – T.C. Middleton
21 – R.A. Smith	16 – C.L. Smith	5 – K.D. James, M.D. Marshall and N.G. Cowley
18 – C.G. Greenidge	13 – R.J. Maru and M.C.J. Nicholas	

	M	Inns	NOs	Runs	HS	Av	100s	50s
E.E. Hemmings	21	23	4	330	54*	17.36		1
R.K. Illingworth	18	15	4	191	39	17.36		
S.T. Clarke	14	13	4	156	32*	17.33		
K.J. Kerr	14	12	5	120	45*	17.14		
A. Needham	11	17	2	256	52	17.06		1
G.R. Cowdrey	18	26	1	425	75	17.00		3
G.J. Parsons	21	24	5	322	58*	16.94		1
M.J. Weston	8	12	2	167	30	16.70		
J. Garner	18	15	4	182	47	16.54		
M.A. Holding	14	20	2	295	36*	16.38		
G.C. Small	25	26	7	304	45*	16.00		
N.G. Cowans	21	21	7	223	44*	15.92		
A.C. Storie	8	11	—	171	38	15.54		
J.E. Davidson	9	10	3	108	41*	15.42		
I.P. Butcher	12	19	1	273	58	15.16		2
D.G. Price	8	15	1	207	60	14.78		1
N.G.B. Cook	27	27	3	351	45	14.62		
P.H. Edmonds	17	19	5	202	31	14.42		
K.T. Medlycott	14	15	1	197	61	14.07		1
A.A.G. Mee	8	14	1	183	51	14.07		1
W.W. Daniel	16	16	6	140	33	14.00		
N.V. Radford	20	16	3	178	30	13.69		
J.H. Childs	22	23	7	214	34	13.37		
I.R. Payne	11	12	4	106	30*	13.25		
K.E. Cooper	17	13	5	105	19	13.12		
C. Gladwin	8	15	—	195	73	13.00		1
J.P. Agnew	19	20	6	181	35*	12.92		
R.A. Pick	19	17	1	206	55	12.87		1
C.H. Dredge	17	21	3	227	40	12.61		

v. Warwickshire (Portsmouth) 19-22 July		v. Derbyshire (Portsmouth) 23-25 July		v. Gloucestershire (Cheltenham) 2-5 August		v. Kent (Canterbury) 6-8 August		v. Sussex (Southampton) 9-12 August		v. Middlesex (Lord's) 16-19 August		v. Worcestershire (Bournemouth) 20-22 August		v. Yorkshire (Bournemouth) 23-26 August		v. Northamptonshire (Northampton) 27-29 August		v. Derbyshire (Derby) 30 Aug.-2 Sept.		v. Sussex (Hove) 10-12 September		v. Lancashire (Southampton) 13-16 September		M	Inns	NOs	Runs	H/S	Av
		24	144*	38	26	26	17	78	79	17	70*	16	42	0	—	222	—	103	180*	126	30			20	34	4	2035	222	67.83
12	—	8	2	0	13					18	2	74	23	21*	—	55	—	12	—	48	0			23	36	4	896	80	28.00
73	—	12	—	25	23	39	55*	30	128*	39	2	7	5	5	—	16*	—	—	—	39	87*			25	38	8	1237	128*	41.23
58	—	19	—	72*	5							36	6*	7	—	23*	—	54*	33*	31	114*			19	28	8	1027	114*	51.35
2	—	55	—	25	7	4	15	6	13*	6	—			—	—	—	—	—	32	7	—			23	31	2	544	55	18.75
—*		8	—	3	5	0	—	11*	—	13	—	22	0					—	1					23	23	2	263	51*	12.52
6*	—			78*	—	22	—	2	—											65*	—			19	21	7	360	78*	25.71
11*	—	1	—	52	3	20	5*	59*	—	42*	28*	2	1*	10*	—									21	23	12	322	59*	29.27
		2	80	0	4	13	—			0*	—	20	—											25	23	5	420	80	23.33
												9*	—							13*	—			17	10	6	116	23	29.00
		2*	—	0	0*	0	—					1	—											19	13	5	41	16	5.12
																								7	5	2	15	7	5.00
																								3	2	1	6	3*	6.00
96	—					12	33	79	—															10	14	1	472	96	36.30
62	—	16	—	1	6	0	0					9	—							36	—			12	13	2	275	62	25.00
		33	8*	27	1	23	49	30	6			10	22	24	—	13	—							8	14	3	316	68*	28.72
										—	—													1					

v. Warwickshire		v. Derbyshire (P)		v. Gloucestershire		v. Kent		v. Sussex (S)		v. Middlesex		v. Worcestershire		v. Yorkshire		v. Northamptonshire		v. Derbyshire (D)		v. Sussex (H)		v. Lancashire	
12			8	8				4		5		5						2		3		1	3
11		3	8	9		5		4	11	3	5	8	14	1				15		1	7	10	6
		1	2			5	1	3		3		6						1		5		4	
7		2		10	5	9	2	1				6		1				5		5	1	4	5
350		184	254	270	98	234	181	320	242	158	129	237	91	58		338	0	176	257	385	245	Ab.	
6		10	2	10	10	10	5	6	2	7	3	10	4	4		2	0	2	1	7	2	0	
W		W		L		D		D		D		D		D		W		W		D			
24		21		7		4		5		5		6		4		20		21		6			

3 – C.A. Connor, S.J.W. Andrew and subs.
2 – D.R. Turner and T.M. Tremlett

	M	Inns	NOs	Runs	HS	Av	100s	50s
T.D. Topley	9	11	2	113	45	12.55		
M.D. Marshall	23	23	2	263	51*	12.52		1
S.P. Hughes	23	26	2	296	47	12.33		
C.A. Walsh	23	24	6	221	52	12.27		1
G.R. Dilley	18	26	8	218	30	12.11		
T. Gard	20	25	6	228	36	12.00		
N.A. Mallender	22	20	10	119	37	11.90		
K.R. Pont	7	13	1	142	36	11.83		
D.L. Underwood	24	26	5	243	29	11.57		
A.N. Hayhurst	10	14		156	31	11.14		

(Qualification – 100 runs, average 10.00)

BOWLING

	Overs	Mds	Runs	Wkts	Av	Best	10/m	5/inn
M.D. Marshall	656.5	171	1508	100	15.08	6/51		5
R.J. Hadlee	547.3	150	1215	76	15.98	6/31	2	7
J.H. Childs	642.1	212	1449	89	16.28	8/58	3	5
S.T. Clarke	341.3	95	806	48	16.79	5/31		3
C.A. Walsh	789.5	193	2145	118	18.17	9/72	4	10
A.H. Gray	342.3	69	966	51	18.94	7/23	1	3
T.M. Alderman	610	139	1882	98	19.20	8/46	3	9
M.A. Holding	388.1	110	1045	52	20.09	7/97		4
J. Simmons	230.5	52	762	36	21.16	7/79	1	2
P.W. Jarvis	428.4	82	1332	60	22.20	7/55	2	5
M.P. Bicknell	196	43	600	27	22.22	3/27		
P.B. Clift	413.3	120	1002	45	22.26	4/35		

	Overs	Mds	Runs	Wks	Av	Best	10/m	5/inn
J.E. Emburey	473.3	170	872	39	22.35	5/51		1
N.A. Foster	806.2	177	2349	105	22.37	6/57	2	10
W.W. Daniel	402.1	52	1387	62	22.37	4/27		
P.A.J. de Freitas	742.5	133	2171	94	23.09	7/44	1	7
G.C. Small	636.3	156	1781	77	23.12	5/35		2
A.N. Babington	117.5	16	348	15	23.20	4/18		
J. Garner	419	95	1091	47	23.21	5/56		1
C.C. Ellison	127	41	325	14	23.21	5/82		2
T.D. Topley	249.4	55	744	32	23.25	5/52		2
Imran Khan	313.2	72	866	37	23.40	8/34		2
A.R. Butcher	111	28	305	13	23.46	4/25		
O.H. Mortensen	416.2	111	1082	46	23.52	5/35		1
A.P. Pridgeon	536	134	1396	59	23.66	6/52		2
N.G. Cowans	436.2	94	1380	58	23.79	5/61		1
K.E. Cooper	410.5	106	1026	43	23.86	5/102		1
N. Gifford	564.3	158	1409	59	23.88	6/27		2
D.R. Pringle	506.3	128	1348	56	24.07	7/46		2
P.J.W. Allott	405.1	106	1053	43	24.48	5/32		2
P.J. Newport	632.3	90	2146	85	25.24	6/48	1	5
C.E.B. Rice	413.2	115	1111	44	25.25	4/54		
P.M. Such	231.3	69	566	22	25.72	5/36		1
G.R. Dilley	505.2	86	1634	63	25.93	6/57	1	3
S.P. Hughes	530.4	123	1652	63	26.22	7/35		1
D.L. Underwood	639.1	259	1371	52	26.36	7/11		1
N.F. Williams	79.3	9	264	10	26.40	3/44		
N.G. Cowley	385.2	78	1060	40	26.50	5/17		1
P.J. Hartley	321.1	49	1095	41	26.70	6/68		1
N.V. Radford	665.4	132	2164	81	26.71	9/70	3	6
A. Sidebottom	226.1	37	671	25	26.84	8/72		2

Hampshire C.C.C — First-Class Matches – Bowling, 1986

	M.D. Marshall	C.A. Connor	R.J. Maru	T.M. Tremlett	N.G. Cowley	C.L. Smith	M.C.J. Nicholas	R.A. Smith	S.J.W. Andrew
v. Nottinghamshire (Trent Bridge) 26–28 April	24–7–48–2 / 7–2–26–0	16–3–54–0 / 19–4–41–1	31–8–71–4 / 17–3–50–0	24–8–48–1 / 8–2–19–0	19.4–4–37–2 / 10–1–29–2	/ 1–0–6–0			
v. Glamorgan (Southampton) 30 April–2 May	20.5–5–46–2 / 15–5–42–0	29–9–57–3 / 27–13–45–3	6–1–30–0 / 35–19–67–1	27–11–40–3 / 27–9–78–2	5–0–13–0 / 21–7–59–1	/ 5–2–21–0	4–0–11–0	/ 3–2–2–0	
v. Lancashire (Old Trafford) 7–9 May									
v. Indians (Southampton) 17–19 May			17–1–51–0 / 9–1–48–1	15–4–48–1	14–3–57–2 / 7–1–22–1		7–2–27–1		17–3–50–1 / 7–5–5–1
v. Cambridge University (Cambridge) 21–23 May			21.2–9–38–5 / 12–3–22–1	14–3–40–2	6–1–10–1 / 13–4–22–3	3–3–0–0		6–3–8–1	10–4–17–1 / 10–3–16–1
v. Gloucestershire (Bournemouth) 24–27 May	20–4–42–1 / 23–5–51–6		34–9–64–2 / 7–2–19–0	22–4–69–1 / 7–2–31–0			5–3–2–0		16–3–58–2 / 8–1–26–0
v. Nottinghamshire (Southampton) 31 May–3 June	13–3–38–5	18–5–53–1	2–2–0–0		2.1–1–5–2		3–1–19–0		9–0–47–2
v. Somerset (Bournemouth) 7–9 June	19–4–49–1 / 8.5–5–11–2	20–3–60–5 / 11–5–34–2	18–6–37–0 / 21–5–88–2		11.2–2–43–1 / 13–1–51–1		2–0–3–0		18–2–65–0 / 8–3–15–1
v. Essex (Ilford) 14–17 June	17–6–60–2 / 21–7–26–4	17–5–54–4 / 12–3–33–1	13–4–34–2 / 25.2–5–74–3		14–3–39–2 / 12–1–36–1	/ 1–0–3–0			
v. Surrey (Basingstoke) 18–20 June	17–7–26–4 / 6–2–15–3	17–4–77–3 / 10–0–34–2	3–1–8–1	8–4–17–2 / 4.1–0–14–4	4–1–11–0				
v. Kent (Southampton) 21–24 June	17–4–38–2 / 13–2–34–1	20–4–58–2 / 11–2–36–0		11–4–33–0 / 12–3–26–0	17.4–7–17–5 / 20–4–38–1			1–0–4–0	11–3–33–1 / 8–0–25–3
v. Worcestershire (Worcester) 28 June–1 July	23–2–70–4 / 15–6–29–4	19–2–42–2 / 8–1–34–0		16–5–29–1 / 6–2–16–0	11–2–26–1 / 2–0–2–0				
v. Leicestershire (Leicester) 2–4 July	15–5–32–0 / 21–4–53–3	21–3–63–1 / 18–2–45–2		24–4–77–1 / 20–4–61–1	15–2–57–0 / 13–3–35–1	1–0–6–0	8–2–27–1		
v. Somerset (Taunton) 5–8 July	21–7–40–5 / 11–0–29–0	14–2–51–0 / 14.4–3–37–0		17–3–43–3			16–3–38–0	9–4–28–0	18–3–58–1 / 1.2–0–4–0
v. Warwickshire (Portsmouth) 19–22 July	15–6–22–5 / 19–4–51–2	15.4–4–34–4 / 16–8–60–1		6–1–27–0 / 18–5–54–2					
v. Derbyshire (Portsmouth) 23–25 July	19–4–46–1 / 17–1–54–4	25–8–71–1 / 10–0–54–2			22.4–8–46–5 / 11.1–0–52–3	4–0–20–0			
v. Gloucestershire (Cheltenham) 2–5 August	19–4–42–3 / 22–6–44–4	20–4–63–2 / 12–0–44–1		15–2–55–3 / 15–4–43–0					
v. Kent (Canterbury) 6–8 August	26–8–34–2	28.5–1–138–1		22–1–88–2	25.1–3–70–2		2–1–9–0		
v. Sussex (Bournemouth) 9–12 August	16–3–43–0 / 13.5–4–26–1	18–8–34–2 / 9–1–30–0	30.1–6–87–1 / 21–3–92–3		18–1–74–0 / 16–3–59–3		15–1–54–1		
v. Middlesex (Lord's) 16–19 August	16–2–38–3 / 4.2–1–4–0	10–2–35–1 / 6–1–19–0	11.1–3–27–3 / 12–3–34–1	19–5–31–2 / 3–0–16–0	6–2–16–1 / 9–1–36–1			10–0–48–0	
v. Worcestershire (Bournemouth) 20–22 August	22–11–30–3 / 12–3–32–3	10–3–23–1 / 6–3–22–0	14–4–33–4 / 17–8–49–2	6–1–13–0 / 9–1–34–0		1–1–0–0			
v. Yorkshire (Bournemouth) 23–26 August	19–6–52–3	10.3–3–14–1	15–2–58–2	11–2–37–1					
v. Northamptonshire (Northampton) 27–29 August	17.4–3–41–4		24–8–47–4	16–2–39–2	9–5–6–0	1–0–7–0			
v. Derbyshire (Derby) 30 August–2 September	21–5–49–5 / 7–4–12–2		17–8–36–0 / 12–9–5–0	12.4–3–34–1 / 5–2–5–0	23–8–54–2 / 8–4–10–0		15–1–60–0	2–0–8–0 / 18.4–1–102–2	
v. Sussex (Hove) 10–12 September	14–3–41–2 / 9–1–42–2	20–4–56–0 / 3–0–11–0	28–4–96–2 / 24.5–9–71–4		24.2–1–77–3 / 16–2–49–1	/ 8–0–54–1		1–0–5–0	
v. Lancashire (Southampton) 13–16 September									
Totals	656.3–171–1508–100 av. 15–08	541.2–123–1616–49 av. 32.97	497.5–146–1336–48 av. 27.83	453.4–110–1263–43 av. 29.37	385.2–78–1060–40 av. 26.50	39–7–177–1 av. 177.00	64–13–198–3 av. 66.00	48.4–10–197–3 av. 65.66	141.2–30–419–14 av. 29.92

a T.A. Lloyd absent hurt   b R. Sharma retired hurt

P.J. Bakker	K.D. James	V.P. Terry	T.C. Middleton	R.J. Parks	D.R. Turner	Byes	Leg-byes	Wides	No-balls	Total	Wkts
							7			265	10
							10			181	3
							4	3	1	201	10
						4	24	3	1	342	7
											Ab.
16–3–85–1						3	3		3	297	6
8–3–27–1							3		5	132	5
12–6–20–1							4		2	129	10
6.5–3–15–2						6	9		5	98	8
18–3–51–1						1	9	2	11	296	7
6–2–22–0							1	1	4	150	6
								2	5	162	10
							5	3	2	262	7
							1	2		200	8
						1	10		10	198	10
						4	9	1	3	185	10
							5	3	5	144	10
							1	1	1	64	10
							10		5	189	10
						3	6	1	3	172	5
	9–1–27–0					1	9	1	10	204	9
	3.4–0–22–0					3	6	4	1	112	4
	22.4–5–74–1					3	1	3	14	313	3
	4–1–17–0	1–1–0–0				6	7	1	12	251	8
	9–0–34–1					1	4	5	18	231	10
	13–2–44–0		6–1–26–0	13–0–54–0	3–1–6–0	5	2	2	6	273	0
	5–1–25–0					1	1	1	2	110	9
	7.5–3–16–4					8	8		2	197	9a
	16–5–44–2						9	1	6	216	10
	9–2–33–0					1	3		6	217	10
	9.4–3–33–2					2	6	2	7	201	10
	16–4–34–5					1	18		2	184	10
	19.5–2–78–1						14		6	431	8
						4	6	5		302	4
							2			209	8
							8	1	8	155	10
			2–0–13–1	10–1–56–0				1		226	3
	12–4–17–2						4		5	120	10
	2–0–12–0						11		2	160	5
	19–7–45–2					1	5	3	7	212	10
										0	0
	11–5–21–0					2	6			169	10
	13–4–28–1					7	1		6	209	9b
	6–2–10–0						10		1	222	4
	18–3–67–0					1	7		5	350	7
	3–1–11–0						5		5	243	8
											Ab.
66.5–20– 220–6 *av.* 36.66	228.4–55– 629–21 *av.* 32.95	1–1– 0–0 —	8–1– 39–1 *av.* 39.00	25–1– 110–0 —	3–1– 6–0 —						

Kent C.C.C. — First-Class Matches – Batting, 1986

	v. Leicestershire (Leicester) 26–28 April	v. Northamptonshire (Canterbury) 30 April–2 May	v. Essex (Chelmsford) 7–9 May	v. Indians (Canterbury) 21–23 May	v. Worcestershire (Tunbridge Wells) 31 May–3 June	v. Sussex (Tunbridge Wells) 4–6 June	v. Oxford University (Oxford) 7–10 June	v. Somerset (Bath) 14–17 June	v. Gloucestershire (Gloucester) 18–20 June	v. Hampshire (Southampton) 21–24 June	v. Glamorgan (Maidstone) 28 June–1 July	v. Somerset (Maidstone) 2–4 July	v. Derbyshire (Derby) 5–8 July	v. Surrey (The Oval) 16–18 July
M.R. Benson	14 39	10 15	64 30	128 —	1 —	31 20	40 —	55 8	13 42	90 97*	46 37			
S.G. Hinks	6 14	43 8	67 9	21 —	86 —	15 8	14 —	20 25	27 19*		22 0	21 103	33 7	24 7
C.J. Tavare	3 33	14 105	29 4	58 —	75* —	6 40*	123 —	38 39	0 1	0 12	93 2	0 80	15 6	39 23
N.R. Taylor	4 4	41 3	9 14	64 —	37* —	3 6*	106 —	20 4	44 11	17 6	19 82*	50 60	9 13	12 3
G.R. Cowdrey	6 59	0 75	13 10	42 —	— —	33* —	30 —	0 3	61 4	14 4	2 7	0 2	11 4	13 0
E.A.E. Baptiste	9 80	3 2		26 —	— —		113 —							
R.M. Ellison	6 0	62* 22*	4 15		— —		— —	10 6		10 22*			57 42	
C.S. Cowdrey	1 24	48 10	9 70*			23 —	53 —	6 43	51 6		2 5	1 49*	23 15	8 16
S.A. Marsh	12* 21*	46* 1	27 0	21* —		52* —	7* —	43 35	0 12	0	55 0	11 1	39 60	0 1
G.R. Dilley	12 4	— 1*	26* 0	4* —	— —			8 0				0 4*	1 28	
D.L. Underwood	1 0	— —	6 16	— —	— —			6* 5	19 5	4 —	1 —	25 —	19 3	29 10*
T.M. Alderman			10* —	— —	— —			2 0*	9 0	2 —	13 —	8 —	1* 2*	25 0
C.S. Dale				— —										
K.B.S. Jarvis				— —					0* 4	0* —	1* —			0* 4
D.G. Aslett				— —					8 6			21 13	17 39	53 0
C. Penn						9 —	84* —				0 0		0 2*	
T.R. Ward												29 12		
A.P. Igglesden												5* —		7 0
R.P. Davis														
Byes		1	1	2		1	6	14 8	3 3		3	4	5 1	4 5
Leg-byes	9 6	3 5	4 1	8	4	5 7	3	2 10	2 10	6 7	2 4	8 9	3 2	
Wides	1	2 1	1 1		2		1	7	1	1		5	11 4	
No-balls	1 14	2 1	4 5	1	1	1 4	1	4 5	3 12	4 9	1 4	4	1 3	
Total	85 299	272 250	272 170	378	208	178 77	590	226 183	238 113	189 172	282 143	155 324	249 231	217 72
Wickets	10 10	7 8	9 9	6	2	6 2	7	10 10	10 10	10 5	10 6	10 6	10 10	10 10
Results	D	D	W	D	D	D	D	L	L	W	D	D	L	L
Points	3	3	22	—	2	5	—	4	6	21	7	5	6	6

Catches: 51 – S.A. Marsh (ct 48/st 3) | 17 – D.G. Aslett | 9 – T.M. Alderman
31 – C.S. Cowdrey | 14 – S.G. Hinks | 6 – G.R. Dilley
21 – C.J. Tavare | 10 – N.R. Taylor and G.R. Cowdrey | 5 – R.M. Ellison and M.R. Benson

	Overs	Mds	Runs	Wks	Av	Best	10/m	5/inn
E.A.E. Baptiste	146	40	351	13	27.00	4/53		
D.A. Reeve	525.5	127	1411	52	27.13	5/32		1
M. Jean-Jacques	159	16	599	22	27.22	8/77	1	1
B.P. Patterson	391.4	70	1309	48	27.27	6/31	1	2
D.E. Malcolm	216.2	39	765	28	27.32	5/42		1
C. Shaw	300.1	64	848	31	27.35	5/38		1
G.J.F. Ferris	104	20	356	13	27.38	4/54		
R.A. Harper	825.2	275	1700	62	27.41	5/84		1
P. Bainbridge	414.1	89	1185	43	27.55	8/53		2
D.L. Acfield	401.3	107	912	33	27.63	5/38		1
R.C. Ontong	606.4	153	1774	64	27.71	8/101	1	2
J.P. Agnew	521.5	118	1528	55	27.78	5/27		1
A.C.S. Pigott	390	48	1363	49	27.81	5/50		3
R.J. Maru	497.5	146	1336	48	27.83	5/38		1
T.A. Munton	296.4	68	905	32	28.28	4/60		
J.K. Lever	638.1	154	1990	70	28.42	6/57		3
D.J. Wild	132.3	17	429	15	28.60	4/4		
A.J. Murphy	91	16	288	10	28.80	3/67		
C. Penn	117.3	20	407	14	29.07	5/65		1
K.T. Medlycott	353.4	86	1166	40	29.15	6/63	1	3
P.H. Edmonds	529	161	1111	38	29.23	4/67		
E.E. Hemmings	818.3	259	2134	73	29.23	7/102	2	5
T.M. Tremlett	453.4	110	1263	43	29.37	5/46		1
A.N. Jones	171	25	620	21	29.52	3/36		
N.G.B. Cook	870.2	289	1890	64	29.53	6/72		2
S.J.W. Andrew	141.2	30	419	14	29.92	3/25		
L.B. Taylor	280.3	66	809	27	29.96	4/106		
M.A. Feltham	224	48	781	26	30.03	4/47		
S.J. Dennis	407.3	81	1318	43	30.65	5/71		1
R.A. Pick	469.1	98	1570	50	31.40	6/68		1
L. Potter	113	31	318	10	31.80	3/37		
J.A. Afford	492.4	131	1455	45	32.33	6/81	1	3
D.J. Capel	633.1	131	2044	63	32.44	7/86		2
C.H. Dredge	388	80	1151	35	32.88	3/10		
K.D. James	228.4	55	692	21	32.95	5/34		1
C.A. Conner	541.4	123	1616	49	32.97	5/60		1
J.W. Lloyds	369.2	71	1221	37	33.00	5/111		1
J.E. Davidson	326	54	998	30	33.26	5/35		2
D.A. Graveney	446	137	999	30	33.30	4/17		
W.K.R. Benjamin	465.3	89	1541	46	33.50	6/33		3
C.S. Cowdrey	266.2	45	905	27	33.51	5/69		1
K. Saxelby	284	54	905	27	33.51	4/47		
A.P. Igglesden	125	25	372	11	33.81	4/46		
R.J. Doughty	300	50	1104	32	34.50	4/52		
D.J. Makinson	322.1	65	1044	30	34.80	4/69		
B.J. Griffiths	238.3	54	741	21	35.28	4/59		
G.S. le Roux	302.2	66	928	26	35.69	3/27		
V.J. Marks	744.5	189	2121	59	35.94	8/100	1	2
N.A. Mallender	611	137	1693	47	36.02	5/110		1
I. Folley	349	98	1046	29	36.06	4/42		
D.V. Lawrence	588.1	85	2299	63	36.49	5/84		1
P.I. Pocock	394.5	107	1095	30	36.50	4/45		
S.J. Base	222.5	39	774	21	36.85	4/74		
A.R.C. Fraser	156	40	370	10	37.00	3/19		
R. Sharma	140.5	33	407	11	37.00	3/72		
S.R. Barwick	292.4	61	964	26	37.07	3/25		
C.M. Wells	458.2	103	1373	37	37.10	4/23		
R.S. Rutnagur	164	34	528	14	37.71	3/50		

	Lancs (Canterbury) 19-22 July	Yorks (Scarborough) 23-25 July	Leics (Canterbury) 2-5 Aug	Hants (Canterbury) 6-8 Aug	Warks (Edgbaston) 9-12 Aug	Sussex (Hove) 16-19 Aug	Surrey (Dartford) 20-22 Aug	Glam (Cardiff) 23-26 Aug	Notts (Trent Bridge) 27-29 Aug	Essex (Folkestone) 30 Aug-2 Sept	Warks (Folkestone) 3-5 Sept	Middx (Canterbury) 13-16 Sept	M	Inns	NOs	Runs	H/S	Av
	16 37	94 23	29 0	94 —	13 82	0 31	123 22	— —	7 20	12 25	2 —	— —	22	37	2	1410	128	40.28
	4 0	46 17	34 8	131 —	8* 38	12 12	2 0	— —	15 10		— —		23	38	2	936	131	26.00
	37 90*	62* 23	35 27	14 —	— 14	1 3	32 5	— —	4 21	17 1	43		26	42	4	1267	123	33.34
	16 36*	21* 34	40 4	42 —	— 81	13 0	88 65	— —	7 6	27 20	10		26	42	5	1151	106	31.10
										16 9	7		18	26	1	425	75	17.00
				18 —							22		7	8	—	273	113	34.12
	3 —	— 25*	26 17	44* —	— 14	6 10	32 26*	— —	23 26	4 1	8		19	27	6	521	62*	24.80
	19 —		— 0	60 7	38	— 20	31 34	10 24*	— —		60 7	100	21	33	3	873	100	29.10
	6 —		— 4	52* 2	30	— 12*	32 20	47 —	— —	61 32	7 38	70	26	36	8	857	70	30.60
	7 —		0 3*			23* 13*				0 7	30 12		14	21	7	183	30	13.07
		— 10	26* 0	— —		— 3*	9 16	— —		5 15	7* 2	1	24	26	5	243	29	11.57
	15* —		— 0	— 0			5 0			7* 2*	1 0*		20	21	8	102	25	7.84
								0* —		2 16			3	3	1	18	16	9.00
													7	6	4	9	4	4.50
	11 —		— 26	4 16	0 —	— 13	44 1	17 57	— —	7 40	24 37	63	17	23	—	517	63	22.47
						— 0							6	7	2	95	84*	19.00
													1	2	—	41	29	20.50
	2 —		— 8*	— —							0* —		5	5	2	22	8*	7.33
											0* —		1	1	1	0	0*	—

	Lancs	Yorks	Leics	Hants	Warks(E)	Sussex	Surrey	Glam	Notts	Essex	Warks(F)	Middx
		5 2				6		15 8		7	9 1	12
	9	10 16	14 1	14		2 7	7 3	2 4		2 6	9 6	21
	1	1					2		1		1	
	11 8	11 4	8 2	6		9	6 2	11 2				1 3
	157 171	250 192	329 87	431	23 299	191 145	379 214	—	140 209	224 160	362	
	10 2	2 9	8 10	8	0 8	10 10	8 5		10 10	10 10	10	
	W	D	W	D	D	L	D	D	L	L	W	D
	21	6	24	8	2	5	6	3	4	6	22	0

2 – A.P. Igglesden, C. Penn, K.B.S. Jarvis,
    D.L. Underwood and subs.
1 – R.P. Davis and E.A.E. Baptiste

	Overs	Mds	Runs	Wks	Av	Best	10/m	5/inn
R.J. Finney	322.4	62	1057	28	37.75	7/54		1
G.J. Parsons	371.1	72	1179	31	38.03	5/24		2
I.R. Payne	215.1	58	576	15	38.40	3/48		
C.D. Fraser-Darling	120	16	461	12	38.41	5/84		1
J.G. Thomas	476.5	77	1746	45	38.80	4/56		
K.J. Kerr	316	52	955	24	39.79	5/47		1
A. Walker	422	76	1314	33	39.81	6/50		1
S.M. McEwan	179.1	31	638	16	39.87	3/33		
K.B.S. Jarvis	155.2	42	487	12	40.58	5/24		
E.A. Moseely	124.3	14	447	11	40.63	4/70		
J. Derrick	262.2	47	897	22	40.77	3/37		
S.D. Fletcher	413.5	82	1273	31	41.06	5/90		1
G.E. Sainsbury	169.1	46	498	12	41.50	4/146		
I.T. Botham	311.1	65	1043	25	41.72	6/125		1
D.N. Patel	453.2	115	1254	30	41.80	5/88		1
G. Monkhouse	233.1	69	589	14	42.07	4/37		
N.S. Taylor	342.2	62	1222	29	42.13	4/40		
G. Miller	634.2	188	1406	33	42.60	5/37		2
A.E. Warner	349.1	71	1200	28	42.85	4/38		
A.N. Hayhurst	114.1	13	429	10	42.90	4/69		
P. Carrick	621.3	186	1550	36	43.05	4/111		
J.D. Inchmore	221.1	48	562	13	43.23	2/41		
A.M.G. Scott	273	71	814	18	45.22	4/100		
G.C. Holmes	131	21	499	11	45.36	2/22		
D.J. Hickey	281.5	39	1102	24	45.91	5/57		1
B.M. McMillan	220	34	808	17	47.52	3/47		
R.M. Ellison	386.4	90	1103	23	47.95	4/36		1
R.K. Illingworth	564.2	189	1361	28	48.60	5/64		1

	Overs	Mds	Runs	Wks	Av	Best	10/m	5/inn
D.J. Thomas	166.3	29	588	12	49.00	2/44		
T.A.J. Dawson	195	39	649	13	49.92	3/65		
M. Watkinson	504.4	87	1753	35	50.08	5/90		1
R.V.J. Coombs	255.5	58	844	16	52.75	3/60		
A.M. Ferreira	178	47	532	10	53.20	2/61		
D.A. Thorne	239.3	70	591	11	53.72	3/42		
C.S. Mays	212.5	45	706	13	54.30	3/77		
P.A. Smith	159	19	743	13	57.15	3/36		
M.R. Davis	167.3	21	631	11	57.36	2/43		
A.K. Golding	252	51	685	10	68.50	3/51		

(Qualification 10 wickets)

LEADING FIELDERS

83 – D.E. East (ct 64/st 19); 81 – R.J. Parks (ct 73/st 8); 66 – S.J. Rhodes (ct 58/st 8); 50 – R.C. Russell (ct 56/st 3); 51 – S.A. Marsh (ct 48/st 3); 49 – P.R. Downton (ct 44/st 5) and G.W. Humpage (ct 41/st 8); 48 – B.N. French (ct 44/st 4); 44 – C.J. Richards (ct 39/st 5); 43 – D.L. Bairstow (ct 40/st 3); 39 – T. Davies (ct 38/st 1); 38 – M.A. Lynch; 37 – S.N.V. Waterton (ct 32/st 5) and I.J. Gould (ct 36/st 1); 36 – T. Gard (ct 30/st 6); 35 – C. Marples (ct 31/st 4); 32 – R.A. Harper and C. Maynard; 31 – C.S. Cowdrey; 29 – K.M. Curran; 27 – C.E.B. Rice; 25 – K.W.R. Fletcher; 24 – K.J. Barnett, P. Gill, P. Whitticase (ct 23/st 1), P. Johnson and J.D. Birch (ct 23/st 1); 23 – R.J. Bailey and B.J.M. Maher; 22 – G.A. Gooch; 21 – J.W. Lloyds, C.W.J. Athey, R.A. Smith, C.J. Tavare and N.G.B. Cook; 20 – D.A. Graveney.

Kent C.C.C. First-Class Matches – Bowling, 1986	G.R. Dilley	R.M. Ellison	E.A.E. Baptiste	D.L. Underwood	C.S. Cowdrey	N.R. Taylor	T.M. Alderman	K.B.S. Jarvis	C. Penn
v. Leicestershire (Leicester) 26–28 April	31–9–74–3 2–0–3–0	23–11–37–1 1–1–0–1	29–10–58–4	24–12–33–2	7–1–25–0				
v. Northamptonshire (Canterbury) 30 April–2 May	14–2–38–2	16–5–43–0	24–7–67–0	21–6–56–0	12–3–29–1	7–0–16–0			
v. Essex (Chelmsford) 7–9 May	13.5–0–69–5 15.5–1–81–1	5–0–19–0 14–3–30–0		10–2–37–1	7–1–21–0 8–2–31–3			13–1–59–4 17–3–46–5	
v. Indians (Canterbury) 21–23 May									
v. Worcestershire (Tunbridge Wells) 31 May–3 June									
v. Sussex (Tunbridge Wells) 4–6 June				29.3–9–58–1 21–5–59–4	2–0–11–0	1–1–0–0 18.3–1–73–1	20–2–70–6 7–0–18–0	22–7–61–2 2–1–2–0	12–1–55–0
v. Oxford University (Oxford) 7–10 June			9–2–24–0	11–8–31–1	8–2–19–1	1–1–0–0		16–9–15–2	16.4–6–38–0
v. Somerset (Bath) 14–17 June	20–4–83–1	15–3–65–1		20–3–59–0	13–1–63–0	7–0–30–0	23.5–3–122–4		
v. Gloucestershire (Gloucester) 18–20 June				22–7–35–0			21.4–8–49–6 26–4–86–4	12–2–48–2 20–8–39–1	7–0–27–2 16.5–3–59–1
v. Hampshire (Southampton) 21–24 June		15.4–3–54–1 3–1–12–0		22–13–30–4 17–10–21–3			23.1–4–71–3 27.1–8–56–6	16–5–57–2 13–3–45–1	
v. Glamorgan (Maidstone) 28 June–1 July	21–2–66–3 6–2–16–0			14–6–23–1 24–11–36–2	15–5–35–1 11–0–43–0	3–0–13–0 30–6–84–1	26.1–9–57–5 12–3–31–1	19–3–71–0 10.2–1–31–1	
v. Somerset (Maidstone) 2–4 July				5.3–2–10–2 17–4–80–2	21–5–55–3 8–0–34–0		26–10–76–1 14–3–58–2		17–3–30–2 14–1–65–5
v. Derbyshire (Derby) 5–8 July	8–2–21–1 29–2–112–4	11–3–33–0 18–0–86–0		18.4–5–58–2	4–2–17–1 14–3–43–1		15–2–46–8 20–2–84–3		
v. Surrey (The Oval) 16–18 July				15–6–30–2 23–8–63–1	11–3–37–2 10–0–48–1	6–0–19–0	17–5–40–2 13–4–44–3	7–1–46–0 16–2–72–1	
v. Lancashire (Canterbury) 19–22 July	22–4–57–6 17.4–3–53–4	7.4–4–7–1 15–4–36–4					24–7–59–2 14–5–36–1		
v. Yorkshire (Scarborough) 23–25 July		18–3–51–2		16–6–50–1 12–2–60–0	24–2–81–3 7–0–23–0		21–4–69–0 11–2–39–1		
v. Leicestershire (Canterbury) 2–5 August	18–4–54–2 21–2–59–1	8–1–56–0 13–3–46–0		9–4–12–0 19–9–27–3	2–0–5–0		21–5–70–8 32–8–74–6		
v. Hampshire (Canterbury) 6–8 August		23–5–58–1 4–0–12–0	25–5–70–3 16–2–41–1	8–5–9–1 23–13–32–1	29–8–69–5 12–3–48–0	1–0–3–0 3–0–14–1			
v. Warwickshire (Edgbaston) 9–12 August		17–3–47–0		24–9–49–0	3–0–19–0		24–5–89–1		23–5–94–3
v. Sussex (Hove) 16–19 August	24–3–101–5 11.5–1–47–2	21.5–6–53–4		2–0–7–0	4–0–23–0		22–6–56–0 11–2–38–2		
v. Surrey (Dartford) 20–22 August		15–1–61–1 1–0–2–0		22.4–6–70–1 8–1–37–2	4–0–16–0		17–1–89–3 10–0–63–2		
v. Glamorgan (Cardiff) 23–26 August		25.1–8–50–1		24–14–24–2			30–12–41–3		11–1–39–1
v. Nottinghamshire (Trent Bridge) 27–29 August	26–2–81–2 13–1–41–0	9.2–3–18–3 6–1–24–0		18–6–39–0 20–5–73–0			21–6–84–5 18–3–47–1		
v. Essex (Folkestone) 30 August–2 September	20.2–4–57–1 6–1–21–1	23–6–63–0 8–0–24–1		40–13–96–4 8–2–30–0	12–3–24–4 0.2–0–4–0		9–2–15–0		
v. Warwickshire (Folkestone) 3–5 September		12–1–26–0	26–9–53–4 8–3–12–0	32–18–48–2 36.5–29–11–7	12–1–49–1				
v. Middlesex (Canterbury) 13–16 September	10–2–22–0	3–0–10–0	9–2–26–1	2–0–6–0	6–0–33–0				
	350.3–51– 1156–44 av. 26.27	351.4–79– 1023–22 av. 46.50	146–40– 351–13 av. 27.00	639.1–259– 1371–52 av. 26.36	266.2–45– 905–27 av. 33.51	77.3–9– 252–3 av. 84.00	607–139– 1882–98 av. 19.20	153.2–42– 487–12 av. 40.58	117.3–20– 407–14 av. 29.07

a G.S. le Roux retired hurt   b I.J. Gould absent hurt   c P. Davis 28.5–4–83–3 31–18–38–3

S.G. Hinks	G.R. Cowdrey	A.P. Igglesden	D.G. Aslett	C.J. Tavare	C.S. Dale	M.R. Benson	Byes	Leg-byes	Wides	No-balls	Total	Wkts
							5	10	1	13	242	10
								2			5	1
								1	3	5	250	3
							4	2	1	21	174	10
							1	17	3	6	243	10
											Ab.	
											Ab.	
								2	2	5	246	9a
							8	2	3	2	173	5
8–2–10–1	3–2–1–0						5	5	1		120	5
							1	10	1	6	433	6
								1			125	10
								8	1	5	227	6
								2		1	214	10
								9			143	10
	4–1–17–1						8	4	6	7	277	10
							1	5		8	264	6
		20–3–59–2					4	15	7	1	249	10
		14–4–31–0						4	1	4	272	9
								1		4	117	10
							4	4	1	9	391	10
		17–6–46–4					1	1		4	201	10
		23–8–46–2	5–1–15–0				1	14	1	4	322	9
		10–1–27–1					1	11		5	162	10
		11–2–32–1						8	1	5	165	10
		18–1–86–1						4		8	341	7
		7–0–25–0	9–1–56–1				2	1	3	6	206	2
								2	1	4	199	10
							1	5		4	212	10
		5–0–20–0						5	5	9	234	10
			9–1–27–1	5–2–3–1			4		1	2	181	5
			2–0–10–1	7–2–8–0			1	9		3	326	5
			4–0–33–0	3–0–21–0			1	2			57	0
							4	8		9	252	9b
										1	85	4
					13–2–59–0			5		5	300	5
			6–0–64–1		3–0–21–0	7–0–55–2	2	1		3	245	8
			1–1–0–0					3	3	3	157	7
					6–1–7–0		1	10			240	10
					12–2–55–0			1			241	1
	3–0–9–0			3–0–7–0				9	1	8	280	10
			6–0–46–1					2		4	127	3
							3	5	2	2	267	10c
				2–1–4–0						1	65	10
							4		5	7	101	1

S.G. Hinks	G.R. Cowdrey	A.P. Igglesden	D.G. Aslett	C.J. Tavare	C.S. Dale	M.R. Benson
8–2– 10–1 *av.* 10.00	10–3– 27–1 *av.* 27.00	125–25– 372–11 *av.* 33.81	35–3– 187–4 *av.* 46.75	27–6– 107–2 *av.* 53.50	34–5– 142–0 —	7–0– 55–2 *av.* 27.50

Lancashire C.C.C. First-Class Matches – Batting, 1986

Batsman	v. Sussex (Hove) 26–28 April		v. Leicestershire (Old Trafford) 20 April–2 May		v. Hampshire (Old Trafford) 7–9 May		v. Worcestershire (Worcester) 21–23 May		v. Yorkshire (Leeds) 24–27 May		v. Warwickshire (Old Trafford) 31 May–3 June		v. Oxford University (Oxford) 4–6 June		v. Middlesex (Old Trafford) 7–10 June		v. Worcestershire (Old Trafford) 14–17 June		v. Glamorgan (Swansea) 21–24 June		v. Derbyshire (Liverpool) 28 June–1 July		v. Essex (Old Trafford) 5–8 July		v. Northamptonshire (Northampton) 14–16 July		v. Kent (Canterbury) 19–22 July	
G.D. Mendis	0	11*	0	28	—	—	15	11*	8	62	44	25	98	—	66	—	66	27	100		35	20	86		9	69	47	44
G. Fowler	180	0	72	56	—	—	3	21			4	8	16	37*	0	—	22	—	14		8	88*	21		50	14	3	21
D.W. Varey	25	11*	72	15	—	—			0	8																		
N.H. Fairbrother	84	—	1	64*	—	—	54	—	20	16	25*	36	59*	—	42	—	131	10*	1		0	52	3		20	20	36	7
S.J. O'Shaughnessy	50*	—	4	14																					10	74	0	5
J. Abrahams	73*	—	3	0	—	—	43	3*	3	21	6	0	117	—	28	—	100*	73*	189*		0	29	30		0	10	4	4
M. Watkinson	—	—	13	39*	—	—	40	—	24	44	—	0	12*	—	0	—			28		7	—	35		2	1	0	25
D.J. Makinson	—	—	11*	—			5	—	14	—	—	2*			4	—					5	—	1*		1*	43		
C. Maynard	—	—	59	37	—	—	26	—	132*	12	7*	64			0	—	0*	—	60		0	4*	9		1*	19	6	3
P.J.W. Allott	—	—	42	16	—	—	22	—	65	21*	—	22*			9*	—			46		5	—	3				35*	5
B.P. Patterson			1*	—					0	—											5	—	1		0*	0*	4	12*
I. Folley	—	—	—	—																	13*	—	20		0	6	9	13
C.H. Lloyd							2	—					—	19*	79	—			14		14	—						
J. Simmons							42	—	0	38*	—	44			61	—			1		1	—						
S. Henriksen							6*	—																				
M.R. Chadwick									13	26	61	47					28	48			6	48	20		38	5	1	12
A.N. Hayhurst													10	0														
J. Stanworth																	1*	—										
A.J. Murphy																												
K.A. Hayes																												
W.K. Hogg																												
Byes			5	2			4		4	2	4		4		2		5	2			14		4		1	4	1	
Leg-byes	12	1	12	4			5	6	6	6	3	11	3	1	12		5	6	8		1	3	4		5	6	11	8
Wides				2			4	1	1	4			5	1			5	2	7		1	5					5	
No-Balls		7	6	7			8	1	7	8	2	2	1		9		5	2	7		8	7	3		7	17	5	5
Total	431	23	301	284			279	43	296	268	152	265	320	63	313		367	170	475		94	270	240		144	288	162	165
Wickets	4	1	9	7			10	1	10	7	4	8	4	1	9		4	2	8		10	4	10		9†	10	10	10
Results	W		D		D		W		D		D		W		D		D		D		D		W		L		L	
Points	24		6		1		19		7		3		—		4		7		5		2		22		1		5	

Catches

32 – C. Maynard (ct 29/st 3)	10 – Subs. and I. Folley	6 – M.R. Chadwick
14 – M. Watkinson	9 – P.J.W. Allott and G. Fowler	5 – S.J. O'Shaughnessy
13 – J. Abrahams	7 – D.W. Varey (ct 6/st 1),	4 – B.P. Patterson, W.K. Hogg (ct 2/st 2)
11 – N.H. Fairbrother	D.J. Makinson and J. Simmons	and J. Stanworth

Review of the Season

The disasters that attended England's Test team are fully documented and commented upon elsewhere in this volume so that there is no need to dwell on them again here and cast a shadow over another entertaining domestic season. The weather was not kind, but the cricket prospered in spite of off-field rumblings.

Once again Essex emerged as the leading county, taking the Britannic Assurance County Championship, being runners-up in the Sunday League and reaching the quarter-finals of the Benson and Hedges Cup. More than any other team in the country they have a belief in their own ability and a positive approach to the game. They set out for victory even if that means flirting with defeat, and one can think of no other county who would have achieved the victories that they did at Taunton and Folkestone in the last weeks of the season. Those wins were decisive. Essentially, they are a team without stars. The signing of Border caused raised eyebrows in many quarters, but he was an invaluable team-man, gave good support and advice to the younger players, and was an excellent public relations man, but it must be remembered that Essex played the last month of the season without him, and that was when the title was decided. Foster and Childs were outstanding in the attack, and Lever (though showing signs of wear in the last weeks of the season), Pringle, Acfield and Topley all performed well. Essex were one of the few counties who were capable of bowling a side out twice, and that is the key factor in winning the championship. Moreover, their bread and butter cricketers, Hardie, Lilley, Fletcher, still the brains behind the team, and Prichard serve them better than any other county is served in this respect.

Indeed, this could be seen as the great difference between Essex and Notts. Notts had the best and most consistent opening pair in the country in Broad and Robinson, both in the first-class and one-day game, and in Hadlee and Rice two of the best all-rounders that have graced English cricket for many years. Rice was one of the very best of captains, but Notts won nothing after coming close in everything, and some of their lesser players and younger players should look to their laurels to see if they are giving all that they are capable of giving. There is still no substitute for hard work.

Gloucestershire, having lost all interest in the one-day competitions, failed bravely in the championship, but realistically they were never quite good enough. Their batting was

v. Nottinghamshire (Southport) 23-25 July	v. Warwickshire (Edgbaston) 26-29 July	v. Yorkshire (Old Trafford) 2-5 August	v. Surrey (The Oval) 6-8 August	v. Derbyshire (Buxton) 9-12 August	v. Nottinghamshire (Trent Bridge) 16-19 August	v. Glamorgan (Lytham) 20-22 August	v. Gloucestershire (Old Trafford) 23-26 August	v. Middlesex (Lord's) 27-29 August	v. Somerset (Old Trafford) 10-12 September	v. Hampshire (Southampton) 13-16 September	M	Inns	NOs	Runs	H/S	Av
13 69	0 —	54 25	2 25	5 65	108 —		61* —	7 28	9 21		23	37	3	1363	108	40.08
30 37	76 —	35 0	20 68	41 86	57 —			5 70			20	32	2	1163	180	38.76
				17 15*					25 83		6	10	2	271	83	33.87
	0 —	1 116*	0 55	45 4*	97 28*	8 2			65 115*		22	33	8	1217	131	48.68
			43 —		4 12*	27 27*		17 4			10	14	3	291	74	26.45
20 16	2 —	4 80	28 81*	4 —	3 2	99 17	13* —	0 45	9 92		24	38	7	1251	189*	40.35
3 58*	3 —	0 1	29 —					18 3	2 2*		21	25	4	389	58*	18.52
				2 —	2* —	0* 6					15	13	6	96	43	13.71
59 13	26 —			11 —	6 —			0 6	36 66		19	26	5	662	132*	31.52
6 17*	21 —	36 —	5 —					4 2			17	19	5	382	65	27.28
	6* —	0 —				0 4	0* 9	12 —			18	15	5	54	12*	5.40
3 —	20* —	1 1	13 5	2 —		2 1		10 17	5 18		17	19	2	159	20*	9.35
19 75	128 —			11 —					2 —		7	8	1	347	128	49.57
		7 8*	23 36*	18* —	1 —	0 1		5 13*	2 —		13	17	5	300	61	25.00
				1 —							2	2	1	7	6*	7.00
3 0						2 50	15 —				10	18	—	423	61	23.50
22 3	0 —	8 14			29 —	19 16		0 3	1 31		10	14	—	156	31	11.14
		2 —	11* —								3	2	1	13	11*	13.00
0* —	— —								1* —		4	3	3	2	1*	—
						17 —					1	1	—	17	17	17.00
						0 4					2	2	—	4	4	2.00
4 1		8	4 14	1 2	6	2 12	1		1							
3 4	11	7 3	4 3	5 1	9	8 8	1	4 2	1 14							
1			1	2	2				2							
5 5		1 2	10 5	10 3	2	6 1	2	1 1	3 1							
182 301	293	170 251	192 292	173 178	324 42	192 149	93	71 204	171 445							
10 7	9	10 6	10 4	10 2	8 0	10 9	1	10 10	10 6							
D	D	D	L	D	L	D	D	L	W	Ab.						
4	7	1	5	1	3	4	2	2	21	0						

2 – G.D. Mendis, A.J. Murphy
    and A.N. Hayhurst
1 – S. Henriksen
†C. Maynard retired hurt

thin and their bowling relied heavily on Walsh. Russell was splendid behind the stumps and, like David East of Essex, must have felt a little aggrieved that he was not on the plane to Australia.

In spite of their Sunday League victory, Hampshire were a disappointment. They failed to reach the final of the Benson and Hedges Cup or the NatWest Trophy, a dream they covet, and they were still short of a bowler to support Marshall. Greenidge finished strongly, but was uneven and injured earlier on, and the batting, Robin Smith, Terry and Nicholas in particular was very disappointing. One had thought Robin Smith would have been on the verge of the England side by now, but he has failed to develop the stability one had hoped for.

Middlesex used more players than any other county save Somerset and slipped down the table alarmingly. They won the Benson and Hedges Cup when they and Kent, two sides out of form, found themselves rather surprisingly in the final and conjured up an exciting one. Indeed, both sides suffered from the same weakness, a lack of strength in batting. In Terry Alderman, Kent possessed the bowler who was most probably the best and most effective in the country, and one wonders whether they can really afford the luxury of a West Indian Test player on their staff who is only used on Sunday afternoons. Middlesex's cause would be served better if they could return to a more consistent line up. When they achieved stability late in the season their fortunes improved dramatically.

Lancashire reached the final of the NatWest Trophy in fine style and were, for a time, leading the championship, but they fell away dreadfully. The bizarre position over the captaincy could have helped nobody, but the county's attack, with Patterson bitterly disappointing after his triumphs in the Caribbean, was woefully weak. Mendis will settle down to become a very useful opening batsman, but there were doubts as to Fowler's future, and the season ended with the dismissal of Bond and Lever from their positions as manager and coach, dismissals that were justified in light of the lack of progress, and Old Trafford was shrouded in mystery.

There was the ususal end of season mystery across the Pennines too, but Yorkshire should take hope from the development of Paul Jarvis, who looked one of the best pace bowlers in the country until injured, and of Ashley Metcalfe. There was promise too in Peter Hartley, but the great problem at Yorkshire in the past decade is the amount of promise that has never been fulfilled. One is wary of hoping too much.

The promise at Worcester, however, was undeniable. They

Lancashire C.C.C. First-Class Matches – Bowling, 1986	B.P. Patterson	P.J.W. Allott	D.J. Makinson	M. Watkinson	S.J. O'Shaughnessy	J. Abrahams	I. Folley	S. Henriksen	J. Simmons
v. Sussex (Hove) 26–28 April	13–2–55–3 / 15–3–62–2	17–4–32–5 / 20–4–54–2	11–4–36–2 / 13–1–48–1	13–6–32–0 / 26.1–5–90–5	9–2–20–0				
v. Leicestershire (Old Trafford) 30 April–2 May	17–6–43–2	23.2–5–74–1 / 6–4–5–1	9–2–51–0 / 9–5–14–1	16–3–62–0 / 7–3–9–0	12–3–45–2 / 4–0–12–0	7–0–22–0			
v. Hampshire (Old Trafford) 7–9 May	12–2–38–1	19–4–65–2		14–0–46–0	6–2–20–0		17–3–72–0		
v. Worcestershire (Worcester) 21–23 May		22.2–4–88–2	24–4–80–4	23–1–91–2				9–2–24–0	8–2–30–1
v. Yorkshire (Leeds) 24–27 May	20–4–67–2	21.4–4–68–4 / 6–1–10–0	13–2–56–1 / 10–4–23–1	19–2–69–2 / 12–1–49–0					14–5–39–1
v. Warwickshire (Old Trafford) 31 May–3 June	21–2–85–0	23–6–44–1 / 5–1–13–2	24–3–69–4 / 5–1–14–0	16–3–41–0					10–0–47–0 / 2–1–2–0
v. Oxford University (Oxford) 4–6 June	17.4–6–31–6 / 18–2–56–2		7–2–7–0 / 30–9–74–0	19–9–44–3 / 31–8–77–2		7–1–14–2	3–1–5–1 / 19–7–32–2		
v. Middlesex (Old Trafford) 7–10 June		10–3–19–0	6–1–23–1	2–0–4–0					4–2–6–0
v. Worcestershire (Old Trafford) 14–17 June	16–5–27–1 / 11–5–23–0	20–7–41–2 / 11–1–45–2		24–5–92–3 / 16–3–51–1		2–0–6–0			20.3–5–53–3 / 8–3–16–0
v. Glamorgan (Swansea) 21–24 June		12.2–5–22–0	16–0–61–2	24–10–59–2			32–11–84–0		
v. Derbyshire (Liverpool) 28 June–1 July	20.1–1–77–2	30–8–91–0	25–3–105–4	23–2–86–0		2–0–14–0	28–11–69–3		
v. Essex (Old Trafford) 5–8 July	12.4–2–46–6 / 13–1–43–4	12–7–10–2 / 11–3–31–3	8–2–11–2 / 8–2–23–0	9.4–2–36–3					
v. Northamptonshire (Northampton) 16–18 July	18–4–69–0 / 2–0–19–0		15–2–69–1 / 1.3–0–15–0	31–6–106–1	11–3–58–0	9.3–0–51–1	15–5–42–0		
v. Kent (Canterbury) 19–22 July	17.4–3–43–4 / 12–1–41–1	18–5–42–4 / 17–4–50–1		10–2–35–0 / 6–1–32–0	9–2–28–2	5–1–29–0	8–3–19–0		
v. Nottinghamshire (Southport) 23–25 July		24–8–63–1		23–0–88–0			30–8–73–3		
v. Warwickshire (Edgbaston) 26–29 July		21.3–5–55–5 / 9–2–17–1		15–2–48–3 / 22–1–96–0		4.2–0–25–0	20–6–59–2		
v. Yorkshire (Old Trafford) 2–5 August	18–2–76–1	29–6–84–1		22–2–77–0			8–0–35–0		15–2–43–0
v. Surrey (The Oval) 6–8 August	15.1–1–80–3 / 16–1–99–2	8–4–20–1		3–1–7–0 / 11–0–64–1	8–1–22–0		9–3–31–1 / 13–2–62–2		11–4–21–4 / 10.5–1–56–3
v. Derbyshire (Buxton) 9–12 August			13–4–32–0 / 10.4–1–49–1			3–2–2–0	19–5–44–3	6–0–26–1 / 2–0–11–0	7–1–11–0 / 22–7–56–3
v. Nottinghamshire (Trent Bridge) 16–19 August	8–1–20–2 / 17–4–59–1		9–2–20–0 / 15–2–57–1		12–1–68–0		1–0–4–0 / 14–1–39–0		8–2–20–1
v. Glamorgan (Lytham) 20–22 August	10–3–15–0 / 1–0–2–0		12–3–22–1			3–1–8–0	22–8–42–4 / 19–3–65–1		21–4–66–3 / 22–5–79–7
v. Gloucestershire (Old Trafford) 23–26 August	16–2–33–2		28–6–85–3	22–3–89–0	12–2–42–1	2–0–4–0	20–7–50–2		
v. Middlesex (Lord's) 27–29 August	17–4–56–1	9–1–10–0		22–1–95–2	14–2–48–0		22–4–74–1		21.4–5–56–3
v. Somerset (Old Trafford) 10–12 September	17–3–44–0			20.5–5–59–4 / 2–0–19–1			23–10–90–2 / 7–0–55–2		17–2–108–2 / 8.5–1–53–5
v. Hampshire (Southampton) 13–16 September									
	391.2–70–1309–48 av. 27.27	405.1–106–1053–43 av. 24.48	322.1–65–1044–30 av. 34.80	504.4–87–1753–35 av. 50.08	97–18–363–5 av. 72.60	44.5–5–175–3 av. 58.33	349–98–1046–29 av. 36.06	17–2–61–1 av. 61.00	230.5–52–762–36 av. 21.16

a G. Monkhouse retired hurt

N.H. Fairbrother	M.R. Chadwick	G. Fowler	A.N. Hayhurst	A.J. Murphy		Byes	Leg-byes	Wides	No-balls	Total	Wkts
							5		5	160	10
						9	10		9	293	10
						4	2	4	7	303	5
							2			40	2
							10		7	251	3
										0	0
							6		6	319	10
3–2–3–0						6	9	1	5	314	10
							5			90	1
2–1–2–0	5–0–51–0	4–0–34–2				1	14		5	301	5
							4	1	1	120	4
1–1–0–0			8–5–11–2			5	4	1	1	96	10
						7	14	2	3	285	10
						4	2			58	1
			8–1–28–1			4	2		7	253	10
3–1–6–0						1	4	1		146	4
						2	2	1	5	230	4
1–0–6–0						9	8	1	22	465	9
							4	1	5	71	10
						4	10	5	6	147	10
						4	1	1	14	400	3
										34	0
							9	1	11	157	10
									8	171	2
			12–1–45–1	21–5–67–3		5	9	2	1	350	8
				14–3–29–2			6		2	138	10
2–0–11–0			6–0–22–0	5–1–17–0		4	4	1	1	255	3
3–1–7–0			26–3–69–4			1	7	2	1	399	7
						4	5		3	190	9a
						5	9	2	1	295	8
							3			72	1
8–3–13–0						3	1	2	7	179	7
			5–0–26–0				2	2	1	72	2
			6.1–0–50–0				2	1	7	295	3
			2–0–12–0			1	6	1		164	8
							2			156	8
			11–1–36–0			5	10		2	354	8
			19–2–77–0			2	14		3	432	8
			5–0–25–1	19–3–69–1		2	11		3	408	10
			6–0–28–1	5–1–21–1		1	5		2	182	10
											Ab.
23–9– 48–0 —	5–0– 51–0 —	4–0– 34–2 av. 17.00	114.1–13– 429–10 av. 42.90	64–13– 203–7 av. 29.00							

Leicestershire C.C.C. — First-Class Matches – Batting, 1986

Each match cell shows the two innings (1st / 2nd) where played. Matches (left→right):
1. v. Cambridge Univ. (Cambridge) 19–22 April
2. v. Kent (Leicester) 26–28 April
3. v. Lancashire (Old Trafford) 30 April–2 May
4. v. Middlesex (Lord's) 7–9 May
5. v. Nottinghamshire (Trent Bridge) 21–23 May
6. v. Northamptonshire (Northampton) 24–27 May
7. v. Gloucestershire (Leicester) 31 May–3 June
8. v. Surrey (Hinckley) 4–6 June
9. v. Sussex (Hove) 7–10 June
10. v. Indians (Leicester) 14–16 June
11. v. Warwickshire (Edgbaston) 21–24 June
12. v. Nottinghamshire (Leicester) 28 June–1 July
13. v. Hampshire (Leicester) 2–4 July
14. v. Yorkshire (Middlesbrough) 5–8 July

Batsman	Camb	Kent	Lancs	Middx	Notts (TB)	Northants	Gloucs	Surrey	Sussex	Indians	Warwick	Notts (L)	Hants	Yorks
I.P. Butcher	58 —	6 —	39 10	4 —	9 —	32 —	— —	26 14	9 11	0 80	78 4	0 4	12 13	8 23
R.A. Cobb	30 —	74 —	4 5	34 —	4 —	41 —	66 68*	16 2	7 67	3 55	12 65	9 68	4 47	2 0
L. Potter	24 —	4 0*	0 17*	1 —	3 —	— —	2 81*	14 5					2 0	63 —
T.J. Boon	16 —	11 —	— 6*	22 —		38 —		41 5*	49 1	18 26	32 22*	4 12*	20* 9	117 29*
J.J. Whitaker	57 —	57 0	102* —	60 —	76 —	27 —	4* —	6 88*	18 26	18 47*	90 5	200* 11	6 13*	
N.E. Briers	3 —				1 —	83 —	81 —	15 23	17* —					
P.B. Clift	43* —	11 —		17 —	4 —	12 —	23 —	43 —	27 0	16 —	16 —		49 —	8 —
P.A.J. de Freitas	10 —	4 —		9 —	55 —	4 —	5 —	63 —	25 21*	5 —	7 —	— 36*	— 66	8 —
P. Whitticase	0 —		60 —	5* —	36 —	57 —	30 —		7 1	95* —	0 —	1 —	12 —	55 11
W.K.R. Benjamin	0 —	29* —	5* —	11* —	34* —	43* —		52* —	7 18		95* —	1 —	12 0	3* —
J.P. Agnew	5* —	1 —	5* —		16 —		1* —	2 —	5* 18	18 —	1 —		0 —	1 —
D.I. Gower		3 3*	76 —	83 —	82 —		4 —		2 —	4* 0	8 —	23 80*	4* —	
P. Gill		13 —						2 —				0* —	4* —	
L.B. Taylor					1* —						0* —		0* —	
J.C. Balderstone						2 —								3 7
P. Willey							12 —	21 0	59 3	12 —	0 34*	119 5	172* 6	17 4*
P. Bowler												100* 62		4 0
L. Tennant														
G.J.F. Ferris														
K. Higgs														
G.A.R. Harris														
Byes	4	5	4	2		4	2	1 4			5 4	9 12	3 6	1 3
Leg-byes	3	10 2	2 4		5	10	3	4 1	11 7		4 3	6 2	8 6 / 1 7	15 2
Wides	1	1	4			1		1			1	1	3 1	2
No-balls		13	7 2	7	2	2		8 3	5	18 9	3 2	2 5	14 12	11 1
Total	254	242 5	303 40	259	312	371	239 149	288 131	236 199	269 244	218 150	376 204	313 251	314 82
Wickets	9	10 1	5 2	8	9	10	8† 0	10 4	8‡ 9	10 3	10 4	4 5	3 8	10 4
Results	D	D	D	D	L	D	L	W	W	D	D	W	D	D
Points		6	8	3	4	5	4	23	22		3	24	7	5

Catches
24 – P. Gill and P. Whitticase (ct 23/st 1)
17 – L. Potter
15 – J.J. Whitaker
13 – P.B. Clift
12 – T.J. Boon
11 – I.P. Butcher
9 – R.A. Cobb and W.K.R. Benjamin
7 – D.I. Gower (ct 6/st 1) and P. Willey
6 – P.A.J. de Freitas and subs.
4 – G.J.F. Ferris
3 – J.C. Balderstone and L.B. Taylor

---

are a happy and eager side. In Hick they had the outstanding batsman of the season, and of many another season, and Curtis played admirably. Smith was rather fitful, perhaps he would be better in the middle order, and d'Oliveira very disappointing, but there is enterprise in the side, if not total self-belief. Rhodes hopefully will survive the over-praise and over-publicity he was given by Press and television and will develop into a keeper of international class. His batting showed signs of improving, and he is a likeable young man who has the potential to go far if he is not destroyed by the media who would have rushed him before he was ready. He is still below two or three other keepers in consistency and the fire which lifts a side, but that could come. What Worcestershire really lack is penetration in their bowling. Radford was again a tower of strength, and Pridgeon and Newport did well, but the spinners failed to grasp what opportunities they had, and but for this failing, Worcestershire might well have won one of the competitions in which they came so close.

Sussex need more variety in attack, but Ian Gould did a marvellous job in revitalising them. He has breathed a sense of youth and urgency into the side. There is some batting which could still come good, and we have not yet seen the best of Jones or Reeve as bowlers. Bredin and Mays are the players who could provide the extra dimension that would make Sussex the team of 1987 even without Imran.

Derbyshire leaned heavily on Kim Barnett, a good captain and a pleasant man, but their team selection was not always easy to understand. It has long since been apparent that Mortensen and Holding are one of the best opening attacks in the country, but too often the new ball was entrusted to others. Hill did well in his own solid way, and Morris batted excitingly, but Warner and the rest need to do more with the ball in support of Mortensen and Holding if Derbyshire are to prosper.

Northants flattered briefly in the Sunday League, but one cannot see their present attack bowling them to a title. The batting is quite strong, with Bailey and Lamb outstanding, but the next few years may see a need for rebuilding and more scope given to players like Wild and Capel who is a very promising all-rounder.

Warwickshire achieved some stability towards the end of the season, but, in spite of the fine form shown by Small, their attack never looked likely to bowl them to success. McMillan proved an ironic failure. Preferred to Kallicharran and Ferreira in the hope that he would strengthen the bowling, he had little success with the ball, but batted excitingly on several occasions and scored 999 runs before returning to South Africa. Like Kerr, the off-spinner, he is unlikely to return. Moles, a dedicated young cricketer and an excellent

v. Essex (Southend) 16–18 July		v. Sussex (Leicester) 19–22 July		v. Glamorgan (Leicester) 23–25 July		v. Kent (Canterbury) 2–5 August		v. Yorkshire (Leicester) 6–8 August		v. Essex (Leicester) 9–12 August		v. Worcestershire (Worcester) 16–19 August		v. Derbyshire (Chesterfield) 20–22 August		v. Northamptonshire (Leicester) 23–26 August		v. Derbyshire (Leicester) 27–29 August		v. Somerset (Leicester) 30 August–2 Sept.		v. Surrey (The Oval) 13–16 September		M	Inns	NOs	Runs	H/S	Av
23*	1	0	1	19	7			47	5	29*	0	13	25	24	—	91	—	17	45	29	7	—	5	12	19	1	273	58	15.16
13	—	10	15	3*	77			7	—	—	0	1	—									—	8	25	41	3	1092	91	28.73
25	—	0	10	—	15																	—	8	20	30	3	545	81*	20.18
46	—	3	29*	—	80	0	1	9	78*	12*	7	63	4	6	—	37	—	25	42	83	41*	—	3	23	36	10	1003	117	38.57
						100*	82*			—	5	18	14	175		51	—	0	106*	31	—	—	11	21	31	9	1504	200*	68.36
																								6	7	1	223	83	37.16
46	—	0	22	—	49																			15	16	1	370	49	24.66
19	—	15	17	—	14	106	16	5	—	—	22	25	26	11	—	19	—	17	0	9	—	—	6	26	30	2	645	106	23.03
				41*	1	0	—			—	55*	26	26	2	—	8	—	4	45	67*	—	—	24	18	21	4	554	67*	32.58
25	—											6	1	5*	—	57*	—	8	—	10	—			20	20	10	404	95*	40.40
35*	1*			—	4	9	27*			—	21			0	—	0	—	16	—					19	20	6	181	35*	12.92
		39	6			6	29							0	2									9	14	2	436	83	36.33
17	0*	6	6*	—	8																			8	11	4	68	17	9.71
			5	—	5																			15	15	6	48	10	5.33
7	—	7	115	13	4	14	11	14	48	7	18	11	2	29	—	37	—	8	12	16	18*	—	7	14	23	1	410	115	18.63
5	—	41	57			10	104			3	31	19	6			40	—	168*	0*	7	—	—	76	17	28	5	1031	172*	44.82
14	—			—	0											21	—	2	—	22	6	18	—	8	11	1	249	100*	24.90
		12*	—																			—	1	2	2	1	13	12*	13.00
		17	—			6	1	16	—	—	10											—	17*	5	6	1	67	17*	13.40
						3*	—															8	—	2	2	1	11	8	11.00
										6	0*											1		1	2	1	6	6	6.00
	5	4	2				1	1	7					2		5				1		7							
7		7	11	2	7	2	5	9	9			1		4	4	5		8		3	2	12	1	2						
		1	2			1				1		3				1		1		1	4		1							
5		4	6	2	6	4	4	4	2	4	10	13	2	11		7		3		2	2									
264	1	162	301	47	273	199	212	235	239	55	190	209	114	293		367		292	262	293	70	0	180						
10	0	10	7	1	10	10	10	9	3	2	10	10	10	10		9		10	6	10	1	0	10						
W		D		L		L		W		L		L		D		D		D		D		L							
23		5		4		4		22		4		2		6		3		7		7		1							

2 – P. Bowler and J.P. Agnew
1 – K. Higgs and N.E. Briers
†J.J. Whitaker and W.K.R. Benjamin absent ill
‡N.E. Briers, P. Gill retired hurt N.E. Briers absent hurt

example to others who aspire to make the grade, and Smith proved to be a fine opening pair.

With an all pace attack, Leicestershire should have done better in the one-day competitions than they did. In de Freitas, they had the find of the season, and Benjamin was a very useful acquisition, but their batting was vulnerable, and they seemed in search of a reliable pair of openers. Leicestershire have not done themselves justice in the past two seasons and one wonders why, for there is much talent in the county.

Another side to disappoint was Surrey who were many people's favourites to win at least one title. They had two overseas pace bowlers of quality in Gray and Clarke who could be used alternately, and in Bicknell they had the most promising of the younger pace bowlers in the country although it is very early days for him at present. Richards kept well and batted well. Stewart, if not quite fulfilling his immense promise, scored many exciting runs, and Jesty played some good innings after a bad spell. There was a lack of stability in the team, however, and no one was ever quite sure about the structure of the side, and this did not help their cause. Medlycott is a spinner of great talent and could well replace Edmonds in the England side within two years.

Glamorgan had too many players trying to establish themselves in the side to be serious contenders for any of the titles. They struggled painfully for much of the time, but

Morris is an intelligent young man and one wishes him well. The next three years will not be easy. One hopes that Greg Thomas can find the consistency and control to ally to his speed. England needs him.

The Richards-Garner-Botham saga overshadowed all else at Somerset. The bowling is weak and the heart lacking in the West country and the action of the cricket committee in deciding not to renew the contracts of Garner and Richards was correct in every detail, except perhaps in the way in which it was announced. Botham's reaction was as predictable as it was unwise and unjustified. His statements on television, radio and in the Press did nothing to help the cause of the county who had made all possible for him, and they did nothing to enhance his own reputation. The reappearance in his affairs of Tim Hudson who, having once stated that county cricket was dead and he intended to start a travelling circus of players, *Hudson's Heroes*, now stated that he wanted to take over at Lancashire and buy the three Somerset players, left one saddened that cricket is seemingly now being attacked by the *malaise* that has destroyed football. Dignity is still an essential part of the game.

Hopefully sanity will prevail at Somerset, at Lancashire and within Ian Botham. The game will survive them all. There is too much joy and hope elsewhere for it to be otherwise.

Leicestershire C.C.C.
First-Class Matches – Bowling, 1986

	J.P. Agnew	W.K.R. Benjamin	P.B. Clift	P.A.J. de Freitas	L. Potter	K. Higgs	L.B. Taylor	N.E. Briers	J.C. Balderstone
v. Cambridge University (Cambridge) 19–22 April	8–4–10–1	8–1–31–2	6–3–7–0	5.2–1–14–1	1–1–0–0				
v. Kent (Leicester) 26–28 April	16–6–27–5 34.4–12–74–3	15–8–21–1 23–7–64–1	8–3–11–2 16–3–52–1	9–3–17–2 29–6–61–4	 9–2–41–1				
v. Lancashire (Old Trafford) 30 April–2 May	19–7–38–3 16–3–58–2	28–4–93–2 23–4–92–1	34–9–87–4 29–10–49–2	19–3–66–0 27–6–74–1	 2–1–1–0				
v. Middlesex (Lord's) 7–9 May									
v. Nottinghamshire (Trent Bridge) 21–23 May		22.5–4–101–1	20–3–71–2	25–4–68–1			21–5–57–0	2–0–6–0	
v. Northamptonshire (Northampton) 24–27 May	25.1–4–81–4 4–0–12–0	20–3–74–1 3–0–18–0	29–11–60–0 19–2–58–1	26–5–54–5 2–0–15–0				11–0–54–2	39–6–120–2
v. Gloucestershire (Leicester) 31 May–3 June	15–5–45–2 13–1–63–0	 10–2–50–1	12–2–24–2 9.3–1–37–1	16–3–66–2 8–0–50–1	 4–0–17–1				
v. Surrey (Hinckley) 4–6 June	18–7–41–0 21–5–61–4	19–3–50–2 19.2–6–41–5	30–10–70–4 8–2–19–0	28–5–67–4 15–5–30–1	2–0–3–0 1–0–6–0				
v. Sussex (Hove) 7–10 June	17–2–49–1 21–5–68–2	19–5–59–2 18–2–62–0	19–8–29–3 18–8–45–3	11.4–3–17–3 19–3–61–5					
v. Indians (Leicester) 14–16 June	20–0–83–1 8–0–38–0	14–4–35–2 5–1–26–0	15.1–3–54–4 8–1–40–2	19–4–52–1 5–1–30–0					
v. Warwickshire (Edgbaston) 21–24 June	20–1–55–3 13–4–40–2	21–2–74–1 3–0–18–0		16–3–49–0 5–0–39–0	26–9–45–3 3–1–11–1		14–3–43–1 12–3–28–2		
v. Nottinghamshire (Leicester) 28 June–1 July	19–2–62–1 11–4–19–3	20–2–66–3 11.5–2–33–6		21–2–73–5					
v. Hampshire (Leicester) 2–4 July	22–4–57–1	18–6–53–1 10–7–3–0	15–5–36–1	5–0–32–0	6–2–13–0 14–9–9–0	19–7–34–3			
v. Yorkshire (Middlesbrough) 5–8 July	34–7–88–2	13–4–32–1	21.3–8–35–4	31–2–97–1	7–1–25–1				
v. Essex (Southend) 16–18 July	13–5–40–1 13–2–37–3	8.4–2–21–2	14–4–45–1 15–4–30–0	17.5–2–42–6 16.1–5–44–7					
v. Sussex (Leicester) 19–22 July			23.2–9–45–3 19–4–52–1	24–5–64–3 20–4–49–1	3–0–10–0				
v. Glamorgan (Leicester) 23–25 July	8–0–28–1		13–3–22–3 12–2–24–1	23.5–4–44–4 10–2–26–1	3–0–15–0 14–4–37–3		19–1–65–2 11–4–24–0		
v. Kent (Canterbury) 2–5 August	27–6–79–1 13–2–46–2			21–4–87–3 10.4–0–21–6			15–2–55–1		
v. Yorkshire (Leicester) 6–8 August				22.4–3–94–4 17–4–63–1	 17–1–81–10	11–4–22–5	10–2–32–0 14–7–18–2		3–0–23–0
v. Essex (Leicester) 9–12 August	22–6–55–3			20–6–50–1			17.2–3–36–2		
v. Worcestershire (Worcester) 16–19 August		12–2–36–1 17–1–70–3		13–3–31–1 11.5–2–38–1			16–6–41–0 17.1–63–2		
v. Derbyshire (Chesterfield) 20–22 August	34–8–133–3 8–4–8–1	20–2–70–0 4–1–7–0		31–6–100–2 5–11–1–0	1–0–4–0		24–7–57–3 4–0–10–0		3–3–0–0
v. Northamptonshire (Leicester) 23–26 August									
v. Derbyshire (Leicester) 27–29 August	9–2–33–0	24–1–104–1		27–4–92–5		7–3–6–0	18–4–76–2		
v. Somerset (Leicester) 30 August–2 September		11.5–1–45–5 24–2–92–1		7–0–23–2 40.3–8–96–3		7–3–6–0 18–3–43–0	12–2–28–2 25–5–106–4		
v. Surrey (The Oval) 13–16 September				24–1–66–3			12–4–36–1		
	521.5–118– 1528–55 *av.* 27.78	465.3–89– 1541–46 *av.* 33.50	413.3–118– 1002–45 *av.* 22.26	703.5–123– 2073–91 *av.* 22.78	113–31– 318–10 *av.* 31.80	36–10– 71–5 *av.* 14.20	280.3–66– 809–27 *av.* 29.96	13–0– 60–2 *av.* 30.00	45–9– 143–2 *av.* 71.50

a I.P. Butcher 2–0–4–0   b R.T. Robinson absent hurt   c D.L. Bairstow retired hurt   d G.A.R. Harris 5–0–18–0 3–1–16–0

T.J. Boon	J.J. Whitaker	P. Willey	P. Bowler	R.A. Cobb	G.J.F. Ferris	L. Tennant	Byes	Leg-byes	Wides	No-balls	Total	Wkts
								2		3	64	4
								9	1	1	85	10
							1	6		14	299	10
							5	12		6	301	9
							2	4	2	7	284	7a
												Ab.
											0	0
								12	9	7	315	5
								4		2	273	10
11–1–28–0	1–0–6–0						2	5			318	5
		5–1–15–0						3	1	8	153	6
							8	11		7	236	4
		3–1–5–0					1	17	5	8	254	10
							2	5		3	164	10
							2	2		6	158	10
							13	7		1	256	10
		10–1–41–0						7		8	272	8
		0.3–0–5–1					1	5			145	4
		20–6–43–0					4	9	1	6	322	8
								6	5		142	5
		6–1–31–0					5	10	1	4	247	10
								6		1	58	9
		16–2–50–1	1–1–0–0				8	12		16	295	7
			9–7–5–0	4–3–8–0			4	1			30	0
		13–3–18–0						14		11	309	9
							1	4	2	3	153	10
									1	3	111	10
					14–3–54–4		9	10	3	3	182	10
		29–9–40–1			7–2–18–0	4–1–11–0	4	2	3	2	186	3
							2	7	2	14	183	10
			7.4–0–38–0				1			6	150	5
		17–5–36–0			20–4–58–3			14	1	8	329	8
		1–1–0–0			6–2–19–2			1		2	87	10
					21–6–62–1			6		8	216	10
8.3–0–40–3					8–1–23–1		1	7	1	7	256	7
		9–4–9–1			15–1–58–2		5	3		5	216	10
8–1–81–2	4.2–0–41–1			6–0–33–0			2	2		1	159	3
		2–2–0–0						2		4	128	2d
1–0—4–0								8		3	199	6
								14	5	15	378	9
							2	1	1	6	39	1
												Ab.
		14.5–3–25–2	2–0–4–0					2		9	336	10
							1	10	1	14	113	9e
		22–9–51–1	6–2–10–0				2	16	6	17	416	9
2–0–17–0		13–1–49–0			13–1–64–0	4–0–24–0	6	8		11	270	4
												0	0
30.3–2–170–5 av. 34.00	5.2–0–47–1 av. 47.00	181.2–49–418–7 av. 59.71	25.4–10–57–0 —	10–3–71–0 —	104–20–356–13 av. 27.38	8–1–35–0 —						

e M.R. Davis absent hurt

Middlesex C.C. First-Class Matches – Batting, 1986

	v. MCC (Lord's) 23–25 April		v. Derbyshire (Lord's) 26–29 April		v. Oxford University (Oxford) 30 April–2 May		v. Leicestershire (Lord's) 7–9 May		v. Glamorgan (Lord's) 21–23 May		v. Sussex (Lord's) 24–27 May		v. Surrey (The Oval) 31 May–3 June		v. Worcestershire (Worcester) 4–6 June		v. Lancashire (Old Trafford) 7–10 June		v. Yorkshire (Lord's) 14–17 June		v. Nottinghamshire (Trent Bridge) 18–20 June		v. Essex (Lord's) 21–24 June		v. New Zealanders (Lord's) 28–30 June		v. Surrey (Uxbridge) 2–4 July	
G.D. Barlow	16	52*	4	—							107	3	12															
W.N. Slack	96	9	59	0*									27	—	9	14	11	—	12	30					10	—	4	0
M.W. Gatting	43	—	41	—					35	—			31	—					29	37					135	—		
R.O. Butcher	34	60	45*	8					18*	—	50	23	1	—	27	0	—	—	0	23	1	17	86	0	30	—	171	0
C.T. Radley	103*	—			—	12			5*	—	4	2			22	30			14	16	9	58	1	9	42	—	12	22
P.R. Downton	—	—			126	—							11*	—					2	22	1	53	7	36	77*	—	0	0
J.E. Emburey	—	—			10	0			0	—			4	—					49	11					15	—		
P.H. Edmonds	—	—											7*	—					5	3			1	11	31	—		
N.F. Williams	—	—			16	23*					1	11																
N.G. Cowans	—	—			—	28					5*	0*							7*	0	6	26	17	3	0	—	17*	24
W.W. Daniel	—	—													0	16	—	—			0*	8*	17*	13*			11	0*
S.P. Hughes					—	21					3*	4			30	0			18	11	1	26	14	2	20	—	4	6
A.R.C. Fraser					—	2									3	13					12	7*	0	4				
A.J.T. Miller									3	—	73	10	62	—	9	21	16*	—	5	17	5	6	12	13	56	—	7	34
K.R. Brown									9	—	31	1			9	23	25*	—			32	4	6	0				
J.D. Carr											23	1			84*	40*	—	—	57	31			1	3			34	3
G.D. Rose											7	0																
C.P. Metson											15	5			8	1												
P.C.R. Tufnell															8	9	—	—									2	1
G.K. Brown																					14	3						
M.A. Roseberry																							36	0			3	59
A.G.J. Fraser																									2	—		
J.F. Sykes																												
Byes			1	5	1	11						4			8		4		4	3	1	10		3	1		1	
Leg-byes			5	3	5	3			3		11	3	2		25		2		12	6	4	20	6	4	7		11	4
Wides						1			3		7	2	2		5	1					1	5	2				2	5
No-balls			8	2	2				5		5	1			5				4	1	3	6	2		10		6	1
Total			306	131	309	109			81		342	70	162		244	176	58		173	187	135	277	208	97	436		285	159
Wickets			4	1	5	6			4		9	10	6		10	10	1		10	10	10	10	10	10	10		10	10
Results	Ab.		D		W		D		D		L		D		L		D		L		L		L		D		L	
Points	—		7		—		3		4		6		5		3		4		3		4		6		—		7	

Catches

48 – P.R. Downton (ct 43/st 5)	13 – P.H. Edmonds and A.J.T. Miller	8 – M.W. Gatting and K.R. Brown
16 – C.T. Radley	12 – J.E. Emburey	4 – N.G. Cowans
15 – W.N. Slack and R.O. Butcher	11 – J.D. Carr	3 – W.W. Daniel, S.P. Hughes and C.P. Metson

v. Warwickshire (Uxbridge) 5–8 July	v. Somerset (Lord's) 16–18 July	v. Derbyshire (Derby) 19–22 July	v. Northamptonshire (Northampton) 26–29 July	v. Northamptonshire (Lord's) 2–5 August	v. Essex (Chelmsford) 6–8 August	v. Gloucestershire (Cheltenham) 9–12 August	v. Hampshire (Lord's) 16–19 August	v. Yorkshire (Leeds) 20–22 August	v. Sussex (Hove) 23–26 August	v. Lancashire (Lord's) 27–29 August	v. Warwickshire (Edgbaston) 30 August–2 Sept.	v. Kent (Canterbury) 13–16 September	M	Inns	NOs	Runs	H/S	Av
													5	6	1	194	107	38.80
3 —	92 57	8 100	0 106	0	15 92	47 17	1 49	105* —	46 —	83 —	51 41*	11 —	22	33	3	1205	106	40.16
				158						8	56 50*		12	12	1	628	158	57.09
13 —	9 10*	66 58	12 25*	42	3 3	33	3 4	4 —	69 —	53 —	15 0		26	37	4	1016	171	30.78
2 —	113* 8*	1 25	25 —	50	14 9	15	14 5*	13 —	15* —	71 —	28 23		25	33	4	792	113*	29.33
104 —	56 —	21 16	7 18	50	15 2	46	33* —	2 —	0 —	84 —	35* 47		23	27	5	871	126*	39.59
		0 —			15 —		21 —				8 23		13	13	1	188	49	15.66
		25 23*			8* —		5 —				6 —		12	11	3	125	31	15.62
													5	4	1	51	23*	17.00
		8 0	14	44* —	7 0*	8* —	0 —				9		21	21	7	223	44*	15.92
		0* 33	18	3	0 1	0 —		20 —					16	16	6	140	33	14.00
47 —		5 0	12* —	23	0 2	5 —	10 —	4 —		4 —	24 —		23	26	2	296	47	12.33
													6	7	1	41	13	6.83
4 —	14 78	4 29	92	39	0 5	32 32*	9 111*	2 —	44 —	44 —	38 7	30* —	23	35	4	963	111*	31.06
					32 16	66 17*		36 —	60 —				10	16	2	367	66	26.21
17 —	75 14	0 22			11 12	66	37 56	38 —	32 —	34 —	33 14	44* —	17	26	3	782	84*	34.00
52 —						9 —		6 —	0* —				5	6	1	74	52	14.80
													3	4	—	29	15	7.25
6 6*			0										6	7	1	32	9	5.33
													1	2	—	17	14	8.50
4 —	0 —		2 70*										5	8	1	174	70*	24.85
19* 11*													4	3	2	32	19*	32.00
			10		12* 26			15 —					3	4	1	63	26	21.00
8	5	2 2	6 3	7	5 1					2	1 9	4						
19 1	4 11	2 14	6 4	4	1 4	13	8	4	7	14	14 15	4 5						
1		1		12	1 1	2 2	1 1	1		3	1 2	7						
13	13 1		12	4	1	7	3	10		3								
312 18	376 184	142 323	216 226	447	116 174	349 68	155 226	252	284	432	319 231	101						
10 0	6 3	10 9†	10 2	9	10 10	10 1	10 3	10	6	8	10 6	1						
D	D	L	L	W	L	W	D	D	D	W	W	D						
4	4	4	6	24	3	20	4	6	3	24	22	0						

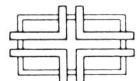

2 – G.D. Barlow, G.K. Brown and subs.
1 – P.C.R. Tufnell and M.A. Roseberry
†J.E. Emburey absent hurt

Middlesex C.C.C.
First-Class Matches –
Bowling, 1986

	N.G. Cowans	W.W. Daniel	N.F. Williams	P.H. Edmonds	J.E. Emburey	M.W. Gatting	A.R.C. Fraser	S.P. Hughes	G.D. Rose
v. M.C.C. (Lord's) 23–25 April									
v. Derbyshire (Lord's) 26–29 April	18–4–64–4	9–1–43–1	12.3–1–44–3	18–7–28–1	21–10–20–0	2–2–0–0			
v. Oxford University (Oxford) 30 April–2 May	5–1–20–0 11–4–17–2		13–2–30–1 7–0–20–1		31–21–20–4 14.5–7–12–3	2–0–5–0 7–2–21–0	17–5–25–2 8–3–18–0	12.1–4–18–3 16–4–28–3	
v. Leicestershire (Lord's) 7–9 May	20–8–47–2	20–3–79–2	20–1–86–3	7–2–11–0	2–0–10–0	11–5–20–0			
v. Glamorgan (Lord's) 21–23 May	10–3–18–0	16–4–34–4	16–4–43–2	14–3–26–0	7–3–11–2	9–4–18–2			
v. Sussex (Lord's) 24–27 May	24–5–58–0 5–1–11–0		11–1–41–0					24–4–81–2 11–2–34–1	19–5–66–1 8–1–40–2
v. Surrey (The Oval) 31 May–3 June		9–0–31–2		2–0–5–0			12–2–34–1	11.2–2–35–7	
v. Worcestershire (Worcester) 4–6 June		35–5–123–2					28–11–72–0	36–7–115–3	
v. Lancashire (Old Trafford) 7–10 June		25–2–98–4					29–5–60–0	27–6–77–4	
v. Yorkshire (Lord's) 14–17 June	13–5–26–1 13–3–49–4			40.4–10–71–4 12–3–35–1	33–6–74–3 8–0–29–1	4–2–7–1	23–5–48–1 9–2–19–3	13–7–30–0 6–2–18–1	
v. Nottinghamshire (Trent Bridge) 18–20 June	11.2–4–22–4 18–2–72–1	15–0–58–2 19–0–88–2					13–4–34–2 17–3–60–1	14–1–71–2 18–3–56–0	
v. Essex (Lord's) 21–24 June	16–2–61–5 18–4–65–2	14.2–2–27–4 18–2–60–2		11–7–5–0 2–0–7–0				4–1–21–1 17–7–35–1	
v. New Zealanders (Lord's) 28–30 June	14–2–43–3 9–2–35–1			20.2–5–31–3 29–8–67–0	20–2–53–0	11–0–36–2 10–4–25–1		8–3–27–2 15–3–57–1	
v. Surrey (Uxbridge) 2–4 July	9–3–35–0 16–3–64–2	22–4–65–4 20–0–84–2						25–7–71–3 15–1–81–0	
v. Warwickshire (Uxbridge) 5–8 July								20–4–61–2	11–2–39–2
v. Somerset (Lord's) 16–18 July	19–3–82–1 11–3–19–2	12–0–36–1 9–3–20–1						24–7–50–1 9–0–33–0	
v. Derbyshire (Derby) 19–22 July	16–2–40–3 14–2–51–2	14.5–1–52–3 20.3–4–89–4		13–5–19–1 33–10–91–2	10–3–17–1			13–1–42–2 17–4–42–1	
v. Northamptonshire (Northampton) 26–29 July	14–2–35–3 15–1–65–2	16–0–76–4 21–2–81–3						2.3–1–7–2 17–2–78–0	
v. Northamptonshire (Lord's) 2–5 August	10–0–52–0 6–2–20–1	16.3–3–50–4 18–4–55–4		9–3–15–0 34–14–57–1	8–3–10–2 33–12–75–3	2–0–9–0 1–1–0–0		11–5–20–3 7–3–27–0	
v. Essex (Chelmsford) 6–8 August	21–6–54–1	21–1–73–1						24–2–93–2	
v. Gloucestershire (Cheltenham) 9–12 August	7–1–19–0 13–4–60–3	8–1–15–2 6–1–17–1						4–1–11–0 11.4–4–40–4	4–0–16–1 4–0–32–0
v. Hampshire (Lord's) 16–19 August	18–3–63–1 6–0–19–0			21–9–24–3 16–3–54–1	14–3–26–0 15–5–38–2			17–6–37–3 6–3–13–0	
v. Yorkshire (Leeds) 20–22 August			17–9–33–3					34–10–92–4	18–2–84–1
v. Sussex (Hove) 23–26 August									
v. Lancashire (Lord's) 27–29 August	9–13–12–2 15–4–36–4				13–9–16–1 23–11–26–3	4–2–8–2 6–1–26–0		9–2–19–3 21–4–80–2	
v. Warwickshire (Edgbaston) 30 August–2 September	10–2–41–2 2–0–5–0			23–5–108–2 27–9–67–4	37–6–102–1 27–8–51–5	3–1–11–0		8–0–35–0 3–0–17–0	
v. Kent (Canterbury) 13–16 September									
	436.2–94 1380–58 av. 23.79	402.1–52 1387–52 av. 22.37	79.3–9 264–10 av. 26.40	343–103 721–23 av. 31.34	316.5–109 590–31 av. 19.03	72–24 186–8 av. 23.25	156–40 370–10 av. 37.00	530.4–125 1652–63 av. 26.22	64–10 277–7 av. 39.57

a G. Miller absent ill   b K.R. Brown 0.4–0–10–0   c G. Cook retired hurt

J.D. Carr	A.J.T. Miller	J.F. Sykes	P.C.R. Tufnell	W.N. Slack	R.O. Butcher	A.G.J. Fraser	Byes	Leg-byes	Wides	No-balls	Total	Wkts
												Ab.
								3	1	9	202	9a
							4			2	122	10
								3	4	2	119	10
							2	4		7	259	8
								9	3	7	159	10
21.2–4–46–1								8	1	3	300	5
2–0–11–0	1–0–5–0							2	1		113	3b
								4	1	2	109	10
1–0–11–0			13–3–76–0	3–0–14–1			1	9	2	10	421	6
			18–3–64–0				2	12		9	313	9
							4	16		2	276	10
							1	2	6	1	153	10
							4	3	3	4	192	10
17–1–51–0							8	11	3	9	346	4
							5	11		7	130	10
					0.4–0–5–0		4	3	1	4	179	5
						11–2–37–0	2	3		3	232	10
	1–0–1–0					9–1–46–3	6	2	3		239	6
10–5–24–0			30–10–83–1	1–0–4–0				6	1	7	288	10
11–2–30–0			25–5–81–2				2	11		11	353	6
											0	0
3–3–0–0			18–4–47–2			14.5–6–37–2		14	1	5	198	8
11–1–36–0			24–3–73–0	6–2–18–0			5	4	1	5	304	4
6–1–22–0			13–2–28–0		1–1–0–0		3	1			126	3
							1	6	1	1	177	10
							1	16	1	13	290	9
			1–1–0–0				1	6	4	4	125	10
		17.3–1–59–1	7–0–27–0				8	3		13	321	6
							1	2	1		159	9c
					1–0–3–0		5	3		6	245	10
		26–4–102–4		8–1–43–0			8	9		1	382	8
										4	61	3
11–0–53–0					9–0–37–2		6	7		3	252	10
					1–1–0–0		5	3	3		158	7
								5			129	3
							2	5		3	216	8
												Ab.
						9.5–4–12–2		4		1	71	10
						12–2–33–1	1	2		1	204	10
								3		3	300	5
							5	5			150	10
												Ab.
93.2–17	2–0	43.3–5	149–31	17–3	13.4–2	56.4–15						
284–1	6–0	161–5	479–5	75–1	49–2	166–8						
av. 284.00	av. —	av. 32.20	av. 95.80	av. 75.00	av. 24.50	av. 20.62						

Northamptonshire C.C.C. First-Class Matches – Batting, 1986

	v. Cambridge Univ. (Cambridge) 26–29 April	v. Kent (Canterbury) 30 April–2 May	v. Gloucestershire (Northampton) 7–9 May	v. Essex (Northampton) 17–19 May	v. Warwickshire (Edgbaston) 21–23 May	v. Leicestershire (Northampton) 24–27 May	v. Indians (Northampton) 31 May–2 June	v. Worcestershire (Northampton) 7–10 June	v. Warwickshire (Northampton) 14–17 June	v. Somerset (Bath) 18–20 June	v. Yorkshire (Luton) 21–24 June	v. Sussex (Hastings) 28 June–1 July	v. Surrey (The Oval) 5–8 July	v. Lancashire (Northampton) 16–18 July
G. Cook	27 —	109*	82 —	81 —	6 43	3 —		38 2		5 70			32	183 7*
A.C. Storie	13 4	26 —	0 —	9 —			1 1		32 38		29 18			
R.J. Boyd-Moss	61 18	4 —	4 —	29 —	16 18	16 53	0 79	2 0	66* 11	36 37	67 58	17 0	77 —	155
R.J. Bailey	55 42*	30* —	25 —	26 —	83 16	88 106	37 14	4 9	9 6	69 1	200* 19	7 57	5 —	17*
R.G. Williams	26 7					0 17				18 0				
D.J. Capel	45 2	— —	22 —	8 —	— 18	111 60*	0 67*	28 0	— 13	103* 10	18* 2	13 54	5 —	8*
D.J. Wild	10* 101						0 41*	0 68		85 29		36 16*		
D. Ripley	0* 14	— —	43 —	14 —		— 0	2 16*							
N.A. Mallender		— 3*	2 —					4 1*	— 4		— 4	7* 8*		
N.G.B. Cook	— 3	— —	17* —	16 —	— 16	19 —	5 —	10 7	— 3	— 2	— 13	18 1		
B.J. Griffiths			6 —	7 —		— 0*		0 —	— 5*	— 0*				
A.J. Lamb		72	50 —	1 —	12* 52		0 33			79* 8		20 157	83* —	
R.A. Harper			234 —	40 —	— 55*	10 49	12 —	47 4	— 39	2 11	— 41*	22 0	10 —	
A. Walker				— 1*		— 0*	10 40*					1 13*		
W. Larkins							8 10				12 0	11 2	9 0	17 19*
S.N.V. Waterton							0 —	36 58*	— 41	24* 11	— 4	9 3	37* —	
G. Smith							4 —							
M.R. Gouldstone														
A. Fordham														
Byes	4 5		5	7	1	2		2	6	9 4	4 8	3 1	6	4
Leg-byes	6 8	1	6	5	4 4	4 5	6	2 6	4 7	5 12	7 10	7 6	6	1
Wides			3				1 2		1			2		1 1
No-balls	2 1		5	7	3 5	2	12 2	5	5 2	5 4	11 2	3 3	2	14 7
Total	248 205	250	503	244	124 232	273 318	118 239	191 160	202 177	355 195	385 193	136 321	330 0	400 34
Wickets	6 7	3	10	10	3 7	10 5	10 4	10 8	2 10	6 10	4 7	10 9	6 0	3 0
Results	D	D	D	D	D	D	D	D	L	D	D	W	W	W
Points		6	5	2		4	—	5	5	8	6	19	20	24

Catches

37 – S.N.V. Waterton (ct 32/st 5)	16 – D. Ripley (ct 12/st 4) and G. Cook	7 – R.J. Boyd-Moss
32 – R.A. Harper	13 – W. Larkins	6 – A. Walker
22 – R.J. Bailey	12 – A.J. Lamb	4 – N.A. Mallender
21 – N.G.B. Cook	11 – D.J. Capel	3 – A.C. Storie

WOMEN'S CRICKET
Rachael Heyhoe Flint

India's first tour of England was anticipated with great interest and excitement for the visitors had a reputation of great expertise despite being the newcomers among the world's women's cricketing nations; they formed an Association in 1973.

Sadly this anticipation was soured by a series of incidents early on in the tour which upset relations between the English Women's Cricket Association officials and those of the touring Indian team..

The upsets occurred during the First Test which was staged at the picturesque club ground of Collingham outside Leeds. The day before the match, India complained that the pitch was too small for Tests – they play all their Internationals on the vast Test arenas in India.

The second incident however was far more serious than just a complaint. On the fourth and final day, England in their second innings were chasing 254 for victory and were going really well thanks to an opening partnership of 149 between England captain Carole Hodges and Test débutante Lesley Cooke – both Lancs and Cheshire players.

The trouble started in the penultimate hour; India adopted none-too subtle time wasting tactics and succeeded in bowling only 8 overs which put a dramatic halt to England's progress; the Indian players demanded that all the cars parked adjacent to the pavilion should be moved – they were dazzling them – (yet the batsmen never complained!) They sat down on the pitch and refused to play until *all* the cars were moved; they also took an interminable amount of time to set their field – although the presence of a left- and right-handed batsman did cause slight time problems.

In the last hour England needed 104 to win in the statutory 20 overs but were 25 runs short at the end.

In the immediate post match ceremonies, England chairman Cathy Mowat in her first year as head of the WCA, criticised the Indians over the microphone to the crowd and inferred that in 1987, the spectators would see 'real cricket' when the Australians came to tour England. Understandably such comments deeply upset the Indians and the manner in which the criticism was levelled hardly won the Gold Rose Award for Diplomacy!

In the week which followed before the Second Test at Blackpool, India's manager Ashutosh Sharma threatened that his team would pull out of the series if Cathy Mowat did

v. Glamorgan (Swansea) 19–22 July	v. Middlesex (Northampton) 26–29 July	v. New Zealanders (Northampton) 30 July–1 August	v. Middlesex (Lord's) 2–5 August	v. Glamorgan (Northampton) 6–8 August	v. Somerset (Wellingborough) 9–12 August	v. Essex (Colchester) 16–19 August	v. Nottinghamshire (Northampton) 20–22 August	v. Leicestershire (Leicester) 23–26 August	v. Hampshire (Northampton) 27–29 August	v. Derbyshire (Derby) 3–5 September	v. Yorkshire (Scarborough) 10–12 September	v. Nottinghamshire (Trent Bridge) 13–16 September	M	Inns	NOs	Runs	H/S	Av
14 —	6 21	— —	26* 2	120 —	12 10	8 9	3 27*	— —	— —	34 31	47 26		22	30	4	1084	183	41.69
													8	11	—	171	38	15.54
68 0	2 34	1	6 3	148* —	0 11*	10 7	9	—		25 0	10 4	25 5	27	42	3	1192	155	30.56
224* 74*	1 38	95 —	5 13	9* —	11* —	63 5	98 —	—		10 114	47 18	16 39	27	41	8	1805	224*	54.69
		93 —											5	7	—	161	93	23.00
48 —	18 0	48* —	0 27			40 11	17 —			2 5	14 20	3 7	27	35	6	847	111	29.20
5 —		8 —					12 —				6 74	19 13	14	21	3	608	101	33.77
		1* —					1		4 26*	1 134*	20 25		13	15	5	301	134*	30.10
	1		10* 0			10 3*	1* —		0 2	11 11*	37 0*		22	20	10	119	37	11.90
8* —	1		37 2		4	17 23	17* —		30 4	5 45	22 6		27	27	3	351	45	14.62
													10	6	3	18	7	6.00
	12 160*		0 117	56 —	83 —	81 27			32 159	1 14	19 24		15	22	4	1294	160*	71.88
88 —	30 3		27 20*	— 12*		13 39	4		24 35				25	30	4	933	234	35.88
	0* —		12 0			0* 2			0*	1* —	7* 0*		19	15	10	87	40*	17.40
5* 40*	26 28		16 43	86 —	59 47	29 34	2 20*		0	40 40	20 27		17	29	4	664	86	26.56
10 —	13 13*		16 4			24 11			0 14				14	17	4	314	58*	24.15
		35 —											2	2	—	7	4	3.50
		4 —								3 —			1	1	—	35	35	35.00
												5 17	2	3	—	26	17	8.66
5	1 8		1 5	2		1 7	4 1		2	5	3 13	6 12						
6	6 3	3	2 3	7	5	6 3	6 1		6	11	6 13	6 10						
3	4	1	1	1			1				1 3	1						
5	4 13	11	6	12	11	4				11	4 7	10 1						
489 114	125 321	300	159 245	441	185 80	302 181	179 49		0 169	421	197 422	216 186						
6 1	10 6	6	9† 10	3	5 2	10 10	8 0		0 10	10	10 8	10 9						
D	W	D	L	D	D	W	D	D	L	D	D	D						
5	20	—	2	6	5	24	4	2	0	7	3	6						

2 – B.J. Griffiths, D.J. Wild and subs.

1 – R.G. Williams and G. Smith

not offer a public apology. Ms Mowat refused to apologise commenting that she stood by what she said so it was left to the placatory diplomacy of Audrey Collins, the WCA president to cool the whole upset – and the tour continued. The Indian players were deeply upset by the whole affair although there was never any animosity between the players of the two sides.

The one day series for the Micro-Diet Cup went to England 3-0; the Indians always admit that the one day game is not their strength.

For the first one day international at Leicester England welcomed the return of Janette Brittain who missed last season, through choice, to concentrate on golf; two Yorkshire newcomers came into the England team – Amanda Stinson, 20-year-old wicket-keeper and left arm seamer Gill Smith (21).

India made 190 for 6 in 48 overs (3 hours) with a stylish 72 from Sandyha Aggarwal who was to score prolifically throughout the tour; Jackie Court, England's vice captain hit an agressive 67, augmented by 44 from Brittain to guide England to a five wicket win with 1.4 overs to spare.

The second one day international at the Indian Gymkhana Club, Osterley, which England won by six wickets, produced more controversy because the pitch turned out to be totally unsuitable for a match of international status – and again the Indians were understandably upset; they were bowled out for 65 in 33.2 overs but the ball reared and shot alarmingly making batting a dangerous game. India's last 7 wickets fell for 18 runs as they lost heart on such an appalling wicket.

The final one day game at Banstead CC started late because the coach sent to collect the Indians went to the wrong hotel; many of the crowd left before the game started not knowing what was happening; a more efficient PA system would have prevented this exodus.

The match was reduced to 40 overs; England made 140 for 9 in the 2¼ hours batting (37 overs), Hodges and Brittain put on 56 for the second wicket in 16 overs, and Court contributed an entertaining 32.

India's target was 3.78 runs per over but skilful bowling by left arm spinner Gill McConway (3 for 21) and four run outs completed England's whitewash in the series as England won by 41 runs.

In the three four-day Tests for the Uni-Vite Trophy India seemed intent on not losing; they had promises of great financial support from the Government of India for their future cricket development if they returned home with creditable results, so this perhaps accounted for their safety first tactics which hardly made for attractive cricket.

Northamptonshire C.C.C
First-Class Matches – Bowling, 1986

Match	N.A. Mallender	B.J. Griffiths	N.G.B. Cook	D.J. Capel	R.G. Williams	D.J. Wild	R.J. Bailey	R.A. Harper	R.J. Boyd-Moss
v. Cambridge University (Cambridge) 26–29 April	12–5–35–1 / 14–4–22–1	17–5–55–1 / 12–4–20–1	21–14–18–1 / 12–8–12–1	10–5–18–2 / 12–1–56–1	10–7–12–0 / 7–2–10–0	6.3–4–4–4 / 4–2–4–0	1–1–0–0		
v. Kent (Canterbury) 30 April–2 May	25–5–69–1 / 17–3–38–1	18–7–58–1 / 18–5–45–1	24–11–30–2 / 24–8–51–2	19–7–42–1 / 13–2–43–1			3–1–8–1	28–7–70–2 / 27–13–39–2	5–0–20–0
v. Gloucestershire (Northampton) 7–9 May	25–9–61–1	22.3–3–72–1 / 4–1–5–0	15–3–48–0	23–7–61–0 / 4–1–9–0			4–3–2–0	24–7–49–2	5–0–14–0
v. Essex (Northampton) 17–19 May		7–3–18–2						4–2–2–0	
v. Warwickshire (Edgbaston) 21–23 May		9–1–36–1 / 11–2–35–1	21–6–39–3 / 14–0–37–0	16–5–39–3 / 5–0–34–0				9.3–4–10–2 / 11–5–9–0	13–3–39–3
v. Leicestershire (Northampton) 24–27 May		17–1–56–1	46–13–83–2	13–4–36–0	21–5–52–1			44–17–84–5	0.3–0–0–1
v. Indians (Northampton) 31 May–2 June			20–2–89–1	10–3–34–1		11–2–42–1		10–2–30–0	1.3–0–13–0
v. Worcestershire (Northampton) 7–10 June	8–6–5–0 / 10–0–40–0	10.2–3–19–1 / 18–5–59–4	39–18–72–6 / 26–10–50–2	4–1–12–0	15–2–59–2	6–1–27–0		25–5–58–1 / 3–0–12–0	
v. Warwickshire (Northampton) 14–17 June	21–4–41–2 / 7–1–14–1	20–4–46–1 / 8–2–34–0	36–16–48–0 / 14–3–48–2	18–2–49–1 / 7–1–29–1		6–0–15–1 / 10–0–58–1		34–10–52–2 / 12–1–38–0	5–1–6–0
v. Somerset (Bath) 18–20 June	20–6–68–2 / 15–5–64–2	13.4–4–33–2 / 15–3–62–2	15–6–29–2 / 7–4–9–2	11–3–40–2 / 11.5–0–50–0		9–2–36–2 / 4–0–13–1		7–3–11–0 / 21–6–45–1	
v. Yorkshire (Luton) 21–24 June	19–6–58–3 / 13–0–57–1	14–1–67–1 / 4–0–21–0	7.5–1–33–1 / 6–1–25–1	11–1–57–1 / 12–0–73–2		10–0–35–0		20–7–52–0 / 12.5–0–60–3	
v. Sussex (Hastings) 28 June–1 July	13.5–3–28–1 / 12–5–26–0		34–11–72–3 / 16–6–30–0	12–0–30–2 / 12–0–48–2		3–0–10–0 / 6–0–17–1		29–8–79–3 / 5–1–9–0	4–1–14–0
v. Surrey (The Oval) 5–8 July	16–6–34–1		12–2–44–2	20–4–70–3		11–1–28–1		16–8–32–2	
v. Lancashire (Northampton) 16–18 July	11–3–39–2 / 24–5–49–0		13–10–6–0 / 30.1–9–56–2	6–2–10–1 / 23–4–62–3		2–0–11–0		18–8–33–0 / 34–18–41–3	
v. Glamorgan (Swansea) 19–22 July	29–8–67–2 / 13–3–30–4		24–9–37–0 / 5–0–30–0	24–5–63–1 / 7–1–40–0		7–0–24–0		41–16–71–3 / 18–7–39–4	
v. Middlesex (Northampton) 26–29 July	16–3–37–2 / 17–3–54–1		23–10–38–3 / 21–5–42–0	9–1–28–1 / 11–0–35–1				21–4–51–1 / 13–3–25–0	
v. New Zealanders (Northampton) 30 July–1 Aug.			10–2–25–0	11–2–25–1	21–6–57–0	24–4–50–3	3–0–35–0		3.1–1–7–0
v. Middlesex (Lord's) 2–5 August	30–4–96–2		26–6–74–2	25–4–110–2				26–6–71–1	
v. Glamorgan (Northampton) 6–8 August	21–5–63–2 / 7–1–13–0		39–12–77–3 / 16–5–27–0	15–2–33–1 / 3–3–0–0			4.5–2–2–1	43.3–15–83–4 / 14–7–20–0	14–8–23–1
v. Somerset (Wellingborough) 9–12 August	17–6–35–1 / 11–3–40–0		8–3–17–0 / 11–2–25–1	24–8–42–3 / 19–3–61–5				18.4–5–50–3 / 12–4–32–0	
v. Essex (Colchester) 16–19 August	27–1–110–5 / 9.1–0–22–4		32–7–76–4 / 10–4–14–5	9–1–55–0				24–7–52–1 / 1–0–5–0	
v. Nottinghamshire (Northampton) 20–22 August	25–4–81–1		13–5–26–1 / 10–2–33–2	31.5–9–84–2 / 7–1–28–0		4–0–21–0 / 9–1–34–0		29–12–50–4	
v. Leicestershire (Leicester) 23–26 August	23–4–64–0		31.2–10–69–4	22–4–72–1				29–11–77–3	
v. Hampshire (Northampton) 27–29 August	13–1–33–1		25–6–81–0	12–4–33–0				25–5–66–0	8–1–21–0
v. Derbyshire (Derby) 3–5 September	22–8–57–0 / 10–1–33–1		29–16–43–1 / 33–10–71–1	26–5–86–7 / 15–4–37–1				29–14–37–2 / 10–4–27–0	2–0–5–0 / 19–4–70–2
v. Yorkshire (Scarborough) 10–12 September	21–3–67–0		24–7–78–1	25–4–89–2				25–6–48–1	
v. Nottinghamshire (Trent Bridge) 13–16 September	11–3–33–1 / 6–0–30–0		6–3–4–1 / 21–3–74–0	16–6–49–2 / 8–0–35–0				7.5–4–10–3 / 44–13–71–4	
	611–137–1693–47 av. 36.02	238.3–54–741–21 av. 35.28	870.2–289–1890–64 av. 29.53	592.4–120–1907–57 av. 33.45	74–22–190–3 av. 63.33	132.3–17–429–15 av. 28.60	15.5–7–47–2 av. 23.50	825.2–275–1700–62 av. 27.41	80.1–19–232–7 av. 33.14

c Maynard retired hurt   d P.H. Edmonds retired hurt

A.J. Lamb	A. Walker	G. Cook	G. Smith		Byes	Leg-byes	Wides	No-balls	Total	Wkts
						8	2	2	150	10
					4	1		3	129	4
						3	2		272	7
2–2–0–0					1	5	1	1	250	8
						10		1	301	4
									30	0
	3–1–3–0								23	2
	13–5–33–1				3	5	3		165	10
	13–1–40–1	10–1–28–1			3	6			231	7
	17–1–46–0				4	10		2	371	10
	15–2–49–1		17–4–38–1		4	2		1	301	5
					6	14		2	272	10
					4	3	1	1	168	6
					2	7		4	266	8
					4	5	1		230	6
						11	5		228	10
					10	8	1	1	241	8
						12	2	1	314	6
						4			240	8
	11–2–37–0				8	5		5	283	9
	13–4–42–0					1			173	3
									0	0
	14–5–14–1					8			230	10
	23–6–50–6				1	5		7	144	9c
	22–4–59–2				4	6		17	288	10
	19–1–71–0					7	3	11	340	6
	12–1–52–1				4	1		7	196	9
	21–6–50–3				6	6		12	216	10
	15–2–63–0				3	4			226	2
	13–2–41–0					6	1		246	5
	19–3–85–2				7	4		4	447	9d
	6–2–11–0	1–1–0–0			4	11	1	15	282	10
	10–2–34–1	6–2–10–0			4	5		3	138	3
	18–3–60–3				3	3		1	210	10
	6–0–31–0				1	5		5	195	6
	9–0–36–0					8		19	337	10
					2	1		7	44	10
	22–6–55–2				4	7	1	10	328	10
	7–1–19–0					4		1	118	2
	19–3–72–1				5	8	1	7	367	9
	18–0–87–1				2	15		5	338	2
									0	0
			9–0–33–0			6	10	5	267	10
			14–4–61–1		5	8	1		312	6
	19–4–56–2				6	8		3	352	7
	17–6–40–2				2	7	1		145	10
	28–3–78–3				11	14		1	313	8
2–2–	422–76–	17–4–	30–8–							
0–0	1314–33	38–0	132–2							
–	av. 39.81	—	av. 66.00							

Nottinghamshire C.C.C.
First-Class Matches – Batting, 1986

	v. Hampshire (Trent Bridge) 26–28 April	v. Surrey (The Oval) 30 April–2 May	v. Oxford University (Oxford) 7–9 May	v. Leicestershire (Trent Bridge) 21–23 May	v. Derbyshire (Derby) 24–26 May	v. Hampshire (Southampton) 31 May–3 June	v. Somerset (Trent Bridge) 4–6 June	v. Essex (Chelmsford) 7–10 June	v. Surrey (Trent Bridge) 14–17 June	v. Middlesex (Trent Bridge) 18–20 June	v. Leicestershire (Leicester) 28 June–1 July	v. Warwickshire (Trent Bridge) 2–4 July	v. Worcestershire (Worcester) 5–8 July	v. Yorkshire (Worksop) 16–18 July
R.T. Robinson	65 48	7 4		— 104	5 31	8 —			52 —	17 67	12 —			105 —
B.C. Broad	18 68*	37 8		— 4	9 34	12 —	52 2	8 11	2 —	22 4	0 0	116 —	23 23	122 —
D.W. Randall	18 7	5 4	101* —	— 26	43 31	17 —	21 10	25 60	46 —	0 8	9 11	8 —	34 4	
C.E.B. Rice	76 31			— 86	120 1	11 —	8 87*	30 27	3 —	17 156*	10 2	70 —	3 37*	49 —
P. Johnson	11 17*	33 46	— 91	— 22	9 71	25 —	51 —	128 20	11 —	29 26	80 5	44 —	15 38*	105* —
J.D. Birch	24 —	62 37	— 26*	— 36*		11 —	79* —	0 17	67* —	46 54*				
R.J. Hadlee	1 —	105* 8		— 9*	30* 20	44 —	129* —	43 3	32 —			41 —	76 —	
B.N. French	12 —	37* 5				16 —	— —	30 17*	36 —		11 11			
E.E. Hemmings	23 —	— 6			3 —			10 1	1 —	16 —	3 17	1 —	13 —	
K.E. Cooper	10* —				0 —	6 —		5 17	9 —	14* —				
J.A. Afford	0 —	— 0*			0 —	0* —		9* 0						
R.A. Pick		29 8*				5 —				7 —	55 0	10 —	1 —	
K. Saxelby		— 5								32* 0*	34 —	1* —		
M. Newell			112* —		28 26*		4 51*	0 43				17 —	80 15	3* —
D.J.R. Martindale			— 88								9 4	14 —		
K.P. Evans														
C.W. Scott					11 7*						10 —	69* —	38* —	
P.M. Such									2 —		0 —		6 1	
C.D. Fraser-Darling														
Byes		8	1		4		2	8 7		4 8	5	8	6	4
Leg-byes	7 10	11 13	13 4	12	17 7	2	2 2	3 8	20	3 11	10 6	5	16 1	11
Wides		1	1 1		9	2	1 3	2	3	3 3	1	4	10 4	2
No-balls		1	1	7	4 3	5	3		10	4 9	4 1	10	10 4	3
Total	265 181	327 152	228 211	0 315	279 235	162	350 157	299 233	294	192 346	247 58	451	310 128	404
Wickets	10 3	6 9	0 2	0 5	10 6	10	5 2	10 10	10	10 4	10 9	10	8 3	3
Results	L	D	W	W	D	D	D	D	W	W	L	D	D	W
Points	5	7	—	20	7	3	5	7	23	21	3	8	8	24

Catches
36 – B.N. French (ct 32/st 4)
27 – C.E.B. Rice
24 – P. Johnson, J.D. Birch and C.W. Scott (ct 23/st 1)
19 – B.C. Broad
16 – M. Newell (ct 15/st 1)
15 – R.T. Robinson
14 – D.W. Randall
7 – E.E. Hemmings
6 – R.J. Hadlee
5 – R.A. Pick
4 – K. Saxelby, K.E. Cooper and J.A. Afford

On cricketing matters, the Collingham Test produced a maiden Test century for India's acting captain Shubhangi Kulkarni – a partner in a sports shop business in Poona with Sunil Gavaskar. India were depleted by the absence of their captain Diana Edulji who broke a finger in practice the day before the Test.

India made 323 in their first innings; England in reply made 198 for 9 – Lesley Cooke chipped in with 72, Sarah Potter-back in favour with the selectors made 86 not out and Janette Brittain could not bat – she had a broken finger sustained while fielding, which also prevented her playing in the Second Test.

England did well to bowl out India for 128 in their second innings; Avril Starling took 3-63 to give her 7 wickets in the match; the target of 254 was quite manageable, in even time, but England did not cater for the unsporting tactics of the Indians which incensed the sizeable Yorkshire crowd. No overall number of overs per day had been written into the Tour's Special Regulations to counteract this occurrence.

The second Test turned into a boring batting exercise on the superb Blackpool wicket; India occupied the crease until tea on the second day in accumulating 426 for 9; Sandyha Aggarwal made 132 but the go-slow condemned the match to a draw once England had avoided the follow-on.

Janet Powell, Yorkshire's captain brought back for the Blackpool Test made 115 not out in England's reply of 350 for 6 declared – the closure of their innings came at the start of the last day – 76 runs behind. India were not prepared to throw out a challenge by a quick declaration and the match ended in a drab draw,

England showed how quick runs should be scored on the first day of the Third Test at Worcester; superb centuries from Carole Hodges and Janette Brittain put England at 332 for 7 at the close; the overnight declaration put the onus on India; but they failed to respond and batted for the whole of the second day in reaching 232 for 6 with Aggarwal 114 not out; she was dropped in the last over – a costly miss in hindsight. Aggarwal carried on where she had left off on the third day, she crawled to 190 in 563 minutes receiving 523 deliveries thus beating the 51-year-old record of Betty Snowball who scored 189 for England against New Zealand in Christchurch in the first ever Test between the two countries in 1935.

By coincidence, at the moment Aggarwal broke the long standing record, Betty Snowball, now 78 years old, was just 8 miles away in her cottage in Colwall quite oblivious of Aggarwal's feat at the County Ground at New Road. Betty Snowball's comment later was 'About time it was broken!'

	v. New Zealanders (Trent Bridge) 19–21 July	v. Lancashire (Southport) 23–25 July	v. Yorkshire (Sheffield) 26–29 July	v. Gloucestershire (Cheltenham) 6–8 August	v. Lancashire (Trent Bridge) 16–19 August	v. Northamptonshire (Northampton) 20–22 August	v. Derbyshire (Trent Bridge) 23–26 August	v. Kent (Trent Bridge) 27–29 August	v. Sussex (Hove) 30 August–1 Sept.	v. Glamorgan (Cardiff) 3–5 September	v. Essex (Trent Bridge) 10–12 September	v. Northamptonshire (Trent Bridge) 13–16 September	M	Inns	NOs	Runs	H/S	Av
	7 26	97 —	4 90*	108 —	0 23*		47* —	52 159*	4 0*	45 47	10 64	1 43	20	32	5	1352	159*	50.07
	47 70	51 —	7 15	105 —	12 66	92 43	0 —	8 47	116 4*	0 56	120 20	27 112	25	42	2	1593	122	39.82
						5 —							14	22	1	493	101*	23.47
		43 —	47 65*	33* —	— —			0 —	41* —	4 15	5 4	20 17	22	31	6	1118	156*	44.72
	3 0	23 —	15 —	— —	36*120*	24 1		4 —	65 —	37 0	23 7	15 0	26	37	5	1250	128	39.06
	31 25	0 —	18 18	— —	— 15	3 16*		44 —	23* —	20 24	0 5	6 11	21	28	7	718	79*	34.19
								88 —		0 15	21 55*		14	18	5	720	129*	55.38
	5 32*							17 —		1 58	18 0		15	16	3	306	58	23.53
	20 10*	26* —	9 —			31 —		0 —		0 19*	25 19	23 54*	21	23	4	330	54*	17.36
	0 —	5* —	0* —								19 —	3 17*	17	13	5	105	19	13.12
						4 —		0* —		0* 4	2* —	0* —	16	12	7	19	9*	3.80
	26 0	14 —	19 —			16* —		16 —		6 9		0 1	19	17	1	206	55	12.87
	25* —		11 —										10	8	5	124	34	41.33
	53 26	33 —	47 —	23* —	19* 61	29 53*	26* —	0 34*	46 —	2 0	14 6	0 11	19	30	9	862	112*	41.04
													3	4	—	115	88	28.75
	0 14		4 —			1 —							4	3	—	15	14	5.00
		41 —				40 —							10	8	3	220	69*	44.00
	— —												5	4	—	9	6	2.25
				20 —		61 —						40 21	5	4	—	142	61	35.50

	NZ	Lancs(S)	Yorks	Gloucs	Lancs(TB)	Northants(N)	Derbys	Kent	Sussex	Glam	Essex	Northants(TB)
	4 8	5 —	4 —	4 —		4 —	1 —	1 —	12 —	2 13	2 —	2 11
	3 6	9 —	4 —	4 —	2 2	7 4	2 —	10 1		7 —	6 2	7 14
	1 —	2 —			2 1	1 —			5	1 1	2 —	1 —
	2 2	1 —	2 —	3 —	1 7	10 1	2 —			3 2		1 —
	227 219	350	191 188	300	72 295	328 118	78	240 241	312 4	121 260	267 184	145 313
	10 7	8	10 2	3	2 3	10 2	1	10 1	4 0	10 10	10 8	10 8
	D	D	D	D	W	D	D	W	D	W	W	D
	—	8	5	7	17	5	3	22	8	20	7	4

3 – P.M. Such and C.D. Fraser-Darling
1 – K.P. Evans and sub.

Her innings was scored at a run a minute and after she had scored her century Miss Snowball was trying to get out 'because I thought the crowd would like to see someone else batting!' The Worcester crowd longed for a similar reaction from Aggarwal.

Aggarwal's record breaking innings earned her the Sunday Telegraph Cricketer of the Week Award of a case of Moët et Chandon champagne; such a shame in a way, because Aggarwal is a teetotaller; it was also a shame that her innings was largely instrumental in another yawning draw which did little for the image of women in cricket, who long to offer to sponsors an attractive alternative in the game.

In India's lengthy first innings, Gill McConway produced remarkable figures of 7 for 34 off 42 overs which included 27 maidens as India progressed gingerly to 374 all out. Only a frustrated head-high beamer from Gill Smith brought to an end Aggarwal's remarkable concentration. England made 253 for 7 in the second knock, highlighted by a superb maiden century from Sarah Potter who improved match by match throughout the summer.

Sandyha Aggarwal was named Player of the Series but it was questionable whether her ability to accumulate runs slowly really was sufficient criteria to give her the ultimate award.

Australia tour England in 1987 and it is the pious hope that this will produce more attractive cricket. Australia has made great strides in development in the last five years with an enormous upsurge in sponsorship, growth of clubs and media coverage; the Australian Women's Cricket Council now has a paid Executive Director, Ray Snedden – a professional at his role; such an appointment for the England Women's Cricket Association would benefit the game greatly for still, after 60 years, they suffer from lack of publicity and sponsorship with consequently dwindling numbers at school and club level.

Uni-Vite Tests and One Day International Series 1986
ENGLAND v. INDIA

Leicester, 22 June

One Day International

England won the toss

India 190 for 6 (48 overs innings closed 3 hours) (S. Agarwal 72, S. Kulkarni 31, S. Shah 28, A. Starling 2 for 28)
England 191 for 5 (46.2 overs) (J. Court 67, J. Brittain 44, S. Potter 30, S. Gupta 2 for 21)

England won by 5 wickets

Nottinghamshire C.C.C. First-Class Matches – Bowling, 1986	R.J. Hadlee	K.E. Cooper	C.E.B. Rice	E.E. Hemmings	J.A. Afford	K. Saxelby	R.A. Pick	P. Johnson	R.T. Robinson
v. Hampshire (Trent Bridge) 26–28 April	18–4–54–1 5–0–19–0	24–13–30–3 5–0–33–0	17–4–54–4 5–0–32–0	21–9–24–0 15.1–2–67–1	28–9–71–0 10–0–54–0				
v. Surrey (The Oval) 30 April–2 May	20–3–60–0			29–10–83–2 26–7–95–4	19.5–4–88–1 20.4–3–75–1	16–5–62–2 5–1–18–0	16–2–65–1 10–2–45–1	2–0–18–0	2–0–18–0
v. Oxford University (Oxford) 7–9 May					16–9–18–3 10–3–11–1	8–3–15–0 13–2–44–0	8–3–13–1 17–7–26–4		
v. Leicestershire (Trent Bridge) 21–23 May	17–5–41–5	19–3–42–1	14–2–60–1		14–1–47–0		15–2–84–1	2–1–16–0	
v. Derbyshire (Derby) 24–26 May	18.5–6–31–6 17–3–43–1	13–4–32–2 10–5–17–2	10–3–16–1	18–9–19–0 34–10–90–0	23–5–63–2 38–15–71–5				
v. Hampshire (Southampton) 31 May–3 June	11–7–14–1	8–3–18–1	6–3–10–2				8–1–37–1		
v. Somerset (Trent Bridge) 4–6 June	27–8–38–0 4–2–3–0	28–0–96–2 9–2–26–3	17–1–63–0		31–3–140–0 17–0–98–1		33–11–110–2 3–0–15–0	7–0–35–0	
v. Essex (Chelmsford) 7–10 June	21.2–6–36–2 11–3–31–1	10–3–23–0 6–0–23–0	12–5–17–0 5–2–12–1	42–15–102–7 35–9–62–3	13–4–49–0 26–7–78–0				
v. Surrey (Trent Bridge) 14–17 June	17–4–39–4 15.3–6–33–6	8–1–22–3 10–2–22–0	9–2–23–2 15–3–40–1	1.2–0–8–1 16–3–47–0					
v. Middlesex (Trent Bridge) 18–20 June		14–5–26–3 25.1–11–43–3	10–0–32–1 8–3–16–1	6.3–4–12–4 32–10–57–1			13–4–39–2 27–4–85–3		
v. Leicestershire (Leicester) 28 June–1 July			16–5–43–2 9–3–23–0	24–6–72–0 18–4–47–0		18–4–69–1 7–1–23–2	16.5–3–96–0 17–2–58–3		
v. Warwickshire (Trent Bridge) 2–4 July	18–6–42–6 25–7–44–3		9–3–16–0 14–3–45–0	8.3–4–19–3 39–18–61–2		6–1–15–0 24–3–72–3	10–3–35–1 18–3–73–0		
v. Worcestershire (Worcester) 5–8 July	16–7–24–4 12–1–38–2		19–5–54–1	1–0–10–0 33–4–154–2	36–10–113–1	21–3–47–4 8–0–38–0	12–4–36–1 10–1–28–0		
v. Yorkshire (Worksop) 16–18 July		14–4–30–1 12–2–19–2	9–4–28–0 10–5–21–1	27–15–50–3 8.5–3–13–1		14–2–48–0 11–2–35–3	21.1–4–68–6 17–6–41–3		
v. New Zealanders (Trent Bridge) 19–21 July		21–5–49–2 15–3–37–0		27–11–90–2 11–4–30–0		17–2–75–2 6–2–8–1	14.5–2–54–2 10–1–22–1		
v. Lancashire (Southport) 23–25 July		7–5–4–0 11–2–38–0	10–4–12–0	28–12–70–5 43–14–105–5			15.3–4–48–3 12–0–48–0		
v. Yorkshire (Sheffield) 26–29 July		14–4–34–3 10–2–38–0	15–5–34–2 12–2–34–3	15–0–67–3		9–1–22–1 8–0–32–0	20–7–50–3 9–0–40–0		
v. Gloucestershire (Cheltenham) 6–8 August		39.4–8–102–5 12–2–37–2	9–2–33–0 14–3–40–2			25–8–81–3 11–3–50–0	18–5–45–1	3–0–25–0	
v. Lancashire (Trent Bridge) 16–19 August		11–3–12–0	17–6–31–2	32–9–90–1		26–5–89–2		5–0–19–0	
v. Northamptonshire (Northampton) 20–22 August				2–2–0–0 1–0–6–0	1–0–1–0	25–5–49–3 6–1–13–0			
v. Derbyshire (Trent Bridge) 23–26 August		18–4–45–1	17–5–32–2	42–10–107–5	18–4–44–1		12–4–19–1		
v. Kent (Trent Bridge) 27–29 August	11–2–16–3 11–3–20–0		4–0–16–0 2–1–8–0	18–4–51–2 26–8–59–4	10–2–22–4 33.2–11–81–6		10–3–33–1 7–2–28–0		
v. Sussex (Hove) 30 August–1 September	15–7–18–3 26–4–60–1		12–4–35–3 16–2–84–1	15–4–52–1 26.2–6–96–2			10.2–3–38–1 19–1–76–2		
v. Glamorgan (Cardiff) 3–5 September	15–5–19–2 10–5–5–0		14–5–32–1 6–1–10–0	19–4–51–0 25.5–10–45–6	30–7–80–5 29–7–71–4		15.3–3–27–2 3–0–8–0		
v. Essex (Trent Bridge) 10–12 September	16–3–51–6 16–1–46–0	5–0–39–0 12–5–28–1	9.2–3–18–3 20–9–34–2	7–4–20–0 25–7–42–2	6–2–10–1 14–2–72–1				
v. Northamptonshire (Trent Bridge) 13–16 September		10–3–28–1 10–2–33–2	14–4–33–3 8–3–20–2	5–2–18–0 15–6–43–1	25.5–11–43–4 23–12–55–4		19–1–67–2 2–0–13–0		
	393.4–108– 825–57 av. 14.47	410.5–106– 1026–43 av. 23.86	413.2–115– 1111–44 av. 25.25	818.3–259– 2134–73 av. 29.23	492.4–131– 1455–45 av. 32.33	284–54– 905–27 av. 33.51	469.1–98– 1570–50 av. 31.40	19–1– 113–0 —	2–0– 18–0 —

K.P. Evans	P.M. Such	D.W. Randall	B.C. Broad	C.D. Fraser-Darling	J.D. Birch	M. Newell	Byes	Leg-byes	Wides	No-balls	Total	Wkts
							3	5	1	3	241	8
							2	2			209	1
								7	2	8	365	7
								3		1	272	6
4–0–12–0	19.3–10–36–5						2	2	3		98	10
10.2–3–19–1	19–10–20–4						1	10	1		131	10
		3–0–17–0						5		2	312	9
											0	0
								6			151	10
							1	10	1		248	9
								1		3	80	5
							1	11		3	459	4
							5	3		1	185	4
							3	10		2	240	10
							4	12			222	5
								3		3	95	10
	16–7–39–3						4	7	1	2	192	10
	9–2–21–0						1	4	1	3	135	10
	20–7–46–2						10	20	5	6	277	10
	27–4–82–1		1–0–6–0					8		2	376	4
	14–4–47–0							6	1	5	204	5
								2		1	129	10
								8	2		303	8
							1	20	1	3	192	10
							2	7	1	2	380	5
3–0–16–0								3			243	10
3–1–22–0								2		3	153	10
11–2–53–0								5			326	8
11–1–61–0							2	5	3		165	2
	20–6–57–2							3	1		182	10
	26–3–90–2						4	4		5	301	7
								6		4	146	10
							5	17		1	233	9
				14–1–70–1				14	1	4	345	10
			6–1–35–0	14–1–55–1	3–0–4–0			3		1	249	5
				24.2–4–87–2			6	9		2	324	8
					3–1–4–1	2–0–19–0					42	1
9–1–35–0				25.4–6–84–5			4	6	1	4	179	8
				7–0–28–0			1	1			49	0
							9	19			275	10
								2			140	10
							7	6	1		209	10
				7–1–36–1			3			2	182	10
				23–3–86–2	5–0–16–0		4	8		7	430	8
								10	3	2	219	10
							3	6			148	10
								1		1	139	10
							1	9	4	1	232	6
				5–0–15–0			6	6	1	10	216	10
							12	10		1	186	9
51.2–8–218–1	170.3–53–438–19	3–0–17–0	7–1–41–0	120–16–461–12	11–1–24–1	2–0–19–0						
av. 218.00	av. 23.05	—	—	av. 38.41	av. 24.00	—						

Somerset C.C.C. — First-Class Matches – Batting, 1986

Each cell shows first-innings and second-innings scores (— = did not bat).

Batsman	v. Oxford University (Oxford) 19-22 April	v. Yorkshire (Taunton) 26-28 April	v. Derbyshire (Chesterfield) 30 April-2 May	v. Glamorgan (Taunton) 7-9 May	v. Gloucestershire (Taunton) 21-23 May	v. Glamorgan (Cardiff) 24-27 May	v. Sussex (Horsham) 31 May-3 June	v. Nottinghamshire (Trent Bridge) 4-6 June	v. Hampshire (Bournemouth) 7-9 June	v. Kent (Bath) 14-17 June	v. Northamptonshire (Bath) 18-20 June	v. Indians (Taunton) 28-30 June	v. Kent (Maidstone) 2-4 July	v. Hampshire (Taunton) 5-8 July
P.M. Roebuck	0 —	60	14	76*	10	40 4*		221* —	6 10	2 —	0 62	23 4	5 5	33 102*
J.G. Wyatt	40 —													
J.J.E. Hardy	39 —	79	73	24 —	28	8 —		46 0	59 37	33 —	50 50	11 34		65 —
N.A. Felton	0 —	29	24	55				51 37	9 56	26 —	7 5	28 104	30 6	25 156
R.J. Bartlett	117* —			18*								0 19		
B.C. Rose	0 —	18	28					43* 24	37 14	107* —	18 34		5 5	
V.J. Marks	9 —	16	27	12*	65	0 16		15*	83* 14*	68	20 35*	19 0*	24 61	19
R.J. Blitz	0 —									18 0				
M.R. Davis	3 —		3								19* 21*			
N.S. Taylor	3 —			—	24*	3					17*		13 0*	0
C.H. Dredge	12* —	24	5		5	4			11* 4				40 1	5 —
I.V.A. Richards		25	22	102	4	136 15		6 65	9 29	128	59 0		29 31	12
I.T. Botham		30	61		61	49 47								
R.V.J. Coombs		4*									1	1		
T. Gard		1	0*	4*	36	30 5*					0	23 10		4* —
J. Garner		1	16						1*		6		20* 26*	6
R.J. Harden				8	81	42 10		77 35*	20 32	51	17 14	4 36	20 102	30
M.S. Turner				—										
G.V. Palmer					11	17 0					1 0	2 —		
J.C.M. Atkinson												10 12*	13 16	4
M.D. Harman														
D.J. Foster														
N.J. Pringle														
P.A.C. Bail														
Byes	3	5	4		3	1 4		1 5		1		1 1	4	1 5
Leg-byes	3	8	16	4	12	10 6		11 3	5 1	10	11 8	8	15 4	4 2
Wides	1		3	3	2	1 1		3 2		1	5 1	1	7 1	5 2
No-balls	6	18	13	10	5	13 2		3 1	2	6		1	3 3	18 6
Total	236	0 318	309	300 16	348 0	359 111	Ab.	459 185	262 200	433	228 241	128 213	249 272	231 273
Wickets	9	0 10	10	4 0	10 0	10 6		4 4	7 8	6	10 8	10 5	10 9	10 0
Results	D	L	D	D	W	D	Ab.	D	D	W	D	D	D	D
Points		1	8	4	20	6	0	6	7	24			6	3

Catches 36 – T. Gard (ct 30/st 6)
19 – I.V.A. Richards
12 – J.J.E. Hardy, R.J. Harden and P.M. Roebuck
8 – J. Garner, I.T. Botham, N.A. Felton, R.J. Blitz and V.J. Marks
7 – C.H. Dredge
4 – R.J. Bartlett and subs.
3 – R.V.J. Coombs and B.C. Rose
2 – M.R. Davis and N.S. Taylor

Collingham, Leeds, 26, 27, 29, 30 June

First Test

India won the toss and batted

India 323 (S. Kulkarni 118, M. Desai 54, G. Banerji 38, A. Starling 4 for 61, S. Potter 3 for 52, G. McConway 2 for 56) and 128 (K. Venkatachar 34, S. Gupta 33*, A. Starling 3 for 26, G. McConway 2 for 11, S. Potter 2 for 17, G. Smith 2 for 30)

England 198 for 9 (innings closed J. Brittain absent hurt) (S. Potter 86*, L. Cooke 72, S. Rangaswamy 4 for 24, S. Gupta 3 for 57) and 229 for 5 (L. Cooke 117, C. Hodges 68, S. Rangaswamy 2 for 72)

Match drawn England 25 runs short, India bowled only 7 overs in the penultimate hour

Blackpool, 3, 4, 6, 7 June

Second Test

India won the toss and batted

India first innings 426 for 9 dec (S. Aggarwal 132, G. Banerji 60, S. Kulkarni 78, R. Venugopal 55, R. Punekar 47, G. McConway 2 for 38, A. Starling 2 for 69) and 176 for 2 dec (G. Banerji 75, S. Shah 62 n.o.)

England 350 for 6 dec (J. Powell 115 n.o. L. Cooke 64, S. Potter 49, J Court 42, D. Edulji 3 for 92, S. Kulkarni 2 for 97) and 54 for 2 (C. Hodges 25)

Match drawn

Worcester, 12, 13, 14, 15 July

Third Test

England won the toss and batted

England first innings 332 for 7 dec (J. Brittain 125, C. Hodges 121 n.o. D. Edulji 4 for 94, S. Sridhar 2 for 46) and 253 for 7 dec (S. Potter 102, C. Hodges 46, J. Court 42, S. Gupta 3 for 50)

India 374 (S. Aggarwal 190, S. Kulkarni 35, M. Singhal 35, G. McConway 7 for 34, G. Smith 2 for 68) and 54 for 1 (S. Aggarwal 24 n.o.)

Match drawn S. Aggarwal's 190 world record in women's Tests

Osterley, 26 July

Second One Day International

(55 overs)

India 65 (33.2 overs) (S. Potter 3 for 11, G. McConway 3 for 12)
England 68 for 4 (34 overs) (C. Hodges 25)

Banstead, 27 July

Third One Day International

(Reduced to 40 overs)

England 140 for 9 (2¼ hours 37 overs) (J. Court 32, C. Hodges 31, A. Gosh 4 for 17, D. Edulji 3 for 40)
India 99 (36.3 overs) (S. Aggarwal 23, G. McConway 3 for 21)

Batting and bowling averages (County matches)

	v. Middlesex (Lord's) 16–18 July	v. Gloucestershire (Bristol) 19–22 July	v. Worcestershire (Weston-s-Mare) 2–5 August	v. Warwickshire (Weston-s-Mare) 6–8 August	v. Northamptonshire (Wellingborough) 9–12 August	v. Surrey (Taunton) 16–19 August	v. Sussex (Taunton) 20–22 August	v. Essex (Taunton) 27–29 August	v. Leicestershire (Leicester) 30 August–2 Sept.	v. Worcestershire (Worcester) 3–5 September	v. Lancashire (Old Trafford) 10–12 September	v. Derbyshire (Taunton) 13–16 September	M	Inns	NOs	Runs	H/S	Av
	128* 3		68 147*	4*		14 5	31* 9	39 —	10 24	2 72	22 33		22	35	8	1288	221*	47.70
		0 13		20 5			3 —						4	6	—	81	40	13.50
	2 5	11 0							11 19	19 8	24 5	52 —	19	29	—	863	79	29.75
	5 53*	4 19	52* 0	— 1		28 14		— 37	4 110	16 8	40 6	41 —	23	37	3	1030	156*	30.29
			6 56						23 11	35 43			6	9	2	307	117*	43.85
	129 —		— 71*		76* 96*	1 17	48* 3	110	4 56	2 23*	43* 33	4 —	14	23	5	784	129	43.55
	2* 7*	18 26				76* 33	— 37		2 7				25	36	12	1057	110	44.04
													5	5	—	33	18	6.60
		14* 0				3 —			6* 1	13 1*		1 —	9	7	3	63	21*	15.75
							— 2	12 —	2 2	0* 7		1 —	16	18	6	107	24*	8.91
		11 8						24 4*	23 7	14 0	0 25	0 —	17	21	3	227	40	12.61
		35	36 4	74* 115		0 43	— 7	53 94		10 74	0 17		18	28	1	1174	136	43.48
		18 0*	104* 17			16 0	— 34	67 41		0 17	139 1	36 —	12	19	1	804	139	44.66
		1 0				8 —	— 0*			— 0*			9	6	3	31	18	10.33
		14 47				13 19*	— 16	5 —	0 0	3 3	6 0	17 —	20	25	6	228	36	12.00
						11 —	— 27	— 0	3 3	0 32*			18	15	4	182	47	16.54
	23 54	1 28	10 28	— 8*		33 53*	— 16	108	14 4	8 63	21 6 / 22 13	1 —	22	36	3	1093	108	33.12
													1	—	—	—	—	—
												16* —	4	6	—	31	17	5.16
							8* —	4* 0		15 0			4	6	2	71	16*	17.75
							0 —						3	5	2	27	15	9.00
													1	1	—	0	0	0.00
									10 11				1	2	—	21	11	10.50
										55 47	0 —		2	3	—	102	55	34.00

Bowling (wickets)

	Mid	Glo	Wor	War	Nor	Sur	Sus	Ess	Lei	Woc	Lan	Der
	5 3		1	1	2 1	3 1	4 3	1		4	1 2	3 / 2 1
	4 1	12 5	5 13	7 1	3 5	1 1	1 2	1 8	10 16	2 2	11 5	8
	1			1 1	1 1				1 6		2	
	5	8 7	5 4	2 4	1 5	3 4	4	1	14 17	7 13	3 2	2

Team totals

	Mid	Glo	Wor	War	Nor	Sur	Sus	Ess	Lei	Woc	Lan	Der
	304 126	147 154	286 341	186 232	210 195	83 166	333	200 263	113 416	127 209	408 182	182
	4 3	10 10	4 5	1 3	10 6	0 10	10	10 10	9† 9	10 10	10 10	10
	D	L	W	D	D	L	D	L	D	L	L	L
	6	4	20	2	4	4	3	6	4	2	8	0

1 – G.V. Palmer and M.D. Harman
†M.R. Davis absent hurt

India tour of England 1986 – County and Representative matches

Ealing, 11 June (45 overs)

India 147 for 9 (42 overs) (S. Rangaswamy 47, K. Jobling 3 for 28)
President's XI 144 for 8 (42 overs) (L. Cooke 73, S. Rangaswamy 3 for 26)

India won by 3 runs

Teddington, 13 June (40 overs)

India 166 for 7 (38 overs) (S. Aggarwal 73, S. Kulkarni 33, A. Wright 2 for 29, J Green 2 for 31 J. Hall 2 for 35)
Civil Service 91 for 8 (38 overs) (D. Edulji 2 for 14)

India won by 75 runs

Osterley, 14 June

India 135 for 5 dec (S. Shah 48*)
Middlesex 107 (J. Court 47, D. Edulji 4 for 16, S. Kulkarni 3 for 20)

India won by 28 runs

Woking, 15 June

India 263 for 3 dec (M. Desai 120*, S. Rangaswamy 99)
Surrey 201 for 1 (J. Brittain 124*, G. Davis 60*)

Match drawn

Gravesend, 17 June (55 overs)

India 210 for 3 (55 overs) (S. Aggarwal 111*, S. Kulkarni 69)
South East England 163 for 7 (55 overs) (M. de Boer 62*)

India won by 47 runs

Gravesend, 18 June (55 overs)

South East England 62 (39 overs) S. Rangaswamy 3 for 14, A. Ghosh 4 for 11)
India 65 for 2 (29 overs) (G. Banerji 36*)

India won by 8 wickets

Tring, 20 June

India 198 for 7 dec (G. Banerji 44, S. Shah 40, G. McConway 3 for 28)
East Anglia 83 for 3 (E. Wulcko 43*)

India batted from 11.30 a.m. until 4.02 p.m. E. Anglia had 18 minutes plus 20 overs batting time

Nottingham, 24 June (55 overs)

India 147 for 6 (52 overs) (G. Banerji 35, S. Kulkarni 36*, A. Goacher 3 for 23)
East Midlands 89 (47 overs) (S. Rangaswamy 3 for 12, G. Banerji 3 for 8)

India won by 58 runs

Somerset C.C.C. First-Class Matches – Bowling, 1986	M.R. Davis	N.S. Taylor	V.J. Marks	C.H. Dredge	J. Garner	I.T. Botham	R.V.J. Coombs	I.V.A. Richards	P.M. Roebuck
v. Oxford University (Oxford) 19–22 April	4–3–1–1	2–2–0–0	4–2–4–0	4–2–5–1					
v. Yorkshire (Taunton) 26–28 April			38–9–90–2	25–7–64–2	10–2–27–0	10–4–20–0	31–8–95–0	6–0–11–0	
v. Derbyshire (Chesterfield) 30 April–2 May	9–0–44–0 22–3–73–1		27–9–83–1	12–0–47–1 21–6–49–0	14–1–34–2 21–5–45–1	18–1–61–3 13–1–45–0		11–3–36–4 18–5–56–1	12–2–30–1
v. Glamorgan (Taunton) 7–9 May		7–3–8–0 19–4–59–1	12–1–38–2		7.5–0–18–2 23–3–53–3			15–4–25–1	
v. Gloucestershire (Taunton) 21–23 May		3–1–4–0 10–1–41–3	10–2–28–0	12.4–3–36–3	16–3–35–4	8–0–27–0		3–1–7–0	
v. Glamorgan (Cardiff) 24–27 May		12–2–35–0 3–0–20–0	43–11–112–6 31.3–7–100–8	13–1–40–0 11–4–21–1	15–4–41–0 18–6–36–1	12–3–29–1 13–4–28–0		10–1–31–0 5–0–23–0	
v. Sussex (Horsham) 31 May–3 June									
v. Nottinghamshire (Trent Bridge) 4–6 June		13–4–57–0 10–2–39–0	33–8–108–1 18–1–65–0	11–2–58–2 7–3–30–1	20–4–85–2 6–0–16–1			9–0–40–0 3–1–3–0	
v. Hampshire (Bournemouth) 7–9 June		17.4–2–78–3 24–7–84–2	12–4–30–1 12–1–40–0	24–4–90–3 19.5–3–68–2	19–6–49–3 14–8–14–0			8–1–25–0	
v. Kent (Bath) 14–17 June			30.3–12–65–2 32.1–20–43–3	18–6–42–1 15–2–26–0	18–9–29–4 22–7–56–5		28–7–60–3 21–11–48–2		
v. Northamptonshire (Bath) 18–20 June	18.1–2–67–2 17–2–49–2		29–10–73–1 13.2–5–28–3		15–1–57–1 12–2–25–1			18–2–55–2	
v. Indians (Taunton) 28–30 June		26–3–81–1	21–5–71–2				9–2–37–0		
v. Kent (Maidstone) 2–4 July		10–2–38–2 22–3–88–1	10.1–4–15–2 25.5–3–87–0	14–4–35–2 20–1–51–3	17–2–56–4 20–4–52–1			2–0–7–0 7–4–7–0	
v. Hampshire (Taunton) 5–8 July		14–2–50–2	11–2–40–0	18–3–48–1	6–3–5–0			14–6–30–1	5–1–15–0
v. Middlesex (Lord's) 16–18 July	21–3–76–0 6–0–23–0		32.1–10–73–1 17–2–76–1	17–2–55–1 6–1–16–0	23–7–57–1 5–2–7–0		29–8–101–2 12–0–46–2		
v. Gloucestershire (Bristol) 19–22 July	16–1–66–2		6.3–3–18–2	20–5–88–1	20–6–59–4		10–2–36–0	8–2–17–0	
v. Worcestershire (Weston-super-Mare) 2–5 August	11–3–55–1 2.4–0–9–0		33–13–66–0 4–0–17–0		13–3–37–1	20–3–70–1 8–1–55–0	24–3–87–1 4–1–19–0	8–1–41–0 6–0–40–0	7–0–75–0
v. Warwickshire (Weston-super-Mare) 6–8 August	18–2–62–0 9–0–63–0		29–6–79–1 31–9–74–2		16–1–40–1 3–0–7–0		24.5–6–82–2 30–6–82–0	4–0–10–0 3–1–6–0	
v. Northamptonshire (Wellingborough) 9–12 August			1.5–1–3–1 7–1–47–1		17–3–73–3 3–2–1–0	12–1–73–0 3–1–7–0	5–1–31–1 7–0–25–1		
v. Surrey (Taunton) 16–19 August		13–1–75–2	24–5–88–2		19.1–0–62–2	14–2–58–1	21–3–95–2	3–0–30–0	
v. Sussex (Taunton) 20–22 August		3–0–6–0	3–1–16–1		6–1–15–0				
v. Essex (Taunton) 27–29 August		15–5–40–4 25–9–58–2	39–10–99–2	5.3–1–10–3 21–6–51–1		21–5–77–3 7–2–32–0			
v. Leicestershire (Leicester) 30 Aug.–2 Sept.	13.4–2–43–2	11–2–39–0 7–0–38–1	12–2–37–1	14–3–36–1 6–1–26–0		43–12–125–6 2–2–0–0			
v. Worcestershire (Worcester) 3–5 September		19–1–85–0	29–4–106–2	16–4–32–1		22.1–4–65–2			
v. Lancashire (Old Trafford) 10–12 September		21.4–3–66–2 26–3–102–2	12–4–41–4 38–1–103–1	8–3–20–0 20–2–67–1		21–8–43–3 25–5–98–2			
v. Derbyshire (Taunton) 13–16 September		9–0–31–1	12.5–1–58–3	9–1–40–3		13–2–48–0			
	167.3–21– 631–11 av. 57.36	342.2–62– 1222–29 av. 42.13	744.5–189– 2121–59 av. 35.94	388–80– 1151–35 av. 32.88	419–95– 1091–47 av. 23.21	285.1–61– 961–22 av. 43.68	255.5–58– 844–16 av. 52.75	161–32– 500–9 av. 55.55	24–3– 120–1 av. 120.00

a J.J.E. Hardy 1–0–5–0 N.A. Felton 1–0–8–0   b N.J. Pringle 10–0–48–0

D.J. Foster	B.C. Rose	M.D. Harman	M.S. Turner	G.V. Palmer	R.J. Harden	J.C.M. Atkinson	Byes	Leg-byes	Wides	No-balls	Total	Wkts
							1		3		11	2
							1	15		2	323	5
											0	0
5–0–29–0								1		3	223	10
							6	14	2	6	438	5a
			15–3–55–2							3	26	2
										12	230	9
				4–0–14–0	2–2–0–0			1	1		19	0
				4–0–22–0			8	7	1	6	211	10
				8–0–15–0	1–0–3–0		3	5	2	1	314	7
				5–1–14–0				1	4	8	243	10
												Ab.
								2	1	3	350	5
							2	2	3		157	2
					3–1–15–0			11		5	298	10
					8–0–35–0			4		2	245	4
					2–0–13–0		14	3		1	226	10
							8	2	1	4	183	10
			20–2–89–0				9	5		5	355	6
			22–4–77–4				4	12		4	195	10
			18–2–59–1		15–2–55–2	24–6–80–2	2	4	5	2	389	8
								4		9	155	10
					4–0–8–0	4–0–18–0	5	8		1	324	6
						6–1–34–0	4	9	2	2	220	4
					4–0–24–2			2			41	2
					3–0–10–0			4		13	376	6
							5	11		1	184	3
							16	8	1	4	308	10
					3–0–8–0		1	14		4	379	4
					1–0–4–0					1	247	2
	6–0–28–2				4–0–21–0		2	6	2	7	302	4
							6	1	1	2	239	2
								5		11	185	5
											80	2
					2–0–7–0		8	4		5	427	9
											0	0
5–0–29–0										5	66	1
		39.3–11–88–1						2		2	129	10
							6	9			343	7
							1	12		2	293	10
					2–0–5–0			1	1	2	70	1
							2	7		1	345	5b
								1		3	171	10
		21–1–61–0						14	2	1	445	6
							1	6		3	184	7
5–0– 29–0 —	11–0– 57–2 av. 28.50	60.3–12– 149–1 av. 149.00	15–3– 55–2 av. 27.50	81–9– 290–5 av. 58.00	54–5– 208–4 av. 52.00	34–7– 132–2 av. 66.00						

Surrey C.C.C. — First-Class Matches – Batting, 1986

Batsman	Worcs (Worcester) 1	2	Notts (Oval) 1	2	Warwick (Oval) 1	2	Sussex (Hove) 1	2	Middx (Oval) 1	2	Leics (Hinckley) 1	2	Derby (Oval) 1	2	Notts (Trent Br.) 1	2	Hants (Basingstoke) 1	2	Camb U (Camb.) 1	2	Gloucs (Bristol) 1	2	Middx (Uxbridge) 1	2	Northants (Oval) 1	2	Kent (Oval) 1	2
A.R. Butcher	15	71	7	11	0	—	50	—							1	21	0	7	157	—	7	26	34	2				
G.S. Clinton	19	28	6	61	60	—	98	—	20	—	73	31	7	—	5	18	22	20	23	—	5*	34	7	16*		28	34	5
A.J. Stewart	53	4	19	76	76	—	37	—	10	—	56	20	1	1*	18	15	8	4	36	—	65*	52	8	144		18	55	166
M.A. Lynch	3	22	152	27	128*	—	59	—	7	—	1	8	3	45	10	1	0	0	33	—	13	23	8	48		36	23	10
T.E. Jesty	17	18	99	9	9	—	6	—	15	—			3	—	5	55	0	0	43	—							0	39
A. Needham	52	0			2	—	18	—	34*	—	44*	27			5	48	7	0	0	—	8	8				0		
C.J. Richards	27	31	14	50*	31*	—	18	—	4	—	1	7	49	—	25	2	56*	13			16	0	20	100		3		
D.J. Thomas	0	35																										
G. Monkhouse	10	1*			—		34*	—	0	—	0	1*	51	—									14*	—			31	24
S.T. Clarke	5	0	—	—			4		0				0						0*	—			14*	—				
P.I. Pocock	0*	0*	—	—			14		1		11	7	5*		0*	4	10	0*			9	0	0			6		
D.M. Ward			3	34									9	0					20*	—			20	8*		28		
M.A. Feltham			23*	0*																	20*	—				0		
R.J. Doughty			25*	—			14		5		8	18	61	—	1	5	16	17	21	—	17	9				41*	24	4
A.H. Gray			—	—									0	7	18	0	11	0			2	4				10	28	4*
N.J. Falkner							6				20	28	14	46*					1	9*	9	40*	102	4		45	0	48
M.P. Bicknell													2	—					1	0	0	0	0	—		7		
K.T. Medlycott																			27	—			61	7			0	0
G. Winterborne																												
G.E. Browne																											0*	2*
Byes	6	2			4						1	2	7	1	4				8			1	2				1	1
Leg-byes	10	14	7	3	22		9		4		17	5	11	1	3	7	5	1	4		5	6	6	11		8	1	14
Wides	3		2						1		5		1		1		3	1	1		1		1				4	1
No-balls	6	2	8	1	4		4		2		8	3	8	2	3	2	5	1	2		2	12	7	11				4
Total	226	218	365	272	336		365		109		254	164	223	96	95	192	144	64	375		158	215	288	353	0	230	201	322
Wickets	10	9	7	6	5		10		10		10	10	10	1	10	10	10	10	8		9†	10	10	6	0	10	10	9
Results	D		D		W		D		D		L		W		L		L		D		L		W		L		W	
Points	6		6		24		4		2		7		22		4		2		—		5		23		2		22	

Catches

44 – C.J. Richards (ct 39/st 5)
38 – M.A. Lynch
15 – A.J. Stewart
12 – R.J. Doughty
10 – T.E. Jesty and G.S. Clinton
9 – S.T. Clarke and K.T. Medlycott
7 – N.J. Falkner and subs.
6 – P.I. Pocock, G. Monkhouse, A.R. Butcher and A. Needham

Nelson, 9 July (50 overs)

India 152 for 9 (50 overs) (S. Rangaswamy 42, C. Hodges 5 for 24)
Lancs & Cheshire 92 (48 overs) (G. Banerji 3 for 9, S. Shah 3 for 17)

India won by 60 runs

West Whitkirk, 10 July (50 overs)

India 174 for 4 (47 overs) (S. Aggarwal 85, S. Gupta 38, J. Aspinall 2 for 23)
Yorkshire 147 for 8 (47 overs) (H. Plimmer 45, S. Rangaswamy 3 for 12)

Ross on Wye, 17 July (55 overs)

India 187 for 8 (47 overs) (M. Singhal 48, S. Sridhar 63*, C. Handley 3 for 51)
West 157 for 6 (47 overs) (S. Potter 67)

India won by 30 runs

Maidenhead, 19 July

India 186 for 5 dec (S. Kulkarni 78*, R. Venugopal 64*, M. Leath 3 for 22)
West Midlands/Thames Valley Combined XI 141 for 5 (R. Flint 53, B. Daniels 30*, A. Ghosh 2 for 16)

Match drawn

Slough, 20 July (55 overs)

India 211 for 8 (55 overs) (S. Shah 69*, G. Banerji 55, T. Britton 3 for 39, R. Flint 2 for 16)
Thames Valley/West Midlands Combined XI 123 for 8 (R. Flint 52, S. Shah 3 for 32, A. Ghosh 2 for 16)

India won by 88 runs

Cheltenham, 22 July

Young England 107 (A. Ghosh 6 for 47 off 18 overs)
India 108 for 2 (G. Banerji 68)

India won by 8 wickets

Cheltenham 23 July (55 overs)

India 192 for 5 (49 overs) G. Banerji 47, S. Aggarwal 45)
Young England (Rain reduced, 35 overs, target 138) 116 (34.1 overs) (S. Potter 52, D. Edulji 5 for 33)

India won by 22 runs

Match columns (each match has two innings sub-columns, 1 and 2):
Y = v. Yorkshire (Leeds) 19–21 July · E-O = v. Essex (The Oval) 23–25 July · Su = v. Sussex (Guildford) 26–29 July · La = v. Lancashire (The Oval) 6–8 August · Wo = v. Worcestershire (The Oval) 9–12 August · So = v. Somerset (Taunton) 16–19 August · Ke = v. Kent (Dartford) 20–22 August · E-C = v. Essex (Chelmsford) 23–26 August · Gl = v. Glamorgan (Swansea) 27–29 August · Go = v. Gloucestershire (The Oval) 3–5 September · Le = v. Leicestershire (The Oval) 13–16 September

Y1	Y2	E-O1	E-O2	Su1	Su2	La1	La2	Wo1	Wo2	So1	So2	Ke1	Ke2	E-C1	E-C2	Gl1	Gl2	Go1	Go2	Le1	Le2	M	Inns	NOs	Runs	H/S	Av
				11	26			45	—	29	—	8	12	23	—	69	—	2	0			16	25	—	634	157	25.36
26	84*			31	12			2	—	117	—	23	1	55	—	44	—	0*	1	11	—	23	35	4	1027	117	33.12
90	0	67	—	7	12	13	69	24	—	78	—	61	105	4	—	23	—	3	86*	81	—	25	39	3	1665	166	46.25
0	14	85	—	28*	63	72	7	77	—	14	—	119*	47	16	—	11	—	0	4	17	—	25	39	3	1234	152	34.27
4	0	221	—	27*	1	24	71	179	—			11	4	23	—	13	—	7	38	56	—	20	30	1	997	221	34.37
		3	—																			11	17	2	256	52	17.06
24	16	40*	—	—	35*	33	46*	60	—	70*	—	21	4	3	—	18*	—	115	0	54*	—	23	34	9	1006	115	40.24
		0*	—	—	45*	0	10	34	—	27	—	47*	0	19*	—	5	—					9	12	4	222	47*	27.75
2	1			—	—	7*	—															10	12	4	162	51	20.25
				—	—	13	29			21	—	—	32*			16*	—	22	—			14	13	4	156	32*	17.33
0*	10			—	—	0*	0*	16*	—			—	—									21	20	9	93	16*	8.45
																				26*	—	4	6	1	100	34	20.00
				0	15			16	—	11	—	—	25*	5	—			76	18	—	—	12	14	5	237	76	26.33
48	28	—	—															25	—			15	19	2	387	61	22.76
6	6	—	—					12*	—													11	14	2	108	28	9.00
0	0	5	—			95	68			37	—											11	18	2	567	102	35.43
																		1*	—			9	10	2	21	9*	2.62
47	1	—	—	—	—	5	5	0	—	3	—					9	—	0	23	—	—	14	15	1	197	61	14.07
														9*	—							1					
																						1	2	2	2	2*	—

Bowling / fielding block:

Y1	Y2	E-O	Su1	Su2	La1	La2	Wo	So	Ke1	Ke2	E-C	Gl	Go1	Go2	Le
9	4	2	1	3	4	5	7	8	2		7	6	8		6
9	5	20	8	8	5	9	20	4	5	1	2	5	3	7	8
2		5	3	2	3	1	7		5	3			2	5	1
2	2		5		3	2	3	1	7	5	3				11

Match totals:

Y	E-O	Su	La	Wo	So	Ke	E-C	Gl	Go	Le
269 171	448	200 249	190 295	500	427 0	300 245	166	210	256 191	270
10 10	5	3 5	9‡ 8	9	9 0	5 8	7	6	9† 6	4
L	D	W	W	D	W	D	D	D	D	W
5	8	22	21	6	20	6	5	0	7	19

5 – G.E. Browne (ct 4/st 1)   1 – D.M. Ward, D.J. Thomas
4 – A.H. Gray and *M.P. Bicknell   and M.A. Feltham
†G.S. Clinton retired hurt   ‡G. Monkhouse retired hurt

Book Reviews

PLAYING DAYS: *Tony Lewis*: Stanley Paul: 251 pp, £9.95
This book is one of the year's great delights. It is elegant, witty and honest. At times critical, but never vindictive, it is an objective account of fourteen years in first-class cricket and a few in top class rugby. Above all, it throbs with the fun of a life enjoyed in sport, and it gives the warmest and most revealing of pictures of cricket at the highest level. The anecdote concerning Boycott's leaving the field before lunch in an exhibition game in Hong Kong because of bad light tells more about that complex Yorkshire character than any vehement volume has done, and the Test match diary of the series in India and Pakistan is more compelling than any cricketer's diary which has been elongated into a book and presented to us in recent years. The revelations concerning Javed Miandad and Glamorgan are as fascinating as they are sad, and the assessment of players throughout is honest and objective. All is presented with an ease of writing which makes this the most readable cricket book of the year. It should be made compulsory reading for any cricketer who suffers memoirs, revelations or diary to be published in his name.

AN AUSTRALIAN SUMMER: *Patrick Eagar*: Kingswood Press: 125 pp, £9.95
A collection of photographs of the Texaco Trophy and Cornhill Test matches of 1985, *An Australian Summer* is a fine black and white pictorial record of the main matches of the season. The photographs reveal both character and incident and are ably supported by Alan Ross's commentary which, if limited, is always lucid and apposite. In splendour, the book does not compare with the same author's book on Botham, but it is still an interesting record.

BOTHAM: *Patrick Eagar*: Kingswood Press: 159 pp, £9.95
An exciting collection of photographs of one of the most exciting cricketers the game has known is a recipe for success, and this book does not disappoint. Patrick Eagar is one of the four best cricket photographers in the world, and I do not think that he has put together a better collection than these studies of the great all-rounder over the past decade. It is interesting to note the change in style, fashion and appearance. There are many moments of joy and exhilaration, very few of anguish and several of leisure and other pursuits. The reproduction in both colour and black and white is excellent. This is, indeed, a lovely book and a beautiful record of a great player in his happiest moments.

THE CRICKET COACHING MANUAL: *Frank Tyson*: Pelham Books: 207 pp, £8.95
There can be few people more qualified to write a coaching manual than an experienced and intelligent teacher who has played cricket at the highest level and has coached in both England and Australia, again at the highest level. Frank Tyson can muster these qualifications and his manual is a credit to his good sense and lucidity as well

Surrey C.C.C.
First-Class Matches – Bowling, 1986

	S.T. Clarke	D.J. Thomas	G. Monkhouse	P.I. Pocock	T.E. Jesty	A.R. Butcher	R.J. Doughty	M.A. Feltham	A.H. Gray
v. Worcestershire (Worcester) 26–28 April	24–8–57–3 27–6–69–5	24–7–64–2 9–0–40–0	21.5–10–37–4 14–0–60–1	11–2–25–0 5.4–3–18–1	8–6–3–0 13–3–56–1	3–1–14–1			
v. Nottinghamshire (The Oval) 30 April–2 May	23–11–32–1 18–4–38–3			26.1–5–79–0 23–5–45–4	4–0–27–0	2–1–4–1	24–6–101–2 13–5–19–1	18–1–77–3 6–2–25–0	
v. Warwickshire (The Oval) 7–9 May			13–2–41–1 9–3–15–2	1–1–0–0	5–2–3–1		12.1–5–44–2 11–5–39–1		17–2–83–6 13.3–4–30–6
v. Sussex (Hove) 21–23 May	5–3–7–1						3–0–12–1		
v. Middlesex (The Oval) 31 May–3 June	16–3–46–2		16–3–46–1	4–0–17–0	7–1–14–2		13–0–37–1		
v. Leicestershire (Hinckley) 4–6 June			31–10–87–1 13–4–25–1	15–7–48–1			21.3–5–52–4 10–1–43–2		29–6–92–4 15–4–58–1
v. Derbyshire (The Oval) 7–10 June	18–3–43–5 13.4–5–30–3		12–2–44–0 9–3–31–1	5–1–29–0 6–4–8–1	4–3–3–0		9.2–2–17–3 11–3–38–1		
v. Nottinghamshire (Trent Bridge) 14–17 June				20–7–44–1	3–0–18–1	5–1–12–0	15–1–54–1		23–3–59–4
v. Hampshire (Basingstoke) 18–20 June				23–3–81–1		14–2–52–0	17–3–76–2		19–3–59–1
v. Cambridge University (Cambridge) 21–24 June						20–6–31–3 23–10–25–4	3–0–6–0 18–4–42–1	28–13–36–3 5–3–4–0	
v. Gloucestershire (Bristol) 28 June–1 July			6.5–2–27–2 24–6–48–0			5–0–25–0 4–1–8–1	12–1–55–2 14–3–50–2		15–4–36–3 31.2–6–68–2
v. Middlesex (Uxbridge) 2–4 July	10–2–45–1			9–1–35–1 23.1–11–45–4				6–1–34–0 7–3–17–0	
v. Northamptonshire (The Oval) 5–8 July							20–1–100–2	18–1–74–3	23–1–66–1
v. Kent (The Oval) 16–18 July			7–3–11–0		2–1–7–0		13–1–41–1 3–1–7–0		24–3–61–2 10.4–3–23–7
v. Yorkshire (Leeds) 19–21 July			20–5–59–0 8–3–8–1	16–6–40–1 7–3–17–1			15–0–57–0 5–1–18–0		14–3–36–3 11–1–56–1
v. Essex (The Oval) 23–25 July		12–2–44–2 13–1–44–2	27.2–8–57–1 9–4–16–0				10–0–70–1 11–1–40–1		28–9–50–4 24–2–73–1
v. Sussex (Guildford) 26–27 July	22.3–7–60–4 5–0–22–0	21–6–52–1 7–1–29–0		18–2–66–0 5–0–20–0	11–4–23–0				
v. Lancashire (The Oval) 6–8 August	24.5–7–51–4 17–5–36–1	8–1–23–1 12–4–34–0	23–9–52–0	3–2–1–0 28–13–36–2				17–4–47–4 14–2–52–1	
v. Worcestershire (The Oval) 9–12 August		11.3–0–71–0 9–1–33–0		17–4–56–0 2–1–6–0		13–2–40–2		16–0–69–0 7–1–16–1	21–8–57–1 8–1–27–0
v. Somerset (Taunton) 16–19 August	5–1–11–0 12.3–1–31–5	4–0–18–0 6–1–25–1		1–1–0–0 9–1–51–2		2–0–14–0		5–0–41–1	
v. Kent (Dartford) 20–22 August	28.1–16–37–2 6–0–14–0	17–4–65–1 8–1–15–1		26–7–61–2 4–0–20–0		8–2–27–0		24–3–110–3 5–0–36–1	
v. Essex (Chelmsford) 23–26 August	12.5–3–37–2	5–0–31–1		21–4–65–2				8–3–22–1	
v. Glamorgan (Swansea) 27–29 August	12–4–29–0			17–5–41–1		3–2–4–0		4–4–0–2	
v. Gloucestershire (The Oval) 3–5 September	26–3–81–3 15–3–30–3				2–1–1–0	6–0–17–1 3–0–32–0	9–1–49–1 7–0–37–0	22–4–75–2 10–1–36–1	
v. Leicestershire (The Oval) 13–16 September				18–0–66–3				4–2–10–0	16–6–32–2
	341.3–95– 806–48 av. 16.79	166.3–29– 588–12 av. 49.00	233.1–69– 589–14 av. 42.07	394.5–107– 1095–30 av. 36.50	59–21– 155–5 av. 31.00	111–28– 305–13 av. 23.46	300–50– 1104–32 av. 34.50	224–48– 781–26 av. 30.03	342.3–69– 966–51 av. 18.94

a G.C. Small retired hurt   b I.R. Payne retired hurt   c N.J. Falkner 3–1–3–1

G.S. Clinton	A.J. Stewart	A. Needham	M.P. Bicknell	G. Winterbourne	K.T. Medlycott	M.A. Lynch	Byes	Leg-byes	Wides	No-balls	Total	Wkts
							16	15	1	6	231	10
							1	10		4	254	8
								11	1		327	6
							8	13			152	9
							3		1	9	174	10
							2	3		4	89	9a
2–1–5–0	1–0–13–0							1			38	2
								2	2	3	162	6
		2–0–4–0					1	4		8	288	10
							4	1		3	131	4
			13–5–23–2				5	15	1	1	179	10
			11–6–30–3				1			2	138	10
		7–2–15–2	18–0–72–3					20	3	10	294	10
		10–1–52–0	17–4–55–1				11	15	4	10	401	5
		30–13–47–1		14–3–34–0	24.4–10–43–3		13	13	4	8	213	10
		12–5–17–0		6–2–13–0	22–5–46–1	1–1–0–0	10	3	1		160	7
			11–0–41–2				1		1	9	185	9b
		18–6–26–0	19–5–48–3				12	24	1	6	284	8
			22–4–88–3		19.3–3–71–5		1	11	2	6	285	10
			7–3–9–1		27–9–84–5			4	5	1	159	10
			22–1–78–0				6	6		2	330	6
											0	0
		9–3–28–0			22–8–63–6		4	2		1	217	10
					7–1–37–3		5			3	72	10
					33–6–101–2		9	5		12	307	6
					3–0–24–0		6	5		2	134	3
		15–8–16–0			3–0–7–0			6	1	12	250	10
		6–1–22–0			21–2–69–1	3–0–8–0		4	1	18	276	7
			20–7–41–3		16–2–67–2		3	5	3	3	294	10
			5–1–18–1		10–5–19–3	4.2–1–18–1		1	1	3	153	6c
					7–4–10–0		4	4		10	192	10
					27–7–117–0		14	3		5	292	4
					18–4–77–2		2	9	1	7	381	5
	2–0–8–0				7–3–17–0	2–1–6–0	2	8		5	123	1
	2–0–34–0					1–0–9–0	4	1	1	3	83	0d
							3	1	1	4	166	10
					14–3–62–0		15	2		11	379	8
					8–1–35–1	6–0–48–1	8	4	1	2	214	5e
					17–3–58–3			9		4	222	10
					9–1–40–1		2	1	1		117	4
			17–4–38–2		3.5–0–21–1		6	10	3	1	297	10
1–0–7–0			7–0–32–0		22–5–62–0	7–0–30–0	1	1	4	8	269	4
											0	0
			7–3–27–3		13.2–4–36–1		7	2			180	10
3–1–12–0 —	5–0–55–0 —	109–39–227–1 av. 227.00	196–43–600–27 av. 22.22	20–5–47–0 —	353.4–86–1166–40 av. 29.15	24.2–3–119–2 av. 59.50						

d N.J. Falkner 1–0–6–0   e C.J. Richards 5–0–34–1

Sussex C.C.C. — First-Class Matches – Batting, 1986

	v. Lancashire (Hove) 26–28 April		v. Yorkshire (Leeds) 7–9 May		v. Surrey (Hove) 21–23 May		v. Middlesex (Lord's) 24–27 May		v. Somerset (Horsham) 31 May–3 June		v. Kent (Tunbridge Wells) 4–6 June		v. Leicestershire (Hove) 7–10 June		v. Cambridge Univ. (Hove) 14–16 June		v. Essex (Ilford) 18–20 June		v. Worcestershire (Worcester) 21–24 June		v. Northamptonshire (Hastings) 28 June–1 July		v. Glamorgan (Cardiff) 2–4 July		v. New Zealanders (Hove) 5–7 July		v. Gloucestershire (Bristol) 16–18 July	
N.J. Lenham	1	22	75	7	1	—	1	5			4	33	13	40	0*													
A.M. Green	35	27	3	34*	23*	—	88	24			0	10	25	20	132	47	4	6	5	22	55	28	179	15	34	24	0	35
P.W.G. Parker	8	78	0	10*	3	—	107	13			79	36	13	1	109	—	0	7	125	22	26	54	75	1*	7*	20*	0	120
C.M. Wells	7	17			10*	—	3	25*			29	43*	0	46	69	—	0	39	2	36*	11	12*	27*	—	—	35*	13	50
A.P. Wells	5	10	36	—	—	—	22*	—			35	0	34	76	1	48*	0	35	3	0	44	—	43*	—			19	0
D.K. Standing	15	14	2	—	—	—					2	—			11	38*	7	3	2	8	22	16	16	3	29*	13	16	9
J.R.T. Barclay	4	28	4	—																								
I.J. Gould	32	42	0	—			7*	—			60*	36	5	8	25*	—			3	68	30	25	1	—			2	5
G.S. le Roux	34	22	0	—							5*	—																
D.A. Reeve	7*	1	35*	—							5	—	15	3					0	51	0	9*	10	—	7*	—	27	31
A.N. Jones	2	4*	11	—									7*	13					0	—								
A.C.S. Pigott			10	—							16	—	31	20			19*	0	19*	—	10	—					3	17
A.N. Babington					—	—							4	8*			3	2	7*	—			—	—			1	0*
A.M. Bredin					—	—					2	—																
Imran Khan							60	43*									49	28					59	62*	—	1	0	47
R.I. Alikhan															22*	13	25	27*	39	2	27*	—						
I.C. Waring																	—	—										
C.S. Mays																											8*	4
C.P. Phillipson																												
A.M.G. Scott																												
M.P. Speight																												
Byes			9	2							8		2	13	4	1			9		8		8				5	
Leg-byes	5	10	10	1	1		8	2			2	2	2	7	3	2	2	6	12	17	5	1	3	1			5	5
Wides							1	1			2	3	3	2			3	2	4	1			1		1		5	5
No-balls	5	9	7	3	3						5	2	6	1			2		5	9	5		7		4	2	8	8
Total	160	293	195	55	38		300	113			246	173	158	256	379	153	112	290	250	158	283	173	351	27	75	95	102	341
Wickets	10	10	10	1	2		5	3			9†	5	10	10	5	3	10	10	9	6	9	3	3	2	1	3	10	10
Results	L		L		D		W		Ab.		D		L		D		L		D		L		D		D		L	
Points	2		1		4		22		0		4		4		—		4		7		7		5		—		2	

Catches:
37 – I.J. Gould (ct 36/st 1)
18 – P.W.G. Parker
13 – subs.
12 – A.M. Green
11 – A.P. Wells
10 – D.A. Reeve
9 – D.K. Standing
7 – R.I. Alikhan
6 – G.S. le Roux, N.J. Lenham and M.P. Speight
5 – C.M. Wells and A.N. Jones
4 – A.N. Babington

as his command of his subject. The book is well illustrated with pictures and diagrams clearly depicting the points raised by the coach in the text. A most useful and praiseworthy publication for the younger, and older, reader.

THE COURAGE BOOK OF GREAT SPORTING TEAMS: *edited Chris Rhys*: Stanley Paul: 128 pp, £6.95
Another in the series sponsored by Courage who last year offered us individuals and this year concerns itself with teams. As with the previous book, there is controversy in who has been included and who has been omitted. Cricket is represented by England, 1932–33; Australia, 1948; West Indies, 1950; Surrey, 1952–58; South Africa, 1969–70; and West Indies, 1984. But there is no Yorkshire of the 1930s, nor Essex of the 1980s, and, arguably, the Hutton – Tyson side was the equal of the Jardine – Larwood side. One of the delights of this well illustrated book, however, is the argument and discussion that it stimulates. Chris Rhys has done his customary fine job, and the book is good value, entertaining and attractive. It makes an ideal gift, and it is especially strong on soccer while cricket, as we have mentioned above, is well represented.

PAKISTAN BOOK OF CRICKET, 1983–84: *edited Qamar Ahmed*: Sportsman Publications: 184 pp
This is a really splendid little book covering all aspects of cricket in Pakistan, and cricket in which the Pakistan national side was involved. There are Pakistan Test records, statistics of domestic cricket, pictures and comment. It is a credit to the editor.

THE COLLINS WHO'S WHO OF ENGLISH FIRST CLASS CRICKET 1945–1984: *compiled Robert Brooke*: Collins Willow: 411 pp, £25
There must have been some misgiving about publishing this book so soon after the *Who's Who of Cricketers* which came out last year and which covered all who had played in first-class cricket in England. Robert Brooke's book covers the period from the end of the second world war until the present day. It is well produced, pleasant to look at and delightfully compiled. It is precise, yet it transcends the merely factual and statistical to give personal details and comment which help to crystallise a man for us more clearly. We learn, for example, that William Lawton, who played twice for Lancashire in 1948, is the husband of actress Dora Bryan and that the wife of William Ashmore who played twice for Middlesex just after the war is the first lady to have been a scorer at Lord's. I cannot agree with all the spellings of foreign players' names. The men concerned would suggest Vinothen John, and not Vinodhan, and it is Ranatunga, not Ranatunge, but those are quibbles, and one should not quibble with this fine work.

ANOTHER WORD FROM ARLOTT: *selected by David Rayvern Allen*: Pelham Books: 312 pp, £12.95
This is Mr Rayvern Allen's third offering of Arlott in the past two years, and if one includes his collection for the BBC in which, doubtless, Arlott also appears, it is his fourth. I feared then that we had reached the point of indigestion and I was even anticipating an *Arlott meets Abbot and Costello*, or something of the sort, which is why I was rather pleasantly surprised. I am not totally convinced

v. Leicestershire (Leicester) 19–22 July	v. Worcestershire (Hove) 23–25 July	v. Surrey (Guildford) 26–29 July	v. Essex (Eastbourne) 2–5 August	v. Derbyshire (Eastbourne) 6–8 August	v. Hampshire (Southampton) 9–12 August	v. Kent (Hove) 16–19 August	v. Somerset (Taunton) 20–22 August	v. Middlesex (Hove) 23–26 August	v. Nottinghamshire (Hove) 30 August–1 Sept.	v. Hampshire (Hove) 10–12 September	v. Warwickshire (Edgbaston) 13–16 September	M	Inns	NOs	Runs	H/S	Av
0 35	4 24	41 0*	68 8	25* 77	— 4	22 11*			0 3	3 17	— —	18	29	4	544	77	21.76
9 23	60 9	15 28	8 5	3 13	17 40	39 15	27* —		3 11	114 0	29 0	25	46	3	1343	179	31.23
48 —	33 97	4 39	7 0	100* 1	83 36	0 51*	19* —		0 111	51 0	1 —	25	43	7	1595	125	44.30
52 39*	0 18	26 0	106 59	— 50	56* 41	82 5			10 —	20 24	2 34	24	38	9	1098	106	37.86
1 14	15 42*	33 17		13* 25*	0 2				63 150*	39 28	19 19	23	34	7	891	150*	33.00
18* —		31 21		— 4					23 5	65 19		17	26	3	412	65	17.91
												2	3	—	36	28	12.00
9 —	4 35*	54 —	1 43*	— 78*	— 13				6 2	12* 37*	— 4	20	24	6	586	78*	32.55
	7* —	36 —	44* 72*	— 7		10 —				— 34*	— 30*	14	16	6	298	72*	29.80
2 —		9 —		— 6*	22* —		3		7 1*			19	21	9	307	51	25.58
												11	10	3	55	13	7.85
		7 —	35 —	— 3		35			40* 80	75* 40	18* 104*	19	18	6	572	104*	47.66
0 —												6	3	1	1	1	0.50
												7	6	2	26	8*	6.50
		55 24		104 31					11 20		135* —	11	18	3	730	135*	48.66
16 64*	67 56	7 40	19 59	64 72	14 14	18 0	15 —		33 16	0 48	5 61	18	28	4	843	72	35.12
												1					
2 —	0 —	0* —	5 —									8	6	2	19	8*	4.75
	6 —											1	1	—	6	6	6.00
	0 —											1	1	—	0	0	0.00
									4 17			5	2	—	21	17	10.50

Bowling:

v. Leics	v. Worcs	v. Surrey	v. Essex	v. Derby	v. Hants (S)	v. Kent	v. Somerset	v. Middlesex	v. Notts	v. Hants (H)	v. Warwick
9 4		3			6	4	4		3 4	1	4
10 2	2 6	5 1	12 2	7 3	6 2	8			8	7 5	13 7
3 3		3 1	3 1		5				2 7	5 5	1
3 2	5 5	2		6 2	9 1	5			7	5 5	11

Team totals:

v. Leics	v. Worcs	v. Surrey	v. Essex	v. Derby	v. Hants (S)	v. Kent	v. Somerset	v. Middlesex	v. Notts	v. Hants (H)	v. Warwick
182 186	203 292	294 153	346 272	205 319	302 209	252 85	66		182 430	350 243	303 278
10 3	10 5	10 6	10 6	2 7	4 8	9‡ 4	1		10 8	7 8	6 6
D	W	L	D	W	D	W	D	D	D	D	D
5	20	3	6	21	6	23	1	2	2	7	7

2 – C.S. Mays
1 – J.R.T. Barclay, A.M. Bredin, I.C. Waring, Imran Khan, C.P. Phillipson and A.M.G. Scott

†G.S. le Roux retired hurt
‡I.J. Gould absent hurt

about the radio scripts. They are meant to be *heard* rather than read, but if one can imagine that rich Hampshire throb as one reads the page, then the words glow with warmth. This collection is certainly as good as the first, *A Word from Arlott*, and the important thing is that we have the words of the man captured between covers so that on long winter nights we can summon up remembrance of joys past.

HEDLEY VERITY: *Alan Hill*: Kingswood Press: 176 pp £12
Hedley Verity was a fine cricketer, England's best left-arm bowler of spin between the two wars, and he was a gentle man to whom no hint of scandal nor misdemeanour was ever attached. He worked hard to win his place as successor to Rhodes in the Yorkshire side and he came late to first-class cricket. He established records which may never be beaten. His domestic life, though not without its sadness, was normal to the common lot. His life ended when he died of wounds received in action in Italy, and this part of the story is well told by Alan Hill. The author has had his problem in that Verity's life was that of a hard working, honest man, and it was not rich in dramatic incident that would make the stuff of an exciting tale. Rightly, Alan Hill has given his subject honest treatment, from the days in the Lancashire League to the death in Italy. It is a faithful reflection of a fine cricketer and a fine man.

A GAME ENJOYED: *Peter May*: Stanley Paul: 224 pp, £9.95
Peter May has reached the pinnacle of every aspect of cricket, captain of the champion county, captain of England, chairman of the Test selectors and President of MCC, so that his reminiscences

have been excitedly awaited. Sadly, the eagerness of anticipation has been followed by bitter disappointment. *A Game Enjoyed* is a gentle book, but the only characteristic of the man it reveals is his reticence.

He has moved through historic, changing, dramatic times in the growth of the game, but we are given none of the fire, only a placid account of games played, and more readable accounts of these matches can be found in several other publications. The collaborator of the book, Michael Melford, has obviously bowed to May's wishes as to the emphasis on fact rather than on opinion, comment and anecdote, and the result is that the reader is left with the sense of opportunity missed, a lifeless object.

The advertising department of the publisher concerned avowed that a 'ghosted' book had been sought rather than an objective, stimulating biography because that was what the *media* wanted. Is all quality and vitality to be sacrificed to this end? One shudders for the future of cricket literature.

CHAMPIONS OF ONE-DAY CRICKET: *ed Khalid Ansari*: Longman Orient: 72 pp, £4.95
Subtitled 'Wills Tribute to Excellence', this book is an attractive record of India in one-day cricket, and contains articles for and against limited-over cricket. There are seventeen chapters by seventeen different contributors, and although some of the contributions are something less in quality than one would hope for from people of reputation, there is enough here of interest and literary merit to make this a very worthwhile publication. Dom Moraes has a fine piece and there are some interesting observations from Abbas

Warwickshire C.C.C. — First-Class Matches – Batting, 1986

Batsman	v. Essex (Edgbaston) 26-28 April	v. Cambridge Univ. (Cambridge) 30 April-2 May	v. Surrey (The Oval) 7-9 May	v. Northamptonshire (Edgbaston) 21-23 May	v. Worcestershire (Edgbaston) 24-27 May	v. Lancashire (Old Trafford) 31 May-3 June	v. Gloucestershire (Bristol) 4-6 June	v. Glamorgan (Edgbaston) 7-10 June	v. Northamptonshire (Northampton) 14-17 June	v. Glamorgan (Swansea) 18-20 June	v. Leicestershire (Edgbaston) 21-24 June	v. Yorkshire (Leeds) 28-30 June	v. Nottinghamshire (Trent Bridge) 2-4 July	v. Middlesex (Uxbridge) 5-8 July
T.A. Lloyd	5 22	1 1	27 0	2 64	70 11	17 0	56 15	99 —	2 2	39 57	70 23	15 100	3 40	— 0
R.I.H.B. Dyer	28 17*	9 13*	9 14	0 0	0 1								17 0	
G.J. Lord	10 11	1 24*												
D.L. Amiss	16 108*	16* —	20 26	21 7	46 1	30 37*	10 104	0 —	12 62	110 48	54 10	83 18	5 46	— 14
G.W. Humpage	22 22	125 —	20 10	41 32	31 1	130 0	75 23	43 —	26 10	55 —	34 56	39 10	14 6	— 21
B.M. McMillan	33 64		58 17	10 50*	9* 29				39 83	9 —	0* —	134 —	0 136	— 63
P.A. Smith	88 3*		3 4	34 51	119 4	20 9	13 3	79 —	58* 11*	24* 47	5 1	19 63	3 5	— 44
G.J. Parsons	42* —		1* 2	25 9	— 24		— 0	22 —				0 —	0 3	— 4
G.C. Small	17 —		8 1*	13 0*	— 7			— 5*	25 —	13 —	0 —	43 —	30 45*	— 12*
T.A. Munton	— —	3 —	0 1	4* —			— 0*					8* —	1 11*	
N. Gifford	— —		1 5*	0 —	— 0*				0 —			8 —	0* —	
A.I. Kallicharran		121 —				14 28	132* 76	163* —	0 16	6 102*	2 0*			
A.M. Ferreira		— —							19 11*	6 —	68 7*			
M. Asif Din			14 0	4 9	8* 27	69* 40*	3* 2	21 —	30 25	0 22*	61 31	16 2*	53 1	— 16
K.J. Kerr					— 12					1 —	8* 3*	4 —		— 4
A.J. Moles						1* —	— 6							
A.R.K. Pierson									42* —					
D.A. Thorne														— 0*
S. Monkhouse														
Byes			3 2	3 3	5	1		4	2 4	5	4			
Leg-byes	6 3	13 1	3	5 6	8 5	14 4	6 10	8	7 5	8 6	9 6	8 7	2 8	14
Wides	3	2 1	1		3 2		1	4 2	2	1	7 1	1 5	1	1
No-balls	1		9 4		7 5	5 q	1 3	2	4	18 7	6	7 1	1	5
Total	271 250	291 40	174 89	165 231	301 134	301 120	300 249	443	266 230	301 290	322 142	385 201	129 303	0 198
Wickets	8 4	6 1	10 9†	10 7	5 10	5 4	4 8	6	8 6	10 3	8 5	10 4	10 8	0 8
Results	D	W	L	D	L	D	D	D	W	W	D	D	D	D
Points	6		3	2	7	5	8	8	17	24	7	5	3	4

Catches
49 – G.W. Humpage (ct 41/st 8)   11 – B.M. McMillan   7 – P.A. Smith
13 – A.I. Kallicharran   10 – M. Asif Din   6 – T.A. Lloyd
12 – D.L. Amiss   8 – A.M. Ferreira   5 – K.J. Kerr, A.J. Moles and R.I.H.B. Dyer

---

Ali Baig. The picture content is excellent and there is a good statistical section by B.B. Mama. The book is obtainable in England from Sangam Books Ltd, 36 Molyneux Street, London W1H 6DS

ASHES '85: *Matthew Engel*: Pelham Books: 216 pp, £10.95
Matthew Engel's reports in *The Guardian* are among the most entertaining pieces of literature ever written about cricket. His writing is witty, perceptive and lucid. This, his first book, is, in fact, a collection of the pieces he wrote about the Australians when they toured England in 1985, and they have been only slightly amended. Those who read about the game will be delighted that at last we have Matthew Engel's writing firmly bound between solid covers. He has always deserved to be something more than a ten-minute read on the train on the way to work. We should be grateful to the publishers for capturing him at last.

MIDDLESEX COUNTY CRICKET CLUB REVIEW 1985/86. *Edited Alvan Seth-Smith*: pp. 128, £4.00
Neat, compact, splendidly produced and very well illustrated, the *Middlesex Review* retains its usual high standard in its sixth year of publication. The score-cards and statistics are presented in a clear and precise manner, and there are excellent literary contributions from Paul Downton and the late Terence Prittie. It is fitting that one of Terence Prittie's last pieces of writing should be about the county about whom he wrote so memorably in *Mainly Middlesex* more than forty years ago. It is pleasing also to note that much news and coverage is given to young Middlesex cricketers. The editor has again done a splendid job, and the book is available, post free, from the Middlesex office at Lord's.

THE WISDEN BOOK OF OBITUARIES. *Compiled by Benny Green*: Queen Anne Press, pp 1029, £29.50
Eagerly awaited, Benny Green's collection of obituaries from *Wisden* from 1892, the year in which the almanack first carried the notices, until 1985 is no disappointment. As Mr Green points out in his most delightful introduction, there have been 8,614 obituary notices in *Wisden*, but almost one fifth of these have been omitted. Those omitted are exclusively men who did not play first-class cricket and invariably are young men who, fresh from public school, fell in the First World War. It is sad that they have had to be omitted, but pressures of space told, and Mr Green's reasoning cannot be faulted. What we are left with is the most readable, most fascinating and most useful directory of first-class cricketers that has ever been published. The compiler's infectious delight in his task is transmitted undiluted to the reader. The book is expensive, but it is a noble publication, and no one who cares for the game, or for life and literature, should be without it.

THE PAVILION LIBRARY –
TWO SUMMERS AT THE TESTS. *John Arlott*; pp 320, £5.95
HIRST AND RHODES. *A.A. Thomson*: pp 211, £5.95
THROUGH THE CARIBBEAN. *Alan Ross*: pp 296, £5.95
LIFE WORTH LIVING. *C.B. Fry*: pp 424, £5.95

Match columns (two innings each): v. New Zealanders (Edgbaston) 12–14 July · v. Derbyshire (Edgbaston) 16–18 July · v. Hampshire (Portsmouth) 19–22 July · v. Lancashire (Edgbaston) 26–29 July · v. Somerset (Weston-s-Mare) 6–8 August · v. Kent (Edgbaston) 9–12 August · v. Gloucestershire (Nuneaton) 16–19 August · v. Worcestershire (Worcester) 23–26 August · v. Yorkshire (Edgbaston) 27–29 August · v. Middlesex (Edgbaston) 30 August–2 Sept. · v. Kent (Folkestone) 3–5 September · v. Sussex (Edgbaston) 13–16 September

NZ		Derby		Hants		Lancs		Som		Kent		Glos		Worc		Yorks		Middx		KentF		Sussex		M	Inns	NOs	Runs	H/S	Av
		46	6	—	—																			16	28	—	793	100	28.32
																								5	10	2	91	28	11.37
																								3	6	1	63	24*	12.60
0	16	66	38	2	33	33	101*	53	1*	5	—	8	—	33	—	8*	—	7	2	73	5	25	37	26	45	6	1450	110	37.17
100*	21	2	9	4	30	0	38*	32*	—	59	—	44	—	28	—	—	—	81	37	19	23	32	57*	26	42	4	1462	130	38.47
65	39	6*	35	0	61	—	—	36	48*	106	—													12	21	4	999	136	58.76
77	0	39	20	11	23	4	10	87	78	55	17*	32	70*	45	—	55	—	24	79	11	14	52	10	25	44	4	1508	119	37.70
—	13	—	0	14	0	8	—							13	—	9	—							21	24	5	322	58*	16.94
—	10	—	3	0	7	6	—					13	—					—	0	28	2	2*	—	23	24	6	290	45*	16.11
—	11*			19	0							0	—					—	0	0	0*	—	—	19	15	6	58	19	6.44
—	—			0	0	4	—					3*	—					—	2*	2*	2	—	—	25	14	6	27	8	3.37
						2	29					19	—	31	—	103*	—	73	1	2	2	41	42	14	23	5	1005	163*	55.83
31*	28					69*	—					47	—	5	—			36*	0	26	0	60*	—	12	15	6	413	69*	45.88
21	17	0*	7*	50*	14*	3	—			40*	—	47	—	12*	—			62*	7	11	5	10	28*	24	38	14	788	69*	32.83
—	33*											45*	—	6*	—			—	0	1	3			14	12	5	120	45*	17.14
		—	0*			1	67	66	102	44	37*	100	29*	26	—	91	—	11	12	82	8	55	0	11	18	3	738	102	49.20
																						10	—	2	2	2	42	42*	
18	2	58	8	5	11			11*	—	4*	—													7	10	3	127	58	18.14
						0	—																	1	1	—	0	0	0.00

Bowling:

NZ		Derby		Hants		Lancs		Som		Kent		Glos		Worc		Yorks		Middx		KentF		Sussex	
4	9	8		1	8		4	2	6	1	1	4		8		2		5		3		6	2
12	7	7	10	1	8	6	4	6	1	9	2	16	2	4		10		3	5	5		9	3
		2	5	1			1	2	1			3		2		4				2			
2	4	6	3	2	2	2	1	7	2	3		3		6		9		3		2	1		

Totals / results:

NZ		Derby		Hants		Lancs		Som		Kent		Glos		Worc	Yorks	Middx		KentF		Sussex	
330	210	240	144	110	197	138	255	302	239	326	57	381	102	215	282	300	150	267	64	302	179
5	9	5	8	9‡	9	10	3	4	2	5	0	9	0	7	2	5	10	10	10	7	4
D		D		L		D		D		D		W		D	W	L		L		D	
—		4		2		4		4		4		20		2	19	8		4		6	

4 – G.C.Small
3 – G.J. Parsons
2 – G.J. Lord, N. Gifford and subs.

1 – D.A. Thorne and T.A. Munton
†G.C. Small retired hurt
‡T.A. Lloyd absent hurt

THE ASHES CROWN THE YEAR. *Jack Fingleton*: pp 320, £5.95
BATTER'S CASTLE. *Ian Peebles*: pp 191, £5.95

The most exciting cricket publishing venture of the past two or three years has been the advent of the Pavilion Library. Six more titles were added in 1986 to bring this handsome collection to its first dozen. Each of the books selected is an established work on the game, and it is fascinating to read again Alan Ross's account of England in the West Indies in 1960 and wonder if very much ever changes. *Hirst and Rhodes* is my personal favourite from this year's half-dozen. A.A. Thomson was one of the greatest of cricket writers, and it is fitting that J.M. Kilburn, another fine writer, should provide the introduction to this, probably the best of Thomson's books. It is a beautifully judged study. Who was the greatest all-rounder after W.G.? 'He batted right-hand and bowled left; and he came from Kirkheaton.' It was good to turn again to Fry's autobiography. My fascination for it remains undiminished as does my conviction that the great sportsman was a rather conceited man. The account of the 1953 Test series by Jack Fingleton evokes the happiest of memories. It mattered so much then, and there is a lovely piece of vintage Arlott. *Two Summers at The Tests* issues two books in one, *Gone to the Cricket*, which covers the South African series of 1947, and *Gone to the Test Match*, which covers the series against Australia the following summer. This is vintage writing of vintage years. The books run together make a most treasured record. Lastly, *Batter's Castle* is a ramble through cricket from a man who was witty and joyful. It is a pleasing addition to the series.

This library of cricket books should form the basis of every follower of the game's collection. Tremendous value, and something to treasure.

GOOD ENOUGH? *Chris Cowdrey and Jonathan Smith*: Pelham Books, pp 187, £10.95

Although there are two authors credited to this book, it is a little difficult to understand the need for Mr Smith's contribution, and one can only conjecture that it was felt that Chris Cowdrey himself had insufficient material to sustain a complete book. I found Mr Smith's comments unnecessary and distracting to the main line of the book which, in itself, is a rather rambling affair, suggesting towards the close that the authors were looking for some extra pages. Having said this, I found the book, for the main part, most enjoyable. The enjoyment lies in the attitudes and comments of Chris Cowdrey who shines through these pages as an eminently likeable man. He has suffered from the burden of a famous father. He is not as good a batsman as his father, but he is a better bowler than many have given him credit for being, and although he is unlikely ever to lead England, he has proved himself to be a more dynamic captain than his father. He needs no excuses any more. He has not been found wanting at the highest level, and he has made a success of a career in the game. As a person, he is a delight, and happily that is reflected in these pages, and that is more important than being the best batsman in the world.

Warwickshire C.C.C. First-Class Matches – Bowling, 1986	G.C. Small	B.M. McMillan	G.J. Parsons	T.A. Munton	N. Gifford	P.A. Smith	A.M. Ferreira	T.A. Lloyd	G.J. Lord
v. Essex (Edgbaston) 26–28 April	22–8–58–2	23–5–64–2	14–3–49–0	14–4–41–1	17–5–33–2	8–0–44–1			
v. Cambridge University (Cambridge) 30 April–2 May	10–3–17–2 13–7–14–1		23.3–7–64–3 17–6–24–5	20–4–42–2 11–7–9–2	15–7–20–1 7–2–12–0		25–6–65–1 14–6–21–1	1–0–4–0	1–0–6–0
v. Surrey (The Oval) 7–9 May	23–4–75–1	25–0–113–0	18–2–70–2	17–6–52–2					
v. Northamptonshire (Edgbaston) 21–23 May	6–0–36–0 12.5–0–73–1	9–1–35–2 14–1–56–2	4–0–31–0 6–0–20–0	1.5–1–3–1	4–1–15–0 17–0–78–4				
v. Worcestershire (Edgbaston) 24–27 May	16–1–53–2 17.3–4–35–5	14–3–44–0	22–0–108–3 9–2–24–0		20–6–50–0 24–9–34–4	5–0–29–1			
v. Lancashire (Old Trafford) 31 May–3 June	15–4–41–3 14–1–60–3		12–4–18–0 5–0–28–1	8–2–22–0 7–2–32–0	12–3–25–0 16–1–74–1	2.4–0–13–1 8–0–36–3			
v. Gloucestershire (Bristol) 4–6 June	21–1–90–1 11–3–15–1		26.2–6–75–5 4–1–16–0	23–4–76–3 4–0–10–0	9–0–31–0 2–0–4–0	5–0–27–1		11–0–80–0	
v. Glamorgan (Edgbaston) 7–10 June	23–6–71–3		20–4–55–3	7–1–47–1	2–0–6–0	10–2–57–1			
v. Northamptonshire (Northampton) 14–17 June	10–4–26–1 17–6–42–3		10–2–22–0 5–1–24–0		14–6–25–1 21.5–11–27–6	4–0–26–0 1–0–13–0	9–3–32–0 3–0–16–0		
v. Glamorgan (Swansea) 18–20 June	21–5–60–3 13–3–40–2		7–2–18–1 4–2–12–0		18.1–8–42–4 5–1–17–3	2–0–12–0	9–4–10–0		
v. Leicestershire (Edgbaston) 21–24 June	21.5–9–41–4 9.2–2–32–0		12–4–29–1 3–2–8–0		6–0–30–0 26–14–26–3		10–2–32–1 6–0–20–0		
v. Yorkshire (Leeds) 28–30 June	15–0–50–3 15–2–38–3	12–3–54–0 10–3–22–2	12–2–26–1	12–5–24–0	22–3–60–2 14–4–21–1	6–1–29–0			
v. Nottinghamshire (Trent Bridge) 2–4 July	22–7–65–2	17–3–71–1	26–3–104–1	20.5–3–78–3	25–9–59–2	11–0–61–1			
v. Middlesex (Uxbridge) 5–8 July	24–5–41–3	16–2–68–2	10.2–3–23–2		29–5–76–2 2–0–8–0	4–2–7–0			
v. New Zealanders (Edgbaston) 12–14 July	9–2–25–0 6–0–18–2	9–0–45–0 4–0–11–0	11–0–53–0 3–1–10–0	14–4–35–3 6–2–16–0		3–1–18–0	14–4–55–0		
v. Derbyshire (Edgbaston) 16–18 July	24–7–67–3 3–2–1–1	18–4–51–1 2–0–4–0	17–5–44–0		48–24–72–4 3–2–2–0	6.1–0–22–1		4–0–29–0	
v. Hampshire (Portsmouth) 19–22 July	23–3–71–1	13–3–54–2	15–4–43–1	16–2–52–0	18–5–54–2	3–0–18–0			
v. Lancashire (Edgbaston) 26–29 July	27–5–85–5		19–2–76–1		2–1–1–0	5–0–24–0	20–5–61–2		
v. Somerset (Weston-super-Mare) 6–8 August		6–2–14–0 10–1–47–3	11–1–28–1 9–0–34–0	8–0–61–0 9–0–40–0	13–0–46–0	9–3–24–0 7–1–31–0			
v. Kent (Edgbaston) 9–12 August		18–3–55–0	4–2–9–0 12–1–34–0	29–9–60–4	15–1–81–2	3–0–12–0 5–1–16–0			
v. Gloucestershire (Nuneaton) 16–19 August	7–3–16–0 10–3–49–3			11–3–25–1 9–0–31–1	3–0–6–0 12–1–56–3	6–0–33–0 6–0–17–0	9–4–16–1 8–2–19–1		
v. Worcestershire (Worcester) 23–26 August									
v. Yorkshire (Edgbaston) 27–29 August	17–6–56–3			10–2–34–2	5–2–15–1	9.1–2–46–3	14–2–70–1		
v. Middlesex (Edgbaston) 30 Aug.–2 Sept.	13–3–47–0 11–6–8–1			16–5–43–3	27.4–7–61–3 25–3–78–3	9–0–46–0 7–3–13–0	14–3–42–1		
v. Kent (Folkestone) 3–5 September	21–4–64–3			2–0–4–0	49.5–15–96–5	2–0–13–0	9–2–32–0		
v. Sussex (Edgbaston) 13–16 September	22–6–42–1 7–1–25–1			17–2–48–2 4–0–20–1	8–1–28–0 7–1–40–0	6–0–31–0 6–3–25–0	14–4–41–1		
	572.3–136– 1647–73 av. 22.56	220–34– 808–17 av. 47.52	371.1–72 1179–31 av. 38.03	296.4–68– 905–32 av. 28.28	564.3–158– 1409–59 av. 23.88	159–19– 743–13 av. 57.15	178–47– 532–10 av. 53.20	16–0– 113–0 —	1–0– 6–0 —

a C.C. Ellison absent hurt

M. Asif Din	K.J. Kerr	A.J. Moles	A.R.K. Pierson	D.A. Thorne	S. Monkhouse	A.I. Kallicharran	Byes	Leg-byes	Wides	No-balls	Total	Wkts
								14	2	6	303	8
							8	10		4	226	9
							6	8		5	104	9a
							4	22		4	336	5
								4		3	124	3
1–1–0–0							1	4		5	232	7
	22–3–97–2						4	4		5	360	8
	5–3–15–0						7	2	1	5	146	10
		7–0–30–0						3		2	152	4
3–0–20–0							4	11		2	265	8
		11–2–32–0					5	16	2	5	352	10
24–1–93–2		13–1–40–1						4			262	4
5–1–19–0	9–1–43–1							2		3	300	9
6–0–26–0			10–2–35–0				6	4	1	5	202	2
12–2–48–1								7		2	177	10
	23–9–44–1								1	5	186	10
	13.5–2–47–5						4	1		2	121	10
1–0–4–0	32–6–67–3						9	6	1	3	218	10
1–0–4–0	18–4–46–1						12	2		2	150	4
	24–4–73–0						6	7		2	300	6
2–1–3–0	8–1–30–1						4	7	4		154	7
							8	5	4	10	451	10
	5–1–26–0			12–2–44–1			8	19	1	13	312	10
1–0–4–0				2–0–5–0				1			18	0
1.4–1–0–1	20–6–42–0			2–0–14–0				2		4	271	4
14–4–51–0				5–2–10–0				2		1	136	2
1–0–1–0			18–3–65–1	8–2–35–0			1	16		15	374	10
12–0–54–0			8–0–33–1	3–0–5–0			2	10		5	140	2
				9–0–35–0			12	11		7	350	6
					10–4–34–1		1	11		5	293	9
1–0–8–0	15–2–42–0						2	7	1	2	186	1
	7–0–32–0						1	1	1	4	232	3
								2			23	0
	8–3–22–1	5–0–18–1					6	7		9	299	8
	7–1–15–0							4		2	105	2
	6.1–0–31–2							2	1	1	205	10
												Ab.
											0	0
								7	5	6	228	10
	19–4–55–3	3–1–10–0					1	14	1		319	10
	28–0–108–2						9	15		2	231	6
	46–2–120–2						12	21		3	362	10
		21.3–5–57–2		12–1–39–0			4	13	1	11	303	6
17–2–74–1		5–1–11–1		7–1–11–0		9–0–65–2		7			278	6
102.4–13–409–5 av. 81.80	316–52–955–24 av. 39.79	65.3–10–198–5 av. 39.60	36–5–133–2 av. 66.50	60–8–198–1 av. 148.00	10–4–34–1 av. 34.00	9–0–65–2 av. 32.50						

Worcestershire C.C.C. First-Class Matches – Batting, 1986

	v. Surrey (Worcester) 26–28 April		v. Indians (Worcester) 6–8 May		v. Lancashire (Worcester) 21–23 May		v. Warwickshire (Edgbaston) 24–27 May		v. Kent (Tunbridge Wells) 31 May–3 June		v. Middlesex (Worcester) 4–6 June		v. Northamptonshire (Northampton) 7–10 June		v. Lancashire (Old Trafford) 14–17 June		v. Yorkshire (Worcester) 18–20 June		v. Sussex (Worcester) 21–24 June		v. Hampshire (Worcester) 28 June–1 July		v. Derbyshire (Derby) 2–4 July		v. Nottinghamshire (Worcester) 5–8 July		v. Glamorgan (Neath) 16–18 July	
T.S. Curtis	9	0	24	23*		10			—		45		39	27	29	55*	122*	37	6	43*	14	21	67	4*	18	13	66*	63*
D.B. d'Oliveira	22	4	12	27*		89	9	35	—		2		47	29	6	24	42	22	10	14	33	6	0	43*	2	2	7	7
G.A. Hick	5	103	70	—		18	62	53	—		70		39	1	13	9	36*	60			21	0	94	—	0	227*	219*	52
D.N. Patel	7	39	14	—		23	12	11	—		108		1	18	94	35*		26	15	—			0	49*	21	—	51	46
M.J. Weston	4	29	49	—			30	4	—								0	—					0	—	1	8		
P.A. Neale	32	3	8	—		35	84*	5	—		118*		76*	27	23	13		30	37	28*	0	13	17	—	42	57		70*
S.J. Rhodes	77*	42*	3	—		61	42	8	—		8		0	40*	5	—		7	0	—		16*	0	3*	28	—	7	15*
P.J. Newport	26	9	4	—		22			—		22*				9	—		16*	3	—			31	—	68	—		
N.V. Radford	0	0*	21	—		26	4	0	—				10	0	22	17*	24	—			6	—	23*	—	29	—		
R.K. Illingworth	3	10	6*	—		7	2	3	—				22	17*	18*	—			39	—			14	—	8	—		
A.P. Pridgeon	8	—						4*	—				3	—					4*	—			3	—	10*	—		
R.M. Ellcock			0*	—																								
D.M. Smith						3	102	8	—		26		1	—	18	0	82	15	6	—			44	6*				9
J.D. Inchmore						13*		0	—				12	—	1	—							1*	—				
S.M. McEwan																5*												
S.R. Lambitt																												
L.K. Smith																												
Byes	16	1	4	2			4	7			1		6	4	4	1	2				1	3	17	4	1	2	1	4
Leg-byes	15	10	2	2		6	4	2			9		14	3	2	4	4	24	8	8	9	6	10		20	7	5	17
Wides	1							1			2			1	1	1	1	1	1	1	4	11			1	1	1	1
No-balls	6	4	13	2			6	5			5		2	1	7	4	11	3	13	8	10	1	4	2	3	2	1	2
Total	231	254	230	56	0	319	360	146			421		272	168	253	146	300	246	148	102	204	112	349	55	192	380	300	225
Wickets	10	8	9	0	0	10	8	10			6		10	6	10	4	2	7	10	1	10	4	10	0	10	5	1	3
Results	D		D		L		W		D		W		D		D		D		D		W		D		D		W	
Points	6		—		4		22		0		24		7		4		6		4		22		8		4		23	

Catches

66 – S.J. Rhodes (ct 58/st 8)	12 – N.V. Radford	8 – P.J. Newport
28 – G.A. Hick	10 – R.K. Illingworth	7 – P.A. Neale and S.M. McEwan
16 – D.B. D'Oliveira	9 – T.S. Curtis, D.M. Smith and A.P. Pridgeon	6 – D.N. Patel

ESSEX COUNTY CRICKET CLUB 1986 HANDBOOK. *Edited by Peter Edwards*: pp 232, £3.00

The energetic and exuberant Peter Edwards has again produced a year-book of which the supporters of the currently most successful side in the country can be proud. Mr Edwards' enthusiasm pervades the book, and he has the happy knack of cajoling contributions from critics of the game like Tony Lewis, Ray Illingworth and Trevor Bailey, and the publication is the better for it. It is packed with information and Leslie Newnham's excellent statistics which have for so long been a feature of Essex publication. Above all, it is readable, packed with interesting features concerning the earliest days of cricket in the county right up to the 'double' of 1985. The book is free to members and at £3.00 to the general public is one of the bargains of the year. It is no accident that the playing success of Essex is mirrored by administration of the highest order, and this handbook is testimony to that.

WICKETS, CATCHES AND THE ODD RUN: *Trevor Bailey*: Collins Willow: 240 pp, £9.95

Outstanding all-rounder who played first-class cricket for over twenty years, a soccer player of distinction, writer, journalist and broadcaster, Trevor Bailey now gives us an autobiography which is the best book he has written and certainly one of the best autobiographies by a cricketer in recent years. Its main quality is its honesty, for the book speaks with the voice of the man. Occasionally rambling, sometimes searching hard for facts only half-remembered, it puts to shame some of the ghosted offerings of the past few years. There are things that the author does not like and these are made apparent, but above all there is the consistent feeling of one who has been part of the game for a very long time, who has given pleasure and derived from it as much as he has given. The honesty is in the observation. When he talks of Derbyshire's Les Jackson, the best six-days-a-week, day-in-day-out paceman in county cricket since the war who played only twice for England, he reflects 'The look of disbelief on the faces of his colleagues—we were playing them at Southend—when they heard that John Warr had been chosen for the 1950–51 tour of Australia ahead of "Big Les" was unforgettable.' This is a lovely book, a just monument to one of the great characters of the game and for a bonus it has the best jacket design that I have ever seen.

ENGLAND V AUSTRALIA: TEST MATCH RECORDS, 1877–1985: *ed David Frith*: Collins Willow: 256 pp, £6.95

The compiler has chosen a subject close to his heart, and the result is a splendid little handbook, packed with information, an invaluable companion to students of clashes between the oldest rivals.

THE PROTEA CRICKET ANNUAL OF SOUTH AFRICA: VOL 32: 1985: *ed Ted Partridge, Frank Heydenrych and Peter Sichel*

The fullest possible guide to the South African season, 1984–85, with complete statistics of every match and player, career records, profiles

v. Essex (Southend) 19–22 July	v. Sussex (Hove) 23–25 July	v. Gloucestershire (Worcester) 26–29 July	v. Somerset (Weston-s-Mare) 2–5 August	v. Surrey (The Oval) 9–12 August	v. Leicestershire (Worcester) 16–19 August	v. Hampshire (Bournemouth) 20–22 August	v. Warwickshire (Worcester) 23–26 August	v. Gloucestershire (Bristol) 27–29 August	v. Somerset (Worcester) 3–5 September	v. Glamorgan (Worcester) 10–12 September	M	Inns	NOs	Runs	H/S	Av
4 22	92 36	10 0	64 74	51 64*	48* 4	33 9	— —	42 —	153 —	50 7*	24	40	10	1498	153	49.93
35 4	62 19	6 21	30 91	42 —	14 1	8 26		146* —	34 —	12 49	25	41	3	1094	146*	28.78
51 29	4 100	4* 134	30 43*	31 —	45* 34	0 81		85 —	13 —	61 107	24	37	6	2004	227*	64.64
128 0		— 21	1* —	132* —	— 43*	28 10*		1* —	40 —	29* 2*	24	30	9	1005	132*	47.85
					— 9	16* 17*					8	12	2	167	49	16.70
2 11	7 4	— 7	70 —	5 —	— 16	6 2		14 —	43* —	22 60*	25	34	7	987	118*	36.55
0 33*	16 19*	— 9		67* 2	— 5*	5 —			7* —		25	27	10	509	77*	29.94
34 5	15* 6*	— 10				2 —					23	17	4	285	68	21.92
21 30		13* 0									18	13	2	165	30	15.00
		— 6*									18	15	4	191	39	17.36
3 0						4 —					20	10	3	44	10*	6.28
											2	2	2	4	4*	—
21 16	63 21	— 6	165* 38*	34 42*	15 76			5 —	52 —	100 67	20	28	4	1041	165*	43.37
23* 2	— —	— 0									9	8	2	55	23*	9.16
	11* —					7 —					8	3	2	13	7	13.00
	11* —										1	1	1	11	11*	—
						2 2					1	2	—	4	2	2.00
		1	8 1	2 2				3	2	7 3						
1 6	4 4	1 5	14	9 8	2 8	4 11		3	7	13 3						
1		1		1						1						
	5 3	4 6	4 1	7 5	4 3	5 2		1	1	2 4						
323 158	280 213	38 234	379 247	381 123	128 199	120 160		300	345	304 302						
10 10	6 5	2 10	4 2	5 1	2 6	10 5		4	5	5 3						
L	L	L	L	D	W	D	D	D	W	W						
6	7	4	5	6	20	4	2	8	24	21						

4 – Subs.
3 – J.D. Inchmore
1 – L.K. Smith

and everything that one could ever wish to know about South African cricket. There are 447 pages, and it is a massive achievement. A truly outstanding publication.

ICC TROPHY 1986 – OLD EDWARDIANS C.C. V HONG KONG, EAST AFRICA V DENMARK: *Old Edwardians C.C.,* 50p

A worthy publication to mark the game between East Africa and Denmark at Old Edwardians, Shirley, a most beautiful ground. Generous hosts and spirited cricket are marked by this fine effort.

THE JOURNAL OF THE CRICKET SOCIETY: *ed C.W. Porter*

Members of the Cricket Society need no introduction to this excellent publication which, under Mr Porter's editorship, goes from strength to strength. Richie Benaud and Geoff Howarth are among the most recent contributors, and all is erudite and literary, but never stuffy. It comes free with Cricket Society membership. All who love the game should join.

SEASONS PAST: THE CRICKETER DIARIES: *edited by Christopher Martin-Jenkins:* Stanley Paul: 223 pp, £16.95

There are many cricket books on the market at present, and this publication, a collection of diaries dealing with seasons from 1967 to 1985, does not add much of value to what we have already. Arlott, Gibson and Lewis deserve to be remembered for better than is recorded in this book. This is not a publication to be recommended, particularly at the price. There is some very thin writing here.

THE CRICKETERS' WHO'S WHO 1986: *compiled and edited by Iain Sproat:* Queen Anne Press: 473 pp: £8.95

One sees so many young people clutching this book at cricket grounds eagerly seeking to get autographs for the pictures of the players that one presumes it must be exceedingly popular, which is why its continued inaccuracies and omissions sadden me. At first sight I thought it was better this year than it had been in the past, but when a book is founded on facts and figures then those facts and figures must be right, and in Mr Sproat's book they are so often wrong. Although Wilf Slack, for example, is listed as being qualified for both England and West Indies, there is no mention that he played for Windward Islands from 1981 to 1983. The statistics, particularly for one-day games, need an overhaul. It is better to stick to *Playfair*. It is more accurate and a lot cheaper.

PLAYFAIR CRICKET ANNUAL: *edited by Bill Frindall:* Queen Anne Press: 256 pp, £1.75

Bill Frindall has succeeded the late Gordon Ross as editor of the pocket annual which, as *The Daily News Annual*, goes back over sixty years. Mr Frindall has tightened the work, and it is very good to see one-day international records included. One is sad to note that the names of several long-standing contributors to the statistical section are missing, but this remains the indispensable pocket companion.

Worcestershire C.C.C. First-Class Matches – Bowling, 1986	N.V. Radford	A.P. Pridgeon	P.J. Newport	M.J. Weston	D.N. Patel	R.K. Illingworth	D.B. d'Oliveira	R.M. Ellcock	J.D. Inchmore
v. Surrey (Worcester) 26–28 April	24–9–66–4 14–2–62–2	4–1–10–0 13–1–43–0	20–6–39–2 12.1–2–58–4	14–5–36–1 7–0–29–2	6–1–18–1 6–3–20–0	21.1–7–41–2	1–1–0–0		
v. Indians (Worcester) 6–8 May	18–3–63–2		15–2–65–2	9–1–22–0	2.2–0–4–2	13–1–51–1		17–1–77–3	
v. Lancashire (Worcester) 21–23 May	29.2–8–77–5 6–2–16–0		20–3–59–1		16–2–50–1 1–0–2–0	10–2–43–1 2–2–0–0			19–5–41–2 5–0–19–1
v. Warwickshire (Edgbaston) 24–27 May	22–2–81–0 6–2–9–1	15–2–37–1 6–0–21–0		5–1–13–0	21–6–64–1 22–9–37–4	23–6–52–2 19.2–8–47–3			13–2–46–0 10–5–10–1
v. Kent (Tunbridge Wells) 31 May–3 June	24–6–75–1	17–7–20–1	12–1–42–0		11–3–27–0	21–7–40–0			
v. Middlesex (Worcester) 4–6 June	27.1–5–80–5 27–14–50–2	18–3–40–1 25–8–52–6	19–3–69–2 19.4–4–66–2		4–0–13–0	10–6–17–0			
v. Northamptonshire (Northampton) 7–10 June	25.3–6–66–5 17–3–63–5	3–1–9–0 8.5–2–10–3			10–3–22–1 10–3–24–0	27–10–72–3 12–3–32–0	2–0–12–0		14–7–18–1 3–0–13–0
v. Lancashire (Old Trafford) 14–17 June	9.2–2–40–0		25.2–3–98–0 5–0–30–0		35–9–82–2 13–2–42–1	29.4–9–82–1 17–2–68–1			27–6–55–1 6–0–17–0
v. Yorkshire (Worcester) 18–20 June		32–6–89–2 8–4–17–0	27.5–5–87–2 8–0–34–0		18–6–27–1 6–0–20–0		8–0–60–2		24–6–82–2 6–0–13–0
v. Sussex (Worcester) 21–24 June	25.5–3–94–7 24–5–75–3		13–4–27–0 12–3–22–2	7–3–11–0 14–6–35–1	15–4–30–0	22–10–36–0 1–0–1–0		15–1–40–1	
v. Hampshire (Worcester) 28 June–1 July	18–7–36–1 15–3–44–1	16.1–3–46–3 14.2–6–19–3	18–3–52–5 17–1–48–6		1–0–5–0	16–12–16–1 13–8–26–0			
v. Derbyshire (Derby) 2–4 July		19–6–74–2 24–5–61–1	17.5–4–49–6 28–5–106–3	15–6–48–1 4–1–13–0	2–1–3–0 2–0–6–0	8–2–23–0 44–22–64–5			
v. Nottinghamshire (Worcester) 5–8 July		21–3–57–3 11–2–38–0	21–2–62–3 8–0–22–1	13–1–48–0 5–0–21–0	15–4–44–0	15–7–36–1 8–4–23–0			18–4–47–1 6–1–17–1
v. Glamorgan (Neath) 16–18 July	26–5–57–3 29–4–72–4	15–5–20–1 19.4–9–25–3	17–2–44–1 14–4–20–1		26–6–86–1 13–3–32–1	26–5–54–1 35–12–84–0	1–0–1–0		
v. Essex (Southend) 19–22 July	23–2–113–2 17–2–74–2	22–5–58–3 14–1–59–3	20–4–83–0 9.5–1–42–4		13–2–48–0				19–3–58–0 6–0–17–1
v. Sussex (Hove) 23–25 July		16–5–43–3 16–3–57–2	15–3–57–2 15–0–73–3			30.5–12–54–4 29–2–120–0	0.4–0–4–0		14–6–26–1 14–4–32–0
v. Gloucestershire (Worcester) 26–29 July		20–2–60–4 5.4–1–24–1	22–5–66–3 5–0–26–0		23–6–75–1	13–3–31–0			17.1–2–51–1
v. Somerset (Weston-super-Mare) 2–5 August	22–3–77–2 18–0–89–3	10–3–34–0 21–3–93–0	13.4–2–72–1 13–0–50–2		16–2–58–1 13–1–43–0	12–3–40–0 12.2–2–52–0			
v. Surrey (The Oval) 9–12 August	10–2–27–0	15–4–41–2	36–0–136–4		24–7–71–0				
v. Leicestershire (Worcester) 16–19 August		18–6–36–2 16–6–33–3	20.4–3–76–5 12.5–3–30–4	15–2–40–0 7–2–14–0	1–1–0–0				
v. Hampshire (Bournemouth) 20–22 August		21.2–9–33–3 4–0–15–1	26–3–74–5 6–0–41–1	20–9–46–0	12–3–31–0				
v. Warwickshire (Worcester) 23–26 August	22–1–80–2	14–2–35–1	19–2–64–3						
v. Gloucestershire (Bristol) 27–29 August	16–6–48–1 6–1–21–1	9–6–12–1 4–1–10–0	6–1–13–0 2–0–3–0		25–7–88–5 7–1–18–0	24–7–39–2 17–6–41–0	10–5–17–2		
v. Somerset (Worcester) 3–5 September	19.2–4–70–9 14–1–59–2	12–3–31–0 8–0–34–0	7–0–24–1 10.4–4–22–3		23–9–56–4				
v. Glamorgan (Worcester) 10–12 September	38.1–11–130–3 10–1–31–0		12–0–41–0 11–2–54–1		31–10–83–2 10–1–25–1	22–8–44–0 11–1–32–0	5–0–24–1		
	602.2–125– 1945–78 av. 24.93	536–134– 1396–59 av. 23.66	632.3–90– 2146–85 av. 25.24	135–37– 376–5 av. 75.20	453.2–115– 1254–30 av. 41.80	564.2–189– 1361–28 av. 48.60	27.4–6– 118–5 av. 23.60	32–2– 117–4 av. 29.25	221.1–48– 562–13 av. 43.23

G.A. Hick	S.M. McEwan	S.R. Lampitt	D.M. Smith	Byes	Leg-byes	Wides	No-balls	Total	Wkts
				6	10	3	6	226	10
				2	14		2	228	9
					15		7	297	10
				4	5	4	8	279	10
					6	1	1	43	1
					8	3	7	301	5
				5	5	2	5	134	10
					4		5	208	2
					25	5	5	244	10
				8			1	176	10
				2	2			191	10
					6		5	160	8
				5	5	5	5	367	4
2–0–5–0				2	6	2	2	170	2
	29–3–96–2			8	16	2	4	405	10
3–0–24–2	7–2–23–0				5		1	196	4
					12	1	5	250	9
				8	17		9	158	6
					8		3	158	10
				1	13		5	156	10
	15–3–52–1				11	1	2	260	10
	14–2–51–0			8	5	2		314	9
					16		10	310	8
				6	1		4	128	3
				2	5	5	3	268	8
3–1–6–0				12	4	3		256	10
					10		1	370	5
				4	6		3	202	10
		7–1–21–0			2		5	203	10
					6		5	292	5
				2	15	1	7	300	9
								50	2
					5		5	286	4
				1	13		4	341	5
20.4–4–74–1	19–4–89–0		10–2–35–2	7	20	1	7	500	9
	17–1–53–3		1–1–0–0		4		13	209	10
	10–1–33–3				4		2	114	10
	19–2–45–2				8	3	6	237	10
	4–0–21–1				14			91	4
	12–5–24–1			8	4	2	6	215	7
				4	5		1	209	9
								110	3
					2		7	127	10
	9–2–38–1			3	2	2	13	209	10
	15–2–89–2			5	7	4	19	399	7
	9.1–4–29–0			2	9	1	1	206	3
28.4–5–109–3 av. 36.33	1791.1–31–638–16 av. 39.87	7–1–21–0 —	11–3–35–2 av. 17.50						

Yorkshire C.C.C. — First-Class Matches – Batting, 1986

Player	v. Somerset (Taunton) 26–28 Apr	v. Sussex (Leeds) 7–9 May	v. Essex (Chelmsford) 21–23 May	v. Lancashire (Leeds) 24–27 May	v. Derbyshire (Sheffield) 4–6 June	v. Gloucestershire (Harrogate) 7–10 June	v. Middlesex (Lord's) 14–17 June	v. Worcestershire (Worcester) 18–20 June	v. Northamptonshire (Luton) 21–24 June	v. Warwickshire (Leeds) 28–30 June	v. Gloucestershire (Bristol) 2–4 July	v. Leicestershire (Middlesbrough) 5–8 July	v. Indians (Scarborough) 12–14 July	v. Nottinghamshire (Worksop) 16–18 July
M.D. Moxon	73 —	— 28	25* 2	1 36*	10 9		20 13	1 82		13 1	55 0	8	123 112*	14 1
A.A. Metcalfe	55 —	— 9	— 57	42 27	67 10	3 —	7 29	108 17	151 35	30 0	0 8	44	92 0	12 6
K. Sharp	96 —	— 7	25* 6	1 22*	74 2	181 —	11 2	4 12*	0 26	114* 6	71 3*	31	1 9	56 37
J.D. Love	46 —	— 12	— 0	41 —	8 2	14 —	8 16	24 43*	46 28*	37 0	9 —		22 87	7 28
S.N. Hartley	31 —	— 24		34 —	78 —		56 10	48 —		11 19	6 —	14		
D.L. Bairstow	4* —	— 0	— 0	41 —	4 41	40 —	46 25	15 0	88 1	47 6	43 —		6* —	20 25
A. Sidebottom	— —	— 18	— 2	6 —	15* 2	— —	9 0	12 —			1* —			
P. Carrick	0* —	— 51	— 16	50 —	43 25	30 —	11 8*	50* —	0* 1	26 38*	19 7*	19	24* —	0 21
G.B. Stevenson		— 58*												
P.J. Hartley		— 15	— 87*	31 —	1* 7	15* —	— 54	— 61*						
I.G. Swallow				41 —						14* 1			3 8*	26 13
G. Boycott		— 12			22 69	81 —	69 31	76 36	3 68	4 26	8 —	127		56 6
P.W. Jarvis		— 16*	— 47	5* —	— 1*	0 —	9* 0	29 —	— 0	10 —	8 —	—		28 2
S.D. Fletcher			— 3								2* —	5		16 1
S.J. Dennis					— 0	0* —	8 15	8 —	— 4*					
C. Shaw											0 —	21		5* 8*
R.J. Blakey													44 0	
P.E. Robinson													15 4	
D. Byas														
P.J. Berry														
Byes	1		1 4	6	4 5	1	4 1	8		6 4	12		5 3	
Leg-byes	15	7	4	9 5	4 6	5	16 2	16 5	12 4	7 7	18	14	7 8	3 2
Wides			1	1	4 1		2	2		4 4	4		1	
No-balls	2	18	5	5	3	2	2 1	4 1	1	2	12 2	11	6 5	3
Total	323 0	0 251	51 252	314 90	259 180	450	276 153	405 196	314 240	300 154	269 20	309	343 236	243 153
Wickets	5 0	0 9	0 10	10 1	7 10	8	10 10	10 4	6 8	6 7	10 2	9†	7 5	10 10
Results	W	W	L	D	L	D	W	D	D	D	D	D	L	L
Points	19	20	4	8	7	6	22	4	5	5	7	5	—	3

Catches
43 – D.L. Bairstow (ct 40/st 3)
12 – M.D. Moxon
11 – P. Carrick
10 – A.A. Metcalfe, K. Sharp and P.W. Jarvis
7 – P.E. Robinson, J.D. Love and P.J. Hartley
5 – S.N. Hartley
4 – S.J. Dennis and R.J. Blakey
3 – A. Sidebottom, G. Boycott and S.D. Fletcher

THE WISDEN BOOK OF ONE-DAY INTERNATIONAL CRICKET, 1971–85: *compiled by Victor H. Isaacs and Bill Frindall:* John Wisden: 372 pp, £16.95

As the present writer compiled *The Book of One-Day Internationals*, published in 1983, he was interested to learn that Messrs Frindall and Isaacs had updated it although no credit is given to the earlier publication. The new publication, though very much over-priced, is an excellent work. Not only does it give complete score-cards (lacking the break-down of extras for Pakistan *v.* India, 1979, with which the present writer also experienced difficulties), but it also contains complete one-day international records. It must now be considered the essential work of reference on the subject and a credit to its compilers.

WISDEN CRICKETERS' ALMANACK: *edited by John Woodcock:* John Wisden: 1295 pp, £14.60

This is the last *Wisden* to be edited by John Woodcock, and one should not let him pass from the scene without offering congratulations and thanks for the fine work he accomplished in his term of office. He revitalised and strengthened what was an ailing publication. He raised the literary standard of the almanack and brought it back to the level when it was once more accepted as the undisputed reference work on the game. His successor, Graeme Wright, has much to live up to, and he inherits a problem which is hard to solve—with so much cricket being played throughout the world, it is becoming increasingly difficult to cover it all and maintain standards. The section allocated to Peter Hargreaves for cricket in Denmark, for example, is so limited, a third of a page, as to mock the achievements of the cricketing enthusiasts of that country. It is difficult to break with tradition, but, as we indicated in our review last year, the time has come to reconsider the *Five Cricketers of the Year* section. One last point in criticism concerns the price which has leapt 21% in a year, but you will get plenty for your money, and nobody who loves the game can be without this book. Well done, John, and thank you. Best of luck to Graeme Wright.

BARCLAYS WORLD OF CRICKET: *The Game from A to Z: general editor E.W. Swanton: editor George Plumptre:* Collins Willow: 724 pp, £25

When I heard that *Barclays World of Cricket* was to be revised and republished I was sceptical. I believed that it was too soon after the 1980 edition and that a revision was not yet necessary. I was wrong. The latest edition is bigger and better than anything that has gone before. It is splendidly edited, magnificently produced and there is a consistency in the quality of contribution which is most pleasing. The book really does tell you about cricket from A to Z. You can read about cricket in Thailand, the literature of cricket, the art of cricket, the Packer revolution, broadcasting, the leagues, the public schools and every other aspect of the game, yet to classify the book as an encyclopaedia would be to do it scant justice, for it is a book to be read. It is a lively, warm, human story. It throbs with the genial guidance of Jim Swanton. His passion for the game has not diminished with the years. None has served it better. *Barclays World of Cricket* will remain a testimony to his endeavours.

v. Surrey (Leeds) 19-21 July		v. Kent (Scarborough) 23-25 July		v. Nottinghamshire (Sheffield) 26-29 July		v. Lancashire (Old Trafford) 2-5 August		v. Leicestershire (Leicester) 6-8 August		v. Glamorgan (Leeds) 9-12 August		v. Derbyshire (Chesterfield) 16-19 August		v. Middlesex (Leeds) 20-22 August		v. Hampshire (Bournemouth) 23-26 August		v. Warwickshire (Edgbaston) 27-29 August		v. Northamptonshire (Scarborough) 10-12 September		M	Inns	NOs	Runs	H/S	Av
3	42*					147	—					0	33	5	—	1	—	—	13			18	29	4	871	147	34.84
55	20	123	26	0	108	151	—	60	35	149	—	20	7	39	—	47	—	—	10	15	—	25	39	—	1674	151	42.92
76	4	0	25*									15	—	15	—			8		33		19	31	6	958	181	38.32
		9	1*	59	8	53*	—	8	10	88	—	32		65*	—	31	—	—	24	109		21	29	5	831	109	34.62
0	11	40	51*	33	7	11	—	23	22	2	—	8	41*	39	—	12	—	—	10			21	30	2	785	87	28.03
0	44*	4	—	0	22	3	—	15	52*	42	—	17	—	42	—	9	—	57		37		24	33	4	796	88	27.44
																						10	9	2	65	18	9.28
12	—	5	—	31	5	14	—	25	27	1	—	9	—	5	—	17	—	—	1	46		25	33	7	637	51	24.50
																						2	1	1	58	58*	—
		27	—	0	3	5	—	30	15			10	—			0	—	—	80			15	17	4	441	87*	33.92
0*	—							3*	—			0	—			43*	—					9	11	5	152	43*	25.33
135*	—																	61	—			12	18	1	890	135*	52.35
																						15	17	7	183	47	18.30
		17*	—	6	2*	3*	—					24	—			10	—	—	4*	—		15	10	3	67	24	9.57
				0*	—			2	—	5*	—	9	—	4	—	11	—	—	0	18*		16	12	4	82	18*	10.25
		—	—	5	1			0	—	7*	—	7*	—					—	3			14	10	4	57	21	9.50
				1	46			32	8											12	—	4	7	—	143	46	20.42
		104*	91	1	8	1	—	2	71	2	—	23	70*	0	—							8	13	2	392	104*	35.63
								0														1	1	—	0	0	0.00
																				4*	—	1	1	1	4	4*	—
9	6			2		5		1		1		1				2		1	6								
5	5	4	1	6	17	7		6	7	10		14	7	5		5		7	8								
12	2	8	6	4	1	1		8	7	6		2	2	3		7		6	3								
307	134	341	206	146	233	399		216	256	310		177	162	216		212		0	228	352							
6	3	7	2	10	9	7		10	7	7		10	2	8		10		0	10	7							
W		D		D		D		L		D		D		D		D		L		D							
23		4		12		8		6		8		1		6		3		0		7							

2 – C. Shaw, P.J. Berry and subs.
1 – D. Byas
†D.L. Bairstow retired hurt

LIMITED OVERS: *Mike Gatting:* Queen Anne Press: 192 pp, £9.95
One has the feeling that as Mike Gatting was one of the very few members of the England party not to have had a book published it was thought that it was about time he joined the gravy train. As it was published just as he was elevated to the England captaincy, the timing was perfect. Of the 192 pages, 27 are given over to statistics and index. The statistics are the records of the various one-day competitions. Of the remaining pages, 31 are filled with a selection of a 'dream team', the ideal eleven – Gooch, Richards, Botham etc. There is some autobiography, a few tactics, and *forty-eight* pages on great one-day matches. It all suggests that Alan Lee, Gatting's 'ghost', had hard work in making a book out of the England captain.

A MAIDAN VIEW: *The Magic of Indian Cricket: Mihir Bose:* George Allen & Unwin: 179 pp: £11.95
What does he know of cricket, who only cricket knows? Not only is this one of the best books of the year, but it is also an important contribution to the history of the game. Like all histories it has its own bias, and while Mihir Bose is quick to criticise the romantic view of India expounded by writers like Paul Scott he himself is guilty of sweeping generalisations about the British Empire and English cricket. Yet to take him to task on this is to pay him a compliment, for this is a book that must be taken seriously. It is a fascinating appraisal of cricket in India, and more, for it presents us with statements which we have failed to assimilate: 'In modern India the word Indian represents all Indians of whatever religion. The country is secular, every religious group has full religious and political rights and Mohammed Azharuddin would be most upset if you called him a Hindu. He is a Muslim and an Indian.' It is a simple statement that England has tended to ignore. Our cricketers learned the truth of it in the summer of 1986.

FLAT JACK: *Jack Simmons:* Queen Anne Press: 192 pp, £8.95
This is the autobiography (with Brian Bearshaw's help) of one of county cricket's most loyal and popular servants. Jack Simmons was dubbed 'flat Jack' because he learned to bowl with a flat trajectory in league cricket. The recipient of a record benefit and a folk hero in Tasmania where he shaped the state side into a Gillette Cup winning team and took them into the Sheffield Shield, Jack Simmons is an honest and hard working cricketer. He also comes through as a good business man and a straightforward companion. The book is an honest reflection of the man.

BRITANNIC ASSURANCE 1985 COUNTY CHAMPIONSHIP REVIEW: *edited by Christopher Martin-Jenkins:* The Cricketer: 128 pp: £2.95
This is the first issue of an annual covering the county championship. It is published within weeks of the end of the season. There are teething problems, and a week by week arrangement would be an improvement on the county segregation. Nevertheless, the publication has promise, and it is sure to improve. It is interesting to note that the photograph used on the cover is from a Benson and Hedges Cup match and not a county championship match, and from 1983.

Yorkshire C.C.C. First-Class Matches – Bowling, 1986	A. Sidebottom	P.J. Hartley	P. Carrick	G.B. Stevenson	I.G. Swallow	P.W. Jarvis	K. Sharp	A.A. Metcalfe	S.D. Fletcher
v. Somerset (Taunton) 26–28 April	24–5–71–3	20–1–90–3	11–0–65–2	13–2–48–0	7–0–31–0				
v. Sussex (Leeds) 7–9 May	19–3–47–2	17.1–2–46–3	6–1–19–0	16–6–27–2		20–6–44–3	5–1–36–1	4.1–0–18–0	
v. Essex (Chelmsford) 21–23 May	16–4–38–2	12–2–50–0	24–6–66–1			21.5–2–78–6 3–0–30–0			15–1–43–1
v. Lancashire (Leeds) 24–27 May	26–4–70–2 5–1–19–0	13.2–2–51–2 8–3–15–0	13–0–42–0 47–13–111–4		14–4–37–1 41–12–109–3	28–5–86–5			
v. Derbyshire (Sheffield) 4–6 June	27–3–103–1	25–3–83–1 2–0–6–0	19–9–21–1			32–6–82–3	10–1–74–1	9–0–52–0	
v. Gloucestershire (Harrogate) 7–10 June		20–3–52–2	28–11–51–2			18–5–82–0			
v. Middlesex (Lord's) 14–17 June	18–5–39–2 16–2–43–2		14–4–38–1 29–6–58–2			17–2–45–5 18.2–7–47–6			
v. Worcestershire (Worcester) 18–20 June	15–1–54–1 13–1–57–1		15–4–40–0 5–4–2–0			13–2–49–0 15.4–1–73–2			
v. Northamptonshire (Luton) 21–24 June	20–4–58–1	22–6–92–2 11–0–61–2	23–5–61–1 13–3–27–2			20–3–72–0 15–4–49–1			
v. Warwickshire (Leeds) 28–30 June		20–1–69–3 3–0–22–0	38–6–123–1 21–5–50–1		19–4–48–1 6–0–36–0				26–5–74–3 13–1–64–3
v. Gloucestershire (Bristol) 2–4 July			1–0–4–0 1.5–0–8–1			20.5–1–75–4 19–3–64–2			16–0–72–2 18–3–58–3
v. Leicestershire (Middlesbrough) 5–8 July	27.1–4–72–8		22–6–55–0 20–12–21–1			19–4–48–2		5–4–5–0	25–8–75–0 5–2–13–0
v. Indians (Scarborough) 12–14 July			20–2–68–3 11–0–70–2		23–1–93–1 7–0–31–0				15–2–52–1 10–1–49–1
v. Nottinghamshire (Worksop) 16–18 July			22–3–62–0		12–2–32–0	22–3–92–1			22–1–97–1
v. Surrey (Leeds) 19–21 July			26–8–66–3 25–9–49–2		16–3–41–0 11–4–17–0	22–5–53–3 25–7–55–7			
v. Kent (Scarborough) 23–25 July		12–2–43–0 18–3–45–4	10–7–8–0 16–11–20–1			17–3–58–2 15–0–72–3			
v. Nottinghamshire (Sheffield) 26–29 July		22.3–2–68–6 1–1–0–0	9–2–16–1			13–3–30–0 1–0–5–0			14–0–43–1
v. Lancashire (Old Trafford) 2–5 August		11–1–31–3 21–8–42–2	10–4–21–0 33–16–67–2			18–6–36–4 18–4–37–1			19–8–29–1 19–5–39–0
v. Leicestershire (Leicester) 6–8 August		21–5–61–3 6–0–46–1	2–1–2–0 17–2–56–0						19–5–47–1 12–1–40–1
v. Glamorgan (Leeds) 9–12 August			11–4–32–1		4–1–14–0 3–2–2–0				21–6–51–3 19–2–64–0
v. Derbyshire (Chesterfield) 16–19 August		6–1–22–0 17–2–57–4	9.4–4–38–0						2–0–4–0 14–2–48–0
v. Middlesex (Leeds) 20–22 August			7–1–30–0		9–4–19–0				28.5–6–90–5
v. Hampshire (Bournemouth) 23–26 August		8–1–27–0	2–1–1–0						6–3–10–0
v. Warwickshire (Edgbaston) 27–29 August		4–0–16–0					4–0–32–0		17–3–61–1
v. Northamptonshire (Scarborough) 10–12 September			7–0–24–0 33–16–58–1				7–2–20–1		12–2–45–1 46–15–105–2
	226.1–37– 671–25 av. 26.84	321–49– 1095–41 av. 26.70	621.3–186– 1550–36 av. 43.05	29–8– 75–2 av. 37.50	172–37– 510–6 av. 85.00	428.4–82– 1332–60 av. 22.20	29–4– 192–3 av. 64.00	18.1–4– 75–0 —	413.5–82– 1273–31 av. 41.06

a D.L. Bairstow 5–3–7–0   b R.J. Blakey 10.3–1–68–1 P.E. Robinson 11–0–115–0

J.D. Love	S.J. Dennis	S.N. Hartley	C. Shaw	M.D. Moxon	D. Byas	P.J. Berry	Byes	Leg-byes	Wides	No-balls	Total	Wkts
											0	0
							5	8		18	318	10
							2	10		7	195	10
								1		3	55	1
							3	17		11	295	10
2.2–0–4–0											34	0
							4	6		7	296	10
2–0–6–0							2	6	4	8	268	7
4–1–11–0	26.5–4–89–4							9		20	398	10
	3–1–4–1							4		2	140	2
5–1–18–0	14–2–44–2	2–1–2–0					8	1		4	257	6
	8–2–35–1						4	12		4	173	10
	9–1–30–0						3	6		1	187	10
8–2–26–0	17–2–62–0	14.2–63–1					2	4	1	11	300	2
	6–0–31–1	13–1–59–3						24	1	3	246	7
9–1–41–0	16–5–50–0						4	7	2	11	385	4
	12–2–38–2						8	10		2	193	7
			22–3–63–2					8	1	7	385	10
			5–1–22–0					7		1	201	4
		4–1–21–0	14–1–47–3	9–4–18–1			1	8		6	246	10
			19–3–39–3					4	1		173	10
			18–6–33–0	4–1–15–0			1	15		11	314	10
			7–2–9–1	8–2–22–1			3	2	2	1	82	4a
	11–2–37–0	3–1–11–0	10–1–25–1	8–1–23–0			6	10		8	325	6
	12–2–51–1		9–3–50–1					6		1	257	5
		4–0–28–0	20–1–78–1				4	11	2	3	404	3
	23.5–7–57–3		16–5–34–1				9	9	2	2	269	10
	13–2–34–1		2–1–7–0				4	5		2	171	10
	17–3–81–0		11.1–0–45–0				5	10	1	11	250	2
1–0–10–0	8–3–23–1		2–1–4–0				2	16		4	192	9
			10–2–26–2				4	4		2	191	10
											188	2b
	17.3–2–38–2						8	7		1	170	10
4–0–16–0	19–2–47–1							3	1	2	251	6
	25.4–6–85–3		15–6–30–2				1	9		4	235	9
1–0–8–0	14.4–3–58–1		4–1–15–0				7	9	1	2	239	3
	18–7–26–4	5–2–10–0	13–6–22–3				4	7		3	134	10
	15–2–39–0		13–2–51–2		2–0–15–0		1	8	3	9	212	3
	6–1–19–0		3–1–12–0				4	7		9	68	0
	14–2–53–2		15–3–38–1				5	5		5	244	7
	25–5–71–5		14–4–38–0					4		3	252	10
	8.4–5–19–3							1		1	58	4
3–2–6–0	19–5–63–0	3.2–1–12–0	11–3–45–1	6.4–2–35–0			2	10	4	9	282	2
											0	0
	16.2–3–71–3		17–3–38–5			4–1–10–1	3	6	1	4	197	10
	12–0–63–2		30–5–77–2			35–12–73–0	13	13	3	7	422	8
39.2–7–146–0	407.3–81–1318–43	48.4–9–206–4	300.1–64–848–31	35.4–10–113–2	2–0–15–0	39–13–83–1						
—	av. 30.65	av. 51.50	av. 27.35	av. 56.50	—	av. 83.00						

Nick Falkner batted well for Surrey and is likely to get more opportunities with the departure of Allan Butcher. (Mike Powell)

Jon Hardy made a useful start with Somerset in a season of trials and tribulations. (Mark Leech)

TWIN AMBITIONS: *Alec Bedser:* Stanley Paul: 217 pp, £9.95
In co-operation with his friend and long associate Alex Bannister, Alec Bedser has produced an autobiography which is one of the most interesting publications of the year. It abounds in anecdote, and opinion is free and honest. Bedser assesses modern players and their attitudes to the game and its ethics. He is forthright on limited-over cricket, over-rates and intimidatory bowling. Above all, he tells an honest and enjoyable story of a lifetime in cricket. He and twin brother Eric tossed up to see who would bowl fast and who would bowl slow. The book is eminently readable and is highly recommended.

BICENTENARY SCOTTISH CRICKET GUIDE: *edited by Neil Leitch:* 148 pp: £1.00
A superb handbook with all the facts and figures about cricket in Scotland, history and records. There are full details of all the leagues. At the price of £1 it is a bargain.

THE BIG HITTERS: *Brian Bearshaw:* Queen Anne Press: 200 pp, £12.95
This is a collection of forty essays on big hitters and fast scorers from Bonnar to Botham. The essays are brief and do not always capture the essence of their subject. The piece on Jim Smith, for example, is pallid reading beside Prittie's essay in *Mainly Middlesex* which was written over forty years ago. Nevertheless, the book is usually entertaining and interesting.

THE CHARACTER OF CRICKET: *Tim Heald: illustrated by Paul Cox:* Pavilion Books: 207 pp: £12.95
This is rather delightful. Tim Heald takes us around the county grounds, and a few club ones, and most expertly assisted by the drawings of Paul Cox, he captures the character and characters of each. He does not always succeed completely, but then it is necessary to avoid monotony, and that is a pitfall in such a book. What Tim Heald does succeed in doing, however, is to give us a warm and leaisurely book which will be much loved by those who have the true interests of the game at heart. This is a happy venture.

THE ASDA CRICKET CHALLENGE SOUVENIR PROGRAMME: *edited by David Arnold:* Dennis Fairey & Associates: 88 pp, £2.00
The cricket in this lavish programme for the Scarborough Festival is rather swamped by some garish advertisements, and one could wish that the quality of writing from such a distinguished collection of names was of a higher standard. Nevertheless, there is plenty for your money and many photographs.

BEYOND THE FAR PAVILIONS: *compiled by Lee Cooper and Allen Synge:* Pavilion Books: 158 pp, £10.95
This is the second collection of items about cricket in far and strange places. It confirms Pelham Warner's view that wherever British men and women are gathered together there will the stumps be pitched; only on the evidence provided by Allen Synge and Lee Cooper, the men and women don't have to be British. What is conveyed in this collection is that wherever the game is played there is a pulsating spirit of friendship and fun in spite of the lions, tigers and bears. A fascinating book.